P. M. Roget

ROGET'S THESAURUS

OF

ENGLISH WORDS AND PHRASES CLASSIFIED AND ARRANGED SO AS TO FACILITATE THE EXPRESSION OF IDEAS AND ASSIST IN LITERARY COMPOSITION

EDITED BY

C. O. SYLVESTER MAWSON, Litt.D., M.R.A.S., F.S.A.

Associate Editor of the Standard English Dictionary; Consulting Specialist to the Oxford English Dictionary; Revising Editor of Webster's New International Dictionary; Revising Editor of Sanskrit and Anglo-Indian Terms in the Century Dictionary; Member of the London Philological Society, American Oriental Society, Société Asiatique of France, etc.

A BOOK OF SYNONYMS AND ANTONYMS

NEW YORK

THOMAS Y. CROWELL COMPANY

PUBLISHERS

1921

EDITOR'S PREFACE

THERE is perhaps no more striking testimony to the usefulness of Roget's *Thesaurus* (on which this work is based) than the many editions which have been periodically demanded. This very popularity lays an added responsibility upon the publishers, and makes the editor's task one of no slight undertaking. A treasury of words and ideas must keep pace with the growth of knowledge and language or lose its place in the forerank of indispensable volumes. To enhance the value of the book and bring it abreast of modern culture and requirements was the aim of the present editor. The original plan of the work has been followed in the main, for that which has stood the test of over half a century, and made the name of Roget of almost classic worth, is not one to be lightly abandoned. But while the labors of the author have been embodied in their entirety, so many new features have been introduced and the time-honored structure has been so much enlarged and modernized that this edition may not unreasonably claim to be a new work, and not a revision in the usual significance of the term. A comparison of the new Index with the old will afford some idea of the extended scope of the present work.

Briefly the new features are these:—

1. All *obsolete* words are so characterized. The editor's first inclination was to eliminate them, but realizing that their retention might be of service to many writers, and the more so if clearly indicated, the method of marking common to many dictionaries was adopted. The Oxford English Dictionary was the final authority for determining these obsoletisms.

2. *Slang* and *cant* expressions are specially marked, so as to increase the usefulness of the book to the playwright, the novelist, and the writer generally. In every instance the leading dictionaries (Oxford, Webster's, Century, and Standard) have been followed in distinguishing such terms from those of unchallenged acceptance.

3. *Americanisms* have been introduced for the first time in any edition of the *Thesaurus*. Just as no English dictionary would be complete which did not embody these virile specimens of our language, so is their inclusion all the more incumbent in a work of this nature. Great care was called for in the selection and grouping of these New World expressions. The list, though by no means exhaustive, is probably more representative and complete than any collection of Americanisms outside a modern dictionary. What is an *Americanism?* The answer is essentially complex. The term includes (1) English words employed differently to what they are in Great Britain; (2) words that are archaic or obsolescent in England, but of everyday usage in America; (3) English provincialisms in general use on this side of the Atlantic; (4) words which have changed their meaning in England, but still retain their original meaning here; (5) words assimilated from European and Indian languages; (6) negroisms; (7) words of strictly American coinage. In treading on such debatable ground the ordinary dictionary of Americanisms is not found to be very reliable, for it frequently includes as " Americanisms " many words by no means peculiar to this country and which are as much British as American. Webster's New International Dictionary proved itself a safer guide, and in characterizing the various Americanisms its lead was invariably followed. The innovation should be one of undoubted utility, besides preventing confusion in the choice of true American terms.

4. Numerous *phrases* and *quotations* have been added, and their authors cited. In making these selections the needs of the average individual and of the scholar were alike borne in mind.

5. The *Index* has been thoroughly revised and enlarged, the numerous errors and

omissions of the old edition being duly rectified ; while all new words and phrases have been included.

The *New Thesaurus* presents a wider range of discriminated synonyms than has ever been attempted in a similar work. The writer at a loss for a word, none the less than the purist and the scholar who seek the finer shades of language, will find here the expression which exactly fits the need. The professional man, the orator, the statesman, the minister, as well as the journalist and *littérateur*, should find the *Thesaurus* an invaluable and inspiring aid. Its use to the student and the teacher needs no emphasizing, for there are few institutions where "Roget" is not freely employed. Its value in assisting and stimulating the writing of essays and theses has been recognized by educators throughout the English-speaking world, and it is hoped the present volume will prove of still greater service.

C. O. Sylvester Mawson.

CONTENTS

INTRODUCTION

THE present Work is intended to supply, with respect to the English language, a desideratum hitherto unsupplied in any language; namely, a collection of the words it contains and of the idiomatic combinations peculiar to it, arranged, not in alphabetical order as they are in a Dictionary, but according to the *ideas* which they express.[1] The purpose of an ordinary dictionary is simply to explain the meaning of words; and the problem of which it professes to furnish the solution may be stated thus: — The word being given, to find its signification, or the idea it is intended to convey. The object aimed at in the present undertaking is exactly the converse of this: namely, — The idea being given, to find the word, or words, by which that idea may be most fitly and aptly expressed. For this purpose, the words and phrases of the language are here classed, not according to their sound or their orthography, but strictly according to their *signification*.

The communication of our thoughts by means of language, whether spoken or written, like every other object of mental exertion, constitutes a peculiar art, which, like other arts, cannot be acquired in any perfection but by long-continued practice. Some, indeed, there are more highly gifted than others with a facility of expression, and naturally endowed with the power of eloquence; but to none is it at all times an easy process to embody, in exact and appropriate language, the various trains of ideas that are passing through the mind, or to depict in their true colors and proportions, the diversified and nicer shades of feeling which accompany them. To those who are unpracticed in the art of composition, or unused to extempore speaking, these difficulties present themselves in their most formidable aspect. However distinct may be our views, however vivid our conceptions, or however fervent our emotions, we cannot but be often conscious that the phraseology we have at our command is inadequate to do them justice. We seek in vain the words we need, and strive ineffectually to devise forms of expression which shall faithfully portray our thoughts and sentiments. The appropriate terms, notwithstanding our utmost efforts, cannot be conjured up at will. Like "spirits from the vasty deep," they come not when we call; and we are driven to the employment of a set of words and phrases either too general or too limited, too strong or too feeble, which suit not the occasion, which hit not the mark we aim at; and the result of our prolonged exertion is a style at once labored and obscure, vapid and redundant, or vitiated by the still graver faults of affectation or ambiguity.

It is to those who are thus painfully groping their way and struggling with the difficulties of composition, that this Work professes to hold out a helping hand. The assistance it gives is that of furnishing on every topic a copious store of words and phrases, adapted to express all the recognizable shades and modifications of the general idea under which those words and phrases are arranged. The inquirer can readily select, out of the ample collection spread out before his eyes in the following pages, those expressions which are best suited to his purpose, and which might not have occurred to him without such assistance. In order to make this selection, he scarcely ever need engage in any critical or elaborate study of the subtle distinctions existing between synonymous terms; for if the materials set before him be sufficiently abundant, an instinctive tact will rarely fail to lead him to the proper choice. Even while glancing over the columns of this Work, his eye may chance to light upon a particular term, which may save the cost of a clumsy paraphrase, or spare the labor of a tortuous circumlocution. Some felicitous turn

[1] See note on p. xviii.

of expression thus introduced will frequently open to the mind of the reader a whole vista of collateral ideas, which could not, without an extended and obtrusive episode, have been unfolded to his view; and often will the judicious insertion of a happy epithet, like a beam of sunshine in a landscape, illumine and adorn the subject which it touches, imparting new grace and giving life and spirit to the picture.

Every workman in the exercise of his art should be provided with proper implements. For the fabrication of complicated and curious pieces of mechanism, the artisan requires a corresponding assortment of various tools and instruments. For giving proper effect to the fictions of the drama, the actor should have at his disposal a well-furnished wardrobe, supplying the costumes best suited to the personages he is to represent. For the perfect delineation of the beauties of nature, the painter should have within reach of his pencil every variety and combination of hues and tints. Now, the writer, as well as the orator, employs for the accomplishment of his purposes the instrumentality of words; it is in words that he clothes his thoughts; it is by means of words that he depicts his feelings. It is therefore essential to his success that he be provided with a copious vocabulary, and that he possess an entire command of all the resources and appliances of his language. To the acquisition of this power no procedure appears more directly conducive than the study of a methodized system such as that now offered to his use.

The utility of the present Work will be appreciated more especially by those who are engaged in the arduous process of translating into English a work written in another language. Simple as the operation may appear, on a superficial view, of rendering into English each of its sentences, the task of transfusing, with perfect exactness, the sense of the original, preserving at the same time the style and character of its composition, and reflecting with fidelity the mind and the spirit of the author, is a task of extreme difficulty. The cultivation of this useful department of literature was in ancient times strongly recommended both by Cicero and by Quintilian, as essential to the formation of a good writer and accomplished orator. Regarded simply as a mental exercise, the practice of translation is the best training for the attainment of that mastery of language and felicity of diction, which are the sources of the highest oratory, and are requisite for the possession of a graceful and persuasive eloquence. By rendering ourselves the faithful interpreters of the thoughts and feelings of others, we are rewarded with the acquisition of greater readiness and facility in correctly expressing our own; as he who has best learned to execute the orders of a commander, becomes himself best qualified to command.

In the earliest periods of civilization, translators have been the agents for propagating knowledge from nation to nation, and the value of their labors has been inestimable; but, in the present age, when so many different languages have become the depositories of the vast treasures of literature and of science which have been accumulating for centuries, the utility of accurate translations has greatly increased, and it has become a more important object to attain perfection in the art.

The use of language is not confined to its being the medium through which we communicate our ideas to one another; it fulfills a no less important function as an *instrument of thought;* not being merely its vehicle, but giving it wings for flight. Metaphysicians are agreed that scarcely any of our intellectual operations could be carried on to any considerable extent, without the agency of words. None but those who are conversant with the philosophy of mental phenomena, can be aware of the immense influence that is exercised by language in promoting the development of our ideas, in fixing them in the mind, and in detaining them for steady contemplation. Into every process of reasoning, language enters as an essential element. Words are the instruments by which we form all our abstractions, by which we fashion and embody our ideas, and by which we are enabled to glide along a series of premises and conclusions with a rapidity so great as to leave in the memory no trace of the successive steps of the process; and we remain uncon-

scious how much we owe to this potent auxiliary of the reasoning faculty. It is on this ground, also, that the present Work founds a claim to utility. The review of a catalogue of words of analogous signification, will often suggest by association other trains of thought, which, presenting the subject under new and varied aspects, will vastly expand the sphere of our mental vision. Amidst the many objects thus brought within the range of our contemplation, some striking similitude or appropriate image, some excursive flight or brilliant conception, may flash on the mind, giving point and force to our arguments, awakening a responsive chord in the imagination or sensibility of the reader, and procuring for our reasonings a more ready access both to his understanding and to his heart.

It is of the utmost consequence that strict accuracy should regulate our use of language, and that every one should acquire the power and the habit of expressing his thoughts with perspicuity and correctness. Few, indeed, can appreciate the real extent and importance of that influence which language has always exercised on human affairs, or can be aware how often these are determined by causes much slighter than are apparent to a superficial observer. False logic, disguised under specious phraseology, too often gains the assent of the unthinking multitude, disseminating far and wide the seeds of prejudice and error. Truisms pass current, and wear the semblance of profound wisdom, when dressed up in the tinsel garb of antithetical phrases, or set off by an imposing pomp of paradox. By a confused jargon of involved and mystical sentences, the imagination is easily inveigled into a transcendental region of clouds, and the understanding beguiled into the belief that it is acquiring knowledge and approaching truth. A misapplied or misapprehended term is sufficient to give rise to fierce and interminable disputes; a misnomer has turned the tide of popular opinion; a verbal sophism has decided a party question; an artful watchword, thrown among combustible materials, has kindled the flame of deadly warfare, and changed the destiny of an empire.

In constructing the following system of classification of the ideas which are expressible by language, my chief aim has been to obtain the greatest amount of practical utility. I have accordingly adopted such principles of arrangement as appeared to me to be the simplest and most natural, and which would not require, either for their comprehension or application, any disciplined acumen, or depth of metaphysical or antiquarian lore. Eschewing all needless refinements and subtleties, I have taken as my guide the more obvious characters of the ideas for which expressions were to be tabulated, arranging them under such classes and categories as reflection and experience had taught me would conduct the inquirer most readily and quickly to the object of his search. Commencing with the ideas expressing abstract relations, I proceed to those which relate to space and to the phenomena of the material world, and lastly to those in which the mind is concerned, and which comprehend intellect, volition, and feeling; thus establishing six primary Classes of Categories.

1. The first of these classes comprehends ideas derived from the more general and ABSTRACT RELATIONS among things, such as *Existence, Resemblance, Quantiy, Order, Number, Time, Power.*

2. The second class refers to SPACE and its various relations, including *Motion,* or change of place.

3. The third class includes all ideas that relate to the MATERIAL WORLD; namely, the *Properties of Matter,* such as *Solidity, Fluidity, Heat, Sound, Light,* and the *Phenomena* they present, as well as the simple *Perceptions* to which they give rise.

4. The fourth class embraces all ideas of phenomena relating to the INTELLECT and its operations; comprising the *Acquisition,* the *Retention,* and the *Communication of Ideas.*

5. The fifth class includes the ideas derived from the exercise of VOLITION; embracing the phenomena and results of our *Voluntary and Active Powers;* such as *Choice, Intention, Utility, Action, Antagonism, Authority, Compact, Property,* &c.

6. The sixth and last class comprehends all ideas derived from the operation of

our SENTIENT AND MORAL POWERS; including our *Feelings, Emotions, Passions,* and *Moral and Religious Sentiments.*[1]

The further subdivisions and minuter details will be best understood from an inspection of the Tabular Synopsis of Categories prefixed to the Work, in which are specified the several *topics* or *heads of signification,* under which the words have been arranged. By the aid of this table, the reader will, with a little practice, readily discover the place which the particular topic he is in search of occupies in the series; and on turning to the page in the body of the Work which contains it, he will find the group of expressions he requires, out of which he may cull those that are most appropriate to his purpose. For the convenience of reference, I have designated each separate group or heading by a particular number; so that if, during the search, any doubt or difficulty should occur, recourse may be had to the copious alphabetical Index of words at the end of the volume, which will at once indicate the number of the required group.[2]

The object I have proposed to myself in this Work would have been but imperfectly attained if I had confined myself to a mere catalogue of words, and had omitted the numerous phrases and forms of expression composed of several words, which are of such frequent use as to entitle them to rank among the constituent parts of the language.[3] Very few of these verbal combinations, so essential to the knowledge of our native tongue, and so profusely abounding in its daily use, are to be met with in ordinary dictionaries. These phrases and forms of expression I have endeavored diligently to collect and to insert in their proper places, under the general ideas that they are designed to convey. Some of these conventional forms, indeed, partake of the nature of proverbial expressions; but actual proverbs, as such, being wholly of a didactic character, do not come within the scope of the present Work; and the reader must therefore not expect to find them here inserted.[4]

For the purpose of exhibiting with greater distinctness the relations between words expressing opposite and correlative ideas, I have, whenever the subject admitted of such an arrangement, placed them in two parallel columns in the same page, so that each group of expressions may be readily contrasted with those which occupy the adjacent column, and constitute their antithesis. By carrying the eye from the one to the other, the inquirer may often discover forms of expression, of which he may avail himself advantageously, to diversify and infuse vigor into his phraseology. Rhetoricians, indeed, are well aware of the power derived from the skillful introduction of antitheses in giving point to an argument, and imparting force and brilliancy to the diction. A too frequent and indiscreet employment of this figure of rhetoric may, it is true, give rise to a vicious and affected style; but

---

[1] It must necessarily happen in every system of classification framed with this view, that ideas and expressions arranged under one class must include also ideas relating to another class; for the operations of the *Intellect* generally involve also those of the *Will*, and *vice versâ;* and our *Affections* and *Emotions*, in like manner, generally imply the agency both of the *Intellect* and of the *Will*. All that can be effected, therefore, is to arrange the words according to the principa or dominant idea they convey. *Teaching*, for example, although a Voluntary act, relates primarily to the Communication of Ideas, and is accordingly placed at No. **537**, under Class IV, Division (II). On the other hand, *Choice, Conduct, Skill*, &c., although implying the coöperation of Voluntary with Intellectual acts, relate principally to the former, and are therefore arranged under Class V.

[2] It often happens that the same word admits of various applications, or may be used in different senses. In consulting the Index the reader will be guided to the number of the heading under which that word, in each particular acceptation, will be found, by means of *supplementary words* printed in Italics; which words, however, are not to be understood as explaining the meaning of the word to which they are annexed, but only as assisting in the required reference. I have also, for shortness' sake, generally omitted words immediately derived from the primary one inserted, which sufficiently represents the whole group of correlative words referable to the same heading. Thus the number affixed to *Beauty* applies to all its derivatives, such as *Beautiful, Beauteous, Beautifulness, Beautifully,* &c., the insertion of which was therefore needless.

[3] For example: — To take time by the forelock; — to turn over a new leaf; — to show the white feather; — to have a finger in the pie; — to let the cat out of the bag; — to take care of number one; — to kill two birds with one stone, &c., &c.

[4] See Trench, *On the Lessons in Proverbs.*

it is unreasonable to condemn indiscriminately the occasional and moderate use of a practice on account of its possible abuse.

The study of correlative terms existing in a particular language, may often throw valuable light on the manners and customs of the nations using it. Thus, Hume has drawn important inferences with regard to the state of society among the ancient Romans, from certain deficiencies which he remarked in the Latin language.[1]

In many cases, two ideas which are completely opposed to each other, admit of an intermediate or neutral idea, equidistant from both; all these being expressible by corresponding definite terms. Thus, in the following examples, the words in the first and third columns, which express opposite ideas, admit of the intermediate terms contained in the middle column, having a neutral sense with reference to the former.

Identity,	*Difference,*	*Contrariety.*
Beginning,	*Middle,*	*End.*
Past,	*Present,*	*Future.*

In other cases, the intermediate word is simply the negative to each of two opposite positions; as, for example, —

Convexity,	*Flatness,*	*Concavity.*
Desire,	*Indifference,*	*Aversion.*

Sometimes the intermediate word is properly the standard with which each of the extremes is compared; as in the case of

Insufficiency,	*Sufficiency,*	*Redundance;*

for here the middle term, *Sufficiency,* is equally opposed, on the one hand to *Insufficiency,* and on the other to *Redundance.*

These forms of correlative expressions would suggest the use of triple, instead of double, columns, for tabulating this threefold order of words; but the practical inconvenience attending such an arrangement would probably overbalance its advantages.

It often happens that the same word has several correlative terms, according to the different relations in which it is considered. Thus, to the word *Giving* are opposed both *Receiving,* and *Taking;* the former correlation having reference to the *persons* concerned in the transfer, while the latter relates to the *mode* of transfer. *Old* has for opposite both *New* and *Young,* according as it is applied to *things* or to *living beings. Attack* and *Defense* are correlative terms; as are also *Attack* and *Resistance. Resistance,* again, has for its other correlative *Submission. Truth in the abstract* is opposed to *Error;* but the opposite of *Truth communicated* is *Falsehood. Acquisition* is contrasted both with *Deprivation* and with *Loss. Refusal* is the counterpart both of *Offer* and of *Consent. Disuse* and *Misuse* may either of them be considered as the correlative of *Use. Teaching,* with reference to what is taught,

[1] "It is an universal observation," he remarks, "which we may form upon language, that where two related parts of a whole bear any proportion to each other, in numbers, rank, or consideration, there are always correlative terms invented which answer to both the parts, and express their mutual relation. If they bear no proportion to each other, the term is only invented for the less, and marks its distinction from the whole. Thus, *man* and *woman, master* and *servant, father* and *son, prince* and *subject, stranger* and *citizen,* are correlative terms. But the words *seaman, carpenter, smith, tailor,* &c., have no correspondent terms, which express those who are no seamen, no carpenters, &c. Languages differ very much with regard to the particular words where this distinction obtains; and may thence afford very strong inferences concerning the manners and customs of different nations. The military government of the Roman emperors had exalted the soldiery so high that they balanced all the other orders of the state: hence *miles* and *paganus* became relative terms; a thing, till then, unknown to ancient, and still so to modern languages." — "The term for a slave, born and bred in the family was *verna.* As *servus* was the name of the genus, and *verna* of the species without any correlative, this forms a strong presumption that the latter were by far the least numerous: and from the same principles I infer that if the number of slaves brought by the Romans from foreign countries had not extremely exceeded those which were bred at home, *verna* would have had a correlative, which would have expressed the former species of slaves. But these, it would seem, composed the main body of the ancient slaves, and the latter were but a few exceptions." — HUME, *Essay on the Populousness of Ancient Nations.*

The warlike propensity of the same nation may, in like manner, be inferred from the use of the word *hostis* to denote both *a foreigner* and *an enemy.*

is opposed to *Misteaching;* but with reference to the act itself, its proper reciprocal is *Learning.*

Words contrasted in form do not always bear the same contrast in their meaning. The word *Malefactor,* for example, would, from its derivation, appear to be exactly the opposite of *Benefactor:* but the ideas attached to these two words are far from being directly opposed; for while the latter expresses one who confers a benefit, the former denotes one who has violated the laws.

Independently of the immediate practical uses derivable from the arrangement of words in double columns, many considerations, interesting in a philosophical point of view, are presented by the study of correlative expressions. It will be found, on strict examination, that there seldom exists an exact opposition between two words which may at first sight appear to be the counterparts of one another; for, in general, the one will be found to possess in reality more force or extent of meaning than the other with which it is contrasted. The correlative term sometimes assumes the form of a mere negative, although it is really endowed with a considerable positive force. Thus *Disrespect* is not merely the absence of *Respect;* its signification trenches on the opposite idea, namely, *Contempt.* In like manner, *Untruth* is not merely the negative of *Truth;* it involves a degree of *Falsehood.* *Irreligion,* which is properly *the want of Religion,* is understood as being nearly synonymous with *Impiety.* For these reasons, the reader must not expect that all the words which stand side by side in the two columns shall be the precise correlatives of each other; for the nature of the subject, as well as the imperfections of language, renders it impossible always to preserve such an exactness of correlation.

There exist comparatively few words of a general character to which no correlative term, either of negation or of opposition, can be assigned, and which therefore require no corresponding second column. The correlative idea, especially that which constitutes a sense negative to the primary one, may, indeed, be formed or conceived; but, from its occurring rarely, no word has been framed to represent it; for, in language, as in other matters, the supply fails when there is no probability of a demand. Occasionally we find this deficiency provided for by the contrivance of prefixing the syllable *non;* as, for instance, the negatives of *existence, performance, payment,* &c., are expressed by the compound words, *nonexistence, nonperformance, nonpayment,* &c. Functions of a similar kind are performed by the prefixes *dis-,*[1] *anti-, contra-, mis-, in-,* and *un-.*[2] With respect to all these, and especially the last, great latitude is allowed according to the necessities of the case; a latitude which is limited only by the taste and discretion of the writer.

On the other hand, it is hardly possible to find two words having in all respects the same meaning, and being therefore interchangeable; that is, admitting of being employed indiscriminately, the one or the other, in all their applications. The investigation of the distinctions to be drawn between words apparently synonymous, forms a separate branch of inquiry, which I have not presumed here to enter upon; for the subject has already occupied the attention of much abler critics than myself, and its complete exhaustion would require the devotion of a whole life. The purpose of this Work, it must be borne in mind, is, not to explain the signification of words, but simply to classify and arrange them according to the sense in which they are now used, and which I presume to be already known to the reader. I enter into no inquiry into the changes of meaning they may have undergone in the course of time.[3] I am content to accept them at the value of their present cur-

---

[1] The words *disannul* and *dissever,* however, have the same meaning as *annul* and *sever; to unloose* is the same as *to loose,* and *inebriety* is synonymous with *ebriety.*

[2] In the case of adjectives, the addition to a substantive of the terminal syllable *less,* gives it a negative meaning: as *taste, tasteless; care, careless; hope, hopeless; friend, friendless; fault, faultless;* &c.

[3] Such changes are innumerable: for instance, the words *tyrant, parasite, sophist, churl, knave, villain,* anciently conveyed no opprobrious meaning. *Impertinent* merely expressed *irrelative;* and implied neither *rudeness* nor *intrusion,* as it does at present. *Indifferent* originally meant *impartial; extravagant* was simply *digressive;* and *to prevent* was properly *to precede* and *assist.* The old translations of the Scriptures furnish many striking examples of the alterations which

rency, and have no concern with their etymologies, or with the history of their transformations; far less do I venture to thrid the mazes of the vast labyrinth into which I should be led by any attempt at a general discrimination of synonyms. The difficulties I have had to contend with have already been sufficiently great, without this addition to my labors.

The most cursory glance over the pages of a Dictionary will show that a great number of words are used in various senses, sometimes distinguished by slight shades of difference, but often diverging widely from their primary signification, and even, in some cases, bearing to it no perceptible relation. It may even happen that the very same word has two significations quite opposite to one another. This is the case with the verb *to cleave*, which means *to adhere tenaciously*, and also *to separate by a blow*. *To propugn* sometimes expresses *to attack;* at other times *to defend*. *To let* is *to hinder*, as well as *to permit*. *To ravel* means both *to entangle* and *to disentangle*. *Shameful* and *shameless* are nearly synonymous. *Priceless* may either mean *invaluable* or *of no value*. *Nervous* is used sometimes for *strong*, at other times for *weak*. The alphabetical Index at the end of this Work sufficiently shows the multiplicity of uses to which, by the elasticity of language, the meaning of words has been stretched, so as to adapt them to a great variety of modified significations in subservience to the nicer shades of thought, which, under peculiarity of circumstances, require corresponding expression. Words thus admitting of different meanings, have therefore to be arranged under each of the respective heads corresponding to these various acceptations. There are many words, again, which express ideas compounded of two elementary ideas belonging to different classes. It is therefore necessary to place these words respectively under each of the generic heads to which they relate. The necessity of these repetitions is increased by the circumstance, that ideas included under one class are often connected by relations of the same kind as the ideas which belong to another class. Thus we find the same relations of *order* and of *quantity* existing among the ideas of *Time* as well as those of *Space*. Sequence in the one is denoted by the same terms as sequence in the other; and the measures of time also express the measures of space. The cause and the effect are often designated by the same word. The word *Sound*, for instance, denotes both the impression made upon the ear by sonorous vibrations, and also the vibrations themselves, which are the cause or source of that impression. *Mixture* is used for the act of mixing, as well as for the product of that operation. *Taste* and *Smell* express both the sensations and the qualities of material bodies giving rise to them. *Thought* is the act of thinking; but the same word denotes also the idea resulting from that act. *Judgment* is the act of deciding, and also the decision come to. *Purchase* is the acquisition of a thing by payment, as well as the thing itself so acquired. *Speech* is both the act of speaking and the words spoken; and so on with regard to an endless multiplicity of words. Mind is essentially distinct from Matter; and yet, in all languages, the attributes of the one are metaphorically transferred to those of the other. Matter, in all its forms, is endowed by the figurative genius of every language with the functions which pertain to intellect; and we perpetually talk of its phenomena and of its powers, as if they resulted from the voluntary influence of one body on another, acting and reacting, impelling and being impelled, controlling and being controlled, as if animated by spontaneous energies and guided by specific intentions. On the other hand, expressions, of which the primary signification refers exclusively to the properties and actions of matter, are metaphorically applied to the phenomena of thought and volition, and even to the feelings and passions of the soul; and in speaking of a *ray of hope*, a *shade of doubt*, a *flight of fancy*, a *flash of wit*, the *warmth of emotion*, or the *ebullitions of anger*, we are scarcely conscious that we are employing metaphors which have this material origin.

As a general rule, I have deemed it incumbent on me to place words and phrases which appertain more especially to one head, also under the other heads to which

time has brought in the signification of words. Much curious information on this subject is contained in Trench's *Lectures on the Study of Words*.

they have a relation, whenever it appeared to me that this repetition would suit the convenience of the inquirer, and spare him the trouble of turning to other parts of the work; for I have always preferred to subject myself to the imputation of redundance, rather than incur the reproach of insufficiency.[1] When, however, the divergence of the associated from the primary idea is sufficiently marked, I have contented myself with making a reference to the place where the modified signification will be found. But in order to prevent needless extension, I have, in general, omitted *conjugate words*[2] which are so obviously derivable from those that are given in the same place, that the reader may safely be left to form them for himself. This is the case with adverbs derived from adjectives by the simple addition of the terminal syllable -*ly*; such as *closely, carefully, safely*, &c., from *close, careful, safe,* &c., and also with adjectives or participles immediately derived from the verbs which are already given. In all such cases, an "&c." indicates that reference is understood to be made to these roots. I have observed the same rule in compiling the Index; retaining only the primary or more simple word, and omitting the conjugate words obviously derived from them. Thus I assume the word *short* as the representative of its immediate derivatives *shortness, shorten, shortening, shortened, shorter, shortly,* which would have had the same references, and which the reader can readily supply.

The same verb is frequently used indiscriminately either in the active or transitive, or in the neuter or intransitive sense. In these cases, I have generally not thought it worth while to increase the bulk of the Work by the needless repetition of that word; for the reader, whom I suppose to understand the use of the words, must also be presumed to be competent to apply them correctly.

There are a multitude of words of a specific character which, although they properly occupy places in the columns of a dictionary, yet, having no relation to general ideas, do not come within the scope of this compilation, and are consequently omitted.[3] The names of objects in Natural History, and technical terms belonging exclusively to Science or to Art, or relating to particular operations, and of which the signification is restricted to those specific objects, come under this category. Exceptions must, however, be made in favor of such words as admit of metaphorical application to general subjects, with which custom has associated them, and of which they may be cited as being typical or illustrative. Thus, the word *Lion* will find a place under the head of *Courage,* of which it is regarded as the type. *Anchor,* being emblematic of *Hope,* is introduced among the words expressing that emotion; and in like manner, *butterfly* and *weathercock,* which are suggestive of fickleness, are included in the category of *Irresolution.*

With regard to the admission of many words and expressions, which the classical reader might be disposed to condemn as vulgarisms, or which he, perhaps, might stigmatize as pertaining rather to the slang than to the legitimate language of the day, I would beg to observe, that, having due regard to the uses to which this Work was to be adapted, I did not feel myself justified in excluding them solely on that ground, if they possessed an acknowledged currency in general intercourse. It is obvious that, with respect to degrees of conventionality, I could not have at-

---

[1] Frequent repetitions of the same series of expressions, accordingly, will be met with under various headings. For example, the word *Relinquishment,* with its synonyms, occurs as a heading at No. **624,** where it applies to *intention,* and also at No. **782,** where it refers to *property.* The word *Chance* has two significations, distinct from one another: the one implying the *absence of an assignable cause;* in which case it comes under the category of the relation of Causation, and occupies the No. **156:** the other, the *absence of design,* in which latter sense it ranks under the operations of the Will, and has assigned to it the place No. **621.** I have, in like manner, distinguished *Sensibility, Pleasure, Pain, Taste,* &c., according as they relate to *Physical,* or to *Moral Affections;* the former being found at Nos. **375, 377, 378, 390,** &c., and the latter at Nos. **822, 827, 828, 850,** &c.

[2] By "*conjugate* or *paronymous* words is meant, correctly speaking, different parts of speech from the same root, which exactly correspond in point of meaning."—*A Selection of English Synonyms,* edited by Archbishop Whately.

[3] [This rule was not in all cases rigorously observed by the author; and the present editor has used his discretion in including such words in the interest of the general writer. C. O. S. M.]

tempted to draw any strict lines of demarcation; and far less could I have presumed to erect any absolute standard of purity. My object, be it remembered, is not to regulate the use of words, but simply to supply and to suggest such as may be wanted on occasion, leaving the proper selection entirely to the discretion and taste of the employer. If a novelist or a dramatist, for example, proposed to delineate some vulgar personage, he would wish to have the power of putting into the mouth of the speaker expressions that would accord with his character; just as the actor, to revert to a former comparison, who had to personate a peasant, would choose for his attire the most homely garb, and would have just reason to complain if the theatrical wardrobe furnished him with no suitable costume.

Words which have, in process of time, become obsolete, are of course rejected from this collection.[1] On the other hand, I have admitted a considerable number of words and phrases borrowed from other languages, chiefly the French and Latin, some of which may be considered as already naturalized; while others, though avowedly foreign, are frequently employed in English composition, particularly in familiar style, on account of their being peculiarly expressive, and because we have no corresponding words of equal force in our own language.[2] The rapid advances which are being made in scientific knowledge, and consequent improvement in all the arts of life, and the extension of those arts and sciences to so many new purposes and objects, create a continual demand for the formation of new terms to express new agencies, new wants, and new combinations. Such terms, from being at first merely technical, are rendered, by more general use, familiar to the multitude, and having a well-defined acceptation, are eventually incorporated into the language, which they contribute to enlarge and to enrich. *Neologies* of this kind are perfectly legitimate, and highly advantageous; and they necessarily introduce those gradual and progressive changes which every language is destined to undergo.[3] Some modern writers, however, have indulged in a habit of arbitrarily fabricating new words and a newfangled phraseology, without any necessity, and with manifest injury to the purity of the language. This vicious practice, the offspring of indolence or conceit, implies an ignorance or neglect of the riches in which the English language already abounds, and which would have supplied them with words of recognized legitimacy, conveying precisely the same meaning as those they so recklessly coin in the illegal mint of their own fancy.

A work constructed on the plan of classification I have proposed might, if ably executed, be of great value, in tending to limit the fluctuations to which language has always been subject, by establishing an authoritative standard for its regulation. Future historians, philologists, and lexicographers, when investigating the period when new words were introduced, or discussing the import given at the present time to the old, might find their labors lightened by being enabled to appeal to such a standard, instead of having to search for data among the scattered writings of the age. Nor would its utility be confined to a single language; for the principles of its construction are universally applicable to all languages, whether living or dead. On the same plan of classification there might be formed a French, a German, a Latin, or a Greek Thesaurus, possessing, in their respective spheres, the same advantages as those of the English model.[4] Still more useful would be a

---

[1] [An appreciable number of obsolete terms have nevertheless found their way into the *Thesaurus*, but these in the present edition have been specially characterized, thus rendering the book of enhanced value to the dramatist and *littérateur*. C. O. S. M.]

[2] All these words and phrases are printed in Italics.

[3] Thus, in framing the present classification, I have frequently felt the want of substantive terms corresponding to abstract qualities or ideas denoted by certain adjectives; and have been often tempted to invent words that might express these abstractions: but I have yielded to this temptation only in the four following instances; having framed from the adjectives *irrelative, amorphous, sinistral,* and *gaseous,* the abstract nouns *irrelation, amorphism, sinistrality,* and *gaseity.* I have ventured also to introduce the adjective *intersocial,* to express the active voluntary relations between man and man.

[4] [Similar works in other languages have since appeared, notably *Dictionnaire Idéologique* by T. Robertson (Paris, 1859); *Deutscher Sprachschatz* by D. Sanders (Hamburg, 1878), and *Deutscher Wortschatz, oder Der passende Ausdruck* by A. Schelling (Stuttgart, 1892). C. O. S. M.]

conjunction of these methodized compilations in two languages, the French and English, for instance; the columns of each being placed in parallel juxtaposition. No means yet devised would so greatly facilitate the acquisition of the one language, by those who are acquainted with the other: none would afford such ample assistance to the translator in either language; and none would supply such ready and effectual means of instituting an accurate comparison between them, and of fairly appreciating their respective merits and defects. In a still higher degree would all those advantages be combined and multiplied in a *Polyglot Lexicon* constructed on this system.

Metaphysicians engaged in the more profound investigation of the Philosophy of Language will be materially assisted by having the ground thus prepared for them, in a previous analysis and classification of our ideas; for such classification of ideas is the true basis on which words, which are their symbols, should be classified.[1] It is by such analysis alone that we can arrive at a clear perception of the relation which these symbols bear to their corresponding ideas, or can obtain a correct knowledge of the elements which enter into the formation of compound ideas, and of the exclusions by which we arrive at the abstractions so perpetually resorted to in the process of reasoning, and in the communication of our thoughts.

Lastly, such analyses alone can determine the principles on which a strictly *Philosophical Language* might be constructed. The probable result of the construction of such a language would be its eventual adoption by every civilized nation; thus realizing that splendid aspiration of philanthropists, — the establishment of a Universal Language. However utopian such a project may appear to the present generation, and however abortive may have been the former endeavors of Bishop Wilkins and others to realize it,[2] its accomplishment is surely not beset with greater difficulties than have impeded the progress to many other beneficial objects, which in former times appeared to be no less visionary, and which yet were successfully achieved, in later ages, by the continued and persevering exertions of the human intellect. Is there at the present day, then, any ground for despair, that at some future stage of that higher civilization to which we trust the world is gradually

[1] The principle by which I have been guided in framing my verbal classification is the same as that which is employed in the various departments of Natural History. Thus the sectional divisions I have formed, correspond to Natural Families in Botany and Zoölogy, and the filiation of words presents a network analogous to the natural filiation of plants or animals.

The following are the only publications that have come to my knowledge in which any attempt has been made to construct a systematic arrangement of ideas with a view to their expression. The earliest of these, supposed to be at least nine hundred years old, is the AMERA CÓSHA, or *Vocabulary of the Sanscrit Language,* by Amera Sinha, of which an English translation, by the late Henry T. Colebrooke, was printed at Serampoor, in the year 1808. The classification of words is there, as might be expected, exceedingly imperfect and confused, especially in all that relates to abstract ideas or mental operations. This will be apparent from the very title of the first section, which comprehends "*Heaven, Gods, Demons, Fire, Air, Velocity, Eternity, Much:*" while *Sin, Virtue, Happiness, Destiny, Cause, Nature, Intellect, Reasoning, Knowledge, Senses, Tastes, Odors, Colors,* are all included and jumbled together in the fourth section. A more logical order, however, pervades the sections relating to natural objects, such as *Seas, Earth, Towns, Plants,* and *Animals,* which form separate classes; exhibiting a remarkable effort at analysis at so remote a period of Indian literature.

The well-known work of Bishop Wilkins, entitled, *An Essay towards a Real Character and a Philosophical Language,* published in 1668, had for its object the formation of a system of symbols which might serve as a universal language. It professed to be founded on a "scheme of analysis of the things or notions to which names were to be assigned;" but notwithstanding the immense labor and ingenuity expended in the construction of this system, it was soon found to be far too abstruse and recondite for practical application.

In the year 1797, there appeared in Paris an anonymous work, entitled "PASIGRAPHIE, *ou Premiers Éléments du nouvel Art-Science d'écrire et d'imprimer une langue de manière à être lu et entendu dans toute autre langue sans traduction,*" of which an edition in German was also published. It contains a great number of tabular schemes of categories; all of which appear to be excessively arbitrary and artificial, and extremely difficult of application, as well as of apprehension.

[2] "The Languages," observes Horne Tooke, "which are commonly used throughout the world, are much more simple and easy, convenient and philosophical, than Wilkins's scheme for a *real character;* or than any other scheme that has been at any other time imagined or proposed for the purpose." — Ἔπεα Πτερόεντα, p. 125.

INTRODUCTION

tending, some new and bolder effort of genius towards the solution of this great problem may be crowned with success, and compass an object of such vast and paramount utility? Nothing, indeed, would conduce more directly to bring about a golden age of union and harmony among the several nations and races of mankind than the removal of that barrier to the interchange of thought and mutual good understanding between man and man, which is now interposed by the diversity of their respective languages.

P. M. ROGET.

PLAN OF CLASSIFICATION

TABULAR SYNOPSIS OF CATEGORIES

Class I. ABSTRACT RELATIONS

TABULAR SYNOPSIS OF CATEGORIES

4. DISTRIBUTIVE...............
- 75. Class
- 76. Inclusion
- 77. Exclusion
- 78. Generality
- 79. Speciality

5. CATEGORICAL...............
- 80. Rule
- 81. Multiformity
- 82. Conformity
- 83. Unconformity

V. NUMBER

1. ABSTRACT...................
- 84. Number
- 85. Numeration
- 86. List

2. DETERMINATE...............
- 87. Unity
- 88. Accompaniment
- 89. Duality
- 90. Duplication
- 91. Bisection
- 92. Triality
- 93. Triplication
- 94. Trisection
- 95. Quaternity
- 96. Quadruplication
- 97. Quadrisection
- 98. Five, &c.
- 99. Quinquesection, &c.
- 100. Plurality
- 100a. Fraction
- 101. Zero

3. INDETERMINATE.............
- 102. Multitude
- 103. Fewness
- 104. Repetition
- 105. Infinity

VI. TIME

- 106. Time
- 107. Neverness

1. ABSOLUTE..................
- *Definite*
- *Indefinite*
- 108. Period
- 109. Course
- 108a. Contingent Duration
- 110. Diuturnity
- 111. Transientness
- 112. Perpetuity
- 113. Instantaneity
- 114. Chronometry
- 115. Anachronism

2. RELATIVE

1. to Succession.....
- 116. Priority
- 117. Posteriority
- 118. Present time
- 119. Different time
- 120. Synchronism

2. to a Period.......
- 121. Futurity
- 122. Preterition
- 123. Newness
- 124. Oldness
- 125. Morning
- 126. Evening
- 127. Youth
- 128. Age
- 129. Infant
- 130. Veteran
- 131. Adolescence

3. to an Effect or Purpose..........
- 132. Earliness
- 133. Lateness
- 134. Occasion
- 135. Intempestivity

3. RECURRENT..................
- 136. Frequency
- 137. Infrequency
- 138. Periodicity
- 139. Irregularity

VII. CHANGE

1. SIMPLE.....................
- 140. Change
- 141. Permanence
- 142. Cessation
- 143. Continuance
- 144. Conversion
- 145. Reversion
- 146. Revolution
- 147. Substitution
- 148. Interchange

2. COMPLEX...................
- 149. Changeableness
- 150. Stability
- *Present*
- *Future*
- 151. Eventuality
- 152. Destiny

VIII. CAUSATION

1. CONSTANCY OF SEQUENCE.......
- 153. { *Constant Antecedent* Cause.
- 154. { *Constant Sequent* Effect
- 155. { *Assignment of* Cause Attribution
- 156. { *Absence of Assignment* Chance

2. CONNECTION BETWEEN CAUSE AND EFFECT................
- 157. Power.
- 158. Impotence
- *Degrees of Power*
- 159. Strength
- 160. Weakness
- 161. Production
- 162. Destruction
- 163. Reproduction

3. POWER IN OPERATION..........
- 164. Producer
- 165. Destroyer
- 166. Paternity
- 167. Posterity
- 168. Productiveness
- 169. Unproductiveness
- 170. Agency
- 171. Energy
- 172. Inertness
- 173. Violence
- 174. Moderation

xxii

TABULAR SYNOPSIS OF CATEGORIES

IV. MOTION

	264. Motion	265. Quiescence
	266. Journey	267. Navigation
1. MOTION IN GENERAL.........	268. Traveler	269. Mariner
	270. Transference	
	271. Carrier	
	272. Vehicle	273. Ship
2. DEGREES OF MOTION.........	274. Velocity	275. Slowness
3. CONJOINED WITH FORCE	276. Impulse	277. Recoil
	278. Direction	279. Deviation
	280. Precession	281. Sequence
	282. Progression	283. Regression
	284. Propulsion	285. Traction
	286. Approach	287. Recession
	288. Attraction	289. Repulsion
	290. Convergence	291. Divergence
	292. Arrival	293. Departure
	294. Ingress	295. Egress
	296. Reception	297. Ejection
4. WITH REFERENCE TO DIRECTION	298. Food	299. Excretion
	300. Insertion	301. Extraction
	302. Passage	
	303. Transcursion	304. Shortcoming
	305. Ascent	306. Descent
	307. Elevation	308. Depression
	309. Leap	310. Plunge
	311. Circuition	
	312. Rotation	313. Evolution
	314. Oscillation	
	315. Agitation	

CLASS III. MATTER

I. MATTER IN GENERAL.........	316. Materiality	317. Immateriality
	318. World	
	319. Gravity	320. Levity

II. INORGANIC MATTER

		321. Density	322. Rarity
		323. Hardness	324. Softness
		325. Elasticity	326. Inelasticity
1. SOLIDS....................		327. Tenacity	328. Brittleness
		329. Texture	
		330. Pulverulence	
		331. Friction	332. Lubrication
	1. In General.........	333. Fluidity	334. Gaseity
		335. Liquefaction	336. Vaporization
		337. Water	338. Air
		339. Moisture	340. Dryness
2. FLUIDS	2. Specific...........	341. Ocean	342. Land
		343. { Gulf / Lake	
			344. Plain
		345. Marsh	346. Island
		347. Stream	
	3. In Motion........	348. River	349. Wind
		350. Conduit	351. Air pipe
		352. Semiliquidity	353. Bubble
3. IMPERFECT FLUIDS		354. Pulpiness	355. Unctuousness
			356. Oil
			356a. Resin

III. ORGANIC MATTER

		357. Organization	358. Inorganization
		359. Life	360. Death
	1. In General.......		361. Killing
			362. Corpse
			363. Interment
1. VITALITY		364. Animality	365. Vegetability
		366. Animal	367. Vegetable
	2. Special ...	368. Zoölogy	369. Botany
		370. Cicuration	371. Agriculture
		372. Mankind	
		373. Man	374. Woman

TABULAR SYNOPSIS OF CATEGORIES

CLASS VI. AFFECTIONS

TABULAR SYNOPSIS OF CATEGORIES

953. Temperance	954. Intemperance
	954a. Sensualist
955. Asceticism	
4. PRACTICE. ...... 956. Fasting	957. Gluttony
958. Sobriety	959. Drunkenness
960. Purity	961. Impurity
	962. Libertine
963. Legality	964. Illegality
965. Jurisprudence	
966. Tribunal	
967. Judge	
968. Lawyer	
5. INSTITUTIONS ...... 969. Lawsuit	
970. Acquittal	971. Condemnation
	972. Punishment
973. Reward	974. Penalty
	975. Scourge

V. RELIGIOUS

	976. Deity
1. SUPERHUMAN BEINGS AND REGIONS	977. Angel — 978. Satan
	979. Jupiter — 980. Demon
	981. Heaven — 982. Hell
	983. Theology
2. DOCTRINES	983a. Orthodoxy — 984. Heterodoxy
	985. Revelation — 986. Pseudo-revelation
	988. Impiety
3. SENTIMENTS	987. Piety — 989. Irreligion
	990. Worship — 991. Idolatry
	992. Sorcery
4. ACTS.	993. Spell
	994. Sorcerer
	995. Churchdom
	996. Clergy — 997. Laity
5. INSTITUTIONS	998. Rite
	999. Canonicals
	1000. Temple

ABBREVIATIONS, ETC.

Adj.	*adj.*	Adjectives, Participles, and Words having the power of Adjectives
Adv.	*adv.*	Adverbs and Adverbial Expressions
Am. Hist.		American History
Aust.		Australian
Can.		Canadian
Cic.		Cicero
Hor.		Horace
Int.	*int*	Interjections
Juv.		Juvenal
L. L. L.		*Love's Labor's Lost*
Luc.		Lucretius
Mar.		Martial
M. for M.		*Measure for Measure*
M. N. D.		*Midsummer Night's Dream*
N.	*n.*	Nouns
N. Am.		North American
Nfld.		Newfoundland
Phr.	*phr.*	Phrases
P. L.		*Paradise Lost*
Plut.		Plutarch
Quin.		Quintilian
Sal.		Sallust
Sen.		Seneca
Tac.		Tacitus
Ter.		Terence
Tertul.		Tertullian
U. S.		United States
V.	*v.*	Verbs
Ver.		Vergil

The numbers are those of the headings or categories.

Words in Italics within parentheses are nct intended to explain the meanings of the words which precede them, but to indicate the nature of allied groups of words under the numbers which follow them.

Obsolete words are indicated by a dagger; thus: abludet.

Slang or *Cant* terms are marked with an asterisk; thus: rhino*.

Authors or works quoted are given in brackets; thus: [Ovid]; [*M. for M.*].

SPACE–SAVING DEVICES

Dashes and hyphens are used to avoid the repetition of some syllable or term common to each word or phrase in the same group.   For example: —

"abs-, ex-, re-cision;" = "abscision," "excision," "recision"

"over –, above- the mark;" = "over the mark," "above the mark"

"on the -verge, – brink, – skirts- of;" = "on the verge of," "on the brink of," "on the skirts of"

"brush –, whisk –, turn –, send- -off, – away;" = "brush off," "brush away," "whisk off," "whisk away," "turn off," "turn away," "send off," "send away"

"quick-, keen-, clear-, sharp--eyed, -sighted, -witted;" = "quick-eyed," "quick-sighted," "quick-witted," "keen-eyed," "keen-sighted," "keen-witted," "clear-eyed," "clear-sighted," "clear-witted," "sharp-eyed," "sharp-sighted," "sharp-witted"

"away from –, foreign to –, beside- the -purpose, – question, – transaction, – point;" = "away from the purpose," "away from the question," "away from the transaction," "away from the point," "foreign to the purpose," &c., "beside the purpose," &c.

"fall, – to the ground;" = "fall, "fall to the ground"

"shortness &c. adj.;" "shortly &c. adj.;" "shortening &c. v.;" = in a similar manner form other words from the groups of adjectives or verbs in the same category

[See also "How to use the Book." p xxxiv.]

HOW TO USE THE BOOK

I. To find a synonym or antonym for any given WORD:

Turn to the Index and find the particular word or any simple term of kindred meaning; then refer to the category indicated. Under the part of speech sought for [**N., V., Adj., Adv.**] will be found a wide choice of synonymous and correlative terms, with their antitheses in the adjoining column. For example:— "distinction."

In the Index we find — " **distinction**
difference 15
discrimination 465
fame 873
rank 875"

the italicized words denoting the general sense of the affinitive terms in the respective categories. Turning to No. **873** (supposing *fame* is the desired significance) we select the most appropriate expression from the comprehensive list presented: "mark, name, figure; repute, reputation; good –, high- repute; note, notability, notoriety, éclat, 'the bubble reputation,' vogue, celebrity; fame, famousness, renown; popularity, *aura popularis;*" and so on. In the parallel column, viz., **874,** are grouped the antonymous terms: "disrepute, discredit; ill-, bad- -repute, -name, -odor, -favor; disapprobation; ingloriousness; derogation," etc.

II. To find a suitable word to express a given IDEA:

Find in the Index some word relating to the idea, and proceed as above. For example:— "hope." The Index refers us to category **858,** where there are words and phrases bearing on "hope" sufficient to satisfy the most exacting writers and the most diverse tastes; while **859** contains a systematic grouping of all opposite terms, as "hopelessness," etc.

III. To find appropriate words or new ideas on any given SUBJECT:

Turn up the subject or any branch of it. The Index itself will suggest various lines of thought, while reference to the indicated groups will provide a banquet of ideas and apt expressions. For example:—"drama." Turning to **599** we find idea-groups covering the entire range of the subject, besides incidental references to other helpful categories.

N.B. To grasp the underlying principle of the classification study the *Tabular Synopsis of Categories* (pp. xxi–xxxi). Reference may be made direct from this Synopsis to the body of the work; but it is usually found more convenient to consult the Index first.

[See also " *Abbreviations, etc.,*" p. xxxii, and " *Space-Saving Devices,*" p. xxxiii.]

ROGET'S THESAURUS

OF

ENGLISH WORDS AND PHRASES

CLASS I

WORDS EXPRESSING ABSTRACT RELATIONS

SECTION I. EXISTENCE

1. BEING, IN THE ABSTRACT

1. Existence. — **N.** existence, being, entity, *ens, esse,* subsistence.

reality, actuality; positiveness &c. *adj.*; fact, matter of fact, sober reality; truth &c. 494; actual existence.

presence &c. (*existence in space*) 186; coexistence &c. 120.

stubborn fact; not a -dream &c. 515; no joke.

center of life, essence, inmost nature, inner reality, vital principle.

[Science of existence], ontology.

V. exist, be; have -being &c. *n.*; subsist, live, breathe, stand, obtain, be the case; occur &c. (*event*) 151; have place, prevail; find oneself, pass the time, vegetate.

consist in, lie in; be -comprised in, -contained in, -constituted by.

come into -existence &c. *n.*; arise &c. (*begin*) 66; come forth &c. (*appear*) 446.

become &c. (*be converted*) 144; bring into existence &c. 161.

abide, continue, endure, last, remain.

Adj. existing &c. *v.*; existent, under the sun; in -existence &c. *n.*; extant; afloat, on foot, current, prevalent; undestroyed.

real, actual, positive, absolute; true &c. 494; substan-tial, -tive; self-exist-ing, -ent; essential.

2. Inexistence.—**N.** inexistence; non-existence, -subsistence; nonentity, *nil;* negativeness &c. *adj.*; nullity; nihil-ity, -ism; *tabula rasa,* blank; abeyance; absence &c. 187; no such thing &c. 4; non-being, nothingness, oblivion.

annihilation; extinction &c. (*destruction*) 162; extinguishment, extirpation, Nirvana, obliteration.

V. not -exist &c. 1; have no -existence &c. 1; be null and void; cease to -exist &c. 1; pass away, perish; be -, become -extinct &c. *adj.*; die out; disappear &c. 449; melt away, dissolve, leave not a rack behind; go, be no more; die &c. 360.

annihilate, render null, nullify; abrogate &c. 756; destroy &c. 162; take away; remove &c. (*displace*) 185; obliterate, extirpate.

Adj. inexistent, nonexistent &c. 1; negative, blank; missing, omitted; absent &c. 187; insubstantial, shadowy, spectral, visionary.

unreal, potential, virtual; baseless, *in nubibus;* unsubstantial &c. 4; vain.

un-born, -created, -begotten, -conceived, -produced, -made.

perished, annihilated, &c. *v.*; extinct, exhausted, gone, lost, departed; defunct &c. (*dead*) 360.

well-founded, -grounded; un-ideal, -imagined; not -potential &c. 2; authentic.

Adv. actually &c. *adj.*; in -fact, – point of fact, – reality; indeed; *de –, ipso - facto.*

Phr. *ens rationis; ergo sum cogito;* "think'st thou existence doth depend on time?" [Byron].

fabulous, ideal &c. (*imaginary*) 515; supposititious &c. 514.

Adv. negatively, virtually &c. *adj.*

Phr. *non ens.*

2. Being, in the Concrete

3. Substantiality. — N. substantiality, hypostasis; person, thing, object, article; something, a being, an existence; creature, body, substance, flesh and blood, stuff, substratum; matter &c. 316; corporeity, element, essential nature, groundwork, materiality, substantialness, vital part.

[Totality of existences], world &c. 318; *plenum.*

Adj. substan-tive, -tial; hypostatic; personal, bodily, tangible &c. (*material*) 316; corporeal.

Adv. substantially &c. *adj.*; bodily, essentially.

4. Unsubstantiality. — N. un-, in substantiality; nothingness, nihility; no -degree, -part, -quantity, -thing.

nothing, naught, *nil*, nullity, zero, cipher, no one, nobody; never –, ne'er -a one; no such thing, none in the world; nothing -whatever, – at all, – on earth; not a -particle &c. (*smallness*) 32; all -talk, – mŏonshine, – stuff and nonsense; matter of no -importance, – consequence.

thing of naught, man of straw, John Doe and Richard Roe, faggot voter; *nominis umbra*, nonentity; flash in the pan, *vox et prœterea nihil.*

shadow; phantom &c. (*fallacy of vision*) 443; dream &c. (*imagination*) 515; *ignis fatuus* &c. (luminary) 423; "such stuff as dreams are made of" [*Tempest*]; air, thin air; bubble &c. 353; "baseless fabric of a vision" [*Tempest*]; mockery.

hollowness, blank; void &c. (*absence*) 187.

inanity, fool's paradise.

V. vanish, evaporate, fade, dissolve, melt away; disappear &c. 449.

Adj. unsubstantial; base-, ground-less; ungrounded; without –, having no-foundation.

visionary &c. (*imaginary*) 515; immaterial &c. 137; spectral &c. 980; dreamy; shadowy; ethereal, airy; cloud -built, -formed; gossamery, illusory, insubstantial, unreal.

vacant, vacuous; empty &c. 187; eviscerated; blank, hollow; nominal; null; inane.

Phr. there's nothing in it; "an ocean of dreams without a sound" [Shelley].

3. Formal Existence

Internal conditions

5. Intrinsicality.—N. intrinsicality, inbeing, inherence, inhesion; subjectiveness; ego; egohood; essence; essentialness &c. *adj.*; essential part, quintessence, incarnation, quiddity, gist, pith, marrow, sap, lifeblood, backbone, heart, soul; important part &c. (*importance*) 642.

principle, nature, constitution, character, type, quality, crasis, diathesis.

habit; temper, -ament; spirit, humor, grain; disposition.

External conditions

6. Extrinsicality.—N. extrinsicality, objectiveness, *non ego;* extraneousness &c. 57; accident.

Adj. derived from without; objective; extrin-sic, -sical; extraneous &c. (*foreign*) 57; modal, adventitious; a-, ad-scititious; incidental, accidental, nonessential; contingent, fortuitous.

implanted, ingrafted; inculcated, infused.

outward &c. (*external*) 220.

Adv. extrinsically &c. *adj.*

endowment, capacity; capability &c. (*power*) 157.

moods, declensions, features, aspects; peculiarities &c. (*speciality*) 79; idio-syncrasy; idiocrasy &c. (*tendency*) 176; diagnostics.

V. be -, run- in the blood; be born so; be -intrinsic &c. *adj.*

Adj. derived from within, subjective; intrin-sic, -sical; fundamental, nor-mal; implanted, inherent, essential, natural; in-nate, -born, -bred, -grained, -wrought; coeval with birth, genetous, hæmatobious, syngenic; radical, in-carnate, thoroughbred, hereditary, inherited, immanent; congen-ital, -ite †; connate, running in the blood; in-generate, -genite †; indigenous; in the -grain &c. *n.*; bred in the bone, instinctive; inward, internal &c. 221; to the manner born; virtual.

characteristic &c. (*special*) 79, (*indicative*) 550; invariable, incurable, inerad-icable, fixed.

Adv. intrinsically &c. *adj.*; at bottom, in the main, in effect, practically, vir-tually, substantially, *au fond;* fairly.

Phr. " character is higher than intellect " [Emerson]; " come give us a taste of your qual-ity " [*Hamlet*]; *magnos homines virtute metimur non fortunâ* [Nepos]; *non numero hœc judi-cantur sed pondere* [Cicero]; " vital spark of heavenly flame " [Pope].

4. Modal Existence

Absolute	*Relative*

7. State. — N. state, condition, cate-gory, estate, lot, case, trim, mood, pickle, plight, temper; aspect &c. (*ap-pearance*) 448; dilemma, pass, predica-ment.

constitution, habitude, diathesis; frame, fabric &c. 329; stamp, set, fit, mold, mould.

mode, modality, schesis; form &c. (*shape*) 240.

tone, tenor, turn; trim, guise, fash-ion, light, complexion, style, character.

V. be in -, possess -, enjoy -, labor under- a -state &c. *n.*; be on a footing, do, fare; come to pass.

Adj. conditional, modal, formal; structural, organic.

Adv. conditionally &c. *adj.*; as -the matter stands, - things are; such being the case &c. 8.

8. Circumstance. — N. circum-stance, situation, phase, position, pos-ture, attitude, place, point; terms; *ré-gime;* footing, standing, status.

occasion, juncture, conjunctive; con-tingency &c. (*event*) 151.

predicament; emergen-ce, -cy; exi-gency, crisis, pinch, pass, push; occur-rence; turning point.

bearings, how the land lies.

Adj. circumstantial; given, condi-tional, provisional; critical; modal; con-tingent, incidental; adventitious &c. (*extrinsic*) 6; limitative.

Adv. in -, under- the -circumstances &c. *n.*, - conditions &c. 7; thus, in such wise.

accordingly; that -, such- being the case; that being so, sith, since, seeing that.

as matters stand; as -things, - times-go.

conditionally, provided, if, in case; if -so, - so be, - it be so; if it so -happen, - turn out; in the event of; in such a -contingency, - case, - event; provi-sionally, unless, without.

according to -circumstances, - the occasion; as it may -happen, - turn out, - be; as the -case may be, - wind blows; *pro re natâ.*

Phr. " yet are my sins not those of circumstance " [Lytton].

Section II. RELATION

1. Absolute Relation

9. Relation. — N. relation, bearing, reference, connection, concern, cogna-tion; correlation &c. 12; analogy; simi-

10. [Want, or absence of relation.] **Irrelation. — N.** irrelation, dissocia-tion; misrelation; inapplicability; in-

larity &c. 17; affinity, homology, alliance, homogeneity, association; approximation &c. (*nearness*) 197; filiation &c. (*consanguinity*) 11; interest; relevancy &c. 23; dependency, relationship, relative position.

comparison &c. 464; ratio, proportion.

link, tie, bond of union.

V. be-related &c. *adj.*; have a relation &c. *n.*; relate –, refer- to; bear upon, regard, concern, touch, affect, have to do with; pertain –, belong –, appertain-to; answer to; interest.

bring -into relation with, – to bear upon; connect, associate, draw a parallel; link &c. 43.

Adj. relative; correlative &c. 12; cognate; relating to &c. *v.*; relative to, in relation with, referable *or* referrible to; belonging to &c. *v.*; appurtenant to, in common with.

related, connected; implicated, associated, affiliated, allied to; *en rapport*, in touch with.

approxima-tive, -ting; proportion-al, -ate, -able; allusive, comparable.

in the same -category &c. 75; like &c. 17; relevant &c. (*apt*) 23; applicable, equiparant.

Adv. relatively &c. *adj.*; pertinently &c. 23.

thereof; as -to, – for, – respects, – regards; about; concerning &c. *v.*; anent; relating –, as relates- to; with -relation, – reference, – respect, – regard- to; in respect of; while speaking –, *à propos-* of; in connection with; by the -way, – by; whereas; for –, in- as much as; in point of, as far as; on the -part, – score- of; *quoad hoc; pro re natâ;* under the -head &c. (*class*) 75 - of; in the matter of, *in re.*

Phr. " thereby hangs a tale " [*Taming of the Shrew*].

connection; multifariousness; disconnection &c. (*disjunction*) 44; inconsequence, independence; incommensurability; irreconcilableness &c. (*disagreement*) 24; heterogeneity; unconformity &c. 83; irrelevancy, impertinence, *nihil ad rem;* intrusion &c. 24; non-pertinence.

V. have no -relation &c. 9 to, – bearing upon, – concern &c. 9 with, – business with; not -concern &c. 9; have -nothing to do with, – no business there; intrude &c. 24.

bring –, drag –, lug- in head and shoulders.

Adj. irrelative, irrespective, unrelated; arbitrary; independent, unallied; un-, dis-connected; adrift, isolated, insular; extraneous, strange, alien, foreign, outlandish, exotic.

not comparable, incommensurable, heterogeneous; unconformable &c. 83.

irrelevant, inapplicable; not -pertinent, – to the purpose; impertinent, inapposite, beside the mark, *à propos de bottes;* aside from –, away from –, foreign to –, beside- the -purpose, – question, – transaction, – point; misplaced &c. (*intrusive*) 24; traveling out of the record.

remote, far-fetched, out of the way, forced, neither here nor there, quite another thing; detached, segregate; disquiparant.

multifarious; discordant &c. 24.

incidental, parenthetical, *obiter dictum*, episodic.

Adv. parenthetically &c. *adj.*; by the -way, – by; *en passant*, incidentally; irrespectively &c. *adj.*; without -reference, – regard- to; in the abstract &c. 87; *a se.*

11. [Relations of kindred.] **Consanguinity. — N.** consanguinity, relationship, kindred, blood; parentage &c. (*paternity*) 166; filiation, affiliation; lineage, agnation, connection, alliance; family -connection, – tie; ties of blood; nepotism.

kins-man, -folk; kith and kin; rela-tion, -tive; connection; sib; next of kin; uncle, aunt, nephew, niece; cousin, -german; first –, second- cousin; cousin -once, – twice &c.- removed; near –, distant- relation; brother, sister, one's own flesh and blood.

family, fraternity; brother-, sister-, cousin-hood.

race, stock, generation; sept &c. 166; stirps, side; strain; breed, clan, tribe.

V. be -related &c. *adj.* – to; claim -relationship &c. *n.*- with.

Adj. related, akin, consanguineous, of the blood, family, allied, collateral; cog-, ag-, con-nate; kindred; affiliated; fraternal.

intimately –, nearly –, closely –, remotely –, distantly- related, – allied; german.

12. [Double or reciprocal relation.] **Correlation. — N.** reciprocalness &c. *adj.*; recipro-city, -cation; mutuality, correlation, interdependence; interchange &c. 148; exchange, barter.

reciprocitist.

V. reciprocate, alternate; interchange &c. 148; exchange; counterchange.

Adj. reciprocal, mutual, commutual, correlative; alternate; interchangeable; international; complemental, complementary.

Adv. *mutatis mutandis; vice versâ;* each other; by turns &c. 148; reciprocally &c. *adj.*

Phr. "happy in our mutual help" [Milton].

13. Identity. — N. identity, sameness; coincidence, coalescence; convertibility; equality &c. 27; selfness, self, oneself; identification.

monotony, tautology &c. (*repetition*) 104.

facsimile &c. (*copy*) 21; homoousia: *alter ego* &c. (*similar*) 17; *ipsissima verba* &c. (*exactness*) 494; same; self –, very –, one and the- same; very –, actual- thing; no other.

V. be -identical &c. *adj.*; coincide, coalesce.

treat as –, render- -the same, – identical; identify; recognize the identity of.

Adj. identical; self, ilk; the -same &c. *n.*; selfsame, homoousian, one and the same.

coincid-, coalesc-ent, -ing; indistinguishable; one; equivalent &c. (*equal*) 27; much ⁓the same, – of a muchness; unaltered.

Adv. identically &c. *adj.*; on all fours.

14. [Noncoincidence.] **Contrariety. — N.** contrariety, contrast, foil, antithesis, oppositeness; contradiction; antagonism &c. (*opposition*) 708; clashing, repugnance.

inversion &c. 218; the -opposite, – reverse, – inverse, – converse, – antipodes, – other extreme.

V. be -contrary &c. *adj.*; contrast with, oppose; differ *toto cœlo*.

invert, reverse, turn the tables; turn -topsy-turvy, – end for end, – upside down.

contra-dict, -vene; antagonize &c. 708.

Adj. contrar-y, -ious, -iant; opposite, counter, dead against; con-, re-verse; opposed, antithetical, contrasted, antipodean, antagonistic, opposing; conflicting, inconsistent, contradictory, at cross purposes; negative; hostile &c. 703.

differing toto cœlo; diametrically opposite; as opposite as -black and white, – light and darkness, – fire and water,

– the poles; "Hyperion to a satyr" [*Hamlet*]; quite the -contrary, – reverse; no such thing, just the other way, *tout au contraire.*

Adv. contrarily &c. *adj.*; contra, contrariwise, *per contra*, on the contrary, nay rather; *vice versâ;* on the other hand &c. (*in compensation*) 30.

Phr. "all concord's born of contraries" [B. Jonson].

15. Difference. — N. difference; vari-ance, -ation, -ety; diversity, dissimilarity &c. 18; disagreement &c. 24; disparity &c. (*inequality*) 28; distinction, contradistinction; alteration.

modification, moods and tenses.

nice –, fine –, delicate –, subtle- distinction; shade of difference, *nuance;* discrimination &c. 465; differentia.

different thing, something else, apple off another tree, another pair of shoes; this that or the other.

V. be -different &c. *adj.*; differ, vary, ablude †, mismatch, contrast; divaricate; differ -*toto cœlo*, – *longo intervallo*.

vary, modify &c. (*change*) 140.

discriminate &c. 465.

Adj. differing &c. *v.*; different, diverse, heterogeneous; distinguishable; varied, modified; diversified, various, divers, all manner of; variform &c. 81; dædal.

other, another, not the same; unequal &c. 28; unmatched; widely apart. distinctive, characteristic; discriminative; distinguishing.

Adv. differently &c. *adj.*

Phr. *il y a fagots et fagots.*

2. Continuous Relation

16. Uniformity. — N. uniformity; homogene-ity, -ousness; consistency; connatural-ity, -ness; homology; accordance; conformity &c. 82; agreement &c. 23; consonance, uniformness.

regularity, constancy, even tenor, routine; monotony.

V. be -uniform &c. *adj.*; accord with &c. 23; run through.

become -uniform &c. *adj.*; conform to &c. 82.

render uniform &c. *adj.*; assimilate, level, smooth, dress.

Adj. uniform; homo-geneous, -logous; of a piece, consistent, connatural; monotonous, even, invariable; regular, unchanged, undeviating, unvaried, unvarying.

Adv. uniformly &c. *adj.*; uniformly with &c. (*conformably*) 82; in harmony with &c. (*agreeing*) 23.

always, invariably, without exception, never otherwise; by clockwork.

Phr. *ab uno disce omnes.*

16a. [Absence or want of uniformity.] **Nonuniformity. — N.** diversity, irregularity, unevenness; multiformity &c. 81; unconformity &c. 83; roughness &c. 256; dissimilarity, dissimilitude, divarication, divergence.

Adj. diversified, varied, irregular, uneven, rough &c. 256; multifarious; multiform &c. 81; of various kinds; all -manner, – sorts, – kinds- of.

Adv. in all manner of ways, here there and everywhere.

3. Partial Relation

17. Similarity. — N. similarity, resemblance, likeness, similitude, semblance; affinity, approximation, parallelism; agreement &c. 23; ana-logy, -logicalness; correspondence, homoiousia, parity.

connatural-ness, -ity; brotherhood, family likeness.

alliteration, rhyme, pun.

repetition &c. 104; sameness &c. (*identity*) 13; uniformity &c. 16; isogamy.

analogue; the like; match, pendant, fellow, companion, pair, mate, twin, double, counterpart, brother, sister; one's second self, *alter ego*, chip of the old block, *par nobile fratrum*, *Arcades ambo*, birds of a feather, *et hoc genus omne*; *gens de même famille.*

parallel; simile; type &c. (*metaphor*) 521; image &c. (*representation*) 554; photograph; close -, striking -, speaking -, faithful &c. *adj.* - likeness, - resemblance.

V. be -similar &c. *adj.*; look like, resemble, bear resemblance; savor -, smack- of; approximate; parallel, match, rhyme with; take after; imitate &c. 19; favor, span [U. S.].

18. Dissimilarity. — N. dissimil-arity, -itude; unlikeness, diversity, disparity, dissemblance; divergence, variation; difference &c. 15; novelty, originality; creativeness; oögamy.

V. be -unlike &c. *adj.*; vary &c. (*differ*) 15; bear no resemblance to, differ *toto cœlo.*

render -unlike &c. *adj.*; vary &c. (*diversify*) 140.

Adj. dissimilar, unlike, disparate; divergent; of a different kind &c. (*class*) 75; unmatched, unique; new, novel; unprecedented &c. 83; original.

nothing of the kind; no such -, quite another- thing; far from it, cast in ε different mold, *tertium quid*, as like a dock as a daisy, " very like a whale " [*Hamlet*]; as different as -chalk from cheese, - Macedon and Monmouth; *lucus a non lucendo.*

diversified &c. 16a.

Adv. otherwise.

Phr. *diis aliter visum;* " no more like my father than I to Hercules" [*Hamlet*].

render -similar &c. *adj.*; assimilate, approximate, bring near; connaturalize, make alike; rhyme, pun.

Adj. similar; resembling &c. *v.*; like, alike; twin.

analog-ous, -ical; parallel, of a piece; such as, so; homoiousian.

connatural, congener, allied to; akin to &c. (*consanguineous*) 11.

approximate, much the same, near, close, something like, such like; a show of; mock, pseudo, simulating, representing.

exact &c. (*true*) 494; lifelike, faithful; true to -nature, – the life; the -very image, – picture- of; for all the world like, *comme deux gouttes d'eau;* as like as -two peas, – it can stare; *instar omnium,* cast in the same mold, ridiculously like.

Adv. as if, so to speak; as –, as if- it were; *quasi,* just as, *veluti in speculum.*

Phr. *et sic de similibus; tel maître tel valet; tel père tel fils.*

19. Imitation. — N. imitation; copying &c. *v.*; transcription; repetition, duplication, reduplication; quotation; reproduction; mimeography.

mockery, mimicry; simulation, personation; representation &c. 554; semblance; copy &c. 21; assimilation.

paraphrase, parody &c. 21.

plagiarism; forgery &c. (*falsehood*) 544; celluloid.

imitator, echo, cuckoo, parrot, ape, monkey, mocking bird, mimic; copyist.

V. imitate, copy, mirror, reflect, reproduce, repeat; do like, echo, re-echo, catch; transcribe; match, parallel.

mock, take off, mimic, ape, simulate, personate; act &c. (*drama*) 599; represent &c. 554; counterfeit, parody, travesty, caricature, burlesque.

follow -, tread- in the- -steps, – footsteps, – wake- of; take pattern by; follow -suit, – the example of; walk in the shoes of, take a leaf out of another's book, strike in with, follow suit; take -, model- after; emulate.

Adj. imitated &c. *v.*; mock, mimic; modelled after, molded on.

paraphrastic; literal; imitative; secondhand; imitable; aping, apish, mimicking.

Adv. literally, to the letter, verbatim, *literatim, sic, totidem verbis,* word for word, *mot à mot;* exactly, precisely.

Phr. like master like man; " like — but oh! how different! " [Wordsworth]; " genius borrows nobly " [Emerson]; " pursuing echoes calling 'mong the rocks " [A. Coles]; " quotation confesses inferiority " [Emerson].

20. Nonimitation. — N. no imitation; originality; creativeness.

Adj. unimitated, uncopied; unmatched, unparalleled; inimitable &c. 13; unique, original; creative, untranslated; exceptional, rare, *sui generis,* uncommon, unexampled.

20a. Variation. — N. variation; alteration &c. (*change*) 140.

modification, moods and tenses; discrepance, discrepancy.

divergency &c. 291; deviation &c. 279; aberration; innovation.

V. vary &c. (*change*) 140; deviate &c. 279; diverge &c. 291; alternate, swerve.

Adj. varied &c. *v.*; modified; diversified &c. 16a.

21. [Result of imitation.] Copy. — N. copy, facsimile, counterpart, *effigies,* effigy, form, likeness, similitude, semblance, cast, tracing, ectype; imitation &c. 19; model, representation, adumbration, study; portrait &c. (*representment*) 554; resemblance.

duplicate; transcript, -ion; reflex, -ion; shadow, echo; chip of the old block; reprint, reproduction; second edition &c. (*repetition*) 104; *réchauffé;* apograph, fair copy, revise.

22. [Thing copied.] Prototype. — N. prototype, original, model, pattern, precedent, standard, scantling, type; arche-, anti-type; protoplast, module, exemplar, example, ensample, paradigm; lay-figure.

text, copy, design; fugleman, keynote.

die, mold; matrix, last, plasm; pro-, proto-plasm; mint; seal, punch, intaglio, negative; stamp.

V. be -, set- an example; set a copy.

Phr. " a precedent embalms a principle " [Disraeli]; *exempla sunt odiosa.*

parody, caricature, burlesque, travesty, *travestie*, paraphrase.

servile -copy, – imitation; counterfeit &c. (*deception*) 545; *pasticcio*.

Adj. faithful; lifelike &c. (*similar*) 17; close, conscientious.

4. GENERAL RELATION

23. Agreement. — N. agreement; ac-cord, -cordance; unison, harmony; concord &c. 714; concordance, concert; understanding, mutual understanding.

conformity &c. 82; conformance; uniformity &c. 16; consonance, consentaneousness, consistency; congru-ity, -ence; keeping; congeniality; correspondence, parallelism, apposition, union.

fitness, aptness &c. *adj.*; relevancy; pertinen-ce, -cy; sortance †; case in point; aptitude, coaptation, propriety, applicability, admissibility, commensurability, compatibility; cognation &c. (*relation*) 9.

adaption, adjustment, graduation, accommodation; reconcil-iation, -ement; assimilation.

consent &c. (*assent*) 488; concurrence &c. 178; coöperation &c. 709.

right man in the right place, very thing; quite –, just- the thing.

V. be -accordant &c. *adj.*; agree, accord, harmonize; correspond, tally, respond; meet, suit, fit, befit, do, adapt itself to; fall in –, chime in –, square –, quadrate –, consort –, comport- with; dovetail, assimilate; fit like a glove; fit to a -tittle, – T; match &c. 17; become one; homologate.

consent &c. (*assent*) 488.

render -accordant &c. *adj.*; fit, suit, adapt, accommodate; graduate; adjust &c. (*render equal*) 27; dress, regulate, readjust; accord, harmonize, reconcile; fadge, dovetail, square.

Adj. agreeing, suiting &c. *v.*; in accord, accordant, concordant, consonant, congruous, consentaneous, correspondent, congenial; coherent; becoming; harmonious, reconcilable, conformable; in -accordance, – harmony, – keeping, – unison, &c. *n.*- with; at one with, of one mind, of a piece; consistent, compatible, proportionate; commensurate; on all fours.

apt, apposite, pertinent, pat; to the -point, – purpose; happy, felicitous, germane, *ad rem*, in point, bearing upon, applicable, relevant, admissible.

fit, adapted, *in loco*, *à propos*, appropriate, seasonable, sortable, suitable, idoneous, deft; meet &c. (*expedient*) 646.

24. Disagreement. — N. disagreement; dis-cord, -cordance; dissonance, dissidence, discrepancy; unconformity &c. 83; incongru-ity, -ence; discongruity, *mésalliance*; jarring &c. *v.*; dissension &c. 713; conflict &c. (*opposition*) 708; bickering, clashing, misunderstanding, wrangle.

disparity, mismatch, disproportion; dissimilitude, inequality; disproportionateness &c. *adj.*; variance, divergence, repugnance.

unfitness &c. *adj.*; inaptitude, impropriety; inapplicability &c. *adj.*; inconsistency, inconcinnity; irrelevancy &c. (*irrelation*) 10.

misjoin-ing, -der; syncretism, intrusion, interference; *concordia discors*.

fish out of water.

V. disagree; clash, jar &c. (*discord*) 713; interfere, intrude, come amiss; not concern &c. 10; mismatch; *humano capiti cervicem jungere equinam*.

Adj. disagreeing &c. *v.*; discordant, discrepant; at -variance, – war; hostile, antagonistic, repugnant, incompatible, irreconcilable, inconsistent with; unconformable, exceptional &c. 83; intrusive, incongruous; disproportion-ate, -ed; unharmonious; unconsonant; divergent, repugnant to.

inapt, unapt, inappropriate, improper; unsuit-ed, -able; inapplicable; un-fit, -fitting, -befitting; unbecoming; ill-timed, unseasonable, *mal à propos*, inadmissible; inapposite &c. (*irrelevant*) 10.

uncongenial; ill-assorted, -sorted; mis-matched, -joined, -placed; unaccommodating, irreducible, uncommensurable; unsympathetic.

out of -character, – keeping, – proportion, – joint, – tune, – place, – season, – its element; at -odds, – variance with.

Adv. in -defiance, – contempt, – spite- of; discordantly &c. *adj.*; *à tort et à travers*.

Phr. *asinus ad lyram.*

at home, in one's proper element.

Adv. *à propos* of; pertinently &c. *adj.*

Phr. *rem acu tetigisti;* the cap fits; *auxilia humilia firma consensus facit* [Syrus]; *discors concordia* [Ovid].

Section III. QUANTITY

1. Simple Quantity

25. [Absolute quantity.] **Quantity.** — **N.** quantity, magnitude; size &c. (*dimensions*) 192; amplitude, mass, amount, quantum, measure, substance, strength.

[Science of quantity.] mathematics, mathesis.

[Logic.] category, general conception, universal predicament.

[Definite or finite quantity.] arm-, hand-, mouth-, spoon-, cap-ful; stock, batch, lot, dose; yaffle.

V. quantify.

Adj. quantitative, some, any, more or less.

Adv. to the tune of.

26. [Relative quantity.] **Degree.** — **N.** degree, grade, extent, measure, amount, ratio, stint, standard, height, pitch; reach, amplitude, range, scope, caliber; gradation, shade; tenor, compass; sphere, station, rank, standing; rate, way, sort.

point, mark, stage &c. (*term*) 71; intensity, strength &c. (*greatness*) 31.

Adj. comparative; gradual, shading off; within the bounds &c. (*limit*) 233.

Adv. by degrees, gradually, inasmuch, *pro tanto;* how-ever, -soever; step by step, bit by bit, little by little, inch by inch, drop by drop; by -inches, – slow degrees, – little and little; in some -degree, – measure; to some extent; *di grado in grado.*

2. Comparative Quantity

27. [Sameness of quantity or degree.] **Equality.** — **N.** equality, parity, co-extension, symmetry, balance, poise; evenness, monotony, level.

equivalence; equi-pollence, -poise, -librium, -ponderance; par, quits; not a pin to choose; distinction without a difference, six of one and half a dozen of the other; identity &c. 13; similarity &c. 17.

equalization, equation; equilibration, coördination, adjustment, readjustment.

drawn -game, -battle; neck and neck race; tie, dead heat.

match, peer, compeer, equal, mate, fellow, brother; equivalent.

28. [Difference of quantity or degree.] **Inequality.** — **N.** inequality; dis-, imparity; odds; difference &c. 15; uneven-ness; inclination of the balance, partiality; shortcoming; casting –, make-weight; superiority &c. 33; inferiority &c. 34; inequation.

V. be -unequal &c. *adj.*; countervail; have –, give- the advantage; turn the scale; kick the beam; topple, -over; over-match &c. 33; not come up to &c. 34.

Adj. unequal, uneven, disparate, partial; un-, over-balanced; top-heavy, lopsided; disquiparant.

Adv. *haud passibus æquis* [Vergil].

V. be -equal &c. *adj.*; equal, match, reach, keep pace with, run abreast; come –, amount –, come up- to; be –, lie- on a level with; balance; cope with; come to the same thing.

render -equal &c. *adj.*; equalize, level, dress, balance, equate, handicap, give points, trim, adjust, poise; fit, accommodate; adapt &c. (*render accordant*) 23; strike a balance; establish –, restore- equality, – equilibrium; readjust; stretch on the bed of Procrustes.

Adj. equal, even, level, monotonous, coequal, symmetrical, coördinate; on a -par, – level, – footing- with; up to the mark; equiparant.

equivalent, tantamount; quits; homologous; synonymous &c. 522; resolv-able into, convertible, much at one, as broad as long, neither more nor less;

much the same –, the same thing –, as good- as; all -one, – the same; equipollent, -ponderant, -ponderous, -balanced; equalized &c. *v.*; drawn; half and half; isochron-al, -ous; isoperimetric, -al; isobath, -ic.

Adv. equally &c. *adj.*; *pari passu, ad eundem, cæteris paribus; in equilibrio;* to all intents and purposes.

Phr. it -comes, – amounts- to the same thing; what is sauce for the goose is sauce for the gander.

29. Mean. — N. mean, medium, intermedium, average, balance; mediocrity, generality; golden mean &c. (*mid-course*) 628; middle &c. 68; compromise &c. 774; middle -course, – state; neutrality.

V. split the difference; take the -average &c. *n.*; reduce to a -mean &c. *n.*; strike a balance, pair off.

Adj. mean, intermediate; middle &c. 68; average; neutral.
mediocre, middle-class; commonplace &c. (*unimportant*) 643.

Adv. on an average, in the long run; taking -one with another, – all things together, – it for all in all; *communibus annis*, in round numbers.

Phr. *medium tenuere beati.*

30. Compensation. — N. compensation, equation; commutation; indemnification; compromise &c. 774; neutralization, nullification; counteraction &c. 179; reaction; measure for measure; retaliation &c. 718; equalization &c. 27; robbing Peter to pay Paul.

set-off, offset; make-, casting-weight; counterpoise, ballast; indemnity, equivalent, *quid pro quo;* bribe, hush money; amends &c. (*atonement*) 952; counterbalance, – claim; cross -debt, – demand.

V. make compensation; com-pensate, -pense; indemnify; counter-act, -vail, -poise; balance; out-, over-, counter-balance; set off; hedge, square, give and take; make up -for, – lee way; cover, fill up, neutralize, nullify; equalize &c. 27; make good; redeem &c. (*atone*) 952.

Adj. compensat-ing, -ory; countervailing &c. *v.*; in the opposite scale; equivalent &c. (*equal*) 27.

Adv. in -return, – consideration; but, however, yet, still, notwithstanding; neverthe-, nath-less; although, though; al-, how-beit; mauger; at -all events, – any rate; be that as it may, for all that, even so, on the other hand, at the same time, *quoad minus, quand même*, however that may be; after all, – is said and done; taking one thing with another &c. (*average*) 29.

Phr. " light is mingled with the gloom " [Whittier]; *primo avulso non deficit alter* [Vergil]; *saepe creat molles aspera spina rosas* [Ovid].

QUANTITY BY COMPARISON WITH A STANDARD

31. Greatness. — N. greatness &c. *adj.*; magnitude; size &c. (*dimensions*) 192; multitude &c. (*number*) 102; immensity; enormity; infinity &c. 105; might, strength, intensity, fullness; importance &c. 642.

great quantity, quantity, deal, power, sight, pot, volume, world; mass, heap &c. (*assemblage*) 72; stock &c. (*store*) 636; peck, bushel, load, cargo; cart -, wagon –, ship- load; flood, spring tide; abundance &c. (*sufficiency*) 639.

principal –, chief –, main –, greater –, major –, best –, essential- part; bulk, mass &c. (*whole*) 50.

V. be -great &c. *adj.*; run high, soar, tower, transcend; rise –, carry- to a

32. Smallness. — N. smallness &c. *adj.*; littleness &c. (*small size*) 193; tenuity; paucity; fewness &c (*small number*) 103; meanness, insignificance &c. (*unimportance*) 643; mediocrity, moderation.

small quantity, modicum, minimum; vanishing point; material point, atom, particle, molecule, corpuscle, point, speck, dot, mote, jot, iota, ace; minutiæ, details; look, thought, idea, *soupçon*, dab, dight, whit, tittle, shade, shadow; spark, scintilla, gleam; touch, cast; grain, scruple, granule, globule, minim, sup, sip, sop, spice, drop, droplet, sprinkling, dash, *morceau*, screed, smack, tinge, tincture; inch, patch, scantling,

great height; know no bounds; ascend, mount.

enlarge &c. (*increase*) 35, (*expand*) 194.

Adj. great; greater &c. 33; large, considerable, fair, above par; big, huge &c. (*large in size*) 192; Herculean, cyclopean; ample; abundant &c. (*enough*) 639; full, intense, strong, sound, passing, heavy, plenary, deep, high; signal, at its height, in the zenith.

world-wide, widespread, far-famed, extensive; wholesale; many &c. 102.

goodly, noble, precious, mighty; sad, grave, serious; far gone, arrant, downright; utter, -most; crass, gross, arch, profound, intense, consummate; rank, unmitigated, red-hot, desperate; glaring, flagrant, stark staring; thorough-paced, -going; roaring, thumping; extraordinary; important &c. 642; unsurpassed &c. (*supreme*) 33; complete &c. 52.

august, grand, dignified, sublime, majestic &c. (*repute*) 873.

vast, immense, enormous, extreme; inordinate, excessive, extravagant, exorbitant, outrageous, preposterous, unconscionable, swinging, monstrous, overgrown; towering, stupendous, prodigious, astonishing, incredible; marvelous &c. (*wonder*) 870.

unlimited &c. (*infinite*) 105; unapproachable, unutterable, indescribable, ineffable, unspeakable, inexpressible, beyond expression, fabulous.

un-diminished, -abated, -reduced, -restricted.

absolute, positive, stark, decided, unequivocal, essential, perfect, finished.

remarkable, of mark, marked, pointed, veriest; noteworthy; renowned.

Adv. [in a positive degree] truly &c. (*truth*) 494; decidedly, unequivocally, purely, absolutely, seriously, essentially, fundamentally, radically, downright, in all conscience; for the most part, in the main.

[in a complete degree] entirely &c. (*completely*) 52; abundantly &c. (*sufficiently*) 639; widely, far and wide.

[in a great or high degree] greatly &c. adj.; much, muckle, well, indeed, very, very much, a deal, no end of, most, not a little; pretty, – well; enough, in a great measure, richly; to a -large, – great, – gigantic- extent; on a large scale; so; never –, ever- so; ever so dole; scrap, shred, tag, splinter, rag,

tatter, cantlet, flitter, gobbet, mite, bit, morsel, crumb, seed, fritter, shive; snip, -pet; snick, snack, snatch, slip, scrag; chip, -ping; shiver, sliver, driblet, clipping, paring, shaving, hair.

nutshell; thimble-, spoon-, hand-, cap-, mouth-ful; fragment; fraction &c. (*part*) 51; drop in the ocean.

animalcule &c. 193.

trifle &c. (*unimportant thing*) 643; mere –, next to- nothing; hardly anything; just enough to swear by; the shadow of a shade.

finiteness, finite quantity.

V. be -small &c. *adj.*; lie in a nutshell.

diminish &c. (*decrease*) 36; (*contract*) 195.

Adj. small, little; diminutive &c. (*small in size*) 193; minute; fine; inconsiderable, paltry &c. (*unimportant*) 643; faint &c. (*weak*) 160; slender, light, slight, scanty, scant, limited; meager &c. (*insufficient*) 640; sparing; few &c. 103; low, so-so, middling, tolerable, no great shakes; below –, under- -par, – the mark; at a lów ebb; halfway; moderate, modest; tender, subtle.

inappreciable, evanescent, infinitesimal, homeopathic, very small; atomic, corpuscular, microscopic, molecular.

mere, simple, sheer, stark, bare; near run.

dull, petty, shallow, stolid, ungifted, unintelligent.

Adv. [in a small degree] to a small extent, on a small scale; a -little, – wee bit; slightly &c. *adj.*; imperceptibly; miserably, wretchedly; insufficiently &c. 640; imperfectly; faintly &c. 160; passably, pretty well, well enough.

[in a certain or limited degree] partially, in part; in -, to- a certain degree; to a certain extent; comparatively; some, rather; in some -degree, – measure; some-thing, -what; simply, only, purely, merely; at -, at the- -least, – most; ever so little, as little as may be, *tant soit peu*, in ever so small a degree; thus far, *pro tanto*, within bounds, in a manner, after a fashion.

almost, nearly, well-nigh, short of, not quite, all but; near -, close- upon; *peu s'en faut*, near the mark; within an -ace, – inch- of; on the brink of; scarcely, hardly, barely, only just, no more than.

[in an uncertain degree] about, there-

much; by wholesale, mighty, powerfully; with a witness, *ultra*, in the extreme, extremely, exceedingly, intensely,
exquisitely, acutely, indefinitely, im-
measurably; beyond -compare, – comparison, – measure, – all bounds; incal-
culably, infinitely.

[in a supreme degree] preëminently,
superlatively &c. (*superiority*) 33.

[in a too great degree] immoderately,
monstrously, preposterously, inordi-
nately, exorbitantly, excessively, enor-
mously, out of all proportion, with a vengeance.

[in a marked degree] particularly, remarkably, singularly, curiously, un-
commonly, unusually, peculiarly, notably, signally, strikingly, pointedly,
mainly, chiefly; famously, egregiously, prominently, glaringly, emphatically,
κατ' ἐξοχήν, strangely, wonderfully, amazingly, surprisingly, astonishingly, in-
credibly, marvelously, awfully, stupendously.

[in an exceptional degree] peculiarly &c. (*unconformity*) 83.

[in a violent degree] furiously &c. (*violence*) 173; severely, desperately, tremendously, extravagantly, confoundedly, deucedly, devilishly, with a vengeance; *à –, à toute- outrance.*

[in a painful degree] painfully, sadly, grossly, sorely, bitterly, piteously,
grievously, miserably, cruelly, woefully, lamentably, shockingly, frightfully,
dreadfully, fearfully, terribly, horribly.

Phr. *a maximis ad minima;* " greatness knows itself " [*Henry IV*]; " mightiest powers by
deepest calms are fed " [B. Cornwall]; *minimum decet libere cui multum licet* [Seneca]; " some
are born great, some achieve greatness, and some have greatness thrust upon them " [*Twelfth
Night*].

abouts, somewhere about, nearly, say;
be the same -more, – little more- or less.

[in no degree] no- ways, – wise; not
-at all, – in the least, – a bit, – a bit of it,
– a whit, – a jot, – a shadow; in no -wise,
– respect; by no -means, – manner of
means; on no account, at no hand.

Phr. *dare pondus idonea fumo* [Persius];
magno conatu magnas nugas [Terence]; " small
sands the mountain, moments make the year "
[Young].

QUANTITY BY COMPARISON WITH A SIMILAR OBJECT

33. Superiority. [Supremacy.] — **N.**
superiority, majority; greatness &c.
31; advantage; pull *; preponder-ance,
-ation; vantage ground, prevalence,
partiality; personal superiority; nobility &c. (*rank*) 875; Triton among the
minnows, *primus inter pares, nulli secundus,* captain; crackajack * [U. S.].

supremacy, preëminence; lead; *maximum;* record; τρικυμία, climax; culmination &c. (*summit*) 210; transcendence;
ne plus ultra; lion's share, Benjamin's
mess; excess, surplus &c. (*remainder*) 40;
(*redundance*) 641.

V. be -superior &c. *adj.*; exceed, excel, transcend; out-do, -balance, -weigh,
-rank, -rival, -Herod; pass, surpass,
get ahead of; over-top, -ride, -pass,
-balance, -weigh, -match; top, o'er-
top, cap, beat, cut out; beat hollow;
outstrip &c. 303; eclipse, throw into
the shade, take the shine out of, put
one's nose out of joint; have the -upper
hand, – whip hand of, – advantage;
turn the scale, kick the beam; play first
fiddle &c. (*importance*) 642; prepon-

34. Inferiority. — **N.** inferiority, minority, subordinacy; shortcoming, deficiency; minimum; smallness &c. 32;
imperfection; lower -quality, – worth.

[personal inferiority] commonalty &c.
876.

V. be -inferior &c. *adj.*; fall –, come-
short of; not -pass, – come up to; want.

become –, render- -smaller &c. (*decrease*) 36, (*contract*) 195; hide its diminished head, retire into the shade,
yield the palm, play second fiddle, take
a back seat.

Adj. inferior, smaller; small &c. 32;
minor, less, lesser, deficient, minus,
lower, subordinate, secondary; second-
rate &c. (*imperfect*) 651; sub, subaltern;
thrown into the shade; weighed in the
balance and found wanting; not fit to
hold a candle to.

least, smallest &c. (*see* little, small
&c. 193); lowest.

diminished &c. (*decreased*) 36; reduced &c. (*contracted*) 195; unimportant
&c. 643.

Adv. less; under –, below- -the mark,

derate, predominate, prevail; precede, take precedence, come first; come to a head, culminate; beat &c. all others, bear the palm; break the record; take the cake * [U. S.].

– par; at -the bottom of the scale, – a low ebb, – a disadvantage; short of, under.

become –, render- -larger &c. (*increase*) 35, (*expand*) 194.

Adj. superior, greater, major, higher; exceeding &c. *v.*; great &c. 31; distinguished, ultra; vaulting; more than a match for.

supreme, greatest, utmost, paramount, preëminent, foremost, crowning; first-rate &c. (*important*) 642, (*excellent*) 648; unrivaled; peer-, match-less; none such, second to none, *sans pareil*; un-paragoned, -paralleled, -equalled, -approached, -surpassed; superlative, inimitable, *facile princeps*, incomparable, sovereign, without parallel, *nulli secundus, ne plus ultra*; beyond -compare, – comparison; culminating &c. (*topmost*) 210; transcend-ent, -ental; *plus royaliste que le Roi.*

increased &c. (*added to*) 35; enlarged &c. (*expanded*) 194.

Adv. beyond, more, over; over –, above- the mark; above par; upwards –, in advance- of; over and above; at the top of the scale, at its height.

[in a superior or supreme degree] eminently, egregiously, preëminently, surpassing, prominently, superlatively, supremely, above all, of all things, the most, to crown all, κατ᾽ ἐξοχήν, *par excellence*, principally, especially, particularly, peculiarly, *à fortiori*, even, yea, still more.

Phr. " I shall not look upon his like again " [*Hamlet*]; *deos fortioribus adesse* [Tacitus].

Changes in Quantity

35. Increase. — N.

increase, augmentation, enlargement, extension; dilatation &c. (*expansion*) 194; increment, accretion; accession &c. 37; development, growth; aggrandizement, aggravation; rise; ascent &c. 305; ex-aggeration, -acerbation; spread &c. (*dispersion*) 73; flood tide; gain, produce, product, profit.

V. increase, augment, add to, enlarge; dilate &c. (*expand*) 194; grow, wax, get ahead, gain strength; advance; run –, shoot- up; rise; ascend &c. 305; sprout &c. 194.

aggrandize; raise, exalt; deepen, heighten; strengthen; intensify, enhance, magnify, redouble; aggravate, exaggerate; ex-asperate, -acerbate; add fuel to the flame, *oleum addere camino*, superadd &c. (*add*) 37; spread &c. (*disperse*) 73.

Adj. increased &c. *v.*; on the increase, undiminished; additional &c. (*added*) 37.

Adv. crescendo.

Phr. *vires acquirit eundo* [Vergil].

36. Nonincrease, Decrease. — N.

decrease, diminution; lessening &c. *v.*; subtraction &c. 38; reduction, abatement, declension; shrinking &c. (*contraction*) 195; coarctation †; abridgment &c. (*shortening*) 201; extenuation.

subsidence, wane, ebb, decline; ebbing; descent &c. 306; decrement, reflux, depreciation; deterioration &c. 659; anticlimax; mitigation &c. (*moderation*) 174.

V. decrease, diminish, lessen; abridge &c. (*shorten*) 201; shrink &c. (*contract*) 195; drop –, fall –, tail- off; fall away, waste, wear; wane, ebb, decline; descend &c. 306; subside; melt –, die- away; retire into the shade, hide its diminished head, fall to a low ebb, run low, languish, decay, crumble.

bate, abate, dequantitate †; discount; depreciate; extenuate, lower, weaken, attenuate, fritter away; mitigate &c. (*moderate*) 174; dwarf, throw into the shade; reduce &c. 195; shorten &c. 201; subtract &c. 38.

Adj. unincreased &c. (*see* increase &c. 35); decreased &c. *v.*; decreasing &c. *v.*; on the -wane &c. n.

Phr. " a gilded halo hovering round decay " [Byron]; " fine by degrees and beautifully less " [Prior].

3. Conjunctive Quantity

37. Addition. — N. addition, annexation, adjection; junction &c. 43; super-position, -addition, -junction, -fetation; accession, reinforcement; increase &c. 35; increment, supplement; accompaniment &c. 88; interposition &c. 228; insertion &c. 300.

V. add, annex, affix, superadd, sub-join, superpose; clap –, saddle– on; tack to, append, tag; ingraft; saddle with; sprinkle; introduce &c. (*interpose*) 228; insert &c. 300.

become added, accrue; ad-, supervene.

re-enforce, -strengthen; reinforce, swell the ranks of; augment &c. 35.

Adj. added &c. *v.*; additional; supplement, -al, -ary; suppletory, subjunctive; adjec-, adsci-, asci-titious; additive, extra, accessory.

Adv. *au reste;* in addition, more, plus, extra; and, also, likewise, too, furthermore, further, item; and -also, – eke; else, besides, to boot, et cætera; &c.; and so -on, – forth; into the bargain, *cum multis aliis*, over and above, moreover.

with, withal; including, inclusive, as well as, not to mention, let alone; together –, along –, coupled –, in conjunction- with; conjointly; jointly &c. 43.

Phr. *adde parvum parvo magnus acervus erit.*

38. Nonaddition. Subduction. — N. sub-duction, -traction; deduction, retrenchment; removal; ab-, sub-lation; abstraction &c. (*taking*) 789; garbling &c. *v.*; mutilation, detruncation; amputation; abs-, ex-, re-cision; curtailment &c. 201; minuend, subtrahend; decrease &c. 36; abrasion.

V. sub-duct, -tract; de-duct, -duce; bate, retrench; remove, withdraw; take -from, – away; detract.

garble, mutilate, amputate, detruncate; cut -off, – away, – out; abscind, excise; pare, thin, prune, decimate; abrade, scrape, file; geld, castrate; eliminate.

diminish &c. 36; curtail &c. (*shorten*) 201; deprive of &c. (*take*) 789; weaken.

Adj. subtracted &c. *v.*; subtractive.

Adv. in -deduction &c. *n.*; less; short of; minus, without, except, excepting, with the exception of, barring, save, exclusive of, save and except, with a reservation.

---

39. [Thing added.] Adjunct. — N. adjunct; addit-ion, -ament; *additum*, affix, appendage, annexe, annex; augment, -ation; increment, reinforcement, supernumerary, accessory, item; garnish, sauce; accompaniment &c. 88; adjective, addendum; complement, supplement; continuation.

rider, offshoot, episode, side issue, corollary; piece; flap, lappet, skirt, embroidery, trappings, *cortège;* tail, suffix &c. (*sequel*) 65; wing.

Adj. additional &c. 37.

alate, -d; winged.

Adv. in addition &c. 37.

40. [Thing remaining.] Remainder. — N. remainder, residue; remains, remanet, remnant, rest, relic; leavings, heeltap, odds and ends, cheeseparings, candle ends, orts; residuum; dregs &c. (*dirt*) 653; refuse &c. (*useless*) 645; stubble, result, educt; fag-end; ruins, wreck, skeleton, stump; alluvium.

surplus, overplus, excess; balance, complement; superplus, surplusage; superfluity &c. (*redundance*) 641; surviv-al, -ance.

V. remain; be -left &c. *adj.*; exceed, survive; leave.

Adj. remaining, left; left -behind, – over; residu-al, -ary; over, odd; uncon-sumed, sedimentary; surviving; net; exceeding, over and above; out-lying, -standing; cast off &c. 782; superfluous &c. (*redundant*) 641.

40a. [Thing deducted.] Decrement. — N. decrement, discount, defect, loss, deduction; afterglow; eduction; waste.

41. [Forming a whole without coherence.] Mixture. — N. mix-, admix-, commix-ture, -tion; commixion, inter-

42. [Freedom from mixture.] Simpleness. — N. simpleness &c. *adj.*; purity, homogeneity.

mixture, alloyage, matrimony; junction &c. 43; combination &c. 48; miscegenation.

impregnation; in-, dif-, suf-, transfusion; infiltration; seasoning, sprinkling, interlarding; interpolation &c. 228; adulteration, sophistication.

[Thing mixed] tinge, tincture, touch, dash, smack, sprinkling, spice, seasoning, infusion, soupçon.

[Compound resulting from mixture] alloy, amalgam; brass, chowchow, pewter; magma, half-and-half, mélange, tertium quid, miscellany, ambigu †, medley, mess, hotchpot, pasticcio, patchwork, odds and ends, all sorts; jumble

elimination; sifting &c. v.; purification &c. (cleanness) 652.

V. render -simple &c. adj.; simplify.

sift, winnow, bolt, eliminate; exclude, get rid of; clear; purify &c. (clean) 652; disentangle &c. (disjoin) 44.

Adj. simple, uniform, of a piece, homogeneous, single, pure, clear, sheer, neat.

un-mixed, -mingled, -blended, -combined, -compounded; elementary, undecomposed; un-adulterated, -sophisticated, -alloyed, -tinged, -fortified; pur et simple; incomplex.

free -, exempt- from; exclusive.

Adv. simple &c. adj.; only.

&c. (disorder) 59; salad, sauce, mash, omnium gatherum, gallimaufry, olla-podrida, olio, salmagundi, potpourri, Noah's ark, caldron; texture, mingled yarn; mosaic &c. (variegation) 440.

half-blood, -caste; mulatto; terc-, quart-, quint-eron &c.; quad-, octoroon; griffo, zambo; cafuzo; Eurasian; fust-ee, -ie; griffe, ladino, marabou, mestee, mestizo, quintroon, sacatra [U. S.]; zebrule; catalo; cross, hybrid, mongrel.

V. mix; join &c. 43; combine &c. 48; com-, im-, inter-mix; mix up with; mingle; com-, inter-, be-mingle; shuffle &c. (derange) 61; pound together; hash -, stir- up; knead, brew; impregnate with; interlard &c. (interpolate) 228; inter-twine, -weave &c. 219; associate with; miscegenate.

be mixed &c.; get among, be entangled with.

instil, imbue; in-, suf-, trans-fuse; infiltrate, dash, tinge, tincture, season, sprinkle, besprinkle, attemper, medicate, blend, cross; alloy, amalgamate, compound, adulterate, sophisticate, infect.

Adj. mixed &c. v.; implex, composite, half-and-half, linsey-woolsey, chowchow, hybrid, mongrel, heterogeneous; motley &c. (variegated) 440; miscellaneous, promiscuous, indiscriminate; miscible.

Adv. among, amongst, amid, amidst; with; in the midst of, in the crowd.

43. Junction. — **N.** junction; joining &c. v.; joinder, union; con-nection, -junction, -jugation; annex-ion, -ation, -ment; astriction, attachment, compagination, vincture, ligation, alligation; accouplement; marriage &c. (wedlock) 903; infibulation, inosculation, symphysis, anastomosis, confluence, communication, concatenation; meeting, reunion; assemblage &c. 72.

coition, copulation; sexual -congress, - conjunction, - intercourse.

joint, joining, juncture, pivot, hinge, articulation, commissure, seam, gore, gusset, suture, stitch; link &c. 45; miter, mortise.

closeness, tightness, &c. adj.; coherence &c. 46; combination &c. 48.

annexationist.

V. join, unite; con-join, -nect; associate; put -, lay -, clap -, hang -, lump -,

44. Disjunction. — **N.** dis-junction, -connection, -unity, -union, -association, -engagement; discontinuity &c. 70; abjunction; cataclasm; inconnection; abstract-ion, -edness; isolation; insul-arity, -ation; oasis; island; separateness &c. adj.; severalty; disjecta membra; dispersion &c. 73; apportionment &c. 786.

separation; parting &c. v.; circumcision; detachment, segregation; divorce, sejunction †, seposition †, diduction, diremption, discerption; elision; cæsura; division, subdivision, break, fracture, rupture; compartition †; dis-member-ment, -integration, -location; luxation; sever-, dissever-ance; scission; re-, abscission; lacer-, dilacer-ation; dis-, abruption; avulsion, divulsion; section, resection, cleavage; fission; partibility separability.

hold –, piece –, tack –, fix –, bind up- together; embody, reëmbody; roll into one.

attach, fix, affix, saddle on, fasten, bind, secure, clinch, twist, make -fast &c. *adj.*; tie, pinion, string, strap, sew, lace, stitch, tack, knit, button, buckle, hitch, lash, truss, bandage, braid, splice, swathe, gird, tether, moor, picket, harness, chain; fetter &c. (*restrain*) 751; lock, latch, belay, brace, hook, grapple, leash, couple, accouple, link, yoke, bracket; marry &c. (*wed*) 903; bridge over, span.

braze; pin, nail, bolt, hasp, clasp, clamp, screw, rivet; impact, solder, set; weld –, fuse- together; wedge, rabbet, mortise, miter, jam, dovetail, enchase; graft, ingraft, inosculate; en-, in-twine; inter-link, -lace, -twine, -twist, -weave; entangle; twine round, belay; tighten; trice -, screw- up.

be -joined &c.; hang –, hold- together; cohere &c. 46.

Adj. joined &c. *v.*; joint; con-joint, -junct; corporate, compact; hand in hand.

firm, fast, close, tight, taut, taught, secure, set, intervolved †; in-separable, -dissoluble, -secable, -severable.

Adv. jointly &c. *adj.*; in conjunction with &c. (*in addition to*) 37; fast, firmly, &c. *adj.*; intimately.

Phr. *tria juncta in uno.*

fissure, breach, rent, split, rift, crack, slit, incision.

dissection, anatomy; decomposition &c. 49; cutting instrument &c. (*sharpness*) 253; buzz-, circular-saw.

separatist.

V. be -disjoined &c.; come –, fall- -off, – to pieces; peel off; get loose.

dis-join, -connect, -engage, -unite, -sociate, -pair; divorce, part, dispart, detach, separate, cut off, rescind, segregate; set -, keep- apart; insulate, isolate; throw out of gear; cut adrift; loose; unloose, -do, -bind, -chain, -lock &c. (*fix*) 43, -pack, -ravel; disentangle; set free &c. (*liberate*) 750.

sunder, divide, subdivide, sever, dissever, abscind; circumcise; cut; in-cide †, -cise; saw, snip, nib, nip, cleave, rive, rend, slit, split, splinter, chip, crack, snap, break, tear, burst; rend &c. -asunder, – in twain; wrench, rupture, shatter, shiver, cranch, crunch, craunch, chop; cut -, rip- up; hack, hew, slash; whittle; haggle, hackle, discind †, lacerate, scamble, mangle, gash, hash, slice.

cut up, carve, dissect, anatomize; dislimb; take -, pull -, pick -, tear- to pieces; tear -to tatters, – piecemeal; divellicate; skin &c. 226; dis-integrate, -member, -branch, -band; disperse &c. 73; dis-locate, -joint; break up; mince; comminute &c. (*pulverize*) 330; apportion &c. 786.

part, – company; separate, leave.

Adj. disjoined &c. *v.*; discontinuous &c. 70; multipartite, abstract; disjunctive; secant; isolated &c. *v.*; insular, separate, disparate, discrete, apart, asunder, far between, loose, free; un-attached, -annexed, -associated, -connected; distinct; adrift; straggling; rift, reft.

[capable of being cut] scissile, divisible, discerptible, partible, separable.

Adv. separately &c. *adj.*; one by one, severally, apart; adrift, asunder, in twain; in the abstract, abstractedly.

45. [Connecting medium.] **Vinculum. — N.** vinculum, link; connec-tive, -tion; junction &c. 43; bond of union, copula, intermedium, hyphen; bracket; bridge, stepping-stone, isthmus.

bond, tendon, tendril; fiber; cord, -age; ribband, ribbon, rope, guy, cable, line, halser †, hawser, painter, moorings, wire, chain; string &c. (*filament*) 205.

fastening, tie; liga-ment, -ture; strap; tackle, rigging; standing –, running-rigging; traces, harness; yoke; band ,-age; brace, roller, fillet; inkle; with, withe, withy; thong, braid; girder, tiebeam; girth, girdle, cestus, garter, halter, noose, lasso, surcingle, knot, running knot; cabestro [U. S.], cinch [U. S.], lariat, *legadero*, oxreim; suspenders.

pin, corking pin, nail, brad, tack, skewer, staple, clamp; cramp, cramp iron, detent, *larigo*, pawl, terret, treenail, screw, button, buckle, clasp, hasp, hinge, hank, catch, latch, bolt, latchet, tag; tooth; hook, – and eye; lock, holdfast, padlock, rivet; anchor, grappling iron, trennel, stake, post.

cement, glue, gum, paste, size, wafer, solder, lute, putty, birdlime, mortar, stucco, plaster, grout; viscum.

shackle, rein &c. (*means of restraint*) 752; prop &c. (*support*) 215.

V. bridge over, span; connect &c. 43; hang &c. 214.

46. Coherence. — N. co-, ad-her-ence, -hesion, -hesiveness; concretion, accretion; con-, ag-glutination, -glomeration; aggregation; consolidation, set, cementation; sticking, soldering &c. *v.*; connection; dependence.

tenacity, toughness; stickiness &c. 352; insepara-bility, -bleness; bur, remora.

conglomerate, concrete &c. (*density*) 321.

V. cohere, adhere, stick, cling, cleave, hold, take hold of, hold fast, close with, clasp, hug; grow -, hang- together; twine round &c. (*join*) 43.

stick like -a leech, - wax; stick close; cling like -ivy, - a bur; adhere like -a remora, - Dejanira's shirt.

glue; ag-, con-glutinate; cement, lute, paste, gum; solder, weld; cake, consolidate &c. (*solidify*) 321; agglomerate.

Adj. co-, ad-hesive, -hering &c. *v.*; tenacious, tough; sticky &c. 352.

united, unseparated, sessile, inseparable, inextricable, infrangible; compact &c. (*dense*) 321.

47. [Want of adhesion, nonadhesion, immiscibility.] **Incoherence. — N.** nonadhesion; immiscibility; incoherence; looseness &c. *adj.*; laxity; relaxation; loosening &c. *v.*; freedom; disjunction &c. 44; rope of sand.

V. make -loose &c. *adj.*; loosen, slacken, relax; un-glue &c. 46; detach &c. (*disjoin*) 44.

Adj. nonadhesive, immiscible; incoherent, detached, loose, baggy, slack, lax, relaxed, flapping, streaming; disheveled; segregated, like grains of sand; un-consolidated &c. 231, -combined &c. 48; noncohesive.

48. Combination. — N. combination; mixture &c. 41; junction &c. 43; union, unification, synthesis, incorporation, amalgamation, embodiment, coalescence, crasis, fusion, blending, absorption, centralization.

alloy, compound, amalgam, composition, *tertium quid;* resultant, impregnation.

V. combine, unite, incorporate, amalgamate, embody, absorb, reëmbody, blend, merge, fuse, melt into one, consolidate, coalesce, centralize, impregnate; put -, lump- together; cement a union, marry.

Adj. combined &c. *v.*; impregnated with, ingrained; imbued, inoculated.

49. Decomposition. — N. decomposition, analysis, dissection, resolution, catalysis, dissolution; corruption &c. (*uncleanness*) 653; dispersion &c. 73; disjunction &c. 44; disintegration.

V. decom-pose, -pound; analyze, disembody, dissolve; resolve -, separate-into its elements; electrolyze; dissect, decentralize, break up; disperse &c. 73; unravel &c. (*unroll*) 313; crumble into dust.

Adj. decomposed &c. *v.*; catalytic, analytical; resolvent, separative, solvent.

4. Concrete Quantity

50. Whole. [Principal part.] **— N.** whole, totality, integrity; totalness &c. *adj.*; entirety, *ensemble*, collectiveness; unity &c. 87; completeness &c. 52; indivisibility, indiscerptibility; integration, embodiment; integer.

all, the whole, total, aggregate, one and all, gross amount, sum, sum total, *tout ensemble*, length and breadth of,

51. Part. — N. part, portion; dose; item, particular; aught, any; division, ward; subdivision, section; chapter, verse; article, clause, count, paragraph, passage; sector, segment; fraction, fragment; cantle, -t; frustum; detachment, parcel.

piece, lump, bit; cut, -ting; chip, chunk, collop, slice, scale; lamina &c.

Alpha and Omega, " be all and end all "; complex, *complexus;* lock stock and barrel.

bulk, mass, lump, tissue, staple, body, compages; trunk, torso, bole, hull, hulk, skeleton; greater –, major –, best –, principal –, main- part; essential part &c. (*importance*) 642; lion's share, Benjamin's mess; the long and the short; nearly –, almost- all.

V. form –, constitute- a whole; integrate, embody, amass; aggregate &c. (*assemble*) 72; amount to, come to.

Adj. whole, total, integral, entire; complete &c. 52; one, individual.

un-broken, -cut, -divided, -severed, -clipped -cropped, -shorn; seamless; undiminished; un-demolished, -dissolved, -destroyed, -bruised.

in-divisible, -dissoluble, -dissolvable, -discerptible.

wholesale, sweeping; comprehensive.

Adv. wholly, altogether; totally &c. (*completely*) 52; entirely, all, all in all, wholesale, in a body, collectively, all put together; in the -aggregate, – lump, – mass, – gross, – main, – long run; *en masse*, on the whole, bodily, *en bloc, in extenso*, throughout, every inch; substantially.

Phr. *tout bien ou rien.*

204; small part; morsel, particle &c. (*smallness*) 32; installment, dividend; share &c. (*allotment*) 786.

débris, odds and ends, oddments, *detritus; excerpta;* member, limb, lobe, lobule, arm, wing, scion, branch, bough, joint, link, offshoot, ramification, twig, bush, spray, sprig; runner; leaf, -let; stump; component part &c. 56; sarmentum.

compartment; department &c. (*class*) 75; county &c. (*region*) 181.

V. part, divide, break &c. (*disjoin*) 44; partition &c. (*apportion*) 786.

Adj. fractional, fragmentary; sectional, aliquot; divided &c. *v.*; in compartments, multifid; disconnected; partial.

Adv. partly, in part, partially; piecemeal, part by part; by -installments, – snatches, – inches, – driblets; bit by bit, inch by inch, foot by foot, drop by drop; in -detail, – lots.

52. Completeness. — N.
completeness &c. *adj.*; completion &c. 729; integration; allness.

entirety; perfection &c. 650; solid-ity, -arity; unity; all; *ne plus ultra*, ideal, limit.

complement, supplement, make-weight; filling up &c. *v.*

impletion; satur-ation, -ity †; high water; high –, flood –, spring- tide; fill, load, bumper, bellyful; brimmer; sufficiency &c. 639.

V. be –complete &c. *adj.*; come to a head.

render -complete &c. *adj.*; complete &c. (*accomplish*) 729; fill, charge, load, replenish; make -up, – good; piece –, eke- out; supply deficiencies; fill -up, – in, – to the brim, – the measure of; saturate.

go the whole -hog, – length; go all lengths.

Adj. complete, entire; whole &c. 50; perfect &c. 650; full, good, absolute, thorough, plenary; solid, undivided; with all its parts; all-sided.

exhaustive, radical, sweeping, thorough-going; dead.

53. Incompleteness. — N.
incompleteness &c. *adj.*; deficiency, short measure; shortcoming &c. 304; insufficiency &c. 640; imperfection &c. 651; immaturity &c. (*nonpreparation*) 674; half measures.

[part wanting] defect, deficit, defalcation, omission; caret; shortage; interval &c. 198; break &c. (*discontinuity*) 70; noncompletion &c. 730; missing link.

V. be -incomplete &c. *adj.*; fall short of &c. 304; lack &c. (*be insufficient*) 640; neglect &c. 460.

Adj. incomplete; imperfect &c. 651; unfinished; uncompleted &c. (*see complete &c. 729*); defective, deficient, wanting, failing; in -default, – arrear; short, – of; hollow, meager, lame, half-and-half, perfunctory, sketchy; crude &c. (*unprepared*) 674.

mutilated, garbled, docked, lopped, truncated.

in -progress, – hand; going on, proceeding.

Adv. incompletely &c. *adj.*; by halves.

Phr. *cœtera desunt; caret.*

regular, consummate, unmitigated, sheer, unqualified, unconditional, free; abundant &c. (*sufficient*) 639.

brimming; brim-, top-ful; chock –, choke- full; as full as -an egg is of meat, – a vetch; saturated, crammed; replete &c. (*redundant*) 641; fraught, laden; full-laden, -fraught, -charged; heavy laden.

completing &c. *v.*; supplement-al, -ary; ascititious.

Adv. completely &c. *adj.*; altogether, outright, wholly, totally, *in toto*, quite; all out; over head and ears; effectually, for good and all, nicely, fully, through thick and thin, head and shoulders; neck and -heel, – crop; in -all respects, – every respect; at all points, out and out, to all intents and purposes; *toto cœlo;* utterly; clean, – as a whistle; to the -full, – utmost, – backbone; hollow, stark; heart and soul, root and branch, down to the ground.

to the top of one's bent, as far as possible, *à outrance*.

throughout; from -first to last, – beginning to end, – end to end, – one end to the other, – Dan to Beersheba, – head to foot, – top to toe, – top to bottom; *de fond en comble; à fond, a capite ad calcem, ab ovo usque ad mala*, fore and aft; every -whit, – inch; *cap-à-pie*, to the end of the chapter; up to the -brim, – ears, – eyes; as . . . as can be.

on all accounts; *sous tous les rapports;* with a -vengeance, – witness.

Phr. *falsus in uno falsus in omnibus; omnem movere lapidem; una scopa nuova spazza bene.*

---

54. Composition. — N. composition, constitution, crasis; combination &c. 48; inclusion, admission, comprehension, reception; embodiment; formation.

V. be -composed, – made, – formed, – made up- of; consist of, be resolved into.

include &c. (*in a class*) 76; contain, hold, comprehend, take in, admit, embrace, embody; involve, implicate; drag into.

compose, constitute, form, make; make –, fill –, build- up; enter into the composition of &c. (*be a component*) 56.

Adj. containing, constituting &c. *v.*

55. Exclusion. — N. exclusion, nonadmission, omission, exception, rejection, repudiation; exile &c. (*seclusion*) 893; noninclusion, preclusion, prohibition.

separation, segregation, seposition †, elimination, expulsion; cofferdam.

V. be excluded from &c.

exclude, bar; leave –, shut –, bar- out; reject, repudiate, blackball; lay –, put –, set- -apart, – aside; relegate, segregate; throw overboard; strike -off, – out; neglect &c. 460; banish &c. (seclude) 893; separate &c. (*disjoin*) 44.

pass over, omit; garble; eliminate, weed, winnow.

Adj. excluding &c. *v.*; exclusive.

---

excluded &c. *v.*; unrecounted, not included in; inadmissible.

Adv. exclusive of, barring; except; with the exception of; save; bating.

---

56. Component. — N. component; component -, integral -, integrant- part; element, constituent, ingredient, leaven; part and parcel; contents; appurtenance; feature; member &c. (*part*) 51; personnel.

V. enter into, – the composition of; be a -component &c. *n.*; be –, form- part &c. 51 of; merge –, be merged- in; be implicated in; share in &c. (*participate*) 778; belong –, appertain- to; combine, inhere in, unite.

form, make, constitute, compose.

Adj. forming &c. *v.*; inclusive.

57. Extraneousness. — N. extraneousness &c. *adj.*; extrinsicality &c. 6; exteriority &c. 220; alienage, alienism.

foreign -body, – substance, – element; alien, stranger, intruder, interloper, foreigner, *novus homo*, newcomer, immi-, emi-grant; creole, Africander; outsider; Dago *, Easterner [U. S.], Dutchman, tenderfoot.

Adj. extraneous, foreign, alien, ulterior; tra-, ultra-montane.

excluded &c. 55; inadmissible; exceptional.

Adv. in foreign -parts, – lands; abroad, beyond seas; over sea; on one's travels.

Section IV. ORDER

1. ORDER IN GENERAL

58. Order. — **N.** order, regularity, uniformity, symmetry, *lucidus ordo;* music of the spheres.

gradation, progression; series &c. (*continuity*) 69.

subordination; course, even tenor, routine; method, disposition, arrangement, array, system, economy, discipline; orderliness &c. *adj.*

rank, place &c. (*term*) 71.

V. be —, become- in order &c. *adj.;* form, fall in, draw up; arrange –, range –, place- itself; fall into –, take- -one's place, – rank; rally round.

adjust, methodize, regulate, systematize.

Adj. orderly, regular; in -order, – trim, – apple-pie order, – its proper place; neat, tidy, *en règle,* well regulated, correct, methodical, uniform, symmetrical, shipshape, businesslike, systematic; unconfused &c. (*see* confuse &c. 61); arranged &c. 60.

Adv. in order; methodically &c. *adj.;* in -turn, – its turn; step by step; by regular -steps, – gradations, – stages. – intervals; *seriatim,* systematically, by clockwork, *gradatim;* at stated periods &c. (*periodically*) 138.

Phr. *natura non facit saltum;* "order is heaven's first law" [Pope]; "order from disorder sprung" [*Paradise Lost*]; *ordo est parium dispariumque rerum sua loca tribuens dispositio* [St. Augustine].

59. [Absence, or want of Order, &c.] **Disorder.** — **N.** disorder; derangement &c. 61; irregularity; anomaly &c. (*unconformity*) 83; anar-chy, -chism; want of method; untidiness &c. *adj.;* disunion; discord &c. 24.

confusion; confusedness &c. *adj.;* mishmash, mix; disarray, jumble, huddle, litter, lumber; *cahotage;* farrago; mess, mash, muddle, muss [U. S.], hash, hodgepodge; hotch-potch, -pot; imbroglio, chaos, *omnium gatherum,* medley; mere -mixture &c. 41; fortuitous concourse of atoms, *disjecta membra, rudis indigestaque moles* [Ovid].

complexity; complexness &c. *adj.; complexus;* com-, im-plication; intricacy, -cation; perplexity; network, labyrinth; wilderness, jungle; involution, raveling, entanglement; coil &c. (*convolution*) 248; sleave, tangled skein, knot, Gordian knot, wheels within wheels; kink, knarl; webwork.

turmoil; ferment &c. (*agitation*) 315; to do, trouble, pudder, pother, row, disturbance, convulsion, tumult, uproar, riot, rumpus, stour, scramble, fracas, embroilment, *mêlée,* spill and pelt, rough and tumble; whirlwind &c. 349; bear garden, Babel, Saturnalia, Donnybrook Fair, confusion worse confounded, most admired disorder, *concordia discors;* Bedlam –, hell- broke loose; bull in a china shop; all the fat in the fire, *diable à quatre,* Devil to pay; pretty kettle of fish; pretty piece of -work,– business.

slattern, slut.

V. be -disorderly &c. *adj.;* ferment, play at cross-purposes.

put out of order; derange &c. 61; ravel &c. 219; ruffle, rumple.

Adj. disorderly, orderless; out of -order, – place, – gear; irregular, desultory; anomalous &c. (*unconformable*) 83; acephalous; aimless; disorganized; straggling; un-, im-methodical; unsymmetric, unsystematic; untidy, slovenly; dislocated; out of sorts; promiscuous, indiscriminate; chaotic, anarchical; unarranged &c. (*see* arrange &c. 60); confused; deranged &c. 61; topsy-turvy &c. (*inverted*) 218; shapeless &c. 241; disjointed, out of joint; knarled.

com-plex, -plexed; intricate, complicated, perplexed, involved, raveled, entangled, knotted, tangled, inextricable; irreducible.

troublous; riotous &c. (*violent*) 173.

Adv. irregularly &c. *adj.;* by fits, -and -snatches, – starts; pellmell; higgledy-piggledy; helter-skelter, harum-scarum; in a ferment; at -sixes and sevens, – cross-purposes; upside down &c. 218.

Phr. the cart before the horse; ὕστερον πρότερον; chaos is come again; "the wreck of matter and the crush of worlds" [Addison].

60. [Reduction to Order.] **Arrangement. — N.** arrangement; plan &c. 626; preparation &c. 673; dispos-al, -ition; col-, al-location; distribution; sorting &c. *v.*; assortment, allotment, apportionment, taxis, taxonomy, syntaxis, graduation, organization; grouping.

analysis, classification, division, digestion.

[Result of arrangement] digest; synopsis &c. (*compendium*) 596; syntagma, table, atlas; register &c. (*record*) 551; organism, architecture.

[Instrument for sorting] sieve, riddle, screen.

V. reduce to –, bring into– order; introduce order into; rally.

arrange, dispose, place, form; put –, set –, place– in order; set out, collocate, pack, marshal, range, size, rank, group, parcel out, allot, distribute, deal; cast –, assign– the parts; dispose of, assign places to; assort, sort; sift, riddle; put –, set– -to rights, – into shape, – in trim, – in array; apportion.

class, -ify; divide; file, string together, thread; register &c. (*record*) 551; catalogue, tabulate, index, graduate, digest, grade.

methodize, regulate, systematize, coördinate, organize, settle, fix.

unravel, disentangle, ravel, card; disembroil; feaze.

Adj. arranged &c. *v.*; embattled, in battle array; cut and dried; methodical, orderly, regular, systematic.

61. [Subversion of Order; bringing into disorder.] **Derangement. — N.** derangement &c. *v.*; disorder &c. 59; evection, discomposure, disturbance; dis-, de-organization; dislocation; perturbation, interruption; shuffling &c. *v.*; inversion &c. 218; corrugation &c. (*fold*) 258; involvement.

V. derange; dis-, mis-arrange; dis-, mis-place; mislay, discompose, disorder; de-, dis-organize; embroil, unsettle, disturb, confuse, trouble, perturb, jumble, tumble; huddle, shuffle, muddle, toss, hustle, fumble, riot; bring –, put –, throw- into -disorder &c.59; muss [U.S.]; break the ranks, disconcert, convulse; break in upon.

unhinge, dislocate, put out of joint, throw out of gear.

turn topsy-turvy &c. (*invert*) 218; bedevil; complicate, involve, perplex, confound; im-, em-brangle, tangle, entangle, ravel, tousle, towzle, dishevel, ruffle; rumple &c. (*fold*) 258.

litter, scatter; mix &c. 41.

Adj. deranged &c. *v.*; syncre-tic, -tistic; mussy [U. S.].

2. CONSECUTIVE ORDER

62. **Precedence. — N.** precedence; coming before &c. *v.*; the lead, *le pas;* superiority &c. 33; importance &c. 642; anteced-ence, -ency; anteriority &c. (*front*) 234; precursor &c. 64; priority &c. 116; precession &c. 280; anteposition; epacme; preference.

V. precede; come -before, – first; head, lead, take the lead; lead the -way, – dance; introduce, usher in; have the *pas;* set the fashion &c. (*influence*) 175; open the ball; take –, have- precedence; have the start &c. (*get before*) 280.

place before; prefix; premise, prelude, preface.

Adj. preceding &c. *v.*; pre-, antecedent; anterior; prior &c. 116; before; former, foregoing; before-, above-, aforementioned; aforesaid, said; precursory, -ive; prevenient, preliminary, pref-

63. **Sequence. — N.** sequence, coming after; going after &c. (*following*) 281; consecution, succession; posteriority &c. 117.

continuation; order of succession; successiveness; paracme.

secondariness; subordinancy &c. (*inferiority*) 34.

after-birth, -burden; placenta, secundines.

V. succeed; come -after, – on, – next; follow, ensue, step into the shoes of; alternate.

place after, suffix, append.

Adj. succeeding &c. *v.*; sequent; sub-, con-sequent; sequacious, proximate, next; consecutive &c. (*continuity*) 69; alternate, amœbean.

latter; posterior &c. 117.

Adv. after, subsequently; behind &c. (*rear*) 235.

atory, introductory; prelus-ive, -ory; proemial, preparatory.

Adv. before; in advance &c. (*precession*) 280.

Phr. *seniores priores; prior tempore prior jure.*

64. Precursor. — N. precursor, antecedent, precedent, predecessor; forerunner, vancourier, *avant-coureur*, pioneer, prodrome †, *prodromos*, prodromus, outrider; leader, bellwether; herald, harbinger; dawn; avant-courier, bellmare, forelooper, foreloper, *voorlooper*, *voortrekker*.

prelude, preamble, preface, prologue, foreword, *avant-propos*, protasis, proemium, prolusion, proem, prolepsis, prolegomena, prefix, introduction; heading, frontispiece, groundwork; preparation &c. 673; overture, exordium, symphony; premises.

prefigurement &c. 511; omen &c. 512.

Adj. precursory; prelu-sive, -sory, -dious; proemial, introductory, prefatory, prodromous, inaugural, preliminary; precedent &c. (*prior*) 116.

Phr. " a precedent embalms a principle " [Disraeli].

65. Sequel. — N. sequel, suffix, successor; tail, queue, train, wake, trail, rear; retinue, suite; appendix, postscript; epilogue; peroration; codicil; continua-, tion, sequela; appendage; tail -, heelpiece; tag, more last words; colophon.

after-come, -growth, -part, -piece, -course, -thought, -game; *arrière pensée*, second thoughts; outgrowth.

66. Beginning.—N. beginning, commencement, opening, outset, incipience, inception, inchoation; introduction &c. (*precursor*) 64; alpha, initial; inauguration, début, *le premier pas*, embarcation, rising of the curtain; maiden speech; outbreak, onset, brunt; initiative, move, first move; narrow -, thinend of the wedge; fresh start, new departure.

origin &c. (*cause*) 153; source, rise; bud, germ &c. 153; egg, rudiment; genesis, birth, nativity, cradle, infancy; start, starting point &c. 293; dawn &c. (*morning*) 125.

title-page; head, -ing; van &c. (*front*) 234; caption, *fatihah*.

en-trance, -try; inlet, orifice, mouth, chops, lips, porch, portal, portico, propylon, door; gate, -way; postern, wicket, threshold, vestibule; propylæum; skirts, border &c. (*edge*) 231.

first -stage, - blush, - glance, - impression, - sight.

rudiments, elements, outlines, grammar, alphabet, ABC.

V. begin, commence, inchoate, rise, arise, originate, conceive, initiate, open, dawn, set in, take its rise, enter upon, enter; set out &c. (*depart*) 293; embark in; incept.

usher in; lead -off, - the way; take the -lead, - initiative; inaugurate, head; stand -at the head, - first, - for; lay the foundations &c. (*prepare*) 673; found

67. End. — N. end, close, termination; desinence, conclusion, finis, finale, period, term, terminus, last, omega; extreme, -tremity; gable -, butt -, fagend; tip, nib, point; tail &c. (*rear*) 235; verge &c. (*edge*) 231; tag, peroration; *bonne bouche;* bottom dollar, tail end.

consummation, *dénouement;* finish &c. (*completion*) 729; fate; doom, -sday; crack of doom, day of Judgment, fall of the curtain; goal, destination; limit, determination; expiration, expiry; death &c. 360; end of all things; finality; eschatology.

break up, *commencement de la fin*, last stage, turning point; *coup de grâce*, deathblow; knock-out, - blow; sockdolager * [U. S.].

V. end, close, finish, terminate, conclude, be all over; expire; die &c. 360; come -, draw- to a -close &c. *n.;* have run its course; run out, pass away.

bring to an -end &c. *n.;* put an end to, make an end of; determine; get through; achieve &c. (*complete*) 729; stop &c. (*make to cease*) 142; shut up shop; hang up one's fiddle.

Adj. ending &c. *v.;* final, terminal, definitive; crowning &c. (*completing*) 729; last, ultimate; hindermost; rear &c. 235; caudal; vergent.

contermin-ate †, -ous, -able.

ended &c. *v.;* at an end; settled, decided, over, played out, set at rest; conclusive.

&c. (*cause*) 153; set -up, – on foot, – agoing, – abroach, – the ball in motion; apply the match to a train; launch, broach; open -up, – the door to; set -about, – to work; make a -beginning, – start; handsel; take the first step, lay the first stone, cut the first turf; break -ground, – the ice, – cover; pass –, cross- the Rubicon; open -fire, – the ball; ventilate, air; undertake &c. 676.

come into -existence, – the world; make one's *début*, take birth; burst forth, break out; spring –, crop- up.

begin -at the beginning, – *ab ovo*, – again, – *de novo;* start afresh, make a fresh start, shuffle the cards, resume, recommence.

Adj. beginning &c. *v.*; initi-al, -atory, -ative; inceptive, introductory, incipient; proemial, inaugural; incho-ate, -ative; embryonic, rudimental; primogenial; primeval &c. (*old*) 124; aboriginal; natal, nascent.

first, foremost, leading; maiden.

begun &c. *v.*; just -begun &c. *v.*

Adv. at –, in- the beginning &c. *n.*; first, in the first place, *imprimis*, first and foremost; *in limine;* in -the bud, – embryo, – its infancy; from -the beginning, – its birth; *ab -initio, – ovo, – incunabilis, – origine.*

Phr. *aller Anfang ist schwer; dimidium facti qui coepit habet* [Cicero]; *omnium rerum principia parva sunt* [Cicero].

penultimate; last but -one, – two, &c. unbegun, uncommenced; fresh.

Adv. finally &c. *adj.*; in fine; at the last; once for all.

Phr. " as high as Heaven and as deep as hell " [Beaumont & Fletcher]; *deficit omne quod nascitur* [Quintilian]; *en toute chose il faut considérer la fin; finem respice; ultimus Romanorum.*

68. Middle. — **N.** middle, midst, mediety †; mean &c. 29; medium, middle term; center &c. 222, mid-course &c. 628; *mezzo termine; juste milieu* &c. 628; halfway house, nave, navel, omphalos; nucle-us, -olus.

equidistance, bisection, half distance; equator, diaphragm, midriff; interjacence &c. 228.

Adj. middle, medial, mesial, mean, mid; middle-, mid-most; mediate; intermediate &c. (*interjacent*) 228; equidistant; central &c. 222; mediterranean, equatorial; homocentric.

Adv. in the middle; mid-, half-way; midships, amidships, *in medias res.*

69. [Uninterrupted sequence.] Continuity. — **N.** continuity; consecu-tion, -tiveness &c. *adj.*; succession, round, suite, progression, series, train, chain; cat-, concat-enation; scale; gradation, course; ceaselessness, constant flow, unbroken extent.

procession, column; retinue, *cortège*, cavalcade, rank and file, line of battle, array.

pedigree, genealogy, lineage, race; ancestry, descent, family, house; line, – of ancestors; strain.

rank, file, line, row, range, tier, string, thread, team; suit; colonnade.

V. follow in –, form- a series &c. *n.*; fall in.

arrange in a -series &c. *n.*; string together, file, thread, graduate, tabulate.

Adj. continu-ous, -ed; consecutive; progressive, gradual; serial, successive; immediate, unbroken, entire; linear; in

70. [Interrupted sequence.] Discontinuity. — **N.** discontinuity; disjunction &c. 44; anacoluthon; interruption, break, fracture, flaw, fault, crack, cut; gap &c. (*interval*) 198; solution of continuity, cæsura; broken thread; parenthesis, episode, rhapsody, patchwork; intermission; alternation &c. (*periodicity*) 138; dropping fire.

V. be -discontinuous &c. *adj.*; alternate, intermit.

discontinue, pause, interrupt; intervene; break, – in upon, – off; interpose &c. 228; break –, snap- the thread; disconnect &c. (*disjoin*) 44; dissever.

Adj. discontinuous, unsuccessive, broken, interrupted, *décousu*; dis-, unconnected; discrete, disjunctive; fitful &c. (*irregular*) 139; spasmodic, desultory; intermit-ting &c. *v.*, -tent; alternate; recurrent &c. (*periodic*) 138.

Adv. at intervals; by -snatches, –

a -line, – row &c. *n.*; uninter-rupted, -mitting; unremitting; perennial, ever-green; constant.

Adv. continuously &c. *adj.*; *seriatim;* in a -line &c. *n.*; in -succession, – turn; running, gradually, step by step, gradatim, at a stretch; in -file, – column, – single file, – Indian file.

jerks, – skips, – catches, – fits and starts; skippingly, *per saltum; longo intervallo.*

Phr. like "angel visits few and far be-tween" [Campbell].

71. Term. — N. term, rank, station, stage, step; degree &c. 26; scale, re-move, grade, link, peg, round of the ladder, status, position, place, point, mark, *pas*, period, pitch; stand, -ing; footing, range.

V. hold –, occupy –, find –, fall into- a place &c. *n.*

3. Collective Order

72. Assemblage. — N. assemblage; col-lection, -location, -ligation; com-pilation, levy, gathering, ingathering, muster, *attroupement;* team; con-course, -flux, -gregation, -tesseration †, -verg-ence &c. 290; meeting, levée, reunion, drawing room, at home; conversazione &c. (*social gathering*) 892; assembly, congress; conven-tion, -ticle; gemote; conclave &c. (*council*) 696; posse, *posse comitatus;* Noah's ark.

miscellany, *collectanea;* museum, me-nagerie &c. (*store*) 636; museology.

crowd, throng; flood, rush, deluge; rabble, mob, press, crush, *cohue*, horde, body, tribe; crew, gang, knot, squad, band, party; swarm, shoal, school, covey, flock, herd, drove; *atajo;* bunch, drive, force, *mulada* [U. S.]; *remuda;* round-up [U. S.]; array, bevy, galaxy; corps, com-pany, troop, troupe; army, regiment &c. (*combatants*) 726; host &c. (*multitude*) 102; populousness.

clan, brotherhood, association &c. (*party*) 712.

volley, shower, storm, cloud.

group, cluster, Pleiades, clump, pen-cil; set, batch, lot, pack; budget, assort-ment, bunch; parcel; pack-et, -age; bundle, fascine, bale; ser-on, -oon; fagot, wisp, truss, tuft; shock, rick, fardel, stack, sheaf, haycock; fascicle, fascicule, fasciculus, gavel, hattock, stook.

accumulation &c. (*store*) 636; congeries, heap, lump, pile, rouleau, tissue, mass, pyramid; bing; drift; snow-ball, -drift; acervation, cumulation; glom-, agglom-eration; conglobation; conglomer-ation, -ate; coacervation, coag-mentation, aggregation, concentration, congestion, *omnium gatherum, spicile-gium,* black hole of Calcutta; quantity &c. (*greatness*) 31.

collector, gatherer; whip, -per in.

V. [be or come together] assemble, collect, muster; meet, unite, join, rejoin; cluster, flock, swarm, surge, stream, herd, crowd, throng, associate; con-gre-gate, -glomerate, -centrate; center round, rendezvous, resort; come –, flock –, get –, pig- together; forgather; huddle; reassemble.

[get or bring together] assemble, muster; bring –, get –, put –, draw –,

73. Nonassemblage. Dispersion. — N. dispersion; disjunction &c. 44; divergence &c. 291; aspersion; scattering &c. *v.*; dissemination, diffusion, dissi-pation, distribution; apportionment &c. 786; spread, respersion †, circumfusion, interspersion, spargefaction †; affusion.

waifs and estrays, flotsam and jet-sam, *disjecta membra,* [Hor.]; waveson.

V. disperse, scatter, sow, disseminate, diffuse, shed, spread, bestrew, over-spread, dispense, disband, disembody, dismember, distribute; apportion &c. 786; blow off, let out, dispel, cast forth, draught off; strew, straw, strow; ted; spirtle, cast, sprinkle; issue, deal out, re-tail, utter; re-, inter-sperse; set abroach, circumfuse.

turn –, cast- adrift; scatter to the winds; sow broadcast.

spread like wildfire, disperse them-selves.

Adj. unassembled &c. (*see* assemble &c. 72); dispersed &c. *v.*; sparse, dis-pread, broadcast, sporadic, widespread; epidemic &c. (*general*) 78; adrift, stray; disheveled, streaming.

Adv. *sparsim*, here and there, *passim.*

scrape –, lump- together; col-lect, -locate, -ligate; get –, whip- in; gather; hold a meeting; con-vene, -voke, -vocate; rake up, dredge; heap, mass, pile; pack, put up, truss, cram; acervate †; ag-glcmerate, -gregate; compile; group, aggroup, concentrate, unite; collect –, bring- into a focus; amass, accumulate &c. (*store*) 636; collect in a dragnet; heap Ossa upon Pelion.

Adj. assembled &c. *v.*; closely packed, dense, serried, crowded to suffocation, teeming, swarming, populous; as thick as hops; all of a heap, fasciculated; cumulative.

Phr. the plot thickens; *acervatim; tibi seris tibi metis.*

74. [Place of meeting.] **Focus.** — **N.** focus; point of- convergence &c. 290; corradiation; center &c. 222; gathering place, resort; haunt; retreat; venue; rendezvous; rallying point, headquarters, home, club; depot &c. (*store*) 636; trysting place; place of -meeting, – resort, – assignation; *point de réunion;* issue.

V. bring to -a point, – a focus, – an issue.

4. Distributive Order

75. **Class.** — **N.** class, division, category, *categorema*, head, order, section; department, province, domain.

kind, sort, genus, species, variety, family, race, tribe, caste, sept, clan, breed, type, kit, sect, set; assortment; feather, kidney; suit; range; gender, sex, kin.

manner, description, denomination, designation, character, stamp; predicament; indication, particularization, selection, specification.

similarity &c. 17.

76. **Inclusion.** [Comprehension under, or reference to a class.] — **N.** inclusion, admission, comprehension, reception.

composition &c. (*inclusion in a compound*) 54.

V. be -included in &c.; come –, fall –, range- under; belong –, pertain- to; range with; merge in.

include, comprise, comprehend, contain, admit, embrace, receive; inclose &c. (*circumscribe*) 229; embody, encircle.

reckon –, enumerate –, number- among; refer to; place –, arrange- -under, – with; take into account.

Adj. includ-ed, -ing &c. *v.*; inclusive; congen-er, -erous; of the same -class &c. -75; encircling.

Phr. *a maximis ad minima, et hoc genus omne, &c., etc.; et cœtera.*

77. **Exclusion.**[1] — **N.** exclusion &c. 55.

78. **Generality.** — **N.** general-ity, -ization; universality; catholic-ity, -ism; miscel-lany, -laneousness; dragnet; common run; worldwideness.

every-one, -body; all hands, all the world and his wife; anybody, N or M, all sorts.

prevalence, run.

V. be -general &c. *adj.*; prevail, be going about, stalk abroad.

render -general &c. *adj.*; generalize.

Adj. general, generic, collective; broad, comprehensive, sweeping; ency-

79. **Speciality.** — **N.** speciality, *spécialité;* individ-uality, -uity †; particularity, peculiarity; idiocrasy &c. (*tendency*) 176; personality, characteristic, mannerism, idiosyncrasy; specificness &c. *adj.*; singularity &c. (*unconformity*) 83; reading, version, lection; state; trait; distinctive feature; technicality; differentia.

particulars, details, items, counts; minutiæ.

I, self, I myself; my-, him-, her-, itself.

---

[1] The same set of words are used to express *Exclusion from a class* and *Exclusion from a compound*. Reference is therefore made to the former at 55. This identity does not occur with regard to *Inclusion*, which therefore constitutes a separate category.

clopedical, widespread &c. (*dispersed*) 73.

universal; catho-lic, -lical; common, world-wide; œ-, e-cumenical; transcendental; prevalent, prevailing, rife, epidemic, besetting; all over, covered with.

Pan-American, -Anglican, -Hellenic, -Germanic, -slavic; panharmonic.

every, all; unspecified, impersonal.

customary &c. (*habitual*) 613.

Adv. what-ever, -soever; to a man, one and all.

generally &c. *adj.*; always, for better for worse; in general, generally speaking; speaking generally; for the most part; in the long run &c. (*on an average*) 29.

V. specify, particularize, individualize, realize, specialize, designate, determine; denote, indicate, point out, select.

descend to particulars, enter into detail, come to the point.

Adj. special, particular, individual, specific, proper, personal, original, private, respective, definite, determinate, especial, certain, esoteric, endemic, partial, party, peculiar, appropriate, several, characteristic, diagnostic, exclusive; singular &c. (*exceptional*) 83; idiomatic; typical.

this, that; yon, -der.

Adv. specially &c. *adj.*; in particular, *in propriâ personâ; ad hominem;* for my part.

each, apiece, one by one; severally, respectively, each to each; *seriatim,* in detail, bit by bit; *pro -hac vice, – re natâ.* namely, that is to say, *videlicet,* viz.; to wit.

Phr. *le style est l'homme même.*

5. Order as Regards Categories

80. Rule. — N. regularity, uniformity, constancy, clock-work precision; punctuality &c. (*exactness*) 494; even tenor; system; routine &c. (*custom*) 613; formula; rule &c. (*form, regulation*) 697; keynote, standard, model; precedent &c. (*prototype*) 22; conformity &c. 82.

nature, principle; law; order of things; normal –, natural –, ordinary –, model--state, – condition; standing -dish, – order; Procrustean law; law of the Medes and Persians; hard and fast rule.

Adj. regular, uniform, constant, steady; according to rule &c. (*conformable*) 82; customary &c. 613; methodical, orderly.

81. Multiformity. — N. multi-, omni-formity; variety, diversity; multifariousness &c. *adj.*; varied assortment.

Adj. multi-form, -fold, -farious, -generous, -plex; variform, manifold, many-sided; omni-form, -genous, -farious; heterogeneous, motley, mosaic; epicene, indiscriminate, desultory, irregular, diversified, different, divers; all manner of; of -every description, – all sorts and kinds; *et hoc genus omne;* and what not? *de omnibus rebus et quibusdam aliis.*

Phr. "harmoniously confused" [Pope]; "variety's the very spice of life" [Cowper].

82. Conformity. — N. conform-ity, -ance; observance; habituation.

naturalization; conventionality &c. (*custom*) 613; agreement &c. 23.

example, instance, specimen, sample, quotation; exemplification, illustration, case in point; object lesson; elucidation.

pattern &c. (*prototype*) 22.

V. conform to, – rule; accommodate -, adapt- oneself to; rub off corners.

be -regular &c. *adj.*; move in a groove; follow –, observe –, go by –, bend to –, obey- -rules, – precedents; comply –, tally –, chime in –, fall in- with; be -guided, – regulated- by; fall into a -custom, – usage; follow the -fashion,

83. Unconformity. — N. nonconformity &c. 82; un-, dis-conformity; unconventionality, informality, abnormity, anomaly; anomalousness &c. *adj.*; exception, peculiarity; infraction –, breach –, violation –, infringement- of -law, – custom, – usage; teratism, eccentricity, *bizarrerie,* oddity, *je ne sais quoi,* monstrosity, rarity; freak of Nature; rouser, snorter * [U. S.].

individuality, idiosyncrasy, originality, mannerism.

aberration; irregularity; variety; singularity; exemption; salvo &c. (*qualification*) 469.

nonconformist; nondescript, charac-

- multitude; pass muster, do as others do, *hurler avec les loups;* do at Rome as the Romans do; go –, swim- with the -stream, – current, – tide; tread the beaten track &c. (*habit*) 613; keep one in countenance.

exemplify, illustrate, cite, quote, put a case; produce an -instance &c. *n.;* elucidate, explain.

Adj. conformable to rule; regular &c. 80; according to -regulation, – rule, – Cocker, – Gunter; *en règle, selon les règles,* well regulated, orderly; symmetric &c. 242.

conventional &c. (*customary*) 613; of -daily, – everyday- occurrence; in the natural order of things; ordinary, common, habitual, usual.

in the order of the day; naturalized.

typical, normal, formal; canonical, orthodox, sound, strict, rigid, positive, uncompromising, Procrustean.

secundum artem, shipshape, technical. exemplary, illustrative, in point.

Adv. conformably &c. *adj.;* by rule; agreeably to; in -conformity, – accordance, – keeping- with; according to; consistently with; as usual, *ad instar, instar omnium; more -solito, – majorum.*

for the sake of conformity; of –, as a matter of- course; *pro formâ,* for form's sake, by the card.

invariably &c. (*uniformly*) 16.

for -example, – instance; *exempli gratiâ; e. g.; inter alia.*

Phr. *cela va sans dire; ex pede Herculem; noscitur a sociis; ne e quovis ligno Mercurius fiat* [Erasmus]; "they are happy men whose natures sort with their vocations" [Bacon].

ter, original, nonsuch, monster, prodigy, wonder, miracle, curiosity, flying fish, black swan, *lusus naturæ, rara avis,* queer fish; mongrel; half-caste, -blood, -breed; métis, crossbreed, hybrid, mule, mulatto; *tertium quid,* hermaphrodite.

phœnix, chimera, hydra, sphinx, minotaur; griff-in, -on; centaur; xiphopagus; hippo-griff, -centaur; saggittary; kraken, cockatrice, wyvern, roc, dragon, sea serpent; mermaid; unicorn; Cyclops, "men whose heads do grow beneath their shoulders" [*Othello*]; teratology.

fish out of water; neither -one thing nor another, – fish flesh nor fowl nor good red herring; one in a -way, – thousand; out-cast, -law; oasis.

V. be -uncomformable &c. *adj.;* abnormalize; leave the beaten -track, – path; infringe –, break –, violate- a -law, – habit, – usage, – custom; drive a coach and six through; stretch a point; have no business there; baffle –, beggar- all description.

Adj. uncomformable, exceptional; abnorm-al, -ous; anomal-ous, -istic; out of -order, – place, – keeping, – tune, – one's element; irregular, arbitrary; teratogenic; lawless, informal, aberrant, stray, wandering, wanton; peculiar, exclusive, unnatural, eccentric, egregious; out of the -beaten track, – common, – common run, – pale of; misplaced; funny.

un-usual, -accustomed, -customary, -wonted, -common; rare, singular, unique, curious, odd, extraordinary, strange, monstrous; wonderful &c. 870; unexpected, unaccountable; *outré,* out of the way, remarkable, noteworthy; queer,

quaint, nondescript, none such, *sui generis;* original, unconventional, unfashionable; un-described, -precedented, -paralleled, -exampled, -heard of, -familiar; fantastic, newfangled, grotesque, bizarre; outlandish, exotic, *tombé des nues,* preternatural; denaturalized.

heterogeneous, heteroclite, amorphous, mongrel, amphibious, epicene, half blood, hybrid; androgyn-ous, -al; unsymmetric &c. 243; adelomorphous, bisexual, hermaphrodite, monoclinous.

qualified &c. 469.

Adv. unconformably &c. *adj.;* except, unless, save, barring, beside, without, save and except, let alone.

however, yet, but.

Int. what -on earth! – in the world!

Phr. never was -seen, – heard, – known- the like.

Section V. NUMBER

1. Number, in the Abstract

84. Number. — **N.** number, symbol, numeral, figure, cipher, digit, integer; counter; round number; formula; function; series.

sum, difference, complement, subtrahend; product; multipli-cand, -er, -cator; coefficient, multiple; dividend, divisor, factor, quotient, submultiple, fraction; mixed number; numerator, denominator; decimal, circulating decimal, repetend; common measure, aliquot part; reciprocal; prime number; totient.

permutation, combination, variation; election.

ratio, proportion; progression; arithmetical –, geometrical –, harmonical-progression; percentage.

figurate –, pyramidal –, polygonal- numbers.

power, root, exponent, index, logarithm, antilogarithm; modulus.

differential, integral, fluxion, fluent.

Adj. numeral, complementary, divisible, aliquot, reciprocal, prime, fractional, decimal, figurate, incommensurable.

proportional, exponential, logarithmic, logometric, differential, fluxional, integral, totitive.

positive, negative; rational, irrational; surd, radical, real, imaginary, impossible.

85. Numeration. — **N.** numeration; numbering &c. *v.*; pagination; tale, recension, enumeration, summation, reckoning, computation, supputation†; calcu-lation, -lus; algorithm†, algorism, rhabdology, dactylonomy; measurement &c. 466; statistics.

arithmetic, analysis, algebra, fluxions; differential –, integral –, infinitesimal-calculus; calculus of differences.

[Statistics] dead reckoning, muster, poll, census, capitation, roll call, recapitulation; account &c. (*list*) 86.

[Operations] notation, addition, subtraction, multiplication, division, rule of three, practice, equations, extraction of roots, reduction, involution, evolution, approximation, interpolation, differentiation, integration.

[Instruments] abacus, suan-pan, logometer, sliding rule, tallies, Napier's bones, calculating machine, difference engine; adding machine; cash register.

arithmetician, calculator, abacist, algebraist, mathematician.

V. number, count, tell; call –, run- over; take an account of, enumerate, muster, poll, recite, recapitulate; sum; sum –, cast- up; tell off, score, cipher, compute, calculate, suppute†, add, subtract, multiply, divide, extract roots. algebraize.

check, prove, demonstrate, balance, audit, overhaul, take stock; affix numbers to, page.

amount –, come- to.

Adj. numer-al, -ical; arithmetical, analytic, algebraic, statistical, numerable, computable, calculable; commensur-able, -ate; incommensur-able, -ate.

86. List. — **N.** list, catalog(ue), inventory, schedule; register &c. (*record*) 551; account; bill, – of costs; syllabus; terrier, tally, file; calendar, index, table, atlas, contents; book, ledger; synopsis, *catalogue raisonné;* tableau; invoice, bill of lading; prospectus, program(me); bill of fare, menu, carte; score, census, statistics, returns; Red –, Blue –, Domesday- book; *cadastre;* directory, gazetter.

almanac; army –, clergy –, civil service –, navy-list; *Almanach de Gotha,* cadaster, card index, dictionary, Lloyd's register, nautical almanac, who's who.

roll; check –, checker –, bead- roll; muster -roll, – book; roster, panel; cartulary, diptych.

Adj. cadastral.

2. DETERMINATE NUMBER

87. Unity. — N. unity; oneness &c. *adj.*; individuality; solitude &c. (*seclusion*) 893; isolation &c. (*disjunction*) 44; unification &c. 48.

one, unit, ace; individual; none else, no other.

V. be -one, – alone &c. *adj.*; dine with Duke Humphrey.

isolate &c. (*disjoin*) 44.

render one; unite &c. (*join*) 43, (*combine*) 48.

Adj. one, sole, single, solitary; individual, apart, alone; kithless.

un-accompanied, -attended; *solus*, single-handed; singular, odd, unique, unrepeated, azygous, first and last; isolated &c. (*disjoined*) 44; insular.

monospermous; uni-fic, -florous, -foliate, -genital, -literal, -locular, -modular.

lone; lone-ly, -some; desolate, dreary.

in-secable†, -severable, -discerptible; compact, irresolvable.

Adv. singly &c. *adj.*; alone, by itself, *per se*, only, apart, in the singular number, in the abstract; one -by one, – at a time; simply; one and a half, *sesqui-*.

Phr. *natura il fece, e poi roppe la stampa; du fort au faible;* "two souls with but a single thought, two hearts that beat as one."

88. Accompaniment. — N. accompaniment; adjunct &c. 39; context; appendage, appurtenance.

coexistence, concomitance, company, association, companionship; part-, co-part-nership; coefficiency.

concomitant, accessory, coefficient; companion, attendant, fellow, associate, consort, spouse, colleague; part-, co-part-ner; satellite, hanger on, shadow; escort, *cortège;* attribute.

V. accompany, coexist, attend; hang -, wait- on; go hand in hand with; synchronize &c. 120; bear -, keep- company; row in the same boat; bring in its train; associate -, couple- with.

Adj. accompanying &c. *v.*; concomitant, fellow, twin, joint; associated -, coupled- with; accessory, attendant, obbligato.

Adv. with, withal; together -, along -, in company- with; hand in hand, side by side; cheek by -jowl, – jole; arm in arm; there-, here-with; and &c. (*addition*) 37.

together, in a body, collectively.

Phr. *noscitur a sociis; virtutis fortuna comes.*

89. Duality. — N. dual-ity, -ism; duplicity; bi-plicity, -formity; polarity.

two, deuce, couple, brace, pair, cheeks, twins, Castor and Pollux, gemini, Siamese twins; fellows; yoke, conjugation; dispermy, doublets, dyad, span.

V. [unite in pairs] pair, couple, bracket, yoke; conduplicate; mate, span [U. S.].

Adj. two, twain; dual, -istic; binary, binomial; twin, biparous; dyadic; conduplicate; duplex &c. 90; biduous, binate, diphyletic, dispermic, unijugate; *tête-à-tête.*

coupled &c. *v.*; conjugate.

both, – the one and the other.

90. Duplication. — N. duplication; doubling &c. *v.*; gemi-, ingemi-nation; reduplication; iteration &c. (*repetition*) 104; renewal.

V. double; re-double, -duplicate; geminate; repeat &c. 104; renew &c. 660.

Adj. double; doubled &c. *v.*; bi-cipital, -cephalous, -dental, -labiate, -valve, -valvular, -fold, -form, -lateral, -farious, -facial; two-fold, -sided; disomatous; duplex; double-faced, -headed; twin, duplicate, ingeminate; second.

91. [Division into two parts.] Bisection. — N. bi-section, -partition; di-, subdi-chotomy; halving &c. *v.*; dimidiation.

bifurcation, forking, branching, ramification, divarication; fork, prong; fold.

half, moiety.

V. bisect, halve, divide, split, cut in two, cleave, dimidiate, dichotomize.

go halves, divide with.

separate, fork, bifurcate; branch -off, – out; ramify.

Adj. bisected &c. *v.*; cloven, cleft;

Adv. twice, once more; over again &c. *repeatedly*) 104; as much again, twofold. secondly, in the second place, again.

bipartite, biconjugate, bicuspid, bifid; bifur-cous, -cate, -cated; distichous, dichotomous, furcular; semi-, demi-, hemi-.

92. Triality. — N. triality, trinity; [1] triunity.

three, triad, triplet, trey, trio, ternion, leash; shamrock, tierce, spike-team [U. S.], trefoil; tri-angle, -dent, -ennium, -gon, -nomial, -onym, -plopia, -pod, -reme, -seme, -skele, -skelion, -sula.

third power, cube.

Adj. three; tri-form, -nal, -nomial; tertiary; triune; triarch, triadic.

Phr. *tria juncta in uno.*

93. Triplication. — N. tripli-cation, -city; trebleness, trine.

V. treble, triple, triplicate, cube.

Adj. treble, triple; tern, -ary; tripli-cate, threefold, trilogistic; third; trinal, trine.

Adv. three -times, – fold; thrice, in the third place, thirdly; trebly &c. *adj.*

94. [Division into three parts.] Tri-section. — N. tri-section, -partition, -chotomy; third, – part.

V. trisect, divide into three parts.

Adj. trifid; trisected &c.*v.*; tri-partite, -chotomous, -sulcate.

tri-adelphous, -angular, -cuspid, -cap-sular, -dental, -dentate, -dentiferous, -foliate, -furcate, -gonal, -grammic, -grammatic, -petalous, -podal, -podic, -quetral, -quetrous.

95. Quaternity. — N. quaternity, four, tetrad, quartet, quaternion, square, quarter; tetract, tetragon.

quad-rangle, -rature, -rifoil, -riform, -ruplet; quatrefoil.

V. reduce to a square, square.

Adj. four; quat-ernary, -ernal; quadratic; quartile; tetract, -ic, -inal; tetrad, tetragonal.

96. Quadruplication. — N. quad-ruplication.

V. multiply by four, quadruplicate, biquadrate.

Adj. fourfold; quad-rable, -ruma-nous, -ruple, -ruplicate, -rible; fourth.

quadri-foliate, -foliolate, -geminal, -geminate, -planar, -serial.

Adv. four times; in the fourth place, fourthly.

97. [Division into four parts.] Quad-risection. — N. quadri-section, -parti-tion; quartering &c. *v.*; fourth; quart, -er, -ern; farthing (*i. e.* fourthing).

V. quarter, divide into four parts.

Adj. quartered &c. *v.*; quadri-fid, -partite.

98. Five, &c. — N. five, cinque, quint, quincunx; six, half-a-dozen; seven; eight; nine, three times three; dicker; ten, decade; eleven; twelve, dozen; thirteen; long –, baker's- dozen; quintuplet; twenty, score; twenty-four, four and twenty, two dozen; twenty-five, five and twenty, quarter of a hundred; forty, two score; fifty, half a hundred; sixty, three score; seventy, three score and ten; eighty, four score; ninety, fourscore and ten; sestiad.

hundred, centenary, hecatomb, century; hundredweight, cwt.; one hundred and forty-four, gross.

thousand, chiliad; myriad, ten thousand; lac, one hundred thousand, plum; million; thousand million, milliard.

99. Quinquesection, &c. — N. di-vision by -five &c. 98; quinquesection &c.; decimation; fifth &c.

V. decimate; quinquesect.

Adj. quinque-fid, -literal, -partite; quinquarticular; octifid; decimal, tenth, tithe; duodecimal, twelfth; sexa-gesimal, -genary; hundredth, centesimal; millesi-mal &c.

___

[1] *Trinity* is hardly ever used except in a theological sense; *see* Deity 976.

billion, trillion &c.

V. centuriate†; quintuplicate.

Adj. five, quinary, quintuple; fifth; senary, sextuple; sixth; seventh; septuple; octuple; eighth; ninefold, ninth; tenfold, decimal, denary, decuple, tenth; eleventh; duo-denary, -denal; twelfth; in one's 'teens, thirteenth.

vices-, viges-imal; twentieth; twenty-fourth &c. *n.*; vicenary, vicennial.

cent-uple, -uplicate, -ennial, -enary, -urial; secular, hundredth; thousandth, &c.

3. Indeterminate Number

100. [More than one.] Plurality. —
N. plurality; a -number, – certain number; one or two, two or three &c.; a few, several; multitude &c. 102; majority.

Adj. plural, more than one, upwards of, some, certain; not -alone &c. 87.

Adv. et cetera, &c., etc.

Phr. *non deficit alter.*

100a. [Less than one.] Fraction. —
N. fraction, fractional part; part &c. 51.

Adj. fractional, fragmentary, inconsiderable.

101. Zero.—N. zero, nothing; naught, nought; cipher, none, nobody; *nichts,* nixie *, nix *; not a soul; *âme qui vive;* absence &c. 187; unsubstantiality &c. 4.

Adj. not -one, – any.

102. Multitude. — N. multitude; numerousness &c. *adj.*; numer-osity, -ality; multiplicity; profusion &c. (*plenty*) 639; legion, host; great –, large –, round –, enormous- number; a quantity, numbers, array, sight, army, sea, galaxy; scores, peck, bushel, shoal, swarm, draught, bevy, cloud, flock, herd, drove, flight, covey, hive, brood, litter, farrow, fry, nest; crowd &c. (*assemblage*) 72; lots; all the world and his wife.

[Increase of number] greater number, majority; multiplication, multiple.

V. be -numerous &c. *adj.*; swarm –, teem –, creep -with; crowd, swarm, come thick upon; outnumber, multiply; people; swarm like -locusts, – bees.

Adj. many, several, sundry, divers, various, not a few; Briarean; a -hundred, – thousand, – myriad, – million, – quadrillion, – nonillion, – thousand and one; some -ten or a dozen, – forty or fifty &c.; half a -dozen, – hundred &c.; very –, full –, ever so- many; numer-ous, -ose; profuse, in profusion; manifold, multiplied, multitudinous, multiple, multinomial, teeming, populous, peopled, crowded, thick, studded; galore.

thick coming, many more, more than one can tell, a world of; no end -of, – to; *cum multis aliis;* thick as -hops, – hail; plenty as blackberries; numerous as the -stars in the firmament, – sands on the seashore, – hairs on the head; and -what not, – heaven knows what; endless &c. (*infinite*) 105.

Phr. their name is " Legion "; *acervatim; en foule;* " many-headed multitude " [Sidney]; " numerous as glittering gems of morning dew " [Young]; *vel prece vel pretio.*

103. Fewness. — N. fewness &c. *adj.*; paucity, small number; small quantity &c. 32; rarity; infrequency &c. 137; handful, maniple; minority; exiguity.

[Diminution of number] reduction; weeding &c. *v.*; elimination, sarculation†, decimation; eradication.

V. be -few &c. *adj.*

render -few &c. *adj.*; reduce, diminish the number, weed, eliminate, thin, decimate.

Adj. few; scant, -y; thin, rare, thinly scattered, few and far between; exiguous; infrequent &c. 137; *rari nantes;* hardly –, scarcely- any; to be counted on one's fingers; reduced &c. *v.*; unrepeated.

Adv. here and there.

---

104. Repetition. — N. repetition, iteration, reiteration, harping, recurrence, succession, run; batto-, tauto-logy; monotony, tautophony; rhythm &c. 138; diffuseness, pleonasm, redundancy.

chimes, repetend, echo, *ritornello,* burden of a song, refrain; rehearsal; *réchauffé, rifacimento,* recapitulation.

cuckoo &c. (*imitation*) 19; reverberation &c. 408; drumming &c. (*roll*) 407; renewal &c. (*restoration*) 660.

twice-told tale; old -story, – song; second –, new- edition; reappearance, re production; periodicity &c. 138.

V. repeat, iterate, reiterate, reproduce, echo, reëcho, drum, harp upon, battologize, hammer, redouble.

recur, revert, return, reappear; renew &c. (*restore*) 660.

rehearse; do –, say- over again; ring the changes on; harp on the same string; din –, drum- in the ear; conjugate in all its moods tenses and inflexions, begin again, go over the same ground, go the same round, never hear the last of; re-sume, return to, recapitulate, reword.

Adj. repeated &c. *v.*; repetition-al, -ary; recur-rent, -ring; ever recurring, thick coming; frequent, incessant; redundant, pleonastic.

monotonous, harping, iterative, unvaried; mocking, chiming; retold; afore-said, -named; above-mentioned, said; habitual &c. 613; another.

Adv. repeatedly, often, again, anew, over again, afresh, once more; ding-dong, ditto, encore, *de novo*, bis, *da capo.*

again and again; over and over, – again; many times over; time- and again, – after time; year after year; day by day &c.; many –, several –, a number of-times; many –, full many- a time; frequently &c. 136.

Phr. *ecce iterum Crispinus; toujours perdrix;* " cut and come again " [Crabbe]; " to-morrow and to-morrow and to-morrow " [*Macbeth*]; *cantilenam eandem canis* [Terence]; *nullum es. jam dictum quod non dictum sit prius* [Terence].

105. Infinity. — N. infini-ty, -tude, -teness &c. *adj.*; perpetuity &c. 112; boundlessness.

V. be -infinite &c. *adj.*; know –, have- no -limits, – bounds; go on for ever.

Adj. infinite; immense; number-, count-, sum-, measure-less; innumer-, immeasur-, incalcul-, illimit-, intermin-, unfathom-, unapproach-able; ex-haustless, indefinite; without -number, – measure, – limit, – end; incompre-hensible; limit-, end-, bound-, term-less; un-told, -numbered, -measured, -bounded, -limited; illimited; perpetual &c. 112.

Adv. infinitely &c. *adj.*; *ad infinitum.*

Phr. " as boundless as the sea " [*Romeo and Juliet*].

Section VI. TIME

1. Absolute Time

106. Time. — N. time, duration; period, term, stage, space, span, spell, season; the whole -time, – period; course &c. 109; snap.

intermediate time, while, interim, in-terval, pendency; inter-vention, -mis-sion, -mittence, -regnum, -lude; respite.

era, epoch; time of life, age, year, date; decade &c. (*period*) 108; moment, &c. (*instant*) 113.

glass –, ravages –, whirligig –, noiseless foot- of time; scythe.

V. continue, last, endure, go on, remain, persist; intervene; elapse &c. 109; hold out.

take –, take up –, fill –, occupy- time.

pass –, pass away –, spend –, while away –, consume –, talk against- time; tide over; use –, employ- time; seize an opportunity &c. 134; waste time &c. (*be inactive*) 683.

Adj. continuing &c. *v.*; on foot; permanent &c. (*durable*) 110.

107. Neverness.[1] — N. " neverness "; absence of time, no time; *dies non;* Tib's eve; Greek Kalends.

Adv. never; at no -time, – period; on no occasion, never in all one's born days, nevermore, *sine die;* in no degree.

---

[1] A term introduced by Bishop Wilkins.

Adv. while, whilst, during, pending; during the -time, – interval; in the course of; for the time being, day by day; in the time of, when; mean-time, -while; in the -meantime, – interim; *ad interim, pendente lite; de die in diem;* from -day to day, – hour to hour &c.; hourly, always; for a -time, – season; till, until, up to, yet; the whole –, all the- time; all along; throughout &c. (*completely*) 52; for good &c. (*diuturnity*) 110.

here-, there-, where-upon; then; *anno, – Domini;* A.D.; *ante Christum;* A.C.; before Christ; B.C.; *anno urbis conditæ;* A.U.C.; *anno regni;* A.R.; once upon a time, one fine morning.

Phr. time -runs, – runs against.
ad calendas Græcas; " panting Time toileth after him in vain " [Johnson]; " 'gainst the tooth of time and razure of oblivion " [*Measure for Measure*]; " rich with the spoils of time " [Gray]; *tempus edax rerum* [Horace]; " the long hours come and go " [C. G. Rossetti]; " the time is out of joint " [*Hamlet*]; " Time rolls his ceaseless course " [Scott]; " Time the foe of man's dominion " [Peacock]; " time wasted is existence, used is life " [Young]; *truditur dies die* [Horace]; *volat hora per orbem* [Lucretius].

---

108. [Definite duration, or portion of time.] **Period.** — **N.** period; second, minute, hour, day, week, month, quarter, year, decade, decennium, lustrum, quinquennium, lifetime, generation; epoch, ghurry, lunation, moon.

century, age, millennium; *annus magnus.*

Adj. horary; hourly, annual &c. (*periodical*) 138.

108a. Contingent Duration.—Adv. during -pleasure, – good behavior; *quandiu se bene gesserit.*

109. [Indefinite duration.] **Course.** — **N.** corridors –, sweep –, vesta –, course –, progress –, process –, succession –, lapse –, flow –, flux –, stream –, tract –, current –, tide –, march –, step –, flight- of time; duration &c. 106.

[Indefinite time] aorist.

V. elapse, lapse, flow, run, proceed, advance, pass; roll –, wear –, press- on; flit, fly, slip, slide, glide; run -its course. out; expire; go –, pass- by; be -past &c. 122.

Adj. elapsing &c. *v.*; aoristic; progressive.

Adv. in due -time, – season; in

-course, – process, – the fullness- of time; in time.

Phr. *labitur et labetur* [Horace]; *truditur dies die* [Horace]; *fugaces labuntur anni* [Horace] " to-morrow and to-morrow creeps in this petty pace from day to day " [*Macbeth*].

---

110. [Long duration.] **Diuturnity.** — **N.** diuturnity; a -long –, length of- time; an age, a century, an eternity; slowness &c. 275; perpetuity &c. 112; blue moon, coon's age [U. S.], dog's age.

dura-bleness, -bility; persistence, last-ingness &c. *adj.*; continuance, standing; permanence &c. (*stability*) 150; survi-val, -vance; longevity &c. (*age*) 128; distance of time.

protraction –, prolongation –, extension- of time; delay &c. (*lateness*) 133.

V. last, endure, stand, remain, abide, continue, brave a thousand years.

tarry &c. (*be late*) 133; drag -on, – its slow length along, – a lengthening chain; protract, prolong; spin –, eke –, draw –, lengthen- out; temporize; gain –, make –, talk against- time.

out-last, -live; survive; live to fight again.

Adj. durable; lasting &c. *v.*; of long -duration, – standing; permanent, chron-

111. [Short duration.] **Transient-ness.** — **N.** transientness &c. *adj.*; eva-nescence, impermanence, fugacity, cadu-city, mortality, span; nine days' wonder, bubble, May-fly; spurt; temporary ar-rangement, interregnum.

velocity &c. 274; suddenness &c. 113; changeableness &c. 149.

transient, – boarder, – guest [U. S.].

V. be -transient &c. *adj.*; flit, pass away, fly, gallop, vanish, fade, evapo-rate; pass away like a -cloud, – summer cloud, – shadow, – dream.

Adj. transi-ent, -tory, -tive; passing, evanescent, fleeting; flying &c. *v.*; fug-acious, -itive; shifting, slippery; spas-modic.

tempor-al, -ary; provis-ional, -ory; cursory, short-lived, ephemeral, decidu-ous; perishable, mortal, precarious; im-permanent.

brief, quick, brisk, extemporaneous, summary; pressed for time &c. (*haste*)

ic, long-standing; intransi-ent, -tive; intransmutable, persistent; life-, livelong; longeval, long-lived, macrobiotic, diuturnal, evergreen, perennial; sempervirent, -virid; uninter-, unre-mitting; perpetual &c. 112.

lingering, protracted, prolonged, spun out &c. v.; long-pending, -winded; slow &c. 275.

Adv. long; for -a long time, – an age, – ages, – ever so long, – many a long day; long ago &c. (*in a past time*) 122; *longo intervallo*.

all the -day long, – year round; the livelong day, as the day is long, morning noon and night; hour after hour, day after day, &c.; for good; permanently &c. adj.

684; sudden, momentary &c. (*instantaneous*) 113.

Adv. temporarily &c. adj.; *pro tempore;* for -the moment, – a time; awhile, *en passant, in transitu;* in a short time; soon &c. (*early*) 132; briefly &c. adj.; at short notice; on the -point, – eve -of; *in articulo;* between cup and lip.

Phr. one's days are numbered; the time is up; here to-day and gone to-morrow; *non semper erit æstas; eheu! fugaces labuntur anni; sic transit gloria mundi;* " a schoolboy's tale, the wonder of the hour! " [Byron]; *dum loquimur fugerit invidia ætas; fugit hora.*

---

112. [Endless duration.] Perpetuity. — N. perpetuity, eternity, everness,[1] aye, sempiternity, immortality, athanasia; everlastingness &c. adj.; perpetuation; continued –, uninterrupted-existence; perennity.

V. last –, endure –, go on- for ever; have no end.

eternize, perpetuate.

Adj. perpetual, eternal; ever-during, -lasting, -living, -flowing; continual, sempiternal; coeternal; endless, unending; ceaseless, incessant, uninterrupted, indesinent†, unceasing; interminable, having no end; unfading, evergreen, amaranthine; never-ending, -dying, -fading; deathless, immortal, undying, imperishable.

Adv. perpetually &c. adj.; always, ever, evermore, aye; for -ever, – aye, – evermore, – ever and a day, – ever and ever; in all ages, from age to age; without end; world –, time- without end; *in secula seculorum;* to the -end of time, – crack of doom, – " last syllable of recorded time " [*Macbeth*]; till doomsday; constantly &c. (*very frequently*) 136.

Phr. *esto perpetuum; labitur et labetur in omne volubilis ævum* [Horace]; " but thou shall flourish in immortal youth " [Addison]; " Eternity! thou pleasing, dreadful thought " [Addison]; " her immortal part with angels lives " [*Romeo and Juliet*]; *ohne Hast aber ohne Rast* [Goethe's motto]; *ora e sempre.*

113. [Point of time.] Instantaneity. — N.-instantane-ity, -ousness; sudden-, abrupt-ness.

moment, instant, second, minute; twinkling, trice, flash, breath, crack, jiffy, *coup,* burst, flash of lightning, stroke of time.

epoch, time; time of -day, – night; hour, minute; very -minute &c., – time, – hour; present –, right –, true –, exact –, correct- time.

V. be -instantaneous &c. adj.; twinkle, flash.

Adj. instantaneous, momentary, sudden, instant, abrupt; subitaneous†, hasty; quick as -thought,[2] – lightning; rapid as electricity.

Adv. instantaneously &c. adj.; in –, in less than- no time; presto, *subito,* instanter, suddenly, at a stroke, like a shot; in a -moment &c. n.; in the twinkling of -an eye, – a bedpost; in one's tracks; right away; *toute à l'heure;* at one jump, in the same breath, *per saltum, uno saltu;* at –, all at- once; plump; slap; " at one fell swoop"; at the same -instant &c. n.; immediately &c. (*early*) 132; extempore, on the -moment, – spot, – spur of the moment; just then; slap-dash &c. (*haste*) 684.

Phr. touch and go; no sooner said than done.

---

114. [Estimation, measurement, and record of time.] Chronometry. — N. chrono-, horo-metry, -logy; date, epoch; style, era.

almanac, calendar, ephemeris; regis-

115. [False estimate of time.] Anachronism. — N. ana-, meta-, para-, pro-chronism; prolepsis, misdate; anticipation, antichronism.

disregard –, neglect –, oblivion- of time

---

[1] Bishop Wilkins.   [2] See note on 264.

ter, -try; chronicle, annals, journal, diary, chronogram.

[Instruments for the measurement of time] clock, watch; chrono-meter, -scope, -graph; repeater; time-keeper, -piece; dial, sundial, gnomon, horologe, pendulum, hourglass, clepsydra; ghurry.

chrono-grapher, -loger, -logist; annalist.

V. fix -, mark- the time; date, register, chronicle; measure -, beat -, mark- time; bear date.

Adj. chrono-logical, -metrical, -grammatical; cinque-, quattro-, tre-cento.

Adv. o'clock.

intempestivity &c. 135.

V. mis-, ante-, post-, over-date; anticipate; take no note of time; anachronize.

Adj. misdated &c. *v.*; undated; overdue; out of date.

2. RELATIVE TIME

1. *Time with reference to Succession*

116. Priority. — N. priority, antecedence, anteriority, precedence, preexistence; precession &c. 280; precursor &c. 64; the past &c. 122; premises.

V. precede, come before; forerun; go before &c. (*lead*) 280; preëxist; dawn; presage &c. 511; herald, usher in.

be -beforehand &c. (*be early*) 132; steal a march upon, anticipate, forestall; have -, gain- the start.

Adj. prior, previous; preced-ing, -ent; anterior, antecedent; pre-existing, -existent; former, foregoing; before-, abovementioned; aforesaid, said; introductory &c. (*precursory*) 64.

Adv. before, prior to; earlier; previously &c. *adj.*; afore, aforehand, ere, theretofore, erewhile; ere -, before-then, - now; erewhile, already, yet, beforehand; on the eve of.

Phr. *prior tempore prior jure.*

117. Posteriority. — N. posteriority; succession, sequence; following &c. 281; subsequence; supervention; futurity &c. 121; successor; sequel &c. 65; remainder, reversion.

V. follow &c. 281 -, come -, go- after; succeed, supervene; ensue, occur; step into the shoes of.

Adj. subsequent, posterior, following, after, later, succeeding, postliminious, postnate †; postdiluvi-al, -an; puisne; posthumous; future &c. 121; afterdinner, postprandial.

Adv. subsequently, after, afterwards, since, later; at a -subsequent, - laterperiod; next, in the sequel, close upon, thereafter, thereupon, upon which, eftsoons †; from that -time, -moment; after a -while, - time; in process of time.

118. The Present Time. — N. the present -time, - day, - moment, - juncture, - occasion; the times, existing time, time being; twentieth century; nonce, crisis, epoch, day, hour.

age, time of life.

Adj. present, actual, instant, current, existing, that is.

Adv. at this -time, - moment &c. 113; at the -present time &c. *n.*; now, at present; at hand.

at this time of day, to-day, now-a-days; already; even -, but -, just- now; on the present occasion; for the -time being, - nonce; *pro hâc vice;* on the -nail, - spot; on the spur of the -moment, - occasion.

until now; to -this, - the present- day.

Phr. "the present hour alone is man's" [Johnson].

119. [Time different from the present.] **Different time. — N.** different -, other- time.

[Indefinite time] aorist.

Adj. aoristic; indefinite.

Adv. at that -, at which- -time, - moment, - instant; then, on that occasion, upon.

when; when-ever, -soever; upon which, on which occasion; at -another, - a different, - some other, - any- time; at various times; some -, one- -of these days, - fine morning; sooner or later; some time or other; once upon a time

120. Synchronism. — **N.** synchronism; coexistence, coincidence; simultaneousness &c. *adj.*; concurrence, concomitance, unity of time, interim.

[Having equal times] isochronism.

contemporary, coetanian †.

V. coexist, concur, accompany, go hand in hand, keep pace with; synchronize.

Adj. synchron-ous, -al, -ical, -istical; simultaneous, coexisting, coincident, concomitant, concurrent; coev-al, -ous; contempora-ry, -neous; coetaneous; coeternal; isochronous.

Adv. at the same time; simultaneously &c. *adj.*; together, in concert, during the same time; in the same breath; *pari passu;* in the interim.

at the -very moment &c. 113; just as, as soon as; meanwhile &c. (*while*) 106.

---

121. [Prospective time.] Futurity.— **N.** futur-ity, -ition; future, hereafter, time to come; approaching –, coming –, subsequent –, after- -time, – age, – days, – hours, – years, – ages, – life; morrow; millennium, doomsday, day of judgment, crack of doom, remote future.

approach of time, advent, time drawing on, womb of time; destiny &c. 152; eventuality.

heritage, heirs, posterity.

prospect &c. (*expectation*) 507; foresight &c. 510.

V. look forwards; anticipate &c. (*expect*) 507, (*foresee*) 510; forestall &c. (*be early*) 132.

come –, draw- on; draw near; approach, await, threaten; impend &c. (*be destined*) 152.

Adj. future, to come; coming &c. (*impending*) 152; next, near; near –, close- at hand; eventual, ulterior; in prospect &c. (*expectation*) 507.

Adv. prospectively, hereafter, in future; *kal,* to-morrow, the day after to-morrow; in -course, – process, – the fullness- of time; eventually, ultimately, sooner or later; proximo; *paulo post futurum;* in after time; one of these days; after a -time, – while.

from this time; hence-forth, -forwards; thence; thence-forth, -forward; whereupon, upon which.

soon &c. (*early*) 132; on the -eve, – point, – brink- of; about to; close upon.

Phr. *quid sit futurum cras fuge quœrere* [Horace].

122. [Retrospective time.] Preterition. — **N.** preterition; priority &c. 116; the past, past time; days –, times- -of yore, – of old, – past, – gone by; bygone days; old –, ancient –, former- times; fore time; the olden –, good old- time; lang syne; eld †.

antiquity, antiqueness, *status quo;* time immemorial; distance of time; remote -age, – time; remote past; rust of antiquity.

pale-ontology, -ography, -ology; palœtiology,[1] archœology; archaism, antiquarianism, medievalism, Pre-Raphaelitism; retrospection, looking back, memory &c. 505.

laudator temporis acti; medievalist, Pre-Raphaelite; antiqu-ary, -arian; archœologist &c.; Oldbuck, Dryasdust.

ancestry &c. (*paternity*) 166.

V. be -past &c. *adj.*; have -expired &c. *adj.*, – run its course, – had its day; pass; pass –, go- -by, – away, – off; lapse, blow over.

look –, trace –, cast the eyes- back; exhume.

Adj. past, gone, gone by, over, passed away, bygone, foregone; elapsed, lapsed, preterlapsed, expired, no more, run out, blown over, that has been, extinct, never to return, exploded, forgotten, irrecoverable; obsolete &c. (*old*) 124.

former, pristine, quondam, *ci-devant,* late; ancestral.

foregoing; last, latter; recent, over-night; preter-perfect, -pluperfect.

looking back &c. *v.*; retro-spective, -active; archœological &c. *n.*

Adv. formerly; of -old, – yore; erst; whilom, erewhile, time was, ago, over; in -the olden time &c. *n.*; anciently, long -ago, – since; a long -while, – time- ago; years -, ages- ago; some time -ago, – since, – back.

yesterday, the day before yesterday; last -year, – season, – month &c.; ultimo; lately &c. (*newly*) 123.

[1] Whewell.

retrospectively; ere –, before –, till- now; hitherto, heretofore; no longer; once, – upon a time; from time immemorial; in the memory of man; time out of mind; already, yet, up to this time; *ex post facto*.

Phr. time was; the time -has, – hath- been; *fuimus Troës* [Vergil]; *fuit Ilium* [Vergil]; *hoc erat in more majorum;* " O call back yesterday, bid time return " [*Richard II*]; *tempi passati;* " the eternal landscape of the past " [Tennyson]; *ultimus Romanorum;* " what's past is prologue " [*Tempest*]; " whose yesterdays look backward with a smile " [Young].

2. Time with reference to a particular Period

123. Newness. — N. newness &c. *adj.*; novelty, recency; immaturity; youth &c. 127; gloss of novelty.

innovation; renovation &c. (*restoration*) 660.

modernism; mushroom, parvenu; latest fashion.

V. renew &c. (*restore*) 660; modernize.

Adj. new, novel, recent, fresh, green; young &c. 127; evergreen; raw, immature; virgin; un-tried, -handseled, -trodden, -beaten; fire-new, span-new.

late, modern, neoteric; new-born, -fashioned, -fangled, -fledged; of yesterday; just out, brand-new, up to date; vernal, renovated; semper-virent, -virid.

fresh as -a rose, – a daisy, – paint; spick and span.

Adv. newly &c. *adj.*; afresh, anew, lately, just now, only yesterday, the other day; latterly, of late.

not long –, a short time- ago.

Phr. *di novello tutto par bello; nullum est jam dictum quod non dictum est prius; una scopa nuova spazza bene.*

124. Oldness. — N. oldness &c. *adj.*; age, antiquity; cobwebs of antiquity.

maturity; decline, decay; senility &c. 128.

seniority, eldership, primogeniture.

archaism &c. (*the past*) 122; thing –, relic- of the past; megatherium; Sanskrit.

tradition, prescription, custom, immemorial usage, common law.

V. be -old &c. *adj.*; have -had, – seen- its day; become -old &c. *adj.*; age, fade.

Adj. old, ancient, antique; of long standing, time-honored, venerable; elder, -est; firstborn.

prime; prim-itive, -eval, -igenous; paleoanthropic; primordi-al, -nate; aboriginal &c. (*beginning*) 66; diluvian, antediluvian; protohistoric; prehistoric; patriarchal, preadamite; paleocrystic; fossil, paleozoic, preglacial, antemundane; archaic, classic, medieval, Pre-Raphaelite, ancestral, black-letter.

immemorial, traditional, prescriptive, customary, whereof the memory of man runneth not to the contrary; inveterate, rooted.

antiquated, of other times, rococo, of the old school, after-age, obsolete; out of -date, – fashion; stale, old-fashioned, behind the age; old-world; exploded; gone -out, – by; *passé*, run out; senile &c. 128; time-worn; crumbling &c. (*deteriorated*) 659; secondhand.

old as -the hills, – Methuselah, – Adam, – history.

Adv. since the -world was made, – year one, – days of Methuselah.

Phr. *vetera extollimus recentium incuriosi* [Tacitus].

125. Morning. [Noon.] **— N.** morning, morn, forenoon, *a. m.*, prime, dawn, daybreak; dayspring, foreday, sun-up; peep –, break- of day; aurora; first blush –, first flush –, prime- of the morning; twilight, crepuscule, sunrise; cockcrow, -ing; the small hours.

spring; vernal equinox.

noon; mid-, noon-day; noontide, meridian, prime; nooning, noontime.

summer, midsummer.

Adj. matin, matutinal; vernal.

126. Evening. [Midnight.] **— N.** evening, eve; decline –, fall –, close- of day; candlelight, -ing; eventide, nightfall, curfew, dusk, twilight, eleventh hour; sun-set, -down; going down of the sun, cock- shut †, dewy eve, gloaming, bedtime.

afternoon, postmeridian, *p. m.*

autumn; fall, – of the leaf; autumnal equinox; Indian –, St. Luke's –, St. Martin's – summer.

midnight; dead –, witching hour –,

Adv. at -sunrise &c. *n.*; with the lark, when the morning dawns.

Phr. " at shut of evening flowers " [*Paradise Lost*]; *entre chien et loup;* " flames in the forehead of the morning sky " [Milton]; " the breezy call of incense-breathing morn " [Gray].

witching time- of night; winter; killing time.

Adj. vespertine, autumnal, nocturnal.

Phr. " midnight, the outpost of advancing day " [Longfellow]; " sable-vested Night " [Milton]; " this gorgeous arch with golden worlds inlay'd " [Young].

127. Youth. — N. youth; juven-ility, -escence; juniority; infancy; baby-, child-, boy-, girl-, youth-hood; incunabula; minority, nonage, teens, tender age, bloom.

cradle, nursery, leading strings, pupilage, puberty, pucelage.

prime -, flower -, springtide -, seed-time -, golden season- of life; heyday of youth, school days; rising generation.

Adj. young, youthful, juvenile, green, callow, budding, sappy, puisne, beardless, under age, in one's teens; *in statu pupillari;* younger, junior; hebetic, unfledged.

Phr. " youth on the prow and pleasure at the helm " [Gray]; " youth . . . the glad season of life " [Carlyle].

128. Age. — N. age; oldness &c. *adj.*; old -, advanced- age; sen-ility, -escence; years, anility, gray hairs, climacteric, grand climacteric, declining years, decrepitude, hoary age, caducity, superannuation; second child-hood, -ishness; dotage; vale of years, decline of life, " sear and yellow leaf " [*Macbeth*]; threescore years and ten; green old age, ripe age; longevity; time of life.

seniority, eldership; elders &c. (*veteran*) 130; firstling; *doyen*, father; primogeniture.

[Science of old age.] nostology.

V. be -aged &c. *adj.*; grow -, get- old &c. *adj.*; age; decline, wane; senesce.

Adj. aged; old &c. 124; elderly, senile; matronly, anile; in years; ripe, mellow, run to seed, declining, waning, past one's prime; gray, -headed; hoar, -y; venerable, time-worn, antiquated, *passé*, effete, decrepit, superannuated; advanced in -life, - years; stricken in years; wrinkled, marked with the crow's foot; having one foot in the grave; doting &c. (*imbecile*) 499; like the last of pea time.

old-, eld-er, -est; senior; firstborn.

turned of, years old; of a certain age, no chicken, old as Methuselah; ancestral; patriarchal &c. (*ancient*) 124; gerontic.

Phr. " give me a staff of honor for my age " [Titus Andronicus]; *bis pueri senes; peu de gens savent être vieux; plenus annis abiit plenus honoribus* [Pliny the Younger]; " old age is creeping on apace " [Byron]; " slow-consuming age " [Gray]; " the hoary head is a crown of glory " [*Proverbs xvi*, 31]; " the silver livery of advised age " [*II Henry VI*]; to grow old gracefully; " to vanish in the chinks that Time has made " [Rogers].

129. Infant. — N. infant, babe, baby; nurse-, suck-, year-, wean-ling; papoose, *bambino;* kid *; vagitus.

child, bairn, little one, brat, chit, pickaninny, urchin; bant-, brat-ling; elf.

youth, boy, lad, stripling, youngster, younker, callant, whipster, whippersnapper, whiffet [U. S.], schoolboy, hobbledehoy, hopeful, cadet, minor, master.

scion; sap-, seed-ling; tendril, olivebranch, nestling, chicken, larva, chrysalis, tadpole, whelp, cub, pullet, fry, callow; codlin, -g; fœtus, calf, colt, pup, foal, kitten; lamb, -kin; aurelia, caterpillar, cocoon, nymph, nympha, orphan, pupa, staddle.

girl; lass, -ie; wench, miss, damsel, demoiselle; maid, -en; virgin; hoyden.

Adj. infant-ine, -ile; puerile; boy-, girl-, child-, baby-, kitten-ish; baby; newborn, unfledged, new-fledged, callow.

in -the cradle, - swaddling clothes, - long clothes, - arms, - leading strings; at the breast; in one's teens.

130. Veteran. — N. veteran, old man, seer, patriarch, graybeard; grandfather, -sire; grandam; gaffer, gammer; crone; pantaloon; sexage-, octoge-, nonage-, cente-narian; old stager; dotard &c. 501.

preadamite, Methuselah, Nestor, old Parr; elders; forefathers &c. (*paternity*) 166.

Phr. " superfluous lags the veteran on the stage " [Johnson].

131. Adolescence. — N. adolescence, pubescence, majority; adultism; adultness &c. *adj.*; manhood, virility, maturity; full –, ripe- age; flower of age; prime –, meridian –, spring- of life.

man &c. 373; woman &c. 374; adult, no chicken.

V. come -of age, – to man's estate, – to years of discretion; attain majority, assume the *toga virilis;* have -cut one's eyeteeth, – sown one's wild oats.

Adj. adolescent, pubescent, of age; of -full, – ripe- age; out of one's teens, grown up, mature, full grown, in one's prime, middle-aged, manly, virile, adult; womanly, matronly; marriageable, nubile.

3. Time with reference to an Effect or Purpose

132. Earliness. — N. earliness &c. *adj.*; morning &c. 125.

punctuality; promptitude &c. (*activity*) 682; haste &c. (*velocity*) 274; suddenness &c. (*instantaneity*) 113.

prematurity, precocity, precipitation, anticipation; a stitch in time.

V. be -early &c. *adj.*, – beforehand &c. *adv.*; keep time, take time by the forelock, anticipate, forestall; have –, gain- the start; steal a march upon; gain time, draw on futurity; bespeak, secure, engage, preëngage.

accelerate; expedite &c. (*quicken*) 274; make haste &c. (*hurry*) 684.

Adj. early, prime, timely, seasonable, in time, punctual, forward; prompt &c. (*active*) 682; summary.

premature, precipitate, precocious; prevenient, anticipatory; rath.

sudden &c. (*instantaneous*) 113; unexpected &c. 508; near, – at hand; immediate.

Adv. early, soon, anon, betimes, rath; eft, -soons; ere –, before- long; punctually &c. *adj.*; to the minute; in time; in -good, – military, – pudding, – due- time; time enough.

beforehand; prematurely &c. *adj.*; precipitately &c. (*hastily*) 684; too soon; before -its, – one's- time; in anticipation; unexpectedly &c. 508.

suddenly &c. (*instantaneously*) 113; before one can say " Jack Robinson," at short notice, extempore; on the spur of the -moment, – occasion [Bacon]; at once; on the -spot, – instant; at sight; off –, out of- hand; *à vue d'œil;* straight, -way, -forth; forthwith, incontinently, -way, -forth; forthwith, incontinently, summarily, immediately, briefly, shortly, quickly, speedily, apace, before the ink is dry, almost immediately, presently, at the first opportunity, in no long time, by and by, in a while, directly.

Phr. touch and go, no sooner said than done; *tout vient à temps pour qui sait attendre.*

133. Lateness. — N. lateness &c. *adj.*; tardiness &c. (*slowness*) 275.

de-lay, -lation; cunctation, procrastination; deferring &c. *v.*; postponement, adjournment, prorogation, retardation, respite; protraction, prolongation; Fabian policy, *médecine expectante,* chancery suit; leeway; high time.

V. be -late &c. *adj.*; tarry, wait, stay, bide, take time; dawdle &c. (*be inactive*) 683; linger, loiter; bide –, take- one's time; gain time; hang fire; stand –, lie- over.

put off, defer, delay; lay over, suspend; shift –, stave- off; waive, retard, remand, postpone, adjourn; procrastinate; dally; prolong, protract; spin –, draw –, lengthen- out; prorogue; keep back; tide over; push –, drive- to the last; let the matter stand over; reserve &c. (*store*) 636; temporize; consult one's pillow, sleep upon it.

lose an opportunity &c. 135; be kept waiting, dance attendance; kick –, cool- one's heels; *faire antichambre;* wait impatiently; await &c. (*expect*) 507; sit up, – at night.

Adj. late, tardy, slow, behindhand, serotine, belated, postliminious, posthumous, backward, unpunctual; dilatory &c. (*slow*) 275; delayed &c. *v.*; in abeyance.

Adv. late; late-, back-ward; late in the day; at -sunset, – the eleventh hour, – length, – last; ultimately; after –, behind- time; too late; too late for &c. 135.

slowly, leisurely, deliberately, at one's leisure; *ex post facto; sine die.*

Phr. *nonum prematur in annum* [Horace]; " against the sunbeams serotine and lucent " [Longfellow]; *è meglio tardi che mai; deliberando sæpe perit occasio* [Syrus].

134. Occasion. — **N.** occasion, opportunity, opening, room; suitable -, proper- -time, - season; high time; opportuneness &c. *adj.*; tempestivity.

crisis, turn, juncture, conjuncture; turning point, given time.

nick of time; golden -, well timed -, fine -, favorable- opportunity; clear stage, fair field; *mollia tempora; fata Morgana;* spare time &c. (*leisure*) 685.

V. seize &c. (*take*) 789 -, use &c. 677 -; give &c. 784- an -opportunity, - occasion; improve the occasion.

suit the occasion &c. (*be expedient*) 646.

strike the iron while it is hot, *battre le fer sur l'enclume,* make hay while the sun shines, seize the present hour, take time by the forelock, *prendre la balle au bond.*

Adj. opportune, timely, well-timed, timeful, seasonable.

providential, lucky, fortunate, happy, favorable, propitious, auspicious, critical; suitable &c. 23; *obiter dicta.*

Adv. opportunely &c. *adj.*; in -proper, - due- -time, - course, - season; for the nonce; in the -nick, - fullness- of time; all in good time; just in time, at the eleventh hour, now or never.

by the -way, - by; *en passant, à propos; pro -re natâ, - hac vice; par parenthèse,* parenthetically, by way of parenthesis; while -speaking of, - on this subject; extempore; on the spur of the -moment, - occasion; on the spot &c. (*early*) 132.

Phr. *carpe diem* [Horace]; *occasionem cognosce;* one's hour is come, the time is up; that reminds me; *bien perdu bien connu; è sempre l'ora; ex quovis ligno non fit Mercurius; nosce tempus; nunc aut nunquam.*

135. Intempestivity. — **N.** intempestivity; unsuitable -, improper- time; unreasonableness &c. *adj.*; evil hour; *contretemps;* intrusion; anachronism &c. 115.

V. be -ill timed &c. *adj.*; mistime, intrude, come amiss, break in upon; have other fish to fry; be -busy, - occupied.

lose -, throw away -, waste -, neglect &c. 460- an opportunity; allow -, suffer- the -opportunity, - occasion- to -pass, - slip, - go by, - escape, - lapse; waste time &c. (*be inactive*) 683; let slip through the fingers, lock the stable door when the steed is stolen.

Adj. ill-, mis-timed; ill-fated, -omened, -starred; untimely, intrusive, unseasonable; out of -date, - season; inopportune, timeless, untoward, *mal à propos,* unlucky, inauspicious, unpropitious, unfortunate, unfavorable; unsuited &c. 24; inexpedient &c. 647.

unpunctual &c. (*late*) 133; too late for; premature &c. (*early*) 132; too soon for; wise after the event.

Adv. inopportunely &c. *adj.*; as ill luck would have it, in an evil hour, the time having gone by, a day after the fair.

Phr. After meat mustard, after death the doctor.

3. RECURRENT TIME

136. Frequency. — **N.** frequency, oftness, oftenness; repetition &c. 104.

V. recur &c. 104; do nothing but; keep, - on.

Adj. frequent, many times, not rare, thickcoming, incessant, perpetual, continual, constant, repeated &c. 104; habitual &c. 613.

Adv. often, oft; oft-, often-times; frequently; repeatedly &c. 104; unseldom, not unfrequently; in -quick, - rapid-succession; many a time and oft; daily, hourly &c.; every -day, - hour, - moment &c.

perpetually, continually, constantly, incessantly, without ceasing, at all times, daily and hourly, night and day, day and night, day after day, morning noon and night, ever and anon.

137. Infrequency. — **N.** infrequency, rareness, rarity; fewness &c. 103; seldomness; uncommonness.

V. be -rare &c. *adj.*

Adj. un-, in-frequent; rare, - as a blue diamond; few &c. 103; scarce; almost unheard of, unprecedented, which has not occurred within the memory of the oldest inhabitant, not within one's previous experience.

Adv. seldom, rarely, scarcely, hardly; not often, unfrequently, unoften; scarcely -, hardly- ever; once in a blue moon.

once; once -for all, - in a way; *pro hac vice.*

Phr. *ein mal kein mal.*

most often; commonly &c. (*habitually*) 613.

sometimes, occasionally, at times, now and then, from time to time, there being times when, *toties quoties*, often enough, again and again.

138. Regularity of recurrence. **Periodicity. — N.** periodicity, intermittence; beat; oscillation &c. 314; pulse, pulsation; rhythm; alter-nation, -nateness, -nativeness, -nity.

bout, round, revolution, rotation, turn, say.

anniversary, jubilee, centenary.

catamenia, courses, menses, menstrual flux.

[Regularity of return] rota, cycle, period, stated time, routine; days of the week; Sunday, Monday &c.; months of the year; January &c.; feast, fast &c.; Christmas, Easter, New Year's day &c.

Allhallows, Allhallowmas, All Saints' Day; All Souls', – Day; Ash Wednesday, bicentennial, birthday, bissextile, Candlemas, Dewali, ground-hog day [U. S.], Halloween, Hallowmas, Lady day, leap year, Midsummer day, Muharram, woodchuck day [U. S.], St. Swithin's day, natal day; yearbook; yuletide.

punctuality, regularity, steadiness.

V. recur in regular -order, – succession; return, revolve; come -again, – in its turn; come round, – again; beat, pulsate; alternate; intermit.

Adj. periodic, -al; serial, recurrent, cyclical, rhythmical; recurring &c. *v.*; inter-, re-mittent; alternate, every other.

hourly; diurnal, daily; quotidian, tertian, weekly; hebdomad-al, -ary; bi-weekly, fortnightly; bimonthly; catamenial; monthly, menstrual; yearly, annual; biennial, triennial, &c.; centennial, secular; paschal, lenten, &c.

regular, steady, punctual, regular as clockwork.

Adv. periodically &c. *adj.*; at -regular intervals, – stated times; at -fixed, – established- periods; punctually &c. *adj.*; *de die in diem;* from day to day, day by day.

by turns; in -turn, – rotation; alternately, every other day, off and on, ride and tie, round and round.

139. Irregularity of recurrence. — **N.** irregularity, uncertainty, unpunctuality; fitfulness &c. *adj.*; capriciousness, ecrhythmus.

Adj. irregular, uncertain, unpunctual, capricious, desultory, fitful, flickering; rambling, rhapsodical; spasmodic; im-methodical, variable.

Adv. irregularly &c. *adj.*; by fits and starts &c. (*discontinuously*) 70.

Section VII. C H A N G E

1. Simple Change

140. [Difference at different times.] **Change. — N.** change, alteration, mutation, permutation, variation, modification, modulation, inflexion, mood, qualification, innovation, metastasis, deviation, turn; diversion; break.

transformation, transfiguration; metamorphosis; transmutation; deoxidization; transubstantiation; metagenesis, transanimation, transmigration, metempsychosis; avatar; alterative.

conversion &c. (*gradual change*) 144; revolution &c. (*sudden or radical change*) 146; inversion &c. (*reversal*) 218; displacement &c. 185; transference &c. 270.

141. [Absence of change.] **Permanence. — N.** stability &c. 150; quiescence &c. 265; obstinacy &c. 606.

permanence, persistence, endurance; durability; standing, *status quo;* maintenance, preservation, conservation; conservatism; law of the Medes and Persians; standing dish.

V. let -alone, – be; persist, remain, stay, tarry, rest; hold, – on; last, endure, bide, abide, aby, dwell, maintain, keep; stand, – still, – fast; subsist, live, outlive, survive; hold -, keep- one's -ground, – footing; hold good.

Adj. stable &c. 150; persisting &c. *v.*; permanent; established; unchanged

changeableness &c. 149; tergiversation &c. (*change of mind*) 607.

V. change, alter, vary, wax and wane; modulate, diversify, qualify, tamper with; turn, shift, veer, tack, chop, shuffle, swerve, warp, deviate, turn aside, evert, intervert; pass to, take a turn, turn the corner, resume.

work a change, modify, vamp, superinduce; trans-form, -figure, -mute, -mogrify, -ume; metamorphose, ring the changes.

innovate, introduce new blood, shuffle the cards; give a -turn, – color- to; influence, turn the scale; shift the scene, turn over a new leaf.

recast &c. 146; reverse &c. 218; disturb &c. 61; convert into &c. 144.

Adj. changed &c. *v.*; newfangled; changeable &c. 149; transitional; modifiable; alterative.

Adv. *mutatis mutandis.*

Int. *quantum mutatus!*

Phr. " a change came o'er the spirit of my dream " [Byron]; *nous avons changé tout cela* [Molière]; *tempora mutantur nos et mutamur in illis; non sum qualis eram* [Horace]; *casaque tourner; corpora lente augescent cito extinguuntur* [Tacitus]; *in statu quo ante bellum;* " still ending and beginning still " [Cowper]; *vox audita perit littera scripta manet.*

&c. (change &c. 140); renewed; intact, inviolate; persistent; monotonous, uncheckered; unfailing.

un-destroyed, -repealed, -suppressed; conservative, *qualis ab incepto;* prescriptive &c. (*old*) 124; stationary &c. 265.

Adv. *in statu quo;* for good, finally; at a stand, -still; *uti possidetis;* without a shadow of turning.

Phr. *esto perpetua; nolumus leges Angliæ mutari; j'y suis et j'y reste.*

---

142. [Change from action to rest.] **Cessation. — N.** cessation, discontinuance, desistance, desinence.

inter-, re-mission; sus-pense, -pension; interruption; stop; stopping &c. *v.*; closure, stoppage, halt; arrival &c. 292.

pause, rest, lull, respite, truce, drop; interregnum, abeyance.

dead -stop, – stand, – lock; comma, colon, semicolon, period, full stop; end &c. 67; death &c. 360.

V. cease, discontinue, desist, stay; break –, leave- off; hold, stop, pull up, stop short; stick, hang fire; halt; pause, rest.

have done with, give over, surcease, shut up shop; give up &c. (*relinquish*) 624.

hold –, stay- one's hand; rest on one's oars, repose on one's laurels.

come to a -stand, – standstill, – deadlock, – full stop; arrive &c. 292; go out, die away; wear -away, – off; pass away &c. (*be past*) 122; be at an end.

intromit, interrupt, suspend, interpel †; inter-, re-mit; put -an end, – a stop, – a period- to; derail; bring to a stand, -still; stop, cut short, arrest, stem the -tide, – torrent; pull the check-string.

Int. hold! stop! enough! avast! have done! a truce to! soft! leave off! *tenez!*

Phr. " I pause for a reply " [*Julius Cæsar*].

143. Continuance in action. — **N.** continu-ance, -ation; run; perpetuation, prolongation; persistence &c. (*perseverance*) 604a; repetition &c. 104.

V. continue, persist; go –, jog –, keep –, run –, hold- on; abide, keep, pursue, stick to; take –, maintain- its course; carry on, keep up.

sustain, uphold, hold up, keep on foot; follow up, perpetuate; maintain; preserve &c. 604a; harp upon &c. (*repeat*) 104

keep -going, – alive, – the pot boiling, – up the ball; die in harness; hold on –, pursue- the even tenor of one's way.

let be; *stare super antiquas vias; quieta non movere;* let things take their course.

Adj. continuing &c. *v.*; uninterrupted, unintermitting, unvarying, unshifting; unreversed, unstopped, unrevoked, unvaried; sustained; undying &c. (*perpetual*) 112; inconvertible.

Int. right away!

Phr. *nolumus leges Angliæ mutari; vestigia nulla retrorsum* [Horace]; *labitur et labetur* [Horace].

---

144. [Gradual change to something different.] **Conversion. — N.** conversion, reduction, transmutation, resolution, assimilation; assumption; naturalization; transportation.

chemistry, alchemy; progress, growth, lapse, flux.

passage; transit, -ion; transmigration, shifting &c. *v.*; phase; conjugation; convertibility.

crucible, alembic, caldron, retort.

convert, pervert, renegade, apostate.

V. be converted into; become, get, wax; come –, turn- -to, – into; turn out, lapse, shift; run –, fall –, pass –, slide –, glide –, grow –, ripen –, open –, resolve itself –, settle –, merge- into; melt, grow, come round to, mature, mellow; assume the -form, – shape, – state, – nature, – character- of; illapse; assume a new phase, undergo a change.

convert –, resolve- into; make, render; mold, form &c. 240; remodel, new model, refound, reform, reorganize; assimilate –, bring –, reduce- to.

Adj. converted into &c. *v.*; convertible, resolvable into; transitional; naturalized.

Adv. gradually &c. (*slowly*) 275; *in transitu* &c. (*transference*) 270.

145. Reversion. — N. reversion, return; revulsion.

turning point, turn of the tide; *status quo ante bellum;* calm before a storm. alternation &c. (*periodicity*) 138; inversion &c. 219; recoil &c. 277; regression &c. 283; restoration &c. 660; relapse &c. 661; atavism; vicinism.

V. revert, turn back; relapse &c. 661; recoil &c. 277; retreat &c. 283; restore &c. 660; undo, unmake; turn the -tide, – scale.

Adj. reverting &c. *v.*; revulsive, reactionary; retrorse.

Adv. *à rebours.*

146. [Sudden or violent change.] **Revolution. — N.** revolution, *bouleversement,* subversion, break up; destruction &c. 162; sudden –, radical –, sweeping –, organic- change; clean sweep, *coup d'état,* counter revolution.

transilience, jump, leap, plunge, jerk, start; explosion; spasm, convulsion, throe, revulsion; storm, earthquake, cataclysm.

legerdemain &c. (*trick*) 545.

V. revolutionize; new model, remodel, recast; strike out something new, break with the past; change the face of, unsex.

Adj. unrecognizable; revolutionary.

147. [Change of one thing for another.] **Substitution. — N.** substitution, commutation;· supplanting &c. *v.,* supersession, metonymy &c. (*figure of speech*) 521.

[Thing substituted] substitute, succedaneum, makeshift, temporary expedient; shift, *pis aller,* stop-gap, jury mast, *locum tenens,* warming pan, dummy, scapegoat; double; changeling; *quid pro quo,* alternative; representative &c. (*deputy*) 759; palimpsest.

price, purchase money, consideration, equivalent.

V. substitute, put in the place of, change for; make way for, give place to; supply –, take- the place of; supplant, supersede, replace, cut out, serve as a substitute; step into –, stand in the shoes of; make a shift –, put up- with; borrow of Peter to pay Paul; commute, redeem, compound for.

148. [Double or mutual change.] **Interchange. — N.** inter-, ex-change; com-, per-, inter-mutation; reciprocation, transposition, shuffling; alternation, reciprocity; castling [at chess]; hocus-pocus.

interchange-ableness, -ability.

barter &c. 794; tit for tat &c. (*retaliation*) 718; cross fire, battledore and shuttlecock; *quid pro quo.*

V. inter-, ex-, counter-change; bandy, transpose, shuffle, change hands, swap, permute, reciprocate, commute; give and take, return the compliment; play at -puss in the corner, – battledore and shuttlecock; retaliate &c. 718; requite.

Adj. interchanged &c. *v.*; reciprocal, mutual, commutative, interchangeable, intercurrent.

Adv. in exchange, *vice versâ, mutatis mutandis,* backwards and forwards, by turns, turn and turn about; each –, every one- in his turn.

Adj. substituted &c. *v.*; vicarious, subdititious.

Adv. instead; in -place, – lieu, – the stead, – the room- of; *faute de mieux.*

2. Complex Change

149. Changeableness. — N. changeableness &c. *adj.*; mutability, inconstancy; versatility, mobility; instability, unstable equilibrium; vacillation &c. (*irresolution*) 605; fluctuation, vicissitude; alternation &c. (*oscillation*) 314.

restlessness &c. *adj.*; fidgets, disquiet; dis-, in-quietude; unrest; agitation &c. 315.

moon, Proteus, chameleon, quicksilver, shifting sands, weathercock, harlequin, Cynthia of the minute, April showers; wheel of Fortune; transientness &c. 111.

V. fluctuate, vary, waver, flounder, flicker, flitter, flit, flutter, shift, shuffle, shake, totter, tremble, vacillate, wamble, turn and turn about, ring the changes; sway –, shift- to and fro; change and change about; oscillate &c. 314; vibrate –, oscillate- between two extremes; alternate; have as many phases as the moon.

Adj. change-able, -ful; changing &c. 140; mutable, variable, checkered, ever changing; prote-an, -iform; versatile.

unstaid, inconstant; un-steady, -stable, -fixed, -settled; fluctuating &c. *v.*; restless; agitated &c. 315; erratic, fickle; irresolute &c. 605; capricious &c. 608; touch and go; inconsonant, fitful, spasmodic; vibratory; vagrant, wayward; desultory; afloat; alternating; alterable, plastic, mobile; transient &c. 111; wavering.

Adv. seesaw &c. (*oscillation*) 314; off and on.

Phr. " a rolling stone gathers no moss "; *pietra mossa non fa muschis; honores mutant mores; varium et mutabile semper femina* [Vergil].

150. Stability. — N. stability; immutability &c. *adj.*; unchangeableness &c. *adj.*; constancy; stable equilibrium, immobility, soundness, vitality, stabiliment, stiffness, ankylosis, solidity, *aplomb.*

establishment, fixture; rock, pillar, tower, foundation, leopard's spots, Ethiopian's skin.

permanence &c. 141; obstinacy &c. 606.

V. be -firm &c. *adj.*; stick fast; stand –, keep –, remain- firm; weather the storm.

settle, establish, stablish, ascertain, fix, set, stabilitate; retain, keep hold; make -good, – sure; fasten &c. (*join*) 43; set on its legs, float; perpetuate.

settle down; strike –, take- root; take up one's abode &c. 184; build one's house on a rock.

Adj. unchangeable, immutable; unalter-ed, -able; not to be changed, constant; permanent &c. 141; invariable, undeviating; stable, durable; perennial &c. (*diuturnal*) 110.

fixed, steadfast, firm, fast, steady, balanced; confirmed, valid; fiducial; immovable, irremovable, riveted, rooted; settled, established &c. *v.*; vested; incontrovertible, stereotyped, indeclinable.

tethered, anchored, moored, at anchor, on a rock, firm as a rock; firmly -seated, – established &c. *v.*; deep-rooted, ineradicable; inveterate; obstinate &c. 606.

transfixed, stuck fast, aground, high and dry, stranded.

indefeasible, irretrievable, intransmutable, incommutable, irresoluble, irrevocable, irreversible, reverseless, inextinguishable, irreducible; indissol-uble, -vable; indestructible, undying, imperishable, indelible, indeciduous; insusceptible, – of change.

Int. *stet.*

Phr. *littera scripta manet.*

Present Events

151. Eventuality. — N. eventuality, event, occurrence, incident, affair, transaction, proceeding, fact; matter of –, naked- fact; phenomenon; advent.

business, concern; circumstance, par-

Future Events

152. Destiny. — N. destiny &c. (*necessity*) 601; future –, post- existence; hereafter; future state, next world, world to come, after life; futurity &c. 121; everlasting -life, – death; life –

ticular, casualty, accident, adventure, passage, crisis, pass, emergency, contingency, consequence.

the world, life, things, doings, affairs; things –, affairs- in general; the times, state of affairs, order of the day; course –, tide –, stream –, current –, run –, march- of -things, – events; ups and downs of life; chapter of accidents &c. (*chance*) 156; situation &c. (*circumstances*) 8.

V. happen, occur; take -place, – effect; come, become of; come -off, – about, – round, – into existence, – forth, – to pass, – on; pass, present itself; fall; fall –, turn- out; run, be on foot, fall in; be-fall, -tide, -chance; prove, eventuate, draw on; turn –, crop –, spring –, cast- up; super-, sur-vene; issue, arrive, ensue, arise, start, hold, take its course; pass off &c. (*be past*) 122.

meet with; experience; fall to the lot of; be one's -chance, – fortune, – lot; find; encounter, undergo; pass –, go- through; endure &c. (*feel*) 821.

Adj. happening &c. *v.*; going on, doing, current; in the wind, afloat; on -foot, – the tapis; at issue, in question; incidental.

eventful, stirring, bustling, full of incident; memorable, momentous, signal.

Adv. eventually; in -the event of, – case; in the course of things; in the -natural, – ordinary- course of things; as -things, – times- go; as the world -goes, – wags; as the -tree falls, – cat jumps; as it may -turn out, – happen.

Phr. the plot thickens; " breasts the blows of circumstance " [Tennyson]; " so runs the round of life from hour to hour " [Tennyson]; " sprinkled along the waste of years " [Keble].

world- beyond the grave; prospect &c. (*expectation*) 507.

V. impend; hang –, lie- over; threaten, loom, await, come on, approach, stare one in the face; fore-, pre-ordain; pre-destine, doom, have in store for.

Adj. impending &c. *v.*; destined; about to -be, – happen; coming, in store, to come, going to happen, instant, at hand, near; near –, close- at hand; over-hanging, hanging over one's head, imminent; brewing, preparing, forth-coming; in the wind, on the cards, in reserve; that -will, – is to- be; in prospect &c. (*expected*) 507; looming in the -distance, – horizon, – future; unborn, in embryo; in the womb of -time, – futurity; pregnant &c. (*producing*) 161.

Adv. in -time, – the long run; all in good time; eventually &c. 151; whatever may happen &c. (*certainly*) 474; as -chance &c. 156- would have it.

Section VIII. CAUSATION

1. Constancy of Sequence in Events

153. [Constant antecedent.] **Cause.** — **N.** cause, origin, source, principle, element; occasioner, prime mover, *primum mobile; vera causa;* author &c. (*producer*) 164; mainspring, agent; leaven; groundwork, foundation &c. (*support*) 215.

spring, fountain, well, font; fountain –, spring- head; *fons et origo*, genesis; descent &c. (*paternity*) 166; remote cause; influence.

pivot, hinge, turning point, lever; key; proximate cause, *causa causans;* last straw that breaks the camel's back.

ground; reason, – why; why and wherefore, rationale, occasion, derivation; final cause &c. (*intention*) 620; *les dessous des cartes;* undercurrents.

rudiment. egg, germ, embryo, bud,

154. [Constant sequent.] **Effect.** — **N.** effect, consequence; after-growth, -come; deriva-tive, -tion; result; resultant, -ance; upshot, issue, dénouement; end &c. 67; development, outgrowth, fruit, crop, harvest, product, bud.

production, produce, work, handi-work, fabric, performance; creature, creation; off-spring, -shoot; first-fruits, -lings; heredity, telegony; premices †; primices †.

V. be the -effect &c. *n.*- of; be -due, – owing- to; originate -in, – from; rise –, arise –, take its rise –, spring –, proceed –, emanate –, come –, grow –, bud –, sprout –, germinate –, issue –, flow –, result –, follow –, derive its origin –, accrue- from; come -to, – of, – out of; depend –, hang –, hinge –, turn- upon.

root, radix, radical, etymon, nucleus, seed, stem, stock, stirps, trunk, tap-root, gemmule, radicle, semen, sperm.

nest, cradle, nursery, womb, nidus, birthplace, hotbed.

caus-ality, -ation; origination; production &c. 161.

V. be the -cause &c. *n.*- of; originate; give -origin, – rise, – occasion- to; cause, occasion, sow the seeds of, kindle, suscitate †; bring -on, – to pass, – about; produce; create &c. 161; set -up, – afloat, – on foot; found, broach, institute, lay the foundation of; lie at the root of.

procure, induce, draw down, open the door to, superinduce, evoke, entail, operate; elicit, provoke.

conduce to &c. (*tend to*) 176; contribute; have a -hand in, – finger in- the pie; determine, decide, turn the scale; have a common origin; derive its origin &c. (*effect*) 154.

Adj. caused &c. *v.*; causal, original; prim-ary, -itive, -ordial; aboriginal; protogenal; radical; embry-onic, -otic; *in -embryo, – ovo;* seminal, germinal; at the bottom of; connate, having a common origin.

Adv. because &c. 155; behind the scenes.

Phr. *causa latet vis est notissima* [Ovid]; *felix qui potuit rerum cognoscere causas* [Vergil].

take the consequences, sow the wind and reap the whirlwind.

Adj. owing to; resulting from &c. *v.*; derivable from; due to; caused &c. 153- by; dependent upon; derived –, evolved- from; derivative; hereditary; telegonous.

Adv. of course, it follows that, naturally, consequently; as a –, in- consequence; through, all along of, necessarily, eventually.

Phr. *cela va sans dire,* " thereby hangs a tale " [*Taming of the Shrew*].

---

155. [Assignment of cause.] **Attribution. — N.** attribution, theory, etiology, ascription, reference to, rationale; accounting for &c. *v.*; palætiology,[1] imputation, derivation from.

fil-, affil-iation; pedigree &c. (*paternity*) 166.

explanation &c. (*interpretation*) 522; reason why &c. (*cause*) 153.

V. attribute –, ascribe –, impute –, refer –, lay –, point –, trace –, bring home- to; put –, set- down- to; blame; charge –, ground- on; invest with, assign as cause, lay at the door of, father upon; account for, derive from, point out the -reason &c. 153; theorize; tell how it comes; put the saddle on the right horse.

Adj. attributed &c. *v.*; attributable &c. *v.*; refer-able, -rible; due to, derivable from; owing to &c. (*effect*) 154; putative; ecbatic.

Adv. hence, thence, therefore, for, since, on account of, because, owing to; on that account; from -this, – that- cause; thanks to, forasmuch as; whence, *propter hoc.*

why? wherefore? whence? how -comes,

156. [Absence of assignable cause.] **Chance.**[2] **— N.** chance, indetermination, accident, fortune, hazard, hap, haphazard, chance medley, random, luck, raccroc, casualty, contingence, adventure, hit; fate &c. (*necessity*) 601; equal chance; lottery; tombola; toss up &c. 621; turn of the -table, – cards; hazard of the die, chapter of accidents; cast –, throw- of the dice; heads or tails, wheel of Fortune; *sortes, – Virgilianæ.*

probability, possibility, contingency, odds, long odds, run of luck; accidentalness; main chance.

theory of -Probabilities, – Chances; bookmaking; assurance; speculation, gaming &c. 621.

V. chance, hap, turn up; fall to one's lot; be one's -fate &c. 601; stumble on, light upon; take one's chance &c. 621.

Adj. casual, fortuitous, accidental, adventitious, causeless, incidental, contingent, uncaused, undetermined, indeterminate; possible &c. 470; unintentional &c. 621.

Adv. by -chance, – accident; casually; perchance &c. (*possibly*) 470; for aught

---

[1] Whewell, *History of the Inductive Sciences,* book xviii. vol. iii. p. 397 (3d edit.).

[2] The word *Chance* has two distinct meanings: the first, the absence of assignable *cause,* as above; and the second, the absence of *design* — for the latter see 621.

– is, – happens- it? how does it happen?

in -some, – some such- way; somehow, – or other.

Phr. that is why; *hinc illæ lachrymæ* [Horace].

one knows; as -good, – bad, – ill-luck &c. *n.*- would have it; as it may -be, – chance, – turn up, – happen; as the case may be.

Phr. "grasps the skirts of happy chance" [Tennyson]; "the accident of an accident" [Lord Thurlow].

2. CONNECTION BETWEEN CAUSE AND EFFECT

157. Power. — **N.** power; poten-cy, -tiality; *jiva;* puissance, might, force; energy &c. 171; dint; right -hand, – arm; ascendency, sway, control; pre-potency, -pollence; almightiness, omnipotence; authority &c. 737; strength &c. 159.

ability; ableness &c. *adj.*; competency; effi-ciency, -cacy; validity, cogency; enablement; vantage ground; influence &c. 175.

pressure; conductivity; elasticity; gravity, electricity, magnetism, galvanism, voltaic electricity, voltaism, electro-magnetism; attraction; *vis -inertiæ, – mortua, – viva;* potential –, dynamic- energy; friction, suction; live-circuit, -rail, -wire.

capability, capacity; *quid valeant humeri quid ferre recusent;* faculty, quality, attribute, endowment, virtue, gift, property, qualification, susceptibility.

V. be -powerful &c. *adj.*; gain -power &c. *n.*

belong –, pertain- to; lie –, be- in one's power; can.

give –, confer –, exercise- power &c. *n.*; empower, enable, invest; in-, en-due; endow, arm; strengthen &c. 159; compel &c. 744.

Adj. powerful, puissant; potent, -ial; capable, able; equal –, up- to; cogent, valid; effect-ive, -ual; efficient, efficacious, adequate, competent; multi-, pleni-, omni-potent; almighty.

forcible &c. *adj.* (*energetic*) 171; influential &c. 175; productive &c. 168.

Adv. powerfully &c. *adj.*; by -virtue, – dint- of.

Phr. *à toute force;* δός μοι ποῦ στῶ καὶ κινῶ τὴν γῆν; *eripuit cælo fulmen sceptrumque tyrannis; fortis cadere cedere non potest.*

158. Impotence. — **N.** impotence; in-, dis-ability; disablement, impuissance, imbecility; incapa-city, -bility; inapt-, inept-itude; indocility; invalidity, inefficiency, incompetence, disqualification.

telum imbelle, brutum fulmen, blank cartridge, flash in the pan, *vox et præterea nihil,* dead letter, bit of waste paper, dummy; Quaker gun.

inefficacy &c. (*inutility*) 645; failure &c. 732.

helplessness &c. *adj.*; prostration, paralysis, palsy, apoplexy, syncope, sideration †, deliquium, collapse, exhaustion, softening of the brain, emasculation, inanition; orchotomy.

cripple, old woman, muff, mollycoddle.

V. be -impotent &c. *adj.*; not have a leg to stand on.

vouloir -rompre l'anguille au genou, – prendre la lune avec les dents.

collapse, faint, swoon, fall into a swoon, drop; go by the board; end in smoke &c. (*fail*) 732.

render -powerless &c. *adj.*; deprive of power; dis-able, -enable; disarm, incapacitate, disqualify, unfit, invalidate, deaden, cramp, tie the hands; double up, prostrate, paralyze, muzzle, cripple, becripple, maim, lame, hamstring, draw the teeth of; throttle, strangle, garrotte, garrote; ratten, silence, sprain, clip the wings of, put *hors de combat*, spike the guns; take the wind out of one's sails, scotch the snake, put a spoke in one's wheel; break the -neck, – back; unhinge, -fit; put out of gear.

unman, unnerve, enervate; emasculate, castrate, geld, alter.

shatter, exhaust; weaken &c. 160.

Adj. powerless, impotent, unable, incapable, incompetent; ineff-icient, -ective; inept; un-fit, -fitted; un-, disqualified; unendowed; in-, un-apt; crippled, disabled &c. *v.*; armless.

harmless, unarmed, weaponless, defenseless, *sine ictu*, unfortified, indefensible, vincible, pregnable, untenable.

para-lytic, -lyzed; palsied, imbecile; nerve-, sinew-, marrow-, pith-, lust-less; emasculate, disjointed; out of -joint, – gear; un-nerved, -hinged; water-logged, on one's beam ends, rudderless; laid on one's back; done up, dead beat, exhausted, shattered, demoralized; graveled &c. (*in difficulty*) 704; helpless, unfriended, fatherless; without a leg to stand on, *hors de combat*, laid on the shelf.

null and void, nugatory, inoperative, good for nothing; ineffectual &c. (*failing*) 732; inadequate &c. 640; inefficacious &c. (*useless*) 645.

Phr. *der kranke Mann;* " desirous still but impotent to rise " [Shenstone].

159. [Degree of power.] **Strength.** — **N.** strength; power &c. 157; energy &c. 171; vigor, force; main –, physical –, brute- force; spring, elasticity, tone, tension, tonicity.

stoutness &c. *adj.*; lustihood, stamina, nerve, muscle, sinew, thews and sinews, physique; pith, -iness; virility, vitality.

athlet-ics, -icism; gymnastics, feats of strength.

adamant, steel, iron, oak, heart of oak; iron grip; grit, bone.

athlete, gymnast, acrobat; Atlas, Hercules, Antæus, Samson, Cyclops, Goliath; tower of strength; giant refreshed.

strengthening &c. *v.*; invigoration, refreshment, refocillation †.

[Science of forces] dynamics, statics.

V. be -strong &c. *adj.*, – stronger; overmatch.

render -strong &c. *adj.*; give -strength &c. *n.*; strengthen, invigorate, brace, nerve, fortify, sustain, harden, case-harden, steel, gird; screw –, wind –, set- up; gird –, brace- up one's loins; recruit, set on one's legs; vivify; refresh &c. 689; refect; reënforce &c. (*restore*) 660.

Adj. strong, mighty, vigorous, forcible, hard, adamantine, stout, robust, sturdy, hardy, powerful, potent, puissant, valid.

resistless, irresistible, invincible, proof against, impregnable, unconquerable, indomitable, inextinguishable, unquenchable; incontestable; more than a match for; over-powering, -whelming; all-powerful, -sufficient; sovereign.

able-bodied; athletic; Herculean, Cyclopean, Atlantean; muscular, brawny, wiry, well-knit, broad-shouldered, sinewy, strapping, stalwart, gigantic.

man-ly, -like, -ful; masculine, male, virile.

un-weakened, -allayed, -withered, -shaken, -worn, -exhausted: in full

160. Weakness. — **N.** weakness &c. *adj.*; debility, atony, relaxation, languor, enervation; impotence &c. 158; infirmity; effeminacy, feminality; fragility, flaccidity; inactivity &c. 683.

anæmia, bloodlessness, deficiency –, poverty- of blood.

declension –, loss –, failure- of strength; delicacy, invalidation, decrepitude, asthenia, adynamy, cachexy, cachexia, sprain, strain.

reed, thread, rope of sand, house of cards.

soft-, weak-ling; infant &c. 129; youth &c. 127.

V. be -weak &c. *adj.*; drop, crumble, give way, totter, tremble, shake, halt, limp, fade, languish, decline, flag, fail, have one leg in the grave.

render -weak &c. *adj.*; weaken, enfeeble, debilitate, shake, deprive of strength, relax, enervate; un-brace, -nerve; cripple, unman &c. (*render powerless*) 158; cramp, reduce, sprain, strain, blunt the edge of; dilute, impoverish; decimate; extenuate; reduce -in strength, – the strength of; *mettre de l'eau dans son vin.*

Adj. weak, feeble, debile †; impotent &c. 158; relaxed, unnerved, &c. *v.*; sap-, strength-, power-less; weakly, unstrung, flaccid, adynamic, asthenic; nervous.

soft, effeminate, feminate, womanly.

frail, fragile, shattery; flimsy, unsubstantial, gimcrack, gingerbread; rickety, cranky; craichy; drooping, tottering &c. *v.*; broken, lame, withered, shattered, shaken, crazy, shaky; palsied &c. 158; decrepit.

languid, poor, infirm; faint, -ish; sickly &c. (*disease*) 655; dull, slack, evanid †, spent, short-winded, effete; weather-beaten; decayed, rotten, worn, seedy, languishing, wasted, washy, laid low, pulled down, the worse for wear.

-force, – swing; in the plenitude of power.

stubborn, thick-ribbed, made of iron, deep-rooted; strong as -a lion, – a horse, – brandy; sound as a roach; in -fine, – high- feather; like a giant refreshed.

Adv. strongly &c. *adj.*; by -force &c. *n.*; by main force &c. (*by compulsion*)744.

Phr. " our withers are unwrung " [*Hamlet*].

Blut und Eisen; cœlitus mihi vires; du fort au diable; en habiles gens; ex vi termini; flecti non frangi; " he that wrestles with us strengthens our nerves and sharpens our skill " [Burke]; " inflexible in faith invincible in arms " [Beattie].

un-strengthened &c. 159, -supported, -aided, -assisted; aidless, defenseless &c. 158.

on its last legs; weak as a -child, – baby, – chicken, – cat, – rat; weak as -water, – water gruel, – gingerbread, – milk and water; colorless &c. 429.

Phr. *non sum qualis eram.*

---

3. Power in Operation

161. Production. — **N.** production, creation, construction, formation, fabrication, manufacture; building, architecture, erection, edification; coinage; diaster; organization; *nisus formativus;* putting together &c. *v.*; establishment; workmanship, performance; achievement &c. (*completion*) 729.

flowering, fructification; inflorescence.

bringing forth &c. *v.*; parturition, birth, birth-throe, childbirth, delivery, confinement, *accouchement*, travail, labor, midwifery, obstetrics; geniture; gestation &c. (*maturation*) 673; assimilation; evolution, development, growth; entelechy; fertilization, gemination, germination, heterogamy, genesis, generation, epigenesis, pro-creation, -generation, -pagation; fecundation, impregnation; albumen &c. 357.

spontaneous generation; arche-genesis, -biosis; bio-, abio-, di-, dysmero-, eumero-, hetero-, oö-, mero-, meto-, mono-, partheno-, homo-, xeno-genesis;[1] authorship, publication; works, *œuvre.*

bio-, disso-, xeno-geny; tocogony, vacuolization.

edifice, building, structure, fabric, erection, pile, tower, flower, fruit.

V. produce, perform, operate, do, make, gar, form, construct, fabricate, frame, contrive, manufacture; weave, forge, coin, carve, chisel; build, raise, edify, rear, erect, put together; set –, run- up; establish, constitute, compose, organize, institute; achieve, accomplish &c. (*complete*) 729.

flower, bear fruit, fructify, teem, ean, yean, farrow, drop, pup, kitten, kindle;

162. [Nonproduction.] Destruction. — **N.** destruction; waste, dissolution, breaking up; di-, dis-ruption; consumption; disorganization.

fall, downfall, ruin, perdition, crash, *éboulement*, smash, havoc, *délabrement, débâcle;* break -down, – up; prostration; desolation, *bouleversement*, wreck, wrack, shipwreck, cataclysm; washout.

extinction, annihilation; destruction of life &c. 361; knock-down blow; doom, crack of doom.

destroying &c. *v.*; demo-lition, -lishment; overthrow, subversion, suppression; abolition &c. (*abrogation*) 756; biblioclasm; sacrifice; ravage, devastation, razzia; incendiarism; revolution &c. 146; extirpation &c. (*extraction*) 301; *commencement de la fin*, road to ruin; dilapidation &c. (*deterioration*) 659; *sabotage.*

V. be -destroyed &c.; perish; fall, – to the ground; tumble, topple; go –, fall- to pieces; break up; crumble, – to dust; go to -the dogs, – the wall, – smash, – shivers, – wreck, – pot, – wrack and ruin; go -by the board, – all to smash; be all -over, – up- with; totter to its fall.

destroy; do –, make- away with; nullify; annul &c. 756; sacrifice, demolish; tear up; over-turn, -throw, -whelm; upset, subvert, put an end to; seal the doom of, do for, dish*, undo; break –, cut- up; break –, cut –, pull –, mow –, blow –, beat- down; suppress, quash, put down; cut short, take off, blot out; dispel, dissipate, dissolve; consume.

---

[1] Huxley.

bear, lay, bring forth, give birth to, lie in, be brought to bed of, evolve, pullulate, usher into the world.

make productive &c. 168; create; beget, get, generate, fecundate, impregnate; pro-create, -generate, -pagate; engender; bring -, call- into -being, - existence; breed, hatch, develop, bring up.

induce, superinduce; suscitate †; cause &c. 153; acquire &c. 775.

Adj. produc-ed, -ing &c. *v.*; productive of; prolific &c. 168; creative; formative; gen-etic, -ial, -ital; pregnant; *enceinte*, big -, fraught- with; in the family way, teeming, parturient, in the straw, brought to bed of; puerper-al, -ous.

di-, hetero-, oö-, xeno-genetic; ectogenous, gamic, hæmatobious, sporogenous, sporophorous.

architectonic.

Phr. *ex nihilo nihil; fiat lux; materiam superabat opus* [Ovid].

smash, crash, quell, squash, squelch, crumple up, shatter, shiver; batter; tear -, crush -, cut -, shake -, pull -, pick- to pieces; laniate; nip; tear to -rags, - tatters; crush-, knock- to atoms; ruin; strike out; throw -, knock- -down, - over; fell, sink, swamp, scuttle, wreck, shipwreck, ingulf, submerge; lay in -ashes, - ruins; sweep away, erase, expunge, raze; level, - with the -ground, - dust.

deal destruction, lay waste, ravage, gut; disorganize; dismantle &c. (*render useless*) 645; devour, swallow up, desolate, devastate, sap, mine, blast, confound; exterminate, extinguish, quench, annihilate; snuff -, put -, stamp -, trample- out; lay -, trample- in the dust; prostrate; tread -, crush -, trample- under foot; lay the ax to the root of; make -short work, - clean sweep, - mincemeat- of; cut up root and branch; fling -, scatter- to the winds; throw overboard; strike at the root of, sap the foundations of, spring a mine, blow up;

ravage with fire and sword; cast to the dogs; eradicate &c. 301.

Adj. destroyed &c. *v.*; perishing &c. *v.*; trembling -, nodding -, tottering- to its fall; in course of -destruction &c. *n.*; extinct; all-destroying, -devouring, -engulfing.

destructive, subversive, ruinous, incendiary, deletory †; destroying &c. *n.*; suicidal; deadly &c. (*killing*) 361.

Adv. with -crushing effect, - a sledge hammer.

Phr. *delenda est Carthago; dum Roma deliberat Saguntum perit; écrasez l'infâme* [Voltaire].

163. Reproduction. — N. reproduction, renovation; restoration &c. 660; renewal; new edition, reprint, revival, regeneration, palingenesis, revivification; apotheosis; resuscitation, reanimation, resurrection, reappearance; regrowth; Phœnix.

generation &c. (*production*) 161; multiplication.

V. reproduce; restore &c. 660; revive, renovate, renew, regenerate, revivify, resuscitate, reanimate, refashion, stir the embers, put into the crucible; multiply, repeat; resurge.

crop up, spring up like mushrooms.

Adj. reproduced &c. *v.*; renascent, reappearing; reproductive; suigenetic.

164. Producer. — N. producer, originator, inventor, author, founder, generator, mover, architect; maker &c. (*agent*) 690; prime mover.

165. Destroyer. — N. destroyer &c. (destroy &c. 162); cankerworm &c. (*bane*) 663; assassin &c. (*killer*) 361; executioner &c. (*punish*) 975; biblio-, eidolo-, icono-, idolo-clast; nihilist.

166. Paternity. — N. paternity; parentage; consanguinity &c. 11.

parent, father, sire, dad, papa, paterfamilias, abba; genitor, progenitor, procreator; ancestor; grand-sire, -father; great-grandfather; father-ship, -hood; *mabap.*

167. Posterity. — N. posterity, progeny, breed, issue, offspring, brood, litter, seed, farrow, spawn, spat; family, grandchildren, heirs; great-grandchild.

child, son, daughter; butcha; bantling, scion; acrospire, plumule, shoot, sprout, olive-branch, sprit, branch; off-shoot

house, stem, trunk, tree, stock, stirps, pedigree, lineage, line, family, tribe, sept, race, clan; genealogy, descent, extraction, birth, ancestry; forefathers, forbears, patriarchs.

motherhood, maternity; mother, dam, mamma, materfamilias; grandmother.

Adj. paternal, parental; maternal; family, ancestral, linear, patriarchal.

Phr. *avi numerantur avorum;* " *happy he with such a mother* " [Tennyson]; *hombre bueno no le busquen abolengo; philosophia stemma non inspicit* [Seneca].

-set; ramification; descendant; heir, -ess; heir -apparent, – presumptive; chip of the old block; heredity; rising generation.

straight descent, sonship, line, lineage, filiation, primogeniture.

Adj. filial; diphyletic.

Phr. " *the child is father of the man* " [Wordsworth].

168. Productiveness. — N. productiveness &c. *adj.*; fecundity, fertility, luxuriance, uberty †.

pregnancy, pullulation, fructification, multiplication, propagation, procreation; superfetation.

milch cow, rabbit, hydra, warren, seed plot, land flowing with milk and honey; second crop, aftermath; aftercrop, -growth; arrish, eddish, rowen; protoplasm; fertilization.

V. make -productive &c. *adj.*; fructify; procreate, generate, fertilize, spermatize, impregnate; fecund-ate, -ify; teem, multiply; produce &c. 161; conceive.

169. Unproductiveness. — N. unproductiveness &c. *adj.*; infertility, sterility, infecundity; impotence &c. 158; unprofitableness &c. (*inutility*) 645.

waste, desert, Sahara, wild, wilderness, howling wilderness.

V. be -unproductive &c. *adj.*; hang fire, flash in the pan, come to nothing.

Adj. unproductive, acarpous, inoperative, barren, addle, unfertile, unprolific, arid, sterile, unfruitful, infecund; *sine prole;* fallow; teem- issue-, fruit-less; unprofitable &c. (*useless*) 645; null and void, of no effect.

Adj. productive, prolific; teem-ing, -ful; fertile, fruitful, frugiferous, fruit-bearing; fecund, luxuriant; pregnant, uberous.

procre-ant, -ative; generative, life-giving, spermatic; multiparous; omnific; propagable.

parturient &c. (*producing*) 161; profitable &c. (*useful*) 644.

170. Agency. — N. agency, operation, force, working, strain, function, office, maintenance, exercise, work, swing, play; inter-working, -action; procurement.

causation &c. 153; instrumentality &c. 631; influence &c. 175; action &c. (*voluntary*) 680; *modus operandi* &c. 627.

quickening –, maintaining –, sustaining- power; home stroke.

V. be -in action &c. *adj.*; operate, work; act, – upon; perform, play, support, sustain, strain, maintain, take effect, quicken, strike.

come –, bring- into -operation, – play; have -play, – free play; bring to bear upon.

Adj. operative, efficient, efficacious, practical, effectual.

at work, on foot; acting &c. (*doing*) 680; in -operation, – force, – action, – play, – exercise; acted –, wrought- upon.

Adv. by the -agency &c. *n.*- of; through &c. (*instrumentality*) 631; by means of &c. 632.

Phr. " I myself must mix with action lest I wither by despair " [Tennyson].

171. Physical Energy. — N. energy, physical energy, force; keenness &c. *adj.*; intensity, vigor, strength, elasticity; go; high pressure; fire; rush.

acri-mony, -tude; causticity, viru-

172. Physical Inertness. — N. inertness, dullness &c. *adj.*; inertia, *vis inertiæ*, inertion, inactivity, torpor, languor; quiescence &c. 265; latency, inaction; passivity.

lence, poignancy; harshness &c. *adj.*; severity, edge, point; pungency &c. 392.

cantharides; seasoning &c. (*condiment*) 393.

activity, agitation, effervescence; ferment, -ation; ebullition, splutter, perturbation, stir, bustle; voluntary ehergy &c. 682; quicksilver.

resolution &c. (*mental energy*) 604; exertion &c. (*effort*) 686; excitation &c. (*mental*) 824.

V. give -energy &c. *n.*; energize, stimulate, kindle, excite, exert; sharpen, intensify; inflame &c. (*render violent*) 173; wind up &c. (*strengthen*) 159.

strike, – into, – hard, – home; make an impression.

Adj. strong, energetic, forcible, active; intense, deep-dyed, severe, keen, vivid, sharp, acute, incisive, trenchant, brisk.

rousing, irritating; poignant; virulent, caustic, corrosive, mordant, harsh, stringent; double-edged, – shotted, – distilled; drastic, escharotic; racy &c. (*pungent*) 392.

potent &c. (*powerful*) 157; radio-active.

Adv. strongly &c. *adj.*; *fortiter in re;* with telling effect.

Phr. the steam is up; *vires acquirit eundo;* "the race by vigor not by vaunts is won" [Pope].

mental inertness; sloth &c. (*inactivity*) 683; inexcitability &c. 826; irresolution &c. 605; obstinacy &c. 606; permanence &c. 141.

V. be -inert &c. *adj.*; hang fire, smolder.

Adj. inert, inactive, passive; torpid &c. 683; sluggish, dull, heavy, flat, slack, tame, slow, blunt; lifeless, dead, uninfluential.

latent, dormant, smoldering, unexerted.

Adv. inactively &c. *adj.*; in -suspense, -abeyance.

173. Violence. — N. violence, inclemency, vehemence, might, impetuosity; boisterousness &c. *adj.*; effervescence, ebullition; turbulence, bluster; uproar, callithump [U. S.], riot, row, rumpus, *le diable à quatre*, devil to pay, all the fat in the fire.

severity &c. 739; ferocity, rage, fury; exacerbation, exasperation, malignity; fit, paroxysm, orgasm, aphrodisia; force, brute force; outrage; *coup de main;* strain, shock, shog; spasm, convulsion, throe; hysterics, passion, &c. (*state of excitability*) 825.

out-break, -burst; debacle; burst, bounce, dissilience, discharge, volley, explosion, blow up, blast, detonation, rush, eruption, displosion †, torrent.

turmoil &c. (*disorder*) 59; ferment &c. (*agitation*) 315; storm, tempest, rough weather; squall &c. (*wind*) 349; earthquake, volcano, thunderstorm.

berserk, -er; fury, dragon, demon, tiger, beldame, Tisiphone, Megæra, Alecto, madcap, wild beast; fire eater &c. (*blusterer*) 887.

V. be -violent &c. *adj.*; run high; ferment, effervesce; romp, rampage; run -wild, – riot; break the peace; rush, tear; rush head-long, -foremost; run a muck, raise a storm, make a riot; make -, kick up- a row; rough-house *; bluster,

174. Moderation. — N. moderation; lenity &c. 740; temperateness, gentleness &c. *adj.*; sobriety; quiet; mental calmness &c. (*inexcitability*) 826.

moderating &c. *v.*; anaphrodisia; relaxation, remission, mitigation, tranquilization, assuagement, contemperation, pacification.

measure, *juste milieu*, golden mean, ἄριστον μέτρον.

moderator; lullaby, sedative, lenitive, demulcent, antispasmodic, carminative; laudanum; rose water, balm, poppy, opiate, anodyne, milk, opium, "poppy or mandragora"; wet blanket; palliative.

V. be -moderate &c. *adj.*; keep within -bounds, – compass; sober –, settle down; keep the peace, remit, relent; take in sail.

moderate, soften, mitigate, temper, accoy †; at-, con-temper; mollify, lenify, dulcify, dull, take off the edge, blunt, obtund, sheathe, subdue, chasten; sober –, tone –, smooth- down; weaken &c. 160; lessen &c. (*decrease*) 36; check; palliate.

tranquilize, assuage, appease, swage, lull, soothe, compose, still, calm, cool, quiet, hush, quell, sober, pacify, tame, damp, lay, allay, rebate, slacken, smooth, alleviate, rock to sleep, deaden, smother; throw -cold water on, – a wet blanket

rage, roar, riot, storm; boil, – over; fume, foam, come in like a lion, wreak, bear down, ride roughshod, out-Herod Herod; spread like wildfire.

break –, fly –, burst- out; bounce, explode, go off, displode †, fly, detonate, thunder, blow up, flash, flare, burst; shock, strain; break-, force-, prize-open.

render -violent &c. *adj.*; sharpen, stir up, quicken, excite, incite, urge, lash, stimulate; irritate, inflame, kindle, suscitate †, foment; accelerate, aggravate, exasperate, exacerbate, convulse, infuriate, madden, lash into fury; fan –, add fuel to- the flame; *oleum addere camino.*

explode; let -off, – fly; discharge, detonize, fulminate.

Adj. violent, vehement; warm; acute, sharp; rough, rude, ungentle, bluff, boisterous, wild; brusque, abrupt, waspish; impetuous; rampant.

turbulent; disorderly; blustering, raging &c. *v.*; troublous, riotous; tumultuary, -ous; obstreperous, uproarious; extravagant; unmitigated; ravening, tameless; frenzied &c. (*insane*) 503; desperate &c. (*rash*) 863; infuriate, furious, outrageous, frantic, hysteric, in hysterics.

fiery, flaming, scorching, hot, red-hot, ebullient.

savage, fierce, ferocious, fierce as a tiger.

excited &c. *v.*; un-quelled, -quenched, -extinguished, -repressed, -bridled, -ruly; headstrong; un-governable, -appeasable, -mitigable; un-, in-controllable; insup-, irre-pressible; orgastic.

spasmodic, convulsive, explosive; detonating &c. *v.*; volcanic, meteoric; stormy &c. (*wind*) 349.

Adv. violently &c. *adj.*; amain; by -storm, – force, – main force; with might and main; tooth and nail, *vi et armis*, at the point of the -sword, – bayonet; at one fell swoop; with a high hand, through thick and thin; in desperation, with a vengeance; *à –, à toute- outrance;* head-long, -foremost.

Phr. *furor arma ministrat;* "blown with restless violence round about the pendent world" [*Measure for Measure*].

over; slake; curb &c. (*restrain*) 751; tame &c. (*subjugate*) 749; smooth over; pour oil on the -waves, – troubled waters; pour balm into, *mettre de l'eau dans son vin.*

go out like a lamb, "roar you as gently as any sucking dove," [*Midsummer-Night's Dream*].

Adj. moderate; lenient &c. 740; gentle, mild; cool, sober, temperate, reasonable, measured; tempered &c. *v.*; calm, unruffled, quiet, tranquil, still; slow, smooth, untroubled; tame; peaceful, -able; pacific, halcyon.

un-exciting, -irritating; soft, bland, oily, demulcent, lenitive, anodyne; hypnotic &c. 683; sedative; antiorgastic, anaphrodisiac.

mild as mother's milk; milk and water.

Adv. moderately &c. *adj.*; gingerly; piano; under easy sail, at half speed; within -bounds, – compass; in reason.

Phr. *est modus in rebus.*

4. Indirect Power

175. Influence. — N. influence; importance &c. 642; weight, pressure, preponderance, prevalence, sway; predominance, -nancy; ascendency; dominance, reign; control, domination, pull *; authority &c. 737; capability &c. (*power*) 157; interest.

footing; purchase &c. (*support*) 215; play, leverage, vantage ground.

tower of strength, host in himself; protection, patronage, auspices.

V. have -influence &c. *n.*; be -influential &c. *adj.*; carry weight, weigh, tell; have a hold upon, magnetize. bear upon, gain a footing, work upon; take -root, – hold; strike root in

175a. Absence of Influence. — N. impotence &c. 158; powerlessness; inertness &c. 172; irrelevancy &c. 10.

V. have no -influence &c. 175.

Adj. uninfluential; unconduc-ing, -ive, -ting to; powerless &c. 158; irrelevant &c. 10.

run through, pervade; prevail, dominate, predominate; out-, over-weigh; over-ride, -bear; gain head; rage; be -rife &c. *adj.*; spread like wildfire; have -, get -, gain- -the upper hand, – full play.

be -recognized, – listened to; make one's voice heard, gain a hearing; play a -part, – leading part- in; take the lead, pull the strings; turn –, throw one's weight into- the scale; set the fashion, lead the dance.

Adj. influential; important &c. 642; weighty; prevailing &c. *v.*; prevalent, rife, rampant, dominant, regnant, predominant, in the ascendant, hegemonical.

Adv. with telling effect.

Phr. *tel maître tel valet.*

176. Tendency. — N. tendency; apt-ness, -itude; proneness, proclivity, bent, turn, tone, bias, set, leaning to, predisposition, inclination, propensity, susceptibility; conatus, nisus; liability &c. 177; quality, nature, temperament; idio-crasy, -syncrasy; cast, vein, grain; humor, mood; drift &c. (*direction*) 278; con-duciveness, -ducement; applicability &c. (*utility*) 644; subservience &c. (*instrumentality*) 631.

V. tend, contribute, conduce, lead, dispose, incline, verge, bend to, trend, affect, carry, redound to, bid fair to, gravitate towards; promote &c. (*aid*) 707.

Adj. tending &c. *v.*; conducive, working towards, in a fair way to, calculated to; liable &c. 177; subservient &c. (*instrumental*) 631; useful &c. 644; subsidiary &c. (*helping*) 707.

Adv. for, whither.

177. Liability. — N. lia-bility, -bleness; possibility, contingency; susceptivity, -bility.

V. be -liable &c. *adj.*; incur, lay oneself open to; run the –, stand a- chance; lie under, expose oneself to, open a door to.

Adj. liable, subject; in danger &c. 665; open –, exposed –, obnoxious- to; answerable; unexempt from; apt to; dependent on; incident to.

contingent, incidental, possible, on the cards, within range of, at the mercy of.

5. Combinations of Causes

178. Concurrence. — N. concurrence, coöperation, coagency; union; agreement &c. 23; consilience; consent &c. (*assent*) 488; alliance; concert &c. 709; partnership &c. 712.

V. con-cur, -duce, -spire, -tribute; agree, unite; hang –, pull- together &c. (*coöperate*) 709; help to &c. (*aid*) 707.

keep pace with, run parallel; go –, go along –, go hand in hand- with.

Adj. concurring &c. *v.*; concurrent, in alliance with, banded together, of one mind, at one with.

Adv. with one consent.

179. Counteraction. — N. counteraction, opposition; contrariety &c. 14; antagonism, polarity; clashing &c. *v.*; collision, interference, resistance, renitency, friction; reaction; retroaction &c. (*recoil*) 277; counterblast; neutralization &c. (*compensation*) 30; vis inertiæ; check &c. (*hindrance*) 706.

voluntary -opposition &c. 708, – resistance &c. 719; repression &c. (*restraint*) 751.

V. counteract; run counter, clash, cross; interfere –, conflict- with; contravene; jostle; go –, run –, beat –, militate- against; stultify; antagonize, oppose &c. 708; traverse; withstand &c. (*resist*) 719; hinder &c. 706; repress &c. (*restrain*) 751; react &c. (*recoil*) 277.

undo, neutralize; counterpoise &c. (*compensate*) 30; overpoise.

Adj. counteracting &c. *v.*; antagonistic, conflicting, retroactive, renitent, reactionary; contrary &c. 14.

Adv. although &c. 30; in spite of &c. 708; against.

CLASS II

Words relating to SPACE

Section I. SPACE IN GENERAL

1. Abstract Space

180. [Indefinite space.] Space. — N. space, extension, extent, superficial extent, expanse, stretch; room, scope, range, latitude, field, way, expansion, compass, sweep, play, swing, spread.

spare –, elbow –, house- room; stowage, roomage, margin; opening, sphere, arena.

open –, free- space; void &c. (*absence*) 187; waste; wild-, wilder-ness; moor, -land; campagna.

abyss &c. (*interval*) 198; unlimited space; infinity &c. 105; world; ubiquity &c. (*presence*) 186; length and breadth of the land.

proportions, acreage; acres, – roods and perches; square -inches, – yards &c.; ares, arpents.

Adj. spacious, roomy, extensive, expansive, capacious, ample; widespread, vast, world-wide, uncircumscribed; boundless &c. (*infinite*) 105; shore-, track-, path-less; extended.

Adv. extensively &c. *adj.*; wherever; everywhere; far and -near, – wide; right and left, all over, all the world over; throughout the -world, – length and breadth of the land; under the sun, in every quarter; in all -quarters, – lands; here there and everywhere; from -pole to pole, – China to Peru [Johnson], – Indus to the pole [Pope], – Dan to Beersheba, – end to end; on the face of the earth, in the wide world, from all points of the compass; to the -four winds, – uttermost parts of the earth.

180a. Inextension. — N. in-, non-extension, point; dot; atom &c. (*smallness*) 32.

181. [Definite space.] Region. — N. region, sphere, ground, soil, area, realm, hemisphere, quarter, district, beat, orb, circuit, circle; pale &c. (*limit*) 233; com-, de-partment; arch-duchy, -dukedom; clearing; domain, tract, territory, country, canton, county, shire, province, *arrondissement*, mofussil, parish, township, commune, ward, wapentake, hundred, riding, lathe, garth, soke, tithing, bailiwick; principality, duchy, kingdom.

arena, precincts, *enceinte*, walk, march; patch, plot, inclosure, close, enclave, field, court; street &c. (*abode*) 189.

clime, climate, zone, meridian, latitude.

Adj. territorial, local, parochial, provincial, regional.

182. [Limited space.] Place. — N. place, lieu, spot, point, dot; niche, nook &c. (*corner*) 244; hole; pigeonhole &c. (*receptacle*) 191; compartment; premises, precinct, station; area, courtyard, square; abode &c. 189; locality &c. (*situation*) 183.

ins and outs; every hole and corner.

Adv. somewhere, in some place, wherever it may be, here and there, in various places, *passim*.

2. Relative Space

183. Situation. — N. situation, position, locality, *locale*, status, latitude and longitude; footing, standing, standpoint, post; stage; aspect, attitude, posture, pose.

place, site, station, seat, venue, whereabouts; ground; bearings &c. (*direction*) 278; spot &c. (*limited space*) 182.

top-, ge-, chor-ography; map &c. 554.

V. be -situated, - situate; lie; have its seat in.

Adj. situ-ate, -ated; local, topical, topographical &c. *n.*

Adv. *in -situ,* - *loco;* here and there, *passim;* here-, there-, where-abouts; in place, here, there.

in -, amidst- such and such- -surroundings, - environs, - *entourage.*

184. Location. — N. loca-tion, -liza-tion; lodgment; de-, re-position; stow-, pack-age; collocation; packing, lading; establishment, settlement, installation; fixation; insertion &c. 300.

anchorage, mooring, encampment.

plantation, colony, settlement, cantonment; colonization, domestication, situation; habitation &c. (*abode*) 189; cohabitation; " a local habitation and a name " [*Midsummer Night's Dream*]; endenization, naturalization.

V. place, situate, locate, localize, make a place for, put, lay, set, seat, station, lodge, quarter, post, install; house, stow; establish, fix, pin, root; graft; plant &c. (*insert*) 300; shelve, pitch, camp, lay down, deposit, reposit; cradle; moor, tether, picket; pack, tuck in; em-, im-bed; vest, invest in.

billet on, quarter upon, saddle with; load, lade, freight; pocket, put up, bag.

inhabit &c. (*be present*) 186; domesticate, colonize; take -, strike- root; anchor; cast -, come to an- anchor; sit -, settle- down; settle; take up one's -abode, - quarters; plant -, establish -, locate- oneself; squat, perch, hive, *se nicher,* bivouac, burrow, get a footing; encamp, pitch one's tent; put up -at, - one's horses at; keep house.

endenizen, naturalize, adopt.

put back, replace &c. (*restore*) 660.

Adj. placed &c. *v.;* situate, posited, ensconced, imbedded, embosomed, rooted; domesticated; vested in, unremoved.

moored &c. *v.;* at anchor.

185. Displacement. — N. displacement, elocation †, transposition.

ejectment &c. 297; exile &c. (*banishment*) 893; removal &c. (*transference*) 270.

misplacement, dislocation &c. 61; fish out of water.

V. dis-place, -plant, -lodge, -establish; exile &c. (*seclude*) 893; ablegate, set aside, remove; take -, cart- away; take -, draft- off; lade &c. 184.

unload, empty &c. (*eject*) 297; transfer &c. 270; dispel.

vacate; depart &c. 293.

Adj. displaced &c. *v.;* un-placed, -housed, -harbored, -established, -settled; house-, home-less; out of -place, - a situation.

misplaced, out of its element.

---

3. EXISTENCE IN SPACE

186. Presence. — N. presence; occup-ancy, -ation; attendance; whereness.

permeation, pervasion; diffusion &c. (*dispersion*) 73.

ubi-ety, -quity, -quitariness; omnipresence.

bystander &c. (*spectator*) 444.

V. exist in space, be -present &c. *adj.; assister;* make one -of, - at; look on, attend, remain; find -, present- oneself; show one's face; fall in the way of, occur in a place; lie, stand; occupy.

people; inhabit, dwell, reside, stay, sojourn, live, abide, lodge, nestle, roost,

187. [Nullibiety.[1]] Absence. — N. absence; inexistence &c. 2; nonresidence, absenteeism; nonattendance, alibi.

emptiness &c. *adj.;* void, vacuum; vac-uity, -ancy; *tabula rasa;* exemption; hiatus &c. (*interval*) 198; lipotype.

truant, absentee.

nobody; nobody -present, - on earth; not a soul; *âme qui vive.*

V. be -absent &c. *adj.;* keep -away, - out of the way; play truant, absent oneself, stay away; keep -, hold- aloof.

withdraw, make oneself scarce, vacate; go away &c. 293.

Adj. absent, not present, away, non-

[1] Bishop Wilkins.

perch; take up one's abode &c. (*be located*) 184; tenant.

resort to, frequent, haunt; revisit.

fill, pervade, permeate; be -diffused, – disseminated- through; over-spread, -run; run through; meet one at every turn.

Adj. present; occupying, inhabiting &c. *v.*; moored &c. 184; resi-ant †, -dent, -dentiary; domiciled.

ubiquit-ous, -ary; omnipresent; universally present.

peopled, populous, full of people, inhabited.

Adv. here, there, where, everywhere, aboard, on board, at home, afield; on the spot; here there and everywhere &c. (*space*) 180; in presence of, before; under the -eyes, – nose- of; in the face of; *in propriâ personâ*.

Phr. *nusquam est qui ubique est* [Seneca].

resident, gone, from home; missing; lost; wanting; omitted; nowhere to be found; inexistence &c. 2.

empty, void; vac-ant, -uous; untenanted, -occupied, -inhabited; tenantless; desert, -ed; devoid; un-, uninhabitable.

exempt from, not having.

Adv. without, minus, nowhere; elsewhere; neither here nor there; in default of; sans; behind one's back.

Phr. the bird has flown, *non est inventus.*
" absence makes the heart grow fonder " [Bayley]; "absent in body but present in spirit" [*1 Corinthians* v, 3]; *absento nemo ne nocuisse velit* [Propertius]; " Achilles absent was Achilles still " [Homer]; *aux absents les os; briller par son absence;* " conspicuous by his absence " [Russell]; " in the hope to meet shortly again and make our absence sweet " [B. Jonson].

---

188. Inhabitant. — N. inhabitant; resident, -iary; dweller, indweller; addressee; occup-ier, -ant; householder, lodger, inmate, tenant, incumbent, sojourner, *locum tenens*, commorant; settler, squatter, backwoodsman, colonist; islander; denizen, citizen; burgher, oppidan, cockney, cit, townsman, burgess; villager; cot-tager, -tier, -ter; compatriot; backsettler, boarder; hotel-, innkeeper; habitant; paying guest; planter.

native, indigene, aborigines, autochthones; Englishman, John Bull; newcomer &c. (*stranger*) 57.

aboriginal, American, Caledonian, Cambrian, Canadian, Canuck *, downeaster [U. S.], Scot, Scotchman, Hibernian, Irishman, Welshman, Uncle Sam, Yankee, Brother Jonathan.

garrison, crew; population; people &c. (*mankind*) 372; colony, settlement; household; mir.

V. inhabit &c. (*be present*) 186; endenizen &c. (*locate oneself*) 184.

Adj. indigenous; nat-ive, -al; autochthon-al, -ous; British, English; American; Canadian, Irish, Scotch, Scottish, Welsh; domestic; domicil-iated, -ed; naturalized, vernacular, domesticated; domiciliary.

in the occupation of; garrisoned –, occupied- by.

189. [Place of habitation, or resort.] **Abode. — N.** abode, dwelling, lodging, domicile, residence, address, habitation, where one's lot is cast, local habitation, berth, diggings, seat, lap, sojourn, housing, quarters, headquarters, resiance †, tabernacle, throne, ark.

home, fatherland, country; homestead, -stall; fireside; hearth, – stone; chimney corner, ingleside; harem, seraglio, zenana; household gods, *lares et penates*, roof, household, housing, *dulce domum*, paternal domicile; native -soil, – land.

nest, nidus, snuggery; arbor, bower, &c. 191; lair, den, cave, hole, hiding place, cell, sanctum sanctorum, aerie, eyry, rookery, hive; habitat, haunt, covert, resort, retreat, perch, roost; nidification; *kala jagah*.

bivouac, camp, encampment, cantonment, castrametation; barrack, casemate, casern.

tent &c. (*covering*) 223; building &c. (*construction*) 161; chamber &c. (*receptacle*) 191; xenodochium.

tenement, messuage, farm, farmhouse, grange, hacienda, toft.

cot, cabin, hut, châlet, croft, shed, booth, stall, hovel, bothy, shanty, dugout [U. S.], wigwam; pen &c. (*inclosure*) 232; barn, bawn; kennel, sty, doghole, cote, coop, hutch, byre; cow-house,

---

-shed; stable, dovecote, columbar-y, -arium; shippen; igloo, iglu, jacal; lacustrine -, lake-, pile-dwelling; log-cabin, -house; shack, shebang *, tepee, topek.

house, mansion, place, villa, cottage, box, lodge, hermitage, *rus in urbe*; folly, rotunda, tower, *château*, castle, pavilion, hotel, court, manor-house, capital messuage, hall, palace; kiosk, bungalow; *casa*, country seat, apartment-, flat-, frame-, shingle-, tenement-house; temple &c. 1000.

hamlet, village, thorp, dorp, ham, kraal; borough, burgh, town, city, capital, metropolis; suburb; province, country; county-town, -seat; courthouse [U. S.]; ghetto.

street, place, terrace, parade, esplanade, *alameda*, board walk, embankment, road, row, lane, alley, court, quadrangle, quad, wynd, close, yard, passage, rents, buildings, mews.

square, polygon, circus, crescent, mall, piazza, arcade, colonnade, peristyle, cloister; gardens, grove, residences; block of buildings, market place, *place*, plaza.

anchorage, roadstead, roads; dock, basin, wharf, quay, port, harbor.

quarter, parish &c. (*region*) 181.

assembly room, meetinghouse, pump room, spa, watering place; inn; hostel, -ry; hotel, tavern, caravansary, dak bungalow, khan, hospice; public-, ale-, pot-, mug-house; gin palace; bar, -room; barrel house * [U. S.], cabaret, chophouse; club, -house; cookshop, dive [U. S.], exchange [euphemism, U. S.]; grill room, saloon [U. S.], shebeen; coffee-, eating-house; canteen, restaurant, buffet, café, *estaminet*, *posada;* alms-, poor-, town-house [U. S.].

garden, park, pleasure ground, plaisance, demesne.

V. take up one's abode &c. (*locate oneself*) 184; inhabit &c. (*be present*) 186.

Adj. urban, metropolitan; suburban; provincial, rural, rustic; domestic; cosmopolitan; palatial.

Phr. *eigner Herd ist goldes Werth;* "even cities have their graves" [Longfellow]; *ubi libertas ibi patria.*

190. [Things contained.] **Contents.** — **N.** contents; cargo, lading, freight, shipment, load, bale, burden, jag; cart-, ship-load; cup -, basket -, &c. (*receptacle*) 191- of; inside &c. 221; stuffing, ullage.

V. load, lade, ship, charge, fill, stuff.

191. Receptacle. — **N.** receptacle; inclosure &c. 232; recipient, receiver, reservatory.

compartment; cell, -ule; follicle; hole, corner, niche, recess, nook; crypt, stall, pigeonhole, cove, oriel; cave &c. (*concavity*) 252.

capsule, vesicle, cyst, pod, calyx, cancelli, utricle, bladder; pericarp, udder.

stomach, paunch, venter, ventricle, crop, craw, maw, gizzard, breadbasket; mouth.

pocket, pouch, fob, sheath, scabbard, socket, bag, sac, sack, saccule, wallet, cardcase, scrip, poke, knit, knapsack, haversack, sachel, satchel, reticule, budget, net; ditty-bag, -box; housewife, hussif; saddlebags; portfolio; quiver &c. (*magazine*) 636.

chest, box, coffer, caddy, case, casket, pyx, pix, caisson, desk, bureau, reliquary; trunk, portmanteau, band-box, valise; grip, -sack [U. S.]; skippet, vasculum; boot, imperial; *vache;* cage, manger, rack.

vessel, vase, bushel, barrel; canister, jar; pottle, basket, pannier, buck-basket, hopper, maund †, creel, cran, crate, cradle, bassinet, wisket, whisket, *jardinière*, *corbeille*, hamper, dosser, dorser, tray, hod, scuttle, utensil; brazier; cuspidor, spittoon.

[For liquids] cistern &c. (*store*) 636; vat, caldron, barrel, cask, puncheon, keg, rundlet, tun, butt, cag, firkin, kilderkin, carboy, amphora, bottle, jar, decanter, ewer, cruse, caraffe, crock, kit, canteen, flagon; demijohn; flask, -et; stoup, noggin, vial, phial, cruet, caster; urn, épergne, salver, patella, *tazza*, patera; pig-, big-gin; tyg, nipperkin, pocket pistol; tub, bucket, pail, skeel, pot, tankard, jug, pitcher, mug, pipkin; gal-, gall-ipot; matrass, receiver, retort, alembic,

bolthead, capsule, can, kettle; bowl, basin, jorum, punch bowl, cup, goblet, chalice, tumbler, glass, rummer, horn, saucepan, skillet, posnet †, tureen.

bail, beaker, billy, canakin; catch-basin, -drain; chatti, *lota*, mussuk, schooner [U. S.], spider, terrine, toby, *urceus*.

plate, platter, dish, trencher, calabash, porringer, potager, saucer, pan, crucible; glass-, table-ware; vitrics.

shovel, trowel, spoon, spatula, ladle, dipper, tablespoon, watch glass, thimble.

closet, commode, cupboard, cellaret, *chiffonnière*, locker, bin, bunker, buffet, press, clothespress, safe, sideboard, drawer, chest of drawers, till, scrutoire †, *secrétaire*, davenport, bookcase, cabinet, canterbury; escritoire, *étagère*, vargueno, vitrine.

chamber, apartment, room, cabin; office, court, hall, atrium; suite of rooms, apartment [U. S.], flat, story; saloon, *salon*, parlor; by-room, cubicle; presence chamber; sitting-, best-, keeping-, drawing-, reception-, state-room; gallery, cabinet, closet; pew, box; boudoir; adytum, sanctum; bedroom, dormitory; refectory, dining room, *salle-à-manger*; nursery, schoolroom; library, study; studio; billiard-, bath-, smoking-room; den; stateroom, tablinum, tenement.

attic, loft, garret, cockloft, clerestory; cellar, vault, hold, cockpit; cubbyhole; cook house; *entre-sol;* mezzanine floor; ground floor, *rez-de-chaussée;* basement, kitchen, pantry, *bawarchi-khana*, scullery, offices; storeroom &c. (*depository*) 636; lumber room; dairy, laundry, coach house; garage; hangar; out-, pent-house; lean-to.

portico, porch, stoop, stope, veranda, lobby, court, hall, vestibule, corridor, passage; ante-room, -chamber; lounge; piazza [=veranda, U. S.].

conservatory, greenhouse, bower, arbor, summerhouse, alcove, grotto, hermitage.

lodging &c. (*abode*) 189; bed &c. (*support*) 215; carriage &c. (*vehicle*) 272.

Adj. capsular; saccu-lar, -lated; recipient; ventricular, cystic, vascular, vesicular, cellular, camerated, locular, multilocular, polygastric; marsupial; siliqu-ose, -ous.

Section II. DIMENSIONS

1. General Dimensions

192. Size. — **N.** size, magnitude, dimension, bulk, volume; largeness &c. *adj.*; greatness &c. (*of quantity*) 31; expanse &c. (*space*) 180; amplitude, mass; proportions.

capacity; ton-, tun-nage; cordage; caliber, scantling.

turgidity &c. (*expansion*) 194; corpulence, obesity; plumpness &c. *adj.*; *embonpoint*, corporation, flesh and blood, lustihood.

hugeness &c. *adj.*; enormity, immensity, monstrosity.

giant, Brobdingnagian, Antæus, Goliath, Gog and Magog, Gargantua, monster, mammoth, Cyclops; cachalot, whale, porpoise, behemoth, leviathan, elephant, hippopotamus; colossus; tun, cord, lump, bulk, block, loaf, mass, swad, clod, nugget, bushel, thumper,

193. Littleness. — **N.** littleness &c. *adj.*; smallness &c. (*of quantity*) 32; exiguity, inextension; parvi-tude, -ty; duodecimo; Elzevir edition, epitome, microcosm; rudiment; vanishing point; thinness &c. 203.

dwarf, pigmy, Liliputian, chit, pigwidgeon, urchin, elf; atomy, dandiprat: doll, puppet; Tom Thumb, Hop-o'-my-thumb; man-, mann-ikin; homunculus, dapperling, cock-sparrow.

animalcule, monad, mite, insect, emmet, fly, midge, gnat, shrimp, minnow, worm, maggot, entozoön; bacteria; infusoria; microzoa; phytozoaria; microbe; grub; tit, tomtit, runt, mouse, small fry; millet-, mustard-seed; barleycorn; pebble, grain of sand; molehill, button, bubble.

point; atom &c. (*small quantity*) 32;

whooper, spanker, strapper; "Triton among the minnows" [*Coriolanus*].

mountain, mound; heap &c. (*assemblage*) 72.

largest portion &c. 50; full-, life-size.

V. be- large &c. *adj.*; become -large &c. (*expand*) 194.

Adj. large, big; great &c. (*in quantity*) 31; considerable, bulky, voluminous, ample, massive, massy; capacious, comprehensive; spacious &c. 180; mighty, towering, fine, magnificent.

corpulent, stout, fat, plump, squab, full, lusty, strapping, bouncing; portly, burly, well-fed, full-grown; corn-, gramfed; stalwart, brawny, fleshy; goodly; in good -case, – condition; in condition; chopping, jolly; chub-, chubby-faced.

lubberly, hulky, unwieldly, lumpish, gaunt, spanking, whacking, whopping, thumping, thundering, hulking; overgrown; puffy &c. (*swollen*) 194.

huge, immense, enormous, mighty; vast, -y; amplitudinous, stupendous; monst-er, -rous; gigantic; elephantine; giant, -like; colossal, Cyclopean, Brobdingnagian, Gargantuan; infinite &c. 105.

large as life; plump as a -dumpling, – partridge; fat as -a pig, – a quail, – butter, – brawn, – bacon.

194. Expansion. — N. expansion; increase &c. 35 -of size; enlargement, extension, augmentation; ampli-fication, -ation; aggrandizement, spread, increment, growth, development, pullulation, swell, dilatation, rarefaction; turg-escence, -idness, -idity; dispansion†; obesity &c. (*size*) 192; hydrocephalus, -ophthalmus; dropsy, tumefaction, intumescence, swelling, tumor, diastole, distension; puff-ing, -iness; inflation; pandiculation.

dilatability, expansibility.

germination, growth, upgrowth; accretion &c. 35; budding, gemmation.

over-growth, -distension; hypertrophy, tympany.

bulb &c. (*convexity*) 250; plumper; superiority of size.

V. become -larger &c. (large &c. 192); expand, widen, enlarge, extend, grow, increase, incrassate, swell, gather; fill out; deploy, take open order, dilate, stretch, spread; mantle, wax; grow -, spring- up; bud, bourgeon, shoot, sprout,

fragment &c. (*small part*) 51; powder &c. 330; point of a pin, mathematical point; minutiæ &c. (*unimportance*) 643.

micro-graphy, -meter, -scope; vernier; scale.

V. be -little &c. *adj.*; lie in a nutshell; become small &c. (*decrease*) 36, (*contract*) 195.

Adj. little; small &c. (*in quantity*) 32; minute, diminutive, microscopic; microzoal; inconsiderable &c. (*unimportant*) 643; exiguous, puny, tiny, wee, petty, minikin, miniature, pigmy, elfin; undersized; dwarf, -ed, -ish; spare, stunted, limited; cramp, -ed; pollard, Liliputian, dapper, pocket; port-ative, -able; duodecimo; dumpy, squat; short &c. 201.

impalpable, intangible, evanescent, imperceptible, invisible, inappreciable, infinitesimal, homœopathic; atomic, corpuscular, molecular; rudiment-ary, -al; embryonic, vestigial.

weazen,† scant, scraggy, scrubby; thin &c. (*narrow*) 203; granular &c. (*powdery*) 330; shrunk &c. 195; brevipennate.

Adv. in a -small compass, – nutshell; on a small scale.

195. Contraction. — N. contraction, reduction, diminution; decrease &c. 36- of size; defalcation, decrement; lessening, shrinking &c. *v.*; compaction; tabes, collapse, emaciation, attenuation, tabefaction, consumption, marasmus, atrophy; systole, neck, hourglass.

condensation, compression, compactness; compendium &c. 596; squeezing &c. *v.*; strangulation; corrugation; astringency; astringents, sclerotics; contractility, compressibility; coarctation.

inferiority in size.

V. become -small, – smaller; lessen, decrease &c. 36; grow less, dwindle, shrink, contract, narrow, shrivel, collapse, wither, lose flesh, wizen, fall away, waste, wane, ebb; decay &c. (*deteriorate*) 659.

be smaller than, fall short of; not come up to &c. (*be inferior*) 34.

render smaller, lessen, diminish, contract, draw in, narrow, coarctate; boil down; constrict, constringe; condense, compress, squeeze, corrugate, crush,

germinate, put forth, vegetate, pullu-late, open, burst forth; gain –, gather-flesh; outgrow; spread like wildfire, overrun.

be larger than; surpass &c. (*be su-perior*) 33.

render -larger &c. (large &c. 192); expand, spread, extend, aggrandize, distend, develop, amplify, spread out, widen, magnify, rarefy, inflate, puff, blow up, stuff, pad, cram; exaggerate; fatten.

Adj. expanded &c. *v.*; larger &c. (large &c. 192); swollen; expansive; wide-open, -spread; flabelliform; overgrown, exaggerated, bloated, fat, tur-gid, tumid, hypertrophied, dropsical; pot-, swag-bellied †; œdematous, obese, puffy, pursy, blowzy, bigswoln, distended; patulous; bulbous &c. (*convex*) 250; full-blown, -grown, -formed; big &c. 192; abdominous, enchymatous, rhipi-date; tume-facient, -fying.

crumple up, warp, purse up, pack, stow; pinch, tighten, strangle; cramp; dwarf, bedwarf; shorten &c. 201; circumscribe &c. 229; restrain &c. 751.

pare, reduce, attenuate, rub down, scrape, file, grind, chip, shave, shear.

Adj. contracting &c. *v.*; astringent; shrunk, contracted &c. *v.*; strangulated, tabid, wizened, stunted; waning &c. *v.*; neap, compact.

unexpanded &c. (expand &c. 194); contractile; compressible; smaller &c. (small &c. 193).

---

196. Distance. — **N.** distance; space &c. 180; remoteness, farness; far-cry to; longinquity, elongation; offing, back-ground; remote region; removedness; parallax; reach, span, stride.

out-post, -skirt; horizon; aphelion; foreign parts, *ultima Thule, ne plus ultra*, antipodes; long range, giant's stride.

dispersion &c. 73.

V. be -distant &c. *adj.*; extend –, stretch –, reach –, spread –, go –, get –, stretch away- to; range.

remain at a distance; keep –, stand- -away, – off, – aloof, – clear of.

Adj. distant; far -off, – away; remote, telescopic, distal, wide of; stretching to &c. *v.*; yon, -der; ulterior; trans-marine, -pontine, -atlantic, -alpine; tramontane; ultra-montane, -mundane; hyperborean, antipodean; inaccessible, out of the way; unapproach-ed, -able; incontiguous.

Adv. far -off, – away; afar, -off; off; away; a -long, – great, – good- way off; wide away, aloof; wide –, clear- of; out of -the way, – reach; abroad, yonder, farther, further, beyond; *outre mer*, over the border, far and wide, " over the hills and far away " [Gay]; from pole to pole &c. (*over great space*) 180; to the -uttermost parts, – ends- of the earth; out of hearing, nobody knows where, *à perte de vue*, out of the sphere of, wide of the mark; a far cry to.

apart, asunder; wide -apart, – asun-der; *longo intervallo;* at arm's length.

Phr. " distance lends enchantment " [Camp-bell].

197. Nearness. — **N.** nearness &c. *adj.*; proximity, propinquity; vicin-ity, -age; neighborhood, adjacency; con-tiguity &c. 199.

short -distance, – step, – cut; earshot, close quarters, stone's throw; bow –, gun –, pistol- shot; hair's breadth, span.

purlieus, neighborhood, vicinage, en-virons, *alentours*, suburbs, confines, *ban-lieue*, borderland; whereabouts.

bystander; neighbor, borderer.

approach &c. 286; convergence &c. 290; perihelion.

V. be -near &c. *adj.*; adjoin, hang about, trench on; border –, verge- upon; stand by, approximate, tread on the heels of, cling to, clasp, hug; huddle; hang upon the skirts of, hover over; burn.

bring –, draw- -near &c. 286; con-verge &c. 290; crowd &c. 72; place -side by side &c. *adv.*

Adj. near, nigh; close –, near- at hand; close, neighboring; bordering upon, contiguous, adjacent, adjoining; proxim-ate, -al; at hand, handy; near the mark, near run; home, intimate.

Adv. near, nigh; hard –, fast- by; close -to, – upon; hard upon; at the point of; next door to; within -reach, – call, – hearing, – earshot; within an ace of; but a step, not far from, at no great distance; on the -verge, – brink, – skirts- of; in the -environs &c. *n.*; at one's -door, – feet, – elbow, – finger's end, – side; on the tip of one's tongue; under one's nose; within a -stone's throw &c. *n.*; in -sight, – presence- of:

at close quarters; cheek by -jole, – jowl; beside, alongside, side by side, *tête-à-tête;* in juxtaposition &c. (*touching*) 199; yardarm to yardarm; at the heels of; on the confines of, at the threshold, bordering upon, verging to; in the way.

about; here-, there-abouts; roughly, in round numbers; approxim-ately, -atively; as good as, well-nigh.

198. Interval. — N. interval, inter-space; separation &c. 44; break, gap, opening; hole &c. 260; chasm, hiatus, cæsura; inter-ruption, -regnum; inter-stice, lacuna, cleft, mesh, crevice, chink, rime, creek, cranny, crack, chap, slit, fissure, scissure, rift, flaw, breach, rent, gash, cut, leak, dike, ha-ha.

gorge, defile, ravine, cañon, crevasse, abyss, abysm; gulf; inlet, frith, strait, gully; pass; furrow &c. 259; abra; *bar-ran-ca, -co;* clove [U. S.], gulch [U. S.], notch [U. S.]; yawning gulf; *hiatus -maxime, – valde-deflendus;* parenthesis &c. (*interjacence*) 228; void &c. (*ab-sence*) 187; incompleteness &c. 53.

V. gape &c. (*open*) 260.

Adj. with an interval, far between; breachy, rimose, rimulose.

Adv. at intervals &c. (*discontinu-ously*) 70; *longo intervallo.*

199. Contiguity. — N. contiguity, contact, proximity, apposition, abuttal, juxtaposition, touching &c. *v.;* abutment, osculation; meeting, appulse, rencontre, rencounter, syzygy, coincidence, coexist-ence; adhesion &c. 46.

borderland; frontier &c. (*limit*) 233; tangent; abutter.

V. be -contiguous &c. *adj.;* join, ad-join, abut on, march with; graze, touch, meet, osculate, come in contact, coin-cide; coexist; adhere &c. 46.

Adj. contiguous; touching. &c. *v.;* in -contact &c. *n.;* conterminous, end to end, osculatory; pertingent †; tangen-tial.

hand to hand; close to &c. (*near*) 197; with no -interval &c. 198.

2. Linear Dimensions

200. Length. — N. length, longi-tude, span; mileage.

line, bar, rule, stripe, streak, spoke, radius.

lengthening &c. *v.;* pro-longation, -duction, -traction; ten-sion, -sure; ex-tension.

[Measures of length] line, nail, inch, hand, palm, foot, cubit, yard, ell, fath-om, rood, pole, furlong, mile, league; chain; arpent, handbreadth, *jornada* [U. S.], kos, vara.

pedometer, perambulator; scale &c. (*measurement*) 466.

V. be -long &c. *adj.;* stretch out, sprawl; extend –, reach –, stretch- to; make a long arm, " drag its slow length along."

render -long &c. *adj.;* lengthen, ex-tend, elongate; stretch; pro-long, -duce, -tract; let –, draw –, spin- out; drawl.

enfilade, look along, view in perspec-tive.

Adj. long, -some; lengthy, wire-drawn, outstretched; lengthened &c. *v.;*

201. Shortness. — N. shortness &c. *adj.;* brevity; littleness &c. 193; a span.

shortening &c. *v.;* abbrevia-tion, -ture; abridgment, concision, retrenchment, curtailment, decurtation †; reduction &c. (*contraction*) 195; epitome &c. (*com-pendium*) 596.

elision, ellipsis; conciseness &c. (*in style*) 572.

abridger, epitomist, epitomizer.

V. be -short &c. *adj.;* render -short &c. *adj.;* shorten, curtail, abridge, ab-breviate, take in, reduce; compress &c. (*contract*) 195; epitomize &c. 596.

retrench, cut short, obtruncate; scrimp, cut, chop up, hack, hew; cut –, pare- down; clip,. dock, lop, prune, shear, shave, mow, reap, crop; snub; truncate, pollard, stunt, nip, check the growth of; [in drawing] foreshorten.

Adj. short, brief, curt; compendi-ous, compact; stubby, scrimp; shorn, stubbed; stumpy, thickset, pug; chunky [U. S.], decurtate; *retroussé;* stocky; squab, -by; squat, dumpy; little &c.

sesquipedalian &c. (*words*) 577; interminable, no end of; macrocolous.

line-ar, -al; longitudinal, oblong.

as long as -my arm, – to-day and to-
morrow; unshortened &c. (shorten &c.
201).

Adv. lengthwise, at length, longitudinally, endlong, along; tandem; in a line
&c. (*continuously*) 69; in perspective.

from -end to end, – stem to stern, – head to foot, – the crown of the head to
the sole of the foot, – top to toe; fore and aft.

193; curtailed of its fair proportions;
short by; oblate; concise &c. 572; summary.

Adv. shortly &c. *adj.*; in short &c.
(*concisely*) 572.

---

202. Breadth, Thickness. — N.
breadth, width, latitude, amplitude;
diameter, bore, caliber, radius; superficial extent &c. (*space*) 180.

thickness, crassitude; corpulence &c.
(*size*) 192; dilatation &c. (*expansion*)
194.

V. be -broad &c. *adj.*; become –, ren-
der- -broad &c. *adj.*; expand &c. 194;
thicken, widen, calibrate.

Adj. broad, wide, ample, extended;
discous; fanlike; out-spread, -stretched;
" wide as a church-door " [*Romeo and
Juliet*]; latifol-iate, -ous.

thick, dumpy, squab, squat, thickset;
thick as a rope.

203. Narrowness, Thinness. — N.
narrowness &c. *adj.*; closeness, exility;
exiguity &c. (*little*) 193.

line; hair's –, finger's- breadth; strip,
streak, vein.

thinness &c. *adj.*; tenuity; emaciation, macilency, marcor †.

shaving, slip &c. (*filament*) 205;
thread paper, skeleton, shadow, anatomy, spindleshanks, lantern jaws, mere
skin and bone.

middle constriction, stricture, neck,
waist, isthmus, wasp, hourglass; ridge,
ghaut, ghât, pass; ravine &c. 198.

narrowing, coarctation, angustation,
tapering; contraction &c. 195.

V. be -narrow &c. *adj.*; narrow, taper,
contract, &c. 195; render -narrow &c. *adj.*

Adj. narrow, close; slender, thin, fine; thread-like &c. (*filament*) 205;
finespun, taper, slim, slight-made; scant, -y; spare, delicate, incapacious;
contracted &c. 195; unexpanded &c. (expand &c. 194); slender as a thread.

emaciated, lean, meager, gaunt, macilent; lank, -y; weedy, skinny; scrawny
[U. S.] slinky; starv-ed, -eling; attenuated, shriveled, extenuated, tabid,
marcid †, barebone, rawboned; herring gutted; worn to a shadow, lean as
a rake [Chaucer]; thin as a -lath, – whipping post, – wafer; hatchet-faced;
lantern-jawed.

---

204. Layer. — N. layer, stratum,
course, bed, zone, substratum, floor,
flag, stage, story, tier, slab, escarpment;
table, tablet; dess; flagstone; board,
plank; trencher, platter.

plate; lam-ina, -ella; sheet, flake, foil,
wafer, scale, coat, peel, pellicle, mem-
brane, film, leaf, slice, shive, cut, rasher,
shaving, integument &c. (*covering*) 223;
eschar.

stratification, scaliness, nest of boxes,
coats of an onion.

V. slice, shave, pare, peel; delaminate;
plate, coat, veneer; cover &c. 223.

Adj. lamell-ar, -ated, -iform; lamin-
ated, -iferous; micaceous; schist-ose,
-ous; scaly, filmy, membranous, flaky,
squamous; folia-ted, -ceous; strati-fied,
-form; tabular, discoid; spath-ic, -ose.

205. Filament. — N. filament, line;
fiber, fibril; funicle, vein, hair, capillament, cilium, tendril, gossamer; hair
stroke; veinlet, venula, venule.

wire, string, thread, packthread, cot-
ton, sewing silk, twine, twist, whipcord,
tape, ribbon, cord, rope, yarn, hemp,
oakum, jute.

strip, shred, slip, spill, list, band,
fillet, fascia, ribbon, riband, roll, lath,
splinter, shiver, shaving.

beard &c. (*roughness*) 256; ramification; strand.

Adj. fil-amentous, -amentiferous,
-aceous, -iform; fibr-ous, -illous; thread-
like, wiry, stringy, ropy; capill-ary,
-iform; funicular, wire-drawn; anguilli-
form; flagelliform; hairy &c. (*rough*) 256;
tæn-iate, -iform, -ioid; ven-ose, -ous.

206. Height. — **N.** height, altitude, elevation; eminence, pitch; loftiness &c. *adj.*; sublimity.

tallness &c. *adj.*; stature, procerity; prominence &c. 250.

colossus &c. (*size*) 192; giant, grenadier, giraffe, camelopard.

mount, -ain; hill, *alto*, butte [U. S.], monticle, fell, knap; cape; head-, foreland; promontory; ridge, hog's back, dune; rising –, vantage- ground; down; moor, -land; Alp; up-, high-lands; heights &c. (*summit*), 210; knob, *loma*, *pena* [U. S.], *picacho*, tump; knoll, hummock, hillock, barrow, mound, mole; steeps, bluff, cliff, craig, tor, peak, pike, clough; escarpment, edge, ledge, brae; dizzy height.

tower, pillar, column, obelisk, monument, steeple, spire, minaret, campanile, turret, dome, cupola.

pole, pikestaff, maypole, flagstaff; top –, topgallant- mast.

ceiling &c. (*covering*) 223.

high water; high –, flood –, spring- tide.

altimetry &c. (*angle*) 244; batophobia.

V. be -high &c. *adj.*; tower, soar, command; hover; cap, culminate; overhang, hang over, impend, beetle; bestride, ride, mount; perch, surmount; cover &c. 223; overtop &c. (*be superior*) 33; stand on tiptoe.

become -high &c. *adj.*; grow, – higher, – taller; upgrow; rise &c. (*ascend*) 305.

render -high &c. *adj.*; heighten &c. (*elevate*) 307.

Adj. high, elevated, eminent, exalted, lofty; tall; gigantic &c. (*big*) 192; Patagonian; towering, beetling, soaring, hanging [gardens]; elevated &c. 307; upper; highest &c. (*topmost*) 210; high-reaching, insessorial, perching.

up-, moor-land; hilly, knobby [U. S.]; mountainous, alpine, sub-alpine, heaven-kissing; cloud-topt, -capt, -touching; aërial.

overhanging &c. *v.*; incumbent, overlying; super-incumbent, -natant, -imposed; prominent &c. 250.

tall as a -maypole, – poplar, – steeple; lanky &c. (*thin*) 203.

Adv. on high, high up, aloft, up, above, aloof, overhead; airward; up –, above- stairs; in the clouds; on -tiptoe, – stilts, – the shoulders of; over head and ears; breast high.

over, upwards; from top to bottom &c. (*completely*) 52.

Phr. *è meglio cader dalle finistre che dal tetto.*

207. Lowness. — **N.** lowness &c. *adj.*; debasement, depression; prostration &c. (*horizontal*) 213; depression &c. (*concave*) 252.

molehill; lowlands; basement-, ground-floor; *rez de chaussée;* cellar; hold; feet, heels.

low water; low –, ebb –, neap –, spring- tide.

V. be -low &c. *adj.*; lie -low, – flat; underlie; crouch, slouch, wallow, grovel; lower &c. (*depress*) 308.

Adj. low, neap, debased; nether, -most; flat, level with the ground; lying low &c. *v.*; crouched, subjacent, squat, prostrate &c. (*horizontal*) 213.

Adv. under; be-, under-neath; below; down, -wards; adown, at the foot of; under-foot, -ground; down –, below-stairs; at a low ebb; below par.

208. Depth. — **N.** depth; deepness &c. *adj.*; profundity, depression &c. (*concavity*) 252.

hollow, pit, shaft, well, crater; gulf &c. 198; bowels of the earth, bottomless pit, hell.

soundings, depth of water, water, draught, submersion; plummet, sound, probe; sounding-rod, – line; lead.

V. be -deep &c. *adj.*; render -deep &c. *adj.*; deepen.

plunge &c. 310; sound, heave the lead, take soundings; dig &c. (*excavate*) 252.

Adj. deep, -seated; profound, sunk, buried; submerged &c. 310; sub-aqueous, -marine, -terranean, -terrene; underground.

209. Shallowness. — **N.** shallowness &c. *adj.*; shoals; mere scratch.

Adj. shallow, slight, superficial; skin –, ankle –, knee- deep; just enough to wet one's feet; shoal, -y.

bottom-, sound-, fathom-less; unfathom-ed, -able; abysmal; deep as a well; bathycolpian; benth-al, -opelagic: down-reaching, yawning.

knee-, ankle-deep.

Adv. beyond –, out of- one's depth; over head and ears.

210. Summit. — N. summit, -y †; top, vertex, apex, zenith, pinnacle, acme, culmination, meridian, utmost height, ne plus ultra, height, pitch, maximum, climax; culminating –, crowning –, turning- point; turn of the tide, fountain head; water -shed, -parting; sky, pole.

tip, -top; crest, crow's nest, cap, truck, peak, nib; end &c. 67; crown, brow; head, nob, noddle, pate; capsheaf.

high places, heights.

topgallant mast, sky scraper; quarter –, hurricane- deck.

architrave, frieze, cornice, coping stone, zoöphorus, capital, epistyle, sconce, pediment, entablature; tympanum; ceiling &c. (covering) 223.

attic, loft, garret, house top, upper story.

V. culminate, crown, top; overtop &c. (be superior to) 33.

Adj. highest &c. (high &c. 206); top; top-, upper-most; tiptop; culminating &c. v.; meridi-an, -onal; capital, head, polar, supreme, supernal, topgallant.

Adv. atop, at the top of the tree.

Phr. en flûte; fleur d'eau.

211. Base. — N. base, -ment; plinth, dado, wainscot; base-, mop-board; bed-rock, hardpan [U. S.]; foundation &c. (support) 215; substructure, substratum, ground, earth, pavement, floor, paving, flag, carpet, ground floor, deck; footing, ground work, basis; hold, bilge.

bottom, nadir, foot, sole, toe, hoof, keel, root; centerboard.

Adj. bottom, under-, nether-most; fundamental; founded–, based–, grounded –, built- on.

212. Verticality. — N. verticality; erectness &c. adj.; perpendicularity; right angle, normal; azimuth circle.

wall, precipice, cliff.

elevation, erection; square, plumb line, plummet.

V. be -vertical &c. adj.; stand -up, – on end, – erect, – upright; stick –, cock-up.

render -vertical &c. adj.; set –, stick –, raise –, cock- up; erect, rear, raise on its legs.

Adj. vertical, upright, erect, perpendicular, plumb, normal, straight, bolt upright; rampant; standing up &c. v.; rectangular, orthogonal.

Adv. vertically &c. adj.; up, on end; up –, right- on end; à plomb, endwise; on one's legs; at right angles.

213. Horizontality. — N. horizontality; flatness; level, plane; stratum &c. 204; dead -level, – flat; level plane.

recumbency; lying down &c. v.; reclination, decumbence; de-, dis-cumbency †; proneness &c. adj.; accubation, supination, resupination, prostration; azimuth.

plain, floor, platform, bowling green; cricket ground; croquet -ground, – lawn; billiard table; terrace, estrade, esplanade, parterre, table-land, plateau, ledge.

V. be -horizontal &c. adj.; lie, recline, couch; lie -down, – flat, – prostrate; sprawl, loll; sit down.

render -horizontal &c. adj.; lay, – down, – out; level, flatten; prostrate, knock down, floor, fell.

Adj. horizontal, level, even, plane; flat &c. 251; flat as a -billiard table, -

bowling green; alluvial; calm, – as a mill pond; smooth, – as glass.

re-, de-, pro-, ac-cumbent; lying &c. v.; prone, supine, couchant, jacent, prostrate, recubant.

Adv. horizontally &c. adj.; on -one's back, – all fours, – its beam ends.

214. Pendency. — N. pend-, depend-ency; suspension, hanging &c. v.; ped-icel, -icle, -uncle; tail, train, flap, skirt, pigtail, pendulum; hangnail.

215. Support. — N. support, ground, foundation, base, basis; terra firma; bearing, fulcrum, bait [U. S.], caudex crib; point d'appui, ποῦ στῶ, purchase

peg, knob, button, hook, nail, stud, ring, staple, tenterhook; fastening &c. 45; spar, horse.

V. be -pendent &c. *adj.*; hang, depend, swing, dangle; swag; daggle, flap, trail, flow; beetle.

suspend, hang, sling, hook up, hitch, fasten to, append.

Adj. pend-ent, -ulous; pensile; hanging &c. *v.*; beetling, jutting over, overhanging, projecting; dependent; suspended &c. *v.*; loose, flowing.

having a -peduncle &c. *n.*; pedunculate, tailed, caudate.

footing, hold, *locus standi;* landing, − stage, − place; stage, platform; block; rest, resting place; groundwork, substratum, riprap, sustentation, subvention; floor &c. (*basement*) 211.

supporter; aid &c. 707; prop, stand, anvil, fulciment †; cue rest, jigger; monkey; stay, shore, skid, rib, truss, bandage; sleeper; stirrup, stilts, shoe, sole, heel, splint, lap; bar, rod, boom, sprit, outrigger; ratlings.

staff, stick, crutch, alpenstock, bâton, staddle; bourdon, cowlstaff, *lathi*, mahlstick.

post, pillar, shaft, thill, column, pilaster; pediment, pedicle; pedestal; plinth, shank, leg, socle, zocle; buttress, jamb, mullion, abutment; baluster, banister, stanchion; balustrade; headstone.

frame, -work; scaffold, skeleton, beam, rafter, girder, lintel, joist, travis, trave, corner stone, summer, transom; rung, round, step, sill; angle-, hiprafter; cantilever, modillion; crown-, king-post; vertebra.

columella, backbone; keystone; axle, -tree; axis; arch, mainstay.

trunnion, pivot, rowlock; peg &c. (*pendency*) 214; tiebeam &c. (*fastening*) 45; thole pin.

board, ledge, shelf, hob, bracket, trevet, trivet, arbor, rack; mantel, -piece, -shelf; slab, console; counter, dresser; flange, corbel; table, trestle; shoulder; perch; horse; easel, desk; clotheshorse, hatrack; retable; teapoy.

seat, throne, dais; divan, musnud; chair, bench, form, stool, sofa, settee, stall; arm −, easy −, elbow −, rocking- chair; couch, *fauteuil*, woolsack, ottoman, settle, squab, bench; aparejo, faldstool, horn; long −, long-sleeve −, morris- chair; *lamba -chauki, - kursi;* saddle, pannel, pillion; side −, pack-saddle; pommel.

bed, berth, pallet, tester, crib, cot, hammock, shakedown, truckle-bed, cradle, litter, stretcher, bedstead; four-poster, French bed; bunk, kip, *palang;* bedding, *bichhona*, mattress, paillasse; pillow, bolster; mat, rug, cushion.

footstool, hassock; tabouret; tripod.

Atlas, Persides, Atlantes, Caryatides, Hercules.

V. be -supported &c.; lie −, sit −, recline −; lean −, loll −, rest −, stand −, step −, repose −, abut −, bear −, be based &c.- on; have at one's back; bestride, -straddle.

support, bear, carry, hold, sustain, shoulder; hold −, back −, bolster −, shore- up; up-hold, -bear; prop; under-prop, -pin, -set; riprap; bandage &c. 43.

give −, furnish −, afford −, supply −, lend- -support, − foundations; bottom, found, base, ground, imbed, embed.

maintain, keep on foot; aid &c. 707.

Adj. support-ing -ed, &c. *v.*; fundamental; dorsigerous.

Adv. astride on, straddle.

216. Parallelism. — N. parallelism; coextension; equidistance.

Adj. parallel; coextensive; equidistant.

Adv. alongside &c. (*laterally*) 236.

217. Obliquity. — N. obliquity, inclination, slope, slant; crookedness &c. *adj.*; slopeness; leaning &c. *v.*; bevel, tilt; bias, list, twist, swag, cant, lurch; distortion &c. 243; bend &c. (*curve*) 245; tower of Pisa.

acclivity, rise, ascent, gradient, *khudd*, rising ground, hill, bank, declivity, downhill, dip, fall, devexity †; gentle −, rapid- slope; easy -ascent, − descent; shelving beach; *talus; montagne Russe; facilis descensus Averni.*

steepness &c. *adj.*; cliff, precipice &c. (*vertical*) 212; escarpment, scarp.

[Measure of inclination] clinometer; sine, cosine, cotangent, angle, hypothenuse.

diagonal; zigzag.

V. be -oblique &c. *adj.*; slope, slant, lean, incline, shelve, stoop, decline, descend, bend, keel, careen, sag, swag, seel †, slouch, cant, sidle.

render -oblique &c. *adj.*; sway, bias; slope, slant; incline, bend, crook; cant, tilt; distort &c. 243.

Adj. oblique, inclined; sloping &c. *v.*; tilted &c. *v.*; recumbent, clinal, skew, askew, slant, aslant, plagihedral, indirect, wry, awry, ajee, crooked; knock-kneed &c. (*distorted*) 243; bevel, out of the perpendicular; aslope; asquint, backhanded; recubant.

uphill, rising, ascending, acclivous; downhill, falling, descending; declining, declivous, devex †, anticlinal; steep, abrupt, precipitous, breakneck.

diagonal; trans-verse, -versal; athwart, antiparallel; curved &c. 245.

Adv. obliquely &c. *adj.*; on –, all on- one side; askew, askant, askance, edgewise, at an angle; side-long, -ways; slope-, slant-wise; by a side wind.

218. Inversion. — **N.** in-, e-, sub-, re-, retro-, intro-version; contraposition &c. 237; contrariety &c. 14; reversal; turn of the tide.

overturn; somer-sault, -set; summerset; *culbute;* revulsion; pirouette.

transposition, transposal, anastrophy, metastasis, hyperbaton, anastrophe, *hysteron proteron,* hypallage, synchysis, tmesis, parenthesis; metathesis; palindrome.

pronation and supination.

V. be -inverted &c.; turn –, go –, wheel- -round, – about, – to the right about; turn –, go –, tilt –, topple- over; capsize, turn turtle.

in-, sub-, retro-, intro-vert; reverse; up-, over-turn, -set; turn -topsy-turvy &c. *adj.*; *culbuter;* transpose, put the cart before the horse, turn the tables.

Adj. inverted &c. *v.*; wrong side -out, – up; inside out, upside down; bottom –, keel- upwards; supine, on one's head, topsy-turvy, *sens dessus dessous.*

inverse; reverse &c. (*contrary*) 14; opposite &c. 237.

top-heavy.

Adv. inversely &c. *adj.*; hirdy-girdy; heels over head, head over heels.

219. Crossing. — **N.** crossing &c. *v.*; inter-section, -digitation; decussation, transversion; convolution &c. 248; level crossing.

reticulation, network; inosculation, anastomosis, intertexture, mortise.

net, plexus, web, mesh, twill, skein, sleeve, felt, lace; wicker; mat, -ting; plait, trellis, wattle, lattice, grating, grille, gridiron, tracery, fretwork, filigree, reticle; tissue, netting, mokes; rivulation.

cross, chain, wreath, braid, cat's cradle, knot; entanglement &c. (*disorder*) 59.

[woven fabrics] cloth, linen, muslin, cambric &c.

V. cross, decussate; inter-sect, -lace, -twine, -twist, -weave, -digitate, -link.

twine, entwine, weave, inweave, twist, wreathe; anastomose, inosculate, dovetail, splice, link.

mat, plait, plat, braid, felt, twill; tangle, entangle, ravel; net, knot; dishevel, raddle.

Adj. crossing &c. *v.*; crossed, matted &c. *v.*; transverse.

cross, cruciform, crucial; reti-form, -cular, -culated; areolar, cancellated, grated, barred, streaked; textile; crossbarred, cruciate, palmiped, secant; web-footed.

Adv. cross, thwart, athwart, transversely; at grade [U. S.]; crosswise.

3. CENTRICAL DIMENSIONS [1]

1. General

220. Exteriority. — N. exteriority; outside, exterior; surface, superficies; skin &c. (*covering*) 223; superstratum; disk, disc; face, facet; extrados.

excentricity; eccentricity; circumjacence &c. 227.

V. be -exterior &c. *adj.*; lie around &c. 227.

place -exteriorly, – outwardly, – outside; put –, turn out.

Adj. exter-ior, -nal; outer, -most; out-ward, -lying, -side, -door; round about &c. 227; extramural; extra-limitary, -mundane.

superficial, skin-deep; frontal, discoid.

extraregarding; excentric; eccentric; outstanding; extrinsic &c. 6; ecdemic, exomorphic.

Adv. externally &c. *adj.*; out, without, over, outwards, *ab extra*, out of ,doors; *extra muros*.

in the open air; *sub -Jove, – dio; à la belle étoile, al fresco*.

221. Interiority. — N. interiority; inside, interior; interspace, subsoil, substratum; intrados.

contents &c. 190; substance, pith, marrow; backbone &c. (*center*) 222; heart, bosom, breast; abdomen; vitals, viscera, entrails, bowels, belly, intestines, guts, chitterlings, womb, lap; penetralia, recesses, innermost recesses; cave &c. (*concavity*) 252.

V. be -inside &c. *adj.*; – within &c. *adv.*

place –, keep- within; inclose &c. (*circumscribe*) 229; intern; imbed &c. (*insert*) 300.

Adj. inter-ior, -nal; inner, inside, inward, intraregarding; in-, inner-most; deep-seated; intes-tine, -tinal; inland; subcutaneous; abdominal, cœliac, endomorphic; interstitial &c. (*interjacent*) 228; inwrought &c. (*intrinsic*) 5; inclosed &c. *v.*

home, domestic, indoor, intramural, vernacular; endemic.

Adv. internally &c. *adj.*; inwards, within, in, inly; here-, there-, where-in; *ab intra*, withinside; in –, within- doors; at home, in the bosom of one's family.

222. Centrality. — N. centrality, centricalness, center; middle &c. 68; focus &c. 74.

core, kernel; nucleus, nucleolus; heart, pole, axis, bull's eye; nave, navel; umbilicus, backbone, marrow, pith; verte-bra, -bral column; hotbed; concentration &c. (*convergence*) 290; centralization; symmetry.

center of -gravity, – pressure, – percussion, – oscillation, – buoyancy &c.; metacenter.

V. be -central &c. *adj.*; converge &c. 290.

render central, centralize, concentrate; bring to a focus.

Adj. centr-al, -ical; middle &c. 68; azygous, axial, focal, umbilical, concentric; middlemost; rachidian; spinal, vertebral.

Adv. middle; midst; centrally &c. *adj.*

223. Covering. — N. covering, cover; balda-chin, -chino, -quin; canopy, tilt, awning, tent, marquee, *tente d'abri*, umbrella, parasol, sunshade; veil (*shade*) 424; shield &c. (*defense*) 717.

roof, ceiling, thatch, tile; pan-, pentile; tiling, slates, slating, leads; barrack [U. S.], plafond, planchment [U. S.], tiling, shed &c. (*abode*) 189.

top, lid, covercle †, door, operculum; bulkhead [U. S.].

bandage, plaster, lint, wrapping, dossil, finger stall.

224. Lining. — N. lining, inner coating; coating &c. (*covering*) 223; stalactite, -agmite.

filling, stuffing, wadding, padding. wainscot, parietes, wall.

V. line, stuff, incrust, wad, pad, fill.

Adj. lined &c. *v.*

---

[1] That is, Dimensions having reference to a center.

coverlet, counterpane, sheet, quilt, tarpaulin, blanket, rug, drugget; housing; antimacassar, eiderdown, numdah, pillow-case, -slip; linoleum; saddle-blanket, -cloth; tidy; tilpah [U. S.], apishamore [U. S.].

in-, tegument; skin, pellicle, fleece, fell, fur, leather, shagreen, hide; pelt, -ry; cordwain; derm; robe, buffalo robe [U. S.]; cuticle, scarfskin, epidermis.

clothing &c. 225; mask &c. (*concealment*) 530.

peel, crust, bark, rind, cortex, husk, shell, coat; eggshell, glume.

capsule; sheath, -ing; pod, cod; casing, case, theca: elytron; elytrum; involucrum; wrapp-ing, -er; envelope, vesicle; corn-husk, -shuck [U. S.]; dermatology, conchology; testaceology.

veneer, facing; engobe; pavement; scale &c. (*layer*) 204; coating, paint; varnish &c. (*resin*) 356a; anointing &c. *v.*; inunction; incrustation, superposition, obduction †; ground, enamel, whitewash, plaster, stucco, compo; cerement; ointment &c. (*grease*) 356.

V. cover; super-pose, -impose; over-lay, -spread; wrap &c. 225; incase; face, case, veneer, pave, paper; tip, cap, bind; bulkhead, -in; clapboard [U. S.].

coat, paint, varnish, pay, incrust, stucco, dab, plaster, tar; wash; be-, smear; be-, daub; anoint, do over; gild, plate, japan, lacquer, lacker, enamel, whitewash; parget; lay it on thick.

over-lie, -arch; endome; conceal &c. 528.

Adj. covering &c. *v.*; cutaneous, dermal, cortical, cuticular, tegumentary, skinny, scaly, squamous; covered &c. *v.*; imbricated, loricated, armor-plated, ironclad; under cover; cowled, cucullate, dermatoid, encuirassed, hooded, squamiferous, tectiform; vaginate.

---

225. Investment. — N. investment; covering &c. 223; dress, clothing, raiment, drapery, costume, attire, guise, toilet, toilette, trim; habiliment; vesture, -ment; garment, garb, palliament†, apparel, wardrobe, wearing apparel, clothes, things.

array; tailoring, millinery; finery &c. (*ornament*) 847; full dress &c. (*show*) 882; garniture; theatrical properties.

outfit, equipment, trousseau; uniform, regimentals; continentals [Am. Hist.]; canonicals &c. 999; livery, gear, harness, turn-out, accouterment, caparison, suit, rigging, trappings, traps, slops, togs, toggery; masquerade.

dishabille, morning dress, *négligé*, dressing gown, undress; kimono; lungi; shooting-coat; mufti; rags, tatters, old clothes; mourning, weeds; duds; slippers.

robe, tunic, paletot, habit, gown, coat, frock, blouse, toga, smock frock; claw-hammer-, Prince Albert-, sack-, tuxedo-, frock-, dress-, tail-coat.

cloak, pall, mantle, mantlet, mantua, shawl, pelisse, wrapper; veil; cape, tippet, kirtle, plaid, muffler, comforter,

226. Divestment. — N. divestment; taking off &c. *v.*

nudity; bareness &c. *adj.*; undress; dishabille &c. 225; the altogether; nu-, denu-dation; decortication, depilation, excoriation, desquamation; molting; exfoliation; trichosis.

V. divest; uncover &c. (cover &c. 223); denude, bare, strip; disfurnish; undress, disrobe &c. (dress, enrobe &c. 225); uncoif; dismantle; put –, take –, cast- off; doff; peel, pare, decorticate, excoriate, skin, scalp, flay; expose, lay open; exfoliate, molt, mew; cast the skin.

Adj. divested &c. *v.*; bare, naked, nude; un-dressed, -draped; exposed; in dishabille; bald, threadbare, ragged, callow, roofless.

in -a state of nature, – nature's garb, – buff, – native buff, – birthday suit; *in puris naturalibus;* with nothing on, stark naked; bald as a coot, bare as the back of one's hand; out at elbows; bare-foot; bareback, -ed; leaf-, nap-, hair-less.

haik, huke †, chlamys, mantilla, tabard; housing, horse cloth, burnoose, burnous, roquelaure; *houppelande;* sur-, over-, great-coat; surtout, spencer; mackintosh, waterproof, ulster, P-coat, dreadnought, wraprascal, poncho, cardinal, pelerine; barbe, chudder, *jubbah*, oilskins, pajamas, pilot jacket, talma.

jacket, vest, jerkin, waistcoat, doublet, *camisole*, gabardine; stays, corsage, corset, corselet, bodice; stomacher; skirt, petticoat, farthingale, kilt, jupe, crinoline, bustle, panier, apron, pinafore; bloom-er, -ers; *chaqueta*, sontag, *tablier*.

trou-, trow-sers; breeches, pantaloons, inexpressibles, overalls, smalls, smallclothes; pants; shintiyan; shorts; tights, drawers; knickerbockers; phil-, fill-ibeg.

head-dress, -gear; chapeau, crush-, opera-hat; kaffiyeh; sombrero, taj, tam-o'-shanter, tarboosh, topi, sola topi, *pagri*, puggaree; cap, hat, beaver, castor, bonnet, tile, wideawake, billycock; wimple; night-, mob-, skull-cap; hood, coif; capote, calash; kerchief, snood; head, coiffure; crown &c. (*circle*) 247; *chignon*, pelt, wig, front, peruke, periwig; caftan, turban, fez, shako, csako, busby; képi, forage cap, bearskin; helmet &c. 717; mask, domino.

body clothes; linen; hickory shirt [U. S.]; shirt, sark, smock, shift, chemise; night-gown, -shirt; bedgown, *sac de nuit;* jersey; under-clothing, -waistcoat.

neck-erchief, -cloth; tie, ruff, collar, cravat, stock, handkerchief, scarf; bib, tucker; boa; girdle &c. (*circle*) 247; cummerbund, *rumal, rabat.*

shoe, pump, boot, slipper, sandal, galoche, goloshes, patten, clog; high-low; Blucher –, Wellington –, Hessian –, jack –, top- boot; Balmoral; arctics, bootee, bootikin, brogan, *chaparajos; chivar-ras, -ros;* gums [U. S.], larrigan [N. Am.], rubbers, snowshoe, stogy, *veldtschoen*, legging, buskin, greave, galli-gaskin, *gamache*, gamashes, moccasin, gambado, gaiter, spatterdash, brogue, antigropelos; stocking, hose, gaskins, trunk hose, sock; hosiery.

glove, gauntlet, mitten, cuff, wristband, sleeve.

swaddling cloth, baby linen, layette; pocket handkerchief; ice wool; taffeta.

clothier, tailor, milliner, costumier, sempstress, snip; dress-, habit-, breeches-, shoe-maker; Crispin; *friseur;* cordwainer, cobbler, hosier, hatter; draper, linen draper, haberdasher, mercer.

V. invest; cover &c. 223; envelop, lap, involve; in-, en-wrap; wrap; fold –, wrap –, lap –, muffle- up; overlap; sheathe, swathe, swaddle, roll up in, cir-cumvest.

vest, clothe, array, dress, dight, drape, robe, enrobe, attire, apparel, accou-ter, rig, fit out; deck &c. (*ornament*) 847; perk, equip, harness, caparison.

wear; don; put –, huddle –, slip- on; mantle.

Adj. invested &c. *v.*; habited; dight, -ed; barbed, barded; clad, *costumé*, shod, *chaussé; en grande tenue* &c. (*show*) 882.

sartorial.

Phr. " the soul of this man is his clothes " [*All's Well*].

227. Circumjacence. — N. circum-jacence, -ambience; environment, en-compassment; atmosphere, medium; surroundings.

outpost; border &c. (*edge*) 231; girdle &c. (*circumference*) 230; outskirts, boule-vards, suburbs, purlieus, precincts, *fau-bourgs*, environs, entourage, *banlieue;* neighborhood, vicinage, vicinity.

V. lie -around &c. *adv.*; surround, beset, compass, encompass, environ, in-close, enclose, encircle, embrace, circum-vent, lap, gird; belt; begird, engird; skirt, twine round; hem in &c. (*circumscribe*) 229.

Adj. circum-jacent, -ambient, -fluent; ambient; surrounding &c. *v.*; circum-ferential, suburban.

228. Interjacence. — N. inter-ja-cence, -currence, -venience, -location, -digitation, -penetration; permeation.

inter-jection, -polation, -lineation, -spersion, -calation; embolism.

inter-vention, -ference, -position; in-, ob-trusion; insinuation; insertion &c. 300; dovetailing; infiltration.

intermedi-um, -ary; go-between, bod-kin, intruder, interloper; parenthesis, episode; flyleaf.

partition, septum, diaphragm, mid-riff; dissepiment; party wall, panel, half-way house.

V. lie –, come –, get- between; inter-vene, slide in, interpenetrate, permeate.

put between, introduce, import; throw –, wedge –, edge –, jam –, worm –, foist

Adv. around, about; without; on -every side, – all sides; right and left, all round, round about.

–, run –, plow –, work- in; inter-pose, -ject, -calate, -polate, -line, -leave, -sperse, -weave, -lard, -digitate; let in, dovetail, splice, mortise; insinuate, smuggle; infiltrate, ingrain.

interfere, put in an oar, thrust one's nose in; intrude, obtrude; have a finger in the pie; introduce the thin end of the wedge; thrust in &c. (*insert*) 300.

Adj. inter-jacent, -current, -venient, -vening &c. *v.*, -mediate, -mediary, -calary, -stitial; embolismal.

parenthetical, episodic; mediterranean; intrusive; embosomed; merged.

Adv. between, betwixt; 'twixt; among, -st; amid, -st; 'mid, -st; in the thick of; betwixt and between; sandwich-wise; parenthically, *obiter dictum*.

229. Circumscription. — N. circumscription, limitation, inclosure; confinement &c. (*restraint*) 751; circumvallation; encincture; envelope &c. 232.

V. circumscribe, limit, bound, confine, inclose; surround &c. 227; compass about; imprison &c. (*restrain*) 751; hedge –, wall –, rail- in; fence –, hedge-round; picket; corral.

enfold, bury, incase, pack up, enshrine, inclasp; wrap up &c. (*invest*) 225; embay, embosom.

Adj. circumscribed &c. *v.*; begirt, lapt; buried –, immersed- in; embosomed, in the bosom of, imbedded, encysted, mewed up; imprisoned &c. 751; land-locked, in a ring fence.

230. Outline. — N. outline, circumference; peri-meter, -phery; ambit, circuit, lines, *tournure*, contour, profile, silhouette; bounds; coast line.

zone, belt, girth, band, baldric, zodiac, girdle, tyre, cingle, clasp, girt; cordon &c. (*inclosure*) 232; circlet &c. 247.

231. Edge. — N. edge, verge, brink, brow, brim, margin, border, confine, skirt, rim, flange, side, mouth; jaws, chops, chaps, fauces; lip, muzzle.

threshold, door, porch; portal &c. (*opening*) 260; coast, shore.

frame, fringe, flounce, frill, list, trimming, edging, skirting, hem, selvedge, welt; furbelow, valance.

Adj. border, marginal, skirting; labial, labiated, marginated.

232. Inclosure. — N. inclosure, envelope; case &c. (*receptacle*) 191; wrapper; girdle &c. 230.

pen, fold; pen-, in-, sheep-fold; paddock, pound; corral; yard; net, seine net.

wall; hedge, -row; espalier; fence &c. (*defense*) 717; pale, paling, balustrade, rail, railing, quickset hedge, park paling, circumvallation, *enceinte*, ring fence.

barrier, barricade; gate, -way; bent, dingle [U. S.]; door, hatch, cordon; prison &c. 752.

dike, dyke, ditch, fosse, moat.

V. inclose; circumscribe &c. 229.

233. Limit. — N. limit, boundary, bounds, confine, enclave, term, bourn, verge, curbstone, but, pale; termin-ation, -us; stint, frontier, precinct, marches; backwoods.

boundary line, landmark; line of -demarcation, – circumvallation; pillars of Hercules; Rubicon, turning point; *ne plus ultra;* sluice, floodgate.

Adj. definite; contermin-ate †, -able; terminal, frontier; bordering.

Adv. thus far, – and no further.

2. Special

234. Front. — **N.** front; fore, – part; foreground; face, disk, disc, frontage, façade, proscenium, facia, frontispiece; anteriority; obverse [of a medal].

fore –, front- rank; van, -guard; advanced guard; outpost; first line; scout.

brow, forehead, visage, physiognomy, phiz, countenance, mug*; rostrum, beak, bow, stem, prow, prore, jib.

pioneer &c. (*precursor*) 64; metoposcopy.

V. be –, stand- in front &c. *adj.*; front, face, confront; bend forwards; come to the -front, – fore.

Adj. fore, anterior, front, frontal.

Adv. before; in -front, – the van, – advance; ahead, right ahead; fore-, head-most; in the -foreground, – lee of; before one's -face, – eyes; face to face, *vis-à-vis; front à front.*

Phr. *formosa facies muta commendatio est* [Syrus]; *frons est animi janua* [Cicero]; " human face divine " [Milton]; *imago animi vultus est indices oculi* [Cicero]; " sea of upturned faces " [Scott].

235. Rear. — **N.** rear, back, posteriority; rear -rank, – guard; background, hinterland.

occiput, nape, chine; heels; tail, rump, croup, buttock, posteriors, backside, scut, breech, dorsum, loin; dorsal –, lumbar- region; hind quarters; aitchbone; natch, -bone.

stern, poop, after-part, heelpiece, crupper.

wake; train &c. (*sequence*) 281.

reverse; other side of the shield.

V. be -behind &c. *adv.*; fall astern; bend backwards; bring up the rear.

Adj. back, rear; hind, -er, -most, -ermost; post-ern, -erior; dorsal, after; caudal, lumbar; mizzen, tergal.

Adv. behind; in the -rear, – background; behind one's back; at the -heels, – tail, – back- of; back to back.

after, aft, abaft, astern, sternmost, aback, rearward.

Phr. *ogni medaglia ha il suo rovescio.*

236. Laterality. — **N.** laterality; side, flank, quarter, lee; hand; cheek, jowl, jole, wing; profile; temple, parietes, loin, haunch, hip; beam.

gable, -end; broadside; lee side.

points of the compass; East, Orient, Levant; West; orientation.

V. be -on one side &c. *adv.*; flank, outflank; sidle; skirt; orientate.

Adj. lateral, sidelong; collateral; parietal, flanking, skirting; flanked; sideling.

many sided; multi-, bi-, tri-, quadrilateral.

Eastern; orient, -al; Levantine; Western, occidental, Hesperian.

237. Contraposition. — **N.** contraposition, opposition; polarity; inversion &c. 218; opposite side; reverse, inverse; counterpart; antipodes; opposite poles, North and South.

V. be -opposite &c. *adj.*; subtend.

Adj. opposite; reverse, inverse; converse; antipodal, subcontrary; fronting, facing, diametrically opposite.

Northern, septentrional, Boreal, arctic; Southern, Austral, antarctic.

Adv. over, – the way, – against; against; face to face, *vis-à-vis;* as poles asunder.

Adv. side-ways, -long; broadside on; on one side, abreast, alongside, beside, aside; by, – the side of; side by side; cheek by jowl &c. (*near*) 197; to windward, – leeward; laterally &c. *adj.*; right and left; on her beam ends.

Phr. " his cheek the map of days outworn " [Shakespeare].

238. Dextrality. — **N.** dextrality; right, – hand; dexter, offside, starboard.

Adj. dextral, right-handed; dexter, dextrorsal, dextrorse; ambidextral.

Adv. dextrad, dextrally.

239. Sinistrality. — **N.** sinistrality; left, -hand; sinister, nearside, larboard, port.

Adj. left-handed; sinister; sinist-ral, -rorsal, -rorse, -rous.

Adv. sinistrally, sinistrously.

Section III. FORM

1. General Form

240. Form. — N. form, figure, shape; con-formation, -figuration; make, formation, frame, construction, cut, set, build, trim, cut of one's jib; stamp, type, cast, mold; fashion; contour &c. (*outline*) 230; structure &c. 329; plasmature.

feature, lineament, turn; phase &c. (*aspect*) 448; posture, attitude, *pose*.

[Science of form] morphology.

[Similarity of form] isomorphism.

forming &c. *v.*; form-, figur-, efformation; sculpture; plasmation.

V. form, shape, figure, fashion, efform, carve, cut, chisel, hew, cast; rough-hew, -cast; sketch; block –, hammer- out; trim; lick –, put- into shape; model, knead, work up into, set, mold, sculpture; cast, stamp; build &c. (*construct*) 161.

Adj. formed &c. *v.*

[Receiving form] plastic, fictile; formative.

[Giving form] plasmic.

[Similar in form] isomorphous.

241. [Absence of form.] Amorphism. — N. amorphism, informity; unlicked cub; *rudis indigestaque moles;* disorder &c. 59; deformity &c. 243.

disfigure-, deface-ment; mutilation; deforming.

V. [Destroy form] deface, disfigure, deform, mutilate, truncate; derange &c. 61; blemish, mar.

Adj. shapeless, amorphous, formless; un-formed, -hewn, -fashioned, -shapen; rough, rude, Gothic, barbarous, rugged.

242. [Regularity of form.] Symmetry. — N. symmetry, shapeliness, finish; beauty &c. 845; proportion, eurythmy, uniformity, parallelism; bi-, tri-, multi-lateral symmetry; centrality &c. 222.

arborescence, branching, ramification; arbor vitæ.

Adj. symmetrical, shapely, well set, finished; beautiful &c. 845; classic, chaste, severe.

regular, uniform, balanced; equal &c. 27; parallel, coextensive.

arbor-escent, -iform; dendr-iform, -oid; branching; ramous, ramose; filici-form, filicoid; subarborescent; papilionaceous.

243. [Irregularity of form.] Distortion. — N. dis-, de-, con-tortion; twist; crookedness &c. (*obliquity*) 217; grimace; deformity; mal-, malcon-formation; harelip; monstrosity, misproportion, want of symmetry, anamorphosis; ugliness &c. 846; talipes; teratology.

V. distort, contort, twist, warp, wrest, writhe, make faces, deform, misshape.

Adj. distorted &c. *v.*; out of shape, irregular, unsymmetric, awry, wry, askew, crooked; not -true, – straight; on one side, crump, deformed; harelipped; mis-shapen, -begotten; mis-, ill-proportioned; ill-made; grotesque, crooked as a ram's horn; camel-, hump-, hunch-, bunch-, crook-backed; bandy; bandy-, bow-legged; bow-, knock-kneed; splay-, club-footed; round-shouldered; snub-nosed; curtailed of one's fair proportions; stumpy &c. (*short*) 201; gaunt &c. (*thin*) 203; bloated &c. 194; scalene; simous; taliped, -ic.

Adv. all manner of ways.

Phr. crooked as a Virginia fence [U. S.].

2. Special Form

244. Angularity. — N. angular-ity, -ness; aduncity; angle, cusp, bend; fold &c. 258; notch &c. 257; fork, bifurcation.

elbow, knee, knuckle, ankle, groin, crotch, crutch, crane, fluke, scythe, sickle, zigzag, kimbo.

corner, nook, recess, niche, oriel, coign.

right angle &c. (*perpendicular*) 212; obliquity &c. 217; angle of 45°, miter; acute –, obtuse –, salient –, reëntering –, spherical- angle.

angular -measurement, – elevation, – distance, – velocity; trigon-, goniometry; altimetry; clin-, graph-, goni-ometer; theodolite; sextant, quadrant; dichotomy.

triangle, trigon, wedge; rectangle, square, lozenge, diamond; rhomb, -us; quadr-angle, -ilateral; parallelogram; quadrature; poly-, penta-, hexa-, hepta-, octa-, oxy-, deca-gon.

Platonic bodies; cube, rhomboid; tetra-, penta-, hexa-, octa-, dodeca-, icosahedron; prism, pyramid; parallelopiped; curb-, gambrel-, mansard-roof.

V. bend, fork, bifurcate, crinkle.

Adj. angular, bent, crooked, aduncous, uncinated, aquiline, jagged, serrated; falc-iform, -ated; furcated, forked, bifurcate, zigzag; furcular; hooked; dovetailed; knock-kneed, crinkled, akimbo, kimbo, geniculated; oblique &c. 217.

fusiform, wedge-shaped, cuneiform; cuneate, multangular, oxygonal; triangular, -gonal, -lateral; quadr-angular, -ilateral; foursquare; rectangular, square, multilateral; polygonal &c. *n.*; cubical, rhomboidal, pyramidal.

---

245. Curvature. — N. curv-ature, -ity, -ation; incurv-ature, -ity†, -ation; bend; flex-ure, -ion; conflexure†; crook, hook, bought, bending; de-, in-flexion; concameration; arcuation, devexity†, turn; deviation, detour, sweep; curl, -ing; bough; recurv-ity, -ation; sinuosity &c. 248.

curve, arc, arch, arcade, vault, bow, crescent, half-moon, lunule, horseshoe, loop, crane neck; para-, hyper-bola; catenary, festoon; conch-, cardi-oid; caustic; tracery; arched- ceiling, -roof; bay-, bow-window.

V. be -curved &c. *adj.*; sweep, swag, sag; deviate &c. 279; turn; reënter.

render -curved &c. *adj.*; bend, curve,

246. Straightness. — M. straightness, rectilinearity, directness; inflexibility &c. (*stiffness*) 323; straight –, right –, direct- line; short cut.

V. be -straight &c. *adj.*; have no turning; not -incline, – bend, – turn, – deviate- to either side; go straight; steer for &c. (*direction*) 278.

render straight, straighten, rectify; set –, put- straight; un-bend, -fold, -curl &c. 248, -ravel &c. 219, -wrap.

Adj. straight; rectiline-ar, -al; direct, even, right, true, in a line; unbent, virgate &c. *v.*; un-deviating, -turned, -distorted, -swerving; straight as an arrow &c. (*direct*) 278; inflexible &c. 323.

---

incurvate; de-, in-flect; crook; turn, round, arch, arcuate, arch over, concamerate; bow, curl, recurve, frizzle.

Adj. curved &c. *v.*; curvi-form, -lineal, -linear; devex †, devious; recurv-ed, ⌣ous; crump; bowed &c. *v.*; vaulted, hooked; falc-iform, -ated; semicircular, crescentic; lun-iform, -ular; semilunar, conchoidal; cord-iform, -ated; cardioid; heart-, bell-, boat-, crescent-, lens-, moon-, oar-, shield-, sickle-, tongue-, pear-, fig-shaped; reniform; lenti-form, -cular; bow-legged &c. (*distorted*) 243; oblique &c. 217; circular &c. 247.

aduncated, arclike, arcuate, beaked; bicorn, -ed, -uous, -ute; clyp-eate, -eiform; cymbiform, embowed, galeiform; ham-ate, -iform, -ous; hooked; ling-uiform, -ulate; lobiform, lunate, navicular, peltate, remiform, rhamphoid; rostr-ate, -iferous, -oid; scutate, scaphoid, uncate; ungui-culate, -form.

---

247. [Simple circularity.] Circularity. — N. circularity, roundness; rotundity &c. 249.

circle, circlet, ring, areola, hoop, roundlet, annulus, annulet, bracelet, armlet; ringlet; eye, loop, wheel; cycle, orb, orbit, rundle, zone, belt, cordon, band; contrate –, crown- wheel; hub, nave; sash, girdle, cestus, cincture,

248. [Complex circularity.] Convolution. — N. winding &c. *v.*; con-, in-, circum-volution; wave, undulation, tortuosity, anfractuosity; sinu-osity, -ation; meandering, circuit, circumbendibus, twist, twirl, windings and turnings, ambages; torsion; inosculation; reticulation &c. (*crossing*) 219; rivulation.

coil, roll, curl, buckle, spiral, helix,

baldric, fillet, fascia, wreath, garland; crown, corona, coronet, chaplet, snood, necklace, collar; noose, lasso.

ellipse, oval, ovule; ellipsoid, cycloid; epi-cycloid, -cycle; semicircle; quadrant, sextant, sector.

V. make -round &c. *adj.*; round.

go round; encircle &c. 227; describe -a circle &c. 311.

Adj. round, rounded, circular, annular, orbicular; oval, ovate; elliptic, -al; egg-shaped; pear-shaped &c. 245; cycloidal &c. *n.*; spherical &c. 249.

Phr. "I watched the little circles die" [Tennyson].

corkscrew, worm, volute, rundle; tendril; scollop, scallop, escalop; kink; ammonite, snakestone.

serpent, eel, maze, labyrinth.

V. be -convoluted &c. *adj.*; wind, twine, turn and twist, twirl; wave, undulate, meander; inosculate; entwine, intwine; twist, coil, roll; wrinkle, curl; crisp, twill; frizz, -le; crimp, crape, indent, scollop, scallop; wring, intort; contort; wreathe &c. (*cross*) 219.

Adj. convoluted; winding, twisted &c. *v.*; tortile, tortive†; wavy; und-ated, -ulatory; circling, snaky, snake-like, serpentine; serpent-, anguill-, vermiform; vermicular; mazy, tortuous, sinuous, flexuous, anfractuous, reclivate, rivulose, scolecoid; sigmoid, -al; spiriferous, -oid;

involved, intricate, complicated, perplexed; labyrinth-ic, -ian, -ine; peristaltic; dædalian; kinky.

wreathy, frizzly, *crépé*, buckled; raveled &c. (*in disorder*) 59.

spiral, coiled, helical; cochle-ate, -ous; screw-shaped; turbin-ated, -iform.

Adv. in and out, round and round.

249. Rotundity. — N. rotundity; roundness &c. *adj.*; cylindricity; sphericity, -oidity; globosity.

cylin-der, -droid; barrel, drum; roll, -er; rouleau, column, rolling-pin, rundle.

cone, conoid; pear-, egg-, bell-shape.

sphere, globe, ball, boulder, bowlder; spher-, ellips-oid; oblong –, oblate-spheroid; drop, spherule, globule, vesicle, bulb, bullet, pellet, pelote, clew, pill, marble, pea, knob, pommel, horn, knot.

V. render -spherical &c. *adj.*; form into a sphere, sphere, roll into a ball; give -rotundity &c. *n.*; round.

Adj. rotund; round &c. (*circular*) 247; cylindr-ic, -ical, -oid; columnar, lumbriciform; conic, -al; spher-ical, -oidal; glob-ular, -ated, -ous, -ose; egg-, bell-, pear-shaped; ov-oid, -iform; gibbous; rixiform; campan-iform, -ulate, -iliform; fungiform, bead-like, moniliform, pyriform, bulbous; *teres atque rotundus;* round as -an orange, – an apple, – a ball, – a billiard ball, – a cannon ball.

3. Superficial Form

250. Convexity. — N. convexity, prominence, projection, swelling, gibbosity, bilge, bulge, protuberance, protrusion; camber, cahot [N. Am.], thank-ye-ma'am [U. S.[, swell.

intumescence; tumour, tumor; tubercle, -osity; excrescence; hump, hunch, bunch.

tooth, knob, elbow, process, apophysis, condyle, bulb, node, nodule, nodosity, tongue, dorsum, boss, embossment, bump, clump; sugar loaf &c. (*sharpness*) 253; bow; mamelon; hub, hubble [U. S.]; molar.

pimple, wen, wheel, papula, pustule, pock, proud flesh, growth, sarcoma,

251. Flatness. — N. flatness &c. *adj.*; smoothness &c. 255.

plane; level &c. 213; plate, platter, table, tablet, slab.

V. render flat, flatten; level &c. 213.

Adj. flat, plane, even, flush, scutiform, discoid; level &c. (*horizontal*) 213; flat as -a pancake, – a fluke, – a flounder, – a board, – my hand.

252. Concavity. — N. concavity, depression, dip; hollow, -ness; indentation, intaglio, cavity, dent, dint, dimple, follicle, pit, sinus, alveolus, lacuna; excavation; trough &c. (*furrow*) 259; honeycomb.

caruncle, corn, wart, furuncle, polypus, fungus, fungosity, exostosis, bleb, blister, blain; boil &c. (*disease*) 655; airbubble, blob, papule, verruca.

papilla, nipple, teat, pap, breast, dug, mammilla; proboscis, nose, neb, beak, snout, nozzle; belly, corporation; withers, back, shoulder, lip, flange.

peg, button, stud, ridge, rib, jutty, trunnion, snag.

. cupola, dome, arch, balcony, eaves; pilaster.

relief, relievo, cameo; *basso-*, *mezzo-*, *alto-rilievo;* low-, bas-, high-relief.

hill &c. (*height*) 206; cape, promontory, mull; fore-, head-land; point of land, mole, jetty, hummock, ledge, spur; naze, ness.

V. be -prominent &c. *adj.*; project, bulge, protrude, pout, bouge †, bunch; jut –, stand –, stick –, poke- out; stick –, bristle –, start –, cock –, shoot- up; swell –, hang –, bend- over; beetle.

render -prominent &c. *adj.*; raise 307; emboss, chase.

Adj. convex, prominent, protuberant; projecting &c. *v.*; bossed, bossy, nodular, bunchy; clav-ate, -ated, -iform; hummocky, *moutonné*, mammiform; papul-ous, -ose; hemispheric, bulbous; bowed, arched; bold; bellied; tuber-ous, -culous; tumorous; cornute, odontoid; lenti-form, -cular; gibbous; club-shaped, hubby [U. S.], hubbly [U. S.], knobby, papillose, saddle-shaped, selliform, subclavate, torose, ventricose, verrucose.

salient, in relief, raised, *repoussé;* bloated &c. (*expanded*) 194.

cup, basin, crater, punch bowl; cell &c. (*receptacle*) 191; socket.

valley, vale, dale, dell, dingle, combe, bottom, slade, strath, glade, grove, glen, cave, cavern, cove; grot, -to; alcove, cul-de-sac; gully–&c. 198; arch &c. (*curve*) 245; bay &c. (*of the sea*) 343.

excavator, sapper, miner.

V. be -concave &c. *adj.*; retire, cave in.

render -concave &c. *adj.*; depress, hollow; scoop, – out; gouge, dig, delve, excavate, dent, dint, mine, sap, undermine, burrow, tunnel, stave in.

Adj. depressed &c. *v.*; alveolate, calathiform, cup-shaped, dishing; favaginous, -eolate, -ose; scyph-iform, -ose; concave, hollow, stove in; retiring; retreating; cavernous; porous &c. (*with holes*) 260; cellular, spongy, spongious; honeycombed, alveolar; infundibul-ar, -iform; funnel-, bell-shaped; campaniform, capsular; vaulted, arched.

---

253. Sharpness. — N. sharpness &c. *adj.*; acuity, acumination; spinosity.

. point, spike, spine, spiculum; needle, pin; prick, -le; spur, rowel, barb; spit, cusp; horn, antler; snag; tag; thorn, bristle; Adam's needle, bear grass [U. S.], tine, yucca.

254. Bluntness. — N. bluntness &c. *adj.*

V. be –, render- blunt &c. *adj.*; obtund, dull; take off the -point, – edge; turn.

Adj. blunt, obtuse, dull, bluff; edentate, toothless.

nib, tooth, tusk; spoke, cog, ratchet.

crag, crest, *aréte*, cone, peak, sugar loaf, pike, aiguille; spire, pyramid, steeple.

beard, *chevaux de frise*, porcupine, hedgehog, brier, bramble, thistle; comb; awn, beggar's lice, bur, burr, catchweed, cleavers, clivers, goose grass, hairif, hariff, flax comb, hackle, hatchel, heckle.

wedge; knife-, cutting- edge; blade, edge tool, cutlery, knife, penknife, whittle, razor; scalpel, bistoury, lancet; plowshare, colter; hatchet, ax, pickax, mattock, pick, adze, bill; billhook, cleaver, cutter; scythe, sickle, scissors, shears; sword &c. (*arms*) 727; bodkin &c. (*perforator*) 262; *belduque*, bowie-, paring-knife; bushwhacker [U. S.]; drawing-knife, -shave.

sharpener, hone, strop; grind-, whet-stone; novaculite; steel, emery.

V. be -sharp &c. *adj.*; taper to a point; bristle with.

render -sharp &c. *adj.*; sharpen, point, aculeate, whet, barb, spiculate, set, strop, grind.

cut &c. (*sunder*) 44.

Adj. sharp, keen; acute; aci-cular, -form; acu-leated, -minated; pointed;

tapering; conical, pyramidal; mucron-ate, -ated; spindle-, needle-shaped; spiked, spiky, ensiform, peaked, salient; cusp-ed, -idate, -idated; corn-ute, -uted, -iculate; prickly; spiny, spinous; thorny, bristling, muricated, pectinated, studded, thistly, briary; craggy &c. (*rough*) 256; snaggy, digitated, two-edged, fusiform; denti-form, -culated; toothed; odontoid; starlike; stellated, -iform; sagitt-ate, -iform; arrowheaded; arrowy, barbed, spurred.

acinaciform; apicul-ate, -ated; arista:e, awned, awny, bearded, calamiform, cone-shaped, coniform, crestate, echinate, gladiate; lanc-eolate, -iform; awl-, lance-, scimitar-, sword-shaped; set·arious, spinuliferous, subulate, tetrahedral, xiphoid.

cutting; sharp-, knife-edged; sharp –, keen- as a razor; sharp as a needle; sharpened &c. *v.*; set.

255. Smoothness. — N. smoothness &c. *adj.*; polish, gloss; lubric-ity, -ation.

down, velvet, silk, satin; velveteen, velumen; slide; bowling green &c. (*level*) 213; glass, ice; asphalt, wood pavement, flags.

roller, steam roller; sand-, emery-paper; flat-, sad-iron; burnisher, turpentine and beeswax.

V. smooth, -en; plane; file; mow, shave; level, roll; macadamize; polish, burnish, calender, glaze; iron, hot-press, mangle; lubricate &c. (*oil*) 332.

Adj. smooth; polished &c. *v.*; leiodermatous, slick, velutinous; even; level &c. 213; plane &c. (*flat*) 251; sleek, glossy; silken, silky; lanate, downy, velvety; glabrous, slippery, glassy, lubricous, oily, soft; unwrinkled; smooth as -glass, – ice, – monumental alabaster, – velvet, – oil; slippery as an eel; woolly &c. (*feathery*) 256.

256. Roughness.—N. roughness &c. *adj.*; tooth, grain, texture, ripple; asperity, rugosity, salebrosity†, corrugation, nodosity; arborescence &c. 242; pilosity.

brush, hair, beard, shag, mane, whisker, moustache, imperial, tress, lock, curl, ringlet, fimbriæ, cilia, villi; lovelock; beaucatcher; curl paper; goatee; papillote, scalp lock.

plum-age, -osity; plume, panache, crest; feather, tuft, fringe, toupee.

wool, velvet, plush, nap, pile, floss, fur, down; byssus, moss, bur; fluff.

V. be -rough &c. *adj.*; go against the grain.

render -rough &c. *adj.*; roughen, ruffle, crisp, crumple, corrugate, set on edge, stroke the wrong way, rumple.

Adj. rough, uneven; scabrous, knotted; rug-ged, -ose, -ous; knurly; asperous, crisp, salebrous †, gnarled, unpolished, unsmooth, roughhewn; crag-gy, -ged; crankling, scraggy; prickly &c.

(*sharp*) 253; arborescent &c. 242; leafy, well-wooded; feathery; plum-ose, -igerous; lacini-ate, -form, -ose; pappose; pil-eous, -ose; trich-ogenous, -oid; tufted, fimbriated, hairy, ciliated, filamentous, hirsute; crin-ose, -ite; bushy, hispid, villous, pappous, bearded, pilous, shaggy, shagged; fringed, befringed; set-ous †, -ose, -aceous; " like quills upon the fretful porcupine " [*Hamlet*]; rough as a -nutmeg grater, – bear.

downy, velvety, flocculent, woolly; lan-ate, -ated; lanugin-ous, -ose; tomentose; fluffy.

Adv. against the grain.

Phr. *cabello luengo y corto el seso.*

257. Notch. — N. notch, dent, nick, cut; indent, -ation; dimple.

embrasure, battlement, machicolation; saw, tooth, crenelle, scallop, scollop; vandyke; depression; jag.

V. notch, nick, cut, dent, indent, jag, scarify, scotch, crimp, scollop, crenulate, vandyke.

Adj. notched &c. *v.*; crenate, -d; dentate, -d; denticulate, -d; toothed, palmated, serrated.

258. Fold. — N. fold, plicature, plait, ply, crease; tuck, gather; flexion, flexure, joint, elbow, double, doubling, duplicature, gather, wrinkle, rimple,

crinkle, crankle, crumple, rumple, rivel, ruck, ruffle, dog's ear, corrugation, frounce, flounce, lapel; pucker, crow's feet; plication.

V. fold, double, plicate, plait, crease, wrinkle, crinkle, crankle, curl, cockle up, cocker, rimple, rumple, frizzle, frounce, rivel, twill, corrugate, ruffle, crimple †, crumple, pucker; turn –, double- -down, – under; tuck, ruck, hem, gather.

Adj. folded &c. *v.*

259. Furrow. — N. furrow, groove, rut, sulcus, scratch, streak, striæ, crack, score, incision, slit; chamfer, fluting; corduroy road, cradle hole.

channel, gutter, trench, ditch, dike, dyke, moat, fosse, trough, kennel; ravine &c. (*interval*) 198; tajo [U. S.], thank-ye-ma'am [U. S.].

V. furrow &c. *n.*; flute, plow; incise, engrave, etch, bite in.

Adj. furrowed &c. *v.*; ribbed, striated, sulcated, fluted, canaliculated; bisulcous, -ate, -ated; canaliferous; trisulcate; corduroy; unisulcate; costate, rimiform.

260. Opening. — N. hole, foramen; puncture, perforation; fontanel; transforation; pin-, key-, loop-, port-, peep-, mouse-, pigeon-hole; eye, – of a needle; eyelet; slot.

opening; apert-ure, -ness; hiation, yawning, oscitancy, dehiscence, patefaction †, pandiculation; chasm &c. (*interval*) 198.

embrasure, window, casement; *abatjour;* light; sky-, fan-light; lattice; bay-, bow-window; oriel; dormer, lantern.

out-, in-let; vent, vomitory; embouchure; orifice, mouth, sucker, muzzle; throat, gullet, weasand, wizen, nozzle; placket.

portal, porch, gate, ostiary†, postern, wicket, trap-door, hatch, door; arcade; cellar-, drive-, gate-, door-, hatch-, gang-way; lich gate.

way, path &c. 627; thoroughfare; channel; passage, -way; tube, pipe; water pipe &c. 350; air pipe &c. 351;

261. Closure. — N. closure, occlusion, blockade; shutting up &c. *v.*; obstruction &c. (*hindrance*) 706; embolus; contraction &c. 195; infarction; con-, ob-stipation; blind -alley, – corner; keddah; cul-de-sac, cæcum; imper-foration, -viousness &c. *adj.*; -meability; stopper &c. 263.

V. close, occlude, plug; block –, stop –, fill –, bung –, cork –, button –, stuff –, shut –, dam- up; blockade; obstruct &c. (*hinder*) 706; bar, bolt, stop, seal, plumb; choke, throttle; ram down, dam, cram; trap, clinch; put to –, shut- the door.

Adj. closed &c. *v.*; shut, operculated; unopened.

unpierced, imporous, cæcal; closable; imper-forate, -vious, -meable; impenetrable; un-, im-passable; invious† ; path-, way-less; untrodden.

unventilated; air-, water-tight; hermetically sealed; tight, snug.

vessel, tubule, canal, gut, fistula; adjutage, ajutage; ostium; smokestack; chimney, flue, tap, funnel, gully, tunnel, main; mine, pit, adit, shaft; gallery.

alley, aisle, glade, vista.

bore, caliber; pore; blind orifice; fulgurite, thundertube.

por-ousness, -osity; sieve, cullender, colander; cribble, riddle, screen; honeycomb.

apertion, perforation; piercing &c. *v.*; terebration, empalement, pertusion†, puncture, acupuncture, penetration.

opener, key, master key, *passe-partout.*

V. open, ope, gape, yawn, bilge; fly open.

perforate, pierce, empierce†, tap, bore, drill; mine &c. (*scoop out*) 252; tunnel; trans-pierce, -fix; enfilade, impale, spike, spear, gore, spit, stab, pink, puncture, lance, stick, prick, riddle, punch; stave in.

cut a passage through; make -way, – room- for.

un-cover, -close, -rip; lay –, cut –, rip –, throw- open.

Adj. open; perforated &c. *v.*; perforate; wide open, ajar, un-closed, -stopped; oscitant, gaping, yawning; patent.

tubular, cannular, fistulous; per-vious, -meable; foraminous; vesi-, vas-

cular; porous, follicular, cribriform, honeycombed, infundibular, riddled; tubul-ous, -ated; piped, tubate.

opening &c. *v.*; aperient.

Int. open *sesame!*

262. Perforator. — N. perforator, piercer, borer, auger, chisel, gimlet, stylet, drill, wimble, awl, bradawl, scoop, terrier, corkscrew, dibble, trocar, trepan, probe, bodkin, needle, stiletto, rimer, warder, lancet; punch, -eon; spikebit, gouge; spear &c. (*weapon*) 727; puncher; punching-machine, -press; punch pliers.

263. Stopper. — N. stopper, stopple; plug, cork, bung, spike, spill, stopcock, tap; rammer; ram, -rod; piston; stop-gap; wadding, stuffing, padding, stopping, dossil, pledget, tompion, tourniquet.

cover &c. 223; valve, vent peg, spigot, slide valve.

janitor, doorkeeper, porter, warder, beadle, Cerberus, ostiary.

Section IV. MOTION

1. Motion in General

264. [Successive change of place.[1]] **Motion. — N.** motion, movement, move; going &c. *v.*; unrest.

stream, flow, flux, run, course, stir; evolution; kinematics; telekinesis.

step, rate, pace, tread, stride, gait, port, footfall, cadence, carriage, velocity, angular velocity; clip, progress, locomotion; journey &c. 266; voyage &c. 267; transit &c. 270.

restlessness &c. (*changeableness*) 149; mobility; movableness, motive power; laws of motion; mobilization.

V. be -in motion &c. *adj.*; move, go, hie, gang, budge, stir, pass, flit; hover -round, - about; shift, slide, glide; roll, - on; flow, stream, run, drift, sweep along; wander &c. (*deviate*) 279; walk &c. 266; change -, shift- one's -place, - quarters; dodge; keep -going, - moving.

put -, set- in motion; move; impel &c. 276; propel &c. 284; render movable, mobilize.

Adj. moving &c. *v.*; in motion; transitional; motory, motive; shifting, movable, mobile, mercurial, unquiet; restless &c. (*changeable*) 149; nomadic &c. 266; erratic &c. 279.

Adv. under way; on the -move, - wing, - tramp, - march.

Phr. *eppur si muove* [Galileo]; *es bildet ein Talent sich in der Stille, sich ein Charakter in dem Strom der Welt.*

265. Quiescence. — N. rest; stillness &c. *adj.*; quiescence; stag-nation, -nancy; fixity, immobility, catalepsy; indisturbance; quietism.

quiet, tranquillity, calm; repose &c. 687; peace; dead calm, anticyclone; statue-like repose; silence &c. 403; not a -breath of air, - mouse stirring; sleep &c. (*inactivity*) 683.

pause, lull &c. (*cessation*) 142; stand, - still; standing still &c. *v.*; lock; dead -lock, - stop, - stand; full stop; fix; embargo.

resting place; *gite*; bivouac; home &c. (*abode*) 189; pillow &c. (*support*) 215; haven &c. (*refuge*) 666; goal &c. (*arrival*) 292.

V. be -quiescent &c. *adj.*; stand -, lie- still; keep quiet, repose, hold the breath.

remain, stay; stand, lie to, ride at anchor, remain *in situ*, tarry, mark time; bring -, heave -, lay- to; pull -, draw- up; hold, halt; stop, - short; rest, pause, anchor; cast -, come to an- anchor; rest on one's oars; repose on one's laurels, take breath; stop &c. (*discontinue*) 142.

stagnate; *quieta non movere;* let -alone, - well alone; abide, rest and be thankful; keep within doors, stay at home, go to bed.

dwell &c. (*be present*) 186; settle &c. (*be located*) 184; alight &c. (*arrive*) 292 stick, - fast; stand, - like a post; not stir a -peg, - step; be at a -stand &c. *n.*

---

[1] A thing cannot be said to *move* from one place to another, unless it passes in succession through every intermediate place; hence motion is only such a change of place as is *successive.* "Rapid, swift, &c., as thought" are therefore incorrect expressions.

quell, becalm, hush, stay, lull to sleep, lay an embargo on.

Adj. quiescent, still; motion-, move-less; fixed; stationary; immotile; at -rest, – a stand, – a standstill, – anchor; stock still; standing still &c. *v.*; sedentary, untraveled, stay-at-home; becalmed, stagnant, quiet; un-moved, -disturbed, -ruffled; calm, restful; cataleptic; immovable &c. (*stable*) 150; sleeping &c. (*inactive*) 683; silent &c. 403; still as -a statue, – a post, – a mouse, – death.

Adv. at a stand &c. *adj.*; *tout court;* at the halt.

Int. stop! stay! avast! halt! hold hard! whoa! hold! *sabr karo!*

Phr. *requiescat in pace; Deus nobis hæc otia fecit* [Vergil]; " the noonday quiet holds the hill " [Tennyson].

266. [Locomotion by land.] **Journey.** — **N.** travel; traveling &c. *v.* wayfaring, campaigning.

journey, excursion, expedition, tour, trip, grand tour, circuit, peregrination, discursion †, ramble, pilgrimage, *hajj*, trek, course, ambulation, march, walk, promenade, constitutional, stroll, saunter, tramp, jog trot, turn, stalk, perambulation; noctambul-ation, -ism; somnambulism; outing, ride, drive, airing, jaunt.

equitation, horsemanship, riding, manège, ride and tie; basophobia.

roving, vagrancy, pererration†; marching and countermarching; nomadism; vagabond-ism, -age; hoboism [U. S.]; gadding; flit, -ting; migration; e-, im-, de-†, inter-migration; *wanderlust.*

plan, itinerary, guide; hand-, road-book; Baedeker, Bradshaw, Murray.

procession, cavalcade, caravan, file, *cortège*, column.

[Organs and instruments of locomotion] vehicle &c. 272; automobile, trolley, locomotive; legs, feet, pegs, pins, trotters.

traveler &c. 268.

depot [U. S.], railway station, station.

V. travel, journey, course; take –, go a journey; take –, go out for- -a walk &c. *n.*; have a run; take the air.

flit, take wing; migrate, emigrate; trek; rove, prowl, roam, range, patrol, pace up and down, traverse; scour –, traverse- the country; peragrate† ; per-, circum-ambulate; nomadize, wander,

267. [Locomotion by water, or air.] **Navigation.** — **N.** navigation; aquatics; boating, yachting; ship &c. 273; oar, paddle, screw, sail, canvas, aileron.

natation, swimming; fin, flipper, fish's tail.

aëro-station, -statics, -nautics; balloonery; balloon &c. 273; ballooning, aviation, airmanship; flying, flight, volitation; wing, pinion.

voyage, sail, cruise, passage, circumnavigation, periplus; head-, stern-, leeway; fairway.

mariner &c. 269.

V. sail; put to sea &c. (*depart*) 293; take ship, get under way; spread -sail, – canvas; gather way, have way on; make –, carry- sail; plow the -waves, – deep, – main, – ocean; walk the waters.

navigate, warp, luff, scud, boom, kedge; drift, course, cruise, coast; hug the -shore, – land; circumnavigate.

ply the oar, row, paddle, pull, scull, punt, steam.

swim, float; buffet the waves, ride the storm, skim, *effleurer*, dive, wade.

fly, be wafted, hover, soar, flutter; take -wing, – a flight; wing one's -flight, – way; aviate.

Adj. sailing &c. *v.*; volant, aërostatic; seafaring, nautical, maritime, naval; seagoing, coasting; afloat; navigable; aërial, aëronautic; grallatory.

Adv. under -way, – sail, – canvas, – steam; on the wing.

Phr. *bon voyage;* " spread the thin oar and catch the driving gale " [Pope].

ramble, stroll, saunter, hover, go one's rounds, straggle; gad, – about; expatiate.

walk, march, step, tread, pace, plod, wend; promenade; trudge, tramp; stalk, stride, straddle, strut, foot it, stump, bundle, bowl along, toddle; paddle; tread a path.

take horse, ride, drive, trot, amble, canter, prance, fisk, frisk, *caracoler*, caracole; gallop &c. (*move quickly*) 274.

peg –, jog –, wag –, shuffle- on; stir one's stumps; bend one's -steps, – course; make –, find –, wend –, pick –, thread –, plow- one's way; slide, glide, coast, skim, skate; march in procession, file off, defile.

go –, repair –, resort –, hie –, betake oneself- to.

Adj. traveling &c. *v.*; ambulatory, itinerant, peripatetic, roving, rambling, gadding, discursive, vagrant, migratory, nomadic; circumforane-an, -ous; nocti-, mundi-vagrant; locomotive.

way-faring, -worn; travel-stained.

Adv. on -foot, – horseback, – Shanks's mare; by the Marrowbone stage; *in transitu* &c. 270; *en route* &c. 282.

Int. come along!

---

268. Traveler. — N. traveler, way-farer, voyager, itinerant, passenger, commuter.

tourist, excursionist, explorer, adventurer, mountaineer, Alpine Club; peregrinator, wanderer, rover, straggler, rambler; bird of passage; gad-about, -ling; vagrant, scatterling, landloper, waifs and estrays, wastrel, foundling; loafer; tramp, -er; vagabond, nomad, Bohemian, gypsy, Arab, Wandering Jew, Hadji, pilgrim, palmer; peripatetic; somnambulist; emigrant, fugitive, refugee; beach comber, booly; globe-girdler, -trotter; hobo [U. S.], night-, sleep-walker; noctambulist, runabout, straphanger, swag-, swags-man [Aust.]; trecker, trekker, *zinga-no, -ro.*

runner, courier; Mercury, Iris, Ariel, comet.

pedestrian, walker, foot passenger; cyclist; wheelman.

rider, horseman, equestrian, cavalier, jockey, roughrider, trainer, breaker.

driver, coachman, whip, Jehu, charioteer, postilion, postboy, carter, wagoner, drayman; cab-man, -driver; *voiturier, vetturino, condottiere;* engine driver; stoker, fireman, guard; chauffeur, conductor, engineer, gharry-wallah, *gari-wala*, hackman, syce, truckman.

269. Mariner. — N. sailor, mariner, navigator; sea-man, -farer, -faring man; dock walloper *; tar, jack tar, salt, able seaman, A. B.; man-of-war's man, bluejacket, galiongee, galionji, marine, jolly; midshipman, middy; skipper; ship-, boat-, ferry-, water-, lighter-, barge-, longshore-man; bargee, gondolier; oar, -sman; rower; boat-, cockswain; coxswain; steersman, pilot; crew.

aërial navigator, aëronaut, balloonist, Icarus; aëroplanist, airman, aviator, birdman, man-bird, wizard of the air.

---

270. Transference. — N. transfer, -ence; trans-, e-location† ; displacement; meta-stasis, -thesis; removal; re-, a-motion; relegation; de-, as-portation; extradition, conveyance, draft; carrying, carriage; con-vection, -duction, -tagion; transfer &c. (*of property*) 783.

transit, transition; passage, ferry, gestation; portage, porterage, carting, cartage; shoveling &c. *v.*; vect-ion†, -ure†, -itation† ; shipment, freight, wafture; trans-mission, -port, -portation, -umption, -plantation, -lation; shift-, dodg-ing; dispersion &c. 73; transposition &c. (*interchange*) 148; traction &c. 285.

[Thing transferred] drift.

V. trans-fer, -mit, -port, -place, -plant; convey, carry, bear, fetch and carry; carry –, ferry- over; hand, pass, forward; shift; conduct, convoy, bring, fetch, reach; tote [U. S.].

send, delegate, consign, relegate, turn over to, deliver; ship, embark; waft; shunt; transpose &c. (*interchange*) 148; displace &c. 185; throw &c. 284; drag &c. 285; mail, post.

shovel, ladle, decant, draft off, transfuse.

Adj. transferred &c. *v.*; drifted, movable; port-able, -ative; mailable [U. S.] contagious.

Adv. from -hand to hand, – pillar to post.

on –, by- the way; on the -road, – wing; as one goes; *in transitu, en route, chemin faisant, en passant*, in mid-progress.

271. Carrier. — N. carrier, porter, bearer, tranter†, conveyer; *cargador;* express, -man; stevedore; coolie; conductor, locomotive, motor.

beast, -of burden, cattle, horse, steed, nag, palfrey, Arab, blood horse, thoroughbred, galloway, charger, courser, racer, hunter, jument, pony, filly, colt, foal, barb, roan, jade, hack, bidet, pad, cob, tit, punch, roadster, goer; race-, pack-, draft-, cart-, dray-, post-horse; ketch, sheltie; garran, garron; jennet, genet, bayard, mare, stallion, gelding; bronco, broncho, cayuse [U. S.]; creature, critter [rural U. S.]; cow pony, mustang, Narraganset, waler; stud.

Pegasus, Bucephalus, Rocinante.

ass, donkey, jackass, mule, hinny; sumpter -horse, – mule; burro, cuddy, ladino [U. S.]; reindeer; camel, dromedary, llama, elephant; carrier pigeon,

carriage &c. (*vehicle*) 272; ship &c. 273.

Adj. equine, asinine.

272. Vehicle. — N. vehicle, conveyance, carriage, caravan, van; wagon, waggon, wain, dray, cart, lorry.

carriole; truck, tram; limber, tumbrel, pontoon; barrow; wheel-, hand-barrow; perambulator; Bath –, wheel –, sedan-chair; chaise; palan-keen, -quin; litter, brancard, crate, hurdle, stretcher, ambulance; black Maria; conestoga- wagon, -wain; jinrikisha, ricksha, brett, dearborn [U. S.], dump cart, hack, hackery, jigger, kittereen, mail stage, manumotor, rig, rockaway, prairie schooner [U. S.], shay, sloven [Can.], team, tonga, wheel; velocipede, hobbyhorse, gocart; cycle; bi-, tri-, quadri-cycle; bike.

equipage, turn-out; coach, chariot, phaëton, break, mail phaëton, wagonette, drag, curricle, tilbury, whisky, landau, barouche, victoria, brougham, clarence, calash, *calèche*, britzka, araba, kibitka; berlin; sulky, *désobligeant*, sociable, *vis-à-vis, dormeuse;* jaunting –, outside- car; dandi; dool-ie, -y; *munchil*, palki; roller skates, skate; runabout; ski; tonjon; *vettura.*

post chaise; diligence, stage; stage –, mail –, hackney –, glass- coach; stage wagon; car, omnibus, fly, cabriolet, cab, hansom, shofle, four-wheeler, growler, droshki, drosky.

dogcart, trap, whitechapel, buggy, four-in-hand, unicorn, random, tandem; shandredhan, *char-à-bancs.*

motor car, automobile, limousine, motor cycle, taxicab, taxicoach.

bob, -sled, -sleigh; cutter; double-ripper, -runner [U. S.]; jumper, sled, sledge, sleigh, toboggan.

train; accommodation –, passenger –,

273. Ship. — N. ship, vessel, sail; craft, bottom.

navy, marine, fleet, flotilla; shipping. man of war &c. (*combatant*) 726; transport, tender, storeship; merchant ship, merchantman; packet, liner; whaler, slaver, collier, coaster, lighter; fishing –, pilot- boat; trawler, hulk; yacht; baggala; floating -hotel, – palace; ocean greyhound.

ship, bark, barque, brig, snow, hermaphrodite brig; brig-, bark-antine; schooner; topsail –, for and aft –, three masted- schooner; *chasse-marée;* sloop, cutter, corvette, clipper, foist, yawl, dandy, ketch, smack, lugger, barge, hoy, cat, buss; sail-er, -ing vessel; windjammer; steam-er, -boat, -ship; mail –, paddle –, screw- steamer; tug; line of steamers &c.

boat, pinnace, launch; life-, long-, jolly-, bum-, fly-, cock-, ferry-, canalboat; ark, bully [Nfld.], bateau [Can.], battery, broadhorn, dory, droger, drogher, dugout, durham boat, flatboat, galiot; shallop, gig, funny, skiff, dingy, scow, cockleshell, wherry, coble, punt, cog, kedge, lerret; eight-, four-, pairoar; randan; outrigger; float, raft, pontoon; prame; ice-boat, -canoe, -yacht.

catamaran, coracle, gondola, carvel, caravel; felucca, caique, canoe; galley, – foist; bilander, dogger, hooker, howker; argosy, carack; galliass, galleon; polacca, polacre, tartane, junk, lorcha, praam, proa, prahu, saick, sampan, xebec, dhow; dahabeah; nuggah; kayak, keel boat [U. S.], log canoe, pirogue; quadri-, tri-reme; stern-wheeler [U. S.]; wanigan, wangan [U. S.], wharf boat.

express –, special –, corridor –, parliamentary –, luggage –, freight –, goods-train; 1st-, 2nd-, 3rd-class- -train, – carriage, – compartment; rolling stock; horse box, cattle truck; baggage-, express-, freight-, parlor-, Pullman-, sleeping-, surface-, tram-, trolley-car; box-car, -wagon; horse car [U. S.]; lightning express; luggage van; mail, -car, -van.

balloon; airship, aëroplane; bi-, mono-, tri-plane; hydroplane; aërodrome; air –, pilot –, fire- balloon; aërostat, Montgolfier; kite, parachute.

Adv. afloat, aboard; on -board, – ship board; hard-a -lee, -port, – starboard, – weather.

shovel, spoon, spatula, ladle, hod, hoe; spade, spaddle, loy; spud; pitch-fork.

2. DEGREES OF MOTION

274. Velocity. — N. velocity, speed, celerity; swiftness &c. *adj.*; rapidity, eagle speed; expedition &c. (*activity*) 682; pernicity †; acceleration; haste &c. 684.

spurt, rush, dash, race, steeple chase; smart –, lively –, swift &c. *adj.* –, rattling –, spanking –, strapping- -rate, – pace; round pace; flying, flight.

gallop, canter, trot, round trot, run, scamper; hand –, full- gallop; amble.

lightning, light, electricity, wind; cannon ball, rocket, arrow, dart, hydrargyrum, quicksilver; telegraph, express train; torrent.

eagle, antelope, courser, race horse, gazelle, greyhound, hare, doe, squirrel, camel bird, chickaree, chipmunk, hackee [U. S.], ostrich, scorcher*.

Mercury, Ariel, Camilla, Harlequin. [Measurement of velocity] log, -line.

V. move quickly, trip, fisk †; speed, hie, hasten, post, spank, scuttle; scud, -dle; scour, – the plain; scamper; run, – like mad; fly, race, run a race, cut away, shoot, tear, whisk, sweep, skim, brush; cut –, bowl- along; scorch; rush &c. (*be violent*) 173; dash -on, – off, – forward; bolt; trot, gallop, amble, troll, bound, flit, spring, dart, boom; march in -quick, – double- time; ride hard, get over the ground.

hurry &c. (*hasten*) 684; accelerate, put on; quicken; quicken –, mend- one's pace; clap spurs to one's horse; make -haste, – rapid strides, – forced marches, – the best of one's way; put one's best leg foremost, stir one's stumps, wing one's way, set off at a score; carry –, crowd- sail; go off like a shot, go ahead, gain ground; outstrip the wind, fly on the wings of the wind.

keep -up, – pace- with; outstrip &c. 303; outmarch.

275. Slowness. — N. slowness &c. *adj.*; languor &c. (*inactivity*) 683; drawl; creeping &c. *v.*, lentor.

retardation; slackening &c. *v.*; delay &c. (*lateness*) 133; claudication†.

jog-, dog-trot; mincing steps; slow -march, – time.

slow -goer, – coach, – back; lingerer, loiterer, sluggard, tortoise, snail; poke* [U. S.]; dawdle &c. (*inactive*) 683.

V. move -slowly &c. *adv.*; creep, crawl, lag, slug, drawl, linger, loiter, saunter; plod, trudge, stump along, lumber; trail, drag; dawdle &c. (*be inactive*) 683; grovel, worm one's way, steal along; jog –, rub –, bundle- on; toddle, waddle, wabble, slug, traipse, slouch, shuffle, halt, hobble, limp, claudicate†, shamble; flag, falter, totter, stagger; mince, step short; march in -slow time, – funeral procession; take one's time; hang fire &c. (*be late*) 133.

retard, relax; slacken, check, moderate, rein in, curb; reef; strike –, shorten –, take in- sail; put on the drag, apply the brake; clip the wings; reduce the speed; slacken -speed, – one's pace; lose ground.

Adj. slow, slack; tardy; dilatory &c. (*inactive*) 683; gentle, easy; leisurely; deliberate, gradual; insensible, imperceptible; languid, sluggish, slow-paced, tardigrade, snail-like; creeping &c. *v.*; reptatorial.

Adv. slowly &c. *adj.*; leisurely; piano, adagio; *largo, larghetto;* at half speed, under easy sail; at a -foot's, – snail's, – funeral- pace; in slow time; with -mincing steps, – clipped wings; *haud passibus æquis* [Vergil].

gradually &c. *adj.*; gradatim; by -degrees, – slow degrees, – inches, – little and little; step by step; inch by inch,

Adj. fast, speedy, swift, rapid, quick, fleet; aliped; nimble, agile, expeditious; express; active &c. 682; flying, galloping &c. *v.*; light-, nimble-footed; winged, eagle-winged, mercurial, electric, telegraphic; light-legged, light of heel; swift as -an arrow &c. *n.*; quick as -lightning &c. *n.*, – thought.[1]

Adv. swiftly &c. *adj.*; with -speed &c. *n.*; apace; at -a great rate, – full speed, – railway speed; full -drive, – gallop; posthaste, in full sail, tantivy; trippingly; instantaneously &c. 113.

under press of -sail, – canvas, – sail and steam; *velis et remis*, on eagle's wing, in double quick time; with -rapid, – giant- strides; *à pas de géant*; in seven league boots; whip and spur; *ventre à terre*; as fast as one's -legs, – heels- will carry one; as fast as one can lay legs to the ground, at the top of one's speed; by leaps and bounds; with haste &c. 684.

Phr. *vires acquirit eundo;* " I'll put a girdle about the earth in forty minutes " [*M. N. D.*]; " swifter than arrow from the Tartar's bow " [*M. N. D.*]; *tempus fugit.*

bit by bit, little by little, *seriatim;* consecutively.

Phr. *dum Roma deliberat Saguntum perit.*

3. Motion conjoined with Force

276. Impulse. — **N.** impulse, impulsion, impetus; momentum; push, pulsion, thrust, shove, jog, jolt, brunt, booming, boost [U. S.], throw; explosion &c. (*violence*) 173; propulsion &c. 284.

percussion, concussion, collision, occursion†, clash, encounter, cannon, carambole, appulse, shock, crash, bump; impact; *élan;* charge &c. (*attack*) 716; beating &c. (*punishment*) 972.

blow, dint, stroke, knock, tap, rap, slap, smack, pat, dab; fillip; slam, bang; hit, whack, thwack; cuff &c. 972; squash, dowse, whap, swap, punch, thump, pelt, kick, punce†, calcitration; *ruade;* arietation †; cut, thrust, lunge, yerk †; carom, carrom, clip *, jab, plug *, sidewinder * [U. S.], sidewipe * [U. S.].

hammer, sledge hammer, mall, maul, mallet, flail; ram, -mer; battering-ram, monkey, pile-driving engine, punch, bat; cant hook; cudgel &c. (*weapon*) 727; ax &c. (*sharp*) 253.

[Science of mechanical forces] dynamics; seismometer.

V. give an -impetus &c. *n.*; impel, push; start, give a start to, set going; drive, urge, boom; thrust, prod, foin; cant; elbow, shoulder, jostle, justle, hustle, hurtle, shove, jog, jolt, encounter; run –, bump –, butt- against; knock, – run- one's head against; impinge; boost [U. S.]; bunt, carom, clip *; fan, -out; jab, plug *.

strike, knock, hit, tap, rap, slap, flap, dab, pat, thump, beat, bang, slam, dash; punch, thwack, whack; hit –, strike- hard; swap, batter, dowse†, baste; pelt, patter, buffet, belabor; fetch one a blow; poke at, pink, lunge, yerk; kick, calcitrate; butt, strike at &c. (*attack*) 716; whip &c. (*punish*) 972.

come –, enter- into collision; collide; foul; fall –, run- foul of; telescope. throw &c. (*propel*) 284.

Adj. impelling &c. *v.*; im-pulsive, -pellent; booming; dynamic, -al; impelled &c. *v.*

Phr. " a hit, a very palpable hit " [*Hamlet*].

277. Recoil. — **N.** recoil; re-, retro-action; revulsion; rebound, ricochet; re-percussion, -calcitration; kick, *contrecoup;* springing back &c. *v.*; elasticity &c. 325; reflexion, reflex, reflux; reverberation &c. (*resonance*) 408; rebuff, re-pulse; return.

ducks and drakes; boomerang; spring; reactionist.

V. recoil, react; spring –, fly –, bound- back; rebound, reverberate, repercuss, recalcitrate; echo, ricochet.

Adj. recoiling &c. *v.*; re-fluent, -percussive, -calcitrant, -actionary; retroactive.

Adv. on the -recoil &c. *n.*

[1] See note on 264.

4. Motion with reference to Direction

278. Direction. — N. direction, bearing, course, set, drift, tenor; tendency &c. 176; incidence; bending, trending &c. *v.*; dip, tack, aim, collimation; steering, -age.

point of the compass, cardinal points; North, East, South, West; N by E, ENE, NE by N, NE, &c.; rhumb, azimuth, line of collimation.

line, path, road, range, quarter, line of march; a-, al-lignment; air-, beeline; straight shoot.

V. tend -, bend -, point- towards; conduct -, go- to; point -to, - at; bend, trend, verge, incline, dip, determine.

steer -, make- -for, - towards; aim -, level- at; take aim; keep -, hold- a course; be bound for; bend one's steps towards; direct -, steer -, bend -, shape- one's course; align -, allign- one's march; go straight, - to the point; march -on, - on a point.

ascertain one's -direction &c. *n.*; *s'orienter*, see which way the wind blows; box the compass; take the air line.

Adj. directed &c. *v.*, - towards; pointing towards &c. *v.*; bound for; aligned -, alligned- with; direct, straight; un-deviating, -swerving; straightforward; North, -ern, -erly, &c. *n.*

Adv. towards; on the -road, - high road- to; *en avant; versus,* to; hither, thither, whither; directly; straight, - forwards, - as an arrow; point-blank; in a -bee, - direct, - straight- line -to, - for, - with; in a line with; full tilt at, as the crow flies.

before -, near -, close to -, against- the wind; windwards, in the wind's eye.

through, *viâ,* by way of; in all -directions, - manner of ways; *quaquaversum,* from the four winds.

279. Deviation. — N. deviation; swerving &c. *v.*; obliquation†, warp, refraction; flection, flexion; sweep; deflection, -flexure; declination.

diversion, digression, departure from, aberration; divergence &c. 291; zigzag; detour &c. (*circuit*) 629; divagation.

[Desultory motion] wandering &c. *v.*; vagrancy, evagation; bypaths and crooked ways; byroad.

[Motion sideways, oblique motion] sidling &c. *v.*; knight's move at chess.

V. alter one's course, deviate, depart from, turn, trend; bend, curve &c. 245; swerve, heel, bear off; gybe, wear.

intervert; deflect; divert, - from its course; put on a new scent, shift, shunt, draw aside, crook, warp.

stray, straggle; sidle; diverge &c. 291; tralineate †, digress, wander; wind, twist, meander; veer, tack; divagate; sidetrack; turn -aside, - a corner, - away from; wheel, steer clear of; ramble, rove, drift; go -astray, - adrift; yaw, dodge; step aside, ease off, make way for, shy.

fly off at a tangent; glance off; wheel -, face- about; turn -, face- to the right about; waddle &c. (*oscillate*) 314; go out of one's way &c. (*perform a circuit,* 629; lose one's way.

Adj. deviating &c. *v.*; aberrant, errant; ex-, dis-cursive; devious, desultory, loose; rambling; stray, erratic, vagrant, undirected; circuitous, indirect, zigzag; crab-like.

Adv. astray from, round about, wide of the mark; to the right about; all manner of ways; circuitously &c. 629.

obliquely, sideling, like the move of the knight on a chessboard.

280. [Going before.] Precession. — N. precession, leading, heading; precedence &c. 62; priority &c. 116; the lead, *le pas;* van &c. (*front*) 234; precursor &c. 64.

V. go -before, - ahead, - in the van, - in advance; precede, forerun; usher in, introduce, herald, head, take the lead; lead, - the way, - the dance; get -, have- the start; steal a march; get -before, - ahead, - in front of; outstrip &c.

281. [Going after.] Sequence. — N. sequence; coming after &c. (*order*) 63; (*time*) 117; following; pursuit &c. 622.

follower, attendant, satellite, shadow, dangler, train.

V. follow; pursue &c. 622; go -, fly- after.

attend, beset, dance attendance on, dog; tread -in the steps of, - close upon; be -, go -, follow- in the -wake, - trail, - rear- of; follow as a shadow, hang on

303; take precedence &c. (*first in order*) 62.

Adj. leading, precedent &c. *v.*

Adv. in advance, before, ahead, in the van; fore-, head-most; in front.

Phr. *seniores priores.*

the skirts of; tread –, follow- on the heels of; camp on the trail.

lay, get behind.

Adj. following &c. *v.*

Adv. behind; in the -rear &c. 235, – train of, – wake of; after &c. (*order*) 63, (*time*) 117.

282. [Motion forwards; progressive motion.] **Progression. — N.** progress, -ion, -iveness; advancing &c. *v.*; advance, -ment; ongoing; flood tide, headway; march &c. 266; rise; improvement &c. 658.

V. advance; proceed, progress; get -on, – along, – over the ground; gain ground; forge ahead; jog –, rub –, wag-on; go with the stream; keep –, hold on-one's course; go –, move –, come –, get –, pass –, push –, press- -on, – forward, – forwards, – ahead; press onwards, step forward; make –, work –, carve –, push –, force –, edge –, elbow- one's way; make -progress, – head, – way, – head-way, – advances, – strides, – rapid strides &c. (*velocity*) 274; go –, shoot-ahead; distance; make up leeway.

Adj. advancing &c. *v.*; pro-gressive, -fluent; advanced.

Adv. forward, onward; forth, on, ahead, under way, *en route* for, on -one's way, – the way, – the road, – the high road- to; in -progress, – mid progress; *in transitu* &c. 270.

Phr. *vestigia nulla retrorsum;* " westward the course of empire takes its way " [Berkeley].

283. [Motion backwards.] **Regression. — N.** regress, -ion; retro-cession, -gression, -gradation, -action; *reculade;* retreat, withdrawal, retirement, remigration; recession &c. (*motion from*) 287; recess; crab-like motion.

re-fluence, -flux; backwater, regurgitation, ebb, return; resilience; re-flexion (*recoil*) 277; *volte-face.*

counter -motion, – movement, – march; veering, tergiversation, recidivation †, backsliding, fall; deterioration &c. 659; recidivism, recidivity.

turning point &c. (*reversion*) 145.

V. re-cede, -grade, -turn, -vert, -treat, -tire; retro-grade, -cede; back, – out; back down; balk; crawfish * [U. S.], crawl *; withdraw; rebound &c. 277; go –, come –, turn –, hark –, draw –, fall –, get –, put –, run- back; lose ground; fall –, drop- astern; backwater, put about; take the back track; veer, – round; double, wheel, countermarch; ebb, re-gurgitate; jib, shrink, shy.

turn -tail, – round, – upon one's heel, – one's back upon; retrace one's steps, dance the back step; sound –, beat- a retreat; go home.

Adj. receding &c. *v.*; retro-grade, -gressive; re-gressive, -fluent, -flex, -cidivous, -silient; crab-like; balky; re-actionary &c. 277.

Adv. back, -wards; reflexively, to the right about; *à reculons, à rebours.*

Phr. *revenons à nos moutons,* as you were.

284. [Motion given to an object situated in front.] **Propulsion. — N.** pro-pulsion, -jection; propelment; *vis a tergo;* push &c. (*impulse*) 276; e-, jaculation; ejection &c. 297; throw, fling, toss, shot, discharge, shy.

[Science of propulsion] projectiles, ballistics, archery.

propeller, screw, twin screws, turbine.

missile, projectile, ball, discus, quoit, brickbat, shot; arrow, gun, &c. (*arms*) 727.

shooter, shot; archer, toxophilite; bow-, rifle-, marks-man; good –, crack-shot; sharpshooter &c. (*combatant*) 726.

V. propel, project, throw, fling, cast, pitch, chuck, toss, jerk, heave, shy, hurl; flirt, fillip.

285. [Motion given to an object situated behind.] **Traction. — N.** traction; drawing &c. *v.*; draught, pull, haul; rake; " a long pull a strong pull and a pull all together; " towage, haulage.

V. draw, pull, haul, lug, rake, drag, tug, tow, trail, train; take in tow.

wrench, jerk, twitch, touse †; yank [U. S.].

Adj. drawing &c. *v.*; tract-ile, -ive.

dart, lance, tilt; e-, jaculate; rulminate, bolt, drive, sling, pitchfork.

send; send -, let -, fire- off; discharge, shoot; launch, send forth, let fly; dash.

put -, set- in motion; set agoing, start; give -a start, - an impulse- to; impel &c. 276; trundle &c. (*set in rotation*) 312; expel &c. 297.

carry one off one's legs; put to flight.

Adj. propelled &c. *v.*; propelling &c. *v.*; pro-pulsive, -jectile.

286. [Motion towards.] **Approach.** — **N.** approach, approximation, appropinquation; access; appulse; afflux, -ion; advent &c. (*approach of time*) 121; pursuit &c. 622.

V. approach, approximate, appropinquate; near; get -, go -, draw- near; come, - near, - to close quarters; move -, set in- towards; drift; make up to; gain upon; pursue &c. 622; tread on the heels of; bear up; make the land; hug the -shore, - land.

Adj. approaching &c. *v.*; approximative; affluent; impending, imminent &c. (*destined*) 152.

Adv. on the road.

Int. come hither! approach! here! come! come near! forward!

287. [Motion from.] **Recession.** — **N.** recession, retirement, withdrawal; retreat; retrocession &c. 283; departure, &c. 293; recoil &c. 277; flight &c. (*avoidance*) 623.

V. recede, go, move -back, - from, retire, withdraw, shrink; come -, move -, go -, get -, drift- away; depart &c. 293; retreat &c. 283; move -, stand -, sheer- off; fall back, stand aside; run away &c. (*avoid*) 623.

remove, shunt.

Adj. receding &c. *v.*

288. [Motion towards, actively.] **Attraction.** — **N.** attract-ion, -iveness; attractivity; drawing to, pulling towards, adduction, magnetism, gravity, attraction of gravitation.

load-stone, -star; magnet, siderite.

V. attract; draw -, pull -, drag- towards; adduce.

Adj. attracting &c. *v.*; attrahent, attractive, adducent, adductive.

Phr. *ubi mel ibi apes* [Plautus].

289. [Motion from, actively.] **Repulsion.** — **N.** repulsion; driving from &c. *v.*; repulse, abduction.

V. repel; push -, drive -, &c. 276- from; chase, dispel; retrude; abduce, abduct; send away; repulse.

keep at arm's length, turn one's back upon, give the cold shoulder; send -off, - away- with a flea in one's ear.

Adj. repelling &c. *v.*; repellent, repulsive; abducent, abductive.

290. [Motion nearer to.] **Convergence.** — **N.** con-vergence, -fluence, -course, -flux, -gress, -currence, -centration; convergency; appulse, meeting; corradiation.

assemblage &c. 72; resort &c. (*focus*) 74; asymptote.

V. converge, concur; come together, unite, meet, fall in with; close -with, - in upon; center -round, - in; enter in; pour in.

gather together, unite, concentrate, bring into a focus.

Adj. converging &c. *v.*; con-vergent, -fluent, -current; centripetal; asymptotical; confluxible.

291. [Motion further off.] **Divergence.** — **N.** diverg-ence, -ency; divarication, ramification, forking; radiation; separation &c. (*disjunction*) 44; dispersion &c. 73; deviation &c. 279; aberration.

V. diverge, divaricate, radiate; ramify; branch -, glance -, file- off; fly off, - at a tangent; spread, scatter, disperse &c. 73; deviate &c. 279; part &c. (*separate*) 44.

Adj. diverging &c. *v.*; divergent, radiant, centrifugal; aberrant.

292. [Terminal motion at.] **Arrival.** — **N.** arrival, advent; landing; de-,

293. [Initial motion from.] **Departure.** — **N.** departure, decession, de-,

disem-barkation; reception, welcome, *vin d'honneur.*

home, goal; landing-place, -stage; bunder; resting place; destination, harbor, haven, port; terminus; halting -place, – ground; journey's end; anchorage &c. (*refuge*) 666.

return, recursion†, remigration; meeting; ren-, en-counter.

completion &c. 729.

V. arrive; get to, come to; come; reach, attain; come up, – with, – to; overtake; make, fetch; complete &c. 729; join, rejoin.

light, alight, dismount; land, go ashore; debark, disembark; put -in, – into; visit, cast anchor, pitch one's tent; sit down &c. (*be located*) 184; get to one's journey's end; make the land; be in at the death; come –, get- -back, – home; return; come in &c. (*ingress*) 294; make one's appearance &c. (*appear*) 446; drop in; detrain; outspan.

come to hand; come -at, – across; hit; come –, light –, pop –, bounce –, plump –, burst –, pitch- upon; meet; en-, ren-counter; come in contact.

Adj. arriving &c. *v.*; homeward bound.
Adv. here, hither.
Int. welcome! hail! all hail! good-day, – morrow!

campment; embarkation; outset, start; removal; exit &c. (*egress*) 295; exodus, hejira, flight.

leave-taking, valediction, adieu, farewell, good-by; stirrup cup; valedictorian.

starting-point, – post; point –, place-of -departure, – embarkation; port of embarkation.

V. depart; go, – away; take one's departure, set out; set –, march –, put –, start –, be –, move –, get –, whip –, pack –, go –, take oneself- off; start, issue, march out, debouch; go –, sallyforth; sally, set forward; be gone; hail from.

leave a place, quit, vacate, evacuate, abandon; go off the stage, make one's exit; retire, withdraw, remove; vamoose*, vamose* [U. S.]; go -one's way, – along, – from home; take -flight, – wing; spring, fly, flit, wing one's flight; fly –, whip- away; embark; go -on board, – aboard; set sail; put –, go- to sea; sail, take ship; hoist blue Peter; get under way, weigh anchor; strike tents, decamp; walk one's chalks, cut one's stick; take leave; say –, bid- -good-by &c. *n.*; disappear &c. 449; abscond &c. (*avoid*) 623; entrain; inspan.

Adj. departing &c. *v.*; valedictory; outward bound.

Adv. whence, hence, thence; with a foot in the stirrup; on the -wing, – move.

Int. begone! &c. (*ejection*) 297; farewell! adieu! good -by, – day! *au revoir!* fare you well! God -bless you, – speed! all aboard! *auf wiedersehen! au plaisir de vous revoir! bon voyage! glückliche Reise! vive valeque!*

---

294. [Motion into.] **Ingress. — N.**
ingress; entrance, entry; introgression; influx; intrusion, inroad, incursion, invasion, irruption; ingression; pene-, interpene-tration; illapse, import, infiltration; immigration; admission &c. (*reception*) 296; insinuation &c. (*interjacence*) 228; insertion &c. 300.

inlet; way in; mouth, door, &c. (*opening*) 260; barway; path &c. (*way*) 627; conduit &c. 350; immigrant.

V. have the entrée; enter; go –, come –, pour –, flow –, creep –, slip –, pop –, break –, burst- -into, – in; set foot on; ingress; burst –, break- in upon; invade, intrude; insinuate itself; inter-, penetrate; infiltrate; find one's way –, wriggle –, worm oneself- into.

295. [Motion out of.] **Egress. — N.**
egress, exit, issue; emer-sion, -gence; out-break, -burst; e-, pro-ruption; emanation; egression; evacuation; ex-, trans-udation; extravasation, perspiration, sweating, leakage, percolation, distillation, oozing; gush &c. (*water in motion*) 348; outpour, -ing; effluence, effusion; efflux, -ion; drain; dribbling &c. *v.*; defluxion; drainage; out-come, -put; discharge &c. (*excretion*) 299.

export; expatriation; e-, re-migration; debouch, *débouché*; emunctory; exodus &c. (*departure*) 293; emigrant.

outlet, vent, spout, tap, sluice, floodgate; pore; vomitory, outgate, sallyport; way out; mouth, door &c. (*opening*) 260; path &c. (*way*) 627; conduit &c. 350; airpipe &c. 351.

give entrance to &c. (*receive*) 296, insert &c. 300.

Adj. incoming.

through; per-, trans-colate †; egurgitate; strain, distill; perspire, sweat, drain, ooze; filter, filtrate; dribble, gush, spout, flow out; well, – out; pour, trickle, &c. (*water in motion*) 348; effuse, extravasate, disembogue, discharge itself, debouch; come –, break- forth; burst -out, – through; find vent; escape &c. 671.

Adj. effused &c. *v.*; outgoing.

V. emerge, emanate, issue; egress; go –, come –, move –, pass –, pour –, flow-out of; pass off, evacuate.

ex-, trans-ude; leak; run, – out, – through; per-, trans-colate †; egurgitate; strain, distill; perspire, sweat, drain, ooze; filter, filtrate; dribble, gush, spout, flow out; well, – out; pour, trickle, &c.

296. [Motion into, actively.] **Reception. — N.** reception; admission, admittance, entrée, importation; introduction, -mission; immission, ingestion, imbibition, introception, absorption, ingurgitation, inhalation; suction, sucking; eating, drinking &c. (*food*) 298; insertion &c. 300; interjection &c. 228; introit.

V. give -entrance to, – admittance to, – the entrée; intro-duce, -mit; usher, admit, receive, import, bring in, open the door to, throw open, ingest, absorb, imbibe, inhale; let –, take –, suck- in; re-admit, -sorb, -absorb; snuff up, swallow, ingurgitate; engulf, engorge; gulp; eat, drink &c. (*food*) 298.

Adj. admit-ting &c. *v.*, -ted &c. *v.*; admissible; absorbent.

297. [Motion out of, actively.] **Ejection. — N.** ejection, emission, effusion, rejection, expulsion, eviction, extrusion, trajection; discharge; emesis.

egestion, evacuation, vomition; ruc-, eruc-tation; bloodletting, venesection, phlebotomy, paracentesis; expuition, ex-spuition; tapping, drainage; clear-ance, -age.

deportation; banishment &c. (*punishment*) 972; rogue's march; relegation, extradition; dislodgment.

bouncer * [U. S.], chucker-out *.

V. give -exit, – vent- to; let –, give –, pour –, send -out; des-, dis-patch; ex-hale, excern †, excrete; embogue; secrete, secern; extravastate, shed, void, evacu-ate; emit; open the -sluices, – floodgates; turn on the tap; extrude, detrude; effuse, spend, expend; pour forth; squirt, spirt, spill, slop; perspire &c. (*exude*) 295; breathe, blow &c. (*wind*) 349.

tap, draw off; bale –, lade- out; let blood, broach.

eject, reject; expel, discard; cut, send to Coventry, boycott; *chasser;* banish &c. (*punish*) 972; bounce * [U. S.]; fire*, – out *; throw &c. 284 -out, – up, – off, – away, – aside; push &c. 276 -out, – off, – away, – aside; shovel –, sweep- -out, – away; brush –, whisk –, turn –, send- -off, – away; discharge; send –, turn –, cast- adrift; turn –, bundle- out; throw overboard; give the sack to; send -packing, – about one's business, – to the right about; strike off the roll &c. (*abrogate*) 756; turn out -neck and heels, – head and shoulders, – neck and crop; pack off; send away with a flea in the ear; send to Jericho; bow out, show the door to.

turn out of -doors, – house and home; evict, oust; un-house, -kennel; dislodge; un-, dis-people; depopulate; relegate, deport.

empty; drain, – to the dregs; sweep off; clear, – off, – out, – away; suck, draw off; clean out, make a clean sweep of, clear decks, purge.

em-, dis-, disem-bowel; eviscerate, gut; unearth, root -out, – up; aver-runcate †; weed –, get- out; eliminate, get rid of, do away with, shake off; ex-enterate.

vomit, spew, puke †, keck, retch; belch, – out; cast –, bring- up; disgorge; expectorate, clear the throat, hawk, spit, sputter, splutter, slobber, drivel, slaver, slabber; eructate; drool.

unpack, unlade, unload, unship; break bulk; dump.

be let out; ooze &c. (*emerge*) 295.

Adj. emitt-ing, -ed, &c. *v.*

Int. begone! get you gone! get –, go- -away, – along, – along with you! go your way! away, – with! off with you! go, – about your business! be off! avaunt! aroynt! *allez-vous-en! jao! va-t'en!*

298. [Eating.] **Food.** — **N.** eating &c.
v.; deglutition, gulp, epulation, mastica-
tion, manducation, rumination; hippo-,
ichthyo-phagy; gluttony &c. 957.

mouth, jaws, mandible, mazard, chops.

drinking &c. *v.*; potation, draught,
libation; carousal &c. (*amusement*) 840;
drunkenness &c. 959.

food, pabulum; aliment, nourishment,
nutriment; susten-ance, -tation; nurture, subsistence, provender, corn, feed,
fodder, provision, ration, keep, commons,
board; commissariat &c. (*provision*) 637;
prey, forage, pasture, pasturage; fare,
cheer; diet, -ary; regimen; belly timber,
staff of life; bread, -and cheese.

comestibles, eatables, victuals, edi-
bles, ingesta; grub, prog, meat; bread,

299. Excretion. — **N.** excretion, discharge, emanation; exhalation, exudation, extrusion, secretion, effusion, extravasation, ecchymosis, evacuation, dejection, *fæces*, excrement; bloody flux;
cacation; cœliac-flux, -passion; dysentery; perspiration, sweat; sub-†, exudation; diaphoresis; sewage; eccrinology.

saliva, spittle, rheum; ptyalism, sali-
vation, catarrh; diarrhœa; ejecta, egesta,
sputa; excreta; lava; exuviæ &c. (*uncleanness*) 653.

hemorrhage, bleeding; outpouring &c.
(*egress*) 295.

V. excrete &c. (*eject*) 297; emanate
&c. (*come out*) 295.

-stuffs; cerealia; cereals; viands, cates, delicacy, dainty, creature comforts,
contents of the larder, fleshpots; festal board; ambrosia; good -cheer, -
living.

beef, biscuit, bun; cornstarch [U. S.]; cook-ie, -y [U. S.]; cracker, doughnut;
fatling; hard-tack, hoecake [U. S.], hominy [U. S.]; mutton, pilot bread;
pork; *roti*, rusk, ship biscuit; veal; joint, *pièce de résistance*, roast and boiled;
remove, entrée, *entremet, hors d'œuvre; relevé*, hash, *réchauffé*, stew, ragout,
fricassee, mince; pottage, *potage*, broth, soup, *consommé, purée*, spoon-meat;
pie, pasty, *vol-au-vent;* pudding, omelet; pastry; sweets &c. 296; kickshaws;
condiment &c. 393.

alligator pear, apple &c., apple slump; artichoke; ash-, griddle-, pan-cake;
atole, avocado, banana, *bêche de mer*, barbecue, beefsteak; beet root; blackberry, blancmange, bloater, *bouilli*, bouillon, breadfruit, chop suey [U. S.];
chowder, chupatty, clam, compote, damper, fish, flapjack, frumenty, grapes,
hasty pudding, ice cream, lettuce, mango, mangosteen, mince pie, oatmeal,
oyster, pineapple, porridge, porterhouse steak, salmis, sauerkraut, sea slug,
sturgeon ("Albany beef"), succotash [U. S.], supawn [U. S.], trepang, vanilla, waffle, walnut.

table, *cuisine*, bill of fare, menu, *table d'hôte*, ordinary.

meal, repast, feed, spread; mess; dish, plate, course; regale; regale-, re-
fresh-, entertain-ment; refection, collation, picnic, feast, banquet, junket;
breakfast; lunch, -eon; *déjeûner*, bever, tiffin, dinner, supper, snack, whet,
bait, dessert; potluck, *table d'hôte, déjeûner à la fourchette;* hearty -, square -,
substantial -, full- -meal; blowout *; light refreshment; *bara-, chota-hazri;
bara khana.*

mouthful, bolus, gobbet, morsel, sop, sippet.

drink, beverage, liquor, broth, soup; potion, dram, draught, drench, swill *;
nip, sip, sup, gulp.

wine, spirits, liqueur, beer, ale, malt liquor, Sir John Barleycorn, stingo,
heavy wet; grog, toddy, flip, purl, punch, negus, cup, bishop, wassail; gin &c.
(*intoxicating liquor*) 959; coffee, chocolate, cocoa, tea, the cup that cheers but
not inebriates; bock-, lager-, Pilsener-, schenk-beer; Brazil tea, cider, claret,
ice water, maté, mint julep [U. S.].

eating house &c. 189.

V. eat, feed, fare, devour, swallow, take; gulp, bolt, snap; fall to; despatch,
dispatch; discuss; take -, get -, gulp- down; lay -, tuck- * in; lick, pick, peck;
gormandize &c. 957; bite, champ, munch, cranch, craunch, crunch, chew,
masticate, nibble, gnaw, mumble.

live on; feed -, batten -, fatten -, feast- upon; browse, graze, crop, regale;

carouse &c. (*make merry*) 840; eat heartily, do justice to, play a good knife and fork, banquet.

break -bread, – one's fast; breakfast, lunch, dine, take tea, sup.

drink, – in, – up, – one's fill; quaff, sip, sup; suck, – up; lap; swig; swill*, tipple &c. (*be drunken*) 959; empty one's glass, drain the cup; toss -off, – one's glass; wash down, crack a bottle, wet one's whistle.

purvey &c. 637.

Adj. eatable, edible, esculent, comestible, alimentary; cereal, cibarious; dietetic; culinary; nutri-tive, -tious; gastric; succulent; pot-able, -ulent †; bibulous.

omn-, carn-, herb-, gran-, gramin-, phyt-ivorous; ichthyophagous; omo-pha-gic, -gous; pantophagous, phytophagous, xylophagous.

Phr. "across the walnuts and the wine" [Tennyson]; "blesséd hour of our dinners!" [O. Meredith]; "now good digestion wait on appetite, and health on both!" [*Macbeth*]; "who can cloy the hungry edge of appetite?" [*Richard II*].

---

300. [Forcible ingress.] **Insertion.**
— **N.** insertion, implantation, introduc-tion; insinuation &c. (*intervention*) 228; planting &c. *v.*; injection, inoculation, importation, infusion; forcible -ingress &c. 294; immersion; submer-sion, -gence, dip, plunge; bath &c. (*water*) 337; inter-ment &c. 363.

clyster, enema, glyster, lavage, lave-ment.

V. insert; intro-duce, -mit; put –, run- into; import; inject; interject &c. 228; infuse, instill, inoculate, impreg-nate, imbue, imbrue.

graft, ingraft, bud, plant, implant; dovetail.

obtrude; thrust –, stick –, ram –, stuff –, tuck –, press –, drive –, pop –, whip –, drop –, put- in; impact; em-pierce † &c. (*make a hole*) 260.

imbed; immerse, immerge, merge; bathe, soak &c. (*water*) 337; dip, plunge &c. 310.

bury &c. (*inter*) 363.

insert &c.- itself; plunge *in medias res*.

Adj. inserted &c. *v.*

301. [Forcible egress.] **Extraction.**
— **N.** extraction; extracting &c. *v.*; re-moval, elimination, extrication, eradica-tion, evolution.

evulsion, avulsion; wrench; expres-sion, squeezing; extirpation, extermina-tion; ejection &c. 297; export &c. (*egress*) 295.

extractor, corkscrew, forceps, pliers.

V. extract, draw; take –, draw –, pull –, tear –, pluck –, pick –, get- out; wring from, wrench; extort; root –, weed –, grub –, rake- -up, – out; eradicate; pull –, pluck- up by the roots; averrun-cate †; unroot; uproot, pull up, extir-pate, dredge.

remove; educe, elicit; evolve, extri-cate; eliminate &c. (*eject*) 297; eviscer-ate &c. 297.

express, squeeze out, press out.

Adj. extracted &c. *v.*

---

302. [Motion through.] **Passage. — N.** passage, transmission; permeation; pene-, interpene-tration; transudation, infiltration; endosmose, exosmose; endosmosis; intercurrence; ingress &c. 294; egress &c. 295; path &c. 627; con-duit &c. 350; opening &c. 260; journey &c. 266; voyage &c. 267.

V. pass, – through; perforate &c. (*hole*) 260; penetrate, permeate, thread, thrid, enfilade; go -through, – across; go –, pass- over; cut across; ford, cross; pass and repass, work; make –, thread –, worm –, force- one's way; make –, force- a passage; cut one's way through; find its -way, – vent; transmit, make way, clear the course; traverse, go over the ground.

Adj. passing &c. *v.*; intercurrent; endos-mosmic, -motic.

Adv. *en passant* &c. (*transit*) 270.

---

303. [Motion beyond.] **Transcur-sion. — N.** trans-cursion†, -ilience,

304. [Motion short of.] **Shortcom-ing. — N.** shortcoming, failure; falling

-iliency, -gression; trespass; encroach-, infringe-ment; extravagation†, tran-scendence; redundance &c. 641.

V. transgress, surpass, pass; go- be-yond, – by; show in –, come to the-front; shoot ahead of; steal a march –, gain- upon.

over-step, -pass, -reach, -go, -ride, -leap, -jump, -skip, -lap, -shoot the mark; out-strip, -leap, -jump, -go, -step, -run, -ride, -rival, -do; beat, – hollow; distance; leave in the -lurch, – rear; throw into the shade; exceed, transcend, surmount; soar &c. (*rise*) 305.

encroach, trespass, infringe, trench upon, intrench on; strain; stretch –, strain- a point; pass the Rubicon.

Adj. surpassing &c. *v.*

Adv. beyond the mark, ahead.

short &c. *v.*; de-fault, -falcation; leeway; labor in vain, no go.

incompleteness &c. 53; imperfection &c. 651; insufficiency &c. 640; non-completion &c. 730; failure &c. 732.

V. come –, fall –, stop- -short, – short of; not reach; want; keep within -bounds, – the mark, – compass.

break down, stick in the mud, col-lapse, flat out [U. S.], come to nothing; fall -through, – to the ground; cave in, end in smoke, miss the mark, fail; lose ground; miss stays.

Adj. unreached; deficient; short, – of; minus; out of depth; perfunctory &c. (*neglect*) 460.

Adv. within -the mark, – compass, – bounds; behindhand; *re infectâ;* to no purpose; far from it.

Phr. the bubble burst.

305. [Motion upwards.] **Ascent.** — **N.** ascent, ascension; rising &c. *v.*; rise, upgrowth; · leap &c. 309; acclivity, hill &c. 217; flight of -steps, – stairs; ladder.

rocket, lark; sky-rocket, -lark; Al-pine Club.

V. ascend, rise, mount, arise, uprise; go –, get –, work one's way –, start –, spring –, shoot- up; aspire.

climb, clamber, ramp, scramble, esca-lade, surmount; scale, – the heights.

go-, fly- aloft; tower, soar, hover, spire, plane, swim, float, surge; leap &c. 309.

Adj. rising &c. *v.*; scandent, buoyant; super-natant, -fluitant; excelsior.

Adv. uphill.

306. [Motion downwards.] **Descent.** — **N.** descent, descension, declension, declination; fall; falling &c. *v.*; slump; drop, cadence; subsidence, lapse; down-fall, tumble, slip, tilt, trip, lurch; crop-per, *culbute;* titubation, stumble; fate of Icarus.

avalanche, *débâcle*, landslip.

declivity, dip, hill.

V. descend; go –, drop –, come- down; fall, gravitate, drop, slip, slide, settle; decline, set, sink, droop, come down a peg; slump.

dismount, alight, light, get down; swoop; stoop &c. 308; fall prostrate, precipitate oneself; let fall &c. 308.

tumble, trip, stumble, titubate, lurch, pitch, swag, topple; topple –, tumble- -down, – over; tilt, sprawl, plump down, come down a cropper.

Adj. descending &c. *v.*; descendent; decur-rent, -sive; labent, deciduous; nodding to its fall.

Adv. down-hill, -wards.

307. Elevation. — **N.** elevation; rais-ing &c. *v.*; erection, lift; sublevation, up-heaval; sublimation, exaltation; prom-inence &c. (*convexity*) 250.

lever &c. 633; crane, derrick, wind-lass, capstan, winch; dredg-e, -er, -ing machine; dumb-waiter, elevator, es-calator, lift.

V. heighten, elevate, raise, lift, erect; set –, stick –, perch –, perk –, tilt- up; rear, hoist, heave; up-lift, -raise, -rear, -bear, -cast, -hoist, -heave; buoy, weigh,

308. Depression. — **N.** lowering &c. *v.*; depression; dip &c. (*concavity*) 252; abasement; detrusion; reduction.

over-throw, -set, -turn; upset; pros-tration, subversion, precipitation.

bow; courtesy, curtsy; genuflexion, kotow, obeisance, salaam.

V. depress, lower; let –, take- -down, – down a peg; cast; let -drop, – fall; sink, debase, bring low, abase, reduce, detrude, pitch, precipitate.

over-throw, -turn, -set; upset, sub-

mount, give a lift; exalt; sublimate; place –, set- on a pedestal.

take –, drag –, fish- up; dredge.

stand –, rise –, get –, jump- up; spring to one's feet; hold -oneself, – one's head- up; drawn oneself up to his full height.

Adj. elevated &c. *v.*; stilted, attol- lent, rampant.

Adv. on -stilts, – the shoulders of, – one's legs, – one's hind legs.

vert, prostrate, level, fell; cast –, take –, throw –, fling –, dash –, pull –, cut –, knock –, hew- down; raze, – to the ground; trample in the dust, pull about one's ears.

sit, – down; couch, squat, crouch, stoop, bend, bow; courtesy, curtsy; bob, duck, dip, kneel; bend –, bow- the -head, – knee; bow down; cower; recline &c. (*be horizontal*) 213.

Adj. depressed &c. *v.*; at a low ebb;

prostrate &c. (*horizontal*) 213; detrusive.

Phr. *facinus quos inquinat æquat* [Lucan].

309. Leap. — N. leap, jump, hop, spring, bound, vault, saltation.

dance, caper; curvet, caracole; gam- bade, -bado; capriole, demivolt; buck, – jump; hop skip and jump; falcade.

kangaroo, jerboa, chamois, goat, frog, grasshopper, flea; buckjumper; wallaby.

V. leap; jump -up, – over the moon; hop, spring, bound, vault, ramp, cut ca- pers, trip, skip, dance, caper; buck, – jump; curvet, caracole; foot it, bob, bounce, flounce, start; frisk &c. (*amusement*) 840; jump about &c. (*agitation*) 315; trip it on the light fantastic toe, dance oneself off one's legs.

Adj. leaping &c. *v.*; saltatory, frisky.

Adv. on the light fantastic toe.

Phr. *di salto in salto.*

310. Plunge. — N. plunge, dip, dive, header; ducking &c. *v.*; diver.

V. plunge, dip, souse, duck; dive, plump; take a -plunge, – header; make a plunge; bathe &c. (*water*) 337.

sub-merge, -merse; immerse; douse, sink, engulf, send to the bottom.

get out of one's depth; go -to the bottom, – down like a stone; founder, welter, wallow.

311. [Curvilinear motion.] Circuition. — N. circuition, circulation; turn, curvet; excursion; circum-vention, -navigation, -ambulation; northwest pas- sage; circuit &c. 629.

turning &c. *v.*; wrench; evolution; coil, corkscrew.

V. turn, bend, wheel; go –, put- about; heel; go –, turn- -round, – to the right about; turn on one's heel; make –, describe- a -circle, – complete circle; go –, pass- through -180°, – 360°.

circum-navigate, -ambulate, -vent; " put a girdle round about the earth " [*M. N. D.*]; go the round, make the round of.

turn –, round- a corner; double a point.

wind, circulate, meander; whisk, twirl; twist &c. (*convolution*) 248; make a detour &c. (*circuit*) 629.

Adj. turning &c. *v.*; circuitous; circum-foraneous, -fluent.

Adv. round about.

312. [Motion in a continued circle.] Rotation. — N. rotation, revolution, gyration, circulation, roll; circum-rota- tion, -volution, -gyration; volutation, circination†, turbination, pirouette, con- volution.

verticity†; whir, whirl, eddy, vortex, whirlpool, gurge; countercurrent; cy- clone, tornado; surge; vertigo, dizzy round; Maelstrom, Charybdis; Ixion.

wheel, screw, whirligig, rolling stone, windmill; top, teetotum; roller; fly- wheel; jack; caster.

313. [Motion in a reverse circle.] Evolution. — N. evolution, unfolding, development; evolvement; unfoldment; eversion &c. (*inversion*) 218.

V. evolve; un-fold, -roll, -wind, -coil, -twist, -furl, -twine, -ravel; disentangle; develop.

Adj. evolving &c. *v.*; evolved &c. *v*

axis, axle, spindle, pivot, pin, hinge, pole, swivel, gimbals, arbor, bobbin, mandrel.

[Science of rotatory motion] trochilics.

V. rotate; roll, – along; revolve, spin; turn, – round; circumvolve; circulate, gyre, gyrate, wheel, whirl, twirl, trundle, troll, bowl.

roll up, furl; wallow, welter; box the compass; spin like a -top, – teetotum.

Adj. rotating &c. *v.*; rota-tory, -ry; circumrotatory, trochilic, vertiginous, gyratory; vortic-al, -ose.

Adv. head over heels, round and round, like a horse in a mill.

314. [Reciprocating motion, motion to and fro.] **Oscillation. — N.** oscillation; vibration, libration; motion of a pendulum; nutation; undulation; pulsation; pulse.

alternation; coming and going &c. *v.*; ebb and flow, flux and reflux, ups and downs.

fluctuation; vacillation &c. (*irresolution*) 605.

wave, vibratiuncle, swing, beat, shake, wag, seesaw, dance, lurch, dodge; logan, loggan, rocking-stone, vibroscope.

V. oscillate; vi-, li-brate; alternate, undulate, wave; rock, swing; pulsate, beat; wag, -gle; nod, bob, courtesy, curtsy; tick; play; wamble, wabble; dangle, swag.

fluctuate, dance, curvet, reel, quake; quiver, quaver; shake, flicker; wriggle; roll, toss, pitch; flounder, stagger, totter; move –, bob- up and down &c. *adv.*; pass and repass, ebb and flow, come and go; vacillate &c. 605; teeter [U. S.].

brandish, shake, flourish.

Adj. oscillating &c. *v.*; oscill-, undul-, puls-, libr-atory; vibrat-ory, -ile; pendulous.

Adv. to and fro, up and down, backwards and forwards, seesaw, zigzag, wibble-wabble, in and out, from side to side, like buckets in a well.

315. [Irregular motion.] **Agitation. — N.** agitation, stir, tremor, shake, ripple, jog, jolt, jar, jerk, shock, succussion, trepidation, .quiver, quaver, dance; jactitation, quassation; shuffling &c. *v.*; twitter, flicker, flutter.

disquiet, perturbation, commotion, turmoil, turbulence; tumult, -uation †; hubbub, rout, bustle, fuss, racket, subsultus, staggers, megrims, epilepsy, fits; carphology, chorea, floccillation, the jerks, St. Vitus's dance, tilmus.

spasm, throe, throb, palpitation, convulsion.

disturbance &c. (*disorder*) 59; restlessness &c. (*changeableness*) 149.

ferment, -ation; ebullition, effervescence, hurly-burly, *cahotage;* tempest, storm, ground swell, heavy sea, whirlpool, vortex &c. 312; whirlwind &c. (*wind*) 349.

V. be -agitated &c.; shake; tremble, – like an aspen leaf; quiver, quaver, quake, shiver, twitter, twire, writhe, toss, shuffle, tumble, stagger, bob, reel, sway; wag, -gle; wriggle, – like an eel; dance, stumble, shamble, flounder, totter, flounce, flop, curvet, prance, cavort [U. S.]; squirm.

throb, pulsate, beat, palpitate, go pitapat; flutter, flitter, flicker, bicker; bustle.

ferment, effervesce, foam; boil, – over; bubble, – up; simmer.

toss -, jump- about; jump like a parched pea; shake like an aspen leaf; shake to its -center, – foundations; be the sport of the winds and waves; reel to and fro like a drunken man; move –, drive- from post to pillar and from pillar to post; keep between hawk and buzzard.

agitate, shake, convulse, toss, tumble, bandy, wield, brandish, flap, flourish, whisk, jerk, hitch, jolt; jog, -gle; jostle, buffet, hustle, disturb, stir, shake up, churn, jounce, wallop, whip, vellicate.

Adj. shaking &c. *v.*; agitated, tremulous; de-, sub-sultory †; saltatoric; quassative; shambling; giddy-paced, saltatory, convulsive, unquiet, restless, all of a twitter.

Adv. by fits and starts; subsultorily † &c. *adj.*; *per saltum;* hop skip and jump; in -convulsions, – fits.

Phr. *tempête dans un verre d'eau.*

CLASS III

Words relating to MATTER

Section I. MATTER IN GENERAL

316. Materiality. — **N.** material-ity, -ness; corpor-eity, -ality; substantiality, substantialness, flesh and blood, plenum; physical condition.

matter, body, substance, brute matter, stuff, element, principle, parenchyma, material, substratum, hyle, *corpus*, pabulum; frame.

object, article, thing, something; still life; stocks and stones; materials &c. 635.

[Science of matter] physics; somatology, -ics; natural –, experimental-philosophy; physicism; physical science, *philosophie positive*, materialism; materialist; physicist; somatism, somatist.

Adj. material, bodily; corpor-eal, -al; physical; somat-ic, -oscopic; sensible, tangible, ponderable, palpable, substantial.

objective, impersonal, nonsubjective, neuter, unspiritual, materialistic.

317. Immateriality. — **N.** immaterial-ity, -ness; incorporeity, spirituality; inextension; astral plane.

personality; I, myself, me; ego, spirit, &c. (*soul*) 450; astral body; immaterialism; spiritual-ism, -ist.

V. disembody, spiritualize.

Adj. immateri-al, -ate; incorpor-eal, -al; incorporate, unfleshly; supersensible; asomatous, unextended; un-, dis-embodied; extramundane, unearthly; pneumatoscopic; spiritual &c. (*psychical*) 450. personal, subjective, nonobjective.

318. World. — **N.** world, creation, nature, universe; earth, globe, wide world; cosmos; kosmos; terraqueous globe, sphere; macro-, mega-cosm; music of the spheres.

heavens, sky, welkin, empyrean; starry -cope, – heaven, – host; firmament; Midgard; supersensible regions; *varuna;* vault –, canopy- of heaven; celestial spaces.

heavenly bodies, stars, asteroids; nebulæ; galaxy, milky way, galactic circle, *via lactea.*

sun, orb of day, Apollo, Phœbus; photo-, chromo-sphere; solar system; planet, -oid; comet; satellite, moon, orb of night, Diana, silver-footed queen; aërolite, meteor; falling –, shooting- star; meteorite, uranolite.

constellation, zodiac, signs of the zodiac, Charles's wain, Dipper, Great Bear, Southern Cross, Orion's belt, Cassiopea's chair, Pleiades.

colures, equator, ecliptic, orbit.

[Science of heavenly bodies] astronomy; urano-graphy, -logy; cosmo-logy, -graphy, -gony; eidouranion, orrery; geodesy &c. (*measurement*) 466; star-gazing, -gazer; astronomer; observatory; planetarium.

Adj. cosmical, mundane; terr-estrial, -estrious †, -aqueous, -ene, -eous †; telluric, earthly, geotic, under the sun; sub-lunary, -astral.

solar, heliacal; lunar; celestial, heavenly, sphery; starry, stellar; sider-eal, -al; astral; nebular; uranic.

Adv. in all creation, on the face of the globe, here below, under the sun.

Phr. *die Weltgeschichte ist das Weltgesicht;* " earth is but the frozen echo of the silent voice of God " [Hageman]; " green calm below, blue quietness above " [Whittier]; " hanging in a golden chain this pendant World " [*Paradise Lost*]; " nothing in nature is unbeautiful " [Tennyson]; " silently as a dream the fabric rose " [Cowper]; " some touch of nature's genial glow " [Scott]; " this majestical roof fretted with golden fire " [*Hamlet*]; " through knowledge we behold the World's creation " [Spenser].

319. Gravity. — N. gravi-ty, -tation; weight; heaviness &c. *adj.*; specific gravity; ponderosity, pressure, load; bur-den, -then; ballast, counterpoise; lump -, mass -, weight- of.

lead, millstone, mountain, Ossa on Pelion.

weighing, ponderation, trutination †; weights; avoirdupois -, troy -, apothecaries'- weight; grain, scruple, drachma, ounce, pound, lb, arroba, load, stone, hundredweight, cwt, ton, quintal, carat, pennyweight, tod.

[Weighing instrument] balance, scales, steelyard, beam, weighbridge, spring balance.

[Science of gravity] statics.

V. be -heavy &c. *adj.*; gravitate, weigh, press, cumber, load.

[Measure the weight of] weigh, poise.

Adj. weighty; weighing &c. *v.*; heavy, – as lead; ponder-ous, -able; lump-ish, -y; cumber-, burden-some; cumbrous, unwieldy, massive.

in-, superin-cumbent.

320. Levity. — N. levity; lightness &c. *adj.*; imponderability, buoyancy, volatility.

feather, dust, mote, down, thistle down, flue, cobweb, gossamer, straw, cork, bubble; float, buoy; ether, air.

leaven, ferment, barm, yeast.

V. be -light &c. *adj.*; float, swim, be buoyed up.

render -light &c. *adj.*; lighten, leaven.

Adj. light, subtile, airy; imponder-ous, -able; astatic, weightless, ethereal, sublimated; gossamery; suber-ose, -ous; uncompressed, volatile; buoyant, float-ing &c. *v.*; portable.

light as -a feather, – thistle down, – air.

Section II. INORGANIC MATTER

1. Solid Matter

321. Density. — N. density, solidity; solidness &c. *adj.*; impenetra-, impermea-bility; incompressibility; imporosity; cohesion &c. 46; constipation, consistence, spissitude.

specific gravity; hydro-, areo-meter.

condensation; caseation; solid-ation, -ification; consolidation; concretion, co-agulation; petrifaction &c. (*hardening*) 323; crystallization, precipitation; de-posit, precipitate; inspissation; thicken-ing &c. *v.*

indivisibility, indiscerptibility, indis-solvableness.

322. Rarity. — N. rarity; tenuity; absence of -solidity &c. 321; subtility; subtilty; sponginess, compressibility.

rarefaction, expansion, dilatation, in-flation, subtilization.

ether &c. (*gas*) 334.

V. rarefy, expand, dilate, subtilize.

Adj. rare, subtile, thin, fine, tenuous, compressible, flimsy, slight; light &c. 320; cavernous, spongy &c. (*hollow*) 252.

rarefied &c. *v.*; unsubstantial; un-com-pact, -pressed; rarefiable.

solid body, mass, block, knot, lump; con-cretion, -crete, -glomerate; cake, clot, stone, curd, coagulum; bone, gristle, cartilage; casein, crassamentum, legumin.

V. be -dense &c. *adj.*; become -, render- solid &c. *adj.*; solid-ify, -ate; con-crete, set, take a set, consolidate, congeal, coagulate; curd, -le; lopper; fix, clot, cake, candy, precipitate, deposit, cohere, crystallize; petrify &c. (*harden*) 323.

condense, thicken, inspissate, incrassate; compress, squeeze, ram down, constipate.

Adj. dense, solid; solidified &c. *v.*; caseous; *pukka;* cohe-rent, -sive &c. 46; compact, close, serried, thickset; substantial, massive, lumpish; impenetrable, impermeable, imporous; incompressible; constipated; concrete &c. (*hard*) 323; knot-ted, -ty; gnarled; crystal-line, -lizable; thick, grumous, stuffy.

un-dissolved, -melted, -liquefied, -thawed.

in-divisible, -discerptible, -frangible, -dissolvable, -dissoluble, -soluble, -fusible.

323. Hardness. — N. hardness &c. *adj.*; rigidity; reniten-ce, -cy; inflexibility, temper, callosity, durity †.

induration, petrifaction; lapid-ification, -escence; vitri-, ossi-fication; crystallization.

stone, pebble, flint, marble, rock, fossil, crag, crystal, quartz, granite, adamant; bone, cartilage; hardware; heart of oak, block, board, deal board; iron, steel; cast –, decarbonized –, wrought- iron; nail; brick, concrete; cement.

V. render -hard &c. *adj.*; harden, stiffen, indurate, petrify, temper, ossify, vitrify; accrust.

Adj. hard, rigid, stubborn, stiff, firm; starch, -ed; stark, unbending, unlimber, unyielding; inflexible, tense; indurate, -d; gritty, proof.

adamant-ine, -ean; concrete, stony, granitic, calculous, lithic, vitreous; horny, corneous; bony; oss-eous, -ific; cartilaginous; hard as a -stone &c. *n.*; stiff as -buckram, – a poker.

324. Softness. — N. softness, pliableness &c. *adj.*; flexibility; pli-ancy -ability; sequacity, malleability; duct-, tract-ility; extend-, extens-ibility; plasticity; inelasticity, flaccidity, laxity.

clay, wax, butter, dough, pudding; alumina, argil; cushion, pillow, feather bed, down, padding, wadding.

mollification; softening &c. *v.*

V. render -soft &c. *adj.*; soften, mollify, mellow, relax, temper; mash, knead, squash.

bend, yield, relent, relax, give.

Adj. soft, tender, supple; pli-ant, -able; flex-ible, -ile; lithe, -some; lissom, limber, plastic; ductile; tract-ile, -able; malleable, extensile, sequacious. inelastic; aluminous; remollient.

yielding &c. *v.*; flabby, limp, flimsy.

flaccid, flocculent, downy; spongy, œdematous, medullary, doughy, argillaceous, mellow.

soft as -butter, – down, – silk; yielding as wax; tender as a chicken.

325. Elasticity. — N. elasticity, springiness, spring, resilience, renitency, buoyancy.

India(n) rubber, caoutchouc, whalebone, gum elastic, baleen.

V. be -elastic &c. *adj.*; spring back &c. (*recoil*) 277.

Adj. elastic, tensile, springy, resilient, renitent, buoyant.

326. Inelasticity. — N. want of –, absence of- elasticity &c. 325; inelasticity &c. (*softness*) 324.

Adj. inelastic &c. (*soft*) 324; irresilient.

327. Tenacity. — N. tenacity, toughness, strength; cohesion &c. 46; sequacity; stubbornness &c. (*obstinacy*) 606; glutinousness, sequaciousness, viscidity &c. 352.

leather; white-, whit-leather; gristle, cartilage.

V. be -tenacious &c. *adj.*; resist fracture.

Adj. tenacious, tough, strong, resisting, sequacious, stringy, gristly, cartilaginous, leathery, coriaceous, tough as whitleather; stubborn &c. (*obstinate*) 606.

328. Brittleness. — N. brittleness &c. *adj.*; frag-, friab-, frangib-, fissility; house of -cards, – glass.

V. be -brittle &c. *adj.*; live in a glass house.

break, crack, snap, split, shiver, splinter, crumble, break short, burst, fly, give way; fall to pieces; crumble -to, – intodust.

Adj. brittle, brash [U. S.], frangible, fragile, frail, gimcrack, shivery, fissile; splitting &c. *v.*; lacerable, splintery, crisp, crimp, short, brittle as glass.

329. [Structure.] Texture. — N. structure, organization, anatomy, frame, mold, fabric, construction; framework, carcass, architecture; stratification, cleavage.

substance, stuff, compages, parenchyma; constitution, staple, organism.

[Science of structures] organ-, oste-, my-, splanchn-, neur-, angi-, aden-ology; angi-, aden-ography.

texture; inter-, con-texture; tissue, grain, web, surface; warp and -woof, – weft; tooth, nap &c. (*roughness*) 256; fineness –, coarseness- of grain, dry goods.

[Science of textures] histology.

Adj. structural, organic; anatomic, -al.

text-ural, -ile; fine-, coarse-grained; fine, delicate, subtile, gossamery, filmy; coarse; homespun.

330. Pulverulence. — N. [State of powder.] pulverulence; sandiness &c. *adj.*; efflorescence; friability.

powder, dust, sand, shingle; sawdust;· grit; meal, bran, flour, farina, rice, paddy, spore, sporule; crumb, seed, grain; particle &c. (*smallness*) 32; limature †, filings, *débris*, detritus, scobs, magistery, fine powder; flocculi.

smoke; cloud of -dust, – sand, – smoke; puff -, volume- of smoke; sand -, dust- storm.

[Reduction to powder] pulverization, comminution, attenuation, granulation, disintegration, subaction, contusion, trituration, levigation, abrasion, detrition, multure; limation; tripsis; filing &c. *v.*

[Instruments for pulverization] mill, arrastra, gristmill, grater, rasp, file, pestle and mortar, nutmeg grater, teeth, grinder, grindstone, kern, quern.

koniology.

V. come to dust; be -disintegrated, – reduced to powder &c.

reduce -, grind- to powder; pulverize, comminute, granulate, triturate, levigate; scrape, file, abrade, rub down, grind, grate, rasp, pound, bray, bruise; con-tuse, -tund; beat, crush, cranch, craunch, crunch, scranch, crumble, disintegrate; attenuate &c. 195.

Adj. powdery, pulverulent, granular, mealy, floury, farinaceous, branny, furfuraceous, flocculent, dusty, sandy, sabulous, psammous; aren-ose, -arious, -aceous; gritty; efflorescent, impalpable; lentiginous, lepidote, sabuline; sporaceous, -ous.

pulverizable; friable, crumbly, shivery; pulverized &c. *v.*; attrite; in pieces.

331. Friction. — N. friction, attrition; rubbing &c. *v.*; con-frication †, -trition †; affriction, abrasion, arrosion †, limature †, frication, rub; elbow grease; rosin; massage.

V. rub, scratch, scrape, scrub, fray, rasp, graze, curry, scour, polish, rub out, gnaw; file, grind &c. (*reduce to powder*) 330.

set one's teeth on edge; rosin.

Adj. anatriptic; attrite.

332. [Absence of friction. Prevention of friction.] **Lubrication. — N.** smoothness &c. 255; unctuousness &c. 355.

lubri-cation, -fication; anointment; oiling &c. *v.*

synovia; glycerin, oil, &c. 356; saliva; lather.

V. lubri-cate, -citate †; oil, grease, lather, soap; wax.

Adj. lubricated &c. *v.*; lubricous.

2. Fluid Matter

1. Fluids in General

333. Fluidity. — N. fluidity, liquidity; liquidness &c. *adj.*; gaseity &c. 334.

fluid, inelastic fluid; liquid, liquor; lymph, humor, juice, sap, serum, blood, serosity, gravy, rheum, ichor, sanies; chyle.

solu-bility, -bleness.

[Science of liquids at rest] hydro-logy, -statics, -dynamics.

V. be -fluid &c. *adj.*; flow &c. (*water in motion*) 348; liquefy &c. 335.

Adj. liquid, fluid, serous, juicy, suc-

334. Gaseity. — N. gaseity; vaporousness &c. *adj.*; flatu-lence, -lency; volatility; aëration, aërification.

elastic fluid, gas, air, vapor, ether, steam, fume, reek, effluvium, flatus; cloud &c. 353; ammonia, -cal gas; volatile alkali.

[Science of elastic fluids] pneumat-ics, -ostatics; aëro-statics, -dynamics.

gas-, gaso-meter; air-, swimming-bladder, sound (*of a fish*).

V. emit vapor &c. 336.

culent. sappy; ichorous; fluent &c. (*flowing*) 348.

liquefied &c. 335; uncongealed; soluble.

335. Liquefaction. — N. liquefaction; liquescen-ce, -cy; melting &c. (*heat*) 384; colliqu-ation †, -efaction †; thaw; de- †, liquation †; lixiviation, dissolution.

solution, apozem, lixivium, infusion, flux.

solvent, menstruum, alkahest.

V. render -liquid &c. 333; liquefy, run; deliquesce; melt &c. (*heat*) 384; solve; dissolve, resolve; liquate †; hold in solution.

Adj. lique-fied &c. *v.*, -scent, -fiable; deliquescent, soluble, colliquative.

Adj. gaseous, aëriform, ethereal, aërial, airy, vaporous, volatile, evaporable, flatulent.

336. Vaporization. — N. vapor-, volatil-ization; gasification; e-, vaporation; distillation, cupellation, cohobation, sublimation, exhalation; volatility.

vaporizer, still, retort; fumigation, steaming; bay salt, chloride of sodium.

V. render -gaseous &c. 334; vaporize, volatilize; distill, sublime; evaporate, exhale, smoke, transpire, emit vapor, fume, reek, steam, fumigate; cohobate; finestill.

Adj. volatilized &c. *v.*; reeking &c. *v.*; volatile; evaporable, vaporizable.

2. Specific Fluids

337. Water. — N. water; serum, serosity; lymph; rheum; diluent; *agua, aqua, pani.*

dilution, maceration, lotion; washing &c. *v.*; im-, mersion †; humectation, infiltration, spargefaction †, affusion, irrigation, douche, balneation, bath.

deluge &c. (*water in motion*) 348; high water, flood tide.

V. be -watery &c. *adj.*; reek.

add water, water, wet; moisten &c. 339; dilute, dip, immerse; merge; im-, sub-merge; plunge, souse, duck, drown; soak, steep, macerate, pickle, wash, sprinkle, lave, bathe, affuse, splash, swash, douse, drench; dabble, slop, slobber, irrigate, inundate, deluge; syringe, inject, gargle.

Adj. watery, aqueous, aquatic, hydrous, lymphatic; balneal, diluent; drenching &c. *v.*; diluted &c. *v.*; weak; wet &c. (*moist*) 339.

Phr. the waters are out.

338. Air. — N. air &c. (*gas*) 334; common -, atmospheric- air; atmosphere; aërosphere.

open, - air; sky, welkin; blue, - sky; cloud &c. 353.

weather, climate, rise and fall of the barometer, isobar.

[Science of air] aëro-logy, -metry, -scopy, -graphy; meteorology, climatology; pneumatics; eudio-, baro-, aërometer, -scope; aneroid, baroscope; weather-gauge, -glass, -cock.

exposure to the -air, - weather; ventilation; aëro-station, -nautics, -naut.

V. air, ventilate; fan &c. (*wind*) 349.

Adj. containing air, flatulent, effervescent; windy &c. 349.

atmospheric, airy; aëri-al, -form; meteorological; weatherwise.

Adv. in the open air, *à la belle étoile, al fresco; sub -Jove, - dio.*

339. Moisture. — N. moisture; moistness &c. *adj.*; hum-idity, -ectation; madefaction †, dew; *serein;* marsh &c. 345; hygromet-ry, -er.

V. moisten, wet; humect, -ate; sponge, damp, bedew; imbue, imbrue, infiltrate, saturate; soak, drench &c. (*water*) 337.

be -moist &c. *adj.*; not have a dry thread; perspire &c. (*exude*) 295.

Adj. moist, damp; watery &c. 337; madid, roric; undried, humid, wet, dank,

340. Dryness. — N. dryness &c. *adj.*; siccity, aridity, drought, ebb tide, low water.

ex-, de-siccation; arefaction, dephlegmation, drainage; drier, desiccative.

V. be -dry &c. *adj.*; render -dry &c. *adj.*; dry; dry -, soak- up; sponge, swab, wipe; ex-, de-siccate; drain, parch.

be fine, hold up.

Adj. dry, anhydrous, arid; adust, arescent; dried &c. *v.*; undamped; juice-,

muggy, dewy; roral †, rorid †; roscid; juicy.

wringing wet; wet -through, – to the skin; saturated &c. *v.*

swashy, soggy, dabbled; reeking, dripping, soaking, soft, sodden, sloppy, muddy; swampy &c. (*marshy*) 345; irriguous.

sap-less; sear; husky; rainless, without rain, fine; dry as -a bone, – dust, – a stick, – a mummy, – a biscuit; waterproof, -tight.

---

341. Ocean. — N. sea, ocean, main, deep, brine, salt water, waters, waves, billows, high seas, offing, great waters, watery waste, "vasty deep"; wave, tide, &c. (*water in motion*) 348.

hydrograph-y, -er; Neptune, Poseidon, Thetis, Triton, Naiad, Nereid; sea nymph, Siren; trident, dolphin.

Adj. oceanic; mar-ine, -itime; pelagic, -ian; seagoing; hydrographic; bathybic, cotidal.

Adv. at –, on- sea; afloat.

342. Land. — N. land, earth, ground, dry land, *terra firma.*

continent, mainland, peninsula, chersonese, delta; tongue -, neck- of land; isthmus, oasis; promontory &c. (*projection*) 250; highland &c. (*height*) 206.

coast, shore, scar, strand, beach; *playa;* bank, lea; sea-board, -side, -bank, -coast, -beach; ironbound coast; loom of the land; derelict; innings; alluvium alluvion; *ancon.*

soil, glebe, clay, loam, marl, cledge, chalk, gravel, mold, subsoil, clod, clot; rock, crag.

acres; real estate &c. (*property*) 780; landsman.

V. land, come to land; set foot on -the soil, – dry land; come –, go- ashore.

Adj. earthy; continental, midland, littoral, riparian; alluvial; terrene &c. (*world*) 318; landed, predial, territorial; geophilous; ripicolous.

Adv. ashore; on -shore, – land.

---

343. Gulf. Lake. — N. land covered with water, gulf, gulph, bay, inlet, bight, estuary, arm of the sea, bayou [U. S.], fiord, armlet; frith, firth, ostiary †, mouth; lagune, lagoon; indraught; cove, creek; natural harbor; roads; strait; narrows; Euripus; sound, belt, gut, kyles.

lake, loch, lough, mere, tarn, plash, broad, pond, pool, lin, puddle, slab, well, artesian well; standing –, dead –, sheet of- water; fish –, mill- pond; ditch, dike, dyke, dam; reservoir &c. (*store*) 636; *alberca, barachois*, hog wallow [U. S.].

Adj. lacustrine.

344. Plain. — N. plain, table-land, face of the country; open -, champaign-country; basin, downs, waste, weary waste, desert, wild, steppe, pampas, savanna, prairie, heath, common, wold, veldt; moor, -land; bush; plateau &c. (*level*) 213; campagna; alkali flat, llano; mesa, mesilla [U. S.], *playa;* shaking -, trembling- prairie; *vega.*

meadow, mead, haugh, pasturage, park, field, lawn, green, plat, plot, grass-plat, greensward, sward, turf, sod, heather; lea, ley, lay; grounds; *maidan, agostadero.*

Adj. champaign, alluvial; campestral, -rial, -rian, -rine.

---

345. Marsh. — N. marsh, swamp, morass, marish, moss, fen, bog, quagmire, slough, sump, wash; mud, squash, slush; baygall [U. S.], *ciénaga, jhil, vlei.*

Adj. marsh, -y; swampy, boggy, plashy, poachy, quaggy, soft; muddy, sloppy, squashy; paludal; moor-ish, -y; fenny.

346. Island. — N. island, isle, islet, eyot, ait, holm, reef, atoll, breaker; archipelago; islander.

Adj. insular, seagirt; archipelagic.

---

3. Fluids in Motion

347. [Fluid in motion.] **Stream. — N.** stream &c. (*of water*) 348. (*of air*) 349.
V. flow &c. 348; blow &c. 349.

348. [Water in motion.] **River.** — **N.** running water.

jet, spirt, squirt, spout, splash, rush, gush, *jet d'eau;* sluice.

water-spout, -fall; fall, cascade, force, foss; lin, -n; ghyll, Niagara; cata-ract, -dupe †, -clysm; *débâcle,* inundation, deluge; chute, washout.

rain, -fall; *serein;* shower, scud; downpour; driving –, drenching- rain; hyeto-logy, -graphy; predominance of Aquarius, reign of St. Swithin; mizzle, drizzle, stillicidium, plash; dropping &c. *v.;* cloud-burst; falling weather.

stream, course, flux, flow, profluence; effluence &c. (*egress*) 295; defluxion; flowing &c. *v.;* current, tide, race, *coulée.*

spring; fount, -ain; rill, rivulet, gill, gullet, rillet; stream-, brook-let; branch [U. S.]; runnel, sike, burn, beck, brook, stream, river; reach; tributary.

body of water, torrent, rapids, flush, flood, swash; spring –, high –, full- tide; bore; eagre, hygre; fresh, -et; indraught, reflux, undercurrent, eddy, vortex, gurge, whirlpool, Maelstrom, regurgitation, overflow; confluence, corrivation †.

wave, billow, surge, swell, ripple, ἀνήριθμον γέλασμα; beach comber, riffle [U. S.], rollers, ground swell, surf, breakers, white horses; rough –, heavy –, cross –, long –, short –, chopping- sea.

[Science of fluids in motion] hydrodynamics; hydraul-ics, -icostatics; rain gauge; pegology.

irrigation &c. (*water*) 337; pump; watering-pot, – cart; hydrant, syringe; *bhisti, mussuk.*

V. flow, run; meander; gush, pour, spout, roll, jet, well, issue; drop, drip, dribble, plash, spirtle, trill, trickle, distill, percolate; stream, overflow, inundate, deluge, flow over, splash, swash; guggle, murmur, babble, bubble, purl, gurgle, sputter, spurt, regurgitate; ooze, flow out &c. (*egress*) 295.

rain, – hard, – in torrents, – cats and dogs, – pitchforks; pour with rain, drizzle, spit, set in; mizzle.

flow –, fall –, open –, drain- into; discharge itself, disembogue.

[Cause a flow] pour; pour out &c. (*discharge*) 297; shower down; irrigate, drench &c. (*wet*) 337; spill, splash.

[Stop a flow] stanch; dam, -up &c. (*close*) 261; obstruct &c. 706.

Adj. fluent; dif-, pro-, af-fluent; tidal; flowing &c. *v.;* meand-ering, -ry, -rous; fluvi-al, -atile; streamy, showery, rainy, pluvial, stillicidous †; stillatitious.

Phr. " for men may come and men may go but I go on forever " [Tennyson].

349. [Air in motion.] **Wind.** — **N.** wind, draught, flatus, afflatus, efflation; eluvium; air; breath, – of air; puff, whiff, zephyr; blow, drift; aura; stream, current; undercurrent.

gust, blast, breeze, squall, gale, half a gale, storm, tempest, hurricane, whirlwind, tornado, samiel, cyclone, typhoon; sim-oon, -oom; harmattan, monsoon, trade wind, sirocco, mistral, *bise,* tramontane, levanter; capful of wind; fresh –, stiff- breeze; keen blast; blizzard, barber [Can.], *candelia,* chinook, foehn, khamsin, norther, *vendaval,* wuther.

windiness &c. *adj.;* ventosity †; rough –, dirty –, ugly –, stress of- weather; dirty sky, mare's tail; thick –, black –, white- squall.

anemography, aërodynamics; wind-gauge, weather-cock, vane; anemo-meter, -scope.

suf-, insuf-, per-, in-, af-flation; blowing, fanning, &c. *v.;* ventilation.

sneezing &c. *v.;* errhine; sternutative, -ory; sternutation; hic-cup, -cough; catching of the breath.

Eolus, Boreas, Zephyr, cave of Eolus.

air pump, lungs, bellows, blowpipe, fan, véntilator, punkah; branchiæ, gills, *flabellum, ventilabrum.*

V. blow, waft; blow -hard, – great guns, – a hurricane &c. *n.;* wuther; stream, issue.

respire, breathe, puff; whif, -fle; gasp, wheeze; snuff, -le; sniff, -le; sneeze, cough.

fan, ventilate; in-, per-flate †; blow up.

Adj. blowing &c. *v.;* windy, flatulent; breezy, gusty, squally; stormy, tempestuous, blustering; boisterous &c. (*violent*) 173.

pulmon-ic, -ary.

Phr. " lull'd by soft zephyrs " [Pope]; " the storm is up and all is on the hazard " [*Julius Cæsar*]; " the winds were wither'd in the stagnant air " [Byron]; " while mocking winds are piping loud " [Milton]; " winged with red lightning and tempestuous rage " [*Paradise Lost*].

350. [Channel for the passage of water.] **Conduit.** — **N.** conduit, channel, duct, watercourse, race; head -, tail- race; abito, abcideau, aboiteau, bito; *acequia, -dor, – madre;* arroyo; adit, aqueduct, canal, trough, gutter, pantile; flume, ingate, runner; lock-weir, tedge; *vena;* dike, main, gully, moat, ditch, drain, sewer, culvert, cloaca, sough, kennel, siphon; *piscina;* pipe &c. (*tube*) 260; funnel; tunnel &c. (*passage*) 627; water -, waste- pipe; emunctory, gully hole, artery, aorta, pore, spout, scupper; ad-, a-jutage; hose; gar-, gur-goyle; penstock, weir; flood-, water-gate; sluice, lock, valve; rose; waterworks.

Adj. vascular &c. (*with holes*) 260.

351. [Channel for the passage of air.] **Airpipe.** — **N.** air -pipe, – tube; air-, blow-, breathing-, vent-hole; shaft, flue, chimney, funnel, vent, nostril, nozzle, throat, weasand, trachea; bronchus, -ia; larynx, tonsils, windpipe, spiracle; venti-duct, -lator; louvre, Venetian blinds; blowpipe &c. (*wind*) 349; pipe &c. (*tube*) 260; *jhilmil;* smokestack.

3. Imperfect Fluids

352. Semiliquidity. — **N.** semiliquidity; stickiness &c. *adj.*; visc-idity, -osity; gumm-, glutin-, muc-osity; spiss-, crassitude; lentor; adhesiveness &c. (*cohesion*) 46.

imspiss-, incrass-ation; thickening.

jelly, mucilage, gelatin; carlock, fish glue; ichthyocol, -la; isinglass; mucus, phelgm; pituite, lava; glair, starch, gluten, albumen, milk, cream, protein; treacle; gum, size, glue; wax, beeswax; emulsion, soup; squash, mud, slush, slime, ooze; moisture &c. 339; marsh &c. 345.

V. inspiss-, incrass-ate; thicken; mash, squash, churn, beat up.

Adj. semi-fluid, -liquid; tremellose; half-melted, -frozen; milky, muddy &c. *n.*; lact-eal, -ean, -eous, -escent, -iferous; emulsive, curdled, thick, succulent, uliginous.

gelat-, album-, mucilag-, glut-inous; gelatin, mastic, amylaceous, ropy, clammy, clotted; vis-cid, -cous; sticky, tacky; slab, -by; lentous †, pituitous; mu-cid, -culent, -cous.

353. [Mixture of air and water.] **Bubble.** [Cloud.] — **N.** bubble; foam, froth, head, spume, lather, suds, spray, surf, yeast, barm, spindrift.

cloud, vapor, fog, mist, haze, steam; scud, messenger, rack, nimbus; cumulus, woolpack, cirrus, stratus; cirro-, cumulostratus; cirro-cumulus; mackerel sky, mare's tail, dirty sky; curl cloud; frost smoke; thunderhead.

[Science of clouds] nephelognosy; nephograph; nephology.

effervescence, fermentation; bubbling &c. *v.*

nebula; cloudliness &c. (*opacity*) 426; nebulosity &c. (*dimness*) 422.

V. bubble, boil, foam, froth, mantle, sparkle, guggle, gurgle; effervesce, ferment, fizzle.

Adj. bubbling &c. *v.*; frothy, nappy, effervescent, sparkling, *mousseux,* up.

cloudy &c. *n.*; thunder-headed; vaporous, nebulous, overcast.

Phr. " the lowring element scowls o'er the darkened landscip " [*Paradise Lost*].

354. Pulpiness. — **N.** pulpiness &c. *adj.*; pulp, paste, dough, curd, pap, rob, jam, pudding, poultice, grume.

Adj. pulpy &c. *n.*; pultaceous, grumous; baccate.

355. Unctuousness. — **N.** unctuousness &c. *adj.*; unctuosity, lubricity; ointment &c. (*oil*) 356; anointment; lubrication &c. 332.

V. oil &c. (*lubricate*) 332.

Adj. unctuous, oily, oleaginous, adipose, sebaceous; unguinous; fat, -ty; greasy; waxy, butyraceous, soapy, saponaceous, pinguid, lardaceous; slippery.

356. Oil. — **N.** oil, fat, butter, cream, grease, tallow, suet, lard, dripping, exunge †, blubber; glycerin, stearin, elaine, oleagine; soap; soft soap, wax, cerement; paraffin, spermaceti, adipocere; petroleum, mineral -, rock -, crystal-

oil; vegetable –, colza –, olive –, salad –, linseed –, nut- oil; animal –, neat's foot –, train- oil; ointment, unguent, liniment; *aceite*, amole, Barbados tar; fusel –, grain –, rape –, seneca- oil; hydrate of amyl, ghee, kerosene, naphtha, stearin.

356a. Resin. — **N.** resin, rosin; gum; lac, sealing wax; amber, -gris; bitumen, pitch, tar; asphalt, -um; camphor; varnish, copal, mastic, magilp, lacquer, japan.

V. varnish &c. (*overlay*) 223.

Adj. resin-ous, -y; bituminous, pitchy, tarry; asphalt-ic, -ite.

Section III. ORGANIC MATTER

1. Vitality

1. Vitality in general

357. Organization. — **N.** organized -world, – nature; living –, animated-nature; living beings; organic remains, fossils.

prot-oplasm, -ein; albumen; structure &c. 329; organ-ization, -ism.

[Science of living beings] biology; natural history,[1] organic chemistry, anatomy, physiology; zoölogy &c. 368; botany &c. 369; naturalist.

archegenesis &c. (*production*) 161; antherozoid, bioplasm, biotaxy, chromosome, dysmeromorph; ec-, œc-ology; erythroblast, *gametangium*, gamete, germinal matter, invagination; iso-, oö-gamy; karyaster; macro-, micro-gamete; metabolism, metaplasm, ontogeny, ovary, ovum, oxidation, phylogeny, polymorphism, protozoa, spermary, spermatozoön, trophoplasm, vacuole, vertebration, zoöglœa, zygote.

Darwin-, Lamarck-, neo-Lamarck-, Weismann-ism; morphology.

Adj. organ-ic, -ized; karyoplasmic, unsegmentic, vacuolar, zoöglœic, zoöglœoid.

358. Inorganization. — **N.** mineral -world, – kingdom; unorganized –, in-organic –, brute –, inanimate- matter.

[Science of the mineral kingdom] mineralogy; geo-logy, -gnosy, -scopy; metall-urgy, -ography; lithology; oryc-to-logy†, -graphy†.

V. turn to dust.

Adj. in-organic, -animate, -organized; lithoidal; azoic; mineral.

359. Life. — **N.** life; vi-tality, -ability; animation; vital -spark, – flame.

respiration, wind; breath -of life, – of one's nostrils; lifeblood; Archeus; existence &c. 1.

vivification; oxygen; vital -air, – force; vitalization; revivification &c. 163; Prometheus; life to come &c. (*destiny*) 152.

[Science of life] physiology, biology; animal economy.

nourishment, staff of life &c. (*food*) 298.

V. be -alive &c. *adj.*; live, breathe, respire; subsist &c. (*exist*) 1; walk the earth; "strut and fret one's hour upon the stage" [*Macbeth*]; be spared.

see the light, be born, come into the

360. Death. — **N.** death; de-cease, -mise; dissolution, departure, obit, release, rest, quietus, fall; loss, bereavement.

end &c. 67 –, cessation &c. 142 –, loss –, extinction –, ebb- of -life &c. 359.

death-warrant, -watch, -rattle, -bed; stroke –, agonies –, shades –, valley of the shadow –, jaws –, hand- of death; last -breath, – gasp, – agonies; dying -day, – breath, – agonies; *chant du cygne*; *rigor mortis*; Stygian shore.

King -of terrors, – Death; Death, mortality; doom &c. (*necessity*) 601; "Hell's grim Tyrant" [Pope].

euthanasia; break up of the system; natural -death, – decay; sudden –, violent- death; untimely end, watery grave;

---

[1] The term *natural history* is also used as relating to all the objects in Nature whether organic or inorganic, and including therefore *mineralogy, geology, meteorology*, &c.

world; fetch –, draw- -breath, – the breath of life; quicken; revive; come to, – life.

give birth to &c. (*produce*) 161; bring to life, put into life, vitalize; vivi-fy, -ficate; reanimate &c. (*restore*) 660; keep -alive, – body and soul together, – the wolf from the door; support life.

have nine lives like a cat.

Adj. living, alive; in -life, – the flesh, – the land of the living; on this side of the grave, above ground, breathing, quick, animated; animative; lively &c. (*active*) 682; all alive and kicking; tenacious of life.

vital, -ic; vivi-fying, -fied, &c. *v.*; viable, zoëtic; Promethean.

Adv. *vivendi causâ.*

Phr. *atqui vivere militare est* [Seneca]; *non est vivere sed valere vita* [Martial].

debt of .nature; suffocation, asphyxia; fatal disease &c. (*disease*) 655; death-blow &c. (*killing*) 361.

necrology, bills of mortality, obituary; death song &c. (*lamentation*) 839.

V. die, expire, perish; meet one's -death, – end; pass away, be taken; yield –, resign- one's breath; resign one's -being, – life; end one's -days, – life, – earthly career; breathe one's last; cease to -live, – breathe; depart this life; be -no more &c. *adj.*; go –, drop –, pop-off; lose –, lay down –, relinquish –, surrender- one's life; drop –, sink- into the grave; close one's eyes; fall –, drop-dead, – down dead; break one's neck; give –, yield- up the ghost; be all over with one.

pay the debt to nature, shuffle off this mortal coil, take one's last sleep; go the way of all flesh; hand –, pass- -in one's checks, – in one's chips [U. S.]; join the -greater number, – majority; come –, turn- to dust; cross the Stygian ferry; go to -one's long account, – one's last home, – Davy Jones's locker, – the wall; receive one's death warrant, make one's will, step out, die a natural death, go out like the snuff of a candle; come to an untimely end; catch one's death; go off the hooks, kick the bucket, hop the twig, turn up one's toes; die a violent death &c. (*be killed*) 361.

Adj. dead, lifeless; deceased, demised, departed, defunct; late, gone, no more; ex-, in-animate; out of the world, taken off, released; departed this life &c. *v.*; dead and gone; dead as -a doornail, – a doorpost, – mutton, – a herring, – nits; launched into eternity, gathered to one's fathers, numbered with the dead.

dying &c. *v.*; mori-bund, -ent†; hippocratic; *in -articulo, – extremis;* in the -jaws, – agony- of death; going, – off; *aux abois;* on one's -last legs, – death-bed; at -the point of death, – death's door, – the last gasp; near one's end, given over, booked; with one foot in –, tottering on the brink of- the grave.

stillborn; mortuary; deadly &c. (*killing*) 361.

Adv. *post -obit, – mortem.*

Phr. life -ebbs, – fails, – hangs by a thread; one's -days are numbered, – hour is come, – race is run, – doom is sealed; Death -knocks at the door, – stares one in the face; the breath is out of the body; the grave closes over one; *sic itur ad astra* [Vergil]; *de mortuis nil nisi bonum; dulce et decorum est pro patria mori* [Horace]; *honesta mors turpi vitâ potior* [Tacitus]; " in adamantine chains shall death be bound " [Pope]; *mors ultima linea rerum est* [Horace]; *omnia mors æquat* [Claudianus]; " spake the grisly Terror " [*Paradise Lost*]; " the lone couch of his everlasting sleep " [Shelley].

361. [Destruction of life; violent death.] **Killing.** — **N.** killing &c. *v.*; homicide, manslaughter, murder, assassination, trucidation†, occision† ; effusion of blood; blood, -shed; gore, slaughter, carnage, butchery; *battue.*

massacre; fusillade, *noyade;* Thuggism.

deathblow, finishing stroke, *coup de grâce*, quietus; execution &c. (*capital punishment*) 972; judicial murder; martyrdom.

butcher, slayer, murderer, Cain, assassin, cutthroat, garroter, *bravo*, Thug, Moloch, matador, *sabreur; guet-à-pens;* gallows, executioner &c. (*punishment*) 975; man-eater, apache, hatchet man [U. S.], highbinder [U. S.].

regicide, parricide, fratricide, infanticide, feticide, fœticide, uxoricide, vaticide. suicide, *felo de se*, suttee, Juggernath; immolation, holocaust.

suffocation, strangulation, garrote; hanging &c. *v.*; lapidation.

deadly weapon &c. (*arms*) 727; Aceldama.

[Destruction of animals] slaughtering; phthiozoics;[1] sport, -ing; the chase, venery; hunting, coursing, shooting, fishing; pig-sticking; sports-, hunts-, fisher-man; hunter, Nimrod; slaughterhouse, shambles, *abattoir*.

fatal accident, violent death, casualty.

V. kill, put to death, slay, shed blood; murder, assassinate, butcher, slaughter, victimize, immolate; massacre; take away -, deprive of- life; make away with, put an end to; despatch, dispatch; burke, settle, do for.

strangle, garrote, hang, throttle, choke, stifle, suffocate, stop the breath, smother, asphyxiate, drown.

saber; cut -down, - to pieces, - the throat; jugulate; stab, run through the body, bayonet; put to the -sword, - edge of the sword.

shoot, - dead; blow one's brains out; brain, knock on the head; stone, lapidate; give -, deal- a deathblow; give a -quietus, - *coup de grâce*.

behead, bowstring &c. (*execute*) 972.

hunt, shoot &c. *n.*

cut off, nip in the bud, launch into eternity, send to one's last account, sign one's death warrant, strike the death knell of.

give no quarter, pour out blood like water; decimate; run amuck; wade knee-deep -, imbrue one's hands- in blood.

die a violent death, welter in one's blood; dash -, blow- out one's brains; commit suicide; kill -, make away with -, put an end to- oneself.

Adj. killing &c. *v.*; murd-, slaught-erous; sanguin-ary, -olent; blood-stained, -thirsty; homicidal, red-handed; bloody, -minded; ensanguined, gory.

mortal, fatal, lethal; dead-, death-ly; mort-†, leth-iferous; unhealthy &c. 657; internecine; suicidal.

sporting; piscator-ial, -y.

Adv. in at the death.

Phr. "assassination has never changed the history of the world" [Disraeli].

362. Corpse. — N. corpse, corse, carcass, cadaver, bones, skeleton, dry bones; defunct, relics, reliquiæ, remains, mortal remains, dust, ashes, earth, clay; mummy; carrion; food for- worms, - fishes; tenement of clay, this mortal coil.

shade, ghost, manes.

organic remains, fossils.

Adj. cadaverous, corpse-like; unburied &c. 363; sapromyiophyllous.

363. Interment. — N. interment, burial, sepulture; in-, humation†; obs-, ex-equies; funeral, wake, pyre, funeral pile; cremation.

funeral -rite, - solemnity; knell, passing bell, tolling; dirge &c. (*lamentation*) 839; cypress; obit, dead march, muffled drum; undertaker, mute; elegy; funeral -oration, - sermon; epitaph.

graveclothes, shroud, winding sheet, cerecloth; cerement.

coffin, shell, sarcophagus, urn, pall, bier, hearse, catafalque, cinerary urn.

grave, pit, sepulcher, tomb, vault, crypt, catacomb, mausoleum, Golgotha, house of death, narrow house; cemetery, necropolis; burial-place, -ground; grave-, church-yard; God's acre; mortuary, tope, cromlech, barrow, tumulus, cairn; ossuary; bone-, charnel-, dead-house; morgue; lich gate; burning ghât; cremato-rium, -ry; dokhma, *mastaba*, potter's field, *stupa*, Tower of Silence.

sexton, gravedigger.

monument, cenotaph, shrine; grave-, head-, tomb-stone; *memento mori*; hatchment, stone.

exhumation, disinterment; necropsy, autopsy, *post mortem* examination; zoöthapsis.

[1] Bentham, *Chrestomathia*.

V. inter, bury; lay in –, consign to- the -grave, – tomb; en-, in-tomb; inhume; lay out; perform a funeral; embalm, mummify; toll the knell; put to bed with a shovel; inurn.

exhume, disinter, unearth.

Adj. buried &c. *v.*; burial, fune-real, -brial; mortuary, sepulchral, cinerary; elegiac; necroscopic.

Adv. *in memoriam; post-obit, -mortem;* beneath the sod.

Phr. *hic jacet, ci-gît; R. I. P.; requiescat in pace;* " the lone couch of his everlasting sleep " [Shelley]; " without a grave — unknell'd, uncoffin'd, and unknown " [Byron]; " in the dark union of insensate dust " [Byron]; " the deep cold shadow of the tomb " [Moore].

2. Special Vitality

364. Animality. — N. animal life; anima-tion, -lity, -lization; animalness, corporeal nature, human system; breath.

flesh, – and blood; physique; strength &c. 159.

Adj. fleshly, human, corporeal.

366. Animal. — N. animal, – kingdom; fauna; brute creation.

beast, brute, creature, created being; creeping –, living- thing; dumb -animal, – creature.

flocks and herds, live stock; domestic –, wild- animals; game, *feræ naturæ;* beasts of the field, fowls of the air, denizens of the day; black-game, -grouse; blackcock, duck, grouse, plover, rail, snipe.

mammal, quadruped, bird, reptile, fish, crustacean, shellfish, mollusk, worm, insect, zoöphyte; animalcule &c. 193; alligator, crocodile; honeybee; saurian; trout.

horse &c. (*beast of burden*) 271; cattle, kine, ox; bull, -ock; cow, milch cow, calf, heifer, shorthorn; sheep; lamb, -kin; ewe, ram, tup; pig, swine, boar, hog, sow; steer, stot; tag, teg; bison, buffalo, yak, zebu.

dog, hound; pup, -py; whelp, cur, mongrel; house-, watch-, sheep-, shepherd's-, sporting-, fancy-, lap-, toy-, bull-, badger-dog; mastiff; blood-, grey-stag-, deer-, fox-, otter-hound; harrier, beagle, spaniel, pointer, setter, retriever; Newfoundland; water -dog, – spaniel; pug, poodle; turnspit; terrier; fox –, Skye- terrier; Dandie Dinmont; collie.

cat; puss, -y; grimalkin; gib-, tomcat; fox, Reynard, vixen, stag, deer, hart, buck, doe, roe; caribou, coyote, elk, moose, musk ox, sambar.

365. Vegetability†. — N. vegetable life; vegeta-tion, -bility† ; vegetality.

Adj. rank, lush; veget-able, -al, -ive.

367. Vegetable. — N. vegetable, – kingdom; flora, verdure.

plant; tree, shrub, bush; creeper; herb, -age; grass.

annual; per-, bi-, tri-ennial; exotic.

timber, forest; wood, -lands; timber-land; hurst, frith, holt, weald, park, chase, greenwood, brake, grove, copse, coppice, *bocage,* tope, clump of trees, thicket, spinet, spinney; under-, brushwood; scrub; boscage, bosk, *ceja,* chaparral, motte [U. S.]; arboretum &c. 371.

bush, jungle, prairie; heath, -er; fern, bracken; furze, gorse, whin; grass, turf; pas-ture, -turage; turbary; sedge, rush, weed; fungus, mushroom, toadstool; lichen, moss, conferva, mold; growth; alfalfa, alfilaria, banyan; blow, blowth; floret, petiole; pin grass, timothy, yam, yew, zinnia.

foliage, branch, bough, ramage, stem, tigella; spray &c. 51; leaf.

flower, blossom, bine; flowering plant; timber-, fruit-tree; pulse, legume.

Adj. veget-able, -al, -ive, -ous† ; herb-aceous, -al; botanic; sylvan, silvan; arbor-ary, -eous, -escent, -ical† ; woody, grassy; ver-dant, -durous; floral, mossy; lign-ous, -eous; wooden, leguminous; bosky, cespitose, turf-like, turfy; end-, ex-ogenous.

Phr. " green-robed senators of mighty woods " [Keats]; " this is the forest primeval " [Longfellow].

bird; poultry, fowl, cock, hen, chicken, chanticleer, partlet, rooster, dunghill cock, barn-door fowl; feathered -tribes, – songster; singing –, dicky- bird;

canary; finch; aberdevine, cushat, cygnet, ringdove, siskin, swan, wood pigeon.

snake, serpent, viper, eft; asp, -ick; vermin.

Adj. animal, zoölogical.

equine, bovine, vaccine, canine, feline, fishy; piscator-y, -ial; molluscous, vermicular; gallinaceous, rasorial, soli-dungulate, -ped.

368. [The science of animals.] **Zoölogy.** — **N.** zoö-logy, -nomy, -graphy, -tomy; anatomy; comparative anatomy; animal –, comparative- physiology; morphology; mammalogy.

anthrop-, ornith-, ichthy-, herpet-, ophi-, malac-, helminth-, entom-, oryct-, paleont-, mast-, verme-ology; ichthy- &c. -otomy; taxidermy.

zo- &c. -ologist.

Adj. zoölogical &c. *n.*

369. [The science of plants.] **Botany.** — **N.** botany; physiological –, structural –, systematic- botany; phytography, -logy, -tomy; vegetable physiology, herborization, dendr-, myc-, fung-, alg-ology; flora, romona; botanic garden &c. (*garden*) 371; *hortus siccus, herbarium,* herbal.

botanist &c.; herb-ist, -arist, -alist, -orist, -arian.

V. botanize, herborize.

Adj. botanical &c. *n.*; botanic.

370. [The economy or management of animals.] **Circuration** †.— **N.** taming &c. *v.*; circuration†, zoöhygiantics;[1] domestic-ation, -ity; manège, veterinary art; farriery; breeding, pisciculture.

menagerie, vivarium, zoölogical garden; bear pit; aviary, apiary, alveary, beehive; hive; aquarium, fishery; duck-, fish-pond.

[Destruction of animals] phthisozoics[2] &c. (*killing*) 361.

neat-, cow-, shep-herd; grazier, drover, cowkeeper; trainer, breeder; apiarian, apiarist; bull whacker [U. S.], cowboy, cow puncher [U. S.], farrier; horseleech, -doctor; *vaquero,* veterinarian, veterinary surgeon.

cage &c. (*prison*) 752; hencoop, bird cage, cauf; sheepfold, &c. (*inclosure*) 232.

V. tame, domesticate, acclimatize, breed, tend, break in, train; cage, bridle, &c. (*restrain*) 751.

Adj. pastoral, bucolic; tame, domestic.

371. [The economy or management of plants.] **Agriculture.** — **N.** agriculture, cultivation, husbandry, farming; georgics, geoponics; tillage, agronomy, gardening, spade husbandry, vintage; hort-, arbor-, flor-iculture; landscape gardening; viticulture.

husbandman, horticulturist, gardener, florist; agricult-or, -urist; yeoman, farmer, cultivator, tiller of the soil, woodcutter, backwoodsman; granger, habitant, *vigneron,* viticulturist; Triptolemus.

field, meadow, garden; botanic –, winter –, ornamental –, flower –, kitchen –, market –, hop- garden; nursery; green-, hot-house; conservatory, bed, border, seed plot; grassplot, grassplat, lawn; park &c. (*pleasure ground*) 840; parterre, shrubbery, plantation, avenue, arboretum, pinery, pinetum, orchard; vineyard, vinery; orangery; farm &c. (*abode*) 189.

V. cultivate; till, – the soil; farm, garden; sow, plant; reap, mow, cut; manure, dress the ground, dig, delve, dibble, hoe, plough, plow, harrow, rake, weed, lop and top; backset [U. S.].

Adj. agr-icultural, -arian, -estic.

arable; predial, rural, rustic, country; horticultural.

372. Mankind. — **N.** man, -kind; human -race, – species, – kind, – nature; humanity, mortality, flesh, generation.

[Science of man] anthropo-logy, -geny, -graphy, -sophy; ethno-logy, -graphy; humanitarian.

human being; person, -age; individual, creature, fellow creature, mortal, body, somebody, one; such a –, some- one; soul, living soul; earthling; party, head, hand; *dramatis personæ; quidam.*

---

[1] Bentham.   [2] Bentham.

people, persons, folk, public, society, world; community, – at large; general public; nation, -ality; state, realm; common-weal, -wealth; republic, body politic; million &c. (*commonalty*) 876; population &c. (*inhabitant*) 188.

cosmopolite; lords of the creation; ourselves.

Adj. human, mortal, personal, individual, national, civic, public, social; cosmopolitan; anthropoid.

Phr. " am I not a man and a brother? " [Wedgwood].

373. Man. — N. man, male, he; manhood &c. (*adolescence*) 131; gentleman, sir, master; sahib; yeoman, wight, swain, fellow, blade, beau, elf, chap, gaffer, good man; husband &c. (*married man*) 903; Mr., mister; boy &c. (*youth*) 129.

[Male animal] cock, drake, gander, dog, boar, stag, hart, buck, horse, entire horse, stallion; gib-, tom-cat; he-, Billy-goat; ram, tup; bull, -ock; capon, ox, gelding; steer, stot.

Adj. male, he, masculine; manly, virile; un-womanly, -feminine.

Phr. *hominem pagina nostra sapit* [Mar.]; *homo homini aut deus aut lupus* [Erasmus]; *homo vitæ commodatus non donatus est* [Syrus].

374. Woman. — N. woman, she, female, petticoat.

feminality, muliebrity; womanhood &c. (*adolescence*) 131.

womankind; the -sex, – fair; fair –, softer- sex; weaker vessel.

dame, madam, *madame*, mistress, Mrs., lady, donna, belle, matron, dowager, goody, gammer; *Frau*, frow, *Vrouw*, rani; good -woman, – wife; squaw; wife &c. (*marriage*) 903; matron-age, -hood.

bachelor girl, new woman, suffragette, suffragist.

nymph, wench, grisette; girl &c. (*youth*) 129.

[Effeminacy] betty, cot betty [U. S.], cotquean, henhussy, molly coddle, muff, old woman.

[Female animal] hen, bitch, sow, doe, roe, mare; she-, Nanny-goat; ewe, cow; lioness, tigress; vixen.

gynecæum.

Adj. female, she; feminine, womanly, ladylike, matronly, maidenly; womanish, effeminate, unmanly; gynecic, gynæcic.

Phr. " a perfect woman nobly planned " [Wordsworth]; " a lovely lady garmented in white " [Shelley]; *das Ewig-Weibliche zieht uns hinan* [Goethe]; " earth's noblest thing, a woman perfected " [Lowell]; *es de vidrio la mujer;* " she moves a goddess and she looks a queen " [Pope]; " the beauty of a lovely woman is like music " [G. Eliot]; *varium et mutabile semper femina* [Vergil]; " woman is the lesser man " [Tennyson].

2. SENSATION

1. Sensation in general

375. Physical Sensibility. — N. sensibility; sensitiveness &c. *adj.*; physical sensibility, feeling, impressibility, perceptivity, æsthetics; moral sensibility &c. 822.

sensation, impression; consciousness &c. (*knowledge*) 490.

external senses.

V. be -sensible &c. *adj.* -of; feel, perceive.

render -sensible &c. *adj.*; sharpen, cultivate, tutor.

cause sensation, impress; excite –, produce- an impression.

Adj. sens-ible, -itive, -uous; æsthetic, perceptive, sentient; conscious &c. (*aware*) 490.

376. Physical Insensibility. — N. insensibility, physical insensibility; obtuseness &c. *adj.*; palsy, paralysis, anæsthesia; sleep &c. (*inactivity*) 683; moral insensibility &c. 823; hemiplegia, motor paralysis.

anæsthetic agent, opium, ether, chloroform, chloral; nitrous oxide, laughing gas; exhilarating gas, protoxide of nitrogen; refrigeration.

V. be -insensible &c. *adj.*; have a -thick skin, – rhinoceros hide.

render -insensible &c. *adj.*; blunt, pall, obtund, benumb, paralyze; put under the influence of -chloroform &c. *n.*; stupefy, stun.

Adj. insensible, unfeeling, senseless,

acute, sharp, keen, vivid, lively, impressive, thin-skinned.

Adv. to the quick.

Phr. "the touch'd needle trembles to the pole" [Pope].

impercipient, callous, thick-skinned, pachydermatous; hard, -ened; case-hardened; proof; obtuse, dull; anæsthetic; paralytic, palsied, numb, dead.

---

377. Physical Pleasure. — N. pleasure; physical –, sensual –, sensuous-pleasure; bodily enjoyment, animal gratification, hedonism, sensuality; luxuriousness &c. *adj.*; dissipation, round of pleasure; titillation, gusto, creature comforts, comfort, ease; pillow &c. (*support*) 215; luxury, lap of luxury; purple and fine linen; bed of -down, – roses; velvet, clover; cup of Circe &c. (*intemperance*) 954.

treat; refreshment, regale; feast; delice; dainty &c. 394; *bonne bouche.*

source of pleasure &c. 829; happiness &c. (*mental enjoyment*) 827.

V. feel –, experience –, receive- pleasure; enjoy, relish; luxuriate –, revel –, riot –, bask –, swim –, wallow- in; feast on; gloat -over, – on; smack the lips.

live -on the fat of the land, – in comfort &c. *adv.*; bask in the sunshine, *faire ses choux gras.*

give pleasure &c. 829.

Adj. enjoying &c. *v.*; luxurious, voluptuous, sensual, comfortable, cosy, snug, in comfort, at ease.

agreeable &c. 829; grateful, refreshing, comforting, cordial, genial; sensuous; apolaustic, hedonic; palatable &c. 394; sweet &c. (*sugar*) 396; fragrant &c. 400; melodious &c. 413; lovely &c. (*beautiful*) 845.

Adv. in -comfort &c. *n*; on -a bed of roses &c. *n.*; at one's ease.

Phr. *ride si sapis* [Martial]; *voluptates commendat rarior usus* [Juvenal].

378. Physical Pain. — N. pain; suffer-ing, -ance; bodily –, physical--pain, – suffering; mental suffering &c. 828; doulour, ache; aching &c. *v.*; smart; shoot, -ing; twinge, twitch, gripe, headache; hurt, cut; sore, -ness; discomfort, *malaise;* cephalalgia, ear-ache, gout, ischiagra, lumbago, neuralgia, odontalgia, otalgia, podagra, rheumatism, sciatica; tic douloureux, tooth-ache, tormina, torticollis.

spasm, cramp; nightmare, ephialtes; crick, stitch; thrill, convulsion, throe; throb &c. (*agitation*) 315; pang; colic; kink.

sharp –, piercing –, throbbing –, shooting –, gnawing –, burning- pain; anguish, agony.

torment, torture; rack; cruci-ation, -fixion; martyrdom; martyr, toad under a harrow, vivisection.

V. feel –, experience –, suffer –, undergo- pain &c. *n.*; suffer, ache, smart, bleed; tingle, shoot; twinge, twitch, lancinate; writhe, wince, make a wry face; sit on -thorns, – pins and needles.

give –, inflict- pain; lacerate; pain, hurt, chafe, sting, bite, gnaw, gripe; pinch, tweak; grate, gall, fret, prick, pierce, wring, convulse; torment, torture; rack, agonize; crucify; ex-, cruciate †; break on the wheel, put to the rack; flog &c. (*punish*) 972; grate on the ear &c. (*harsh sound*) 410.

Adj. in -pain &c. *n.*, – a state of pain; pained &c. *v.*; gouty, podagric, torminous.

painful; aching &c. *v.*; sore, raw.

---

2. Special Sensation

(1) Touch

379. [Sensation of pressure.] **Touch. — N.** touch; tact, -ion, -ility; feeling; palp-ation, -ability; contrectation; manipulation; massage.

[Organ of touch] hand, finger, forefinger, thumb, paw, feeler, antenna; palpus.

V. touch, feel, handle, finger, thumb, paw, fumble, grope, grabble; twiddle, tweedle; pass –, run- the fingers over; manipulate, wield; throw out a feeler.

Adj. tact-ual, -ile; tangible, palpable; lambent.

380. Sensations of Touch. — N. itching &c. *v.*; titillation, formication, aura; stereognosis.

V. itch, tingle, creep, thrill, sting; prick, -le; tickle, titillate.

Adj. itching &c. *v.*; stereognostic, titillative.

381. [Insensibility to touch.] Numbness. — N. numbness &c. (*physical insensibility*) 376; anæsthesia; pins and needles.

V. benumb &c. 376.

Adj. numb; benumbed &c. *v.*; deadened; intangible, impalpable.

(2) Heat

382. Heat. — N. heat, caloric; temperature, warmth, fervor, calidity; incal-, incand-escence; glow, flush; fever, hectic.

phlogiston; fire, spark, scintillation, flash, flame, blaze; bonfire; firework, pyrotechny; wildfire; sheet of fire, lambent flame; devouring element; adiathermancy; recalescence.

summer, dog days; canicular days; baking &c. 384 –, white –, tropical –, Afric –, Bengal –, summer –, blood- heat; sirocco, simoom; broiling sun; insolation; warming &c. 384.

sun &c. (*luminary*) 423.

[Science of heat] pyrology; thermology, -otics; thermometer &c. 389.

V. be -hot &c. *adj.*; glow, flush, sweat, swelter, bask, smoke, reek, stew, simmer, seethe, boil, burn, broil, blaze, flame; smolder; parch, fume, pant.

heat &c. (*make hot*) 384; recalesce; thaw, give.

Adj. hot, warm, mild, genial, tepid, lukewarm, unfrozen; therm-al, -ic; calorific; ferv-ent, -id; ardent; aglow.

sunny, torrid, tropical, estival, canicular; close, sultry, stifling, stuffy, suffocating, oppressive; reeking &c. *v.*; baking &c. 384.

red –, white —, smoking —, burning &c. *v.* –, piping- hot; like -a furnace, – an oven; hot as -fire, – pepper; hot enough to roast an ox.

fiery; incand-, incal-escent; candent, ebullient, glowing, smoking; live; on fire; blazing &c. *v.*; in -flames, – a blaze; alight, afire, ablaze; un-quenched, -extinguished; smoldering; in a -heat, – glow, – fever, – perspiration, – sweat; sudorific; swelter-ing, -ed; blood-hot, -warm; warm as -a toast, – wool.

volcanic, plutonic, igneous; isother-mal, -mic, -al.

Phr. not a breath of air; " whirlwinds of tempestuous fire " [*Paradise Lost*].

383. Cold. — N. cold, -ness &c. *adj.*; frigidity, inclemency, fresco.

winter; depth of –, hard- winter; Siberia, Nova Zembla.

ice; snow, – flake, – crystal, – drift; sleet; hail, -stone; rime, frost; hoar –, white –, hard –, sharp- frost; *barf*; glaze [U. S.], lolly [N. Am.]; icicle, thick-ribbed ice; fall of snow, heavy fall; ice-berg, -floe; floe berg; glacier; *nevée, serac; pruina.*

[Sensation of cold] chilliness &c. *adj.*; chill; shivering &c. *v.*; goose skin, rigor, horripilation, chattering of teeth.

V. be -cold &c. *adj.*; shiver, starve, quake, shake, tremble, shudder, didder, quiver; perish with cold; chill &c. (*render cold*) 385; horripilate.

Adj. cold, cool; chill, -y; gelid, frigid, algid; fresh, keen, bleak, raw, inclement, bitter, biting, niveous, cutting, nipping, piercing, pinching; clay - cold; starved &c. (*made cold*) 385; shivering &c. *v.*; aguish, *transi de froid;* frostbitten, -bound, -nipped.

cold as -a stone, – marble, – lead, – iron, – a frog, – charity, – Christmas; cool as -a cucumber, – custard.

icy, glacial, frosty, freezing, pruinose, wintry, brumal, hibernal, boreal, arctic, Siberian, hyemal; hyperbore-an, -al; icebound; frozen out.

un-warmed, -thawed; lukewarm, tepid; iso-cheimal, -cheimenal, -cheimic.

Adv. coldly, bitterly &c. *adj.*; *à pierre fendre.*

384. Calefaction. — N. increase of temperature; heating &c. *v.*; cale-, tepe-, torre-faction; melting, fusion;

385. Refrigeration. — N. refrigeration, infrigidation, reduction of temperature; cooling &c. *v.*; con-gelation,

liquefaction &c. 335; burning &c. *v.*; am-, com-bustion; in-†, ac-cension; con-, cremation; scorification; cauter-y, -ization; ustulation, calcination; in-, cineration; carbonization; cupellation.

ignition, inflammation, adustion, flagration† ; de-, con-flagration; empyrosis, incendiarism; arson; *auto da fé*.

boiling &c. *v.*; coction, ebullition, estuation, elixation†, decoction; ebullioscope; geyser.

furnace &c. 386; blanket, flannel, fur; wadding &c. (*lining*) 224; clothing &c. 225.

match &c. (*fuel*) 388; incendiary; *pétroleuse;* caustic, lunar caustic, apozem, moxa; aqua-fortis, -regia; catheretic, nitric acid, nitrochloro-hydric acid, nitromuriatic acid, radium.

sunstroke, *coup de soleil;* insolation.

pottery, ceramics, crockery, porcelain, china; earthen-, stone-ware; pot, mug, terra cotta, brick, clinker; cinder, ash, scoriæ; embers, slag, products of combustion, coke, carbon, charcoal.

inflamma-, combusti-bility.

[Transmission of heat] diathermancy, transcalency.

V. heat, warm, chafe, stive, foment; make -hot &c. 382; sun oneself.

fire; set -fire to, – on fire; kindle, enkindle, light, ignite, strike a light; apply the -match, – torch- to; re-kindle, -lume; fan –, add fuel to- the flame; poke –, stir –, blow- the fire; make a bonfire of.

melt, thaw, fuse; liquefy &c. 335.

burn, inflame, roast, toast, fry, grill, singe, parch, bake, torrefy, scorch; brand, cauterize, sear, burn in; corrode, char, calcine, incinerate; smelt, scorify; reduce to ashes; burn to a cinder; commit –, consign- to the flames.

boil, digest, stew, cook, seethe, scald, parboil, simmer; do to rags.

take –, catch- fire blaze &c. (*flame*) 382.

Adj. heated &c. *v.*; molten, sodden; *réchauffé;* heating &c. *v.*; adust.

inflammable, combustible; diatherm-al, -anous; burnt &c. *v.*; volcanic, radio-active.

-glaciation† ; ice &c. 383; solidification &c. (*density*) 321; ice box.

extincteur; fire annihilator; amianth, -us; earth-, mountain-flax; flexible asbestos; fireman, fire brigade.

incombusti-bility, -bleness &c. *adj.*

V. cool, fan, refrigerate, refresh, ice; congeal, freeze, glaciate; benumb, starve, pinch, chill, petrify, chill to the marrow, regelate, nip, cut, pierce, bite, make one's teeth chatter; damp, slack; quench; put –, stamp- out; extinguish.

go –, burn- out.

Adj. cooled &c. *v.*; frozen out; cooling &c. *v.*; frigorific.

incombustible; un-, unin-flammable; fireproof.

386. Furnace. — N. furnace, stove, kiln, oven; hot-, bake-, wash-house; laundry; conservatory; hearth, focus; athanor, hypocaust, reverberatory; volcano; forge, fiery furnace; limekiln; Dutch oven; tuyère, brasier, salamander, heater, warming pan; boiler, caldron, seething caldron, pot; urn, kettle; chafing-dish; retort, crucible, alembic, still; waffle irons.

fire-place, -dog, -irons; grate, range, kitchener; ca-, cam-boose; poker, tongs, shovel, hob, trivet; and-, grid-iron; frying-, stew-pan, backlog.

sudatory; Turkish –, Russian –, vapor –, warm- bath; vaporarium.

387. Refrigeratory. — N. refrigerator, -y; frigidarium; cold storage; ice-house, -pail, -bag, -box; cooler, damper; wine cooler; freezing mixture.

388. Fuel. — N. fuel, firing, combustible, coal, wallsend, anthracite, culm, coke, carbon, charcoal; turf, peat, firewood, bobbing, faggot, log; cinder &c. (*products of combustion*) 384; ingle, tinder, touchwood; sulphur, brimstone; incense; port-fire; fire-barrel, -ball, -brand; amadou, bavin; blind-, glance-coal; German tinder, pyrotechnic sponge, punk, smudge [U. S.].

brand, torch, fuse; wick; spill, match, light, lucifer, congreve, vesuvian, vesta, fusee, locofoco; linstock.

candle &c. (*luminary*) 423; oil &c. (*grease*) 356.

Adj. carbonaceous; combustible, inflammable.

389. Thermometer. — N. thermo-meter, -metrograph, -pile, -stat, -scope; pyro-, calori-meter.

(3) Taste

390. Taste. — N. taste, flavor, gust, gusto, savor; *goût*, relish; sapor†, sapidity; twang, smack, smatch†; after-taste, tang.

tasting; de-, gustation.

palate, tongue, tooth, stomach.

V. taste, savor, smatch, smack, flavor, twang; tickle the palate &c. (*savory*) 394; smack the lips.

Adj. sapid, saporific; gusta-ble†, -tory; gustful; strong; palatable &c. 394.

391. Insipidity. — N. insipidity; tastelessness &c. *adj.*

V. be -tasteless &c. *adj.*

Adj. void of -taste &c. 390; insipid; taste-, gust-†, savor-less; ingustible†, mawkish, milk and water, weak, stale, flat, vapid, *fade*, wishy-washy, mild; untasted.

392. Pungency. — N. pungency, piquancy, poignancy *haut-goût*, strong taste, twang, race.

sharpness &c. *adj.*; acrimony; roughness &c. (*sour*) 392; unsavoriness &c. 395.

niter, salpeter; mustard, cayenne, caviare; seasoning &c. (*condiment*) 393; brine; carbonate of ammonia; sal-ammoniac, -volatile; smelling salts; hartshorn.

dram, cordial, nip.

nicotine, tobacco, snuff, quid; segar; cigar, -ette; weed; fragrant –, Indian-weed; Cavendish, fid, negro head, old soldier, rappee, stogy.

V. be -pungent &c. *adj.*; bite the tongue.

render -pungent &c. *adj.*; season, spice, salt, pepper, pickle, brine, devil.

smoke, chew, take snuff.

Adj. pungent, strong; high-, full-flavored; high-tasted, -seasoned; gamy; sharp, stinging, rough, piquant, racy; biting, mordant; spicy; seasoned &c. *v.*; hot, – as pepper; peppery, vellicating, escharotic, meracious†; acrid, acrimonious, bitter; rough &c. (*sour*) 397; unsavory &c. 395.

salt, saline, brackish, briny; salt as -brine, – a herring, – Lot's wife.

393. Condiment. — N. condiment, salt, mustard, pepper, cayenne, curry, seasoning, sauce, spice, relish, *sauce piquante*, caviare, pot herbs, onion, garlic, pickle; *achar*, allspice, appetizer; bell-, Jamaica-, red-pepper; capsicum, chutney; cubeb, pimento.

V. season &c. (*render pungent*) 392.

394. Savoriness. — N. savoriness &c. *adj.*; relish, zest; appetizer.

titbit, dainty, delicacy, ambrosia, nectar, *bonne-bouche;* game, turtle, venison; delicatessen.

V. be -savory &c. *adj.*; tickle the -palate, – appetite; flatter the palate.

render -palatable &c. *adj.*

relish, like, smack the lips.

Adj. savory, well-tasted, to one's taste, tasty, good, palatable, nice,

395. Unsavoriness. — N. unsavoriness &c. *adj.*; amaritude; acrimony, -tude; roughness &c. (*sour*) 397; acerbity, austerity; gall and wormwood, rue, quassia, aloes; marah; sickener.

V. be -unpalatable &c. *adj.*; sicken, disgust, nauseate, pall, turn the stomach.

Adj. un-savory, -palatable, -sweet; ill-flavored; bitter, – as gall; acrid, acrimonious; rough.

dainty, delectable; tooth-ful, -some; gustful, appetizing, lickerish, delicate, delicious, exquisite, rich, luscious, ambrosial.

Adv. *per amusare la bocca*

Phr. *cela se laisse manger.*

396. Sweetness. — N. sweetness, dulcitude.

sugar, syrup, treacle, molasses, honey, manna; confection, -ary; sweets, grocery, conserve, preserve, confiture, jam, julep; sugar-candy, -plum; licorice, marmalade, plum, lollipop, bonbon, jujube, comfit, sweetmeat; apple butter, caramel, damson, glucose; maple-sirup, -syrup, -sugar; *mithai*, sorghum, taffy.

nectar; hydromel, mead, metheglin, honeysuckle, liqueur, sweet wine.

pastry, pie, tart, puff, pudding.

dulc-ification†, -oration†.

V. be -sweet &c. *adj.*

render -sweet &c. *adj.*; sweeten; edulcorate; dulc-orate†, -ify†; candy; mull.

Adj. sweet; sacchar-ine, -iferous; dulcet, candied, honied, luscious, lush, nectarious, melliferous; sweetened &c. *v.*

sweet as -a nut, – sugar, – honey.

Phr. *eau sucrée;* " sweets to the sweet " [*Hamlet*].

offensive, repulsive, nasty; sickening &c. *v.*; nauseous; loath-, ful-some; unpleasant &c. 830.

397. Sourness. — N. sourness &c. *adj.*; acid, -ity; acetous fermentation.

vinegar verjuice, crab, alum; acetic acid.

V. be – turn- -sour &c. *adj.*; set the teeth on edge.

render -sour &c. *adj.*; acid-ify, -ulate.

Adj. sour; acid, -ulous, -ulated; tart, crabbed; acet-ous, -ose; acerb, acetic; sour as vinegar, sourish, acescent, subacid; styptic, hard, rough.

(4) Odor

398. Odor. — N. odor, smell, odorament †, scent, effluvium; eman-, exhal-ation; fume, essence, trail, nidor†, redolence.

sense of smell; scent; act of -smelling &c. *v.*; olfaction, olfactories.

V. have an -odor &c. *n.*; smell, – of, – strong of; exhale; give out a -smell &c. *n.*; scent.

smell, scent; snuff, – up; sniff, nose, inhale.

Adj. odor-ant, -ous, -iferous; smelling, strong-scented; redolent, graveolent, nidorous, pungent.

[Relating to the sense of smell] olfactory, quick-scented.

399. Inodorousness. — N. inodorousness; absence –, want- of smell.

deodor-ant, -ization, -izer.

V. be -inodorous &c. *adj.*; not smell.

deodorize.

Adj. inodor-ous, -ate; scentless; without –, wanting- smell &c. 398.

deodor-zed, -ing.

400. Fragrance. — N. fragrance, aroma, redolence, perfume, bouquet; sweet smell, aromatic perfume.

agalloch, -ium; aloes wood; bay rum; calam-bac, -bour; champak, horehound, lign-aloes, marrubium, mint, muskrat, napha water, olibanum, spirit of myrcia.

incense; musk, frankincense; pastil, -le; myrrh, perfumes of Arabia; otto, ottar, attar; bergamot, balm, civet, potpourri, pulvil †; nosegay; scent, -bag; sachet, smelling bottle, vinaigrette; *eau de Cologne;* thurification.

401. Fetor. — N. fetor; bad &c. *adj.* -smell, – odor; stench, stink; foul –, mal- odor; empyreuma; mustiness &c. *adj.*; rancidity; foulness &c. (*uncleanness*) 653.

stoat, polecat, skunk; assafœtida; fungus, garlic; stinkpot; fitchet, fitchew, fourmart, peccary.

V. have a -bad smell &c. *n.*; smell; stink, – in the nostrils, – like a polecat; smell -strong &c. *adj.*, – offensively.

Adj. fetid; strong-smelling; high, bad, strong, fulsome, offensive, noisome,

perfumer.

V. be -fragrant &c. *adj.*; have a -perfume &c. *n.*; smell sweet, scent, perfume, embalm.

Adj. fragrant, aromatic, redolent, spicy, balmy, scented; sweet-smelling, -scented; perfum-ed, -atory; thuriferous; fragrant as a rose, muscadine, ambrosial.

rank, rancid, reasty, tainted, musty, fusty, frouzy; olid, -ous †; nidorous; smell-, stink-ing; putrid &c. 653; suffocating, mephitic; empyreumatic.

(5) *Sound*

(i) Sound in General

402. Sound. — N. sound, noise, strain; accent, twang, intonation, tone; cadence; sonorousness &c. *adj.*; audibility; resonance &c. 408; voice &c. 580; aspirate; ideophone; rough breathing.

[Science of sound] acoustics; phon-ics, -etics, -ology, -ography; dia-coustics, -phonics; phonetism.

V. produce sound; sound, make a noise; give out -, emit- sound; resound &c. 408.

Adj. sounding; soniferous; sonor-ous, -ific; resonant, audible, distinct; stertorous; phonetic; phonic, phonocamptic.

Phr. "a thousand trills and quivering sounds" [Addison]; *forensis strepitus.*

403. Silence. — N. silence; stillness &c. (*quiet*) 265; peace, hush, lull; muteness &c. 581; solemn -, awful -, dead -, deathlike- silence.

V. be -silent &c. *adj.*; hold one's tongue &c. (*not speak*) 585.

render -silent &c. *adj.*; silence, still, hush; stifle, muffle, stop; muzzle, put to silence &c. (*render mute*) 581.

Adj. silent; still, -y; noise-, soundless; hushed &c. *v.*; mute &c. 581.

soft, solemn, awful, deathlike, silent as the grave; inaudible &c. (*faint*) 405.

Adv. silently &c. *adj.*; *sub silentio.*

Int. hush! silence! soft! whist! tush! chut! tut! *pax!* be -quiet! – silent! – still! *chup! chup rao! tace!*

Phr. one might hear a.-feather, – pin- drop; *grosse Seelen dulden still; le silence est la vertu de ceux qui ne sont pas sages; le silence est le parti le plus sûr de celui se défie de soi-même;* "silence more musical than any song" [C. G. Rossetti]; *tacent satis laudant.*

404. Loudness.—N. loudness, power; loud noise, din; blare; clang, -or; clatter, noise, bombilation, roar, uproar, racket, hubbub, bobbery, fracas, charivari, trumpet blast, flourish of trumpets, fanfare, tintamarre, peal, swell, blast, larum, boom; resonance &c. 408.

vociferation, hullabaloo, &c. 411; lungs; Stentor.

artillery, cannon; thunder.

V. be -loud &c. *adj.*; peal, swell, clang, boom, thunder, fulminate, roar; resound &c. 408; speak up, shout &c. (*vociferate*) 411; bellow &c. (*cry as an animal*) 412.

rend the -air, – skies; fill the air; din -, ring -, thunder- in the ear; pierce -, split -, rend- the -ears, – head; deafen, stun; *faire le diable à quatre;* make one's windows shake; awaken-, startle- the echoes.

Adj. loud, sonorous; high-, big-sounding; deep, full, powerful, noisy, blatant, clangorous, multisonous; thundering, deafening &c. *v.*; trumpet-tongued; ear-splitting, -rending, -deafen-

405. Faintness. — N. faintness &c. *adj.*; faint sound, whisper, breath; under-tone, -breath; murmur, hum, susurration; tinkle; "still small voice."

hoarseness &c. *adj.*; raucity.

V. whisper, breathe, murmur, purl, hum, gurgle, ripple, babble, flow; tinkle; mutter &c. (*speak imperfectly*) 583; susurrate.

steal on the ear; melt in -, float on- the air.

Adj. inaudible; scarcely -, just- audible; low, dull, stifled, muffled; hoarse, husky; gentle, soft, faint; floating; purling, flowing &c. *v.*; whispered &c. *v.*; liquid; soothing; dulcet &c. (*melodious*) 413; susurr-ant, -ous.

Adv. in a whisper, with bated breath, *sotto voce,* between the teeth, aside; piano, -issimo; *à la sourdine;* out of earshot, inaudibly &c. *adj.*

ing; piercing; obstreperous, rackety, uproarious; enough to wake the -dead, – seven sleepers.

shrill &c. 410; clamorous &c. (*vociferous*) 411; stentor-ian, -ophonic †.

Adv. loudly &c. *adj.*; aloud; at the top of one's voice. lustily, in full cry.

Phr. the air rings with; " the deep dread-bolted thunder " [*Lear*].

(ii) Specific Sounds

406. [Sudden and violent sounds.] **Snap. — N.** snap &c. *v.*; rapping &c. *v.*; de-, crepitation; report; thud; burst, explosion, discharge, detonation, firing, salvo, volley.

squib, cracker, gun, popgun.

V. rap, snap, tap, knock; click; clash; crack, -le; crash; pop; slam, bang, clap; brustle; burst on the ear; crepitate, flump.

Adj. rapping &c. *v.*

407. [Repeated and protracted sounds.] **Roll. — N.** roll &c. *v.*; drumming &c. *v.*; berloque, bombination, rumbling; tattoo; dingdong; tantara; rataplan; whirr; ratatat; rubadub; pitapat; quaver, clutter, charivari, racket; cuckoo; repetition &c. 104; peal of bells, devil's tattoo; reverberation &c. 408.

V. roll, drum, rumble, rattle, clatter, patter, clack; bombinate.

hum, trill, shake; chime, peal, toll; tick, beat.

drum –, din- in the ear.

Adj. rolling &c. *v.*; monotonous &c. (*repeated*) 104; like a bee in a bottle.

408. Resonance. — N. resonance; ring &c. *v.*; ringing &c. *v.*; reflexion, reflection, reverberation.

low –, base –, bass –, flat –, grave –, deep- note; bass; *basso, – profondo;* bari-, bary-tone; contralto.

V. re-sound, -verberate, -echo; ring, jingle, gingle, chink, clink; tink, -le; chime; gurgle &c. 405; plash, guggle, echo, ring in the ear.

Adj. resounding &c. *v.*; resonant, reverberant, tinnient †, tintinnabulary; deep-toned, -sounding, -mouthed; hollow, sepulchral; gruff &c. (*harsh*) 410.

Phr. " sweet bells jangled, out of time and harsh " [*Hamlet*]

408a. Nonresonance. — N. thud, thump, dead sound; nonresonance; muffled drums, cracked bell; damper; silencer.

V. sound dead; stop –, damp –, deaden-, the -sound, – reverberations.

Adj. nonresonant, dead.

409. [Hissing sounds.] **Sibilation. — N.** sibilation; zip; hiss &c. *v.*; sternutation; high note &c. 410.

goose, serpent.

V. hiss, buzz, whiz, rustle; fizz, -le; wheeze, whistle, snuffle; squash; sneeze; sizzle, swish.

Adj. sibilant; hissing &c. *v.*; wheezy; sternutative.

410. [Harsh sounds.] **Stridor. — N.** creak &c. *v.*; creaking &c. *v.*; discord, &c. 414; stridor; roughness, sharpness, &c. *adj.*; cacophony; cacoëpy.

acute –, high- note; soprano, treble, tenor, alto, falsetto, penny trumpet, *voce aï testa.*

V. creak, grate, jar, burr, pipe, twang, jangle, clank, clink; scream &c. (*cry*) 411; yelp &c. (*animal sound*) 412; buzz &c. (*hiss*) 109.

set the teeth on edge, *écorcher les oreilles;* pierce –, split- the -ears, – head; offend –, grate upon –, jar upon- the ear.

Adj. creaking &c. *v.*; stridulous, harsh, coarse, hoarse, horrisonous †, rough, gruff, grum, sepulchral, hollow.

sharp, high, acute, shrill; trumpet-toned; piercing, ear-piercing, high-pitched, -toned; cracked; discordant &c. 414; cacophonous.

411. Cry. — N. cry &c. *v.*; voice &c. (*human*) 580; hubbub; bark &c. (*animal*) 412.

vociferation, outcry, hullabaloo, chorus, clamor, hue and cry, plaint; lungs; stentor.

V. cry, roar, shout, bawl, brawl, halloo, halloa, hoop, whoop, yell, bellow, howl, scream, screech, screak, shriek, shrill, squeak, squeal, squall, whine, pule, pipe, yaup.

cheer; hoot; grumble, moan, groan.

snore, snort; grunt &c. (*animal sounds*) 412.

vociferate; raise –, lift up- the voice; call –, sing –, cry- out; exclaim; rend the air; thunder –, shout- at the -top of one's voice, – pitch of one's breath; *s'égosiller*; strain the -throat, – voice, – lungs; give a -cry &c.

Adj. crying &c. *v.*; clam-ant, -orous; vociferous; stentorian &c. (*loud*) 404; open-mouthed.

412. [Animal sounds.] Ululation. — N. cry &c. *v.*; crying &c. *v.*; bow-wow, ululation, latration, belling; reboation; woodnote; insect cry, fritiniancy †, drone; screech owl; cuckoo.

V. cry, roar, bellow, blare, rebellow, bark, yelp; bay, – the moon; yap, growl, yarr †, yawl, snarl, howl; grunt, -le; snort, squeak; neigh, bray; mew, mewl; purr, caterwaul, pule; bleat, low, moo; troat, croak, crow, screech, caw, coo, gobble, quack, cackle, gaggle, guggle; chuck, -le; cluck, clack; chirp, cheep, chirrup, twitter, cuckoo; hum, buzz; hiss, blatter.

Adj. crying &c. *v.*; blatant, latrant; re-, mugient; deep-, full-mouthed; re-bellowing, reboant.

Adv. in full cry.

(iii) Musical Sounds

413. Melody. Concord. — N. melody, rhythm, measure; rhyme &c. (*poetry*) 597.

pitch, timbre, intonation, tone.

scale, gamut; diapason; diatonic –, chromatic –, enharmonic- scale; key, clef, chords.

modulation, temperament, syncope, syncopation, preparation, suspension, resolution.

staff, stave, line, space, brace; bar, rest; *appoggia-to, -tura; acciaccatura.*

note, musical note, notes of a scale; sharp, flat, natural; high note &c. (*shrillness*) 410; low note &c. 408; interval; semitone; second, third, fourth &c.; diatessaron.

breve, semibreve, minim, crotchet, quaver; semi-, demisemi-quaver; sustained note, drone, burden.

tonic; key-, leading-, fundamental- note; supertonic, mediant, dominant; sub-mediant, -dominant; octave, tetrachord; major –, minor- -mode, – scale, – key; passage, phrase.

concord, harmony; emmeleia; unison, -ance; chime, homophony; euphon-y, -ism; tonality; consonance; concent; part.

[Science of harmony] harmon-y, -ics; thorough-, fundamental-bass; counterpoint; faburden.

piece of music &c. 415; composer, harmonist, contrapuntist.

V. be -harmonious &c. *adj.*; harmonize, chime, symphonize, transpose; put in tune, tune, accord, string.

Adj. harmoni-ous, -cal; in -concord &c. *n.*, – tune, – concert; unisonant, concentual, symphonizing, isotonic, homophonous, assonant; ariose, consonant.

measured, rhythmical, diatonic, chromatic, enharmonic.

414. Discord. — N. discord, -ance; dissonance, cacophony, want of harmony, caterwauling; harshness &c. 410.

[Confused sounds] Babel; Dutch –, cat's- concert; marrowbones and cleavers.

V. be -discordant &c. *adj.*; jar &c. (*sound harshly*) 410.

Adj. discordant; dis-, ab-sonant; out of tune, tuneless; un-musical, -tunable; un-, im-melodious; un-, in-harmonious; singsong; cacophonous; harsh &c. 410; jarring.

melodious, musical; melic; tuneful, tunable; sweet, dulcet, canorous; mellow, -ifluous; soft, clear, – as a bell; silvery; euphon-ious, -ic, -ical; symphónious; enchanting &c. (*pleasure-giving*) 829; fine-, full-, silver-toned.

Adv. harmoniously &c. *adj.*

Phr. " the hidden soul of harmony " [Milton].

415. Music. — N. music; concert; strain, tune, air; melody &c. 413; aria, arietta; piece of music, sonata; rond-o, -eau; pastorale, cavatina, roulade, fantasia, *concerto*, overture, symphony, variations, cadenza; cadence; fugue, canon, serenade, *notturno*, dithyramb; opera, operetta; oratorio; composition, movement; stave; *passamezzo, toccata, Vorspiel.*

instrumental music; full score; minstrelsy, tweedledum and tweedledee, band, orchestra; concerted piece, potpourri, *capriccio.*

vocal music, vocalism; chaunt, chant; psalm, -ody; hymn; song &c. (*poem*) 597; canticle, canzonet, cantata, bravura, lay, ballad, ditty, carol, pastoral, recitative, recitativo, *solfeggio.*

Lydian measures; slow -music, – movement; adagio &c. *adv.*; minuet; siren strains, soft music, lullaby; dump; dirge &c. (*lament*) 839; pibroch; martial music, march; dance music; waltz &c. (*dance*) 840.

solo, duet, *duo*, trio; quartet, -t; septett; part song, descant, glee, madrigal, catch, round, chorus, chorale; antiphon, -y; accompaniment, second, bass; score; bourdon, drone, *morceau*, terzetto.

composer &c. 413; musician &c. 416.

V. compose, perform &c. 416; attune.

Adj. musical; instrumental, vocal, choral, lyric, operatic; harmonious &c. 413; Wagnerian.

Adv. *adagio; largo, larghetto, andan-te, -tino; alla capella; maestoso, moderato; allegr-o, -etto; spiritoso, vivace, veloce; prest-o, -issimo; con brio; capriccioso; scherz-o, -ando; legato, staccato, crescendo, diminuendo, rallentando, affettuoso; obbligato; pizzicato; desto.*

Phr. " in notes by distance made more sweet " [Collins]; " like the faint exquisite music of a dream " [Moore]; " music arose with its voluptuous swell " [Byron]; " music is the universal language of mankind " [Longfellow]; " music's golden tongue " [Keats]; " the speech of angels " [Carlyle]; " will sing the savageness out of a bear " [*Othello*].

416. Musician. [Performance of Music.] — **N.** musician, *artiste*, performer, player, minstrel; bard &c. (*poet*) 597; accompan-, accordion-, instrumental-, organ-, pian-, violin-, flaut-ist; harper, fiddler, fifer, trumpeter, piper, drummer; catgut scraper.

band, orchestra, waits.

vocal-, melod-ist; singer, warbler; songst-, chaunt-er, -ress; *cantatrice.*

choir, quire, chorister; chorus, – singer; liedertafel.

nightingale, philomel, thrush; siren; bulbul, mavis; Pierides; sacred nine; Orpheus, Apollo, the Muses, Erato, Euterpe, Terpsichore; tuneful -nine, – quire.

composer &c. 413.

performance, execution, touch, expression, solmization.

V. play, pipe, strike up, sweep the chords, tweedle, fiddle; strike the lyre, beat the drum; blow –, sound –, wind- the horn; doodle; grind the organ; touch the -guitar &c. (*instruments*) 417; thrum, strum, beat time.

execute, perform; accompany; sing –, play- a second; compose, set to music, arrange.

sing, chaunt, chant, hum, warble, carol, chirp, chirrup, lilt, purl, quaver, trill, shake, twitter, whistle; sol-fa; intone.

have -an ear for music, – a musical ear, – a correct ear.

Adj. playing &c. *v.*; musical.

Adv. *adagio, andante* &c. (*music*) 415.

417. Musical Instruments. — N. musical instruments; band; string-, brass-band; orchestra; orchestrina.

[Stringed instruments] mono-, poly-chord; harp, lyre, lute, archlute; mandol-a, -in, -ine; guitar; zither; cither, -n; gittern, rebeck, *bandurria*, banjo; bina, vina; xanorphica.

viol, -in; fiddle, kit; viola, - *d'amore*, - *di gamba;* tenor, cremona, violoncello, bass; bass-, base-viol; theorbo, double base, contrabasso, *violone*, psaltery; bow, fiddlestick.

piano, -forte; harpsi-, clavi-, clari-, mani-chord; clavier, spinet, virginals, dulcimer, hurdy-gurdy, vielle, pianino, Eolian harp.

[Wind instruments] organ; harmoni-um, -phon; American-, barrel-, hand-organ; accordian, seraphina, concertina; humming top.

flute, fife, piccolo, flageolet; clari-net, -onet; basset horn, *corno di bassetto*, oboe, hautboy, *cor Anglais, corno Inglese,* bassoon, double bassoon, *contrafagotto*, serpent, bass clarinet; bag-, union-pipes; *musette,* ocarina, Pandean pipes; reed instrument; sirene, pipe, pitch-pipe; sourdet; whistle, catcall; doodlesack, harmoniphone.

horn, bugle, cornet, *cornet-à-pistons,* cornopean†, clarion, trumpet, trombone, ophicleide; French-, bugle-, sax-, flugel-, alt-, helican-, post-horn; sackbut, euphonium, bombardon, tuba.

[Vibrating surfaces] cymbal, bell, gong; tambour, -ine; drum, tom-tom; tab-or, -ret, -ourine, -orin; side-, kettle-drum; *tympani;* tymbal, timbrel, castanet, bones; musical-glasses, -stones; harmonica, sounding-board, rattle; tam-tam, zambomba.

[Vibrating bars] reed, tuning fork, triangle, Jew's harp, musical box, harmonicon, xylophone.

sord-ine, -et; sourd-ine, -et; mute.

(iv) Perception of Sound

418. [Sense of sound.] Hearing. — N. hearing &c. *v.*; audition, auscultation; eavesdropping; audibility.

acute -, nice -, delicate -, quick -, sharp -, correct -, musical -ear; ear for music.

ear, auricle, lug, acoustic organs, audi-tory apparatus, ear-drum, tympanum; ear-, speaking-trumpet; telephone, pho-nograph, microphone; gramophone, meg-aphone, phonorganon.

hearer, auditor, listener, eavesdropper; audi-tory, -ence.

419. Deafness. — N. deafness, hard-ness of hearing, surdity†; inaudibility, inaudibleness.

V. be -deaf &c. *adj.*; have no ear; shut -, stop -, close- one's ears; turn a deaf ear to.

render deaf, stun, deafen.

Adj. deaf, earless, surd; hard -, dull- of hearing; deaf-mute, stunned, deaf-ened; stone deaf; deaf as -a post, - an adder, - a beetle, - a trunkmaker.

inaudible, out of hearing.

V. hear, overhear; hark, -en; list, -en; give -, lend -, bend- an ear; catch a sound, prick up one's ears; give ear, give -a hearing, - audience- to.

hang upon the lips of, be all ear, listen with both ears.

become audible; meet -, fall upon -, catch -, reach- the ear; be heard; ring in the ear &c. (*resound*) 408.

Adj. hearing &c. *v.*; auditory, auricular, acoustic; phonic.

Adv. *arrectis auribus.*

Int. hark, - ye! hear! list, -en! O yes! *Oyez!*

(6) Light

(i) Light in General

420. Light. — **N.** light, ray, beam, stream, gleam, streak, pencil; sun-, moon-beam; aurora.

day; sunshine; light of -day, – heaven; sun &c. (*luminary*) 432-, day-, broad day-, noontide- light; noon-tide, -day.

glow &c. *v.*; glimmering &c. *v.*; glint; play –, flood- of light; phosphorescence, lambent flame.

flush, halo, glory, nimbus, aureola.

spark, scintilla; facula; sparkling &c. *v.*; emication †, scintillation, flash, blaze, coruscation, fulguration; flame &c. (*fire*) 382; lightning, levin, *ignis fatuus,* &c. (*luminary*) 423.

luster, sheen, shimmer, reflexion, reflection; gloss, tinsel, spangle, brightness, brilliancy, splendor; eff-, re-fulgence; ful-gor, -gidity; dazzlement, resplendence, transplendency; luminousness &c. *adj.*; luminosity; lucidity; re-†, nitency; radi-ance, -ation; irradiation, illumination.

actinic rays, actinism; Röntgen-, X-ray; phot-, heli-ography; photometer &c. 445.

[Science of light] optics; photo-logy, -metry; di-, cat-optrics.

[Distribution of light] *chiaroscuro, clairobscur,* clear obscure, breadth, light and shade, black and white, tonality.

reflection, refraction, dispersion; refractivity.

V. shine, glow, glitter; glis-ter, -ten; twinkle, gleam; flare, – up; glare, beam, shimmer, glimmer, flicker, sparkle, scin-tillate, coruscate, flash, blaze; be -bright &c. *adj.*; reflect light, daze, dazzle, be-dazzle, radiate, shoot out beams; ful-gurate.

clear up, brighten.

lighten, enlighten; levin; light, – up; irradiate, shine upon; give –, hang out a-light; cast –, throw –, shed- -luster, -light- upon; illum-e, -ine, -inate; re-lume, strike a light; kindle &c. (*set fire to*) 384.

Adj. shining &c. *v.*; lumin-ous, -iferous; luc-id, -ent, -ulent, -ific, -iferous; light, -some; bright, vivid, splendent, nitid, lustrous, shiny, beamy, scintillant, radiant, lambent; sheen, -y; glossy, burnished, glassy, sunny, orient, merid-

421. Darkness. — **N.** darkness &c. *adj.*; blackness &c. (*dark color*) 431; obscurity, gloom, murk; dusk &c. (*dimness*) 422.

Cimmerian –, Stygian –, Egyptian-darkness; night; midnight; dead of –, witching hour of –, witching time of-night; blind man's holiday; darkness -visible, – that can be felt; palpable obscure; Erebus; "the jaws of darkness" [*Midsummer Night's Dream*]; "sable-vested Night" [Milton].

shade, shadow, umbra, penumbra; sciagraphy.

obscuration; ad-, ob-umbration; ob-tenebration, offuscation †, caligation †; extinction; eclipse, total eclipse; gathering of the clouds.

shading; distribution of shade; *chiaroscuro* &c. (*light*) 420.

noctivagation.

V. be -dark &c. *adj.*

darken, obscure, shade; dim; tone down, lower; over-cast, -shadow; eclipse; ob-, of-† fuscate; ob-, ad-umbrate; cast into the shade; be-cloud, -dim, -darken; cast –, throw –, spread- a -shade, – shadow, – gloom.

extinguish; put –, blow –, snuff- out; doubt.

Adj. dark, -some, -ling; obscure, tenebrious, sombrous, pitch dark, pitchy; caliginous; black &c. (*in color*) 431.

sunless, lightless &c. (*see* sun, light, &c. 423); somber, dusky; unilluminated &c. (*see* illuminate &c. 420); nocturnal; dingy, lurid, gloomy; murk-y, -some; shady, umbrageous; overcast &c. (*dim*) 422; cloudy &c. (*opaque*) 426; darkened &c. *v.*

dark as -pitch, – a pit, – Erebus.

benighted; noctivag-ant, -ous.

Adv. in the -dark, – shade.

Phr. "brief as the lightning in the collied night" [*M. N. D.*]; "eldest Night and Chaos, ancestors of Nature" [*P. L.*]; "the blackness of the noonday night" [Longfellow]; "the prayer of Ajax was for light" [Longfellow].

422. Dimness. — **N.** dimness &c. *adj.*; darkness &c. 421; paleness &c. (*light color*) 429.

half light, *demi-jour;* partial -shadow, – eclipse; shadow of a shade; glim-

ian; noon-day, -tide; cloudless, clear; un-clouded, -obscured.

gair-, gar-ish; re-, tran-splendent; re-, ef-fulgent; ful-gid, -gent; relucent, splendid, blazing, in a blaze, ablaze, rutilant, meteoric, phosphorescent; aglow.

bright as silver; light –, bright- as -day,– noonday, – the sun at noonday.

actinic; photo-genic, -graphic; helio-graphic; heliophagous.

Phr. " a day for gods to stoop and men to soar " [Tennyson]; " dark with excessive bright " [Milton].

mer, -ing; nebulosity; cloud &c. 353; eclipse.

aurora, dusk, twilight, shades of evening, crepuscule, cockshut time †; break of day, daybreak, dawn.

moon-light, -beam, -glade, -shine; star-, owl's-, candle-, rush-, fire-light; farthing candle.

V. be –, grow- -dim &c. *adj.*; flicker, twinkle, glimmer; loom, lower; fade, pale, – its ineffectual fire [*Hamlet*].

render -dim &c. *adj.*; dim, bedim, obscure.

Adj. dim, dull, lackluster, dingy, dark-ish, shorn of its beams, dark 421.

faint, shadowed forth; glassy; cloudy; misty &c. (*opaque*) 426; blear; muggy, fuliginous; nebul-ous, -ar; obnubilated, overcast, crepuscular, muddy, lurid, leaden, dun, dirty; looming &c. *v.*

pale &c. (*colorless*) 429; confused &c. (*invisible*) 447.

423. [Source of light, self-luminous body.] **Luminary.** — **N.** luminary; light &c. 420; flame &c. (*fire*) 382.

spark, scintilla; phosphorescence.

sun, orb of day, Phœbus, Apollo, Aurora; star, orb, meteor; falling –, shooting- star; blazing –, dog- star; Sirius, canicula, Aldebaran; constellation, galaxy; northern light, *aurora borealis*, zodiacal light; anthelion; day –, morning- star; Lucifer; mock sun, parhelion; Phosphor, -us; sundog; Venus; polar lights.

lightning; chain –, fork –, sheet –, summer- lightning; phosphorus; *ignis fatuus*; Jack o' –, Friar's- lantern; will-o'-the-wisp, firedrake, *Fata Morgana*.

glowworm, firefly.

[Artificial light] gas; gas –, lime –, electric- light; lamp; lant-ern, -horn; dark lantern, bull's-eye; candle, bougie, taper, rushlight; oil &c. (*grease*) 356; wick, burner; Argand, moderator, duplex; torch, flambeau, link, brand; gase-, chande-, electro-lier; candelabrum, girandole, sconce, luster, candlestick.

firework, fizgig; pyrotechnics; rocket, lighthouse &c. (*signal*) 550.

V. illuminate &c. (*light*) 420.

Adj. self-luminous; phosphor-ic, -escent; radiant &c. (*light*) 420.

Phr. " blossomed the lovely stars, the forget-me-nots of the angels " [Longfellow]; " the sentinel stars set their watch in the sky " [Campbell]; " the planets in their station list'ning stood " [*Paradise Lost*]; " the Scriptures of the skies " [Bailey]; " that orbed continent, the fire that severs day from night " [*Twelfth Night*].

424. Shade. — **N.** shade; awning &c. (*cover*) 223; parasol, sunshade, umbrella; chick; *portière;* screen, curtain, shutter, blind, gauze, veil, mantle, mask; cloud, mist, gathering of clouds.

umbrage, glade; shadow &c. 421.

V. draw a curtain; put up –, close- a shutter; veil &c. *v.*; cast a shadow &c. (*darken*) 421.

Adj. shady, umbrageous.

Phr. " welcome ye shades! ye bowery thickets hail " [Thomson].

425. Transparency, — **N.** transparen-ce, -cy; translucen-ce, -cy; diaphaneity; luc-, pelluc-, limp-idity; fluorescence; trans-illumination, -lumination.

transparent medium, glass, crystal, lymph, vitrite, water.

V. be -transparent &c. *adj.*; transmit light.

426. Opacity.—**N.** opacity; opaqueness &c. *adj.*

film; cloud &c. 353.

V. be -opaque &c. *adj.*; obstruct the passage of light; ob-, of-† fuscate.

Adj. opaque, impervious to light; adiaphanous; dim &c. 422; turbid, thick, muddy, opacous †, obfuscated, fuligi-

Adj. transparent, pellucid, lucid, diaphanous; trans-, tra-†, re-lucent; limpid, clear, serene, crystalline, clear as crystal, vitreous, transpicuous, glassy, hyaline; hyaloid, vitreform.

inous, cloudy, hazy, misty, foggy, vaporous, nubiferous, muggy.

smoky, fumid, murky, dirty.

427. Semitransparency. — **N.** semi-transparency, opalescence, milkiness, pearliness; gauze, muslin; film; mica, mother-of-pearl, nacre; mist &c. (*cloud*) 353.

    Adj. semi-transparent, -pellucid, -diaphanous, -opacous †, -opaque; opalescent, -ine; pearly, milky; frosted, nacreous.

    V. opalesce.

(ii) Specific Light

428. Color. — **N.** color, hue, tint, tinge, dye, complexion, shade, tincture, cast, livery, coloration, glow, flush; tone, key.

pure –, positive –, primary –, primitive –, complementary- color; three primaries; spectrum, chromatic dispersion; broken –, secondary –, tertiary- color.

local color, coloring, keeping, tone, value, aërial perspective.

[Science of color] chromatics, spectrum analysis; chromat-ism, -ography, -ology; prism, spectroscope.

pigment, coloring matter, paint, dye, wash, distemper, stain; medium; mordant; oil paint &c. (*painting*) 556.

V. color, dye, tinge, stain, tint, tinct, paint, wash, ingrain, grain, illuminate, emblazon, bedizen, imbue; paint &c. (*fine art*) 556.

    Adj. colored &c. *v.*; colorific, tingent, tinctorial; chromatic, prismatic; full-, high-, deep-colored; doubly-dyed; polychromatic; chromatogenous; tingible.

bright, vivid, intense, deep; fresh, unfaded; rich, gorgeous; gay.

gaudy, florid, gai-, ga-rish; showy, flaunting, flashy; raw, crude; glaring, flaring; discordant, inharmonious.

mellow, harmonious, pearly, sweet, delicate, tender, refined.

429. [Absence of color.] Achromatism. — **N.** achromatism; de-, discoloration; pall-or, -idity; paleness &c. *adj.*; etiolation; neutral tint, monochrome, black and white.

V. lose -color &c. 428; fade, fly, go; become -colorless &c. *adj.*; turn pale, pale.

deprive of color, decolorize, bleach, tarnish, achromatize, blanch, etiolate, wash out, tone down.

    Adj. uncolored &c. (*see* color &c. 428); colorless, achromatic, aplanatic; etiolate, -d; hueless, pale, pallid; pale-, tallow-faced; faint, dull, cold, muddy, leaden, dun, wan, sallow, dead, dingy, ashy, ashen, ghastly, cadaverous, glassy, lackluster; discolored &c. *v.*

light-colored, fair, blond; white &c. 430.

pale as -death, – ashes, – a witch, – a ghost, – a corpse.

430. Whiteness. — **N.** whiteness &c. *adj.*; argent.

albification, etiolation; lactescence.

snow, paper, chalk, milk, lily; ivory, silver, alabaster; albata, eburin, German silver, white metal, barium sulphate, *blanc fixe*, ceruse, pearl white; white –, carbonate of- lead.

V. be -white &c. *adj.*

render -white &c. *adj.*; whiten, bleach, blanch, etiolate, whitewash, silver.

    Adj. white; milk-, snow-white; snowy; niveous, candid, chalky; hoar, -y; sil-

431. Blackness. — **N.** blackness &c. *adj.*; darkness &c. (*want of light*) 421; swarthness, lividity, dark color, tone, color; *chiaroscuro* &c. 420.

nigrification, infuscation.

jet, ink, ebony, coal, pitch, soot, charcoal, sloe, smut, raven, crow; negro; blackamoor, man of color, nigger, darkie, Ethiop, black; buck, -nigger [U. S.]; coon * [U. S.], sambo.

[Pigments] lamp –, ivory –, blue-black; writing –, printing –, printer's –, Indian- ink.

very; argent, -ine; canescent, cretaceous, lactescent.

whitish, creamy, pearly, fair, blond; blanched &c. v.; high in tone, light.

white as -a sheet, – driven snow, – a lily, – silver; like -ivory &c. n.

V. be -black &c. adj.

render -black &c. adj.; blacken, infuscate, denigrate; blot, -ch; smutch; smirch; darken &c. 421.

Adj. black, sable, swarthy, somber, dark, inky, ebon, atramentous, jetty; coal-, jet-black; fuliginous, pitchy, sooty, swart, dusky, dingy, murky, Ethiopic; low-toned, low in tone; of the deepest dye.

black as -jet &c. n., – my hat, – a shoe, – a tinker's pot, – November, – thunder, – midnight; nocturnal &c. (*dark*) 421; nigrescent; gray &c. 432; obscure &c. 421.

Adv. in mourning.

432. Gray. — N. gray &c. adj.; neutral tint, silver, pepper and salt, *chiaroscuro*, grisaille.

[Pigments] Payne's gray; black &c. 431.

Adj. gray, grey; iron-gray, dun, drab, dingy, leaden, livid, somber, sad, pearly, russet, roan; calcareous, limy, favillous; silver, -y, -ed; ash-en, -y; ciner-eous, -itious; grizzl-y, -ed; slate-, stone-, mouse-, ash-colored; cool.

433. Brown. — N. brown &c. adj. [Pigments] bister, ocher, sepia, Vandyke brown.

V. render -brown &c. adj.; tan, embrown, bronze.

Adj. brown, bay, dapple, auburn, castaneous, chestnut, nut-brown, cinnamon, russet, tawny, fuscous, chocolate, maroon, foxy, tan, brunette, whitey brown; fawn-, snuff-, liver-colored; brown as -a berry, – mahogany, – the oak leaves; khaki.

sun-burnt; tanned &c. v.

Primitive Colors [1]

434. Redness. — N. red, scarlet, vermilion, carmine, crimson, pink, lake, maroon, carnation, *couleur de rose*, *rose du Barry*; magenta, damask, purple; flesh -color, – tint; color; fresh –, high-color; warmth; gules.

ruby, carbuncle; rose; rust, iron mold. [Dyes and pigments] cinnabar, cochineal; fuchsine; ruddle, madder; Indian –, light –, Venetian- red; red ink, annotto; annatto, realgar, minium, red lead.

redness &c. adj.; rub-escence, -icundity, -ification; erubescence, blush.

V. be –, become- -red &c. adj.; blush, flush, color up, mantle, redden.

render -red &c. adj.; redden, rouge; rub-ify, -ricate; incarnadine; ruddle.

Adj. red &c. n., -dish; rufous, ruddy, florid, incarnadine, sanguine; ros-y, -eate; blow-zy, -ed; burnt; rubi-cund, -form; lurid, stammel, blood red; russet, buff, murrey, carroty, sorrel, lateritious; rub-ineous, -ricate, -ricose; rufulous.

rose-, ruby-, cherry-, claret-, flame-, flesh-, peach-, salmon-, brick-, brick-dust-colored.

blushing &c. v.; erubescent; reddened &c. v.

red as -fire, – blood, – scarlet, – a turkey cock, – a lobster; warm, hot; foxy.

Complementary Colors

435. Greenness. — N. green &c. adj.; blue and yellow; vert.

emerald, verd antique, verdigris, malachite, beryl, aquamarine; absinthe, *crème de menthe*.

[Pigments] *terre verte*, verditer, verdine.

greenness, verdure; virid-ity, -escence; verditure.

Adj. green, verdant; glaucous, olive; green as grass; verdurous.

emerald –, pea –, grass –, apple –, sea –, olive –, bottle- green.

greenish; vir-ent, -escent.

---

[1] The author's classification of colors has been retained, though it does not entirely accord with the theories of modern science.

436. Yellowness. — N. yellow &c. *adj.*; or.

[Pigments] gamboge; cadmium –, chrome –, Indian –, king's –, lemon-yellow; orpiment, yellow ocher, Claude tint, aureolin; xanth-ein, -in; zaöfulvin.

crocus, saffron, topaz; xanthite; yolk. jaundice; London fog; yellowness &c. *adj.*; icterus; xantho-cyanopia, -psia.

Adj. yellow, aureate, golden, flavous†, citrine, fallow; fulv-ous, -id; sallow, luteous, tawny, creamy, sandy; xanth-ic, -ous; jaundiced; auricomous.

gold-, citron-, saffron-, lemon-, sulphur-, amber-, straw-, primrose-, cream-colored; xantho-carpous, -chroid, -pous.

yellow as a -quince, – guinea, – crow's foot.

warm, advancing.

437. Purple. — N. purple &c. *adj.*; blue and red, bishop's purple; aniline dyes, gridelin, amethyst; purpure; heliotrope.

livid-ness, -ity.

V. empurple.

Adj. purple, violet, plum-colored, lavender, lilac, puce, mauve; livid.

---

438. Blueness. — N. blue &c. *adj.*; garter-blue; watchet†.

[Pigments] ultramarine, smalt, cobalt, cyanogen; Prussian –, syenite- blue; bice, indigo; zaffer.

lapis lazuli, sapphire, turquoise; indicolite.

blue-, bluish-ness; bloom.

Adj. blue, azure, cerulean; sky-blue, -colored, -dyed; cerulescent; bluish; atmospheric, retiring; cold.

439. Orange. — N. orange, red and yellow; gold; or; flame &c. color, *adj.*

[Pigments] ocher, Mars orange, cadmium.

cardinal -bird, – flower, – grosbeak, – lobelia.

V. gild, warm.

Adj. orange; ochreous; orange-, gold-, flame-, copper-, brass-, apricot-colored; warm, hot, glowing.

---

440. Variegation. — N. variegation; di-, tri-chroism; iridescence, play of colors, polychrome, maculation, spottiness, striæ.

spectrum, rainbow, iris, tulip, peacock, chameleon, butterfly, tortoise shell; mackerel, – sky; zebra, leopard, cheetah, nacre, ocelot, ophite, mother-of-pearl, opal, marble.

check, plaid, tartan, patchwork; mar-, par-quetry; mosaic, tesseræ, *strigæ;* chessboard, checkers, chequers; harlequin; Joseph's coat; tricolor.

V. be -variegated &c. *adj.*; variegate, stripe, streak, checker, chequer; be-, speckle; be-, sprinkle; stipple, maculate, dot, bespot; tattoo, inlay, damascene; embroider, braid, quilt.

Adj. variegated &c. *v.*; many-colored, -hued; divers-, party-colored; di-, poly-chromatic; bi-, tri-, versi-color; of all- the colors of the rainbow, – manner of colors; kaleidoscopic.

iridescent; opal-ine, -escent; prismatic, nacreous, pearly, shot, *gorge de pigeon,* chatoyant; irisated, pavonine.

pied, piebald; motley; mottled, marbled; pepper and salt, paned, dappled, clouded, cymophanous.

mosaic, tesselated, plaid; tortoise shell &c. *n.*

spott-ed, -y; punctated, powdered; speckled &c. *v.*; freckled, flea-bitten, studded; fleck-ed, -ered; striated, barred, veined; brind-ed, -led; tabby; watered; grizzled; listed; embroidered &c. *v.*; dædal; nævose, stipiform; stri-gose, -olate.

(iii) Perceptions of Light

441. Vision. — N. vision, sight, optics, eyesight.

view, look, espial, glance, ken, *coup d'œil;* glimpse, glint, peep; gaze, stare,

442. Blindness. — N. blindness, cecity, excecation †, *amaurosis,* cataract, ablepsy†, prestriction†; dim-sightedness &c. 443; ablepsia; Braille, -type; *gutta*

leer; perlustration, contemplation; con-spect-ion †, -uity †; regard, survey; in-, intro-spection; reconnaissance, specula-tion, watch, espionage, *espionnage*, au-topsy; ocular -inspection, – demonstra-tion; sight-seeing.

point of view; gazebo, loophole, bel-vedere, watchtower.

field of view; theater, amphitheater, arena, vista, horizon; commanding –, bird's eye- view; periscope.

visual organ, organ of vision; eye; naked –, unassisted- eye; retina, pupil, iris, cornea, white; optics, orbs; saucer –, goggle –, gooseberry- eyes.

short sight &c. 443; clear –, sharp –, quick –, eagle –, piercing –, penetrating--sight, – glance, – eye; perspicacity, dis-cernment; catopsis.

eagle, hawk; cat, lynx; Argus.

evil eye; basilisk, cockatrice.

V. see, behold, discern, perceive, have in sight, descry, sight, make out, dis-cover, distinguish, recognize, spy, espy,

serena (" drop serene "), noctograph, teichopsia.

V. be -blind &c. *adj.*; not see; lose sight of; have the eyes bandaged; grope in the dark.

not look; close –, shut –, turn away –, avert- the eyes; look another way; wink &c. (*limited vision*) ·443; shut the eyes –, be blind- to; wink –, blink- at.

render -blind &c. *adj.*; blind, -fold; hoodwink, dazzle; put one's eyes out; throw dust into one's eyes; *jeter de la poudre aux yeux;* screen from sight &c. (*hide*) 528.

Adj. blind; eye-, sight-, vision-less; dark; stone-, sand-, stark-blind; undis-cerning; dim-sighted &c. 443.

blind as -a bat, – a buzzard, – a beetle, – a mole, – an owl; wall-eyed.

blinded &c. *v.*

Adv. blind-ly, -fold; darkly.

Phr. " O dark, dark, dark, amid the blaze of noon " [Milton].

ken; get –, have –, catch- a -sight, – glimpse- of; command a view of; witness, contemplate, speculate; cast –, set- the eyes on; be a -spectator &c. 444- of; look on &c. (*be present*) 186; see sights &c. (*curiosity*) 455; see at a glance &c. (*intelligence*) 498.

look, view, eye; lift up the eyes, open one's eye; look -at, – on, – upon, – over, – about one, – round; survey, scan, inspect; run the eye -over, – through; reconnoiter, glance -round, – on, – over; turn –, bend- one's looks upon; direct the eyes to, turn the eyes on, cast a glance.

observe &c. (*attend to*) 457; watch &c. (*care*) 459; see with one's own eyes; watch for &c. (*expect*) 507; peep, peer, pry, take a peep; play at bopeep.

look- -full in the face, – hard at, – intently; strain one's eyes; fix –, rivet-the eyes upon; stare, gaze; pore over, gloat on; leer, ogle, glare; goggle; cock the eye, squint, gloat, look askance.

Adj. seeing &c. *v.*; visual, ocular; optic, -al; ophthalmic.

clear-sighted &c. *n.*; eagle-, hawk-, lynx-, keen-, Argus-eyed.

visible &c. 446.

Adv. visibly &c. 446; in sight of, with one's eyes open. ·

at -sight, – first sight, – a glance, – the first blush; *primâ facie.*

Int. look! &c. (*attention*) 457.

Phr. the scales falling from one's eyes; " an eye like Mars to threaten or command " [*Hamlet*]; " her eyes are homes of silent prayer " [Tennyson]; " looking before and after " [*Hamlet*]; " thy rapt soul sitting in thine eyes " [Milton].

443. [Imperfect vision.] **Dim-sightedness.** [Fallacies of vision.] — **N.** dim –, dull –, half –, short –, near –, long –, double –, astigmatic –, failing- sight; dim &c. -sightedness; purblindness, lippitude; my-, presby-opia; confusion of vision; astigmatism; color blindness, chromato-pseudo-blepsis, Daltonism; nyctalopia; strabismus, strabism, squint; blearedness, day blindness, heme-ralopia, nystagmus; xantho-cyanopia, -psia; cast in the eye, swivel eye, goggle-eyes; obliquity of vision.

winking &c. *v.*; nictitation; blinkard, albino.

dizziness, swimming, scotomy; cataract; ophthalmia.

[Limitation of vision] blinker; screen &c. (*hider*) 530.

[Fallacies of vision] *deceptio visûs;* refraction, distortion, illusion, false light, anamorphosis, virtual image, spectrum, mirage, looming, phasma†; phantasm, -asma, -om; vision; specter, apparition, ghost; *ignis fatuus &c. (luminary)* 423; specter of the Brocken; magic mirror; magic lantern &c. *(show)* 448; mirror, lens &c. *(instrument)* 445.

V. be -dim-sighted &c. *n.*; see double; have a -mote in the eye, – mist before the eyes, – film over the eyes; see through a -prism, – glass darkly; wink, blink, nictitate; squint; look ask-ant, -ance; screw up the eyes, glare, glower; nictate. dazzle, loom.

Adj. dim-sighted &c. *n.*; my-, presby-opic; astigmatic; moon-, mope-, blear-, goggle-, gooseberry-, one-eyed; blind of one eye, monoculous; half-, pur-blind; cock-, dim-, mole-eyed; dichroic.

blind as a bat &c. *(blind)* 442; winking &c. *v.*

444. Spectator. — N. spectator, beholder, observer, looker-on, on-looker, witness, eyewitness, bystander, passer by; sight-seer; rubberneck * [U. S.]. spy; sentinel &c. *(warning)* 668.

V. witness, behold &c. *(see)* 441; look on &c. *(be present)* 186; rubber *, -neck * [U. S.].

445. Optical Instruments. — N. optical instruments; lens, meniscus, magnifier; micro-, mega-, tieno-scope; spectacles, glasses, barnacles, goggles, eyeglass, *pince-nez;* periscopic lens; telescope, glass, lorgnette, binocular; spy-, opera-, field-glass; burning glass, convex lens.

mirror, reflector, speculum; looking-, pier-, cheval-glass.

prism; camera-lucida, -obscura; magic lantern &c. *(show)* 448; stereopticon; chro-, thau-matrope; stereo-, pseudo-, poly-, kaleido-scope.

photo-, erio-, actino-, luci-, radio-meter; abdomino-, gastro-, helio-, polari-, polemo-, spectro-scope.

abdominoscopy; gastroscopy; microscop-y, -ist.

446. Visibility. — N. visibility, perceptibility; conspicuousness, distinctness &c. *adj.*; conspicuity; appearance &c. 448; bassetting; exposure; manifestation &c. 525; ocular -proof, – evidence, – demonstration; field of view &c. *(vision)* 441; periscopism.

V. be –, become- -visible &c. *adj.*; appear, open to the view; meet –, catch- the eye; basset; present –, show –, manifest –, produce –, discover –, reveal –, expose –, betray- itself; stand -forth, – out; materialize; show; arise; peep –, peer –, crop- out; start –, spring –, show –, turn –, crop- up; glimmer, loom; glare; burst forth; burst upon the -view, – sight; heave in sight; come -in sight, – into view, – out, – forth, – forward; see the light of day; break through the clouds; make its appearance, show its face, appear to one's eyes, come upon the stage, float before the eyes, speak for itself &c. *(manifest)* 525; attract the attention &c. 457; reappear; live in a glass house.

expose to view &c. 525.

447. Invisibility. — N. invisibility, invisibleness, nonappearance, imperceptibility; indistinctness &c. *adj.*; mystery, delitescence.

concealment &c. 528; latency &c. 526.

V. be -invisible &c. *adj.*; be hidden &c. *(hide)* 528; lurk &c. *(lie hidden)* 526; escape notice.

render -invisible &c. *adj.*; conceal &c. 528; put out of sight.

not see &c. *(be blind)* 442; lose sight of.

Adj. invisible, imperceptible; un-, in-discernible; un-, non-apparent; out of –, not in- sight; *à perte de vue;* behind the -scenes, – curtain; view-, sight-less; in-, un-conspicuous; unseen &c. *(see* see *&c.* 441); covert &c. *(latent)* 526; eclipsed, under an eclipse.

dim &c. *(faint)* 422; mysterious, dark, obscure, confused; indistin-ct, -guishable; shadowy, indefinite, undefined; ill-defined, -marked; blurred, fuzzy, out of focus; misty &c. *(opaque)* 426; veiled &c. *(concealed)* 528; delitescent.

Phr. "full many a flower is born to blush unseen" [Gray].

Adj. visible, perceptible, perceivable, discernible, apparent; in -view, - full view, - sight; exposed to view, *en évidence;* unclouded.

obvious &c. *(manifest)* 525; plain, clear, distinct, definite; well-defined, -marked; in focus; recognizable, palpable, autoptical; glaring, staring, conspicuous; stereoscopic; in -bold, - strong- relief.

periscopic, panoramic.

before -, under- one's eyes; before one, *à vue d'œil*, in one's eye, *oculis subjecta fidelibus*.

Adv. visibly &c. *adj.*; in sight of; before one's eyes &c. *adj.*; *veluti in speculum*.

---

448. Appearance. — N. appearance, phenomenon, sight, spectacle, show, premonstration †, scene, species, view, *coup d'œil;* lookout, outlook, prospect, vista, perspective, bird's-eye view, scenery, landscape, picture, tableau; display, exposure, *mise en scène;* rising of the curtain.

phant-asm, -om &c. *(fallacy of vision)* 443.

pageant, spectacle; peep-, raree-, gallanty-show; *ombres chinoises;* magic lantern, phantasmagoria, dissolving views; biograph, cinematograph, moving pictures; pan-, di-, cosm-, ge-orama; *coup -, jeu- de théâtre;* pageantry &c. *(ostentation)* 882; insignia &c. *(indication)* 550.

aspect, angle, phase, phasis, seeming; shape &c. *(form)* 240; guise, look, complexion, color, image, mien, air, cast, carriage, port, demeanor; presence, expression, first blush, face of the thing; point of view, light.

lineament, feature, trait, lines; out-line, -side; contour, face, countenance, physiognomy, visage, phiz, cast of countenance, profile, *tournure*, cut of one's jib, metoposcopy; outside &c. 220.

V. appear; be -, become- visible &c. 446; seem, look, show; present -, wear -, carry -, have -, bear -, exhibit -, take -, take on -, assume- the -appearance, - semblance- of; look like; cut a figure, figure; present to the view; show &c. *(make manifest)* 525.

Adj. apparent, seeming, ostensible; on view.

Adv. apparently; to all -seeming, - appearance; ostensibly, seemingly, as it seems, on the face of it, *primâ facie;* at the first blush, at first sight; in the eyes of; to the eye.

Phr. *editio princeps.*

449. Disappearance. — N. disappearance, evanescence, eclipse, occultation.

departure &c. 293; exit; vanishing point; dissolving views.

V. disappear, vanish, dissolve, fade, melt away, pass, go, avaunt; be -gone &c. *adj.*; leave -no trace, - " not a rack behind " [*Tempest*]; go off the stage &c. *(depart)* 293; suffer -, undergo- an eclipse; retire from sight; be lost to view, pass out of sight.

lose sight of.

efface &c. 552.

Adj. disappearing &c. *v.*; evanescent; missing, lost; lost to -sight, - view; gone.

Int. vanish! disappear!. avaunt! &c. *(ejection)* 297.

CLASS IV

Words relating to the INTELLECTUAL FACULTIES

Division (I) FORMATION OF IDEAS

Section I. Operations of Intellect in General

450. Intellect. — N. intellect, mind, understanding, reason, thinking principle; rationality; cogitative –, cognitive –, discursive –, reasoning –, intellectual-faculties; faculties, senses, consciousness, observation, percipience, intelligence, intellection, intuition, association of ideas, instinct, conception, judgment, wits, parts, capacity, intellectuality, genius; brains, cognitive –, intellectual- powers; wit &c. 498; ability &c. (*skill*) 698; wisdom &c. 498; *Vernunft, Verstand.*

soul, spirit, ghost, inner man, heart, breast, bosom, *penetralia mentis, divina particula auræ,* heart's core; the Absolute, psyche, subliminal consciousness, supreme principle.

organ –, seat- of thought; sensorium, sensory, brain; head, -piece; pate, noddle, skull, scull, pericranium, cerebrum, cranium, brainpan, sconce, upper story.

[Science of mind] metaphysics; psych-ics, -ology; ideology; mental –, moral- philosophy; philosophy of the mind; pneumat-, phren-ology; craniology, -scopy.

ideal-ity, -ism; transcendental-, spiritual-ism; immateriality &c. 317; universal -concept, – conception.

metaphysician, psychologist &c.

V. note, notice, mark; take -notice, – cognizance- of; be -aware, – conscious- of; realize; appreciate; ruminate &c. (*think*) 451; fancy &c. (*imagine*) 515.

Adj. [Relating to intellect] intellectual, mental, rational, subjective, metaphysical, noöscopic, spiritual; ghostly; psych-ical, -ological; cerebral; animastic; brainy; hyper-, super-physical; subconscious, subliminal.

immaterial &c. 317; endowed with reason.

Adv. *in petto.*

Phr. *ens rationis; frons est animi janua* [Cicero]; *locos y niños dicen la verdad; mens sola loco non exulat* [Ovid]; " my mind is my kingdom " [Campbell]; " stern men with empires in their brains " [Lowell]; " the mind, the music breathing from her face " [Byron]; " thou living ray of intellectual Fire " [Falconer].

450a. Absence or want **of Intellect.** — **N.** absence –, want- of -intellect &c. 450; imbecility &c. 499; brutality; brute -instinct, – force.

Adj. unendowed with –, void of- reason.

---

451. Thought. — N. thought; exercitation –, exercise- of the intellect; intellection; reflection, cogitation, consideration, meditation, study, lucubration, speculation, deliberation, pondering; head-, brain-work; cerebration; deep reflection; close study, application &c. (*attention*) 457.

452. [Absence or want of thought.] Incogitancy. — N. incogitancy, vacancy, inunderstanding; fatuity &c. 499; thoughtlessness &c. (*inattention*) 458; vacuity.

V. not -think &c. 451; not think of; dismiss from the -mind, – thoughts &c. 451.

abstract thought, abstraction, contemplation, musing; brown study &c. (*inattention*) 458; reverie, Platonism; depth of thought, workings of the mind, thoughts, inmost thoughts; self-counsel, -communing, -consultation; philosophy of the -Absolute, – Academy, – Garden, Lyceum, – Porch.

association –, succession –, flow –, train –, current- of -thought, – ideas.

after –, mature- thought; reconsideration, second thoughts; retrospection &c. (*memory*) 505; excogitation; examination &c. (*inquiry*) 461; invention &c. (*imagination*) 515.

thoughtfulness &c. *adj*.

V. think, reflect, cogitate, excogitate, consider, deliberate; bestow -thought, – consideration -upon; speculate, contemplate, meditate, ponder, muse, dream, ruminate; brood –, con- over; animadvert, study; bend –, apply- the mind &c. (*attend*) 457; digest, discuss, hammer at, weigh, perpend; realize, appreciate; fancy &c. (*imagine*) 515; trow.

take into consideration; take counsel &c. (*be advised*) 695; commune with –, bethink- oneself; collect one's thoughts; revolve –, turn over –, run over- in the mind; chew the cud –, sleep- upon; take counsel of –, advise with- one's pillow.

rack –, ransack –, crack –, beat –, cudgel- one's brains; set one's -brain, – wits- to work.

harbor –, entertain –, cherish –, nurture- an -idea &c. 453; take into one's head; bear in mind; reconsider.

occur; present –, suggest- itself; come –, get- into one's head; strike one, flit across the view, come uppermost, run in one's head; enter –, pass in –, cross –, flash on –, flash across –, float in –, fasten itself on –, be uppermost in –, occupy- the mind; have in one's mind.

make an impression; sink –, penetrate- into the mind; engross the thoughts.

Adj. thinking &c. *v.*; thoughtful, pensive, meditative, reflective, museful, wistful, contemplative, speculative, deliberative, studious, sedate, introspective, Platonic, philosophical.

lost in thought &c. (*inattentive*) 458; deep musing &c. (*intent*) 457.

in the mind, under consideration.

Adv. all things considered.

Phr. the mind being on the stretch; the -mind, – head- -turning, – running- upon; " divinely bent to meditation " [*Rich. III*]; *en toute chose il faut considérer la fin;* " fresh-pluckt from bowers of never-failing thought " [O. Meredith]; " go speed the stars of Thought " [Emerson]; " in maiden meditation fancy-free " [*M. N. D.*]; " so sweet is zealous contemplation " [*Rich. III*]; " the power of Thought is the magic of the Mind " [Byron]; " those that think must govern those that toil " [Goldsmith]; " thought is parent of the deed " [Carlyle]; " thoughts in attitudes imperious " [Longfellow]; " thoughts that breathe and words that burn " [Gray]; *vivere est cogitare* [Cicero]; *Volk der Dichter und Denker.*

indulge in reverie &c. (*be inattentive*) 458.

put away thought; unbend –, relax –, divert- the mind.

Adj. vacant, unintellectual, unideal, unoccupied, unthinking, inconsiderate, thoughtless; absent &c. (*inattentive*) 458; diverted; irrational &c. 499; narrow-minded &c. 481.

un-thought of, -dreamt of, -considered; off one's mind; incogitable, not to be thought of.

Phr. absence d'esprit; pabulum pictura pascit inani.

---

453. [Object of thought.] **Idea.** — **N.** idea, notion, conception, thought, apprehension, impression, perception, image, εἴδωλον, sentiment, reflection, observation, consideration; abstract idea; archetype, formative notion; guiding –, organizing- conception; image in the mind, regulative principle.

view &c. (*opinion*) 484; theory &c.

454. [Subject of thought, νοήματα.] **Topic.** — **N.** subject of –, material for- thought; food for the mind, mental pabulum.

subject, -matter; matter, theme, νοήματα, topic, what it is about, thesis, text, business, affair, matter in hand, argument; motion, resolution; head, chapter; case, point; proposition, theorem; field

514; conceit, fancy; phantasy &c. (*imagination*) 515.

point of view &c. (*aspect*) 448; field of view.

Adv. under consideration; in -question, – the mind; on -foot, – the carpet, – the docket, – the *tapis;* relative to &c. 9.

of inquiry; moot point, problem &c. (*question*) 461.

V. float –, pass- in the mind &c. 451.

Adj. thought of; uppermost in the mind; *in petto.*

Section II. Precursory Conditions and Operations

455. [The desire of knowledge.] **Curiosity.** — **N.** interest, thirst for knowledge; curi-osity, -ousness; inquiring mind; inquisitiveness.

sight-seer, quidnunc, newsmonger, Paul Pry, eavesdropper; gossip &c. (*news*) 532; rubberneck * [U. S.].

V. be -curious &c. *adj.*; take an interest in, stare, gape; prick up the ears, see sights, lionize; pry; nose; rubber *, -neck * [U. S.].

Adj. curious, inquisitive, burning with curiosity, overcurious; inquiring &c. 461; prying; inquisitorial; agape &c. (*expectant*) 507.

Phr. what's the matter? what next?

456. [Absence of curiosity.] **Incuriosity.** — **N.** incuriosity; incuriousness &c. *adj.*; insouciance &c. 866; indifference.

V. be -incurious &c. *adj.*; have no -curiosity &c. 455; take no interest in &c. 823; mind one's own business.

Adj. incurious, uninquisitive, indifferent; impassive &c. 823; uninterested.

457. Attention. — **N.** attention; mindfulness &c. *adj.*; intent-ness, -iveness; alertness; thought &c. 451; adverten-ce, -cy; observ-ance, -ation; consideration, reflection, perpension †; heed; heedfulness; particularity; notice, regard &c. *v.*; circumspection &c. (*care*) 459; study, scrutiny; in-, intro-spection; revis-ion, -al.

active –, diligent –, exclusive –, minute –, close –, intense –, deep –, profound –, abstract –, labored –, deliberate- -thought, – attention, – application, – study.

minuteness, attention to detail.

absorption of mind &c. (*abstraction*) 458.

indication, calling attention to &c. *v.*

V. be -attentive &c. *adj.*; attend, advert to, observe, look, see, view, remark, notice, regard, take notice, mark; give –, pay- -attention, – heed- to; incline –, lend- an ear to; trouble one's head about; give a thought –, animadvert- to; occupy oneself with; contemplate &c. (*think of*) 451; look -at, – to, – after, – into, – over; see to; turn –, bend –, apply –, direct –, give- the -mind, – eye, – attention -to; have -an eye to, – in one's eye; bear in mind; take into -account, – consideration; keep in -sight, – view; have

458. Inattention. — **N.** in-attention, -consideration; inconsiderateness &c. *adj.*; oversight; inadverten-ce, -cy; nonobservance, disregard.

supineness &c. (*inactivity*) 683; *étourderie;* want of thought; heedlessness &c. (*neglect*) 460; insouciance &c. (*indifference*) 866.

abstraction; absence –, absorption- of mind; preoccupation, distraction, reverie, brown study, deep musing, fit of abstraction.

V. be -inattentive &c. *adj.*; overlook, disregard; pass by &c. (*neglect*) 460; not -observe &c. 457; think little of.

close –, shut- one's eyes to; pay no attention to; dismiss –, discard –, discharge- from one's -thoughts, – mind; drop the subject, think no more of; set –, turn –, put- aside; turn -away from, – one's attention from, – a deaf ear to, – one's back upon.

abstract oneself, dream, indulge in reverie.

escape -notice, – attention; come in at one ear and go out at the other; forget &c. (*have no remembrance*) 506.

call off –, draw off –, call away –, divert –, distract- the -attention, – thoughts, – mind; put out of one's head; dis-concert, -compose; put out, confuse,

regard to, heed, mind, take cognizance of, entertain, recognize; make –, take-note of; note.

examine cursorily; glance -at, – upon, – over; cast –, pass- the eyes over; run over, turn over the leaves, dip into, per-stringe †; skim &c. (*neglect*) 460; take a cursory view of.

examine, – closely, – intently; scan, scrutinize, consider; give –, bend- one's mind to; overhaul, revise, pore over; inspect, review, pass under review; take stock of; fix –, rivet –, devote- the -eye, – mind, – thoughts, – attention- on *or* to; hear –, think- out; mind one's business.

revert to; watch &c. (*expect*) 507, (*take care of*) 459; hearken –, listen- to; prick up the ears; have –, keep- the eyes open; come to the point.

meet with attention; fall under one's -notice, – observation; be -under consideration &c. (*topic*) 454.

catch –, strike- the eye; attract notice; catch –, awaken –, wake –, invite –, solicit –, attract –, claim –, excite –, engage –, occupy –, strike –, arrest –, fix –, engross –, absorb –, rivet- the -attention, – mind, – thoughts; be -present to, – uppermost in- the mind.

bring under one's notice; point -out, – to, – at, – the finger at; lay the finger on, indigitate †, indicate; direct –, call-attention to; show; put a -mark &c. (*sign*) 550- upon; call soldiers to " attention "; bring forward &c. (*make manifest*) 525.

Adj. attentive, mindful, observant, regardful; alive –, awake- to; observing &c. *v.*; alert; taken up –, occupied- with; engaged –, engrossed –, wrapped-in; absorbed, rapt; breathless; preoccupied &c. (*inattentive*) 458; watchful &c. (*careful*) 459; intent on, open-eyed; breathless, undistracted, upon the stretch; on the watch &c. (*expectant*) 507.

steadfast.

Int. see! look, – here, – you, – to it! mark! lo! behold! soho! hark, – ye! mind! halloo! observe! lo and behold! attention! *nota bene;* N.B.; *, †; I'd have you to know; notice! O yes! *Oyez! dekko! ecco!* yoho!

Phr. this is –, these are- to give notice; *dictum sapienti sat est; finem respice.*

perplex, bewilder, moider, fluster, muddle, dazzle; throw a sop to Cerberus.

Adj. inattentive; un-observant, -mindful, -heeding, -discerning; inadvertent; mind-, regard-, respect-less; listless &c. (*indifferent*) 866; blind, deaf; bird-witted; hand over head; cur-, percur-sory; giddy-, scatter-, hare-brained; unreflecting, *écervelé*, inconsiderate, offhand, thoughtless, dizzy, muzzy, brainsick; giddy, – as a goose; wild, harum-scarum, rantipole, high-flying; heed-, care-less &c. (*neglectful*) 460.

absent, abstracted, *distrait;* absent-minded, lost; lost –, wrapped- in thought; rapt, in the clouds, bemused; dreaming –, musing- on other things; preoccupied, engrossed &c. (*attentive*) 457; in a -reverie &c. *n.*; off one's guard &c. (*inexpectant*) 508; napping; dreamy; caught napping.

disconcerted, put out &c. *v.*

Adv. inattentively, inadvertently &c. *adj.; per incuriam, sub silentio.*

Int. stand -at ease, – easy!

Phr. the attention wanders; one's wits gone a -woolgathering, – bird's nesting; it never entered into one's head; the mind running on other things; one's thoughts being elsewhere; had it been a bear it would have bitten you.

---

459. Care. — [Vigilance.] — **N.** care, solicitude, heed; heedfulness &c. *adj.;* scruple &c. (*conscientiousness*) 939.

watchfulness &c. *adj.;* vigilance, *surveillance,* eyes of Argus, watch, vigil, look out, watch and ward, *l'œil du maître.*

alertness &c. (*activity*) 682; attention &c. 457; prudence &c., circumspection &c. (*caution*) 864; anxiety; forethought &c. 510; precaution &c. (*preparation*) 673; tidiness &c. (*order*) 58, (*cleanliness*)

460. Neglect. — **N.** neglect; carelessness &c. *adj.;* trifling &c. *v.;* negligence; omission, laches, default; supineness &c. (*inactivity*) 683; inattention &c. 458; nonchalance &c. (*insensibility*) 823; imprudence, recklessness &c. 863; slovenliness &c. (*disorder*) 59, (*dirt*) 653; improvidence &c. 674; noncompletion &c. 730; inexactness &c. (*error*) 495.

paraleipsis [in rhetoric].

trifler, waiter on Providence; Micawber.

652; accuracy &c. (*exactness*) 494; minuteness, attention to detail.

V. be -careful &c. *adj.*; reck; take care &c. (*be cautious*) 864; pay attention to &c. 457; take care of; look -, see- -to, - after; keep -an eye, - a sharp eye- upon; chaperon, matronize, play goose- berry; keep -watch, - watch and ward; mount guard, set watch, watch; keep in -sight, - view; mind, - one's busi- ness.

look -sharp, - about one; look with one's own eyes; keep a -good, - sharp- lookout; have all one's -wits, - eyes- about one; watch for &c. (*expect*) 507; keep one's eyes -, have the eyes -, sleep with one eye- open.

take precautions &c. 673; protect &c. (*render safe*) 664.

do one's best &c. 682; mind one's Ps and Qs, speak by the card, pick one's steps.

Adj. care-, regard-, heed-ful; taking care &c. *v.*; particular; prudent &c. (*cautious*) 864; considerate; thoughtful &c. (*deliberative*) 451; provident &c. (*prepared*) 673; alert &c. (*active*) 682; sure-footed.

guarded, on one's guard; on the -*qui vive*, - alert, - watch, - look out; awake, broad awake, vigilant; watch-, wake-, wist-ful; Argus-eyed; wide awake &c. (*intelligent*) 498; on the watch for &c. (*expectant*) 507.

tidy &c. (*orderly*) 58, (*clean*) 652; accurate &c. (*exact*) 494; scrupulous &c. (*conscientious*) 939; *cavendo tutus* &c. (*safe*) 664.

Adv. carefully &c. *adj.*; with care, gingerly.

Phr. *quis custodiet istos custodes?* "care will kill a cat" [Wither]; *ni bebas agua que no veas;* "O polished perturbation! golden care!" [*Henry IV.*]; "the incessant care and labor of his mind" [*Henry IV.*].

V. be -negligent &c. *adj.*; take no care of &c. (take care of &c. 459); neg- lect; let -slip, - go; lay -, set -, cast -, put- aside; keep -, leave- out of sight; lose sight of.

overlook, disregard; pass -over, - by; let pass; blink; wink -, connive- at; gloss over; take no -note, - notice, - thought, - account- of; pay no regard to; *laisser aller.*

scamp; trifle, fribble; do by halves; cut; slight &c. (*despise*) 930; play -, trifle- with; slur; skim, - the surface; *effleurer;* take a cursory view of &c. 457.

slur -, slip -, skip -, jump- over; pre- termit, miss, skip, jump, omit, give the go-by to, push aside, pigeonhole, throw into the background, shelve, sink; ig- nore, shut one's eyes to, refuse to hear, turn a deaf ear to; leave out of one's calculation; not -attend to &c. 457, - mind; not trouble -oneself, - one's head- -with, - about; forget &c. 506; be caught napping &c. (*not expect*) 508; leave a loose thread; let the grass grow under one's feet.

render -neglectful &c. *adj.*; put -, throw- off one's guard.

Adj. neglecting &c. *v.*; unmindful, negligent, neglectful; heedless, careless, thoughtless; perfunctory, remiss.

inconsiderate; un-, in-circumspect; off one's guard; un-wary, -watchful, -guarded; offhand.

supine &c. (*inactive*) 683; inattentive &c. 458; insouciant &c. (*indifferent*) 823; imprudent, reckless &c. 863; slovenly &c. (*disorderly*) 59, (*dirty*) 653; inexact &c. (*erroneous*) 495; improvident &c. 674.

neglected &c. *v.*; un-heeded, -cared for, -perceived, -seen, -observed, -no- ticed, -noted, -marked, -attended to, -thought of, -regarded, -remarked, -missed; shunted, shelved.

un-examined, -studied, -searched, -scanned, -weighed, -sifted, -explored. abandoned; buried in a napkin, hid under a bushel.

Adv. negligently &c. *adj.*; hand over head, anyhow; in an unguarded moment &c. (*unexpectedly*) 508; *per incuriam.*

Int. never mind, no matter, let it pass.

---

461. Inquiry. [Subject of Inquiry. Question.] — **N.** inquiry; request &c. 765; search, research, quest; pursuit &c. 622.

462. Answer. — **N.** answer, response, reply, replication, riposte, rejoinder, surrejoinder, rebutter, surrebutter, re- tort, repartee; rescript, -ion; antiphon,

examination, review, scrutiny, investigation, indagation †; per-quisition, -scrutation, -vestigation †; inqu-est, -isition; exploration; exploitation, ventilation.

sifting; calculation, analysis, dissection, resolution, induction; Baconian method.

strict -, close -, searching -, exhaustive- inquiry; narrow -, strict- search; study &c. (*consideration*) 451.

scire facias, ad referendum; trial.

questioning &c. *v.;* interroga-tion, -tory; interpellation; challenge, examination, cross-examination, catechism; feeler, Socratic method, zetetic philosophy; leading question; discussion &c. (*reasoning*) 476.

reconnoitering, reconnaissance; prying &c. *v.;* espionage, *espionnage;* domiciliary visit, peep behind the curtain; lantern of Diogenes.

-y; acknowledgment; password; echo; counter statement.

discovery &c. 480*a;* solution &c. (*explanation*) 522; rationale &c. (*cause*) 153; clue &c. (*indication*) 550.

Œdipus; oracle &c. 513; return &c. (*record*) 551.

V. answer, respond, reply, rebut, retort, rejoin; give -, return for- answer; acknowledge, echo.

explain &c. (*interpret*) 522; solve &c. (*unriddle*) 522; discover &c. 480*a;* fathom, hunt out &c. (*inquire*) 461; satisfy, set at rest, determine.

Adj. answering &c. *v.;* respon-sive, -dent; conclusive.

Adv. because &c. (*cause*) 153; on the -scent, - right scent.

Int. eureka!

question, query, problem, desideratum, point to be solved, porism; subject -, field- of -inquiry, - controversy; point -, matter- in dispute; moot point; issue, question at issue; bone of contention &c. (*discord*) 713; plain -, fair -, open- question; enigma &c. (*secret*) 533; knotty point &c. (*difficulty*) 704; *quodlibet;* threshold of an inquiry.

inquirer, investigator, inquisitor, inspector, querist, examiner, catechist; scrut-ator, -ineer, -inizer; analyst; quidnunc &c. (*curiosity*) 455.

V. make -inquiry &c. *n.;* inquire, seek, search; look -for, - about for, - out for; scan, reconnoiter, explore, sound, rummage, ransack, pry, peer, look round; look -, go- -over, - through; spy, overhaul.

scratch the head, slap the forehead.

look -, peer -, pry- into every hole and corner; nose; trace up; hunt -, fish -, ferret- out; unearth; leave no stone unturned.

seek a -clue, - clew; hunt, track, trail, mouse, dodge, trace; follow the -trail, - scent; pursue &c. 662; beat up one's quarters; fish for; feel for &c. (*experiment*) 463.

investigate; take up -, institute -, pursue -, follow up -, conduct -, carry on -, prosecute- -an inquiry &c. *n.;* look -at, - into; preëxamine; discuss, canvass, agitate.

examine, study, consider, calculate; dip-, dive -, delve -, go deep- into; make sure of, probe, sound, fathom; probe to the -bottom, - quick; scrutinize, analyze, anatomize, dissect, parse, resolve, sift, winnow; view -, try- in all its phases; thresh out.

bring in question, subject to examination; put to the proof &c. (*experiment*) 463; audit, tax, pass in review; take into consideration &c. (*think over*) 451; take counsel &c. 695.

ask, question, demand; put -, pop -, propose -, propound -, moot -, start -, raise -, stir -, suggest -, put forth -, ventilate -, grapple with -, go into- a question.

put to the question, interrogate, catechize, pump; cross-question, -examine; dodge; require an answer; pick -, suck- the brains of; feel the pulse.

be -in question &c. *adj.;* undergo examination.

Adj. inquiry &c. *v.;* inquisitive &c. (*curious*) 455; requisit-ive †, -ory; catechetical, inquisitorial, analytic; in -search, - quest- of; on the lookout for, interrogative, zetetic; all-searching.

un-determined, -tried, -decided; in -question, - dispute, - issue, - course

of inquiry; under -discussion, – consideration, – investigation &c. *n.*; *sub judice*, moot, proposed; doubtful &c. (*uncertain*) 475.

Adv. what? why? wherefore? whence? whither? where? *quære?* how -comes, – happens, – is- it? what is the reason? what's -the matter, – in the wind? what on earth? when? who? *nicht wahr?*

463. Experiment. — N. experiment; essay &c. (*attempt*) 675; analysis &c. (*investigation*) 461; trial, tentative method, *tâtonnement*.

verification, probation, *experimentum crucis*, proof, criterion, diagnostic, test, crucial test.

crucible, reagent, check, touchstone, pix; assay, ordeal; ring; curcuma –, turmeric- paper.

empiricism, rule of thumb.

feeler; pilot –, messenger- balloon; pilot engine; scout; straw to show the wind.

speculation, random shot, leap in the dark.

analy-zer, -st; adventurer; experiment-er, -ist, -alist.

V. experiment; essay &c. (*endeavor*) 675; try, assay; make -an experiment, – trial of; give a trial to; put upon –, subject to- trial; experiment upon; rehearse; put –, bring –, submit- to the -test, – proof; prove, verify, test, touch, practice upon, try one's strength.

grope; feel –, grope- -for, – one's way; fumble, *tâtonner, aller à tâtons;* put –, throw- out a feeler; send up a pilot balloon; see how the -land lies, – wind blows; consult the barometer; feel the pulse; fish –, bob- for; cast –, beat- about for; angle, trawl, cast one's net, beat the bushes.

try one's fortune &c. (*adventure*) 675; explore &c. (*inquire*) 461.

Adj. experimental; probat-ive, -ory, -ionary; analytic, docimastic; tentative; empirical.

under probation, on one's trial.

464. Comparison. — N. comparison, collation, contrast; identification; comparative –, relative- estimate.

sim-ile, -ilitude; allegory &c. (*metaphor*) 521.

V. compare -to, – with; collate, confront; place side by side &c. (*near*) 197; set –, pit- against one another; contrast, balance.

identify, draw a parallel, parallel.

compare notes; institute a comparison; *parva componere magnis.*

Adj. comparative; metaphorical &c. 521.

compared with &c. *v.*; comparable; judged by comparison.

Adv. relatively &c. (*relation*) 9; as compared with &c. *v.*

Phr. comparisons are odious; " comparisons are odorous " [*Much Ado*].

465. Discrimination. — N. discrimination, distinction, differentiation, diagnosis, diorism; nice perception; perception –, appreciation- of difference; estimation &c. 466; nicety, refinement; taste &c. 850; critique, judgment; tact; discernment &c. (*intelligence*) 498; acuteness, penetration; *nuances.*

dope *, past performances.

V. discriminate, distinguish, severalize; separate; draw the line, sift; separate –, winnow- the chaff from the wheat; split hairs.

estimate &c. (*measure*) 466; know -which is which, – what is what, – " a hawk from a handsaw " [*Hamlet*].

take into -account, – consideration; give –, allow- due weight to; weigh carefully.

465a. Indiscrimination. — N. indiscrimination; indistinct-ness, -ion; uncertainty &c. (*doubt*) 475.

V. not -discriminate &c. 465; overlook &c. (*neglect*) 460- a distinction; con-found, -fuse.

Adj. indiscriminate; undistinguish-ed, -able; unmeasured; promiscuous, undiscriminating.

Phr. *valeat quantum valere potest.*

Adj. discriminating &c. *v.*; dioristic, discriminative, distinctive; nice.

Phr. *il y a fagots et fagots; rem acu tetigisti; la critique est aisée et l'art est difficile.*

466. Measurement. — N.

measurement, admeasurement, mensuration, survey, valuation, appraisement, assessment, assize; estim-ate, -ation; dead reckoning; reckoning &c. (*numeration*) 85; gauging &c. *v.*; horse power.

metrology, weights and measures, compound arithmetic.

measure, yard measure, standard, rule, foot rule, compass, calipers; gage, gauge; meter, line, rod, check; dividers; velo.

flood –, high water- mark; index &c. 550.

scale; gradu-ation, -ated scale; nonius; vernier &c. (*minuteness*) 193; batho-, galvano-, helio-, interfero-, odo-, ombro-, panto-, pluvio-, pneumato-, pneumo-, radio-, refracto-, respiro-, rheo-, spiro-, tele-, udo-, vacuo-, vario-, via-, thermo(*heat* &c. 382)-, baro(*air* &c. 338)-, anemo(*wind* 349)-, dynamo-, gonio (*angle* 244)-meter; landmark &c. (*limit*) 233; balance &c. (*weight*) 319; mari-, pneumato-, stetho-graph; rain gauge, rain gage.

coördinates, ordinate and abscissa, polar coördinates, latitude and longitude, declination and right ascension, altitude and azimuth.

geo-, stereo-, hypso-metry; metage; surveying, land surveying; geo-desy, -detics, -desia; ortho-, alti-metry; cadastre.

astrolabe, armillary sphere.

land surveyor; geometer.

V. measure, mete; value, assess, rate, appraise, estimate, form an estimate, set a value on; appreciate; standardize.

span, pace, step; apply the -compass &c. *n.*; gauge, plumb, probe, sound, fathom; heave the -log, – lead; survey.

take an average &c. 29; graduate.

Adj. measuring &c. *v.*; metric, -al; measurable; geodetical.

Section III. Materials for Reasoning

467. Evidence [On one side.] — N.

evidence; facts, premises, data, *præcognita*, grounds.

indication &c. 550; criterion &c. (*test*) 463.

testi-mony, -fication; attestation; deposition &c. (*affirmation*) 535; examination.

admission &c. (*assent*) 488; authority, warrant, credential, diploma, voucher, certificate, doquet, docket; *testamur;* record &c. 551; document; *pièce justificative;* deed, warranty &c. (*security*) 771; signature, seal &c. (*identification*) 550; exhibit.

witness, indicator; eye-, ear-witness; deponent; sponsor; cojuror.

oral –, documentary –, hearsay –, external –, extrinsic –, internal —, intrinsic –, circumstantial –, cumulative –, *ex parte* –, presumptive –, collateral –, constructive- evidence; proof &c. (*demonstration*) 478; evidence in chief.

secondary evidence; confirmation, corroboration, support; ratification &c. (*as-*

468. [Evidence on the other side, on the other hand.] Counter Evidence. —

N. counter evidence; evidence on the other -side, – hand; disproof; refutation &c. 479; negation &c. 536; conflicting evidence.

plea &c. 617; vindication &c. 937; counter protest; *tu quoque* argument; other side –, reverse- of the shield.

V. countervail, oppose; rebut &c. (*refute*) 479; subvert &c. (*destroy*) 162; check, weaken; contravene; contradict &c. (*deny*) 536; tell another story, turn the scale, alter the case; turn the tables; cut both ways; prove a negative.

audire alteram partem.

Adj. countervailing &c. *v.*; contradictory.

un-attested, -authenticated, -supported by evidence; supposititious.

Adv. *per contra.*

469. Qualification. — N.

qualification, limitation, modification, coloring.

allowance, grains of allowance, con-

sent) 488; authentication; compurgation, wager of law, comprobation†.

citation, reference.

V. be -evidence &c. *n.*; evince, show, betoken, tell of; indicate &c. (*denote*) 550; imply, involve, argue, bespeak, breathe.

have –, carry- weight; tell, speak volumes; speak for itself &c. (*manifest*) 525.

rest –, depend- upon; repose on.

bear -witness &c. *n.*; give -evidence &c. *n.*; testify, depose, witness, vouch for; sign, seal, undersign, set one's hand and seal, sign and seal, deliver as one's act and deed, certify, attest; acknowledge &c. (*assent*) 488.

make absolute, confirm, ratify, corroborate, indorse, countersign, support, bear out, uphold, warrant.

adduce, attest, cite, quote; refer –, appeal- to; call, – to witness; bring -forward, – into court; allege, plead; produce –, confront- witnesses; collect –, bring together –, rake up- evidence.

have –, make out- a case; establish, authenticate, substantiate, verify, make good, quote chapter and verse; bring -home to, – to book.

Adj. showing &c. *v.*; indica-tive, -tory; deducible &c. 478; grounded –, founded –, based- on; corroborative, confirmatory.

Adv. by inference; according to, witness, *a fortiori;* still -more, – less; *raison de plus;* in corroboration &c. *n.* of; *valeat quantum;* under -seal, – one's hand and seal.

Phr. *dictum de dicto.*

sideration, extenuating circumstances; mitigation.

condition, proviso, exception; exemption; salvo, saving clause; discount &c. 813; restriction.

V. qualify, limit, modify, leaven, give a color to, introduce new conditions, narrow, temper.

allow –, make allowance- for; admit exceptions, take into account; modulate.

take exception.

Adj. qualifying &c. *v.*; conditional; exceptional &c. (*unconformable*) 83.

hypothetical &c. (*supposed*) 514; contingent &c. (*uncertain*) 475.

Adv. provided, – always; if, unless, but, yet; according as; conditionally, admitting, supposing; on the supposition of &c. (*theoretically*) 514; with the understanding, even, although, though, for all that, after all, at all events.

with grains of allowance, *cum grano salis; exceptis excipiendis;* wind and weather permitting; if possible &c. 470.

subject to; with this -proviso &c. *n.*

Degrees of Evidence

470. Possibility. — N. possibility, potentiality; what -may be, – is possible &c. *adj.*; compatibility &c. (*agreement*) 23.

practicability, feasibility; practicableness &c. *adj.*

contingency, chance &c. 156.

V. be -possible &c. *adj.*; stand a chance; admit of, bear.

render -possible &c. *adj.*; put in the way of.

Adj. possible; on the -cards, – dice; *in posse,* within the bounds of possibility, conceivable, credible; compatible &c. 23; likely.

practicable, feasible, performable, achievable; within -reach, – measurable distance; accessible, superable, surmountable; at-, ob-tainable; contingent &c. (*doubtful*) 475.

471. Impossibility. — N. impossibility &c. *adj.*; what -cannot, – can never- be; sour grapes; hopelessness &c. 859.

V. be -impossible &c. *adj.*; have no chance whatever.

attempt impossibilities; square the circle, wash a blackamoor white; skin a flint; make -a silk purse out of a sow's ear, – bricks without straw; have nothing to go upon; weave a rope of sand, build castles in the air, *prendre la lune avec les dents,* extract sunbeams from cucumbers, set the Thames on fire, milk a he-goat into a sieve, catch a weasel asleep, *rompre l'anguille au genou,* be in two places at once.

Adj. impossible; not -possible &c. 470; absurd, contrary to reason; unlikely; unreasonable &c. 477; incredible

Adv. possibly, by possibility; per-haps, -chance, -adventure; may be, haply, mayhap.

if possible, wind and weather permit-ting, God willing, *Deo volente*, D. V.; as luck may have it.

Phr. *misericordia Domini inter pontem et fontem;* "the glories of the Possible are ours" [B. Taylor].

&c. 485; beyond the bounds of -reason, – possibility; from which reason recoils; visionary; inconceivable &c. (*improb-able*) 473; prodigious &c. (*wonderful*) 870; un-, in-imaginable; unthinkable.

impracticable, unachievable; un-, in-feasible; insuperable; un-, in-surmount-able; unat-, unob-tainable; out of -reach, – the question; not to be -had, – thought of; beyond control; desperate &c. (*hope-less*) 859; incompatible &c. 24; inaccessible, uncomeatable, impassable, im-pervious, innavigable, inextricable; self-contradictory.

out of –, beyond- one's -power, – depth, – reach, – grasp; too much for; *ultra crepidam.*

Phr. the grapes are sour; *non possumus; non nostrum tantas componere lites* [Vergil]; *chercher une aiguille dans une botte de foin; il a le mer à boire.*

472. Probability. — N.
probability, likelihood; credibleness; likeliness &c. *adj.*

vraisemblance, verisimilitude, plausi-bility; color, semblance, show of; pre-sumption; presumptive –, circumstan-tial- evidence; credibility.

reasonable –, fair –, good –, favorable--chance, – prospect; prospect, well-grounded hope; chance &c. 156.

V. be -probable &c. *adj.*; give –, lend-color to; point to; imply &c. (*evidence*) 467; bid fair &c. (*promise*) 511; stand fair for; stand –, run- a good chance.

think likely, dare say, flatter one-self; expect &c. 507; count upon &c. (*believe*) 484.

473. Improbability. — N.
improb-ability, unlikelihood; unfavorable –, bad –, ghost of a –, little –, small –, poor –, scarcely any –, no- chance; bare possibility; long odds; incredibility &c. 485.

V. be -improbable &c. *adj.*; have a -small chance &c. *n.*

Adj. improbable, unlikely, contrary to all reasonable expectation.

rare &c. (*infrequent*) 137; unheard of, inconceivable; un-, in-imaginable; in-credible &c. 485; more than doubtful.

Phr. the chances are against; *aquila non capit muscas; pedir peras al olmo.*

Adj. probable, likely, hopeful, to be expected, in a fair way.

plausible, specious, ostensible, colorable, *ben trovato*, well-founded, reason-able, credible, easy of belief, presumable, presumptive, apparent.

Adv. probably &c. *adj.*; belike; in all -probability, – likelihood; very –, most- likely; like enough; ten &c. to one; apparently, seemingly, according to every reasonable expectation; *primâ facie;* to all appearance &c. (*to the eye*) 448.

Phr. the -chances, – odds- are; appearances –, chances- are in favor of; there is reason to -believe, – think, – expect; I dare say; all Lombard Street to a China orange.

474. Certainty. — N.
certainty; ne-cessity &c. 601; certitude, surety, as-surance; dead –, moral- certainty; in-fallibleness &c. *adj.*; infallibility, relia-bility; indubitableness, inevitableness, unquestionableness.

gospel, scripture, church, pope, court of final appeal; *res judicata*, ultimatum.

positiveness; dogmat-ism, -ist, -izer; doctrinaire, bigot, opinionist, Sir Oracle; *ipse dixit.*

fact; positive –, matter of- fact; *fait accompli.*

475. Uncertainty. — N.
uncertainty, incertitude, doubt; doubtfulness &c. *adj.*; dubi-ety, -tation, -tancy†, -ous-ness.

hesitation, suspense; perplexity, em-barrassment, dilemma, bewilderment; timidity &c. (*fear*) 860; vacillation &c. 605; diaporesis, indetermination.

vagueness &c. *adj.*; haze, fog; ob-scurity &c. (*darkness*) 421; ambiguity &c. (*double meaning*) 520; contingency, double contingency, possibility upon a possibility; open question &c. (*question*)

V. be -certain &c. *adj.*; stand to reason.

render -certain &c. *adj.*; in-, en-, assure; clinch, make sure; determine, decide, set at rest, " make assurance double sure " [*Macbeth*]; know &c. (*believe*) 484.

dogmatize, lay down the law.

Adj. certain, sure; assured &c. *v.*; solid, well-founded.

unqualified, absolute, positive, determinate, definite, clear, unequivocal, categorical, unmistakable, decisive, decided, ascertained.

inevitable, unavoidable, avoidless; ineluctable.

unerring, infallible; unchangeable &c. 150; to be depended on, trustworthy, reliable, bound.

un-impeachable, -deniable, -questionable; in-disputable, -contestable, -controvertible, -dubitable; irrefutable &c. (*proven*) 478; conclusive, without power of appeal.

indubious; without –, beyond a –, without a shade or shadow of- -doubt, – question; past dispute; clear as day; beyond all -question, – dispute; undoubted, -contested, -questioned, -disputed; question-, doubt-less.

authoritative, authentic, official.

sure as -fate, – death and taxes, – a gun.

evident, self-evident, axiomatic; clear, – as day, – as the sun at noonday.

Adv. certainly &c. *adj.*; for certain, certes, sure, no doubt, doubtless, and no mistake, *flagrante delicto*, sure enough, to be sure, of course, as a matter of course, *à coup sur*, to a certainty; in truth &c. (*truly*) 494; at -any rate, – all events; without fail; *coûte -que coûte, – qu'il coûte;* whatever may happen, if the worst come to the worst; come –, happen- what -may, – will; sink or swim; rain or shine.

Phr. *cela va sans dire;* there is -no question, – not a shadow of doubt; the die is cast &c. (*necessity*) 601; " facts are stubborn things " [Smollett].

461; *onus probandi;* blind bargain, pig in a poke, leap in the dark, something or other; needle in a bottle of hay; roving commission.

precariousness &c. *adj.*; fallibility.

V. be -uncertain &c. *adj.*; wonder whether.

lose the -clue, – clew, – scent; miss one's way.

not know -what to make of &c. (*unintelligibility*) 519, – which way to turn, – whether one stands on one's head or one's heels; float in a sea of doubt, hesitate, flounder; lose -oneself, – one's head; muddle one's brains.

render -uncertain &c. *adj.*; put out, pose, puzzle, perplex, embarrass; confuse, -found; bewilder, bother, moider, addle the wits, throw off the scent, *ambiguas in vulgus spargere voces;* keep in suspense.

doubt &c. (*disbelieve*) 485; hang –, tremble- in the balance; depend.

Adj. uncertain; casual; random &c. (*aimless*) 621; changeable &c. 149.

doubtful, dubious; indecisive; unsettled, -decided, -determined; in suspense, open to discussion; controvertible; in question &c. (*inquiry*) 461.

vague; in-determinate, -definite; ambiguous, equivocal; undefin-ed, -able; confused &c. (*indistinct*) 447; mystic, oracular; dazed.

perplexing &c. *v.*; enigmatic, paradoxical, apocryphal, problematical, hypothetical; experimental &c. 463.

fallible, questionable, precarious, slippery, ticklish, debatable, disputable; un-reliable, -trustworthy.

contingent, – on, dependent on; subject to; dependent on circumstances; occasional; provisional.

unauth-entic, -enticated, -oritative; un-ascertained, -confirmed; undemonstrated; un-told, -counted.

in a -state of uncertainty, – cloud, – maze; bushed, off the track; ignorant &c. 491; afraid to say; out of one's reckoning, astray, adrift; at -sea, – fault, – a loss, – one's wit's end, – a *nonplus;* puzzled &c. *v.*; lost, abroad, *désorienté;* dis-

tracted, -traught.

Adv. *pendente lite; sub spe rati.*

Phr. Heaven knows; who can tell? who shall decide when doctors disagree? *ambiguas in vulgum spargere voces.*

Section IV. Reasoning Processes

476. Reasoning. — **N.** reasoning; ratio-cination, -nalism; dialectics, induction, generalization.

discussion, comment; ventilation; inquiry &c. 461.

argumentation, controversy, debate; polemics, wrangling; contention &c. 720; logomachy; dis-putation, -ceptation; paper war.

art of reasoning, logic.

process –, train –, chain- of reasoning; de-, in-duction; synthesis, analysis.

argument; case, *plaidoyer*, opening; *lemma*, proposition, terms, premises, postulate, data, starting point, principle; inference &c. (*judgment*) 480.

pro-, syllogism; enthymeme, sorites, dilemma, *perilepsis*, *à priori* reasoning, *reductio ad absurdum*, horns of a dilemma, *argumentum ad hominem*, comprehensive argument; empirema, epagoge.

reasoner, logician, dialectician; disputant; controver-sialist, -tist; wrangler, arguer, debater, polemic, casuist, rationalist; scientist; eristic.

logical sequence; good case; correct –, just –, sound –, valid –, cogent –, logical –, forcible –, persuasive –, persuasory –, consectary † –, conclusive &c. 478 –, subtle- reasoning; force of argument; strong -point, – argument.

arguments, reasons, pros and cons.

V. reason, argue, discuss, debate, dispute, wrangle; argufy, bandy -words, – arguments; chop logic; hold –, carry on- an argument; controvert &c. (*deny*) 536; canvass; comment –, moralize- upon; spiritualize; consider &c. (*examine*) 461.

open a -discussion, – case; try conclusions; join –, be at- issue; moot; come to the point; stir –, agitate –, ventilate –, torture- a question; take up a -side, – case.

contend, take one's stand upon, insist, lay stress on; infer &c. 480.

follow from &c. (*demonstration*) 478.

Adj. reasoning &c. *v.*; rationalistic; argumentative, controversial, dialectic, polemical; discurs-ory, -ive; disputatious; Aristotelian, eristic, -al.

debatable, controvertible.

logical; relevant &c. 23.

Adv. for, because, hence, whence, seeing that, since, sith, then, thence, so; for -that, – this, – which- reason; for-,

477. [The absence of reasoning.] **Intuition.** [False or vicious reasoning; show of reason.] **Sophistry.** — **N.** intuition, instinct, association; presentiment; rule of thumb.

sophistry, paralogy, perversion, casuistry, jesuitry, equivocation, evasion; chicane, -ry; quiddet, quiddity; mystification; special pleading; speciousness &c. *adj.*; nonsense &c. 497; word-, tongue-fence.

false –, vicious- reasoning; *petitio principii, ignoratio elenchi; post hoc ergo propter hoc; non sequitur, ignotum per ignotius.*

misjudgment &c. 481; false teaching &c. 538.

sophism, solecism, paralogism; quibble, quirk, *elenchus*, elench, fallacy, *quodlibet*, subterfuge, subtlety, quillet; inconsistency, antilogy; " a delusion, a mockery, and a snare " [Denman]; claptrap, mere words; " lame and impotent conclusion " [*Othello*].

meshes –, cobwebs- of sophistry; flaw in an argument; weak point, bad case.

overrefinement; hairsplitting &c. *v.*

V. judge -intuitively, – by intuition; hazard a proposition, talk at random.

reason -ill, falsely &c. *adj.*; misjudge &c. 481; paralogize.

pervert, quibble; equivocate, mystify, evade, elude; gloss over, varnish; misteach &c. 538; mislead &c. (*error*) 495; cavil, refine, subtilize, split hairs; misrepresent &c. (*lie*) 544.

beg the question, reason in a circle, cut blocks with a razor, beat about the bush, play fast and loose, blow hot and cold, prove that black is white and white black, travel out of the record, *parler à tort et à travers*, put oneself out of court, not have a leg to stand on.

Adj. intuitive, instinctive, impulsive; independent of –, anterior to- reason; gratuitous, hazarded; unconnected.

unreasonable, illogical, false, unsound, invalid; unwarranted, not following; inconsequent, -ial; inconsistent; absonous †, -ant; unscientific; untenable, inconclusive, incorrect; fall-acious, -ible; groundless, unproved.

deceptive, sophistical, jesuitical; illusive, -ory; specious, hollow, plausible, *ad captandum*, evasive; irrelevant &c. 10.

inasmuch as; whereas, *ex concesso*, considering, in consideration of; there-, where-fore; consequently, *ergo*, thus, accordingly; *a fortiori*.

in -conclusion, – fine; finally, after all, *au bout du compte*, on the whole, taking one thing with another.

Phr. *ab actu ad posse valet consecutio: per troppo dibatter la verità si perde; troppo disputare la verità fa errare.*

478. Demonstration. — N.

demonstration, proof; conclusiveness &c. *adj.*; apodeixis, apodixis, probation, comprobation †.

logic of facts &c. (*evidence*) 467; *experimentum crucis* &c. (*test*) 463; argument &c. 476; rigorous –, absolute- establishment.

V. demonstrate, prove, establish, make good; show, evince &c. (*be evidence of*) 467; verify &c. 467; settle the question, reduce to demonstration, set the question at rest.

make out, – a case; prove one's point, have the best of the argument; draw a conclusion &c. (*judge*) 480.

follow, – of course; stand to reason; hold -good, – water.

Adj. demonstra-ting &c. *v.*, -tive, -ble; probative, unanswerable, conclusive; apodeictic, -al; irre-sistible, -futable, -fragable.

categorical, decisive, crucial.

demonstrated &c. *v.*; proven; un-confuted, -answered, -refuted; evident &c. 474.

deducible, consequential, consectary, inferential, following.

Adv. of course, in consequence, consequently, as a matter of course.

Phr. *probatum est;* there is nothing more to be said, Q.E.D., it must follow; *exitus acta probat.*

weak, feeble, poor, flimsy, loose, vague, irrational; nonsensical &c. (*absurd*) 497; foolish &c. (*imbecile*) 499; frivolous, pettifogging, quibbling; finespun, overrefined.

at the end of one's tether, *au bout de son latin.*

Adv. intuitively &c. *adj.*; by intuition; illogically &c. *adj.*

Phr. *non constat;* that goes for nothing.

479. Confutation. — N.

con-, refutation; answer, complete answer; disproof, conviction, redargution, invalidation; expos-ure, -ition; clincher; retort; *reductio ad absurdum;* knock down –, *tu quoque*- argument; sockdolager * [U. S.].

V. con-, re-fute; parry, negative, disprove, redargue, expose, show the fallacy of, rebut, defeat; demolish &c. (*destroy*) 162; over-throw, -turn; scatter to the winds, explode, invalidate; silence; put –, reduce- to silence; clinch -an argument, – a question; give one a setdown, stop the mouth, shut up; have, – on the hip.

not leave a leg to stand on, cut the ground from under one's feet.

be confuted &c.; fail; expose –, show- one's weak point.

Adj. confut-ing, -ed, &c. *v.*; capable of refutation; re-, con-futable.

condemned -on one's own showing, – out of one's own mouth.

Phr. the argument falls to the ground, *cadit quæstio*, it does not hold water, " *suo sibi gladio hunc jugulo* " [Terence].

Section V. RESULTS OF REASONING

480. Judgment. [Conclusion.] — N.

result, conclusion, upshot; deduction, inference, ergotism†, illation; corollary, porism; moral.

estimation, valuation, appreciation, judication; di-, ad-judication; arbitrament, -ement, -ation; assessment, ponderation; valorization.

award, estimate; review, criticism, critique, notice, report.

decision, determination, judgment, finding, verdict, sentence, decree; *res judicata.*

481. Misjudgment. — N.

misjudgment, obliquity of judgment; mis-calculation, -computation, -conception &c. (*error*) 495; hasty conclusion.

prejud-gment, -ication, -ice; foregone conclusion; pre-notion, -vention, -conception, -dilection, -possession, -apprehension, -sumption, -sentiment; fixed –, preconceived- idea; *idée fixe; mentis gratissimus error;* fool's paradise.

esprit de corps, party spirit, partisanship, clannishness, prestige.

bias, warp, twist; hobby, fad, quirk,

plebiscite, voice, casting vote; vote &c. (*choice*) 609; opinion &c. (*belief*) 484; good judgment &c. (*wisdom*) 498.

judge, umpire; arbi-ter, -trator; assessor, referee; censor, reviewer, critic; connoisseur; commentator &c. 524; inspector, inspecting officer.

V. judge, conclude; come to –, draw –, arrive at- a conclusion; ascertain, determine, make up one's mind.

deduce, derive, gather, collect, draw an inference, make a deduction, weet†, ween.

form an estimate, estimate, appreciate, value, count, assess, rate, rank, account; regard, consider, think of; look upon &c. (*believe*) 484; review; size up *.

settle; pass –, give- an opinion; decide, try, pronounce, rule; pass -judgment, – sentence; sentence, doom; find; give –, deliver- judgment; adjud-ge, -icate; arbitrate, award, report; bring in a verdict; make absolute, set a question at rest; confirm &c. (*assent*) 488.

comment, criticize; pass under review &c. (*examine*) 457; investigate &c. (*inquire*) 461.

hold the scales, sit in judgment; try –, hear- a cause.

Adj. judging &c. *v.*; judicious &c. (*wise*) 498; determinate, conclusive.

Adv. on the whole, all things considered.

Phr. " a Daniel come to judgment " [*Merchant of Venice*]; " and stand a critic, hated yet caress'd " [Byron]; " it is much easier to be critical than to be correct " [Disraeli]; *la critique est aisée et l'art est difficile;* " nothing if not critical" [*Othello*]; " O most lame and impotent conclusion " [*Othello*].

crotchet, partiality, infatuation, blind side, mote in the eye.

one-sided –, partial –, narrow –, confined –, superficial- -views, – ideas, – conceptions, – notions; narrow mind; bigotry &c. (*obstinacy*) 606; *odium theologicum;* pedantry; hypercriticism.

doctrinaire &c. (*positive*) 474.

V. mis-judge, -estimate, -think, -conjecture, -conceive &c. (*error*) 495; fly in the face of facts; mis-calculate, -reckon, -compute.

overestimate &c. 482; underestimate &c. 483.

pre-, fore-judge; pre-suppose, -sume, -judicate; dogmatize; have a -bias &c. *n.*; have only one idea; *jurare in verba magistri*, run away with the notion; jump –, rush- to a conclusion; look only at one side of the shield; view -with jaundiced eye, – through distorting spectacles; not see beyond one's nose; *dare pondus fumo;* get the wrong sow by the ear &c. (*blunder*) 699.

give a -bias, – twist; bias, warp, twist; pre-judice, -possess.

Adj. misjudging &c. *v.*; ill-judging, wrong-headed; prejudiced &c. *v.*; jaundiced; shortsighted, purblind; partial, one-sided, superficial.

narrow-minded, -souled; mean-spirited; confined, illiberal, intolerant, besotted, infatuated, fanatical, *entêté*, positive, dogmatic, conceited; opin-, opiniative; opinion-ed, -ate, -ative, -ated; self-opinioned, wedded to an opinion, *opiniâtre;* bigoted &c. (*obstinate*) 606; crotchety, fussy, impracticable; unreason-able, stupid &c. 499; credulous &c 486; warped.

---

misjudged &c. *v.*
Adv. *ex parte.*
Phr. nothing like leather; the wish the father to the thought.

480a. [Result of search or inquiry.] **Discovery.** — **N.** discovery, detection, disenchantment; ascertainment, disclosure, find, revelation.

trover &c. 775.

V. discover, find, determine, evolve; fix upon; find –, trace –, make –, hunt –, fish –, worm –, ferret –, root- out; fathom; bring –, draw- out; educe, elicit, bring to light; dig –, grub –, fish- up; unearth, disinter.

solve, resolve; un-riddle, -ravel, -lock; pick –, open- the lock; find a -clue, – clew- to; interpret &c. 522; disclose &c. 529.

trace, get at; hit it, have it; lay one's -finger, – hands- upon; spot; get –, arrive- at the -truth &c. 494; put the saddle on the right horse, hit the right nail on the head.

be near the truth, burn; smoke, scent, sniff, smell a rat.

open the eyes to; see -through, – daylight, – in its true colors, – the cloven foot; detect; catch, – tripping.

pitch '–, fall –, light –, hit –, stumble –, pop- upon; come across; meet –, fall in- with.

recognize, realize, verify, make certain of, identify.

Int. eureka!

482. Overestimation. — N. overestimation &c. *v.*; exaggeration &c. 549; vanity &c. 880; optim-, pessim-ism, -ist.

much -cry and little wool, – ado about nothing; storm in a teacup; fine talking.

V. over-estimate, -rate, -value, -prize, -weigh, -reckon, -strain, -praise; eulogize; estimate too highly, attach too much importance to, make mountains of molehills, catch at straws; strain, magnify; exaggerate &c. 549; set too high a value upon; think –, make- -much, – too much- of; outreckon; panegyrize.

extol, – to the skies; make the -most, – best, – worst- of; make two bites of a cherry.

have too high an opinion of oneself &c. (*vanity*) 880.

Adj. overestimated &c. *v.*; oversensitive &c. (*sensibility*) 822.

Phr. all his geese are swans; *parturiunt montes.*

483. Underestimation. — N. underestimation; depreciation &c. (*detraction*) 934; pessim-ism, -ist; undervaluing &c. *v.*; modesty &c. 881.

V. under-rate, -estimate, -value, -reckon; depreciate; disparage &c. (*detract*) 934; not do justice to; mis-, disprize; ridicule &c. 856; slight &c. (*despise*) 930; neglect &c. 460; slur over.

make -light, – little, – nothing, – no account- of; belittle; minimize, think nothing of; set -no store by, – at naught; shake off as dewdrops from the lion's mane.

Adj. depreciat-ing, -ed &c. *v.*; unvalued, -prized.

484. Belief. — N. belief; credence; credit; assurance; faith, trust, troth, confidence, presumption, sanguine expectation &c. (*hope*) 858; dependence on, reliance on.

persuasion, conviction, convincement, plerophory, self-conviction; certainty &c. 474; opinion, mind, view; conception, thinking; impression &c. (*idea*) 453; surmise &c. 514; conclusion &c. (*judgment*) 480.

tenet, dogma, principle, way of thinking; popular belief &c. (*assent*) 488.

firm –, implicit –, settled –, fixed –, rooted –, deep-rooted –, staunch –, unshaken –, steadfast –, inveterate –, calm –, sober –, dispassionate –, impartial –, well-founded- -belief,– opinion &c.; *uberrima fides.*

system of opinions, school, doctrine, articles, canons; article –, declaration –, profession- of faith; tenets, *credenda*, creed; thirty-nine articles &c. (*orthodoxy*) 983a; catechism; assent &c. 488; propaganda &c. (*teaching*) 537.

credibility &c. (*probability*) 472.

V. believe, credit; give -faith, – credit, – credence- to; see, realize; assume, receive; set down –, take- for; have –, take- it; consider, esteem, presume.

485. Unbelief. Doubt. — N. un-, dis-, mis-belief; discredit, miscreance; infidelity &c. (*irreligion*) 989; dissent &c. 489; change of -opinion &c. 484; retractation &c. 607.

doubt &c. (*uncertainty*) 475; skepticism, misgiving, demur; dis-, mis-trust; misdoubt, suspicion, jealousy, scruple, qualm; *onus probandi.*

incredib-ility, -leness; incredulity; unbeliever &c. 487.

V. dis-believe, -credit; not -believe &c. 484; misbelieve; refuse to admit &c. (*dissent*) 489; refuse to believe &c. (*incredulity*) 487.

doubt; be -doubtful &c. (*uncertain*) 475; doubt the truth of; be -skeptical as to &c. *adj.*; diffide †; dis-, mis-trust; suspect, smoke, scent, smell a rat; have –, harbor –, entertain- -doubts, – suspicions; have one's doubts.

demur, stick at, pause, hesitate, scruple; stop to consider, waver.

hang in -suspense, – doubt.

throw doubt upon, raise a question; bring –, call- in question; question, challenge; dispute; deny &c. 536; cavil; cause –, raise –, start –, suggest –, awake- a -doubt, – suspicion; ergotize.

count –, depend –, calculate –, pin one's faith –, reckon –, lean –, build –, rely –, rest- upon; lay one's account for; make sure of.

make oneself easy -about, – on that score; take on -trust, – credit; take for -granted, – gospel; allow –, attach- some weight to.

know, – for certain; have –, make- no doubt; doubt not; be –, rest- -assured &c. *adj.*; persuade –, assure –, satisfy- oneself; make up one's mind.

give one credit for; confide –, believe –, put one's trust- in; place –, repose- implicit confidence in; take -one's word for, – at one's word; place reliance on, rely upon, swear by, regard to.

think, hold; take, – it; opine, be of opinion, conceive, trow, ween, fancy, apprehend; have –, hold –, possess –, entertain –, adopt –, imbibe –, embrace –, get hold of –, hazard –, foster –, nur- ture –, cherish- -a belief, – an opinion &c. *n.*

view –, consider –, take –, hold –, conceive –, regard –, esteem –, deem –, look upon –, account –, set down- as; surmise &c. 514.

get –, take- it into one's head; come round to an opinion; swallow &c. (*credulity*) 486.

cause to -be believed &c. *v.*; satisfy, persuade, have the ear of, gain the con- fidence of, assure; con-vince, -vict, -vert; wean, bring round; bring –, win- over; indoctrinate &c. (*teach*) 537; cram down the throat; produce –, carry- conviction; bring –, drive- home to.

go down, find credence, pass current; be -received &c. *v.*, – current &c. *adj.*; possess –, take hold of –, take possession of- the mind.

Adj. believing &c. *v.*; certain, sure, assured, positive, cocksure, satisfied, confident, unhesitating, convinced, secure.

under the impression; impressed –, imbued –, penetrated- with.

confiding, suspectless †; unsusp-ecting, -icious; void of suspicion; credulous &c. 486; wedded to.

believed &c. *v.*; accredited, putative; unsuspected.

worthy of –, deserving of –, commanding- belief; credible, reliable, trust- worthy, to be depended on; satisfactory; probable &c. 472; fiduci-al, -ary; persuasive, impressive.

relating to belief, doctrinal.

Adv. in the -opinion, – eyes- of; *me judice;* me-seems, -thinks; to the best of one's belief; I -dare say, – doubt not, – have no doubt, – am sure; sure enough &c. (*certainty*) 474; depend –, rely- upon it; be –, rest- assured; I'll warrant you &c. (*affirmation*) 535.

Phr. *experto crede* [Vergil]; *fata viam invenient; Justitiæ soror incorrupta Fides;* " live to explain thy doctrine by thy life " [Prior]; " stands not within the prospect of belief " [*Macbeth*]; *tarde quæ credita lædunt credimus* [Ovid]; *vide et crede.*

startle, stagger; shake –, stagger- one's -faith, – belief.

Adj. unbelieving; incredulous –, skep- tical- as to; distrustful –, shy –, suspi- cious- of; doubting &c. *v.*

doubtful &c. (*uncertain*) 475; dispu- table; unworthy –, undeserving- of -belief &c. 484; questionable; sus-pect, -picious; open to -suspicion, – doubt; staggering, hard to believe, incredible, not to be believed, inconceivable.

fallible &c. (*uncertain*) 475; unde- monstrable; controvertible &c. (*untrue*) 495.

Adv. *cum grano salis;* with grains of allowance.

Phr. *fronti nulla fides; nimium ne crede colori* [Vergil]; " *timeo Danaos et dona ferentes* " [Vergil]; *credat Judæus Apella* [Horace]; let those be- lieve who may; *ad tristem partem strenua est suspicio* [Syrus].

---

486. Credulity. — N. credul-ity, -ousness &c. *adj.*; gull-, cull-ibility †; gross credulity, infatuation; self-delu- sion, -deception; superstition; one's blind side; bigotry &c. (*obstinacy*) 606;

487. Incredulity. — N. incredul-ous- ness, -ity; skepticism, pyrrhonism; want of faith &c. (*irreligion*) 989.

suspiciousness &c. *adj.*; scrupulosity; suspicion &c. (*unbelief*) 485.

hyperorthodoxy &c. 984; misjudgment &c. 481.

credulous person &c. (*dupe*) 547.

V. be -credulous &c. *adj.*; *jurare in verba magistri;* follow implicitly; swallow, gulp down; take on trust; take for -granted, – gospel; run away with -a notion, – an idea; jump –, rush- to a conclusion; think the moon is made of green cheese; take –, grasp- the shadow for the substance; catch at straws.

impose upon &c. (*deceive*) 545.

Adj. credulous, gullible; easily -deceived &c. 545; simple, green, soft, childish, silly, stupid; easily convinced; over-credulous, -confident, -trustful; infatuated, superstitious; confiding &c. (*believing*) 484.

Phr. the wish the father to the thought; *credo quia impossibile* [Tertullian]; all is not gold that glitters; *no es oro todo lo que reluce; omne ignotum pro magnifico.*

unbeliever, skeptic; misbeliever,[1] pyrrhonist; heretic &c. (*heterodox*) 984.

V. be -incredulous &c. *adj.*; distrust &c. (*disbelieve*) 485; refuse to believe; shut one's -eyes, – ears- to; turn a deaf ear to; hold aloof; ignore, *nullis jurare in verba magistri.*

Adj. incredulous, skeptical, unbelieving, inconvincible; hard –, shy- of belief; suspicious, scrupulous, distrustful, disposed to doubt, indisposed to believe.

---

488. Assent. — N. assent, -ment; acquiescence, admission; nod; ac-, con-cord, -cordance; agreement &c. 23; affirm-ance, -ation; recognition, acknowledgment, avowal; confession, – of faith.

unanimity, common consent, consensus, acclamation, chorus, *vox populi;* popular –, current- -belief, – opinion; public opinion; concurrence &c. (*of causes*) 178; coöperation &c. (*voluntary*) 709.

ratification, confirmation, corroboration, approval, acceptance, *visa;* indorsement &c. (*record*) 551.

consent &c. (*compliance*) 762.

V. assent; give –, yield –, nod- assent; acquiesce; agree &c. 23; receive, accept, accede, accord, concur, lend oneself to, consent, coincide, reciprocate, go with; be -at one with &c. *adj.*; go along –, chime in –, strike in –, close- with; echo, enter into one's views, agree in opinion; vote –, give one's voice- for; recognize; subscribe –, conform –, defer-to; say -yes, – ditto, – amen, – aye- to.

acknowledge, own, admit, allow, avow, confess; concede &c. (*yield*) 762; come round to; abide by; permit &c. 760.

arrive at-, come to -an understanding, – terms, – an agreement.

con-, af-firm; ratify, approve. indorse, countersign; corroborate &c. 467.

go –, swim- with the stream; be in the fashion, join in the chorus; be in every mouth.

Adj. assenting &c. *v.*; of one -accord,

489. Dissent. — N. dissent; discord-ance &c. (*disagreement*) 24; difference –, diversity- of opinion.

nonconformity &c. (*heterodoxy*) 984; protestantism, recusancy, schism; disaffection; secession &c. 624; recantation &c. 607.

dissension &c. (*discord*) 713; discontent &c. 832; caviling.

protest; contradiction &c. (*denial*) 536; noncompliance &c. (*rejection*) 764.

dissent-ient, -er; non-juror, -content, -conformist; sectary, separatist, recusant, schismatic, protestant, heretic.

V. dissent, demur; call in question &c. (*doubt*) 485; differ in opinion, disagree; say -no &c. 536; refuse -assent, – to admit; cavil, protest, raise one's voice against, repudiate; contradict &c. (*deny*) 536.

have no notion of, differ *toto cœlo;* revolt -at, – from the idea.

shake the head, shrug the shoulders; look -askance, – askant.

secede; recant &c. 607.

Adj. dissenting &c. *v.*; negative &c. 536; diss-ident, -entient; unconsenting &c. (*refusing*) 764; non-content, -jur-ing; protestant, recusant; uncon-vinced, -verted.

unavowed, unacknowledged; out of the question.

discontented &c. 832; unwilling &c. 603; extorted.

sectarian, denominational, schismatic; heterodox; intolerant.

---

[1] The word *miscreant*, which originally meant simply *misbeliever*, has now quite another meaning (949). See Trench, *On the Study of Words*, p. 71.

– mind; of the same mind, at one with, agreed, acquiescent, content; willing &c. 602.

un-contradicted, -challenged, -questioned, -controverted.

carried –, agreed- -*nem. con.* &c. *adv.*; unanimous; agreed on all hands, carried by acclamation.

affirmative &c. 535.

Adv. yes, yea, ay, aye, true; good; well; very -well, – true; well and good; granted; even –, just- so; to be sure, " thou hast said "; truly, exactly, precisely, that's just it, indeed, certainly, certes, *ex concesso;* of course, unquestionably, assuredly, no doubt, doubtless.

be it so; so -be it, – let it be; amen; willingly &c. 602.

affirmatively, in the affirmative.

with one -consent, – voice, – accord; unanimously, *unâ voce,* by common consent, in chorus, to a man, *nem. con.; nemine -contradicente, – dissentiente;* without a dissentient voice; as one man, one and all, on all hands.

Phr. *avec plaisir; chi tace accousente;* " the public mind is the creation of the Master-Writers " [Disraeli].

Adv. no &c. 536; at -variance, – issue- with; under protest.

Int. God forbid! not for the world; I'll be hanged if; never tell me; your humble servant, pardon me.

Phr. many men many minds; *quot homines tot sententiæ* [Terence]; *tant s'en faut; il s'en faut bien.*

---

490. Knowledge. — N. knowledge; cogn-izance, -ition, -oscence †; acquaintance, experience, ken, privity, insight, familiarity; com-, ap-prehension; recognition; appreciation &c. (*judgment*) 480; intuition; consci-ence, -ousness; perception, precognition; acroamatics.

light, enlightenment; glimpse, inkling; glimmer, -ing; dawn; scent, suspicion; impression &c. (*idea*) 453; discovery &c. 480*a.*

system –, body- of knowledge; science, philosophy, pansophy; acroama; theory, ætiology; circle of the sciences; pandect, doctrine, body of doctrine; cy-, encyclopedia; school &c. (*system of opinions*) 484.

tree of knowledge; republic of letters &c. (*language*) 560.

erudition, learning, lore, scholarship, reading, letters; literature; book madness; book learning, bookishness; bibliomania, -latry; information, general information; store of -knowledge &c.; education &c. (*teaching*) 537; culture, menticulture, attainments; acqui-rements, -sitions; accomplishments; proficiency; practical knowledge &c. (*skill*) 698; liberal education; dilettantism; rudiments &c. (*beginning*) 66.

deep –, profound –, solid –, accurate –, acroatic –, acroamatic –, vast –, extensive –, encyclopedical- -knowledge, – learning; omniscience, pantology.

march of intellect; progress –, ad-

491. Ignorance. — N. ignorance, nescience, *tabula rasa,* crass ignorance, *ignorance crasse;* unacquaintance; unconsciousness &c. *adj.*; dark-, blind-ness; incomprehension, inexperience, simplicity.

unknown quantities, $x, y, z.$

sealed book, *terra incognita,* virgin soil, unexplored ground; dark ages.

[Imperfect knowledge] smattering, sciolism, glimmering; bewilderment &c. (*uncertainty*) 475; incapacity.

[Affectation of knowledge] pedantry; charlatan-ry, -ism; *Philister,* Philistine.

V. be -ignorant &c. *adj.*; not -know &c. 490; know -not, – not what, – nothing of; have no -idea, – notion, – conception; not have the remotest idea; not know chalk from cheese.

ignore, be blind to; keep in ignorance &c. (*conceal*) 528.

see through a glass darkly; have a -film over the eyes, – glimmering &c. *n.*; wonder whether; not know what to make of &c. (*unintelligibility*) 519; not pretend –, not take upon oneself- to say.

Adj. ignorant; nescient; un-knowing, -aware, -acquainted, -apprized, -witting, -weeting†, -conscious; wit-, weet †- less; a stranger to; unconversant.

un-informed, -cultivated, -versed, -instructed, -taught, -initiated, -tutored, -schooled, -guided, -enlightened; Philistine; behind the age.

shallow, superficial, green, rude, emp-

vance- of -science, – learning; school-master abroad.

V. know, ken, scan, wot; wot –, be aware &c. *adj.-* of; ween, weet†, trow, have, possess.

conceive; ap-, com-prehend; take, realize, understand, savvy * [U. S.], ap-preciate; fathom, make out; recognize, discern, perceive, see, get a sight-of, experience.

know full well; have –, possess- some knowledge of; be *-au courant* &c. *adj.*; have -in one's head, – at one's fingers' ends; know by -heart, – rote; be master of; *connaître le dessous des cartes*, know what's what &c. 698.

see one's way; discover &c. 480*a*.

come to one's knowledge &c. (*information*) 527.

Adj. knowing &c. *v.*; cognitive; acroamatic.

aware –, cognizant –, conscious- of; acquainted –, made acquainted- with; privy –, no stranger- to; *au -fait, – couran.*; in the secret; up –, alive- to; behind the -scenes, – curtain; let into; apprized –, informed- of; undeceived.

proficient –, versed –, read –, forward –, strong –, at home- in; conversant –, familiar- with.

erudite, instructed, learned, lettered, educated; well-conned, -informed, -read, -grounded, -educated; enlightened, shrewd, *savant*, blue, bookish, scholastic, solid, profound, deep-read, book-learned; accomplished &c. (*skillful*) 698; omniscient; self-taught.

known &c. *v.*; ascertained, well-known, recognized, received, notorious, noted; proverbial; familiar, – as household words, – to every schoolboy; hackneyed, trite, commonplace.

cogn-oscible, -izable.

Adv. to –, to the best of- one's knowledge.

Phr. one's eyes being opened &c. (*disclosure*) 529; *comprendre tout c'est tout pardonner; empta dolore docet experientia;* γνῶθι σεαυτόν; " half our knowledge we must snatch not take " [Pope]; *Jahre lehren mehr als Bücher;* " knowledge comes but wisdom lingers " [Tennyson]; " knowledge is power " [Bacon]; *les affaires font les hommes; nec scire fas est omnia* [Horace]; " the amassed thought and experience cf innumerable minds " [Emerson]; *was ich nicht weiss macht mich nicht heiss.*

ty, half-learned, illiterate; un-read, -in-formed, -educated, -learned, -lettered, -bookish; empty-headed; pedantic.

in the dark; be-nighted, -lated; blind-, ed, -fold; hoodwinked; misinformed; *au bout de son latin*, at the end of his tether, at fault; at sea &c. (*uncertain*) 475; caught tripping.

un-known, -apprehended, -explained, -ascertained, -investigated, -explored, -heard of, -perceived; concealed &c. 528; novel.

Adv. ignorantly &c. *adj.*; unawares; for -anything, – aught- one knows; not that one knows.

Int. God –, Heaven –, the Lord –, nobody- knows.

Phr. " ignorance never settles a question " [Disraeli]; *quantum animis erroris inest !* [Ovid]; " small Latin and less Greek " [B. Jonson]; " that unlettered small-knowing soul " [*Love's Labor's Lost*]; " there is no darkness but ignorance " [*Twelfth Night*].

---

492. Scholar. — N. scholar, connoisseur, *savant*, pundit, schoolman, professor, graduate, wrangler; academician, -ist; master of arts, doctor, licentiate, gownsman; philo-sopher, -math; scientist, clerk; soph -ist, -ister; linguist; glosso-, philo-logist; philologer; lexico-, glosso-grapher; grammarian; *littérateur, literati, dilettanti,* illuminati; fellow, Hebraist, lexicologist, mullah, munshi, Sanskritist; sinolog-ist, -ue; Mezzofanti, admirable Crichton, Mecænas.

bookworm, *helluo librorum;* biblio-phile, -maniac; bluestocking, *bas-bleu;* bigwig, learned Theban, don; *Artium-Baccalaureus, – Magister.*

493. Ignoramus. — N. ignoramus, dunce; wooden spoon; no scholar.

sciolist, smatterer, dabbler, half scholar; charlatan; wiseacre.

novice; greenhorn &c. (*dupe*) 547; tyro &c. (*learner*) 541; numskull.

lubber &c. (*bungler*) 701; fool &c. 501; pedant &c. 492.

Adj. bookless, shallow; ignorant &c. 491.

Phr. " a wit with dunces and a dunce with wits " [Pope].

learned –, literary- man; *homo multarum literarum;* man of -learning, – letters, – education, – genius.

antiquar-ian, -y; archæologist; sage &c. (*wise man*) 500.

pedant, doctrinaire; pedagogue, Dr. Pangloss; pantologist; criminologist. schoolboy &c. (*learner*) 541.

Adj. learned &c. 490; brought up at the feet of Gamaliel.

Phr. " he was a scholar and a ripe and good one " [*Henry VIII*]; " the manifold linguist " [*All's Well That Ends Well*].

494. [Object of knowledge.] **Truth.** — **N.** fact, reality &c. (*existence*) 1; plain matter of fact; nature &c. (*principle*) 5; truth, verity; gospel; orthodoxy &c. 983*a*; authenticity; veracity &c. 543; correctitude.

accuracy, exactitude; exact-, precise-ness &c. *adj.*; precision, delicacy; rigor, mathematical precision, punctuality; clockwork precision &c. (*regularity*) 80; conformity to rule; nicety.

orthology; *ipsissima verba;* realism.

plain –, honest –, sober –, naked –, unalloyed –, unqualified –, stern –, exact –, intrinsic- truth; *nuda veritas;* the very thing; not an -illusion &c. 495; real Simon Pure; unvarnished tale; the truth the whole truth and nothing but the truth; just the thing.

V. be -true &c. *adj.*, – the case; stand the test; have the true ring; hold -good, – true, – water.

render –, prove- -true &c. *adj.*; substantiate &c. (*evidence*) 467.

get at the truth &c. (*discover*) 480*a*.

Adj. real, actual &c. (*existing*) 1; veritable, true; certain &c. 474; substantially –, categorically- true &c.; true -to the letter, – as gospel; unimpeachable; veracious &c. 543; unre-, uncon-futed; un-ideal, -imagined; realistic.

exact, accurate, definite, precise, well-defined, just, right, correct, strict, severe; close &c. (*similar*) 17; literal; rigid, rigorous; scrupulous &c. (*conscientious*) 939; religiously exact, punctual, mathematical, scientific; faithful, constant, unerring; curious, particular, nice, delicate, fine; clean-cut, clear-cut.

genuine, authentic, legitimate; orthodox &c. 983*a*; official, *ex officio*.

pure, natural, sound, sterling; unsophisticated, -adulterated, -varnished, -colored; in its true colors; *pukka*.

well-grounded, -founded; solid, substantial, tangible, valid; undis-torted, -guised; un-affected, -exaggerated, -romantic, -flattering.

495. Error. — **N.** error, fallacy; misconception, -apprehension, -understanding; inexactness &c. *adj.*; laxity; misconstruction &c. (*misinterpretation*) 523; miscomputation &c. (*misjudgment*) 481; *non sequitur* &c. 477; mis-statement, -report; mumpsimus.

mistake; miss, fault, blunder, *quipro-quo*, cross purposes, oversight, misprint, erratum, corrigendum, slip, blot, flaw, loose thread; trip, stumble &c. (*failure*) 732; botchery &c. (*want of skill*) 699; slip of the -tongue, – pen; *lapsus linguæ*, clerical error; bull &c. (*absurdity*) 497; haplography.

il-, de-lusion; false -impression, – idea; bubble; self-deceit, -deception; mists of error.

heresy &c. (*heterodoxy*) 984; hallucination &c. (*insanity*) 503; false light &c. (*fallacy of vision*) 443; dream &c. (*fancy*) 515; fable &c. (*untruth*) 546; bias &c. (*misjudgment*) 481; misleading &c. *v.*

V. be -erroneous &c. *adj.*

cause error; mis-lead, -guide; lead -astray, – into error; beguile, misinform &c. (*misteach*) 538; delude; give a false -impression, – idea; falsify, misstate; deceive &c. 545; lie &c. 544.

err; be -in error &c. *adj.*, – mistaken &c. *v.*; be deceived &c. (*duped*) 547; mistake, receive a false impression, deceive oneself; fall into –, lie under –, labor under- -an error &c. *n.*; be in the wrong, blunder; mis-apprehend, -conceive, -understand, -reckon, -count, -calculate &c. (*misjudge*) 481.

play –, be- at cross purposes &c. (*misinterpret*) 523.

trip, stumble; lose oneself &c. (*uncertainty*) 475; go astray; fail &c. 732; be in the wrong box; take the wrong sow by the ear &c. (*mismanage*) 699; put the saddle on the wrong horse; reckon without one's host; take the shadow for the substance &c. (*credulity*) 486; dream &c. (*imagine*) 515.

Adj. erroneous, untrue, false, devoid

Adv. truly &c. *adj.*; verily, indeed, in reality; with truth &c. (*veracity*) 543; certainly &c. (*certain*) 474; actually &c. (*existence*) 1; in effect &c. (*intrinsically*) 5.

exactly &c. *adj.*; *ad amussim;* verbatim, – *et literatim;* word for word, literally, *literatim, totidem verbis, sic,* to the letter, chapter and verse, *ipsissimis verbis; ad unguem;* to an inch; to a-nicety, – hair, – tittle, – turn, – T; *au pied de la lettre;* neither more nor less; in -every respect, – all respects; *sous tous les rapports;* at -any rate, – all events; strictly speaking.

Phr. the -truth, – fact- is; *rem acu tetigisti; en suivant la verité; ex facto jus oritur; la verità è figlia del tempo; locos y niños dicen la verdad; nihil est veritatis luce dulcius* [Cicero]; *veritas nunquam perit* [Seneca]; *veritatem dies aperit* [Seneca].

of truth, fallacious, apocryphal, unreal, ungrounded, groundless; unsubstantial &c. 4; heretical &c. (*heterodox*) 984; unsound; illogical &c. 477.

in-, un-exact; in-accurate, -correct; indefinite &c. (*uncertain*) 475.

illus-ive, -ory; delusive; mock, ideal &c. (*imaginary*) 515; spurious &c. 545; deceitful &c. 544; perverted.

controvertible, unsustainable; unauthenticated, untrustworthy.

exploded, refuted; discarded.

in –, under an- error &c. *n.*; mistaken &c. *v.*; tripping &c. *v.*; out, – in one's reckoning; aberrant; beside –, wide of the- -mark, – truth; astray &c. (*at fault*) 475; on -a false, – the wrong-scent; in the wrong box; at cross purposes, all in the wrong; all out.

Adv. more or less.

Phr. *errare est humanum; mentis gratissimus error* [Horace]; " on the dubious waves of error tost " [Cowper]; " to err is human, to forgive divine " [Pope]; " you lie — under a mistake " [Shelley].

---

496. Maxim. — N. maxim, aphorism; apo-, apoph-thegm; dictum, saying, adage, saw, proverb; sentence, mot, motto, word, byword, moral, phylactery, protasis.

axiom, theorem, scholium, truism, postulate.

reflection &c. (*idea*) 453; conclusion &c. (*judgment*) 480; golden rule &c. (*precept*) 697; principle, principia; profession of faith &c. (*belief*) 484; settled principle, formula.

wise –, sage –, received –, admitted –, recognized- maxim &c.; true –, common –, hackneyed –, trite –, commonplace- saying &c.

Adj. aphoristic, proverbial, phylacteric; axiomatic, gnomic.

Adv. as -the saying is, – they say.

497. Absurdity. — N. absurd-ity, -ness &c. *adj.*; imbecility &c. 499; alogy†, nonsense, paradox, inconsistency; stultiloqu-y, -ence; nugacity.

blunder, muddle, bull; Irish-, Hibernic-ism; slipslop; anticlimax, bathos; sophism &c. 477.

farce, *galimathias*, amphigouri, rhapsody; farrago &c. (*disorder*) 59; *bêtise;* extravagance, romance; sciamachy.

sell, pun, verbal quibble, macaronic.

jargon, fustian, twaddle &c. (*no meaning*) 517; exaggeration &c. 549; moonshine, stuff; mare's nest, quibble, self-delusion.

vagary, tomfoolery, mummery, monkey trick, *boutade,* escapade.

V. play the fool &c. 499; talk nonsense, *parler à tort et à travers; battre la campagne;* ἀνεμώλια βάζειν; be -absurd &c. *adj.*

Adj. absurd, nonsensical, preposterous, egregious, senseless, inconsistent, ridiculous, extravagant, quibbling; self-annulling, -contradictory; macaronic, punning.

foolish &c. 499; sophistical &c. 477; unmeaning &c. 517; without rhyme or reason; fantastic.

Int. fiddlededee! pish! pho! " in the name of the Prophet — figs! " [Horace Smith].

Phr. *credat Judæus Apella* [Horace]; tell it to the marines.

Faculties

498. Intelligence. Wisdom. — N. intelligence, capacity, comprehension,

499. Imbecility. Folly. — N. want of -intelligence &c. 498, – intellect &c.

understanding; cuteness, sabe * [U. S.], savvy * [U. S.]; intellect &c. 450; nous, parts, sagacity, mother wit, wit, *esprit*, gumption, quick parts, grasp of intellect; acuteness &c. *adj.*; acumen, subtlety, penetration, perspica-cy †, -city; discernment, due sense of, good judgment; discrimination &c. 465; cunning &c. 702; refinement &c. (*taste*) 850.

head, brains, headpiece, upper story, long head; eagle -eye, – glance; eye of a -lynx, – hawk.

wisdom, sapience, sense; good –, common –, horse – [U. S.], plain- sense; rationality, reason; reasonableness &c. *adj.*; judgment; solidity, depth, profundity, caliber; enlarged views; reach –, compass- of thought; enlargement of mind.

genius, inspiration, *geist*, fire of genius, heaven-born genius, soul; talent &c. (*aptitude*) 698.

[Wisdom in action] prudence &c. 864; vigilance &c. 459; tact &c. 698; foresight &c. 510; sobriety, self-possession, *aplomb*, ballast.

a bright thought, not a bad idea.

V. be -intelligent &c. *adj.*; have all one's wits about one; understand &c. (*intelligible*) 518; catch –, take in- an idea; take a -joke, – hint.

see -through, – at a glance, – with half an eye, – far into, – through a millstone; penetrate; discern &c. (*descry*) 441; foresee &c. 510.

discriminate &c. 465; know what's what &c. 698; listen to reason.

Adj. [Applied to persons] intelligent, quick of apprehension, keen, acute, alive, brainy, awake, bright, quick, sharp; quick-, keen-, clear-, sharp- -eyed, -sighted, -witted; wide-awake; canny, shrewd, astute; clear-headed; farsighted &c. 510; discerning, perspicacious, penetrating, piercing; argute; nimble-, needle-witted; sharp as a needle; alive to &c. (*cognizant*) 490; clever &c. (*apt*) 698; arch &c. (*cunning*) 702; *pas si bête;* acute &c. 682.

wise, sage, sapient, sagacious, reasonable, rational, sound, in one's right mind, sensible, *abnormis sapiens*, judicious, strong-minded.

un-prejudiced, -biassed, -bigoted, -prepossessed; un-dazzled, -perplexed; of unwarped judgment, impartial, equitable, fair.

450; shadow-, silli-, foolish-ness &c. *adj.*; imbecility, incapacity, vacancy of mind, poverty of intellect, clouded perception, poor head, apartments to let; stup-, stol-idity; hebetude, dull understanding, meanest capacity, shortsightedness; incompetence &c. (*unskillfulness*) 699.

one's weak side; bias &c. 481; infatuation &c. (*insanity*) 503.

simplicity, puerility, babyhood; dotage, anility, second childishness, fatuity; idio-cy, -tism; driveling.

folly, frivolity, irrationality, trifling, ineptitude, nugacity, inconsistency, lip wisdom, conceit; sophistry &c. 477; giddiness &c. (*inattention*) 458; eccentricity &c. 503; extravagance &c. (*absurdity*) 497; rashness &c. 863.

act of folly &c. 699.

V. be -imbecile &c. *adj.*; have no -brains, – sense &c. 498.

trifle, drivel, *radoter*, dote; ramble &c. (*madness*) 503; play the -fool, – monkey; take leave of one's senses; not see an inch beyond one's nose; stultify oneself &c. 699; talk nonsense &c. 497.

Adj. [Applied to persons] un-intelligent, -intellectual, -reasoning; mind-, wit-, reason-, brain-less; half-baked; having no -head &c. 498; not -bright &c. 498; inapprehensible.

weak-, addle-, puzzle-, blunder-, muddle-, muddy-, pig-, beetle-, buffle-, chuckle-, mutton-, maggoty-, gross-headed; beef-, fat- -witted, -headed.

weak-, feeble-minded; dull-, shallow-, lack-brained; rattle-brained, -headed; half-, lean-, short-, dull-, blunt-witted; shallow-, clod-, addle-pated; dim-, short-sighted; thick-skulled; weak in the upper story.

shallow, *borné*, weak, wanting, soft, sappy, spoony; dull, – as a beetle; stupid, heavy, insulse, obtuse, blunt, stolid, doltish; asinine; inapt &c. 699; prosaic &c. 843; hebetudinous.

child-ish, -like; infant-ine, -ile, baby-, bab-ish; puerile, anile; simple &c. (*credulous*) 486; old-womanish.

fatuous, idiotic, imbecile, driveling; blatant, babbling; vacant; sottish; bewildered &c. 475.

blockish, unteachable; Bœot-ian, -ic; bovine; un-gifted, -discerning, -enlightened, -wise, -philosophical; apish; simious.

cool; cool-, long-, hard-, strong-head-ed; long-sighted, calculating, thought-ful, reflecting; solid, deep, profound.

oracular; heaven-directed, -born.

prudent &c. (*cautious*) 864; sober, staid, solid; considerate, politic, wise in one's generation; watchful &c. 459; provident &c. (*prepared*) 673; in advance of one's age; wise as -a serpent, – Solomon, – Solon.

[Applied to actions] wise, sensible, reasonable, judicious; well-judged, -advised; prudent, politic; expedient &c. 646.

Phr. *aut regem aut fatuum nasci oportet;* "but with the morning cool reflection came" [Scott]; *flosculi sententiarum; les affaires font les hommes; más vale saber que haber; más vale ser necio que porfiado; nemo solus sapit* [Plautus]; *nosce te;* γνῶθι σεαυτόν; *nullum magnum ingenium sine mixtura dementiæ fuit* [Seneca, from Aristotle]; *sapere aude* [Horace]; *victrix fortunæ sapientia* [Juvenal].

foolish, silly, senseless, irrational, insensate, nonsensical, inept; maudlin.

narrow-minded &c. 481; bigoted &c. (*obstinate*) 606; giddy &c. (*thoughtless*) 458; rash &c. 863; eccentric &c. (*crazed*) 503.

[Applied to actions] foolish, unwise, injudicious, improper, unreasonable, without reason, ridiculous, silly, stupid, asinine; ill-imagined, -advised, -judged, -devised; *mal entendu;* inconsistent, irrational, unphilosophical; extravagant &c. (*nonsensical*) 497; sleeveless, idle; useless &c. 645; inexpedient &c. 647; frivolous &c. (*trivial*) 643.

Phr. *Davus sum non Œdipus;* "a fool's bolt is soon shot" [*Henry V.*]; *clitellæ bovi sunt impositæ* [Cicero]; "fools rush in where angels fear to tread" [Pope]; *il n'a ni bouche ni éperon;* "the bookful blockhead, ignorantly read" [Pope]; "to varnish nonsense with the charms of sound" [Churchill].

---

500. Sage. — N. sage, wiseman; master -mind, – spirit of the age; longhead, thinker.

authority, oracle, luminary, shining light, *esprit fort, magnus Apollo,* Solon, Solomon, Nestor, Magi, "second Daniel."

man of learning &c. 492; expert &c. 700; wizard &c. 994.

[Ironically] wiseacre, bigwig.

Adj. venerable, reverenced, *emeritus.*

Phr. *barbâ tenus sapientes.*

501. Fool. — N. fool, idiot, tom-fool, wiseacre, simpleton, witling, diz-zard, donkey, ass; ninny, -hammer; chowder-, chuckle-head; dolt, booby, Tom Noddy, looby, hoddy-doddy †, noddy, nonny, noodle, nizy, owl; goose, -cap; imbecile; gaby, *radoteur,* nincompoop, *badaud,* zany; trifler, babbler; pretty fellow; natural, *niais.*

child, baby, infant, innocent, milksop, sop.

oaf, lout, loon, lown, dullard, doodle †, calf, colt, buzzard, block, put, stick,

---

stock, numps †, tony †.

bull-, dunder-, addle-, block-, dull-, logger-, jolt-, jolter-, beetle-, gross-, mutton-, noodle-, giddy-head; num-, thick-skull; lack-, shallow-brain; half-, lack-wit; dunderpate; lunkhead [U. S.]

sawney, gowk; clod, -hopper; clod-, clot-poll, -pate; bull calf; gawk, Gothamite, lummox, rube [U. S.]; men of Bœotia, wise men of Gotham.

un sot à triple étage, sot; jobbernowl, changeling, mooncalf, *gobemouche.*

dotard, driveler; old -fogey, – woman; crone, grandmother; cotquean, henhussy.

greenhorn &c. (*dupe*) 547; dunce &c. (*ignoramus*) 493; lubber &c. (*bungler*) 701; madman &c. 504.

one who -will not set the Thames on fire, – did not invent gunpowder; *qui n'a pas inventé la poudre;* no conjuror.

Phr. *fortuna favet fatuis; les fous font les festins et les sages les mangent; nomina stultorum parietibus hærent; stultorum plena sunt omnia* [Cicero].

502. Sanity. — N. sanity; soundness &c. *adj.*; rationality, sobriety, lucidity, lucid interval; senses, sober senses, sound mind, *mens sana.*

V. be -sane &c. *adj.*; retain one's senses, – reason.

503. Insanity. — N. disordered -reason, – intellect; diseased –, unsound –, abnormal- mind; derangement, unsoundness.

insanity, lunacy; madness &c. *adj.*, mania, rabies, furor, mental alienation,

become -sane &c. *adj.*; come to one's senses, sober down.

render -sane &c. *adj.*; bring to one's senses, sober.

Adj. sane, rational, reasonable, *compos mentis,* of sound mind; sound, -minded; lucid.

self-possessed; sober, -minded.

in one's -sober senses, – right mind; in possession of one's faculties.

Adv. sanely &c. *adj.*

aberration; paranoia; demen-tation,-tia, -cy; phrenitis, phrensy, frenzy, raving, incoherence, wandering, delirium, calenture of the brain, delusion, hallucination; lycanthropy; brain storm.

vertigo, dizziness, swimming; sunstroke, *coup de soleil,* siriasis.

fanaticism, infatuation, craze; oddity, eccentricity, twist, monomania; klepto-, dipso-mania; hypochondriasis &c. (*low spirits*) 837; melancholia, hysteria; amentia.

screw –, tile –, slate- loose; bee in one's bonnet, rats in the upper story.

dotage &c. (*imbecility*) 499.

V. be –, become- -insane &c. *adj.*; lose one's senses, – reason, – faculties, – wits; go –, run- mad; rave, dote, ramble, wander; drivel &c. (*be imbecile*) 499; have a -screw loose &c. *n.*, – devil; *avoir le diable au corps;* lose one's head &c. (*be uncertain*) 475.

render –, drive- -mad &c. *adj.*; madden, dementate, addle the wits, derange the head, infatuate, befool; turn -the brain, – one's head.

Adj. insane, mad, lunatic; crazy, crazed, *aliéné, non compos mentis;* not right, cracked, touched; bereft of reason; all-possessed, unhinged, unsettled in one's mind; insensate, reasonless, beside oneself, demented, daft; phren-, fren-zied, -etic; possessed, – with a devil; deranged, far gone, maddened, moonstruck; shatter-pated; mad-, scatter-, shatter-, crack-brained; off one's head.

maniacal; delirious, light-headed, incoherent, rambling, doting, wandering; frantic, raving, stark staring mad.

corybantic, dithyrambic; rabid, giddy, vertiginous, wild; haggard, mazed; flighty; distr-acted, -aught; bewildered &c. (*uncertain*) 475.

mad as a -March hare, – hatter; of -unsound mind &c. *n.*; touched –, wrong –, not right- in one's -head, – mind, – wits –, upper story; out of one's -mind, – senses, – wits; not in one's right mind.

fanatical, infatuated, odd, eccentric; hypp-ed, -ish.

imbecile, silly, &c. 499.

Adv. like one possessed.

Phr. the mind having lost its balance; the reason under a cloud; *tête -exaltée, -montée; ira furor brevis est; omnes stultos insanire* [Horace].

504. Madman. — N. madman, lunatic, maniac, bedlamite, candidate for Bedlam, raver, madcap; energumen; auto-, mono-, dipso-, klepto-maniac; hypochondriac &c. (*low spirits*) 837; crank, Tom o' Bedlam.

dreamer &c. 515; rhapsodist, seer, highflier, enthusiast, fanatic, *fanatico; exalté;* knight errant, Don Quixote.

idiot &c. 501.

Section VI. Extension of Thought

1. To the Past

505. Memory. — N. memory, remembrance; reten-tion, -tiveness; tenacity; *veteris vestigia flammæ;* tablets of the memory; readiness.

reminiscence, recognition, recurrence, recollection, rememoration; retrospect, -ion; afterthought.

506. Oblivion. — N. oblivion; forgetfulness &c. *adj.*; obliteration &c. 552 of –, insensibility &c. 823 to- the past.

short –, treacherous –, loose –, slippery –, failing- memory; decay –, failure –, lapse- of memory; waters of -Lethe, – oblivion.

suggestion &c. (*information*). 527; prompting &c. *v*.; hint, reminder, token of remembrance, memento, souvenir, keepsake, relic, memorandum; remembrancer, flapper; memorial &c. (*record*) 551; commemoration &c. (*celebration*) 883.

things to be remembered, memorabilia.

art of –, artificial- memory; *memoria technica;* mnemo-nics, -technics; phrenotypics; Mnemosyne; prompt-book.

retentive –, tenacious –, green –, trustworthy –, capacious –, faithful –, correct –, exact –, ready –, prompt- memory.

celebrity, fame, renown, reputation &c. (*repute*) 873.

V. remember, mind; retain the -memory, – remembrance- of; keep in view.

have –, hold –, bear –, carry –, keep –, retain- in *or* in the -thoughts, – mind, – memory, – remembrance; be in –, live in –, remain in –, dwell in –, haunt –, impress- one's -memory, – thoughts,- mind.

amnesty, general pardon.

V. forget; be -forgetful &c. *adj*.; fall –, sink- into oblivion; have -a short memory &c. *n*., – no head.

forget one's own name, have on the tip of one's tongue, come in at one ear and go out at the other.

slip –, escape –, fade from –, die away from- the memory; lose, – sight of.

unlearn; efface &c. 552 –, discharge- from the memory; consign to -oblivion, – the tomb of the Capulets; think no more of &c. (*turn the attention from*) 458; cast behind one's back, wean one's thoughts from; let bygones be bygones &c. (*forgive*) 918.

Adj. forgotten &c. *v*.; unremembered, past recollection, bygone, out of mind; buried –, sunk- in oblivion; clean forgotten; gone out of one's -head, – recollection.

forgetful, oblivious, mindless, Lethean; insensible &c. 823- to the past; heedless.

Phr. *non mi ricordo;* the memory -failing, – deserting one, – being at (*or* in) fault.

sink in the mind; run in the head; not be able to get it out of one's head; be deeply impressed with; rankle &c. (*revenge*) 919.

recur to the mind; flash -on the mind, – across the memory.

recognize, recollect, bethink oneself, recall, call up, retrace; look –, trace- -back, – backwards; think –, look back- upon; review; call –, recall –, bring- to -mind, – remembrance; carry one's thoughts back; rake up the past.

suggest &c. (*inform*) 527; prompt; put –, keep- in mind; remind; fan the embers; call –, summon –, rip- up; renew; *infandum renovare dolorem;* task –, tax –, jog –, flap –, refresh –, rub up –, awaken- the memory; pull by the sleeve; bring back to the memory, put in remembrance, memorialize.

get –, have –, learn –, know –, say –, repeat- by -heart, – rote; say one's lesson; repeat, – as a parrot; have at one's fingers' ends.

commit to memory; con, – over; fix –, rivet –, imprint –, impress –, stamp –, grave –, engrave –, store –, treasure up –, bottle up –, embalm –, enshrine- in the memory; load –, store –, stuff –, burden- the memory with; memorize.

redeem from oblivion; keep the -memory alive, – wound green; *tangere ulcus;* keep up the memory of; commemorate &c. (*celebrate*) 883.

make a note of &c. (*record*) 551.

Adj. remember-ing, -ed &c. *v*.; mindful, reminiscential; retained in the memory &c. *v*.; pent up in one's memory; fresh; green, – in remembrance; unforgotten, present to the mind; within one's -memory &c. *n*.; indelible; uppermost in one's thoughts; memorable &c. (*important*) 642.

Adv. by -heart, – rote; without book, *memoriter*.

in memory of; *in memoriam; memoriâ in æternâ;* suggestive.

Phr. *manet altâ mente repostum* [Vergil]; *forsan et hæc olim meminisse juvabit* [Vergil]; *absens hæres non erit; beatæ memoriæ;* " briefly thyself remember " [*Lear*]; *mendacem memorem esse oportet* [Quintilian]; " memory the warder of the brain " [*Macbeth*]; *parsque est meminisse doloris* [Ovid]; " to live in hearts we leave behind is not to die " [Campbell]; *vox audita perit littera scripta manet.*

2. To the Future

507. Expectation. — **N.** expect-ation, -ance, -ancy; anticipation, reckoning, calculation; foresight &c. 510.

contemplation, prospection, lookout; prospect, perspective, horizon, vista; destiny &c. 152.

suspense, waiting, abeyance; curiosity &c. 455; anxious –, ardent –, eager –, breathless –, sanguine- expectation; torment of Tantalus.

hope &c. 858; trust &c. (*belief*) 484; auspices &c. (*prediction*) 511; assurance, confidence, presumption, reliance.

V. expect; look -for, – out for, – forward to; hope for, anticipate; have in -prospect, – contemplation; keep in view; contemplate, promise oneself; not -wonder &c. 870 -at, – if.

wait –, tarry –, lie in wait –, watch –, bargain- for; keep a -good, – sharp- lookout for; await; stand at " attention," abide, bide one's time, watch.

foresee &c. 510; prepare for &c. 673; forestall &c. (*be early*) 132; count upon &c. (*believe in*) 484; think likely &c. (*probability*) 472.

lead one to expect &c. (*predict*) 511; have in store for &c. (*destiny*) 152.

prick up one's ears, hold one's breath.

Adj. expectant; expecting &c. *v.*; in -expectation &c. *n.*; on the watch &c. (*vigilant*) 459; open-eyed, -mouthed; agape, gaping, all agog; on -tenter-hooks, – tiptoe, – the tiptoe of expectation; *aux aguets;* ready; curious &c. 455; looking forward to.

expected &c. *v.*; long expected, fore-seen; in prospect &c. *n.*; prospective; in -one's eye, – view, – the horizon; impending &c. (*destiny*) 152.

Adv. on the watch &c. *adj.*; with -breathless expectation &c. *n.*, – bated breath; *arrectis auribus.*

Phr. we shall see; *nous verrons;* " expectation whirls me round " [*Troilus and Cressida*].

508. Inexpectation. — **N.** in-, non-expectation; false expectation &c. (*disappointment*) 509; miscalculation &c. 481.

surprise, sudden burst, thunderclap, blow, shock; bolt out of the blue; wonder &c. 870; eye opener.

V. not -expect &c. 507; be taken by surprise; start; miscalculate &c. 481; not bargain for; come –, fall- upon.

be -unexpected &c. *adj.*; come -unawares &c. *adv.*; turn up, pop, drop from the clouds; come –, burst –, flash –, bounce –, steal –, creep- upon one; come –, burst- like a thunder-clap, -bolt; take –, catch- -by surprise, – unawares, – napping; yach [S. Africa].

pounce –, spring a mine- upon.

surprise, startle, take aback, electrify, stun, stagger, take away one's breath, throw off one's guard; astonish &c. (*strike with wonder*) 870.

Adj. nonexpectant; surprised &c. *v.*; un-warned, -aware; off one's guard; in-attentive &c. 458.

un-expected, -anticipated, -looked for, -foreseen, -hoped for; dropped from the clouds; beyond –, contrary to –, against- expectation; out of one's reck-oning; unheard of &c. (*exceptional*) 83; startling; sudden &c. (*instantaneous*) 113.

Adv. abruptly, unexpectedly, plump, pop, *à l'improviste*, unawares; without -notice, – warning, – saying " by your leave "; like a -thief in the night, – thunderbolt; in an unguarded moment; suddenly &c. (*instantaneously*) 113.

Int. heydey! &c. (*wonder*) 870.

Phr. little did one -think, – expect; nobody would ever -suppose, – think, – expect; who would have thought? it beats the Dutch.

---

509. [Failure of expectation.] Disappointment. — **N.** disappointment; blighted hope, balk; blow; slip 'twixt cup and lip; nonfulfillment of one's hopes; sad –, bitter- disappointment; trick of fortune; afterclap; false –, vain- expecta-tion; miscalculation &c. 481; fool's paradise; much cry and little wool.

V. be disappointed; look -blank, – blue; look –, stand- -aghast &c. (*wonder*) 870; find to one's cost; laugh on the wrong side of one's mouth; find one a false prophet.

disappoint; crush –, dash –, balk –, disappoint –, blight –, falsify –, defeat –,

not realize- one's -hope, – expectation; balk, jilt, bilk; play one -false, – a trick; dash the cup from the lips; tantalize; dumfounder.

Adj. disappointed &c. *v.*; disconcerted, aghast; disgruntled; out of one's reckoning.

Phr. the mountain brought forth a mouse; *parturiunt montes; nascitur ridiculus mus* [Horace]; *diis aliter visum,* the bubble burst; one's countenance falling.

510. Foresight. — N. foresight, prospicience, prevision, long-sightedness; anticipation; providence &c. (*preparation*) 673.

fore-thought, -cast; pre-deliberation, -surmise; foregone conclusion &c. (*prejudgment*) 481; prudence &c. (*caution*) 864.

foreknowledge; prognosis; pre-cognition, -science, -notion, -sentiment; second-sight; sagacity &c. (*intelligence*) 498; antepast, prelibation, prophasis.

prospect &c. (*expectation*) 507; foretaste; prospectus &c. (*plan*) 626.

V. foresee; look -forwards to, – ahead, – beyond; scent from afar; look –, pry –, peep- into the future.

see one's way; see how the -land lies, – wind blows, – cat jumps.

anticipate; expect &c. 507; be beforehand &c. (*early*) 132; predict &c. 511; fore-know, -judge, -cast; presurmise; have an eye to the -future, – main chance; *respicere finem;* keep a sharp lookout &c. (*vigilance*) 459; forewarn &c. 668.

Adj. foreseeing &c. *v.*; prescient; far-seeing, -sighted; sagacious &c. (*intelligent*) 498; weatherwise; provident &c. (*prepared*) 673; prospective &c. 507.

Adv. against the time when.

Phr. *cernit omnia Deus vindex; mihi cura futuri.*

511. Prediction. — N. prediction, announcement; program(me) &c. (*plan*) 626; premonition &c. (*warning*) 668; prognosis, prophecy, vaticination, mantology, prognostication, premonstration †; augur-y, -ation †; a-, ha-riolation †; fore-, a-boding; bode-, abode-ment; omni-ation†, -ousness; auspices, forecast; omen &c. 512; horoscope, nativity; sooth †,-saying; fortune -telling; divination; necromancy &c. 992.

[Divination by the stars] astrology, horoscopy, judicial astrology.[1]

[Place of prediction] adytum.

prefigur-ation, -ement; prototype, type.

V. predict, prognosticate, prophesy, vaticinate, divine, foretell, soothsay, augurate, tell fortunes; cast a -horoscope, – nativity; advise; forewarn &c. 668.

presage, augur, bode; a-, fore-bode; fore-, be-token; pre-figure, -show; portend; fore-show, -shadow; shadow forth, typify, pretypify, ominate†, signify, point to.

---

[1] The following terms, expressive of different forms of divination, have been collected from various sources, and are here given as a curious illustration of bygone superstitions:—

Divination *by oracles*, Theomancy; *by the Bible*, Bibliomancy; *by ghosts*, Psychomancy; *by crystal gazing*, Crystallomancy; *by shadows or manes*, Sciomancy; *by appearances in the air*, Aeromancy, Chaomancy; *by the stars at birth*, Genethliacs; *by meteors*, Meteoromancy; *by winds*, Austromancy; *by sacrificial appearances*, Aruspicy (*or* Haruspicy), Hieromancy, Hieroscopy; *by the entrails of animals sacrificed*, Extispicy, Hieromancy; *by the entrails of a human sacrifice*, Anthropomancy; *by the entrails of fishes*, Ichthyomancy; *by sacrificial fire*, Pyromancy; *by red-hot iron*, Sideromancy; *by smoke from the altar*, Capnomancy; *by mice*, Myomancy; *by birds*, Orniscopy, Ornithomancy; *by a cock picking up grains*, Alectryomancy (*or* Alectoromancy); *by fishes*, Ophiomancy; *by herbs*, Botanomancy; *by water*, Hydromancy; *by fountains*, Pegomancy; *by a wand*, Rhabdomancy; *by dough of cakes*, Crithomancy; *by meal*, Aleuromancy, Alphitomancy; *by salt*, Halomancy; *by dice*, Cleromancy; *by arrows*, Belomancy; *by a balanced hatchet*, Axinomancy; *by a balanced sieve*, Coscinomancy; *by a suspended ring*, Dactyliomancy; *by dots made at random on paper*, Geomancy; *by precious stones*, Lithomancy; *by pebbles*, Pessomancy; *by pebbles drawn from a heap*, Psephomancy; *by mirrors*, Catoptromancy; *by writings in ashes*, Tephramancy; *by dreams*, Oneiromancy; *by the hand*, Palmistry, Chiromancy; *by nails reflecting the sun's rays*, Onychomancy; *by finger rings*, Dactylomancy; *by numbers*, Arithmancy; *by drawing lots*, Sortilege; *by passages in books*, Stichomancy; *by the letters forming the name of the person*, Onomancy, Nomancy; *by the features*, Anthroposcopy; *by the mode of laughing*, Geloscopy; *by ventriloquism*, Gastromancy; *by walking in a circle*, Gyromancy; *by dropping melted wax into water*, Ceromancy; *by currents*, Bletonism; *by the color and peculiarities of wine*, Œnomancy.

usher in, herald, premise, announce; lower.

hold out –, raise –, excite- -expectation, – hope; bid fair, promise, lead one to expect; be the -precursor &c. 64.

Adj. predicting &c. *v.*; predictive, prophetic; fatidic, -al; vaticinal, oracular, fatiloquent, haruspical; Sibylline; weatherwise.

ominous, portentous; augur-ous †, -ial, -al; auspici-al, -ous; prescious, monitory, extispicious, premonitory, significant of, pregnant with, big with the fate of.

Phr. " coming events cast their shadows before " [Campbell]; *dicamus bona verba;* " there buds the promise of celestial worth " [Young].

512. Omen. — N. omen, portent, presage, prognostic, augury, auspice; sign &c. (*indication*) 550; harbinger &c. (*precursor*) 64; yule candle.

bird of ill omen; signs of the times; gathering clouds; warning &c. 668.

prefigurement &c. 511.

Adj. ill-boding.

Phr. *auspicium melioris ævi.*

513. Oracle. — N. oracle; prophet, seer, soothsayer, augur, fortune teller, witch, geomancer, aruspex; a-, ha-ruspice; haruspex; Sibyl; Python, -ess; Pythia; Pythian –, Delphian- oracle; Monitor, Sphinx, Tiresias, Cassandra, Sibylline leaves; Zadkiel, Old Moore; sorcerer &c. 994; interpreter &c. 524.

Section VII. Creative Thought

514. Supposition. — N. supposition, assumption, postulation, condition, presupposition, hypothesis, postulate, postulatum, theory, data; pro-, position; thesis, theorem; proposal &c. (*plan*) 626; assumed position.

bare –, vague –, loose- -supposition, – suggestion; conceit; conjecture; guess, – work; rough guess, shot; conjecturality; surmise, suspicion, inkling, suggestion, association of ideas, hint; presumption &c. (*belief*) 484; divination, speculation.

V. suppose, conjecture, surmise, suspect, guess, divine; theorize; pre-sume, -surmise, -suppose; assume, fancy, wis, take it; give a guess, speculate, believe, dare say, take it into one's head, take for granted.

put forth; pro-pound, -pose; start, put a case, submit, move, make a motion; hazard –, throw out –, put forward- a -suggestion, – conjecture.

allude to, suggest, hint, put it into one's head.

suggest itself &c. (*thought*) 451; run in the head &c. (*memory*) 505; marvel –, wonder- -if, – whether.

Adj. supposing &c. *v.*; given, mooted, postulatory; assumed &c. *v.*; suppositive, -itious; gratuitous, speculative, conjectural, hypothetical, theoretical, academic, supposable, presumptive, putative; suppositional.

suggestive, allusive.

Adv. if, – so be; an; on the -supposition &c. *n.*; *ex hypothesi;* in -case, – the event of; quasi, as if, provided; perhaps &c. (*by possibility*) 470; for aught one knows.

515. Imagination. — N. imagination; originality; invention; fancy; inspiration; verve.

warm –, heated –, excited –, sanguine –, ardent –, fiery –, boiling –, wild –, bold –, daring –, playful –, lively –, fertile- -imagination, – fancy.

" mind's eye "; " such stuff as dreams are made of " [*Tempest*].

ideal-ity, -ism; romanticism, utopianism, castle-building; dreaming; phrensy, frenzy; ecs-, ex-tasy †; calenture &c. (*delirium*) 503; reverie, trance; somnambulism.

conception, *Vorstellung*, excogitation, " a fine frenzy "; cloud-, dream-land;

flight –, fumes- of fancy; " thick-coming fancies " [*Macbeth*]; creation –, coinage- of the brain; imagery.

conceit, maggot, figment, myth, dream, vision, shadow, chimera; phan-tasm, -tasy; fantasy, fancy; whim, -sey, -sy; vagary, rhapsody, romance, gest, geste, extravaganza; air-drawn dagger, bugbear, nightmare; flying Dutchman, great sea serpent, man in the moon, castle in the air, *château en Espagne;* Utopia, Atlantis, happy valley, millennium, fairyland; land of Prester John, kingdom of Micomicon; work of fiction &c. (*novel*) 594; Arabian nights; *le pot au lait;* dream of Alnaschar &c. (*hope*) 858; day –, golden- dream.

illusion &c. (*error*) 495; phantom &c. (*fallacy of vision*) 443; *Fata Morgana* &c. (*ignis fatuus*) 423; vapor &c. (*cloud*) 353; stretch of the imagination &c. (*exaggeration*) 549; mythogenesis.

idealist, romanticist, visionary; mopus; romancer, dreamer; somnambulist; rhapsodist &c. (*fanatic*) 504; castle-builder, fanciful projector.

V. imagine, fancy, conceive; ideal-, real-ize; dream, – of; " give to airy nothing a local habitation and a name " [*Midsummer Night's Dream*].

create, originate, devise, invent, coin, fabricate; improvise, strike out something new.

set one's wits to work; strain –, crack- one's invention; rack –, ransack –, cudgel- one's brains; excogitate.

give -play, – the reins, – a loose- to the- -imagination, – fancy; indulge in reverie.

conjure up a vision; fancy –, represent –, picture –, figure- to oneself; *vorstellen.*

float in the mind; suggest itself &c. (*thought*) 451.

Adj. imagined &c. *v.*; *ben trovato;* air-drawn, -built.

imagin-ing &c. *v.*, -ative; original, inventive, creative, fertile.

romantic, high-flown, flighty, extravagant, fanatic, enthusiastic, Utopian, Quixotic.

ideal, unreal; in the clouds, *in nubibus;* unsubstantial &c. 4; illusory &c. (*fallacious*) 495.

fabulous, legendary; myth-ic, -ological; chimerical; imagin-, vision-ary; notional; fan-cy, -ciful, -tastical; whimsical; fairy, -like; gestic.

Phr. " a change came o'er the spirit of my dream " [Byron]; *ægri somnia vana; dolphinum appingit sylvis in fluctibus aprum* [Horace]; " fancy light from fancy caught " [Tennyson]; " imagination rules the world " [Napoleon]; *l'imagination gallope, le jugement ne va que le pas; musæo contingens cuncta lepore* [Lucretius]; *tous songes sont mensonges; Wahrheit und Dichtung.*

DIVISION (II) COMMUNICATION OF IDEAS

Section I. NATURE OF IDEAS COMMUNICATED

516. [Idea to be conveyed.] **Meaning.** [Thing signified.] — **N.** meaning; signific-ation, -ance; sense, expression; im-, pur-port; force; drift, tenor, spirit, bearing, coloring; scope.

matter; subject, -matter; argument, text, sum and substance; gist &c. 5.

general –, broad –, substantial –, colloquial –, literal –, plain –, simple –, natural –, unstrained –, true &c. (*exact*) 494 –, honest &c. 543 –, *primâ facie* &c. (*manifest*) 525- meaning.

literality; after acceptation; allusion &c. (*latency*) 526; suggestion &c. (*infor-*

517. [Absence of meaning.] **Unmeaningness.** — **N.** unmeaningness &c. *adj.*; scrabble.

empty sound, dead letter, *vox et præterea nihil;* " a tale told by an idiot, full of sound and fury, signifying nothing "; " sounding brass and a tinkling cymbal."

nonsense, jargon, gibberish, jabber, mere words, hocus-pocus, fustian, rant, bombast, balderdash, palaver, flummery, verbiage, babble, *bavardage, baragouin,* platitude, *niaiserie;* inanity; flapdoodle; rigmarole, rodomontade; truism;

mation) 527; synonym; figure of speech &c. 521; acceptation &c. (*interpretation*) 522.

V. mean, signify, express; im-, purport; convey, imply, breathe, indicate, bespeak, bear a sense; tell –, speak- of; touch on; point –, allude- to; drive at; involve &c. (*latency*) 526; declare &c. (*affirm*) 535.

understand by &c. (*interpret*) 522.

Adj. meaning &c. *v.*; expressive, suggestive, allusive; signific-ant, -ative, -atory; pithy; full of –, pregnant with- meaning.

declaratory &c. 535; intelligible &c. 518; literal; synonymous; tantamount &c. (*equivalent*) 27; implied &c. (*latent*) 526; explicit &c. 525.

Adv. to that effect; that is to say &c. (*being interpreted*) 522.

518. Intelligibility. — N. intelligibility; clearness, explicitness &c. *adj.*; lucidity, comprehensibility, perspicuity; legibility, plain speaking &c. (*manifestation*) 525; precision &c. 494; φωνᾶντα συνετοῖσι, a word to the wise.

V. be -intelligible &c. *adj.*; speak -for itself, – volumes; tell its own tale, lie on the surface.

render -intelligible &c. *adj.*; popularize, simplify, clear up; elucidate &c. (*explain*) 522.

understand, comprehend; take, – in; catch, grasp, follow, collect, master, make out; see -with half an eye, – daylight, – one's way; enter into the ideas of; come to an understanding.

Adj. intelligible; clear, – as -day, – noonday; lucid; per-, tran-spicuous; luminous, transparent.

easily understood, easy to understand, for the million, intelligible to the meanest capacity, popularized.

plain, distinct, explicit; positive; definite &c. (*precise*) 494.

graphic; expressive &c. (*meaning*) 516; illustrative &c. (*explanatory*) 522.

un-ambiguous, -equivocal, -mistakable &c. (*manifest*) 525, -confused; legible, recognizable; obvious &c. 525.

Adv. in plain -terms, – words, – English.

Phr. he that runs may read &c. (*manifest*) 525.

nugæ canoræ; twaddle, twattle, fudge, trash; poppy-cock [U. S.]; stuff, – and nonsense; bosh, rubbish, moonshine, wish-wash, fiddle-faddle; absurdity &c. 497; vagueness &c. (*unintelligibility*) 519.

V. mean nothing; be -unmeaning &c. *adj.*; twaddle, quibble, scrabble.

Adj. unmeaning; meaning-, senseless; nonsensical; void of -sense &c. 516.

in-, un-expressive; vacant; not -significant &c. 516; insignificant.

trashy, washy, trumpery, trivial, fiddle-faddle, twaddling, quibbling.

unmeant, not expressed; tacit &c. (*latent*) 526.

inexpressible, undefinable, incommunicable.

519. Unintelligibility. — N. unintelligibility, incomprehensibility, imperspicuity; inconceivableness, vagueness &c. *adj.*; obscurity; ambiguity &c. 520; doubtful meaning; uncertainty &c. 475; perplexity &c. (*confusion*) 59; spinosity; *obscurum per obscurius;* mystification &c. (*concealment*) 528; latency &c. 526; transcendentalism.

paradox; riddle &c. (*secret*) 533; *dignus vindice nodus;* sealed book; steganography, freemasonry.

pons asinorum, asses' bridge; high Dutch, Greek, Hebrew; jargon &c. (*unmeaning*) 517.

V. be -unintelligible &c. *adj.*; require -explanation &c. 522; have a doubtful meaning, pass comprehension.

render -unintelligible &c. *adj.*; conceal &c. 528; darken &c. 421; confuse &c. (*derange*) 61; perplex &c. (*bewilder*) 475.

not -understand &c. 518; lose, – the clue; miss; not know what to make of, be able to make nothing of, give it up; not be able to -account for, – make either head or tail of; be at sea &c. (*uncertain*) 475; wonder &c. 870; see through a glass darkly &c. (*ignorance*) 491.

not understand one another; play at cross purposes &c. (*misinterpret*) 523.

Adj. un-intelligible, -accountable, -decipherable, -discoverable, -knowable, -fathomable; in-cognizable, -explicable, -scrutable; inap-, incom-prehensible; insol-vable, -uble; impenetrable.

illegible, as Greek to one, unexplained, paradoxical; enigmatic, -al; puzzling; indecipherable.

obscure, dark, muddy, clear as mud, seen through a mist, dim, nebulous, shrouded in mystery; undiscernible &c. (*invisible*) 447; misty &c. (*opaque*) 426; hidden &c. 528; latent &c. 526.

indefinite &c. (*indistinct*) 447; perplexed &c. (*confused*) 59; undetermined, vague, loose, ambiguous; mysterious; mystic, -al; acroamatic, -al; metempirical; transcendental; occult, recondite, abstruse, crabbed.

incon-ceivable, -ceptible; searchless; above -, beyond -, past- comprehension; beyond one's depth; unconceived.

inexpressible, undefinable, incommunicable.

520. [Having a double sense.] **Equivocalness. — N.** equivocalness &c. *adj.*; double -meaning &c. 516; ambiguity, *double entente*, pun, paragram, *calembour*, quibble, equivoque, anagram; conundrum &c. (*riddle*) 533; word -play &c. (*wit*) 842; homonym, -y; amphibo-ly, -logy; ambilogy, ambiloquy †.

Sphinx, Delphic oracle.

equivocation &c. (*duplicity*) 544; white lie, mental reservation &c. (*concealment*) 528; paltering.

V. be -equivocal &c. *adj.*; have two -meanings &c. 516; equivocate &c. (*palter*) 544.

Adj. equivocal, ambiguous, amphibolous, homonymous; double-tongued &c. (*lying*) 544; enigmatical, indeterminate.

521. Metaphor. — N. figure of speech: *façon de parler*, way of speaking, colloquialism.

phrase &c. 566; figure, trope, metaphor, metonymy, enallage, catachresis, synecdoche, autonomasia; irony, figurativeness &c. *adj.*; image, -ry; metalepsis, type, anagoge, simile, personification, prosopopœia, allegory, apologue, parable, fable; allusion, adumbration; application.

V. employ -metaphor &c. *n.*; personify, allegorize, adumbrate, shadow forth, apply, allude to.

Adj. metaphorical, figurative, catachrestical, typical, tralatitious, parabolic, allegorical, allusive, anagogical; ironical; colloquial; tropical.

Adv. so to -speak, - say, - express oneself; as it were.

Phr. *mutato nomine de te fabula narratur* [Horace].

522. Interpretation. — N. interpretation, definition; explan-, explic-ation; solution, answer; rationale; plain -, simple -, strict- interpretation; meaning &c. 516.

translation; rend-ering, -ition; reddition; literal -, free- translation; key; secret; clew &c. (*indication*) 550; *clavis*, crib, pony [U. S.].

exegesis; ex-pounding, -position; hermeneutics; comment, -ary; inference &c. (*deduction*) 480; illustration, exemplification; gloss, annotation, scholium, note; e-, di-lucidation †; *éclaircissement*, *mot d'énigme*.

symptomat-, semei-ology; metoposcopy, physiognomy; paleography &c. (*philology*) 560; oneirology

accept-ion, -ation, -ance; light, reading, lection, construction, version.

523. Misinterpretation. — N. misinterpretation, -apprehension, -understanding, -acceptation †, - construction, -application; catachresis; eisegesis; cross -reading, - purposes; mistake &c. 495.

misrepresentation, perversion, exaggeration &c. 549; false -coloring, - construction; abuse of terms; parody, travesty; falsification &c. (*lying*) 544.

V. mis-interpret, -apprehend, -understand, -conceive, -spell, -translate, -construe, -apply; mistake &c. 495.

misrepresent, pervert; explain wrongly, misstate; garble &c. (*falsify*) 544; distort, detort †; travesty, play upon words; stretch -, strain -, wrest- the -sense, - meaning; explain away; put a -bad, - false- construction on; give a false coloring.

be -, play- at cross purposes.

equivalent, – meaning &c. 516; synonym; para-, meta-phrase; convertible terms, apposition; dictionary &c. 562; polyglot.

V. interpret, explain, define, construe, translate, render; do –, turn- into; transfuse the sense of.

find out &c. 480a- -the meaning &c. 516- of; read; spell –, make- out; decipher, unravel, disentangle; find the key of, enucleate, resolve, solve; read between the lines.

account for; find –, tell- the cause &c. 153- of; throw –, shed- -light, –new light, – fresh light- upon; clear up, elucidate.

illustrate, exemplify; unfold, expound, comment upon, annotate; popularize &c. (*render intelligible*) 518.

take –, understand –, receive –, accept- in a particular sense; understand by, put a construction on, be given to understand.

Adj. explanatory, expository; explica-tive, -tory; exegetical; construable.

polyglot; literal; para-, meta-phrastic; consignificative, synonymous; equivalent &c. 27.

Adv. in -explanation &c. *n.*; that is to say, *id est, videlicet,* to wit, namely, in other words.

literally, strictly speaking; in -plain, – plainer- -terms, – words, – English; more simply.

Adj. misinterpreted &c. *v.*; untranslat-ed, -able.

524. Interpreter. — **N.** interpreter; ex-positor, -pounder, -ponent, -plainer; demonstrator.

scholiast, commentator, annotator; meta-, para-phrast; glossarist, prolocutor.

spokesman, speaker, mouthpiece.

dragoman, courier, *valet de place, cicerone,* showman; oneirocritic; Œdipus; oracle &c. 513.

Section II. Modes of Communication

525. Manifestation. — **N.** manifestation; plainness &c. *adj.*; plain speaking; expression; showing &c. *v.*; exposition, demonstration; exhibition, production; display, show, showing off; premonstration †. [Thing shown] exhibit.

indication &c. (*calling attention to*) 457; publicity &c. 531; disclosure &c. 529; openness &c. (*honesty*) 543, (*artlessness*) 703; *épanchement.*

V. make –, render- -manifest &c. *adj.*; bring -forth, – forward, – to the front, – into view; give notice; express; represent, set forth, exhibit; show, – up; expose; produce; hold up –, expose- to view; set –, place –, lay- before -one, – one's eyes; tell to one's face; trot out, put through one's paces, bring to light, display, demonstrate, unroll; lay open; draw –, bring- out; bring out in strong relief; call –, bring- into notice; hold up the mirror; wear one's heart upon his sleeve; show one's -face, – colors; manifest oneself; speak out; make no -mys-

526. Latency. — **N.** latency, inexpression; hidden –, occult- meaning; occultness, mystery, cabala, anagoge; silence &c. (*taciturnity*) 585; concealment &c. 528; more than meets the -eye, – ear; Delphic oracle; *le dessous des cartes,* undercurrent.

allusion, insinuation, implication; innuendo &c. 527; adumbration; " something rotten in the state of Denmark " [*Hamlet*].

snake in the grass &c. (*pitfall*) 667; secret &c. 533.

darkness, invisibility, imperceptibility.

V. be -latent &c. *adj.*; lurk, smolder, underlie, make no sign; escape -observation, – detection, – recognition; lie hid &c. 528.

laugh in one's sleeve; keep back &c. (*conceal*) 528.

involve, imply, understand, allude to, infer, leave an inference; whisper &c. (*conceal*) 528.

tery, – secret- of; unfurl the flag; proclaim &c. (*publish*) 531.

indicate &c. (*direct attention to*) 457; disclose &c. 529; elicit &c. 480a.

be -manifest &c. *adj*.; appear &c. (*be visible*) 446; transpire &c. (*be disclosed*) 529; speak for itself, stand to reason; stare one in the face, rear its head; give -token, – sign, – indication of; tell its own tale &c. (*intelligible*) 518.

Adj. manifest, apparent; salient, striking, demonstrative, prominent, in the foreground, notable, pronounced.

flagrant; notorious &c. (*public*) 531; arrant; stark staring; unshaded, glaring.

defin-ed, -ite; distinct, conspicuous &c. (*visible*) 446; obvious, evident, unmistakable, indubitable, not to be mistaken, plain, clear, palpable, self-evident, autoptical; intelligible &c. 518; clear as -day, – daylight, – noonday; plain as -a pike- staff, – the sun at noonday, – the nose on one's face, – way to parish church.

ostensible; open, – as day; overt, patent, express, explicit; naked, bare, literal, downright, undisguised, exoteric.

unreserved; frank, plain-spoken &c. (*artless*) 703; barefaced.

manifested &c. *v*.; disclosed &c. 529; capable of being shown, producible; in-, un-concealable.

Adv. manifestly, openly &c. *adj*.; before one's eyes, under one's nose, to one's face, face to face, above board, *cartes sur table*, on the stage, in open court, in the open streets; in market overt; in the face of -day, – heaven; in -broad –, open- daylight; without reserve; at first blush, *primâ facie*, on the face of; in set terms.

Phr. *cela saute aux yeux;* he that runs may read; you can see it with half an eye; it needs no ghost to tell us; the meaning lies on the surface; *cela va sans dire; res ipsa loquitur;* " clothing the palpable and familiar " [Coleridge]; *fari quæ sentiat; volto sciolto i pensieri stretti.*

Adj. latent; lurking &c. *v*.; secret &c. 528; occult; implied &c. *v*.; dormant; abeyant.

un-apparent, -known, -seen &c. 441; in the background; invisible &c. 447; indiscoverable, dark; impenetrable &c. (*unintelligible*) 519; un-spied, -suspected.

un-said, -written, -published, -breathed, -talked of, -told &c. 527, -sung, -exposed, -proclaimed, -disclosed &c. 529, -expressed; not expressed, tacit.

un-developed, -solved, -explained, -traced, -discovered &c. 480a, -tracked, -explored, -invented.

indirect, crooked, inferential; by -inference, -implication; implicit; constructive; allusive, covert, muffled; steganographic; under-stood, -hand, -ground; concealed &c. 528; delitescent.

Adv. by a side wind; *sub silentio;* in the background; behind -the scenes, – one's back; on the tip of one's tongue; secretly &c. 528; between the lines.

Phr. " thereby hangs a tale " [*As You Like It*]; *tacitum vivit sub pectore vulnus* [Vergil].

527. Information. — N. information, enlightenment, acquaintance, knowledge &c. 490; publicity &c. 531.

communication, intimation; not-ice, -ification; e-, an-nunciation; announcement; *communiqué;* representation, round robin, presentment.

case, estimate, specification, report, advice, monition; news &c. 532; return &c. (*record*) 551; account &c. (*description*) 594; statement &c. (*affirmation*) 535.

mention; acquainting &c. *v*.; instruction &c. (*teaching*) 537; outpouring; intercommunication, communicativeness.

informant, authority, teller, intelligencer, reporter, exponent, mouthpiece;

528. Concealment. — N. concealment; hiding &c. *v*.; occultation, mystification.

seal of secrecy; screen &c. 530; disguise &c. 530; masquerade; masked battery; hiding place &c. 530; crypt-, stegan-ography; freemasonry.

stealth, -iness; obreption †; slyness &c. (*cunning*) 702.

latit-ancy, -ation; seclusion &c. 893; privacy, secrecy, secretness; incognita.

reticence; reserve; mental –, reservation; *arrière pensée*, suppression, evasion, white lie, misprision; silence &c. (*taciturnity*) 585; suppression of truth &c. 544; underhand dealing; close-, secretive-ness &c. *adj*.; mystery.

informer, eavesdropper, delator, detect-ive; sleuth; *mouchard*, spy, newsmonger; messenger &c. 534; *amicus curiæ*.

valet de place, cicerone, pilot, guide; guide-, hand-book; *vade mecum;* manual; map, plan, chart, gazetteer; itin-erary &c. (*journey*) 266.

hint, suggestion, innuendo, inkling, whisper, passing word, word in the ear, subaudition, cue, byplay; gesture &c. (*indication*) 550; gentle -, broad- hint; *verbum sapienti;* word to the wise; in-sinuation &c. (*latency*) 526.

V. tell; inform, - of; acquaint, - with; impart, - to; make acquainted with, apprise, advise, enlighten, awaken.

let fall, mention, express, intimate,˙ represent, communicate, make known; publish &c. 531; notify, signify, specify, convey the knowledge of.

let one -, have one to- know; give one to understand; give notice; set -, lay -, put- before; point out, put into one's head; put one in possession of; instruct &c. (*teach*) 537; direct the attention to &c. 457.

an-nounce, -nunciate; report, - prog-ress; bring -, send -, leave -, write-word; tele-graph, -phone; wire; retail, render an account; give an account &c. (*describe*) 594; state &c. (*affirm*) 535.

disclose &c. 529; show cause; explain &c. (*interpret*) 522.

hint; give an inkling of; give -, drop -, throw out- a hint; insinuate; allude -, make allusion- to; glance at; tip the wink &c. (*indicate*) 550; suggest, prompt, give the cue, breathe; whisper, - in the ear.

give a bit of one's mind; tell one -plainly, - once for all; speak volumes.

un-deceive, -beguile; set right, cor-rect, open the eyes of, disabuse.

be -informed of &c.; know &c. 490; learn &c. 539; get scent of, gather from; awaken -, open one's eyes- to; become -alive, - awake- to; hear, overhear, un-derstand.

come to one's -ears, - knowledge; reach one's ears.

Adj. informed &c. *v.*; *communiqué;* reported &c. *v.*; published &c. 531.

expressive &c. 516; explicit &c. (*open*) 525, (*clear*) 518; plain-spoken &c. (*art-less*) 703.

nuncupa-tive, -tory †; declara-, ex-posi-tory; enunciative; communicat-ive, -ory.

latency &c. 526; snake in the grass; secret &c. 533; stowaway.

V. conceal, hide, secrete, put out of sight; lock -, seal -, bottle- up.

cover, screen, cloak, veil, shroud; cover up one's tracks; screen from -sight, - observation; draw the veil; draw -, close- the curtain; curtain, shade, eclipse, throw a veil over; be-cloud, -mask; mask, disguise; ensconce, muffle, smother; befog; whisper.

keep -from, - back, - to oneself; keep -snug, - close, - secret, - dark; bury; sink, suppress; keep -from, - out of--view, - sight; keep in -, throw into- the -shade, - background; stifle, hush up, smother, withhold, reserve; fence with a question; ignore &c. 460.

keep -a secret, - one's own counsel; hold one's tongue &c. (*silence*) 585; make no sign, not let it go further; not breathe a -word, - syllable- about; not let the right hand know what the left is doing; hide one's light under a bushel, bury one's talent in a napkin.

keep -, leave- in -the dark, - igno-rance; blind, - the eyes; blindfold, hood-wink, mystify; puzzle &c. (*render un-certain*) 475; bamboozle &c. (*deceive*) 545.

be -concealed &c. *v.*; suffer an eclipse; retire from sight, couch; hide oneself; lie -hid, - in ambush, - perdu, - close; seclude oneself &c. 893; lurk, sneak, skulk, slink, prowl; steal -into, - out of, - by, - along; play at -bopeep, - hide and seek; hide in holes and corners; still-hunt.

Adj. concealed &c. *v.*; hidden; secret, recondite, mystic, cabalistic, occult, dark; cryptic, -al; private, privy, *in petto*, auricular, clandestine, close, invio-late; tortuous.

behind a -screen &c. 530; under -cov-er, - an eclipse; in -ambush, - hiding, - disguise; in a -cloud, - fog, - mist, - haze, - dark corner; in the -shade, - dark; clouded, wrapt in clouds; invis-ible &c. 447; buried, underground, per-du; secluded &c. 893.

un-disclosed &c. 529, -told &c. 527; covert &c. (*latent*) 526; mysterious &c. (*unintelligible*) 519.

irrevealable, inviolable; confidential; esoteric; not to be spoken of.

obreptitious, furtive, stealthy, feline; skulking &c. *v.*; surreptitious, under-hand, hole and corner; sly &c. (*cunning*)

Adv. from information received.

Phr. a little bird told me.

702; secretive, evasive; reserved, reticent, uncommunicative, buttoned up; close, – as wax; taciturn &c. 585.

Adv. secretly &c. *adj.*; in -secret, – private, – one's sleeve, – holes and corners; in the dark &c. *adj.*

januis clausis, with closed doors, *à huis clos;* hugger-mugger, *à la dérobée;* under the -cloak of, – rose, – table; *sub rosâ, en tapinois,* in the background, aside, on the sly, with bated breath, *sotto voce,* in a whisper, without beat of drum, *â la sourdine.*

behind the veil; beyond -mortal ken, – the grave, – the veil; hid from mortal vision; into the -eternal secret, – realms supersensible, – supreme mystery.

in –, in strict- confidence; confidentially &c. *adj.*; between -ourselves, – you and me; *entre nous, inter nos,* under the seal of secrecy; *à couvert.*

underhand, by stealth, like a thief in the night; stealthily &c. *adj.*; behind -the scenes, – the curtain, – one's back, – a screen &c. 530; incognito; *in camerâ.*

Phr. it -must, – will- go no further; " tell it not in Gath," nobody the wiser; *alitur vitium vivitque tegendo;* " let it be tenable in your silence still " [*Hamlet*].

529. Disclosure. — N. disclosure; re-tection †; unveiling &c. *v.*; deterration †, revealment, revelation; expos-ition, -ure; *exposé;* whole truth; telltale &c. (*news*) 532.

acknowledgment, avowal; confession, -al; shrift.

bursting of a bubble; *dénouement.*

V. dis-close, -cover, -mask †; draw –, draw aside –, lift –, raise –, lift up –, re-move –, tear- the -veil, – curtain; un-mask, -veil, -fold, -cover, -seal, -ken-nel; take off –, break- the seal; lay -open, – bare; expose; open, – up; bare, bring to light.

divulge, reveal, break; let into the secret; reveal the secrets of the prison house; tell &c. (*inform*) 527; squeal *; breathe, utter, blab, peach; let -out, – fall, – drop, – the cat out of the bag; betray; tell tales, – out of school; come out with; give -vent, – utterance- to; open the lips, blurt out, vent, whisper about; speak out &c. (*make manifest*) 525; make public &c. 531; unriddle &c. (*find out*) 480a; split.

acknowledge, allow, concede, grant, admit, own, confess, avow, throw off all disguise, turn inside out, make a clean breast; show one's -hand, – cards; unburden –, disburden- one's mind, – conscience, – heart; open –, lay bare –, tell a piece of- one's mind; unbosom oneself, own to the soft impeachment; say –, speak- the truth; turn King's (*or* Queen's) evidence; acknowledge the corn * [U. S.].

raise –, drop –, lift –, remove –, throw off- the mask; expose; lay open; un-deceive, -beguile; disabuse, set right, correct, open the eyes of; *désillusionner.*

be -disclosed &c.; transpire, come to light; come in sight &c. (*be visible*) 446; become known, escape the lips; come --, ooze -, creep -, leak -, peep -, crop-out; show its -face, – colors; discover &c. itself; break through the clouds, flash on the mind.

Adj. disclosed &c. *v.*

530. Ambush. [Means of conceal-ment.] — **N.** hiding place; secret -place, – drawer; recess, hole, holes and cor-ners; closet, crypt, adytum, abditory, *oubliette.*

am-bush, -buscade; stalking-horse; lurking-hole, -place; secret path, back stairs; retreat &c. (*refuge*) 666.

screen, cover, shade, blinker; veil, curtain, blind, cloak, cloud.

mask, visor, vizor, disguise, masquer-ade dress, domino.

pitfall &c. (*source of danger*) 667; trap &c. (*snare*) 545.

V. lie in ambush &c. (*hide oneself*) 528; lie in wait for; set a trap for &c. (*de-ceive*) 545; ambuscade, ambush.

Adv. *aux aguets.*

161

Int. out with it!

Phr. the murder is out; a light breaks in upon one; the scales fall from one's eyes; the eyes are opened.

531. Publication. — N. publication; public -announcement |&c. 527; promulgation, propagation, proclamation, *pronunziamento;* circulation, indiction, edition; hue and cry.

publicity, notoriety, currency, flagrancy, cry, *bruit; vox populi;* report &c. (*news*) 532.

the Press, public press, newspaper, journal, gazette, daily; telegraphy; publisher &c. *v.;* imprint.

circular, - letter; manifesto, advertisement, ad., placard, bill, *affiche,* broadside, poster; notice &c. 527.

V. publish; make -public, - known &c. (*information*) 527; speak -, talk- of; broach, utter; put forward; circulate, propagate, promulgate; spread, - abroad; rumor, diffuse, disseminate, evulgate †; put -, give -, send- forth; emit, edit, get out; issue; bring -, lay -, drag- before the public; give -out, - to the world; put -, bandy -, hawk -, buzz -, whisper -, bruit -, blaze- about; drag into the open day; voice.

proclaim, herald, blazon; blaze -, noise- abroad; sound a trumpet; trumpet -, thunder- forth; give tongue; announce with -beat of drum, - flourish of trumpets; proclaim -from the housetops, - at Charing Cross.

advertise, placard; post, - up; *afficher,* publish in the Gazette, send round the crier.

raise a -cry, - hue and cry, - report; set news afloat.

be -published &c.; be -, become- -public &c. *adj.;* come out; go -, fly -, buzz -, blow- about; get -about, - abroad, - afloat, - wind; find vent; see the light; go forth, take air, acquire currency, pass current; go -the rounds, - the round of the newspapers, - through the length and breadth of the land; *virum volitare per ora;* pass from mouth to mouth; spread; run -, spread- like wildfire.

Adj. published &c. *v.;* current &c. (*news*) 532; in circulation, public; notorious; flagrant, arrant; open &c. 525; trumpet-tongued; encyclical, encyclic, promulgatory; exoteric.

Adv. publicly &c. *adj.;* in open court, with open doors.

Int. Oyez! O yes! notice!

Phr. notice is hereby given; this is -, these are- to give notice; *nomina stultorum parietibus hærent; semel emissum volat irrevocabile verbum.*

532. News. — N. news; information &c. 527; piece -, budget- of -news, - information; intelligence, tidings.

word, advice, aviso, message; dis-, des-patch; telegram, cable, marconigram, wire, communication, errand, embassy; bulletin.

report, rumor, hearsay, *on dit,* flying rumor, news stirring, cry, buzz, bruit, fame; talk, *oui-dire,* scandal, eavesdropping; town -, table- talk; tittle-tattle; canard, topic of the day, idea afloat.

fresh -, stirring -, old -, stale- news; glad tidings; old -, stale- story; chestnut *.

narrator &c. (*describe*) 594; news-, scandal-monger; talebearer, telltale, gossip, tattler.

V. transpire &c. (*be disclosed*) 529; rumor &c. (*publish*) 531.

533. Secret. — N. secret; dead -, profound- secret; arcanum, mystery; latency &c. 526; Asian mystery; sealed book, secrets of the prison house; *le dessous des cartes.*

enigma, riddle, puzzle, nut to crack, conundrum, charade, rebus, logogriph; mono-, ana-gram; Sphinx; *crux criticorum.*

maze, labyrinth, Hyrcynian wood; intricacy, meander.

problem &c. (*question*) 461; paradox &c. (*difficulty*) 704; unintelligibility &c. 519; *terra incognita* &c. (*ignorance*) 491.

Adj. secret &c. (*concealed*) 528; involved &c. 248; labyrinthian, mazy.

Adj. many-tongued; rumored; publicly –, currently- -rumored, – reported; rife, current, floating, afloat, going about, in circulation, in every one's mouth, all over the town.

Adv. as the story -goes, – runs; as they say, it is said; by -telegraph, – wireless.

Phr. " airy tongues that syllable men's names " [Milton].

534. Messenger. — N. messenger, envoy, emissary, legate; nuncio, internuncio; ambassador &c. (*diplomatist*) 758.

marshal, flag bearer, herald, crier, trumpeter, bellman, pursuivant, *parlementaire*, apparitor.

courier, runner, dak, estafette; Mercury, Iris, Ariel.

commissionaire; errand-, chore-, news-boy.

mail; post, -office; letter bag; tele-graph, -phone; cable; wire; carrier pigeon.

reporter; gentleman –, representative- of the press; penny-a-liner; special –, own- correspondent; spy, scout; informer &c. 527.

535. Affirmation. — N. affirm-ance, -ation; statement, allegation, assertion, predication, declaration, word, averment; confirmation.

asseveration, adjuration, swearing, oath, affidavit; deposition &c. (*record*) 551; avouchment, assurance; protest, -ation; profession; acknowledgment &c. (*assent*) 488; legal pledge, pronouncement; solemn -averment, – avowal, – declaration.

vote, voice; ballot, suffrage.

remark, observation; position &c. (*proposition*) 514; saying, dictum, sentence, *ipse dixit*.

emphasis; weight; dogmatism &c. (*certainty*) 474; dogmatist &c. 887.

V. assert; make -an assertion &c. *n.*; have one's say; say, affirm, predicate, declare, state; protest, profess.

put -forth, – forward; advance, allege, propose, propound, enunciate, broach, set forth, hold out, maintain, contend, pronounce, pretend.

depose, depone, aver, avow, avouch, asseverate, swear; make –, take one's- oath; make –, swear –, put in- an affidavit; take one's Bible oath, kiss the book, vow, *vitam impendere vero;* swear till -one is black in the face, – all's blue; be sworn, call Heaven to witness; vouch, warrant, certify, assure, swear by bell book and candle.

swear by &c. (*believe*) 484; insist –, take one's stand- upon; emphasize, lay stress on; assert -roundly, – positively; lay down, – the law; raise one's voice, dogmatize, have the last word; rap out; repeat; re-assert, -affirm.

536. Negation. — N. ne-, abnega-tion; denial; dis-avowal, -claimer; -juration; contra-diction, -vention; -cusation, protest; recusancy &c. (dissent) 489; flat –, emphatic- -contra diction, – denial; *démenti*.

qualification &c. 469; rep... &c. 610; retractation ... cation &c. 479; refusal ... prohibition &c. 761.

V. deny; contra-d... -vene; controvert, give denial to, gainsay, negative, shake the head.

dis-own, -affirm, -claim, -avow; recant &c. 607; revoke &c. (*abrogate*) 756.

dispute, impugn, traverse, rebut, join issue upon; bring –, call- in question &c. (*doubt*) 485; give (one) the lie in his throat.

deny -flatly, – peremptorily, – emphatically, – absolutely, – wholly, – entirely; give the lie to, belie.

repudiate &c. 610; set aside, ignore &c. 460; rebut &c. (*confute*) 479; qualify &c. 469; refuse &c. 764.

Adj. denying &c. *v.*; denied &c. *v.*; contradictory; negat-ive, -ory; recusant &c. (*dissenting*) 489; at issue upon.

Adv. no, nay, not, nowise; not a -bit, – whit, – jot; not -at all, – in the least, – so; no such thing; nothing of the -kind, – sort; quite the contrary, *tout au contraire*, far from it; *tant s'en faut;* on no account, in no respect; by -no, – no manner of- means; negatively.

Phr. there never was a greater mistake; I know better; *non hæc in fœdera.*

announce &c. (*information*) 527; acknowledge &c. (*assent*) 488; attest &c. (*evidence*) 467; adjure &c. (*put to one's oath*) 768.

Adj. asserting &c. *v.*; declaratory, predicatory, pronunciative, affirmative, *soi-disant;* positive; certain &c. 474; express, explicit &c. (*patent*) 525; absolute, emphatic, flat, broad, round, pointed, marked, distinct, decided, confident, trenchant, dogmatic, definitive, formal, solemn, categorical, peremptory; unretracted; predicable.

Adv. affirmatively &c. *adj.*; in the affirmative.

with emphasis, ex-cathedra, without fear of contradiction.

I must say, indeed, i' faith, let me tell you, why, give me leave to say, marry, you may be sure, I'd have you to know; upon my -word, – honor; by my troth, egad, I assure you; by -jingo, – Jove, – George, – &c.; troth, seriously, sadly; in –, in sober- -sadness, – truth, – earnest; of a truth, truly, perdy; in all conscience, upon oath; be assured &c. (*belief*) 484; yes &c. (*assent*) 488; I'll -warrant, – warrant you, – engage, – answer for it, – be bound, – venture to say, – take my oath; in fact, forsooth, joking apart; so help me God; not to mince the matter.

Phr. quoth he; *dixi.*

537. Teaching. — N. teaching &c. v.; instruction; edification; education; tuition; tutor-, tutel-age; direction, guidance; opsimathy.

qualification, preparation; train-, school-ing &c. *v.*; discipline; exer-cise, -citation; drill, practice.

persuasion, proselytism, propagandism, propaganda; in-doctrination, -culcation, -oculation.

explanation &c. (*interpretation*) 522; lesson, lecture, sermon; apologue, parable; discourse, prelection, preachment; chalk talk; Chautauqua [U. S.].

exercise, task; curriculum; course, – of study; grammar, three R's, initiation, A. B. C. &c. (*beginning*) 66.

elementary –, primary –, secondary –, technical –, college –, collegiate –, military –, university –, liberal –, classical –, religious –, denominational –, moral –, secular- education; propædeutics, moral tuition.

gymnastics, calisthenics; physical -drill, – education; sloyd.

V. teach, instruct, edify, school, tutor; cram, prime, coach; enlighten &c. (*inform*) 527.

in-culcate, -doctrinate, -oculate, -fuse, -still, -fix, -graft, -filtrate; im-bue, -pregnate, -plant; graft, sow the seeds of, disseminate.

give an idea of; put -up to, – in the way of; set right.

sharpen the wits, enlarge the mind; give new ideas, open the eyes, bring forward, " teach the young idea how to shoot " [Thomson]; improve &c. 658.

538. Misteaching. — N. mis-teaching, -information, -intelligence, -guidance, -direction, -persuasion, -instruction, -leading &c. *v.*; perversion, false teaching; sophistry &c. 477; college of Laputa; the blind leading the blind.

V. mis-inform, -teach, -describe, -direct, -guide, -instruct, -correct; pervert; put on a false –, throw off the- scent; deceive &c. 545; mislead &c. (*error*) 495; misrepresent; lie &c. 544; *ambiguas in vulgum spargere voces* [Vergil], preach to the wise, teach one's grandmother to suck eggs.

render unintelligible &c. 519; bewilder &c. (*uncertainty*) 475; mystify &c. (*conceal*) 528; unteach.

Adj. misteaching &c. *v.*; unedifying.

Phr. *piscem natare doces.*

539. Learning. — N. learning; acquisition of -knowledge &c. 490, – skill &c. 698; acquirement, attainment; edification, scholarship, erudition; acquired knowledge, lore, wide information; self-instruction; study, reading, perusal; inquiry &c. 461.

ap-, prenticeship; pupil-age, -arity; tutelage, novitiate, matriculation.

docility &c. (*willingness*) 602; aptitud &c. 698.

V. learn; acquire –, gain –, receiv –, take in –, drink in –, imbibe –, pic up –, gather –, get –, obtain –, collect – glean- -knowledge, – information, – learning.

acquaint oneself with, master; mal oneself -master of, – acquainted wit

expound &c. (*interpret*) 522; lecture; read –, give- a -lesson, – lecture, – sermon, – discourse; incept; hold forth, preach; sermon-, moral-ize; point a moral.

train, discipline; bring up, – to; educate, form, ground, prepare, qualify, drill, exercise, practice, habituate, familiarize with, nurture, drynurse, breed, rear, take in hand; break, – in; tame; preinstruct; initiate; inure &c. (*habituate*) 613.

put to nurse, send to school.

direct, guide; direct attention to &c. (*attention*) 457; impress upon the -mind, – memory; beat into, – the head; convince &c. (*belief*) 484.

Adj. teaching &c. *v.*; taught &c. *v.*; educational; scholastic, academic, doctrinal; disciplinal; instructive, didactic; propædeutic, -al.

Phr. the schoolmaster abroad; *a bovi majori discit arare minor; adeo in teneris consuescere multum est* [Vergil]; *docendo discimus; quæ nocent docent; qui docet discit;* " sermons in stones and good in everything " [*As You Like It*].

grind, cram; get –, coach- up; learn by -heart, – rote.

read, spell, peruse; con –, pore –, thumb- over; wade through; dip into; run the eye -over, – through; turn over the leaves.

study; be -studious &c. *adj.*; consume the midnight oil, mind one's book.

go to -school, – college, – the university; serve -an (*or* one's) apprenticeship, – one's time; learn one's trade; be -informed &c. 527; be -taught &c. 537.

Adj. studious; schol-astic, -arly; teachable; docile &c. (*willing*) 602; apt &c. 698, industrious &c. 682.

Adv. at one's books; *in statu pupillari* &c. (*learner*) 541.

Phr. " a lumber-house of books in every head " [Pope]; *ancora imparo!* " hold high converse with the mighty dead " [Thomson]; " lash'd into Latin by the tingling rod " [Gay].

540. Teacher. — N. teacher, trainer, instructor, institutor, master, tutor, director, Corypheus, dry nurse, coach, grinder, crammer, don; governor, bear leader; governess, duenna; disciplinarian.

professor, lecturer, reader, prelector, prolocutor, preacher; chalk talker, *khoja;* pastor &c. (*clergy*) 996; schoolmaster, dominie, usher, pedagogue, abecedarian; schoolmistress, dame, monitor, pupil teacher.

expositor &c. 524; preceptor, guide; guru; mentor &c. (*adviser*) 695; pioneer, apostle, missionary, propagandist, munshi, example &c. (*model for imitation*) 22.

professorship &c. (*school*) 542.

tutelage &c. (*teaching*) 537.

Adj. professorial.

Phr. *qui docet discit.*

541. Learner. — N. learner, scholar, student, alumnus, *élève*, pupil; ap-, pren- tice; articled clerk; schoolboy, beginner, tyro, abecedarian, alphabetarian.

recruit, novice, neophyte, inceptor, *débutant*, catechumen, probationer; chela, fellow-commoner; undergraduate; fresh, freshman; junior –, senior- soph; sophister, sophomore; questionist.

class, form, remove; pupilage &c. (*learning*) 539.

disciple, follower, apostle, proselyte; fellow-student, condisciple.

Adj. *in statu pupillari*, in leading strings.

542. School. — N. school, academy, university, *alma mater*, college, seminary, Lyceum; instit-ute, -ution; *palæstra*, Gymnasium, class, seminar.

day –, boarding –, preparatory –, primary –, infant –, dame's –, grammar –, middle class –, Board –, denominational –, National –, British and Foreign –, collegiate –, art –, continuation –, convent –, County Council –, government –, grant-in-aid –, high –, higher grade –, military –, missionary –, naval –, state-aided –, technical –, voluntary- school; school of art; kindergarten, nursery, *crèche*, reformatory.

pulpit, desk, reading desk, ambo, lecture room, theater, amphitheater, forum, stage, rostrum, platform, hustings, tribune.

school -, horn -, text book; grammar, primer, abecedary, rudiments, manual, *vade mecum;* en-, cyclopedia; Lindley Murray, Cocker; dictionary, lexicon.

professor-, lecture-, reader-, fellow-, tutor-ship; chair.

School Board, Council of Education; Board of Education; Board -, Prefect- of Studies; Textbook Committee; propaganda.

Adj. scholastic, academic, collegiate; educational.

Adv. ex-cathedra.

543. Veracity. — N. veracity; truth-fulness, frankness, &c. *adj.*; truth, sincerity, candor, honesty, fidelity; plain dealing, *bona fides;* love of truth; probity &c. 939; ingenuousness &c. (*artlessness*) 703.

the truth the whole truth and nothing but the truth; honest -, sober- truth &c. (*fact*) 494; unvarnished tale; light of truth.

V. speak -, tell- the truth; speak by the card; paint in its -, show oneself in one's- true colors; make a clean breast &c. (*disclose*) 529; speak one's mind &c. (*be blunt*) 703; not -lie &c. 544, - deceive &c. 545.

Adj. truthful, true; ver-acious, -idical; scrupulous &c. (*honorable*) 939; sincere, candid, frank, open, straightforward, unreserved; open-, true-, simple- hearted; honest, trustworthy; un-dissembling &c. (*dissemble* &c. 544); guileless, pure; truth-loving; unperjured; true blue, as good as one's word; unaffected, unfeigned, *bonâ fide;* outspoken, ingenuous &c. (*artless*) 703; undisguised &c. (*real*) 494.

Adv. truly &c. (*really*) 494; in plain words &c. 703; in -, with -, of a -, in good- truth; as the -dial to the sun, - needle to the pole; honor bright; troth; in good -sooth, - earnest; unfeignedly, with no nonsense, in sooth, sooth to say, *bonâ fide, in foro conscientiæ;* without equivocation; *cartes sur table,* from the bottom of one's heart; by my troth &c. (*affirmation*) 535.

Phr. *di il vero e affronterai il diavolo; Dichtung und Wahrheit; esto quod esse videris; magna est veritas et prævalet;* "that golden key that opes the palace of eternity" [Milton]; *veritas odium parit; veritatis simplex oratio est; verité sans peur.*

544. Falsehood. — N. false-hood, -ness; fals-ity, -ification; deception &c. 545; untruth &c. 546; guile; lying &c. *v.* misrepresentation; mendacity, perjury, false swearing; forgery, invention, fabrication; subreption; covin.

perversion -, suppression- of truth; *suppressio veri;* perversion, distortion, false coloring; exaggeration &c. 549; prevarication, equivocation, shuffling, fencing, evasion, fraud; *suggestio falsi* &c. (*lie*) 546; mystification &c. (*concealment*) 528; simulation &c. (*imitation*) 19; dis-simulation, -sembling; deceit; blague.

sham; pretense, pretending, malingering.

lip -homage, - service; mouth honor; hollowness; mere -show, - outside; duplicity, double dealing, insincerity, hypocrisy, cant, humbug; jesuit-ism, -ry; pharisaism; Machiavelism, "organized hypocrisy"; crocodile tears, mealy-mouthedness, quackery; charlatan-ism, -ry; gammon; bun-kum, -combe, flam; bam *, flimflam, cajolery, flattery; Judas kiss; perfidy &c. (*bad faith*) 940; *il volto sciolto i pensieri stretti.*

unfairness &c. (*dishonesty*) 940; artfulness &c. (*cunning*) 702; misstatement &c. (*error*) 495.

V. be -false &c. *adj.*, - a liar &c. 548; speak -falsely &c. *adv.*; tell -a lie &c. 546; lie, fib; lie like a trooper; swear false, forswear, perjure oneself, bear false witness.

mis-state, -quote, -cite, -report, -represent; belie, falsify, pervert, distort; put a false construction upon &c. (*misinterpret*) 523.

prevaricate, equivocate, quibble; palter, - to the understanding; *répondre en Normand;* trim, shuffle, fence, mince the truth, beat about the bush, blow hot and cold, play fast and loose.

garble, gloss over, disguise, give a color to; give -, put- a -gloss, - false coloring- upon; color, varnish, cook, dress up, embroider; varnish right and puzzle wrong; exaggerate &c. 549; blague.

invent, fabricate; trump -, get- up; forge, fake, hatch, concoct; romance &c. (*imagine*) 515; cry "wolf!"

dis-semble, -simulate; feign, assume, put on, pretend, make believe; play possum; play -false, – a double game; coquet; act –, play- a part; affect &c. 855; simulate, pass off for; counterfeit, sham, make a show of; malinger; say the grapes are sour.

cant, play the hypocrite, sham Abraham, *faire pattes de velours*, put on the mask, clean the outside of the platter, lie like a conjuror; hang out –, hold out –, sail under- false colors; " commend the poisoned chalice to the lips " [*Macbeth*]; *ambiguas in vulgum spargere voces;* deceive &c. 545.

Adj. false, deceitful, mendacious, unveracious, fraudulent, dishonest; faith-, truth-, troth-less; un-fair, -candid; hollow-hearted; evasive; un-, dis-ingenuous; hollow, sincere, *Parthis mendacior;* forsworn.

canting; hypocrit-, jesuit-, pharisa-ical; tartuffish; Machiavelian; double, -tongued, -faced, -handed, -minded, -hearted, -dealing; Janus-faced; smooth-faced, -spoken, -tongued; plausible; mealy-mouthed; affected &c. 855.

collus-ive, -ory; artful &c. (*cunning*) 702; perfidious &c. 940; spurious &c. (*deceptive*) 545; untrue &c. 546; falsified &c. *v.*; covinous.

Adv. falsely &c. *adj.*; *à la Tartufe*, with a double tongue; slily &c. (*cunning*) 702.

Phr. *blandæ mendacia linguæ; falsus in uno falsus in omnibus;* " I give him joy that's awkward at a lie " [Young]; *la mentira tiene las piernas cortas;* " O what a goodly outside falsehood hath! " [*Merchant of Venice*].

545. Deception. — N. deception; falseness &c. 544; untruth &c. 546; im-pos-ition, -ture; fraud, deceit, guile; fraudulen-ce, -cy; covin; knavery &c. (*cunning*) 702; misrepresentation &c. (*falsehood*) 544; bluff; straw-bail, -bid [U. S.]; spoof *.

delusion, gullery; juggl-ing, -ery; sleight of hand, legerdemain; presti-gia-tion †,- digitation; magic &c. 992; conjur-ing, -ation; hocus-pocus, *escamoterie*, jockeyship; trickery, coggery †, chicanery; *supercherie*, cozenage, circumven-tion, ingannation †, collusion; treachery &c. 940; practical joke.

trick, cheat, wile, blind, feint, plant, bubble, fetch, catch, chicane, juggle, reach, hocus, bite; thimblerig, card sharping, artful dodge, swindle; tricks upon travelers; stratagem &c. (*artifice*) 702; confidence trick, fake, hoax; theft &c. 791; ballot-box stuffing [U. S.], barney *; brace * –, bunko –, drop * –, gum * – [U. S.], panel –, shell –, skin *- game [U. S.].

snare, trap, pitfall, decoy, gin; sprin-ge, -gle †; noose, hook; bait, decoy-duck, tub to the whale, baited trap, *guet-à-pens;* cobweb, net, meshes, toils, mouse trap, birdlime; dionæa, Venus's flytrap; ambush &c. 530; trapdoor, slid-ing panel, false bottom; spring-net, -gun; mask, -ed battery; mine; flytrap; green goods [U. S.]; panel house.

Cornish hug; wolf in sheep's clothing &c. (*deceiver*) 548; disguise, -ment; false colors, masquerade, mummery, borrowed plumes; *pattes de velours.*

mockery &c. (*imitation*) 19; copy &c. 21; counterfeit, sham, make-believe, forgery, fraud; lie &c. 546; " a delusion a mockery and a snare " [Denman], hollow mockery.

whited –, painted- sepulcher; tinsel, paste, false jewelry, scagliola, ormolu, German silver, albata, paktong, white metal, Britannia metal, paint; jerry building; man of straw.

illusion &c. (*error*) 495; *ignis fatuus* &c. 423; mirage &c. 443.

V. deceive, take in; defraud, cheat, jockey, do, cozen, diddle, nab, chouse, play one false, bilk, cully, jilt, bite, pluck, swindle, victimize; abuse; mystify; blind -one's eyes; blindfold, hoodwink; throw dust into the eyes, " keep the word of promise to the ear and break it to the hope " [*Macbeth*].

impose –, practice –, play –, put –, palm –, foist- upon; snatch a verdict; bluff, -off; bunko, four flush *, gum * [U. S.], spoof *, stuff (a ballot box) [U. S.].

circumvent, overreach; out-reach, -wit, -maneuver; steal a march upon, give the go-by, to leave in the lurch.

set –, lay- a -trap, – snare- for; bait the hook, forelay †, spread the toils, lime; decoy, waylay, lure, beguile, delude, inveigle; tra-, tre-pan; kidnap; let-, hook-in; trick; en-, in-trap, -snare; nick, springe; nousle †, nousel †; blind a trail, immesh; shanghai; catch, – in a trap; sniggle, entangle, illaqueate, hocus, *escamoter*, practice on one's credulity, dupe, gull, hoax, fool, befool, bamboozle; hum, -bug; gammon, stuff up *, sell; play a -trick, – practical joke- upon one; balk, trip up, throw a tub to a whale; fool to the top of one's bent, send on a fool's errand; make -game, – a fool, – an April fool, – an ass- of; trifle with, cajole, flatter; come over &c. (*influence*) 615; gild the pill, make things pleasant, divert, put a good face upon; dissemble &c. 544.

cog, – the dice; live by one's wits, play at hide and seek; obtain money under false pretenses &c. (*steal*) 791; conjure, juggle, practice chicanery; deacon [U. S.]. play –, palm –, foist –, fob- off.

lie &c. 544; misinform &c. 538; mislead &c. (*error*) 495; betray &c. 940; be -deceived &c. 547.

Adj. deceived &c. *v.*; deceiving &c. *v.*; cunning &c. 702; prestigi-ous †, -atory †; decept-ive, -ious; deceitful, covinous; delus-ive, -ory; illus-ive, -ory; elusive, insidious, *ad captandum vulgus*.

untrue &c. 546; mock, sham, make-believe, counterfeit, snide *, pseudo, spurious, so-called, pretended, feigned, trumped up, bogus, scamped, fraudulent, tricky, factitious, artificial, bastard; surreptitious, illegitimate, contraband, adulterated, sophisticated; unsound, rotten at the core; colorable; disguised; meretricious; tinsel, pinchbeck, plated; catchpenny; Brummagem; simulated &c. 544.

Adv. under -false colors, – the garb of, – cover of; over the left.

Phr. *fronti nulla fides;* " ah that deceit should steal such gentle shapes " [*Rich. III*]; " a quicksand of deceit " [*Hen. VI*]; *decipimur specie recti* [Hor.]; *falsi crimen; fraus est celare fraudem; lupus in fabula;* " so smooth, he daubed his vice with show of virtue " [*Rich. III*].

546. Untruth. — N. untruth, falsehood, lie, story, thing that is not, fib, bounce, crammer, taradiddle, whopper; *jhuth*.

forgery, fabrication, invention; mis-statement, -representation; perversion, falsification, gloss, *suggestio falsi*; exaggeration &c. 549.

invention, fabrication, fiction; fable, nursery tale; romance &c. (*imagination*) 515; absurd –, untrue –, false –, trumped up- -story, – statement; thing devised by the enemy; canard; shave, sell, hum, traveler's tale, Canterbury tale, cock and bull story, fairy tale, fake, press-agent's yarn; claptrap.

myth, moonshine, bosh, all my eye and Betty Martin, mare's-nest, farce.

irony; half truth, white lie, pious fraud; mental reservation &c. (*concealment*) 528.

pretense, pretext; false -plea &c. 617; subterfuge, evasion, shift, shuffle, make-believe; sham &c. (*deception*) 545.

profession, empty words; Judas kiss &c. (*hypocrisy*) 544; disguise &c. (*mask*) 530.

V. have a false meaning.

Adj. untrue, false, trumped up; void of –, without- foundation; fictive, far from the truth, false as dicer's oaths; unfounded, *ben trovato*, invented, fabulous, fabricated, forged; fict-, fact-, supposit-, surrept-itious; e-, il-lusory; ironical; *soi-disant* &c. (*misnamed*) 565.

Phr. *se non e vero è ben trovato;* " where none is meant that meets the ear " [Milton].

547. Dupe. — N. dupe, gull, gudgeon, *gobemouche*, cull *, cully, victim, pigeon, April fool; jay *, sucker *; laughingstock &c. 857; Cyclops, simple Simon, flat, greenhorn; fool &c. 501; puppet, cat's paw.

V. be -deceived &c. 545, – the dupe

548. Deceiver. — N. deceiver &c. (deceive &c. 545); dissembler, hypocrite; sophist, Pharisee, Jesuit, Mawworm, Pecksniff, Joseph Surface, Tartufe, Janus; serpent, snake in the grass, cockatrice, Judas, wolf in sheep's clothing; jilt; shuffler, stool pigeon.

of; fall into a trap; swallow –, nibble at- the bait; bite; catch a Tartar.

Adj. credulous &c. 486; mistaken &c. (*error*) 495.

liar &c. (*lie* &c. 544); story-teller, perjurer, false witness, *menteur à triple étage*, Scapin; bunko steerer * [U. S.], carpetbagger * [U. S.], capper * [U. S.], faker, fraud, four flusher *, horse coper, ringer *, spieler, straw bidder [U. S.].

impostor, pretender, *soi-disant*, humbug; adventurer; Cagliostro, Fernam Mendez Pinto; ass in lion's skin &c. (*bungler*) 701; actor &c. (*stage player*) 599.

quack, charlatan, mountebank, saltimbanco †, *saltimbanque*, empiric, quacksalver, medicaster, Rosicrucian, gypsy; man of straw.

conjuror, juggler, trickster, prestidigitator, jockey; crimp, decoy-duck; rogue, knave, cheat; swindler &c. (*thief*) 792; jobber.

Phr. " saint abroad and a devil at home " [Bunyan].

549. Exaggeration. — N. exaggeration; expansion &c. 194; hyperbole, stretch, strain, coloring; high coloring, caricature, *caricatura;* extravagance &c. (*nonsense*) 497; Baron Munchausen; men in buckram, yarn, fringe, embroidery, traveler's tale; fish story, gooseberry *.

storm in a teacup; much ado about nothing &c. (*over-estimation*) 482; puffery &c. (*boasting*) 884; rant &c. (*turgescence*) 577.

figure of speech, *façon de parler;* stretch of -fancy, – the imagination; flight of fancy &c. (*imagination*) 515.

false coloring &c. (*falsehood*) 544; aggravation &c. 835.

V. exaggerate, magnify, pile up, aggravate; amplify &c. (*expand*) 194; over-estimate &c. 482; hyperbolize; over-charge, -state, -draw, -lay, -shoot the mark, -praise; make -much, – the most- of; strain, – a point; stretch, – a point; go great lengths; spin a long yarn; draw –, shoot with- a longbow; deal in the marvelous.

out-Herod Herod, run riot, talk at random.

heighten, overcolor; color -highly, – too highly; *broder;* flourish; color &c. (*misrepresent*) 544; puff &c. (*boast*) 884.

Adj. exaggerated &c. *v.;* overwrought; bombastic &c. (*magniloquent*) 577; hyperbolical, on stilts; fabulous, extravagant, preposterous, egregious, *outré*, highflying.

Adv. hyperbolically &c. *adj.*

Phr. *excitabat enim fluctus in simpulo* [Cicero].

Section III. Means of communicating Ideas

1. *Natural Means*

550. Indication. — N. indication; symbol-ism, -ization; semeio-logy, -tics; *Zeitgeist*.

lineament, feature, trait, characteristic, diagnostic; divining rod; cloven hoof; footfall; means of recognition.

sign, symbol; ind-ex, -ice †, -icator; point,-er; exponent, note, token, symptom; dollar mark.

type, figure, emblem, cipher, device; representation &c. 554; epigraph, motto, posy.

gest-ure, -iculation; pantomime; wink, glance, leer; nod, shrug, beck; touch, nudge; dactylo-logy, -nomy; freemasonry, telegraphy, chirology, byplay, dumb show; cue; hint &c. 527; clue, clew, key, scent,

signal, -post; rocket, blue light; watch-fire, -tower; telegraph, semaphore, flagstaff; cresset, fiery cross; calumet; heliograph; guidon; headlight.

mark, line, stroke, dash, score, stripe, streak, scratch, tick, dot, point, notch, nick; asterisk, red letter, Italics, sublineation, underlining, jotting; print;

impr-int, -ess, -ession; note, annotation; blaze, cedilla, guillemets, hachure, quotation marks, tilde.

[For identification] badge, criterion; counter-check, -mark, -sign, -foil; duplicate, tally; label, ticket, billet, letter, counter, check, chip, chop; dib; totem; tessera, card, bill; witness, voucher; stamp; *cachet;* trade –, Hall- mark; signature; address –, visiting- card; *carte de visite;* credentials &c. (*evidence*) 467; attestation; hand, – writing, sign manual; cipher; seal, sigil, signet; autograph, -y; paraph, brand; superscription; in-, en-dorsement; title, heading, docket; *mot -de passe, – du guet;* pass-parole; shibboleth; watch-, catch-, pass-word; open *sesame;* timbrology.

insignia; banner, -et, -ol; bandrol; flag, colors, streamer, standard, eagle, labarum, oriflamb, oriflamme; figurehead; ensign; pen-non, -nant, -dant; burgee, blue Peter, jack, ancient, gonfalon, union jack; banderole, " old glory " [U. S.], quarantine flag; vexillum; yellow-flag, – jack; tricolor, stars and stripes; bunting.

heraldry, crest; coat of –, arms; armorial bearings, hatchment; e-, scutcheon; shield, supporters; livery, uniform; cockade, epaulet, chevron; garland, love knot, favor.

[Of locality] beacon, cairn, post, staff, flagstaff, hand, pointer, vane, cock, weathercock; guide-, hand-, finger-, directing-, sign-post; pillars of Hercules, pharos; bale-, beacon-fire; *l'Étoile du Nord;* land-, sea-mark; lighthouse, balize; pole-, load-, lode-star; cynosure, guide; address, direction, name; sign, -board.

[Of the future] warning &c. 668; omen &c. 512; prefigurement &c. 511. [Of the past] trace, record &c. 551. [Of danger] warning &c. 668; alarm &c. 669. [Of authority] scepter &c. 747. [Of triumph] trophy &c. 733. [Of quantity] gauge &c. 466. [Of distance] mile-stone, -post. [Of disgrace] brand, fool's cap. [For detection] check, telltale; test &c. (*experiment*) 463; mileage ticket; milliary.

notification &c. (*information*) 527; advertisement &c. (*publication*) 531.

word of command, call; bugle-, trumpet-call; bell, alarum, cry; battle –, rally-ing- cry; angelus; reveille; sacring-, sanctus-bell.

exposition &c. (*explanation*) 522; proof &c. (*evidence*) 463; pattern &c. (*prototype*) 22.

V. indicate; be the -sign &c. *n.*- of; denote, betoken; argue, testify &c. (*evidence*) 467; bear the -impress &c. *n.*- of; con-note, -notate.

represent, stand for; typify &c. (*prefigure*) 511; symbolize.

put -an indication, – a mark, – &c. *n.*; note, mark, stamp, earmark; blaze; label, ticket, docket; dot, spot, score, dash, trace, chalk; print; im-print, -press; engrave, stereotype.

make a -sign &c. *n.*; signalize; underscore; give –, hang out- a signal; beck, -on; nod; wink, glance, leer, nudge, shrug, tip the wink; gesticulate; raise ⊢, hold up- the -finger, – hand; saw the air, " suit the action to the word " [*Hamlet*].

wave –, unfurl –, hoist –, hang out- a banner &c. *n.*; wave -the hand, – a kerchief; give the cue &c. (*inform*) 527; show one's colors; give –, sound- an alarm; beat the drum, sound the trumpets, raise a cry.

sign, seal, attest &c. (*evidence*) 467; underline &c. (*give importance to*) 642; call attention to &c. (*attention*) 457; give notice &c. (*inform*) 527.

Adj. indicat-ing &c. *v.*, -ive, -ory; de-, con-notative; diacritical, representa-tive, typical, symbolic, pantomimic, pathognomonic, symptomatic, character-istic, demonstrative, diagnostic, exponential, emblematic, armorial; individual &c. (*special*) 79.

known –, recognizable- by; indicated &c. *v.*; pointed, marked.

[Capable of being denoted] denotable; indelible.

Adv. in token of; symbolically &c. *adj.*; in dumb show.

Phr. *ecce signum; ex ungue leonem, ex pede Herculem; vide ut supra; vultus ariete fortior.*

---

551. Record. — N. trace, vestige, relic, remains; scar, cicatrix; foot-step, | **552.** [Suppression of sign.] **Oblitera-tion. — N.** obliteration; erasure, rasure;

-mark, -print; *pug;* track, mark, wake, trail, scent, *piste.*

monument, hatchment, slab, tablet, trophy, achievement; obelisk, pillar, column, monolith; memorial; memento &c. (*memory*) 505; testimonial, medal; commemoration &c. (*celebration*) 883.

record, note, minute; regis-ter, -try; roll &c. (*list*) 86; cartulary, diptych, Domesday book; *catalogue raisonné;* entry, memorandum, indorsement, inscription, copy, duplicate, docket; notch &c. (*mark*) 550; muniment, deed &c. (*security*) 771; document; deposition, *procès verbal;* affidavit; certificate &c. (*evidence*) 467.

note-, memorandum-, pocket-, commonplace-book; portfolio; pigeonholes, *excerpta,* adversaria, jottings, dottings.

gazette, -er; newspaper, daily, magazine; alman-ac, -ack; calendar, ephemeris, diary, log, journal, daybook, ledger; cashbook, petty cashbook.

archive, scroll, state paper, return, blue book; statistics &c. 86; *compte rendu;* Acts –, Transactions –, Proceedings- of; Hansard's Debates; chronicle, annals; legend; history, biography &c. 594; Congressional Records.

registration; registry; en-, in-rollment; tabulation; entry, booking; signature &c. (*identification*) 550; recorder &c. 553; journalism.

V. record; put –, place- upon record; chronicle, calendar, hand down to posterity; keep up the memory &c. (*remember*) 505; commemorate &c. (*celebrate*) 883; report &c. (*inform*) 527; commit to –, reduce to- writing; put –, set down- in writing, – in black and white; put –, jot –, take –, write –, note –, set-down; note, minute, put on paper; take –, make- a -note, – minute, – memorandum; make a return.

mark &c. (*indicate*) 550; sign &c. (*attest*) 467.

enter, book; post, – up; insert, make an entry of; mark –, tick- off; register, enroll, inscroll; file &c. (*store*) 636.

Adv. on record.

Phr. *exegi monumentum ære perennius* [Horace]; " read their history in a nation's eyes " [Gray]; " records that defy the tooth of time " [Young].

cancel, -lation; circumduction; deletion, blot; *tabula rasa;* effacement, extinction.

V. efface, obliterate, erase, rase, expunge, cancel; blot -, take -, rub -, scratch -, strike -, wipe -, wash -, sponge-out; wipe -, rub- off; wipe away; deface, render illegible; draw the pen through, apply the sponge.

be -effaced &c.; leave no -trace &c. 550; " leave not a rack behind."

Adj. obliterated &c. *v.*; out of print; printless; leaving no trace; intestate; un-recorded, -registered, -written.

Int. *dele;* out with it!

Phr. *delenda est Carthago* [Cato].

553. Recorder. — **N.** recorder, notary, clerk; regis-trar, -trary, -ter; prothonotary; amanuensis, secretary, scribe, babu, remembrancer, bookkeeper, *custos rotulorum,* Master of the Rolls.

annalist; histori-an, -ographer; chronicler, journalist; biographer &c. (*narrator*) 594; antiquary &c. (*antiquity*) 122; memorialist; interviewer.

554. Representation. — **N.** represent-ation, -ment; imitation &c. 19; illustration, delineation, depictment; imagery, portraiture, iconography; design, -ing; art, fine arts; painting &c. 556; sculpture &c. 557; engraving &c. 558; photography; radiography, sciagraphy.

person-ation, -ification; impersonation; drama &c. 599.

picture, drawing, sketch, draught, draft; tracing; copy &c. 21; photograph, **daguerreotype,** snapshot.

555. Misrepresentation. — **N.** misrepresentation, distortion, caricatura †, exaggeration; daubing &c. *v.*; bad likeness, daub, sign painting; scratch, caricature; anamorphosis; burlesque, falsification, misstatement, parody, take-off, travesty.

V. misrepresent, distort, overdraw, exaggerate, caricature, daub; burlesque, parody, travesty.

Adj. misrepresented &c. *v.*

image, likeness, icon, portrait; striking –, speaking- likeness; very image; effigy, facsimile.

figure, – head; puppet, doll, figurine, aglet, manikin, lay-figure, model, mammet, marionette, fantoccini, waxwork, bust; statue, -tte.

hieroglyphic, anaglyph; dia-, mono-gram.

map, plan, chart; ground plan, projection, elevation; ichno-, carto-graphy; atlas; outline, scheme; view &c. (*painting*) 556; radio-, scoto-, scia-graph; spectro-gram, -heliogram.

V. represent, delineate; depict, -ure; portray; take –, catch- a likeness &c. *n.*; hit off, photograph, daguerreotype; snapshot; figure, shadow -forth, – out; adumbrate; body forth; describe &c. 594; trace, copy; mold.

dress up; illustrate, symbolize.

paint &c. 556; carve &c. 557; engrave &c. 558.

person-ate, -ify; impersonate; assume a character; pose as; act; play &c. (*drama*) 599; mimic &c. (*imitate*) 19; hold the mirror up to nature.

Adj. represent-ing &c. *v.*, -ative; illustrative; represented &c. *v.*; imitative, figurative; iconic.

like &c. 17; graphic &c. (*descriptive*) 594; cinque-, quattro-, tre-cento.

556. Painting. — N. painting; depicting; drawing &c. *v.*; design; perspective, sci-, ski-agraphy; *chiaroscuro* &c. (*light*) 420; composition; treatment.

historical –, portrait –, miniature –, landscape –, marine –, flower –, scene-painting; scenography.

school, style; the grand style, high art, *genre*, portraiture; ornamental art &c. 847.

mono-, poly-chrome; grisaille.

pallet, palette; easel; brush, pencil, stump; black lead, charcoal, crayons, chalk, pastel; paint &c. (*coloring matter*) 428; water-, body-, oil-color; oils, oil paint; varnish &c. 356*a*; priming; *gouache*, tempera, distemper, fresco, water glass; enamel; encaustic painting; mosaic; tapestry.

photo-, helio-graphy; sun painting.

picture, painting, piece, tableau, canvas; oil &c.- painting; fresco, cartoon; easel –, cabinet- picture; drawing, draught, draft; pencil &c. –, water color-drawing; sketch, outline, study.

photo-, helio-graph; daguerreo-, talbo-, calo-, helio-type.

portrait &c. (*representation*) 554; whole –, full –, half- length; kitcat, head; miniature; shade, silhouette; profile.

landscape, seapiece; view, scene, prospect; pan-, di-orama; still life.

picture gallery; studio, *atelier;* pinacotheca.

V. paint, design, limn, draw, sketch, pencil, scratch, shade, stipple, hatch, dash off, chalk out, square up; color, dead color, wash, varnish; draw in -pencil &c. *n.*; paint in -oils &c. *n.*; stencil; depict &c. (*represent*) 554.

Adj. painted &c. *v.*; pictorial, graphic, picturesque.

pencil, oil &c. *n.*

Adv. in -pencil &c. *n.*

Phr. *fecit, delineavit; mutum est pictura poëma.*

557. Sculpture. — N. sculpture, insculpture †; carving &c. *v.*; statuary.

high –, low –, bas- relief; relief; relievo; *basso-, alto-, mezzo-rilievo;* intaglio, anaglyph; medal, -lion; cameo.

marble, bronze, terra cotta; ceramic ware, pottery, porcelain, china, earthenware; cloisonné, enamel, faïence, Laocoön, satsuma.

statue &c. (*image*) 554; cast &c. (*copy*) 21; glyptotheca.

V. sculpture, carve, cut, chisel, model, mold; cast.

Adj. sculptured &c. *v.*; in relief, anaglyptic, ceroplastic, ceramic; parian; marble &c. *n.*; xanthian.

558. Engraving. — **N.** engraving, chalcography; line -, mezzotint -, stipple -, chalk- engraving; dry point, bur; etching, aquatinta; chiseling; plate -, copperplate -, steel -, wood- engraving; xylo-, ligno-, glypto-, cero-, litho-, chromolitho-, photolitho-, zinco-, glypho- -graphy, -graph.

impression, print, engraving, plate; steel-, copper-plate; etching; mezzo-, aqua-, litho-tint; cut, woodcut; stereo-, grapho-, auto-, helio-type.

graver, burin, etching point, style; plate, stone, wood block, negative; die, punch, stamp.

printing; plate -, copperplate -, anastatic -, color -, lithographic- printing; type printing &c. 591; three-color process.

illustr-, illumin-ation; half tone; photogravure; vignette, initial letter, *cul de lampe*, tailpiece.

V. engrave, grave, stipple, scrape, etch; bite, - in; lithograph &c. *n.*; print.

Adj. insculptured; engraved &c. *v.*

Phr. *sculpsit, imprimit.*

559. Artist. — **N.** artist; painter, limner, drawer, sketcher, designer, engraver; draughtsman; copyist; enamel-er, -ist; caricaturist.

historical -, landscape -, marine -, flower -, portrait -, miniature -, scene -, sign -, coach- painter; engraver; Apelles; sculptor, carver, chaser, modeler, *figuriste*, statuary; Phidias, Praxiteles; Royal Academician.

2. *Conventional Means*

1. *Language generally*

560. Language. — **N.** language; phraseology &c. 569; speech &c. 582; tongue, lingo, vernacular; mother -, vulgar -, native- tongue; household words; King's *or* Queen's English; dialect &c. 563.

confusion of tongues, Babel, *pasigraphie;* pantomime &c. (*signs*) 550; onomatopœia; betacism, mimmation, myatism, nunnation; pasigraphy.

lexic-, phil-, gloss-, glott-ology; linguistics, chrestomathy; paleo-logy, -graphy; comparative grammar.

literature, letters, polite literature, *belles lettres*, muses, humanities, *litœræ humaniores*, republic of letters, dead languages, classics; genius of a language; scholarship &c. (*knowledge*) 490.

linguist &c. (*scholar*) 492.

V. express by words &c. 566.

Adj. lingu-al, -istic; dialectic; vernacular, current; bilingual; di-, hexa-, poly-glot; literary.

Phr. " syllables govern the world " [Selden].

561. Letter. — **N.** letter; character; hieroglyphic &c. (*writing*) 590; type &c. (*printing*) 591; capitals; di-, tri-graph; ideo-gram, -graph; majus-, minus-cule; *majus-, minus-culæ;* alphabet, ABC, abecedary, christcross-row.

consonant, vowel; diph-, triph-thong; mute, liquid, labial, dental, guttural.

syllable; mono-, dis-, poly-syllable; affix, suffix.

spelling, orthograph; phon-ography, -etic spelling; ana-, meta-grammatism.

cipher, monogram, anagram; double -, acrostic.

V. spell.

Adj. literal; alphabetical, abecedarian; syllabic; majus-, minus-cular; uncial &c. (*writing*) 590.

562. Word. — **N.** word, term, vocable; name &c. 564; phrase &c. 566; root, etymon; derivative; part of speech &c. (*grammar*) 567; ideophone.

dictionary, vocabulary, lexicon, in-

563. Neology. — **N.** neolo-gy, -gism; newfangled expression; caconym; barbarism; archaism, black letter, monkish Latin; corruption, missaying, antiphrasis.

dex, glossary, thesaurus, gradus, delectus, concordance.

etymology, derivation; gloss-, termin-, orism-ology; paleology &c. (*philology*) 560.

lexicography; glossographer &c. (*scholar*) 492; lexicologist, verbarian.

Adj. verbal, literal; titular, nominal.

[Similarly derived] conjugate, paronymous; derivative.

Adv. verbally &c. *adj.*; *verbatim* &c. (*exactly*) 494.

Phr. " the artillery of words " [Swift].

paronomasia, play upon words; word play &c. (*wit*) 842; *double-entente* &c. (*ambiguity*) 520; palindrome, paragram, clinch; abuse of -language, – terms.

dialect, brogue, patois, provincialism, broken English, lingua franca; Angl-, Brit-, Gall-, Scott-, Hibern-icism; Americanism; Gypsy lingo, Romany, pigeon English; Volapük, Chinook, Esperanto, Hindustani, kitchen Kaffir.

dog Latin, macaronics, gibberish; confusion of tongues, Babel; jargon; babu English, chi-chi.

colloquialism &c. (*figure of speech*) 521; byword; technicality, lingo, slang, cant, argot, St. Giles's Greek, thieves' Latin, peddler's French, flash tongue, Billingsgate, Wall Street slang.

pseudology.

pseudonym &c. (*misnomer*) 565; Mr. So-and-so; what d'ye call 'em, what's his name; thingum-my, -bob; *je ne sais quoi.*

neologist, coiner of words.

V. coin words; Americanize, Anglicize.

Adj. neologic, -al; archaic; obsolete &c. (*old*) 124; colloquial; *Anglice.*

564. Nomenclature. — N. nomenclature; naming &c. *v.*; nuncupation †, nomination, baptism; orismology; onomatopœia; antonomasia.

name; appela-tion, -tive; designation; title; head, -ing; caption; denomination; by-name, epithet.

style, proper name; præ-, ag-, cognomen; patronymic, surname; cognomination; eponym; compellation, description, antonym; empty -title, – name; handle to one's name; namesake.

term, expression, noun; byword; convertible terms &c. 522; technical term; cant &c. 563.

V. name, call, term, denominate, designate, style, entitle, clepe, dub, christen, baptize, characterize, specify, define, distinguish by the name of; label &c. (*mark*) 550.

be -called &c. *v.*; take –, bear –, go (*or* be known) by –, go (*or* pass) under –, rejoice in- the name of.

Adj. named &c. *v.*; hight, ycleped, known as; what one may -well, – fairly, – properly, – fitly- call.

nuncupa-tory †, -tive; cognominal, titular, nominal, orismological.

Phr. " beggar'd all description " [*Antony and Cleopatra*].

565. Misnomer. — N. misnomer; *lucus a non lucendo;* Mrs. Malaprop; what d'ye call 'em &c. (*neologism*) 563; Hoosier.

nickname, *sobriquet*, by-name; assumed -name, – title; alias; *nom de -course, – theâtre, – guerre, – plume;* pseudonym, -y.

V. mis-name, -call, -term; nickname; assume a name.

Adj. misnamed &c. *v.*; pseudonymous; *soi-disant;* self-called, -styled, -christened; so-called.

nameless, anonymous; without a –, having no- name; innominate, unnamed; unacknowledged.

Adv. in no sense.

566. Phrase. — N. phrase, expression, set phrase; sentence, paragraph; figure of speech &c. 521; idi-om, -otism; turn of expression; style.

paraphrase &c. (*synonym*) 522; periphrase &c. (*circumlocution*) 573; motto &c. (*proverb*) 496.

phraseology &c. 569.

V. express, phrase; word, – it; give -words, – expression -to; voice; arrange in –, clothe in –, put into –, express by- words; couch in terms; find words to express; speak by the card; call, denominate, designate, dub.

Adj. expressed &c. *v.*; idiomatic.

Adv. in -round, – set, – good set- terms; in set phrases.

567. Grammar. — **N.** grammar, accidence, syntax, praxis, punctuation; parts of speech; jussive; syllabication; inflection, case, declension, conjugation; *jus et norma loquendi;* Lindley Murray &c. (*schoolbook*) 542; correct style, philology &c. (*language*) 560.

V. parse, punctuate, syllabicate.

568. Solecism. — **N.** solecism; bad –, false –, faulty- grammar; slip of the -pen, – tongue; *lapsus linguæ;* slipslop; bull; barbarism, impropriety.

V. use -bad, – faulty- grammar; solecize, commit a solecism; murder the -King's – Queen's- English; break Priscian's head.

Adj. ungrammatical; in-correct, -accurate; faulty; improper, incongruous; solecistic, -al.

569. Style. — **N.** style, diction, phraseology, wording; manner, strain; composition; mode of expression, choice of words; mode of speech, literary power, ready pen, pen of a ready writer; command of language &c. (*eloquence*) 582; authorship; *la morgue littéraire.*

V. express by words &c. 566; write.

Phr. *le style c'est de l'homme* [Buffon]; " style is the dress of thoughts " [Chesterfield].

Various Qualities of Style

570. Perspicuity. — **N.** perspicuity &c. (*intelligibility*) 518; plain speaking &c. (*manifestation*) 525; defin-iteness, -ition; exactness &c. 494; explicitness, lucidness.

Adj. lucid &c. (*intelligible*) 518; explicit &c. (*manifest*) 525; exact &c. 494.

571. Obscurity. — **N.** obscurity &c. (*unintelligibility*) 519; involution; hard words; ambiguity &c. 520; unintelligibleness; vagueness &c. 475, inexactness &c. 495; what d'ye call 'em &c. (*neologism*) 563; darkness of meaning.

Adj. obscure &c. *n.*; crabbed, involved, confused.

572. Conciseness. — **N.** conciseness &c. *adj.*; brevity, " the soul of wit," laconism; Tacitus; ellipsis; syncope; abridgment &c. (*shortening*) 201; compression &c. 195; epitome &c. 596; monostich; brunch –, portmanteau- word.

V. be -concise &c. *adj.*; condense &c. 195; abridge &c. 201; abstract &c. 596; come to the point.

Adj. concise, brief, short, terse, close; to the point, exact; neat, compact; compressed, condensed, pointed; laconic, curt, pithy, trenchant, summary; pregnant; compendious &c. (*compendium*) 596; succinct; elliptical, epigrammatic, quaint, crisp; sententious.

Adv. concisely &c. *adj.*; briefly, summarily; in -brief, – short, – a word, – few words; for shortness sake; to -come to the point, – make a long story short, – cut the matter short, – be brief; it comes to this, the long and the short of it is.

Phr. *brevis esse laboro obscurus fio* [Horace].

573. Diffuseness. — **N.** diffuseness &c. *adj.*; amplification &c. *v.*; dilating &c. *v.*; verbosity, verbiage, cloud of words, *copia verborum;* flow of words &c. (*loquacity*) 584; looseness.

poly-, tauto-, batto-, perisso-logy †; pleonasm, exuberance, redundance; thrice-told tale; prolixity; circumlocution, ambages; periphra-se, -sis; roundabout phrases; episode; expletive; penny-a-lining; richness &c. 577.

V. be -diffuse &c. *adj.*; run out on, descant, expatiate, enlarge, dilate, amplify, expand, inflate; launch-, branch-out; rant.

maunder, prose; harp upon &c. (*repeat*) 104; dwell on, insist upon.

digress, ramble, *battre la campagne,* beat about the bush, perorate, spin a long yarn, protract; spin –, swell –, draw-out; battologize.

Adj. dif-, pro-fuse; wordy, verbose, largiloquent †, copious, exuberant, pleonastic, lengthy; long, -some, -winded,

-spun, -drawn out; spun out, protracted, prolix, prosing, maundering; circumlocutory, periphrastic, ambagious, roundabout; digressive; dis-, excursive; loose; rambling, episodic; flatulent, frothy.

Adv. diffusely &c. *adj.*; at large, *in extenso;* about it and about it.

574. Vigor. — N. vigor, power, force; boldness, raciness &c. *adj.*; intellectual force; spirit, point, antithesis, piquancy; verve, glow, fire, warmth; strong language; gravity, sententiousness; elevation, loftiness, sublimity.

eloquence; command of -words, – language.

Adj. vigorous, nervous, powerful, forcible, trenchant, incisive, impressive; sensational.

spirited, lively, glowing, sparkling, racy, bold, slashing; pungent, piquant, antithetical; sententious.

lofty, elevated, sublime; eloquent; poetic.

Adv. in -glowing, – good set, – no measured- terms.

Phr. " thoughts that breathe and words that burn " [Gray].

575. Feebleness. — N. feebleness &c. *adj.*

Adj. feeble, bald, tame, meager, jejune, vapid, trashy, cold, frigid, poor, dull, dry, languid; colorless, enervated; pros-ing, -y, -aic; unvaried, monotonous, weak, washy, wishy-washy; sketchy, slight; careless, slovenly, loose, lax; slip-shod, -slop; inexact; puerile, childish; flatulent; rambling &c. (*diffuse*) 573.

full of point, pointed, pithy, antithetical; vehement, petulant, impassioned;

576. Plainness. — N. plainness &c. *adj.*; simplicity, severity; plain -terms, – English; Saxon English; household words.

V. call a spade " a spade "; plunge *in medias res;* come to the point.

Adj. plain, simple; un-ornamented, -adorned, -varnished; home-ly, -spun; neat; severe, chaste, pure, Saxon; commonplace, matter-of-fact, natural, prosaic.

dry, unvaried, monotonous &c. 575.

Adv. in plain -terms, – words, – English, – common parlance; point-blank.

577. Ornament.—N. ornament; floridness &c. *adj.*; turg-idity, -escence; altiloquence &c. *adj.*; declamation, teratology; well-rounded periods; elegance &c. 578; orotundity.

inversion, antithesis, alliteration, paronomasia; figurativeness &c. (*metaphor*) 521.

flourish; flowers of -speech, – rhetoric; frills, – of style; euph-uism, -emism.

big-, high-sounding words; macrology, *sesquipedalia verba,* Alexandrine; inflation, pretension; rant, bombast, fustian, prose run mad; fine writing; sesquipedality; Minerva press.

phrasemonger; euph-uist, -emist.

V. ornament, overlay with ornament, overcharge; smell of the lamp.

Adj. ornamented &c. *v.*; beautified &c. 847; ornate, florid, rich, flowery; euph-uistic, -emistic; sonorous; high-, big-sounding; inflated, swelling, tumid; turg-id, -escent; pedantic, pompous, stilted; orotund; high-flown, -flowing; sententious, rhetorical, declamatory; grandiose; grand-, magn-, alt-iloquent; sesquipedal, -ian; Johnsonian, mouthy; bombastic; fustian; frothy, flashy, flaming.

antithetical, alliterative; figurative &c. 521; artificial &c. (*inelegant*) 579.

Adv. ore rotundo.

578. Elegance. — N. elegance, purity, grace, ease; gracefulness, readiness &c. *adj.*; concinnity, euphony, numerosity; Atticism, classi-calism, -cism.

well rounded –, well turned –, flowing- periods; the right word in the right place; antithesis &c. 577.

579. Inelegance. — N. inelegance; stiffness &c. *adj.*; " unlettered Muse " [Gray]; barbarism; slang &c. 563; solecism &c. 568; mannerism &c. (*affectation*) 855; euphuism; fustian &c. 577; cacophony; words that -break the teeth, – dislocate the jaw; marinism.

purist.

V. point an antithesis, round a period.

Adj. elegant, polished, classical, Attic, correct, Ciceronian, artistic; chaste, pure, Saxon, academical.

graceful, easy, readable, fluent, flowing, tripping; unaffected, natural, unlabored; mellifluous; euph-onious, -emistic; numerose †, rhythmical.

felicitous, happy, neat; well –, neatly--put, – expressed.

V. be -inelegant &c. *adj.*

Adj. inelegant, graceless, ungraceful; harsh, abrupt; dry, stiff, cramped, formal, *guindé;* forced, labored; artificial, mannered, ponderous; awkward, uncourtly, unpolished; turgid &c. 577; affected, euphuistic; barbarous, uncouth, grotesque, rude, crude, halting; offensive to ears polite.

2. Spoken Language

580. Voice. — N. voice; vocality; organ, lungs, bellows; good –, fine –, powerful &c. (*loud*) 404 –, musical &c. 413- voice; intonation; tone &c. (*sound*) 402- of voice.

vocalization; cry &c. 411; strain, utterance, prolation; exclam-, ejacul-, vocifer-ation, ecphonesis; enunci-, articul-ation; articulate sound, distinctness; clearness, – of articulation; stage whisper; delivery.

accent, -uation; emphasis, stress; broad –, strong –, pure –, native –, foreign- accent; pronunciation.

[Word similarly pronounced] homonym.

orthoëpy; cacoëpy; euphony &c. (*melody*) 413.

gastri-, ventri-loquism; ventriloquist; polyphon-ism, -ist.

[Science of voice] phonology &c. (*sound*) 402.

V. utter, breathe; give -utterance, – tongue; cry &c. (*shout*) 411; ejaculate, rap out; vocalize, prolate †, articulate, enunciate, pronounce, accentuate, aspirate, deliver, mouth; whisper in the ear.

Adj. vocal, phonetic, oral; ejaculatory, articulate, distinct, stertorous; euphonious &c. (*melodious*) 413.

Phr. " how sweetly sounds the voice of a good woman " [Massinger]; " the organ of the soul " [Longfellow]; " thy voice is a celestial melody " [Longfellow].

581. Aphony. — N. aphony, aphonia; dumbness &c. *adj.*; obmutescence; absence –, want- of voice; dysphony; cacoëpy; silence &c. (*taciturnity*) 585; raucity; harsh &c. 410 –, unmusical &c. 414- voice; falsetto, " childish treble "; mute, dummy.

V. keep silence &c. 585; speak -low, – softly; whisper &c. (*faintness*) 405.

silence; render -mute, – silent; muzzle, muffle, suppress, smother, gag, strike dumb, dumfounder; drown the voice, put to silence, stop one's mouth, cut one short.

stick in the throat.

Adj. aphonous, dumb, mute; deaf-mute, – and dumb; mum; tongue-tied; breath-, tongue-, voice-, speech-, word-less; mute as a -fish, – stockfish, – mackerel; silent &c. (*taciturn*) 585; muzzled; in-articulate, -audible.

croaking, raucous, hoarse, husky, dry, hollow, sepulchral, hoarse as a raven; rough.

Adv. with -bated breath, – the finger on the lips; *sotto voce;* in a -low tone, – cracked voice, – broken voice.

Phr. *vox faucibus hæsit* [Vergil].

582. Speech. — N. speech, faculty of speech; locution, talk, parlance, verbal intercourse, prolation, oral communication, word of mouth, parole, palaver, prattle; effusion.

oration, recitation, delivery, say, speech, lecture, harangue, sermon, tirade, formal speech, peroration; speech-ifying; soliloquy &c. 589; allocution &c. 586; interlocution &c. 588; salutatory [U. S.]; screed: valedictory [U. S.].

583. [Imperfect Speech.] Stammering. — N. inarticulateness; stammering &c. *v.*; hesitation &c. *v.*; impediment in one's speech; titubancy, traulism †; whisper &c. (*faint sound*) 405; lisp, drawl, tardiloquence; nasal -tone, – accent; twang; falsetto &c. (*want of voice*) 581; broken -voice, – accents, – sentences.

brogue &c. 563; slip of the tongue, *lapsus linguæ.*

oratory; elo-cution, -quence; rhet-oric, declamation; grandi-, multi-lo-quence; burst of eloquence; facundity; flow –, command- of -words, – language; *copia verborum;* power of speech, gift of the gab; *usus loquendi.*

speaker &c. *v.*; spokesman; pro-, in-ter-locutor; mouthpiece, Hermes; ora-tor, -trix, -tress; Demosthenes, Cicero; rhetorician; stump –, platform- orator; speechmaker, patterer, *improvisatore.*

V. speak, – of; say, utter, pronounce, deliver, give utterance to; utter –, pour-forth; breathe, let fall, come out with; rap –, blurt- out; have on one's lips; have at the -end, – tip- of one's tongue.

break silence; open one's -lips, – mouth; lift –, raise- one's voice; give –, wag the-, tongue; talk, outspeak; put in a word or two.

hold forth; make –, deliver- -a speech &c. *n.*; speechify, harangue, declaim, stump, flourish, spout, rant, recite, lecture, sermonize, discourse, be on one's legs; have –, say- one's say; expatiate &c. (*speak at length*) 573; speak one's mind, go on the –, take the- stump [U. S.].

soliloquize &c. 589; tell &c. (*inform*) 527; speak to &c. 586; talk together &c. 588.

be -eloquent &c. *adj.*; have -a tongue in one's head, – the gift of the gab &c. *n.*

pass –, escape- one's lips; fall from the -lips, – mouth.

Adj. speaking &c., spoken &c. *v.*; oral, lingual, phonetic, not written, un-written, outspoken; elo-quent, -cutionary; orat-, rhet-orical; declamatory; grandiloquent &c. 577; talkative &c. 584; Ciceronian, nuncupative, Tullian.

Adv. orally &c. *adj.*; by word of mouth, *vivâ voce*, from the lips of.

Phr. quoth –, said- he &c.; " action is eloquence " [*Coriolanus*]; " pour the full tide of eloquence along " [Pope]; " she speaks poignards and every word stabs " [*Much Ado About Nothing*]; " speech is but broken light upon the depth of the unspoken " [G. Eliot]; " to try thy eloquence now 'tis time " [*Antony and Cleopatra*].

V. stammer, stutter, hesitate, falter, hammer; balbu-tiate †, -cinate †; haw, hum and haw, be unable to put two words together.

mumble, mutter; maund †, -er; whis-per &c. 405; mince, lisp; jabber, gibber; sp-, spl-utter; muffle, mump; drawl, mouth; croak; speak -thick, – through the nose; snuffle, clip one's words; mur-der the -language, – King's (*or* Queen's) English; mis-pronounce, -say.

Adj. stammering &c. *v.*; inarticulate, guttural, nasal; tremulous; affected.

Adv. *sotto voce* &c. (*faintly*) 405.

---

584. Loquacity. — N. loquac-ity, -iousness; talkativeness &c. *adj.*; gar-rulity; multiloquence, much speaking.

jaw; gab, -ble; jabber, chatter; prate, prattle, cackle, clack; twaddle, twattle, rattle; *caquet, -terie;* blabber, *bavardage,* bibble-babble, gibble-gabble; small talk &c. (*converse*) 588.

fluency, flippancy, volubility, flowing tongue; flow, – of words; *flux de -bouche,* – *mots; copia verborum, cacoëthes lo-quendi; furor loquendi;* verbosity &c. (*diffuseness*) 573; gift of the gab &c. (*eloquence*) 582.

talker; chatter-er, -box; babbler &c. *v.*; rattle; ranter; sermonizer, proser, driveler; blatherskite [U. S.]; gossip &c. (*converse*) 588; magpie, jay, parrot, poll, Babel; *moulin à paroles.*

V. be -loquacious &c. *adj.*; talk glibly, pour forth, patter; prate, palaver, prose, chatter, prattle, clack, jabber, jaw;

585. Taciturnity. — N. silence, mute-ness, obmutescence; taciturnity, paucil-oquy, costiveness †, curtness; reserve, reticence &c. (*concealment*) 528.

man of few words.

V. be -silent &c. *adj.*; keep silence; hold one's -tongue, – peace, – jaw; not speak &c. 582; say nothing; seal –, close –, put a padlock on- the -lips, – mouth; put a bridle on one's tongue; keep one's tongue between one's teeth; make no sign, not let a word escape one; keep a secret &c. 528; not have a word to say; lay –, place- the finger on the lips; render mute &c. 581.

stick in one's throat.

Adj. silent, mute, mum; silent as a -post, – stone, – the grave &c. (*still*) 403; dumb &c. 581; unconversable.

taciturn, sparing of words; close, – tongued; costive †, inconversable †, curt; reserved; reticent &c. (*concealing*) 528.

blather, blatter, blether; rattle, – on; twaddle, twattle; babble, gabble; out-talk; talk oneself -out of breath, – hoarse; expatiate &c. (*speak at length*) 573; gossip &c. (*converse*) 588; din in the ears &c. (*repeat*) 104; talk -at random, – nonsense &c. 497; be hoarse with talking.

Adj. loquacious, talkative, garrulous, linguacious †, multiloquous; largiloquent †; chattering &c. *v.*; chatty &c. (*sociable*) 892; declamatory &c. 582; open-mouthed.

fluent, voluble, glib, flippant; long-tongued, -winded &c. (*diffuse*) 573.

Adv. trippingly on the tongue; glibly &c. *adj.*; off the reel.

Phr. the tongue running -fast, – loose, – on wheels; all talk and no cider; " foul whisperings are abroad " [*Macbeth*]; " what a spendthrift is he of his tongue! " [*Tempest*].

Int. tush! silence! mum! hush! *chut!* hist! tut! *chup!*

Phr. *cave quid dicis quando et cui; volto sciolto i pensieri stretti.*

---

586. Allocution. — N. allocution, alloquy †, address; speech &c. 582; apostrophe, interpellation, appeal, invocation, salutation; word in the ear.

[Feigned dialogue] dialogism.

platform &c. 542; plank; audience &c. (*interview*) 588.

V. speak to, address, accost, make up to, apostrophize, appeal to, invoke; hail, salute; call to, halloo.

take -aside, – by the button; talk to in private.

lecture &c. (*make a speech*) 582.

Int. soho! halloo! hey! hist!

587. Response &c., *see* Answer 462.

---

588. Interlocution. — N. interlocution; collocution, colloquy, converse, conversation, confabulation, talk, discourse, verbal intercourse; oral communication, commerce; dia-, duo-, trialogue.

causerie, chat, chitchat; small –, table –, teatable –, town –, village –, idle- talk; tattle, gossip, tittle-tattle; babble, -ment; *tripotage*, cackle, prittle-prattle, cancan, *on dit;* talk of the -town, – village.

conference, parley, interview, audience, *pourparler; tête-à-tête;* reception, *conversazione;* congress &c. (*council*) 696; powwow [U. S.].

hall of audience, durbar.

palaver, debate, logomachy, war of words.

gossip, tattler; Paul Pry; tabby; chatterer &c. (*loquacity*) 584; interlocutor &c. (*spokesman*) 582; conversationist, dialogist.

" the feast of reason and the flow of soul " [Pope]; *mollia tempora fandi.*

V. talk together, converse, confabulate; hold –, carry on –, join in –, engage in- a conversation; put in a word; shine in conversation; bandy words; parley; palaver; chat, gossip, tattle; prate &c. (*loquacity*) 584; powwow [U. S.].

discourse –, confer –, commune –, commerce- with; hold -converse, – conference, – intercourse; talk it over; be closeted with; talk with one -in private, – tête-à-tête.

Adj. conversing &c. *v.*; interlocutory; convers-ational, -able; dis-cursive, -coursive; chatty &c. (*sociable*) 892; colloquial.

Phr. " with thee conversing I forget all time " [*Paradise Lost*].

589. Soliloquy. — N. soliloquy, monologue, apostrophe; monology.

V. soliloquize; say –, talk- to oneself; say aside, think aloud, apostrophize.

Adj. soliloquizing &c. *v.*

Adv. aside.

3. Written Language

590. Writing. — N. writing &c. *v.*; chiro-, stelo-, cero-graphy; pen-craft, -manship; quill driving; typewriting.

writing, manuscript, MS., *literæ scrip-tæ;* these presents.

stroke –, dash- of the pen; *coup de plume;* line; headline; pen and ink.

letter &c. 561; uncial writing, cuneiform character, arrowhead, Ogham, Runes, hieroglyphic; contraction; Brahmi, Devanagari, Nagari; script.

shorthand; steno-, brachy-, tachy-graphy; secret writing, writing in cipher; crypt-, stegan-ography; phono-, pasi-, poly-, logo-graphy.

copy; tran-, re-script; rough –, fair-copy; handwriting; signature, sign manual; auto-, mono-, holo-graph; hand, fist.

calligraphy; good –, running –, flowing –, cursive –, legible –, bold- hand.

cacography, *griffonage, barbouillage;* bad –, cramped –, crabbed –, illegible-hand; scribble &c. *v.; pattes de mouche;* ill-formed letters; pothooks and hangers.

stationery; pen, quill, goose quill; pencil, style; paper, foolscap, parchment, vellum, papyrus, tablet, slate, marble, pillar, table; blackboard; ink-bottle, -horn, -pot, -stand, -well; typewriter.

transcription &c. (*copy*) 21; inscription &c. (*record*) 551; superscription &c. (*indication*) 550; graphology.

composition, authorship; *cacoëthes scribendi;* graph-oidea, -omania; phrenoia.

writer, scribe, amanuensis, scrivener, secretary, clerk, penman, copyist, transcriber, quill driver; stenographer, typewriter, typist; writer for the press &c. (*author*) 593.

V. write, pen; copy, engross; write out, – fair; transcribe; scribble, scrawl, scrabble, scratch; interline; stain paper; write down &c. (*record*) 551; sign &c. (*attest*) 467; enface.

compose, indite, draw up, draft, formulate; dictate; inscribe, throw on paper, dash off; manifold.

take -up the pen, – pen in hand; shed –, spill –, dip one's pen in- ink.

Adj. writing &c. *v.*; written &c. *v.*; in -writing, – black and white; under one's hand.

uncial, Runic, cuneiform, hieroglyphical.

Adv. *currente calamo;* pen in hand.

Phr. *audacter et sincere; le style est l'homme même;* " nature's noblest gift — my gray goose quill " [Byron]; *scribendi recte sapere et principium et fons* [Horace]; " that mighty instrument of little men " [Byron]; " the pen became a clarion " [Longfellow].

591. Printing. — N. printing; block –, type- printing; plate printing &c. (*engraving*) 558; the press &c. (*publication*) 531; composition.

print, letterpress, text; context, note, page, column.

typography; stereo-, electro-, apro-type; type, black letter, font, fount; pi, pie; capitals &c. (*letters*) 561; brevier, bourgeois, pica &c.

boldface, capitals, caps., catchword; composing-frame, -room, -rule, -stand, -stick; italics, justification, linotype, live matter, logotype; lower –, upper-case; make-up, matrix, matter, mono-type, point system: $4\frac{1}{2}$, 5, $5\frac{1}{2}$, 6, 7, 8 point, etc.; press-room, -work; reglet, roman; running-head, -title; scale, serif, shank, sheet work, shoulder, signature, slug, underlay.

folio &c. (*book*) 593; copy, impression, pull, proof, revise; author's –, galley –, page –, press- proof; press revise.

printer, compositor, reader; printer's devil; copyholder.

V. print; compose; put –, go- to press; pass –, see- through the press; publish &c. 531; bring out; appear in –, rush into- print; distribute, make-up, mortise, offset, overrun, rout.

Adj. printed &c. *v.*; in type; typographical &c. *n.*; solid in galleys.

592. Correspondence. — N. correspondence, letter, epistle, note, billet,

593. Book. — N. book, -let; writing, work, volume, tome, opuscule; tract,

post card, missive, circular, favor, *billet-doux;* chit, chitty, letter card, picture post card; postal [U. S.], – card; des-, dis-patch; bulletin, these presents; re-script, -ion; post &c. (*messenger*) 534.

V. correspond, – with; write –, send a letter- to; keep up a correspondence.

Adj. epistolary.

Phr. *furor scribendi.*

-ate; *livret;* brochure, libretto, hand-book, codex, manual, pamphlet, en-chiridion, circular, publication; chap book.

part, issue, number, *livraison;* album, portfolio; periodical, serial, magazine, ephemeris, annual, journal.

paper, bill, sheet, broadsheet; leaf, -let; fly leaf, page; quire, ream.

chapter, section, head, article, para-graph, passage, clause.

folio, quarto, octavo; duo-, sexto-, octo-decimo.

en-, cyclopedia; compilation; library, bibliotheca; the press &c. (*publication*) 531.

writer, author, *littérateur*, essayist, journalist; pen, scribbler, the scribbling race; literary hack, Grub-street writer; writer for –, gentleman of –, repre-sentative of- the press; adjective jerker, diaskeuast, ghost, hack writer, ink slinger; publicist; reporter, penny-a-liner; editor, subeditor; playwright &c. 599; poet &c. 597.

bookseller, publisher; biblio-pole, -polist; librarian; bookstore, book-seller's shop.

knowledge of books, bibliography; book -learning &c. (*knowledge*) 490.

Phr. " among the giant fossils of my past " [E. B. Browning]; *craignez tout d'un auteur en courroux;* " for authors nobler palms remain " [Pope]; " I lived to write and wrote to live " [Rogers]; " look in thy heart and write " [Sidney]; " there is no Past so long as Books shall live " [Bulwer Lytton]; " the public mind is the creation of the Master-Writers " [Disraeli]; " volumes that I prize above my dukedom " [*Tempest*].

594. Description. — N. description, account, statement, report; *exposé* &c. (*disclosure*) 529; specification, particulars; state –, summary- of facts; brief &c. (*abstract*) 596; return &c. (*record*) 551; catalogue raisonné &c. (*list*) 86; guide-book &c. (*information*) 527.

delineation &c. (*representation*) 554; sketch; monograph; minute –, detailed –, particular –, circumstantial –, graphic- account; narration, recital, rehearsal, relation.

histori-, chron-ography; historic Muse, Clio; history; bi-, autobi-ography; necrology, obituary.

narrative, history; memoir, memorials; annals &c. (*chronicle*) 551; saga; tradition, legend, story, tale, historiette; personal narrative, journal, life, ad-ventures, fortunes, experiences, confessions; anecdote, ana, *trait.*

work of fiction, novel, romance, Minerva press; fairy –, nursery- tale; fable, parable, apologue; dime novel, penny dreadful, shilling shocker *.

relator &c. *v.;* raconteur, historian &c. (*recorder*) 553; biographer, fabulist, novelist.

V. describe; set forth &c. (*state*) 535; draw a picture, picture; portray &c. (*represent*) 554; characterize, particularize; narrate, relate, recite, recount, sum up, run over, recapitulate, rehearse, fight one's battles over again.

unfold &c. (*disclose*) 529- a tale; tell; give –, render- an account of; report, make a report, draw up a statement.

detail; enter into –, descend to- -particulars, – details; itemize.

Adj. descriptive, graphic, narrative, epic, suggestive, well-drawn; historic; tradition-al, -ary; legendary; anecdotic, storied; described &c. *v.*

Phr. *furor scribendi.*

595. Dissertation. — N. dissertation, treatise, essay; thesis, theme; tract, -ate, -ation; discourse, memoir, disquisition, lecture, sermon, homily, pandect; excursus.

commentary, review, *critique*, criticism, article; lead-er, -ing article; editorial; running commentary.

investigation &c. (*inquiry*) 461; study &c. (*consideration*) 451; discussion &c. (*reasoning*) 476; exposition &c. (*explanation*) 522.

commentator, critic, essayist, pamphleteer.

V. dissert –, descant –, write –, touch- upon a subject; treat of –, take up –, ventilate –, discuss –, deal with –, go into –, canvass –, handle –, do justice to- a subject.

Adj. dis-cursive, -coursive; disquisitionary; expository.

596. Compendium. — **N.** compend, -ium; abstract, *précis*, epitome, *multum in parvo;* analysis, pandect, digest, sum and substance, brief, abridgment, summary, *aperçu*, draft, minute, note; excerpt; synopsis, textbook, conspectus, outlines, syllabus, contents, heads, prospectus.

album; scrap –, note –, memorandum –, commonplace- book; extracts, *excerpta*, cuttings; fugitive -pieces, – writings; *spicilegium*, flowers, anthology, collectanea, analecta; compilation.

recapitulation, *résumé*, review.

abbrevia-tion, -ture; contraction; shortening &c. 201; compression &c. 195.

V. abridge, abstract, epitomize, summarize; make –, prepare –, draw–, compile- an abstract &c. *n.*

recapitulate, review, skim, run over, sum up.

abbreviate &c. (*shorten*) 201; condense &c. (*compress*) 195; compile &c. (*collect*) 72.

Adj. compendious, synoptic, analectic; *abrégé*, abridged &c. *v.*; variorum.

Adv. in -short, – epitome, – substance, – few words.

Phr. it lies in a nutshell.

597. Poetry. — **N.** poetry, poetics, poesy, Muse, Calliope, tuneful Nine, Parnassus, Helicon, Pierides, Pierian spring.

versification, rhyming, making verses; prosody, orthometry.

poem; epic, – poem; epopee, *epopœa*, ode, epode, idyl, lyric, eclogue, pastoral,

598. Prose. — **N.** prose, – writer pros-aicism, -aism, -aist, -er.

V. prose.

write -prose, – in prose.

Adj. pros-al, -y, -aic; unpoetical. rhymeless, unrhymed, in prose, not in verse.

bucolic, dithyramb, anacreontic, sonnet, round[elay, rondeau, rondo, madrigal, canzonet, *cento*, monody, elegy; amœbæum, *ghazal*, palinode.

dramatic –, lyric- poetry; opera; posy, anthology; *disjecta membra poetæ*.

song, ballad, lay; love –, drinking –, war –, sea- song; lullaby; music &c. 415; nursery rhymes.

[Bad poetry] doggerel, Hudibrastic verse, prose run mad; macaronics; macaronic –, leonine- verse; runes.

canto, stanza, distich, verse, line, couplet, triplet, quatrain; strophe, antistrophe.

verse, rhyme, assonance, crambo, meter, measure, foot, numbers, strain, rhythm; accentuation &c. (*voice*) 580; dactyl, spondee, trochee, anapest &c.; hex-, pent-ameter; Alexandrine; anacrusis, antispast, blank verse, ictus.

elegiacs &c. *adj.*; elegiac &c. *adj.* -verse, – meter, – poetry.

poet, – laureate; laureate; bard, lyrist, scald, skald, troubadour, trouvère; minstrel; minne-, meister-singer; *improvisatore;* versifier, sonneteer; rhym-er, -ist, -ester; ballad monger, runer; poetaster; *genus irritabile vatum*.

V. poetize, sing, versify, make verses, rhyme, scan.

Adj. poetic, -al; lyric, -al; tuneful; epic; dithyrambic &c. *n.*; metrical; a-, catalectic; elegiac, iambic, trochaic, anapestic; amœbæic, Melibean, skaldic; Ionic, Sapphic, Alcaic, Pindaric.

Phr. " a poem round and perfect as a star " [Alex. Smith]; *Dichtung und Wahrheit; furor poeticus;* " his virtues formed the magic of his song " [Hayley]; " I do but sing because I

must " [Tennyson]; " I learnt life from the poets " [de Staël]; *licentia vatum; mutum est pictura poema;* " O for a muse of fire! " [*Henry V*]; " sweet food of sweetly uttered knowledge " [Sidney]; " the true poem is the poet's mind " [Emerson]; *Volk der Dichter und Denker;* " wisdom married to immortal verse " [Wordsworth].

599. The Drama. — N. the -drama, – stage, – theater, – play; theatricals, dramaturgy, histrionic art, buskin, sock, cothurnus, Melpomene and Thalia, Thespis.

play, drama, stageplay, piece, five-act play, tragedy, comedy, opera, vaudeville, comedietta, *lever de rideau,* interlude, afterpiece, exode, farce, *divertissement,* extravaganza, burletta, harlequinade, pantomime, burlesque, *opéra bouffe,* ballet, spectacle, masque, *drame, comédie drame;* melo-drama, -drame; *comédie larmoyante,* sensation drama; tragi-, farcical-comedy; mono-drame, -logue; duologue; trilogy; charade, *proverbe;* mystery, miracle play.

act, scene, tableau; in-, intro-duction; pro-, epi-logue; libretto.

performance, representation, *mise en scène,* stagery, *jeu de théâtre;* acting; gesture &c. 550; impersonation &c. 554; stage business, gag, buffoonery.

theater; play-, opera-house; house; music hall; amphitheater, circus, hippodrome; puppet show, fantoccini; marionettes, Punch and Judy.

auditory, auditorium, front of the house, stalls, boxes, pit, gallery, parquet; greenroom, coulisses.

flat; drop, – scene; wing, screen, side scene; transformation scene, curtain, act drop; proscenium.

stage, scene, the boards; trap, mezzanine floor; flies; floats, footlights; orchestra.

theatrical -costume, – properties.

part, rôle, character, *dramatis personæ;* répertoire.

actor, player; stage –, strolling- player; stager, performer; mime, -r; artiste; com-, trag-edian; *tragédienne,* Thespian, Roscius, star; ham *, -fatter *; masker.

pantomimist, clown, harlequin, buffo, buffoon, *farceur,* grimacer, pantaloon, columbine; punch, -inello; *pulcinell-o, -a;* mute, *figurante,* general utility; super, -numerary.

mummer, guiser, guisard, gysart †, masque.

mountebank, Jack Pudding; tumbler, posture master, acrobat; contortionist; ballet -dancer, – girl; chorus singer; *coryphée, danseuse.*

company; first tragedian, *prima donna,* protagonist; *jeune premier; débutant, -e;* light –, genteel –, low- -comedy; – comedian; walking gentleman, *amoroso,* heavy father, *ingénue, jeune veuve.*

property man, costumier, machinist; prompter, call boy; manager; stage –, acting- manager; *entrepreneur,* impresario.

dramatic -author, – writer; play-writer, -wright; dramatist, mimographer.

V. act, play, perform; put on the stage; personate &c. 554; mimic &c. (*imitate*) 19; enact; play –, act –, go through –, perform- a part; rehearse, spout, gag, rant; " strut and fret one's hour upon a stage "; tread the -stage, – boards; come out; star it.

Adj. dramatic; theatric, -al; scenic, histrionic, comic, tragic, buskined, farcical, tragi-comic, melodramatic, operatic; stagy.

Adv. on the -stage, – boards; before -the floats, – an audience; behind the scenes.

Phr. *fere totus mundus exercet histrionem* [Petronius Arbiter]; " suit the action to the word, the word to the action " [*Hamlet*]; " the play's the thing " [*Hamlet*]; " to wake the soul by tender strokes of art " [Pope].

CLASS V

WORDS RELATING TO THE VOLUNTARY POWERS [1]

DIVISION (I) INDIVIDUAL VOLITION

Section I. VOLITION IN GENERAL

1. *Acts of Volition*

600. Will. — N. will, volition, conation,[2] velleity; *liberum arbitrium;* will and pleasure, free will; freedom &c. 748; discretion; option &c. (*choice*) 609; voluntariness; spontane-ity, -ousness; originality.

pleasure, wish, mind; desire; frame of mind &c. (*inclination*) 602; intention &c. 620; predetermination &c. 611; self-control &c. determination &c. (*resolution*) 604; force of will.

V. will, list; see –, think- fit; determine &c. (*resolve*) 604; enjoin; settle &c. (*choose*) 609; volunteer.

have a will of one's own; do what one chooses &c. (*freedom*) 748; have it all one's own way; have one's -will, – own way.

use –, exercise- one's discretion; take -upon oneself, – one's own course, – the law into one's own hands; do -of one's own accord, – upon one's own authority; originate &c. (*cause*) 153.

Adj. voluntary, volitional, willful; free &c. 748; optional; discretion-al, -ary; volitient, volitive.

minded &c. (*willing*) 602; prepense &c. (*predetermined*) 611; intended &c. 620; autocratic; unbidden &c. (bid &c. 741); spontaneous; original &c. (*causal*) 153; unconstrained.

Adv. voluntarily &c. *adj.*; at -will, – pleasure; *à -volonté, – discrétion; al piacere; ad -libitum, – arbitrium;* as -one thinks proper, – it seems good to; *a bene-placito.*

of one's own -accord, – free will; *proprio –, suo –, ex mero- motu;* out of

601. Necessity. — N. involuntariness; instinct, blind impulse; inborn –, innate- proclivity; native –, natural-tendency; natural impulse, predetermination.

necessi-ty, -tation; obligation; compulsion &c. 744; subjection &c. 749; stern –, hard –, dire –, imperious –, inexorable –, iron –, adverse- -necessity, – fate; ἀνάγκη, what must be.

desti-ny, -nation; fatality, fate, kismet, doom, foredoom, election, predestination; pre-, fore-ordination; lot, fortune; fatalism; inevitableness &c. *adj.*; spell &c. 993.

star, -s; planet, -s; astral influence; sky, Fates, Parcæ, Sisters three, book of fate; God's will, will of Heaven; wheel of Fortune, Ides of March, Hobson's choice.

last -shift, – resort; *dernier ressort; pis aller* &c. (*substitute*) 147; necessaries &c. (*requirement*) 630.

necess-arian, -itarian; fatalist; automaton.

V. lie under a necessity; be -fated, – doomed, – destined &c., – in for, – under the necessity of; have no -choice, – alternative; be one's -fate &c. *n.*- to; be -pushed to the wall, – driven into a corner, – unable to help.

destine, doom, foredoom, devote; predestine, -ordain; cast a spell &c. 992; necessitate; compel &c. 744.

Adj. necessary; needful &c. (*requisite*) 630.

fated; destined &c. *v.*; elect; spellbound.

---

[1] Conative powers or faculties as distinguished from cognition and feeling (Hamilton).
[2] Hamilton.

one's own head; by choice &c. 609; purposely &c. (*intentionally*) 620; deliberately &c. 611.

Phr. *stet pro ratione voluntas; sic volo sic jubeo; a vostro beneplacito; beneficium accipere libertatem est vendere; Deus vult; was man nicht kann meiden muss man willig leiden.*

compulsory &c. (*compel*) 744; uncontrollable, inevitable, unavoidable, irresistible, irrevocable, inexorable; avoid-, resist-less.

involuntary, instinctive, automatic, blind, mechanical; un-conscious, -witting, -thinking; unintentional &c. (*undesigned*) 621; impulsive &c. 612.

Adv. necessarily &c. *adv.*; of -necessity, – course; *ex necessitate rei;* needs must; perforce &c. 744; *nolens volens;* will he nil he, willy nilly, *bon gré mal gré,* willing or unwilling, *coûte que coûte.*

faute de mieux; by stress of; if need be.

Phr. it cannot be helped; there is no -help for, – helping- it; it -will, – must, – must needs- be, – be so, – have its way; the die is cast; *jacta est alea; che sarà sarà;* " it is written "; one's- days are numbered, – fate is sealed; *Fata obstant; diis aliter visum; actum me invito factus, non est meus actus; aujourd'hui roi demain rien; quisque suos patimur manes* [Vergil].

602. Willingness. — N.

willingness, voluntariness &c. *adj.*; willing mind, heart.

disposition, inclination, leaning, animus; frame of mind, humor, mood, vein; bent &c. (*turn of mind*) 820; *penchant* &c. (*desire*) 865; aptitude &c. 698.

doc-ility, -ibleness; persuasi-bleness, -bility; pliability &c. (*softness*) 324.

geniality, cordiality; goodwill; alacrity, readiness, earnestness, forwardness; eagerness &c. (*desire*) 865.

assent &c. 488; compliance &c. 762; pleasure &c. (*will*) 600; gratuitous service.

labor of love; volunteer, -ing.

V. be -willing &c. *adj.*; incline, lean to, mind, propend; had as lief; lend –, give –, turn- a willing ear; have -a, – half a, – a great- mind to; hold –, cling- to; desire &c. 865.

see –, think- -good, – fit, – proper; acquiesce &c. (*assent*) 488; comply with &c. 762.

swallow –, nibble at- the bait; gorge the hook; have –, make- no scruple of; make no bones of; jump –, catch- at; meet halfway; volunteer.

Adj. willing, minded, fain, disposed, inclined, favorable; favorably-minded, -inclined, -disposed; nothing loth; in the -vein, – mood, – humor, – mind.

ready, forward, earnest, eager; bent upon &c. (*desirous*) 865; predisposed, propense.

docile; persua-dable, -sible; suasible, easily persuaded, facile, easy-going; tractable &c. (*pliant*) 324; genial, gracious, cordial, cheering, hearty; content &c. (*assenting*) 488.

603. Unwillingness. — N.

unwillingness &c. *adj.*; indispos-ition, -edness; disinclination, aversation; nolleity, nolition; renitenc-e, -y; reluctance; indifference &c. 866; backwardness &c. *adj.*; slowness &c. 275; want of -alacrity, – readiness; indocility &c. (*obstinacy*) 606.

scrupul-ousness, -osity; qualms –, twinge- of conscience; delicacy, demur, scruple, qualm, shrinking, recoil; hesitation &c. (*irresolution*) 605; fastidiousness &c. 868.

averseness &c. (*dislike*) 867; dissent &c. 489; refusal &c. 764.

V. be -unwilling &c. *adj.*; nill; dislike &c. 867; grudge, begrudge; not be able to find it in one's heart to, not have the stomach to.

demur, stick at, scruple, stickle; hang fire, run rusty; recoil, shrink, swerve; hesitate &c. 605; avoid &c. 623.

oppose &c. 708; dissent &c. 489; refuse &c. 764.

Adj. unwilling; not in the vein, loth, loath, shy of, disinclined, indisposed, averse, reluctant, not content; adverse &c. (*opposed*) 708; laggard, backward, remiss, slack, slow to; indifferent &c. 866; scrupulous; squeamish &c. (*fastidious*) 868; repugnant &c. (*dislike*) 867; restiff †, -ive; demurring &c. *v.*; unconsenting &c. (*refusing*) 764; involuntary &c. 601.

Adv. unwillingly &c. *adj.*; grudgingly, with a heavy heart; with -a bad, – an ill- grace; against –, sore against- -one's wishes, – one's will, – the grain; *invitâ Minervâ; à contre cœur; malgré soi;* in spite of -one's teeth, – oneself; *nolens volens* &c. (*necessity*) 601; perforce &c.

voluntary, gratuitous, spontaneous; unasked &c. (ask &c. 765); unforced &c. (*free*) 748.

Adv. willingly &c. *adj.*; fain, freely, as lief, heart and soul; with -pleasure, – all one's heart, – open arms; with -good, – right good- will; *de bonne volonté, ex animo; con amore,* heart in hand, nothing loth, without reluctance, of one's own accord, graciously, with a good grace.

à la bonne heure; by all -means, – manner of means; to one's heart's content; yes &c. (*assent*) 488.

744; under protest; no &c. 536; not for the world, far be it from me.

---

604. Resolution. — N.

determination, will; iron –, unconquerable- will; will of one's own, decision, resolution; backbone; clear –, grit [U. S. & Can.]; sand, strength of -mind, – will; resolve &c. (*intent*) 620; firmness &c. (*stability*) 150; energy, manliness, vigor; game, pluck; resoluteness &c. (*courage*) 861; zeal &c. 682; aplomb; desperation; devot-ion, -edness.

mastery over self; self-control, -command, -possession, -reliance, -government, -restraint, -conquest, -denial; moral -courage, – strength; perseverance &c. 604a; tenacity; obstinacy &c. 606; bulldog; British lion.

V. have -determination &c. *n.*; know one's own mind; be -resolved &c. *adj.*; make up one's mind, will, resolve, determine; decide &c. (*judgment*) 480; form –, come to- a -determination, – resolution, – resolve; conclude, fix, seal, determine once for all, bring to a crisis, drive matters to an extremity; take a decisive step &c. (*choice*) 609; take upon oneself &c. (*undertake*) 676.

devote oneself –, give oneself up- to; throw away the scabbard, kick down the ladder, nail one's colors to the mast, set one's back against the wall, set one's teeth, put one's foot down, take one's stand; stand firm &c. (*stability*) 150; steel oneself; stand no nonsense, not listen to the voice of the charmer.

buckle to; buckle oneself; put –, lay –, set- one's shoulder to the wheel; put one's heart into; run the gauntlet, make a dash at, take the bull by the horns; rush –, plunge- *in medias res;* go in for; insist upon, make a point of; set one's -heart, – mind- upon.

stick at nothing; make short work of &c. (*activity*) 682; not stick at trifles; go -all lengths, – the limit *, – the whole hog; persist &c. (*persevere*) 604a; go through fire and water, ride in the whirlwind and direct the storm.

605. Irresolution. — N.

irresolution, infirmity of purpose, indecision; in-, un-determination; unsettlement; uncertainty &c. 475; demur, suspense; hesi-tating &c. *v.*, -tation, -tancy; vacillation; changeableness &c. 149; fluctuation; alternation &c. (*oscillation*) 314; caprice &c. 608.

fickleness, levity, *légèreté;* pliancy &c. (*softness*) 324; weakness; timidity &c. 860; cowardice &c. 862; half measures.

waverer, ass between two bundles of hay; shuttlecock, butterfly; doughface [U. S.].

V. be -irresolute &c. *adj.*; hang –, keep- in suspense; leave "*ad referendum*"; think twice about, pause; dawdle &c. (*inactivity*) 683; remain neuter; dillydally, hesitate, boggle, hover, dacker, hum and haw, demur, not know one's own mind; debate, balance; dally –, coquet- with; will and will not, *chasser-balancer;* go halfway, compromise, make a compromise; be thrown off one's balance, stagger like a drunken man; be afraid &c. 860; let " I dare not " wait upon " I would " [*Macbeth*]; falter, waver.

vacillate &c. 149; change &c. 140; retract &c. 607; fluctuate; pendulate; alternate &c. (*oscillate*) 314; keep off and on, play fast and loose; blow hot and cold &c. (*caprice*) 608.

shuffle, palter, blink; trim.

Adj. irresolute, infirm of purpose, double-minded, half-hearted; un-decided, -resolved, -determined; shilly-shally; fidgety, tremulous; hesitating &c. *v.*; off one's balance; at a loss &c. (*uncertain*) 475.

vacillating &c. *v.*; unsteady &c. (*changeable*) 149; unsteadfast, fickle, without ballast; capricious &c. 608; volatile, frothy; light, -some, -minded; giddy; fast and loose.

weak, feeble-minded, frail; timid &c. 860; cowardly &c. 862; dough-faced

Adj. resolved &c. *v.*; determined; strong-willed, -minded; resolute &c. (*brave*) 861; self-possessed; decided, definitive, peremptory, *tranchant;* un-hesitating, -flinching, -shrinking; firm, iron, gritty [U. S.], indomitable, game to the backbone; inexorable, relentless, not to be -shaken, – put down; *tenax propositi;* inflexible &c. (*hard*) 323; obstinate &c. 606; steady &c. (*persevering*) 604a.

earnest, serious; set –, bent –, intent- upon.

steeled –, proof- against; *in utrumque paratus.*

Adv. *resolutely* &c. *adj.*; in –, in good- earnest; seriously, joking apart, earnestly, heart and soul; on one's mettle; manfully, like a man, with a high hand; with a strong hand &c. (*exertion*) 686.

at any -rate, – risk, – hazard, – price, – cost, – sacrifice; at all -hazards, – risks, – events; *à bis ou à blanc;* cost what it may; *coûte que coûte; à tort et à travers;* once for all; neck or nothing; rain or shine.

Phr. *spes sibi quisque; celui qui veut celui-la peut; chi non s'arrischia non guadagna; frangas non flectes; manu forti; tentanda via est.*

[U. S.]; facile; pliant &c. (*soft*) 324; unable to say " no," easy-going.

revocable, reversible.

Adv. irresolutely &c. *adj.*; irresolvedly; in faltering accents; off and on; from pillar to post; seesaw &c. 314.

Int. " how happy could I be with either! " [Gay].

604a. Perseverance. — N. perseverance; continuance &c. (*inaction*) 143; permanence &c. (*absence of change*) 141; firmness &c. (*stability*) 150.

constancy, steadiness; singleness –, tenacity- of purpose; persistence, plodding, patience; sedulity &c. (*industry*) 682; pertina-cy †, -city, -ciousness; iteration &c. 104.

bottom, game, pluck, stamina, backbone, grit; indefatiga-bility, -bleness; bulldog courage.

V. persevere, persist; hold -on, – out; die in the last ditch, be in at the death; stick –, cling –, adhere- to; stick to one's text, keep on; keep to –, maintain- one's -course, – ground; go -all lengths, – through fire and water; bear –, keep –, hold- up; plod; stick to work &c. (*work*) 686; continue &c. 143; follow up; die -in harness, – at one's post.

Adj. persevering, constant; stead-y, -fast; un-deviating, -wavering, -faltering, -swerving, -flinching, -sleeping, -flagging, -drooping; steady as time; uninter-, unre-mitting; plodding; industrious &c. 682; strenuous &c. 686; pertinacious; persist-ing, -ent.

solid, sturdy, staunch, stanch, true to oneself; unchangeable &c. 150; unconquerable &c. (*strong*) 159; indomitable, game to the last, indefatigable, untiring, unwearied, never tiring.

Adv. through -evil report and good report, – thick and thin, – fire and water; *per fas et nefas;* without fail, sink or swim, at any price, *vogue la galère.*

Phr. never say die; *vestigia nulla retrorsum; aut vincere aut mori; la garde meurt et ne se rend pas; tout vient à temps pour qui sait attendre.*

606. Obstinacy. — N. obstinateness &c. *adj.*; obstinacy, tenacity; cussedness [U. S.]; perseverance &c. 604a; immovability; old school; inflexibility &c. (*hardness*) 323; obdur-acy, -ation; dogged resolution; resolution &c. 604; ruling passion; blind side.

self-will, contumacy, perversity; pervica-cy †, -city; indocility.

bigotry, intolerance, dogmatism; opinia-try †, -tiveness; fixed idea &c. (*pre-*

607. Tergiversation. — N. change of -mind, – intention, – purpose; afterthought.

tergiversation, recantation; palin-ode, -ody; renunciation; abjur-ation, -ement; defection &c. (*relinquishment*) 624; going over &c. *v.*; apostasy; retract-ion, -ation; withdrawal; disavowal &c. (*negation*) 536; revo-cation, -kement; reversal; repentance &c. 950; *redintegratio amoris.*

judgment) 481; fanaticism, zealotry, infatuation, monomania; opinion-atedness, -ativeness.

mule; opin-ionist †, -ionatist, -iator †, -ator †; stickler, dogmatist; bigot; zealot, enthusiast, fanatic.

V. be -obstinate &c. *adj.*; stickle, take no denial, fly in the face of facts; opinionate, be wedded to an opinion, hug a belief; have one's own way &c. (*will*) 600; persist &c. (*persevere*) 604*a*; have –, insist on having- the last word.

die hard, fight against destiny, not yield an inch, stand out.

Adj. obstinate, tenacious, stubborn, obdurate, casehardened; inflexible &c. (*hard*) 323; balky; immovable, not to be moved; inert &c. 172; unchangeable &c. 150; inexorable &c. (*determined*) 604; mulish, obstinate as a mule, pig-headed.

dogged; sullen, sulky; un-moved, -influenced, -affected.

willful, self-willed, perverse; res-ty, -tive, -tiff †; pervicacious, wayward, refractory, unruly; head-y, -strong; *entêté*; contumacious; crossgrained.

arbitrary, dogmatic, positive, bigoted; prejudiced &c. 481; creed-bound; prepossessed, infatuated; stiff-backed, -necked, -hearted; hard-mouthed, hidebound; unyielding; im-pervious, -practicable, -persuasible; unpersuadable; in-, un-tractable; incorrigible, deaf to advice, impervious to reason; crotchety &c. 608.

Adv. obstinately &c. *adj.*

Phr. *non possumus;* no surrender; *ils n'ont rien appris ne rien oublié.*

coquetry; vacillation &c. 605; backsliding; *volte-face.*

turn-coat, -tippet †; rat, apostate, renegade; con-, per-vert; proselyte, deserter; backslider; blackleg, crawfish * [U. S.], scab *, mugwump [U. S.], recidivist.

time-server, -pleaser; timist †, Vicar of Bray, trimmer, ambidexter; weathercock &c. (*changeable*) 149; Janus.

V. change one's- mind, – intention, - purpose, – note; abjure, renounce; withdraw from &c. (*relinquish*) 624; wheel –, turn –, veer- round; turn a pirouette; go over –, pass –, change –, skip- from one side to another; go to the right-about; box the compass, shift one's ground, go upon another tack.

apostatize, change sides, go over, rat; recant, retract; revoke; rescind &c. (*abrogate*) 756; recall; forswear, unsay; come -over, – round- to an opinion; crawfish * [U. S.], crawl * [U. S.].

draw in one's horns, eat one's words; eat –, swallow- the leek; swerve, flinch, back out of, retrace one's steps, think better of it; come back –, return· to one's first love; turn over a new leaf &c. (*repent*) 950.

trim, shuffle, play fast and loose, blow hot and cold, coquet, be on the fence, straddle, hold with the hare but run with the hounds; *nager entre deux eaux;* wait to see how the -cat jumps, – wind blows.

Adj. changeful &c. 149; irresolute &c. 605; ductile, slippery as an eel, trimming, ambidextrous, timeserving; coquetting &c. *v.*

revocatory, reactionary.

Phr. " a change came o'er the spirit of my dream " [Byron].

608. Caprice. — **N.** caprice, fancy, humor; whim, -sey, -wham; crotchet, *capriccio*, quirk, freak, maggot, fad, vagary, prank, fit, flimflam, escapade, boutade, wild-goose chase; capriciousness &c. *adj.*; kink.

V. be -capricious &c. *adj.*; have a maggot in the brain; take it into one's head, strain at a gnat and swallow a camel; blow hot and cold; play -fast and loose, – fantastic tricks; *tourner casaque.*

Adj. capricious; erratic, eccentric, fitful, hysterical; full of -whims &c. *n.*; maggoty; inconsistent, fanciful, fantastic, whimsical, crotchety, kinky [U. S.], particular, humorsome, freakish, skittish, wanton, wayward; contrary; captious; arbitrary; unconformable &c. 83; penny wise and pound foolish; fickle &c. (*irresolute*) 605; frivolous, sleeveless, giddy, volatile.

Adv. by fits and starts, without rhyme or reason.

Phr. *nil fuit unquam sic impar sibi;* the deuce is in him.

609. Choice. — **N.** choice, option; discretion &c. (*volition*) 600; preoption;

609a. Absence of Choice. — **N.** no –, Hobson's- choice; first come first

alternative; dilemma, *embarras de choix;* adoption, coöptation; novation; decision &c. (*judgment*) 480.

election, poll, ballot, vote, voice, suffrage, plumper, cumulative vote; plebiscitum, plebiscite, *vox populi;* electioneering; voting &c. *v.;* elective franchise; straight –, ticket [U. S.].

selection, excerption, gleaning, eclecticism; *excerpta*, gleanings, cuttings, scissors and paste; pick &c. (*best*) 650.

preference, prelation; predilection &c. (*desire*) 865.

V. offer for one's choice, set before; hold out –, present –, offer- the alternative; put to the vote.

use –, exercise –, one's- -discretion, – option; adopt, take up, embrace, espouse; choose, elect; take –, make- one's choice; make choice of, fix upon.

vote, poll, hold up one's hand; divide. settle; decide &c. (*adjudge*) 480; list &c. (*will*) 600; make up one's mind &c. (*resolve*) 604.

select; pick, – and choose; pick –, single- out; cull, glean, winnow; sift –, separate –, winnow- the chaff from the wheat; pick up, pitch upon; pick one's way; indulge one's fancy.

set apart, mark out for; mark &c. 550.

prefer; have -rather, – as lief; fancy &c. (*desire*) 865; be persuaded &c. 615.

take a -decided, – decisive- step; commit oneself to a course; pass –, cross- the Rubicon; cast in one's lot with; take for better or for worse.

Adj. optional; discretional &c. (*voluntary*) 600.

eclectic; choosing &c. *v.;* preferential; chosen &c. *v.;* choice &c. (*good*) 648.

Adv. optionally &c. *adj.;* at pleasure &c. (*will*) 600; either, – the one or the other; or; at the option of; whether or not; once for all; for one's money.

by -choice, – preference; in preference; rather, before.

served; necessity &c. 601; not a pin to choose &c. (*equality*) 27; any, the first that comes; that or nothing.

neutrality, indifference; indecision &c. (*irresolution*) 605.

V. be -neutral &c. *adj.;* have no choice; waive, not vote; abstain –, refrain -from voting; leave undecided; " make a virtue of necessity " [*Two Gentlemen*].

Adj. neu-tral, -ter; indifferent; undecided &c. (*irresolute*) 605.

Adv. either &c. (*choice*) 609.

610. Rejection. — N. rejection, repudiation, exclusion; refusal &c. 764; declination.

V. reject; set –, lay- aside; give up; decline &c. (*refuse*) 764; exclude, except; pluck, spin; cast.

repudiate, scout, set at naught; fling –, cast –, throw –, toss- -to the winds, – to the dogs, – overboard, – away; send to the right-about; disclaim &c. (*deny*) 536; discard &c. (*eject*) 297, (*have done with*) 678.

Adj. rejected &c. *v.;* reject-aneous †, -itious †; not -chosen &c. 609, – to be thought of; out of the question.

Adv. neither, – the one nor the other; no &c. 536.

Phr. *non hæc in fœdera.*

611. Predetermination. — N. pre-destination, -ordination, -meditation, -deliberation, -determination; foregone conclusion; *parti pris;* resolve, propendency †; intention &c. 620; project &c. 626; fate, foredoom, necessity.

V. pre-destine, -ordain, -determine, -meditate, -resolve, -concert; resolve beforehand.

Adj. pre-pense, -meditated &c. *v.,* -designed; advised, studied, designed, calculated; aforethought; intended &c. 620; foregone.

well-laid, -devised, -weighed; maturely considered; cunning.

612. Impulse. — N. impulse, sudden thought; impromptu, improvisation; inspiration, flash, spurt.

improvisatore; creature of impulse.

V. flash on the mind.

say what comes uppermost; improvise, extemporize.

Adj. extemporaneous, impulsive, indeliberate; snap; improvis-ed, -ate, -atory; un-, unpre-meditated; *improvisé;* un-prompted, -guided; natural, unguarded; spontaneous &c. (*voluntary*) 600; instinctive &c. 601.

Adv. extem-pore, -poraneously; offhand, impromptu, *à l'improviste;* im-

Adv. advisedly &c. *adj.*; with pre-meditation, deliberately, all things considered, with eyes open, in cold blood; intentionally &c. 620.

proviso; on the spur of the -moment, -occasion.

613. Habit. — N.

habit, -ude; as-sue-tude †, -faction †; wont; run, way.

common -, general -, natural -, ordinary- -course, - run, - state- of things; matter of course; beaten -path, - track, - ground.

prescription, custom, use, usage, immemorial usage, practice; prevalence, observance; conventional-ism, -ity; mode, fashion, vogue; etiquette &c. (*gentility*) 852; order of the day, cry; conformity &c. 82; consuetude, dustoor.

one's old way, old school, *veteris vestigia flammæ; laudator temporis acti.*

rule, standing order, precedent, routine; red-tape, -tapism; pipe clay; rut, groove.

cacoëthes; bad -, confirmed -, inveterate -, intrinsic &c. 5- habit; addiction, trick.

614. Desuetude. — N.

desuetude, disusage; obsolescence, disuse &c. 678; want of -habit, - practice; inusitation: newness to; new brooms.

infraction of usage &c. (*unconformity*) 83; nonprevalence; " a custom more honored in the breach than the observance " [*Hamlet*].

V. be -unaccustomed &c. *adj.*; leave off -, cast off -, break off -, wean oneself of -, violate -, break through -, infringe- -a habit, - a custom, - a usage; disuse &c. 678; wear off.

Adj. un-accustomed, -used, -wonted, -seasoned, -inured, -habituated, -trained; new; green &c. (*unskilled*) 699; unhackneyed.

unusual &c. (*unconformable*) 83; non-observant; disused &c. 678.

training &c. (*education*) 537; seasoning, hardening, inurement; radication; second nature, acclimatization; knack &c. (*skill*) 698.

V. be -wont &c. *adj.*

fall into a custom &c. (*conform to*) 82; tread -, follow- the beaten -track, - path; *stare super antiquas vias;* move in a rut, run on in a groove, go round like a horse in a mill, go on in the old jog trot way.

habituate, inure, harden, season, caseharden; accustom, familiarize; naturalize, acclimatize; keep one's hand in; train &c. (*educate*) 537.

get into the -way, - knack- of; learn &c. 539; cling -, adhere- to; repeat &c. 104; acquire -, contract -, fall into- a -habit, - trick; addict oneself -, take- to.

be -habitual &c. *adj.*; prevail; come into use, become a habit, take root; gain -, grow- upon one.

Adj. habitual; ac-, customary; prescriptive; accustomed &c. *v.*; of -daily, - everyday- occurrence; consuetudinary; wonted, usual, general, ordinary, common, frequent, everyday, household, jog trot; well-trodden, -known; familiar, vernacular, trite, commonplace, conventional, regular, set, stock, established, stereotyped; pre-vailing, -valent; current, received, acknowledged, recognized, accredited; of course, admitted, understood.

conformable &c. 82; according to -use, - custom, - routine; in -vogue, - fashion; fashionable &c. (*genteel*) 852.

wont; used -, given -, addicted -, attuned -, habituated &c. *v.*- to; in the habit of; *habitué;* at home in &c. (*skillful*) 698; seasoned; imbued with; devoted -, wedded- to.

hackneyed, fixed, rooted, deep-rooted, ingrafted, permanent, inveterate, besetting; naturalized; ingrained &c. (*intrinsic*) 5.

Adv. habitually &c. *adj.*; always &c. (*uniformly*) 16.

as -usual, - is one's wont, - things go, - the world goes, - the sparks fly upwards; *more -suo, - solito; ex more.*

as a rule, for the most part; generally &c. *adj.*; most -often, - frequently.

Phr. *cela s'entend; abeunt studia in mores; adeo in teneris consuescere multum est; consuetudo quasi altera natura* [Cicero]; *hoc erat in more majorum;* " how use doth breed a habit in a man! " [*Two Gentlemen*]; *magna est vis consuetudinis; morem fecerat usus* [Ovid].

2. *Causes of Volition*

615. Motive. — N. motive, springs of action.

reason, ground, call, principle; by-end, -purpose; mainspring, *primum mobile*, keystone; the why and the wherefore; *pro* and *con*, reason why; secret motive, *arrière pensée;* intention &c. 620.

inducement, consideration; attraction; loadstone; magnet, -ism, -ic force; al-lect-ation †, -ive †; temptation, entice-ment, *agacerie*, allurement, witchery; be-witch-ment, -ery; charm; spell &c. 993; fascination, blandishment, cajolery; se-duc-tion, -ement; honeyed words, voice of the tempter, song of the Sirens; for-bidden fruit, golden apple.

persuasi-bility, -bleness; attractabil-ity; impress-, suscept-ibility; softness; persuas-, attract-iveness; tantalization.

influence, prompting, dictate, in-stance; impuls-e, -ion; incit-ement, -ation; press, instigation; provocation &c. (*excitation of feeling*) 824; inspira-tion; per-, suasion; encouragement, ad-vocacy; ex-, hortation; advice &c. 695; solicitation &c. (*request*) 765; lobbyism; pull *.

incentive, stimulus, spur, fillip, whip, goad, *ankus*, rowel, provocative, whet, dram.

bribe, lure; decoy, – duck; bait, trail of a red herring; bribery and corrup-tion; sop, – for Cerberus.

prompter, tempter; seduc-er, -tor; instigator, firebrand, incendiary; Siren, Circe; *agent provocateur;* lobbyist.

V. induce, move; draw, – on; bring in its train, give an -impulse &c. *n.*- to; inspire; put up to, prompt, call up; at-tract, beckon.

stimulate &c. (*excite*) 824; spirit up, inspirit; a-, rouse; animate, incite, provoke, instigate, set on, actuate; act –, work –, operate- upon; encourage; pat –, clap- on the -back, – shoulder.

influence, weigh with, bias, sway, incline, dispose, predispose, turn the scale, inoculate; lead, – by the nose; have –, exercise –, influence- -with, – over, – upon; go –, come- round one; turn the head, magnetize; lobby.

persuade; prevail -with, – upon; overcome, carry; bring -round, – to one's senses; draw –, win –, gain –, come –, talk- over; procure, enlist, engage; invite, court.

tempt, seduce, overpersuade, entice, allure, captivate, fascinate, bewitch, carry away, charm, conciliate, wheedle, coax, lure; inveigle; tantalize; cajole &c. (*deceive*) 545.

tamper with, bribe, suborn, grease the palm. bait with a silver hook, gild the

615a. Absence of Motive. — N. ab-sence of motive; caprice &c. 608; chance &c. (*absence of design*) 621.

V. have no motive; scruple &c. (*be unwilling*) 603.

Adj. without rhyme or reason; aim-less &c. (*chance*) 621.

Adv. out of mere caprice.

616. Dissuasion. — N. dissuasion, de-hortation, expostulation, remonstrance; deprecation &c. 766.

discouragement, damper, wet blan-ket.

cohibition &c. (*restraint*) 751; curb &c. (*means of restraint*) 752; check &c. (*hindrance*) 706.

reluctance &c. (*unwillingness*) 603; contraindication.

V. dissuade, dehort, cry out against, remonstrate, expostulate, warn, contra-indicate.

disincline, indispose, shake, stagger; dispirit; dis-courage, -hearten, -enchant; deter; hold –, keep- back &c. (*restrain*) 751; render -averse &c. 603; repel; turn aside &c. (*deviation*) 279; wean from; act as a drag &c. (*hinder*) 706; throw cold water on, damp, cool, chill, blunt, calm, quiet, quench; deprecate &c. 766.

Adj. dissuading &c. *v.*; dissuasive; dehortatory, expostulatory; monit-ive †, -ory.

dissuaded &c. *v.*; admonitory; unin-duced &c. (induce &c. 615); unpersuad-able &c. (*obstinate*) 606; averse &c. (*un-willing*) 603; repugnant &c. (*dislike*) 867.

pill, make things pleasant,. put a sop into the pan, throw a sop to, bait the hook.

enforce, force; impel &c. (*push*) 276; propel &c. 284; whip, lash, goad, spur, prick, urge; egg -, hound -, hurry- on; drag &c. 285; exhort; advise &c. 695; call upon &c. press &c. (*request*) 765; advocate.

set -an example, – the fashion; keep in countenance.

be -persuaded &c.; yield to temptation, come round; concede &c. (*consent*) 762; obey a call; follow -advice, – the bent, – the dictates of; act on principle.

Adj. impulsive, motive; suas-, persuas-, hortat-ive, -ory; protreptical †; inviting, tempting, &c. *v.*; suas-ive, -ory; seductive, attractive; fascinating &c. (*pleasing*) 829; provocative &c. (*exciting*) 824.

induced &c. *v.*; disposed; persuadable &c. (*docile*) 602; spellbound; instinct -, smitten- with; inspired &c. *v.*- by.

Adv. because, therefore &c. (*cause*) 155; from -this, – that- motive; for -this, – that- reason; for; by reason –, for the sake –, on the score –, on account- of; out of, from, as, forasmuch as.

for all the world; on principle.

Phr. *fax mentis incendium gloriæ;* " temptation hath a music for all ears " [Willis]; " to beguile many and be beguiled by one " [*Othello*].

617. [Ostensible motive, ground, or reason assigned.] **Plea.** — **N.** plea, pretext; allegation, advocation; ostensible -motive, – ground, – reason; excuse &c. (*vindication*) 937; color; gloss, guise.

loop-, starting-hole; how to creep out of, salvo, come off; way of escape.

handle, peg to hang on, room, *locus standi;* stalking-horse, *cheval de bataille,* cue.

pretense &c. (*untruth*) 546; put off, dust thrown in the eyes; blind; moonshine; mere -, shallow- pretext; lame -excuse, – apology; tub to a whale; false plea, sour grapes; makeshift, shift, white lie; special pleading &c. (*sophistry*) 477; soft sawder &c. (*flattery*) 933.

V. plead, allege; shelter oneself under the plea of; excuse &c. (*vindicate*) 937; lend a color to; furnish a -handle &c. *n.*; make a -pretext, – handle- of; use as a -plea &c. *n.*; take one's stand upon, make capital out of; pretend &c. (*lie*) 544.

Adj. ostensibly &c. (*manifest*) 525; alleged, apologetic; pretended &c. 545.

Adv. ostensibly; under -color; – the plea, – the pretense- of.

3. *Objects of Volition*

618. Good. — **N.** good, benefit, advantage; improvement &c. 658; greatest – supreme- good; interest, service, behoof, behalf; weal; main chance, *summum bonum*, common weal; " consummation devoutly to be wished "; gain, boot; profit, harvest.

boon &c. (*gift*) 784; good turn; blessing; world of good; piece of good -luck, – fortune; nuts, prize, windfall, godsend, waif, treasure-trove.

good fortune &c. (*prosperity*) 734; happiness &c. 827.

[Source of good] goodness &c. 648; utility &c. 644; remedy &c. 662; pleasure giving &c. 829.

Adj. commendable &c. 931; useful &c. 644; good &c., beneficial &c. 648.

Adv. well, aright, satisfactorily, fa-

619. Evil. — **N.** evil, ill, harm, hurt, mischief, nuisance; machinations of the devil, Pandora's box, ills that flesh is heir to.

blow, buffet, stroke, scratch, bruise, wound, gash, mutilation; mortal -blow, – wound; *immedicabile vulnus;* damage, loss &c. (*deterioration*) 659.

disadvantage, prejudice, drawback.

disaster, accident, casualty; mishap &c. (*misfortune*) 735; bad job, devil to pay; calamity, bale, catastrophe, tragedy; ruin &c. (*destruction*) 162; adversity &c. 735.

mental suffering &c. 828. [Evil spirit] demon &c. 980. [Cause of evil] bane &c. 663. [Production of evil] badness &c. 649; painfulness &c. 830; evil doer &c. 913.

vorably, not amiss; all for the best; to one's -advantage &c. *n.*; in one's -favor, – interest &c. *n.*

Phr. so far so good; *magnum bonum.*

out of joint; disadvantageous.

    Adv. amiss, wrong, ill, to one's cost.

    Phr. "moving accidents by flood and field" [*Othello*].

outrage, wrong, injury, foul play; bad –, ill- turn; disservice; spoliation &c. 791; grievance, crying evil.

    V. be in trouble &c. (*adversity*) 735.

    Adj. disastrous, bad &c. 649; awry.

Section II. Prospective Volition [1]

1. *Conceptional Volition*

620. Intention. — N. intent, -ion, -ionality; purpose; *quo animo;* project &c. 626; undertaking &c. 676; predetermination &c. 611; design, ambition.

contemplation, mind, animus, view, purview, proposal; study; look out.

final cause; *raison d'être; cui bono;* object, aim, end; "the be all and the end all"; drift &c. (*meaning*) 516; tendency &c. 176; destination, mark, point, butt, goal, target, bull's-eye, quintain; prey, quarry, game.

decision, determination, resolve; fixed –, set –, settled- purpose; ultimatum; resolution &c. 604; wish &c. 865; *arrière pensée;* motive &c. 615.

[Study of final causes] teleology.

    V. intend, purpose, design, mean; have to; propose to oneself; harbor a design; have in -view, – contemplation, – one's eye, – *petto;* have an eye to.

bid –, labor- for; be –, aspire –, endeavor- after; be –, aim –, drive –, point –, level –, aspire- at; take aim; set before oneself; study to.

take upon oneself &c. (*undertake*) 676; take into one's head; meditate, contemplate; think –, dream –, talk- of; premeditate &c. 611; compass, calculate; dest-ine, -inate; propose.

project &c. (*plan*) 626; have a mind to &c. (*be willing*) 602; desire &c. 865; pursue &c. 622.

    Adj. intended &c. *v.*; intentional, advised, express, determinate; prepense &c. 611; bound for; intending &c. *v.*; minded; bent upon &c. (*earnest*) 604; at stake; on the -anvil, – tapis; in -view, – prospect, – the breast of; *in petto;* teleological.

    Adv. intentionally &c. *adj.*; advisedly, wittingly, knowingly, designedly, pur-

621. [Absence of purpose in the succession of events.] **Chance.** [2] **— N.** chance &c. 156; lot, fate &c. (*necessity*) 601; luck; good luck &c. (*good*) 618; mascot.

speculation, venture, stake, game of chance; mere –, random- shot; blind bargain, leap in the dark; pig in a poke &c. (*uncertainty*) 475; fluke, potluck; faro bank; flyer *; limit.

drawing lots; sorti-legy, -tion †; *sortes, – Virgilianæ; rouge et noir*, hazard, ante, chuck-a-luck, crack-loo [U. S.], craps, faro, roulette, pitch and toss, chuck farthing, cup tossing, heads or tails, cross and pile, poker-dice; wager; bet, -ting; gambling; the turf.

gaming-, gambling-, betting-house; bucket shop; joint *; totalizator, totalizer; hell; betting ring; dice, – box; dicer; gam-bler, -ester; man of the turf; adventurer.

    V. chance &c. (*hap*) 156; stand a chance &c. (*be possible*) 470.

toss up; cast –, draw- lots; leave –, trust- -to chance, – to the chapter of accidents; tempt fortune; chance it, take one's chance; run –, incur –, encounter- the -risk, – chance; stand the hazard of the die.

speculate, try one's luck, set on a cast, raffle, put into a lottery, buy a pig in a poke, shuffle the cards.

risk, venture, hazard, stake; ante; lay, – a wager; make a bet, wager, bet, gamble, game, play for; play at chuck farthing.

    Adj. fortuitous &c. 156; unintentional, -ded; accidental; not meant; undesigned, -purposed; unpremeditated &c. 612; never thought of.

indiscriminate, promiscuous; undi-

---

[1] That is, volition having reference to a future object.   [2] See note on 156.

posely, on purpose, by design, studiously, pointedly; with -intent &c. *n.*; deliberately &c. (*with premeditation*) 611; with one's eyes open, in cold blood.

for; with -a view, – an eye- to; in order -to, – that; to the end –, with the intent- that; for the purpose –, with the view –, in contemplation –, on account- of.

in pursuance of, pursuant to; *quo animo;* to all intents and purposes.

Phr. "hell is paved with good intentions" [Johnson]; *sublimi feriam sidera vertice* [Horace].

rected, random; aim-, drift-, design-, purpose-, cause-less; without purpose.

possible &c. 470.

Adv. casually &c. 156; unintentionally &c. *adj.*; unwittingly.

en passant, by the way, incidentally; as it may happen; at -random, – a venture, – haphazard.

Phr. *acierta errando; dextro tempore;* "fearful concatenation of circumstances" [D. Webster]; "fortuitous combination of circumstances" [Dickens]; *le jeu est le fils d'avarice et le père du désespoir;* "the happy combination of fortuitous circumstances" [Scott]; "the fortuitous or casual concourse of atoms" [Bentley].

622. [Purpose in action.] Pursuit. — N. pursuit; pursuing &c. *v.*; prosecution; pursuance; enterprise &c. (*undertaking*) 676; business &c. 625; adventure &c. (*essay*) 675; quest &c. (*search*) 461; scramble, hue and cry, game; hobby; still-hunt.

chase, hunt, *battue*, race, steeple chase, hunting, coursing; ven-ation, -ery; fox chase; sport, -ing; shooting, angling, fishing, hawking; shikar.

pursuer; hunt-er, -sman; shikari, sportsman, Nimrod; hound &c. 366.

V. pursue, prosecute, follow; run –, make –, be –, hunt –, prowl- after; shadow; carry on &c. (*do*) 680; engage in &c. (*undertake*) 676; set about &c. (*begin*) 66; endeavor &c. 675; court &c. (*request*) 765; seek &c. (*search*) 461; aim at &c. (*intention*) 620; follow the trail &c. (*trace*) 461; fish for &c. (*experiment*) 463; press on &c. (*haste*) 684; run a race &c. (*velocity*) 274.

chase, give chase, course, dog, hunt, hound; tread –, follow- on the heels of, &c. (*sequence*) 281.

rush upon; rush headlong &c. (*violence*) 173; ride –, run- full tilt at; make a leap –, jump –, snatch- at; run down; start game.

tread a path; take –, hold- a course; shape –, direct –, bend- one's -steps, – course; play a game; fight –, elbow- one's way; follow up; take -to, – up; go in for; ride one's hobby.

Adj. pursuing &c. *v.*; in quest of &c. (*inquiry*) 461; in -pursuit, – full cry, – hot pursuit; on the scent.

Adv. in pursuance of &c. (*intention*) 620; after.

Int. tallyho! yoicks! soho!

623. [Absence of pursuit.] Avoidance. — N. abst-ention, -inence; forbearance; refraining &c. *v.*; inaction &c. 681; neutrality.

avoidance, evasion, elusion; seclusion &c. 893.

avolation †, flight; escape &c. 671; retreat &c. 287; recoil &c. 277; departure &c. 293; rejection &c. 610.

shirker &c. *v.*; truant; fugitive, refugee; runa-way, -gate; maroon.

V. abstain, refrain, spare, not attempt; not do &c. 681; maintain the even tenor of one's way.

eschew, keep from, let alone, have nothing to do with; keep –, stand –, hold- -aloof, – off; take no part in, have no hand in.

avoid, shun; steer –, keep- clear of; fight shy of; keep -one's, – at a respectful- distance; keep –, get- out of the way; evade, elude, turn away from; set one's face against &c. (*oppose*) 708; deny oneself.

shrink; hang –, hold –, draw- back; recoil &c. 277; retire &c. (*recede*) 287; flinch, blink, blench, shy, shirk, dodge, parry, make way for, give place to.

beat a retreat; turn -tail, – one's back; take to one's heels; run, -away, – for one's life; cut and run; be off, – like a shot; fly, flee; fly –, flee –, run away- from; take –, take to- flight; desert, elope; make –, scamper –, sneak –, shuffle –, sheer- off; break –, burst –, tear oneself –, slip –, slink –, steal- -away, – away from; slip cable, part company, turn on one's heel; sneak out of, play truant, give one the go-by, give leg bail, take French leave, slope, decamp, flit, bolt, abscond, levant, skedaddle, ab-

628. Mid-course. — **N.** middle-, mid-course; mean &c. 29; middle &c. 68; *juste milieu*, *mezzo termine*, golden mean, ἄριστον μέτρον, *aurea mediocritas*.

straight &c. (*direct*) 278 -course, – path; short –, cross- cut; great circle sailing.

neutrality; half –, half and half-measures; compromise.

V. keep in –, preserve- -a middle, – an even- course; go straight &c. (*direct*) 278.

go halfway, compromise, make a compromise.

Adj. straight &c. (*direct*) 278.

Phr. *medium tenuere beati*.

629. Circuit. — **N.** circuit, round-about way, digression, detour, circum-bendibus, ambages, loop; winding &c. (*circuition*) 311; zigzag &c. (*deviation*) 279.

V. perform a circuit; go -round about, – out of one's way; make a detour; meander &c. (*deviate*) 279.

lead a pretty dance; beat about, – the bush; make two bites of a cherry.

Adj. circuitous, indirect, roundabout: zigzag &c. (*deviating*) 279; backhanded.

Adv. by -a side wind, – an indirect course; in a roundabout way; from pillar to post.

630. Requirement. — **N.** requirement, need, wants, necessities; necessaries, – of life; stress, exigency, pinch, *sine quâ non*, matter of necessity; case of -need, – life or death.

needfulness, essentiality, necessity, indispensability, urgency.

requisition &c. (*request*) 765, (*exaction*) 741; run upon; demand –, call- for.

charge, claim, command, injunction, mandate, order, precept.

desideratum &c. (*desire*) 865; want &c. (*deficiency*) 640.

V. require, need, want, have occasion for; not be able to -do without, – dispense with; prerequire.

render necessary, necessitate, create a necessity for, call for, put in requisition; make a requisition &c. (*ask for*) 765, (*demand*) 741.

stand in need of; lack &c. 640; desiderate; desire &c. 865; be -necessary &c. *adj.*

Adj. required &c. *v.*; requisite, needful, necessary, imperative, essential, indispensable, prerequisite; called for; in -demand, – request.

urgent, exigent, pressing, instant, crying, absorbing.

in want of; destitute of &c. 640.

Adv. *ex necessitate rei* &c. (*necessarily*) 601; of necessity.

Phr. there is no time to lose; it cannot be -spared, – dispensed with; *mendacem memorem esse oportet* [Quintilian]; *necessitas non habet legem; nec tecum possum vivere nec sine te* [Martial].

2. Subservience to Ends

1. Actual Subservience

631. Instrumentality. — **N.** instrumentality; aid &c. 707; subservien-ce, -cy; mediation, intervention, medium, intermedium, vehicle, hand; agency &c. 170.

minister, handmaid; midwife, *accoucheur*, *accoucheuse*, obstetrician; go-between; cat's-paw; stepping-stone.

key; master –, pass –, latch- key; " open sesame "; passport, *passe-partout*, safe-conduct.

instrument &c. 633; expedient &c. (*plan*) 626; means &c. 632.

V. subserve, minister, mediate, intervene; be -instrumental &c. *adj.*; pander to; officiate; tend.

Adj. instrumental; useful &c. 644; ministerial, subservient, mediatorial; inter-mediate, -vening; conducive.

Adv. through, by, *per;* where-, there-, here-by; by the -agency &c. 170- of; by dint of; by –, in- virtue of; through the -medium &c. *n.*- of; along with; on the shoulders of; by means of &c. 632; by –, with- -the aid &c. (*assistance*) 707- of.

per fas et nefas, by fair means or foul; somehow, – or other; by hook or by crook.

632. Means. — N. means, resources, wherewithal, ways and means; capital &c. (*money*) 800; revenue; stock in trade &c. 636; provision &c. 637; a shot in the locker; appliances &c. (*machinery*) 633; means and appliances; conveniences; cards to play; expedients &c. (*measures*) 626; two strings to one's bow; sheet anchor &c. (*safety*) 666; aid &c. 707; medium &c. 631.

V. find –, have –, possess- means &c. *n.*

Adj. instrumental &c. 631; mechanical &c. 633.

Adv. by means of, with; by -what, – all, – any, – some- means; where-, here-, there-with; wherewithal.

how &c. (*in what manner*) 627; through &c. (*by the instrumentality of*) 631; with –, by- the aid &c. (*assistance*) 707- of; by the -agency &c. 170- of.

633. Instrument. — N. machinery, mechanism, engineering.

instrument, organ, tool, implement, utensil, machine, engine, lathe, gin, mill; air –, caloric –, heat- engine.

gear; tack-le, -ling; rigging, apparatus, appliances; plant, *matériel;* harness, trappings, fittings, accouterments; barde; equip-ment, -age; appointments, furniture, upholstery; chattels; paraphernalia &c. (*belongings*) 780.

mechanical powers; lever, -age; mechanical advantage; crow, -bar; hand-spike, gavelock, jemmy, arm, limb, wing; oar, paddle; pulley; wheel and axle; wheel-, clock-work; wheels within wheels; pinion, crank, winch; cam; pedal; capstan &c. (*lift*) 307; wheel &c. (*rotation*) 312; inclined plane; wedge; screw; spring, mainspring; can hook, glut, heald, heddle, jenny, parbuckle, sprag, water wheel.

handle, hilt, haft, shaft, heft, shank, blade, trigger, tiller, helm, treadle, key; turnscrew, screwdriver; knocker.

hammer &c. (*impulse*) 276; edge tool &c. (*cut*) 253; borer &c. 262; vice, teeth, &c. (*hold*) 781; nail, rope &c. (*join*) 45; peg &c. (*hang*) 214; support &c. 215; spoon &c. (*vehicle*) 272; arms &c. 727; oar &c. (*navigation*) 267; cardiograph, recapper, snowplow, tenpenny, votograph.

Adj. instrumental &c. 631; mechanical, machinal; brachial.

634. Substitute. — N. substitute &c. 147; deputy &c. 759; *badli.*

635. Materials. — N. material, raw material, stuff, stock, staple; adobe, brown stone; chinking; clapboard; daubing; puncheon; shake; shingle, bricks and mortar; metal; stone; clay, brick; crockery &c. 384; compo, -sition; con-crete; reënforced concrete, cement; wood, ore, timber.

materials; supplies, munition, fuel, grist, household stuff; pabulum &c. (*food*) 298; ammunition &c. (*arms*) 727; contingents; relay, reënforcement; baggage &c. (*personal property*) 780; means &c. 632; calico, cambric, cashmere.

Adj. raw &c. (*unprepared*) 674; wooden &c. *n.*; adobe.

636. Store. — N. stock, fund, mine, vein, lode, quarry; spring; fount, -ain; well, -spring; milch cow.

stock in trade, supply; heap &c. (*collection*) 72; treasure; reserve, *corps de réserve,* reserved fund, nest egg, savings, *bonne bouche.*

crop, harvest, mow, vintage.

store, accumulation, hoard, rick, stack; lumber; relay &c. (*provision*) 637.

store-house, -room, -closet; depository, depot, cache, re-pository, -serva-tory, -pertory; repertorium; promptuary, warehouse, *entrepôt,* magazine; but-tery, larder, spence; garner, granary; cannery, safe-deposit vault, stillroom; thesaurus; bank &c. (*treasury*) 802; armory; arsenal; dock; gallery, museum, conservatory; menag-ery, -erie.

reservoir, cistern, *aljibar*, tank, pond, mill pond; gasometer.

budget, quiver, bandolier, portfolio; coffer &c. (*receptacle*) 191.

conservation; storing &c. *v.*; storage.

V. store; put –, lay –, set- by; stow away; set –, lay- apart; store –, hoard –, treasure –, lay –, heap –, put –, garner –, save- up; bank; cache; accumulate, amass, hoard, fund, garner, save.

reserve; keep –, hold- back; husband, – one's resources.

deposit; stow, stack, load; harvest; heap, collect &c. 72; lay -in store &c. *adj.*; keep, file [papers]; lay in &c. (*provide*) 637; preserve &c. 670.

Adj. stored &c. *v.*; in -store, – reserve, – ordinary; spare, supernumerary.

Phr. *adde parvum parvo magnus acervus erit.*

637. Provision. — **N.** provision, supply; grist, – to the mill; subvention &c. (*aid*) 707; resources &c. (*means*) 632; grocer-ies, -y.

providing &c. *v.*; purveyance; reënforcement; commissariat.

provender &c. (*food*) 298; ensilage; viaticum.

caterer, purveyor, commissary, quartermaster, manciple, feeder, batman, victualer, grocer, comprador, *restaurateur;* jackal, pelican; sutler &c. (*merchant*) 797.

grocery [U. S.], – shop, – store.

V. provide; make -provision, – due provision for; lay in, – a stock, – a store.

sup-ply, -peditate †; furnish; find, – one in; arm.

cater, victual, provision, purvey, forage; beat up for; stock, – with; make good, replenish; fill, – up; recruit, feed.

have in -store, – reserve; keep, – by one, – on foot; have to fall back upon; store &c. 636; provide against a rainy day &c. (*economy*) 817.

638. Waste. — **N.** consumption, expenditure, exhaustion; dispersion &c. 73; ebb; leakage &c. (*exudation*) 295; loss &c. 776; wear and tear; waste, prodigality &c. 818; misuse &c. 679; wasting &c. *v.*; rubbish &c. (*useless*) 645.

mountain in labor.

V. spend, expend, use, consume, swallow up, exhaust; impoverish; spill, drain, empty; disperse &c. 73.

cast –, fool –, muddle –, throw –, fling –, fritter- away; burn the candle at both ends, waste; squander &c. 818.

" waste its sweetness on the desert air " [Gray]; cast -one's bread upon the waters, – pearls before swine; employ a steam engine to crack a nut, waste powder and shot, break a butterfly on a wheel; labor in vain &c. (*useless*) 645; cut blocks with a razor, pour water into a sieve.

leak &c. (*run out*) 295; run to waste; ebb; melt away, run dry, dry up.

Adj. wasted &c. *v.*; at a low ebb.

wasteful &c. (*prodigal*) 818; penny wise and pound foolish.

Phr. *magno conatu magnas nugas; le jeu ne vaut pas la chandelle;* " idly busy rolls their world away " [Goldsmith].

639. Sufficiency. — **N.** sufficiency, adequacy, enough, withal, *quantum sufficit,* satisfaction, competence; no less.

mediocrity &c. (*average*) 29.

fill; fullness &c. (*completeness*) 52; plen-itude, -ty; abundance; copiousness &c. *adj.*; amplitude, galore, lots, profusion; full measure; " good measure pressed down and running over."

luxuriance &c. (*fertility*) 168; affluence &c. (*wealth*) 803; fat of the land; " a land flowing with milk and honey "; cornucopia; horn of -plenty, – Amalthæa; mine &c. (*stock*) 636.

outpouring; flood &c. (*great quantity*) 31; tide &c. (*river*) 348; repletion &c. (*redundance*) 641; satiety &c. 869.

640. Insufficiency. — **N.** insufficiency; inadequa-cy, -teness; incompetence &c. (*impotence*) 158; deficiency &c. (*incompleteness*) 53; imperfection &c. 651; shortcoming &c. 304; paucity; stint; scantiness &c. (*smallness*) 32; none to spare; bare subsistence.

scarcity, dearth; want, need, lack, poverty, exigency; inanition, starvation, famine, drought.

dole, mite, pittance; short -allowance, – commons; half rations; banyan day.

emptiness, poorness &c. *adj.*; depletion, vacancy, flaccidity; ebb tide; low water; " a beggarly account of empty boxes " [*Rom. and Jul.*]; indigence &c. 804; insolvency &c. (*nonpayment*) 808.

V. be -sufficient &c. *adj.*; suffice, do, just do, satisfy, pass muster; have -enough &c. *n.*; eat –, drink –, have- one's fill; roll –, swim- in; wallow in &c. (*superabundance*) 641; wanton.

abound, exuberate, teem, flow, stream, rain, shower down; pour, – in; swarm; bristle with; superabound.

render -sufficient &c. *adj.*; replenish &c .(*fill*) 52.

Adj. sufficient, enough, adequate, up to the mark, commensurate, competent, satisfactory, valid, tangible.

measured; moderate &c. (*temperate*) 953.

full &c. (*complete*) 52; ample; plen-ty, -tiful, -teous; plenty as blackberries; copious, abundant; abounding &c. *v.*; replete, enough and to spare, flush; choke-full; well-stocked, -provided; lib-eral; unstint-ed, -ing; stintless; with-out stint; un-sparing, -measured; lavish &c. 641; wholesale.

rich; luxuriant &c. (*fertile*) 168; af-fluent &c. (*wealthy*) 803; wantless; big with &c. (*pregnant*) 161.

un-exhausted, -wasted; exhaustless, inexhaustible.

Adv. sufficiently, amply &c. *adj.*; full; in -abundance &c. *n.*; with no spar-ing hand; to one's heart's content, *ad libitum*, without stint.

Phr. " cut and come again " [Crabbe]; *das Beste ist gut genug.*

V. be -insufficient &c. *adj.*; not -suf-fice &c. 639; come short of &c. 304; run dry.

want, lack, need, require; *caret;* be in want &c. (*poor*) 804; live from hand to mouth.

render -insufficient &c. *adj.*; drain of resources; impoverish &c. (*waste*) 638; stint &c. (*begrudge*) 819; put on short allowance.

do -insufficiently &c. *adv.*; scotch the snake.

Adj. insufficient, inadequate; too -lit-tle &c. 32; not -enough &c. 639; un-equal to; incompetent &c. (*impotent*) 158; " weighed in the balance and found wanting "; perfunctory &c. (*neglect*) 460; deficient &c. (*incomplete*) 53; wanting &c. *v.*; imperfect &c. 651; ill-furnished, -provided, -stored, -off.

slack, at a low ebb; empty, vacant, bare; short –, out –, destitute –, de-void –, bereft &c. 789 –, denuded- of; dry, drained.

un-provided, -supplied, -furnished; un-replenished, -fed; un-stored, -treas-ured; empty-handed.

meager, poor, thin, scrimp, sparing, spare, stinted; starv-ed, -eling; half-starved, famine-stricken, famished; je-june.

scant &c. (*small*) 32; scarce; not to be had, – for love or money, – at any price; scurvy; stingy &c. 819; at the end of one's tether; without -resources &c. 632; in want &c. (*poor*) 804; in debt &c. 806.

Adv. insufficiently &c. *adj.*; in default –, for want- of; failing.

Phr. *semper avarus eget* [Horace].

641. Redundance. — N. redundance; too -much, – many; super-abund-ance, -fluity, -fluence †, -saturation; nimiety, transcendency, exuberance, pro-fuseness; profusion &c. (*plenty*) 639; repletion, enough in all conscience, *satis superque*, lion's share; more than -enough &c. 639; plethora, engorgement, congestion, load, surfeit, sickener; turgescence &c. (*expansion*) 194; over-dose, -measure, -supply, -flow; inundation &c. (*water*) 348; avalanche.

accumulation &c. (*store*) 636; heap &c. 72; drug, – in the market; glut; crowd; burden.

excess; sur-, over-plus; epact; margin; remainder &c. 40; duplicate; surplus-age, expletive; work of –, supererogation; bonus, bonanza.

luxury; intemperance &c. 954; extravagance &c. (*prodigality*) 818; exorbi-tance, lavishment.

pleonasm &c. (*diffuseness*) 573; too many irons in the fire; *embarras de richesses.*

V. super-, over-abound; know no bounds, swarm; meet one at every turn; creep –, bristle- with; overflow; run –, flow –, well –, brim- over; run riot; over-run, -stock, -lay. -charge, -dose, -feed, -burden, -load, -do, -whelm, -shoot

the mark &c. (*go beyond*) 303; surcharge, supersaturate, gorge, glut, load, drench, whelm, inundate, deluge, flood; drug, – the market; hepatize.

choke, cloy, accloy, suffocate; pile up, lay on thick; impregnate with; lavish &c. (*squander*) 818.

send –, carry- coals to Newcastle, – owls to Athens; teach one's grandmother to suck eggs; *pisces natare docere;* kill the slain, " gild refined gold," " paint the lily "; butter one's bread on both sides, put butter upon bacon; employ a steam engine to crack a nut &c. (*waste*) 638.

exaggerate &c. 549; wallow in; roll in &c. (*plenty*) 639; remain on one's hands, hang heavy on hand, go a begging.

Adj. redundant; too -much, – many; exuberant, inordinate, superabundant, excessive, overmuch, replete, profuse, lavish; prodigal &c. 818; exorbitant; overweening; extravagant; overcharged &c. *v.*; supersaturated, drenched, overflowing; running -over, – to waste, – down.

crammed –, filled- to overflowing; gorged, ready to burst; dropsical, turgid, plethoric; obese &c. 194.

superfluous, unnecessary, needless, supervacaneous †, uncalled for, to spare, in excess; over and above &c. (*remainder*) 40; *de trop;* adscititious &c. (*additional*) 37; supernumerary &c. (*reserve*) 636; on one's hands, spare, duplicate, supererogatory, expletive; *un peu fort.*

Adv. over, too, over and above; over –, too- much; too far; without –, beyond –, out of- measure; with . . . to spare; over head and ears; up to one's -eyes, – ears; extra; beyond the mark &c. (*transcursion*) 303; *acervatim.*

Phr. it never rains but it pours; *fortuna multis dat nimium nulli satis.*

2. Degree of Subservience

642. Importance. — N. importance, consequence, moment, prominence, consideration, mark, materialness.

import, significance, concern; emphasis, interest.

greatness &c. 31; superiority &c. 33; notability &c. (*repute*) 873; weight &c. (*influence*) 175; value &c. (*goodness*) 648; usefulness &c. 644.

gravity, seriousness, solemnity; no -joke, – laughing matter; pressure, urgency, stress; matter of life and death.

memorabilia, notabilia, great doings; red-letter day.

great -thing, – point; main chance, " the be all and the end all " [*Macbeth*]; cardinal point; substance, gist &c. (*essence*) 5; sum and substance, gravamen, head and front; important –, principal –, prominent –, essential- part; half the battle; *sine quâ non;* breath of one's nostrils &c. (*life*) 359; cream, salt, core, kernel, heart, nucleus; key, -note, -stone; corner stone; trump card &c. (*device*) 626; salient points.

top sawyer, first fiddle, prima donna, chief; triton among the minnows; " it " [U. S.].

V. be -important &c. *adj.*, – somebody, – something; import, signify, mat-

643. Unimportance. — N. unimportance, insignificance, nothingness, immateriality.

triviality, levity, frivolity; paltriness &c. *adj.*; poverty; smallness &c. 32; vanity &c. (*uselessness*) 645; matter of -indifference &c. 866; no object.

nothing, – to signify, – worth speaking of, – particular, – to boast of, – to speak of; small –, no great –, trifling &c. *adj.*- matter; mere -joke, – nothing; hardly –, scarcely- anything; nonentity, small beer, cipher; no great shakes, *peu de chose;* child's play.

toy, plaything, popgun, paper pellet, gimcrack, gewgaw, bauble, trinket, bagatelle, kickshaw, knicknack, whim-wham, trifle, " trifles light as air "; yankee-, notions [U. S.].

trumpery, trash, rubbish, stuff, *fatras,* frippery; " leather or prunello "; chaff, drug, froth, bubble, smoke, cobweb; weed; refuse &c. (*inutility*) 645; scum &c. (*dirt*) 653.

joke, jest, snap of the fingers; fudge &c. (*unmeaning*) 517; fiddlestick, – end; pack of nonsense, mere farce.

straw, pin, fig, button, rush; bulrush, feather, halfpenny, farthing, brass farthing, doit, peppercorn, jot, rap, pinch of

ter, boot, be an object; carry weight &c. (*influence*) 175; make a figure &c. (*repute*) 873; be in the ascendant, come to the front, lead the way, take the lead, play first fiddle, throw all else into the shade; lie at the root of; deserve –, merit –, be worthy of- -notice, – regard, – consideration.

attach –, ascribe –, give- importance &c. *n.*- to; value, care for; set store -upon, – by; mark &c. 550; mark with a white stone, underline; write –, put –, print- in -italics, – capitals, – large letters, – large type, – letters of gold; accentuate, emphasize, lay stress on.

make -a fuss, – a stir, – a piece of work, – much ado- about; make -of, – much of.

Adj. important; of -importance &c. *n.*; momentous, material; to the point; not to be -overlooked, – despised, – sneezed at; egregious; weighty &c. (*influential*) 175; of note &c. (*repute*) 873; notable, prominent, salient, signal; memorable, remarkable; worthy of -remark, – notice; never to be forgotten; stirring, eventful.

grave, serious, earnest, noble, grand, solemn, impressive, commanding, imposing.

urgent, pressing, critical, instant.

paramount, essential, vital, all-absorbing, radical, cardinal, chief, main, prime, primary, principal, leading, capital, foremost, overruling; of vital &c. importance.

in the front rank, first-rate; superior &c. 33; considerable &c. (*great*) 31; marked &c. *v.*; rare &c. 137.

significant, telling, trenchant, emphatic, pregnant; *tanti*.

Adv. materially &c. *adj.*; in the main; above all, κατ' ἐξοχήν, *par excellence*, to crown all.

Phr. *expende Hannibalem!* [Juvenal].

snuff, old song; cent, mill, picayune, pistareen, red cent [U. S.].

minutiæ, details, minor details, small fry; dust in the balance, feather in the scale, drop in the ocean, flea-bite, mole-hill.

nine days' wonder, *ridiculus mus;* flash in the pan &c. (*impotence*) 158; much ado about nothing &c. (*overestimation*) 482.

V. be -unimportant &c. *adj.*; not -matter &c. 642; go for –, matter –, signify- -little, – nothing, – little or nothing; not matter a -straw &c. *n.*

make light of &c. (*underestimate*) 483; catch at straws &c. (*overestimate*) 482.

Adj. unimportant; of -little, – small, – no- -account, – importance &c. 642; immaterial; un-, non-essential; indifferent.

subordinate &c. (*inferior*) 34; mediocre &c. (*average*) 29; passable, fair, respectable, tolerable, commonplace; uneventful, mere, common; ordinary &c. (*habitual*) 613; inconsiderable, so-so, insignificant, inappreciable.

trifling, trivial; slight, slender, light, flimsy, frothy, idle; puerile &c. (*foolish*) 499; airy, shallow; weak &c. 160; powerless &c. 158; frivolous, petty, niggling; pid-, ped-dling; fribble, inane, ridiculous, farcical; fini-cal, -kin; fiddle-faddle, fingle-fangle, namby-pamby, wishy-washy, milk and water.

poor, paltry, pitiful; contemptible &c. (*contempt*) 930; sorry, mean, meager, shabby, miserable, wretched, vile, scrubby, scrannel, weedy, niggardly, scurvy, putid, beggarly, worthless, twopenny-halfpenny, cheap, trashy, catchpenny, gimcrack, trumpery; one-horse [U. S.].

not worth -the pains, – while, – mentioning, – speaking of, – a thought, – a curse, – a straw &c. *n.*; beneath –, unworthy of- -notice, – regard, – consideration; *de lanâ caprinâ;* vain &c. (*useless*) 645.

Adv. slightly &c. *adj.*; rather, somewhat, pretty well, tolerably. for aught one cares.

Int. no matter! pish! tush! tut! pshaw! pugh! pooh, -pooh! fudge! bosh! humbug! fiddlestick, – end! fiddlededee! never mind! *n'importe!* what -signifies, – matter, – boots it, – of that, – 's the odds! a fig for! stuff! nonsense! stuff and nonsense!

Phr. *magno conatu magnas nugas; le jeu ne vaut pas la chandelle;* it -matters not, – does not signify; it is of no -consequence, – importance; *elephantus non capit murem; tempête dans un verre d'eau.*

644. Utility. — N. utility; usefulness &c. *adj.*; efficacy, efficiency, adequacy; service, use, stead, avail; help &c. (*aid*) 707; applicability &c. *adj.*; subservience &c. (*instrumentality*) 631; function &c. (*business*) 625; value; worth &c. (*goodness*) 648; money's worth; productiveness &c. 168; *cui bono* &c. (*intention*) 620; utilization &c. (*use*) 677; step in the right direction.

common weal; commonwealth; public -good, — interest; utilitarianism &c. (*philanthropy*) 910.

V. be -useful &c. *adj.*; avail, serve; subserve &c. (*be instrumental to*) 631; conduce &c. (*tend*) 176; answer –, serve- -one's turn, — a purpose.

act a part &c. (*action*) 680; perform –, discharge- -a function &c. 625; do –, render- -a service, — good service, — yeoman's service; bestead, stand one in good stead; be the making of; help &c. 707.

bear fruit &c. (*produce*) 161; bring grist to the mill; profit, remunerate; benefit &c. (*do good*) 648.

find one's -account, — advantage- in; reap the benefit of &c. (*be better for*) 658.

render useful &c. (*use*) 677.

Adj. useful; of -use &c. *n.*; serviceable, proficuous †, good for; subservient &c. (*instrumental*) 631; conducive &c. (*tending*) 176; subsidiary &c. (*helping*) 707.

advantageous &c. (*beneficial*) 648; profitable, gainful, remunerative, worth one's salt; valuable; prolific &c. (*productive*) 168.

adequate; ef-ficient, -ficacious; effective, -ual; expedient &c. 646.

applicable, available, ready, handy, at hand, tangible; commodious, adaptable; of all work.

Adv. usefully &c. *adj.*; *pro bono publico.*

645. Inutility. — N. inutility; uselessness &c. *adj.*; inefficacy, futility; inep-, inap-titude; unsubservience; inadequacy &c. (*insufficiency*) 640; inefficiency &c. (*incompetence*) 158; unskillfulness &c. 699; disservice; unfruitfulness &c. (*unproductiveness*) 169; labor -in vain, — lost, — of Sisyphus; lost -trouble, — labor; work of Penelope; sleeveless errand, wild-goose chase, mere farce.

tautology &c. (*repetition*) 104; supererogation &c. (*redundance*) 641.

vanitas vanitatum, vanity, inanity, worthlessness, nugacity; triviality &c. (*unimportance*) 643.

caput mortuum, waste paper, dead letter; blunt tool.

litter, rubbish, junk, lumber, odds and ends, cast-off clothes; button top; shoddy; rags, orts, trash, refuse, sweepings, scourings, offscourings, waste, rubble, *débris;* stubble, leavings; broken meat; dregs &c. (*dirt*) 653; weeds, tares; rubbish heap, dust hole; *rudera*, deads.

fruges consumere natus [Horace] &c. (*drone*) 683.

V. be -useless &c. *adj.*; go a begging &c. (*redundant*) 641; fail &c. 732.

seek –, strive- after impossibilities; use vain efforts, labor in vain, roll the stone of Sisyphus, beat the air, lash the waves, *battre l'eau avec un bâton, donner un coup d'épée dans l'eau,* fish in the air, milk the ram, drop a bucket into an empty well, sow the sand; bay the moon; preach –, speak- to the winds; whistle jigs to a milestone; kick against the pricks, *se battre contre des moulins;* lock the stable door when the steed is stolen &c. (*too late*) 135; hold a farthing candle to the sun; cast pearls before swine &c. (*waste*) 638; carry coals to Newcastle &c. (*redundance*) 641; wash a blackamoor white &c. (*impossible*) 471.

render -useless &c. *adj.*; dis-mantle, -mast, -mount, -qualify, -able; unrig; cripple, lame &c. (*injure*) 659; spike guns, clip the wings; put out of gear.

Adj. useless, inutile, inefficacious, futile, unavailing, bootless; inoperative &c. 158; inadequate &c. (*insufficient*) 640; in- †, unsub-servient; inept, inefficient &c. (*impotent*) 158; of no -avail &c. (*use*) 644; ineffectual &c. (*failure*) 732; incompetent &c. (*unskillful*) 699; " stale, flat and unprofitable "; superfluous &c. (*redundant*) 641; dispensable; thrown away &c. (*wasted*) 638; abortive &c. (*immature*) 674.

worth-, value-, price-less; unsalable; not worth a straw &c. (*trifling*) 643; dear at any price.

vain, empty, inane; gain-, profit-, fruit-less; un-serviceable, -profitable;

ill-spent; unproductive &c. 169; *hors de combat;* effete, past work &c. (*impaired*) 659; obsolete &c. (*old*) 124; fit for the dust hole; good for nothing; of no earthly use; not worth -having, – powder and shot; leading to no end, uncalled for; un-necessary, -needed.

Adv. uselessly &c. *adj.*; to -little, – no, – little or no- purpose.

Int. *cui bono ?* what's the good!

Phr. *actum ne agas; chercher une aiguille dans une botte de foin; tanto buon che val niente*

646. [Specific subservience.] **Expedience. — N.** expedien-ce, -cy; desirableness, -bility &c. *adj.*; fitness &c. (*agreement*) 23; utility &c. 644; propriety; opportunism; advantage.

high time &c. (*occasion*) 134.

V. be -expedient &c. *adj.*; suit &c. (*agree*) 23; befit; suit –, befit- the -time, – season, – occasion.

conform &c. 82.

Adj. expedient; desir-, advis-, acceptable; convenient; worth while, meet; fit, -ting; due, proper, eligible, seemly, becoming; befitting &c. *v.*; opportune &c. (*in season*) 134; *in loco;* suitable &c. (*accordant*) 23; applicable &c. (*useful*) 644.

Adv. in the right place; conveniently &c. *adj.*

Phr. *operæ pretium est.*

647. Inexpedience. — N. inexpedien-ce, -cy; undesira-bleness, -bility &c. *adj.*; discommodity, impropriety; unfitness &c. (*disagreement*) 24; inutility &c. 645; disadvantage.

V. be -inexpedient &c. *adj.*; come amiss &c. (*disagree*) 24; embarrass &c. (*hinder*) 706; put to inconvenience; pay too dear for one's whistle.

Adj. inexpedient, undesirable; un-, in-advisable; objectionable; in-apt, -eligible, -admissible, -convenient; in-, discommodious; disadvantageous; inappropriate, unfit &c. (*inconsonant*) 24.

ill-contrived, -advised; unsatisfactory; unprofitable &c., unsubservient &c. (*useless*) 645; inopportune &c. (*unseasonable*) 135; out of –, in the wrong-place; improper, unseemly.

clumsy, awkward; cum-brous, -bersome; lumbering, unwieldy, hulky; un-impedient &c. (*in the way*) 706.

manageable &c. (*impracticable*) 704; unnecessary &c. (*redundant*) 641.

Phr. it will never do.

648. [Capability of producing good. Good qualities.] **Goodness. — N.** goodness &c. *adj.*; excellence, merit; virtue &c. 944; value, worth, price.

super-excellence, -eminence; superiority &c. 33; perfection &c. 650; *coup de maître;* masterpiece, *chef d'œuvre,* prime, flower, cream, *élite,* pick, A1, nonesuch, *nonpareil, crème de la crème,* flower of the flock, cock of the roost, salt of the earth; champion; prodigy.

tidbit; gem, – of the first water; *bijou,* precious stone, jewel, pearl, diamond, ruby, brilliant, treasure; good thing; *rara avis,* one in a thousand.

beneficence &c. 906; good man &c. 948.

V. be -beneficial &c. *adj.*; produce –, do- -good &c. 618; profit &c. (*be of use*) 644; benefit; confer a -benefit &c. 618.

be the making of, do a world of good, make a man of.

produce a good effect; do a good turn, confer an obligation; improve &c. 658.

do no harm, break no bones.

649. [Capability of producing evil. Bad qualities.] **Badness. — N.** hurtfulness &c. *adj.*; virulence.

evil doer &c. 913; bane &c. 663; plague spot &c. (*insalubrity*) 657; evil star, ill wind; hoodoo; Jonah; snake in the grass, skeleton in the closet; *amari aliquid,* thorn in the side.

malignity; malevolence &c. 907; tender mercies [ironically].

ill-treatment, annoyance, molestation, abuse, oppression, persecution, outrage; misusage &c. 679; injury &c. (*damage*) 659; knockout drops [U. S.].

badness &c. *adj.*; peccancy, abomination; painfulness &c. 830; pestilence &c. (*disease*) 655; guilt &c. 947; depravity &c. 945.

V. be -hurtful &c. *adj.*; cause –, produce –, inflict –, work –, do- evil &c. 619; damnify, endamage, hurt, harm; injure &c. (*damage*) 659; pain &c. 830.

wrong, aggrieve, oppress, persecute; trample –, tread –, bear hard –. put-

be -good &c. *adj.*; excel, transcend &c. (*be superior*) 33; bear away the bell.

stand the -proof, – test; pass -muster, – an examination.

challenge comparison, vie, emulate, rival.

Adj. harm-, hurt-less; unobnoxious; in-nocuous, -nocent, -offensive.

beneficial, valuable, of value; serviceable &c. (*useful*) 644; advantageous, profitable, edifying; salutary &c. (*healthful*) 656.

favorable; propitious &c. (*hope-giving*) 858; fair.

good, – as gold; excellent; better; superior &c. 33; above par; nice, fine; genuine &c. (*true*) 494.

best, choice, select, picked, elect, *recherché*, rare, priceless; unpara-goned, -lleled &c. (*supreme*) 33; superlatively &c. 33- good; bully *, crackajack *, gilt-edged; super-fine, -excellent; of the first water; first-rate, -class; high-wrought, exquisite, very best, crack, prime, tip-top, capital, cardinal; standard &c. (*perfect*) 650; inimitable.

admirable, estimable; praiseworthy &c. (*approve*) 931; pleasing &c. 829; *couleur de rose*, precious, of great price; costly &c. (*dear*) 814; worth -its weight in gold, – a Jew's eye; priceless, invaluable, inestimable, precious as the apple of the eye.

tolerable &c. (*not very good*) 651; up to the mark, un-exceptionable, -objectionable; satisfactory, tidy.

in -good, – fair- condition; fresh; sound &c. (*perfect*) 650.

Adv. beneficially &c: *adj.*; well &c. 618.

Phr. " jewels five words long " [Tennyson]; " long may such goodness live! " [Rogers]; " the luxury of doing good " [Goldsmith].

upon; overburden; weigh -down, – heavy on; victimize; run down; molest &c. 830.

maltreat, abuse; ill-use, -treat; buffet, bruise, scratch, maul; smite &c. (*scourge*) 972; do -violence, – harm, – a mischief; stab, pierce, outrage.

do –, make- mischief; bring into trouble.

destroy &c. 162.

Adj. hurt-, harm-, scath-, bane-, bale-ful; injurious, deleterious, detrimental, noxious, pernicious, mischievous, full of mischief, mischief-making, malefic, malignant, nocuous, noisome; prejudicial; dis-serviceable, -advantageous; wide-wasting.

unlucky, sinister; obnoxious; untoward, disastrous.

oppressive, burdensome, onerous; malign &c. (*malevolent*) 907.

corrupting &c. (corrupt &c. 659); virulent, venomous, envenomed, corrosive; poisonous &c. (*morbific*) 657; deadly &c. (*killing*) 361; destructive &c. (*destroying*) 162; inauspicious &c. 859.

bad, ill, arrant, as bad as bad can be, dreadful; hor-rid, -rible; dire; rank, peccant, foul, fulsome; rotten, – at the core.

vile, base, villanous; mean &c. (*paltry*) 643; injured &c. deteriorated &c. 659; unsatisfactory, exceptionable, indifferent; below par &c. (*imperfect*) 651; ill-contrived, -conditioned; wretched, sad, grievous, deplorable, lamentable; pitiful, -able, woeful &c. (*painful*) 830.

evil, wrong; depraved &c. 945; shocking; reprehensible &c. (*disapprove*) 932.

hateful, – as a toad; abominable, detestable, execrable, cursed, accursed, confounded; damn-ed, -able; infernal; diabolic &c. (*malevolent*) 907.

unadvisable &c. (*inexpedient*) 647; un-profitable &c. (*useless*) 645; incompetent &c. (*unskillful*) 699; irremediable &c. (*hopeless*) 859.

Adv. badly &c. *adj.*; wrong, ill; to one's cost; where the shoe pinches.

Phr. bad is the best; the worst come to the worst; *herba mala presto cresco;* " wrongs unredressed or insults unavenged " [Wordsworth].

650. Perfection. — **N.** perfection; perfectness &c. *adj.*; indefectibility; impecc-ancy, -ability.

pink, *beau idéal*, phenix, paragon; pink –, acme- of perfection; *ne plus ultra;* summit &c. 210.

cygne noir; philosopher's stone; chrysolite, Koh-i-noor.

651. Imperfection. — **N.** imperfection; imperfectness &c. *adj.*; deficiency; inadequacy &c. (*insufficiency*) 640; peccancy &c. (*badness*) 649; immaturity &c. 674.

fault, defect, weak point; screw loose; flaw &c. (*break*) 70; gap &c. 198; twist &c. 243; taint, attainder; bar sinister,

model, standard, pattern, mirror, admirable Crichton; trump, very prince of.

masterpiece, superexcellence &c. (*goodness*) 648; transcendence &c. (*superiority*) 33.

V. be -perfect &c. *adj.*; transcend &c. (*be supreme*) 33.

bring to perfection, perfect, ripen, mature; complete &c. 729; put in trim &c. (*prepare*) 673; maturate.

Adj. perfect, faultless; inde-fective, -ficient, -fectible; immaculate, spotless, impeccable; free from -imperfection &c. 651; un-blemished, -injured &c. 659; sound, – as a roach; in perfect condition; scathless, intact, harmless; seaworthy &c. (*safe*) 644; right as a trivet; *in seipso totus teres atque rotundus* [Hor.]; consummate &c. (*complete*) 52; finished &c. 729.

best &c. (*good*) 648; model, standard; inimitable, unparagoned, unparalleled &c. (*supreme*) 33; superhuman, divine; beyond all praise &c. (*approbation*) 931; *sans peur et sans reproche.*

Adv. to perfection; perfectly &c. *adj.*; *ad unguem;* clean, – as a whistle.

Phr. " let us go on unto perfection " [*Hebrews* vi, 1]; " the perfection of art is to conceal art " [Quintilian].

hole in one's coat; blemish &c. 848; weakness &c. 160; half blood; shortcoming &c. 304; drawback; seamy side.

mediocrity; no great -shakes, – catch; not much to boast of; one-horse shay.

V. be -imperfect &c. *adj.*; have a -defect &c. *n.*; lie under a disadvantage; spring a leak.

not –, barely- pass muster; fall short &c. 304.

Adj. imperfect; not -perfect &c. 650; de-ficient, -fective; faulty, unsound, tainted; out of -order, – tune; cracked, leaky; sprung; warped &c. (*distort*) 243; lame; injured &c. (*deteriorated*) 659; peccant &c. (*bad*) 649; frail &c. (*weak*) 160; inadequate &c. (*insufficient*) 640; crude &c. (*unprepared*) 674; incomplete &c. 53; found wanting; below par; short-handed; below –, under- its full -strength, – complement.

indifferent, middling, ordinary, mediocre; average &c. 29; so-so; *couci-couci*, milk and water; tolerable, fair, passable; pretty -well, – good; rather –, moderately- good; good –, well-enough; decent; not -bad, – amiss; inobjectionable, admissible, bearable, only better than nothing.

secondary, inferior; second-rate, -best; one-horse [U. S.].

Adv. almost &c.; to a limited extent, rather &c. 32; pretty, moderately; only, considering, all things considered, enough.

Phr. *surgit amari aliquid.*

---

652. Cleanness. — **N.** cleanness &c. *adj.*; purity; cleaning &c. *v.*; purification, defecation &c. *v.*; purgation, lustration; de-, abs-tersion; epuration, mundation †, ablution, lavation, colature †; disinfection &c. *v.*; drain-, sewer-age.

lavatory, laundry, washhouse; washerwoman, laundress, dhobi, laundryman, washerman; scavenger, dustman, sweep; white wings [Local U. S.].

brush; broom, besom, mop, rake, shovel, sieve, riddle, screen, filter; blotter.

napkin, cloth, maukin †, malkin †, handkerchief, towel, sudary; doyley, doily, duster, sponge, mop, swab.

cover, drugget.

wash, lotion, detergent, cathartic, purgative; purifier &c. *v.*; disinfectant; aperient; benz-ene, -ine, -ol, -olin; bleaching powder, chloride of lime, dentifrice, deobstruent, laxative.

V. be –, render- clean &c. *adj.*

653. Uncleanness. — **N.** uncleanness &c. *adj.*; impurity; immundi-ty, -city; impurity &c. [of mind] 961.

defilement, contamination &c. *v.*; defœdation †; soil-ure, -iness †; abomination; leaven; taint, -ure †; fetor &c. 401.

decay; putre-scence, -faction; corruption; mold, must, mildew, dry rot, mucor, rubigo †.

slovenry; slovenliness &c. *adj.*; squalor.

dowdy, drab, slut, malkin, slattern, sloven, slammerkin †, slammock, slummock, scrub, draggle-tail, mudlark, dustman, sweep; beast.

dirt, filth, soil, slop; dust, cobweb, flue; smoke, soot, smudge, smut, grime, raff; sossle, sozzle.

sordes, dregs, grounds, lees; argol; sedi-, settle-ment; heeltap; dross, -iness; mother †, precipitate, *scoriæ*, ashes, cinders, recrement, slag; scum, froth.

clean, -se; mundify †, rinse, wring, flush, full, wipe, mop, sponge, scour, swab, scrub, brush up.

wash, lave, launder, buck; abs-†, deterge; decrassify; clear, purify; depurate, -spumate, -fecate; purge, expurgate, elutriate, lixiviate, edulcorate, clarify, refine, rack; fil-ter, -trate; drain, strain.

disinfect, fumigate, ventilate, deodorize; whitewash; castrate, emasculate.

sift, winnow, pick, weed, comb, rake, brush, sweep.

rout -, clear -, sweep &c.- out; make a clean sweep of.

Adj. clean, -ly; pure; immaculate; spot-, stain-, taint-less; trig; without a stain, un-stained, -spotted, -soiled, -sullied, -tainted, -infected; sweet, – as a nut.

neat, spruce, tidy, trim, gimp, clean as a new penny, like a cat in pattens; cleaned &c. v.; kempt.

abstergent, cathartic, cleansing, purifying.

Adv. neatly &c. adj.; clean as a whistle.

hogwash; ditch-, dish-, bilge-water; rinsings, cheeseparings; sweepings &c. (*useless refuse*) 645; off-, out-scourings; off scum; *caput mortuum*, residuum, sprue, fecula, clinker, draff; scurf, -iness; exuviæ, morphea; fur, -fur; dandruff, tartar.

riffraff; vermin, louse, flea, bug, chinch.

mud, mire, quagmire, alluvium, silt, sludge, slime, slush, slosh, sposh [U. S.].

spawn, offal, gurry [U. S.]; lientery; garbage, carrion; excreta &c. 299; slough, peccant humor, pus, matter, suppuration, lienteria; fæces, excrement, ordure, dung; sew-, sewer-age; muck; coprolite; guano, manure, compost.

dunghill, colluvies, mixen, midden, bog, laystall, sink, privy, jakes; cess, -pool; sump, sough, cloaca, latrines, drain, sewer, common sewer; Cloacina; dust hole.

sty, pigsty, lair, den, Augean stable, sink of corruption; slum, rookery.

V. be -, become- unclean &c. adj.; rot, putrefy, fester, rankle, reek; stink &c. 401; mold, -er; go -bad &c. adj.

render -unclean &c. adj.; dirt, -y; soil, smoke, tarnish, slaver, spot, smear; daub, blot, blur, smudge, smutch, smirch; begrease; d-, dr-abble, -aggle; spatter, slubber; be-smear &c., -mire, -slime, -grime, -foul; splash, stain, distain, maculate, sully, pollute, defile, debase, contaminate, taint, leaven; corrupt &c. (*injure*) 659; cover with -dust &c. n.; drabble in the mud; roil.

wallow in the mire; slob-, slab-ber.

Adj. unclean, dirty, filthy, grimy; soiled &c. v.; not to be handled with kid gloves; dusty, snuffy, smutty, sooty, smoky; thick, turbid, dreggy; slimy; mussy [U. S.].

uncleanly, slovenly, untidy, sluttish, dowdy, draggle-tailed; un-combed, -kempt, -scoured, -swept, -wiped, -washed, -strained, -purified; squalid; lutose, slammocky, slummocky, sozzly.

nasty, coarse, foul, impure, offensive, abominable, beastly, reeky, reechy; fetid &c. 401.

moldy, musty, mildewed, rusty, moth-eaten, mucid, rancid, bad, gone bad, etercoral, lentiginous, touched, fusty, effete, reasty, rotten, corrupt, tainted, high, flyblown, maggoty; putr-id, -efactive, -escent, -efied; saprogen-ic, -ous; purulent, carious, peccant; fec-al, -ulent; stercoraceous, excrementitious; scurfy, impetiginous; gory, bloody; rotting &c. v.; rotten as -a pear, – cheese.

crapulous &c. (*intemperate*) 954; gross &c. (*impure in mind*) 961; fimetarious, fimicolous.

Phr. " they that touch pitch will be defiled " [*Much Ado About Nothing*].

654. Health. — N. health, sanity; soundness &c. adj.; vigor; good -, perfect -, excellent -, rude -, robust- health; bloom. *mens sana in corpore sano;* Hy-

655. Disease. — N. disease; illness, sickness &c. adj.; ailing &c. v.; " all the ills that flesh is heir to " [*Hamlet*]; morb-idity, -osity †; infirmity, ailment,

geia; incorrupti-on, -bility; good state –, clean bill- of health; eupepsia; euphoria, -y; St. Anthony's fire.

V. be in health &c. *adj.*; bloom, flourish.

keep -body and soul together, – on one's legs; enjoy -good, – a good state of- health; have a clean bill of health.

return to health; recover &c. 660; get better &c. (*improve*) 658; take a -new, – fresh- lease of life; recruit; restore to health; cure &c. (*restore*) 660; tinker.

Adj. health-y, -ful; in -health &c. *n.*; well, sound, hearty, hale, fresh, green, whole; florid, flush, hardy, stanch, staunch, brave, robust, vigorous, weatherproof.

un-scathed, -injured, -maimed, -marred, -tainted; sound of wind and limb, safe and sound.

on one's legs; sound as a -roach, – bell; fresh as -a daisy, – a rose, – April; hearty as a buck; in -fine, – high- feather; in -good case, – full bloom; pretty bobbish, tolerably well, as well as can be expected.

sanitary &c. (*health-giving*) 656; sanatory &c. (*remedial*) 662.

Phr. " health that snuffs the morning air " [Grainger]; *non est vivere sed valere vita* [Martial].

indisposition; complaint, disorder, malady; distemper, -ature.

visitation, attack, seizure, stroke, fit.

delicacy, loss of health, invalidation, cachexy; cachexia, atrophy, marasmus; indigestion, dyspepsia; decay &c. (*deterioration*) 659; decline, consumption, palsy, paralysis, prostration.

taint, pollution, infection, septicity; epi-, en-demic; murrain, plague, pestilence, virus, pox.

sore, ulcer, abscess, fester, boil; pimple &c. (*swelling*) 250; carbuncle, gathering, imposthume, peccant humor, issue; rot, canker, cancer, carcinoma, caries, mortification, corruption, gangrene, sphacelus, sphacelation, leprosy, eruption, rash, breaking out.

fever, calenture; inflammation.

ague, angina pectoris, appendicitis; Asiatic –, spasmodic- cholera; biliary calculus, black death; blennorrh-agia, -œa; blood poisoning, bloodstroke, bloody flux, brash; breakbone –, dengue –, malarial- fever; bronchocele, canker rash, cardialgia, carditis; cholera, -asphyxia; chlorosis, chorea, cynanche, dartre; enanthem, -a; erysipelas; exanthem, -a; gallstone, goiter, gonorrhea, green sickness, grip, grippe, hay fever, heartburn, heaves, hernia, hemorrhoids, herpes, itch, king's evil, lockjaw, measles, necrosis, pertussis, phthisis, piles, pneumonia, psora, pyæmia, pyrosis, quinsy, rachitis, ringworm, rubeola, rupture, St. Vitus's dance, scabies, scarlatina, scarlet fever, scrofula, seasickness, struma, syntexis, tetanus, tetter, tonsilitis, tracheocele, trachoma, trismus, varicella, varicosis, variola, water qualm, whooping cough; yellow-fever, -jack.

fatal &c. (*hopeless*) 859- -disease &c.; dangerous illness, galloping consumption, churchyard cough; general breaking up, break up of the system.

[Disease of mind] idiocy &c. 499; insanity &c. 503.

martyr to disease; cripple; " the halt the lame and the blind "; valetudinar-y, -ian; invalid, patient, case; sick-room, -chamber.

[Science of disease] path-, eti-, nos-ology.

[Veterinary] anthrax, bighead; black-leg, -quarter; cattle plague, glanders, mange, milk sickness; quarter-evil, -ill; rinderpest.

V. be -ill &c. *adj.*; ail, suffer, labor under, be affected with, complain of; droop, flag, languish, halt; sicken, peak, pine; gasp.

keep one's bed; feign sickness &c. (*falsehood*) 544.

lay -by, – up; take –, catch- -a disease &c. *n.*, – an infection; break out.

Adj. diseased; ailing &c. *v.*; ill, – of; taken ill, seized with; indisposed, unwell, sick, squeamish, poorly, seedy; affected –, afflicted- with illness; laid up, confined, bedridden, invalided, in hospital, on the sick list; out of -health, – sorts; under the weather [U. S.]; valetudinary.

un-sound, -healthy; sickly, morbose, healthless, infirm, chlorotic, unbraced. drooping, flagging, lame, crippled, halting.

morbid, tainted, vitiated, peccant, contaminated, poisoned, tabid, mangy, leprous, cankered; rotten, – to, – at- the core; withered, palsied, paralytic;

dyspeptic; luetic, pneumonic, pulmonic, phthisic, rachitic; syntectic, -al; tabetic, varicose.

touched in the wind, broken-winded, spavined, gasping; *hors de combat* &c. (*useless*) 645.

weak-ly, -ened &c. (*weak*) 160; decrepit; decayed &c. (*deteriorated*) 659; incurable &c. (*hopeless*) 859; in declining health; cranky; in a bad way, in danger, prostrate; moribund &c. (*death*) 360.

morbific &c. 657; epi-, en-demic; zymotic.

656. Salubrity. — N. salubrity; healthiness &c. *adj.*

fine -air, – climate; eudiometer.

[Preservation of health] hygiene; valetudinarian, -ism; sanitarian; sanitarium, sanitorium.

V. be -salubrious &c. *adj.*; agree with; assimilate &c. 23.

Adj. salu-brious, -tary, -tiferous; wholesome; health-y, -ful; sanitary, prophylactic, benign, bracing, tonic, invigorating, good for, nutritious; hygeian, -ienic.

in-noxious, -nocuous, -nocent; harmless, uninjurious, uninfectious.

sanative &c. (*remedial*) 662; restorative &c. (*reinstate*) 660; useful &c. 644.

658. Improvement. — N. improvement; a-, melioration; betterment; mend, amendment, emendation; mending &c. *v.*; advancement; advance &c. (*progress*) 282; ascent &c. 305; promotion, preferment; elevation &c. 307; increase &c. 35; cultiv-, civiliz-ation; culture, march of intellect; menticulture; race-culture, eugenics.

reform, -ation; revision, radical reform; second thoughts, correction, *limæ labor*, refinement, elaboration; purification &c. 652; oxidation; repair &c. (*restoration*) 660; recovery &c. 660.

revise, new edition.

reformer, radical.

V. improve; be –, become –, get- better; mend, amend.

advance &c. (*progress*) 282; ascend &c. 305; increase &c. 35; fructify, ripen, mature; pick up, come about, rally, take a favorable turn; turn -over a new leaf, – the corner; raise one's head, sow one's wild oats; recover &c. 660.

be -better &c. *adj.*, – improved by; turn to -right, – good, – best- account; profit by, reap the benefit of; make -good use of, – capital out of; place to good account.

render better, improve, mend, amend,

657. Insalubrity. — N. insalubrity; unhealthiness &c. *adj.*; nonnaturals; plague spot; malaria &c. (*poison*) 663; death in the pot, contagion; toxicity.

Adj. insalubrious; un-healthy, -wholesome; noxious, noisome; morbi-fic, -ferous; mephitic, septic, azotic, deleterious; pesti-lent, -ferous, -lential; virulent, venomous, envenomed, poisonous, toxic, toxiferous, narcotic.

contagious, infectious, catching, taking, epidemic, zymotic; epizoötic.

innutritious, indigestible, ungenial; uncongenial &c. (*disagreeing*) 24.

deadly &c. (*killing*) 361.

659. Deterioration. — N. deterioration, debasement; wane, ebb; recession &c. 287; retrogradation &c. 283; decrease &c. 36.

degenera-cy, -tion, -teness; degradation; deprav-ation, -ement; devolution; depravity &c. 945; demoralization, retrogression; masochism.

impairment, inquination †, injury, damage, loss, detriment, delaceration †; outrage, havoc, inroad, ravage, scath; perversion, prostitution, vitiation, discoloration, oxidation, pollution, defœdation †, poisoning, venenation †, leaven, contamination, canker, corruption, adulteration, alloy.

decl-ine, -ension, -ination; decaden-ce, -cy; falling off &c. *v.*; caducity, decrepitude.

decay, dilapidation, ravages of time, wear and tear; cor-, e-rosion; moldiness; rotten-ness; moth and rust, dry rot, blight, marasmus, atrophy, collapse; disorganization; *délabrement* &c. (*destruction*) 162; aphid, Aphis, plant louse, puceron; vine-fretter, -grub.

wreck, mere wreck, honeycomb, *magni nominis umbra;* jade, plug, rackabones [U. S.], skate [U. S.]; tack-ey, -y [U. S.].

better; a-, meliorate; correct; decrassify.

improve -, refine- upon; rectify; enrich, mellow, elaborate, fatten.

promote, cultivate, advance, forward, enhance; bring -forward, - on; foster &c. 707; invigorate &c. (*strengthen*) 159.

touch -, rub -, brush -, furbish -, bolster -, vamp -, brighten -, warm- up; polish, cook, make the most of, set off to advantage; prune; repair &c. (*restore*) 660; put in order &c. (*arrange*) 60.

review, revise; make -corrections, - improvements &c. *n.*; doctor &c. (*remedy*) 662; purify &c. 652.

relieve, refresh, infuse new blood into, recruit.

re-form, -model, -organize; new model.

view in a new light, think better of, appeal from Philip drunk to Philip sober.

palliate, mitigate; lessen &c. 36- an evil.

Adj. improving &c. *v.*; progressive, improved &c. *v.*; better, - off, - for; all the better for; better advised.

reform-, emend-atory; reparatory &c. (*restorative*) 660; remedial &c. 662.

corrigible, improvable; accultural.

Adv. on -consideration, - reconsideration, - second thoughts, - better advice; *ad melius inquirendum*.

Phr. *urbem latericiam invenit marmoream reliquit.*

V. be -, become- -worse, - deteriorated &c. *adj.*; have seen better days, deteriorate, degenerate, fall off; wane &c. (*decrease*) 36; ebb; retrograde &c. 283; decline, droop; go down &c. (*sink*) 306; go -downhill, - on from bad to worse, - farther and fare worse; jump out of the frying pan into the fire.

run to -seed, - waste; swale †, sweal †; lapse, be the worse for; sphacelate; break, - down; spring a leak, crack, start; shrivel &c. (*contract*) 195; fade, go off, wither, molder, rot, rankle, decay, go bad; go to -, fall into- decay; " fall into the sear and yellow leaf," rust, crumble, shake; totter, - to its fall; perish &c. 162; die &c. 360.

[Render less good] deteriorate; weaken &c. 160; put back; taint, infect, contaminate, poison, empoison, envenom, canker, corrupt, exulcerate †, pollute, vitiate, inquinate †; de-, em-base †; denaturalize, leaven; de-flower, -bauch, -file, -prave, -grade; ulcerate; stain &c. (*dirt*) 653; discolor; alloy, adulterate, sophisticate, tamper with, prejudice.

pervert, prostitute, demoralize, brutalize; render vicious &c. 945.

embitter, acerbate, aggravate.

injure, impair, labefy, damage, harm, hurt, shend, scath, spoil, mar, despoil, dilapidate, waste; overrun; ravage; pillage &c. 791.

wound, stab, pierce, maim, lame, surbate †, cripple, hough, hamstring, hit between wind and water, scotch, mangle, mutilate, disfigure, blemish, deface, warp.

blight, rot; cor-, e-rode; wear -away, - out; gnaw, - at the root of; sap, mine, undermine, shake, sap the foundations of, break up; dis-organize, -mantle, -mast; destroy &c. 162.

damnify &c. (*aggrieve*) 649; do one's worst; knock down; deal a blow to; play -havoc, - sad havoc, - the mischief, - the deuce, - the very devil- -with, - among; decimate.

Adj. unimproved &c. (improve &c. 658); deteriorated &c. *v.*; altered, - for the worse; injured &c. *v.*; sprung; withering, spoiling &c. *v.*; on the -wane, - decline; tabid; degenerate; marescent; worse; the -, all the- worse for; out of -repair, - tune; imperfect &c. 651; the worse for wear; battered; weather-ed, -beaten; stale, *passé*, shaken, dilapidated, frayed, faded, wilted, shabby, secondhand, threadbare; worn, - to- -a thread, - a shadow, - the stump, - rags; reduced, - to a skeleton; far gone; tacky [U. S.].

decayed &c. *v.*; moth-, worm-eaten; mildewed, rusty, moldy, spotted, seedy, time-worn, moss-grown; discolored; effete, wasted, crumbling, moldering, rotten, cankered, blighted, tainted; depraved &c. (*vicious*) 945; decrep-id, -it; broken down; done, - for, - up; worn out, used up; fit for the -dust hole, - waste-paper basket; past work &c. (*useless*) 645.

at a low ebb, in a bad way, on one's last legs; undermined, deciduous; nodding to its fall &c. (*destruction*) 162; tottering &c. (*dangerous*) 665; past

cure &c. (*hopeless*) 859; fatigued &c. 688; retrograde &c. (*retrogressive*) 283; deleterious &c. 649.

Phr. out of the frying pan into the fire; *ægrescit medendo;* " what a falling off was there! " [*Hamlet*].

660. Restoration.— N. restor-ation, -al; re-instatement, -placement, -habilitation, -establishment, -constitution, -construction; reproduction &c. 163; renovation, -newal; reviv-al, -escence, -iscence; refreshment &c. 689; re-suscitation, -animation, -vivification, -viction †; Phenix; reorganization.

renaissance, second youth, rejuvenescence, new birth; regenera-tion, -cy, -teness; palingenesis, reconversion.

661. Relapse. — N. relapse, lapse; falling back &c. *v.*; retrogradation &c. (*retrogression*) 283; deterioration &c. 659.

[Return to, or recurrence of a bad state] backsliding, recidivation†; recidivism, -ity; recrudescence.

V. relapse, lapse; fall --, slide –, sinkback; return; retrograde &c. 283; recidivate; fall off &c. 659- again.

redress, retrieval, reclamation, recovery; convalescence; resumption, *ré-sumption;* sanativeness.

recurrence &c. (*repetition*) 104; *réchauffé, rifacimento.*

cure, recure †, sanation †; healing &c. *v.*; redintegration; rectification; instauration.

repair, reparation; recruiting &c. *v.*; cicatrization; disinfection; tinkering.

reaction; redemption &c. (*deliverance*) 672; restitution &c. 790; relief &c. 834.

tinker, cobbler; *vis medicatrix* &c. (*remedy*) 662.

curableness.

V. return to the original state; recover, rally, revive; come -to, – round, – to oneself; pull through, weather the storm, be oneself again; get -well, – round, – the better of, – over, – about; rise from -one's ashes, – the grave; survive &c. (*outlive*) 110; resume, reappear; come to, – life again; live –, rise-again.

heal, skin over, cicatrize; right itself.

restore, put back, place *in statu quo;* re-instate, -place, -seat, -habilitate, -establish, -estate, -install.

re-construct, -build, -organize, -constitute; reconvert; re-new, -novate; regenerate; rejuvenate.

re-deem, -claim, -cover, -trieve; rescue &c. (*deliver*) 672.

redress, recure; cure, heal, remedy, doctor, physic, medicate; break of; bring round, set on one's legs.

re-suscitate, -vive, -animate, -vivify, -call to life; reproduce &c. 163; warm up; reinvigorate, refresh &c. 689.

redintegrate, make whole; recoup &c. 790; make -good, – all square; rectify; put –, set- -right, – to rights, – straight; set up, correct; put in order &c. (*arrange*) 60; refit, recruit; fill up, – the ranks; reinforce.

repair; put in -repair, – thorough repair, – complete repair; retouch, botch, vamp, tinker, cobble; do –, patch, – plaster –, vamp- up; darn, finedraw, heelpiece; stop a gap, stanch, staunch, caulk, calk, careen, splice, bind up wounds.

Adj. restored &c. *v.*; redivivus, convalescent; in a fair way; none the worse; rejuvenated.

restoring &c. *v.*; restorative, recuperative; sana-, repara-tive, -tory; curative, remedial.

restor-, recover-, san-, remedi-, retriev-, cur-able.

Adv. *in statu quo;* as you were.

Phr. *revenons à nos moutons; médecin, guéris-toi toi-même; vestigia nulla retrorsum* [Horace].

662. Remedy. — N. remedy, help, redress; anthelmintic; anti-febrile, -poi-

663. Bane. — N. bane, curse; evil &c. 619; hurtfulness &c. (*badness*) 649;

son, -spasmodic; bracer, faith cure, helminthagogue, lithagogue, pick-me-up, stimulant, tonic, vermifuge, anti-dote, counterpoison, prophylactic, an-tiseptic, corrective, restorative; sedative &c. 174; palliative; febrifuge; alter-ant, -ative; specific; emetic, carminative; Nepenthe, Mithridate.

cure; radical -, perfect -, certain-cure; sovereign remedy.

physic, medicine, Galenicals, simples, drug, potion, draught, dose, pill, bolus, electuary; linct-us, -ure; medicament; pharmacon.

nostrum, receipt, recipe, prescription; catholicon, panacea, elixir, *elixir vitæ*, philosopher's stone; balm, balsam, cor-dial, theriac, ptisan.

agueweed, arnica, benzoin, bitartrate of potash, boneset, calomel, catnip, cin-chona, cream of tartar, Epsom salts; fe-ver-root, -wort; friar's balsam, Indian sage; ipecac, -uanha; jonquil, mercu-rous chloride, Peruvian bark; quin-ine, -quina; sassafras, yarrow.

salve, ointment, cerate, oil, lenitive, lotion, cosmetic; plaster; epithem, embrocation, liniment, cataplasm, sina-pism, arquebusade, traumatic, vulnerary, pepastic, poultice, collyrium, de-pilatory; emplastrum; eyewater, vesicatory.

compress, pledget; bandage &c. (*support*) 215.

treatment, medical treatment, regimen; diet-ary, -etics; *vis medicatrix, – naturæ; médecine expectante;* bloodletting, bleeding, venesection, phlebotomy, cupping, sanguisuge, leeches; operation, surgical operation.

pharma-cy, -cology, -ceutics; acology, Materia Medica, therapeutics, posology; home-, all-, heter-, oste-, hydr-opathy; cold water cure; dietetics; sur-, chirur-gery; healing art, leechcraft; ortho-pedy, -praxy; dentistry, midwifery, obstetrics; tocology; pharmacopœia; sarcology.

hospital, infirmary; pest-, lazar-house; lazaretto; lock hospital; *maison de santé;* ambulance; dispensary; dispensatory, drug store, *Hôtel des Invalides;* sanatarium, spa, pump room, well; hospice; Red Cross.

doctor, physician, surgeon; medical –, general- practitioner ; medical at-tendant, apothecary, druggist; leech; osteopath, -ist; Æsculapius, Hip-pocrates, Galen; *accoucheur, accoucheuse,* midwife, oculist, aurist; operator; nurse, monthly nurse, sister; dresser; bonesetter; pharma-ceutist, -cist, -copolist.

V. apply a -remedy &c. *n.*; doctor, dose, physic, nurse, minister to, attend, dress the wounds, plaster; prevent &c. 706; relieve &c. 834; pal-liate &c. 658; restore &c. 660; drench with physic; bleed, cup, let blood; manicure.

Adj. remedial; restorative &c. 660; corrective, palliative, healing; sana-tory, -tive; prophylactic; salutiferous &c. (*salutary*) 656; medic-al, -inal; therapeutic, chirurgical, epulotic †, paregoric, tonic, corroborant, analeptic, balsamic, anodyne, hypnotic, neurotic, narcotic, sedative, lenitive, demulcent, emollient; depuratory; deter-sive, -gent; abstersive, disinfectant, febrifugal, alterative; traumatic, vulnerary.

all-, heter-, home-, hydr-opathic; anthelmintic; anti-febile, -luetic; aperi-ent, chalybeate, deobstruent, depurative, laxative, roborant.

painfulness &c. (*cause of pain*) 830; scourge &c. (*punishment*) 975; *damnosa hereditas;* white elephant.

sting, fang, thorn, tang, bramble, brier, nettle.

poison, leaven, virus, venom; arsenic, Prussic acid, antimony, tartar emetic, strychnine, nicotine; miasm, mephitis, malaria, azote, sewer gas; pest.

Albany hemp, arsenious -oxide, - acid; bichloride of mercury; carbonic acid, – gas; choke damp, corrosive sublimate, fire damp; hydrocyan-ic acid, -ide; marsh gas, nux vomica, ratsbane.

rust, worm, helminth, moth, moth and rust, fungus, mildew; dry rot; canker, -worm; cancer; torpedo; viper &c. (*evil doer*) 913; demon &c. 980.

hemlock, hellebore, nightshade, bella-donna, henbane, aconite; banewort, bhang, ganja, hashish; Upas tree.

[Science of poisons] toxicology.

Adj. baneful &c. (*bad*) 649; poisonous &c. (*unwholesome*) 657.

Phr. *bibere venenum in auro.*

dietetic, alimentary; nutrit-ious, -ive; peptic; alexi-pharmic, -teric; remedi-, cur-able.

Phr. *aux grands maux les grands remèdes; Dios que da la llaga da la medicina; para todo hay remedio sino para la muerte; temporis ars medicina fere est* [Ovid]; " the remedy is worse than the disease " [Dryden]; " throw physic to the dogs, I'll none of it " [*Macbeth*].

3. Contingent Subservience

664. Safety. — **N.** safety, security, surety, impregnability; invulnera-bility, -bleness &c. *adj.*; danger -past, – over; storm blown over; coast clear; escape &c. 671; means of escape; blow-, safety-, snifting-valve; safeguard, palladium.

guardian-, ward-, warden-ship; tutelage, custody, safe-keeping; preservation &c. 670; protection, auspices.

safe-conduct, escort, convoy; guard, shield &c. (*defense*) 717; guardian angel; tutelary -god, – deity, – saint; *genius loci*.

protector, guardian; ward-en, -er; preserver, custodian, duenna, chaperon, third person.

watch-, ban-dog; Cerberus; watch-, patrol-, police-man; cop *, peeler, zarp; sentinel, sentry, scout &c. (*warning*) 668; garrison; guardship.

[Means of safety] refuge &c. anchor &c. 666; precaution &c. (*preparation*) 673; quarantine, *cordon sanitaire*. [Sense of security] confidence &c. 858.

V. be -safe &c. *adj.*; keep one's head above water, tide over, save one's bacon; ride out –, weather- the storm; light upon one's feet; bear a charmed life; escape &c. 671.

make –, render- -safe &c. *adj.*; protect; take care of &c. (*care*) 459; preserve &c. 670; cover, screen, shelter, shroud, flank, ward; guard &c. (*defend*) 717; secure &c. (*restrain*) 751; intrench, fence round &c. (*circumscribe*) 229; house, nestle, ensconce; take charge of.

escort, convoy; garrison; watch, mount guard, patrol.

make assurance doubly sure &c. (*caution*) 864; take up a loose thread; take precautions &c. (*prepare for*) 673; double reef topsails.

seek safety; take –, find- shelter &c. 666.

Adj. safe, secure, sure; in -safety, – security; on the safe side; under the -shield of, – shade of, – wing of, – shadow of one's wing; under -cover, – lock and key; out of -danger, – the meshes,

665. Danger. — **N.** danger, peril, insecurity, jeopardy, risk, hazard, venture, precariousness, slipperiness; instability &c. 149; defenselessness &c. *adj.*

exposure &c. (*liability*) 177; vulnerability; vulnerable point, heel of Achilles; forlorn hope &c. (*hopelessness*) 859.

[Dangerous course] leap in the dark &c. (*rashness*) 863; road to ruin, *facilis descensus Averni* [Vergil], hairbreadth escape.

cause for alarm; source of danger &c. 667. [Approach of danger] rock –, breakers- ahead; storm brewing; clouds -in the horizon, – gathering; warning &c. 668; alarm &c. 669. [Sense of danger] apprehension &c. 860.

V. be -in danger &c. *adj.*; be exposed to –, run into –, incur –, encounter- -danger &c. *n.*; run a risk; lay oneself open to &c. (*liability*) 177; lean on –, trust to- a broken reed; feel the ground sliding from under one, have to run for it; have the -chances, – odds- against one.

hang by a thread, totter; sleep –, stand- on a volcano; sit on a barrel of gunpowder, live in a glass house.

bring –, place –, put- in -danger &c. *n.*; endanger, expose to danger, imperil; jeopard, -ize; compromise; sail too near the wind &c. (*rash*) 863.

adventure, risk, hazard, venture, stake, set at hazard; run the gauntlet &c. (*dare*) 861; engage in a forlorn hope.

threaten &c. 909- danger; run one hard; lay a trap for &c. (*deceive*) 545.

Adj. in -danger &c. *n.*; endangered &c. *v.*; fraught with danger; danger-, hazard-, peril-, parl-, pericul-ous †; unsafe, unprotected &c. (safe, protect &c. 664); insecure, untrustworthy; built upon sand, on a sandy basis; wild-cat.

defense-, fence-, guard-, harbor-less; unshielded; vulnerable, expugnable, exposed; open to &c. (*liable*) 177.

aux abois, at bay; on -the wrong side of the wall, – a lee shore, – the rocks.

at stake, in question; precarious, critical, ticklish; slip-pery, -py; hanging

– harm's way; on sure ground, at anchor, high and dry, above water; un-threatened, -molested; protected &c. *v.*; *cavendo tutus;* panoplied &c. (*defended*) 717.

snug, seaworthy; weather-, water-, fire-proof.

defensible, tenable, proof against, invulnerable; un-assailable, -attackable; im-pregnable, -perdible †; inexpugnable; Achillean.

safe and sound &c. (*preserved*) 670; harmless; scathless &c. (*perfect*) 650; unhazarded; not -dangerous &c. 665.

protecting &c. *v.*; guardian, tutelary; preservative &c. 670; trustworthy &c. 939.

Adv. *ex abundanti cautelâ;* with impunity.

Phr. all's well; *salva. res est; suave mari magno; à couvert; e terra alterius spectare laborem* [Lucretius]; *Dieu vous garde.*

by a thread &c. *v.*; with a halter round one's neck; between -the hammer and the anvil, – Scylla and Charybdis, – two fires; on the -edge, – brink, – verge of a- -precipice, – volcano; in the lion's den, on slippery ground, under fire; not out of the wood.

un-warned, -admonished, -advised; unprepared &c. 674; off one's guard &c. (*inexpectant*) 508.

tottering; un-stable, -steady; shaky, top-heavy, tumble-down, ramshackle, crumbling, water-logged; help-, guideless; in a bad way; reduced to –, at- the last extremity; trembling in the balance; nodding to its fall &c. (*destruction*) 162.

threatening &c. 909; ominous, ill-omened; alarming &c. (*fear*) 860; explosive.

adventurous &c. (*rash*) 863, (*bold*) 861.

Phr. *incidit in Scyllam qui vult vitare Charybdim; nam tua res agitur paries dum proximus ardet.*

---

666. [Means of safety.] **Refuge.** — **N.** refuge, sanctuary, retreat, fastness; acropolis; keep, last resort; ward; prison &c. 752; asylum, ark, home, refuge for the destitute; almshouse; hiding place &c. (*ambush*) 530; *sanctum sanctorum* &c. (*privacy*) 893.

roadstead, anchorage; breakwater, mole, port, haven; harbor, – of refuge; seaport; pier, jetty, embankment, quay.

covert, shelter, screen, lee wall, wing, shield, umbrella; dashboard, dasher [U. S.].

wall &c. (*inclosure*) 232; fort &c. (*defense*) 717.

anchor, kedge; grap-nel, -pling iron; sheet anchor, killick; mainstay; support &c. 215; check &c. 706; ballast.

jury mast; vent-peg; safety -valve, – lamp; lightning conductor.

means of escape &c. (*escape*) 671; lifeboat, swimming belt, cork jacket; parachute, plank, steppingstone.

safeguard &c. (*protection*) 664.

V. seek –, take –, find- refuge &c. *n.*; seek –, find- safety &c. 664; throw oneself into the arms of; break for taller timber [U. S.].

Phr. *bibere venenum in auro; valet anchora virtus.*

667. [Source of danger.] **Pitfall.** — **N.** rocks, reefs, coral reef, sunken rocks, snags; sands, quicksands; syrt, -is; Goodwin sands, sandy foundation; slippery ground; breakers, shoals, shallows, bank, shelf, flat, lee shore, ironbound coast; rock –, breakers- ahead.

precipice; maelstrom, volcano; ambush &c. 530; pitfall, trapdoor; trap &c. (*snare*) 545.

sword of Damocles; wolf at the door, snake in the grass, death in the pot; latency &c. 526.

ugly customer, dangerous person, *le chat qui dort;* firebrand, hornet's nest.

Phr. *latet anguis in herbâ* [Vergil]; *proximus ardet Ucalegon* [Vergil].

668. Warning. — **N.** warning, caution, caveat; notice &c. (*information*) 527; premoni-tion, -shment; prediction &c. 511; contraindication, lesson, dehortation; admonition, monition; alarm &c. 669.

handwriting on the wall, *tekel upharsin*, yellow flag; fog-signal, -horn; siren; monitor, warning voice, Cassandra, signs of the times, Mother Cary's chickens,

stormy petrel, bird of ill omen, gathering clouds, clouds in the horizon, death watch.

watchtower, beacon, signal post; lighthouse &c. (*indication of locality*) 550.

sent-inel, -ry; watch, -man; watch and ward; watch-, ban-, house-dog; patrol, vedette, picket, bivouac, scout, spy, spial; advanced –, rear- guard; lookout.

cautiousness &c. 864.

V. warn, caution; fore-, pre-warn; ad-, pre-monish; give -notice, – warning; dehort; menace &c. (*threaten*)   09; put on one's guard; sound the alarm &c. 669; croak.

beware, ware; take -warning, – heed at one's peril; keep watch and ward &c. (*care*) 459.

Adj. warning &c. *v.*; premonitory, monitory, cautionary; admoni-tory, -tive; sematic.

warned &c. *v.*; on one's guard &c. (*careful*) 459, (*cautious*) 864.

Adv. *in terrorem* &c. (*threat*) 909.

Int. beware! ware! take care! mind –, take care- what you are about! mind!

Phr. *ne reveillez pas le chat qui dort; fœnum habet in cornu; caveat actor; le silence du peuple est la leçon des rois; verbum sat sapienti; un averti en vaut deux.*

669. [Indication of danger.] **Alarm.** — **N.** alarm; alarum, larum, alarm bell, tocsin, *alerte*, beat of drum, sound of trumpet, note of alarm, hue and cry, fire cross, signal of distress; blue lights; war-cry, -whoop; warning &c. 668; fog-signal, -horn; yellow flag; danger signal; red -light, – flag; fire bell; police whistle.

false alarm, cry of wolf; bug-bear, -aboo.

V. give –, raise –, sound –, turn in –, beat- the *or* an -alarm &c. *n.*; alarm; warn &c. 668; ring the tocsin; *battre la générale;* cry wolf.

Adj. alarming &c. *v.*

Int. *sauve qui peut! qui vive?*

670. Preservation. — **N.** preservation; safe-keeping; conservation &c. (*storage*) 636; maintenance, support, sustentation, conservatism; *vis conservatrix;* salvation &c. (*deliverance*) 672.

[Means of preservation] prophylaxis; preserv-er, -ative; hygi-astics, -antics; cover, drugget; *cordon sanitaire;* canning; ensilage; tinned –, canned- goods.

[Superstitious remedies] charm &c. 993.

V. preserve, maintain, keep, sustain, support; keep -up, – alive; not willingly let die; bank up; nurse; save, rescue; be –, make- -safe &c. 664; take care of &c. (*care*) 459; guard &c. (*defend*) 717.

stare super antiquas vias [Bacon]; hold one's own; hold –, stand- -one's ground &c. (*resist*) 719.

embalm, dry, cure, salt, pickle, season, kyanize, bottle, pot, tin, can; husband &c. (*store*) 636.

Adj. preserving &c. *v.*; conservative; prophylactic; preserva-tory, -tive; hygienic.

preserved &c. *v.*; un-impaired, -broken, -injured, -hurt, -singed, marred; safe, – and sound; intact, with a whole skin.

Phr. *nolumus leges Angliœ mutari.*

671. Escape. — **N.** escape, scape; avolation †, elopement, flight; evasion &c. (*avoidance*) 623; retreat; narrow –, hairbreadth- escape; close call; come off, impunity.

[Means of escape] loophole &c. (*opening*) 260; path &c. 627; refuge &c. 666; vent, – peg; safety valve; drawbridge, fire escape.

reprieve &c. (*deliverance*) 672; liberation &c. 750.

refugee &c. (*fugitive*) 623.

V. escape, scape; make –, effect –, make good- one's escape; break jail; get

-off, – clear off, – well out of; *échapper belle*, save one's bacon; weather the storm &c. (*safe*) 664; escape scot-free.

elude &c., make off &c. (*avoid*) 623; march off &c. (*go away*) 293; give one the slip; slip through the -hands, – fingers; slip the collar, wriggle out of; break -loose, – from prison; break –, slip –, get- away; find -vent, – a hole to creep out of.

Adj. escap-ing, -ed &c. *v.*; stolen away, fled.

Phr. the bird has flown.

672. Deliverance. — **N.** deliverance, extrication, rescue; repriev-e, -al; respite; liberation &c. 750; emancipation; redemption, salvation; riddance; gaol delivery; redeemableness.

V. deliver, extricate, rescue, save, emancipate, redeem, ransom; bring -off, – through; *tirer d'affaire*, get the wheel out of the rut, snatch from the jaws of death, come to the rescue; rid; retrieve &c. (*restore*) 660; be –, get- rid of.

Adj. saved &c. *v.*; extric-, redeem-, rescu-able.

Int. to the rescue!

3. *Precursory Measures*

673. Preparation. — **N.** preparation; providing &c.*v.*; provi-sion, -dence; anticipation &c. (*foresight*) 510; pre-caution, -concertation, -disposition; forecast &c. (*plan*) 626; rehearsal, note of preparation.

[Putting in order] arrangement &c. 60; clearance; adjustment &c. 23; tuning; equipment, outfit, accouterment, armament, array.

ripening &c. *v.*; maturation, evolution; elaboration, concoction, digestion; gestation, hatching, incubation, sitting.

groundwork, first stone, cradle, stepping-stone; foundation, scaffold &c. (*support*) 215; scaffolding, *échafaudage*.

[Preparation -of men] training &c. (*education*) 537; inurement &c. (*habit*) 613; novitiate; [– of food] cook-ing, -ery; brewing, culinary art; [– of the soil] till-, plow-, sow-ing; semination, cultivation.

[State of being prepared] prepared-, readi-, ripe-, mellow-ness; maturity; *un impromptu fait à loisir.*

[Preparer] preparer, trainer, pioneer; *avant-courrier, -coureur; voortrekker;* sappers and miners, pavior, navvy; packer, stevedore; warming pan.

V. prepare; get –, make- ready; make preparations, settle preliminaries, get up, sound the note of preparation.

set –, put- in order &c. (*arrange*) 60; forecast &c. (*plan*) 626; prepare –, plow –, dress- the ground; till –, cultivate- the soil; predispose, sow the seed, lay a train, dig a mine; lay –, fix-

674. Nonpreparation. — **N.** non-, absence of –, want of- preparation; in-culture †, inconcoction †, improvidence.

immaturity, crudity; rawness &c. *adj.*; abortion; disqualification.

[Absence of art] nature, state of nature; virgin soil, unweeded garden; neglect &c. 460.

rough copy &c. (*plan*) 626; germ &c. 153; raw material &c. 635.

improvisation &c. (*impulse*) 612.

V. be -unprepared &c. *adj.*; want –, lack- preparation; lie fallow; *s'embarquer sans biscuits;* live from hand to mouth.

[Render unprepared] dismantle &c. (*render useless*) 645; undress &c. 226.

extemporize, improvise.

Adj. un-prepared &c. [prepare &c. 673]; without -preparation &c. 673; incomplete &c. 53; rudimental, embryonic, abortive; immature, unripe, *kachcha,* raw, green, crude; coarse; rough, -cast, -hewn; in the rough; un-hewn, -formed, -fashioned, -wrought, -labored, -blown, -cooked, -boiled, -concocted, -polished.

un-hatched, -fledged, -nurtured, -licked, -taught, -educated, -cultivated, -trained, -tutored, -drilled, -exercised; deckle-edged; precocious, premature; un-, in-digested; un-mellowed, -seasoned, -leavened.

fallow; un-sown, -tilled; natural, in a state of nature; undressed; in dishabille, *en déshabillé.*

un-, dis-qualified; unfitted; ill-digested; un-begun, -ready, -arranged, -organized, -furnished, -provided, -equip-

the -foundations, – basis, – groundwork; dig the foundations, erect the scaffolding; lay the first stone &c. (*begin*) 66.

roughhew; cut out work; block–, hammer- out; lick into shape &c. (*form*) 240.

elaborate, mature, ripen, mellow, season, bring to maturity; nurture &c. (*aid*) 707; hatch, cook, brew; temper, anneal, smelt; barbecue; infumate; maturate.

equip, arm, man; fit-out, -up; furnish, rig, dress, garnish, betrim, accouter, array, fettle, fledge; dress –, furbish –, brush –, vamp- up; refurbish; sharpen one's tools, trim one's foils, set, prime, attune; whet the -knife, – sword; wind –, screw- up; adjust &c. (*fit*) 27; put in -trim, – train, – gear, – working order, – tune, – a groove for, – harness; pack.

train &c. (*teach*) 537; inure &c. (*habituate*) 613; breed; prepare &c.- for; rehearse; make provision for; take -steps, – measures, – precautions; provide, – against; beat up for recruits; open the door to &c. (*facilitate*) 705.

set one's house in order, make all snug; clear -decks, – for action; close one's ranks; shuffle the cards.

prepare oneself; serve an apprenticeship &c. (*learn*) 539; lay oneself out for, get into harness, gird up one's loins, buckle on one's armor, *reculer pour mieux sauter*, prime and load, shoulder arms, get the steam up, put the horses to.

guard –, make sure- against; forearm, make sure, prepare for the evil day, have a rod in pickle, provide against a rainy day, feather one's nest; lay in provisions &c. 637; make investments; keep on foot.

be -prepared, – ready &c. *adj.*; hold oneself in readiness, keep one's powder dry; lie in wait for &c. (*expect*) 507; anticipate &c. (*foresee*) 510; *principiis obstare; veniente occurrere morbo.*

Adj. preparing &c. *v.*; in -preparation, – course of preparation, – agitation, – embryo, – hand, – train; afoot, afloat; on -foot, – the stocks, – the anvil; under consideration &c. (*plan*) 626; brewing, hatching, forthcoming, brooding; in -store for, – reserve.

precautionary, provident; prepara-tive, -tory; provisional, inchoate, under revision; preliminary &c. (*precedent*) 62.

prepared &c. *v.*; in readiness; ready, – to one's hand, – made, – cut and dried; made to one's hand, handy, on the table; in gear; in working -order, – gear; snug; in practice.

ripe, mature, mellow; *pukka;* practiced &c. (*skilled*) 698; labored, elaborate, highly-wrought, smelling of the lamp, worked up.

in -full feather, – best bib and tucker; in –, at- harness; in -the saddle, – arms, – battle array, – war paint; up in arms; armed -at all points, – to the teeth, – *cap à pie;* sword in hand; booted and spurred.

in utrumque –, semper- paratus; on the alert &c. (*vigilant*) 459; at one's post.

Adv. in -preparation, – anticipation of; against, for; abroach.

Phr. *a bove majori discit arare minor;* "looking before and after" [*Hamlet*], *si vis pacem para bellum.*

ped, -trimmed; out of -gear, – order; dismantled &c. *v.*

shiftless, improvident, unthrifty, thriftless, thoughtless, unguarded; happy-go-lucky; caught napping &c. (*inexpectant*) 508; unpremeditated &c. 612.

Adv. extempore &c. 612.

675. Essay. — **N.** essay, trial, endeavor, attempt; aim, struggle, venture, adventure, speculation, *coup d'essai, début;* probation &c. (*experiment*) 463.

V. try, essay; experiment &c. 463; endeavor, strive; tempt, attempt, make an attempt; venture, adventure, speculate, take one's chance, tempt fortune; try one's -fortune, – luck, – hand; use one's endeavor; feel –, grope –, pick- one's way.

try hard, push, make a bold push, use one's best endeavor; do one's best &c. (*exertion*) 686.

Adj. essaying &c. *v.*; experimental &c. 463; tentative, empirical, probationary.

Adv. experimentally &c. *adj.*; on trial, at a venture; by rule of thumb. if one may be so bold.

Phr. *aut non tentaris aut perfice* [Ovid]; *chi non s'arrischia non guadagna.*

676. Undertaking. — N. undertaking; compact &c. 769; adventure, venture; engagement &c. (*promise*) 768; enter-, em-prise; pilgrimage; matter in hand &c. (*business*) 625; move; first move &c. (*beginning*) 66.

V. undertake; engage –, embark- in; launch –, plunge- into; volunteer; apprentice oneself to; engage &c. (*promise*) 768; contract &c. 769; take upon -oneself, – one's shoulders; devote oneself to &c. (*determination*) 604.

take -up, – in hand; tackle; set –, go- about; set –, fall- -to, – to work; launch forth; set up shop; put in -hand, – execution; set forward; break the neck of a business, be in for; put one's -hand to, – foot in; betake oneself to, turn one's hand to, go to do; begin &c. 66; broach, institute &c. (*orginate*) 153; put –, lay- one's -hand to the plow, – shoulder to the wheel.

have in hand &c. (*business*) 625; have many irons in the fire &c. (*activity*) 682.

Adj. undertaking &c. *v.*; on the anvil &c. 625.

Int. here goes!

677. Use. — N. use; employ, -ment; exer-cise, -citation; appli-cation, -ance; adhibition, disposal; consumption; agen-cy &c. (*physical*) 170; usufruct; usefulness &c. 644; benefit; recourse, resort, avail.

[Conversion to use] utilization, service, wear.

[Way of using] usage.

V. use, make use of, employ, put to use; put in -action, – operation, – practice; set -in motion, – to work.

ply, work, wield, handle, manipulate; play, – off; exert, exercise, practice, avail oneself of, profit by; resort –, have recourse –, recur –, take –, betake one-self- to; take -up with, – advantage of; lay one's hands on, try.

render useful &c. 644; mold; turn to -account, – use; convert to use, utilize; work up; call –, bring- into play; put into requisition; call –, draw- forth; press –, enlist- into the service; bring to bear upon, devote, dedicate, consecrate, apply, adhibit, dispose of; make a -handle, – cat's-paw- of.

fall back upon, make a shift with; make the -most, – best- of.

use –, swallow- up; consume, absorb, expend; tax, task, wear, put to task.

Adj. in use; used &c. *v.*; well-worn, -trodden.

useful &c. 644; subservient &c. (*instrumental*) 631.

678. Disuse. — N. forbearance, abstinence; disuse; relinquishment &c. 782; desuetude &c. (*want of habit*) 614; disusage.

V. not use; do without, dispense with, let alone, not touch, forbear, abstain, spare, waive, neglect; keep back, reserve.

lay -up, – by, – on the shelf, – up in ordinary, – up in a napkin; shelve; set –, put –, lay- aside; disuse, leave off, have done with; supersede; discard &c. (*eject*) 297; dismiss, give warning.

throw aside &c. (*relinquish*) 782; make away with &c. (*destroy*) 162; cast –, heave –, throw- overboard; cast to the -dogs, – winds; dismantle &c. (*render useless*) 645.

lie –, remain- unemployed &c. *adj.*

Adj. not used &c. *v.*; un-employed, -applied, -disposed of, -spent, -exercised, -touched, -trodden, -essayed, -gathered, -culled; uncalled for, not required.

disused &c. *v.*; done with.

679. Misuse. — N. mis-use, -usage, -employment, -application, -appropriation.

abuse, profanation, prostitution, desecration; waste &c. 638.

V. mis-use, -employ, -apply, -appropriate.

desecrate, abuse, profane, prostitute; waste &c. 638; over-task, -tax, -work; squander &c. 818.

cut blocks with a razor, employ a steam engine to crack a nut; catch at a straw.

Adj. misused &c. *v.*

Phr. *ludere cum sacris.*

Section III. VOLUNTARY ACTION

1. *Simple Voluntary Action*

680. Action. — N. action, performance; doing &c. *v.*; perpetration; exercise, -citation; movement, operation, evolution, work; labor &c. (*exertion*) 686; praxis, execution; procedure &c. (*conduct*) 692; handicraft; business &c. 625; agency &c. (*power at work*) 170.

deed, act, overt act, stitch, touch, gest; transaction, job, doings, dealings, proceeding, measure, step, maneuver, bout, passage, move, stroke, blow; *coup, – de main, – d'état; tour de force* &c. (*display*) 882; feat, exploit; achievement &c. (*completion*) 729; handiwork, workmanship; manufacture; stroke of policy &c. (*plan*) 626.

actor &c. (*doer*) 690.

V. do, perform, execute; achieve &c. (*complete*) 729; transact, enact; commit, perpetrate, inflict; exercise, prosecute, carry on, work, practice, play.

employ oneself, ply one's task; officiate, have in hand &c. (*business*) 625; labor &c. 686; be at work; pursue a course; shape one's course &c. (*conduct*) 692.

act, operate; take -action, – steps; strike a blow, lift a finger, stretch forth one's hand; take in hand &c. (*undertake*) 676; put oneself in motion; put in practice; carry into execution &c. (*complete*) 729; act upon.

be -an actor &c. 690; take –, act –, play –, perform- a part in; participate in; have a -hand in, – finger in the pie; have to do with; be a -party to, – participator in; bear –, lend- a hand; pull an oar, run in a race; mix oneself up with &c. (*meddle*) 682.

be in action; come into operation &c. (*power at work*) 170.

Adj. doing &c. *v.*; acting; in action; in harness; on duty; in operation &c. 170.

Adv. in the -act, – midst of, – thick of; red-handed, *in flagrante delicto;* while one's hand is in.

681. Inaction. — N. inaction, passiveness, abstinence from action; non-interference; Fabian –, conservative-policy; neglect &c. 460.

inactivity &c. 683; rest &c. (*repose*) 687; quiescence &c. 265; want of –, inoccupation; idle hours, time hanging on one's hands, *dolce far niente;* sinecure; soft -snap *, – thing *.

V. not -do, – act, – attempt; be -inactive &c. 683; abstain from doing, do nothing, hold, spare; not -stir, – move, – lift- a -finger, – foot, – peg; fold one's -arms, – hands; leave –, let- alone; let -be, – pass, – things take their course, – it have its way, – well alone; *quieta non movere; stare super antiquas vias;* rest and be thankful, live and let live; lie –, rest- upon one's oars; *laisser -aller, – faire;* stand aloof; refrain &c. (*avoid*) 623; keep oneself from doing; remit –, relax- one's efforts; desist &c. (*relinquish*) 624; stop &c. (*cease*) 142; pause &c. (*be quiet*) 265.

wait, lie in wait, bide one's time, take time, tide it over.

cool –, kick- one's heels; while away the -time, – tedious hours; pass –, fil! up –, beguile- the time; talk against time; waste time &c. (*inactive*) 683.

lie -by, – on the shelf, – in ordinary, – idle, – to, – fallow; keep quiet, slug; have nothing to do, whistle for want of thought.

undo, do away with; take -down, – to pieces; destroy &c. 162.

Adj. not doing &c. *v.*; not done &c. *v.*; undone; passive; un-occupied, -employed; out of -employ, – work; fallow; *désœuvré.*

Adv. *re infectâ,* at a stand, *les bras croisés,* with folded arms; with the hands -in the pockets, – behind one's back; *pour passer le temps.*

Int. so let it be!stop!&c.142;hands off!

Phr. *cunctando restituit rem.*

Phr. " action is eloquence " [*Coriolanus*]; actions speak louder than words; *actum aiunt ne agas* [Terence]; " awake, arise, or be forever fall'n " [*Paradise Lost*]; *dii pia facta vident* [Ovid]; *faire sans dire; fare fac; fronte capillata post est occasio calva;* " our deeds are sometimes better than our thoughts " [Bailey]; " the great end of life is not knowledge but action " [Huxley]; " thought is the soul of act " [R. Browning]; *vivre ce n'est pas respirer c'est agir;* " we live in deeds not years " [Bailey].

682. Activity. — N. activity; briskness, liveliness &c. *adj.*; animation, life, vivacity, spirit, dash, energy; snap, vim.

nimbleness, agility; smartness, quickness &c. *adj.*; velocity &c. 274; alacrity, promptitude; des-, dis-patch; expedition; haste &c. 684; punctuality &c. (*early*) 132.

eagerness, zeal, ardor, *perfervidum irgenium, empressement*, earnestness, intentness; *abandon;* vigor &c. (*physical energy*) 171; devotion &c. (*resolution*) 604; exertion &c. 686.

industry, assiduity; assiduousness &c. *adj.*; sedulity; laboriousness; drudgery &c. (*labor*) 686; painstaking, diligence; perseverance &c. 604*a*; indefatigation †; habits of business.

vigilance &c. 459; wakefulness; sleep-, rest-lessness; insomnia; pervigilium, *insomnium;* racketing.

movement, bustle, stir, fuss, ado, bother, pottering; fidget, -iness; flurry &c. (*haste*) 684.

officiousness; dabbling, meddling; inter-ference, -position, -meddling; tampering with, intrigue.

press of business, no sinecure, plenty to do, many irons in the fire, great doings, busy hum of men, battle of life, thick of the action.

housewife, busy bee; new brooms; sharp fellow, blade; devotee, enthusiast, zealot, meddler, intermeddler, intriguer, busybody, pickthank; hummer *, hustler, live man [U. S.], rustler * [U. S.].

V. be -active &c. *adj.*; busy oneself in; stir, -about, – one's stumps; bestir –, rouse- oneself; speed, hasten, peg away, lay about one, bustle, fuss; raise –, kick up- a dust; push; make a -push, – fuss, – stir; go ahead, push forward; fight –, elbow- one's way; make progress &c. 282; toil &c. (*labor*) 686; plod, persist &c. (*persevere*) 604*a*; keep -up the ball, – the pot boiling.

look sharp; have all one's eyes about one &c. (*vigilance*) 459; rise, arouse oneself, hustle, get up early, be about, keep moving, steal a march, kill two birds with one stone; seize the opportunity &c. 134; lose no time, not lose a moment, make the most of one's time, not suffer the grass to grow under one's feet, improve the shining hour, make short work of; dash off; make haste &c. 684; do

683. Inactivity. — N. inactivity; inaction &c. 681; inertness &c. 172; obstinacy &c. 606.

lull &c. (*cessation*) 142; quiescence &c. 265; rust, -iness.

idle-, remiss-ness &c. *adj.*; sloth, indolence, indiligence; dawdling &c. *v.*; ergophobia, otiosity.

dullness &c. *adj.*; languor; segni-ty †, -tude †; lentor; sluggishness &c. (*slowness*) 275; procrastination &c. (*delay*) 133; torp-or, -idity, -escence; stupor &c. (*insensibility*) 823; somnolence; drowsiness &c. *adj.*; nodding &c. *v.*; oscit-ation, -ancy; pandiculation, hypnotism, lethargy; statuvolence; heaviness, heavy eyelids.

sleep, slumber; sound –, heavy –, balmy- sleep; Morpheus; Somnus; coma, trance, ecstasis, dream, hibernation, nap, doze, snooze, siesta, wink of sleep, forty winks, snore; hypnology.

dull work; pottering; relaxation &c. (*loosening*) 47; Castle of Indolence.

[Cause of inactivity] lullaby, sedative &c. 174; torpedo.

idler, drone, droil, dawdle, mopus; do-little, *fainéant*, dummy, sleeping partner; afternoon farmer; truant &c. (*runaway*) 623; bummer [U. S.], lounger, lazzarone, loafer; lub-ber, -bard; slow coach &c. (*slow*) 275; opium –, lotuseater; slug; lag-, slug-gard; slumberer, dormouse, marmot; waiter on Providence, *fruges consumere natus*.

V. be -inactive &c. *adj.*; do nothing &c. 681; move slowly &c. 275; let the grass grow under one's feet; take one's time, dawdle, drawl, droil, lag, hang back, slouch; loll, -op; lounge, poke, loaf, loiter; go to sleep over; sleep at one's post, *ne battre que d'une aile*.

take -it easy, – things as they come; lead an easy life, vegetate, swim with the stream, eat the bread of idleness; loll in the lap of -luxury, — indolence; waste –, consume –, kill –, lose- time; burn daylight, waste the precious hours.

idle –, trifle –, fritter –, fool- away time; spend –, take- time in; ped-, piddle; potter, pudder, dabble, faddle, fribble, fiddle-faddle; dally, dilly-dally.

sleep, slumber, be asleep; hibernate; oversleep; sleep like a -top, – log, – dormouse; sleep -soundly, – heavily; doze, drowze, snooze, nap; take a -nap &c. *n.*; dream; snore; settle –, go –, go

one's best, take pains &c. (*exert oneself*) 686; do –, work- wonders.

have -many irons in the fire, – one's hands full, – much on one's hands; have other -things to do, – fish to fry; be busy; not have a moment -to spare, – that one can call one's own.

have one's fling, run the round of; go all lengths, stick at nothing, run riot.

outdo; over-do, -act, -lay, -shoot the mark; make a toil of a pleasure.

have a hand in &c. (*act in*) 680; take an active part, put in one's oar, have a finger in the pie, mix oneself up with, trouble one's head about, intrigue; agitate.

tamper with, meddle, moil; inter-meddle, -fere, -pose; obtrude; poke –, thrust- one's nose in.

Adj. active, brisk, – as a lark, – as a bee; lively, animated, vivacious; alive, – and kicking; frisky, spirited, stirring.

nimble, – as a squirrel; agile; light –, nimble-footed; featly, tripping.

quick, prompt, yare, instant, ready, alert, spry, sharp, smart; fast &c. (*swift*) 274; quick as a lamplighter, expeditious; awake, broad awake; go-ahead, live [U. S.]; wide-awake &c. (*intelligent*) 498.

forward, eager, strenuous, zealous, enterprising, in earnest; resolute &c. 604.

industrious, assiduous, diligent, sedulous, notable, painstaking; intent &c. (*attention*) 457; indefatigable &c. (*persevering*) 604a; unwearied; unsleeping, never tired; plodding, hardworking &c. 686; businesslike, workaday.

bustling; restless, – as a hyena; fussy, fidgety, pottering; busy, – as a hen with one chicken.

working, at work, on duty, in harness; up in arms; on one's legs, at call; up and -doing, – stirring.

busy, occupied; hard at -work, – it; up to one's ears in, full of business, busy as a bee.

meddling &c. *v.*; meddlesome, pushing, officious, overofficious, intrigant.

astir, stirring; a-going, -foot; on foot; in full swing; eventful; on the alert &c. (*vigilant*) 459.

Adv. actively &c. *adj.*; with -life and spirit, – might and main &c. 686, – haste &c. 684, – wings; full tilt, *in mediis rebus*.

Int. be –, look- -alive, – sharp! move –, push- on! keep moving! go ahead! stir your stumps! *age quod agis! jaldi! – karo!* step lively!

Phr. *carpe diem* &c. (*opportunity*) 134; *nulla dies sine lineâ* [Pliny]; *nec mora nec requies* [Vergil]; the plot thickens; no sooner said than done &c. (*early*) 132; "*veni vidi vici*" [Suetonius]; catch a weasel asleep; *abends wird der Faule fleissig; dictum ac factum* [Terence]; *schwere Arbeit in der Jugend ist sanfte Ruhe im Alter;* "the busy hum of men" [Milton].

off- to sleep; drop off; fall –, drop-asleep; close –, seal up- -the -eyes, – eyelids; weigh down the eyelids; get sleepy, nod, yawn; go to bed, turn in.

languish, expend itself, flag, hang fire; relax.

render -idle &c. *adj.*; sluggardize; mitigate &c. 174.

Adj. inactive; motionless &c. 265; unoccupied &c. (*doing nothing*) 681; unbusied.

indolent, lazy, slothful, idle, lusk, remiss, slack, inert, torpid, sluggish, otiose, languid, supine, heavy, dull, leaden, lumpish; exanimate, soulless; listless; dron-y, -ish; lazy as Ludlam's dog.

dilatory, laggard; lagging &c. *v.*; slow &c. 275; rusty, flagging; lackadaisical, maudlin, fiddle-faddle; pottering &c. *v.*; shilly-shally &c. (*irresolute*) 605.

sleeping &c. *v.*; asleep; fast –, dead –, sound- asleep; in a sound sleep; sound as a top, dormant, comatose; in the -arms, – lap- of Morpheus.

sleep-y, -ful; dozy, drowsy, somnolent, torpescent; lethargic, -al; somnifacient; statuvol-ent, -ic; heavy, – with sleep; napping; somni-fic, -ferous; sopor-ous, -ific, -iferous; hypnotic; balmy, dreamy; un-, una-wakened.

sedative &c. 174.

Adv. inactively &c. *adj.*; at leisure &c. 685.

Phr. the eyes begin to draw straws; "bankrupt of life yet prodigal of ease" [Dryden]; "better 50 years of Europe than a cycle of Cathay" [Tennyson]; "idly busy rolls their world away" [Goldsmith]; "the mystery of folded sleep" [Tennyson]; "the timely dew of sleep" [Milton]; "thou driftest gently down the tides of sleep" [Longfellow]; "tired Nature's sweet restorer, balmy sleep" [Young].

684. Haste. — N. haste, urgency; des-, dis-patch; acceleration, spurt, spirt, forced march, rush, dash; velocity &c. 274; precipit-ancy, -ation, -ousness &c. *adj.*; impetuosity; *brusquerie;* hurry, drive, scramble, bustle, fuss, fidget, flurry, flutter, splutter.

V. haste, hasten; make -haste, – a dash &c. *n.*; hurry –, dash –, whip –, push –, press- -on, – forward; hurry, skurry, scuttle along, bundle on, dart to and fro, bustle, flutter, scramble; plunge, – headlong; dash off; rush &c. (*violence*) 173; express.

bestir oneself &c. (*be active*) 682; lose -no time, – not a moment, – not an instant; make short work of; make the best of one's -time, – way.

be -precipitate &c. *adj.*; jump at, be in -haste, – a hurry &c. *n.*; have -no time, – not a moment- -to lose, – to spare; work against time.

quicken &c. 274; accelerate, expedite, put on, precipitate, urge, whip; railroad.

Adj. hasty, hurried, brusque; scrambling, cursory, precipitate, headlong, furious, boisterous, impetuous, hot-headed; feverish, fussy; pushing.

in -haste, – a hurry &c. *n.*; in -hot, – all- haste; breathless, pressed for time, hard pressed, urgent.

Adv. with -haste, – all haste, – breathless speed; in haste &c. *adj.*; apace &c. (*swiftly*) 274; amain; all at once &c. (*instantaneously*) 113; at short notice &c., immediately &c. (*early*) 132; posthaste; by -cable, – express, – telegraph, – forced marches.

hastily, precipitately &c. *adj.*; helter-skelter, hurry-skurry, holus-bolus; slap-dash, -bang; full-tilt, -drive; heels over head, head and shoulders, headlong, *à corps perdu.*

by -fits and starts, – spurts; hop skip and jump.

Phr. *sauve qui peut,* devil take the hindmost, no time to be lost; no sooner said than done &c. (*early*) 132; a word and a blow; *maggiore frétta minore átto; ohne Hast aber ohne Rast* [Goethe's motto]; " stand not upon the order of your going " [*Macbeth*]; " swift, swift, you dragons of the night " [*Cymbeline*].

685. Leisure. — N. leisure; convenience; spare -time, – hours, – moments; vacant hour; time, – to spare, – on one's hands; holiday &c. (*rest*) 687; *otium cum dignitate* [Cic.], ease.

V. have -leisure &c. *n.*; take one's -time, – leisure, – ease; repose &c. 687; move slowly &c. 275; while away the time &c. (*inaction*) 681; be -master of one's time, – an idle man.

Adj. leisure, -ly; slow &c. 275; deliberate, quiet, calm, undisturbed; at -leisure, – one's ease, – a loose end.

Phr. time hanging heavy on one's hands; *eile mit Weile.*

686. Exertion. — N. exertion, effort, strain, tug, pull, stress, throw, stretch, struggle, spell, spurt, spirt; stroke –, stitch- of work.

" a strong pull a long pull and a pull all together "; dead lift; heft; gymnastics; exer-cise, -citation; wear and tear; ado; toil and trouble; up-hill –, hard –, warm- work; harvest time.

labor, work, toil, travail, manual labor, sweat of one's brow, swink, operoseness, drudgery, slavery, fagging, hammering; *limæ labor;* operosity.

trouble, pains, duty; resolution &c. 604; energy &c. (*physical*) 171.

V. exert oneself; exert –, tax- one's energies; use exertion.

labor, work, toil, moil, sweat, fag,

687. Repose. — N. repose, rest, silken repose; sleep &c. 683.

relaxation, breathing time; halt, stay, pause &c. (*cessation*) 142; respite.

day of rest, *dies non,* Sabbath, Lord's day, holiday, red-letter day, vacation, recess.

V. repose; rest, – and be thankful; take -rest, – one's ease.

relax, unbend, slacken; take breath &c. (*refresh*) 689; rest upon one's oars; pause &c. (*cease*) 142; stay one's hand.

lie down; recline, – on a bed of down, – on an easy chair; go to -rest, – bed, – sleep &c. 683.

take a holiday, shut up shop; lie fallow &c. (*inaction*) 681.

Adj. reposing &c. *v.*; unstrained.

drudge, slave, drag a lengthened chain, wade through, strive, strain; make –, stretch- a long arm; pull, tug, ply; ply –, tug at- the oar; do the work; take the laboring oar.

Adv. at rest.

Phr. " the best of men have ever loved repose " [Thomson]; " to repair our nature with comforting repose " [*Henry VIII*].

bestir oneself (*be active*) 682; take trouble, trouble oneself.

work hard; rough it; put forth -one's strength, – a strong arm; fall to work, bend the bow; buckle to, set one's shoulder to the wheel &c. (*resolution*) 604; work like a -horse, – cart horse, – galley slave, – coal heaver; labor –, work- day and night; redouble one's efforts; do double duty; work double -hours, – tides; sit up, burn the candle at both ends; stick to &c. (*persevere*) 604*a*; work –, fight- one's way; lay about one, hammer at.

take pains; do one's -best, – level best, – utmost; do -the best one can, – all one can, – all in one's power, – as much as in one lies, – what lies in one's power; use one's -best, – utmost- endeavor; try one's -best, – utmost; play one's best card; put one's -best, – right- leg foremost; have one's whole soul in his work, put all one's strength into, strain every nerve; spare no -efforts, pains; go all lengths; go through fire and water &c. (*resolution*) 604; move heaven and earth, leave no stone unturned.

Adj. laboring &c. *v.*

laborious, operose, elaborate; strained; toil-, trouble-, weari-some; uphill; herculean, gymnastic, palestric.

hardworking, painstaking, strenuous, energetic.

hard at work, on the stretch.

Adv. laboriously &c. *adj.*; lustily; *pugnis et calcibus;* with -might and main, – all one's might, – a strong hand; – sledge hammer, – much ado; to the best of one's abilities, *totis viribus, vi et armis, manibus pedibusque,* tooth and nail, *unguibus et rostro,* hammer and tongs, heart and soul; through thick and thin &c. (*perseverance*) 604*a*.

by the sweat of one's brow, *suo Marte.*

Phr. *aide-toi, le ciel t'aidera;* " and still be doing, never done " [Butler]; *buen principio la mitad es hecha; cosa ben fatta è fatta due volte;* " it is better to wear out than to rust out " [Bp. Horne]; *labor omnia vincit* [Vergil]; " labor, wide as the earth, has its summit in Heaven " [Carlyle]; *le travail du corps délivre des peines de l'esprit; manu forti; ora et labora.*

---

688. Fatigue. — N. fatigue; weariness &c. 841; yawning, drowsiness &c. 683; lassitude, tiredness, fatigation †, exhaustion; sweat; dyspnœa.

anhelation, shortness of breath; faintness; collapse, prostration, swoon, fainting, deliquium, syncope, lipothymy; goneness.

V. be -fatigued &c. *adj.*; yawn &c. (*get sleepy*) 683; droop, sink, flag; lose -breath, – wind; gasp, pant, puff, blow, drop, swoon, faint, succumb.

fatigue, tire, weary, irk, flag, jade, harass, exhaust, knock up, wear out, prostrate.

tax, task, strain; over-task, -work, -burden, -tax, -strain.

Adj. fatigued &c. *v.*; weary &c. 841; drowsy &c. 683; drooping &c. *v.*; haggard; toil-, wayworn; footsore, surbated †, weather-beaten; faint; done –,

689. Refreshment. — N. bracing &c. *v.*; recovery of -strength &c. 159; restoration, revival &c. 660; repair, refection, refocillation †, refreshment, regalement, bait; relief &c. 834.

V. brace &c. (*strengthen*) 159; reinvigorate; air, freshen up, refresh, recruit; repair &c. (*restore*) 660; fan, refocillate †; refresh the inner man.

breathe, respire; drink in the ozone; draw –, take –, gather –, take a long –, regain –, recover- breath; get better, raise one's head; recover –, regain –, renew- one's strength &c. 159; perk up.

come to oneself &c. (*revive*) 660; feel like a giant refreshed.

Adj. refreshing &c. *v.*; recuperative &c. 660.

refreshed &c. *v.*; un-tired, -wearied.

used –, knocked- up; bushed * [U. S.]; exhausted, prostrate, spent; over-tired, –spent, -fatigued; unre-freshed, -stored.

worn, – out; battered, shattered, pulled down, seedy, altered.

breath-, wind-less; short of –, out of -breath, – wind; blown, puffing and blowing; short-breathed; anhelose; broken-, short-winded; dyspnœ-al, -ic.

ready to drop, all in, more dead than alive, dog-weary, walked off one's legs, tired to death, on one's last legs, played out, *hors de combat*.

fatiguing &c. *v.*; tire-, irk-, weari-some; weary, trying.

690. Agent. — N. doer, actor, agent, performer, perpetrator, operator; execu-tor, -trix; practitioner, worker, stager.

bee, ant, working bee, termite, white ant; laboring oar, servant of all work, factotum.

workman, artisan; crafts-, handicrafts-man; mechanic, operative; working –, laboring- man; demiurgus, hewers of wood and drawers of water, laborer, navvy; hand, man, day laborer, journeyman, charwoman, hack; mere -tool &c. 633; beast of burden, drudge, fag; lumper, roustabout.

maker, artificer, artist, wright, manufacturer, architect, builder, mason, bricklayer, smith, forger, Vulcan; carpenter; ganger, platelayer; blacksmith, locksmith, sailmaker, wheelwright.

machinist, mechanician, engineer.

semp-, sem-, seam-stress; needle-, work-woman; tailor, cordwainer.

minister &c. (*instrument*) 631; servant &c. 746; representative &c. (*commissioner*) 758, (*deputy*) 759.

coworker, party to, participator in, *particeps criminis, dramatis personæ; personnel*.

Phr. *quorum pars magna fui* [Vergil]; *faber est quisque fortunæ suæ*.

691. Workshop. — N. work-shop, -house; laboratory, manufactory, mill, factory, mint, forge, loom; cabinet, studio, bureau, *atelier;* hive, – of industry; nursery; hot-house, -bed; kitchen; dock, -yard; alveary; armory; beehive, bindery, forcing pit, nailery, *usine*, slip, yard, wharf; found-ry -ery; furnace; vine-yard.

crucible, alembic, caldron, matrix.

2. Complex Voluntary Action

692. Conduct. — N. dealing, transaction &c. (*action*) 680; business &c. 625.

tactics, game, policy, polity; general-, statesman-, seaman-ship; strate-gy, -gics; plan &c. 626.

husbandry; house-keeping, -wifery; stewardship; ménage; régime; econom-y, -ics; political economy; management; government &c. (*direction*) 693.

execution, manipulation, treatment, campaign, career, life, course, walk, race, record.

conduct; behavior; de-, com-portment; carriage, *maintien*, demeanor, guise, bearing, manner, observance.

course –, line- of -conduct, – action, – proceeding; rôle; process, ways, practice, procedure, *modus operandi;* method &c., path &c. 627.

V. transact, execute; des-, dis-patch; proceed with, discharge; carry -on, – through, – out, – into effect; work out; go –, get- through; enact; put into practice; officiate &c. 625.

bear –, behave –, comport –, demean –, carry –, conduct –, acquit- oneself.

run a race, lead a life, play a game; take –, adopt- a course; steer –, shape-one's course; play one's- -part, – cards; shift for oneself; paddle one's own canoe; bail one's own boat.

conduct; manage &c. (*direct*) 693.

squatulate [U. S.], cut one's stick, walk one's chalks, show a light pair of heels, make oneself scarce; escape &c. 671; go away &c. (*depart*) 293; abandon &c. 624; reject &c. 610.

lead one a -dance, – pretty dance; throw off the scent, play at hide and seek.

Adj. unsought, unattempted; avoiding &c. *v.*; neutral; shy of &c. (*unwilling*) 603; elusive, evasive; fugitive, runaway; shy, wild.

Adj. lest, in order to avoid.

Int. forbear! keep –, hands- off! *sauve qui peut!* devil take the hindmost!

Phr. " things unattempted yet in prose or rhyme " [*Paradise Lost*].

624. Relinquishment. — N. relinquish-, abandon-ment; desertion, defection, secession, withdrawal; cave of Adullam; *nolle prosequi.*

discontinuance &c. (*cessation*) 142; renunciation &c. (*recantation*) 607; abrogation &c. 756; resignation &c. (*retirement*) 757; desuetude &c. 614; cession &c. (*of property*) 782.

V. relinquish, give up, abandon, desert, forsake, leave in the lurch; go back on; depart –, secede –, withdraw- from; back out of; leave, quit, take leave of, bid a long farewell; vacate &c. (*resign*) 757.

renounce &c. (*abjure*) 607; forego, have done with, drop; disuse &c. 678; discard &c. 782; wash one's hands of; drop all idea of.

break –, leave- off; desist; stop &c. (*cease*) 142; hold –, stay- one's hand; quit one's hold; give over, shut up shop.

throw up the -game, – cards; give up the -point, – argument; pass to the order of the day, move the previous question.

Adj. unpursued; relinquished &c. *v.*; relinquishing &c. *v.*

Int. avast! &c. (*stop*) 142.

Phr. *aufgeschoben ist nicht aufgehoben; entbehre gern was du nicht hast.*

625. Business. — N. business, occupation, employment; pursuit &c. 622; what one is -doing, – about; affair, concern, matter, case.

matter in hand, irons in the fire; thing to do, agendum, task, work, job, chore [U. S.], errand, commission, mission, charge, care; duty &c. 926.

part, rôle, cue; province, function, lookout, department, capacity, sphere, orb, field, line; walk, – of life; beat, round, routine; race, career.

office, place, post, chargeship, incumbency, living; situation, berth, employ; service &c. (*servitude*) 749; engagement; undertaking &c. 676.

vocation, calling, profession, cloth, faculty; industry, art; industrial arts; craft, mystery, handicraft; trade &c. (*commerce*) 794.

exercise; work &c. (*action*) 680; avocation; press of business &c. (*activity*) 682.

V. pass –, employ –, spend- one's time in; employ oneself -in, – upon; occupy –, concern- oneself with; make it one's -business &c. *n.*; undertake &c. 676; enter a profession; betake oneself to, turn one's hand to; have to do with &c. (*do*) 680.

drive a trade; carry on –, do –, transact- -business, – a trade &c. *n.*; keep a shop; ply one's -task, – trade; labor in one's vocation; pursue the even tenor of one's way; attend to -business, – one's work.

officiate, serve, act; act –, play- one's part; do duty; serve –, discharge –, perform- the -office, – duties, – functions- of; hold –, fill- -an office, – a place, – a situation; hold a portfolio.

be -about, – doing, – engaged in, – employed in, – occupied with, – at work on; have one's hands in, have in hand; have on one's -hands, – shoulders; bear the burden; have one's hands full &c. (*activity*) 682.

be -in the hands of, – on the stocks, – on the anvil; pass through one's hands.

Adj. businesslike; workaday; professional; official, functional; busy &c. (*actively employed*) 682; on –, in- -hand, – one's hands; afoot; on -foot, – the anvil; going on; acting.

Adv. in the course of business, all in one's day's work; professionally &c. *adj.*

Phr. "a business with an income at its heels" [Cowper]; *amoto quæramus seria ludo* [Horace]; *par negotiis neque supra* [Tacitus].

626. Plan. — **N.** plan, scheme, design, project; propos-al, -ition; suggestion; resolution, motion; precaution &c. (*provision*) 673; deep-laid &c. (*premeditated*) 611- plan &c.

system &c. (*order*) 58; organization &c. (*arrangement*) 60; germ &c. (*cause*) 153.

sketch, skeleton, outline, draught, draft, *ébauche, brouillon;* rough -cast, - draft, – draught, – copy; copy; proof, revise.

forecast, program(me), prospectus; *carte du pays;* card; bill, protocol; order of the day, list of agenda; bill of fare &c. (*food*) 298; base of operations; platform, plank, slate [U. S.], ticket [U. S.].

rôle; policy &c. (*line of conduct*) 692.

contrivance, invention, expedient, receipt, nostrum, artifice, device; pipelaying [U. S.]; stratagem &c. (*cunning*) 702; trick &c. (*deception*) 545; alternative, loophole; shift &c. (*substitute*) 147; last shift &c. (*necessity*) 601.

measure, step; stroke, – of policy; master stroke; trump-, court-card; *cheval de bataille*, great gun; *coup, – d'état;* clever -, bold -, good- -move, – hit, – stroke; bright -thought, – idea.

intrigue, cabal, plot, conspiracy, complot, machination; under-, counter-plot.

schem-er, -ist, -atist †; strategist, machinator; projector, artist, promoter, designer &c. *v.*; conspirator; intrigant &c. (*cunning*) 702.

V. plan, scheme, design, frame, contrive, project, forecast, sketch; devise, invent &c. (*imagine*) 515; set one's wits to work &c. 515; spring a project; fall -, hit- upon; strike -, chalk -, cut -, lay -, map- out; lay down a plan; shape -, mark- out a course; predetermine &c. 611; concert, preconcert, preëstablish; prepare &c. 673; hatch, – a plot; concoct; take -steps, – measures.

cast, recast, systematize, organize; arrange &c. 60; digest, mature.

plot; counter-plot, -mine; dig a mine; lay a train; intrigue &c. (*cunning*) 702.

Adj. planned &c. *v.*; strategic, -al; planning &c. *v.*; in course of preparation &c. 673; under consideration; on the -tapis, – carpet.

627. Method. [Path.] — **N.** method, way, manner, wise, gait, form, mode, fashion, tone, guise; *modus operandi;* procedure &c. (*line of conduct*) 692.

path, road, route, course; line of -way, – road; trajectory, orbit, track, beat, tack.

steps; stair, -case; flight of stairs, ladder, stile; perron.

bridge, footbridge, viaduct, pontoon, stepping-stone, plank, gangway; drawbridge; pass, ford, ferry, tunnel; pipe &c. 260.

door; gateway &c. (*opening*) 260; channel, passage, avenue, means of access, approach, adit; artery, lane, alley, aisle, lobby, corridor; back-door, -stairs; secret passage; covert way; vennel.

road-, path-, stair-way; express; thoroughfare; highway; turnpike -, royal -, coach- road; broad -, King's -, Queen's- highway; beaten -track, – path; horse -, bridle- road, – track, – path; walk, *trottoir*, footpath, pavement, flags, sidewalk; by -, cross- -road, – path, – way; cut; short -cut &c. (*mid-course*) 628; *carrefour;* private -, occupation- road; highways and byways; rail-, tram--road, -way; towpath; causeway; canal &c. (*conduit*) 350; street &c. (*abode*) 189; speedway.

Adv. how; in what -way, – manner; by what mode; so, in this way, after this fashion.

one way or another, anyhow; somehow or other &c. (*instrumentality*) 631; by way of; *viâ; in transitu* &c. 270; on the high road to.

Phr. *hæ tibi erunt artes.*

deal –, have to do- with; treat, handle a case; take -steps, – measures.

Adj. conducting &c. *v.*; strategical, businesslike, practical, executive.

693. Direction. — **N.** direction; manage-ment, -ry; government, gubernation, conduct, legislation, regulation, guidance; bossism [U. S.]; legislature; steer-, pilot-age; reins, – of government; helm, rudder, needle, compass; guiding –, load –, lode –, pole- star; cynosure.

super-vision, -intendence; surveillance, oversight; eye of the master; control, charge; board of control &c. (*council*) 696; command &c. (*authority*) 737.

premier-, senator-ship; director &c. 694; chair, portfolio.

statesmanship; state-, king-, queen-craft.

minis-try, -tration; administration; steward-, proctor-ship; agency.

V. direct, manage, govern, conduct; order, prescribe, cut out work for; head, lead; lead –, show- the way; take the lead, lead on; regulate, guide, steer, pilot; take –, be at- the helm; have –, handle –, hold –, take- the reins; drive, tool; tackle.

super-intend, -vise; overlook, control, keep in order, look after, see to, legislate for; administer, ministrate; matronize; have the -care, – charge- of; have –, take- the direction; pull the -strings, – wires; rule &c. (*command*) 737; have –, hold- -office, – the portfolio; preside, – at the board; take –, occupy –, be in- the chair; pull the stroke oar.

Adj. directing &c. *v.*; hegemonic.

Adv. at the -helm, – head of.

694. Director. — **N.** director, manager, governor, rector, comptroller; super-intendent, -visor; intendant; over-seer, -looker; supercargo, husband, inspector, visitor, ranger, surveyor, ædile, moderator; monitor, taskmaster; master &c. 745; leader, ringleader, demagogue, corypheus, conductor, fugleman, precentor, bellwether, agitator; *caporal*, choregus, collector, file leader, flugelman, linkboy.

guiding star &c. (*guidance*) 693; adviser &c. 695; guide &c. (*information*) 527; pilot; helmsman; steers-man, -mate; wire-puller.

driver, whip, Jehu, charioteer; coach-, car-, cab-man; postilion, *vetturino*, muleteer, *arriero*, teamster; whipper in.

head, – man, – center; principal, president, speaker; chair, -man; captain &c. (*master*) 745; superior; mayor &c. (*civil authority*) 745; vice president, prime minister, premier, vizier, grand vizier, eparch.

officer, functionary, minister, official, red-tapist, bureaucrat; man –, Jack- in office; office bearer; person in authority &c. 745.

statesman, strategist, legislator, lawgiver, politician, statist, statemonger; Minos, Draco; arbiter &c. (*judge*) 967; boss * [U. S.], political dictator.

board &c. (*council*) 696.

secretary, – of state; Reis Effendi; vicar &c. (*deputy*) 759; steward, factor; agent &c. 758; bailiff, middleman; foreman, clerk of works; landreeve; factotum, major-domo, seneschal, housekeeper, shepherd, croupier; proctor, procurator.

Adv. *ex officio.*

695. Advice. — **N.** advice, counsel, adhortation †; word to the wise; suggestion, submonition †, recommendation, advocacy; advisement.

exhortation &c. (*persuasion*) 615; expostulation &c. (*dissuasion*) 616; admonition &c. (*warning*) 668; guidance &c. (*direction*) 693.

instruction, charge, injunction, obtestation; Governor's –, President's- message; King's –, Queen's- speech; message, speech from the throne.

adviser, prompter; counsel, -or; monitor, mentor, Nestor, *magnus Apollo*, senator; teacher &c. 540.

guide, manual, chart &c. (*information*) 527.

physician, leech, archiater; arbiter &c. (*judge*) 967.

refer-ence, -ment; consultation, conference, *pourparler*.

V. advise, counsel; give -advice, – counsel, – a piece of advice; suggest, prompt, submonish †, recommend, prescribe, advocate; exhort &c. (*persuade*) 615.

enjoin, enforce, charge, instruct, call; call upon &c. (*request*) 765; dictate.

expostulate &c. (*dissuade*) 616; admonish &c. (*warn*) 668.

advise with; lay heads –, consult- together; compare notes; hold a council, deliberate, be closeted with.

confer, consult, refer to, call in; take –, follow- advice; be advised by, have at one's elbow, take one's cue from.

Adj. recommendatory; hortative &c. (*persuasive*) 615; dehortatory &c. (*dissuasive*) 616; admonitory &c. (*warning*) 668.

Int. go to!

Phr. " give every man thine ear but few thy voice " [*Hamlet*]; " I pray thee cease thy counsel " [*Much Ado About Nothing*]; " my guide, philosopher and friend " [Pope]; " 'twas good advice and meant, my son be good " [Crabbe]; *verbum sat sapienti; vive memor leti;* " we ask advice but we mean approbation " [Colton].

696. Council. — N. council, committee, subcommittee, comitia, court, chamber, cabinet, board, bench, staff.

senate, *senatus*, parliament, chamber of deputies, directory, *reichsrath*, rigsdag, cortes, storthing, witenagemote, junta, divan, musnud, sanhedrim; audience –, council –, state- chamber; classis; Amphictyonic council; duma, house of representatives; legislative -assembly, – council; riksdag, *volksraad*, witan, caput, consistory, chapter, syndicate; court of appeal &c. (*tribunal*) 966; board of -control, – works; vestry; county council, local board.

cabinet –, privy- council; cockpit, convocation, synod, congress, convention, diet, states-general.

assembly, caucus, conclave, clique, conventicle; meeting, sitting, séance, conference, session, palaver, *pourparler*, durbar, house; quorum; council fire [N. Am.], powwow [U. S.], primary [U. S.].

senator; member, – of parliament; councilor, M. P., representative of the people; assemblyman, congressman.

Adj. senatorial, curule; congressional, parliamentary.

697. Precept. — N. precept, direction, instruction, charge; prescript, -ion; recipe, receipt; golden rule; maxim &c. 496.

rule, canon, law, code, *corpus juris, lex scripta*, act, statute, rubric, stage direction, regulation; form, -ula, -ulary; technicality; canon law; norm.

order &c. (*command*) 741.

698. Skill. — N. skill, skillfulness, address; dexter-ity, -ousness; adroitness, expertness &c. *adj.*; proficiency, competence, craft, callidity, facility, knack, trick, sleight; master-y, -ship; excellence, panurgy; ambidext-erity, -rousness; sleight of hand &c. (*deception*) 545.

sea-, air-, marks-, horse-manship; rope-dancing.

accomplish-, acquire-, attain-ment; art, science; techn-icality, -ology; practical –, technical- knowledge.

knowledge of the world, world wisdom, *savoir faire;* tact; mother wit &c. (*sagacity*) 498; discretion &c. (*caution*) 864; finesse; craftiness &c. (*cunning*)

699. Unskillfulness. — N. unskillfulness &c. *adj.*; want of -skill &c. 698; incompeten-ce, -cy; in-ability, -felicity, -dexterity, -experience; disqualification, unproficiency; quackery.

folly, stupidity &c. 499; indiscretion &c. (*rashness*) 863; thoughtlessness &c. (*inattention*) 458 (*neglect*) 460; sabotage.

mis-management, -conduct; impolicy; maladministration; mis-rule, -government, -application, -direction, -feasance; petticoat government.

absence of rule, rule of thumb; bungling &c. *v.*; failure &c. 732; screw loose; too many cooks.

blunder &c. (*mistake*) 495; *étourderie,*

702; management &c. (*conduct*) 692; self-help.

cleverness, talent, ability, ingenuity, capacity, parts, talents, faculty, endowment, forte, turn, gift, genius; intelligence &c. 498; sharpness, readiness &c. (*activity*) 682; invention &c. 515; apt-ness, -itude; turn –, capacity –, genius- for; felicity, capability, *curiosa felicitas*, qualification, habilitation.

proficient &c. 700.

masterpiece, *coup de maître, chef d'œuvre, tour de force;* good stroke &c. (*plan*) 626.

V. be -skillful &c. *adj.;* excel in, be master of; have -a turn for &c. *n.*

know -what's what, – a hawk from a handsaw, – what one is about, – on which side one's bread is buttered, – what's o'clock; have cut one's -eye, – wisdom- teeth.

see -one's way, – where the wind lies, – which way the wind blows; have -all one's wits about one, – one's hand in; *savoir vivre; scire quid valeant humeri quid ferre recusent.*

look after the main chance; cut one's coat according to one's cloth; live by one's wits; exercise one's discretion, feather the oar, sail near the wind; stoop to conquer &c. (*cunning*) 702; play one's -cards well, – best card; hit the right nail on the head, put the saddle on the right horse.

take advantage of, make the most of; profit by &c. (*use*) 677; make a hit &c. (*succeed*) 731; make a virtue of necessity; make hay while the sun shines &c. (*occasion*) 134.

Adj. skillful, dexterous, adroit, expert, apt, handy, quick, deft, ready, gain; slick, smart &c. (*active*) 682; proficient, good at, up to, at home in, master of, a good hand at, *au fait*, thoroughbred, masterly, crack, accomplished; conversant &c. (*knowing*) 490.

experienced, practiced, skilled, hackneyed; up –, well up- in; in -practice, – proper cue; competent, efficient, qualified, capable, fitted, fit for, up to the mark, trained, initiated, prepared, primed, finished.

clever, cute, able, ingenious, felicitous, gifted, talented, endowed; inventive &c. 515; shrewd, sharp &c. (*intelligent*) 498; cunning &c. 702; alive to, un

gaucherie, act of folly, *balourdise;* botch, -ery; bad job, sad work.

sprat sent out to catch a whale, much ado about nothing, wild-goose chase.

bungler &c. 701; fool &c. 501.

V. be -unskillful &c. *adj.;* not see an inch beyond one's nose; blunder, bungle, boggle, fumble, botch, bitch †, flounder, stumble, trip; hobble &c. 275; put one's foot in it; make a -mess, – hash, – sad work- of; overshoot the mark.

play -tricks .with, – Puck; mis-manage, -conduct, -direct, -apply, -send.

stultify –, make a fool of –, commit-oneself; act foolishly; play the fool; put oneself out of court; lose one's -head, – cunning.

begin at the wrong end; do things by halves &c. (*not complete*) 730; make two bites of a cherry; play at cross purposes; strain at a gnat and swallow a camel &c. (*caprice*) 608; put the cart before the horse; lock the stable door when the horse is stolen &c. (*too late*) 135.

not know -what one is about, – one's own interest, – on which side one's bread is buttered; stand in one's own light, quarrel with one's bread and butter, throw a stone in one's own garden, kill the goose which lays the golden eggs, pay dear for one's whistle, cut one's own throat, burn one's fingers; knock –, run- one's head against a stone wall; fall into a trap, catch a Tartar, bring the house about one's ears; have too many -eggs in one basket (*imprudent*) 863, – irons in the fire.

mistake &c. 495; take the shadow for the substance &c. (*credulity*) 486; bark up the wrong tree; be in the wrong box, aim at a pigeon and kill a crow; take –, get- -the wrong pig by the tail, – the wrong sow by the ear, – the dirty end of the stick; put -the saddle on the wrong horse, – a square thing into a round hole, – new wine into old bottles.

cut blocks with a razor; hold a farthing candle to the sun &c. (*useless*) 645; fight with –, grasp at- a shadow; catch at straws, lean on a broken reed, reckon without one's host, pursue a wild-goose chase; go on a fool's –, sleeveless- errand; go further and fare worse; lose –, miss- one's way; fail &c. 732.

Adj. unskillful &c. 698; inexpert;

to snuff, not to be caught with chaff; discreet.

neat-handed, fine-, nimble-fingered, ambidextrous, sure-footed; cut out -, fitted- for.

technical, artistic, scientific, dædalian, shipshape; workman-, business-, states-man-like.

Adv. skillfully &c. *adj.*; well &c. 618; artistically; with -skill, – consummate skill; *secundum artem, suo Marte;* to the best of one's abilities &c. (*exertion*) 686.

Phr. *ars celare artem; artes honorabit; celui qui veut celui-là peut; c'est une grande habilité que de savoir cacher son habilité; expertus metuit* [Horace]; *es bildet ein Talent sich in der Stille sich ein Charakter in dem Strom der Welt; "* heart to conceive, the understanding to direct, or the hand to execute " [Junius].

bungling &c. *v.*; awkward, clumsy, un-handy, lubberly, gauche, maladroit; left-, heavy-handèd; slovenly, slatternly; gawky.

adrift, at fault.

in-, un-apt; inhabile †; un-tractable, -teachable; giddy &c. (*inattentive*) 458; inconsiderate &c. (*neglectful*) 460; stupid &c. 499; inactive &c. 683; incompetent; un-, dis-, ill-qualified; unfit; quackish; raw, green, inexperienced, rusty, out of practice.

un-accustomed, -used, -trained &c. 537, -initiated, -conversant &c. (*igno-rant*) 491; shiftless; unstatesmanlike.

un-, ill-, mis-advised; ill-devised, -imagined, -judged, -contrived, -con-ducted; un-, mis-guided; misconducted, foolish, wild; infelicitous; penny wise and pound foolish &c. (*inconsistent*) 608.

Phr. one's fingers being all thumbs; the right hand forgets its cunning; *il se noyerait dans une goutte d'eau; incidit in Scyllam qui vult vitare Charybdim;* out of the frying pan into the fire; *non omnia possumus omnes* [Vergil].

700. Proficient. — N. proficient, ex-pert, adept, dab; dabster; connoisseur &c. (*scholar*) 492; master, -hand; top sawyer, *prima donna,* first fiddle, *chef de cuisine;* protagonist; past master; mahatma.

picked man; medallist, prizeman.

veteran; old -stager, – campaigner, – soldier, – file, – hand; man of -business, – the world.

nice -, good -, clean- hand; practiced -, experienced- -eye, – hand; marks-man; good -, dead -, crack- shot; rope-dancer, funambulist, acrobat; cunning man; conjuror &c. (*deceiver*) 548; wiz-ard &c. 994.

genius; master -mind, – head, – spirit.

cunning -, sharp- -blade, – fellow; jobber; cracksman &c. (*thief*) 792; politi-cian, tactician, strategist.

pantologist, admirable Crichton, Jack of all trades; prodigy of learning.

701. Bungler. — N. bungler; blun-der-er, -head; marplot, fumbler, lubber, duffer, stick; bad -, poor- -hand, – shot; butter-fingers.

no conjuror, flat, muff, slow coach, looby, lubber, swab; clod, yokel, awk-ward squad, novice, greenhorn, *blanc-bec;* galoot.

land lubber; fresh water -, fair weather- sailor; horse marine; fish out of water, ass in lion's skin, jackdaw in peacock's feathers; quack &c. (*deceiver*) 548; lord of misrule.

sloven, slattern, trapes.

Phr. *il n'a pas inventé la poudre;* he will never set the Thames on fire; *acierta errando; aliquis in omnibus nullus in singulis.*

702. Cunning. — N. cunning, craft; cunningness, craftiness &c. *adj.*; sub-tlety, artificiality; maneuvering &c. *v.*; temporization; circumvention.

chicane, -ry; sharp practice, knavery, jugglery; concealment &c. 528; guile, doubling, duplicity &c. (*falsehood*) 544; foul play.

diplomacy, politics; Machiavelism; jobbery, back-stairs influence.

art, -ifice; device, machination; plot

703. Artlessness. — N. artlessness &c. *adj.*; nature, simplicity; innocence &c. 946; *bonhomie, naïveté, abandon,* candor, sincerity; singleness of -pur-pose, – heart; honesty &c. 939; plain speaking; *épanchement.*

rough diamond, matter of fact man; *le palais de vérité; enfant terrible.*

V. be -artless &c. *adj.*; look one in the face; wear one's heart upon his sleeves for daws to peck at; think aloud;

&c. (*plan*) 626; maneuver, stratagem, dodge, artful dodge, wile; trick, -ery &c. (*deception*) 545; ruse, – *de guerre;* finesse, side blow, thin end of the wedge, shift, go by, subterfuge, evasion; white lie &c. (*untruth*) 546; juggle, *tour de force;* tricks -of the trade, – upon travelers; *espiéglerie;* net, trap &c. 545.

Ulysses, Machiavel, sly boots, fox, reynard; Scotchman; Jew, Yankee; intriguer, intrigant; floater [U. S.], Indian giver [U. S.], keener [U. S.], repeater [U. S. *politics*].

V. be -cunning &c. *adj.*; have cut one's eyeteeth; contrive &c. (*plan*) 626; live by one's wits; maneuver; intrigue, gerrymander, finesse, double, temporize, stoop to conquer, *reculer pour mieux sauter*, circumvent, steal a march upon; overreach &c. 545; throw off one's guard; surprise &c. 508; snatch a verdict; waylay, undermine, introduce the thin end of the wedge; play -a deep game, – tricks with; *ambiguas in vulgum spargere voces;* flatter, make things pleasant; have an ax to grind.

Adj. cunning, crafty, artful; skillful &c. 698; subtle, feline, vulpine; cunning as a -fox, – serpent; deep, – laid; profound; designing, contriving; intriguing &c. *v.*; strategic, diplomatic, politic, Machiavelian, timeserving; artificial; trick-y, -sy; wily, sly, slim, insidious, stealthy; underhand &c. (*hidden*) 528; subdolous; deceitful &c. 545; crooked; arch, pawky, shrewd, acute; sharp, – as a needle; canny, astute, leery, knowing, up to snuff, too clever by half, not to be caught with chaff.

Adv. cunningly &c. *adj.*; slily, on the sly, by a side wind.

Phr. diamond cut diamond; *à bis ou à blanc; fin contre fin;* " something is rotten in the state of Denmark " [*Hamlet*].

speak -out, – one's mind; be free with one, call a spade a spade.

Adj. artless, natural, pure, native, confiding, simple, plain, inartificial, untutored, unsophisticated, *ingénu*, unaffected, naïve; sincere, frank; open, – as day; candid, ingenuous, guileless; unsuspicious, honest &c. 939; innocent &c. 946; Arcadian; undesigning, straightforward, unreserved, aboveboard; simple-, single-minded; frank-, open-, single-, simple-hearted.

free-, plain-, out-spoken; blunt, downright, direct, matter of fact, unpoetical; unflattering.

Adv. in plain -words, – English; without mincing the matter; not to mince the matter &c. (*affirmation*) 535.

Phr. *Davus sum non Œdipus* [Terence]; *liberavi animam meam;* " as frank as rain on cherry-blossoms " [E. B. Browning].

Section IV. ANTAGONISM

1. *Conditional Antagonism*

704. Difficulty. — **N.** difficulty; hardness &c. *adj.*; impracticability &c. (*impossibility*) 471; tough -, hard -, uphill-work; hard –, Herculean –, Augean-task; task of Sisyphus, Sisyphean labor, tough job, teaser, rasper, dead lift.

dilemma, embarrassment; deadlock; perplexity &c. (*uncertainty*) 475; intricacy; entanglement &c. 59; cross fire; awkwardness, delicacy, ticklish card to play, knot, Gordian knot, *dignus vindice nodus*, net, meshes, maze; coil &c. (*convolution*) 248; crooked path; involvement.

nice -, delicate -, subtle -, knotty-point; vexed question, *vexata quæstio*, poser; puzzle &c. (*riddle*) 533; paradox; hard -, nut to crack; bone to pick,

705. Facility. — **N.** facility, ease; easiness &c. *adj.*; capability; feasibility &c. (*practicability*) 470; flexibility, pliancy &c. 324; smoothness &c. 255.

plain -, smooth -, straight- sailing; mere child's play, holiday task; cinch [U. S.].

smooth water, fair wind; smooth -, royal- road; clear -coast, – stage; *tabula rasa;* full play &c. (*freedom*) 748.

disen-cumbrance, -tanglement; deoppilation; permission &c. 760.

V. be -easy &c. *adj.*; go on -, run- smoothly; have -full play &c. *n.*; go -, run- on all fours; obey the helm, work well.

flow -, swim -, drift -, go- with the- -stream, – tide; see one's way; have -it

crux, *pons asinorum*, where the shoe pinches.

nonplus, quandary, strait, pass, pinch, pretty pass, stress, brunt; critical situation, crisis; trial, rub, emergency, exigency, scramble.

scrape, hobble, slough, quagmire, hot water, hornet's nest; sea –, peck- of troubles; pretty kettle of fish; pickle, stew, imbroglio, mess, ado; false position; set fast, stand; dead -lock, – set; fix, horns of a dilemma, *cul de sac;* hitch; stumbling block &c. (*hindrance*) 706.

V. be -difficult &c. *adj.*; run one hard, go against the grain, try one's patience, put one out; put to one's -shifts, – wit's end; go hard with –, try- one; pose, perplex &c. (*uncertain*) 475; bother, nonplus, gravel, bring to a deadlock; be -impossible &c. 471; be in the way of &c. (*hinder*) 706.

meet with –, labor under –, get into –, plunge into –, struggle with –, contend with –, grapple with- difficulties; labor under a disadvantage; be -in difficulty &c. *adj.*

fish in troubled waters, ·buffet the waves, swim against the stream, scud under bare poles.

have -much ado with, – a hard time of it; come to the -push, – pinch; bear the brunt.

grope in the dark, lose one's way, weave a tangled web, walk among eggs.

get into a -scrape &c. *n.*; bring a hornet's nest about one's ears; be put to one's shifts; flounder, boggle, struggle; not know which way to turn &c. (*uncertain*) 475; *perdre son Latin;* stick -at, – in the mud, – fast; come to a -stand, – deadlock; hold the wolf by the ears.

all one's own way, – the game in one's own hands; walk over the course, win at a canter; make -light of, – nothing of, – no bones of; be at home in &c. (*skillful*) 698.

render -easy &c. *adj.*; facilitate, smooth, ease; popularize; lighten, – the labor; free, clear; dis-encumber, -embarrass, -entangle, -engage; deobstruct, unclog, extricate, unravel; untie –, cut- the knot; disburden, unload, exonerate, emancipate, free from, deoppilate; humor &c. (*aid*) 707; lubricate &c. 332; relieve &c. 834.

leave -a hole to creep out of, – a loophole, – the matter open; give -the reins to, – full play, – full swing; make way for; open the -door to, – way; prepare –, smooth –, clear- the -ground, – way, – path, – road; pave the way; bridge over; permit &c. 760.

Adj. easy, facile; feasible &c. (*practicable*) 470; easily -managed, – accomplished; within reach, accessible, easy of access, for the million, open to.

manageable, wieldy; towardly, tractable; submissive; yielding, ductile; suant; pliant &c. (*soft*) 324; glib, slippery; smooth &c. 255; on -friction wheels, – velvet.

un-, dis-burdened, -encumbered, -embarrassed; exonerated; un-loaded, -obstructed, -trammeled; unrestrained &c. (*free*) 748; at ease, light.

at –, quite at- home; in -one's element, –smooth water.

Adv. easily &c. *adj.*; readily, smoothly, swimmingly, on easy terms, single-handed.

Phr. touch and go.

render -difficult &c. *adj.*; enmesh, encumber, embarrass, ravel, entangle; put a spoke in the wheel &c. (*hinder*) 706; lead a pretty dance.

Adj. difficult, not easy, hard, tough; trouble-, toil-, irk-some; operose, laborious, onerous, arduous, Herculean, formidable; sooner –, more easily- said than done; difficult –, hard- to deal with; ill-conditioned, crabbed; not -to be handled with kid gloves, – made with rose water.

awkward, unwieldy, unmanageable; intractable, stubborn &c. (*obstinate*) 606; perverse, refractory, plaguy, trying, thorny, rugged; knot-ted, -ty; invious †; path-, track-less; labyrinthine &c. (*convoluted*) 248; intricate, complicated &c. (*tangled*) 59; impracticable &c. (*impossible*) 471; not -feasible &c. 470; desperate &c. (*hopeless*) 859.

embarrassing, perplexing &c. (*uncertain*) 475; delicate, ticklish, critical; beset with –, full of –, surrounded by –, entangled by –, encompassed with- difficulties.

under a difficulty; in a box; in -difficulty, – hot water, – the suds, – a cleft

stick, – a fix, – the wrong box, – a scrape &c. *n.*, – deep water, – a fine pickle; *in extremis;* between -two stools, – Scylla and Charybdis; surrounded by -shoals, – breakers, – quicksands; at cross purposes; not out of the wood.

reduced to straits; hard –, sorely- pressed; run hard; pinched, put to it, straitened; hard -up, – put to it, – set; put to one's shifts; puzzled, at a loss, &c. (*uncertain*) 475; at -the end of one's tether, – one's wit's end, – a nonplus, – a standstill; graveled, nonplussed, stranded, aground; stuck –, set- fast; up a tree, at bay, *aux abois,* driven -into a corner, – from post to pillar, – to extremity, – to one's wit's end, – to the wall; *au bout de son Latin;* out of one's depth; thrown out.

accomplished with difficulty; hard-fought, -earned.

Adv. with -difficulty, – much ado; hardly &c. *adj.*; uphill; against the -stream, – grain; *à rebours; invitâ Minervâ;* in the teeth of; at –, upon- a pinch; at long odds.

Phr. "ay there's the rub" [*Hamlet*]; *hic labor hoc opus* [Vergil]; things are come to a pretty pass, *ab inconvenienti; ad astra per aspera; aucun chemin de fleurs ne conduit á la gloire.*

2. *Active Antagonism*

706. Hindrance. — N. prevention, preclusion, obstruction, stoppage; embolus; inter-ruption, -ception, -clusion †; hindrance, impedition †; retard-ment, -ation; embarrassment, oppilation; co-arctation, stricture, restriction; infarct; restraint &c. 751; inhibition &c. 761; blockade &c. (*closure*) 261.

inter-ference, -position; obtrusion; dis-couragement, -countenance.

impediment, let, obstacle, obstruction, knot; knag; check, hitch, *contretemps,* screw loose, grit in the oil.

bar, stile, barrier; turn-stile, -pike; gate, portcullis; beaver dam; *trocha;* barricade &c. (*defense*) 717; wall, dead wall, breakwater, groyne; bulkhead, block, buffer; stopper &c. 263; boom, dam, weir, burrock.

drawback, objection; stumbling-block, -stone; lion in the path; snag; snags and sawyers.

en-, in-cumbrance; clog, skid, shoe, spoke; drag, – chain, – weight; stay, stop; preventive, prophylactic; load, burden, fardel, onus, millstone round one's neck, impedimenta; dead weight; lumber, pack; nightmare, Ephialtes, incubus, old man of the sea; remora.

difficulty &c. 704; insuperable &c. 471- obstacle; estoppel; ill wind; head wind &c. (*opposition*) 708; trammel, tether &c. (*means of restraint*) 752; hold back, counterpoise; damper, wet blanket, hinderer, marplot, kill-joy, interloper; trail of a red herring; opponent &c. 710.

707. Aid. — N. aid, -ance; assistance, help, opitulation †, succor; support, lift, advance, furtherance, promotion; co-adjuvancy &c. (*coöperation*) 709.

patronage, championship, countenance, favor, interest, advocacy.

sustentation, subvention, alimentation, nutrition, nourishment; eutrophy; manna in the wilderness; food &c. 298; means &c. 632.

ministr-y, -ation; subministration; accommodation.

relief, rescue; help at a dead lift; supernatural aid; *deus ex machinâ.*

supplies, reënforcements, succors, contingents, recruits; support &c. (*physical*) 215; adjunct, ally &c. (*helper*) 711.

V. aid, assist, help, succor, lend one's aid; come to the -aid &c. *n.*- of; contribute, subscribe to; bring –, give –, furnish –, afford –, supply- -aid &c. *n.*; give –, stretch –, lend –, bear –, hold out- a -hand, – helping hand; give one a -lift, – cast, – turn; take -by the hand, – in tow; help a lame dog over a stile, lend wings to.

relieve, rescue; set -up, – agoing, – on one's legs; bear –, pull- through; give new life to, be the making of; reënforce, recruit; set –, put –, push- forward; give -a lift, – a shove, – an impulse- to; promote, further, forward, advance; speed, expedite, quicken, hasten.

support, sustain, uphold, prop, hold up, bolster.

cradle, nourish; nurture, nurse, dry

V. hinder, impede, filibuster [U. S.], impedite †, embarrass.

keep –, stave –, ward- off; obviate; a-, ante-vert †; turn aside, draw off, prevent, forefend, nip in the bud; retard, slacken, check, let; counter-act, -check; preclude, debar, foreclose, estop; inhibit &c. 761; shackle &c. (*restrain*) 751; restrict.

obstruct, stop, stay, bar, bolt, lock; block, – up; choke off; belay, barricade; block –, stop- the way; forelay; dam up &c. (*close*) 261; put on the -brake &c. *n.*; scotch –, lock –, put a spoke in- the wheel; put a stop to &c. 142; traverse, contravene; inter-rupt, -cept; oppose &c. 708; hedge -in, – round; cut off; interclude †.

inter-pose, -fere, -meddle &c. 682.

cramp, hamper; clog, – the wheels; cumber; en- in-cumber; handicap; choke; saddle –, load- with; overload, lay; lumber, trammel, tie one's hands, put to inconvenience; in-, dis-commode; discompose; hustle, corner, drive into a corner.

run –, fall- foul of; cross the path of, break in upon.

thwart, frustrate, disconcert, balk, foil; faze, feaze, feeze [U. S.]; baffle, snub, override, circumvent; defeat &c. 731; spike guns &c. (*render useless*) 645; spoil, mar, clip the wings of; cripple &c. (*injure*) 659; put an extinguisher on; damp; dishearten &c. (*dissuade*) 616; discountenance, throw cold water on, spoil sport; lay –, throw- a wet blanket on; cut the ground from under one, take the wind out of one's sails, undermine; be –, stand- in the way of; act as a drag; hang like a millstone round one's neck.

Adj. hindering &c. *v.*; obstr-uctive, -uent; impedi-tive, -ent; intercipient †; prophylactic &c. (*remedial*) 662; impedimentary.

in the way of, unfavorable; onerous, burdensome; cumb-rous, -ersome; obtrusive.

hindered &c. *v.*; windbound, water-logged, heavy laden; hard pressed.

unassisted &c. (*see* assist· &c. 707); single-handed, alone; deserted &c. 624.

Phr. *occurrent nubes.*

nurse, suckle, put out to nurse; manure, cultivate, force; foster, cherish, foment; feed –, fan- the flame.

serve; do service to, tender to, pander to; ad-, sub-, minister to; tend, attend, wait on; take care of &c. 459; entertain; smooth the bed of death.

oblige, accommodate, consult the wishes of; humor, cheer, encourage.

second, stand by; back, – up; pay the piper, abet; work –, make interest –, stick up –, take up the cudgels- for; take up –, espouse –, adopt- the cause of; advocate, beat up for recruits, press into the service; squire, give moral support to, keep in countenance, countenance, patronize; lend -oneself, – one's countenance- to; smile –, shine- upon; favor, befriend, take in hand, enlist under the banners of; side with &c. (*coöperate*) 709.

be of use to; subserve &c. (*instrument*) 631; benefit &c. 648; render a service &c. (*utility*) 644; conduce &c. (*tend*) 176.

Adj. aiding &c. *v.*; auxiliary, adjuvant, helpful; coadjuvant &c. 709; subservient, ministrant, ancillary, accessory, subsidiary.

at one's beck; friendly, amicable, favorable, propitious, well-disposed; neighborly; obliging &c. (*benevolent*) 906:

Adv. with –, by- -the aid &c. *n.*- of; on –, in- behalf of; in -aid, – the service, – the name, – favor, – furtheranceof; on account of; for the sake of, on the part of; *non obstante.*

Int. help! save us! to the rescue!

Phr. *alterum alterius auxilio eget* [Sallust]; " God befriend us as our cause is just " [*Henry IV*].

---

708. Opposition. — N. opposition, antagonism; oppug-nancy, -nation; impugnation; contrariety; contravention; counteraction &c. 179; counterplot.

cross fire, undercurrent, head wind.

clashing, collision, conflict.

709. Coöperation. — N. coöperation; coadju-vancy, -tancy; coagency, coefficiency; concert, concurrence, complicity, participation; union &c. 43; combination &c. 48; collusion.

association, alliance, colleagueship,

competition, two of a trade, rivalry, emulation, race.

absence of -aid &c. 707; resistance &c. 719; restraint &c. 751; hindrance &c. 706.

V. oppose, counteract, run counter to; withstand &c. (*resist*) 719; control &c. (*restrain*) 751; hinder &c. 706; antagonize, oppugn, fly in the face of, go dead against, kick against, fall foul of; set -, pit- against; face, confront, cope with; make a -stand, - dead set-against; set -oneself, - one's face-against; protest -, vote -, raise one's voice- against; disfavor, turn one's back upon; set at naught, slap in the face, slam the door in one's face.

be -, play- at cross purposes; counter-work, -mine; thwart, overthwart.

stem, breast, encounter; stem -, breast- the -tide, - current, - flood; buffet the waves; beat up -, make head-against; grapple with; kick against the pricks &c. (*resist*) 719; contend &c. 720 -, do battle &c. (*warfare*) 722- -with, - against.

contra-dict, -vene; belie; go -, run -, beat -, militate- against; come in conflict with.

emulate &c. (*compete*) 720; rival, spoil one's trade.

Adj. oppos-ing, -ed &c. *v.*; adverse, antagonistic; contrary &c. 14; at variance &c. 24; at issue, at war with.

un-favorable, -friendly; hostile, inimical, cross, unpropitious.

in hostile array, front to front, with crossed bayonets, at daggers drawn; up in arms; resistant &c. 719.

competitive, emulous.

Adv. against, *versus*, counter to, in conflict with, at cross purposes.

against the -grain, - current, - stream, - wind, - tide; with a head-wind; with the wind-ahead, - in one's teeth.

in spite, in despite, in defiance; in the -way, - teeth, - face- of; across; a-, over-thwart; where the shoe pinches; in spite of one's teeth.

though &c. 30; even; *quand même*; *per contra*.

Phr. *nitor in adversum.*

joint stock, copartnership; cartel; confederation &c. (*party*) 712; coalition, fusion; a long pull a strong pull and a pull all together; logrolling, freemasonry.

unanimity &c. (*assent*) 488; *esprit de corps*, party spirit; clan-, partisan-ship; concord &c. 714; synergy.

V. coöperate, concur; conduce &c. 178; combine, unite one's efforts; keep -, draw -, pull -, club -, hang -, hold -, league -, band -, be banded- together; pool; stand -, put- shoulder to shoulder; act in concert, join forces, fraternize, cling to one another, conspire, concert, lay one's heads together; confederate, be in league with; collude, understand one another, play into the hands of, hunt in couples.

side -, take side -, go along -, go hand in hand -, join hands -, make common cause -, strike in -, unite -, join -, mix oneself up -, take part -, cast in one's lot- with; join -, enter into- partnership with; rally round, follow the lead of; come to, pass over to, come into the views of; be -, row -, sail- in the same boat; sail on the same tack.

be a party to, lend oneself to; chip in; participate; have a -hand in, - finger in the pie; take -, bear- part in; second &c. (*aid*) 707; take the part of, play the game of; espouse a -cause, - quarrel.

Adj. coöperating &c. *v.*; in -coöperation &c. *n.*, - league &c. (*party*) 712; coadju-vant, -tant; dyed in the wool; synerg-etic, -istic.

favorable &c. 707- to; unopposed &c. 708.

Adv. as one man &c. (*unanimously*) 488; shoulder to shoulder.

Phr. *due tesie valgono piu che una sola.*

710. Opponent. — N. opponent, antagonist, adversary; adverse party, opposition; enemy &c. 891; assailant.

oppositionist, obstructive; brawler, wrangler, brangler, disputant; filibuster [U. S.], obstructionist.

711. Auxiliary. — N. auxiliary; recruit; assistant; adju-vant, -tant; *ayudante*, co-aid; adjunct; help, -er, -mate, -ing hand; midwife; colleague, partner, mate, confrère, coöperator; coadju-tor, -trix; collaborator.

malcontent; Jacobin, Fenian; demagogue, reactionist.

rival, competitor.

inis; *socius criminis.*

aide-de-camp, secretary, clerk, associate, marshal; right-hand; candle-,
bottle-holder; handmaid; servant &c. 746; puppet, cat's-paw, jackal; tool,
âme damnée; satellite, adherent.

votary; secta-rian, -ry; seconder, backer, upholder, abettor, advocate,
partisan, champion, patron, friend at court, mediator; angel *.

friend in need, Jack at a pinch, *deus ex machinâ*, guardian angel, tutelary
genius.

ally; friend &c. 890, confidant, *fidus
Achates*, pal, *alter ego.*

confederate; ac-, complice; accessory, – after the fact; *particeps crim-*

712. Party. — **N.** party, faction, side, denomination, communion, set, crew,
band, horde, posse, phalanx; family, clan, &c. 166; team; *tong.*

community, body, fellowship, sodality, solidarity; con-, fraternity; *familis-
tère*, familistery; brother-, sister-hood.

knot, gang, clique, ring, circle; coterie, club, casino; machine; Tammany,
– Hall [U. S.].

corporation, corporate body, guild; establishment, company; co-, partnership; firm, house; joint concern, joint-stock company; cahoot *, combine [U. S.],
trust.

society, association; instit-ute, -ution; union; trades union; league, syndicate,
alliance, *Verein, Bund, Zollverein*, combination; *Turnverein;* league –, alliance-
offensive and defensive; coalition; federation; confedera-tion, -cy; junto, cabal,
camarilla, camorra, brigue †; freemasonry; party spirit &c. (*coöperation*) 709.

Confederates, Conservatives, Democrats, Federalists, Federals, Freemason,
Knight Templar; Kuklux, – Klan; Liberals, Luddites, Republicans, Socialists,
Tories, Whigs &c.

staff; *dramatis personæ.*

V. unite, join; club together &c. (*coöperate*) 709; cement –, form- a party &c.
n.; associate &c. (*assemble*) 72; enleague, federalize, go cahoots *.

Adj. in -league, – partnership, – alliance &c. *n.*

bonded –, banded –, linked &c. (*joined*) 43- together; embattled; confeder-
ated, federative, joint.

Adv. hand in hand, side by side, shoulder to shoulder, *en masse*, in the same
boat.

713. Discord. — **N.** disagreement &c.
24; dis-cord, -accord, -sidence, -so-
nance; jar, clash, shock; jarring, jost-
ling &c. *v.*; screw loose.

variance, difference, dissension, misunderstanding, cross purposes, odds,
brouillerie; division, split, rupture, dis-
ruption, division in the camp, house divided against itself, disunion, breach;
schism &c. (*dissent*) 489; feud, faction.

quarrel, dispute, tiff, *tracasserie,* squabble, altercation, barney *, *démêlé*, snarl,
spat, towrow, words, high words; wrangling &c. *v.*; jangle, brabble, cross questions and crooked answers, snip-snap;
family jars.

polemics; litigation; strife &c. (*contention*) 720; warfare &c. 722; outbreak,
open rupture, declaration of war.

714. Concord. — **N.** concord, accord,
harmony, symphony; homologue; agreement &c. 23; sympathy &c. (*love*) 897;
response; union, unison, unity; bonds
of harmony; peace &c. 721; unanimity
&c. (*assent*) 488; league &c. 712; happy
family.

rapprochement; reunion; amity &c.
(*friendship*) 888; alliance, *entente cor-
diale*, good understanding, conciliation,
peacemaker; intercessor, mediator.

V. agree &c. 23; accord, harmonize
with; fraternize; be -concordant &c.
adj.; go hand in hand; run parallel &c.
(*concur*) 178; understand one another;
pull together &c. (*coöperate*) 709; put
up one's horses together, sing in chorus.

side –, sympathize –, go –, chime in –,
fall in- with; come round; be pacified

broil, brawl, row, racket, hubbub, rixation †; embroilment, embranglement, imbroglio, fracas, breach of the peace, piece of work, scrimmage, rumpus; breeze, squall; riot, disturbance &c. (*disorder*) 59; commotion &c. (*agitation*) 315; bear garden, Donnybrook Fair.

subject of dispute, ground of quarrel, battle ground, disputed point; bone -of contention, - to pick; apple of discord, *casus belli;* question at issue &c. (*subject of inquiry*) 461; vexed question, *vexata quæstio*, brand of discord.

troublous times; cat-and-dog life; contentiousness &c. *adj.*; enmity &c. 889; hate &c. 898; Kilkenny cats; disputant &c. 710; strange bedfellows.

V. be -discordant &c. *adj.*; disagree, come amiss &c. 24; clash, jar, jostle, pull different ways, conflict, have no measures with, misunderstand one another; live like cat and dog; differ; dissent &c. 489; have a -bone to pick, - crow to pluck- with.

fall out, quarrel, dispute; litigate; controvert &c. (*deny*) 536; squabble, wrangle, jangle, brangle, bicker, nag; spar &c. (*contend*) 720; have -words &c. *n.* with; fall foul of.

split; break -, break squares -, part company- with; declare war, try conclusions; join -, put in- issue; pick a quarrel, fasten a quarrel on; sow -, stir up- -dissension &c. *n.*; embroil, entangle, disunite, widen the breach; set -at odds, - together by the ears; set -, pit- against.

get into hot water, fish in troubled waters, brawl; kick up a -row, - dust; turn the house out of window.

Adj. discordant; disagreeing &c. *v.*; out of tune, ajar, on bad terms, dissentient &c. 489; un-reconciled, -pacified.

quarrelsome, unpacific; gladiatorial, controversial, polemic, disputatious; factious; liti-gious, -gant; pettifogging.

at odds, at loggerheads, at daggers drawn, at variance, at issue, at cross purposes, at sixes and sevens, at feud, at high words; up in arms, together by the ears, in hot water, embroiled.

torn, disunited.

Phr. *quot homines tot sententiæ* [Terence]; no love lost between them, *non nostrum tantas componere lites* [Vergil]; *Mars gravior sub pace latet* [Claudius].

&c. 723; assent &c. 488; enter into the -ideas, - feelings- of; reciprocate.

hurler avec les loups; go -, swim- with the stream.

keep in good humor, render accordant, put in tune; come to an understanding, meet halfway; keep the -, remain at- peace.

Adj. concordant, congenial; agreeing &c. *v.*; in- accord &c. *n.*; harmonious, united, cemented; banded together &c. 712; allied; friendly &c. 888; fraternal; conciliatory; at one with; of one mind &c. (*assent*) 488.

at peace, in still water; tranquil &c. (*pacific*) 721.

Adv. with one voice &c. (*assent*) 488; in concert with, hand in hand; on one's side.

Phr. *commune periculum concordiam parit.*

715. Defiance. — **N.** defiance; daring &.; *v.* dare; challenge, cartel; threat &c. 909; war-cry, -whoop.

V. defy, dare, beard; brave &c. (*courage*) 861; bid defiance to; set at -defiance, - naught; hurl defiance at; dance the war dance; snap the fingers at, laugh to scorn; disobey &c. 742.

show -fight, - one's teeth, - a bold front; bluster, look big, stand akimbo; double -, shake- the fist; threaten &c. 909.

challenge, call out; throw -, fling- down the -gauntlet, - gage, - glove.

Adj. defiant; defying &c. *v.*; with arms akimbo.

Adv. in -defiance, - the teeth- of; under one's very nose.

Int. do your worst! come if you dare! come on! marry come up! hoity toity!

Phr. *noli me tangere; nemo me impune lacessit.*

716. Attack. — **N.** attack; assault, - and battery; onset, onslaught, charge.

717. Defense. — **N.** defense, protection, guard, ward; shielding &c. *v.*; pro-

aggression, offense; incursion, inroad, invasion; irruption; outbreak; estrapade, *ruade; coup de main*, sally, sortie, camisade, raid, foray; run -at, – against; dead set at.

storm, -ing; boarding, escalade; siege, investment, obsession, bombardment, cannonade.

fire, volley; platoon –, file- fire; fusillade; sharpshooting, broadside; raking –, cross- fire; volley of grapeshot, *feu d'enfer.*

cut, thrust, lunge, pass, passado, carte and tierce, home thrust; *coup de bec;* kick, punch &c. (*impulse*) 276.

battue, razzia, *Jacquerie*, dragonnade; devastation &c. 162; *éboulement.*

assailant, aggressor, invader.

base of operations, point of attack; echelon.

V. attack, assault, assail; set –, fall-upon; charge, impugn, break a lance with, enter the lists.

assume –, take- the offensive; be –, become- the aggressor; strike the first blow, throw the first stone at; lift a hand –, draw the sword- against; take up the cudgels; advance –, march-against; march upon, invade, harry; come on, show fight.

strike at, poke at, thrust at; aim –, deal- a blow at; give –, fetch- one a -blow, – kick; have a -cut, – shot, – fling, – shy- at; be down –, pounce-upon; fall foul of, pitch into, launch out against; bait, slap on the face; make a -thrust, – pass, – set, – dead set- at; bear down upon.

close with, come to close quarters, bring to bay.

ride full tilt against; let fly at, dash at, run a tilt at, rush at, tilt at, run at, fly at, hawk at, have at, let out at; make a -dash, – rush at; attack tooth and nail; strike home; drive –, press-one hard; be hard upon, run down, strike at the root of.

lay about one, run amuck.

fire -upon, – at, – a shot at; draw a bead on [U. S.]; shoot at, pop at, level at, let off a gun at; open fire, pepper, bombard, shell, pour a broadside into; fire -a volley, – red-hot shot; spring a mine.

throw -a stone, – stones- at; stone, lapidate, pelt; hurl -at, – against, – at the head of; rock [U. S.].

pugnation ?, preservation &c. 670; guardianship.

self-defense, -preservation; resistance &c. 719.

safeguard &c. (*safety*) 664; balistraria; screen &c. (*shelter*) 666 (*concealment*) 530; fortification; muni-tion, -ment; bulwark, fosse, moat, ditch, intrenchment; *kila;* dike, dyke; parapet, sunk fence, embankment, mound, mole bank; earth-, field-work; fence, wall. dead wall, contravallation; paling &c. (*inclosure*) 232; palisade, haha, stockade, stoccado, *laager*, sangar; barri-er, -cade; boom; portcullis, *chevaux de frise;* aba-, abat-, abba-tis; vallum, circumvallation, battlement, rampart, scarp; e-, counter-scarp; glacis, casemate; vallation, vanfos.

buttress, abutment; shore &c. (*support*) 215.

breastwork, banquette, curtain, mantlet, bastion, redan, ravelin; vauntmure; advanced –, horn –, out- work; barbacan, -ican; redoubt; fort-elage, -alice; lines.

loophole, machicolation; sally port.

hold, stronghold, fastness; asylum &c. (*refuge*) 666; keep, donjon, fortress, citadel, capitol, castle; tower, – of strength; fort, barracoon, pah, sconce, martello tower, peelhouse, blockhouse, rath; wooden walls.

buffer, corner stone, fender, apron, mask, gauntlet, thimble, carapace, armor, shield, buckler, ægis, breastplate, backplate, cowcatcher, face guard, scutum, cuirass, habergeon, mail, coat of mail, brigandine, hauberk, lorication, helmet, helm, bassinet, salade, heaume, morion, murrion, armet, cabaset, vizor, casquetel, siege cap, headpiece, casque, *pickethaube*, vambrace, shako &c. (*dress*) 225; bearskin; panoply; truncheon &c. (*weapon*) 727.

garrison, picket, piquet; defender, protector; guardian &c. (*safety*) 664; bodyguard, champion; knight-errant, Paladin; propugner.

V. defend, forfend, fend; shield, screen, shroud; engarrison; fence round &c. (*circumscribe*) 229; fence, intrench; guard &c. (*keep safe*) 664; guard against; take care of &c. (*vigilance*) 459; bear harmless; fend –, keep –, ward –, beat-off; hinder &c. 706.

parry, repel, propugn †, put to flight;

beset, besiege, beleaguer; lay siege to, invest, open the trenches, plant a battery, sap, mine; storm, board, scale the walls.

cut and thrust, bayonet, butt; kick, strike &c. (*impulse*) 276; whip &c. (*punish*) 972.

Adj. attacking &c. *v.*; aggressive, offensive, obsidional.

up in arms.

Adv. on the offensive.

Int. " up and at them! "

Phr. " the din of arms, the yell of savage rage, the shriek of agony, the groan of death " [Southey]; " their fatal hands no second stroke intend " [*Paradise Lost*]; " thirst for glory quells the love of life " [Addison].

give a warm reception to [ironical]; hold -, keep- at -bay, - arm's length.

stand -, act- on the defensive; show fight; maintain -, stand- one's ground; stand by; hold one's own; bear -, stand- the brunt; fall back upon, hold, stand in the gap.

Adj. defending &c. *v.*; defensive; mural; armed, - at all points, - cap-a-pie, - to the teeth; panoplied; iron-plated, -clad; loopholed, castellated, machicolated, casemated; defended &c. *v.*; proof against; ball-, bullet-proof.

Adv. defensively; on the -defense, - defensive; in defense; at bay, *pro aris et focis.*

Int. no surrender!

Phr. defense not defiance; *Dieu defend le droit; fidei defensor.*

---

718. Retaliation. — N. retaliation, reprisal, retort; counter-stroke, -blast, -plot, -project; retribution, *lex talionis;* reciprocation &c. (*reciprocity*) 12.

tit for tat, give and take, blow for blow, *quid pro quo*, a Roland for an Oliver, measure for measure, diamond cut diamond, the biter bit, a game at which two can play; reproof valiant, retort courteous.

recrimination &c. (*accusation*) 938; revenge &c. 919; compensation &c. 30; reaction &c. (*recoil*) 277.

V. retaliate, retort, turn upon; pay -off, - back; pay in -one's own, - the same- coin; cap; reciprocate &c. 148; turn the tables upon, return the compliment; give -a *quid pro quo* &c. *n.*, - as much as one takes; give and take, exchange fisticuffs; be -quits, - even-with; pay off old scores.

serve one right, be hoist on one's own petard, throw a stone in one's own garden, catch a Tartar.

Adj. retaliating &c. *v.*; retalia-tory, -tive; talionic.

Adv. in retaliation; *en revanche.*

Phr. *mutato nomine de te fabula narratur* [Horace]; *par pari refero* [Terence]; *tu quoque;* you're another; *suo sibi gladio hunc jugulo; à beau jeu beau retour; litem . . . lite resolvit* [Horace].

719. Resistance. — N. resistance, stand, front, oppugnation; oppugnancy; opposition &c. 708; renitenc-e, -y; reluctation, recalcitration; kicking &c. *v.* repulse, rebuff.

insurrection &c. (*disobedience*) 742; strike; turn -, lock -, barring- out; *levée en masse, Jacquerie;* riot &c. (*disorder*) 59.

V. resist; not -submit &c. 725; repugn †, reluctate, withstand; stand up -, strive -, bear up -, be proof -, make head- against; stand, - firm, - one's ground, - the brunt of, - out; hold -one's ground, - one's own, - out.

breast the -wave, - current; stem the -tide, - torrent; face, confront, grapple with; show a bold front &c. (*courage*) 861; present a front; make a -, take one's- stand.

kick, - against; recalcitrate, kick against the pricks; oppose &c. 708; fly in the face of; lift the hand against &c. (*attack*) 716; rise up in arms &c. (*war*) 722; strike, turn out; draw up a round robin &c. (*remonstrate*) 932; revolt &c. (*disobey*) 742; make a riot.

prendre le mors aux dents; take the bit between the teeth; sell one's life dearly, die hard, keep at bay; repel, repulse.

Adj. resisting &c. *v.*; resist-ive, -ant; refractory &c. (*disobedient*) 742; re-calci-trant, -nitent, -pulsive, -pellant; up in arms.

proof against; unconquerable &c. (*strong*) 159; stubborn, unconquered; indomitable &c. (*persevering*) 604a; unyielding &c. (*obstinate*) 606.

Int. hands off! keep off!

720. Contention. — N. contention, strife; contest, -ation; struggle; belligerency; opposition &c. 708.

controversy, polemics; debate &c. (*discussion*) 476; war of words, logomachy, litigation; paper war; high words &c. (*quarrel*) 713; sparring &c. v.

competition, rivalry; corrival-ry, -ship; agonism †, *concours*, match, race, horse racing, heat, steeple chase, handicap; regatta; field day; sham fight, Derby day; turf, sporting, bullfight, tauromachy, gymkhana; boat race, torpids.

wrestling, pugilism, boxing, fisticuffs, spar, mill, set-to, round, bout, event; prize fighting; quarterstaff, single stick; gladiatorship, gymnastics; jiujitsu, ju-jutsu, *kooshti, samo;* athletic-s, – sports; games of skill &c. 840.

shindy; fracas &c. (*discord*) 713; clash of arms; tussle, scuffle, broil, fray; affray, -ment †; velitation †; col- †, luctation; brabble, *brigue* †, scramble, *mêlée*, scrimmage, stramash, bushfighting.

free –, stand up –, hand to hand –, running- fight.

conflict, skirmish; ren-, en-counter; rencontre, collision, affair, brush, fight; battle, – royal; combat, action, engagement, joust, tournament; tilt, -ing; tournay, list; pitched battle.

death struggle, struggle for life or death, Armageddon; hard knocks, sharp contest, tug of war.

naval engagement, naumachia, sea fight.

duel, -lo; single combat, monomachy; satisfaction, *passage d'armes*, passage of arms, affair of honor; triangular duel; hostile meeting, digladiation; appeal to arms &c. (*warfare*) 722.

deeds –, feats- of arms; pugnacity; combativeness &c. *adj.*; bone of contention &c. 713.

V. contend; contest, strive, struggle, scramble, wrestle; spar, square; exchange -blows, – fisticuffs; fib, justle, tussle, tilt, box, stave, fence; skirmish; pickeer; fight &c. (*war*) 722; wrangle &c. (*quarrel*) 713.

contend &c. –, grapple –, engage –, close –, buckle –, bandy –, try conclusions –, have a brush &c. *n.* –, tilt- with; encounter, fall foul of, pitch into, clapperclaw, run a tilt at; oppose &c. 708; reluct.

join issue, come to blows, go to loggerheads, set to, come to the scratch, exchange shots, measure swords, meet hand to hand; take up the -cudgels, – glove, – gauntlet; enter the lists; couch one's lance; give satisfaction; appeal to arms &c. (*warfare*) 722.

lay about one; break the peace.

compete –, cope –, vie –, race- with; outvie, emulate, rival; run a race; contend &c. –, stipulate –, stickle- for; insist upon, make a point of.

Adj. contending &c. *v.*; together by the ears, at loggerheads, at war, at issue.

competitive, rival; belligerent; contentious, combative, bellicose, unpeaceful; warlike &c. 722; quarrelsome &c. 901; pugnacious; pugilistic, gladiatorial; palestric, -al.

Phr. *a verbis ad verbera;* a word and a blow; " a very pretty quarrel as it stands " [Sheridan]; *commune periculum concordiam parit; lis litem generat.*

721. Peace. — N. peace; amity &c. (*friendship*) 888; harmony &c. (*concord*) 714; tranquillity &c. (*quiescence*) 265; truce &c. (*pacification*) 723; pipe –, calumet- of peace.

piping time of peace, quiet life; neutrality.

V. be at peace; keep the peace &c. (*concord*) 714; make peace &c. 723.

Adj. pacific; peace-able, -ful; calm, tranquil, untroubled, halcyon; bloodless; neutral.

Phr. the storm blown over; the lion lies down with the lamb; " all quiet on the Potomac "; *paritur pax bello* [Nepos]; " peace hath her victories no less renowned than war " [Milton].

722. Warfare. — N. warfare; fighting &c. *v.*; hostilities; war, arms, the

723. Pacification. — N. pacification, conciliation; reconcil-iation, -ement

sword; Mars, Bellona, grim visaged war, *horrida bella;* bloodshed.

appeal to -arms, – the sword; ordeal -, wager- of battle; *ultima ratio regum,* arbitrament of the sword.

battle array, campaign, crusade, expedition; mobilization; state of siege; battlefield &c. (*arena*) 728; warpath.

art of war, tactics, strategy, castrametation; general-, soldier-ship; military evolutions, ballistics, gunnery; chivalry; gunpowder, shot.

battle, tug of war &c. (*contention*) 720; service, campaigning, active service, tented field; kriegspiel, *Kriegsspiel;* fire cross, trumpet, clarion, bugle, pibroch, slogan; war-cry, -whoop; battle cry, beat of drum, rappel, tom-tom; calumet of war; word of command; pass-, watch-word; *passage d'armes.*

war to the -death, – knife; *guerre à .-mort, – outrance;* open –, internecine –, civil- war.

V. arm; raise –, mobilize- troops; raise up in arms; take up the cudgels &c. 720; take up –, fly to –, appeal to- -arms, – the sword; draw –, unsheathe- the sword; dig up the -hatchet, – tomahawk; go to –, declare –, wage –, " let slip the dogs of- war " [*Julius Cæsar*]; cry havoc; kindle –, light- the torch of war; raise -one's banner, – the fire cross; hoist the black flag; throw –, fling- away the scabbard; enroll, enlist; take the field; take the law into one's own hands; do –, give –, join –, engage in –, go to- battle; flesh one's sword; set to, fall to, engage, measure swords with, draw the trigger, cross swords; come to -blows, – close quarters; fight; combat; contend &c. 720; battle –, break a lance- with.

serve; see –, be on- -service, – active service; campaign; wield the sword, shoulder a musket, smell powder, be under the fire; spill –, imbrue the hands in- blood; on the warpath.

carry on -war, – hostilities; keep the field; fight the good fight; fight -it out, – like devils, – one's way, – hand to hand; sell one's life dearly.

Adj. conten-ding, -tious &c. 720; armed, – to the teeth, – cap-a-pie; sword in hand; in –, under –, up in- arms; at war with; bristling with arms; in -battle array, – open arms, – the field; embattled; battled.

unpacific, unpeaceful; belligerent, combative, armigerous, bellicose, martial, warlike; mili-tary, -tant; soldier-like, -ly; chivalrous; strategical, internecine.

Adv. *flagrante bello,* in the -thick of the fray, – cannon's mouth; at the -sword's point, – point of the bayonet.

Int. *væ victis!* to arms! to your tents O Israel!

Phr. the battle rages; *à la guerre comme à la guerre; bis peccare in bello non licet; jus gladii;* " my voice is still for war " [Addison]; " my sentence is for open war " [Milton]; " pride, pomp, and circumstance of glorious war " [*Othello*]; " the cannons have their bowels full of wrath " [*King John*]; " the cannons . . . spit forth their iron indignation " [*King John*]; " the fire-eyed maid of smoky war " [*Henry IV*]; *silent leges inter arma* [Cicero]; *si vis pacem para bellum.*

shaking of hands, accommodation, arrangement, adjustment; terms, compromise; amnesty, deed of release.

peace offering; olive branch; calumet -, preliminaries- of peace.

truce, armistice; suspension of -arms, – hostilities; breathing time; convention; *modus vivendi;* flag of truce, white flag, *parlementaire,* cartel.

hollow truce, *pax in bello;* drawn battle.

V. pacify, tranquillize, compose; allay &c. (*moderate*) 174; reconcile, propitiate, placate, conciliate, meet halfway, hold out the olive branch, heal the breach, make peace, restore harmony, bring to terms.

settle –, arrange –, accommodate- -matters, – differences; set straight; make up a quarrel, *tantas componere lites;* come to -an understanding, – terms; bridge over, hush up; make -it, – matters- up; shake hands; mend one's fences [U. S.].

raise a siege; put up –, sheathe- the sword; bury the hatchet, lay down one's arms, turn swords into plowshares; smoke the calumet of peace, close the temple of Janus; keep the peace &c. (*concord*) 714; be -pacified &c.; come round.

Adj. conciliatory; composing &c. *v.;* pacified &c. *v.*

Phr. *requiescat in pace.*

724. Mediation. — N. media-tion, -torship, -tization; inter-vention, -position, -ference, -meddling, -cession; parley, negotiation, arbitration; flag of truce &c. 723; good offices, peace offering; diploma-tics, -cy; compromise &c. 774.

mediator, intercessor, peacemaker, make-peace, negotiator, go-between; diplomatist &c. (*consignee*) 758; moderator; propitiator; umpire.

V. media-te, -tize; inter-cede, -pose, -fere, -vene; step in, negotiate; meet halfway; arbitrate; *magnas componere lites*.

Adj. mediatory.

725. Submission. — N. submission, yielding; nonresistance; obedience &c. 743.

surrender, cession, capitulation, resignation; backdown.

obeisance, homage, kneeling, genuflexion, courtesy, curtsy, kotow, prostration.

V. succumb, submit, yield, bend, resign, defer to.

lay down –, deliver up- one's arms; lower –, haul down –, strike- one's -flag, – colors.

surrender, – at discretion; cede, capitulate, come to terms, retreat, beat a retreat; draw in one's horns &c. (*humility*) 879; give -way, – ground, – in, – up; cave in; suffer judgment by default; bend, – to one's yoke, – before the storm; reel back; bend –, knuckle--down, – to, – under; knock under.

eat -dirt, – the leek, – humble pie; bite –, lick- the dust; be –, fall- at one's feet; craven; crouch before, throw oneself at the feet of; swallow the -leek, – pill; kiss the rod; turn the other cheek; *avaler les couleuvres*, gulp down.

obey &c. 743; kneel to, bow to, pay homage to, cringe to, truckle to; bend the -neck, – knee; kneel, fall on one's knees, bow submission, courtesy, curtsy, kotow.

pocket the affront; make -the best of, – a virtue of necessity; grin and abide, shrug the shoulders, resign oneself; submit with a good grace &c. (*bear with*) 826.

Adj. surrendering &c. *v.*; submissive, resigned, crouching; downtrodden; down on one's marrow bones; on one's bended knee; un-, non-resisting; pliant &c. (*soft*) 324; undefended.

untenable, indefensible; humble &c. 879.

Phr. have it your own way; it can't be helped; amen &c. (*assent*) 488; *da locum melioribus; tempori parendum.*

726. Combatant. — N. combatant; disputant, controversialist, polemic, litigant, belligerent; competitor, rival, corrival; fighter, assailant; champion, Paladin; mosstrooper, swashbuckler, fire eater, duelist, bully, bludgeon man, rough, fighting man, prize fighter, pugilist, boxer, bruiser, the fancy, gladiator, athlete, wrestler; fighting-, game-cock; swordsman, *sabreur*.

warrior, soldier, Amazon, man at arms, armigerent; campaigner, veteran; redcoat, military man, Rajput.

armed force, troops, soldiery, military, forces, sabaoth, the army, standing army, regulars, the line, troops of the line, militia, yeomanry, volunteers, trainband, fencible; auxiliary, *bersagliere*, brave; *garde-nationale, – royale;* minuteman [Am. Hist.]; auxiliary –, reserve- forces; reserves, *posse comitatus*, national guard, *gendarme*, beefeater; guards, -man; yeomen of the guard, life guards, household troops.

janissary; myrmidon; Mama-, Mame-luke; spahee, spahi, Cossack, Croat, Pandor; irregular, franc-tireur, tirailleur, *bashi-bazouk*, guerilla, *condottiere;* mercenary; bushwhacker, free lance, companion; Hessian.

levy, draught; Land-wehr, -sturm; conscript, recruit, cadet, raw levies.

private, – soldier; Tommy Atkins, rank and file, peon, trooper, sepoy, *légionnaire*, legionary, food for powder; officer &c. (*commander*) 745; subaltern, ensign, standard bearer; spear-, pike-man; halberdier, lancer; musketeer, cara-

bineer, rifleman, jäger, sharpshooter, yager, skirmisher; grenadier, fusileer, archer, bowman.

horse and foot; horse –, foot- soldier; cavalry, horse, artillery, horse artillery, infantry, light horse, *voltigeur*, uhlan, mounted rifles, dragoon, hussar; light –, heavy- dragoon; heavy; cuirassier; Foot Guards, Horse Guards; gunner, cannoneer, bombardier, artilleryman, matross †; sapper, – and miner; engineer; light infantry, rifles, chasseur, zouave; military train, coolie.

army, *corps d'armée*, host, division, battalia, column, wing, detachment, garrison, flying column, brigade, regiment, corps, battalion, *sotnia*, squadron, company, platoon, battery, subdivision, section, squad; piquet, picket, guard, rank, file; legion, phalanx, cohort; cloud of skirmishers.

war horse, charger, destrier.

marine, man-of-war's man &c. (*sailor*) 269; navy, wooden walls, naval forces, fleet, flotilla, armada, squadron.

man-of-war; armored –, protected- cruiser; destroyer, dreadnought, submarine; torpedo-boat, – destroyer; torpedo-catcher, war castle, H. M. S.; line of battle ship, ship of the line, ironclad, turret ship, ram, monitor, floating battery; first-rate, frigate, sloop of war, corvette, gunboat, bomb vessel; flagship, guard ship, cruiser; privateer; tender; store –, troop- ship; transport, catamaran.

727. Arms. — N. arm, -s; weapon, deadly weapon; arma-ment, -ture; panoply, stand of arms; armor &c. (*defense*) 717; armory &c. (*store*) 636; *apparatus belli*.

ammunition; powder, – and shot; explosive; gun-powder, -cotton; dynam-, melin-, cord-, lydd-ite; cartridge; ball cartridge, cartouche, fireball; " villanous saltpeter " [*Hen. IV*]; dumdum bullet; pyroxyline.

sword, saber, broadsword, cutlass, falchion, scimitar, cimeter, brand, whinyard, bilbo, glaive, glave, rapier, skean, Toledo, Ferrara, tuck, claymore, adaga, baselard, Lochaber ax, skean dhu, creese, kris, dagger, dirk, hanger, poniard, stiletto, stylet, dudgeon, bayonet; sword-bayonet, -stick; side arms, foil, blade, steel; ax, bill; pole-, battle-ax; gisarme, halberd, partisan, tomahawk, bowie knife; at-, att-, yat-aghan; yatachan; ass-agai, -egai; good –, trusty –, naked- sword; cold steel.

club, mace, truncheon, staff, bludgeon, cudgel, life-preserver, shillelah, sprig; hand-, quarter-staff; bat, cane, stick, knuckle duster; billy, black-jack, sandbag, waddy.

gun, piece; firearms; artillery, ordnance; siege –, battering- train; park, battery; cannon, gun of position, heavy gun, fieldpiece, mortar, howitzer, carronade, culverin, basilisk; falconet, jingal, swivel, pederero, *bouche à feu*; petard, torpedo; *mitrailleu-r, -se*; infernal machine; smooth bore, rifled cannon; Armstrong –, Lancaster –, Paixhan –, Whitworth –, Parrott –, Krupp –, Gatling –, Maxim –, machine- gun; pompom; tenpounder.

small arms; musket, -ry, firelock, fowling piece, rifle, fusil, caliver, carbine, blunderbuss, musketoon, Brown Bess, matchlock, harquebuss, arquebus, haguebut; pistol, -et; petronel; small bore; breach-, muzzle-loader; revolver, repeater; Minié –, Enfield –, Flobert –, Westley Richards –, Snider –, Martini-Henry –, Lee-Metford –, Lee-Enfield –, Mauser –, magazine- rifle; needle gun, *chassepot;* wind-, air-gun; automatic -gun, - pistol; escopet, escopette, gunflint, -lock; hackbut, shooter, shooting iron * [U. S.], six-shooter [U. S.], shotgun.

bow, crossbow, balister, catapult, sling; battering-ram &c. (*impulse*) 276; gunnery; ballistics &c. (*propulsion*) 284.

missile, bolt, projectile, shot, ball; grape; grape –, canister –, bar –, cannon –, langrel –, langrage –, round –, chain- shot; balista, ballista, slung shot, trebuchet, trebucket; bullet, slug, stone, brickbat, grenade, shell, bomb, carcass, rocket; congreve, – rocket; shrapnel, *mitraille;* levin- -bolt. - brand: thunderbolt.

pike, lance, spear, spontoon, javelin, dart, jereed, jerid, arrow, reed, shaft, bolt, boomerang, harpoon, gaff; eelspear, oxgoad, weet-weet, wommerah.

Phr. *en flûte; nervos belli pecuniam infinitam.*

728. Arena. — N. arena, field, platform; scene of action, theater; walk, course; hustings; stage, boards &c. (*playhouse*) 599; amphitheater; Coli-, Colosseum; Flavian amphitheater, hippodrome, circus, race course, *corso,* turf, cockpit, bear garden, playground, gymnasium, palestra, ring, lists; tilt-yard, -ing ground; *Campus Martius, Champ de Mars;* campus [U. S.].

theater -, seat- of war; battle-field, -ground; field of -battle, - slaughter; Aceldama, camp; the enemy's camp; trysting place &c. (*place of meeting*) 74.

Section V. Results of Voluntary Action

729. Completion. — N. completion; accomplish-, achieve-, fulfill-ment; performance, execution; des-, dis-patch; consummation, culmination; finish, conclusion; close &c. (*end*) 67; terminus &c. (*arrival*) 292; winding up; *finale, dénouement,* catastrophe, issue, upshot, result; final -, last -, crowning -, finishing- -touch, - stroke; last finish, *coup de grâce;* crowning of the edifice; coping-, key-stone; missing link &c. 53; superstructure, *ne plus ultra,* work done, *fait accompli.*

elaboration; finality; completeness &c. 52.

V. effect, -uate; accomplish, achieve, compass, consummate, hammer out; bring to -maturity, – perfection; perfect, complete; elaborate.

do, execute, make; go -, get- through; work out, enact; bring -about, – to bear, – to pass, – through, – to a head.

des-, dis-patch; knock -, finish -, polish- off; make short work of; dispose of, set at rest; perform, discharge, fulfill, realize; put in -practice, – force; carry -out, – into effect, – into execution; make good; be as good as one's word.

do thoroughly, not do by halves, go the whole hog; drive home; be in at the death &c. (*persevere*) 604a; carry through, play out, exhaust; fill the bill [U. S.].

finish, bring to a close &c. (*end*) 67; wind up, stamp, clinch, seal, set the seal on, put the seal to; give the -final touch &c. *n.* to; put the -last, – finishing- hand to; crown, – all; cap.

ripen, culminate; come to a -head, – crisis; come to its end; die -a natural death, – of old age; run -its course, – one's race; touch -, reach -, attain- the goal; reach &c. (*arrive*) 292; get in the harvest.

Adj. completing, final; conclu-ding, -sive; crowning &c. *v.;* exhaustive.

done, completed &c. *v.;* done for, sped, wrought out; highly wrought &c. (*preparation*) 673; thorough &c. 52; ripe &c. (*ready*) 673.

Adv. completely &c. (*thoroughly*) 52; to crown all, out of hand.

Phr. the race is run; *actum est; finis coronat opus; consummatum est; c'en est fait;* it is all over; the game is played out, the bubble has burst; *aussitôt dit aussitôt fait; aut non tentaris aut perfice* [Ovid].

730. Noncompletion. — N. noncompletion, -fulfillment; shortcoming &c. 304; incompleteness &c. 53; drawn -battle, – game; work of Penelope.

nonperformance, inexecution; neglect &c. 460.

V. not -complete &c. 729; leave -unfinished &c. *adj.,* – undone; neglect &c. 460; let -alone, – slip; lose sight of.

fall short of &c. 304; do things by halves, scotch the snake not kill it; hang fire; be slow to; collapse &c. 304.

Adj. not completed &c. *v.;* incomplete &c. 53; uncompleted, unfinished, unaccomplished, unperformed, unexecuted; sketchy, addle.

in progress, in hand; going on, proceeding; on one's hands; on the anvil.

Adv. *re infectâ.*

731. Success. — N. success, -fulness; speed; advance &c. (*progress*) 282.

732. Failure. — N. failure; non-success, -fulfillment; dead failure, success

trump card; hit, stroke; lucky –, fortunate –, good- -hit, – stroke; bold –, master- stroke; ten-strike [U. S.]; *coup de maitre*, checkmate; half the battle, prize; profit &c. (*acquisition*) 775.

continued success; good fortune &c. (*prosperity*) 734; time well spent.

advantage over; upper –, whip- hand; ascendancy, mastery; expugnation †, conquest, victory, subdual; subjugation &c. (*subjection*) 749.

triumph &c. (*exultation*) 884; proficiency &c. (*skill*) 698; conqueror, victor; master of the -situation, – position.

V. succeed; be -successful &c. *adj.*; gain one's -end, ᐁ ends; crown with success.

gain –, attain –, carry –, secure –, win- -a point, – an object; get there * [U. S.]; manage to, contrive to; accomplish &c. (*effect, complete*) 729; do –, work- wonders; make a go of it.

come off -well, – successful, – with flying colors; make short work of; take –, carry- by storm; bear away the bell; win -one's spurs, – the battle; win –, carry –, gain- the -day, – prize, – palm; have -the best of it, – it all one's own way, – the game in one's own hands, – the ball at one's feet, – one on the hip; walk over the course; carry all before one, remain in possession of the field; score a success.

speed; make progress &c. (*advance*) 282; win –, make –, work –, find- one's way; strive to some purpose; prosper &c. 734; drive a roaring trade; make profit &c. (*acquire*) 775; reap –, gather- the -fruits, – benefit of, – harvest; strike oil * [U. S.]; make one's fortune, get in the harvest, turn to good account; turn to account &c. (*use*) 677.

triumph, be triumphant; gain –, obtain- -a victory, – an advantage; chain victory to one's car.

surmount –, overcome –, get over- -a difficulty, – an obstacle &c. 706; *se tirer d'affaire;* make head against; stem the -torrent, – tide, – current; weather -the storm, – a point; turn a corner, keep one's head above water, tide over; master; get –, have –, gain- the -better of, – best of, – upper hand, – ascendancy, – whip hand, – start of; distance; surpass &c. (*superiority*) 33.

defeat, conquer, vanquish, discomfit; euchre *; over-come, -throw, -power,

lessness; abortion, miscarriage; *brutum fulmen* &c. 158; labor in vain &c. (*inutility*) 645; no go; inefficacy; inefficaciousness &c. *adj.*; vain –, ineffectual –, abortive- -attempt, – efforts; flash in the pan, " lame and impotent conclusion " [*Othello*]; frustration; slip 'twixt cup and lip &c. (*disappointment*) 509.

blunder &c. (*mistake*) 495; fault, omission, miss, oversight, slip, trip, stumble, claudication †, footfall; false –, wrong- step; *faux pas*, titubation, *bévue, faute*, lurch; botchery &c. (*want of skill*) 699; scrape, mess, fiasco, breakdown; flunk [U. S.].

mishap &c. (*misfortune*) 735; split, collapse, smash, blow, explosion.

repulse, rebuff, defeat, rout, overthrow, discomfiture; beating, drubbing; quietus, nonsuit, subjugation; check-, stale-, fool's-mate.

fall, downfall, ruin, perdition; wreck &c. (*destruction*) 162; deathblow; bankruptcy &c. (*nonpayment*) 808.

losing game, *affaire flambée*.

victim; bankrupt; flunk-er, -y [U. S.].

V. fail; be -unsuccessful &c. *adj.*; not -succeed &c. 731; make -vain efforts &c. *n.*; do –, labor –, toil- in vain; flunk [U. S.]; lose one's labor, take nothing by one's motion; bring to naught, make nothing of; wash a blackamoor white &c. (*impossible*) 471; roll the stone of Sisyphus &c. (*useless*) 645; do by halves &c. (*not complete*) 730; lose ground &c. (*recede*) 283; fall short of &c. 304.

miss, – one's aim, – the mark, – one's footing, – stays; slip, trip, stumble; make a -slip &c., *n.* – blunder &c. 495, – mess of, – botch of; bitch it †, miscarry, abort, go up like a rocket and come down like the stick, reckon without one's host; get the wrong -pig by the tail, – sow by the ear &c. (*blunder, mismanage*) 699.

limp, halt, hobble, titubate; fall, tumble; lose one's balance; fall -to the ground, – between two stools; flounder, falter, stick in the mud, run aground, split upon a rock; run –, knock –, dash- one's head against a stone wall; break one's back; break down, sink, drown, founder, have the ground cut from under one; get into -trouble, – a mess, – a scrape; come to grief &c. (*adversity*) 735; go to -the wall, – the dogs, – pot; lick –, bite- the dust; be -defeated &c. 731; have the worst of it, lose the day, come

-master, -match, -set, -ride, -reach; out-wit, -do, -flank,-maneuver, -general, -vote; take the wind out of one's adversary's sails; beat, – hollow; rout, lick, drub, floor, worst; put -down, – to flight, – to the rout, – *hors de combat*, – out of court.

silence, quell, nonsuit, checkmate, upset, confound, nonplus, stalemate, trump; baffle &c. (*hinder*) 706; circumvent, elude; trip up, – the heels of; drive -into a corner, – to the wall; run hard, put one's nose out of joint.

settle, do for; break the -neck of, – back of; capsize, sink, shipwreck, drown, swamp; subdue; subjugate &c. (*subject*) 749; reduce; make the enemy bite the dust; victimize, roll in the dust, trample under foot, put an extinguisher upon.

answer, – the purpose; avail, prevail, take effect, do, turn out well, work well, take, tell, bear fruit; hit -it, – the mark, – the right nail on the head; nick it; turn up trumps, make a hit; find one's account in.

Adj. succeeding &c. *v.*; successful; prosperous &c. 734; triumphant; flushed –, crowned- with success; victorious; set up; in the ascendant; unbeaten &c. (*see* beat &c. *v.*); well-spent; felicitous, effective, in full swing.

Adv. successfully &c. *adj.*; with flying colors, in triumph, swimmingly; *à merveille*, beyond all hope; to some –, to good- purpose; to one's heart's content.

Phr. *veni vidi vici*, the day being one's own, one's star in the ascendant; *omne tulit punctum. bis vincit qui se vincit in victoria; cede repugnanti cedendo victor abibis* [Ovid]; *chacun est l'artisan de sa fortune; dies faustus; l'art de vaincre est celui de mépriser la mort; omnia vincit amor;* " peace hath her victories no less renowned than war " [Milton]; " the race by vigor not by vaunts is won " [Pope]; *vincit qui patitur; vincit qui se vincit.*

off second best, lose; fall a prey to; succumb &c. (*submit*) 725; not have a leg to stand on.

come to nothing, end in smoke; flat out [U. S.]; fall -to the ground, – through, – dead, – stillborn, – flat; slip through one's fingers; hang –, miss- fire; flash in the pan, collapse; topple down &c. (*descent*) 305; go to wrack and ruin &c. (*destruction*) 162.

go amiss, go wrong, go cross, go hard with, go on a wrong tack; go on –, come off –, turn out –, work- ill; take -a wrong, – an ugly- term.

be all -over with, – up with; explode; dash one's hopes &c. (*disappoint*) 509; defeat the purpose; sow the wind and reap the whirlwind, jump out of the frying pan into the fire.

Adj. unsuccessful, successless; failing, tripping &c. *v.*; at fault; unfortunate &c. 735.

abortive, addle, stillborn; fruitless, bootless; ineffect-ual, -ive; inefficient &c. (*impotent*) 158; inefficacious; lame, hobbling, *décousu*; insufficient &c. 640; unavailing &c. (*useless*) 645; of no effect.

aground, grounded, swamped, stranded, cast away, wrecked, foundered, capsized, shipwrecked, nonsuited; foiled; defeated &c. 731; struck –, borne –, broken- down; downtrodden; over-borne, -whelmed; all up with; ploughed, plowed, plucked.

lost, undone, ruined, broken; bankrupt &c. (*not paying*) 808; played out; done -up, – for; dead beat, ruined root and branch, *flambé*, knocked on the head; destroyed &c. 162.

frustrated, crossed, unhinged, disconcerted, dashed; thrown -off one's balance, – on one's back, – on one's beam ends; unhorsed, in a sorry plight; hard hit.

stultified, befooled, dished, hoist on one's own petard; victimized, sacrificed.

wide of the mark &c. (*error*) 495; out of one's reckoning &c. (*inexpectation*) 508; left in the lurch; thrown away &c. (*wasted*) 638; unattained; uncompleted &c. 730.

Adv. unsuccessfully &c. *adj.*; to little or no purpose, in vain, *re infectâ*.

Phr. the bubble has burst, " the game is up " [*Cymbeline*]; all is lost; the devil to pay; *parturiunt montes* &c. (*disappointment*) 509; *dies infaustus; tout est perdu hors l'honneur.*

733. Trophy. — N. trophy; medal, prize, palm; laurel, -s; bays, crown, chaplet, wreath, civic crown; insignia &c. 550; feather in one's cap &c. (*honor*) 873; decoration &c. 877; garland, triumphal arch, Victoria Cross, Iron Cross.

triumph &c. (*celebration*) 883; flying colors &c. (*show*) 882.

monumentum œre perennius [Hor.].

Phr. "for valor."

734. Prosperity.— N. prosperity, welfare, well-being; affluence &c. (*wealth*) 803; success &c. 731; thrift, roaring trade; good –, smiles of- fortune; blessings, godsend.

luck; good –, run of- luck; sunshine; fair -weather, – wind; palmy –, bright –, halcyon- days; piping times, tide, flood, high tide.

Saturnia regna, Saturnian age; golden -time, – age; bed of roses; fat of the land, milk and honey, loaves and fishes.

made man, lucky dog, *enfant gâté*, spoiled child of fortune.

upstart, parvenu, skipjack, mushroom.

V. prosper, thrive, flourish; be -prosperous &c. *adj.*; drive a roaring trade; go on -well, – smoothly, – swimmingly; sail before the wind, swim with the tide; run -smooth, – smoothly, – on all fours.

rise –, get on- in the world; work –, make- one's way; look up; lift –, raise- one's head, make one's fortune, feather one's nest, make one's pile *.

flower, blow, blossom, bloom, fructify, bear fruit, fatten.

keep oneself afloat; keep –, hold- one's head above water; light –, fall- on one's -legs, – feet; drop into a good thing; bear a charmed life; bask in the sunshine; have a -good, – fine- time of it; have a run, – of luck; have the -good fortune &c. *n.* to; take a favorable turn; live -on the fat of the land, – in clover.

Adj. prosperous; thriving &c. *c.*; in a fair way, buoyant; well -off, – to do, – to do in the world; set up, at one's ease; rich &c. 803; in good case; in -full, – high- feather; fortunate, lucky, in luck; born -with a silver spoon in one's mouth, – under a lucky star; on the sunny side of the hedge.

auspicious, propitious, providential.

palmy, halcyon; agreeable &c. 829; *couleur de rose*.

Adv. prosperously &c. *adj.*; swimmingly; as good luck would have it; beyond all hope.

Phr. one's star in the ascendant, all for the best, one's course runs smooth.

chacun est l'artisan de sa fortune; donec eris felix multos numerabis amicos [Ovid]; *felicitas multos habet amicos; felix se nescit amari* [Lucan]; "good luck go with thee" [*Henry V*]; *nulli est homini perpetuum bonum* [Plautus].

735. Adversity. — N. adversity, evil &c. 619; failure &c. 732; bad –, ill –, evil –, adverse –, hard- -fortune, – hap, – luck, – lot; frowns of fortune; evil -dispensation, – star, – genius; ups and downs of life, broken fortunes; hard -case, – lines, – life; sea –, peck- of troubles; hell upon earth; slough of despond.

trouble, hardship, curse, blight, blast, load, pressure.

pressure of the times, iron age, evil day, time out of joint; hard –, bad –, sad- times; rainy day, cloud, dark cloud, gathering clouds, ill wind; visitation, infliction; affliction &c. (*painfulness*) 830; bitter pill; care, trial; the sport of fortune.

mis-hap, -chance, -adventure, -fortune; disaster, calamity, catastrophe; accident, casualty, cross, reverse, check, *contretemps*, rub; backset, comedown, setback [U. S.].

losing game; falling &c. *v.*; fall, downfall; ruin-ation, -ousness; undoing; extremity; ruin &c. (*destruction*) 162.

V. be -ill off &c. *adj.*; go hard with; fall on evil, – days; go on ill; not -prosper &c. 734.

go -downhill, – to rack and ruin &c. (*destruction*) 162, – to the dogs; fall, – from one's high estate; decay, sink, decline, go down in the world; have seen better days; bring down one's gray hairs with sorrow to the grave; come to grief; be all -over, – up- with; bring a -wasp's, – hornet's- nest about one's ears.

Adj. unfortunate, unblest, unhappy, unlucky; im-, un-prosperous; hoodooed [U. S.]; luck-, hap-less; out of luck; in trouble, in a bad way, in an evil plight; under a cloud; clouded; ill –, badly- off; in adverse circumstances; poor &c. 804; behindhand, down in the world, decayed, undone; on the road to ruin, on its last legs, on the wane; in one's utmost need.

planet-struck, devoted; born -under an evil star, – with a wooden ladle in one's mouth; ill-fated, -starred, -omened.

adverse, untoward; disastrous, calamitous, ruinous, dire, deplorable.

Adv. if the worst come to the worst, as ill luck would have it, from bad to worse, out of the frying pan into the fire.

Phr. one's star is on the wane; one's luck -turns, – fails; the game is up, one's doom is sealed, the ground crumbles under one's feet, *sic transit gloria mundi, tant va la cruche à l'eau qu'à la fin elle se casse.*

" adversity's sweet milk, philosophy " [*Romeo and Juliet*]; *amici probantur rebus adversis; bien vengas mal si vienes solo;* εὐτυχῶν μὲν μέτριος ἴσθι ἀτυχῶν δὲ φρόνιμος [Periander]; *gaudet tentamine virtus; curæ leves loquuntur ingentes stupent;* " in the shadow of a great affliction " [Whittier]; *res est sacra miser* [Ovid]; *sempre il mal non vien per nuocere; væ victis* [Livy]; " sweet are the uses of adversity " [*As You Like It*].

736. Mediocrity. — N. moderate –, average- circumstances; respectability; middle classes; mediocrity; golden mean &c. (*mid-course*) 628, (*moderation*) 174.

V. jog on; go –, get on- -fairly, – quietly, – peaceably, – tolerably, – respect- ably.

DIVISION (II) I N T E R S O C I A L   V O L I T I O N[1]

Section I. GENERAL INTERSOCIAL VOLITION

737. Authority. — N. authority; in- fluence, patronage, power, preponder- ance, credit, prestige, prerogative, ju- risdiction; right &c. (*title*) 924.

divine right, dynastic rights, authori- tativeness; absolut-eness, -ism; despo- tism; *jus nocendi; jus divinum.*

command, empire, sway, rule; domin- ion, -ation; sovereignty, supremacy, su- zerainty; lord-, head-ship; chiefdom; seignior-y, -ity; master-y, -ship, -dom; government &c. (*direction*) 693; dicta- tion, control.

hold, grasp; grip, -e; reach; iron sway &c. (*severity*) 739; fangs, clutches, tal- ons; rod of empire &c. (*scepter*) 747.

reign, *régime*, dynasty; director-, dic- tator-ship; protector-ate, -ship; cali- phate, pashalic, electorate; presiden -cy, -tship; administration; pro-, consul- ship; prefecture; seneschalship; magis- tra-ture, -cy.

empire; monarchy; king-hood, -ship; royalty, regality; arist-archy, -ocracy; oligarchy, democracy, demagogy; het- eronomy; republic, -anism; socialism; collectivism; mob law, mobocracy, och-

738. [Absence of authority] **Laxity. — N.** laxity; lax-, loose-, slack-ness; toleration &c. (*lenity*) 740; freedom &c. 748.

anarchy, interregnum; relaxation; loosening &c. *v.*; remission; dead letter, *brutum fulmen,* misrule; license, licen- tiousness; insubordination &c. (*diso- bedience*) 742; lynch law &c. (*illegality*) 964; nihilism, reign of violence.

[Deprivation of power] dethronement, deposition, usurpation, abdication.

V. be -lax &c. *adj.*; *laisser -faire, – aller;* hold a loose rein; give -the reins to, – rope enough, – a loose to; tolerate; relax; misrule.

go beyond the length of one's tether; have one's -swing, – fling; act without -instructions, – authority; act on one's own responsibility, usurp authority.

dethrone, depose; abdicate.

Adj. lax, loose; slack; remiss &c. (*careless*) 460; weak.

relaxed; licensed; reinless, unbridled; anarchical; unauthorized &c. (*unwar- ranted*) 925; adespotic.

locracy; *vox populi, imperium in imperio;* bureaucracy; beadle-, bumble-dom; stratocracy; military -power, – government; feodality, feudal system, feu- dalism.

Thearchy, dinarchy; du-, tri-, heter-archy; du-, tri-umvirate; auto-cracy, -nomy; limited monarchy; constitutional -government, – monarchy; home rule; representative government; monocracy, pantisocracy.

gyn-archy, -ocracy, -æocracy; petticoat government.

[Vicarious authority] commission &c. 755; deputy &c. 759; permission &c. 760.

state, realm, body politic, *posse comitatus.*

---

[1] Implying the action of the will of one mind over the will of another.

person in authority &c. (*master*) 745; judicature &c. 965; cabinet &c. (*council*) 696; seat of -government, – authority; headquarters.

[Acquisition of authority] accession; installation &c. 755.

V. authorize &c. (*permit*) 760; warrant &c. (*right*) 924; dictate &c. (*order*) 741; have –, hold –, possess –, exercise –, exert –, wield- -authority &c. *n.*

be -at the head of &c. *adj.*; hold –, be in –, fill an- office; hold –, occupy- a post; be -master &c. 745.

rule, sway, command, control, administer; govern &c. (*direct*) 693; lead, preside over, reign; possess –, be seated on –, occupy- the throne; sway –, wield- the scepter; wear the crown.

have –, get- the -upper, – whip- hand; gain a hold upon, preponderate, dominate, rule the roast; boss [U. S.]; over-ride, -rule, -awe; lord it over, hold in hand, keep under, make a puppet of, lead by the nose, turn round one's little finger, bend to one's will, hold one's own, wear the breeches; have -the ball at one's feet, – it all one's own way, – the game in one's own hand, – on the hip, – under one's thumb; be master of the situation; take the lead, play first fiddle, set the fashion; give the law to; carry with a high hand; lay down the law; " ride in the whirlwind and direct the storm " [Addison]; rule with a rod of iron &c. (*severity*) 739.

ascend –, mount- the throne; take the reins, – into one's hand; assume -authority &c. *n.*, – the reins of government; take –, assume the- command.

be governed by, be in the power of.

Adj. ruling &c. *v.*; regnant, at the head, dominant, paramount, supreme, predominant, preponderant, in the ascendant, influential; gubernatorial; imperious; authoritative, executive, administrative, clothed with authority, official, departmental, *ex officio*, imperative, peremptory, overruling, absolute; hegemonic, -al; arbitrary; compulsory &c. 744: stringent.

regal, sovereign; royal, -ist; monarchical, kingly; imperi-al, -atorial; princely; feudal; aristo-, auto-cratic; oligarchic &c. *n.*; republican, dynastic.

at one's command; in one's -power, – grasp; under control; authorized &c. (*due*) 924.

Adv. in the name of, by the authority of, *de par le Roi*, in virtue of; under the auspices of, in the hands of.

at one's pleasure; by a -dash, – stroke- of the pen; *ex mero motu; ex cathedrâ.*

Phr. the gray mare the better horse; " every inch a king " [*Lear*].

" a dog's obeyed in office " [*Lear*]; *cada uno tiene su alguazil; le Roi le veut; regibus esse manus en nescio longas; regnant populi;* " the demigod Authority " [*Measure for Measure*]; " the right divine of kings to govern wrong " [Pope]; " uneasy lies the head that wears a crown " [*Henry IV*].

---

739. Severity. — **N.** severity; strictness, harshness &c. *adj.*; rigor, stringency, austerity; inclemency &c. (*pitilessness*) 914a; arrogance &c. 885; precisianism.

arbitrary power; absolut-, despotism; dictatorship, autocracy, tyranny, domineering, oppression; assumption, usurpation; inquisition, reign of terror, martial law; iron -heel, – rule, – hand, – sway; tight grasp; brute -force, – strength; coercion &c. 744; strong –, tight- hand.

hard -lines, – measure; tender mercies [ironical]; sharp practice; pipe-clay, officialism.

tyrant, disciplinarian, precisian, martinet, stickler, bashaw, despot, hard

740. Lenity. — **N.** leni-ty, -ence-, -ency; moderation &c. 174; toler-ance, -ation; mildness, gentleness; favor; indulgen-ce, -cy; clemency, mercy, forbearance, quarter; compassion &c. 914.

V. be -lenient &c. *adj.*; tolerate, bear with; *parcere subjectis*, give quarter.

indulge, allow one to have his own way, spoil.

Adj. lenient; mild, – as milk; gentle, soft; tolerant, indulgent, easy-going; clement &c. (*compassionate*) 914; forbearing; long-suffering.

master, Draco, oppressor, inquisitor, extortioner, harpy, vulture; accipitres, birds of prey, raptorials, raptors.

V. be -severe &c. *adj.*

assume, usurp, arrogate, take liberties; domineer, bully &c. 885; tyrannize, inflict, wreak, stretch a point, put on the screw; be hard upon; bear –, lay- a heavy hand on; be –, come- down upon; illtreat; deal -hardly with, – hard measure to; rule with a rod of iron, chastise with scorpions; dye with blood; oppress, override; trample –, tread- -down, – upon, – under foot; crush under an iron heel, ride roughshod over; rivet the yoke; hold –, keep- a tight hand; force down the throat; coerce &c. 744; give no quarter &c. (*pitiless*) 914a.

Adj. severe; strict, hard, harsh, dour, rigid, stiff, stern, rigorous, uncompromising, exacting, exigent, *exigeant*, inexorable, inflexible, obdurate, austere, hard-headed, hard-shell [U. S.], relentless, Spartan, Draconian, stringent, strait-laced, searching, unsparing, iron-handed, peremptory, absolute, positive, arbitrary, imperative; coercive &c. 744; tyrannical, extortionate, grinding, withering, oppressive, inquisitorial; inclement &c. (*ruthless*) 914a; cruel &c. (*malevolent*) 907; haughty, arrogant &c. 885; precisian.

Adv. severely &c. *adj.*; with a -high, – strong, – tight, – heavy- hand. at the point of the -sword, – bayonet.

Phr. *Delirant reges plectuntur Achivi; manu forti; ogni debole ha sempre il suo tiranno.*

741. Command. — N. command, order, ordinance, act, fiat, *hukm*, bidding, dictum, hest, behest, call, beck, nod.

des-, dis-patch; message, direction, injunction, charge, instructions; appointment, fixture.

demand, exaction, imposition, requisition, claim, reclamation, revendication; ultimatum &c. (*terms*) 770; request &c. 765; requirement.

dictation; dict-, mand-ate; caveat, decree, *senatus consultum;* precept; pre-, re-script; writ, ordination, bull, edict, decretal, dispensation, prescription, brevet, placit, ukase, firman, hatti-sherif, warrant, passport, mittimus, mandamus, summons, subpœna, *nisi prius*, interpellation, citation; word, – of command; *mot d'ordre;* bugle –, trumpet- call; beat of drum, tattoo; order of the day; enactment &c. (*law*) 963; plebiscite &c. (*choice*) 609.

V. command, order, decree, enact, ordain, dictate, direct, give orders.

prescribe, set, appoint, mark out; set –, prescribe –, impose- a task; set to work, put in requisition.

bid, enjoin, charge, call upon, instruct; require, – at the hands of; exact, impose, tax, task; demand; insist on &c. (*compel*) 744.

claim, lay claim to, revendicate, reclaim.

cite, summon; call –, send- for; subpœna; beckon.

issue a command; make –, issue –, promulgate- -a requisition, – a decree, – an order &c. *n.*; give the -word of command, – word, – signal; call to order; give –, lay down- the law; assume the command &c. (*authority*) 737; remand.

be -ordered &c.; receive an order &c. *n.*

Adj. commanding &c. *v.*; authoritative &c. 737; decret-ory, -ive, -al; callable, jussive.

Adv. in a commanding tone; by a -stroke, – dash- of the pen; by order, at beat of drum, on the first summons.

Phr. the decree is gone forth; *sic volo sic jubeo; le Roi le veut; boutez en avant.*

742. Disobedience. — N. disobedience, insubordination, contumacy; infraction, -fringement; violation, noncompliance; nonobservance &c. 773.

revolt, rebellion, mutiny, outbreak, rising, uprising, insurrection, *émeute;* riot, tumult &c. (*disorder*) 59; strike &c.

743. Obedience. — N. obedience; observance &c. 772; compliance; submission &c. 725; subjection &c. 749; nonresistance; passiveness, resignation.

allegiance, loyalty, fealty, homage, deference, devotion; constancy, fidelity. submiss-ness, -iveness; ductility &c

(*resistance*) 719; barring out; defiance &c. 715.

mutinousness &c. *adj.*; mutineering; sedition, treason; high –, petty –, misprision of- treason; premunire; *lèse-majesté;* violation of law &c. 964; defection, secession.

insurgent, mutineer, rebel, revolter, rioter, traitor, *carbonaro*, sansculottes, red republican, *bonnet rouge*, communist, Fenian, *frondeur;* seceder, runagate, brawler, anarchist, demagogue; Spartacus, Masaniello, Wat Tyler, Jack Cade; ringleader.

V. disobey, violate, infringe; shirk; set at defiance &c. (*defy*) 715; set authority at naught, run riot, fly in the face of; take the law into one's own hands; kick over the traces.

turn –, run- restive; champ the bit; strike &c. (*resist*) 719; rise, – in arms; secede; mutiny, rebel.

(*softness*) 324; obsequiousness &c. (*servility*) 886.

V. be -obedient &c. *adj.*; obey, bear obedience to; submit &c. 725; comply, answer the helm, come at one's call; do -one's bidding, – what one is told, – suit and service; attend to orders, serve faithfully.

follow, – the lead of, – to the world's end; serve &c. 746; play second fiddle.

Adj. obedient; compl-ying, -iant; loyal, faithful, devoted; at one's -call, – command, – orders, – beck and call; under -beck and call, – control.

restrainable; resigned, passive; submissive &c. 725; henpecked; pliant &c. (*soft*) 324.

unresisted.

Adv. obediently &c. *adj.*; in compliance with, in obedience to. ·

Phr. to hear is to obey; as –, if- you please.

Adj. disobedient; uncompl-ying, -iant; unsubmissive, unruly, ungovernable; breachy, insubordinate, impatient of control; rest-iff †, -ive; refractory, contumacious; recusant &c. (*refuse*) 764; recalcitrant; resisting &c. 719; lawless, mutinous, seditious, insurgent, riotous.

unobeyed; unbidden.

Phr. *seditiosissimus quisque ignavus* [Tacitus]; " unthread the rude eye of rebellion " [*King John*].

744. Compulsion. — N. compulsion, coercion, coaction, constraint, duress, enforcement, press, conscription.

force; brute -, main -, physical- force; the sword, *ultima ratio;* club -, lynch -, mob- law, *argumentum baculinum, le droit du plus fort*, martial law.

restraint &c. 751; necessity &c. 601; *force majeure;* Hobson's choice.

V. compel, force, make, drive, coerce, constrain, enforce, necessitate, oblige.

force upon, press; cram -, thrust -, force- down the throat; say it must be done, make a point of, insist upon, take no denial; put down, dragoon.

extort, wring from; put -, turn- on the screw; drag into; bind, – over; pin -, tie- down; require, tax, put in force; commandeer; restrain &c. 751.

Adj. compelling &c. *v.*; coercive, coactive; inexorable &c. 739; compuls-ory, -atory; obligatory, stringent, peremptory.

forcible, not to be trifled with; irresistible &c. 601; compelled &c. *v.*; fain to.

Adv. by -force &c. *n.*, – force of arms; on compulsion, perforce; *vi et armis*, under the lash; at the point of the -sword, – bayonet; forcibly; by a strong arm.

under protest, in spite of one's teeth; against one's will &c. 603; *nolens volens* &c. (*of necessity*) 601; by stress of -circumstances, – weather; under press of; *de rigueur.*

745. Master. — N. master, *padrone;* lord, – paramount; command-er, -ant; captain; chief, -tain; sirdar, sachem, sheik, head, senior, governor, ruler, dictator; leader &c. (*director*) 694; boss, cockarouse, sagamore, werowance.

lord of the ascendant; cock of the -walk, – roost; gray mare; mistress.

746. Servant. — N. subject, liegeman; servant, retainer, follower, henchman, servitor, domestic, menial, help, lady help, employé, *attaché;* official.

retinue, suite, *cortège*, staff, court.

attendant, squire, usher, page, donzel, footboy; train-, cup-bearer; waiter, tapster, butler, livery servant, lackey,

potentate; liege, – lord; suzerain, sovereign, monarch, autocrat, despot, tyrant, oligarch.

crowned head, emperor. king, anointed king, majesty, imperator, protector, president, stadholder, judge.

cæsar, kaiser, czar, sultan, soldan †, grand Turk, caliph, imaum, shah, padishah, sophi, mogul, great mogul, khan, lama, tycoon, mikado, inca, cazique; voivode; landamman; seyyid; Abuna, cacique, czarowitz, grand seignior, tsar.

prince, duke &c. (*nobility*) 875; archduke, doge, elector; seignior; mar-, landgrave; rajah, emir, nizam, nawab.

empress, queen, sultana, czarina, princess, infanta, duchess, margravine; czarevna, -ita; maharani, rani, rectrix.

regent, viceroy, exarch, palatine, khedive, hospodar, beglerbeg, three-tailed bashaw, pasha, bashaw, bey, beg, dey, scherif, tetrarch, satrap, mandarin, subahdar, nabob, maharajah; burgrave; laird &c. (*proprietor*) 779; collector, commissioner, deputy commissioner, woon.

the -authorities, – powers that be, – government; staff, *état major*, aga, official, man in office, person in authority; sircar, sirkar, Sublime Porte.

[Military authorities] marshal, field marshal, *maréchal;* general, -issimo; commander in chief, seraskier, hetman; lieutenant-, major-general; colonel, lieutenant colonel, major, captain, centurion, skipper, lieutenant, sublieutenant, officer, staff officer, aide-de-camp, brigadier, brigade major, adjutant, jemidar, ensign, cornet, cadet, subaltern, noncommissioned officer; sergeant, -major; color sergeant; corporal, -major; lance-, acting-corporal; drum major; captain general, *dizdar*, knight marshal, naik, pendragon.

footman, flunkey, valet, *valet de chambre;* equerry, groom; jockey, hostler, ostler, tiger, orderly, messenger, cad, gillie, herdsman, swineherd; bar-keeper, -tender; bell boy, boots, boy, counter-jumper; khansam-ah, -an; khitmutgar; yardman.

bailiff, castellan, seneschal, chamberlain, major-domo, groom of the chambers.

secretary; under –, assistant- secretary; clerk; subsidiary; agent &c. 758; subaltern; under-ling, -strapper; man.

maid, -servant; handmaid; *confidente*, lady's maid, abigail, soubrette; amah, biddy, nurse, *bonne*, ayah; nurse-, nursery-, house-, parlor-, waiting-, chamber-, kitchen-, scullery-maid; *femme –, fille- de chambre; camarista; chef de cuisine, cordon bleu,* cook, scullion, Cinderella; potwalloper; maid –, servant- of all work; laundress, bedmaker; journeyman, charwoman &c. (*worker*) 690; bearer, chokra, gyp [Cambridge], *hamal*, scout [Oxford].

serf, vassal, slave, negro, helot; bondsman, -woman; bondslave; *âme damnée*, odalisque, ryot, *adscriptus glebæ;* villain, -ein; bead-, bede-sman; sizar; pension-er, -ary; client; depend-ant, -ent; hanger on, satellite; parasite &c. (*servility*) 886; led captain; *protégé*, ward, hireling, mercenary, puppet, creature.

badge of slavery; bonds &c. 752.

V. serve; wait –, attend –, dance attendance –, pin oneself- upon; squire, tend, hang on the sleeve of; chore [U. S.].

Adj. in the train of; in one's -pay, – employ; at one's call &c. (*obedient*) 743; in bonds.

[Civil authorities] mayor, -alty; prefect, chancellor, archon, provost, magistrate, syndic; alcalde, alcaid; burgomaster, *corregidor*, seneschal, alderman, warden, constable, portreeve; lord mayor; officer &c. (*executive*) 965; dewan, *fonctionnaire*.

[Naval authorities] admiral, -ty; rear-, vice-, port-admiral; commodore, captain, commander, lieutenant, skipper, mate, master; navarch.

Phr. *da locum melioribus; der Fürst ist der erste Diener seines Staats;* "lord of thy presence and no land beside " [*King John*].

747. [Insignia of authority.] **Scepter.** — **N.** scepter, regalia, caduceus; Mercury's-rod, -staff, -wand; rod of empire, mace, fasces, wand; staff, – of office; baton, truncheon; flag &c. (*insignia*) 550; ensign –, emblem –, badge –, insignia- of authority.

throne, chair, musnud, divan, dais, woolsack.

toga, pall, mantle, robes of state, ermine, purple.

crown, coronet, diadem, tiara, cap of maintenance; decoration; title &c. 877; portfolio.

key, signet, seals, talisman; helm; reins &c. (*means of restraint*) 752.

748. Freedom. — N. freedom, liberty, independence; license &c. (*permission*) 760; facility &c. 705.

scope, range, latitude, play; free -, full- -play, – scope; free stage and no favor; swing, full swing, elbowroom, margin, rope, wide berth; Liberty Hall.

franchise, denization; free -, freed-, livery- man; denizen.

autonomy, self-government, liberalism, free trade; noninterference &c. 706; Monroe Doctrine [U. S.].

immunity, exemption; emancipation &c. (*liberation*) 750; en-, af-franchisement.

free land, freehold; allodium; frankalmoigne, mortmain.

bushwhacker; free-lance, -thinker, -trader; independent.

V. be -free &c. *adj.*; have -scope &c. *n.*, – the run of, – one's own way, – a will of one's own, – one's fling; do what one -likes, – wishes, – pleases, – chooses; go at large, feel at home, paddle one's own canoe; stand on one's -legs, – rights; shift for oneself.

take a liberty; make -free with, – oneself quite at home; use a freedom; take -leave, – French leave.

set free &c. (*liberate*) 750; give a loose to &c. (*permit*) 760; allow -, give -scope &c. *n.* to; give a horse his head.

make free of; give the -freedom of, – franchise; en-, af-franchise.

laisser -faire, – aller; live and let live; leave to oneself; leave -, let- alone.

Adj. free, – as air; out of harness, independent, at large, loose, scot-free; left -alone, – to oneself.

in full swing; uncaught, unconstrained, unbuttoned, unconfined, unrestrained, unchecked, unprevented, unhindered, unobstructed, unbound, uncontrolled, untrammeled.

unsubject, ungoverned, unenslaved, unenthralled, unchained, unshackled, unfettered, unreined, unbridled, uncurbed, unmuzzled.

unrestricted, unlimited, unconditional; absolute; discretionary &c. (*optional*) 600.

unassailed, unforced, uncompelled. unbiassed, spontaneous.

749. Subjection. — N. subjection; depend-ence, -ency; subordination; thrall, thraldom, enthrallment, subjugation, bondage, serfdom; feudal-ism, -ity; vassalage, villenage; slavery, enslavement, involuntary servitude; conquest.

service; servi-tude, -torship; tendence, employ, tutelage, clientship; liability &c. 177; constraint &c. 751; oppression &c. (*severity*) 739; yoke &c. (*means of restraint*) 752; submission &c. 725; obedience &c. 743.

V. be -subject &c. *adj.*; be -, lie- at the mercy of; depend -, lean -, hang- upon; fall -a prey to, – under; play second fiddle.

be a -mere machine, – puppet, – football; not dare to say one's soul is his own; drag a chain.

serve &c. 746; obey &c. 743; submit &c. 725.

break in, tame; subject, subjugate; master &c. 731; tread -down, – under foot; weigh down; drag at one's chariot wheels; reduce to -subjection, – slavery; en-, in-, be-thrall; enslave, lead captive; take into custody &c. (*restrain*) 751; rule &c. 737; drive into a corner, hold at the sword's point; keep under; hold in -bondage, – leading strings, – swaddling clothes.

Adj. subject, dependent, subordinate; feud-al, -atory; in subjection to, under control; in -leading strings, – harness; subjected, enslaved &c. *v.*; constrained &c. 751; downtrodden; over-borne, -whelmed; under the lash, on the hip, led by the nose, henpecked; the -puppet, – sport, – plaything- of; under one's -orders, – command, – thumb; a slave to; at the mercy of; in the -power, – hands, – clutches- of; at the feet of; at one's beck and call &c. (*obedient*) 743; liable &c. 177; parasitical; stipendiary.

Adv. under.

Phr. " slaves — in a land of light and law " [Whittier].

free and easy; at –, at one's- ease; *dégagé*, quite at home; wanton, rampant, irrepressible, unvanquished.

exempt; freed &c. 750; freeborn; autonomous, freehold, allodial; gratis &c. 815; eleutherian.

unclaimed, going a begging.

Adv. freely &c. *adj.*; *ad libitum* &c. (*at will*) 600.

Phr. *ubi libertas ibi patria.*

750. Liberation. — N. liberation, disengagement, release, enlargement, emancipation; disenthral(l)ment; af-, enfranchisement; manumission; discharge, dismissal.

deliverance &c. 672; redemption, extrication, acquittance, absolution; acquittal &c. 970; escape &c. 671.

V. liberate, free; set -free, – clear, – at liberty; render free, emancipate, release; en-, af-franchise; manumit; enlarge; dis-band, -charge, -enthral(l), -miss; let -go, – loose, – out, – slip; cast –, turn- adrift; deliver &c. 672; absolve &c. (*acquit*) 970.

unfetter &c. 751, untie &c. 43; loose &c. (*disjoin*) 44; loosen, relax; un-bolt, -bar, -close, -cork, -clog, -hand, -bind, -chain, -harness; dis-engage, -entangle; clear, extricate, unloose.

gain –, obtain –, acquire- one's -liberty &c. 748; get -rid, – clear- of; deliver oneself from; shake off the yoke, slip the collar; break -loose, – prison; tear asunder one's bonds, cast off trammels; escape &c. 671.

Adj. liberated &c. *v.*; out of harness &c. (*free*) 748.

Int. unhand me! let me go!

751. Restraint. — N. restraint; hindrance &c. 706; coercion &c. (*compulsion*) 744; cohibition, constraint, repression; discipline, control.

confinement; durance, duress; imprisonment; incarceration, coarctation †, entombment, mancipation, durance vile, limbo, captivity; blockade.

arrest, -ation; custody, keep, care, charge, ward, restringency.

curb &c. (*means of restraint*) 752; *lettres de cachet*.

limitation, restriction, protection, monopoly; prohibition &c. 761.

prisoner &c. 754; repressionist.

V. restrain, check; put –, lay- under restraint; en-, in-, be-thral(l); restrict; debar &c. (*hinder*) 706; constrain; coerce &c. (*compel*) 744; curb, control; hold –, keep- -back, – from, – in, – in check, – within bounds; hold in -leash, – leading strings; withhold.

keep under; repress, suppress; smother; pull in, rein in; hold, – fast; keep a tight hand on; prohibit &c. 761; in-, cohibit.

enchain; fasten &c. (*join*) 43; fetter, shackle; en-, trammel; bridle, muzzle, hopple, gag, pinion, manacle, handcuff, tie one's hands, hobble, bind hand and foot; swathe, swaddle; pin down, tether; picket; tie, – up, – down; secure; forge fetters.

confine; shut -up, – in; clap up, lock up, box up, mew up, bottle up, cork up, seal up, button up; hem in, bolt in, wall in, rail in; impound, pen, coop; inclose &c. (*circumscribe*) 229; cage; in-, en-cage; close the door upon, cloister; imprison, immure; incarcerate, entomb; clap –, lay- under hatches; put in -irons, – a strait-waistcoat; throw –, cast- into prison; put into bilboes.

arrest; take -up, – charge of, – into custody; take –, make- -prisoner, – captive; captivate; lead -captive, – into captivity; send –, commit- to prison; commit; give in -charge, – custody; subjugate &c. 749.

Adj. re-, con-strained; imprisoned &c. *v.*; pent up; jammed in, wedged in; under -restraint, – lock and key, – hatches; in swaddling clothes; on parole; in custody &c. (*prisoner*) 754; cohibitive; coactive &c. (*compulsory*) 744.

stiff, restringent, strait-laced, hidebound, barkbound.

ice-, wind-, weather-bound; " cabined cribbed confined " [*Macbeth*]; in Lob's pound, laid by the heels.

752. [Means of restraint.] Prison. — N. prison, -house; jail, gaol, cage, coop, den, cell; stronghold, fortress, keep, donjon, dungeon, Bastille, *oubliette*,

bridewell, house of correction, hulks, tollbooth, panopticon, penitentiary, guardroom, lockup, hold; round –, watch –, station –, sponging- house; station; house of detention, black hole, pen, fold, pound; inclosure &c. 232; penal settlement; bilboes, stocks, limbo, quod *; calaboose, *chauki*, choky, *thana;* workhouse [U. S.].

Newgate, Fleet, Marshalsea; King's (*or* Queen's) Bench.

bond; bandage; irons, pinion, gyve, fetter, shackle, trammel, manacle, handcuff, strait-waistcoat, hopples; vice, vise.

yoke, collar, halter, harness; muzzle, gag, bit, brake, curb, snaffle, bridle; rein, -s; bearing rein; martingale; leading string; tether, picket, band, guy, chain; cord &c. (*fastening*) 45; cavesson, hackamore [U. S.], headstall, jaquima [U. S.], lines, ribbons.

bolt, bar, lock, padlock, rail, wall; paling, palisade; fence; barrier, barricade.

drag &c. (*hindrance*) 706.

---

753. Keeper. — N. keeper, custodian, *custos*, ranger, warder, jailer, gaoler, turnkey, castellan, guard; watch, -dog, -man; Charley; chokidar, durwan, hayward; sen-try, -tinel; watch and ward; *concierge*, coastguard, *guarda costa*, gamekeeper.

escort, bodyguard.

protector, governor, duenna; guardian; governess &c. (*teacher*) 540; nurse, *bonne*, ayah.

---

754. Prisoner. — N. prisoner, captive, *détenu*, close prisoner.

jail bird, ticket of leave man, *chevronné*.

V. stand committed; be -imprisoned &c. 751.

Adj. imprisoned &c. 751; in -prison, – quod *, – durance vile, – limbo, – custody, – charge, – chains; under -lock and key, – hatches; on parole.

---

755. [Vicarious authority.] Commission. — N. commission, delegation; con-, as-signment; procuration; deputation, legation, mission, embassy; agency, agentship; power of attorney; clerkship.

errand, charge, brevet, diploma, exequatur, permit &c. (*permission*) 760.

appointment, nomination, return; charter; ordination; installation, inauguration, investiture; accession, coronation, enthronement.

vicegerency; regency, regentship.

viceroy &c. 745; consignee &c. 758; deputy &c. 759.

V. commission, delegate, depute; consign, assign; charge; in-, en-trust; commit, – to the hands of; authorize &c. (*permit*) 760.

put in commission, accredit, engage, hire, bespeak, appoint, name, nominate, return, ordain; install, induct, inaugurate, invest, crown; en-roll, -list; give power of attorney to.

employ, empower; set –, place- over; send out.

be commissioned, be accredited; represent, stand for; stand in the -stead, – place, – shoes- of.

Adj. commissioned &c. *v.*

Adv. *per procurationem.*

---

756. Abrogation. — N. abrogation, annulment, nullification; *vacatur;* canceling &c. *v.*; cancel; revo-cation, -kement; repeal, rescission, defeasance.

dismissal, *congé*, demission †; bounce * [U. S.]; depos-al, -ition; dethronement; disestablish-, disendow-ment; deconsecration; sack *, walking-papers, -ticket; yellow cover *.

aboli-tion, -shment; dissolution.

counter-order, -mand; repudiation, retractation; recantation &c. (*tergiversation*) 607; abolitionist.

V. abrogate, annul, cancel; destroy &c. 162; abolish; revoke, repeal, rescind, reverse, retract, recall; abolitionize; over-rule, -ride; set aside; disannul, dissolve, quash, nullify, declare null and void; dis-establish, -endow; deconsecrate.

disclaim &c. (*deny*) 536; ignore, repudiate; recant &c. 607; divest oneself, break off.

counter-mand, -order; do away with; sweep –, brush- away; throw -overboard, – to the dogs; scatter to the winds, cast behind.

dismiss, discard; cast –, turn- -off, – out, – adrift, – out of doors, – aside, – away; send -off, – away, – about one's

business; discharge, get rid of &c. (*eject*) 297; bounce * [U. S.]; fire *, - out *; sack *.

cashier; break; oust; un-seat, -saddle; un-, de-, disen-throne; depose, uncrown; unfrock, strike off the roll; dis-bar, -bench.

be -abrogated &c.; receive its quietus.

Adj. abrogated &c. *v.*; *functus officio.*

Int. get along with you! begone! go about your business! away with!

757. Resignation. — N. resignation, retirement, abdication, renunciation, abjuration; abandonment, relinquishment.

V. resign; give -, throw- up; lay down, throw up the cards, wash one's hands of, abjure, renounce, forego, disclaim, retract; deny &c. 536.

abrogate &c. 756; desert &c. (*relinquish*) 624; get rid of &c. 782.

abdicate; vacate, - one's seat; accept the stewardship of the Chiltern Hundreds; retire; tender one's resignation.

Adj. abdicant.

Phr. "Othello's occupation's gone " [*Othello*].

758. Consignee. — N. consignee, trustee, nominee, committee.

delegate; commiss-ary, -ioner; emissary, envoy, commissionaire; messenger &c. 534.

diplomatist, diplomat(e), *corps diplomatique,* embassy; am-, em-bassador; representative, resident, consul, legate, nuncio, internuncio, *chargé d'affaires, attaché.*

vicegerent &c. (*deputy*) 759; plenipotentiary.

functionary, placeman, curator; treasurer &c. 801; agent, factor, bailiff, clerk, secretary, attorney, solicitor, proctor, broker, underwriter, commission agent, auctioneer, one's man of business; factotum &c. (*director*) 694; caretaker; dalal, dubash, garnishee, *gomashta.*

negotiator, go-between; middleman; under agent, employé; servant &c. 746.

traveler, bagman, *commis-voyageur,* touter, commercial traveler, drummer [U. S.], traveling man.

newspaper -, own -, special- correspondent.

759. Deputy. — N. deputy, substitute, vice, proxy, *locum tenens, badli,* delegate, representative, next friend, surrogate, secondary.

regent, vicegerent, vizier, minister, vicar; premier &c. (*director*) 694; chancellor, prefect, provost, warden, lieutenant, archon, consul, proconsul; viceroy &c. (*governor*) 745; commissioner &c. 758; Tsung-li Yamen, Wai Wu Pu; plenipotentiary, *alter ego.*

team, eight, eleven; champion.

V. be -deputy &c. *n.*; stand -, appear -, hold a brief -, answer- for; represent; stand -, walk- in the shoes of; stand in the stead of.

ablegate, accredit.

Adj. acting; vice, -regal; accredited to.

Adv. in behalf of.

Section II. Special Intersocial Volition

760. Permission. — N. permission, leave; allow-, suffer-ance; toler-ance, -ation; liberty, law, license, concession, grace; indulgence &c. (*lenity*) 740; favor, dispensation, exemption, release; connivance; vouchsafement.

authorization, warranty, accordance, admission.

761. Prohibition. — N. pro-, in-hibition; *veto,* disallowance; interdict, -ion; injunction; embargo, ban, taboo, proscription; *index expurgatorius;* restriction &c. (*restraint*) 751; hindrance &c. 706; forbidden fruit; Maine law [U. S.].

V. pro-, in-hibit; forbid, put one's

permit, warrant, brevet, precept, sanction, authority, firman; *hukm;* pass, -port; furlough, license, *carte blanche,* ticket of leave; grant, charter, patent.

V. permit; give -permission &c. *n.,* – power; let, allow, admit; suffer, bear with, tolerate, recognize; concede &c. 762; accord, vouchsafe, favor, humor, gratify, indulge, stretch a point; wink at, connive at; shut one's eyes to.

grant, empower, charter, enfranchise, privilege, confer a privilege, license, authorize, warrant; sanction; intrust &c. (*commission*) 755.

give -*carte blanche,* – the reins to, – scope to &c. (*freedom*) 748; leave -alone, – it to one, – the door open; open the -door to, – flood gates; give a loose to.

let off; absolve &c. (*acquit*) 970; release, exonerate, dispense with.

ask –, beg –, request- -leave, – permission.

veto upon, disallow; bar; debar &c. (*hinder*) 706, forefend.

keep -in, – within bounds; restrain &c. 751; cohibit, withhold, limit, circumscribe, clip the wings of, restrict; interdict, taboo; put –, place- under -an interdiction, – the ban; proscribe; exclude, shut out; shut –, bolt –, show- the door; warn off; dash the cup from one's lips; forbid the banns.

Adj. prohibit-ive, -ory; proscriptive; restrictive, exclusive; forbidding &c. *v.*

prohibited &c. *v.;* not -permitted &c. 760; unlicensed, contraband, under the ban of; illegal &c. 964; unauthorized, not to be thought of.

Adv. on no account &c. (*no*) 536.

Int. forbid it heaven! &c. (*deprecation*) 766.

hands –, keep- off! hold! stop! avast!

Phr. that will never do.

Adj. permitting &c. *v.;* permissive, indulgent; permitted &c. *v.;* patent, chartered, permissible, allowable, lawful, legitimate, legal; legalized &c. (*law*) 963; licit; unforbid, -den; unconditional.

Adv. by –, with –, on- -leave &c. *n.; speciali gratiâ;* under favor of; *pace; ad libitum* &c. (*freely*) 748, (*at will*) 600; by all means &c. (*willingly*) 602; yes &c. (*assent*) 488.

Phr. *avec permission; brevet d'invention.*

762. Consent. — N. consent; assent &c. 488; acquiescence; approval &c. 931; compliance, agreement, concession; yield-ance †, -ingness; accession, acknowledgment, acceptance, agnition †.

settlement, ratification, confirmation, adjustment.

permit &c. (*permission*) 760; promise &c. 768.

V. consent; assent &c. 488; yield assent, admit, allow, concede, grant, yield; come -over, – round; give into, acknowledge, agnize, give consent, comply with, acquiesce, agree to, fall in with, accede, accept, embrace an offer, close with, take at one's word, have no objection.

satisfy, meet one's wishes, settle, come to terms &c. 488; not -refuse &c. 764; turn a willing ear &c. (*willingness*) 602; jump at; deign, vouchsafe; promise &c. 768.

Adj. consenting &c. *v.;* squeezable; agreed &c. (*assent*) 488; unconditional.

Adv. yes &c. (*assent*) 488; by all means &c. (*willingly*) 602; if –, as- you please; be it so, so be it, well and good, of course.

Phr. *chi tace accousente.*

763. Offer. — N. offer, proffer, presentation, tender, bid, overture; proposal, -ition; motion, invitation; candidature; offering &c. (*gift*) 784.

V. offer, proffer, present, tender; bid; propose, move; make -a motion, – advances; start; invite, hold out, place in one's way, put forward.

hawk about; offer for sale &c. 796; press &c. (*request*) 765; lay at one's feet.

764. Refusal. — N. refusal, rejection; non-, in-compliance; denial; declining &c. *v.;* declension; declinature; peremptory –, flat –, point blank- refusal; repulse, rebuff; discountenance.

recusancy, abnegation, protest, disclaimer; dissent &c. 489; revocation &c. 756.

V. refuse, reject, deny, decline; nill, negative; refuse –, withhold- one's as-

offer –, present- oneself; volunteer, come forward, be a candidate; stand –, bid- for; seek; be at one's service; go a begging; bribe &c. (*give*) 784.

Adj. offer-ing, -ed &c. *v.*; in the market, for sale, to let, disengaged, on hire.

sent; shake the head; close the -hand, – purse; grudge, begrudge, be slow to, hang fire; pass [at cards].

be deaf to; turn -a deaf ear to, – one's back upon; set one's face against, discountenance, not hear of, have nothing to do with, wash one's hands of, stand aloof, forswear, set aside, cast behind one; not yield an inch &c. (*obstinacy*) 606.

resist, cross; not -grant &c. 762; repel, repulse; shut –, slam- the door in one's face; rebuff; send -back, – to the right about, – away with a flea in the ear; deny oneself, not be at home to; discard &c. (*repudiate*) 610; rescind &c. (*revoke*) 756; disclaim, protest; dissent &c. 489.

Adj. refusing &c. *v.*; rest-ive, -iff †; recusant; uncomplying, unconsenting; not willing to hear of, deaf to.

refused &c. *v.*; ungranted, out of the question, not to be thought of, impossible.

Adv. no &c. 536; on no account, not for the world; no thank you.

Phr. *non possumus;* [ironically] your humble servant; *bien obligé;* not on your life [U. S.].

765. Request. — N. requ-est, -isition; claim &c. (*demand*) 741; petition, suit, prayer; begging letter, round robin.

motion, overture, application, canvass, address, appeal, apostrophe; imprecation; rogation; proposal, proposition.

orison &c. (*worship*) 990; incantation &c. (*spell*) 993.

mendicancy; asking, begging &c. *v.*; postulation, solicitation, invitation, entreaty, importunity, supplication, instance, impetration, imploration, obsecration, obtestation, invocation, interpellation.

V. request, ask; beg, crave, sue, pray, petition, solicit, invite, pop the question, make bold to ask; beg -leave, – a boon; apply to, call to, put to; call -upon, – for; make –, address –, prefer –, put up- a -request, – prayer, – petition; make -application, – a requisition; ask –, trouble- one for; claim &c. (*demand*) 741; offer up prayers &c. (*worship*) 990; whistle for.

beg hard, entreat, beseech, plead, supplicate, implore; conjure, adjure; obtest; cry to, kneel to, appeal to; invoke, evoke; impetrate, imprecate, ply, press, urge, beset, importune, dun, tax, clamor for; cry -aloud, – for help; fall on one's knees; throw oneself at the feet of; come down on one's marrowbones.

beg from door to door, send the hat round, go a begging; mendicate, mump, cadge, beg one's bread.

dance attendance on, besiege, knock at the door.

bespeak, canvass, tout, make interest, court; seek, bid for &c. (*offer*) 763; publish the banns.

Adj. requesting &c. *v.*; precatory; suppli-ant, -cant, -catory; postulant; obsecratory.

importunate, clamorous, urgent; cap in hand: on one's -knees, – bended knees, – marrowbones.

766. [Negative request.] **Deprecation. — N.** deprecation, expostulation; intercession, mediation, protest, remonstrance.

V. deprecate, protest, expostulate, enter a protest, intercede for; remonstrate.

Adj. deprecatory, expostulatory, intercessory, mediatorial.

deprecated, protested.

un-, unbe-sought; unasked &c. (*see* ask &c. 765).

Int. cry you mercy! God forbid! forbid it Heaven! Heaven -forefend, – forbid! far be it from! hands off! &c. (*prohibition*) 761.

Adv. prithee, do, please, pray; be so good as, be good enough; have the goodness, vouchsafe, will you, I pray thee, if you please.

Int. for -God's, – heaven's, – goodness', – mercy's- sake!

Phr. *Dieu vous garde; dirige nos Domine.*

767. Petitioner. — N. petitioner, solicitor, applicant; suppli-ant, -cant; suitor, candidate, claimant, postulant, aspirant, competitor, bidder; place – pot- hunter; prizer.

beggar, mendicant, mumper, sturdy beggar, cadger; hotel runner, runner, steerer [U. S.], tout, touter.

canvasser, bagman &c. 758; salesman.

Section III. Conditional Intersocial Volition

768. Promise. — N. promise, under-taking, word, troth, plight, pledge, parole, word of honor, vow; oath &c. (*affirmation*) 535; profession, assurance, warranty, guarantee, insurance, obligation; contract &c. 769; stipulation.

engagement, preëngagement; affiance; betroth, -al, -ment.

V. promise; give a -promise &c. *n.*; undertake, engage; make –, form- an engagement; enter -into, – on- an engagement; bind –, tie –, pledge –, commit –, take upon- oneself; vow; swear &c. (*affirm*) 535, give –, pass –, pledge –, plight- one's -word, – honor, – credit, – troth; betroth, plight faith.

assure, warrant, guarantee; covenant &c. 769; attest &c. (*bear witness*) 467.

hold out an expectation; contract an obligation; become -bound to, – sponsor for; answer –, be answerable- for; secure; give security &c. 771; underwrite.

adjure, administer an oath, put to one's oath, swear a witness.

Adj. promising &c. *v.*; promissory; votive; under hand and seal, upon oath.

promised &c. *v.*; affianced, pledged, bound; committed, compromised; in for it.

Adv. as one's head shall answer for.

Phr. in for a penny in for a pound; *ex voto; gage d'amour.*

768a. Release from engagement. — **N.** release &c. (*liberation*) 750.

Adj. absolute; unconditional &c. (*free* 748.

769. Compact. — N. compact, contract, agreement, bargain; affidation; pact, -ion; bond, covenant, indenture; *bundobast*, deal.

stipulation, settlement, convention; compromise, cartel.

protocol, treaty, concordat, *Zollverein, Sonderbund*, charter, Magna Charta Pragmatic Sanction.

negotiation &c. (*bargaining*) 794; diplomacy &c. (*mediation*) 724; negotiatoi &c. (*agent*) 758.

ratification, completion, signature, seal, sigil, signet.

V. contract, covenant, agree for; engage &c. (*promise*) 768.

treat, negotiate, stipulate, make terms; bargain &c. (*barter*) 794.

make –, strike- a bargain; come to -terms, – an understanding; compromise &c. 774; set at rest; close, – with; conclude, complete, settle; confirm, ratify, clench, subscribe, underwrite; en-, in-dorse; put the seal to; sign, seal &c (*attest*) 467; indent.

take one at one's word, bargain by inch of candle.

Adj. agreed &c. *v.*; conventional; under hand and seal.

Phr. *caveat emptor.*

770. Conditions. — N. conditions, terms; articles, – of agreement; memorandum.

clauses, provisions; proviso &c. (*qualification*) 469; covenant, stipulation, obligation, ultimatum, *sine quâ non; casus fœderis.*

V. make –, come to- -terms &c. (*contract*) 769; make it a condition, stipulate, insist upon, make a point of; bind, tie up.

Adj. conditional, provisional, guarded, fenced, hedged in.

Adv. conditionally &c. (*with qualification*) 469; provisionally, *pro re natâ;* on condition; with a string to it.

771. Security. — N. security; guaran-ty, -tee; gage, warranty, bond, tie, pledge, plight, mortgage, debenture, hypothecation, bill of sale, lien, pawn, ṕignoration; real security; vadium.

stake, deposit, earnest, handsel, caution.

promissory note; bill, – of exchange; I.O.U.; personal security, covenant, specialty; parole &c. (*promise*) 768.

acceptance, indorsement, signature, execution, stamp, seal.

spon-sor, -sion, -sorship; surety, bail; mainpernor, hostage; god-chiid, -father, -mother.

recognizance; deed –, covenant- of idemnity.

authentication, verification, warrant, certificate, voucher, doquet; record &c. 551; probate, attested copy.

receipt; ac-, quittance; discharge, release.

muniment, title deed, instrument; deed, – poll; assurance, indenture; charter &c. (*compact*) 769; charter poll; paper, parchment, settlement, will, testament, last will and testament, codicil.

V. give -security, – bail, – substantial bail; go bail; pawn, impawn, spout, mortgage, hypothecate, impignorate.

guarantee, warrant, assure; accept, indorse, underwrite, insure.

execute, stamp; sign, seal &c. (*evidence*) 467.

let, sett; grant –, take –, hold- a lease; hold in pledge; lend on security &c. 787.

Phr. *bonis avibus;* " gone where the woodbine twineth."

772. Observance. — N. observance, performance, compliance, acquiescence, concurrence; obedience &c. 743; fulfillment, satisfaction, discharge; acquittance, -tal.

adhesion, acknowledgment; fidelity &c. (*probity*) 939; exact &c. 494- observance.

V. observe, comply with, respect, acknowledge, abide by; cling to, adhere to, be faithful to, act up to; meet, fulfill; carry -out, – into execution; execute, perform, keep, satisfy, discharge; do one's office.

perform –, fulfill –, discharge –, acquit oneself of- an obligation; make good; make good –, keep- one's -word, – promise; redeem one's pledge; keep faith with, stand to one's engagement.

Adj. observant, faithful, true, loyal; honorable &c. 939; true as the -dial to the sun, – needle to the pole; punct-ual, -ilious; literal &c. (*exact*) 494; as good as one's word.

Adv. faithfully &c. *adj.*

Phr. *ignoscito sæpe alteri nunquam tibi; tempori parendum;* " to God, thy country, and thy friend be true " [Vaughan].

773. Nonobservance. — N. nonobservance &c. 772; evasion, inobservance, failure, omission, neglect, laches, laxity, informality.

infringement, infraction; violation, transgression; piracy.

retractation, repudiation, nullification; protest; forfeiture.

lawlessness; disobedience &c. 742; bad faith &c. 940.

V. fail, neglect, omit, elude, evade, give the go-by to, set aside, ignore; shut –, close- one's eyes to.

infringe, transgress, violate, pirate, break, trample under foot, do violence to, drive a coach and six through.

discard, protest, repudiate, fling to the winds, set at naught, nullify, declare null and void; cancel &c. (*wipe off*) 552.

retract, go back from, be off, forfeit, go from one's word, palter; stretch –, strain- a point.

Adj. violating &c. *v.;* lawless, transgressive; elusive, evasive.

unfulfilled &c. (*see* fulfill &c. 772).

774. Compromise. — N. com-promise, -mutation, -position; middle term, *mezzo termine;* compensation &c. 30; abatement of differences, adjustment, mutual concession.

V. com-promise, -mute, -pound; take the mean; split the difference, meet one halfway, give and take; come to terms &c. (*contract*) 769; submit to –, abide by- arbitration; patch up, bridge over, arrange; straighten out, adjust, – differences; agree; make -the best of, – a virtue of necessity; take the will for the deed.

Section IV. Possessive Relations [1]

1. *Property in general*

775. Acquisition. — N. acquisition; gaining &c. *v.*; obtainment; procuration, -ement; purchase, descent, inheritance; gift &c. 784.

recovery, retrieval, revendication, replevin; redemption, salvage, trover; find, *trouvaille*, foundling.

gain, thrift; money-making, -grubbing; lucre filthy lucre, loaves and fishes, the main chance, pelf; emolument &c. (*remuneration*) 973.

profit, earnings, winnings, innings, pickings, net profit; avails; income &c. (*receipt*) 810; pro-ceeds, -duce, -duct; out-come, -put; return, fruit, crop, harvest; second crop, aftermath; benefit &c. (*good*) 618.

sweepstakes, trick, prize, pool; pot; wealth &c. 803.

[Fraudulent acquisition] subreption; obreption; stealing &c. 791.

776. Loss. — N. loss; de-, perdition; forfeiture, lapse.

privation, bereavement; deprivation &c. (*dispossession*) 789; riddance; damage, squandering, waste.

V. lose; incur –, experience –, meet with- a loss; miss; mislay, let slip, allow to slip through the fingers; be without &c. (*exempt*) 777a; forfeit.

get rid of &c. 782; waste &c. 638.

be lost, lapse.

Adj. losing &c. *v.*; not having &c. 777a.

shorn of, deprived of; denuded, bereaved, bereft, minus, cut off; dispossessed &c. 789; rid of, quit of; out of pocket.

lost &c. *v.*; long lost; irretrievable &c. (*hopeless*) 859; off one's hands.

Int. farewell to! adieu to.

V. acquire, get, gain, win, earn, obtain, procure, gather; collect &c. (*assemble*) 72; pick, – up; glean.

find; come –, pitch –, light- upon; scrape -up, – together; get in, reap and carry, net, bag, sack, bring home, secure; derive, draw, get in the harvest.

profit; make –, draw- profit; turn to -profit, – account; make -capital out of, – money by; obtain a return, reap the fruits of; reap –, gain- an advantage; turn -a penny, – an honest penny; make the pot boil, bring grist to the mill; make –, coin –, raise- money; raise -funds, – the wind; fill one's pocket &c. (*wealth*) 803.

treasure up &c. (*store*) 636; realize, clear; produce &c. 161; take &c. 789.

get back, recover, regain, retrieve, revendicate, replevy, redeem, come by one's own.

come -by, – in for; receive &c. 785; inherit; step into, – a fortune, – the shoes of; succeed to.

get -hold of, – between one's finger and thumb, – into one's hand, – at; take –, come into –, enter into- possession.

be -profitable &c. *adj.*; pay, answer.

accrue &c. (*be received*) 785.

Adj. acquir-ing, -ed &c. *v.*; profitable, advantageous, gainful, remunerative, paying, lucrative.

Phr. *lucri causa.*

---

[1] That is, relations which concern property.

777. Possession. — N. possession, seizin, seisin; ownership &c. 780; occupancy; hold, -ing; tenure, tenancy, feodality, dependency; vill-enage, -einage; socage, chivalry, knight service.

exclusive possession, impropriation, monopoly, retention &c. 781; pre-possession, -occupancy; nine points of the law; corner, usucaption.

future possession, heritage, inheritance, heirship, reversion, fee, seigniority; primo-, ultimo-geniture.

bird in hand, *uti possidetis*, chose in possession.

V. possess, have, hold, occupy, enjoy; be -possessed of &c. *adj.*; have -in hand &c. *adj.*; own &c. 780; command.

inherit; come -to, – in for.

engross, monopolize, forestall, regrate, impropriate, have all to oneself; corner; have a firm hold of &c. (*retain*) 781; get into one's hand &c. (*acquire*) 775.

belong to, appertain to, pertain to; be -in one's possession &c. *adj.*; vest in.

Adj. possessing &c. *v.*; worth; possessed of, seized of, master of, in possession of; usucapient; endowed –, blest –, instinct –, fraught –, laden –, charged- with.

possessed &c. *v.*; on hand, by one; in hand, in store, in stock; in one's -hands, – grasp, – possession; at one's -command, – disposal; one's own &c. (*property*) 780.

unsold; unshared.

Phr. *entbehre gern was du nicht hast; meum et tuum; tuum est.*

777a. Exemption. — N. exemption; absence &c. 187; exception, immunity, privilege, release.

V. not -have &c. 777; be -without &c. *adj.*; excuse.

Adj. exempt from, devoid of, without, unpossessed of, unblest with; immune from.

not -having &c. 777; unpossessed; untenanted &c. (*vacant*) 187; without an owner.

unobtained, unacquired.

778. [Joint possession.] Participation. — N. participation; co-, joint-tenancy; occupancy –, possession –, tenancy- in common; joint –, common-stock; co-, partnership; communion; community of -possessions, – goods; communism, socialism; coöperation &c. 709.

snacks, coportion †, picnic, hotchpot; co-heirship, -parceny, -parcenary; gavelkind.

participator, sharer; co-, partner; shareholder; co-, joint-tenant; tenants in common; co-heir, -parcener.

communist, socialist.

V. par-ticipate, -take; share, – in; come in for a share; go -shares, – snacks, – halves; share and share alike.

have –, possess –, be seized- -in common, – as joint tenants &c. *n.*

join in; have a hand in &c. (*coöperate*) 709.

Adj. partaking &c. *v.*; communistic.

Adv. share and share alike.

779. Possessor. — N. possessor, holder; occup-ant, -ier; tenant; person –, man- -in possession &c. 777; renter, lodger, lessee, underlessee; zemindar, ryot; tenant -on sufferance, – at will, – from year to year, – for years, – for life.

owner; propriet-or, -ress, -ary; impropriator, master, mistress, lord.

land-holder, -owner, -lord, -lady; lord -of the manor, – paramount; heritor, laird, vavasour, landed gentry, mesne lord; planter.

cestui-que-trust, beneficiary, mortgagor.

grantee, feoffee, releasee, devisee; legat-ee, -ary.

trustee; holder &c.- of the legal estate; mortgagee

right –, rightful- owner.

[Future possessor] heir, – apparent, – presumptive; heiress; inherit-or, -ress, -rix; reversioner, remainder-man.

780. Property. — N. property, possession, *suum cuique, meum et tuum.*

owner-, proprietor-, lord-ship; seignority; empire &c. (*dominion*) 737.

interest, stake, estate, right, title, claim, demand, holding; tenure &c. (*possession*) 777; vested –, contingent –, beneficial –, equitable- interest; use, trust, benefit; legal –, equitable- estate; seizin, seisin.

absolute interest, paramount estate, freehold; fee, – simple, – tail; estate -in fee, – in tail, – tail; estate in tail -male, – female, – general.

limitation, term, lease, settlement, strict settlement, particular estate; estate -for life, – for years, – *pur autre vie;* remainder, reversion, expectancy, possibility.

dower, dowry, jointure, appanage, inheritance, heritage, patrimony alimony; legacy &c. (*gift*) 784; Falcidian law, paternal estate, thirds.

assets, belongings, means, resources, circumstances; wealth &c. 803; money &c. 800; what one -is worth, – will cut up for; estate and effects.

landed –, real- -estate, – property; realty; land, -s; tenements; hereditaments; corporeal –, incorporeal- hereditaments; acres; ground &c. (*earth*) 342; acquest, messuage, toft.

territory, state, kingdom, principality, realm, empire, protectorate, sphere of influence.

manor, honor, domain, demesne; farm, plantation, hacienda; allodium &c. (*free*) 748; fieff, feoff, feud, zemindary, dependency; *arado,* merestead, ranch.

free-, copy-, lease-holds; folkland; chattels real; fixtures, plant, heirloom; easement; right of -common, – user.

personal -property, – estate, – effects; personalty, chattels, goods, effects, movables; stock, – in trade; things, traps, rattletraps, paraphernalia; equipage &c. 633.

parcels, appurtenances.

impedimenta; lug-, bag-gage; bag and baggage; pelf; cargo, lading.

rent roll; income &c. (*receipts*) 810; maul and wedges [U. S.].

patent, copyright; chose in action; credit &c. 805; debt &c. 806.

V. possess &c. 777; be the -possessor &c. 779- of; own; have for one's -own, – very own; come in for, inherit.

savor of the realty.

be one's -property &c. *n.*; belong to; ap-, pertain to.

Adj. one's own; landed, predial, manorial, allodial; free-, copy-, lease-hold; feu-, feo-dal.

Adv. to one's -credit, – account; to the good.

to one and -his heirs for ever, – the heirs of his body, – his heirs and assigns, – his executors administrators and assigns.

781. Retention. — N. retention; retaining &c. *v.*; keep, detention, custody; tenacity, firm hold, grasp, gripe, grip, iron grip.	**782. Relinquishment. — N.** relinquishment, abandonment &c. (*of a course*) 624; renunciation, expropriation, dereliction; cession, surrender, dispensation; resignation &c. 757; riddance.
fangs, teeth, claws, talons, nail, unguis, hook, tentacle, tenaculum; bond &c. (*vinculum*) 45.	derelict &c. *adj.*; foundling; jetsam, waif.
clutches, tongs, forceps, pincers, nippers, pliers, vice.	**V.** relinquish, give up, surrender, yield, cede; let -go, – slip; spare, drop, resign, forego, renounce, abandon, expropriate, give away, dispose of, part with; lay -aside, – apart, – down, – on the shelf &c. (*disuse*) 678; set -, put- aside;
paw, hand, finger, wrist, fist, neaf, neif. bird in hand; captive &c. 754.	
V. retain, keep; hold, – fast, – tight, one's own, – one's ground; clinch,	

clench, clutch, grasp, gripe, hug, have a firm hold of.

secure, withhold, detain; hold –, keepback; keep close; husband &c. (*store*) 636; reserve; have –, keep- in stock &c. (*possess*) 777; entail, tie up, settle.

Adj. retaining &c. *v.*; retentive, tenacious.

unforfeited, undeprived, undisposed, uncommunicated.

incommunicable, inalienable; in mortmain; in strict settlement.

Phr. *uti possidetis.*

culled; left &c. (*residuary*) 40.
Int. away with!

make away with, cast behind; discard cast off, dismiss; maroon.

give -notice to quit, – warning; supersede; be –, get- -rid of, – quit of; eject &c. 297.

rid –, disburden –, divest –, dispossess- oneself of; wash one's hands of.

cast –, throw –, pitch –, fling- -away, – aside, – overboard, – to the dogs; cast –, throw –, sweep- to the winds; put –, turn –, sweep- away; jettison.

quit one's hold.

Adj. relinquished &c. *v.*; cast off, derelict; unowned, unappropriated, un-

2. *Transfer of Property*

783. Transfer. — **N.** transfer, conveyance, assignment, alienation, abalienation; demise, limitation; conveyancing; transmission &c. (*transference*) 270; enfeoffment, bargain and sale, lease and release; exchange &c. (*interchange*) 148; barter &c. 794; substitution &c. 147.

succession, reversion; shifting -use, – trust; devolution.

V. transfer, convey; alien, -ate; assign; grant &c. (*confer*) 784; consign; make –, hand- over; pass, hand, transmit, negotiate; hand down; exchange &c. (*interchange*) 148.

change -hands, – from one to another; devolve, succeed; come into possession &c. (*acquire*) 775.

abalienate; disinherit; dispossess &c. 789; substitute &c. 147.

Adj. alienable, negotiable.

Phr. estate coming into possession.

784. Giving. — **N.** giving &c. *v.*; bestowal, bestowment, donation; presentation, -ment; accordance; con-, cession; delivery, consignment, dispensation, communication, endowment; investment, -iture; award.

almsgiving, charity, liberality, generosity.

[Thing given] gift, donation, present, *cadeau;* fairing; free gift, boon, favor, benefaction, grant, offering, oblation, sacrifice, immolation; lagniappe [U. S.], pilon [U. S.].

grace, act of grace, bonus.

allowance, contribution, subscription, subsidy, tribute, subvention.

bequest, legacy, devise, will, dotation, dot, appanage; voluntary -settlement, – conveyance &c. 783; amortization.

alms, largess, bounty, dole, sportule †, donative, help, oblation, offertory, honorarium, gratuity, Peter pence, sportula, Christmas box, Easter offering, vail,

785. Receiving. — **N.** receiving &c. *v.*; acquisition &c. 775; reception &c. (*introduction*) 296; suscipiency, acceptance, admission.

re-, ac-cipient; assignee, devisee; lega-tee, -tary; grantee, feoffee, donee, relessee, lessee; receiver.

sportulary †, stipendiary; beneficiary; pension-er, -ary; almsman.

income &c. (*receipt*) 810.

V. receive; take &c. 789; acquire &c. 775; admit.

take in, catch, touch; pocket; put into one's -pocket, – purse; accept; take off one's hands.

be received; come -in, – to hand; pass –, fall- into one's hand; go into one's pocket; fall to one's -lot, – share; come –, fall- to one; accrue; have -given &c. 784 to one.

Adj. receiving &c. *v.*; re-, sus-cipient.

received &c. *v.*; given &c. 784; secondhand.

douceur, drink money, *pourboire, trink-geld*, bakshish; fee &c. (*recompense*) 973; consideration.

bribe, bait, ground bait; peace offering, handsel; boodle *, graft, grease *.

giver, grantor &c. *v.*; donor, feoffer, settlor.

V. deliver, hand, pass, put into the hands of; hand –, make –, deliver –, pass –, turn- over; assign dower.

present, give away, dispense, dispose of; give –, deal –, dole –, mete –, fork –, squeeze- out.

pay &c. 807; render, impart, communicate.

concede, cede, yield, part with, shed, cast; spend &c. 809.

give, bestow, confer, grant, accord, award, assign. -

intrust, consign, vest in.

make a present; allow, contribute, subscribe, furnish its quota.

invest, endow, settle upon; bequeath, leave, devise.

furnish, supply, help; ad-, minister to; afford, spare; accommodate –, indulge –, favor- with; shower down upon; lavish, pour on, thrust upon; tip, bribe; tickle –, grease- the palm; offer &c. 763; sacrifice, immolate.

Adj. giving &c. *v.*; given &c. *v.*; allow-ed, -able; concessional; communicable; charitable, eleemosynary, sportulary †, tributary; gratis &c. 815; donative.

Phr. *auctor pretiosa facit; ex dono; res est ingeniosa dare* [Ovid].

not given, unbestowed &c. (*see* give, bestow &c. 784).

---

786. Apportionment. — **N.** apportion-, allot-, consign-, assign-, appointment; appropriation; dis-pensation, -tribution; division, deal; re-, partition; administration.

dividend, portion, contingent, share, allotment, lot, measure, dose; dole, meed, pittance; *quantum*, ration; ratio, proportion, quota, modicum, mess, allowance; *suerte*.

V. apportion, divide; distribute, administer, dispense; billet, allot, detail, cast, share, mete; portion –, parcel –, dole- out; deal, carve.

partition, assign, appropriate, appoint.

come in for one's share &c. (*participate*) 778.

Adj. apportioning &c. *v.*; respective.

Adv. respectively, each to each.

787. Lending. — **N.** lending &c. *v.*; loan, advance, accommodation, feneration †; mortgage &c. (*security*) 771; investment.

mont de piété, pawnshop, my uncle's.

lender, pawnbroker, money lender, usurer.

V. lend, advance, accommodate with; lend on security; loan; pawn &c. (*security*) 771.

intrust, invest; place –, put- out to interest.

let, demise, lease, sett, underlet.

Adj. lending &c. *v.*; lent &c. *v.*; unborrowed &c. (*see* borrowed &c. 788).

Adv. in advance; on -loan, – security.

788. Borrowing. — **N.** borrowing, pledging.

borrowed plumes; plagiarism &c. (*thieving*) 791.

replevin.

V. borrow, desume †.

hire, rent, farm; take a -lease, – demise; take –, hire- by the -hour, – mile, – year &c.; adopt, apply, appropriate, imitate, make use of, take.

raise –, take up- money; raise the wind; fly a kite, borrow of Peter to pay Paul; run into debt &c. (*debt*) 806.

replevy.

789. Taking. — **N.** taking &c. *v.*; reception &c. (*taking in*) 296; deglutition &c. (*taking food*) 298; appropriation, prehension, prensation †; capture, cap-

790. Restitution. — **N.** restitution, return; ren-, red-dition; restoration; reinvestment, recuperation; rehabilitation &c. (*reconstruction*) 660; reparation,

tion; ap-, de-prehension †; abreption †, seizure; ab-duction, -lation; subtraction &c. (*subduction*) 38; abstraction, ademption; androlepsy.

dispossession; depriv-ation, -ement; bereavement; divestment; disherison; distraint, distress; sequestration, confiscation; eviction &c. 297.

rapacity, rapaciousness, extortion, vampirism; theft &c. 791.

resumption; repris-e, -al; recovery &c. 775.

clutch, swoop, wrench; grip &c. (*retention*) 781; haul, take, catch; scramble.

taker, captor.

V. take, catch, hook, nab, bag, sack, pocket, put into one's pocket; receive; accept.

reap, crop, cull, pluck; gather &c. (*get*) 775; draw.

ap-, im-propriate; assume, possess oneself of; take possession of; commandeer; lay –, clap- one's hands on; help oneself to; make free with, dip one's hands into, lay under contribution; intercept; scramble for; deprive of.

take –, carry –, bear- -away, – off; adeem; abstract; hurry off –, run away-with; abduct; steal &c. 791; ravish; seize; pounce –, spring- upon; swoop -to, – down upon; take by -storm, – assault; snatch, reave.

snap up, nip up, whip up, catch up; kidnap, crimp, capture, lay violent hands on.

get –, lay –, take –, catch –, lay fast –, take firm- hold of; lay by the heels, take prisoner; fasten upon, grip, grapple, embrace, gripe, clasp, grab, clutch, collar, throttle, take by the throat, claw, clinch, clench, make sure of.

catch at, jump at, make a grab at, snap at, snatch at; reach, make a long arm, stretch forth one's hand.

take -from, – away from; disseize; deduct &c. 38; retrench &c. (*curtail*) 201; dispossess, ease one of, snatch from one's grasp; tear –, tear away –, wrench –, wrest –, wring- from; extort; deprive of, bereave; disinherit, cut off with a shilling.

oust &c. (*eject*) 297; divest; levy, distrain, confiscate; sequest-er, -rate; accroach; usurp; despoil, strip, fleece, shear, displume, impoverish, eat out of house and home; drain, – to the dregs; gut, dry, exhaust, swallow up; absorb &c. (*suck in*) 296; draw off; suck, – like a leech, – the blood of.

retake, resume; recover &c. 775.

Adj. taking &c. *v.*; privative, prehensile; pred-aceous, -al, -atory, -atorial; lupine, rap-acious, -torial; ravenous; parasitic.

bereft &c. 776.

Adv. at one fell swoop.

Phr. give an inch and take an ell.

atonement; compensation, indemnification.

release, replevin, redemption; recovery &c. (*getting back*) 775; remitter, reversion.

V. return, restore; give –, carry –, bring- back; render, – up; give up; let go, unclutch; dis-, re-gorge; regurgitate; recoup, reimburse, compensate, indemnify, reinvest, remit, rehabilitate; repair &c. (*make good*) 660.

redeem, recover &c. (*get back*) 775; take back again; revest, revert.

Adj. restoring &c. *v.*; recuperative &c. 660.

Phr. *suum cuique.*

791. Stealing. — N. stealing &c. *v.*; theft, thievery, robbery, latrociny †, direption; abstraction, appropriation; plagiar-y, -ism; autoplagiarism; rape, depredation; raid; *latrocinium.*

spoilation, plunder, pillage; sack, -age; rapine, brigandage, foray, razzia; blackmail; piracy, privateering, buccaneering; filibuster-ing, -ism; burglary; housebreaking; badger game *, hold-up * [U. S.].

peculation, embezzlement; fraud &c. 545; larceny, petty larceny, shoplifting.

thievishness, rapacity, kleptomania, Alsatia; den of -Cacus, – thieves; Black Hand [U. S.].

license to plunder, letters of marque.

V. steal, thieve, rob, purloin, pilfer, filch, prig, bag, nim †, crib, cabbage, palm; abstract; appropriate, plagiarize.

convey away, carry off, abduct, kidnap, crimp; make –, walk –, run- off with; run away with; spirit away, seize &c. (*lay violent hands on*) 789.

plunder, pillage, rifle, sack, loot, ransack, spoil, spoliate, despoil, strip, sweep, gut, forage, levy blackmail, pirate, pickeer †, maraud, lift cattle, poach, smuggle, run; badger *; bail –, hold –, stick- up; bunco, bunko, filibuster.

swindle, peculate, embezzle; sponge, mulct, rook, bilk, pluck, pigeon, fleece; defraud &c. 545; obtain under false pretenses; live by one's wits.

rob –, borrow of– Peter to pay Paul; set a thief to catch a thief.

disregard the distinction between *meum* and *tuum*.

Adj. thieving &c. *v.*; thievish, light-fingered; fur-acious, -tive; piratical; pred-aceous, -al, -atory, -atorial; raptorial &c. (*rapacious*) 789.

stolen &c. *v.*

Phr. *sic vos non vobis.*

792. Thief. — N. thief, robber, *homo trium literarum*, pilferer, rifler, filcher, plagiarist.

spoiler, depredator, pillager, marauder; harpy, shark *, land shark, falcon, mosstrooper, bushranger, Bedouin, brigand, freebooter, bandit, thug, dacoit, pirate, corsair, viking, Paul Jones; buccan-eer, -ier; piqu-†, pick-eerer †; rover, ranger, privateer, filibuster; rapparee, wrecker, picaroon; smuggler, poacher; abductor, badger *, bunko man, cattle thief, *chor*, contrabandist, crook *, hawk, hold-up * [U. S.], jackleg * [U. S.], kidnaper, rustler * [U. S.], sandbagger, sea king, skin *, sneak thief, spieler, strong-arm man [U. S.].

highwayman, Dick Turpin, Claude Duval, Macheath, footpad, sturdy beggar.

cut-, pick-purse; pickpocket, light-fingered gentry; sharper; card-, skittle-sharper; thimblerigger; rook *, Greek, blackleg, leg, welsher *; defaulter; Autolycus, Jeremy Diddler, Robert Macaire, artful dodger, trickster; swell mob *, *chevalier d'industrie;* shoplifter.

swindler, peculator; forger, coiner; fence, receiver of stolen goods, duffer; smasher.

burglar, housebreaker; cracks-, mags-man *; Bill Sikes, Jack Sheppard, Jonathan Wild.

793. Booty. — N. booty, spoil, plunder, prize, loot, swag *, pickings; *spolia opima*, prey; blackmail; stolen goods.

Adj. manubial †.

3. *Interchange of Property*

794. Barter. — N. barter, exchange, scorse †, truck system; interchange &c. 148.

a Roland for an Oliver; *quid pro quo;* com-mutation, -position; Indian gift [U. S.].

trade, commerce, mercature †, buying and selling, bargain and sale; traffic, business, nundination †, custom, shopping; commercial enterprise, speculation, jobbing, stockjobbing, agiotage, brokery.

dealing, transaction, negotiation, bargain.

free trade.

V. barter, exchange, truck, scorse †, swop; interchange &c. 148; commutate &c. (*substitute*) 147; compound for.

trade, traffic, buy and sell, give and take, nundinate †; carry on –, ply –, drive- a trade; be in -business, – the city; keep a shop, deal in, employ one's capital in.

trade –, deal –, have dealings- with; transact –, do- business with; open –, keep- an account with.

bargain; drive –, make- a bargain; negotiate, bid for; haggle, higgle; dicker [U. S.]; chaffer, huckster, cheapen, beat down; stickle, – for; out-, under-bid; ask, charge; strike a bargain &c. (*contract*) 769.

speculate, give a sprat to catch a herring; buy in the cheapest and sell in the dearest market; rig –, stag- the market.

Adj. commercial, mercantile, trading; interchangeable, marketable, staple, in the market, for sale.

wholesale, retail.

Adv. across the counter.

Phr. *cambio non è furto.*

795. Purchase. — N. purchase, emption; buying, purchasing, shopping; preëmption, refusal.

coemption, bribery; slave trade.

buyer, purchaser, *emptor*, vendee; patron, employer, client, customer, *clientèle.*

V. buy, purchase, invest in, procure; rent &c. (*hire*) 788; repurchase, buy in.

keep in one's pay, bribe, suborn; pay &c. 807; spend &c. 809.

make –, complete- a purchase; buy over the counter.

shop, market, go a shopping.

Adj. purchased &c. *v.*

Phr. *caveat emptor.*

796. Sale. — N. sale, vent, disposal; auction, roup, Dutch auction; outcry, vendue; custom &c. (*traffic*) 794.

vendi-bility, -bleness.

seller; vender, vendor; merchant &c. 797; auctioneer.

V. sell, vend, dispose of, effect a sale; sell -over the counter, – by auction &c. *n.*; dispense, retail; deal in &c. 794; sell -off, – out; turn into money, realize; bring -to, – under- the hammer; put up to auction; offer –, put up- for sale; hawk, bring to market; offer &c. 763; undersell.

let; mortgage &c. (*security*) 771.

Adj. under the hammer, in the market, for sale.

salable, marketable, vendible; unsalable &c., unpurchased, unbought; on one's hands.

Phr. *chose qui plaît est à demi vendue.*

797. Merchant. — N. merchant, trader, dealer, monger, chandler, salesman; changer; regrater; shop-keeper, -man; trades-man, -people, -folk.

retailer; chapman, hawker, huckster, higgler; pedlar, colporteur, cadger, Autolycus; sutler, vivandière; coster-man, -monger; tallyman; *camelot;* faker; vintner.

money-broker, -changer, -lender; cambist, usurer, moneyer, banker.

jobber; broker &c. (*agent*) 758; buyer &c. 795; seller &c. 796; bear, bull.

concern; firm &c. (*partnership*) 712.

798. Merchandise. — N. merchandise, ware, commodity, effects, goods, article, stock, produce, staple commodity; stock in trade &c. (*store*) 636; cargo &c. (*contents*) 190.

799. Mart. — N. mart; market, -place; fair, bazaar, staple, exchange, change, bourse, hall, guildhall; tollbooth, customhouse; Tattersall's.

shop, stall, booth; wharf; office, chambers, countinghouse, bureau; coun-, comp-ter.

ware-house, -room; depot, interposit, *entrepôt*, emporium, establishment; store &c. 636; department store, finding store [U. S.], grindery warehouse.

market-overt.

4. *Monetary Relations*

800. Money. — N. money -matters, – market; finance; accounts &c. 811; funds, treasure; capital, stock; assets &c. (*property*) 780; wealth &c. 803; supplies, ways and means, wherewithal, sinews of war, almighty dollar, needful, cash.

sum, amount; balance, -sheet; sum total; proceeds &c. (*receipts*) 810.

currency, circulating medium, specie, coin, piece, hard cash, dollar, sterling coin; pounds shillings and pence; £ s. d.; pocket, breeches pocket, purse; money in hand; ready, – money; rhino *, blunt *, dust *, mopus *, tin *, salt *, chink *; *argent comptant;* bottom-, buzzard-dollar *; cent, checks, dibs *, dime, double eagle, dough *, eagle; Federal –, fractional –, postal- currency; long-, short-bit [U. S.]; moss, nickel, pile *, pin money, quarter [U. S.], red cent, roanoke, rock *; seawan, -t; slug [U. S.], wad * [U. S.].

precious metals, gold, silver, copper, bullion, ingot, nugget.

petty cash, pocket money, change, small coin; doit, stiver, rap, mite, farthing, sou, penny, shilling, tester, groat, guinea; rouleau; wampum; good –, round –, lump- sum; power of money, plum, lac of rupees.

[Science of coins] numismatics, chrysology.

paper money; money –, Post Office- order; note, – of hand; bank –, promissory- note; I O U, bond; bill, – of exchange; draft, check, cheque, order, warrant, coupon, debenture, exchequer bill, assignat, greenback; blueback [U. S.], *hundi*, shinplaster * [U. S.].

remittance &c. (*payment*) 807; credit &c. 805; liability &c. 806.

draw-er, -ee; oblig-or, -ee; moneyer, coiner.

false –, bad- money; base coin, flash note, slip †, kite *; fancy stocks; Bank of Elegance.

argumentum ad crumenam.

V. amount to, come to, mount up to; touch the pocket; draw, – upon; indorse &c. (*security*) 771; issue, utter; discount &c. 813; back; de-, re-monetize; fiscalize, monetize.

Adj. monetary, pecuniary, crumenal †, fiscal, financial, sumptuary, numismatical; sterling; nummary.

Phr. *barbarus ipse placet dummodo sit dives* [Ovid]; " but the jingling of the guinea helps the hurt that honor feels " [Tennyson]; *Gelt regiert die Welt; nervos belli pecuniam infinitam* [Cicero]; *redet Geld so schweigt die Welt.*

801. Treasurer. — N. treasurer; bursar, -y; purser, purse bearer; cashkeeper, banker; depositary; questor, receiver, steward, trustee, accountant, Accountant General, almoner, liquidator, paymaster, cashier, teller; cambist; money changer &c. (*merchant*) 797.

financier, Chancellor of the Exchequer, minister of finance.

802. Treasury. — N. treasury, bank, exchequer, fisc, hanaper; cash register, kutcherry, bursary; strong-box, -hold, -room; coffer; chest &c. (*receptacle*) 191; safe; depository &c. 636; till, -er; purse; money-bag, -box; *porte-monnaie.*

purse strings; pocket, breeches pocket.

sinking fund; stocks; public –, parliamentary- -stocks, – funds, – securities; Consols, *crédit mobilier;* bonds.

803. Wealth. — N. wealth, riches, fortune, handsome fortune, opulence, affluence; good –, easy- circumstances; independence; competence &c. (*sufficiency*) 639; solvency.

provision, livelihood, maintenance; alimony, dowry; means, resources, substance; property &c. 780; command of money.

income &c. 810; capital, money; round sum &c. (*treasure*) 800; mint of money, mine of wealth, El Dorado, bonanza, Pactolus, Golconda, Potosi.

804. Poverty. — N. poverty, indigence, penury, pauperism, destitution, want; need, -iness; lack, necessity, privation, distress, difficulties, wolf at the door.

bad –, poor –, needy –, embarrassed –, reduced –, straightened- circumstances; slender –, narrow- means; straits; hand to mouth existence, *res angusta domi,* low water, impecuniosity.

beggary; mendi-cancy, -city; broken –, loss of- fortune; insolvency &c. (*nonpayment*) 808.

long -, full -, well lined -, heavy-purse; purse of Fortunatus; *embarras de richesses.*

pelf, Mammon, lucre, filthy lucre; loaves and fishes.

rich -, moneyed -, warm- man; man of substance; capitalist, millionaire, tippybob *, Nabob, Crœsus, Midas, Plutus, Dives, Timon of Athens; Timo-, Plutocracy; Danaë.

V. be -rich &c. *adj.*; roll -, wallow-in -wealth, - riches.

afford, well afford; command -money, - a sum; make both ends meet, hold one's head above water.

become -rich &c. *adj.*; fill one's -pocket &c. (*treasury*) 802; feather one's nest, make a fortune; make money &c. (*acquire*) 775.

enrich, imburse.

worship - Mammon, - the golden calf.

Adj. wealthy, rich, affluent, opulent, moneyed, monied, worth much; well -to do, - off; warm; well -, provided for.

made of money; rich as -Crœsus, - a Jew; rolling in -riches, - wealth.

flush, - of -cash, - money, - tin *; in -funds, - cash, - full feather; solvent, pecunious, out of debt, all straight.

Phr. one's ship coming in.

amour fait beaucoup mais argent fait tout; aurea rumpunt tecta quietem [Seneca]; *magna servitus ist magna fortuna;* " mammon, the least erected spirit that fell from Heaven " [*Paradise Lost*]; *opum furiata cupido* [Ovid]; *vera prosperità è non aver necessità; wie gewonnen so zerronnen.*

empty -purse, - pocket; light purse; beggarly account of empty boxes.

poor man, pauper, mendicant, mumper, beggar, starveling; *pauvre diable;* fakir, schnorrer.

V. be -poor &c. *adj.*; .want, lack, starve, live from hand to mouth, have seen better days, go down in the world, come upon the parish; go to -the dogs, - wrack and ruin; not have a -penny &c. (*money*) 800, - shot in one's locker; beg one's bread; *tirer le diable par la queue;* run into debt &c. (*debt*) 806.

render -poor &c. *adj.*; impoverish; reduce, - to poverty; pauperize, fleece, ruin, bring to the parish.

Adj. poor, indigent; poverty-stricken; badly -, poorly -, ill- off; poor as -a rat, - a church mouse, - Job; fortune-, dower-, money-, penni-less; unportioned, unmoneyed; impecunious; out -, short- of -money, - cash; without -, not-worth- a rap &c. (*money*) 800; *qui n'a pas le sou,* out of pocket, hard up; out at -elbows, - heels; seedy, bare-footed; beggar-ly, -ed; destitute; fleeced, stripped; bereft, bereaved; reduced.

in -want &c. *n.*; needy, necessitous, distressed, pinched, straitened; put to one's -shifts, - last shifts; unable to -keep the wolf from the door, - make both ends meet; embarrassed, under hatches; involved &c. (*in debt*) 806; insolvent &c. (*not paying*) 808.

Adv. in formâ pauperis.

Phr. *zonam perdidit;* " a penniless lass wi' a lang pedigree " [Lady Nairne]; *à pobreza no hay vergüenza;* " he that is down can fall no lower " [Butler]; *poca roba poco pensiero;* " steeped . . . in poverty to the very lips " [Othello]; " the short and simple annals of the poor " [Gray].

805. Credit. — **N.** credit, trust, tick, score, tally, account.

letter of credit, circular note; duplicate; mortgage, lien, debenture, paper credit, floating capital; draft, *lettre de créance,* securities.

creditor, lender, lessor, mortgagee; dun; usurer.

V. keep -, run up- an account with; intrust, credit, accredit.

place to one's -credit, - account; give -, take- credit; fly a kite.

Adj. credit-ing, -ed; accredited.

Adv. on -credit &c. *n.*; to the -account, - credit- of; *à compte.*

806. Debt. — **N.** debt, obligation, liability, indebtment, debit, score.

arrears, deferred payment, deficit, default; insolvency &c. (*nonpayment*) 808; bad debt.

interest; premium; usance, usury; floating -debt, - capital.

debtor, debitor; mortgagor; defaulter &c. 808; borrower.

V. be -in debt &c. *adj.*; owe; incur -, contract- a debt &c. *n.*; run up -a bill, - a score, - an account; go on tick; borrow &c. 788; run -, get- into debt; outrun the constable.

answer -, go bail- for.

Adj. indebted; liable, chargeable, answerable for.

in -debt, – embarrassed circumstances, – difficulties; incumbered, involved; involved –, plunged –, deep –, over head and ears- in debt; deeply involved; fast tied up; insolvent &c. (*not paying*) 808; minus, out of pocket.

unpaid; unrequited, unrewarded; owing, due, in arrear, outstanding.

Phr. *æs alienum debitorem leve gravius inimicum facit;* " neither a borrower nor a lender be " [*Hamlet*].

807. Payment. — N.

pay-, defrayment; discharge; ac-, quittance; settlement, clearance, liquidation, satisfaction, reckoning, arrangement.

acknowledgment, release; receipt, – in full, – in full of all demands; voucher.

repayment, reimbursement, retribution; pay &c. (*reward*) 973; money paid &c. (*expenditure*) 809.

ready money &c. (*cash*) 800; stake, remittance, installment.

payer, liquidator &c. 801.

V. pay, defray, make payment; pay -down, – on the nail, – ready money, – at sight, – in advance; cash, honor a bill, acknowledge; redeem; pay in kind.

pay one's -way, – shot, – footing; pay -the piper, – sauce for all, – costs; do the needful; shell –, fork- out; come down with, – the dust; tickle –, grease- the palm; expend &c. 809; put –, lay- down.

discharge, settle, quit, acquit oneself of; foot the bill; account –, reckon –, settle –, be even –, be quits- with; strike a balance; settle –, balance –, square- accounts with; quit scores; wipe –, clear- off old scores; satisfy; pay in full; satisfy –, pay in full of- all demands; clear, liquidate; pay -up, – old debts.

disgorge, make repayment; repay, refund, reimburse, retribute; make compensation &c. 30.

Adj. paying &c. paid &c. *v.*; owing nothing, out of debt, all straight; unowed, never indebted.

Adv. to the tune of; on the nail, money down.

808. Nonpayment. — N.

nonpayment; default, defalcation; protest, repudiation; application of the sponge; whitewashing.

insolvency, bankruptcy, failure; insufficiency &c. 640; run upon a bank; overdrawn account.

waste paper bonds; dishonored –, protested- bills; bogus check (cheque).

bankrupt, insolvent debtor, lame duck, man of straw, welsher, stag, defaulter, levanter.

V. not -pay &c. 807; fail, break, stop payment; become -insolvent, – bankrupt; be gazetted.

protest, dishonor, repudiate, nullify.

pay under protest; button up one's pockets, draw the purse strings; apply the sponge; pay over the left shoulder, get whitewashed; swindle &c. 791; run up bills, fly kites.

Adj. not paying; in debt &c. 806; behindhand, in arrear; beggared &c. (*poor*) 804; unable to make both ends meet, minus; worse than nothing.

insolvent, bankrupt, in the gazette, gazetted.

unpaid &c. (*outstanding*) 806; gratis &c. 815; unremunerated.

809. Expenditure. — N.

expenditure, money going out; out-goings, -lay; expenses, disbursement; prime cost &c. (*price*) 812; circulation; run upon a bank.

[Money paid] payment &c. 807; pay &c. (*remuneration*) 973; bribe &c. 973; fee, footing, garnish; subsidy; tribute; contingent, quota; donation &c. 784.

pay in advance, earnest, handsel, deposit, installment.

investment; purchase &c. 795.

V. expend, spend; run –, get- through; pay, disburse; ante, -up; pony up *

810. Receipt. — N.

receipt, value received, money coming in; income, incomings, innings, revenue, return, proceeds; gross receipts, net profit; earnings &c. (*gain*) 775; *accepta*, avails.

rent, – roll; rent-al, -age; rack-rent.

premium, bonus; sweepstakes, tontine.

pension, annuity; jointure &c. (*property*) 780; alimony, pittance; emolument &c. (*remuneration*) 973.

V. receive &c. 785; take money; draw –, derive- from; acquire &c. 775; take &c. 789.

[U. S.]; open –, loose –, untie- the purse strings; lay –, shell * –, fork * - out; bleed; make up a sum, invest, sink money.

fee &c. (*reward*) 973; pay one's way &c. (*pay*) 807; subscribe &c. (*give*) 784; subsidize.

Adj. expend-ing, -ed &c. *v.*; sumptuary.

Phr. *vectigalia nervos esse reipublicæ* [Cicero].

bring in, yield, afford, pay, return; accrue &c. (*be received from*) 785.

Adj. receiv-ing, -ed &c. *v.*; profitable &c. (*gainful*) 775.

811. Accounts. — N. accounts, accompts; commercial –, monetary- arithmetic; statistics &c. (*numeration*) 85; money matters, finance, budget, bill, score, reckoning, account.

books, account book, ledger; day –, cash –, pass- book; journal; debtor and creditor –, cash –, running- account; account current; balance, – sheet; *compte rendu*, account settled; *acquit*, assets, expenditure, liabilities, outstanding accounts; profit and loss -account, – statement; receipts.

bookkeeping, audit, double entry, reckoning.

accountant, auditor, actuary, bookkeeper; financier &c. 801; accounting party; chartered accountant.

V. keep accounts, enter, post, book, credit, debit, carry over; take stock; balance –, make up –, square –, settle -, wind up –, cast up- accounts; make accounts square.

bring to book, audit, tax, surcharge and falsify.

falsify –, garble –, cook –, doctor- an account.

Adj. monetary &c. 800; account-able, -ing.

812. Price. — N. price, amount, cost, expense, prime cost, charge, figure, demand, damage, fare, hire; wages &c. (*remuneration*) 973.

dues, duty, toll, tax, impost, cess, sess, tallage, levy; *abkari;* capitation –, poll- tax; doomage [U. S.], *likin;* gabel, gabelle; gavel, *octroi*, custom, excise, assessment, benevolence, tithe, tenths, exactment, ransom, salvage, tariff; broker-, wharf-, freight-age.

worth, rate, value, par value, valuation, appraisement, money's worth; penny &c. -worth; price current, market price, quotation; what it will -fetch &c. *v.*

bill &c. (*account*) 811; shot.

V. bear –, set –, fix- a price; appraise, assess, doom [U. S.], price, charge, demand, ask, require, exact, run up; distrain; run up a bill &c. (*debt*) 806; have one's price; liquidate.

amount to, come to, mount up to; stand one in.

fetch, sell for, cost, bring in, yield, afford.

Adj. priced &c. *v.*; to the tune of, *ad valorem;* dutiable; mercenary, venal.

Phr. no penny no paternoster; *point d'argent point de Suisse*, no longer pipe no longer dance, no song no supper.

one may have it for; *à bon marché*.

813. Discount. — N. discount, abatement, concession, reduction, depreciation, allowance, qualification, set-off, drawback, poundage, agio, percentage; rebate, -ment; backwardation, contango; salvage; tare and tret.

V. discount, bate; a-, re-bate; reduce, take off, allow, give, make allowance; tax.

Adj. discounting &c. *v.*

Adv. at a discount, below par.

814. Dearness. — N. dearness &c. *adj.*; high –, famine –, fancy- price; overcharge; extravagance; exorbitance, extortion; heavy pull upon the purse.

V. be -dear &c. *adj.*; cost -much, – a pretty penny; rise in price, look up.

overcharge, bleed, fleece, extort.

815. Cheapness. — N. cheapness, low price; depreciation; bargain; good penny &c.- worth; snap [U. S.].

[Absence of charge] gratuity; free -quarters, – seats, – admission, -warren; run of one's teeth; nominal price. peppercorn rent; labor of love.

pay -too much, – through the nose, –
too dear for one's whistle.

Adj. dear; high, – priced; of great
price, expensive, costly, precious, worth
a Jew's eye, dear bought; unreasonable,
extravagant, exorbitant, extortionate.

at a premium; not to be had, – for
love or money; beyond –, above- price;
priceless, of priceless value.

Adv. dear, -ly; at great –, heavy-
cost; *à grands frais.*

Phr. prices looking up; *le jeu ne vaut pas la
chandelle; le coût en ôte le goût; vel prece vel
pretio.*

drug in the market; deadhead.

V. be -cheap &c. *adj.*; cost little;
come down –, fall- in price.

buy for -a mere nothing, – an old
song; have one's money's worth.

Adj. cheap; low, – priced; moderate,
reasonable; in-, un-expensive; well –,
worth the money; *magnifique et pas cher;*
good –, cheap- at the price; dirt –, dog-
cheap; cheap, -as dirt, – and nasty;
catchpenny.

half-price, depreciated, unsalable.

gratuitous, gratis, free, for nothing;
cost-, expense-less; without charge, not
charged, untaxed; scot –, shot –, rent-
free; free of -cost, – expense; honorary, unbought, unpaid.

Adv. for a mere song; at -cost price, – prime cost, – a reduction; *à bon
marché.*

816. Liberality. — **N.** liberality, generosity, munificence; bount--y, --eous-
ness, -ifulness; hospitality; charity &c.
(*beneficence*) 906.

V. be -liberal &c. *adj.*; spend –, bleed-
freely; shower down upon; open one's
purse strings &c. (*disburse*) 809; spare
no expense, give *carte blanche.*

Adj. liberal, free, generous; charitable &c. (*beneficent*) 906; hospitable;
bount-iful, -eous; handsome; unsparing,
ungrudging; unselfish; open-, free-,
full-handed; open-, large-, free-hearted;
munificent, princely.

overpaid.

Phr. " handsome is that handsome does "
[Goldsmith].

817. Economy. — **N.** economy, frugality; thrift, -iness; care, husbandry,
good housewifery, savingness, retrenchment.

savings; prevention of waste, save-all;
cheese parings and candle ends; parsimony &c. 819.

V. be -economical &c. *adj.*; practice
economy; economize, save; retrench;
cut one's coat according to one's cloth,
make both ends meet, keep within compass, meet one's expenses, pay one's
way; husband &c. (*lay by*) 636; save –,
invest- money; put out to interest;
provide –, save- -for, – against- a rainy
day; feather one's nest; look after the
main chance.

Adj. economical, frugal, careful,
thrifty, saving, chary, spare, sparing; parsimonious &c. 819.
underpaid.

Adv. sparingly &c. *adj.*; *ne quid nimis.*

Phr. *adde parvum parvo magnus acervus erit; magnum est vectigal parsimonia* [Cicero].

818. Prodigality. — **N.** prodi-gality,
-gence †; unthriftiness, waste; profusion, -eness; extravagance; squandering
&c. *v.*; malversation.

prodigal; spend-, waste-thrift; losel,
squanderer, locust; high roller * [U. S.].

V. be -prodigal &c. *adj.*; squander,
lavish, sow broadcast; pour forth like
water; blow in *; pay through the nose
&c. (*dear*) 814; spill, waste, dissipate, exhaust, drain, eat out of house and home,
overdraw, outrun the constable; run
-out, – through; misspend; throw -good
money after bad, – the helve after the
hatchet; burn the candle at both ends;

819. Parsimony. — **N.** parsimony,
parcity †; parsimoniousness, stinginess
&c. *adj.*; stint; illiberality, avarice, tenacity, avidity, rapacity, extortion, venality, cupidity; selfishness &c. 943;
auri sacra fames.

miser, niggard, churl, screw, skinflint,
crib, codger, muckworm, scrimp, lickpenny, hunks, curmudgeon, Harpagon,
harpy, extortioner, Jew, usurer; Hessian
[U. S.]; pinch-fist, -penny.

V. be -parsimonious &c. *adj.*; grudge,
begrudge, stint, pinch, gripe, screw, dole
out, hold back, withhold, starve, famish, live upon nothing, skin a flint.

make ducks and drakes of one's money; fool –, potter –, muddle –, fritter –, throw– away one's money; pour water into a sieve, kill the goose that lays the golden eggs; *manger son blé en herbe.*

Adj. prodigal, profuse, thriftless, unthrifty, improvident, wasteful, losel, extravagant, lavish, dissipated, overliberal; full-handed &c. (*liberal*) 816.

penny wise and pound foolish.

Adv. with an unsparing hand; money burning one's pocket.

Phr. *amor nummi; facile largiri de alieno; wie gewonnen so zerronnen; les fous font les festins et les sages les mangent;* "spendthrift alike of money and of wit" [Cowper]; "squandering wealth was his peculiar art" [Dryden].

drive a -bargain, – hard bargain; cheapen, beat down; stop one hole in a sieve; have an itching palm, grasp, grab.

Adj. parsimonious, penurious, stingy, miserly, mean, shabby, peddling, scrubby, penny wise, near, niggardly, close; fast-, close-, strait-handed; close-, hard-, tight-fisted; tight, sparing; chary; grudging, griping &c. *v.*; illiberal, ungenerous, churlish, hidebound, sordid, mercenary, venal, covetous, usurious, avaricious, greedy, extortionate, rapacious.

Adv. with a sparing hand.

Phr. *desunt inopiæ multa avaritiæ omnia* [Syrus]; "hoards after hoards his rising raptures fill" [Goldsmith]; "the unsunn'd heaps of miser's treasures" [Milton].

CLASS VI

Words relating to the SENTIENT and MORAL POWERS

Section I. AFFECTIONS IN GENERAL

820. Affections. — N. affections, character, qualities, disposition, nature, spirit, tone; temper, -ament; diathesis, idiosyncrasy; cast -, habit -, frame- of -mind, – soul; predilection, turn; natural -, turn of mind; bent, bias, predisposition, proneness, proclivity; propen-sity, -seness, -sion, -dency †; vein, humor, mood, grain, mettle; sympathy &c. (*love*) 897.

soul, heart, breast, bosom, inner man; heart's -core, – strings, – blood; heart of hearts, *penetralia mentis;* secret and inmost recesses of the –, cockles of one's- heart; inmost- heart, – soul; backbone.

passion, pervading spirit; ruling –, master- passion; *furore;* fullness of the heart, heyday of the blood, flesh and blood, flow of soul.

energy, fervor, fire, force.

V. have –, possess- -affections &c. *n.*; be of a -character &c. *n.*; be -affected &c. *adj.*; breathe.

Adj. affected, characterized, formed, molded, cast; at-, tempered; framed; pre-, disposed; prone, inclined; having a -bias &c. *n.*; tinctured –, imbued –, penetrated –, eaten up- with.

inborn, inbred, ingrained; deep-rooted, ineffaceable, inveterate; pathoscopic; congenital, dyed in the wool, implanted by nature, inherent, in the grain.

Adv. in one's -heart &c. *n.*; at heart; heart and soul &c. 821.

Phr. " affection is a coal that must be cool'd else suffer'd it will set the heart on fire " [*Venus and Adonis*].

821. Feeling. — N. feeling; suffering &c. *v.*; endurance, tolerance, sufferance, supportance, experience, response; sympathy &c. (*love*) 897; impression, inspiration, affection, sensation, emotion, pathos, deep sense.

warmth, glow, unction, gusto, vehemence; ferv-or, -ency; heartiness, cordiality; earnestness, eagerness; *empressement,* gush, ardor, zeal, passion, enthusiasm, verve, *furore,* fanaticism; excitation of feeling &c. 824; fullness of the heart &c. (*disposition*) 820; passion &c. (*state of excitability*) 825; ectasy &c. (*pleasure*) 827.

blush, suffusion, flush; hectic; tingling, thrill, turn, shock; agitation &c. (*irregular motion*) 315; quiver, heaving, flutter, flurry, fluster, twitter, tremor; throb, -bing; pulsation, palpitation, panting; trepid-, perturb-ation; ruffle, hurry of spirits, pother, stew, ferment; state of excitement.

V. feel; receive an -impression &c. *n.*; be -impressed with &c. *adj.*; entertain –, harbor –, cherish- -feeling &c. *n.*

respond; catch the -flame, – infection; enter the spirit of.

bear, suffer, support, sustain, endure, thole, aby; abide &c. (*be composed*) 826; experience &c. (*meet with*) 151; taste, prove; labor –, smart- under; bear the brunt of, brave, stand.

swell, glow, warm, flush, blush, change color, mantle; turn -color, – pale, – red, – black in the face; tingle, thrill, heave, pant, throb, palpitate, go pitapat, tremble, quiver, flutter, twitter; shake &c. 315; be -agitated, – excited &c. 824; look -blue, – black; wince, draw a deep breath.

impress &c. (*excite the feelings*) 824.

Adj. feeling &c. *v.*; sentient; sensuous; sensor-ial, -y; emo-tive, -tional; of -, with -feeling &c. *n.*

warm, quick, lively, smart, strong, sharp, acute, cutting, piercing, incisive; keen, – as a razor; trenchant, pungent, racy, piquant, poignant, caustic.

impressive, deep, profound, indelible; deep-, home-, heart-felt; swelling, soul-stirring, deep-mouthed, heart-expanding, electric, thrilling, rapturous, ecstatic.

earnest, wistful, eager, breathless; fer-vent, -vid; gushing, passionate, warm-hearted, hearty, cordial, sincere, zealous, enthusiastic, glowing, ardent, burning, red-hot, fiery, flaming; boiling, – over.

pervading, penetrating, absorbing; rabid, raving, feverish, fanatical, hysterical; impetuous &c. (*excitable*) 825.

impressed -, moved -, touched -, affected -, penetrated -, seized -, imbued &c. 820- with; devoured by; wrought up &c. (*excited*) 824; struck all of a heap; rapt; in a -quiver &c. *n.*; enraptured &c. 829.

Adv. heart and soul, from the bottom of one's heart, *ab imo pectore*, at heart, *con amore*, heartily, devoutly, over head and ears.

Phr. the heart -big, – full, – swelling, – beating, – pulsating, – throbbing, – thumping, – beating high, – melting, – overflowing, – bursting, – breaking.

---

822. Sensibility. — N. sensi-bility, -bleness, -tiveness; moral sensibility; impress-, affect-ibility; suscepti-bleness--bility, -vity; mobility; viva-city, -ciousness; tender-, soft-ness; sentimental-ity, -ism.

excitability &c. 825; fastidiousness &c. 868; physical sensibility &c. 375.

sore -point, – place; where the shoe pinches.

V. be -sensible &c. *adj.*; have a -tender, – warm, – sensitive- heart.

take to -, treasure up in the- heart; shrink.

" die of a rose in aromatic pain " [Pope]; touch to the quick; touch on the raw.

Adj. sensi-ble, -tive; impressi-ble, -onable; suscepti-ve, -ble; alive to, impassionable, gushing; warm-, tender-, soft-hearted; tender -, as a chicken; soft, sentimental, romantic; enthusiastic, highflying, spirited, mettlesome, vivacious, lively, expressive, mobile, tremblingly alive; excitable &c. 825; over-sensitive, without skin, thin-skinned; fastidious &c. 868.

Adv. sensibly &c. *adj.*; to the -quick, - inmost core.

Phr. *mens æqua in arduis.*

823. Insensibility. — N. insensi-bility, -bleness; moral insensibility; inertness, inertia, *vis inertiæ;* impassi-bility, -bleness; inappetency, apathy, phlegm, dullness, hebetude, supineness, lukewarmness.

cold -fit, – blood, – heart; cold-, coolness; frigidity, *sang froid;* stoicism, imperturbation &c. (*inexcitability*) 826; nonchalance, unconcern, dry eyes; insouciance &c. (*indifference*) 866; recklessness &c. 863; callousness; heart of stone, stock and stone, marble, deadness.

torp-or, -idity; obstupefaction †, lethargy, coma, trance; sleep &c. 683; suspended animation; stup-or, -efaction; paralysis, palsy; numbness &c. (*physical insensibility*) 376.

neutrality; quietism, vegetation.

V. be -insensible &c. *adj.*; have a rhinoceros hide; show -insensibility &c. *n.*; not -mind, – care, – be affected by; have no desire for &c. 866; have -, feel -, take- no interest in; *nil admirari;* not care a -straw &c. (*unimportance*) 643 for; disregard &c. (*neglect*) 460; set at naught &c. (*make light of*) 483; turn a deaf ear to &c. (*inattention*) 458; vegetate.

render -insensible, – callous; blunt, obtund, numb, benumb, paralyze, chloroform, deaden, hebetate, stun, stupefy; brut-ify, -alize; assify.

inure; harden, – the heart; steel, caseharden, sear.

Adj. insensible, unconscious; impassi-ve, -ble; blind to, deaf to, dead to; un-, in-susceptible; unimpress-ionable, -ible; passion-, spirit-, heart-, soulless; unfeeling; unmoral.

apathetic; leuco- †, phlegmatic; dull, frigid; cold, -blooded, -hearted; cold as charity; flat, maudlin, obtuse, inert, supine, sluggish, torpid, torpedinous, torporific; sleepy &c. (*inactive*) 683; languid, half-hearted, tame; numb, -ed; comatose; anæsthetic &c. 376; stupefied, chloroformed, palsy-stricken.

indifferent, lukewarm; careless, mindless, regardless; inattentive &c. 458; neglectful &c. 460; disregarding.

unconcerned, nonchalant, pococurante, insouciant, *sans souci;* unambitious &c. 866.

un-affected, -ruffled, -impressed, -inspired, -excited, -moved, -stirred, -touched, -shocked, -struck; unblushing &c. (*shameless*) 885; unanimated; vegetative.

callous, thick-skinned, pachydermatous, impervious; hard, -ened; inured, casehardened; steeled -, proof- against; imperturbable &c. (*inexcitable*) 826; unfelt.

Adv. insensibly &c. *adj.*; *æquo animo;* without being -moved, – touched, – impressed; in cold blood; with -dry eyes, – withers unwrung.

Phr. never mind; it is of no consequence &c. (*unimportant*) 643; it cannot be helped; nothing coming amiss; it is all -the same, – one- to.

824. Excitation. — **N.** excitation of feeling; mental –, excitement; suscitation, galvanism, stimulation, piquancy, provocation, inspiration, calling forth, infection; animation, agitation, perturbation; subjugation, fascination, intoxication; en-, ravishment; entrancement, high pressure.

unction, impressiveness &c. *adj.*

trial of temper, *casus belli;* irritation &c. (*anger*) 900; passion &c. (*state of excitability*) 825; thrill &c. (*feeling*) 821; repression of feeling &c. 826; sensationalism, yellow journalism.

V. excite, affect, touch, move, impress, strike, interest, animate, inspire, impassion, smite, infect; stir –, fire –, warm- the blood; set astir; a-, wake; a-, waken; call forth; e-, pro-voke; raise up, summon up, call up, wake up, blow up, get up, light up; raise; get up the steam, rouse, arouse, stir, fire, kindle, enkindle, apply the torch, set on fire, inflame.

stimulate; ex-, suscitate †; inspirit; spirit up, stir up, work up; infuse life into, give new life to; bring –, introduce- new blood; quicken; sharpen, whet; work upon &c. (*incite*) 615; hurry on, give a fillip, put on one's mettle.

fan the -fire, – flame; blow the coals, stir the embers; fan, – into a flame; foster, heat, warm, foment, raise to a fever heat; keep -up, – the pot boiling; revive, rekindle; rake up, rip up.

stir –, play on –, come home to- the feelings; touch -a string, – a chord, – the soul, – the heart; go to one's heart, penetrate, pierce, go through one, touch to the quick; possess –, pervade –, penetrate –, imbrue –, absorb –, affect –, disturb- the soul.

absorb, rivet the attention; sink into the -mind, – heart; prey on the mind; intoxicate; over-whelm, -power; *bouleverser,* upset, turn one's head.

fascinate; enrapture &c. (*give pleasure*) 829.

agitate, perturb, ruffle, fluster, shake, disturb, startle, shock, stagger; give one a -shock, – turn; strike all of a heap; stun, astound, electrify, galvanize, petrify.

irritate, sting; cut, – to the -heart, – quick; try one's temper; fool to the top of one's bent, pique; infuriate, madden, make one's blood boil; lash into fury &c. (*wrath*) 900.

be -excited &c. *adj.*; flash up, flare up; catch the infection; thrill &c. (*feel*) 821; mantle; work oneself up; seethe, boil, simmer, foam, fume, flame, rage, rave; run mad &c. (*passion*) 825.

Adj. excited &c. *v.*; wrought up, on the *qui vive,* astir, sparkling; in a -quiver &c. 821, – fever, – ferment, – blaze, – state of excitement; in hysterics; black in the face, overwrought; hot, red-hot, flushed, feverish; all -of a twitter, – in a pucker; with -quivering lips, – tears in one's eyes.

flaming; boiling, – over; ebullient, seething; foaming, – at the mouth; fuming, raging, carried away by passion, wild, raving, frantic, mad, distracted, beside oneself, out of one's wits, ready to burst, *bouleversé*, demoniacal.

lost, *éperdu*, tempest-tossed; haggard; ready to sink.

stung to the quick, up, on one's high ropes.

exciting &c. *v.*; impressive, warm, glowing, fervid, swelling, imposing, spirit-stirring, thrilling; high-wrought; soul-stirring, -subduing; heart-stirring, -swelling, -thrilling; agonizing &c. (*painful*) 830; telling, sensational, hysterical; over-powering, -whelming; more than flesh and blood can bear; yellow.

piquant &c. (*pungent*) 392; spicy, appetizing, provocative, *provoquant*, tantalizing.

Adv. till one is black in the face.

Phr. the heart -beating high, – going pitapat, – leaping into one's mouth; the blood -being up, – boiling in one's veins; the eye -glistening, – " in a fine frenzy rolling "; the head turned.

---

825. [Excess of sensitiveness.] **Excitability. — N.** excitability, impetuosity, vehemence; boisterousness &c. *adj.*; turbulence; impatience, intolerance, non-endurance; irritability &c. (*irascibility*) 901; itching &c. (*desire*) 865; wincing; disquiet, -ude; restlessness; fidget-s, -tiness; agitation &c. (*irregular motion*) 315.

trepidation, perturbation, ruffle, hurry, fuss, flurry; fluster, flutter; pother, stew, ferment; whirl; buck fever; hurry-skurry, thrill &c. (*feeling*) 821; state –, fever- of excitement; transport.

passion, excitement, flush, heat; fever, -heat; fire, flame, fume, blood boiling; tumult; effervescence, ebullition; boiling, – over; whiff, gust, storm, tempest; scene, breaking out, burst, fit, paroxysm, explosion; out-break, -burst; agony.

violence &c. 173; fierceness &c. *adj.*; rage, fury, furor, *furore*, desperation, madness, distraction, raving, delirium; phrensy, frenzy, hysterics; intoxication; tearing –, raging- passion; anger &c. 900.

fascination, infatuation, fanaticism; Quixot-ism, -ry; *tête montée*.

V. be -impatient &c. *adj.*; not be able to -bear &c. 826; bear ill, wince, chafe, champ the bit; be in a -stew &c. *n.*; be out of all patience, fidget, fuss, not have a wink of sleep; toss, – on one's pillow.

lose one's temper &c. 900; break –, burst –, fly- out; go –, fly- -off, – off at a tangent; explode; flare up, flame up, fire up, burst into a flame, take fire, fire, burn; boil, – over; foam, fume, rage, rave, rant, tear; go –, run- -wild, – mad;

826. [Absence of excitability, or of excitement.] **Inexcitability. — N.** inexcit-, imperturb-, inirrit-ability; even temper, tranquil mind, dispassion; tolerance, patience.

passiveness &c. (*physical inertness*) 172; hebet-ude, -ation; impassibility &c. (*insensibility*) 823; stupefaction.

coolness, calmness &c. *adj.*; composure, placidity, indisturbance, imperturbation, *sang froid*, tranquillity, serenity; quiet, -ude; peace of mind, mental calmness.

staidness &c. *adj.*; gravity, sobriety, Quakerism; philosophy, equanimity, stoicism, command of temper; self-possession, -control, -command, -restraint; presence of mind.

submission &c. 725; resignation; suffer-, support-, endur-, longsuffer-, forbear-ance; longanimity; fortitude; patience -of Job, – " on a monument " [*Twelfth Night*], – " sovereign o'er transmuted ill " [Johnson]; moderation; repression –, subjugation- of feeling; restraint &c. 751.

tranquillization &c. (*moderation*) 174.

V. be -composed &c. *adj.*

laisser -faire, – aller; take things -easily, – as they come; take it easy, rub on, live and let live; take -easily, – coolly, – in good part; *æquam servare mentem.*

bear, – well, – the brunt; go through, support, endure, brave, disregard.

tolerate, suffer, stand, bide; abide, aby; bear –, put up –, take up –, abide-with; acquiesce; submit &c. (*yield*) 725; submit with a good grace; resign –, reconcile- oneself to; brook, digest, eat, swallow, pocket, stomach; make -light of, – the best of, – " a virtue of neces-

go into hysterics; run -riot, – a muck; *battre la campagne, faire le diable à quatre,* play the deuce.

Adj. excitable, easily excited, in an excitable state; high-strung; irritable &c. (*irascible*) 901; impatient, intolerant.

feverish, febrile, hysterical; delirious, mad, moody, maggoty-headed.

unquiet, mercurial, electric, galvanic, hasty, hurried, restless, fidgety, fussy; chafing &c. *v.*

startlish, mettlesome, high-mettled, skittish.

vehement, demonstrative, violent, wild, furious, fierce, fiery, hot-headed, madcap.

overzealous, enthusiastic, impassioned, fanatical; rabid &c. (*eager*) 865.

rampant, clamorous, uproarious, turbulent, tempestuous, tumultuary, boisterous.

impulsive, impetuous, passionate; un-controll-ed, -able; ungovernable, irrepressible, stanchless, inextinguishable, burning, simmering, volcanic, ready to burst forth.

excit-ed, -ing &c. 824.

Int. pish! pshaw!

Phr. *noli me tangere;* " filled with fury, rapt, inspir'd " [Collins]; *maggiore fretta minore atto.*

sity " [Chaucer]; put a good face on, keep one's countenance; check &c. 751- oneself.

compose, appease &c. (*moderate*) 174; propitiate; repress &c. (*restrain*) 751; render insensible &c. 823; overcome –, allay –, repress- one's -excitability &c. 825; master one's feelings.

make -oneself, – one's mind- easy; set one's mind at -ease, – rest.

calm –, cool- down; gentle; thaw, grow cool.

be -borne, – endured; go down.

Adj. in-, un-excitable; imperturbable; unsusceptible &c. (*insensible*) 823; un-, dis-passionate; cold-blooded, inirritable; enduring &c. *v.*; stoical, Platonic, philosophic, staid, stayed; sober, – minded; grave; sober –, grave- as a judge; sedate, demure, cool-headed.

easy-going, peaceful, placid, calm; quiet, – as a mouse; tranquil, serene; cool, – as -a cucumber, – custard; undemonstrative.

temperate &c. (*moderate*) 174; composed, collected; un-excited, -stirred, -ruffled, -disturbed, -perturbed, -impassioned; unoffended; unresisting.

meek, tolerant; patient, – as Job; submissive &c. 725; tame; content, resigned, chastened, subdued, lamblike; gentle, – as a lamb; *suaviter in modo;* mild, – as mother's milk; soft as peppermint; armed with patience, bearing with, clement, long-suffering.

Adv. " like patience on a monument smiling at grief " [*Twelfth Night*]; *æquo animo,* in cold blood &c. 823; more in sorrow than in anger.

Int. patience! and shuffle the cards.

Phr. " adversity's sweet milk, philosophy " [*Romeo and Juliet*]; *mens æqua in arduis; philosophia stemma non inspicit* [Seneca]; *quo me cumque rapit tempestas deferor hospes* [Horace]; " they also serve who only stand and wait " [Milton].

Section II. PERSONAL AFFECTIONS[1]

1. Passive Affections

827. Pleasure. — **N.** pleasure, gratification, enjoyment, fruition; ob-, delectation; relish, zest; gusto &c. (*physical pleasure*) 377; satisfaction &c. (*content*) 831; complacency.

well-being; good &c. 618; snugness, comfort, ease; cushion &c. 215; *sans souci,* mind at ease.

joy, gladness, delight, glee, cheer, sunshine; cheerfulness &c. 836.

treat, refreshment; amusement &c. 840; luxury &c. 377.

828. Pain. — **N.** mental suffering, pain, dolor; suffer-ing, -ance; ache, smart &c. (*physical pain*) 378; passion.

displeasure, dissatisfaction, discomfort, discomposure, disquiet; *malaise;* inquietude, uneasiness, vexation of spirit; taking; discontent &c. 832.

dejection &c. 837; weariness &c. 841; anhedonia.

annoyance, irritation, worry, infliction, visitation; plague, bore; bother,

[1] Or those which concern one's own state of feeling.

mens sana in corpore sano [Juvenal].

happiness, felicity, bliss; beati-tude, -fication; enchantment, transport, rapture, ravishment ecstasy; *summum bonum;* paradise, elysium &c. (*heaven*) 981; third –, seventh- heaven; unalloyed -happiness &c.; hedonics, hedonism.

honeymoon; palmy –, halcyon- days; golden -age, – time; Dixie, Dixie's land; *Saturnia regna*, Arcadia, happy valley, Agapemone.

V. be pleased &c. 829; feel –, experience- -pleasure &c. *n.*; joy; enjoy –, hug- oneself; be in -clover &c. 377, – elysium &c. 981; tread on enchanted ground; fall –, go- into raptures.

feel at home, breathe freely, bask in the sunshine.

be -pleased &c. 829- with; receive –, derive- pleasure &c. *n.*- from; take -pleasure &c. *n.*- in; delight in, rejoice in, indulge in, luxuriate in; gloat over &c. (*physical pleasure*) 377; enjoy, relish, like; love &c. 897; take -to, – a fancy to; have a liking for; enter into the spirit of.

take in good part.

treat oneself to, solace oneself with.

Adj. pleased &c. 829; not sorry; glad, -some; pleased as Punch.

happy, blest, blessed, blissful, beatified; happy as -a clam at high water [U. S.], – a king, – the day is long; thrice happy, *ter quaterque beatus;* enjoying &c. *v.*; joyful &c. (*in spirits*) 836; hedonic.

in -a blissful state, – paradise &c. 981, – raptures, – ecstasies, – a transport of delight.

comfortable &c. (*physical pleasure*) 377; at ease; content &c. 831; *sans souci*.

overjoyed, entranced, enchanted; en-, raptured; en-, ravished; transported; fascinated, captivated.

with -a joyful face, – sparkling eyes.

pleasing &c. 829; ecstatic, beatic; painless, unalloyed, without alloy, cloudless.

Adv. happily &c. *adj.*; with pleasure &c. (*willingly*) 602; with -glee &c. *n.*

Phr. one's heart leaping with joy. "a wilderness of sweets" [*P. L.*]; "I wish you all the joy that you can wish" [*M. of Venice*]; *jour de ma vie;* "joy ruled the day and love the night" [Dryden]; "joys season'd high and tasting strong of guilt" [Young]; "oh happiness, our being's end and aim!" [Pope]; "there is a pleasure that is born of pain" [O. Meredith]; "throned on highest bliss" [*P. L.*]; *vedi Napoli e poi muori; zwischen Freud und Leid ist die Brücke nicht weit.*

-ation; stew, vexation, mortification, chagrin, *esclandre; mauvais quart d'heure*.

care, anxiety, solicitude, trouble, trial, ordeal, fiery ordeal, shock, blow, cark, dole, fret, burden, load.

concern, grief, sorrow, distress, affliction, woe, bitterness, heartache; carking cares; heavy –, aching –, bleeding –, broken- heart; heavy affliction, gnawing grief.

unhappiness, infelicity, misery, tribulation, wretchedness, desolation; despair &c. 859; extremity, prostration, depth of misery.

nightmare, ephialtes, incubus.

pang, anguish, agony; tor-ture, -ment; purgatory &c. (*hell*) 982.

hell upon earth; iron age, reign of terror; slough of despond &c. (*adversity*) 735; peck –, sea- of troubles; "ills that flesh is heir to" [*Hamlet*] &c. (*evil*) 619; miseries of human life; "unkindest cut of all" [*Julius Cæsar*].

sufferer, victim, prey, martyr, object of compassion, wretch, shorn lamb.

V. feel –, suffer –, experience –, undergo –, bear –, endure- pain &c. *n.*, smart, ache &c. (*physical pain*) 378; suffer, bleed, ail; be the victim of.

labor under afflictions; bear the cross; quaff the bitter cup, have a bad time of it; fall on evil days &c. (*adversity*) 735; go hard with, come to grief, fall a sacrifice to, drain the cup of misery to the dregs, "sup full of horrors" [*Macbeth*].

sit on thorns, be on pins and needles, wince, fret, chafe, worry oneself, be in a taking, fret and fume; take -on, – to heart; cark.

grieve; mourn &c. (*lament*) 839; yearn, repine, pine, droop, languish, sink; give way; despair &c. 859; break one's heart; weigh upon the heart &c. (*inflict pain*) 830.

Adj. in –, in a state of –, full of- pain &c. *n.*; suffering &c. *v.*; pained, afflicted, worried, displeased &c. 830; aching, griped, sore &c. (*physical pain*) 378; on the rack, in limbo; between hawk and buzzard.

un-comfortable, -easy; ill at ease; in a -taking, – way; disturbed; discontented &c. 832; out of humor &c. 901*a*; weary &c. 841.

heavy laden, stricken, crushed, a prey to, victimized, ill-used.

unfortunate &c. (*hapless*) 735; to be pitied, doomed, devoted, accursed, undone, lost, stranded; fey.

unhappy, infelicitous, poor, wretched, miserable, woe-begone; cheerless &c. (*dejected*) 837; careworn.

concerned, sorry; sorrow-ing, -ful; cut up, chagrined, horrified, horror-stricken; in –, plunged in –, a prey to- grief &c. *n.*; in tears &c. (*lamenting*) 839; steeped to the lips in misery; heart-stricken, -broken, -scalded; broken-hearted; in despair &c. 859.

Phr. " the iron entered into our soul "; *hæret lateri lethalis arundo* [Vergil]; one's heart bleeding; " down, thou climbing sorrow " [*Lear*]; " mirth cannot move a soul in agony " [*Love's Labor's Lost*]; *nessun maggior dolore che ricordarsi del tempo felice nella miseria;* " sorrow's crown of sorrow is remembering happier things " [Tennyson]; " the niobe of Nations " [Byron].

829. [Capability of giving pleasure; cause or source of pleasure.] **Pleasurableness.** — **N.** pleasurable-, pleasant-, agreeable-ness &c. *adj.*; pleasure giving, jucundity, delectability; amusement &c. 840.

attraction &c. (*motive*) 615; attractiveness, -ability; invitingness &c. *adj.*; harm, fascination, enchantment, witchery, seduction, winning ways, amenity, amiability; winsomeness.

loveliness &c. (*beauty*) 845; sunny –, bright- side; sweets &c. (*sugar*) 396; goodness &c. 648; manna in the wilderness, land flowing with milk and honey; bittersweet; fair weather.

treat; regale &c. (*physical pleasure*) 377; dainty; tit-, tid-bit; nuts, *sauce piquante.*

V. cause –, produce –, create –, give –, afford –, procure –, offer –, present –, yield- pleasure &c. 827.

please, charm, delight, becharm, imparadise; gladden &c. (*make cheerful*) 836; take, captivate, fascinate; enchant, entrance, enrapture, transport, bewitch; en-, ravish.

bless, beatify; satisfy; gratify, – desire &c. 865; slake, satiate, quench; indulge, humor, flatter, tickle; tickle the palate &c. (*savory*) 394; regale, refresh; enliven; treat; amuse &c. 840; take –, tickle –, hit- one's fancy; meet one's wishes; win –, gladden –, rejoice –, warm the cockles of- the heart; do one's heart good.

attract, allure &c. (*move*) 615; stimulate &c. (*excite*) 824; interest.

make things pleasant, popularize, gild the pill, sweeten.

Adj. causing pleasure &c. *v.*; lætificant; pleasure-giving; pleas-ing, -ant, -urable; agreeable; grat-eful, -ifying; leef †, lief, acceptable; welcome, – as the

830. [Capability of giving pain; cause or source of pain.] **Painfulness.** — **N.** painfulness &c. *adj.*; trouble, care &c. (*pain*) 828; trial; af-, in-fliction; blow, stroke, burden, load, curse; bitter -pill, – draught; waters of bitterness.

annoyance, grievance, nuisance, vexation, mortification, sickener; bore, bother, pother, hot water, " sea of troubles " [*Hamlet*], hornet's nest, plague, pest.

cancer, ulcer, sting, thorn; canker &c. (*bane*) 663; scorpion &c. (*evil doer*) 913; dagger &c. (*arms*) 727; scourge &c. (*instrument of punishment*) 975; carking –, canker worm of- care.

mishap, misfortune &c. (*adversity*) 735; *désagrément, esclandre,* rub.

source of -irritation, – annoyance; wound, sore subject, skeleton in the closet; thorn in -the flesh, – one's side; where the shoe pinches, gall and wormwood.

sorry sight, heavy news, provocation; affront &c. 929; " head and front of one's offending " [*Othello*].

infestation, molestation; malignity &c. (*malevolence*) 907.

V. cause –, occasion –, give –, bring –, induce –, produce –, create –, inflict- pain &c. 828; pain, hurt, wound.

pinch, prick, gripe &c. (*physical pain*) 378; pierce, lancinate, cut.

hurt –, wound –, grate upon –, jar upon- the feelings; wring –, pierce –, lacerate –, break –, rend- the heart; make the heart bleed; tear –, rend- the heart-strings; draw tears from the eyes.

sadden; make -unhappy &c. 828; plunge into sorrow, grieve, fash, afflict, distress; cut -up, – to the heart.

displease, annoy, incommode, discompose, trouble, disquiet; faze, feaze, feeze [U. S.]; disturb, cross, perplex, molest, tease, tire, irk, vex, mortify, wher-

roses in May; welcomed; favorite; to one's taste, – mind, – liking; satisfactory &c. (*good*) 648.

refreshing; comfortable; cordial; genial; glad, -some; sweet, delectable, nice, dainty; delic-ate, -ious; dulcet; luscious &c. 396; palatable &c. 394; luxurious, voluptuous; sensual &c. 377.

attractive &c. 615; inviting, prepossessing, engaging; win-ning, -some; taking, fascinating, captivating, killing; seduc-ing, -tive; heart-robbing; alluring, enticing; appetizing &c. (*exciting*) 824; cheering &c. 836; bewitching; enchanting, entrancing, enravishing.

charming; delightful, felicitous, exquisite; lovely &c. (*beautiful*) 845; ravishing, rapturous; heartfelt, thrilling, ecstatic; beat-ic, -ific; seraphic; empyrean; elysian &c. (*heavenly*) 981.

palmy, halcyon, Saturnian.

Phr. *decies repetita placebit;* " charms strike the sight but merit wins the soul " [Pope]; " sweetness and light " [Swift].

ret †, worry, plague, bother, pester, bore, pother, harass, harry, badger, heckle, bait, beset, infest, persecute, importune.

wring, harrow, torment, torture; bullyrag; put to the -rack, – question; break on the wheel, rack, scarify; cruciate, -fy; convulse, agonize; barb the dart; plant a -dagger in the breast, – thorn in one's side.

irritate, provoke, sting, nettle, try the patience, pique, fret, rile, tweak the nose, chafe, gall; sting –, wound –, cut- to the quick; aggrieve, affront, enchafe, enrage, ruffle, sour the temper; give offense &c. (*resentment*) 900.

maltreat, bite, snap at, assail; smite &c. (*punish*) 972.

sicken, disgust, revolt, nauseate, disenchant, repel, offend, shock, stink in the nostrils; go against –, turn- the stomach; make one sick, set the teeth on edge, go against the grain, grate on the ear; stick in one's -throat, – gizzard; rankle, gnaw, corrode, horrify, appal, freeze the blood; make the -flesh creep, – hair stand on end; make the blood -curdle, – run cold; make one shudder.

haunt, – the memory; weigh –, prey- on the -heart, – mind, – spirits; bring one's gray hairs with sorrow to the grave; add a nail to one's coffin.

Adj. causing pain, hurting &c. *v.*; hurtful &c. (*bad*) 649; painful; dolor-ific, -ous; unpleasant; un-, dis-pleasing; disagreeable, unpalatable, bitter, distasteful; uninviting; unwelcome; undesir-able, -ed; obnoxious; unacceptable, unpopular, thankless.

unsatisfactory, untoward, unlucky, uncomfortable.

distressing; afflict-ing, -ive; joy-, cheer-, comfort-less; dismal, disheartening; depress-ing, -ive; dreary, melancholy, grievous, piteous; woeful, rueful, mournful, deplorable, pitiable, lamentable; sad, affecting, touching, pathetic.

irritating, provoking, stinging, annoying, aggravating, mortifying, galling; unaccommodating, invidious, vexatious; trouble-, tire-, irk-, weari-some; plagu-ing, -y; awkward.

importunate; teas-, pester-, bother-, harass-, worry-, torment-, carking.

in-toler-, -suffer-, -support-able; un-bear-, -endur-able; past bearing; not to be -borne, – endured; more than flesh and blood can bear; enough to -drive one mad, – provoke a saint, – make a parson swear.

shocking, terrific, grim, appalling, crushing; dreadful, fearful, frightful; thrilling, tremendous, dire; heart-breaking, -rending, -wounding, -corroding, -sickening; harrowing, rending.

odious, hateful, execrable, repulsive, repellent, abhorrent; horri-d, -ble, -fic, -fying; offensive; nause-ous, -ating; disgust-, sicken-, revolt-ing; nasty; loath-some, -ful; fulsome; vile &c. (*bad*) 649; hideous &c. 846.

sharp, acute, sore, severe, grave, hard, harsh, cruel, biting, caustic; cutting, corroding, consuming, racking, excruciating, searching, grinding, grating, agonizing; envenomed; catheretic, pyrotic.

ruinous, disastrous, calamitous, tragical; desolating, withering; burdensome, onerous, oppressive; cumb-rous, -ersome.

Adv. painfully &c. *adj.*; with -pain &c. 828; deuced.

Int. *hinc illæ lachrymæ!*

Phr. *surgit amari aliquid;* the place being too hot to hold one; the iron entering into the soul; " he jests at scars that never felt a wound " [*Romeo and Juliet*]; " I must be cruel only to be kind " [*Hamlet*]; " what deep wounds ever closed without a scar? " [Byron].

831. Content. — **N.** content, -ment, -edness; complacency, satisfaction, entire satisfaction, ease, heart's ease, peace of mind; serenity &c. 826; cheerfulness &c. 836; ray of comfort; comfort &c. (*well-being*) 827.

re-, conciliation; resignation &c. (*patience*) 826.

waiter on Providence.

V. be -content &c. *adj.*; rest -satisfied, – and be thankful; take the good the gods provide, let well alone, feel oneself at home, hug oneself, lay the flattering unction to one's soul.

take -up with, – in good part; assent &c. 488; be reconciled to, make one's peace with; get over it; take -heart, – comfort; put up with &c. (*bear*) 826.

render -content &c. *adj.*; set at ease, comfort; set one's -heart, – mind- at -ease, – rest; speak peace; conciliate, reconcile, win over, propitiate, disarm, beguile; content, satisfy; gratify &c. 829.

be -tolerated &c. 826; go down, – with; do.

Adj. content, -ed; satisfied &c. *v.*; at -ease, – one's ease, – home; with the mind at ease, *sans souci, sine curâ,* easygoing, not particular; conciliatory; unrepining, of good comfort; resigned &c. (*patient*) 826; cheerful &c. 836.

un-afflicted, -vexed, -molested, -plagued; serene &c. 826; at rest; snug, comfortable; in one's element.

satisfactory, tolerable.

Adv. to one's heart's content; *à la bonne heure;* all for the best.

Int. amen &c. (*assent*) 488; very well, all –, so much- the better, well and good; it –, that- will do; it cannot be helped.

Phr. nothing comes amiss.

" a heart with room for every joy " [Bailey]; *ich habe genossen das irdische Glück ich habe gelebt und geliebet* [Schiller]; " nor cast one longing ling'ring look behind " [Gray]; " shut up in measureless content " [*Macbeth*]; " sweet are the thoughts that savor of content " [R. Greene]; " their wants but few their wishes all confined " [Goldsmith].

832. Discontent. — **N.** discontent, -ment; dissatisfaction; dissent &c. 489.

disappointment, mortification; cold comfort; regret &c. 833; repining, taking on &c. *v.*; inquietude, vexation of spirit, soreness; heart-burning, -grief; querulousness &c. (*lamentation*) 839; hypercriticism.

malcontent, grumbler, growler, croaker, *laudator temporis acti;* censurer, complainer, fault-finder, murmurer.

cave of Adullam, indignation meeting, " winter of our discontent " [*Henry VI*].

V. be -discontented &c. *adj.*; quarrel with one's bread and butter; repine; regret &c. 833; wish one at the bottom of the Red Sea; take -on, – to heart; shrug the shoulders; make a wry –, pull a long- face; knit one's brows; look -blue, – black, – black as thunder, – blank, – glum.

take -in bad part, – ill; fret, chafe, make a piece of work; grumble, croak; lament &c. 839.

cause -discontent &c. *n.*; dissatisfy, disappoint, mortify, put out, disconcert; cut up; dishearten.

Adj. discontented; dissatisfied &c. *v.*; unsatisfied, ungratified; dissident; dissentient &c. 489; malcontent, exigent, exacting, hypercritical.

repining &c. *v.*; regretful &c. 833; down in the mouth &c. (*dejected*) 837.

in -high dudgeon, – a fume, – the sulks, – the dumps, – bad humor; glum, sulky; sour, – as a crab; soured, sore; out of -humor, – temper.

disappointing &c. *v.*; unsatisfactory.

Int. so much the worse!

Phr. that –, it- will never do; *curtæ nescio quid semper abest rei* [Horace]; *ne Jupiter quidem omnibus placet;* " poor in abundance, famished at a feast " [Young].

833. Regret. — **N.** regret, repining; homesickness, nostalgia; *mal –, maladie -du pays;* lamentation &c. 839; penitence &c. 950.

bitterness, heartburning.

laudator temporis acti &c. (*discontent*) 832.

V. regret, deplore; bewail &c. (*lament*) 839; repine, cast a longing lingering look behind; rue, – the day; repent &c. 950; *infandum renovare dolorem.*

prey –, weigh –, have a weight- on the mind; leave an aching void.

Adj. regretting &c. *v.*; regretful; homesick.

regretted &c. *v.*; much to be regretted, regrettable; lamentable &c. (*bad*) 649.

Int. what a pity! hang it!

Phr. 'tis -pity, – too true; " sigh'd and look'd and sigh'd again " [Dryden].

---

834. Relief. — N. relief; deliverance; refreshment &c. 689; easement, softening, alleviation, mitigation, palliation, soothing, lullaby.

solace, consolation, comfort, encouragement.

lenitive, restorative &c. (*remedy*) 662; cushion &c. 215; crumb of comfort, balm in Gilead.

V. relieve, ease, alleviate, mitigate, palliate, soothe; salve; soften, – down; foment, stupe, poultice; assuage, allay.

cheer, comfort, console; enliven; encourage, bear up, pat on the back, give comfort, set at ease; gladden –, cheer- the heart; inspirit, invigorate.

remedy; cure &c. (*restore*) 660; refresh; pour -balm into, – oil on.

smooth the ruffled brow of care, temper the wind to the shorn lamb, lay the flattering unction to one's soul.

disburden &c. (*free*) 705; take off a load of care.

be relieved; breathe more freely, draw a long breath; take comfort; dry –, wipe- the -tears, – eyes.

Adj. relieving &c. *v.*; consolatory, soothing; assua-ging, -sive; bal-my, -samic; lenitive, palliative; anodyne &c. (*remedial*) 662; curative &c. 660.

Phr. " here comes a man of comfort " [*Measure for Measure*].

835. Aggravation. — N. aggravation, heightening; exacerbation; exasperation; overestimation &c. 482; exag-geration &c. 549.

V. aggravate, render worse, heighten, embitter, sour; ex-, acerbate; exasperate, envenom; enrage, provoke, tease.

add fuel to the -fire, – flame; fan the flame &c. (*excite*) 824; go from bad to worse &c. (*deteriorate*) 659.

Adj. aggravated &c. *v.*; worse, unrelieved; aggravable; aggravating &c. *v.*

Adv. out of the frying pan into the fire, from bad to worse, worse and worse

Int. so much the worse!

---

836. Cheerfulness.—N. cheerfulness &c. *adj.*; geniality, gayety, *l'allegro*, cheer, good humor, spirits; high –, animal –, flow of- spirits; glee, high glee, light heart; sunshine of the -mind, – breast; *gaieté de cœur, bon naturel.*

liveliness &c. *adj.*; life, alacrity, vivacity, animation, *allegresse;* jocundity, joviality, jollity; levity; jocularity &c. (*wit*) 842.

mirth, merriment, hilarity, exhilaration; laughter &c. 838; merrymaking &c. (*amusement*) 840; heyday, rejoicing &c. 838; marriage bell.

nepenthe, Euphrosyne.

optimism &c. (*hopefulness*) 858; self-complacency; hedonics, hedonism.

V. be -cheerful &c. *adj.*; have the mind at ease, smile, put a good face upon, keep up one's spirits; view -the bright side of the picture, – things *en couleur de rose; ridentem dicere verum,* cheer up, brighten up, light up bear up; chirp,

837. Dejection. — N. dejection; dejectedness &c. *adj.*; depression, prosternation †; lowness –, depression- of spirits; weight –, oppression –, damp- on the spirits; low –, bad –, drooping –, depressed- spirits; heart sinking; heaviness –, failure- of heart.

heaviness &c. *adj.*; infestivity, gloom; weariness &c. 841; *tœdium vitœ,* disgust of life; *mal du pays* &c. (*regret*) 833; anhedonia.

melancholy; sadness &c. *adj.*; *il penseroso,* melancholia, dismals, blues, lachrymals, mumps, dumps, blue devils, doldrums, vapors, megrims, spleen, horrors, hypochondriasis, pessimism; *la maladie sans maladie;* despondency, slough of Despond; disconsolateness &c. *adj.*; hope deferred, blank despondency; voiceless woe.

prostration, – of soul; broken heart; despair &c. 859; cave of -despair, – Trophonius.

take heart, cast away care, drive dull care away, perk up; keep a stiff upper lip *.

rejoice &c. 838; carol, chirrup, lilt; frisk, rollick, give a loose to mirth.

cheer, enliven, elate, exhilarate, gladden, inspirit, animate, raise the spirits, inspire; perk up; put in good humor; cheer –, rejoice- the heart; delight &c. (*give pleasure*) 829.

Adj. cheerful; happy &c. 827; cheer-y, -ly; of good cheer, smiling; blithe; in –, in good- spirits; breezy, bully, chipper [U. S.]; in high -spirits, – feather; happy as -the day is long, – a king; gay, – as a lark; *allegro;* debonair; light, -some, -hearted; buoyant, *débonnaire*, bright, free and easy, airy; janty, jaunty, canty; hedonic; riant; spright-ly, -ful; spry; spirit-ed, -full; lively, animated, vivacious; brisk, – as a bee; sparkling; sportive; full of -play, – spirit; all alive.

sunny, palmy; hopeful &c. 858.

merry, – as a -cricket, – grig, – marriage bell; joyful, joyous, jocund, jovial; jolly, – as a thrush, – as a sand-boy; blithesome; glee-ful, -some; hilarious, rattling.

winsome, bonny, hearty, buxom.

play-ful, -some; *folâtre*, playful as a kitten, tricksy, frisky, frolicsome; gamesome; jocose, jocular, waggish; mirth-, laughter-loving; mirthful, rollicking.

elate, -d; exulting, jubilant, flushed; rejoicing &c. 838; cock-a-hoop.

cheering, inspiriting, exhilarating; cardiac, -al; pleasing &c. 829; palmy.

Adv. cheerfully &c. *adj.*

Int. never say die! come! cheer up! hurrah! &c. 838; " hence loathed melancholy! " begone dull care! away with melancholy!

Phr. "a merry heart goes all the day " [*A Winter's Tale*]; " as merry as the day is long " [*Much Ado*]; *ride si sapis* [Martial].

demureness &c. *adj.*; gravity, solemnity; long, – grave- face.

hypochondriac, seek-sorrow, self-tormentor, *heautontimorumenos*, *malade imaginaire*, *médecin tant pis;* croaker, pessimist; mope, mopus.

[Cause of dejection] affliction &c. 830; sorry sight; *memento mori;* damper, wet blanket, Job's comforter.

V. be -dejected &c. *adj.*; grieve; mourn &c. (*lament*) 839; take on, give way, lose heart, despond, droop, sink.

lower, look downcast, frown, pout; hang down the head; pull –, make- a long face; laugh on the wrong side of the mouth; grin a ghastly smile; look -blue, – like a drowned man; lay –, take- to heart.

mope, brood over; fret; sulk; pine, – away; yearn; repine &c. (*regret*) 833; despair &c. 859.

refrain from laughter, keep one's countenance; be –, look- grave &c. *adj.*; repress a smile.

depress; dis-courage, -hearten; dispirit; damp, dull, deject, lower, sink, dash, knock down, unman, prostrate, break one's heart; frown upon; cast a -gloom, – shade- on; sadden; damp –, dash –, wither- one's hopes; weigh –, lie heavy –, prey- on the -mind, – spirits; damp –, depress- the spirits.

Adj. cheer-, joy-, spirit-less; uncheer-ful, -y; unlively; unhappy &c. 828; melancholy, dismal, somber, dark, gloomy, *triste*, clouded, murky, lowering, frowning, lugubrious, funereal, mournful, lamentable, dreadful.

dreary, flat; dull, – as -a beetle, – ditchwater; depressing &c. *v.*

" melancholy as a gib cat "; oppressed with –, a prey to- melancholy; downcast, -hearted; down -in the mouth, – on one's luck; heavy-hearted; in the -dumps, – suds, – sulks, – doldrums; in doleful dumps, in bad humor; sullen; mumpish, dumpish, mopish, moping; moody, glum; sulky &c. (*discontented*) 832; out of -sorts, – humor, – heart, – spirits; ill at ease, low-spirited, in low spirits, a cup too low; weary &c. 841; dis-couraged, -heartened; desponding; chap-, chop-, jaw-, crest-fallen.

sad, pensive, *penseroso*, tristful; dole-some, -ful; woe-begone, lachrymose, in tears, melancholic, hypped, hypochondriacal, bilious, jaundiced, atrabilious, saturnine, splenetic; lackadaisical.

serious, sedate, staid, stayed; grave, – as -a judge, – an undertaker, – a mustard pot; sober, solemn, demure; grim; grim-faced, -visaged; rueful, wan, long-faced

disconsolate; un-, in-consolable; forlorn, comfortless, desolate, *désolé;* sick at heart; soul-, heart-sick; *au désespoir;* in despair &c. 859; lost.

overcome; broken-, borne-, bowed-down; heartstricken &c. (*mental suffering*) 828; cut up, dashed, sunk; unnerved, unmanned; down-fallen, -trodden; broken-hearted; careworn.

Adv. with -a long face, – tears in one's eyes; sadly &c. *adj.*

Phr. the countenance falling; the heart -failing, – sinking within- one; " a plague of sighing and grief " [*Henry IV*]; "thick-ey'd musing and curs'd melancholy " [*Henry IV*]; " the sickening pang of hope deferred " [Scott].

---

838. [Expression of pleasure.] **Rejoicing. — N.** rejoicing, exultation, triumph, jubilation, heyday, flush, revelling; merrymaking &c. (*amusement*) 840; jubilee &c. (*celebration*) 883; pæan, *Te Deum* &c. (*thanksgiving*) 990; congratulation &c. 896.

smile, simper, smirk, grin; broad –, sardonic- grin.

laughter, giggle, titter, snigger, crow, cheer, chuckle, shout; horse –, hearty-laugh; guffaw; burst –, fit –, shout –, roar –, peal- of laughter; cachinnation; Kentish fire; tiger.

risibility; derision &c. 856.

Momus; Democritus the Abderite; rollicker.

V. rejoice; thank –, bless- one's stars; congratulate –, hug- oneself; rub –, clap-one's hands; smack the lips, fling up one's cap; dance, skip; sing, carol, chirrup, chirp; hurrah; cry for –, leap with-joy; exult &c. (*boast*) 884; triumph; hold jubilee &c. (*celebrate*) 883; make merry &c. (*sport*) 840.

smile, simper, smirk; grin, – like a Cheshire cat; mock, laugh in one's sleeve; laugh, – outright; giggle, titter, snigger, crow, smicker †, chuckle, cackle; burst -out, – into a fit of laughter; shout, split, roar.

shake –, split –, hold both- one's sides; roar –, die- with laughter.

raise laughter &c. (*amuse*) 840.

Adv. rejoicing &c. *v.*; jubilant, exultant, triumphant; flushed, elated; laughing &c. *v.*; risible; ready to -burst, – split, – die with laughter; convulsed with laughter.

laughable &c. (*ludicrous*) 853.

Int. hurrah! huzza! aha! hail! tolder-olloll! Heaven be praised! *io triumphe! tant mieux!* so much the better.

Phr. the heart leaping with joy; *ce n'est pas être bien aisé que de rire;* " Laughter holding both his sides " [Milton]; θάλαττα! θάλαττα! le roi est mort, vive le roi; " with his eyes in flood with laughter " [*Cymbeline*].

---

839. [Expression of pain.] **Lamentation. — N.** lament, -ation; wail, complaint, plaint, murmur, mutter, grumble, groan, moan, whine, whimper, sob, sigh, suspiration, heaving, deep sigh.

cry &c. (*vociferation*) 411; scream, howl; outcry, wail of woe, frown, scowl.

tear; weeping &c. *v.*; flood of tears, fit of crying, lachrymation, melting mood, weeping and gnashing of teeth.

plaintiveness &c. *adj.*; languishment; condolence &c. 915.

mourning, weeds, willow, cypress, crape, deep mourning; sackcloth and ashes; lachrymatory; knell &c. 363; dump, death song, dirge, coronach, nenia, requiem, elegy, epicedium; threne; mon-, thren-ody; jeremi-ad, -ade; ulla-lulla.

mourner; grumbler &c. (*discontent*) 832; Niobe; Heraclitus.

V. lament, mourn, deplore, grieve, weep over; be-wail, -moan; condole with &c. 915; fret &c. (*suffer*) 828; wear –, go into –, put on- mourning; wear -the willow, – sackcloth and ashes; *infandum renovare dolorem* [Vergil] &c. (*regret*) 833; give sorrow words.

sigh; give –, heave –, fetch- a sigh; " waft a sigh from Indus to the pole " [Pope]; sigh " like a furnace " [*As You Like It*]; wail.

cry, weep, sob, greet, blubber, pipe, snivel, bibber, whimper, pule; pipe one's eye; drop –, shed- -tears, – a tear; melt –, burst- into tears; *fondre en larmes;* cry -oneself blind, – one's eyes out; yammer.

scream &c. (*cry out*) 411; mew &c. (*animal sounds*) 412; groan, moan, whine; roar; roar –, bellow- like a bull; cry out lustily, rend the air.

frown, scowl, make a wry face, gnash one's teeth, wring one's hands, tear one's hair, beat one's breast, roll on the ground, burst with grief.

complain, murmur, mutter, grumble,

growl, clamor, make a fuss about, croak, grunt, maunder; deprecate &c. (*disapprove*) 932.

cry out before one is hurt, complain without cause.

Adj. lamenting &c. *v.*; in mourning, in sackcloth and ashes; sorrow-ing, -ful &c. (*unhappy*) 828; mourn-, tear-ful; lachrymose; plaint-ive, -ful; quer-ulous, -imonious; in the melting mood; threnetic.

in tears, with tears in one's eyes; with -moistened, – watery- eyes; bathed –, dissolved- in tears; "like Niobe all tears" [*Hamlet*].

elegiac, epicedial.

Adv. *de profundis; les larmes aux yeux.*

Int. heigh-ho! alas! alack! O dear! ah –, woe is- me! lackadaisy! well –, lack -, alack- a day! wellaway! alas the day! *O tempora O mores!* what a pity! *miserabile dictu!* O lud lud! too true!

Phr. tears -standing in, – starting from- the eyes; eyes -suffused, – swimming, – brimming, – overflowing- with tears; "if you have tears prepare to shed them now" [*Julius Cæsar*]; *interdum lacrymæ pondera vocis habent* [Ovid]; "strangled his language in his tears" [*Henry VIII*]; "tears such as angels weep" [*Paradise Lost*].

---

840. Amusement. — N.

amuse-, entertain-ment; diver-sion, -tissement; reaction, relaxation, solace; pastime, *passetemps*, sport; labor of love; pleasure &c. 827.

fun, frolic, merriment, jollity; joviality, -ness; heyday; laughter &c. 838; jocos-ity, -eness; droll-, buffoon-, tomfool-ery; mummery, pleasantry; wit &c. 842; quip, quirk.

play; game, – at romps; gambol, romp, prank, antic, rig, lark, spree, skylarking, vagary, monkey trick, gambade, *fredaine*, escapade, *échappée*, bout, *espièglerie;* practical joke &c. (*ridicule*) 856.

dance, hop, reel, rigadoon, saraband, hornpipe, bolero, fandango, cancan, minuet, waltz, polka; bayadere; breakdown, cake-walk, cornwallis [U. S.]; nautch-girl; shindig * [U. S.]; skirt-dance, stag dance, Virginia reel; galop, -ade; jig, fling, strathspey; *allemande;* gavot, -te; mazurka, morisco †, morris dance; quadrille, country dance, *cotillon*, Sir Roger de Coverley; ballet &c. (*drama*) 599; ball; *bal, – masqué, – costumé;* masquerade; Terpsichore.

festivity, merrymaking; party &c. (*social gathering*) 892; bat * [U. S.], bum * [U. S.], bust *, clambake [U. S.], donation party [U. S.], fish fry [U. S.], jamboree *, kantikoy, nautch, randy, squantum [U. S.], tear *, *Turnerfest,* yule log; *fête,* festival, gala, *ridotto;* revel-s, -ry, -ing; carnival, brawl, saturnalia, high jinks; feast, banquet &c. (*food*) 298; regale, symposium, wassail; carous-e, -al; jollification, junket, wake, picnic, *fête champêtre,* regatta, field day; treat.

841. Weariness. — N.

weariness, defatigation †, ennui; lassitude &c. (*fatigue*) 688; drowsiness &c. 683.

disgust, nausea, loathing, sickness; satiety &c. 869; *tædium vitæ* &c. (*dejection*) 837; boredom.

wearisome-, tedious-ness &c. *adj.*; dull work, tedium, monotony, twice-told tale.

bore, buttonholer, proser, wet blanket; pill *, stiff *; heavy hours, "the enemy" [time].

V. weary; tire &c. (*fatigue*) 688; bore; bore –, weary –, tire- -to death, – out of one's life, – out of all patience; set –, send- to sleep; buttonhole.

pall, sicken, nauseate, disgust.

harp on the same string; drag its -slow, – weary- length along.

never hear the last of; be- tired &c. *adj.* -of, – with; yawn; die with *ennui.*

Adj. wearying &c. *v.*; wearing; weari-, tire-, irk-some; uninteresting, stupid, bald, devoid of interest, dry, monotonous, dull, arid, tedious, humdrum, mortal, flat; pros-y, -ing; slow; soporific, somniferous.

disgusting &c. *v.*; unenjoyed.

weary; tired &c. *v.*; drowsy &c. (*sleepy*) 683; uninterested, flagging, used up, worn out, *blasé*, life-weary, weary of life; sick of.

Adv. wearily &c. *adj.*; *usque ad nauseam.*

Phr. time hanging heavily on one's hands: *toujours perdrix; crambe repetita.*

round of pleasures, dissipation, a short life and a merry one, racketing, holiday making.

rejoicing &c. 838; jubilee &c. (*celebration*) 883.

bonfire, fireworks, *feu-de-joie*, firecracker.

holiday; gala –, red letter –, play- day; high days and holidays; high –, Bank- holiday; May –, Derby- day; Saint –, Easter –, Whit- Monday; Bairam; wayz-goose, bean feast; Arbor –, Declaration –, Independence –, Labor –, Memorial –, Thanksgiving- Day; Mardi gras, *mi-carême, feria, fiesta.*

place of amusement, theater; concert-, ball-, assembly-room; music hall.

park, plaisance; arbor; garden &c. (*horticulture*) 371; pleasure-, play-, cricket-, croquet-, archery-, hunting-ground; tennis-, racket-court; bowling-green, -alley; croquet lawn, rink, glaciarum, skating rink; roundabout, merry-go-round; swing; *montagne Russe.*

game, – of -chance, – skill; athletic sports, gymnastics; archery, rifle shooting; tournament, pugilism &c. (*contention*) 720; sporting &c. 622; horse racing, the turf; aquatics &c. 267; skating, sliding; cricket, tennis, lawn tennis, rackets, fives, trap bat and ball, battledore and shuttlecock, *la grâce;* pall-mall, tipcat, croquet, golf, curling, hockey, football, pallone, polo; tent pegging, tilting at the ring, quintain, greasy pole; quoits, discus; knurr and spell; leapfrog, hop skip and jump; French and English, tug of war; blindman's buff, hunt the slipper, hide and seek, kiss in the ring; snapdragon; cross questions and crooked answers; rounders, baseball, lacrosse; crisscross, hopscotch, jackstones, mumblety-peg, pingpong, pushball, shinney, shinny, tag, tobogganing, water polo; &c.

billiards, pool, pyramids, bagatelle; bowls, skittles, ninepins, kail, American bowls; tenpins [U. S.], tivoli.

cards; whist, rubber; round game; loo, cribbage, *bésique*, euchre, drole, écarté, picquet, allfours, quadrille, omber, reverse, Pope Joan, commit; bo-, boa-ston; *vingt-un;* quinze, thirty-one, put, speculation, connections, brag, cassino, lottery, commerce, snip-snap-snorem, lift smoke, blind hookey, Polish bank, Earl of Coventry, Napoleon, patience, pairs; banker; blind –, draw –, straight –, stud- poker; bluff; bridge, -whist; lotto, monte, nap, penny-ante, poker, reversis, squeezers, old maid, fright, beggar-my-neighbor; *baccarat.*

ace, king, queen, knave, jack, joker; bower; right –, left- bower; dummy; jackpot; trump; deck; flush, full-house, straight; *misère* &c.

chess, draughts, checkers, chequers, backgammon, dominos, merelles, nine men's morris, gobang, solitaire; game of –, fox and- goose; loto &c.[1]

morra; gambling &c. (*chance*) 621.

toy, plaything, bauble; doll &c. (*puppet*) 554; teetotum; knicknack &c. (*trifle*) 643; magic lantern &c. (*show*) 448; peep-, puppet-, raree-, gallanty-show; toy-shop; " quips and cranks and wanton wiles, nods and becks and wreathed smiles" [Milton].

sportsman, gamester, reveler; master of the -ceremonies, – revels; *arbiter elegantiarum; arbiter bibendi,* archer, fan [U. S.], toxophilite, turfman.

V. amuse, entertain, divert, enliven; tickle, – the fancy; titillate, raise a smile, put in good humor; cause –, create –, occasion –, raise –, excite –, produce –, convulse with- laughter; set the table in a roar, be the death of one.

recreate, solace, cheer, rejoice; please &c. 829; interest; treat, regale.

amuse oneself; game; play, – a game, – pranks, – tricks; sport, disport, toy, wanton, revel, junket, feast, carouse, banquet, make merry, drown care; drive dull care away; frolic, gambol, frisk, romp; caper; dance &c. (*leap*) 309; keep up the ball; run a rig, sow one's wild oats, have one's fling, take one's pleasure; paint the town red *; see life; *desipere in loco,* play the fool.

make –, keep- holiday; go a Maying.

while away –, beguile- the time; kill time, dally.

---

[1] A curious list of games is given in Sir Thomas Urquhart's translation of Rabelais. — *Life of Gargantua,* book i. chapter 22.

Adj. amusing, entertaining, diverting &c. *v.*; recreative, lusory; pleasant &c. (*pleasing*) 829; laughable &c. (*ludicrous*) 853; witty &c. 842; fest-ive, -al; jovial, jolly, jocund, roguish, rompish; playful, – as a kitten; sportive, ludibrious †.

amused &c. *v.*; " pleased with a rattle, tickled with a straw " [Pope].

Adv. " on the light fantastic toe " [Milton], at play, in sport.

Int. *vive la bagatelle! vogue la galère!*

Phr. *Deus nobis hæc otia fecit: dum vivimus vivamus; dulce est desipere in loco* [Horace]; " (every room) hath blazed with lights and brayed with minstrelsy " [*Timon of Athens*]; *misce stultitiam consiliis brevem* [Horace].

842. Wit. — N. wit, -tiness; attic

-wit, – salt; atticism; salt, *esprit*, point, fancy, whim, humor, drollery, pleasantry.

farce, buffoonery, fooling, tomfoolery; shenanigan [U. S.], harlequinade &c. 599; broad -farce, – humor; fun, *espiéglerie; vis comica.*

jocularity; jocos-ity, -eness; facetiousness; wagg-ery, -ishness; whimsicality; comicality &c. 853.

smartness, ready wit, banter, badinage, retort, repartee, *qui-pro-quo;* ridicule &c. 856.

facetiæ, quips and cranks; jest, joke, capital joke; *canoræ nugæ;* standing -jest, – joke; conceit, quip, quirk, crank, quiddity, *concetto, plaisanterie,* brilliant idea; merry -, bright -, happy- thought; sally; flash, – of wit, – of merriment; scintillation; *mot, – pour rire;* witticism, smart saying, *bon-mot, jeu d'esprit,* epigram; jest book; dry joke, *quodlibet,* cream of the jest.

word-play, *jeu de mots;* play -of, – upon- words; pun, -ning; *double entente* &c. (*ambiguity*) 520; quibble, verbal quibble; conundrum &c. (*riddle*) 533; anagram, acrostic, double acrostic, trifling, idle conceit, turlupinade †.

old joke, Joe Miller.

V. joke, jest, cut jokes; crack a joke; perpetrate a -joke, – pun; make -fun of, – merry with; set the table in a roar &c. (*amuse*) 840.

retort; banter &c. (*ridicule*) 856; *ridentem dicere verum;* joke at one's expense.

Adj. witty, attic; quick-, nimble-witted; smart; jocular, jocose, waggish, facetious, whimsical, humorous; playful &c. 840; merry and wise; pleasant, sprightly, *spirituel,* sparkling, epigrammatic, full of point, *ben trovato;* comic &c. 853.

Adv. in joke, in jest, in sport, in play.

Phr. *adhibenda est in jocando moderatio;* " gentle dullness ever loves a joke " [Pope]; " leave this keen encounter of our wits " [*Richard III*].

843. Dullness. — N. dullness, heavi-

ness, flatness; infestivity &c. 837, stupidity &c. 499; want of originality; dearth of ideas.

prose, matter of fact; heavy book, *conte à dormir debout;* platitude.

V. be -dull &c. *adj.*; prose, take *au sérieux,* be caught napping.

render -dull &c. *adj.*; damp, depress, throw cold water on, lay a wet blanket on; fall flat upon the ear.

Adj. dull, – as ditch water; unentertaining, uninteresting, unlively, logy [U. S.]; unimaginative; insulse; dry as dust; pros-y, -ing, -aic; matter of fact, commonplace, pointless; " weary stale flat and unprofitable " [*Hamlet*].

stupid, slow, flat, humdrum, monotonous; melancholic &c. 837; stolid &c. 499; plodding.

Phr. *Davus sum non Œdipus.*

844. Humorist. — N. humorist, wag, wit, reparteeist, epigrammatist,

punster; *bel esprit,* life of the party; wit-snapper, -cracker, -worm; joker, jester, Joe Miller, *drôle de corps,* gaillard, spark; *bon diable.*

buffoon, *farceur,* merry-andrew, mime, tumbler, acrobat, mountebank, charlatan, posturemaster, harlequin, punch, pulcinella, scaramouch, clown; wearer of the -cap and bells, – motley; motley fool; pantaloon, gypsy; jack -pudding, – in the green, – a dandy; zany; madcap, pickle-herring, witling, caricaturist, grimacier; *persifleur.*

2. Discriminative Affections

845. Beauty. — N. beauty, the beautiful, τὸ καλόν, le beau idéal.

[Science of the perception of beauty] callæsthetics.[1]

form, elegance, grace, beauty unadorned; symmetry &c. 242; comeliness, fairness &c. *adj.*; pulchritude, polish, gloss; good -effect, – looks; *belle tournure;* trigness; bloom, brilliancy, radiance, splendor, gorgeousness, magnificence; sublimi-ty, -fication †.

concinnity, delicacy, refinement; charm, *je ne sais quoi*, style.

Venus, Aphrodite, Hebe, the Graces, Peri, Houri, Cupid, Apollo, Hyperion, Adonis, Antinous, Narcissus.

peacock, butterfly; flower, flow'ret gay, rose, lily, garden; flower of, pink of; *bijou;* jewel &c. (*ornament*) 847; work of art.

anemone, asphodel, buttercup, crane's-bill, daffodil, geranium, lily of the valley, ranunculus, rhododendron, windflower.

pleasurableness &c. 829.

beautifying; landscape gardening; decoration &c. 847; calisthenics.

V. be -beautiful &c. *adj.*; shine, beam, bloom; become one &c. (*accord*) 23; set off, grace.

render -beautiful &c. *adj.*; beautify; polish, burnish; gild &c. (*decorate*) 847; set out.

" snatch a grace beyond the reach of art " [Pope].

Adj. beaut-iful, -eous; handsome; pretty; lovely, graceful, elegant; delicate, dainty, refined; fair, personable, comely, seemly; bonny; good-looking; well-favored, -made, -formed, -proportioned; proper, shapely; symmetrical &c. (*regular*) 242; harmonious &c. (*color*) 428; sightly.

fit to be seen, passable, not amiss.

goodly, dapper, tight, jimp; gimp; janty, jaunty; trig, natty, quaint, trim, tidy, neat, spruce, smart, tricksy.

bright, -eyed; rosy-, cherry-cheeked; rosy, ruddy; blooming, in full bloom.

brilliant, shining; beam-y, -ing; sparkling, splendid, resplendent, dazzling, glowing; glossy, sleek.

showy, specious; rich, gorgeous, superb, magnificent, grand, fine, sublime.

artistic, -al; æsthetic; pict-uresque, -orial; *fait à peindre;* well-composed, -grouped, -varied; curious.

846. Ugliness. — N. ugliness &c. *adj.*; deformity, inelegance; acomia; disfigurement &c. (*blemish*) 848; want of symmetry, inconcinnity; distortion &c. 243; squalor &c. (*uncleanness*) 653.

forbidding countenance, vinegar aspect, hanging look, wry face, " *spretæ injuria formæ*" [Vergil].

eyesore, object, figure, sight, fright, octopus, specter, scarecrow, hag, harridan, satyr, witch, toad, baboon, monster, Caliban, Æsop, " *monstrum horrendum informe ingens cui lumen ademptum* " [Vergil].

V. be -ugly &c. *adj.*; look ill, grin horribly a ghastly smile, make faces.

render -ugly &c. *adj.*; deface; dis-, de-figure †; distort &c. 243; blemish &c. (*injure*) 659; soil &c. (*render unclean*) 653.

Adj. ugly, – as -sin, – a toad, – a scarecrow, – a dead monkey; plain, bald; homely &c. (*unadorned*) 849; ordinary, unornamental, inartistic; unsightly, unseemly, uncomely, unshapely, unlovely; sightless, seemless; not fit to be seen; unbeaut-eous, -iful; beautiless; shapeless &c. (*amorphous*) 241.

mis-shapen, -proportioned; monstrous; gaunt &c. (*thin*) 203; dumpy &c. (*short*) 201; curtailed of its fair proportions; ill-made, -shaped, -proportioned; crooked &c. (*distorted*) 243; hard-featured, -visaged; ill-, hard-, evil-favored; ill-looking; unprepossessing.

graceless, inelegant; ungraceful, ungainly, uncouth; stiff; rugged, rough, gross, rude, awkward, clumsy, slouching, rickety; gawky; lump-ing, -ish; lumbering; hulk-y, -ing; unwieldy.

squalid, haggard; grim, -faced, -visaged; grisly, ghastly; ghost-, death-like; cadaverous, grewsome.

frightful, hideous, odious, uncanny, forbidding, repellant, repulsive; horri-d, -ble; shocking &c. (*painful*) 830.

foul &c. (*dirty*) 653; dingy &c. (*colorless*) 429; gaudy &c. (*color*) 428; dis figured &c. *v.*; discolored.

[1] Whewell, *Philosophy of the Inductive Sciences.*

enchanting &c. (*pleasure-giving*) 829; attractive &c. (*inviting*) 615; becoming &c. (*accordant*) 23; ornamental &c. 847.

undeformed, undefaced, unspotted; spotless &c. (*perfect*) 650.

Phr. *auxilium non leve vultus habet* [Ovid]; " beauty born of murmuring sound " [Wordsworth]; " flowers preach to us if we will hear " [C. G. Rossetti]; *gratior ac pulchro veniens in corpore virtus* [Vergil]; " none but the brave deserve the fair " [Dryden]; " thou who hast the fatal gift of beauty " [Byron].

847. Ornament. — N. ornament,
-ation, -al art; ornat-ure, -eness; adornment, decoration, embellishment; architecture.

garnish, polish, varnish, French polish, gilding, japanning, lacquer, ormolu, enamel; cosmetics.

pattern, diaper, powdering, paneling, graining, pargeting; detail; texture &c. 329; richness; tracery, molding, fillet, listel, strapwork, *coquillage*, flourish, *fleur-de-lis*, arabesque, fret, anthemion; egg and -tongue, – dart; astragal, zigzag, acanthus, cartouche; pilaster &c. (*projection*) 250; bead, beading; *champlevé -*, *cloisonné-* ware; frostwork, Moresque, Morisco, tooling.

em-, broidery; brocade, brocatelle, galloon, lace, fringe, trapping, border, edging, trimming; hanging, tapestry, arras; millinery, ermine; *drap d'or*.

wreath, festoon, garland, chaplet, flower, nosegay, bouquet, posy, " daisies pied and violets blue " [*L. L. L.*].

tassel, knot; shoulder knot, epaulette, epaulet, aigulet, frog; star, rosette, bow; feather, plume, panache, aigrette.

jewel, -ry, -lery; bijoutry; *bijou -terie*; trinket, locket, necklace, bracelet, anklet, ear-ring, carcanet, chain, chatelaine, brooch, torque.

gem, precious stone; diamond, brilliant, beryl, emerald, chalcedony, agate, heliotrope; girasol, -e; onyx, plasma; sard, -oynx; garnet, lapis lazuli, opal, peridot, chrysolite, sapphire, ruby; spinel, -le; balais; oriental -, topaz; turquois, -e; zircon, jacinth, hyacinth, carbuncle, amethyst; pearl, coral; alexandrite, cat's-eye, bloodstone, hematite, jasper, moonstone, sunstone.

finery, frippery, gewgaw, gimcrack, tinsel, spangle, clinquant, pinchbeck, paste; excess of ornament &c. (*vulgarity*) 851; gaud, pride.

illustration, illumination, vignette; *fleuron;* head-, tail-piece; *cul-de-lampe;* flowers of rhetoric &c. 577; work of art.

V. ornament, embellish, enrich, decorate, adorn, bead, beautify, adonize.

smarten, furbish, polish, gild, varnish, whitewash, enamel, japan, lacquer, paint, grain.

garnish, trim, dizen, bedizen, prink, prank; trick -, fig- out; deck, bedeck, dight, bedight, array; begawd, titivate; dress, – up; spangle, bespangle, powder; embroider, work; chase, emboss, fret; emblazon, illuminate; illustrate.

become &c. (*accord with*) 23.

Adj. ornamented, beautified &c. *v.*; ornate, rich, gilt, begilt, tesselated, festooned; *champlevé, cloisonné,* topiary.

848. Blemish. — N. blemish, disfigurement, deformity; adactylism; defect &c. (*imperfection*) 651; flaw; injury &c. (*deterioration*) 659; spots on the sun; eyesore.

stain, blot; spot, -tiness; speck, -le, blur, freckle, mole, macula, patch, blotch, birthmark; blobber-, blubberlip; blain, maculation, tarnish, smudge; dirt &c. 653; scar, wem†; pustule; whelk; excrescence, pimple &c. (*protuberance*) 250.

V. disfigure &c. (*injure*) 659; speckle.

Adj. pitted, freckled, discolored; imperfect &c. 651; blobber-lipped, bloodshot; injured &c. (*deteriorated*) 659.

849. Simplicity. — N. simplicity;
plain-, homeli-ness; undress, chastity.

V. be -simple &c. *adj.*

render -simple &c. *adj.*; simplify.

Adj. simple, plain; home-ly, -spun; ordinary, household.

unaffected; free from -affectation, – ornament; *simplex munditiis* [Horace]; *sans façon, en déshabillé.*

chaste, inornate, severe.

un-adorned, -ornamented, -decked, -garnished, -arranged, -trimmed, -varnished.

bald, flat, dull.

Phr. *veritatis simplex oratio est.*

smart, gay, tricksy, flowery, glittering; new-gilt, -spangled; fine, – as -a Mayday queen, – fivepence, – a carrot fresh scraped; pranked out, bedight, well-groomed.

in full dress &c. (*fashion*) 852; *en grande -tenue, – toilette;* in best bib and tucker, in Sunday best, *endimanché;* dressed to advantage.

showy, flashy; gaudy &c. (*vulgar*) 851; ga-, gai-rish; gorgeous.

ornamental, decorative; becoming &c. (*accordant*) 23.

850. [Good taste.] Taste. — N. taste; good –, refined –, cultivated- taste; delicacy, refinement, fine feeling, gust, gusto, tact, finesse; nicety &c. (*discrimination*) 465; τὸ πρέπον, polish, elegance, grace.

virtu; dilettanteism; fine art; cult-ure, -ivation.

[Science of taste] æsthetics.

man of -taste &c.; connoisseur, judge, critic, conoscente, virtuoso, amateur, dilettante, Aristarchus, Corinthian, *arbiter elegantiarum,* stagirite, euphemist.

" caviare to the general" [*Hamlet*].

V. appreciate, judge, criticise, discriminate &c. 465.

Adj. in good taste; cute; tasteful, tasty; unaffected, pure, chaste, classical, attic; cultivated, refined; dainty; æsthetic, artistic; elegant &c. 578; euphemistic.

to one's -taste, – mind; after one's fancy; *comme il faut; tiré à quatre épingles.*

Adv. elegantly &c. *adj.*

Phr. *nihil tetigit quod non ornavit* [from Johnson's epitaph on Goldsmith]; *chacun à son goût; oculi picturâ tenentur aures cantibus* [Cicero].

852. Fashion. — N. fashion, style, ton, *bon ton,* society; good –, polite-society; *monde;* drawing-room, civilized life, civilization, town, *beau monde,* high life, court; world; fashionable –, gay-world; Vanity Fair; show &c. (*ostentation*) 822.

manners, breeding &c. (*politeness*) 894; air, demeanor &c. (*appearance*) 448; *savoir faire;* gentlemanliness, gentility, decorum, propriety, bienséance; conventions of society; Mrs. Grundy; punctilio; form, -ality; etiquette, point of etiquette; custom &c. 613; mode, vogue, go; rage &c. (*desire*) 865; prevailing taste; dress &c. 225.

man –, woman- of -fashion, – the world; height –, pink –, star –, glass –, leader- of fashion; *arbiter elegantiarum* &c. (*taste*) 850; upper ten thousand &c. (*nobility*) 875; *élite* &c. (*dis-*

851. [Bad taste.] Vulgarity. —N. vulgar-ity, -ism; barbar-, Vandal-, Gothic-ism; *mauvais goût,* bad taste; *gaucherie,* awkwardness, want of tact; ill-breeding &c. (*discourtesy*) 895.

coarseness &c. *adj.*; indecorum, misbehavior.

low-, homeli-ness; low life, *mauvais ton,* rusticity; boorishness &c. *adj.*; brutality; rowdy-, blackguard-ism; ribaldry; slang &c. (*neology*) 563.

bad joke, *mauvaise plaisanterie.*

[Excess of ornament] gaudi-, tawdriness; false ornament; finery, frippery, trickery, tinsel, gewgaw, clinquant.

rough diamond, tomboy, hoyden, cub, unlicked cub; clown &c. (*commonalty*) 876; Goth, Vandal, Bœotian; snob, cad, gent; parvenu &c. 876 frump, dowdy; slattern &c. 653.

V. be -vulgar &c. *adj.*; misbehave; talk –, smell of the- shop.

Adj. in bad taste, vulgar, unrefined.

coarse, indecorous, ribald, gross; unseemly, unbeseeming, unpresentable; *contra bonos mores;* ungraceful &c. (*ugly*) 846.

dowdy; slovenly &c. (*dirty*) 653; ungenteel, shabby genteel; low &c. (*plebeian*) 876; uncourtly; uncivil &c. (*discourteous*) 895; ill-bred, -mannered; underbred; ungentleman-ly, -like; unladylike, unfeminine; wild, – as an unbacked colt.

unkempt, uncombed, untamed, unlicked, unpolished, uncouth; plebeian; incondite; heavy, rude, awkward; homely, -spun, -bred; provincial, countrified, rustic; boorish, clownish; savage, brutish, blackguard, rowdy, snobbish; barbar-ous, -ic; Gothic, unclassical, doggrel, heathenish, tramontane, outlandish; uncultivated; Bohemian.

obsolete &c. (*antiquated*) 124; unfashionable; newfangled &c. (*unfamiliar*) 83; odd &c. (*ridiculous*) 853.

particular; affected &c. 855; meretricious; extravagant, monstrous, horrid; shocking &c. (*painful*) 830.

tinction) 873; smart set; the four hundred [U. S.].

V. be -fashionable &c. *adj.*, – the rage &c. *n.*; have a run, pass current.

follow –, conform to –, fall in with- the fashion &c. *n.*; go with the stream &c. (*conform*) 82; *savoir -vivre, – faire;* keep up appearances, behave oneself.

set the –, bring into- fashion; give a tone to –, cut a figure in- society; keep one's carriage.

Adj. fashionable; in -fashion &c. *n.*; *à la mode, comme il faut;* admitted –, admissible- in -society &c. *n.*; presentable; conventional &c. (*customary*) 613; genteel; well-bred, -mannered, -behaved, -spoken; gentleman-like, -ly; lady-like; civil, polite &c. (*courteous*) 894.

polished, refined, thoroughbred, courtly; *distingué;* unembarrassed, *dégagé;* ja-, jau-nty; dashing, fast.

modish, stylish, *recherché;* newfangled &c. (*unfamiliar*) 83; all the -rage, – go.

in -court, – full, – evening- dress; *en grande tenue* &c. (*ornament*) 847.

Adv. fashionably &c. *adj.*; for fashion's sake.

Phr. *à la -française, – parisienne; à l' -anglaise, – américaine; autre temps autre mœurs; chaque pays a sa guise.*

gaudy, tawdry, bedizened, tricked out, gingerbread; obtrusive.

---

853. Ridiculousness. — N. ridiculousness &c. *adj.*; comical-, odd-ity &c. *adj.*; extravagance, drollery.

farce, comedy; burlesque &c. (*ridicule*) 856; buffoonery &c. (*fun*) 840; frippery; doggrel verses; absurdity &c. 497; bombast &c. (*unmeaning*) 517; anti-climax, bathos; monstrosity &c. (*unconformity*) 83; laughingstock &c. 857.

V. be -ridiculous &c. *adj.*; pass from the sublime to the ridiculous; make one laugh; play the fool, make a fool of oneself, commit an absurdity.

Adj. ridiculous, ludicrous; comic, -al; droll, funny, laughable, *pour rire,* grotesque, farcical, odd; whimsical, – as a dancing bear; fanciful, fantastic, queer, rum, quizzical, quaint, bizarre; screaming; eccentric &c. (*unconformable*) 83; strange, outlandish, out of the way, baroque; awkward &c. (*ugly*) 846.

extravagant, *outré,* monstrous, preposterous, bombastic, inflated, stilted, burlesque, mock heroic.

drollish; serio-, tragi-comic; gimcrack, contemptible &c. (*unimportant*) 643; doggrel; ironical &c. (*derisive*) 856; risible.

Phr. *risum teneatis amici?* [Horace]; *rideret Heraclitus; du sublime au ridicule il n'y a qu'un pas* [Napoleon].

---

854. Fop. — N. fop, fine gentleman; swell; dand-y, -iprat; exquisite, cox-comb, beau, macaroni, blade, blood, buck, man about town, fast man; fribble, jemmy, spark, popinjay, puppy, prig, *petit maître;* jacka-napes, -dandy; man milliner; Jemmy Jessamy, carpet knight; masher, dude.

fine lady, coquette.

---

855. Affectation. — N. affectation; affectedness &c. *adj.*; acting a part &c. *v.*; pretense &c. (*falsehood*) 544, (*ostentation*) 882; boasting &c. 884.

charlatanism, quackery, shallow profundity; pretension, airs, pedantry, purism, precisianism, euphuism; teratology &c. (*altiloquence*) 577.

mannerism, *simagrée,* grimace.

conceit, foppery, dandyism, man millinery, coxcombry, puppyism.

stiffness, formality, buckram; prudery, demureness, coquetry, mock modesty, *minauderie,* sentimentalism; *mauvaise honte,* false shame.

affector, performer, actor; pedant, pedagogue, doctrinaire, purist, euphuist, mannerist; grimacier; lump of affectation, *précieuse ridicule, bas bleu,* blue stocking, poetaster; prig; charlatan &c. (*deceiver*) 548; *petit maître* &c. (*fop*) 854; flatterer &c. 935; coquette, prude, puritan.

V. affect, act a part, put on; give oneself airs &c. (*arrogance*) 885; boast &c. 884; coquet; simper, mince, attitudinize, pose; flirt a fan; over-act, -do.

Adj. affected, full of affectation, pretentious, pedantic, stilted, stagy, theatrical, big-sounding, *ad captandum;* canting, insincere.

not natural, unnatural; self-conscious; *maniéré;* artificial; over-wrought, -done, -acted; euphuistic &c. 577.

stiff, starch, formal, prim, smug, demure, *tiré à quatre épingles*, quakerish, puritanical, prudish, pragmatical, priggish, conceited, coxcomical, foppish, dandified; fini-cal, -kin; mincing, simpering, namby-pamby, sentimental.

Phr. " conceit in weakest bodies strongest works " [*Hamlet*].

856. Ridicule. — N. ridicule, derision; sardonic -smile, - grin; irrision; scoffing &c. (*disrespect*) 929; mockery, quiz, banter, irony, persiflage, raillery, chaff, badinage; quizzing &c. *v.*; asteism.

squib, satire, skit, quip, quib, grin.

parody, burlesque, travesty, *travestie;* farce &c. (*drama*) 599; caricature.

buffoonery &c. (*fun*) 840; practical joke; horseplay.

V. ridicule, deride; laugh at, grin at, smile at; snigger; laugh in one's sleeve; banter, rally, chaff, joke, twit, quiz, poke fun at, roast; haze [U. S.]; tehee; fleer; play -, play tricks- upon; fool, - to the top of one's bent; show up.

satirize, parody, caricature, burlesque, travesty.

turn into ridicule; make merry with; make -fun, - game, - a fool, - an April fool- of; rally; scoff &c. (*disrespect*) 929.

raise a laugh &c. (*amuse*) 840; play the fool, make a fool of oneself.

Adj. deris-ory, -ive; mock; sarcastic, ironical, quizzical, burlesque, Hudibrastic; scurrilous &c. (*disrespectful*) 929.

Adv. in -ridicule &c. *n.*

857. [Object and cause of ridicule.] **Laughingstock. — N.** laughing-jesting-, gazing-stock; butt, game, fair game; April fool &c. (*dupe*) 547.

original, oddity; queer -, odd- fish; quiz, square toes; old -, fogey *or* fogy monkey; buffoon &c. (*jester*) 844; pantomimist &c. (*actor*) 599.

jest &c. (*wit*) 842.

Phr. *dum vitant stulti vitia in contraria currunt.*

3. Prospective Affections

858. Hope. — N. hope, -s; desire &c. 865; fervent hope, sanguine expectation, trust, confidence, reliance; faith &c. (*belief*) 484; affiance, assurance; secur-eness, -ity; reassurance.

good -omen, - auspices; promise, well-grounded hopes; good -, bright- prospect; clear sky.

as-, pre-sumption; anticipation &c. (*expectation*) 507.

hopefulness, buoyancy, optimism, enthusiasm, heart of grace, aspiration; optimist, utopist.

castles in the air, *châteaux en Espagne, le pot au lait,* Utopia, millennium; day -, golden- dream; dream of Alnaschar; airy hopes, fool's paradise; mirage &c. (*fallacies of vision*) 443; fond hope.

beam -, ray -, gleam -, glimmer -, dawn -, flash -, star- of hope; cheer;

859. [Absence, want, or loss of hope.] **Hopelessness. — N.** hopelessness &c. *adj.*; despair, desperation; despondency &c. (*dejection*) 837; pessim-ism, -ist; Job's comforter; bird of -bad, - ill- omen.

hope deferred, dashed hopes; vain expectation &c. (*disappointment*) 509.

airy hopes &c. 858; forlorn hope; gone -case, - coon * [U. S.]; goner *; bad -job, - business; *enfant perdu;* gloomy -, black spots in the- horizon; slough of Despond, cave of Despair; *immedicabile vulnus.*

V. despair; lose -, give up -, abandon -, relinquish- -all hope, - the hope of; give -up, - over; yield to despair; falter; despond &c. (*be dejected*) 837; *jeter le manche après la cognée.*

inspire -, drive to- despair &c. *n.*;

bit of blue sky, silver lining of the cloud, bottom of Pandora's box, balm in Gilead.

anchor, sheet anchor, mainstay; staff &c. (*support*) 215; heaven &c. 981.

V. hope, trust, confide, rely on, put one's trust in, lean upon; pin one's -hope, – faith- upon &c. (*believe*) 484.

feel –, entertain –, harbor –, indulge –, cherish –, feed –, foster –, nourish –, encourage –, cling to –, live in- hope &c. *n.*; see land; feel –, rest- -assured, – confident &c. *adj.*

presume; promise oneself; expect &c. (*look forward to*) 507.

hope for &c. (*desire*) 865; anticipate.

be -hopeful &c. *adj.*; look on the bright side of, view on the sunny side, *voir en couleur de rose*, make the best of it, hope for the best; put -a good, – a bold, – the best- face upon; keep one's spirits up; take heart, – of grace; be of good -heart, – cheer; flatter oneself, "lay the flattering unction to one's soul" [*Hamlet*].

catch at a straw, hope against hope, reckon one's chickens before they are hatched.

give –, inspire –, raise –, hold out- hope &c. *n.*; raise expectations; encourage, cheer, assure, reassure, buoy up, embolden; promise, bid fair, augur well, be in a fair way, look up, flatter, tell a flattering tale.

Adj. hoping &c. *v.*; in -hopes &c. *n.*; hopeful, confident; secure &c. (*certain*) 484; sanguine, in good heart, buoyed up, buoyant, elated, flushed, exultant, enthusiastic; heartsome; utopian.

unsus-pecting, -picious; fearless, free –, exempt from- -fear, – suspicion, – distrust, – despair; undespairing, self-reliant.

probable, on the high road to; within sight of -shore, – land; promising, propitious; of –, full of- promise; of good omen; auspicious, *de bon augure;* reassuring; encouraging, cheering, inspiriting, looking up, bright, roseate, *couleur de rose*, rose-colored.

Adv. hopefully &c. *adj.*

Int. God speed!

Phr. *nil desperandum* [Horace]; never say die, *dum spiro spero, latet scintillula forsan*, all is for the best, *spero meliora;* "the wish being father to the thought" [*Henry IV*]; "hope told

disconcert; dash –, crush –, destroy-one's hopes; hope against hope.

Adj. hopeless, desperate, despairing, gone, in despair, *au désespoir*, forlorn; inconsolable &c. (*dejected*) 837; broken-hearted.

out of the question, not to be thought of; impracticable &c. 471; past -hope, – cure, – mending, – recall; at one's last gasp &c. (*death*) 360; given -up, – over.

incurable, cureless, immedicable, remediless, beyond remedy; incorrigible; irre-parable, -mediable, -coverable, -versible, -trievable, -claimable, -deemable, -vocable; ruined, undone; immitigable.

unpromising, unpropitious; inauspicious, ill-omened, threatening, clouded over.

Phr. "*lasciate ogni speranza voi ch' entrate*" [Dante]; its days are numbered; the worst come to the worst; "no change, no pause, no hope, yet I endure" [Shelley]; "O dark, dark, dark, amid the blaze of noon" [Milton].

860. Fear. — N. fear, timidity, diffidence, want of confidence; apprehensive-, fearful-ness &c. *adj.*; solicitude, anxiety, care, apprehension, misgiving; feeze [U. S.]; mistrust &c. (*doubt*) 485; suspicion, qualm; hesitation &c. (*irresolution*) 605.

nervous-, restless-ness &c. *adj.*; in-, dis-quietude; batophobia; heartquake; flutter, trepidation, fear and trembling, perturbation, tremor, quivering, shaking, trembling, throbbing heart, palpitation, ague fit, cold sweat; abject fear &c. (*cowardice*) 862; mortal funk, heart-sinking, despondency; despair &c. 859.

fright; affright, -ment; boof [U. S.]; alarm, dread, awe, terror, horror, dismay, consternation, panic, scare, stampede [of horses].

intimidation, terrorism, reign of terror.

[Object of fear] bug-bear, -aboo; scarecrow; hobgoblin &c. (*demon*) 980; nightmare, Gorgon, mormo, ogre, Hurlothrumbo, raw head and bloody bones, fee-faw-fum, *bête noire, enfant terrible.*

alarmist &c. (*coward*) 862.

V. fear, stand in awe of; be -afraid &c. *adj.*; have -qualms &c. *n.*; apprehend, sit upon thorns, eye askance; distrust &c. (*disbelieve*) 485.

hesitate &c. (*be irresolute*) 605; falter,

a flattering tale "; *rusticus expectat dum defluat amnis.*

at spes non fracta; ego spem pretio non emo [Terence]; *en Dieu est ma fiance;* "hope! thou nurse of young desire" [Bickerstaff]; *in hoc signo spes mea; in hoc signo vinces; la speranza è il pan de'miseri; l'espérance est le songe d'un homme éveillé;* "the mighty hopes that make us men" [Tennyson]; "the sickening pang of hope deferred" [Scott].

funk, cower, crouch; skulk &c. (*cowardice*) 862; let "I dare not" wait upon "I would"; take -fright, – alarm; start, wince, flinch, shy, shrink; fly &c. (*avoid*) 623.

tremble, shake; shiver, – in one's shoes; shudder, flutter; shake –, tremble- -like an aspen leaf, – all over; quake, quaver, quiver, quail.

grow –, turn- pale; blench, stand aghast; not dare to say one's soul is one's own.

inspire –, excite- -fear, – awe; raise apprehensions; be in a daze, bulldoze [U. S.]; faze, feeze [U. S.]; give —, raise –, sound- an alarm; alarm, startle, scare, cry "wolf," disquiet, dismay; fright, -en; affright, terrify; astound; fright from one's propriety; fright out of one's -wits, – senses, – seven senses; awe; strike -all of a heap, – an awe into, – terror; harrow up the soul, appall, unman, petrify, horrify; pile on the agony.

make one's -flesh creep, – hair stand on end, – blood run cold, – teeth chatter; take away –, stop- one's breath; make one -tremble &c.

haunt; prey –, weigh- on the mind.

put in -fear, – bodily fear; terrorize, intimidate, cow, daunt, overawe, abash, deter, discourage; browbeat, bully; threaten &c. 909.

Adj. fearing &c. *v.*; frightened &c. *v.*; in -fear, – a fright &c. *n.*; haunted with the -fear &c. *n.*- of; afeard.

afraid, fearful; tim-id, -orous; nervous, diffident, coy, faint-hearted, tremulous, shaky, afraid of one's shadow, apprehensive, restless, fidgety; more frightened than hurt.

aghast; awe-, horror-, terror-, panic- -struck, -stricken; frightened to death, white as a sheet; pale, – as -death, – ashes, – a ghost; breathless, in hysterics.

inspiring fear &c. *v.*; alarming; formidable, redoubtable; perilous &c. (*danger*) 665; portentous; fearful; dread, -ful; fell; dire, -ful; shocking; terri-ble, -fic; tremendous; horri-d, -ble, -fic; ghastly; awful, awe-inspiring; revolting &c. (*painful*) 830; Gorgonian.

Adv. *in terrorem.*

Int. "angels and ministers of grace defend us!" [*Hamlet*].

Phr. *ante tubam trepidat; horresco referens,* one's heart failing one, *obstupui steteruntque comæ et vox faucibus hæsit* [Vergil].

"a dagger of the mind" [*Macbeth*]; *expertus metuit* [Horace]; "fain would I climb but that I fear to fall" [Raleigh]; "fear is the parent of cruelty" [Froude]; "Gorgons and hydras and chimeras dire" [*Paradise Lost*]; *omnia tuta timens* [Vergil]; "our fears do make us traitors" [*Macbeth*].

861. [Absence of fear.] **Courage.** — **N.** courage, bravery, valor; resolute-, bold-ness &c. *adj.*; spirit, daring, gallantry, intrepidity; contempt –, defiance- of danger; derring-do; audacity; rashness &c. 863; dash; defiance &c. 715; confidence, self-reliance.

man-liness, -hood; nerve, pluck, mettle, game; heart, – of grace; spunk, face, virtue, hardihood, fortitude; firmness &c. (*stability*) 150; heart of oak; bottom, backbone &c. (*perseverance*) 604a.

resolution &c. (*determination*) 604; bulldog courage.

prowess, heroism, chivalry.

862. [Excess of fear.] **Cowardice.** — **N.** cowardice, pusillanimity; cowardliness &c. *adj.*; timidity, effeminacy.

poltroonery, baseness; dastard-ness, -y; abject fear, funk; Dutch courage; fear &c. 860; white feather, faint heart; cold feet * [U. S.], yellow streak *.

coward, poltroon, dastard, sneak, recreant; shy –, dunghill- cock; coistril, milksop, white-liver, nidget, one that cannot say "Bo" to a goose; slink; Bob Acres, Jerry Sneak.

alarm-, terror-, pessim-ist; runagate &c. (*fugitive*) 623.

V. quail &c. (*fear*) 860; be -cowardly

exploit, feat, achievement; heroic -deed, – act; bold stroke.

man, – of mettle; hero, demigod, Amazon, Hector; lion, tiger, panther, bulldog; game-, fighting-cock; bully, fire eater &c. 863.

V. be -courageous &c. *adj.*; dare, venture, make bold; face –, front –, affront –, confront –, brave –, defy –, despise –, mock- danger; look in the face; look -full, – boldly, – danger- in the face; face; meet, – in front; brave, beard; defy &c. 715.

take –, muster –, summon up –, pluck up- courage; nerve oneself, take heart; take –, pluck up- heart of grace; hold up one's head, screw one's courage to the sticking place; come -to, – up to- the scratch; stand, – to one's guns, – fire, – against; bear up, – against; hold out &c. (*persevere*) 604a.

put a bold face upon; show –, present- a bold front; show fight; face the music.

bell the cat, take the bull by the horns, beard the lion in his den, march up to the cannon's mouth, go through fire and water, run the gantlet.

give –, infuse –, inspire- courage; reassure, encourage, embolden, inspirit, cheer, nerve, put upon one's mettle, rally, raise a rallying cry; pat on the back, make a man of, keep in countenance.

Adj. courageous, brave; val-iant, -orous; gallant, intrepid; spirit-ed, -ful; high-spirited, -mettled; mettlesome, plucky; man-ly, -ful; resolute; stout, -hearted; iron-, lion-hearted; heart of oak; Penthesilean.

bold, – spirited; daring, audacious; fear-, daunt-, dread-, awe-less; un-daunted, -appalled, -dismayed, -awed, -blenched, -abashed, -alarmed, -flinching, -shrinking, -blenching, -apprehensive; confident, self-reliant; bold as -a lion, – brass.

enterprising, adventurous; ventur-ous, -esome; dashing, chivalrous; soldierly &c. (*warlike*) 722; heroic.

fierce, savage; pugnacious &c. (*bellicose*) 720.

strong-minded, hardy, doughty; firm &c. (*stable*) 150; determined &c. (*resolved*) 604; dogged, indomitable &c. (*persevering*) 604a.

up to, – the scratch; upon one's mettle; reassured &c. *v.*; unfeared, undreaded.

Phr. one's blood being up; *courage sans peur; fortes fortuna adjuvat* [Terence]; "have I not in my time heard lions roar" [*Taming of the Shrew*]; "I dare do all that may become a man" [*Macbeth*]; *male vincetis sed vincite* [Ovid]; *omne solum forti patria;* "self-trust is the essence of heroism" [Emerson]; *stimulos dedit æmula virtus* [Lucan]; "strong and great, a hero" [Longfellow]; *teloque animus præstantior omni* [Ovid]; "there is always safety in valor" [Emerson]; *virtus ariete fortior.*

&c. *adj.*, – a coward &c. *n.*; funk; cower, skulk, sneak; flinch, shy, fight shy, slink, turn tail; run away &c. (*avoid*) 623; show the white feather.

Adj. coward, -ly; fearful, shy; tim-id, -orous; skittish; poor-spirited, spiritless, soft, effeminate.

weak-minded; infirm of purpose &c. 605; weak-, faint-, chicken-, hen-, lily-, pigeon-hearted; white-, lily-, milk-livered; milksop, smock-faced; unable to say "Bo" to a goose.

dastard, -ly; base, craven, sneaking, dunghill, recreant; unwar-, unsoldierlike.

"in face a lion but in heart a deer."

unmanned; frightened &c. 860.

Int. *sauve qui peut!* devil take the hindmost!

Phr. *ante tubam trepidat*, one's courage oozing out; *degeneres animos timor arguit* [Vergil].

---

863. Rashness. — N. rashness &c. *adj.*; temerity, want of caution, imprudence, indiscretion; over-confidence, presumption, audacity.

precipit-ancy, -ation; impetuosity; levity; foolhardi-hood, -ness; heed-, thought-lessness &c. (*inattention*) 458; carelessness &c. (*neglect*) 460; despera-

864. Caution. — N. caution; cautiousness &c. *adj.*; discretion, prudence, cautel †, heed, circumspection, calculation, deliberation.

foresight &c. 510; vigilance &c. 459; warning &c. 668.

coolness &c. *adj.*; self-possession, -command; presence of mind, *sang froid;*

tion; Quixotism, knight-errantry; fire eating.

gam-ing, -bling; blind bargain, leap in the dark, fool's paradise; too many eggs in one basket.

desperado, rashling, madcap, daredevil, Hotspur, fire eater, bully, bravo, Hector, scapegrace, *enfant perdu;* Don Quixote, knight-errant, Icarus; adventurer; gam-bler, -ester; dynamitard; boomer [U. S.].

V. be -rash &c. *adj.;* stick at nothing, play a desperate game; run into danger &c. 665; play with -fire, – edge tools.

carry too much sail, sail too near the wind, ride at single anchor, go out of one's depth.

take a leap in the dark, buy a pig in a poke.

donner tête baissée; knock one's head against a wall &c. (*be unskillful*) 699; rush on destruction; kick against the pricks, tempt Providence, go on a forlorn hope.

reckon -one's chickens before they are hatched, – without one's host; catch at straws; trust to –, lean on- a broken reed.

Adj. rash, incautious, indiscreet; imprudent, improvident, temerarious; uncalculating; heedless; careless &c. (*neglectful*) 460; without ballast, heels over head; giddy &c. (*inattentive*) 458; wanton, reckless, wild, madcap; desperate, devil-may-care.

hot-blooded, -headed, -brained; headlong, -strong; breakneck; foolhardy; harebrained; precipitate, impulsive.

over-confident, -weening; venturesome, -ous; adventurous, Quixotic; fire eating, cavalier; janty, jaunty, free and easy.

off one's guard &c. (*inexpectant*) 508.

Adv. post haste, *à corps perdu*, hand over head, *tête baissée*, headforemost; happen what may.

Phr. neck or nothing, the devil being in one; *non semper temeritas est felix* [Livy]; *paucis temeritas est bono multis malo* [Phædrus].

well-regulated mind; worldly wisdom, Fabian policy.

V. be -cautious &c. *adj.*; take -care, – heed, – good care; have a care, mind, – what one is about; be on one's guard &c. (*keep watch*) 459; "make assurance doubly sure" [*Macbeth*].

bespeak &c. (*be early*) 132.

think twice, look before one leaps, count the cost, look to the main chance, cut one's coat according to one's cloth; feel one's -ground, – way; see how the land lies &c. (*foresight*) 510; wait to see how the cat jumps; bridle one's tongue; *reculer pour mieux sauter* &c. (*prepare*) 673; let well alone, *ne pas reveiller le chat qui dort.*

keep out of -harm's way, – troubled waters; keep at a respectful distance, stand aloof; keep -, be- on the safe side.

husband one's resources &c. 636.

caution &c. (*warn*) 668.

Adj. cautious, wary, guarded; on one's guard &c. (*watchful*) 459; *cavendo tutus; in medio tutissimus;* vigilant.

care-, heed-ful; cautelous †, stealthy, chary, shy of, circumspect, prudent, discreet, politic; sure-footed &c. (*skillful*) 698.

unenterprising, unadventurous, cool. steady, self-possessed; overcautious.

Adv. cautiously &c. *adj.*

Int. have a care!

Phr. *timeo Danaos* [Vergil]; *festina lente.*

ante victoriam ne canas triumphum; "give every man thine ear but few thy voice" [Hamlet]; *il rit bien qui rit le dernier; ni firmes carta que no leas ni bebas agua que no veas; nescit vox missa reverti* [Horace]; "love all, trust a few" [*All's Well*]; *noli irritare leones;* safe bind safe find.

865. Desire. — **N.** desire, wish, fancy, fantasy; want, need, exigency.

mind, inclination, leaning, bent, animus, partiality, *penchant*, predilection; propensity &c. 820; willingness &c. 602; liking, love, fondness, relish.

longing, hankering, inkling; solicitude, anxiety; yearning, coveting; aspiration, ambition, vaulting ambition; eagerness, zeal, ardor, *empressement*,

866. Indifference. — **N.** indifference, neutrality; coldness &c. *adj.*; anaphrodisia; unconcern, insouciance, nonchalance; want of -interest, – earnestness; anorexy, inappetency; apathy &c. (*insensibility*) 823; supineness &c. (*inactivity*) 683; disdain &c. 930; recklessness &c. 863; inattention &c. 458.

ana-, anta-phrodisiac; lust-quencher, passion-queller.

breathless impatience, overanxiety; impetuosity &c. 825.

appet-ite, -ition, -ence, -ency; sharp appetite, keenness, hunger, stomach, twist; thirst, -iness; drouth, mouth-watering; itch, -ing; prurience, cacoëthes, cupidity, lust, concupiscence.

edge of -appetite, – hunger; torment of Tantulus; sweet –, lickerish- tooth; itching palm; longing –, wistful –, sheep's- eye.

avidity; greed, -iness; covetous-, ravenous-ness &c. adj.; grasping, craving, canine appetite, rapacity; voracity &c. (gluttony) 957.

passion, rage, furore, mania, manie †; inextinguishable desire; dips-, kleptomania.

[Person desiring] lover, amateur, votary, devotee, aspirant, solicitant, candidate; cormorant &c. 957.

[Object of desire] desideratum; want &c. (requirement) 630; " consummation devoutly to be wished "; attraction, magnet, allurement, fancy, temptation, seduction, fascination, prestige, height of one's ambition, idol; whim, -sey; maggot; hobby, -horse.

Fortunatus's cap; wishing -cap, – stone, – well.

V. desire; wish, – for; be -desirous &c. adj.; have a -longing &c. n.; hope &c. 858.

care for, affect, like, list; take to, cling to, take a fancy to; fancy; prefer &c. (choose) 609.

have -an eye, – a mind- to; find it in one's heart &c. (be willing) 602; have a fancy for, set one's eyes upon; cast a sheep's eye –, look sweet- upon; take into one's head, have at heart, be bent upon; set one's -cap at, – heart upon, – mind upon; covet.

want, miss, need, feel the want of; would fain -have, – do; would be glad of.

be -hungry &c. adj.; have a good appetite, play a good knife and fork; hunger -, thirst -, crave -, lust -, itch -, hanker -, run mad- after; raven -, die- for; burn to.

desiderate; sigh -, cry -, gape -, gasp -, pine -, pant -, languish -, yearn -, long -, be on thorns -, hope- for; aspire after; catch at, grasp at, jump at.

woo, court, solicit; fish -, spell -, whistle -, put up- for; ogle.

cause -, create -, raise -, excite -,

V. be -indifferent &c. adj.; stand neuter; take no interest in &c. (insensibility) 823; have no -desire &c. 865, – taste, – relish- for; not care for; care nothing -for, – about; not care a -straw &c. (unimportance) 643 -about, – for; not mind.

set at naught &c. (make light of) 483; spurn &c. (disdain) 930.

Adj. indifferent, cold, frigid, lukewarm; cool, – as a cucumber; unconcerned, insouciant, phlegmatic, pococurante, easy-going, devil-may-care, careless, listless, lackadaisical; half-hearted; un-ambitious, -aspiring, -desirous, -solicitous, -attracted.

un-attractive, -alluring, -desired, -desirable, -cared for, -wished, -valued, all one to.

insipid &c. 391; vain.

Adv. for aught one cares.

Int. never mind.

867. Dislike. — N. dis-like, -taste, -relish, -inclination, -placency.

reluctance; backwardness &c. (unwillingness) 603.

repugnance, disgust, queasiness, turn, nausea, loathing; avers-eness, -ation †, -ion; abomination, antipathy, abhorrence, horror; mortal –, rooted- -antipathy, – horror; hatred, detestation; hate &c. 898; animosity &c. 900; hydrophobia; canine madness; byssa, xenophobia.

sickener; gall and wormwood &c. (unsavory) 395; shuddering, cold sweat.

V. dis-, mis-like, -relish; mind, object to; have rather not, not care for; have -, conceive -, entertain -, take- -a dislike, – an aversion- to; have no -taste, – stomach- for.

shun, avoid &c. 623; eschew; withdraw -, shrink -, recoil- from; not be able to -bear, – abide, – endure; shrug the shoulders at, shudder at, turn up the nose at, look askance at; make a -mouth, – wry face, – grimace; make faces.

loathe, nauseate, abominate, detest, abhor; hate &c. 898; take amiss &c. 900; have enough of &c. (be satiated) 869.

cause -, excite- dislike; disincline, repel, sicken; make -, render- sick; turn one's stomach, nauseate, wamble, disgust, shock, stink in the nostrils; go against the -grain, – stomach; stick in

provoke- desire; whet the appetite; appetize, titillate, allure, attract, take one's fancy, tempt; hold out -temptation, – allurement; tantalize, make one's mouth water, *faire venir l'eau à la bouche.*

gratify desire &c. (*give pleasure*) 829.

Adj. desirous; desiring &c. *v.*; inclined &c. (*willing*) 602; partial to; fain, wishful, optative; anxious, wistful, curious; at a loss for, sedulous, solicitous.

craving, hungry, sharp-set, peckish, ravening, with an empty stomach, esurient, lickerish, thirsty, athirst, parched with thirst, pinched with hunger, famished, dry, drouthy; hungry as a -hunter, – hawk, – horse, – church mouse.

greedy, – as a hog; overeager, voracious; ravenous, – as a wolf; open-mouthed, covetous, rapacious, grasping, extortionate, exacting, sordid, *alieni appetens;* insati-able, -ate; unquenchable, quenchless; omnivorous.

unsatisfied, unsated, unslaked.

eager, avid, keen; burning, fervent, ardent; agog; all agog; breathless; impatient &c. (*impetuous*) 825; bent –, intent –, set- -on, – upon; mad after, *enragé,* rabid, dying for, devoured by desire.

aspiring, ambitious, vaulting, sky-aspiring, high-reaching.

desirable; desired &c. *v.*; in demand; pleasing &c. (*giving pleasure*) 829; appeti-zing, -ble; tantalizing.

Adv. wistfully &c. *adj.*; fain.

Int. would -that, – it were! O for! *esto perpetua!*

Phr. the wish being father to the thought; *sua cuique voluptas; hoc erat in votis,* the mouth watering, the fingers itching; *aut Cæsar aut nullus.*
" Cassius has a lean and hungry look " [*Jul. Cæsar*]; " hungry as the grave " [Thomson]; " I was born to other things " [Tennyson]; "not what we wish but what we want " [Merrick]; " such joy ambition finds " [*P. L.*]; " the sea hath bounds but deep desire hath none " [*Venus and Adonis*]; *ubi mel ibi apes.*

the throat; make one's blood run cold &c. (*give pain*) 830; pall.

Adj. disliking &c. *v.*; averse from, loth, adverse; shy of, sick of, out of conceit with; disinclined; heart-, dog-sick; queasy.

dislike &c. *v.*; uncared for, unpopular; out of favor; repulsive, repugnant, repellant; abhorrent, insufferable, fulsome, nauseous; loath-some, -ful; offensive; disgusting &c. *v.*; disagreeable &c. (*painful*) 830.

Adv. *usque ad nauseam.*

Int. faugh! foh! ugh!

Phr. *non libet.*

868. Fastidiousness. — N. fastidiousness &c. *adj.*; nicety, hypercriticism, difficulty in being pleased, *friandise,* epicurism, *omnia suspendens naso.*

epicure, gourmet.

[Excess of delicacy] prudery.

V. be -fastidious &c. *adj.*; have a sweet tooth.

mince the matter; turn up one's nose at &c. (*disdain*) 930; look a gift horse in the mouth, see spots on the sun.

Adj. fastidious, nice, delicate, *délicat,* finical, difficult, dainty, lickerish, squeamish, thin-skinned; s-, queasy; hard –, difficult- to please; querulous, particular, strait-laced, scrupulous; censorious &c. 932; hypercritical; overcritical.

Phr. *noli me tangere.*

869. Satiety. — N. satiety, satisfaction, saturation, repletion, glut, surfeit; cloyment, satiation; weariness &c. 841.

spoiled child; *enfant gâté;* too much of a good thing, *toujours perdrix; crambe repetita.*

V. sate, satiate, satisfy, saturate; cloy, quench, slake, pall, glut, gorge, surfeit; bore &c. (*weary*) 841; tire &c. (*fatigue*) 688; spoil.

have -enough of, – quite enough of, – one's fill, – too much of; be -satiated &c. *adj.*

Adj. satiated &c. *v.*; overgorged; *blasé,* used up, sick of, heartsick.

Int. enough! hold! *eheu jam satis!*

4. CONTEMPLATIVE AFFECTIONS

870. Wonder. — N. wonder, marvel; astonish-, amaze-, wonder-, bewilderment; amazedness &c. *adj.*; admiration,

871. [Absence of wonder.] **Expectance. — N.** expectance &c. (*expectation*) 507.

awe; stup-or, -efaction; stound †, fascination; sensation; surprise &c. (*inexpectation*) 508.

note of admiration; thaumaturgy &c. (*sorcery*) 992.

V. wonder, marvel, admire; be -surprised &c. *adj.*; start; stare; open -, rub -, turn up- one's eyes; gloar †; gape, open one's mouth, hold one's breath; look -, stand- -aghast, - agog; look blank &c. (*disappointment*) 509; *tomber des nues;* not believe one's -eyes, - ears, - senses.

not be able to account for &c. (*unintelligible*) 519; not know whether one stands on one's head or one's heels.

surprise, astonish, amaze, astound; dumfound, -er; startle, dazzle; daze; strike, - with -wonder, - awe; electrify; stun, stupefy, petrify, confound, bewilder, flabbergast; stagger, throw on one's beam ends, fascinate, turn the head, take away one's breath, strike dumb; make one's -hair stand on end, - tongue cleave to the roof of one's mouth; make one stare.

take by surprise &c. (*be unexpected*) 508.

be -wonderful &c. *adj.*; beggar -, baffle- description; stagger belief.

Adj. surprised &c. *v.*; aghast, all agog, breathless, agape; open-mouthed; awe-, thunder-, moon-, planet-struck; spellbound; lost in -amazement, - wonder, - astonishment; struck all of a heap, unable to believe one's senses, like a duck in thunder.

wonderful, wondrous; surprising &c. *v.*; unexpected &c. 508; unheard of; mysterious &c. (*inexplicable*) 519; miraculous.

in-describable, -expressible, -effable; un-utterable, -speakable.

monstrous, prodigious, stupendous, marvelous; in-conceivable, -credible; in-, un-imaginable; strange &c. (*uncommon*) 83; passing strange.

striking &c. *v.*; overwhelming; wonder-working.

Adv. wonderfully &c. *adj.*; fearfully; for a -, in the name of- wonder; strange to say; *mirabile -dictu, - visu;* to one's great surprise.

with -wonder &c. *n.*, - gaping mouth, - open eyes, - upturned eyes.

Int. lo, - and behold! O! heyday! halloo! what! indeed! really! surely! humph! hem! good -lack, - heavens, - gracious! gad so! welladay! dear me! only think! lackadaisy! my -stars, - goodness! gracious goodness! goodness gracious! mercy on us! heavens and earth! God bless me! bless -us, - my heart! odzookens! *O gemini!* adzooks! hoity-toity! strong! Heaven save -, bless- the mark! can such things be! zounds! 'sdeath! what -on earth, - in the world! who would have thought it! &c. (*inexpectation*) 508; you don't say so! what do you say to that! *nous verrons!* how now! where am I?

Phr. *vox faucibus hæsit;* one's hair standing on end.

nine days' wonder.

V. expect &c. 507; not -be surprised, - wonder &c. 870; *nil admirari,* make nothing of.

Adj. expecting &c. *v.*; unamazed, astonished at nothing; *blasé* &c. (*weary*) 841; expected &c. *v.*; foreseen.

common, ordinary &c. (*habitual*) 613.

Int. no wonder; of course.

872. Prodigy. — **N.** prodigy, phenomenon; wonder, -ment; marvel, miracle; monster &c. (*unconformity*) 83; curiosity, lion, sight, spectacle; *jeu -, coup- de théâtre;* gazingstock; sign; St. Elmo's -fire, - light; portent &c. 512.

bursting of a -shell, - bomb; volcanic eruption, peal of thunder; thunder-clap, -bolt.

what no words can paint; wonders of the world; *annus mirabilis; dignus vindice nodus.*

Phr. *natura il fece e poi roppe la stampa.*

5. Extrinsic Affections [1]

873. Repute. — **N.** distinction, mark, name, figure, repute, reputation; good -, high- repute; note, notability, notoriety, éclat, "the bubble reputation" [*As You Like It*], vogue, celebrity; fame, famousness; renown; popularity, *aura popularis;* approbation &c. 931; credit, *succès d'estime*, prestige, talk of the town; name to conjure with.

glory, honor; luster &c. (*light*) 420; illustriousness &c. adj.

account, regard, respect; reputableness &c. adj.; respectability &c. (*probity*) 939; good -name, - report; fair name.

dignity; stateliness &c. adj.; solemnity, grandeur, splendor, nobility, majesty, sublimity.

rank, standing, brevet rank, precedence, *pas*, station, place, status; position, - in society; order, degree, baccalaureate, *locus standi*, caste, condition.

greatness &c. adj.; eminence; height &c. 206; importance &c. 642; pre-, supereminence; high mightiness, primacy; top of the -ladder, - tree.

elevation; ascent &c. 305; super-, exaltation; dignification, aggrandizement.

dedication, consecration, enthronement, canonization, celebration, enshrinement, glorification.

hero, man of mark, great card, celebrity, worthy, lion, *rara avis*, notability, somebody; classman; man of rank &c. (*nobleman*) 875; pillar of the -state, - church.

chief &c. (*master*) 745; first fiddle &c. (*proficient*) 700; cynosure, mirror; flower, pink, pearl; paragon &c. (*perfection*) 650; choice and master spirits of the age; *élite;* star, sun, constellation, galaxy.

ornament, honor, feather in one's cap, halo, aureole, nimbus; halo -, blaze- of glory; blushing honors; laurels &c. (*trophy*) 733.

memory, posthumous fame, niche in the temple of fame; immor-tality, -tal name; *magni nominis umbra* [Lucan].

V. be conscious of glory; be proud of &c. (*pride*) 878; exult &c. (*boast*) 884; be vain of &c. (*vanity*) 880.

be -distinguished &c. adj.; shine &c. (*light*) 420; shine forth, figure; make -, cut- a -figure, - dash, - splash.

rival, surpass; out-shine, -rival, -vie,

874. Disrepute. — **N.** disrepute, discredit; ill-, bad- -repute, -name, -odor, -favor; disapprobation &c. 932; ingloriousness, derogation; a-, de-basement; abjectness &c. adj.; degradation dedecoration; "a long farewell to all my greatness" [*Henry VIII*]; odium, obloquy, opprobrium, ignominy.

dishonor, disgrace; shame, humiliation; scandal, baseness, vileness; turpitude &c. (*improbity*) 940; infamy.

tarnish, taint, defilement, pollution.

stain, blot, spot, blur, stigma, brand, reproach, imputation, slur.

crying -, burning- shame; *scandalum magnatum*, badge of infamy, blot in one's escutcheon; bend -, bar- sinister; champain, point champain; byword of reproach; Ichabod.

argumentum ad verecundiam; sense of shame &c. 879.

V. be -inglorious &c. adj.; incur -disgrace &c. n.; have -, earn- a bad name; put -, wear- a halter round one's neck; disgrace -, expose- oneself.

play second fiddle; lose caste; pale one's ineffectual fire; recede into the shade; fall from one's high estate; keep in the background &c. (*modesty*) 881; be conscious of disgrace &c. (*humility*) 879; look -blue, - foolish, - like a fool; cut a -poor, - sorry- figure; laugh on the wrong side of the mouth; make a sorry face, go away with a flea in one's ear, slink away.

cause -shame &c. n.; shame, disgrace, put to shame, dishonor; throw -, cast -, fling -, reflect- dishonor &c. n. upon; be a -reproach &c. n. to; derogate from.

tarnish, stain, blot, sully, taint; discredit; degrade, debase, defile; beggar; expel &c. (*punish*) 972.

impute shame to, brand, post, stigmatize, vilify, defame, slur, cast a slur upon, hold up to shame, send to Coventry; tread -, trample- under foot; show up, drag through the mire, heap dirt upon; reprehend &c. 932.

bring low, put down, snub; take down a peg, - lower, - or two.

obscure, eclipse, outshine, take the shine out of; throw -, cast- into the shade; overshadow; leave -, put- in the background; push into a corner, put

[1] Or personal affections derived from the opinions or feelings of others.

-jump; emulate, eclipse; throw –, cast- into the shade; overshadow.

live, flourish, glitter; flaunt, gain –, acquire- honor &c. *n.*; play first fiddle &c. (*be of importance*) 642, bear the -palm, – bell; lead the way; take -pre- cedence, – the wall of; gain –, win- -laurels, – spurs, – golden opinions &c. (*approbation*) 931; take one's degree, pass one's examination.

make -a, – some- -noise, – noise in the world; leave one's mark, exalt one's horn, star it, have a run, be run after; come -into vogue, – to the front; raise one's head.

enthrone, signalize, immortalize, deify, exalt to the skies; hand one's name down to posterity.

consecrate; dedicate to, devote to; en- shrine, inscribe, blazon, lionize, blow the trumpet, crown with laurel.

confer –, reflect- honor &c. *n.* on; shed a luster on; redound to one's honor, en- noble.

give –, do –, pay –, render- honor to; honor, accredit, pay regard to, dignify, glorify; sing praises to &c. (*approve*) 931; look up to; exalt, aggrandize, elevate, nobilitate.

Adj. distinguished, *distingué*, noted; of -note &c. *n.*; honored &c. *v.*; popular; fashionable &c. 852.

in good odor in; –, in high- favor; re- put-, respect-, credit-able.

remarkable &c. (*important*) 642; notable, notorious; celebrated, renowned, in every one's mouth, talked of; fam-ous, -ed; far-famed; conspicuous, to the front; foremost; in the -front rank, – ascendant.

imperishable, deathless, immortal, never fading, *ære perennius;* time- honored.

illustrious, glorious, splendid, brilliant, radiant; bright &c. 420; full-blown; honorific.

eminent, prominent; high &c. 206; in the zenith; at the -head of, – top of the tree; peerless, of the first water; superior &c. 33; super-, pre-eminent.

great, dignified, proud, noble, honorable, worshipful, lordly, grand, stately, august, princely, imposing, solemn, transcendent, majestic, sacred, sublime, heaven-born, heroic, *sans peur et sans reproche;* sacrosanct.

Int. hail! all hail! *ave! viva! vive!* long life to! glory –, honor- be to!

Phr. one's name -being in every mouth, – living for ever; *sic itur ad astra, fama volat, aut Cæsar aut nullus;* not to know him argues oneself unknown; none but himself could be his parallel, *palmam qui meruit ferat* [Nelson's motto].

" above all Greek above all Roman fame " [Pope]; *cineri gloria sera est* [Martial]; "great is the glory for the strife is hard " [Wordsworth]; *honor virtutis præmium* [Cicero]; *immensum gloria calcar habet* [Ovid]; " the glory dies not and the grief is past " [Brydges]; *vivit post funera virtus.*

one's nose out of joint; put out, – of countenance.

upset, throw off one's center; discom- pose, disconcert; put to the blush &c. (*humble*) 879.

Adj. disgraced &c. *v.*; blown upon; " shorn of -its beams " [Milton], – one's glory; overcome, downtrodden; loaded with -shame &c. *n.*; in -bad repute &c. *n.*; out of -repute, – favor, – fashion, – countenance; at a discount; under -a cloud, – an eclipse; unable to show one's face; in the -shade, – background; out at elbows, down in the world.

inglorious; nameless, renownless; ob- scure; unknown to fame; un-noticed, -noted, -honored, -glorified.

shameful; dis-graceful, -creditable, -reputable; despicable; questionable; unbecoming, unworthy; derogatory; de- grading, humiliating, *infra dignitatem,* dedecorous; scandalous, infamous, too bad, unmentionable; ribald, opprobri- ous; arrant, shocking, outrageous, noto- rious.

ignominious, scrubby, dirty, abject, vile, beggarly, pitiful, low, mean, shabby; base &c. (*dishonorable*) 940.

Adv. to one's shame be it spoken.

Int. fie! shame! for shame! *proh pu- dor! O tempora! O mores!* ough! *sic transit gloria mundi!*

---

875. Nobility. — N. nobility, rank, condition, distinction, optimacy, blood, *pur sang,* birth, high descent, order;

876. Commonalty. — N. common- alty, democracy; obscurity; low -con- dition, – life, – society, – company;

quality, gentility; blue blood of Castile; *ancien régime.*

high life, *haute monde;* upper -classes, – ten thousand; the four hundred [U. S.]; *élite,* aristocracy, great folks; fashionable world &c. (*fashion*) 852.

peer, -age; house of -lords, – peers; lords, – temporal and spiritual; noblesse; noble, -man; lord, -ling; grandee, magnifico, hidalgo; daimio, samurai, *shizoku;* don, -ship; aristocrat, swell, three-tailed bashaw; gentleman, squire, squireen, patrician, laureate.

gentry, gentlefolk; squirarchy, better sort, magnates, primates, optimates; pantisocracy.

king &c. (*master*) 745; atheling; prince, duke; marquis, -ate; earl, viscount, baron, thane, banneret; baronet, -cy; knight, -hood; count, armiger, laird; sig-, seig-nior; esquire, boyar, margrave, vavasour, emir, ameer, scherif, effendi, sahib; chevalier, maharaja, nawab, palsgrave, pasha, rajah, waldgrave.

princess, begum, duchess, marchioness; countess &c.; lady, dame; memsahib; Doña, maharani, rani.

personage –, man- of -distinction, – mark, – rank; nota-bles, -bilities; celebrity, bigwig, magnate, great man, star; big bug; big-, great-gun; gilded rooster * [U. S.]; *magni nominis umbra* [Lucan]; " every inch a king " [*Lear*].

V. be -noble &c. *adj.*

Adj. noble, exalted; of -rank &c. *n.*; princely, titled, patrician, aristocratic; high-, well-born; of gentle blood; genteel, *comme il faut,* gentlemanlike, courtly &c. (*fashionable*) 852; highly respectable.

Adv. in high quarters.

Phr. *Adel sitzt im Gemüthe nicht im Geblüte; adelig und edel sind zweierlei; noblesse oblige.*

877. Title. — N. title, honor; knighthood &c. (*nobility*) 875.

highness, excellency, grace; lordship, worship; rever-ence, -end; esquire, sir, master, Mr., *signor, señor, Mein Herr,* mynheer; your –, his- honor; serene highness; handle to one's name.

decoration, laurel, palm, wreath, garland, bays, medal, ribbon, riband, blueribbon, cordon, cross, crown, coronet, star, garter; feather, – in one's cap; epaulet, epaulette, colors, cockade; livery; order, arms, shield, scutcheon; reward &c. 973.

bourgeoisie; mass of -the people, – society; Brown Jones and Robinson; lower –, humbler- -classes, – orders; vulgar –, common- herd; rank and file, *hoc genus omne;* the -many, – general, – crowd, – people, – populace, – multitude, – million, – masses, – mobility, – peasantry; king Mob; proletariat; *fruges consumere nati,* δῆμος, οἱ πολλοί, great unwashed; man in the street.

mob; rabble, – rout; chaff, rout, horde, canaille; scum –, residuum –, dregs- of -the people, – society; swinish multitude, *fœx populi;* trash· *profanum –, ignobile- vulgus;* vermin, riffraff, rag-tag and bobtail; small fry.

commoner, one of the people, democrat, plebeian, republican, proletary, proletaire, *roturier,* Mr. Snooks, bourgeois, *épicier,* Philistine, cockney; grisette, demimonde.

peasant, countryman, boor, carle, churl; vill-ain, -ein; *terræ filius;* serf, kern, tyke, tike, chuff, ryot, fellah; longshoreman; swain, clown, hind; clod, -hopper; hobnail, yokel, bog-trotter, bumpkin; plow-man, -boy; rustic, hayseed *, lunk-head [U. S.], chaw-bacon *, tiller of the soil; hewers of wood and drawers of water, groundling; gaffer, loon, put, cub, Tony Lumpkin, looby, rube * [U. S.], lout, underling; gamin; rough; pot-wallopper, slubberdegullion†; vulgar –, low- fellow; cad, curmudgeon.

upstart, parvenu, skipjack; nobody, – one knows; *hesterni quirites, pessoribus orti; bourgeois gentilhomme, novus homo,* snob, gent, mushroom, no one knows who, adventurer; man of straw.

beggar, gaberlunzie, muckworm, mudlark, *sans culotte,* raff, tatterdemalion, caitiff, ragamuffin, Pariah, outcast of society, tramp, vagabond, bezonian, panhandler *, sundowner, *chiffonnier,* Cinderella, cinderwench, scrub, jade; gossoon.

Goth, Vandal, Hottentot, Zulu, savage, barbarian, Yahoo; unlicked cub, rough diamond.

barbar-ousness, -ism; Bœotia.

V. be -ignoble &c. *adj.,* – nobody &c. *n.*

Adj. ignoble, common, mean, low, base, vile, sorry, scrubby, beggarly, below pår; no great shakes &c. (*unimportant*) 643; home-ly, -spun; vulgar, low-minded; snobbish.

plebeian, proletarian; of -low, –

mean- -parentage, – origin, – extraction; low-, base-, earth-born; mushroom, dunghill, risen from the ranks; unknown to fame, obscure, untitled.

rustic, uncivilized; lout-, boor-, clown-, churl-, brut-, raff-ish; rude, unlicked.

barbar-ous, -ian, -ic, -esque; cockney, born within sound of Bow bells.

underling, menial, subaltern.

Adv. below the salt.

Phr. *dummodo sit dives Barbarus ipse placet* [Ovid].

878. Pride. — N. dignity, self-respect, *mens sibi conscia recti* [Vergil].

pride; haughtiness &c. *adj.*; high notions, hauteur; vainglory, crest; arrogance &c. (*assumption*) 885.

proud man, highflier; fine -gentleman, - lady.

V. be -proud &c. *adj.*; put a good face on; look one in the face; stalk abroad, perk oneself up; think no small beer of oneself; presume, swagger, strut; rear –, lift up –, hold up- one's head; hold one's head high, look big, take the wall, " bear like the Turk no rival near the throne " [Pope], carry with a high hand; ride the –, mount on one's- high horse; set one's back up, bridle, toss the head; give oneself airs &c. (*assume*) 885; boast &c. 884.

pride oneself on; glory in, take a pride in; pique –, plume –, hug- oneself; stand upon, be proud of; put a good face on; not -hide one's light under a bushel, – put one's talent in a napkin; not think small beer of oneself &c. (*vanity*) 880.

Adj. dignified; stately; proud, -crested; lordly, baronial; lofty-minded; high-souled, -minded, -mettled, -handed, -plumed, -flown, -toned.

haughty, lofty, high, mighty, swollen, puffed up, flushed, blown; vainglorious; purse-proud, fine; proud as -a peacock, - Lucifer; bloated with pride.

supercilious, disdainful, bumptious, magisterial, imperious, high and mighty, overweening, consequential; arrogant &c. 885; unblushing &c. 880.

stiff, -necked; starch; perked –, stuck- up; in buckram, strait-laced; prim &c. (*affected*) 855.

on one's -dignity, – high horses, – tight ropes, – high ropes; on stilts; *en grand seigneur.*

Adv. with head erect.

Phr. *odi profanum vulgus et arceo* [Horace]. " a duke's revenues on her back " [*Henry VI*]; " disdains the shadow which he treads on at noon " [*Coriolanus*]; " pride in their port, defiance in their eye " [Goldsmith].

879. Humility. — N. hum-ility, -bleness; meek-, low-ness; lowli-ness, -hood; abasement, self-abasement; submission &c. 725; resignation.

condescension; affability &c. (*courtesy*) 894.

modesty &c. 881; verecundity †, blush, suffusion, confusion; sense of -shame, – disgrace; humiliation, mortification; let –, set- down.

V. be -humble &c. *adj.*; deign, vouchsafe, condescend; humble –, demean-oneself; stoop, – to conquer; carry coals; submit &c. 725; submit with a good grace &c. (*brook*) 826; yield the palm.

lower one's -tone, – note; sing small, draw in one's horns, sober down; hide one's -face, – diminished head; not dare to show one's face, take shame to oneself, not have a word to say for oneself; feel –, be conscious of- -shame, – disgrace; drink the cup of humiliation to the dregs.

blush -for, – up to the eyes; redden, change color; color up; hang one's head, look foolish, feel small.

render humble; humble, humiliate; let –, set –, take –, tread –, frown-down; snub, abash, abase, make one sing small, strike dumb; teach one his distance; take down a peg, – lower; throw –, cast- into the shade &c. 874; stare –, put- out of countenance; put to the blush; confuse, ashame, mortify, disgrace, crush; send away with a flea in one's ear.

get a setdown.

Adj. humble, lowly, meek; modest &c. 881; humble-, sober-minded; un-offended; submissive &c. 725; servile &c. 886.

condescending; affable &c. (*courteous*) 894.

humbled &c. *v.*; bowed down, resigned; abashed, ashamed, dashed; out of countenance; down in the mouth; down on one's -knees, – marrowbones, – uppers; humbled in the dust, browbeaten; chap-, crest-fallen; dumfoundered, flabbergasted.

shorn of one's glory &c. (*disrepute*) 874.

Adv. with -downcast eyes, – bated breath, – bended knee; on all fours, on one's feet.

under correction, with due deference.

Phr. I am your -obedient, – very humble- servant; my service to you; *da locum melioribus* [Terence]; *parvum parva decent* [Horace].

880. Vanity. — N.

vanity; conceit, -edness; self-conceit, -complacency, -confidence, -sufficiency, -esteem, -love, -approbation, -praise, -glorification, -laudation, -gratulation, -applause, -admiration; *amour propre;* selfishness &c. 943.

airs, affected manner, pretensions, mannerism; egotism; prigg-ism, -ish-ness; coxcombery, gaudery, vainglory, elation; pride &c. 878; ostentation &c. 882; assurance &c. 885.

vox et præterea nihil; cheval de bataille. coxcomb &c. 854; Sir Oracle &c. 887.

V. be -vain &c. *adj.*, – vain of; pique oneself &c. (*pride*) 878; lay the flattering unction to one's soul.

have -too high, – an overweening-opinion of -oneself, – one's talents; blind oneself as to one's own merit; not think -small beer, – *vin ordinaire-* of oneself; put oneself forward; fish for compliments; give oneself airs &c. (*assume*) 885; boast &c. 884.

render -vain &c. *adj.*; inspire with -vanity &c. *n.*; inflate, puff up, turn up, turn one's head.

Adj. vain, – as a peacock; conceited, overweening, pert, forward; vainglorious, high-flown; ostentatious &c. 882; puffed up, inflated, flushed.

self-satisfied, -confident, -sufficient, -flattering, -admiring, -applauding, -glorious, -opinionated; *entêté* &c. (*wrongheaded*) 481; wise in one's own conceit, pragmatical, overwise, pretentious, priggish; egotistic, -al; *soi-disant* &c. (*boastful*) 884; arrogant &c. 885.

un-abashed, -blushing; un-constrained, -ceremonious; free and easy.

Adv. vainly &c. *adj.*

Phr. "how we apples swim!" [Swift]; "prouder than rustling in unpaid-for silk" [*Cymbeline*].

881. Modesty. — N.

modesty; humility &c. 879; diffidence, timidity; retiring disposition; unobtrusiveness; bashfulness &c. *adj.*; *mauvaise honte;* blush, -ing; verecundity †; self-knowledge.

reserve, constraint; demureness &c. *adj.*; "blushing honors" [*Henry VIII*].

V. be -modest &c. *adj.*; retire, reserve oneself; give way to; draw in one's horns &c. 879; hide one's face.

keep -private, – in the background, – one's distance; pursue the noiseless tenor of one's way, "do good by stealth and blush to find it fame" [Pope], hide one's light under a bushel, cast a sheep's eye.

Adj. modest, diffident; humble &c. 879; timid, timorous, bashful; shy, nervous, skittish, coy, sheepish, shamefaced, blushing, overmodest.

unpreten-ding, -tious; un-obtrusive, -assuming, -ostentatious, -boastful, -aspiring; poor in spirit.

out of countenance &c. (*humbled*) 879. reserved, constrained, demure.

Adv. humbly &c. *adj.*; quietly, privately; without -ceremony, – beat of drum; *sans façon.*

Phr. "not stepping o'er the bounds of modesty" [*Romeo and Juliet*]; "thy modesty's a candle to thy merit" [Fielding].

882. Ostentation. — N.

ostentation, display, show, flourish, parade, *étalage*, pomp, array, state, solemnity; dash, splash, splurge, glitter, strut, pomposity; preten-ṣe, -sions; showing off; fuss.

magnificence, splendor; *coup d'œil;* grand doings.

coup de théâtre; stage -effect, – trick; claptrap; *mise en scène; tour de force; chic.*

demonstration, flying colors; tomfoolery; flourish of trumpets &c. (*celebration*) 883; pageant, -ry; spectacle, exhibition, exposition, procession; turn -, set- out; grand function; fête, gala, field day, review, march past, promenade, insubstantial pageant.

dress; court -, full -, evening -, ball -, fancy- dress; tailoring, millinery, man millinery, frippery; foppery, equipage.

ceremon-y, -ial; ritual; form, -ality; etiquette; punct-o, -ilio, -ilious-ness; starched-, stateli-ness.

mummery, solemn mockery, mouth honor.

attitudinarian; fop &c. 854.

V. be -ostentatious &c. *adj.*; come -, put oneself- forward; attract attention, star it.

make -, cut- a -figure, - dash, - splash, - splurge; figure, - away; make a show, - display; glitter.

show -off, - one's paces; parade, march past; display, exhibit, put forward, hold up; trot -, hand- out; sport, brandish, blazon forth; dangle, - before the eyes.

cry up &c. (*praise*) 931; *prôner*, flaunt, emblazon, prink, set off, mount, have framed and glazed.

put a -good, - smiling- face upon; clean the outside of the platter &c. (*disguise*) 544.

Adj. ostentatious, showy, dashing, pretentious; ja-, jau-nty; grand, pompous, palatial; high-sounding; turgid &c. (*big-sounding*) 577; gai-, ga-rish; gaudy, - as a -peacock, - butterfly, - tulip; flaunting, flashing, flaming, glittering; gay &c. (*ornate*) 847.

splendid, magnificent, sumptuous.

theatrical, dramatic, spectacular; ceremonial, ritual.

solemn, stately, majestic, formal, stiff, ceremonious, punctilious, starched.

en grande tenue, in best bib and tucker, in Sunday best, *endimanché, chic.*

Adv. with -flourish of trumpet, - beat of drum, - flying colors.

ad captandum vulgus.

Phr. *honores mutant mores.*

883. Celebration. — N. celebration, solemnization, jubilee, commemoration, ovation, pæan, triumph, jubilation; china -, diamond -, golden -, silver -, tin- -anniversary, - jubilee, - wedding.

triumphal arch, bonfire, salute; salvo, - of artillery; *feu de joie*, flourish of trumpets, fanfare, colors flying, illuminations.

inauguration, installation, presentation; coronation; Lord Mayor's show; harvest-home, red-letter day; trophy &c. 733; *Te Deum* &c. (*thanksgiving*) 990; fête &c. 882; holiday &c. 840; Forefathers' Day [U. S.].

V. celebrate, keep, signalize, do honor to, commemorate, solemnize, hallow, mark with a red letter.

pledge, drink to, toast, hob and nob.

inaugurate, install, chair.

rejoice &c. 838; kill the fatted calf, hold jubilee, roast an ox.

Adj. celebrating &c. *v.*; commemorative, celebrated, immortal.

Adv. in -honor, - commemoration- of.

Int. hail! all hail! *io -pæan, - triumphe!* " see the conquering hero comes! "

884. Boasting. — N. boasting &c. *v.*; boast, vaunt, crake †; preten-se, -sions; puff, -ery; flourish, fanfaronade; gasconade; blague, bluff, gas *; highfalut-in, -ing; hot air *, spread-eagleism [U. S.]; brag, -gardism; bravado, bunkum, Buncombe; jact-itation, -ancy; bounce; venditation †, vaporing, rodomontade, bombast, fine talking, tall talk, magniloquence, teratology †, heroics; Chauvinism; exaggeration &c. 549.

vanity &c. 880; *vox et præterea nihil;* much cry and little wool, *brutum fulmen.*

exultation; gloria-tion †, -fication; flourish of trumpets: triumph &c. 883.

boaster; bragg-art, -adocio; Gascon, fanfaron, pretender, *soi-disant;* blower * [U. S.], bluffer, Foxy Quiller; blusterer &c. 887; charlatan, jackpudding, trumpeter; puppy &c. (*fop*) 854.

V. boast, make a boast of, brag, vaunt, puff, show off, flourish, crake †, crack, trumpet, strut, swagger, vapor; blague, blow *, four-flush *, bluff.

exult, crow over, neigh, chuckle, triumph; throw up one's cap; talk big, *se faire valoir*, *faire claquer son fouet*, take merit to oneself, make a merit of, sing *Io triumphe*, holloa before one is out of the wood.

Adj. boasting &c. *v.*; magniloquent, flaming, Thrasonic, stilted, gasconading, braggart, boastful, pretentious, *soi-disant;* vainglorious &c. (*conceited*) 880; highfalut-in, -ing; spread-eagle [U. S.].

elate, -d; jubilant, triumphant, exultant; in high feather; flushed, – with victory; cock-a-hoop; on stilts.

vaunted &c. *v.*

Adv. vauntingly &c. *adj.*

Phr. " let the galled jade wince " [*Hamlet*]; *facta non verba.*

---

885. [Undue assumption of superiority.] **Insolence. — N.** insolence; haughtiness &c. *adj.*; arrogance, airs; overbearance; domineering &c. *v.*; tyranny &c. 739.

impertinence; sauciness &c. *adj.*; flippancy, dicacity †, petulance, procacity, bluster; swagger, -ing &c. *v.*; bounce; terrorism.

as-, pre-sumption; beggar on horseback; usurpation.

impudence, assurance, audacity, hardihood, front, face, brass; shamelessness &c. *adj.*; effrontery, hardened front, face of brass.

assumption of infallibility.

saucebox &c. (*blusterer*) 887.

V. be -insolent &c. *adj.*; bluster, vapor, swagger, swell, give oneself airs, snap one's fingers, kick up a dust; swear &c. (*affirm*) 535; rap out oaths; roister.

arrogate; as-, pre-sume; make -bold, – free; take a liberty, give an inch and take an ell.

domineer, bully, dictate, hector; lord it over; *traiter –*, *regarder- de haut en bas;* exact; snub, huff, beard, fly in the face of; put to the blush; bear –, beat-down; browbeat, intimidate; trample –, tread- -down, – under foot; dragoon, ride roughshod over.

out-face, -look, -stare, -brazen, -brave; stare. out of countenance; brazen out; lay down the law; teach one's grandmother to suck eggs; assume a lofty bearing; talk –, look- big; put on big looks, act the *grand seigneur;* mount –, ride- the high horse; toss the head, carry with a high hand.

tempt Providence, want snuffing.

Adj. insolent, haughty, arrogant, imperious, magisterial, dictatorial, arbitrary; high-handed, high and mighty;

886. Servility. — N. servility; slavery &c. (*subjection*) 749; obsequiousness &c. *adj.*; subserviency; abasement; prostration, -ternation †; genuflection &c. (*worship*) 990; fawning &c. *v.*; tuft-hunting, timeserving, flunkeyism; sycophancy &c. (*flattery*) 933; humility &c. 879.

sycophant, parasite; toad, -y, -eater; tufthunter; snob, flunkey, lapdog, spaniel, lick-spittle, smell-feast, *Græculus esuriens*, hanger on, *cavaliere servente*, led captain, carpet knight; timeserver, fortune hunter, Vicar of Bray, Sir Pertinax Mac Sycophant, pickthank; flatterer &c. 935; doer of dirty work; *âme damnée*, tool; reptile; slave &c. (*servant*) 746; courtier; beat *, dead beat *, dough-face * [U. S.], heeler [U. S.], *homme de cour*, sponger, sucker *, tagtail, truckler.

V. cringe, bow, stoop, kneel, bend the knee; fall on one's knees, prostrate oneself; worship &c. 990.

sneak, crawl, crouch, cower, sponge, truckle to, grovel, fawn, lick the feet of, kiss the hem of one's garment.

pay court to; feed on, fatten on, dance attendance on, pin oneself upon, hang on the sleeve of, *avaler les couleuvres*, keep time to, fetch and carry, do the dirty work of.

go with the stream, worship the rising sun, hold with the hare and run with the hounds.

Adj. servile, obsequious; supple, – as a glove; soapy, oily, pliant, cringing, abased, dough-faced, fawning, slavish, groveling, sniveling, mealy-mouthed; beggarly, sycophantic, parasitical; abject, prostrate, down on one's marrowbones; base, mean, sneaking; crouching &c. *v.*

Adv. hat –, cap- in hand.

contumelious, supercilious, overbearing, intolerant, domineering, overweening, high-flown.

flippant, pert, fresh [U. S.], cavalier, saucy, forward, impertinent, malapert.

precocious, assuming, would-be, bumptious.

bluff; brazen, shameless, aweless, unblushing, unabashed; bold-, bare-,
brazen-faced; dead –, lost- to shame.

impudent, audacious, presumptuous, free and easy, devil-may-care, rollicking; jaunty, janty; roistering, blustering, hectoring, swaggering, vaporing;
thrasonic, fire eating, " full of sound and fury " [*Macbeth*].

Adv. with a high hand; *ex cathedrâ*.

Phr. one's bark being worse than his bite; " beggars mounted run their horse to death "
[*Henry VI*]; *quid times ? Cæsarem vehis* [Plutarch].

887. Blusterer. — N. bluster-, swagger-, vapor-, roister-, brawl-er; fanfaron; braggart &c. (*boaster*) 884; bully, terrorist, rough; bulldozer [U. S.],
hoodlum, hooligan *, larrikin, roarer *; Mo-hock, -hawk; drawcansir, swashbuckler, Captain Bobadil, Sir Lucius O'Trigger, Thraso, Pistol, Parolles, Bombastes Furioso, Hector, Chrononhotonthologos; jingo; desperado, dare-devil,
fire eater; fury &c. (*violent person*) 173; rowdy; slang-whanger *, tough [U. S.].

puppy &c. (*fop*) 854; prig; Sir Oracle, dogmatist, doctrinaire, jack-in-office;
saucebox, malapert, jackanapes, minx; bantam-cock.

Section III. SYMPATHETIC AFFECTIONS

1. Social Affections

888. Friendship. — N. friendship,
amity; friendliness &c. *adj.*; brotherhood, fraternity, sodality, confraternity; harmony &c. (*concord*) 714; peace
&c. 721.

firm –, staunch –, intimate –, familiar
–, bosom –, cordial –, tried –, devoted –,
lasting –, fast –, sincere –, warm –, ar-
dent- friendship.

cordiality, fraternization, *entente cor-
diale*, good understanding, *rapprochement*, sympathy, fellow-feeling, response,
welcomeness.

affection &c. (*love*) 897; favoritism;
good will &c. (*benevolence*) 906.

acquaintance, familiarity, intimacy,
intercourse, fellowship, knowledge of;
introduction.

V. be -friendly &c. *adj.*, – friends &c.
890, – acquainted with &c. *adj.*; know;
have the ear of; keep company with &c. (*sociality*) 892; hold communication
–, have dealings –, sympathize- with; have a leaning to; bear good will &c. (*benevolent*) 906; love &c. 897; make much of; befriend &c. (*aid*) 707; introduce to.

set one's horses together; have the latchstring out [U. S.]; hold out –, ex-
tend- the right hand of -friendship, – fellowship; become -friendly &c. *adj.*;
make -friends &c. 890 with; break the ice, be introduced to; make –, pick –,
scrape- acquaintance with; get into favor, gain the friendship of.

shake hands with, fraternize, embrace; receive with open arms, throw oneself into the arms of; meet halfway, take in good part.

Adj. friendly; amic-able, -al; well-affected, unhostile, neighborly, brotherly,
fraternal, sympathetic, harmonious, hearty, cordial, warm-hearted.

889. Enmity. — N. enmity, hostility; unfriendliness &c. *adj.*; discord &c.
713; bitterness, rancor.

alienation, estrangement; dislike &c.
867; hate &c. 898.

heartburning; animosity &c. 900;
malevolence &c. 907.

V. be -inimical &c. *adj.*; keep –, hold-
at arm's length; be at loggerheads; bear
malice &c. 907; fall out; take umbrage
&c. 900; harden the heart, alienate, estrange.

Adj. inimical, unfriendly, hostile; at
-enmity, – variance, – daggers drawn, –
open war with; up in arms against; in
bad odor with.

on bad –, not on speaking- terms;
cool; cold, -hearted; estranged, alien-
ated, disaffected, irreconcilable.

friends –, well –, at home –, hand in hand- with; on -good, – friendly, –
amicable, – cordial, – familiar, – intimate- --terms, – footing; on -speaking,
– visiting- terms; in one's good -graces, – books.

acquainted, familiar, intimate, thick, hand and glove, hail fellow well met,
free and easy; welcome.

Adv. amicably &c. *adj.*; with open arms; *sans cérémonie;* arm in arm.

Phr. *amicitia semper prodest* [Seneca]; " a mystic bond of brotherhood makes all men
one " [Carlyle]; " friendship is love without either flowers or veil " [Hare]; *vulgus amicitias
utilitate probat* [Ovid].

890. Friend. — N. friend, – of one's
bosom; acquaintance, neighbor, wellwisher; *alter ego;* bosom –, fast- friend;
*amicus usque ad aras; fidus Achates;
persona grata.*

favorer, fautor, patron, Mecænas;
tutelary saint, good genius, advocate,
partisan, sympathizer; ally; friend in
need &c. (*auxiliary*) 711.

associate, compeer, comrade, mate, companion, confrère, *camarade,* confidante; old –, crony; chum; pal; play-fellow, -mate; schoolfellow; bed-fellow,
-mate; chamber fellow; class-fellow, -man, -mate; fellow-man, stable companion; maid of honor.

compatriot; fellow –, countryman.

room-, shop-, ship-, mess-mate; fellow –, boon –, pot- companion; co-,
partner.

Arcades ambo, Pylades and Orestes, Castor and Pollux, Nisus and Euryalus,
Damon and Pythias, *par nobile fratrum.*

host, Amphitryon, Boniface; guest, visitor, *protégé.*

Phr. *amici probantur rebus adversis; ohne Bruder kann man leben nicht ohne Freund;*
" best friend, my well-spring in the wilderness " [G. Eliot]; *conocidos muchos amigos pocos;*
" friend more divine than all divinities " [G. Eliot]; *vida sin amigo muerte sin testigo.*

891. Enemy. — N. enemy; antagonist; foe, -man; open –, bitter- enemy;
opponent &c. 710; back friend.

public enemy, enemy to society.

Phr. every hand being against one; " he
makes no friend who never made a foe " [Ten-
nyson].

892. Sociality. — N. soci-ality, -abil-
ity, -ableness &c. *adj.*; social intercourse; consociation; inter-course, -com-
munity; consort-, companion-, com-
rade-ship; clubbism; *esprit de corps.*

conviviality; good- fellowship, – company; joviality, jollity, *savoir vivre,*
festivity, festive board, merrymaking;
loving cup; hospitality, heartiness;
cheer.

welcome, -ness; greeting; hearty –,
warm –, welcome- reception; urbanity
&c. (*courtesy*) 894; familiarity.

good –, jolly- fellow; *bon enfant,* bawcock.

social –, family- circle; circle of acquaintance, coterie, society, company.

social -gathering; – reunion; assembly
&c. (*assemblage*) 72; barbecue [U. S.],
bee; corn-husking [U. S.], -shucking
[U. S.]; hen party; house raising; husking, -bee [U. S.]; infare; smoker, -party;
sociable [U.S.], stag, tamasha; tea-party,
-fight *; party, entertainment, reception, levee, at home, conversazione,

893. Seclusion. Exclusion. — N.
seclusion, privacy; retirement; reclu-
sion, recess; snugness &c. *adj.*; delitescence; rustication, *rus in urbe;* solitude;
solitariness &c. (*singleness*) 87; isolation; loneliness &c. *adj.*; estrangement
from the world, voluntary exile; aloofness.

cell, hermitage; convent &c. 1000;
sanctum sanctorum.

depopulation, desertion, desolation;
wilderness &c. (*unproductive*) 169; howling wilderness; rotten borough, Old
Sarum.

exclusion, excommunication, banishment, exile, ostracism, proscription; cut,
– direct; dead cut.

inhospit-ality, -ableness &c. *adj.*; dis-
sociability; domesticity, Darby and
Joan.

recluse, hermit, eremite, cenobite;
anchor-et, -ite; Simon Stylites; troglo-
dyte, Timon of Athens, Santon, solitaire, ruralist, disciple of Zimmermann,
closet cynic, Diogenes; outcast, Pariah,

soirée, matinée; evening –, morning –, afternoon –, garden –, surprise- party; kettle-, drum; *partie carrée*, dish of tea, *ridotto*, rout, housewarming; ball, festival &c. (*amusement*) 840; "the feast of reason and the flow of soul" [Pope].

visit, -ing; round of visits; call, morning call; interview &c. (*interlocution*) 588; assignation; tryst, -ing place; appointment.

club &c. (*association*) 712.

V. be -sociable &c. *adj.*; know; be -acquainted &c. *adj.*; associate –, sort –, keep company –, walk hand in hand -with; eat off the same trencher, club together, consort, bear one company, join; make acquaintance with &c. (*friendship*) 888; make advances, fraternize, embrace.

be –, feel –, make oneself- at home with; make free with; crack a bottle with; receive hospitality, live at free quarters; find the latchstring out [U. S.].

visit, pay a visit; interchange -visits, – cards; call -at, – upon; leave a card; drop in, look in; look one up, beat up one's quarters.

entertain; give a -party &c. *n.*; be at home, see one's friends, hang out, keep open house, do the honors; receive, – with open arms; welcome; give a warm reception &c. *n.* to; kill the fatted calf.

Adj. sociable, companionable, clubbable, conversable, cosy, cosey, chatty, conversational; homiletical.

convivial; fest-ive, -al; jovial, jolly, hospitable.

welcome, – as the roses in May; fêted, entertained.

free and easy, hail fellow well met, familiar, on visiting terms, acquainted.

social, neighborly; international; gregarious.

Adv. *en famille*, in the family circle; *sans -façon, – cérémonie*; arm in arm.

Phr. "a crowd is not company" [Bacon]; "be bright and jovial among your guests tonight" [*Macbeth*]; "his worth is warrant for his welcome" [*Two Gentlemen*]; "let's be red with mirth" [*Winter's Tale*]; "welcome the coming speed the parting guest" [Pope].

castaway, pilgarlic; wastrel, foundling; wilding.

V. be –, live- secluded &c. *adj.*; keep –, stand –, hold oneself- -aloof, – in the background; keep snug; shut oneself up; deny –, seclude- oneself; creep into a corner, rusticate, *aller planter ses choux;* retire, – from the world; take the veil; abandon &c. 624; sport one's oak *.

cut, – dead; refuse to -associate with, – acknowledge; look cool –, turn one's back –, shut the door- upon; repel, blackball, excommunicate, exclude, exile, expatriate; banish, outlaw, maroon, ostracize, proscribe, cut off from, send to Coventry, keep at arm's length, draw a cordon round.

depopulate; dis-, un-people.

Adj. secluded, sequestered, retired, delitescent, private, bye; out of the -world, -way; "the world forgetting by the world forgot" [Pope].

snug, domestic, stay-at-home.

unsociable; un-, dis-social; inhospitable, cynical, inconversable †, unclubbable, *sauvage*, troglodytic.

solitary; lone-ly, -some; isolated, single.

estranged; unfrequented; uninhabitable, -ed; tenantless; abandoned; deserted, – in one's utmost need; unfriended; kith-, friend-, home-less; lorn, forlorn, desolate.

un-visited, -introduced, -invited, -welcome; under a cloud, left to shift for oneself, derelict, outcast.

banished &c. *v.*

Phr. *noli me tangere.*

"among them but not of them" [Byron]; "and homeless near a thousand homes I stood" [Wordsworth]; "far from the madding crowd's ignoble strife" [Gray]; "makes a solitude and calls it peace" [Byron]; *magna civitas magna solitudo;* "never less alone than when alone" [Rogers]; "O sacred solitude! divine retreat!" [Young].

---

894. Courtesy. — N. courtesy; respect &c. 928; good- manners, – behavior, – breeding; manners; politeness &c. *adj.*; bienséance, urbanity, comity, gentility, breeding, polish, presence; civili-ty, -zation; amenity, suavity; good -temper, – humor; amiability,

895. Discourtesy. — N. discourtesy; ill-breeding; ill –, bad –, ungainly- manners; insuavity; uncourteousness &c. *adj.*; rusticity, inurbanity; illiberality, incivility, displacency.

disrespect &c. 929; procacity, impudence; barbar-ism, -ity; misbehavior,

easy temper, complacency, soft tongue, mansuetude; condescension &c. (*humility*) 879; affability, complaisance, *prévenance*, amability, gallantry; pink of -politeness, – courtesy.

compliment; fair -, soft -, sweet-words; honeyed phrases, ceremonial; salutation, reception, presentation,, introduction, *accueil*, greeting, recognition; welcome, abord †, respects, *devoir*, regards, remembrances; kind -regards, – remembrances; love, best love, duty; empty encomium, flattering remark, hollow commendation; salaams.

obeisance &c. (*reverence*) 928; bow, courtesy, curtsy, scrape, salaam, kotow, bowing and scraping; kneeling; genuflection &c. (*worship*) 990; obsequiousness &c. 886; capping, shaking hands, &c. *v.*; grip of the hand, embrace, hug, squeeze, accolade, loving cup, *vin d'honneur*, pledge; love token &c. (*endearment*) 902; kiss, buss, salute.

mark of recognition, nod; " nods and becks and wreathed smiles " [Milton]; valediction &c. 293; condolence &c. 915.

V. be -courteous &c. *adj.*; show -courtesy &c. *n.*

mind one's P's and Q's, behave oneself, be all things to all men, conciliate, speak one fair, take in good part; make –, do the amiable; look as if butter would not melt in one's mouth; mend one's manners.

receive, do the honors, usher, greet, hail, bid welcome; welcome, – with open arms; shake hands; hold out -, press -, squeeze- the hand; bid Godspeed; speed the parting guest; cheer, serenade.

salute; embrace &c. (*endearment*) 902; kiss, – hands; drink to, pledge, hob and nob; move to, nod to; smile upon.

uncover, cap; touch -, take off- the hat; doff the cap; present arms; make way for; bow; make -one's bow, – a leg; scrape, curtsy, courtesy; bob a -curtsy, – courtesy; kneel; bow -, bend- the knee.

visit, wait upon, present oneself, pay one's respects, pay a visit &c. (*sociability*) 892; dance attendance on &c. (*servility*) 886; pay attentions to; do homage to &c. (*respect*) 928.

prostrate oneself &c. (*worship*) 990.

give -, send- one's duty &c. *n.* to.

render -polite &c. *adj.*; polish, civilize, humanize.

Adj. courteous, polite, civil, mannerly, urbane; well-behaved, -mannered,

brutality, blackguardism, conduct unbecoming a gentleman, *grossièreté, brusquerie;* vulgarity &c. 851.

churlishness &c. *adj.*; spinosity, perversity; moroseness &c. (*sullenness*) 901a.

sternness &c. *adj.*; austerity; moodishness, captiousness &c. 901; cynicism; tartness &c. *adj.*; acrimony, acerbity, virulence, asperity.

scowl, black looks, frown; short answer, rebuff; hard words, contumely; unparliamentary language, personality.

bear, bruin, brute, blackguard, beast; unlicked cub; frump, crosspatch; saucebox &c. 887; crooked stick; grizzly.

V. be -rude &c. *adj.*; insult &c. 929; treat with discourtesy; take a name in vain; make -bold, – free- with; take a liberty; stare out of countenance, ogle, point at, put to the blush.

cut; turn -one's back upon, – on one's heel; give the cold shoulder; keep at -a distance, – arm's length; look -cool, – coldly, – black- upon; show the door to, send away with a flea in the ear.

lose one's temper &c. (*resentment*) 900; sulk &c. 901a; frown, scowl, glower, pout; snap, snarl, growl.

render -rude &c. *adj.*; brut-alize, -ify.

Adj. dis-, un-courteous; uncourtly; ill-bred, -mannered, -behaved, -conditioned; unbred; unmanner-ly, -ed; im-, un-polite; un-polished, -civilized, -genteel; ungentleman-like, -ly; unladylike; blackguard; vulgar &c. 851; dedecorous; foul-mouthed -spoken; abusive.

un-civil, -gracious, -ceremonious; cool; pert, forward, obtrusive, impudent, rude, saucy, precocious.

repulsive; un-complaisant, -accommodating, -neighborly, -gallant; inaffable; un-gentle, -gainly; rough, rugged, bluff, blunt, gruff; churl-, boor-, bear-ish; brutal, brusque; stern, harsh, austere; cavalier.

tart, sour, crabbed, sharp, short, trenchant, sarcastic, biting, doggish, caustic, virulent, bitter, acrimonious, venomous, contumelious; snarling &c. *v.*; surly, – as a bear; perverse; grim, sullen &c. 901a; peevish &c. (*irascible*) 901.

Adv. discourteously &c. *adj.*; with -discourtesy &c. *n.*, – a bad grace.

-bred, -brought up; good-mannered, polished, civilized, cultivated; refined &c. (*taste*) 850; gentlemanlike &c. (*fashion*) 852; gallant; on one's good behavior.

fine -, fair -, soft- spoken; honey-mouthed, -tongued; oily, bland; obliging, conciliatory, complaisant, complacent; obsequious &c. 886.

ingratiating, winning; gentle, mild; good-humored, cordial, gracious, affable, familiar; neighborly.

Adv. courteously &c. *adj.*; with a good grace; with -open, – outstretched- arms; *à bras ouverts; suaviter in modo*, in good humor.

Int. hail! welcome! well met! *ave!* all hail! good -day, – morrow! Godspeed! *pax vobiscum!* may your shadow never be less!

Phr. *rien de plus estimable que la cerémonie;* " the very pink of courtesy " [*Romeo and Juliet*].

896. Congratulation. — N. con-, gratulation; felicitation; salute &c. 894; condolence &c. 915; compliments of the season.

V. con-, gratulate; felicitate; give -, wish one- joy; compliment; tender -, offer- one's congratulations; wish -many happy returns of the day, – a merry Christmas and a happy new year.

congratulate oneself &c. (*rejoice*) 838.

Adj. con-, gratulatory.

Phr. " I wish you all the joy that you can wish " [*Merchant of Venice*].

897. Love. — N. love; fondness &c. *adj.*; liking; inclination &c. (*desire*) 865; regard, dilection †, admiration, fancy.

affection, sympathy, fellow-feeling; tenderness &c. *adj.*; heart, brotherly love; benevolence &c. 906; attachment.

yearning, ἔρως, tender passion, amour; gyneolatry; gallantry, passion, flame, devotion, fervor, enthusiasm, transport of love, rapture, enchantment, infatuation, adoration, idolatry.

Cupid, Venus; myrtle; true lover's knot; love -token, – suit, – affair, – tale, – story; the old story, plighted love; courtship &c. 902; amourette; free-love.

maternal love, στοργή.

attractiveness; popularity; favorite &c. 899.

lover, suitor, follower, admirer, adorer, wooer, amoret, beau, sweetheart, inamorato, swain, young man, flame, love, truelove; leman, Lothario, gallant, paramour, *amoroso, cavaliere servente,* captive, *cicisbeo; caro sposo.*

inamorata, ladylove, idol, darling, duck, Dulcinea, angel, goddess, *cara sposa.*

betrothed, affianced, fiancée.

flirt, coquette; amorette; pair of turtle-doves; abode of love, agapemone.

V. love, like, affect, fancy, care for, take an interest in, be partial to, sympathize with; affection; be -in love &c. *adj.*- with; have -, entertain -, harbor -,

898. Hate. — N. hate, hatred, vials of hate.

dis-affection, -favor; alienation, estrangement, coolness; enmity &c. 889; animosity &c. 900.

umbrage, pique, grudge; dudgeon, spleen; bitterness, – of feeling; ill -, bad-blood; acrimony; malice &c. 907; implacability &c. (*revenge*) 919.

repugnance &c. (*dislike*) 867; demono-, gyne-, negro-phobia; odium, unpopularity; detestation, antipathy; object of -hatred, – execration; abomination, aversion, *bête noire;* enemy &c. 891; bitter pill; source of annoyance &c. 830.

V. hate, detest, abominate, abhor, loathe; recoil -, shudder- at; shrink from, view with horror, hold in abomination, revolt against, execrate; scowl &c. 895; disrelish &c. (*dislike*) 867.

owe a grudge; bear -spleen, – a grudge, – malice &c. (*malevolence*) 907; conceive an aversion to.

excite -, provoke- hatred &c. *n.*; be -hateful &c. *adj.*; stink in the nostrils; estrange, alienate, repel, set against, sow dissension, set by the ears, envenom, incense, irritate, rile; horrify &c. 830; roil.

Adj. hating &c. *v.*; abhorrent; averse from &c. (*disliking*) 867; set against.

bitter &c. (*acrimonious*) 895; implacable &c. (*revengeful*) 919.

un-loved, -beloved, -lamented, -de-

cherish- a -love &c. *n.* for; regard, revere; take to, bear love to, be wedded to; set one's affections on; make much of, feast one's eyes on; hold dear, prize; hug, cling to, cherish, pet.

burn; adore, idolize, love to distraction, *aimer éperdument;* dote- on, – upon.

take a fancy to, look sweet upon; become -enamored &c. *adj.*; fall in love with, lose one's heart; desire &c. 865.

excite love; win –, gain –, secure –, engage- the -love, – affections, – heart; take the fancy of; have a place in –, wind round- the heart; attract, attach, endear, charm, fascinate, captivate, bewitch, seduce, enamor, enrapture, turn the head.

get into favor; ingratiate –, insinuate –, worm- oneself; propitiate, curry favor with, pay one's court to, *faire l'aimable*, set one's cap at, flirt.

Adj. loving &c. *v.*; fond of; taken –, struck- with; smitten, bitten; attached to, wedded to; enamored; charmed &c. *v.*; in love; love-sick; over head and ears in love.

affectionate, tender, sweet upon, sympathetic, loving; amorous, amatory; fond, erotic, uxorious, ardent, passionate, rapturous, devoted, motherly.

loved &c. *v.*; beloved; well –, dearly- beloved; dear, precious, darling, pet, little; favorite, popular.

congenial; to –, after- one's -mind, – taste, – fancy, – own heart.

in one's good -graces &c. (*friendly*) 888; dear as the apple of one's eye, nearest to one's heart.

lovable, adorable; lovely, sweet; attractive, seductive, winning; charming, engaging, interesting, enchanting, captivating, fascinating, bewitching; amiable, like an angel.

Phr. *amantes amentes* [Terence]; *credula res amor est* [Ovid]; *militat omnis amasius* [Ovid]; *omnia vincit amor* [Vergil]; *si vis amari ama* [Seneca]; "the sweetest joy, the wildest woe" [Bailey].

plored, -mourned, -cared for, -endeared, -valued; disliked &c. 867.

crossed in love, forsaken, rejected, lovelorn, jilted.

obnoxious, hateful, odious, abominable, repulsive, offensive, shocking; disgusting &c. (*disagreeable*) 830; reprehensible.

invidious, spiteful; malicious &c. 907.

insulting, irritating, provoking.

[Mutual hate] at daggers drawn; not on speaking terms &c. (*enmity*) 889; at loggerheads.

Phr. no love lost between.

899. Favorite. — N. favorite, pet, cosset, minion, idol, jewel, spoiled child, *enfant gâté;* led captain; crony; fondling; apple of one's eye, man after one's own heart; *persona grata.*

love, dear, darling, duck, honey, jewel; mopsey, moppet; sweetheart &c. (*love*) 897.

general –, universal- favorite; idol of the people.

900. Resentment. — N. resentment, displeasure, animosity, anger, wrath, indignation; exasperation, bitter resentment, wrathful indignation.

pique, umbrage, huff, miff, soreness, dudgeon, acerbity, virulence, bitterness, acrimony, asperity, spleen, gall; heart-burning, -swelling; rankling.

ill –, bad- -humor, – temper; irascibility &c. 901; ill blood &c. (*hate*) 898; revenge &c. 919.

excitement, irritation; warmth, bile, choler, ire, fume, pucker, dander, ferment, ebullition; towering passion, *acharnement*, angry mood, taking, pet, tiff, passion, fit, tantrums.

burst, explosion, paroxysm, storm, rage, fury, desperation; violence &c. 173; fire and fury; vials of wrath; gnashing of teeth, hot blood, high words.

scowl &c. 895; sulks &c. 901*a*.

[Cause of umbrage] affront, provocation, offense; indignity &c. (*insult*) 929; grudge, crow to pluck, sore subject, *casus belli;* ill turn, outrage.

Furies, Eumenides.

buffet, slap in the face, box on the ear, rap on the knuckles.

V. resent; take -amiss, – ill, – to heart, – offense, – umbrage, – huff, – exception; take in -ill part, – bad part, – dudgeon; *ne pas entendre raillerie;* breathe revenge, cut up rough.

fly –, fall –, get- into a -rage, – passion; bridle –, bristle –, froth –, fire –, flare- up; open –, pour out- the vials of one's wrath.

pout, knit the brow, frown, scowl, lower, snarl, growl, gnarl, gnash, snap; redden, color; look -black, – black as thunder, – daggers; bite one's thumb; show –, grind- one's teeth; champ the bit.

chafe, mantle, fume, kindle, fly out, take fire; boil, – over; boil with- indignation, – rage; rage, storm, foam; vent one's -rage, – spleen; lose one's temper, stand on one's hind legs, stamp the foot; stamp –, quiver –, swell –, foam- with rage; burst with anger; raise Cain.

have a fling at; bear malice &c. (*revenge*) 919.

cause –, raise- anger; affront, offend; give -offense, – umbrage; anger; hurt the feelings; insult, discompose, fret, ruffle, nettle, huff, pique; excite &c. 824; irritate, stir the blood, stir up bile; sting, – to the quick; rile, provoke, chafe, wound, incense, inflame, enrage, aggravate, add fuel to the flame, fan into a flame, widen the breach, envenom, embitter, exasperate, infuriate, kindle wrath; stick in one's gizzard; rankle &c. 919; hit –, rub –, sting –, strike- on the raw.

put out of -countenance, – humor; put one's -monkey, – back -up; raise one's -gorge, – dander, – choler; work up into a passion; make -one's blood boil, – the ears tingle; throw into a ferment, madden, drive one mad; lash into -fury, – madness; fool to the top of one's bent; set by the ears.

bring a hornet's nest about one's ears.

Adj. angry, wrath, irate; ire-, wrath-ful; cross &c. (*irascible*) 901; Achillean; sulky &c. 901*a*; bitter, virulent; acrimonious &c. (*discourteous*) &c. 895; violent &c. 173.

warm, burning; boiling, – over; fuming, raging; foaming, – at the mouth; convulsed with rage.

offended &c. *v.*; waxy, *acharné;* wrought, worked up; indignant, hurt, sore; set against.

fierce, wild, rageful, furious, mad with rage, fiery, infuriate, rabid, savage; relentless &c. 919.

flushed with -anger, – rage; in a -huff, – stew, – fume, – pucker, – passion, – rage, – fury, – taking, – way; on one's high ropes, up in arms; in high dudgeon.

Adv. angrily &c. *adj.*; in the height of passion; in the heat of -passion, – the moment.

Int. *tantæne animis cœlestibus iræ* [Vergil]! marry come up! zounds! 'sdeath!

Phr. one's -blood, – back, – monkey- being up; *fervens difficili bile jecur;* the gorge rising, eyes flashing fire; the blood -rising, – boiling; *hæret lateri lethalis arundo* [Vergil]; " beware the fury of a patient man " [Dryden]; *furor arma ministrat* [Vergil]; *ira furor brevis est* [Horace]; *quem Jupiter vult perdere dementat prius;* " what, drunk with choler? " [*Henry IV*].

901. Irascibility. — **N.** irascibility, irascibleness, temper; crossness &c. *adj.*; susceptibility, procacity, petulance, irritability, tartness, acerbity, protervity; pugnacity &c. (*contentiousness*) 720.

excitability &c. 825; bad -, fiery -, crooked -, irritable &c. *adj.*- temper; *genus irritabile*, hot blood.

ill humor &c. (*sullenness*) 901*a*; asperity &c., churlishness &c. (*discourtesy*) 895.

huff &c. (*resentment*) 900; a word and a blow.

Sir Fretful Plagiary; brabbler, Tartar; shrew, vixen, virago, termagant, dragon, scold, Xantippe; porcupine; spitfire; fire eater &c. (*blusterer*) 887; fury &c. (*violent person*) 173.

V. be -irascible &c. *adj.*; have a -temper &c. *n.*, – devil in one; fire up &c. (*be angry*) 900.

Adj. irascible; bad-, ill-tempered; irritable, susceptible; excitable &c. 825; thin-skinned &c. (*sensitive*) 822; fretful, fidgety; on the fret.

hasty, overhasty, quick, warm, hot, testy, touchy, techy, tetchy; like -touchwood, – tinder; huffy; pet-tish, -ulant; waspish, snappish, peppery, fiery, passionate, choleric, shrewish, " sudden and quick in quarrel " [*As You Like It*].

querulous, captious, moodish; quarrelsome, contentious, disputatious; pugnacious &c. (*bellicose*) 720; cantankerous, exceptious; restiff &c. (*perverse*) 901*a*; churlish &c. (*discourteous*) 895.

cross, – as -crabs, – two sticks, – a cat, – a dog, – the tongs; fractious, peevish, *acariâtre*.

in a bad temper; sulky &c. 901*a*; angry &c. 900.

resent-ful, -ive; vindictive &c. 919.

Int. pish!

Phr. *à vieux comptes nouvelles disputes; quamvis tegatur proditur vultu furor* [Seneca]; *vino tortus et irâ* [Horace].

901a. Sullenness. — N. sullenness &c. *adj.*; morosity, spleen; churlishness &c. (*discourtesy*) 895; irascibility &c. 901.

moodiness &c. *adj.*; perversity; obstinacy &c. 606; torvity †, spinosity; crabbedness &c. *adj.*

ill -, bad- -temper, – humor; sulks, dudgeon, mumps, dumps, doldrums, fit of the sulks, bouderie, black looks, scowl; grouch; huff &c. (*resentment*) 900.

V. be -sullen &c. *adj.*; sulk; frown, scowl, lower, glower, gloam, pout, have a hangdog look, glout.

Adj. sullen, sulky; ill-tempered, -humored, -affected, -disposed; grouty [U. S.]; in -an ill, – a bad, – a shocking- -temper, – humor; out of -temper, – humor; knaggy, torvous, crusty, crabbed; sour, – as a crab; surly &c. (*discourteous*) 895.

moody; spleen-ish, -ly; splenetic, cankered.

cross, -grained; perverse, wayward, humorsome; rest-iff, -ive; cantankerous, intractable, exceptious, sinistrous, deaf to reason, unaccommodating, rusty, froward; cussed [U. S.].

dogged &c. (*stubborn*) 606.

grumpy, glum, grim, grum, morose, frumpish; in the -sulks &c. *n.*; out of sorts; scowl-, glower-, growl-ing; grouchy.

peevish &c. (*irascible*) 901.

902. [Expression of affection or love.] Endearment. — N. endearment, caress; blandish-, blandi-ment †; *épanchement*, fondling, billing and cooing, dalliance; caressing.

embrace, salute, kiss, buss, smack, osculation, deosculation †; amorous glances.

courtship, wooing, suit, addresses, the soft impeachment; love-making; serenading; caterwauling.

flirting &c. *v.*; flirtation, gallantry; coquetry.

true lover's knot, plighted love; love -tale, – token, – letter; *billet-doux*, valentine.

honeymoon; Strephon and Chloe.

V. caress, fondle, pet, dandle; pat, – on the -head, – cheek; chuck under the chin, smile upon, coax, wheedle, cosset, coddle, cocker, cockle; make -of, – much of; cherish, foster, kill with kindness.

clasp, hug, cuddle; fold -, strain- in one's arms; nestle, nuzzle; embrace, kiss, buss, smack, blow a kiss; salute &c. (*courtesy*) 894; fold to the heart, press to the bosom.

bill and coo, spoon, toy, dally, flirt, coquet; galli-, gala-vant; philander; make love; pay one's -court, – addresses. – attentions- to; serenade; court,

woo; set one's cap at; be –, look- sweet upon; ogle, cast sheep's eyes upon; *faire les yeux doux*.

fall in love with, win the affections &c. (*love*) 897; die for.

propose; make –, have- an offer; pop the question; plight one's -troth, – faith.

Adj. caressing &c. *v.*; "sighing like furnace" [Shakespeare]; love-sick, spoony.

caressed &c. V.

Phr. "faint heart ne'er won fair lady"; "kisses honeyed by oblivion" [G. Eliot].

903. Marriage. — N. marriage, mat-
rimony, wedlock, union, intermarriage, miscegenation, *vinculum matrimonii*, nuptial tie.

married state, coverture, bed, cohabitation.

match; betrothment &c. (*promise*) 768; wedding, nuptials, Hymen, bridal; e-, spousals; leading to the altar &c. *v.*; nuptial benediction, epithalamium; sealing.

torch –, temple- of Hymen; hymeneal altar; honeymoon.

brides-maid, -man; bride, bridegroom.

married -man, – woman, – couple; neogamist, Benedict, partner, spouse, mate, yokemate; husband, man, consort, baron; old –, good- man; wife, – of one's bosom; helpmate, rib, better half, gray mare, old woman, good wife; feme, – coverte; squaw, lady; matron, -age, -hood; man and wife; wedded pair, Darby and Joan; spiritual wife.

mono-, bi-, di-, deutero-, tri-, polygamy; mormonism; levirate; spiritual wife-ry, -ism; polyandrism; Turk, Bluebeard.

unlawful –, left-handed –, morganatic –, ill-assorted- marriage; *mésalliance; mariage de convenance*.

marriage broker; matrimonial -agency, – agent, – bureau; schatchen.

V. marry, wive, take to oneself a wife; be -married, – spliced; go –, pair-off; wed, espouse, lead to the hymeneal altar, take "for better for worse," give one's hand to, bestow one's hand upon.

marry, join, handfast; couple &c. (*unit*) 43; tie the nuptial knot; give -away, – in marriage; seal; affy, affiance; betroth &c. (*promise*) 768; publish –, bid- the banns; be asked in church.

Adj. married &c. *v.*; one, – bone and one flesh.

marriageable, nubile.

engaged, betrothed, affianced.

matrimonial, marital, conjugal, connubial, wedded; nuptial, hymeneal, spousal, bridal.

Phr. the gray mare the better horse; "a world-without-end bargain" [*Love's Labor's Lost*]; "marriages are made in Heaven" [Tennyson]; "render me worthy of this noble wife" [*Julius Cæsar*]; *si qua voles apte nubere nube pari* [Ovid].

904. Celibacy. — N. celibacy, singleness, single blessedness; bachelor-hood, -ship; miso-gamy, -gyny.

virginity, pucelage; maiden-hood, -head.

unmarried man, bachelor, Cœlebs, agamist, old bachelor; miso-gamist, -gynist; monogamist; monk.

unmarried woman, spinster; maid, -en; virgin, *feme sole*, old maid; bachelor-girl, girl-bachelor; nun.

V. live single.

Adj. un-married, -wedded; wife-, spouse-less; single.

905. Divorce. — N. divorce, -ment; separation; judicial separation, separate maintenance; *separatio a -mensâ et thoro, – vinculo matrimonii*.

widowhood, viduity, weeds.

widow, -er; relict; dowager; *divorcée*; cuckold; grass widow, -er.

V. live separate; separate, divorce disespouse, put away; wear the horns.

2. Diffusive Sympathetic Affections

906. Benevolence. — N. benevo-
lence, Christian charity; God's -love, –

907. Malevolence. — N. malevo-
lence; bad intent, -ion; un-, dis-kind-

grace; good will; philanthropy &c. 910; unselfishness &c. 942.

good -nature, – feeling, – wishes; kind-, kindli-ness &c. *adj.*; loving-kindness, benignity, brotherly love, charity, humanity, fellow- feeling, sympathy; goodness –, warmth- of heart; bonhomie; kind-heartedness; amiability, milk of human kindness, tenderness; love &c. 897; friendship &c. 888.

toleration, consideration, generosity; mercy &c. (*pity*) 914.

charitableness &c. *adj.*; bounty, almsgiving; good works, beneficence, " the luxury of doing good " [Goldsmith].

acts of kindness, a good turn; good –, kind- -offices, – treatment.

good Samaritan, sympathizer, *bon enfant;* altruist.

V. be -benevolent &c. *adj.*; have one's heart in the right place, bear good will; wish -well, – Godspeed; view –, regard- with an eye of favor; take in good part; take –, feel- an interest in; be –, feel- interested- in; sympathize with, feel for; fraternize &c. (*be friendly*) 888.

enter into the feelings of others, do as you would be done by, meet halfway.

treat well; give comfort, smooth the bed of death; do -good, – a good turn; benefit &c. (*goodness*) 648; render a service, be of use; aid &c. 707.

Adj. benevolent; kind, -ly; well-meaning; amiable; obliging, accommodating, indulgent, gracious, complacent, good-humored.

warm-, kind-, tender-, large-, broad-hearted; merciful &c. 914; charitable, beneficent, humane, benignant; bounteous, -iful.

good-, well-natured; spleenless; sympath-izing, -etic; complaisant &c. (*courteous*) 894; well-meant, -intentioned.

fatherly, motherly, brotherly, sisterly; pat-, mat-, frat-ernal; sororal; friendly &c. 888.

Adv. with -a good intention, – the best intentions.

Int. Godspeed! much good may it do!

. Phr. " act a charity sometimes " [Lamb]; " a tender heart, a will inflexible " [Longfellow]; *de mortuis nil nisi bonum;* " kind words are more than coronets " [Tennyson]; *quando amigo pide no hay mañana;* " the social smile, the sympathetic tear " [Gray].

ness; ill -nature, – will, – blood; bad blood; enmity &c. 889; hate &c. 898; malignity; malice, – prepense; maliciousness &c. *adj.*; spite, despite; resentment &c. 900.

uncharitableness &c. *adj.*; incompassionateness &c. 914a; gall, venom, rancor, rankling, virulence, mordacity, acerbity; churlishness &c. (*discourtesy*)895.

hardness of heart, heart of stone, obduracy; cruelty; cruelness &c. *adj.*; brutality, savagery; fer-ity, -ocity; barbarity, inhumanity, immanity †, truculence, ruffianism; evil eye, cloven foot; torture, vivisection.

ill –, bad- turn; affront &c. (*disrespect*) 929; outrage, atrocity; ill usage; intolerance, persecution; tender mercies [ironical]; " unkindest cut of all " [*J. Cæsar*].

V. be -malevolent &c. *adj.*; bear –, harbor- -spleen, – a grudge, – malice; betray –, show- the cloven foot.

hurt &c. (*physical pain*) 378; annoy &c. 830; injure, harm, wrong; do -harm, – an ill office- to; outrage; disoblige, malign, plant a thorn in the breast.

molest, worry, harass, haunt, harry, bait, tease; throw stones at; play the devil with; hunt down, dragoon, hound; persecute, oppress, grind; maltreat; ill-treat, -use.

wreak one's malice on, do one's worst, break a butterfly on the wheel; dip –, imbrue- one's hands in blood; have no mercy &c. 914a.

Adj. male-, unbene-volent; unbenign; ill-disposed, -intentioned, -natured, -conditioned, -contrived; evil-minded, -disposed; black-browed.

malicious; malign, -ant; rancorous; de-, spiteful; mordacious, caustic, bitter, envenomed, acrimonious, virulent; un-amiable, -charitable; maleficent, venomous, grinding, galling.

harsh, disobliging; un-kind, -friendly, -gracious; inofficious; invidious; uncandid; churlish &c. (*uncourteous*) 895; surly, sullen &c. 901a.

cold, -blooded, -hearted; black-, hard-, flint-, marble-, stony-hearted; hard of heart, unnatural; ruthless &c. (*unmerciful*) 914a; relentless &c. (*revengeful*) 919.

cruel; brut-al, -ish; savage, – as a -bear, – tiger; fer-ine, -ocious; inhuman;

barbarous, fell, untamed, tameless, truculent, incendiary; bloodthirsty &c (*murderous*) 361; atrocious; bloodyminded.

fiend-ish, -like; demoniacal; diabolic, -al; devilish, infernal, hellish, Satanic; Tartarean.

Adv. malevolently &c. *adj.*; with -bad intent &c. *n.*

Phr. cruel as death; " hard unkindness' alter'd eye " [Gray]; *homo homini lupus* [Plautus]; *mala mens malus animus* [Terence]; " rich gifts wax poor when givers prove unkind " [*Hamlet*]; " sharp-tooth'd unkindness " [*Lear*].

908. Malediction. — N. malediction, malison, curse, imprecation, denunciation, execration, anathema, ban, proscription, excommunication, commination, thunders of the Vatican, fulmination, maranatha; aspersion, disparagement, vilification, vituperation.

abuse; foul -, bad -, strong -, unparliamentary- language; billingsgate, sauce, evil speaking; cursing &c. *v.*; profane swearing, oath; foul invective, ribaldry, rude reproach, scurrility.

threat &c. 909; more bark than bite; invective &c. (*disapprobation*) 932.

V. curse, accurse, imprecate, damn, swear at; curse with bell book and candle; invoke -, call down- curses on the head of; devote to destruction.

execrate, beshrew, scold; anathematize &c. (*censure*) 932; hold up to execration, denounce, proscribe, excommunicate, fulminate, thunder against; threaten &c. 909.

curse and swear; swear, - like a trooper; fall a cursing, rap out an oath, damn.

Adj. curs-ing, -ed &c. *v.*

Int. woe to! beshrew! *ruat cœlum!* ill -, woe- betide; confusion seize! damn! confound! blast! curse! devil take! hang! out with! a plague -, out- upon! aroynt! *honi soit! parbleu!*

Phr. *delenda est Carthago.*

909. Threat. — N. threat, menace; defiance &c. 715; abuse, minacity, intimidation; denunciation; fulmination; commination &c. (*curse*) 908; gathering clouds &c. (*warning*) 668.

V. threat, -en; menace; snarl, growl, gnarl, mutter, bark, bully.

defy &c. 715; intimidate &c. 860; keep -, hold up -, hold out- *in terrorem;* shake -, double -, clinch- the fist at; thunder, talk big, fulminate, use big words, bluster, look daggers.

Adj. threatening, menacing; mina-tory, -cious; comminatory, abusive; *in terrorem;* ominous &c. (*predicting*) 511; defiant &c. 715; under the ban.

Int. *væ victis!* at your peril! do your worst!

910. Philanthropy. — N. philanthropy; humanit-y, -arianism; universal benevolence; endæmonism, *deliciæ humani generis;* cosmopolitanism, utilitarianism, the greatest happiness of the greatest number, social science, sociology.

common weal; socialism, communism; Fourierism, phalansterianism, Saint Simonianism.

911. Misanthropy. — N. misanthropy, incivism; egotism &c. (*selfishness*) 943; moroseness &c. 901a; cynicism.

misanthrope, misanthropist, egotist, cynic, man hater, Timon, Diogenes. woman hater, misogynist.

Adj. misanthropic, antisocial, unpatriotic; egotistical &c. (*selfish*) 943; morose &c. 901a.

patriotism, civism, nationality, love of country, *amor patriæ*, public spirit. chivalry, knight errantry; generosity &c. 942.

philanthropist, endæmonist, utilitarian, Benthamite, socialist, communist, cosmopolite, citizen of the world, *amicus humani generis;* knight errant; patriot.

Adj. philanthropic, humanitarian, utilitarian, cosmopolitan; public-spirited, patriotic; humane, large-hearted &c. (*benevolent*) 906; chivalric; generous &c. 942.

Adv. *pro -bono publico, - aris et focis* [Cicero].

Phr. *humani nihil a me alienum puto* [Terence]; *omne solum forti patria* [Ovid]; *un bien fait n'est jamais perdu*

912. Benefactor. — N. benefactor, savior, good genius, tutelary saint, guardian angel, good Samaritan; *pater patriæ;* salt of the earth &c. (*good man*) 948; auxiliary &c. 711.

913. [Maleficent being.] Evil doer. — N. evil -doer, – worker; wrongdoer &c. 949; mischief-maker, marplot; oppressor, tyrant; firebrand, incendiary, fire bug [U. S.], pyromaniac; anarchist, destroyer, Vandal, iconoclast; communist; terrorist.

savage, brute, ruffian, barbarian, semibarbarian, caitiff, desperado; Apache, hoodlum, plug-ugly * [U. S.], Red Skin, tough [U. S.]; Mo-hock, -hawk; bludgeon man, bully, rough, hooligan,* larrikin, dangerous classes, ugly customer; thief &c. 792.

cockatrice, scorpion, hornet; viper, adder; snake, – in the grass; serpent, cobra, asp, rattlesnake, anaconda; canker-, wire-worm; locust, Colorado beetle; *alacran,* alligator, caymon, crocodile, mosquito, mugger, octopus; torpedo; bane &c. 663.

cannibal; anthropophag-us, -ist; bloodsucker, vampire, ogre, ghoul, gorilla; vulture; gyr-, ger-falcon.

wild beast, tiger, hyena, butcher, hangman; cutthroat &c. (*killer*) 361; blood-, hell-, sleuth-hound; catamount [U. S.], cougar, jaguar, puma.

hag, hellhag, beldam, Jezebel.

monster; fiend &c. (*demon*) 980; devil incarnate, demon in human shape; Frankenstein's monster.

harpy, siren; Furies, Eumenides.

Attila, scourge of the human race.

Phr. *fœnum habet in cornu.*

3. Special Sympathetic Affections

914. Pity. — N. pity, compassion, commiseration; bowels, – of compassion; sympathy, fellow-feeling, tenderness, yearning, forbearance, humanity, mercy, clemency; leniency &c. (*lenity*) 740; charity, ruth, long-suffering.

melting mood; *argumentum ad misericordiam;* quarter, grace, *locus pœnitentiæ.*

sympathizer; advocate, friend, partisan, patron, wellwisher.

914a. Pitilessness. — N. pitilessness &c. *adj.*; inclemency; severity &c. 739; malevolence &c. 907.

V. have no –, shut the gates of mercy &c. 914; give no quarter.

Adj. piti-, merci-, ruth-, bowel-less; unpitying, unmerciful, inclement; grimfaced, -visaged; in-, un-compassionate; inexorable; harsh &c. 739; cruel &c. 907; unrelenting &c. 919.

V. pity; have –, show –, take- pity &c. *n.*; commiserate, compassionate; condole &c. 915; sympathize; feel –, be sorry –, yearn- for; weep, melt, thaw, enter into the feelings of.

forbear, relent, relax, give quarter, wipe the tears, *parcere subjectis*, give a *coup de grâce*, put out of one's misery.

raise –, excite- pity &c. *n.*; touch, soften; melt, – the heart; propitiate, disarm.

ask for -mercy &c. *n.*; supplicate &c. (*request*) 765; cry for quarter, beg one's life, kneel; deprecate.

Adj. pitying &c. *v.*; pitiful, compassionate, sympathetic, touched.

merciful, clement, ruthful; humane; humanitarian &c. (*philanthropic*) 910; tender, – hearted, – as a chicken; soft, – hearted; unhardened; lenient &c. 740; exorable, forbearing; melting &c. *v.*; weak.

Int. for pity's sake! mercy! have –, cry you- mercy! God help you! poor -thing, – dear, – fellow! woe betide! *quis talia fando temperet a lachrymis!* [Ver.].

Phr. one's heart bleeding for; *haud ignara mali miseris succurrere disco* [Vergil]; " a fellow feeling makes one wondrous kind " [Garrick]; *onor di bocca assai giova e poco costa.*

915. Condolence. — N. condolence; lamentation &c. 839; sympathy, consolation.

V. condole with, console, sympathize; express –, testify- pity; afford –, supply- consolation; lament &c. 839- with; express sympathy for; feel -grief, – sorrow- in common with; share one's sorrow.

4. RETROSPECTIVE SYMPATHETIC AFFECTIONS

916. Gratitude. — N. gratitude, thankfulness, feeling of –, sense of- obligation.

acknowledgment, recognition, thanksgiving, giving thanks; thankful good will.

thanks, praise, benediction; pæan; *Te Deum* &c. (*worship*) 990; grace, – before, – after- meat; thank offering.

requital.

V. be -grateful &c. *adj.*; thank; give –, render –, return –, offer –, tender- thanks &c. *n.*; acknowledge, requite.

feel –, be –, lie- under an obligation; *savoir gré;* not look a gift horse in the mouth; never forget, overflow with gratitude; thank –, bless- one's stars; fall on one's knees.

Adj. grateful, thankful, obliged, beholden, indebted to, under obligation.

Int. thanks! many thanks! gramercy! much obliged! thank you! thank Heaven! Heaven be praised!

917. Ingratitude. — N. ingratitude, thanklessness, oblivion of benefits, unthankfulness.

" benefits forgot "; thankless -task, – office.

V. be -ungrateful &c. *adj.*; forget benefits; look a gift horse in the mouth.

Adj. un-grateful, -mindful, -thankful; thankless, ingrate, wanting in gratitude, insensible of benefits.

forgotten; un-acknowledged, -thanked, -requited, -rewarded; ill-requited.

Int. thank you for nothing! " *et tu Brute!* " [*Julius Cæsar*].

Phr. " ingratitude! thou marble-hearted fiend " [*Lear*].

918. Forgiveness. — N. forgiveness, pardon, condonation, grace, remission, absolution, amnesty, oblivion; indulgence; reprieve.

conciliation; reconcilement; reconciliation &c. (*pacification*) 723; propitiation.

excuse, exoneration, quittance, release, indemnity; bill –, act –, covenant –, deed- of indemnity; exculpation &c. (*acquittal*) 970.

longanimity, placability; *amantium iræ; locus pœnitentiæ;* forbearance.

V. forgive, – and forget; pardon, condone, think no more of, let bygones be bygones, shake hands; forget an injury.

excuse, pass over, overlook; wink at &c. (*neglect*) 460; bear with; allow –, make allowances- for; let one down easily, not be too hard upon, pocket the affront.

let off, remit, absolve, give absolution, reprieve; acquit &c. 970.

beg –, ask –, implore- pardon &c. *n.*; conciliate, propitiate, placate; make up

919. Revenge. — N. revenge, -ment; vengeance; avenge-ment, -ance †, sweet revenge, vendetta, death feud, blood for blood; retaliation &c. 718; day of reckoning.

rancor, vindictiveness, implacability; malevolence &c. 907; ruthlessness &c. 914*a*.

avenger, vindicator, Nemesis, Eumenides.

V. re-, a-venge; vindicate; take –, have one's- revenge; breathe -revenge, – vengeance; wreak one's -vengeance, – anger.

have -accounts to settle, – a crow to pluck, – a rod in pickle.

keep the wound green; harbor -revenge, – vindictive feeling; bear malice; rankle, – in the breast.

Adj. revenge-, venge-ful; vindictive, rancorous; pitiless &c. 914*a*; ruthless, rigorous, avenging.

unforgiving, unrelenting; inexorable, stony-hearted, implacable; relent-, remorse-less.

319

a quarrel &c. (*pacify*) 723; let the wound heal.

Adj. forgiving, placable, conciliatory.

forgiven &c. *v.*; un-resented, -avenged, -revenged.

Adv. cry you mercy.

Phr. *veniam petimusque damusque vicissim* [Horace]; more in sorrow than in anger; *comprendre tout c'est tout pardonner;* "the offender never pardons" [Herbert].

æternum servans sub pectore vulnus; rankling, immitigable.

Phr. *manet -cicatrix, – altâ mente repostum; dies iræ dies illa;* "in high vengeance there is noble scorn" [G. Eliot]; *inhumanum verbum est ultio* [Seneca]; *malevolus animus abditos dentes habet* [Syrus]; "now infidel I have thee on the hip" [*Merchant of Venice*].

920. Jealousy. — **N.** jealous-y, -ness; jaundiced eye; envious suspicion, suspicion; "green-eyed monster" [*Othello*]; yellows; Juno.

V. be -jealous &c. *adj.*; view with -jealousy, – a jealous eye.

Adj. jealous, – as a Barbary pigeon; jaundiced, yellow-eyed, envious, horn-mad.

921. Envy. — **N.** envy; enviousness &c. *adj.*; rivalry; *jalousie de métier;* ill-will, spite.

V. envy, covet, burst with envy.

Adj. envious, invidious, covetous; *alieni appetens.*

Phr. "base envy withers at another's joy" [Thomson]; *cæca invidia est* [Livy]; *multa petentibus desunt multa* [Horace]; *summa petit livor* [Ovid].

Section IV. MORAL AFFECTIONS

1. MORAL OBLIGATIONS

922. Right. — **N.** right; what -ought to, – should- be; fitness &c. *adj.*; *summum jus.*

justice, equity; equitableness &c. *adj.*; propriety; fair play, impartiality, measure for measure, give and take, *lex talionis.*

Astræa, Nemesis, Themis.

scales of justice, evenhanded justice, karma; *suum cuique;* clear stage –, fair field- and no favor.

morals &c. (*duty*) 926; law &c. 963; honor &c. (*probity*) 939; virtue &c. 944.

V. be -right &c. *adj.*; stand to reason.

see -justice done, – one righted, – fair play; do justice to; recompense &c. (*reward*) 973; hold the scales even, give and take; serve one right, put the saddle on the right horse; give -every one, – the devil- his due; *audire alteram partem.*

deserve &c. (*be entitled to*) 924.

Adj. right, good; just, reasonable; fit &c. 924; equ-al, -able, -itable; even-handed; fair.

legitimate, justifiable, rightful; as it -should, – ought to- be; lawful &c. (*permitted*) 760, (*legal*) 963.

deserved &c. 924.

923. Wrong. — **N.** wrong; what -ought not to, – should not- be; *malum in se;* unreasonableness, grievance; shame.

injustice; unfairness &c. *adj.*; iniquity, foul play, partiality, leaning; favor, -itism; nepotism, party spirit; undueness &c. 925; unlawfulness &c. 964.

robbing Peter to pay Paul &c. *v.*; the wolf and the lamb; vice &c. 945.

"a custom more honored in the breach than the observance" [*Hamlet*].

V. be -wrong &c. *adj.*; cry to heaven for vengeance.

do -wrong &c. *n.*; be -inequitable &c. *adj.*; favor, lean towards; encroach; impose upon; reap where one has not sown; give an inch and take an ell; rob Peter to pay Paul.

Adj. wrong, -ful; bad, too bad; un-just, -fair; in-, un-equitable; unequal, partial, one-sided; injurious.

objectionable; un-reasonable, -allowable, -warrantable, -justifiable; improper, unfit; unjustified &c. 925; illegal &c. 964; iniquitous; immoral &c 945.

in the wrong, – box.

Adv. rightly &c. *adj.*; *à -*, *au-bon droit*, in -justice, – equity, – reason.

without -distinction of, – regard to, – respect to- persons; upon even terms.

Int. all right!

Phr. *Dieu et mon droit;* " in equal scale weighing delight and dole " [*Hamlet*]; *justitia cuum cuique distribuit* [Cicero]; *justitiæ soror incorrupta fides; justitia virtutem regina;* " thrice is he armed that hath his quarrel just " [*Henry VI*].

Adv. wrongly &c. *adj*

Phr. it will not do.

---

924. Dueness. — N. due, -ness; right, privilege, prerogative, prescription, title, claim, pretension, demand, birthright.

immunity, license, liberty, franchise; vested -interest, – right.

sanction, authority, warranty, charter; warrant &c. (*permission*) 760; constitution &c. (*law*) 963; tenure; bond &c. (*security*) 771.

claimant, appellant; plaintiff &c. 938.

V. be -due &c. *adj.* to, – the due &c. *n.* of; have -right, – title, – claim- to; be entitled to; have a claim upon; belong to &c. (*property*) 780.

deserve, merit, be worthy of, richly deserve.

demand, claim; call upon –, come upon –, appeal to- for; re-vendicate, -claim; exact; insist -on, – upon; challenge; take one's stand, make a point of, require, lay claim to, assert, assume, arrogate, make good; substantiate; vindicate a -claim, – right; fit –, qualify- for; make out a case.

give –, confer- a right; entitle; authorize &c. 760; sanctify, legalize, ordain, prescribe, allot.

give every one his due &c. 922; pay one's dues; have one's -due, – rights.

use a right, assert, enforce, put in force, lay under contribution.

Adj. having a right to &c. *v.*; entitled to; claiming; deserving, meriting, worthy of.

privileged, allowed, sanctioned, warranted, authorized; ordained, prescribed, constitutional, chartered, enfranchised.

prescriptive, presumptive; absolute, indefeasible; un-, in-alienable; imprescriptible, inviolable, unimpeachable, unchallenged; sacrosanct.

due to, merited, deserved, condign, richly deserved.

allowable &c. (*permitted*) 760; lawful, licit, legitimate, legal; legalized &c. (*law*) 963.

square, unexceptionable, right; equitable &c. 922; due, *en règle;* fit, -ting; correct, proper, meet, befitting, becoming, seemly; decorous; creditable, up to the mark, right as a trivet; just –, quite- the thing; *selon les règles.*

Adv. duly, *ex officio, de jure;* by -right, – divine right; *jure divino, Dei gratiâ,* in the name of.

Phr. *civis Romanus sum* [Cicero]; *à chaque saint sa chandelle.*

---

925. [Absence of right.] **Undueness — N.** undueness &c. *adj.*; *malum prohibitum;* impropriety; illegality &c. 964.

falseness &c. *adj.*; emptiness –, invalidity- of title; illegitimacy.

loss of right, disfranchisement, forfeiture. .

usurpation, tort, violation, breach, encroachment, presumption, assumption, seizure; stretch, exaction, imposition, lion's share.

usurper, pretender.

V. be -undue &c. *adj.*; not be -due &c. 924.

infringe, encroach, trench on, exact; arrogate, – to oneself; give an inch and take an ell; stretch –, strain- a point; usurp, violate, do violence to.

dis-franchise, -entitle, -qualify; invalidate.

relax &c. (*be lax*) 738; misbehave &c. (*vice*) 945; misbecome.

Adj. undue; unlawful &c. (*illegal*) 964; unconstitutional; illicit; un-authorized, -warranted, -allowed, -sanctioned, -justified; un-, dis-entitled, -qualified; un-privileged, -chartered.

illegitimate, bastard, spurious, false; usurped, tortious.

un-deserved, -merited, -earned; unfulfilled.

forfeited, disfranchised.

improper; un-meet, -fit, -befitting, -seemly; un-, mis-becoming; seemless; *contra bonos mores;* not the thing, out of the question, not to be thought of; preposterous, pretentious, would-be.

Phr. *filius nullius.*

926. Duty. — N.

duty, what ought to be done, moral obligation, accountableness, liability, onus, responsibility; bounden -, imperative- duty; call, - of duty; accountability.

allegiance, fealty, tie; engagement &c. (*promise*) 768; part; function, calling &c. (*business*) 625.

morality, morals, decalogue; case of conscience; conscientiousness &c. (*probity*) 939; conscience, inward monitor, still small voice within, sense of duty, tender conscience; the hell within [*P. L.*].

dueness &c. 924; propriety, fitness, seemliness, amenability, decorum, τὸ πρέπον; the -thing, - proper thing; the -right, - proper- thing to do.

[Science of morals] eth-ics, -ology; deon-, are-tology; moral -, ethical-philosophy; casuistry, polity.

observance, fulfillment, discharge, performance, acquittal, satisfaction, redemption; good behavior.

V. be -the duty of, - incumbent &c. *adj.* on, - responsible &c. *adj.*; behoove, become, befit, beseem; belong -, pertain- to; fall to one's lot; devolve on; lie -upon, - on one's head, - at one's door; rest -with, - on the shoulders of.

take upon oneself &c. (*promise*) 768; be -, become- -bound to, - sponsor for; incur a -responsibility &c. *n.*; be -, stand -, lie- under an obligation; have to answer for, owe to it oneself.

impose a -duty &c. *n.*; enjoin, require, exact; bind, - over; saddle with, prescribe, assign, call upon, look to, oblige.

enter upon -, perform -, observe -, fulfill -, discharge -, adhere to -, acquit oneself of -, satisfy- -a duty, - an obligation; act one's part, redeem one's pledge, do justice to, be at one's post; do duty; do one's duty &c. (*be virtuous*) 944.

be on one's good behavior, mind one's P's and Q's.

Adj. obligatory, binding; imperative, peremptory; stringent &c. (*severe*) 739; behooving &c. *v.*; incumbent -, chargeable- on; under obligation; obliged -, bound -, tied- by; saddled with.

due -, beholden -, bound -, indebted- to; tied down; compromised &c. (*promised*) 768; in duty bound.

amenable, liable, accountable, responsible, answerable.

right, meet &c. (*due*) 924; moral, ethical, casuistical, conscientious, ethological.

Adv. with a safe conscience, as in duty bound, on one's own responsibility, at one's own risk, *suo periculo; in foro conscientiæ; quamdiu se bene gesserit.*

Phr. *dura lex sed lex; dulce et decorum est pro patria mori: honos habet onus; leve fit quod bene fertur onus* [Ovid]; *loyauté m'oblige;* "simple duty hath no place for fear" [Whittier]; "stern daughter of the voice of God" [Wordsworth]; "there is a higher law than the Constitution" [Wm. Seward].

927. Dereliction of Duty. — N.

dereliction of duty; fault &c. (*guilt*) 947; sin &c. (*vice*) 945; non-observance, -performance; neglect, relaxation, infraction, violation, transgression, failure, evasion; dead letter.

V. violate; break, - through; infringe; set -aside, - at naught; encroach -, trench- upon; trample -on, - under foot; slight, neglect, evade, renounce, forswear, repudiate; wash one's hands of; escape, transgress, fail.

call to account &c. (*disapprobation*) 932.

927a. Exemption. — N.

exemption, freedom, irresponsibility, immunity, liberty, license, release, exoneration, excuse, dispensation, absolution, franchise, renunciation, discharge; exculpation &c. 970.

V. be -exempt &c. *adj.*

exempt, release, acquit, discharge, quitclaim, remise, remit; free, set at liberty, let off, pass over, spare, excuse, dispense with, give dispensation, license; stretch a point; absolve &c. (*forgive*) 918; exonerate &c. (*exculpate*) 970; save the necessity.

Adj. exempt, free, immune, at liberty, scot-free; released &c. *v.*; unbound, unencumbered; irresponsible, unaccountable, not answerable; excusable.

Phr. *bonis nocet quisquis pepercerit malis* [Syrus].

2. MORAL SENTIMENTS

928. Respect. — N. respect, regard, consideration; courtesy &c. 894; attention, deference, reverence, honor, esteem, estimation, veneration, admiration; approbation &c. 931.

homage, fealty, obeisance, genuflection, kneeling, prostration; obsequiousness &c. 886; salaam, kotow, bow, presenting arms, salute.

respects, regards, duty, *devoirs, égards.* devotion &c. (*piety*) 987.

V. respect, regard; revere, -nce; hold in reverence, honor, venerate, hallow; esteem &c. (*approve of*) 931; think much of; entertain –, bear- respect for; look up to, defer to; have –, hold- a high opinion of; pay -attention, – respect &c. *n.*- to; do –, render- honor to; do the honors, hail; show courtesy &c. 894; salute, present arms; do –, pay- homage to; pay tribute to, kneel to, bow to, bend the knee to; fall down before, prostrate oneself, kiss the hem of one's garment; worship &c. 990.

keep one's distance, make room, observe due decorum, stand upon ceremony.

command –, inspire- respect; awe, impose, overawe, dazzle.

Adj. respecting &c. *v.*; respectful, deferential, decorous, reverential, obsequious, ceremonious, bareheaded, cap in hand, on one's knees; prostrate &c. (*servile*) 886.

respected &c. *v.*; in high -esteem, – estimation; time-honored, venerable, *emeritus.*

Adv. in deference to; with -all, – due, – the highest- respect; with submission.

saving your -grace, – presence; *salva sit reverentia; pace tanti nominis.*

Int. hail! all hail! *esto perpetua!* may your shadow never be less!

Phr. " and pluck up drowned honor by the locks " [*Henry IV*]; " his honor rooted in dishonor stood " [Tennyson]; " honor pricks me on " [*Henry IV*].

929. Disrespect. — N. dis-respect, -esteem, -estimation; disparagement &c. (*dispraise*) 932, (*detraction*) 934.

irreverence; slight, neglect; *spretæ injuria formæ* [Vergil], superciliousness &c. (*contempt*) 930.

vilipendency †, contumely, affront, dishonor, insult, indignity, outrage, discourtesy &c. 895; practical joking; scurrility, scoffing, sibilation; ir-, de-rision; mockery; irony &c. (*ridicule*) 856; sarcasm.

hiss, hoot, gibe, flout, jeer, scoff, gleek †, taunt, sneer, quip, fling, wipe, slap in the face.

V. hold in disrespect &c. (*despise*) 930; misprize, disregard, slight, trifle with, set at naught, pass by, push aside, overlook, turn one's back upon, laugh in one's sleeve; be -disrespectful &c. *adj.*, – discourteous &c. 895; treat with -disrespect &c. *n.*; set down, browbeat.

dishonor, desecrate; insult, affront, outrage.

speak slightingly of; disparage &c. (*dispraise*) 932; vilipend, call names; throw –, fling- dirt; drag through the mud, point at, indulge in personalities; make -mouths, – faces; bite the thumb; take –, pluck- by the beard; toss in a blanket, tar and feather.

have –, hold- in derision; deride, scoff, barrack, sneer, laugh at, snigger, ridicule, gibe, mock, jeer, taunt, twit, niggle, gleek, gird, flout, fleer; roast, turn into ridicule; burlesque &c. 856; laugh to scorn &c. (*contempt*) 930; smoke; fool; make -game, – a fool, – an April fool- of; play a practical joke; lead one a dance, run the rig upon, have a fling at, scout, hiss, hoot, mob.

Adj. disrespectful; aweless, irreverent; disparaging &c. 934; insulting &c. *v.*; supercilious &c. (*scornful*) 930; rude, derisive, sarcastic; scurri-le, -lous; contumelious.

un-respected, -worshiped, -envied, -saluted; un-, dis-regarded.

Adv. disrespectfully &c. *adj.*

930. Contempt. — N. contempt, disdain, scorn, sovereign contempt; despisal, -ciency; despisement; vilipendency, contumely; slight, sneer, spurn, byword; despect.

contemptuousness &c. *adj.*; scornful eye; smile of contempt; derision &c. (*disrespect*) 929.

[State of being despised] despisedness.

V. despise, contemn, scorn, disdain, feel contempt for, view with a scornful eye; disregard, slight, not mind; pass by &c. (*neglect*) 460.

look down upon; hold -cheap, – in contempt, – in disrespect; think -nothing, – small beer- of; make light of; underestimate &c. 483; esteem -slightly, – of small or no account; take no account of, care nothing for; set no store by; not care a -straw &c. (*unimportance*) 643; set at naught, laugh in one's sleeve, snap one's fingers at, shrug one's shoulders, turn up one's nose at, pooh-pooh, "damn with faint praise" [Pope]; sneeze –, whistle –, sneer- at; curl up one's lip, toss the head, *traiter de haut en bas;* laugh at &c. (*be disrespectful*) 929.

point the finger of –, hold up to –, laugh to- scorn; scout, hoot, flout, hiss, scoff at.

turn -one's back, – a cold shoulder- upon; tread –, trample- -upon, – under foot; spurn, kick; fling to the winds &c. (*repudiate*) 610; send away with a flea in the ear.

Adj. contemptuous; disdain-, scorn-ful; withering, contumelious, supercilious, cynical, haughty, bumptious, cavalier; derisive.

contemptible, despicable; pitiable; pitiful &c. (*unimportant*) 643; despised &c. *v.*; downtrodden; unenvied.

Adv. contemptuously &c. *adj.*

Int. a fig for &c. (*unimportant*) 643; bah! never mind! away with! hang it! fiddlededee!

Phr. "a dismal universal hiss, the sound of public scorn" [*Paradise Lost*]; "I had rather be a dog and bay the moon than such a Roman" [*Julius Cæsar*].

931. Approbation. — N. approbation; approv-al, -ement; sanction, advocacy; nod of approbation; esteem, estimation, good opinion, golden opinions, admiration; love &c. 897; appreciation, regard, account, popularity, κῦδος, credit; repute &c. 873; best seller.

commendation, praise; laud, -ation; good word; meed –, tribute- of praise; encomium; eulog-y, -ium; *éloge*, panegyric; homage, hero worship; benediction, blessing, benison.

applause, plaudit, clap; clapping, – of hands; accl-aim, -amation; cheer; pæan, hosannah; shout –, peal –, chorus –, thunders- of -applause &c.; Prytaneum.

V. approve; approbate,[1] think -good, – much of, – well of, – highly of; esteem, value, prize; set great store -by, – on.

do justice to, appreciate; honor, hold in esteem, look up to, admire; like ·&c. 897; be in favor of, wish Godspeed; hail, – with satisfaction.

stand –, stick- up for; uphold, hold up, countenance, sanction; clap –, pat- on the back; keep in countenance, indorse; give credit, recommend; mark with a white -mark, – stone.

commend, belaud, praise, laud, compliment, pay a tribute, bepraise; clap, –

932. Disapprobation. — N. disapproba-tion, -val; improbation †; dis-esteem, -valuation, -placency; odium; dislike &c. 867.

dis-praise, -commendation; blame, censure, obloquy; detraction &c. 934; disparagement, depreciation; denunciation; condemnation &c. 971; ostracism; black list.

animadversion, reflection, stricture, objection, exception, criticism; sardonic -grin, – laugh; sarcasm, insinuation, innuendo; bad –, poor –, left-handed- compliment.

satire; sneer &c. (*contempt*) 930; taunt &c. (*disrespect*) 929; cavil, carping, censoriousness; hypercriticism &c. (*fastidiousness*) 868.

reprehension, remonstrance, expostulation, reproof, reprobation, admonition, increpation, reproach; rebuke, reprimand, castigation, jobation, lecture, curtain lecture, blow up, wigging, dressing, rating, scolding, trimming; correction, set down, rap on the knuckles, *coup de bec*, rebuff; slap, – on the face; home thrust, hit; frown, scowl, black look.

diatribe; jeremi-ad, -ade; tirade, philippic.

---

[1] [Obsolete in England except in legal writings, but surviving in the United States chiefly in a technical sense for *license*. C. O. S. M.].

the hands; applaud, cheer, acclamate, encore; panegyrize, eulogize, cry up, *prôner*, puff; extol, – to the skies; magnify, glorify, exalt, swell, make much of; flatter &c. 933; bless, give a blessing to; have –, say- a good word for; speak -well, – highly, – in high terms- of; sing –, sound –, chaunt –, resound- the praises of; sing praises to; cheer –, applaud- to the -echo, – very echo.

redound to the -honor, – praise, – credit- of; do credit to; deserve -praise &c. *n.*; recommend itself; pass muster.

be -praised &c.; receive honorable mention; be in -favor, – high favor- with; ring with the praises of, win golden opinions, gain credit, find favor with, stand well in the opinion of; *laudari à laudato viro*.

Adj. approving &c. *v.*; in favor of; lost in admiration.

commendatory, complimentary, benedictory, laudatory, panegyrical, eulogistic, encomiastic, lavish of praise, uncritical.

approved, praised &c. *v.*; un-censured, -impeached; popular, in good odor; in high esteem &c. (*respected*) 928; in –, in high- favor.

deserving –, worthy of- praise &c. *n.*; praiseworthy, commendable, of estimation; good &c. 648; meritorious, estimable, creditable, plausible, unimpeachable; beyond all praise.

Adv. with credit, to admiration; well &c. 618; with three times three.

Int. hear hear! bully for you! * well done! *bravo! bravissimo! euge! macte virtute!* so far so good, that's right, quite right; *optime!* one cheer more; may your shadow never be less! *esto perpetua!* long life to! *viva! evviva!* Godspeed! *valete et plaudite! encore! bis!*

Phr. *probatum est; tacent satis laudant;* " servant of God, well done! " [*Paradise Lost*].

clamor, outcry, hue and cry; hiss, -ing; sibilation, catcall; execration &c. 908.

chiding, upbraiding &c. *v.*; exprobration, abuse, vituperation, invective, objurgation, contumely; hard –, cutting –, bitter- words.

evil-speaking; bad language &c. 908; personality.

V. disapprove; dislike &c. 867; lament &c. 839; object to, take exception to; be scandalized at, think ill of; view with -disfavor, – dark eyes, – jaundiced eyes; *nil admirari*, disvalue, improbate. †

frown upon, look grave; bend –, knit- the brows; shake the head at, shrug the shoulders; turn up the nose &c. (*contempt*) 930; look -askance, – black upon; look with an evil eye; make a wry -face, – mouth- at; set one's face against.

dis-praise, -commend, -parage; deprecate, speak ill of, not speak well of; condemn &c. (*find guilty*) 971.

blame; lay –, cast- blame upon; censure, *fronder*, reproach, pass censure on, reprobate, impugn.

remonstrate, expostulate, recriminate.

reprehend, chide, admonish; berate, betongue; bring –, call- -to account, – over the coals, – to order; take to task, reprove, lecture, bring to book; read a -lesson, – lecture- to; rebuke, correct.

reprimand, chastise, castigate, lash, blow up, trounce, trim, *laver la tête*, overhaul; give it one, – finely; gibbet.

accuse &c. 938; impeach, denounce; hold up to -reprobation, – execration; expose, brand, gibbet, stigmatize; show –, pull –, take- up; cry " shame " upon; be outspoken; raise a hue and cry against.

execrate &c. 908; exprobate, speak daggers, vituperate; abuse, – like a pickpocket; scold, rate, objurgate, upbraid, fall foul of; jaw; rail, – at, – in good set terms; bark at; anathematize, call names; call by -hard, – ugly- names; a-†, re-vile; vili-fy, -pend; bespatter; backbite; clapperclaw; rave –, thunder –, fulminate- against; load with reproaches.

exclaim –, protest –, inveigh –, declaim –, cry out –, raise one's voice- against.

decry; cry –, run –, frown- down; clamor, hiss, hoot, mob, ostracize, blacklist; draw up –, sign- a round robin.

animadvert –, reflect- upon; glance at; cast -reflection, – reproach, – a slur- upon; insinuate, damn with faint praise; " hint a fault and hesitate dislike "; not to be able to say much for.

scoff at, point at; twit, taunt &c. (*disrespect*) 929; sneer at &c. (*despise*) 230; satirize, lampoon; defame &c. (*detract*) 934; depreciate, find fault with,

criticize, cut up; pull –, pick- to pieces; take exception; cavil; peck –, nibble –, carp- at; be -censorious &c. *adj.*; pick -holes, – a hole, – a hole in one's coat; make a fuss about.

take –, set- down; snub, snap one up, give a rap on the knuckles; throw a stone -at, – in one's garden; have a -fling, – snap- at; have words with, pluck a crow with; give one a -wipe, – lick with the rough side of the tongue.

incur blame, excite disapprobation, scandalize, shock, revolt; get a bad name, forfeit one's good opinion, be under a cloud, come under the ferule, bring a hornet's nest about one's ears.

take blame, stand corrected; have to answer for.

Adj. disapproving &c. *v.*; scandalized.

disparaging, condemnatory, damnatory, denunciatory, reproachful, abusive, objurgatory, clamorous, vituperative; defamatory &c. 934.

satirical, sarcastic, sardonic, cynical, dry, sharp, cutting, biting, severe, withering, trenchant, hard upon; censorious, critical, captious, carping, hypercritical; fastidious &c. 868; sparing of –, grudging -praise.

disapproved, chid &c. *v.*; in bad odor, blown upon, unapproved; unblest; at a discount, exploded; weighed in the balance and found wanting.

blameworthy, reprehensible &c. (*guilt*) 947; to –, worthy of- blame; answerable, uncommendable, exceptionable, not to be thought of; bad &c. 649; vicious &c. 945.

un-lamented, -bewailed, -pitied.

Adv. with a wry face; reproachfully &c. *adj.*

Int. it is too bad! it -won't, – will never- do! marry come up! Oh! come! 'sdeath!

forbid it Heaven! God –, Heaven- forbid! out –, fie- upon it! away with! tut! *O tempora! O mores!* shame! fie, – for shame! out on you!

tell it not in Gath!

933. Flattery. — N. flattery, adulation, gloze; bland-ishment, -iloquence; cajolery; fawning, wheedling &c. *v.*; captation, coquetry, obsequiousness, sycophancy, flunkeyism, toadeating, tufthunting; snobbishness.

incense, honeyed words, flummery; bun-kum, -combe; blarney, placebo, butter; soft -soap, – sawder; rose water.

voice of the charmer, mouth honor; lip homage; euphemism; unctuousness &c. *adj.*

V. flatter, praise to the skies, puff; wheedle, cajole, glaver, coax; fawn, – upon; humor, gloze, soothe, pet, coquet, slaver, butter; jolly [U. S.]; be-spatter, -slubber, -plaster, -slaver; lay it on thick, overpraise; earwig, cog, collogue; truckle –, pander *or* pandar –, pay court- to; court; creep into the good graces of, curry favor with, hang on the sleeve of; fool to the top of one's bent; lick the dust.

lay the flattering unction to one's soul, gild the pill, make things pleasant.

overestimate &c. 482; exaggerate &c. 549.

Adj. flattering &c. *v.*; adulatory;

934. Detraction. — N. detraction, disparagement, depreciation, vilification, obloquy, scurrility, scandal, defamation, aspersion, traducement, slander, calumny, obtrectation †, evil-speaking, backbiting, *scandalum magnatum.*

personality, libel, lampoon, skit, pasquinade; *chronique scandaleuse*; roorback [U. S.].

sarcasm, cynicism; criticism (*disapprobation*) 932; invective &c. 932; envenomed tongue; *spretæ injuria formæ.*

detractor &c. 936.

V. detract, derogate, decry, depreciate, disparage; run –, cry- down; backcap [U. S.]; belittle; sneer at &c. (*contemn*) 930; criticize, pull to pieces, pick a hole in one's coat, asperse, cast aspersions, blow upon, bespatter, blacken, vili-fy, -pend; avile †; give a dog a bad name, brand, malign; muckrake; backbite, libel, lampoon, traduce, slander, defame, calumniate, bear false witness against; speak ill of behind one's back.

fling dirt &c. (*disrespect*) 929; anathematize &c. 932; dip the pen in gall, view in a bad light.

Adj. detracting &c. *v.*; defamatory,

mealy-, honey-mouthed; honeyed; smooth, – tongued; soapy, oily, unctuous, blandiloquent, specious; fine-, fair-spoken; plausible, servile, sycophantic, fulsome; courtier-ly, -like.

Adv. *ad captandum.*

detractory, derogatory; disparaging, libelous; scurril-e, -ous; abusive; foulspoken, -tongued, -mouthed; slanderous; calumni-ous, -atory; sar-castic, -donic; satirical, cynical.

Phr. " damn with faint praise, assent with civil leer; and without sneering, teach the rest to sneer" [Pope]; another lie nailed to the counter; " cut men's throats with whisperings " [B. Jonson]; " foul whisperings are abroad " [*Macbeth*]; " soft-buzzing slander " [Thomson]; " virtue itself 'scapes not calumnious strokes " [*Hamlet*].

---

935. Flatterer. — N. flatterer, adulator; eu-logist, -phemist; optimist, encomiast, laudator, whitewasher.

toad-y, -eater; sycophant, courtier, Sir Pertinax MacSycophant; *flâneur, prôneur;* puffer, touter, *claqueur;* clawback, earwig, doer of dirty work; parasite, hanger-on &c. (*servility*) 886.

Phr. *pessimum genus inimicorum laudantes* [Tacitus].

936. Detractor. — N. detractor, reprover; cens-or, -urer; cynic, critic, caviler, carper, word-catcher, *frondeur;* barracker.

defamer, backbiter, slanderer, Sir Benjamin Backbite, lampooner, satirist, traducer, libeler, calumniator, dawplucker, Thersites; Zoilus; good-natured friend [satirically]; reviler, vituperator, castigator; shrew &c. 901; muckraker.

disapprover, *laudator temporis acti* [Horace].

Adj. black-mouthed, abusive &c. 934.

937. Vindication. — N. vindication, justification, warrant; exoneration, exculpation; acquittal &c. 970; whitewashing.

extenuation; pallia-tion, -tive; softening, mitigation.

reply, defense; recrimination &c. 938.

apology, gloss, varnish; plea &c. 617; salvo; excuse, extenuating circumstances; allowance, – to be made; *locus pœnitentiæ.*

apologist, vindicator, justifier; defendant &c. 938.

justifiable charge, true bill.

V. justify, warrant; be an -excuse &c. *n.-* for; lend a color, furnish a handle; vindicate; ex-, dis-culpate; acquit &c. 970; clear, set right, exonerate, whitewash; clear the skirts of.

extenuate, palliate, excuse, soften, apologize, varnish, slur, gloze; put a -gloss, – good face- upon; mince; gloss over, bolster up, help a lame dog over a stile.

advocate, defend, plead one's cause; stand –, stick –, speak- up for; contend –, speak- for; bear out, keep in countenance, support; plead &c. 617; say in defense; plead ignorance; confess and avoid, propugn †, put in a good word for.

take the will for the deed, make allow-

938. Accusation. — N. accusation, charge, imputation, slur, inculpation, exprobration, delation; crimination; in-, ac-, re-crimination; *tu quoque* argument; invective &c. 932.

de-nunciation, -nouncement; libel, challenge, citation, arraignment; im-, ap-peachment †; indictment, bill of indictment, true bill; lawsuit &c. 969; condemnation &c. 971.

gravamen of a charge, head and front of one's offending, *argumentum ad hominem;* scandal &c. (*detraction*) 934; *scandalum magnatum.*

accuser, prosecutor, plaintiff; relator, informer; appellant.

accused, defendant, prisoner, panel, respondent; litigant.

V. accuse, charge, tax, impute, twit, taunt with, reproach.

brand with reproach; stigmatize, slur; cast a -stone at, – slur on; in-, criminate; inculpate, implicate; call to account &c. (*censure*) 932; take to -blame, – task; put in the black book.

inform against, indict, denounce, arraign; im-, ap-peach†; have up, show up, pull up; challenge, cite, lodge a complaint; prosecute, bring an action against &c. 969; blow upon.

charge –, saddle- with; lay to one's

ance for, do justice to; give -one, – the Devil- his due.

make good; prove -the truth of, – one's case; be justified by the event.

Adj. vindicat-ed, -ing &c. *v.*; vindicat-ive, -ory; palliative; exculpatory; apologetic.

excusable, defensible, pardonable; veni-al, -able; specious, plausible, justifiable.

Phr. " *honi soit qui mal y pense;*" "good wine needs no bush."

-door, – charge; lay the blame on, bring home to; cast –, throw- in one's teeth; cast the first stone at.

have –, keep- a rod in pickle for; have a crow to pluck with.

trump up a charge.

Adj. accusing &c. *v.*; accusat-ory, -ive; imputative, denunciatory; re-, criminatory.

accused &c. *v.*; suspected; under -suspicion, – a cloud, – surveillance; in -custody, – detention; in the -lockup, – watch-house, – house of detention.

accusable, imputable; in-defensible, -excusable; un-pardonable, -justifiable; vicious &c. 845.

Int. look at home; *tu quoque* &c. (*retaliation*) 718.

Phr. " the breath of accusation kills an innocent name " [Shelley]; " thou can'st not say I did it " [*Macbeth*].

3. MORAL CONDITIONS

939. Probity. — N. probity, integrity, rectitude; uprightness &c. *adj.*; honesty, faith; honor; *bonne foi,* good faith, *bona fides;* purity, clean hands.

fairness &c. *adj.*; fair play, justice, equity, impartiality, principle; grace.

constancy; faithfulness &c. *adj.*; fidelity, loyalty; incorrupt-ion, -ibility.

trustworthiness &c. *adj.*; truth, candor, singleness of heart; veracity &c. 543; tender conscience &c. (*sense of duty*) 926.

punctilio, delicacy, nicety; scrupulosity, -ousness &c. *adj.*; scruple; point, – of honor; punctuality.

dignity &c. (*repute*) 873; respectability, -bleness &c. *adj.*; *gentilhomme,* gentleman; man of -honor, – his word; *fidus Achates, preux chevalier, galantuomo;* true-penny, trump, brick; true Briton; white man * [U. S.].

court of honor, a fair field and no favor; *argumentum ad verecundiam.*

V. be -honorable &c. *adj.*; deal -honorably, – squarely, – impartially, – fairly; speak the truth &c. (*veracity*) 543; draw a straight furrow; tell the truth and shame the Devil, *vitam impendere vero;* show a proper spirit, make a point of; do one's duty &c. (*virtue*) 944.

redeem one's pledge &c. 926; keep –, be as good as- one's -promise, – word; keep faith with, not fail.

give and take, *audire alteram partem,* give the Devil his due, put the saddle on the right horse.

940. Improbity. — N. improbity; dishon-esty, -or; deviation from rectitude; disgrace &c. (*disrepute*) 874; fraud &c. (*deception*) 545; lying &c. 544; bad –, Punic- faith; *mala –, Punica- fides;* infidelity; faithlessness &c. *adj.*; Judas kiss, betrayal.

breach of -promise, – trust, – faith; prodition †, disloyalty, treason, high treason; apostacy &c. (*tergiversation*) 607; nonobservance &c. 773.

shabbiness &c. *adj.*; villany; baseness &c. *adj.*; abjection, debasement, turpitude, moral turpitude, laxity, trimming, shuffling.

perfidy; perfidiousness &c. *adj.*; treachery, double dealing; unfairness &c. *adj.*; knavery, roguery, rascality, foul-play; jobb-ing, -ery; graft; venality, nepotism; corruption, job, shuffle, fishy transaction; barratry, sharp practice, heads I win tails you lose; mouth honor &c. (*flattery*) 933.

V. be -dishonest &c. *adj.*; play false; break one's -word, – faith, – promise; jilt, betray, forswear; shuffle &c. (*lie*) 544; live by one's wits, sail near the wind.

disgrace –, dishonor –, demean –, degrade- oneself; derogate, stoop, grovel, sneak, lose caste; sell oneself, go over to the enemy; seal one's infamy.

Adj. dishon-est, -orable; un-conscientious, -scrupulous; fraudulent &c. 545; knavish; disgraceful &c. (*disreputable*) 974; wicked &c. 945.

redound to one's honor.

Adj. upright; honest, – as daylight; veracious &c. 543; virtuous &c. 944; honorable; fair, right, just, equitable, impartial, evenhanded, square; fair –, open- and aboveboard; white * [U. S.].

constant, – as the northern star; faithful, loyal, staunch; true, – blue, – to one's colors, – to the core, – as the needle to the pole; " marble-constant " [*Antony and Cleopatra*]; true-hearted, trust-y, -worthy; as good as one's word, to be depended on, incorruptible.

straightforward &c. (*ingenuous*) 703; frank, candid, open-hearted.

conscientious, tender-conscienced, right-minded; high-principled, -minded; scrupulous, religious, strict; nice, punctilious, correct, punctual; respect-, reput-able; gentlemanlike.

inviol-able, -ate; un-violated, -broken, -betrayed; un-bought, -bribed.

innocent &c. 946; pure, stainless; unstained, -tarnished, -sullied, -tainted, -perjured; uncorrupt, -ed; unde-filed, -praved, -bauched; *integer vitœ sceleris-que purus* [Horace]; *justus et tenax propositi* [Horace].

chivalrous, jealous of honor, *sans peur et sans reproche;* high-spirited.

supramundane, unworldly, over-scrupulous.

Adv. honorably &c. *adj.*; *bonâ fide;* on the square, in good faith, honor bright, *foro conscientiœ,* with clean hands.

Phr. " a face untaught to feign " [Pope]; *bene qui latuit bene vixit* [Ovid]; *mens sibi conscia recti; probitas laudatur et alget* [Juvenal]; *fidelis ad urnam;* " his heart as far from fraud as heaven from earth " [*Two Gentlemen*]; *loyauté m'oblige; loyauté n'a honte;* " what stronger breastplate than a heart untainted? " [*Henry VI*].

false-hearted, disingenuous; unfair, one-sided; double, -hearted, -tongued, -faced; timeserving, crooked, tortuous, insidious, Machiavelian, dark, slippery; fishy; perfidious, treacherous, perjured.

infamous, arrant, foul, base, vile, ignominious, blackguard.

contemptible, abject, mean, shabby, little, paltry, dirty, scurvy, scabby, sneaking, groveling, scrubby, rascally, pettifogging; beneath one.

low-minded, -thoughted; base-minded.

undignified, indign †; unbe-coming, -seeming, -fitting; de-rogatory, -grading; *infra dignitatem;* ungentleman-ly, -like; un-knightly, -chivalric, -manly, -handsome; recreant, inglorious.

corrupt, venal; debased, mongrel.

faithless, of bad faith, false, unfaithful, disloyal; untrustworthy; trust-, trothless; lost to shame, dead to honor; barratrous.

Adv. dishonestly &c. *adj.*; *malâ fide,* like a thief in the night, by crooked paths.

Int. *O tempora! O mores!* [Cicero].

Phr. *corruptissimâ respublicâ plurimœ leges* [Tacitus].

---

941. Knave. — N. knave, rogue; Scapin, rascal; Lazarillo de Tormes; bad man &c. 949; blackguard &c. 949; barrat-er, -or; shyster [U. S.].

traitor, betrayer, archtraitor, conspirator, Judas, Catiline; reptile, serpent, snake in the grass, wolf in sheep's clothing, sneak, Jerry Sneak, squealer *, telltale, mischief-maker; trimmer, renegrade &c. (*tergiversation*) 607; truant, recreant; sycophant &c. (*servility*) 886.

942. Disinterestedness. — N. disinterestedness &c. *adj.*; generosity; liberal-ity, -ism; altruism; benevolence &c. 906; elevation, loftiness of purpose, exaltation, magnanimity; chival-ry, -rous spirit; heroism, sublimity.

self-denial, -abnegation, -sacrifice, -immolation, -control &c. (*resolution*) 604; stoicism, devotion, martyrdom, suttee.

labor of love.

V. be -disinterested &c. *adj.*; make a sacrifice, lay one's head on the block;

943. Selfishness. — N. selfishness &c. *adj.*; self-love, -indulgence, -worship, -interest; ego-tism, -ism; *amour propre* &c. (*vanity*) 880; nepotism.

worldliness &c. *adj.*; world wisdom.

illiberality; meanness &c. *adj.*

time-pleaser, -server; tuft-, fortune-hunter; jobber, worldling; egotist, egoist, monopolist, nepotist; dog in the manger, charity that begins at home; *canis in prœsepi,* " foes to nobleness," temporizer, trimmer.

V. be -selfish &c. *adj.*; please –, in-

put oneself in the place of others, do as one would be done by, do unto others as we would men should do unto us.

Adj. disinterested; unselfish; self-denying, -sacrificing, -devoted; generous.

handsome, liberal, noble; noble-, high-minded; princely, great, high, elevated, lofty, exalted, spirited, stoical, magnanimous; great-, large-hearted; chivalrous, heroic, sublime.

un-bought, -bribed; uncorrupted &c. (*upright*) 939.

Phr. *non vobis solum.*

interested; *alieni appetens sui profusus.*

Adv. ungenerously &c. *adj.*; to gain some private ends, from interested motives.

Phr. *après nous le déluge.*

dulge -, coddle- oneself; consult one's own -wishes, - pleasure; look after one's own interest; feather one's nest; take care of number one, have an eye to the main chance, know on which side one's bread is buttered; give an inch and take an ell.

Adj. selfish; self-seeking, -indulgent, -interested; wrapt up -, centered- in self; egotistic, -al; egoistical.

illiberal, mean, ungenerous, narrow-minded; mercenary, venal; covetous &c. 819.

unspiritual, earthly, -minded; mundane; worldly, -minded, -wise; time-serving.

944. Virtue. — **N.** virtue; virtuousness &c. *adj.*; morality; moral rectitude; integrity &c. (*probity*) 939; nobleness &c. 873.

morals; ethics &c. (*duty*) 926; cardinal virtues.

merit, worth, desert, excellence, credit; self-control &c. (*resolution*) 604; self-denial &c. (*temperance*) 953.

well-doing; good -actions, - behavior; discharge -, fulfillment -, performance- of duty; well-spent life; innocence &c. 946.

V. be -virtuous &c. *adj.*; practice -virtue &c. *n.*; do -, fulfill -, perform -, discharge- one's duty; redeem one's pledge &c. 926; act well, - one's part; fight the good fight; acquit oneself well; command -, master- one's passions; keep in the right path.

set -an, - a good-example; be on one's -good, - best- behavior.

Adj. virtuous, good; innocent &c. 946; meritorious, deserving, worthy, desertful, correct; dut-iful, -eous; moral; right, -eous, -minded; well-intentioned, creditable, laudable, commendable, praiseworthy; above -, beyond- all praise; excellent, admirable; sterling, pure, noble; whole-souled.

exemplary; match-, peer-less; saint-ly, -like; heaven-born, angelic, seraphic, godlike.

Adv. virtuously &c. *adj.*; *e merito.*

Phr. *esse quam videri bonus malebat* [Sallust]; *Schönheit vergeht Tugend besteht;* " virtue the greatest of all monarchies " [Swift]; *virtus laudatur et alget* [Juvenal]; *virtus vincit invidiam.*

945. Vice. — **N.** vice; evil -doing, - courses; wrongdoing; wickedness, viciousness &c. *adj.*; iniquity, peccability, demerit; sin, Adam; old -, offending-Adam.

immorality, impropriety, indecorum, scandal, laxity, looseness of morals; endo-, exo-phagy; want of -principle, - ballast; obliquity, backsliding, infamy, demoralization, pravity, depravity, pollution; hardness of heart; brutality &c. (*malevolence*) 907; corruption &c. (*debasement*) 659; knavery &c. (*improbity*) 940; profligacy; flagrancy, atrocity; cannibalism; lesbianism, Sadism.

infirmity; weakness &c. *adj.*; weakness of the flesh, frailty, imperfection, error; weak side; foible; fail-ing, -ure; crying -, besetting- sin; defect, deficiency; cloven foot.

lowest dregs of vice, sink of iniquity, Alsatian den; *gusto picaresco.*

fault, crime; criminality &c. (*guilt*) 947.

sinner &c. 949.

[Resorts] brothel &c. 961; gambling house &c. 621; joint *, opium den.

V. be -vicious &c. *adj.*; sin, commit sin, do amiss, err, transgress; misdemean -, forget -, misconduct- oneself; mis-do, -behave; fall, lapse, slip, trip, offend, trespass; deviate from the -line of duty, - path of virtue &c. 944; take a wrong course, go astray; hug a -sin, - fault; sow one's wild oats.

render -vicious &c. *adj.*; demoralize, brutalize; corrupt &c. (*degrade*) 659.

Adj.[1] vicious; sinful; sinning &c. *v.*; wicked, iniquitous, immoral, unrighteous, wrong, criminal; naughty, incorrect; undut-eous, -iful.

unprincipled, lawless, disorderly, *contra bonos mores*, indecorous, unseemly, improper; dissolute, profligate, scampish; unworthy; worth-, desert-less; disgraceful, recreant; reprehensible, blameworthy, uncommendable; discreditable, -reputable; Sadistic.

base, sinister, scurvy, foul, gross, vile, black, grave, facinorous †, felonious, nefarious, shameful, scandalous, infamous, villanous, of a deep dye, heinous; flag-rant, -itious; atrocious, incarnate, accursed.

Mephistophelian, satanic, diabolic, hellish, infernal, stygian, fiendlike, hell-born, demoniacal, devilish, fiendish.

mis-created, -begotten; demoralized, corrupt, depraved.

evil-minded, -disposed; ill-conditioned; malevolent &c. 907; heart-, grace-, shame-, virtue-less; abandoned, lost to virtue; unconscionable; sunk -, lost -, deep -, steeped- in iniquity.

incorrigible, irreclaimable, obdurate, reprobate, past praying for; culpable, reprehensible &c. (*guilty*) 947.

unjustifiable; in-defensible, -excusable; inexpiable, unpardonable, irremissible.

weak, frail, lax, infirm, imperfect, indiscreet; demoralizing, degrading.

Adv. wrong; sinfully &c. *adj.*; without excuse.

Int. *O tempora! O mores!*

Phr. *alitur vitium vivitque tegendo* [Vergil]; *genus est mortis male vivere* [Ovid]; *mala mens malus animus* [Terence]; *nemo repente fuit turpissimus;* " the trail of the serpent is over them all " [Moore]; " to sanction vice and hunt decorum down" [Bryon].

946. Innocence. — N. innocence; guiltlessness &c. *adj.*; incorruption, impeccability.

clean hands, clear conscience, *mens sibi conscia recti* [Vergil].

innocent, lamb, dove.

V. be -innocent &c. *adj.*; *nil conscire sibi nullâ pallescere culpâ* [Horace].

acquit &c. 970; exculpate &c. (*vindicate*) 937.

Adj. innocent, not guilty; unguilty; guilt-, fault-, sin-, stain-, blood-, spotless; clear, immaculate; *rectus in curiâ;* un-spotted, -blemished, -erring; undefiled &c. 939; unhardened, Saturnian; Arcadian &c. (*artless*) 703.

in-, un-culpable; unblam-ed, -able; blameless, unfallen, inerrable, above suspicion; irrepr-oachable, -ovable, -ehensible; un-exceptionable, -objectionable, -impeachable; salvable; venial &c. 937.

harmless; in-offensive, -noxious, -nocuous; dove-, lamb-like; pure, harmless as doves; innocent as -a lamb, – the babe unborn; " more sinned against than sinning " [Lear].

virtuous &c. 944; un-reproved, -impeached, -reproached.

Adv. innocently &c. *adj.*; with clean hands; with a -clear, – safe- conscience.

Phr. *murus aëneus conscientia sana* [Horace].

947. Guilt. — N. guilt, -iness; culpability; crimin-ality, -ousness; deviation from rectitude &c. (*improbity*) 940; sinfulness &c. (*vice*) 945.

mis-conduct, -behavior, -doing, -deed; malpractice, fault, sin, error, transgression; dereliction, delinquency; indiscretion, lapse, slip, trip, *faux pas*, peccadillo; flaw, blot, omission; fail-ing, -ure; break, bad break [U. S.], capital crime, *delicium.*

offense, trespass; mis-demeanor, -feasance, -prision; mal-efaction, -feasance, -versation; crime, felony.

enormity, atrocity, outrage; deadly -, mortal- sin; " deed without a name " [*Macbeth*].

corpus delicti.

Adj. guilty, to blame, culpable, peccable, in fault, censurable, reprehensible, blameworthy, uncommendable, illaudable; weighed in the balance and found wanting; exceptionable.

Adv. *in flagrante delicto;* red-handed, in the very act.

Phr. *cui prodest scelus is fecit* [Seneca]; *culpam pœna premit comes* [Horace]; " O would the deed were good! " [*Richard II*]; " responsibility prevents crimes " [Burke;] *se judice nemo nocens absolvitur* [Juvenal]; " so many laws argues so many sins " [*Paradise Lost*].

---

[1] Most of these adjectives are applicable both to the act and to the agent.

948. Good Man. — N. good man, worthy.

model, paragon &c. (*perfection*) 650; good example; hero, demigod, seraph, angel; innocent &c. 946; saint &c. (*piety*) 987; benefactor &c. 912; philanthropist &c. 910; Aristides; noble liver, pattern.

brick *, trump *, rough diamond, ugly duckling.

salt of the earth; one in ten thousand; a man among men.

Phr. *si sic omnes!*

949. Bad Man. — N. bad man, wrongdoer, worker of iniquity; evildoer &c. 913; sinner; the -wicked &c. 945; bad example.

rascal, scoundrel, villain, miscreant, budmash, caitiff; wretch, reptile, viper, serpent, cockatrice, basilisk, urchin; tiger, monster; devil &c. (*demon*) 980; devil incarnate; demon in human shape, Nana Sahib; hell-hound, -cat; rakehell.

bad woman, jade, Jezebel.

scamp, scapegrace, rip, runagate, ne'er-do-well, reprobate, *roué*, rake; Sadist, scal(l)awag; skeesicks *, skeezix * [U. S.]; limb; one who has sold himself to the devil, fallen angel, *âme damnée, vaurien, mauvais sujet*, loose fish, sad dog; rounder *; lost -, black- sheep; castaway, recreant, defaulter; prodigal &c. 818.

rough, rowdy, ugly customer, ruffian, bully; Jonathan Wild; hangman; incendiary; fire bug [U. S.]; thief &c. 792; murderer &c. 361.

culprit, delinquent, criminal, malefactor, misdemeanant; felon; convict, jail bird, ticket of leave man; outlaw.

blackguard, *polisson*, loafer, sneak; raps-, ras-callion; cullion, mean wretch, varlet, kern †, *âme-de-boue, drôle*; cur, dog, hound, whelp, mongrel; lown, loon, runnion, outcast, vagabond; rogue &c. (*knave*) 941; ronian; scum of the earth, riffraff; *Arcades ambo.*

Int. sirrah!

Phr. *Acherontis pabulum; gibier de potence.*

950. Penitence. — N. penitence, contrition, compunction, repentance, remorse; regret &c. 833.

self-reproach, -reproof, -accusation, -condemnation, -humiliation; stings -, pangs -, qualms -, prickings -, twinge -, twitch -, touch -, voice- of conscience; compunctious visitings of nature.

acknowledgment, confession &c. (*disclosure*) 529; apology &c. 952; recantation &c. 607; penance &c. 952; resipiscence.

awakened conscience, deathbed repentance, *locus pœnitentiæ*, stool of repentance, cuttystool.

penitent, repentant, Magdalen, prodigal son, " a sadder and a wiser man " [Coleridge].

951. Impenitence. — N. impenitence, irrepentance, recusance; lack of contrition.

hardness of heart, seared conscience, induration, obduracy.

V. be -impenitent &c. *adj.*; steel -, harden- the heart; die -game, - and make no sign.

Adj. impenitent, uncontrite, obdurate; hard, -ened; seared, recusant; unrepentant; relent-, remorse-, graceshrift-less.

lost, incorrigible, irreclaimable.

unre-claimed, -formed; unrepented, unatoned.

V. repent, be sorry for; be -penitent &c. *adj.*; rue; regret &c. 833; think better of; recant &c. 607; knock under &c. (*submit*) 725; plead guilty; sing -miserere, – de profundis; cry peccavi; own oneself in the wrong; acknowledge, confess &c. (*disclose*) 529; humble oneself; beg pardon &c. (*apologize*) 952; turn over a new leaf, put on the new man, turn from sin; reclaim; repent in sackcloth and ashes &c. (*do penance*) 952; learn by experience.

Adj. penitent; repenting &c. *v.*; repentant, contrite; conscience-smitten, -stricken; self-accusing, -convicted.

penitenti-al, -ary; reclaimed; not hardened; unhardened.

Adv. *meâ culpâ.*

Phr. *peccavi; erubuit; salva res est* [Terence]; *Tu l'as voulu, Georges Dandin;* " and wet his grave with my repentant tears " [*Richard III*].

952. Atonement. — N. atonement, reparation; compromise, composition; compensation &c. 30; quittance, quits; expiation, redemption, reclamation, conciliation, propitiation; indemnification, redress.

amends, apology, *amende honorable*, satisfaction; peace –, sin –, burnt- offering; scapegoat, sacrifice.

penance, fasting, maceration, sackcloth and ashes, white sheet, shrift, flagellation, lustration; purga-tion, -tory.

V. atone, – for; expiate; propitiate; make -amends, – good; reclaim, redeem, repair, ransom, absolve, purge, shrive, do penance, stand in a white sheet, repent in sackcloth and ashes.

set one's house in order, wipe off old scores, make matters up; pay the -forfeit, – penalty.

apologize, beg pardon, *faire l'amende honorable*, give satisfaction; come –, fall- down on one's -knees, – marrow bones.

Adj. propitiatory, expiatory; sacrific, -ial, -atory; piacul-ar, -ous.

4. MORAL PRACTICE

953. Temperance. — N. temperance, moderation, sobriety, soberness.

forbearance, abnegation; self-denial, -restraint, -control &c. (*resolution*) 604.

frugality; vegetarianism, teetotalism, total abstinence; abst-inence, -emiousness; Encratism, prohibition; system of -Pythagoras, – Cornaro; Pythagorism, Stoicism.

vegetarian; Pythagorean, gymnosophist; teetotaler &c. 958; abstainer; Encratite, fruitarian, hydropot.

V. be -temperate &c. *adj.*; abstain, forbear, refrain, deny oneself, spare; know when one has had enough; take the pledge.

Adj. temperate, moderate, sober, frugal, sparing; abst-emious, -inent; within compass; measured &c. (*sufficient*) 639. Pythagorean; vegetarian; teetotal.

Phr. *appetitus rationi obediant* [Cic.]; *l'abstenir pour jouir c'est l'épicurisme de la raison* [Rousseau]; *trahit sua quemque voluptas* [Vergil].

954. Intemperance. — N. intemperance; sensuality, animalism, carnality; tragalism; pleasure; effeminacy, silkiness; luxur-y, -iousness; lap of -pleasure, – luxury; free-living.

indulgence; high living, inabstinence, self-indulgence; voluptuousness &c. *adj.*; epicur-ism, -eanism; sybaritism; drug habit.

dissipation; licentiousness &c. *adj.*; debauchery; crapulence.

revel-s, -ry; debauch, carousal, jollification, drinking bout, wassail, saturnalia, orgies; excess, too much.

Circean cup; bhang, hashish, opium, cocaine.

V. be -intemperate &c. *adj.*; indulge, exceed; live -well, – high, – on the fat of the land; give a loose to -indulgence &c. *n.*; wallow in -voluptuousness &c. *n.*; plunge into dissipation.

revel, rake, live hard, run riot, sow one's wild oats; slake one's -appetite, – thirst; swill; pamper.

Adj. intemperate, inabstinent; sensual, self-indulgent; voluptuous, luxurious, licentious, wild, dissolute, rakish, fast, debauched.

brutish, crapulous, swinish, piggish.

Paphian, Epicurean, Sybaritical; bred –, nursed- in the lap of luxury; indulged, pampered; full –, high- fed.

Phr. " being full of supper and distempering draughts " [*Othello*].

954a. Sensualist. — N. Sybarite, voluptuary, Sardanapalus, man of pleasure, carpet knight; epicure, -an; *gourm-et, -and;* pig, hog; votary –, swine- of Epicurus; sensualist; Heliogabalus; free –, hard- liver; libertine &c. 962; hedonist; tragalist.

955. Asceticism. — N. asceticism, puritanism, sabbatarianism; cynicism, austerity; total abstinence; nephalism.

mortification, maceration, sackcloth and ashes, flagellation; penance &c. 952; fasting &c. 956; martyrdom.

ascetic; anchor-et, -ite; martyr; *Heautontimorumenos;* hermit &c. (*recluse*) 893; puritan, sabbatarian, cynic, sanyasi, yogi.

Adj. ascetic, austere, puritanical; cynical; over-religious; acerbic.

956. Fasting. — N. fasting; xerophagy; famishment, starvation.

fast, *jour maigre;* fast -, banyan- day; Lent, quadragesima; Rama-dan, -zan; spare -, meager- diet; lenten -diet, – entertainment; *soupe maigre*, short commons, Barmecide feast; short rations.

V. fast, starve, clem †, famish, perish with hunger; dine with Duke Humphrey; make two bites of a cherry.

Adj. lenten, quadragesimal; unfed; starved &c. *v.;* half-starved; fasting &c. *v.;* hungry &c. 865.

957. Gluttony. — N. gluttony; greed; greediness &c. *adj.;* voracity.

epicurism; good -, high- living; edacity, gulosity, crapulence; gutt-, guzzling; pantophagy.

good cheer, blow out *; feast &c. (*food*) 298; gastronomy, *batterie de cuisine.*

epicure, *bon-vivant*, gourmand; glutton, cormorant, hog, belly-god, Apicius, gastronome.

V. gormandize, gorge; over-gorge, -eat- oneself; engorge, eat one's fill, cram, stuff; gutt-, guzz-le; bolt, devour, gobble up; gulp &c. (*swallow food*) 298; raven, eat out of house and home.

have the stomach of an ostrich; play a good knife and fork &c. (*appetite*) 865.

pamper.

Adj. gluttonous, greedy; gormandizing &c. *v.;* edacious, omnivorous, crapulent, swinish.

pampered; over-fed, -gorged.

Phr. *jejunus raro stomachus vulgaria temnit* [Horace].

958. Sobriety. — N. sobriety; teetotalism.

water-drinker; hydropot; prohibitionist; teetotal-er, -ist; abstainer, Good Templar, band of hope.

V. take the pledge.

Adj. sober, – as a judge.

959. Drunkenness. — N. drunkenness &c. *adj.;* intemperance; drinking &c. *v.;* inebri-ety, -ation; ebri-ety, -osity; insobriety; intoxication; temulency, bibacity, winebibbing; com-, potation; deep potations, bacchanals, bacchanalia, libations; bender * [U. S.].

oino-, dipso-mania; delirium tremens; alcohol, -ism; *mania a potu.*

drink; alcoholic drinks; blue ruin *, grog, port wine; punch, -bowl; cup, rosy wine, flowing bowl; drop, – too much; dram; beer &c. (*beverage*) 298; *aguardiente;* apple-brandy -jack; brandy, -smash [U. S.]; chain lightning *, champagne, cocktail; gin, -sling; highball [U. S.], peg, rum, rye, schnapps [U. S.], sherry, sling [U. S.], usquebaugh, whisky, xeres.

drunkard, sot, toper, tippler, bibber, winebibber; hard -, gin -, dram-drinker; soaker *, sponge, tun; love-, toss-pot; thirsty soul, reveler, carouser, Bacchanal, -ian; Bacch-al, -ante; devotee to Bacchus; bum * [U. S.], guzzler, tavern haunter.

V. get -, be- drunk &c. *adj.;* see double; take a -drop, – glass- too much; drink, tipple, tope, booze, bouse, guzzle, swill *, soak *, sot, bum * [U. S.], besot, have a jag on *, lush *, bib, swig, carouse; sacrifice at the shrine of Bacchus; take to drinking; drink -hard, – deep, – like a fish; have one's swill *, drain the cup, splice the main brace, take a hair of the dog that bit you.

liquor. – up; wet one's whistle, take a whet; crack a -, pass the- bottle; toss off &c. (*drink up*) 298; go to the -ale, – public-house.

make one -drunk &c. *adj.;* inebriate, fuddle, befuddle, fuzzle, get into one's head.

Adj. drunk, tipsy; intoxicated; inebri-ous, -ate, -ated; in one's cups; in a

state of -intoxication &c. *n.*; temulent, -ive; fuddled, mellow, cut, boozy, fou, fresh, merry, elevated; flush, -ed; flustered, disguised, groggy, beery; top-heavy; potvaliant, glorious; potulent †; squiffy *; over-come, -taken; whittled, screwed *, tight *, primed, corned, raddled, sewed up *, lushy *, nappy, muddled, muzzy, obfuscated, maudlin; crapulous, dead drunk.[1]

inter pocula; in –, the worse for- liquor; having had a drop too much, half seas over, three sheets in the wind; under the table.

drunk as -a piper, – a fiddler, – a lord, – Chloe, – an owl, – David's sow, – a wheelbarrow.

drunken, bibacious, sottish; given –, addicted- to -drink, – the bottle; toping &c. *v.*

Phr. *nunc est bibendum;* " Bacchus ever fair and young " [Dryden]; " drink down all unkindness " [*Merry Wives*]; " O that men should put an enemy in their mouths to steal away their brains " [*Othello*].

960. Purity. — **N.** purity; decency, decorum, delicacy; continence, chastity, honesty, virtue, modesty, shame; pudicity, pucelage, virginity.

vestal, virgin, Joseph, Hippolytus; Lucretia, Diana; prude.

Adj. pure, undefiled, modest, delicate, decent, decorous; *virginibus puerisque;* chaste, continent, virtuous, honest, Platonic.

Phr. " as chaste as unsunn'd snow " [*Cymbeline*]; " a soul as white as heaven " [Beaumont & Fl.]; " 'tis Chastity, my brother, Chastity " [Milton]; " to the pure all things are pure " [Shelley].

961. Impurity. — **N.** impurity; uncleanness &c. (*filth*) 653; immodesty; grossness &c. *adj.*; indelicacy, indecency; impudicity; obscenity, ribaldry, Fescennine, smut, bawdry, *double entente, équivoque.*

concupiscence, lust, carnality, flesh, salacity; pruriency, lechery, lasciviency, lubricity; Sadism, sapphism.

incontinence, intrigue, *faux pas;* amour, -ette; gallantry; debauchery, libertinism, libertinage, fornication; *liaison;* wenching, venery, dissipation.

seduction; defloration, defilement, abuse, violation, rape; incest.

social evil, harlotry, stupration, whoredom, concubinage, cuckoldom, adultery, advoutry, crim. con.; free-love.

seraglio, harem; brothel, bagnio, stew, bawdyhouse, lupanar, house of ill fame, bordel.

V. be -impure &c. *adj.*; intrigue; debauch, defile, seduce; prostitute; abuse, violate, deflower; commit -adultery &c. *n.*

Adj. impure; unclean &c. (*dirty*) 653; not to be mentioned to ears polite; immodest, shameless; in-decorous, -delicate, -decent; Fescennine; loose, *risqué*, coarse, gross, broad, free, equivocal, smutty, fulsome, ribald, obscene, bawdy, pornographic.

concupiscent, prurient, lickerish, rampant, lustful; carnal, -minded; lewd, lascivious, lecherous, libidinous, erotic, ruttish, salacious; Paphian; voluptuous; goatish; *must,* musty.

unchaste, light, wanton, licentious, debauched, dissolute; of -loose character, – easy virtue; frail, gay, riggish, incontinent, meretricious, rakish, gallant, dissipated; no better than she should be; on the -town, - streets, - pavé, – loose.

adulterous, incestuous, bestial.

962. Libertine. — **N.** libertine; voluptuary &c. 954a; rake, debauchee, loose fish, rip, rakehell, fast man; intrigant, gallant, seducer, fornicator, lecher, satyr, goat, whoremonger, *paillard,* adulterer, gay deceiver, Lothario, Don Juan, Bluebeard; chartered libertine.

adultress, advoutress, courtesan, prostitute, strumpet, harlot, whore, punk, *fille de joie;* woman, – of the town; streetwalker, Cyprian, miss, piece; frail

---

[1] More than three hundred slang expressions coming under this category are given in Farmer and Henley's *Dictionary of Slang and Colloquial English.* C. O S. M.l.

sisterhood; demirep, wench, trollop, trull, baggage, hussy, drab, bitch, jade, skit, rig, quean, mopsy, slut, minx, harridan; unfortunate, – female, – woman; woman -of easy virtue &c. (*unchaste*) 961; wanton, fornicatress; Jezebel, Messalina, Delilah, Thais, Phryne, Aspasia, Lais, *lorette, cocotte, petite dame*, grisette; demimonde; chippy * [U. S.]; sapphist; spiritual wife; white slave.

concubine, mistress, doxy, *chère amie, bona roba*.

pimp; pand-er, -ar; bawd, *conciliatrix*, procuress, mackerel, wittol †.

5. INSTITUTIONS

963. Legality. — N. legality; legitima-cy, -teness.

legislature; law, code, *corpus juris*, constitution, pandect, charter, enactment, statute, rule; canon &c. (*precept*) 697; ordinance, institution, regulation; by-, bye-law; decree &c. (*order*) 741; ordonnance; standing order; plebiscite &c. (*choice*) 609.

legal process; form, -ula, -ality; rite, arm of the law; *habeas corpus; fieri facias*.

[Science of law] jurisprudence, nomology; legislation, codification.

equity, common law; *lex –, lex non-scripta;* law of nations, *droit des gens,* international law, *jus gentium; jus civile;* civil –, canon –, crown –, criminal –, statute –, ecclesiastical- law; *lex mercatoria.*

constitutional-ism, -ity; justice &c. 922.

V. legalize; enact, ordain; decree &c. (*order*) 741; pass a law; legislate; codify, formulate.

Adj. legal, legitimate; according to law; vested, constitutional, chartered, legalized; lawful &c. (*permitted*) 760; statut-able, -ory; legislat-orial, -ive.

Adv. legally &c. *adj.*; in the eye of the law; *de jure.*

Phr. *ignorantia legis neminem excusat;* "where law ends tyranny begins" [Earl of Chatham].

964. [Absence or violation of law.] **Illegality. — N.** lawlessness; illicitness; breach –, violation- of law; disobedience &c. 742; unconformity &c. 83.

arbitrariness &c. *adj.*; antinomy, violence, brute force, despotism, outlawry.

mob –, lynch –, club –, Lydford –, martial –, drumhead- law; *coup d'état; le droit du plus fort; argumentum baculinum.*

illegality, informality, unlawfulness, illegitimacy, bar sinister.

trover and conversion; smuggling, poaching; simony.

V. offend against –, violate- the law; set the law at defiance, ride roughshod over, drive a coach and six through a statute; make the law a dead letter, take the law into one's own hands.

smuggle, run, poach.

Adj. illegal; prohibited &c. 761; not allowed, unlawful, illegitimate, illicit, contraband, actionable.

unchartered, unconstitutional; unwarrant-ed, -able; unauthorized; informal, unofficial; in-, extra-judicial.

lawless, arbitrary; despotic, -al; summary, irresponsible; un-answerable, -accountable.

null and void; a dead letter.

Adv. illegally &c. *adj.*; with a high hand, in violation of law.

965. Jurisdiction. [Executive.] **— N.** jurisdiction, judicature, administration of justice, soc; executive, commission of the peace; magistracy &c. (*authority*) 737.

judge &c. 967; tribunal &c. 966; municipality, corporation, bailiwick, shrievalty; lord lieutenant, sheriff, shrieve, constable; selectman; police, – force; constabulary, bumbledom.

officer, bailiff, tipstaff, bum-bailiff, catchpoll, beadle; police-man, -constable, -sergeant; *sbirro*, alguazil, *gendarme*, kavass, lictor, mace bearer, *huissier*, bedel; tithingman.

press gang; exciseman, ga(u)ger, customhouse officer, *douanier*.

coroner, edile, ædile, portreeve, paritor †; *posse comitatus*.

bureau, cutcherry, department, secretariat.

V. judge, sit in judgment.

Adj. executive, administrative, municipal; inquisitorial, causidical; judicatory, -iary, -ial; juridical.

Adv. *coram judice.*

966. Tribunal. — **N.** tribunal, court, board, bench, judicatory; court of -justice, – law, – arbitration; inquisition; guild.

justice –, judgment –, mercy- seat; woolsack; bar, – of justice; dock; forum, hustings, bureau, drumhead; jury-, witness-box.

senate-house, town hall, theater; House of- Commons, – Lords; statehouse [U. S.], townhouse.

assize, eyre; ward-, burgh-mote; barmote; superior courts of Westminster; court of -record, – oyer and terminer, – assize, – appeal, – error; High court of -Judicature, – Appeal; Judicial Committee of the Privy Council; Star-Chamber; Court of -Chancery, – King's *or* Queen's Bench, – Exchequer, – Common Pleas, – Probate, – Arches, – Admiralty; Lords Justices' –, Rolls –, Vice Chancellor's –, Stannary –, Divorce –, Palatine –, county –, district –, police- court; sessions; quarter –, petty- sessions; court -leet, – baron, – of pie poudre, – of common council; board of green cloth.

court-martial; drumhead court-martial; durbar, divan; Areopagus; *rota.*

Adj. judicial &c. 965; appellate.

Phr. *die Weltgeschichte ist das Weltgericht.*

967. Judge. — **N.** judge; justi-ce, -ciar, -ciary; chancellor; justice –, judge, of assize; recorder, common serjeant; puisne –, assistant –, county court-judge; conservator –, justice- of the peace; J. P.; court &c. (*tribunal*) 966; jury; magistrate, police magistrate, beak*; his -worship, – honor, – lordship; twelve men in a box.

Lord -Chancellor, – Justice; Master of the Rolls, Vice Chancellor; Lord Chief -Justice, – Baron; Mr. Justice; Baron, – of the Exchequer.

jurat, assessor; arbi-ter, -trator; umpire; refer-ee, -endary; revising barrister; domesman; censor &c. (*critic*) 480; barmaster, ephor; grand-juror, -juryman; juryman, talesman.

archon, tribune, prætor, syndic, podesta, mollah, ulema, mufti, cadi, kadi; Rhadamanthus.

litigant &c. (*accusation*) 938.

V. adjudge &c. (*determine*) 480; try a -case, – prisoner.

Adj. judicial &c. 965.

Phr. " a Daniel come to judgment " [*Merchant of Venice*].

968. Lawyer. — **N.** lawyer, jurist, legist, civilian, pundit, publicist, jurisconsult, legal adviser, advocate; barrister, – at law; counsel, -lor; King's *or* Queen's counsel; K. C.; Q. C.; silk gown, leader, serjeant-at-law, bencher; tubman, judge &c. 967.

bar, legal profession, gentleman of the long robe; junior –, outer –, inner- bar; equity draftsman, conveyancer, pleader, special pleader.

solicitor, attorney, proctor; notary, – public; scrivener, cursitor; writer, – to the signet; S.S.C.; limb of the law; pettifogger; vakil.

V. practice -at, – within- the bar; plead; call –, be called- -to, – within- the bar; take silk.

Adj. learned in the law; at the bar; forensic

Phr. *banco regis.*

969. Lawsuit. — **N.** lawsuit, suit, action, cause; litigation; suit in law; dispute &c. 713.

citation, arraignment, prosecution, impeachment; accusation &c. 938; presentment, true bill, indictment.

apprehension, arrest; committal; imprisonment &c. (*restraint*) 751.

writ, summons, subpœna, latitat, *nisi prius; venire, - facias.*

pleadings; declaration, bill, claim; *procès-verbal*, bill of right, information, *corpus delicti*; affidavit, state of facts; answer, replication, plea, demurrer, re-butter, rejoinder; surre-butter, -joinder.

suitor, party to a suit; litigant &c. 938.

hearing, trial; verdict &c. (*judgment*) 480; appeal, – motion; writ of error; certiorari.

case, decision, precedent; decided case, reports.

V. go to –, appeal to the- law; bring to -justice, – trial, – the bar; put on trial, pull up; accuse &c. 938; prefer –, file- a claim &c. *n.*; take the law of, inform against.

serve with a writ, cite, apprehend, arraign, sue, prosecute, bring an action against, indict, impeach, attach, distrain, commit; arrest; summon, -s; give in charge &c. (*restrain*) 751.

empanel a jury, implead, join issue; close the pleadings; set down for hearing. try, hear a cause; sit in judgment; adjudicate &c. 480.

Adj. litigious &c. (*quarrelsome*) 713; *qui tam; coram –, sub- judice.*

Adv. *pendente lite.*

Phr. *adhuc sub judice lis est; accedas ad curiam; transeat in exemplum.*

---

970. Acquittal. — N. acquit-tal, -ment; clearance, exculpation; acquit-tance, clearance, exoneration; discharge &c. (*release*) 750; *quietus*, absolution, compurgation, reprieve, respite; pardon &c. (*forgiveness*) 918.

[Exemption from punishment] im-punity.

V. acquit, exculpate, exonerate, clear; absolve, whitewash, assoil; discharge, release; liberate &c. 750.

reprieve, respite; pardon &c. (*forgive*) 918; let off, – scot-free.

Adj. acquitted &c. *v.*; un-condemned, -punished, -chastised.

Phr. *nemo bis punitur pro eodem delicto.*

971. Condemnation. — N. condem-nation, conviction, judgment, penalty. sentence; proscription, damnation; death warrant.

attain-der, -ture, -tment.

V. condemn, convict, cast, bring home to, find guilty, damn, doom, sign the death warrant, sentence, pass sentence on, attaint, confiscate, proscribe, seques-trate; nonsuit.

disapprove &c. 932; accuse &c. 938.

stand condemned.

Adj. condem-, dam-natory; con-demned &c. *v.*; nonsuited &c. (*failure*) 732; self-convicted.

Phr. *mutato nomine de te fabula narratur;* " unrespited, unpitied, unreprieved " [*P. L.*].

---

972. Punishment. — N. punishment, punition; chast-isement, -ening, correction, castigation.

discipline, infliction, trial; judgment; penalty &c. 974; retribution; thunder-bolt, Nemesis; requital &c. (*reward*) 973; penology; retributive justice.

lash, scaffold &c. (*instrument of punishment*) 975; imprisonment &c. (*re-straint*) 751; transportation, banishment, expulsion, exile, involuntary exile, ostracism; penal servitude, hard labor; galleys &c. 975; beating &c. *v.*; flagel-lation, fustigation, gantlet, strappado, estrapade, bastinado, *argumentum baculinum*, stick law, rap on the knuckles, box on the ear; blow &c. (*impulse*) 276; stripe, cuff, kick, buffet, pummel; slap, – in the face; wipe, douse; *coup de grâce;* torture, rack; picket, -ing; dragonnade; capital punishment; execu-tion; hanging &c. *v.*; electrocution, rail-riding, scarpines; de-capitation, -colla-tion; *garrot-te, -to;* crucifixion, impalement; martyrdom, *auto-da-fé; noyade;* hara-kiri, seppuku, happy dispatch.

V. punish; chast-ise, -en; castigate, correct, inflict punishment, administer correction, deal retributive justice; cowhide, lambaste *.

visit upon, pay; pay -, serve- out; do for; make short work of, give a lesson to, serve one right, make an example of; have a rod in pickle for; give it one.

strike &c. 276; deal a blow to, administer the lash, smite; slap, - the face; smack, cuff, box the ears, spank, thwack, thump, beat, lay on, swinge, buffet;

thresh, thrash, pummel, drub, leather, trounce, sandbag, baste, belabor; lace, – one's jacket; dress, give a dressing, trim, warm, wipe, tund †, cob, bang, strap, comb, lash, lick, larrup, wallop, whop †, flog, scourge, whip, birch, cane, give the stick, switch, flagellate, horsewhip, bastinado, towel, rub down with an oaken towel, rib roast, dust one's jacket, fustigate, pitch into, lay about one, beat black and blue; beat to a -mummy, – jelly; give a black eye.

tar and feather; pelt, stone, lapidate; masthead, keelhaul.

execute; bring to the -block, – gallows; behead; de-capitate, -collate; guillotine; hang, turn off, gibbet, bowstring, hang draw and quarter; shoot; decimate; burn; break on the wheel, crucify; em-, im-pale; flay; lynch; electrocute.

torture; put -on, – to- the rack; picket.

banish, exile, transport, expel, ostracize; rusticate; drum out; dis-miss, -bar, -bench; strike off the roll, unfrock; post.

suffer, – for, – punishment; be -flogged, – hanged &c.; come to the gallows, dance upon nothing, die in one's shoes; be rightly served.

Adj. punishing &c. *v.*; penal; puni-tory, -tive; inflictive, castigatory; punished &c. *v.*

Int. *à la lanterne!*

Phr. *culpam pœna premit comes* [Horace]; "eating the bitter bread of banishment" [*Richard II*]; *gravis ira regum est semper* [Seneca]; *sera tamen tacitis pœna venit pedibus* [Tibullus]; *suo sibi gladio hunc jugulo* [Terence].

973. Reward. — N. reward, recompense, remuneration, meed, guerdon, reguerdon †; price; indemni-ty, -fication; quittance; compensation; reparation, redress; retribution, reckoning, acknowledgment, requital, amends, sop; atonement; consideration, return, *quid pro quo*; salvage, perquisite; vail &c. (*donation*) 784; *douceur*, bribe; hush-, smart-money; blackmail; carcelage †; solatium.

allowance, salary, stipend, wages; pay, -ment; emolument; tribute; batta, shot, scot; premium, fee, honorarium; hire; dasturi, dustoori; mileage.

crown &c. (*decoration of honor*) 877.

V. re-ward, -compense, -pay, -quite; re-, munerate; compensate; fee; pay one's footing &c. (*pay*) 807; make amends, indemnify, atone; satisfy, acknowledge.

get for one's pains, reap the fruits of.

Adj. remunerat-ive, -ory; munerary, compensatory, retributive, reparatory.

Phr. *fideli certa merces; honor virtutis præmium* [Cicero]; *tibi seris tibi metis.*

974. Penalty. — N. penalty; retribution &c. (*punishment*) 972; pain, pains and penalties; weregild, wergild; *peine forte et dure;* penance &c. (*atonement*) 952; the devil to pay.

fine, mulct, amercement; forfeit, -ure; escheat, damages, deodand, sequestration, confiscation, premunire; doomage [U. S.].

V. fine, mulct, amerce, sconce, confiscate; sequest-rate, -er; escheat; estreat, forfeit.

975. [Instrument of punishment.] Scourge. — N. scourge, rod, cane, stick; ra-, rat-tan; birch, – rod; *azote*, blacksnake, bullwhack [U. S.], *chicote*, kurbash, quirt, rawhide, sjambok; rod in pickle; switch, ferule, cudgel, truncheon.

whip, lash, strap, thong, cowhide, knout; cat, – o' nine tails; rope's end.

pillory, stocks, whipping post; cuck-, duck-ing stool; brank; trebuchet, trebucket; triangle, wooden horse, maiden, thumbscrew, boot, rack, wheel, iron heel; treadmill, crank, galleys.

scaffold; block, ax, guillotine; stake; cross; gallows, gibbet, tree, drop, noose, rope, halter, bowstring; death -, electric- chair; *mecate.*

house of correction &c. (*prison*) 752.

gaol-, jail-er; executioner; electrocutioner; lyncher; hang-, heads-man; Jack Ketch.

Section V. RELIGIOUS AFFECTIONS

1. Superhuman Beings and Regions

976. Deity. — **N.** Deity, Divinity; God-head, -ship; Omnipotence, Providence.

[Quality of being divine] divin-eness, -ity.

God, Lord, Jehovah; The -Almighty, – Supreme Being, – First Cause; *Ens Entium;* Author –, Creator- of all things; Author of our being; Cosmoplast; El; The -Infinite, – Eternal; The All-powerful, -wise, -merciful, -holy.

[Attributes and perfections] infinite -power, – wisdom, – goodness, – justice, – truth, – mercy; omni-potence, -science, -presence; unity, immutability, holiness, glory, majesty, sovereignty, infinity, eternity.

The -Trinity, – Holy Trinity, – Trinity in Unity, – Triune God.

God the Father; The -Maker, – Creator, – Preserver.

[Functions] creation, preservation, divine government; The-ocracy, -archy; providence; ways –, dealings –, dispensations –, visitations- of Providence.

God the Son, Jesus, Christ; The -Messiah, – Anointed, – Saviour, – Redeemer, – Mediator, – Intercessor, – Advocate, – Judge; The Son of -God, – Man, –David; The Lamb of God, The Word; Logos; Em-, Im-manuel; The -King of Kings and Lord of Lords, – King of Glory, – Prince of Peace, – Good Shepherd, – Way, – Truth, – Life, – Bread of Life, – Light of the World; The -Lord our, – Sun of- Righteousness; " The Pilot of the Galilean lake " [Milton].

The -Incarnation, – Hypostatic Union.

[Functions] salvation, redemption, atonement, propitiation, mediation, intercession, judgment.

God the Holy Ghost, The Holy Spirit, Paraclete; The -Comforter, – Spirit of Truth, – Dove.

[Functions] inspiration, unction, regeneration, sanctification, consolation.

eon, æon, special providence, *deus ex machinâ;* avatar.

V. create, uphold, preserve, govern &c.

atone, redeem, save, propitiate, mediate &c.

predestinate, elect, call, ordain, bless, justify, sanctify, glorify &c.

Adj. almighty, holy, hallowed, sacred, divine, heavenly, celestial; sacrosanct; all-knowing, -seeing, -wise; omniscient.

super-human, -natural; ghostly, spiritual, hyperphysical, unearthly; theistic, -ocratic; anointed; soterial.

Adv. *jure divino,* by divine right.

Phr. *Domine dirige nos; en Dieu est ma fiance; et sceleratis sol oritur* [Seneca]; " He mounts the storm and walks upon the wind " [Pope]; " Thou great First Cause, least understood " [Pope]; *sans Dieu rien.*

---

977. [Beneficent spirits.] Angel. — **N.** angel, archangel; guardian angel; heavenly host, host of heaven, sons of God; seraph, -im; cherub, -im; ministering spirit, morning star; saint, Madonna; invisible helpers.

Adj. angelic, seraphic.

978. [Maleficent spirits.] Satan. — **N.** Satan, the Devil, Lucifer, Ahriman, Belial; Samael, Zamiel, Beelzebub, the Prince of the Devils.[1]

the tempter; the evil -one, – spirit; the Adversary; the archenemy; the -author of evil, – wicked one, – old Serpent; the Prince of -darkness, – this world, – the power of the air; the -foul, – arch- fiend; the devil incarnate; the -common enemy, – angel of the bottomless pit; Abaddon, Apollyon.

fallen angels, unclean spirits, devils; the -rulers, – powers- of darkness; inhabitants of Pandemonium; demon &c. 980.

---

[1] The slang expressions " the -deuce, – dickens, – old Gentleman; old -Nick, – Scratch, – Horny, – Harry, – Gooseberry," have not been inserted in the text.

diabolism; devil-ism, -ship; diabolology; satanism, manicheism; the cloven foot.

Adj. satanic, diabolic, devilish; infernal, hellborn.

Mythological and other fabulous Deities and Powers

979. Jupiter. — N. god, -dess; heathen gods and goddesses; deva; Jupiter, Jove &c.; pantheon.

Allah, Bathala, Brahm, Brahmă, Brahmā, cloud-compeller, Devi, Durga, Kali, oread, the Great Spirit, Ushas; water -, wood- nymph; Yama, Varuna, Zeus, Vishnu, Siva, Shiva, Krishna, Juggernath, Buddha; Isis, Osiris; Belus, Bel, Baal, Asteroth &c.; Thor, Odin; Mumbo Jumbo; good -, tutelary- genius; demiurge, familiar; sibyl; fairy, fay; sylph, -id; Ariel, peri, nymph, nereid, dryad, sea-maid, banshee, benshie, Ormuzd; Oberon, Mab, hamadryad, naiad, mermaid, kelpie, Ondine, nixie, sprite; denizens of the air; pixy &c. (*bad spirit*) 980.

mythology; heathen -, fairy- mythology; Lemprière, folklore.

Adj. fairy-, sylph-like; sylphic.

Phr. " you moonshine revelers and shades of night " [*Merry Wives*].

980. Demon. — N. demon, -ry, -ology; evil genius, fiend, familiar, dæva, devil; bad -, unclean- spirit; cacodemon, incubus, Frankenstein's monster, Eblis, *shaitan*, succubus and succuba, Titan, Shedim, Mephistopheles, Asmodeus, Moloch, Belial, Ahriman, fury, harpy; Friar Rush.

vampire, ghoul; afreet, barghest, Loki; ogre, -ss; gnome, gin, jinn, imp, deev, lamia; bo-gie, -gle; nis, kobold, flibbertigibbet, fairy, brownie, pixy, elf, dwarf, urchin, Puck, Robin Goodfellow; leprechaun, Cluricaune, troll, dwerger, sprite, ouphe, bad fairy, nix, nixie, pigwidgeon, will-o'-the-wisp.

[Supernatural appearance] ghost, revenant, specter, apparition, spirit, shade, shadow, vision; hob-, goblin; wraith, spook, boggart, banshee, *loup-garou*, lemures; evil eye.

mer-man, -maid, -folk; siren; satyr, faun; manit-o, -ou, -u.

Adj. supernatural, weird, uncanny, unearthly, spectral; ghost-ly, -like; elf-in, -ish, -like; fiend-ish, -like; impish, demoniacal; haunted; pokerish [U. S.].

981. Heaven. — N. heaven; kingdom of -heaven, - God; heavenly kingdom; throne -, presence- of God; inheritance of the saints in light.

Paradise, Eden, Zion, abode of the blessed; celestial bliss, glory.

[Mythological -heaven] Olympus; [- paradise] Elysium, Elysian fields, Arcadia, bowers of bliss, garden of the Hesperides, third heaven; Val-, Walhalla (Scandinavian); Nirvana (Buddhist); happy hunting grounds; *Alfardaws, Assama; Falak al aflak* " the highest heaven " (Mohammedan).

future state, eternal home, resurrection, translation; resuscitation &c. 660; apotheosis, deification.

Adj. heavenly, celestial, supernal, unearthly, from on high, paradisiacal, beatific, elysian.

Phr. " looks through nature up to nature's god " [Pope]; " the great world's altarstairs, that slope through darkness up to God " [Tennyson]; " the treasury o. everlasting joy " [*Henry VI*]; *vigeur de dessus.*

982. Hell. — N. hell, bottomless pit, place of torment; habitation of fallen angels; Pandemonium, Abaddon, Domdaniel; *jahannan*, sheol.

hell fire; everlasting -fire, - torment; lake of fire and brimstone; fire that is never quenched, worm that never dies.

purgatory, limbo, gehenna, abyss.

[Mythological hell] Tartarus, Hades, Avernus, Styx, Stygian creek, pit of Acheron, Cocytus; infernal regions, inferno, shades below, realms of Pluto.

Pluto, Rhadamanthus, Erebus; Tophet.

Adj. hellish, infernal, stygian.

Phr. *dies iræ dies illa;* " the hue of dungeons and the scowl of night " [*Love's Labor's Lost*].

2. Religious Doctrines

983. [Religious Knowledge.] **Theology. — N.** theology (natural and revealed); theo-gony, -sophy; divinity; hagio-logy, -graphy; Caucasian mystery; monotheism; religion; religious -persuasion, – sect, – denomination; creed &c. (belief) 484; articles –, declaration –, profession –, confession- of faith.

theolog-ue, -ian; scholastic, divine, schoolman, canonist, theologist; the Fathers.

Adj. theological, religious; denominational; sectarian &c. 984.

983a. Orthodoxy. — N. orthodoxy; strictness, soundness, religious truth, true faith; truth &c. 494; soundness of doctrine.

Christian-ity, -ism; Catholic-ism, -ity; "the faith once delivered to the saints"; hyperorthodoxy &c. 984; iconoclasm.

the Church; Catholic –, Universal –, Apostolic –, Established- Church; temple of the Holy Ghost; Church –, body –, members –, disciples –, followers- of Christ; Christian, – community; true believer; canonist &c. (theologian) 983; Christendom, collective body of Christians.

canons &c. (belief) 484; thirty-nine articles; Apostles' –, Nicene –, Athanasian- Creed; Church Catechism; textuary.

Adj. orthodox, sound, strict, faithful, catholic, schismless, Christian, evangelical, scriptural, divine, monotheistic; true &c. 494.

Phr. of the true faith.

984. Heterodoxy. [Sectarianism.] — **N.** heterodoxy; error &c. 495; false doctrine, heresy, schism; schismatic-ism, -alness; recusancy, backsliding, apostasy; atheism &c. (irreligion) 989.

bigotry &c. (obstinacy) 606; fanaticism, iconoclasm; hyperorthodoxy, precisianism, bibliolatry, sabbatarianism, puritanism; anthropomorphism; idolatry &c. 991; superstition &c. (credulity) 486; dissent &c. 489.

sectar-ism, -ianism; nonconformity; secularism; syncretism, religious sects.

protestant-, Arian-, Advent-, Jansen-, Stund-, Erastian-, Calvin-, quaker-, method-, anabapt-, Pusey-, tractarian-, ritual-, Origen-, Sabellian-, Socinian-, De-, The-, material-, positiv-, latitudinarian-ism &c.

High –, Low –, Broad –, Free- Church; ultramontanism; pap-ism, -istry; monkery; papacy; Anglican-, Catholic-, Roman-ism; popery, Scarlet Lady, Church of Rome, Greek Church.

pagan-, heathen-, ethic-ism; mythology; poly-, di-, tri-, pan-theism; dualism; heathendom.

Juda-, Gentil-, Islam-, Mohammedan-, Bab-, Sufi-, Neoplaton-, Turc-, Brahmin-, Hindu-, Buddh-, Sabian-, Gnostic-, Hylothe-, Mormon-ism; Christian Science.

heretic, antichrist; pagan, heathen; pai-, pay-nim; giaour; gentile; pan-, poly-theist; idolator.

bigot &c. (obstinacy) 606; fanatic, abdal, iconoclast.

latitudinarian, Deist, Theist, Unitarian; positivist, materialist; Homoiousian, Homoousian, limitarian, theosophist, ubiquitarian; skeptic &c. 989.

schismatic; sectar-y, -ian, -ist; seceder, separatist, recusant, dissenter; non-conformist, -juror; Huguenot, Protestant; orthodox dissenter, Congregationalist, Independent; Episcopalian, Presbyterian; Lutheran, Calvinist, Methodist, Wesleyan; Ana-, Baptist; Mormon, Latter-day Saint, Irvingite, Sandemanian, Glassite, Erastian; Sub-, Supra-lapsarian; Gentoo, Antinomian, Swedenborgian; Adventist, Bible Christian, Bryanite, Brownian, Christian Scientist, Dunker, Ebionite, Eusebian; Faith Cur-er, -ist; Familist, Jovinianist, Libadist, Quaker, Restitutionist, Shaker, Stundist, Tunker &c.

Catholic, Roman Catholic, Romanist, ultramontane; Anglican, Oxford School; tractarian, Puseyite, ritualist; Puritan.

Jew, Hebrew, Rabbinist, Rabbist; Babist, Motazilite, Shiah, Sunni, Wahabi, Mohammedan, Mussulman, Moslem, Osmanli; Brahm-in, -an; Parsee, Sufi,

Buddhist; Magi, Gymnosophist, fire worshiper, Sabian, Gnostic, Sadducee, Rosicrucian &c.

Adj. heterodox, heretical; un-orthodox, -scriptural, -canonical; anti-scriptural, apocryphal; un-, anti-christian; schismatic, recusant, iconoclastic; sectarian; dis-senting, -sident; secular &c. (*lay*) 997.

pagan; heathen, -ish; ethnic, -al; gentile, paynim; pan-, poly-theistic.

Judaical, Mohammedan, Brahminical, Buddhist &c. *n.*; Romish, Protestant &c. *n.*

bigoted &c. (*prejudiced*) 481, (*obstinate*) 606; superstitious &c. (*credulous*) 486; fanatical; idolatrous &c. 991; visionary &c. (*imaginative*) 515.

Phr. " slave to no sect " [Pope]; *superstitione tollendâ religio non tollitur* [Cicero].

985. Revelation. — N. revelation, inspiration, *afflatus;* theophany, theopneusty.

Word, – of God; Scripture; the -Scriptures, – Bible; Holy -Writ, – Scriptures; inspired writings, Gospel.

Old Testament, Septuagint, Vulgate, Pentateuch; Octateuch; the -Law, – Jewish Law, – Prophets; major –, minor-Prophets; Hagio-grapha, -logy; Hierographa; Apocrypha.

New Testament; Gospels, Evangelists, Acts, Epistles, Apocalypse, Revelations.

Talmud; Mishna, Masorah.

prophet &c. (*seer*) 513; evangelist, apostle, disciple, saint; the –, the Apostolical- Fathers; Holy Men of old, inspired penmen.

Adj. scriptural, biblical, sacred, prophetic; evangel-ical, -istic; apostolic, -al; inspired, theopneustic, theopneusted, apocalyptic, ecclesiastical, canonical, textuary.

986. Pseudo-Revelation. — N. the -Koran, – Alcoran; Ly-king, Vedas, Zendavesta, Avesta, Sastra, Shastra, Tantra, Upanishads, Purana, Edda; Book of Mormon.

[Non-Biblical prophets and religious founders] Gautama, Buddha; Zoroaster, Confucius, Bab-ed-Din, Mohammed.

[Idols] golden calf &c. 991; Baal, Moloch, Dagon.

3. Religious Sentiments

987. Piety. — N. piety, religion, theism, faith; religiousness, holiness &c. *adj.*; saintship; religionism; sanctimony &c. (*assumed piety*) 988; reverence &c. (*respect*) 928; humility, veneration, devotion; prostration &c. (*worship*) 990; grace, unction, edification; sancti-ty, -tude; consecration.

spiritual existence, odor of sanctity, beauty of holiness.

theopathy, beatification, adoption, regeneration, conversion, justification, sanctification, salvation, inspiration, bread of life; Body and Blood of Christ.

believer, convert, theist, Christian, devotee, pietist; the -good, – righteous, – just, – believing, – elect; Saint, Madonna, *Notre Dame*, Our Lady.

the children of -God, – the kingdom, – light.

V. be -pious &c. *adj.*; have -faith &c. *n.*; believe, receive Christ; revere &c. 928; be -converted &c.

988. Impiety. — N. impiety; sin &c. 945; irreverence; profan-eness &c. *adj.*, -ity, -ation; blasphemy, desecration, sacrilege; scoffing &c. *v.*

[Assumed piety] hypocrisy &c. (*falsehood*) 544; pietism, cant, pious fraud; lip-devotion, -service, -reverence; mis-devotion, formalism, austerity; sancti-mon-y, -iousness &c. *adj.*; pharisaism, precisianism; sabbat-ism, -arianism; *odium theologicum*, sacerdotalism; bigo-try &c. (*obstinacy*) 606, (*prejudice*) 481; blue laws.

hardening, backsliding, declension, perversion, reprobation.

sinner &c. 949; scoffer, blasphemer, sacrilegist; sabbath breaker; worldling; hypocrite &c. (*dissembler*) 548; Tartufe, Mawworm.

bigot; saint [ironically]; Pharisee, sabbatarian, formalist, methodist, puritan, pietist, precisian, religionist, devotee, ranter, fanatic; *juramentado*.

convert, edify, sanctify, keep holy, beatify, regenerate, inspire, consecate, enshrine.

Adj. pious, religious, devout, devoted, reverent, godly, heavenly-minded, humble, pure, holy, spiritual, pietistic; saintly, -like; seraphic, sacred, solemn.

believing, faithful, Christian, Catholic.

elected, adopted, justified, sanctified, regenerated, inspired, consecrated, converted, unearthly, not of the earth.

Phr. *ne vile fano;* "pure-eyed Faith . . . thou hovering angel girt with golden wings" [Milton].

the -wicked, – evil, – unjust, – reprobate; sons of -men, – Belial, – the wicked one; children of darkness.

V. be -impious &c. *adj.*; profane, desecrate, blaspheme, revile, scoff; swear &c. (*malediction*) 908; commit sacrilege.

snuffle; turn up the whites of the eyes; idolize.

Adj. impious; irreligious &c. 989; desecrating &c. *v.*; profane, irreverent, sacrilegious, blasphemous.

· un-hallowed, -sanctified, -regenerate; hardened, perverted, reprobate.

hypocritical &c. (*false*) 544; canting, pietistical, sanctimonious, unctuous, pharisaical, overrighteous, righteous over much.

bigoted, fanatical; priest-ridden.

Adv. under the -mask, – cloak, – pretense, – form, -guise- of religion.

Phr. *giovane santo diavolo vecchio.*

989. Irreligion. — N. irreligion, indevotion; ungodliness &c. *adj.*; laxity, quietism.

skepticism, doubt; un-, dis-belief; incredul-ity, -ousness &c. *adj.*; want of -faith, – belief; pyrrhonism; doubt &c. 485; agnosticism.

atheism, deism; hylotheism; materialism; positivism; nihilism.

infidelity, freethinking, antichristianity, rationalism; neology.

atheist, skeptic, unbeliever, deist, infidel, pyrrhonist; *giaour*, heathen, alien, gentile, Nazarene; *esprit fort*, freethinker, latitudinarian, rationalist; materialist, positivist, nihilist, agnostic, somatist, theophobist.

V. be -irreligious &c. *adj.*; disbelieve, lack faith; doubt, question &c. 485. dechristianize.

Adj. irreligious; in-, un-devout; devout-, god-, grace-less; un-godly, -holy, -sanctified, -hallowed; atheistic, without God.

skeptical, freethinking; un-believing, -converted; incredulous, faithless, lacking faith; deistical; un-, anti-christian.

worldly, mundane, earthly, carnal; worldly &c.- minded.

Adv. irreligiously &c.- *adj.*

4. Acts of Religion

990. Worship. — N. worship, adoration, devotion, aspiration, homage, service, humiliation; kneeling, genuflection, prostration.

prayer, invocation, supplication, rogation, intercession, orison, holy breathing; petition &c. (*request*) 765; collect, litany, Lord's prayer, paternoster; beadroll; latria, dulia, hyperdulia, vigils; revival; cult; anxious - camp- meeting; ebenezer, virginal.

thanksgiving; giving –, returning- thanks; grace, praise, glorification, benediction, doxology, hosanna; h-, allelujah; *Te Deum, non nobis Domine, nunc dimittis;* pæan; *benschen; Ave Maria, O Salutaris,* Sanctus, The Annunciation, Tersanctus, Trisagion.

psalm, -ody; hymn, plain song, chant, chaunt, response, anthem, motet; antiphon, -y.

oblation, sacrifice, incense, libation; burnt –, heave –, votive- offering; offertory.

discipline; self-discipline, -examination, -denial; fasting.

divine service, office, duty; exercises; morning prayer; mass, matins, evensong, vespers; undernsong, tierce; holyday &c. (*rites*) 998.

worshiper, congregation, communicant, celebrant.

V. worship, lift up the heart, aspire; revere &c. 928; adore, do service, pay homage; humble oneself, kneel; bow –, bend- the knee; fall -down, – on one's knees; prostrate oneself, bow down and worship.

pray, invoke, supplicate; put –, offer- up -prayers, – petitions; beseech &c. (*ask*) 765; say one's prayers, tell one's beads.

return –, give- thanks; say grace, bless, praise, laud, glorify, magnify, sing praises; give benediction, lead the choir, intone; deacon, -off [U. S.].

propitiate, offer sacrifice, fast, deny oneself; vow, offer vows, give alms.

work out one's salvation; go to church; attend -service, – mass; communicate &c. (*rite*) 998.

Adj. worshiping &c. *v.*; devout, devotional, reverent, pure, solemn; fervid &c. (*heartfelt*) 821.

Int. h-, allelujah! hosanna! glory be to God! O Lord! pray God that! God -grant, – bless, – save, – forbid! *sursum corda.*

Phr. "making their lives a prayer" [Whitter]; *ora et labora;* "prayers ardent open heaven" [Young].

991. Idolatry. — N. idol-atry, -ism; demon-ism -olatry; idol –, demon –, devil –, fire- worship; zoölatry, fetichism; ecclesi-, heli-, hier-, Mari-, Bibliolatry.

deification, apotheosis, canonization; hero worship.

sacrifices, hecatomb, holocaust; human sacrifices, immolation, mactation, infanticide, self-immolation, suttee.

idol, golden calf, graven image, fetich, avatar, Juggernath, *lares et penates;* Baal &c. 986.

V. worship -idols, – pictures, – relics; deify, canonize.

Adj. idolatrous.

Phr. *adorer le veau d'or.*

992. Sorcery. — N. sorcery; occult -art, – sciences; magic, the black art, necromancy, theurgy, thaumaturgy; demon-ology, -omy, -ship; diablerie, bedevilment; witch-craft, -ery; glamor; fetic-hism, -ism; ghost dance, hoodoo; obi, -ism; voodoo, -ism; Shamanism [Esquimaux], vampirism; conjuration; bewitchery, exorcism, enchantment, mysticism, second sight, mesmerism, animal magnetism; od –, odylic- force; electrobiology, clairvoyance; spiritualism, spirit rapping, table turning.

divination &c. (*prediction*) 511; sortilege, ordeal, *sortes Virgilianæ;* hocuspocus &c. (*deception*) 545.

V. practice -sorcery &c. *n.*; cast a nativity, conjure, exorcise, charm, enchant; be-witch, -devil; hoodoo, voodoo; entrance, mesmerize, magnetize; fascinate &c. (*influence*) 615; taboo; wave a wand; rub the -ring, – lamp; cast a spell; call up spirits, – from the vasty deep; raise spirits from the dead.

Adj. magic, -al; mystic, weird, cabalistic, talismanic, phylacteric, incantatory; charmed &c. *v.*; Circean, odyllic, voodoo.

993. Spell. — N. spell, charm, incantation, exorcism, weird, cabala, exsufflation †, cantrap, runes, abracadabra, open sesame, countercharm, Ephesian letters, bell book and candle, Mumbo Jumbo, evil eye, fee-faw-fum.

talisman, amulet, periapt, telesm, phylactery, philter; fetich, fetish; *agnus Dei;* furcula, madstone; mascot, -te; merrythought; Om, Aum; scarab, -æus; sudarium, triskelion, veronica, wishbone; swastika, fylfot, gammadion.

wand, caduceus, rod, divining rod, lamp of Aladdin; wishing –, Fortunatus's-cap.

994. Sorcerer. — N. sorcerer, magician; thaumat-, the-urgist; conjuror, necromancer, seer, wizard, witch; hoodoo, voodoo; fairy &c. 980; lamia, hag

warlock, charmer, exorcist, mage; cunning –, medicine- man; Shaman, figure flinger, ecstatica, medium, clairvoyant, mesmerist; *deus ex machinâ;* sooth-sayer &c. 513.

Katerfelto, Cagliostro, Mesmer, Rosicrucian; Circe, siren, weird sisters.

5. RELIGIOUS INSTITUTIONS

995. Churchdom. — N. church, -dom; ministry, apostleship, priesthood, prelacy, hierarchy, church government, christendom, pale of the church.

clerical-, sacerdotal-, episcopalian-, ultramontan-ism; theocracy; ecclesi-olog-y, -ist; priestcraft, *odium theologicum.*

monach-ism, -y; monasticism, monkhood.

[Ecclesiastical offices and dignities] pontificate, primacy, archbishopric, archiepiscopacy; prelacy; bishop-ric, -dom; episcop-ate, -acy; see, diocese; deanery, stall; canon-ry, -icate; prebend, -aryship; benefice, incumbency, glebe, advowson, living, cure; rectorship; vicar-iate, -ship; deacon-ry, -ship; curacy; chaplain, -cy, -ship; cardinal-âte, -ship; abbacy, presbytery.

holy orders, ordination, institution, consecration, induction, reading in, pre-ferment, translation, presentation.

popedom; the -Vatican, – apostolic see; religious sects &c. 984.

council &c. 696; conclave, convocation, synod, consistory, chapter, vestry; sanhedrim, *congé d'élire;* ecclesiastical courts, consistorial court, court of Arches.

V. call, ordain, induct, prefer, translate, consecrate, present.

take -orders, – the veil, – vows.

Adj. ecclesi-astical, -ological; clerical, sacerdotal, priestly, prelatical, pas-toral, ministerial, capitular; theocratic; hierarchical, archiepiscopal; episcopal, -ian; canonical; mon-astic, -achal; monkish; abbati-al, -cal; Anglican; pontif-ical, papal, apostolic; ultramontane, priest-ridden.

996. Clergy. — N. clergy, clericals, ministry, priesthood, presbytery, the cloth, the desk.

clergyman, divine, ecclesiastic, church-man, priest, presbyter, hierophant, pas-tor, shepherd, minister; father, – in Christ; padre, *abbé, curé;* patriarch; reverend; black coat; confessor.

dignitaries of the church; ecclesi-, hier-arch; ebdomarius; eminence, rever-

997. Laity. — N. laity, flock, fold, congregation, assembly, brethren, peo-ple; society [U. S.].

temporality, secularization.

layman, civilian; parishioner, cate-chumen; secularist.

V. secularize.

Adj. secular, lay, laical, civil, tempo-ral, profane.

ence, elder, primate, metropolitan, archbishop, bishop, prelate, diocesan, suf-fragan, dean, subdean, archdeacon, prebendary, canon, rural dean, rector, parson, vicar, perpetual curate, residentiary, beneficiary, incumbent, chap-lain, curate; deacon, -ess; preacher, reader, lecturer; capitular; missionary, propagandist, Jesuit, revivalist, field preacher.

churchwarden, sidesman; clerk, precentor, choir; almoner, *suisse,* verger, beadle, sexton, sacristan; acol-yth, -othyst, -yte; chorister.

[Roman Catholic priesthood] Pope, *Papa,* pontiff, high priest, cardinal; ancient –, flamen; confessor, penitentiary; spiritual director.

cenobite, conventual, abbot, prior, monk, friar, lay brother, beadsman, mendicant, pilgrim, palmer; canon-regular, -secular; Franciscan, Friars mi-nor, Minorites; Observant, Capuchin, Dominican, Carmelite; Augustinian; Gilbertine; Austin-, Black-, White-, Gray-, Crossed-, Crutched-Friars; Bon-homme, Carthusian, Benedictine, Cistercian, Trappist, Cluniac, Premon-stratensian, Maturine; Templar, Hospitaler; Bernardine, Lorettine, pillarist, stylite.

abb-, prior-, canon-ess; *religieuse,* nun, novice, postulant.

[Under the Jewish dispensation] prophet, priest, high priest, Levite; Rabbi, -n; scribe.

[Mohammedan &c.] mullah, ulema, imaum, sheik; sufi; *kahin, kassis;* mufti, hadji, muezzin, dervish; fa-kir, -quir; brahmin, guru, kaziaskier, poonghie, sanyasi; druid, bonze, santon, abdal, Lama, talapoin, caloyer.

V. take orders &c. 995.

Adj. the -, the very -, the Right- Reverend; ordained, in orders, called to the ministry.

998. Rite. — N. rite; ceremon-y, -ial; ordinance, observance, function, duty; form, -ulary; solemnity, sacrament; incantation &c. (*spell*) 993; service, psalmody &c. (*worship*) 990.

ministration; preach-ing, -ment; predication, sermon, homily, lecture, discourse, pastoral.

baptism, christening, chrism; circumcision; baptismal regeneration; font.

confirmation; imposition -, laying on- of hands; ordination &c. (*churchdom*) 995; excommunication.

Eucharist, Lord's supper, communion; the -, the holy- sacrament; celebration, high celebration; *missa cantata; asperges;* offertory; introit; consecration; con-, tran-substantiation; real presence; elements; mass; high -, low -, drymass.

matrimony &c. 903; burial &c. 363; visitation of the sick.

seven sacraments, impanation, subpanation, extreme unction, viaticum, invocation of saints, canonization, transfiguration, auricular confession; maceration, flagellation, sackcloth and ashes; penance &c. (*atonement*) 952; telling of beads, processional; thurification, incense, holy water, aspersion.

relics, rosary, beads, reliquary, host, cross, rood, crucifix, pax, pix, pyx, *agnus Dei*, censer, thurible, patera; eileton, Holy Grail; prayer-machine, -wheel; Sangraal, urceus.

ritual, rubric, canon, ordinal; liturgy, prayer book, book of common prayer, pietas, euchology, litany, lectionary; missal, breviary, mass book, beadroll; farse.

psalter; psalm -, hymn- book; hymn-al, -ology.

ritual-, ceremonial-ism; sabbat-ism, -arianism; ritualist, sabbatarian.

holyday, feast, fast; Sabbath, Passover, Pentecost; Advent, Christmas, Epiphany, Lent; Passion -, Holy- week; Easter, Whitsuntide; agape, Ascension Day, Candlemas, Good Friday, Holy Thursday; Lam-, Martin-, Michael-mas; Rama-dan, -zan; Bairam &c., &c.

V. perform service, do duty, minister, officiate, baptize, dip, sprinkle; confirm, lay hands on; give -, administer -, take -, receive -, attend -, partake of- the -sacrament, - communion; communicate; administer -, receive- extreme unction; anele.

excommunicate, ban with bell book and candle.

preach, sermonize, predicate, lecture.

Adj. ritual, -istic; ceremonial; baptismal, eucharistical; paschal.

Phr. " what art thou, thou idol ceremony ? " [*Henry V*].

999. Canonicals. — N. canonicals, vestments; robe, gown, Geneva gown frock, pallium, surplice, cassock, dalmatic, scapulary, cope, mozetta, scarf, tunicle, chasuble, alb, alba, stole; fan-on, -nel; tonsure, cowl, hood; calo-te, -tte; bands; capouch, amice; vagas, vakas, vakass; apron, lawn sleeves, pontificals, pall; miter, tiara, triple crown; shovel -, cardinal's- hat; biretta; crosier; pastoral staff, thurifer; costume &c. 225.

1000. Temple. — N. place of worship; house of -God, - prayer.

temple, cathedral, minster, church, kirk, chapel, meetinghouse, bethel, tabernacle, conventicle, basilica, fane, holy place, chantry, oratory.

synagogue; mosque; marabout; pantheon; pagoda; joss house; dagobah, tope; kiosk; kiack, masjid.

parsonage, rectory, vicarage, manse, deanery, glebe; Vatican; bishop's palace; Lambeth.

altar, shrine, sanctuary, Holy of Holies, *sanctum sanctorum*, sacristy; sacrarium; communion –, holy –, Lord's– table; table of the Lord; pyx; baptistery, font; piscina, stoup; aumbry; sedile; reredos; rood -loft, – screen.

chancel, quire, choir, nave, aisle, transept, vestry, crypt, cloisters, churchyard, golgotha, calvary, Easter sepulcher; stall, pew; pulpit, ambo, lectern, reading desk, confessional, prothesis, credence, baldachin, *baldacchino;* apse, belfry; chapter house; presbytery; anxious-bench, -seat; *diaconicum,* jube; mourners'-bench, -seat.

monastery, priory, abbey, friary, convent, nunnery, cloister.

Adj. claustral, cloistered; monast-ic, -erial; conventual.

Phr. *ne vile fano;* " there's nothing ill can dwell in such a temple " [*Tempest*].

INDEX

INDEX

N. B. The numbers refer to the headings under which the words or phrases occur. When the same word or phrase may be used in various senses, the several headings under which it, or its synonyms, will be found, according to those meanings, are indicated by the words printed in *Italics*. These words in Italics are not intended to explain the meaning of the word or phrase to which they are annexed, but only to assist in the required reference.

When a number or word of reference is placed within parentheses, the actual word or phrase will not be found under the heading referred to, although it may sometimes be useful to consult the category thus indicated.

When the word given in the Index is itself the title or heading of a category, the number of reference is printed in bold-face type, thus: **abode 189.**

nearly 32
near 197
around 227
- it and about it 573
- to 121
- to be 152
be - *busy with* 625
 active 682
beat - 629
come - 658
get - *public* 531
 recover 660
go - *turn* 311
going - *news* 532
not know what one
 is - 699
put -
 turn round 283
round - 311
send - one's business
 756
set - 676
turn - *invert* 218
what it is - 454
what one is - 625
above 206
- all *superior* 33
 important 642
- board
 manifest 525
 artless 703
 fair 939
- comprehension 519
- ground
 alive 359
- par *great* 31
 good 648
- praise 944
- price 814
- stairs 206
- suspicion 946
- the mark 33
- water *safe* 664
above-mentioned
 preceding 62
 repeated 104
 prior 116
a bovi majori discit
 537, 673
abra 198
abracadabra 993
Abraham,
 sham - 544
abrasion
 paring 38
 filing 330, 331
abreast 236
abregé 596
abreption 789
abri, tente d' - 233
abridge *lessen* 36
 shorten 201
 - *in writing* 572, 596
abridger 201
abridgment
 compendium 596
abroach 673
abroad
 extraneous 57
 distant 196
 uncertain 475

get - *public* 531
abrogation 756
abrupt *sudden* 113
 violent 173
 steep 217
 unexpected 508
 style 579
abruption 44
abscess 655
abscind 44
abscissa 466
abscission
 retrenchment 38
 division 44
abscond 623
absence
 nonpresence **187**
 - d'esprit 452
 - of choice 609a
 - of influence 175a
 - of intellect 450a
 - of mind 458
 - of motive 615a
absens hæres non
 erit 505
absentee 187
absent-minded 458
absento nemo ne
 nocuisse velit 187
absinthe 435
absolute
 not relative **1**
 great 31
 complete 52
 certain 474
 affirmative 535
 authoritative 737
 severe 739
 free 748
 unalienable 924
 - establishment 478
 - interest
  property 980
 make -
  confirm 467
  adjudge 480
Absolute, the 450
absolution 918
absolutism 739
absolve
 liberate 750
 forgive 918
 exempt 927a
 shrive 952
 acquit 970
absonant
 discordant 414
 unreasonable 477
absorb *combine* 48
 take in 296
 consume 677
 - the mind
  attention 457
  inattention 458
 - the soul 824
absorbing
 exigent 630
 impressive 821
absorption 296
absquatulate 623
abstain

refrain 623
disuse 678
temperance 953
- from action 681
- from voting 609a
abstainer 953, 958
abstemious 953
abstention 623
absterge 652
abstersive 662
abstinence [*see* ab-
 stain]
 total - 953, 955
abstract
 separate 44
 abridge 596
 take 789
 steal 791
 - idea 453
 - oneself
  inattention 458
 - thought 451
  attention 457
 in the - *apart* 44
 alone 87
abstracted
 inattentive 458
abstruse 519
absurdity
 impossible 471
 nonsense **497**
 ridiculous 853
absurd statement
 546
Abuna 745
abundance
 poor in - 832
abundant *great* 31
 enough 639
abundanti cautelâ,
 ex - 664
abuse *deceive* 545
 illtreat 649
 misuse 679
 malediction 908
 threat 909
 upbraid 932
 violate 961
 - of language 563
 - of terms 523
abusive
 uncourteous 895
 defamatory 934, 936
abut *touch* 199
 rest on 215
abutment
 defense 717
abutter 199
aby *remain* 141
 endure 821, 826
abysm 198
abysmal *deep* 208
abyss *space* 180
 interval 198
 hell 982
A. C. 106
academic
 theory 514
 teaching 537, 542
academical
 style 578

academician 492
 Royal - 559
academy 542
acanthus 847
a capite ad calcem
 52
acariâtre 901
acarpous 169
acatalectic 597
accede *assent* 488
 consent 762
accelerate
 early 132
 stimulate 173
 velocity 274
 hasten 684
accension 384
accent *sound* 402
 tone of voice 580
 rhythm 597
accentuate 642
accentuation 580
accept *assent* 488
 consent 762
 receive 785
 take 789
accepta 810
acceptable
 expedient 646
 agreeable 829
acceptance
 security 771
acceptation
 interpretation 522
acception 522
access
 approach 286
 easy of - 705
 means of - 627
accessible
 possible 470
 easy 705
accession
 increase 35
 addition 37
 - to *office* 737, 755
 consent 762
accessory
 additive 37
 adjunct 39
 accompanying 88
 aid 707
 auxiliary 711
acciaccatura 413
accidence 567
accident *event* 151
 chance 156
 disaster 619
 misfortune 735
 - of an accident 15
 -s by flood and fi
  619
 fatal - 361
accidental
 extrinsic 6
 fortuitous 156
 undesigned 621
accidents
 trust to the chap
  of - 621
accipient 785

accipitres 739
acclamation
  assent 488
  approbation 931
acclimatize
  domesticate 370
  inure 613
acclivity 217
accloy 641
accolade 894
accommodate
  suit 23
  adjust 27
  aid 707
  reconcile 723
  give 784
  lend 787
  - oneself to
  conform 82
accommodating
  kind 906
accommodation
  train 272
accompaniment
  adjunct 39
  coexistence **88**
  musical 415
accompanist 416
accompany
  add 37
  coexist 88
  concur 120
  music 416
accompli, fait - 729
accomplice 711
accomplish
  execute 161
  complete 729
  succeed 731
accomplishment
  learning 490
  talent 698
accompts 811
accord
  uniform 16
  agree 23
  music 413
  assent 488
  concord 714
  grant 760
  give 784
  of one's own - 602
accordance 23
according
  - as *qualification* 469
  - to *evidence* 467
  - to circumstances 8
  - to Gunter 82
  - to law 963
  - to rule
  conformably 82
accordingly
  logically 476
accordion 417
accordionist 416
accost 586
accouchement 161
accoucheur
  minister 631
  doctor 662
accoucheuse 662

account *list* 86
  adjudge 480
  description 594
  credit 805
  money - 811
  fame 873
  approbation 931
  - as *deem* 484
  - for
  attribution 155
  interpret 522
  - with *trade* 794
  pay 807
  call to -
  censure 932
  find one's - in
  useful 644
  success 731
  make no - of
  undervalue 483
  despise 930
  not - for
  unintelligible 519
  on - of
  cause 155
  motive 615
  behalf 707
  on no - 536
  send to one's -
  kill 361
  small - 643
  take into -
  attend to 457
  qualify 469
  to one's -
  property 780
  turn to -
  improve 658
  use 677
  success 731
  gain 775
accountable
  debit 811
  duty 926
accountant
  treasurer 801
  auditor 811
  - general 801
accounting 811
accounts 811
accouple 43
accouterment
  dress 225
  appliance 633
  equipment 673
accoy 174
accredit
  commission 755, 759
  money 805
  honor 873
accredited
  believed 484
  recognized 613
  - to 755, 759
accretion
  increase 35
  coherence 46
accrimination 938
accroach 789
accrue *add* 37
  result 154

  acquire 775
  be received 785, 810
accrust 323
accubation 213
accueil 894
accultural 658
accumbent 213
accumulate
  collect 72
  store 636
  redundance 641
accurate 494
  - knowledge 490
accurse 908
accursed
  disastrous 649
  undone 828
  vicious 945
accusation 938
accuse
  disapprove 932
  charge 938
  lawsuit 969
accustom
  habit 613
ace *small quantity* 32
  unit 87
  cards 840
  within an - 197
aceite 356
aceldama *kill* 361
  arena 728
acephalous 59
acequiador 350
acerb 397
acerbate
  embitter 659
  aggravate 835
acerbic 955
acerbity
  acrimony 395
  rudeness 895
  spleen 900, 901
  malevolence 907
acervate 72
acervatim 72, 102, 641
acetic 397
  - acid 397
acetous 397
achar 393
acharné 900
Achates, fidus -
  friend 890
  faithful 939
ache *physical* 378
  mental 828
Acheron
  pit of - 982
Acherontis pabulum
  949
achievable 470
achieve *end* 67
  produce 161
  do 680
  accomplish 729
achievement
  sign 551
  feat 861
Achillean 664, 900
Achilles
  - absent 187

  heel of -
  vulnerable 665
achromatism 429
acicular 253
acid 397
acidify 397
acierta errando 621, 701
aciform 253
acinaciform 253
acknowledge
  answer 462
  assent 488
  disclose 529
  avow 535
  consent 762
  observe 772
  pay 807
  thank 916
  repent 950
  reward 973
  - the corn 529
acknowledged
  custom 613
acme 210
  - of perfection 650
acology 662
acolyte 996
acomia 846
à compte 805
aconite 663
acoustic 418
  - organs 418
acoustics 402
à couvert 528, 664
acquaint
  - oneself with 539
  - with 527
acquaintance
  knowledge 490
  information 527
  friend 890
  make - with 888
acquest 780
acquiesce
  assent 488
  willing 488
  consent 762
  tolerate 826
acquiescence 488, 772
acquire
  develop 161
  get 775
  receive 785
  - a habit 613
  - learning 539
acquirement
  knowledge 490
  learning 539
  talent 698
  receipt 810
acquisition
  knowledge 490
  gain **775**
acquit
  liberate 750
  accounts 811
  exempt 927a
  vindicate 937
  innocent 946
  absolve 970

affected 583
- manner 880
affected with
 feeling 821
 disease 655
affectibility 822
affecting
 pathetic 830
affection *feeling* 821
 love 897
affections 820
affettuoso
 music 415
affiance *promise* 768
 trust 858
affianced *love* 897
 marriage 903
affiche 531
affidation 769
affidavit
 affirmation 535
 record 551
 lawsuit 969
affiliation
 relation 9
 kindred 11
 attribution 155
affinity *relation* 9
 similarity 17
affirmation
 assert **535**
 assent 488
affix *add* 37
 sequel 39
 fasten 43
 letter 561
afflation 349
afflatus *wind* 349
 inspiration 985
afflict 830
- with illness 655
affliction *pain* 828
 infliction 830
 adversity 735
affluence
 sufficiency 639
 prosperity 734
 wealth 803
affluent *river* 348
afflux 286
afford *supply* 784
 wealth 803
 yield 810
 sell for 812
- aid &c. 707
affranchise
 make free of 748
 liberate 750
affray 720
affriction 331
affright 860
affront *molest* 830
 provocation 900
 insult 929
- danger 861
affuse 337
affusion 73
afield 186
afire 382
afloat *extant* 1
 unstable 149

going on 151
ship 273
navigation 267
ocean 341
news 532
preparing 673
keep oneself - 734
set - *publish* 531
à fond 52
afoot *on hand* 625
 preparing 673
 astir 682
afore 116
aforehand 116
afore-mentioned 62
aforesaid
 preceding 62
 repeated 104
 prior 116
aforethought 611
a fortiori 33
afraid 860
- to say *uncertain* 475
be - *irresolute* 605
afreet 980
afresh *repeated* 104
 new 123
Afric heat 382
Afrikander 57
aft 235
after *in order* 63
 in time 117
 too late 135
 rear 235
 pursuit 622
- all *for all that* 30
 qualification 469
 on the whole 476
- time 133
be - *intention* 620
 pursuit 622
go - *follow* 281
after acceptation 516
after-age 124
afterbirth 63
afterburden 63
afterclap 509
aftercome 65, 154
aftercrop 168
afterdinner 117
afterglow 40a
aftergrowth 65, 154
afterlife 152
aftermath
 fertile 168
 profit 775
afternoon 126
- farmer 683
after-part
 sequel 65
 rear 235
afterpiece 599
aftertaste 390
afterthought
 thought 451
 memory 505
 change of mind 607
aftertime 121
afterwards 117
aga 745
agacerie 615

again *duplicate* 90
 repeated 104
- and again 136
come - *periodic* 138
fall off - 661
live - 660
against
 counteraction 179
 anteposition 237
 provision 673
 voluntary opposition 708
- one's expectation 508
- one's will 744
- one's wishes 603
- the grain *difficult* 704
 painful 830
 dislike 867
- the stream 704
- the time when 510
chances - 473
declaim - 932
false witness - 934
go - 708
raise &c. one's voice - 489
set - *actively* 898
set one's face - *refuse* 764
 disapprove 932
stand up - *resist* 719
agalloch 400
agamist 904
agape *curious* 455
 expectant 507
 wonder 870
agape *love feast* 998
Agapemone
 pleasure 827
 love 897
agate 847
age *time* 106
 period 108
 long time 110
 present time 118
 oldness 124
 advanced life **128**
from age to - 112
of - 131
agency
 physical **170**
 instrumentality 631
 means 632
 employment 677
 voluntary action 680
 direction 693
 commission 755
agenda 625
list of - 626
agent *physical* 153
 voluntary **690**
 consignee 758
- *provocateur* 615
agentship 755
age quod agis! 682
ages: - ago 122
for - 110
agglomerate
 cohere 46

assemble 72
agglutinate 46
aggrandize
 in degree 35
 in bulk 194
 honor 873
aggravate
 increase 35
 vehemence 173
 exaggerate 549
 render worse 659
 distress 835
 exasperate 900
aggravating
 painful 830
aggravation 835
aggregate
 whole 50
 collect 72
aggregation 46
aggression 716
aggrieve *injure* 649
 distress 830
aggroup 72
aghast
 disappointed 509
 fear 860
 wonder 870
agile *swift* 274
 active 682
agio 813
agiotage 794
agitate *move* 315
 inquire 461
 activity 682
 excite the feelings 824
- a question 476
agitation [see agitate]
 changeableness 149
 energy 171
 motion **315**
in - *preparing* 673
agitator
 leader 694
aglet 554
aglow
 warm 382
 shine 420
agnate 11
agnition 762
agnomen 564
agnosticism 989
agnus Dei *spell* 993
 rite 998
ago 122
not long - 123
agog *expectant* 507
 desire 865
 wonder 870
 (*envious* 455)
agoing 682
set - 707
agonism 720
agonizing
 thrilling 824
 painful 830
agony
 physical 378
 mental 828
- of death 360

- of excitement 825
à soul in - 828
agostadero 344
agrarian 371
agree *accord* 23
  concur 178
  assent 488
  concord 714
  consent 762
  compact 769
  compromise 774
- in opinion 488
- with *salubrity* 656
agreeable
  physically 377
  mentally 829
agreeably to
  conformably 82
agreement 23 [*see*
  agree]
  compact 769
agrestic 371
agriculture 371
agronomy 371
aground *fixed* 150
  in difficulty 704
  failure 732
agua 337
aguardiente 959
ague 655
ague fit 860
aguets, aux -
  expectation 507
  ambush 530
agueweed 662
aguish *cold* 383
aha! *rejoicing* 838
ahead *in front* 234
  procession 280
  go - *progression* 282
  rock - *danger* 665
  pitfall 667
  shoot - *transcursion*
    303
  activity 682
ah me! 839
Ahriman 978, 980
aid *help* **707**
  charity 906
  by the - of
    instrument 631
    means 632
aid-de-camp
  auxiliary 711
  officer 745
aide-toi, le ciel t'ai-
  dera 686
aidless 160
aigrette 847
aiguille 253
aiguille: chercher une
  - dans une botte
  de foin 644
aigulet 847
ail *sick* 655
  pain 828
aileron 267
ailment 655
aim *direction* 278
  purpose 620
  essay 675

- a blow at 716
aimable, faire l' -
  897
aimer éperdument
  897
aimless *without design*
  59, 621
  without motive 615a
air *unsubstantial* 4
  broach 66
  lightness 320
  gas 334
  atmospheric **338**
  wind 349
  tune 415
  appearance 448
  refresh 689
  fashionable 852
  beat the - 645
  fill the - 404
  fine - *salubrity* 656
  fish in the - 645
  fowls of the - 366
  rend the - 404
  take - 531
air balloon 273
air bladder 334
air bubble 250
air-drawn 515
air engine 633
air gun 727
air hole 351
airing 266
air line 278
airman 269
airmanship 267, 698
air pipe 351
air pump 349
airs *affectation* 855
  pride 878
  vanity 880
  arrogance 885
airship 273
air-tight 261
airward 206
airy [*see* air]
  unimportant 643
  gay 836
  - hopes 858, 859
  - tongues 532
  give to - nothing a lo-
    cal habitation &c.
    515
aisle *passage* 260
  way 627
  in a church 1000
ait 346
aitchbone 235
ajar *open* 260
  discordant 713
ajee 217
ajutage *opening* 260
  pipe 350
akimbo *angular* 244
  stand - 715
akin *consanguineous*
  11
  similar 17
à la
  - française 852
  - guerre 722

- parisienne 852
alabaster *white* 430
alack! 839
alacran 913
alacrity *willing* 602
  active 682
  cheerful 836
Aladdin's lamp 993
alameda 189
à l'américaine 852
à l'anglaise 852
alarm *warning* 668
  notice of danger **669**
  fear 860
  cause for - 665
  give an - *indicate* 550
alarmist 862
alarum
  indication 550
  notice of danger 669
alas! 839
alate 39
alb 999
alba 999
Albany
  - beef 298
  - hemp 663
albata 430, 545
albeit 30
alberca 343
albification 430
albino 443
album *book* 593
  compendium 596
albumen
  semiliquid 352
  protein 161, 357
Alcaic 597
alcaid 745
alcalde 745
alchemy 144
alcohol
  drinking 959
alcoholism 959
Alcoran 986
alcove *bower* 191
  hollow 252
Aldebaran 423
alderman 745
ale 298
alea, jacta est - 601
Alecto 173
alectromancy 511
alehouse 189
  go to the - 959
alembic
  conversion 144
  vessel 191
  furnace 386
  laboratory 691
alentours 197
alert *watchful* 459
  active 682
alerte 669
alertness 457
aleuromancy 511
Alexandrine
  ornate style 577
  verse 597
  (*length* 200)
alexandrite 847

alexipharmic 662
alexiteric 662
alfalfa 367
Alfardaws 981
alfilaria 367
algebra 85
algebraist 85
algid 383
algology 369
algorism 85
algorithm 85
alguazil 965
alias 565
alibi 187
alien *irrelevant* 10
  foreign 57
  transfer 783
  gentile 989
alienable 783
alienage 57
alienate
  transfer 783
  estrange 889
  set against 898
alienation
  mental - 503
aliéné 503
alieni appetens
  grasping 865
  envious 921
  selfish 943
alienism 57
align 278
alight *stop* 265
  arrive 292
  descend 306
  on fire 382
alike 17
  share and share -
    778
aliment *food* 298
  (*materials* 635)
alimentary
  regimen 662
alimentation
  aid 707
alimony
  property 780
  provision 803
  income 810
aliped 274
aliquis in omnibus
  701
aliquot *part* 51
  number 84
aliter visum, diis -
  601
alitur vitium vivit-
  que tegendo 528,
  945
alive
  living 359
  intelligent 498
  active 682
  cheerful 836
  - to *attention* 457
  cognizant 490
  informed 527
  able 698
  sensible 822
  keep - *continue* 143

keep the memory -
505
aljibar 636
alkahest 335
alkali 344
all *whole* 50
  complete 52
  generality 78
  - aboard 293
  - absorbing 642
  - agog 865
  - along 106
  - along of 154
  - at once 113
  - but 32
  - colors 440
  - considered
    thought 451
    judgment 480
  - day long 110
  - fours *easy* 705
    cards 840
  - hail! *welcome* 292
    honor to 873
    celebration 883
    courtesy 894
  - hands *everybody* 78
  - in 688
  - in all 50
  - in good time 152
  - in one's power 686
  - manner of *different*
    15
    multiform 81
  - of a heap 72
  - one *equal* 27
    indifferent 866
  - out *completely* 52
    error 495
  - over *end* 67
    universal 78
    destruction 162
    space 180
  - powerful
    mighty 159
    God 976
    completely 52
    truly 494
  - right! 922
  - searching 461
  - sorts *diverse* 16a
    mixed 41
    multiform 81
  - talk 4
  - the better 831
  - the go 852
  - the rage 852
  - the time 106
  - the world and his
    wife 78
  - things to all men
    894
  - together 50
  - ways
    distortion 243
    deviation 279
  at - events *compen-*
    sation 30
    qualification 469
    true 494
    resolve 604

  at - points 52
  at - times 136
  in - ages 112
  in - directions 278
  in - quarters 180
  in - respects
  of - work •
    useful 644
    maid - 746
  on - hands 488
  on - sides 227
  with - one's might 686
  with - respect 928
Allah 979
allay
  moderate 174
  pacify 723
  relieve 834
  - excitability 826
all-destroying 162
all-devouring 162
allective 615
allege *evidence* 467
  assert 535
  plea 617
allegiance
  obedience 743
  duty 926
allegory
  similitude 464
  metaphor 521
allegresse 836
allegro *music* 415
  cheerful 836
allelujah 990
allemande 840
all-engulfing 162
aller Anfang ist
  schwer 66
aller à tâtons 463
alleviate
  moderate 174
  relieve 834
alley *court* 189
  passage 260
  way 627
allez-vous-en 297
Allhallowmas 138
alliance *relation* 9
  kindred 11
  physical coöperation
    178
  voluntary coöpera-
    tion 709
  party 712
  union 714
allied to *like* 17
alligation 43
alligator 366, 913
  - pear 298
allign 278
alliteration
  similarity 17
  style in writing 577
all-knowing 976
allness 52
allocation 60
allocution 586
allodium *free* 748
  property 780
allopathy 662

alloquy 586
allot *arrange* 60
  distribute 786
  due 924
allow *assent* 488
  admit 529
  permit 760
  consent 762
  give 784
  - to have one's own
    way 740
allowable
  permitted 760
  due 924
allowance
  qualification 469
  gift 784
  allotment 786
  discount 813
  salary 973
  make - for *forgive* 918
  vindicate 937
  with grains of - 485
alloy *mixture* 41, 48
  debase 659
all-possessed 503
All Saint's Day 138
all-seeing 976
all-sided 52
All Soul's Day 138
allspice 393
all-sufficient 159
allude *hint* 514
  mean 516
  refer to 521
  latent 526
  inform 527
allure *move* 615
  create desire 865
alluring
  pleasurable 829
allusive
  relative 9
alluvial *level* 213
  land 342
  plain 344
alluvium
  deposit 40
  land 342
  soil 653
all-wise 976
ally *auxiliary* 711
  friend 890
alma mater 542
almanac
  chronometry 114
  record 86, 551
  - de Gotha 86
almighty 157
Almighty, the - 976
almoner
  treasurer 801
  church officer 996
almost *nearly* 32
  not quite 651
  - all 50
  - immediately 132
alms *gift* 784
  benevolence 906
  worship 990
almshouse 189, 666

almsman 785
Alnaschar's dream
  imagination 515
  hope 858
aloes 395
aloes wood 400
aloft 206
alogy 497
alone *single* 87
  unaided 706
  let - *not use* 678
  not restrain 748
  never less - 893
along 200
  - of *caused by* 154
  - with *added* 37
  together 88
  by means of 631
  get - *progress* 282
  go - *depart* 293
  go - with *concur* 178
  assent 488
  coöperate 709
alongside *near* 197
  parallel 216
  laterally 236
aloof *distant* 196
  high 206
  secluded 893
  stand - *inaction* 681
  refuse 764
  cautious 864
aloofness 893
aloud 404
  think - *soliloquy* 589
  naïveté 703
Alp 206
alpenstock 215
Alpha 66
  - and Omega 50
alphabet
  beginning 66
  letters 561
alphabetarian 541
alphitomancy 511
alpine *high* 206
Alpine Club
  traveler 268
  ascent 305
already
  antecedently 116
  even now 118
  past time 122
Alsatia
  thieving 791
Alsatian den 945
also 37
altar *marriage* 903
  church 1000
  world's - *stairs* 981
alter 140
  emasculate 158
  - one's course 279
  - the case 468
alterable 149
alteram partem, au-
  dire -
  counter evidence 468
  just 922
alterant 662
alteration 15

annotto 434
announce
 predict 511
 inform 527
 publish 531
 assert 535
annoy
 molest 649, 907
 disquiet 830
annoyance 828
source of - 830
annual periodic 138
 plant 367
 book 593
annuity 810
annul
 destroy 162
 abolish 756
annular 247
annulet 247
annunciate
 inform 527
 (publish 531)
Annunciation, the -
 990
annus magnus 108
anodyne
 lenitive 174
 remedial 662
 relief 834
anoint coat 223
anointed
 deity 976
 king 745
anointment
 lubrication 332
 oil 355
anomaly
 disorder 59
 irregularity 83
anon 132
anonymous 565
anorexy 866
another
 different 15
 repetition 104
- time 119
go upon - tack 607
tell - story 468
answer
 to an inquiry 462
 confute 479
 solution 522
 succeed 731
 pecuniary profit 775
 pleadings 969
- for deputy 759
 promise 768
 go bail 806
- one's turn 644
- the helm 743
- the purpose 731
- to correspond 9
I'll - for it 535
require an - 461
answerable
 liable 177
 bail 806
 duty 926
 censurable 392
ant 690

Antæus
 strength 159
 size 192
antagonism
 difference 14
 physical 179
 voluntary 708
antagonist 710
antagonistic 24
antaphrodisiac 866
antarctic 237
ante 621
 expend 809
- up 809
antecedence
 in order 62
 in time 116
antecedent 64
antechamber 191
ante Christum 106
antedate 115
antediluvian 124
antelope 274
antemundane 124
antenna 379
antepast 510
anteposition 62
anterior
 in order 62
 in time 116
 in place 234
- to reason 477
anteroom 191
antevert 706
ante victoriam 864
anthelion 423
anthelmintic 662
anthem 990
anthemion 847
antherozoid 357
anthology
 collection 596
 poem 597
anthracite 388
anthrax 655
anthropogeny 372
anthropoid 372
anthropology
 zoölogy 368
 mankind 372
anthropomancy 511
anthropomorphism
 984
anthropophagus 913
anthroposcopy 511
anthroposophy 372
antic 840
antichambre, faire -
 133
antichristian
 heterodox 984
 irreligious 989
antichronism 115
anticipate
 anachronism 115
 priority 116
 future 121
 early 132
 expect 507
 foresee 510
 prepare 673

 hope 858
anticlimax
 decrease 36
 bathos 497, 853
anticlinal 217
anticyclone 265
antidote 662
antigropelos 225
antifebrile 662
antilogarithm 84
antilogy 477
antiluctic 662
antimacassar 223
antimony 663
Antinomian 984
antinomy 964
Antinous 845
antiorgastic 174
antiparallel 217
antipathy
 dislike 867
 hate 898
antiphon music 415
 answer 462
 worship 990
antiphrasis 563
antipodes
 difference 14
 distance 196
 contraposition 237
antipoison 662
antiquary
 past times 122
 scholar 492
 historian 553
antiquas vias, stare
 super -
 habit 613
 conservative 670
antiquated
 aged 128
 (cut of fashion 851)
antique 124
antiquity 122
antiscriptural 984
antiseptic 662
antisocial 911
antispasmodic 174,
 662
antispast 597
antistrophe 597
antithesis
 contrast 14
 style 574, 577
antitype 22
antler 253
antonomasia
 metaphor 521
 nomenclature 564
anvil support 215
on the -
 intended 620
 in hand 625, 730
 preparing 673
anxiety
 solicitude 459
 pain 828
 fear 860
 desire 865
anxious
- bench 1000

- expectation 507
- meeting 1000
- seat 1000
any some 25
 part 51
 no choice 609a
at - price 604a
at - rate
 certain 474
 true 494
 at all hazards 604
anybody 78
anyhow
 careless 460
 in some way 627
anything one knows,
 for - 491
aorist
 indefinite time 109,
 119
aorta 350
apace early 132
 swift 274
apache assassin 361
Apache 913
aparejo 215
apart separate 44
 singleness 87
set - 636
wide - 196
apartment 191
- house 189
-s to let
 imbecile 499
apathy 823
ape imitate 19
Apelles 559
aperçu 596
aperient 652, 662
aperture 260
apex 210
aphelion 196
aphid 659
Aphis 659
aphony 581
aphorism 496
aphrodisia 173
Aphrodite 845
apiarist 370
apiary 370
Apicius 957
apiculate 253
apiece 79
apish 19, 499
apishamore 223
aplanatic 429
à plomb 212
aplomb
 stability 150
 self-possession 498
 resolution 604
Apocalypse 985
Apocrypha 985
apocryphal
 uncertain 475
 erroneous 495
 heterodox 984
apodeictic 478
apodeixis 478
apograph 21
apolaustic 377

Apollo *sun* 318
  music 416
  luminary 423
  beauty 845
  magnus -
  sage 500
  adviser 695
Apollyon 978
apologue
  metaphor 521
  teaching 537
  description 594
apology *excuse* 617
  vindication 937
  penitence 950
  atonement 952
apophthegm 496
apophysis 250
apoplexy 158 .
apostasy
  recantation 607
  dishonor 940
  heterodoxy 984
apostate
  convert 144
  turncoat 607
  (recreant 941)
apostle *teacher* 540
  disciple 541
  inspired 985
  -'s creed 983*a*
apostolic 985
  - church 983*a*
  - see 995
apostrophe
  address 586
  soliloquy 589
  appeal 765
apothecary 662
  -'s weight 319
apothegm 496
apotheosis
  resuscitation 163
  heaven 981
  hero worship 991
apozem *liquefy* 335
  fuse 384
appal *pain* 830
  terrify 860
appanage
  property 780
  gift 784
apparatus 63°
  - belli 727
apparel 225
apparent
  visible 446
  appearing 448
  probable 472
  manifest 525
  heir - 779
apparition
  fallacy of vision 443
  spirit 980
  (appearance 448)
apparitor 534
appeach 938
appeal
  address 586
  request 765
  - from Philip

362

drunk to Philip
  sober 658
  - motion 969
  - to *call to witness* 467
  - to arms 722
  - to for *(claim)* 924
  court of - 966
appear *come in sight*
  446
  show itself 525
  (come into being 1)
  - for 759
  - in print 591
appearance 448
  make one's -
  arrive 292
  to all - *to the eye* 448
  probable 472
appearances
  keep up - 852
appease 174
appellant
  claimant 924
  accuser 938
appellate 966
appellation 564
append *add* 37
  sequence 63
  hang 214
appendage 39, 88
appendicitis 655
appendix 65
appertain
  related to 9
  component 56
  belong 777
  property 780
appetence 865
appetite 865
  hungry edge of - 298
  tickle the -
  savory 394
appetitus rationi
  obediant 953
appetizer 393, 394
appetizing 865
  exciting 824
applaud 931
apple 298
  - brandy 959
  - butter 396
  - jack 959
  - of discord 713
  - off another tree 15
  - of one's eye *good*
  648
  love 897
  favorite 899
  - slump 298
  golden -
  allurement 615
  how we -s swim! 880
apple green 435
apple-pie order 58
appliance *use* 677
  -s *means* 632
  machinery 633
applicable *relevant* 9,
  23
  useful 644
  expedient 646

applicant 767
application *study* 457
  metaphor 521
  use 677
  request 765
apply
  appropriate 788
  - a match 384
  - the match to a
  train 66
  - the mind 457
  - a remedy 662
appoggiato 413
appoggiatura 413
appointment *order*
  741
  charge 755
  assignment **786**
  interview 892
appointments
  gear 633
apportion *arrange* 60
  disperse 73
  allot 786
  (portion 51)
apportionment 786
apposition
  relevancy 23
  closeness 199
  paraphrase 522
appraise
  estimate 466
  value 812
appreciate
  realize 450, 451
  measure 466
  judge 480
  know 490
  taste 850
  approve 931
apprehend
  believe 484
  know 490
  fear 860
  seize 969
apprehension
  idea 453
  taking 789
apprentice 541
  - oneself 676
apprenticeship
  learning 539
  training 673
appris
  ils n'ont rien - 606
apprize 527
apprized of 490
approach
  of time 121
  impend 152
  nearness 197
  move **286**
  path 627
approbation 931
appropinquation
  286
à propos *relative* 9
  apt 23
  occasion 134
  (expedient 646)
  - de bottes 10

appropriate *fit* 23
  peculiar 79
  assign 786
  borrow 788
  take 789
  steal 791
  (expedient 646)
approval *assent* 488
  commend 931
approximate
  related to 9
  resemble 17
  in mathematics 85
  nearness 197
  approach 286
appulse *meeting* 199
  collision 276
  approach 286
  convergence 290
appurtenance
  adjunct 88
  component 56
  belonging 780
  (part 51)
appurtenant
  relating 9
après nous le deluge
  943
apricot *color* 439
April
  - fool *dupe* 547
  laughingstock 857
  - showers 149
  make an - fool of 545
apron *clothing* 225
  defense 717
  canonicals 999
apropos [see à propos]
aprotype 591
apse 1000
apt *consonant* 23
  tendency 176, 177
  docile 539
  willing 602
  clever 698
  (intelligent 498)
  (expedient 646)
aqua 337
  - fortis 384
  - regia 384
aquamarine 435
aquarium 370
Aquarius *rain* 348
aquatic *water* 337
aquatics 267
aquatinta 558
aqueduct 350
aqueous 337
aquila non capit
  muscas 473
aquiline 244
A. R. 106
Arab *wanderer* 268
  horse 271
araba 272
arabesque 847
Arabian
  - nights 515
  - perfumes 400
arable 371
arado 780

Arbeit
  schwere - in der Jugend 682
arbiter *critic* 480
  director 694
  adviser 695
  judge 967
  - bibendi 840
  - elegantiarum
  revels 840
  taste 850
  fashion 852
arbitrament
  judgment 480
  (*choice* 609)
  - of the sword 722
arbitrary
  without relation 10
  irregular 83
  willful 606
  capricious 608
  authoritative 737
  severe 739
  insolent 885
  lawless 964
  - power 739
arbitrate
  adjudicate 480
  mediate 724
arbitration
  court of - 966
  submit to - 774
arbitrium, ad - 600
arbor *abode* 189
  summerhouse 191
  support 215
  rotation 312
  plaisance 840
  - vitæ 242
Arbor Day 840
arborescent
  ramifying 242
  rough 256
  trees 367
arboriculture 371
arboriform 242
arc 245
arcade *street* 189
  curve 245
  gateway 260
Arcades ambo
  alike 17
  friends 890
  bad men 949
Arcadia
  pleasure 827
  paradise 981
Arcadian
  artless 703
  innocent 946
arcanum 533
arch *great* 31
  support 215
  curve 245
  convex 250
  concave 252
  clever 498
  cunning 702
  this gorgeous - 126
  triumphal -
  trophy 733

celebration 883
archæologist
  antiquary 122
  scholar 492
archæology 122
archaic *old* 124
archaism
  past times 122
  obsolete phrase 563
archangel 977
archbishop 996
archbishopric 995
archdeacon 996
archduchy 181
archduke 745
archdukedom 180
archebiosis 161
arched roof 245
archegenesis 161, 357
archenemy, the - 978
archer 726, 840
archery 840
Arches, court of -
  tribunal 966
  churchdom 995
archetype 22, 453
Archeus 359
archfiend 978
archiater 695
archiepiscopal 995
archipelago 346
architect
  constructor 164
  agent 690
architectonic 161
architecture
  arrangement 60
  construction 161
  fabric 329
  ornament 847
architrave 210
archive 551
archlute 417
archon *ruler* 745
  deputy 759
  judge 967
archtraitor 941
arclike 245
arctic *northern* 237
  cold 383
arctics 225
arcuation 245
ardent *fiery* 382
  feeling 821
  loving 897
  - expectation 507
  - imagination 515
ardet, proximus -
  665, 667
ardor *activity* 682
  feeling 821
  desire 865
arduous 704
area 181, 182
arefaction 340
arena *space* 180
  region 181
  field of view 441
  field of battle **728**
arenaceous 330
areola 247

areolar 219
areometer 321
Areopagus 966
ares 180
arescent 340
arête 253
aretology 926
Argand lamp 423
argent 430
  - comptant 800
argil 324
argillaceous 324
argol 653
argosy 273
argot 563
argue *evidence* 467
  reason 476
  indicate 550
argufy 476
argument *topic* 454
  discussion 476
  meaning 516
  have the best of an -
  478
argumentum
  - ad crumenam 800
  - ad hominem
  reasoning 476
  accuse 938
  - ad verecundiam 939
  - baculinum
  compel 744
  lawless 964
  punish 972
Argus-eyed
  sight 441
  vigilant 459
argute 498
aria 415
Arianism 984
arid
  unproductive 169
  dry 340
  uninteresting 841
Ariel *courier* 268
  swift 274
  messenger 534
  spirit 979
arietation 276
arietta 415
aright *well* 618
  (*skillful* 698)
ariolation 511
ariose 413
arise *exist* 1
  begin 66
  happen 151
  mount 305
  appear 446
  - from 154
aris et focis, pro -
  defense 717
  philanthropy 910
Aristarchus 850
aristate 253
Aristides
  good man 948
aristocracy
  power 737
  nobility 875
ἄριστον μέτρον 628

Aristotelian 476
arithmancy 511
arithmetic 85
ark *abode* 189
  asylum 666
  boat 273
arm *part* 51
  power 157
  instrument **633**
  provide 637
  prepare 673
  war 722
  weapon 727
  - chair 215
  - in arm
  together 88
  friends 888
  sociable 892
  - of the law 963
  - of the sea 343
  make a long - 200
armada 726
Armageddon 720
armament
  preparation 673
  arms 727
armed
  defence 717
  - at all points 673
  - force 726
armet 717
armful 25
armiger 875
armigerent 726
armigerous 722
armillary sphere 466
armistice 723
armless 158
armlet *ring* 247
  gulf 343
armorial 550
armory 636, 691
armor *defense* 717
  arms 727
  - plated 223
  buckle on one's - 673
arm's length
  at - 196
  keep at -
  repel 289
  defense 717
  enmity 889
  seclusion 893
  discourtesy 895
arms 727 [see arm]
  heraldry 550
  war 722
  honors 877
  clash of - 720
  deeds of - 720
  in - *infant* 129
  throw oneself into
  the - of
  refuge 666
  friendship 888
  under - 722
  up in - *active* 682
  discord 713
  resistance 719
  resentment 900
  enmity 889

maps 554
Atlas *strength* 159
  support 215
atmosphere
  circumambience 227
  air 338
atmospheric blue
  438
atole 298
atoll 346
atom
  small in degree 32
  small in size 193
atoms
  crush to - 162
atomy 193
atonement
  restitution 790
  expiation **952**
  amends 973
  religious 976
atony 160
à toute force 157
atqui vivere militaire est 359
atrabilious 837
atramentous 431
atrium 191
atrocity
  malevolence 907
  vice 945
  guilt 947
atrophy
  shrinking 195
  disease 655
  decay 659
at spes non fracta
  858
attach *join* 43
  love 897
  legal 969
  - importance to 642
attaché
  employé 746
  diplomatic 758
attack *disease* 655
  assault **716**
attaghan 727
attain *arrive* 292
  succeed 731
  - majority 131
attainable
  possible 470
  (easy 705)
attainder
  taint 651
  at law 971
attainment
  knowledge 490
  learning 539
  skill 698
attar 400
attemper *mix* 41
  moderate 174
attempered
  affected 820
attempt 675
  - impossibilities 471
  vain - 732
attend
  accompany 88

be present 186
follow 281
apply the mind 457
medically 662
aid 707
serve 746
- to business 625
- to orders 743
attendance on
  dance - 886
attendant
  [*see* attend]
attention 457
  care 459
  respect 928
  attract - 882
  call - to 550
  call to - 457
  pay -s to 894
  pay one's -s to 902
attenuate
  decrease 36
  reduce 195
attenuated 203
attest
  bear testimony 467
  affirm 535
  adjure 768
attested copy 771
attic *garret* 191
  summit 210
  style 578
  wit 842
  taste 850
  - salt 842
Atticism 578
Attila 913
attire 225
attitude
  circumstance 8
  situation 183
  posture 240
attitudinarian 882
attitudinize 855
attollent 307
attorney
  consignee 758
  at law 968
  power of - 755
attract
  bring towards 288
  induce 615
  allure 865
  excite love 897
  - the attention 457
  visible 446
attraction
  [*see* attract]
  natural power 157
  bring towards **288**
attractive
  [*see* attract]
  pleasing 829
  beautiful 845
attractivity 288
attrahent 288
attribute
  power 157
  -s of the Deity 976
  - to 155

attribute *accompaniment* 88
attribution 155
attrite 330, 331
attrition 331
attroupement 72
attune *music* 415
  prepare 673
attuned to
  habit 613
au bon droit 922
auburn 433
A. U. C. 106
auction 796
auctioneer
  agent 758
  seller 796
auctor pretiosa facit
  784
audacity
  courage 861
  rashness 863
  insolence 885
audacter et sincere
  590
audible 402
  become - 418
  scarcely - 405
audience
  hearing 418
  conversation 588
  - chamber 696
  before an - 599
audire alteram partem
  counter evidence 468
  right 922
  justice 939
audit
  numeration 85
  examination 461
  accounts 811
auditor
  hearer 418
  accountant 811
auditory
  hearing 418
  theater 599
  - apparatus 418
au fait 698
aufgeschoben ist nicht aufgehoben 624
au fond 5
Augean
  - stable 653
  - task 704
auger 262
aught 51
  for - one cares
  unimportant 643
  indifferent 866
  for - one knows
  ignorance 491
  conjecture 514
augment
  increase 35
  thing added 39
  expand 194
augur
  soothsayer 513

- well 858
augural 511
augurate 511
augury 512
august 31, 873
Augustinian 996
aujourd'hui roi demain rien 601
Aum 993
aumbry 1000
aunt 11
aura *wind* 349
  sensation 380
aurea mediocritas
  628
aurea rumpunt tecta quietam
  803
aureate 436
aurelia 129
aureola 420
aureole 873
aureolin 436
au reste 37
auribus, arrectis -
  418
auricle 418
auricomous 436
auricular *hearing* 418
  clandestine 528
  - confession 998
auri sacra fames 819
aurist 662
aurora
  dawn 125
  light 420, 423
  twilight 422
  - borealis 423
auscultation 418
auspice *omen* 512
auspices
  influence 175
  prediction 511
  protection 664
  under the - of **737**
auspicious
  opportune 134
  prosperous 734
  hopeful 858
  (*expedient* 646)
auspicium melioris ævi 512
aussitôt dit aussitôt fait 729
austerity
  harsh taste 395
  severe 739
  discourteous 895
  ascetic 955
  pietism 988
Austral 237
austromancy 511
authentic
  well-founded 1
  certain 474
  true 484
authentication
  evidence 467
  security 771
author
  producer 164

B

barbarian
  uncivilized 876
  evil doer 913
barbaric vulgar 851
  rude 876
barbarism
  neology 563
  solecism 568
  bad style 579
  vulgarity 851
  discourtesy 895
barbarous
  unformed 241
  plebeian 876
  maleficent 907
barbarus ipse placet
  800
barbâ tenus sapien-
  tes 500
barbe 225
barbecue
  repast 298, 892
  cook 673
barbed 225
barber wind 349
barbican 717
barbouillage 590
bard musician 416
  poet 597
barde 633
barded 225
bare mere 32
  nude 226
  manifest 525
  disclose 529
  scanty 640
  - bone 203
  - faced insolent 885
  - foot 226
  poor 804
  - headed respect 928
  - possibility 473
  - supposition 514
  scud under - poles
  704
bareback 226
bargain
  compact 769
  barter 794
  cheap 815
  - and sale transfer of
  property 783
  - for 507
  into the - 37
barge 273
bargee 269
barghest 980
barf 383
baritone 408
barium sulphate 430
bark rind 223
  ship 273
  yelp 412
  - at threaten 909
  censure 932
  - up the wrong tree
  699
  - worse than bite 885
  more - than bite 908
barkantine 273
barkbound 751

barkeeper 746
barleycorn
  little 193
Barleycorn, Sir John
  - 298
barm leaven 320
  bubbles 353
barmaster 967
Barmecide feast 956
barmote 966
barn 189
barnacles 445
barndoor fowl 366
barney 545, 713
barometer air 338
  measure 466
  consult the - 463
baron peer 875
  husband 903
  - of the Exchequer
  967
  court - 966
baronet 875
baronial 878
baroque 853
baroscope 338
barouche 272
barque 273
barrack 189
  shed 223
  jibe 929
barracker 936
barracoon 717
barranca 198
barrator 941
barratrous 940
barratry 940
barred crossed 219
  striped 440
barrel vessel 191
  cylinder 249
  - organ 417
barrel house 189
barren 169
barricade fence 232
  obstacle 706
  defense 717
  prison 752
barrier [see barricade]
barrin save 38
  excluding 55
  except 83
  - out resist 719
  disobey 742
barrister 968
  revising - 967
barrow
  mound 206
  vehicle 272
  grave 363
barter
  reciprocate 12
  interchange 148
  commerce 794
barway 294
barytone 408
bas bleu
  scholar 492
  affectation 855
base
  lowest part 211

support 215
  bad 649
  cowardly 862
  shameful 874
  servile 886
  dishonorable 940
  vicious 945
  - board 211
  - born 876
  - coin 800
  - note 408
  - of operations
  plan 626
  attack 716
  - viol 417
baseball 840
based on ground of
  belief 467
baselard 727
baseless unreal 2
  unsubstantial 4
basement cellar 191
  lowest part 207, 211
bashaw tyrant 739
  ruler 745
bashful 881
bashi bazouk 726
basilica 1000
basilisk sight 441
  cannon 737
  serpent 949
basin dock 189
  vessel 191
  hollow 252
  plain 344
basis
  lowest part 211
  support 215
  preparation 673
bask physical enjoy-
  ment 377
  warmth 382
  prosperity 734
  moral enjoyment 827
basket 191
  - of 190
basophobia 266
bas-relief
  convex 250
  sculpture 557
bass music 415
  - clarinet 417
  - note 408
  - viol 417
basset 446
basset horn 417
bassinet cradle 191
  helmet 717
bassoon 417
basso profondo 408
basso-rilievo
  convex 250
  sculpture 557
bastard
  spurious 545
  illegitimate 925
baste beat 276
  punish 972
Bastille 752
bastinado 972
bastion 717

bat strike 276
  club 727
  spree 840
batch quantity 25
  collection 72
bate diminish 36
  subtract 38
  reduce price 813
bateau 273
bated breath
  with - faint sound 405
  expecting 507
  hiding 528
  whisper 581
  humble 879
bath 337
  - room 191
  warm - 386
Bathala 979
Bath chair 272
bathe immerse 300
  plunge 310
  water 337
bathometer 466
bathos
  anticlimax 497
  (ridiculous 853)
bathybic 341
bathycolpian 208
bating 55
batman 637
bâton support 215
  scepter 747
batophobia 206, 860
batta 973
battalia 726
battalion 726
batten 298
batter destroy 162
  beat 276
battered
  worse for wear 659
  tired 688
batterie de cuisine
  957
battering-ram 276
battering train 727
battery
  boat 273
  artillery 726
  guns 727
  floating - 726
  plant a - 716
battle 720, 722
  - array order 60
  prepare 673
  war 722
  - ax 727
  - cry sign 550
  war 722
  - field arena 728
  - ground discord 713
  - with oppose 708
  half the - 642
  win the - 731
battled 722
battledore and shut
  tlecock
  interchange 148
  game 840
battlement

embrasure 257
defense 717
battologize 573
battology
  repeat 104
  diffuse style 573
battre
  - la campagne
  nonsense 497
  diffuse style 573
  excitable 825
  - la générale 669
  - l'eau avec un bâton
  645
  - le fer sur l'enclume
  134
  ne - que d'une aile
  683
  se - contre des mou-
  lins 645
battue
  kill 361
  pursuit 622
  attack 716
bauble *trifle* 643
  toy 840
bavardage
  unmeaning 517
  chatter 584
bavin 388
bawarchi-khana 191
bawcock 892
bawd 962
bawdy, -house 961
bawl 411
bawn 189
bay *concave* 252
  gulf 343
  cry 412
  brown 433
  at - *danger* 665
  difficulty 604
  defense 717, 719
  - *rum* 400
  - *salt* 336
  - the moon
  useless 645
  - window 245, 260
  bring to - 716
bayadere 840
bayard 271
baygall 345
bayonet *kill* 361
  attack 716
  weapon 727
  at the point of the -
  war 722
  severity 739
  coercion 744
  crossed -s 708
bayou 343
bays *trophy* 733
  crown 877
bazaar 799
B. C. 106
be 1
  - all and end all!
  whole 50
  intention 620
  importance 642
  - off *depart* 293

eject 297
retract 773
- it so 488
- that as it may 30
beach 342
beach comber 268,
  348
beacon *sign* 550
  warning 668
  (*light* 423)
  - fire 550
bead 249, 847
beading 847
beadle *janitor* 263
  law officer 965
  church 996
beadledom 737
beadroll *list* 86
  prayers 990
  ritual 998
beads
  tell one's - 990, 998
beadsman
  servant 746
  clergy 996
beagle 366
beak *face* 234
  nose 250
  magistrate 967
beaked 245
beaker 191
beam *support* 215
  quarter 236
  weigh 319
  light 420
  on - ends
  powerless 158
  horizontal 213
  side 236
  fail 732
  wonder 870
beaming
  beautiful 845
bean feast 840
bear *produce* 161
  sustain 215
  carry 270
  admit of 470
  stock exchange 797
  suffer 821
  endure 826
  - a hand 680
  - a sense 516
  - away 789
  - away the bell
  best 648
  success 731
  - company 88
  - date 114
  - down *violent* 173
  insolent 885
  - down upon 716
  - false witness 544
  - fruit *produce* 161
  useful 644
  success 731
  prosper 734
  - hard upon 649
  - harmless 717
  - ill 825
  - off *deviate* 279

- on 215
- oneself 692
- out *evidence* 467
  vindicate 937
- pain 828
- the brunt
  difficult 704
  defense 717
- the burden 625
- the cross 828
- the palm
  supreme 33
- through 707
- up *approach* 286
  persevere 604a
  relieve 834
  cheerful 836
- up against
  resist 719
  brave 861
- upon
  relevant 9, 23
  influence 175
- with
  tolerate 740
  permit 760
  take coolly 826
  forgive 918
  bring to - 677
  more than flesh and
  blood can - 824
  unable to -
  excited 825
  dislike 867
bear
  savage 907
  surly 895
  - garden
  disorder 59
  discord 713
  arena 728
  - leader 540
  - pit 370
  - skin *cap* 225
  helmet 717
  had it been a - it
  would have bitten
  you
  inattention 458
bearable 651
beard *hair* 205
  prickles 253
  rough 256
  defy 715
  brave 861
  insolence 885
  pluck by the -
  disrespect 929
beardless 127
bearer 271
  servant 746
bear grass 253
bearing *relation* 9
  support 215
  direction 278
  meaning 516
  demeanor 692
  - rein 752
bearings
  circumstances 8
  situation 183

bearish 895
beast *animal* 366
  unclean 653
  discourteous 895
  - of burden
  carrier 271
  laborer 690
beat *be superior* 33
  periodic 138
  region 181
  impulse 276
  surpass 303
  oscillate 314
  agitation 315
  crush 330
  sound 407
  line of pursuit 625
  path 627
  overcome 731
  sponger 886
  strike 972
  - about
  circuit 629
  - about the bush
  try for 463
  evade the point 477
  prevaricate 544
  diffuse style 573
  - against 708
  - a retreat
  retire 283
  avoid 623
  submit 725
  - down *destroy* 162
  cheapen 794, 819
  insolent 885
  - hollow 33
  - into *teach* 537
  - of drum
  music 416
  publish 531
  alarm 669
  war 722
  command 741
  pomp 882
  - off 717
  - one's breast 839
  - the air 645
  - the Dutch 508
  - time *clock* 114
  music 416
  - up *churn* 352
  - up against
  oppose 708
  - up for *cater* 637
  - up for recruits
  prepare 673
  aid 707
  - up one's quarters
  seek 461
  visit 892
  without - of drum
  528
beatæ memoriæ 505
beaten track
  habit 613
  way 627
  leave the - 83
  tread the - 82
beatic 827
beatific *pleasing* 829

371

bésique 840
beslaver 933
beslime 652
beslubber 933
besmear *cover* 223
   dirt 653
besom 652
besot 959
besotted 481
bespangle 847
bespatter *dirt* 653
   disapprove 932
   flatter 933
   detract 934
bespeak *early* 132
   evidence 467
   indicate 516
   engage 755
   ask for 765
bespeckle 440
bespot 440
besprinkle *mix* 41
   variegate 440
best *good* 648
   perfect 650
all for the -
   good 618
   prosper 734
   content 831
   hope 858
bad is the - 649
- bib and tucker
   prepared 673
   ornament 847
   ostentation 882
- intentions 906
- part *great* 31
   nearly all 50
- room 191
- seller 931
do one's -
   care 459
   try 675
   activity 682
   exertion 686
have the - of it 731
make the - of it
   overestimate 482
   use 677
   submit 725
   compromise 774
   take easily 826
   hope 858
make the - of one's
   time 684
to the - of one's be-
   lief 484
bestead 644
Beste ist gut genug
   639
bestial 961
bestir oneself
   activity 682
   haste 684
   exertion 686
bestow 784
- one's hand 903
- thought 451
bestraddle 215
bestrew 73
bestride *mount* 206

374

   ride 215
bet 621
betacism 560
betake oneself to
   journey 266
   business 625
   use 677
bête, pas si - 498
bête noire *fear* 860
   hate 898
bethel 1000
bethink *think* 451
   remember 505
bethral
   subjection 749
   restraint 751
betide 151
betimes 132
bêtise 497
betoken
   evidence 467
   predict 511
   indicate 550
betongue 932
betray
   disclose 529
   deceive 545
   dishonor 940
- itself *visible* 446
betrayer 941
betrim 673
betroth
   promise 768
   marriage 903
betrothed 897
better *good* 648
   improve 658
- half 903
- sort
   beau monde 875
for - for worse
   choice 609
   marriage 903
get - *health* 654
   improve 658
   refreshment 689
   restoration 660
get the - of 731
only - than nothing
   651
seen - days
   deteriorate 659
   adversity 735
   poor 804
think - of
   correct 658
   repent 950
betting house 621
betty 374
Betty Martin, all my
   eye and - 546
between 228
- cup and lip 111
- ourselves 528
- the lines 526
- two fires 665
far - 198
lie - 228
vibrate - two ex-
   tremes 149
betwixt 228

bevel 217
bever 298
beverage 298
bévue 732
bevy *assemblage* 72
   multitude 102
bewail *regret* 833
   lament 839
beware 668
- fury of a patient
   man 900
bewilder
   put out 458
   uncertain 475
   astonish 870
bewitch
   fascinate 615
   please 829
   excite love 897
   exorcise 992
bey 745
beyond *superior* 33
   distance 196
- compare 31, 33
- control 471
- expression 31
- hope 731, 734
- measure 641
- mortal ken 528
- one's depth
   deep 208
   unintelligible 519
- one's grasp 471
- possibility 471
- praise
   perfect 650
   approbation 931
   virtue 944
- price 814
- question 474
- reason 471
- remedy 859
- seas 57
- the grave 528
- the mark
   transcursion 303
   redundance 641
- the veil 528
go - 303
bezonian 876
bhang 663, 954
bhisti 348
bias *tendency* 176
   slope 217
   prepossession 481
   disposition 820
   (*motive* 615)
bib *pinafore* 225
   drink 959
bibber *weep* 839
   tope 959
bibble-babble 584
bibendum, nunc est
   - 959
bibere venenum in
   auro 663, 666
Bible 985
- Christian 984
- oath 535
biblioclasm 162
biblioclast 165

bibliography 593
bibliolatry
   learning 490
   heterodoxy 984
   idolatry 991
bibliomancy 511
bibliomania 490
bibliomaniac 492
bibliophile 492
bibliopole 593
bibliotheca 593
bibulous 298
bice 438
bicentennial 138
bicephalous 90
bichhona 215
bichloride of mer-
   cury 663
bicipital 90
bicker *flutter* 315
   quarrel 713
   (*contend* 720)
bickering 24
bicolor 440
biconjugate 91
bicorn 245
bicuspid 91
bicycle 272
bid *order* 741
   offer 763
- a long farewell 624
- defiance 715
- fair *tend* 176
   probable 472
   promise 511
   hope 858
- for *intend* 620
   offer 763
   request 765
   bargain 794
- the banns 903
bidder 767
biddy 746
bide *wait* 133
   remain 141
   take coolly 826
- one's time 133
   watch 507
   inactive 681
bidental 90
bidet 271
biduous 89
bien
- perdu - connu 134
un - fait 910
biennial
   periodic 138
   plant 367
bienséance
   polish 852
   manners 894
bier 363
bifacial 90
bifarious 90
bifid 91
bifold 90
biform *double* 90
   (*two* 89)
bifurcate *bisect* 91
   angle 244
big *in degree* 31

- sheep 949
- spots in the horizon 859
- swan 83
look - *feeling* 821
  discontent 832
  angry 900
prove that - is white 477
blackamoor 431
  wash a - white 471
blackball
  exclude 55
  banish 893
blackberry 298
blackboard 590
blackcoat 996
blackcock 366
blacken [*see* black]
  defame 934
Black friar 996
blackguard
  vulgar 851
  rude 895
  base 940
  vagabond 949
Black Hand 791
black-jack 727
blackleg
  apostate 607
  disease 655
  thief 792
blacklist 932
blackmail *theft* 791
  booty 793
  bribe 973
blackness 431
  - of the noonday night 421
blacksmith 690
black snake
  whip 975
bladder 191
blade *edge tool* 253
  man 373
  instrument 633
  sharp fellow 682
  proficient 700
  sword 727
  fop 854
blague 544, 884
blain *lump* 250
  blotch 848
blame 155, 932
  lay - on 938
  take - 932
blameless 946
blameworthy
  disapprove 932
  vice 945
  guilt 947
blanc-bec 701
blanc fixe 430
blanch 429, 430
blancmange 298
bland *mild* 174
  courteous 894
blandæ mendacia linguæ 544
blandiloquence 933
blandishment

inducement 615
endearment 902
flattery 933
blank *inexistent* 2
  unsubstantial 4
  - *cartridge* 158
  - *verse* 597
  look -
    disappointed 509
    discontent 832
    wonder 870
  point - 576
blanket *cover* 223
  warm 384
  toss in a - 929
  wet - 174
blare 404, 412
blarney 933
blasé *weary* 841
  satiated 869
blasphemy 988
blast *destroy* 162
  explosion 173
  wind 349
  sound 404
  adversity 735
  curse 908
blatant
  loud 404
  cry 412
  silly 499
blather 584
blatherskite 584
blatter 412, 584
blaze *heat* 382
  light 420
  mark 550
  excitement 824
  amid the - of noon 859
  - abroad 531
  -d with lights 840
blazing
  luminary 423
blazon *publish* 531
  repute 873
  ostentation 882
blé: manger son - en herbe 818
bleach 429, 430
  - ing powder 652
bleak 383
blear 422
blear-eyed 443
bleat 412
bleb 250
bleed
  physical pain 378
  remedy 662
  spend money 809
  extort money 814
  moral pain 828
  - freely *liberal* 816
  make the heart - 830
bleeding
  hemorrhage 299
  remedy 662
  - heart 828
blemish
  deface 241
  imperfection 651

injure 659
ugly 846
defect **848**
blench *avoid* 623
  fear 860
blend *mix* 41
  combine 48
blennorrhagia 655
blennorrhœa 655
bless
  give pleasure 829
  approve 931
  divine function 976
  worship 990
  - my heart 870
  - one's stars
    rejoice 838
    thanks 916
blessed 827
  abode of the - 981
blessedness
  single - 904
blessing *good* 618
  approval 931
blessings
  prosperity 734
blest 827
  - with
    possessed of 777
blether 584
Bletonism 511
blight
  deteriorate 659
  adversity 735
  - hope 509
blind *shade* 424
  cecity 442
  inattentive 458
  ignorant 491
  conceal 528
  screen 530
  deception 545
  instinctive 601
  pretext 617
  insensible 823
  - alley 261
  - a trail 545
  - bargain
    uncertain 475
    purposeless 621
    rash 863
  - coal 388
  - hookey 840
  - lead the blind 538
  - man's buff 840
  - man's holiday 421
  - of one eye 443
  - poker 840
  - side *prejudice* 481
    credulity 486
    obstinacy 606
  - the eyes *hide* 528
    deceive 545
  - to one's own merit 880
blindfold 528
blindness 442
blink *wink* 443
  neglect 460
  falter 605
  avoid 623

(*overlook* 458)
  - at *blind to* 442
blinkard 443
blinker 530
bliss 827
  celestial 981
blister 250
blithe 836
blizzard 349
bloated
  expanded 194
  misshapen 243
  convex 250
  - with pride 878
bloater 298
blob 250
blobber 848
  - lip 848
block *mass* 192
  support 215
  dense 321
  hard 323
  fool 501
  hinder 706
  execution 975
  - of buildings 189
  - out *shape* 240
  prepare 673
  - printing 591
  - up *close* 261
  obstruct 706
  bring to the - 972
  cut -s with a razor 638
  wood - 558
blockade *close* 261
  restrain 751
blockhead 501
  the bookful - 499
blockhouse 717
blockish 499
blonde 429, 430
blood
  consanguinity 11
  fluid 333
  kill 361
  fop 854
  nobility 875
  - boil *excite* 824, 825
  anger 900
  - for blood 919
  - heat 382
  - horse 271
  - hound 913
  - letting
    ejection 297
    remedy 662
  - poisoning 655
  - red 434
  - run cold
    painful 830
    fear 860
  - stained 361
  - sucker 913
  - thirsty
    murderous 361
    cruel 907
  - up *excited* 824
    angry 900
  dye with -
    severe 739

- clothes 225
- color 556
- forth 554
- guard
  defense 717
  keeper 753
- of doctrine 490
- of knowledge 490
- of water 348
- politic
  mankind 372
  authority 737
in a - *together* 88
keep - and soul to-
  gether 654
Bœotian *stupid* 499
  fool 501
  vulgar 851
  ignoble 876
bog *swamp* 345
  dunghill 653
- trotter 876
boggart 980
boggle *hesitate* 605
  awkward 699
  difficulty 704
bogie 980
bogle 980
bogus 545
- check 808
Bohemian 268
  ungenteel 851
boil *violence* 173
  effervesce 315
  bubble 353
  heat 382, 384
  ulceration 665
  excitement 824, 825
  anger 900
- down 195
boiler 386
boisterous
  violent 173
  hasty 684
  excitable 825
bold *prominent* 250
  vigorous 574
  brave 861
- faced 885
- push *essay* 675
- relief *visible* 446
- stroke *plan* 626
  success 731
make - with
  discourtesy 895
show a - front
  defy 715
  brave 861
bold face
  type 591
bole 50
bolero 840
bolster *support* 215
  repair 658
  aid 707
- up *vindicate* 937
bolt *sift* 42
  fasten 43
  fastening 45
  close 261
  move rapidly 274

378

propel 284
run away 623
escape 671
hindrance 706
shaft 727
shackle 752
- food *swallow* 298
  gormandize 957
- in 751
- out of the blue 508
- the door 761
- upright 212
thunder - 872
bolthead 191
bolus *mouthful* 298
  remedy 662
bomb 727
- vessel 726
bombard 716
bombardier 726
bombardon 417
bombast
  unmeaning 517
  magniloquence 577
  ridiculous 853
  boasting 884
  (*exaggeration* 549)
Bombastes Furioso
  887
bombilation 404
bombinate 407
bon: *diable* 844
- enfant *social* 892
  kindly 906
- gré mal gré 601
- mot 842
- naturel 836
- ton 852
- vivant 957
- voyage 267
de - augure 858
bona - fides
  veracity 543
  probity 939
- roba 962
bonanza *extra* 641
  wealth 803
bonbon 396
bond *tie* 45
  compact 769
  security 771
  money 800
  right 924
- of union 9, 45
bondage 749
bonded together 712
bonds [*see* bond]
  fetters 752
  securities 802
- of harmony 714
in - *service* 746
tear asunder one's -
  750
bondsman 746
bone *dense* 321
  hard 323
  strength 159
- of contention 713,
  720
- to pick *difficulty* 704
  discord 713

bred in the - 5
one - and one flesh
  903
bonehouse 363
bones [*see* bone]
  corpse 362
  music 417
break no - 648
make no - *willing* 602
  easy 705
bonesetter 662
bonfire 382
  festivity 840
  celebration 883
make a - of 384
bonhomie
  candor 703
  kindness 906
bonhomme 996
Boniface 890
bonis avibus 771
bonis nocet 927a
bonne *servant* 746
  nurse 753
à la - heure
  willing 602
  content 831
- bouche *end* 67
  pleasant 377
  savory 394
  saving 636
- foi 939
de - volonté 602
bonnet 225
- rouge 742
bonny
  cheerful 836
  pretty 845
bono: cui -
  intention 620
  utility 644
  inutility 645
pro - publico
  useful 644
  philanthropy 910
bonus *extra* 641
  gift 784
  money 810
bony 323
bonze 996
booby 501
boodle 784
boof 860
book *register* 86
  record 551
  volume 593
  enter accounts 811
at one's -s 539
- learning 490
- madness 490
- of fate 601
bring to -
  evidence 467
  account 811
  reprove 932
mind one's - 539
school - 542
without -
  by heart 505
bookcase 191
booked *dying* 360

bookish 490
bookkeeper 553
bookkeeping 811
bookless
  unlearned 493
bookmaking 156
bookseller 593
bookstore 593
bookworm 492
booly 268
boom
  support 215
  sail 267
  rush 274
  impulse 276
  sound 404
  obstacle 706
  defense 717
boomer 863
boomerang
  recoil 277
  weapon 727
boon 784
beg a - 765
- companion 890
boor *clown* 876
boorish
  ridiculous 851
  uncourteous 895
boost 276
boot *box* 191
  dress 225
  advantage 618
  important 642
  punishment 975
to - *added* 37
booted and spurred
  673
bootee 225
booth *stall* 189
  shop 799
bootikin 225
bootless *useless* 645
  failing 732
boots *dress* 225
  servant 746
what - it? 643
booty 793
booze 959
bo-peep *peep* 441
  hide 528
bordel 961
border *edge* 231
  flower bed 371
  ornament 847
- upon 197, 199
borderer 197
bordering 233
- upon 197
bore *diameter* 202
  hole 260
  tide 348
  trouble 828
  plague 830
  weary 841
Boreal
  Northern 237
  cold 383
Boreas 349
boredom 841
borer 262

born 359
- so 5
- to other things 865
- under a lucky star 734
- under an evil star 735
borne 826
- down *failure* 732
defection 837
borné 499
borough 189
rotten - 893
borrow 788
- of Peter, &c. 147
borrowed plumes
deception 545
borrower 806
neither a - nor a lender be 806
borrowing 788
boscage 367
bosh
unmeaning 517
untrue 546
trifling 643
bosk 367
bosom *breast* 221
mind 450
affections 820
- friend 890
- of one's family 221
in the - of 229
boss
knob 250
politician 694
rule 737
master 745
bossism 693
boston 840
botanic 369
- garden 369, 371
botanomancy 511
botany 367, 369
botch *mend* 660
unskillful 699
fail 732
both 89
burn the candle at - ends 641
butter one's bread on - sides 641
listen with - ears 418
bother
uncertainty 475
bustle 682
difficulty 704
trouble 828
harass 830
botheration 828
bothy 189
bottle
receptacle 191
preserve 670
bee in a - 407
- green 435
- holder
auxiliary 177
mediator 724
- up *remember* 505
hide 528

restrain 751
crack a - 298
pass the - 959
smelling - 400
bottom
lowest part 211
support 215
combe 252
ship 273
pluck 604a
courage 861
at - 5
at the - of
cause 153
- dollar 67, 800
- upwards 218
from the - of one's heart *veracity* 543
feeling 821
go to the - 310
probe to the - 461
bottomless 208
angel of the - pit 978
- pit 982
bouche:
- à feu 727
bonne - *end* 67
savory 394
saving 636
pleasant 829
ni - ni éperon 499
bouderie 901a
boudoir 191
bouffe, opéra 599
bouge 250
bough *part* 51
curve 245
tree 367
bought *flexure* 245
bougie 423
bouilli 298
boulder 249
boulevards 227
bouleversement
revolution 146
destruction 162
excite 824
bounce *violence* 173
eject 297
jump 309
lie 546
dismiss 756
boast 884
insolence 885
- upon *arrive* 292
surprise 508
bouncer
ejection 297
bouncing *large* 192
bound
circumscribe 229
swift 274
leap 309
certain 474
- back *recoil* 277
- by 926
- for *direction* 278
destination 620
- to *promise* 768
responsible 926
I'll be - 535

boundary 233
bounden duty 926
boundless
infinite 105
space 180
bounds 233
outline 230
- of modesty 881
- of possibility 470
keep within -
moderation 174
shortcoming 304
restrain 751
prohibit 761
bountiful
liberal 816
benevolent 906
bounty *gift* 784
bouquet
fragrant 400
beauty 847
bourdon *staff* 215
drone 415
bourgeois *type* 591
commoner 876
bourgeon 194
bourn 233
bourse 799
bouse 959
bout *turn* 138
job 680
fight 720
prank 840
drinking - 954
bout
au - de son latin
sophistry 477
ignorance 491
difficulty 704
au - du compte 476
boutade
absurdity 497
caprice 608
boutez en avant 741
bovine *ox* 366
beef-witted 499
bow *fore part* 234
curve 245
projection 250
stoop 308
fiddlestick 417
weapon 727
ornament 847
servility 886
reverence 894
respect 928
bend the - 686
- down *worship* 990
- out 297
- submission 725
- window 245, 260
Bow bells
born within sound of - 876
bowed down
lament 837
humble 879
bowelless 914a
bowels *inside* 221
- full of wrath 722
- of compassion 914

- of the earth 208
bower *abode* 189
alcove 191
cards 840
-s of bliss 981
bowie knife 253, 727
bowl *vessel* 191
rotate 312
- along *walk* 266
swift 274
flowing - 959
bowlder 249
bow-legged 243
bowling green
level 213
bowls 840
bowman 726
bowshot 197
bowstring
execution 972, 975
bowwow 412
box *house* 189
chest 191
theater 599
fight 720
- car 272
- the compass
direction 278
rotation 312
change of mind 607
- the ear *anger* 900
strike 972
- up 751
horse - 272
in a - 704
musical - 417
wrong - *error* 495
unskillful 699
dilemma 704
boxer 726
boy 129
servant 746
boyar 875
boycott 297
boyhood 127
brabble *discord* 713
contest 720
brabbler 901
brace *tie* 43
fasten 45
two 89
strengthen 159
music 413
refresh 689
- game 545
bracelet *circle* 247
ornament 847
bracer 662
brachial 633
brachygraphy 590
bracing
salubrious 656
bracken 367
bracket *tie* 43, 45
couple 89
support 215
brackish 392
brad 45
bradawl 262
Bradshaw 266
brae 206

brag *cards* 840
  boast 884
braggadocia 884
Brahma 979
Brahmi 590
Brahmin
  religion 984
  priest 996
braid *tie* 43
  ligature 45
  net 219
  variegate 440
Braille 442
brain *kill* 361
  intellect 450
  skill 498
  blow one's -s out 361
  coinage of the - 515
  rack one's -s 451, 515
  suck one's -s 461
brainless 499
brainpan 450
brainsick 458
brain storm 503
brainwork 451
brainy 450, 498
brake *copse* 367
  curb 752
  apply the - *slower* 275
  hinder 706
  [see also break]
bramble *thorn* 253
  bane 663
bran 330
brancard 272
branch *member* 51
  posterity 167
  stream 348
  tree 367
  - off *bifurcate* 91
  diverge 291
  - out *ramify* 91
  diffuse style 573
branchiæ 349
branching
  symmetry 242
brand *burn* 384
  fuel 388
  torch 423
  mark 550
  sword 727
  disrepute 874
  censure 932
  stigmatize 934
  - new 123
  - of discord 713
  - with reproach 938
brandish
  oscillate 314
  flourish 315
  display 882
brandy smash 959
brangle 713
brangler 710
brank 975
bras
  à - ouverts 894
  les - croisés 681
brash *brittle* 328
  sickness 655
brasier 386

brass
  alloy 41
  insolence 885
  bold as - 861
  - band 417
  - colored 439
  - farthing 643
brat 129
bravado 884
brave *healthy* 654
  defy 715
  warrior 726
  bear 821, 826
  courage 861
  - a thousand years 110
  - deserve the fair 845
bravo
  assassin 361
  desperado 863
  applause 931
bravura 415
brawl *cry* 411
  discord 713
  revel 840
brawler
  disputant 710
  rioter 742
  blusterer 887
brawny
  strong 159
  stout 192
bray *grind* 330
  cry 412
Bray, Vicar of -
  tergiversation 607
  servility 886
braze 43
brazen
  insolent 885
brazier 191
Brazil tea 298
breach *crack* 44
  gap 198
  quarrel 713
  violation 925
  - of faith 940
  - of law
  unconformity 83
  illegal 964
  - of the peace 713
  custom honored in the - 614
breachloader 727
breachy 198
  unruly 742
bread 298
  beg - 765
  selfish 943
  - of idleness 683
  - of life *Christ* 976
  piety 987
  - upon the waters 638
  quarrel with - and butter 699
breadbasket 191
breadfruit 298
breadth 202
  chiaroscuro 420
break
  fracture 44

  discontinuity 70
  change 140
  gap 198
  carriage 272
  crumble 328
  disclose 529
  cashier 756
  violate 773, 927
  bankrupt 808
  faux pas 947
  - a habit 614
  - a lance *attack* 716
  battle 722
  - a law 83
  - away 623
  - bread 298
  - bulk 297
  - down *destroy* 162
  fall short 304
  decay 659
  fail 732
  - for taller timber 666
  - forth 295
  - ground 66
  - in *ingress* 294
  domesticate 370
  teach 537
  tame 749
  - in upon *derange* 61
  inopportune 135
  hinder 706
  - jail 671
  - loose *escape* 671
  get free 750
  - no bones 648
  - of 660
  - of day *morning* 125
  twilight 422
  - off *cease* 70, 142
  relinquish 624
  abrogate 756
  - one's neck
  powerless 158
  die 360
  - on the wheel
  physical pain 378
  mental pain 830
  punishment 972
  - open 173
  - out *begin* 66
  violent 173
  disease 655
  excited 825
  - Priscian's head 568
  - prison 750
  - short 328
  - silence 582
  - the heart *pain* 828, 830
  dejection 837
  - the ice 888
  - the neck of
  task 676
  success 731
  - the peace
  violence 173
  contest 720
  - the ranks 61
  - the teeth
  hard words 579
  - the thread 70

  - through a custom 614
  - through the clouds
  visible 446
  disclose 529
  - up *disjoin* 44
  decompose 49
  end 67
  revolution 146
  destroy 162
  - up of the system
  death 360
  disease 655
  - with 713
  - with the past 146
  - word *deceive* 545
  improbity 940
breakbone fever 655
breakdown 840
breaker
  of horses 268
  reef 346
  wave 348
breakers *surf* 348
  shallow 667
  - ahead 665
  surrounded by - 704
breakfast 298
breakneck
  precipice 217
  rash 863
breakwater
  refuge 666
  obstruction 706
breast *interior* 221
  convex 250
  mind 450
  oppose 708
  soul 820
  at the - 129
  - high 206
  - the current 719
  in the - of 620
breastplate 717
breastwork 717
breath *instant* 113
  breeze 349
  life 359
  animality 364
  faint sound 405
  - of accusation 938
  hold - *quiet* 265
  expect 507
  wonder 870
  in the same - 120
  not a - of air *quiet* 265
  hot 382
  out of - 688
  shortness of -
  fatigue 688
  take away one's -
  unexpected 508
  fear 860
  wonder 870
  take - *rest* 265
  refresh 689
  with bated - 581
breathe *exist* 1
  blow 349
  live 359
  faint sound 405

evince 467
mean 516
inform 527
disclose 529
utter 580
speak 582
refresh 689
- freely *pleasure* 827
relief 834
- one's last 360
not - a word 528
breathing-hole 351
breathing time
repose 687
truce 723
breathless
voiceless 581
out of breath 688
feeling 821
fear 860
eager 865
wonder 870
- attention 457
- expectation 507
- impatience 865
- speed 684
breech 235
breeches 225
- maker 225
- pocket
money 800, 802
wear the - 737
breed
race 11
kind 75
multiply 161
progeny 167
animals 370
rear 537
(*prepare* 673)
breeding *style* 852
politeness 894
breeze *wind* 349
discord 713
breezy 836
brethren 997
brett 272
breve 413
brevet
warrant 741
commission 755
permit 760
- rank 873
brevet d'invention
760
breviary 998
brevier 591
brevipennate 193
brevis esse laboro 572
brevity *short* 201
concise 572
brew *mix* 41
prepare 673
brewing
impending 152
storm - 665
Briarean 102
bribe *equivalent* 30
tempt 615
offer 763
gift 784

buy 795
reward 973
brick *hard* 323
pottery 384
material 635
trump 939, 948
- color 434
make -s without
straw 471
brickbat 727
bricklayer 690
bridal 903
bridewell 752
bridge
intermedium 45
way 627
card game 840
- over *join* 43
facilitate 705
make peace 723
compromise 774
bridle *restrain* 751
rein 752
- one's tongue
silent 585
cautious 864
- road 627
- up 900
brief *time* 111
space 201
concise 572
compendium 596
hold a - for 759
briefly *anon* 132
- thyself remember
505
brier *sharp* 253
bane 663
brig 273
brigade 726
brigadier 745
brigand 792
brigandage 791
brigandine 717
brigantine 273
bright *shine* 420
color 428
intelligent 498
cheery 836
beauty 845
glory 873
- days 734
- eyed 845
- prospect 858
- side 829
- thought
sharp 498
good stroke 626
wit 842
look at the - side
cheer 836
hope 858
brighten up
furbish 658
brigue *party* 712
contention 720
**briller par son ab-
sence** 187
brilliant
shining 420
good 648

beautiful 845
gem 847
glorious 873
- idea 842
brim 231
- over 641
brimful 52
brimstone 388
brindled 440
brine *sea* 341
salt 392
bring 270
- about *cause* 153
achieve 729
- back 790
- back to the memory
505
- forth 161
- forward
evidence 467
manifest 525
teach 537
improve 658
- gray hairs to the
grave
adversity 735
pain 830
- grist to the mill 644
- home 775
- home to 155
- in *receive* 296
income 810
price 812
- in a verdict 480
- in its train 88
- in question 461
- into being 161
- into play 677
- low 874
- off 672
- out
discover 480a
manifest 525
publish 591
- over
persuade 484
- round
persuade 615
restore 660
- to *convert* 144
halt 265
- to a crisis 604
- to a point 74
- to bear upon
relation 9
action 170
- together 72
- to life 359
- to light 480a
- to maturity
prepare 673
complete 729
- to mind 505
- to perfection 677
- to terms 723
- to trial 969
- under one's notice
457
- up *develop* 161
vomit 297
educate 537

- up the rear 235
- word 527
brink 231
- of the grave 360
on the -
almost 32
coming 121
near 197
briny 392
brio *music* 415
brisk *prompt* 111
energetic 171
active 682
cheery 836
bristle 253
- up *stick up* 250
angry 900
- with plenty 639
too much 641
- with arms 722
Britannia metal 545
Briticism 563
British 188
- lion 604
Briton, true - 939
brittleness 328
britzka 272
broach *begin* 66
found 153
tap 297
publish 531
assert 535
broad *general* 78
space 202
lake 343
emphatic 535
indelicate 961
- accent 580
- awake
vigilant 459
brisk 682
- daylight
light 420
manifest 525
- farce 842
- grin 838
- highway 627
- hint 527
- meaning 516
broadcast 73
sow - 818
broadhearted 906
broadhorn 273
broadsheet 593
broad-shouldered
159
broadside
lateral 236
publication 531
cannonade 716
broadsword 727
Brobdingnagian 192
brocade 847
brocatelle 847
brochure 593
**Brocken, specter of
the** 443
broder 549
brogan 225
brogue *boot* 225
dialect 563

C

capability
endowment 5
power 157
skill 698
facility 705
capacious *space* 180
- *memory* 505
capacity
endowment 5
power 157
space 180
size 192
intellect 450
wisdom 498
office 625
talent 698
cap-à-pie
complete 52
armed -
prepared 673
defense 717
war 722
caparison 225
cape *height* 206
cloak 225
projection 250
(*land* 342)
capella, alla - 415
caper *leap* 309
dance 840
capful *quantity* 25
small 32
- *of wind* 349
capillament 205
capillary
hairlike 205
(*thin* 203)
capital *city* 189
top 210
letter 561
important 642
excellent 648
money 800
wealth 803
- *crime* 947
- *messuage* 189
- *punishment* 972
make - *out of*
pretext 617
acquire 775
print in -s 642
capitalist 803
capitals 591
capitation 85
- *tax* 812
capitol 717
capitular 995, 996
capitulate 725
capnomancy 511
capon 373
caporal 694
capote 225
capouch 999
capper 548
capriccio *music* 415
whim 608
caprice 608
out of - 615a
capricious
irregular 139
changeable 149

irresolute 605
whimsical 608
capriole 309
capsheaf 210
capsicum 393
capsize
inversion 218
wreck 731
capsized 732
capstan *lift* 307
machine 633
capsular
concave 252
capsule *vessel* 191
tunicle 223
captain 745
captandum, ad -
sophistry 477
deception 545
affectation 855
ostentation 882
flattery 933
captation 933
caption 789
heading 66, 564
captious
capricious 608
irascible 901
censorious 932
captivate
induce 615
restrain 751
please 829
captivated
fascinated 827
captivating
pleasing 829
lovable 897
captive
prisoner 754
adorer 897
lead - 749
make - 751
captivity 751
capture 789
Capuchin 996
caput 696
- *mortuum*
useless 645
dirt 653
(*residue* 40)
caquet 584
car 272
carabineer 726
carack 273
caracole 309
caracoler 266
caraffe 191
carambole 276
caramel 396
carapace 717
cara sposa 897
carat 319
caravan
journey 266
vehicle 272
caravansary 189
caravel 273
carbine 727
carbon 388
carbonaro 742

carbonate
- *of ammonia* 392
- *of lead* 430
carbonic acid 663
carbonization 384
carboy 191
carbuncle *red* 434
abscess 655
jewel 847
carcanet 847
carcass
structure 329
corpse 362
bomb 727
carcelage 973
carcinoma 655
card *unravel* 60
ticket 550
plan 626
address - 550
by the - 82
- *index* 86
-s *to play* 632
great - 873
house of -s 328
leave a - 892
on the -s *liable* 177
destiny 152
possible 470
playing -s 840
play one's best - 686
play one's - 692
play one's -s *well* 698
shuffle the -s
begin again 66
change 140
chance 621
prepare 673
speak by the -
care 459
veracity 543
phrase 566
throw up the -s 757
ticklish - 704
trump - 626
cardcase 191
cardiac 836
cardialgia 655
cardinal *dress* 225
important 642
excellent 648
priest 995, 996
- *bird* 439
- *flower* 439
- *points*
compass 278
- *virtues* 944
cardinalate 995
cardiograph 633
cardioid 245
carditis 655
card-sharper 792
card-sharping 545
care *attention* 459
business 625
adversity 735
custody 751
economy 817
pain 828
fear 860
begone dull - 836

- *for important* 642
desire 865
love 897
- *will kill a cat* 459
drive - *away* 840
for aught one -s
unimportant 643
indifferent 866
have the - *of* 693
incessant - *and labor*
459
take - 864
take - *of* 459
careen *slope* 217
repair 660
career *business* 625
conduct 692
careless
inattentive 458
neglectful 460
feeble 575
insensible 823
indifferent 866
caress 902
caret *incomplete* 53
want 640
caretaker 758
careworn *pain* 828
dejection 837
cargador 271
cargo
large quantity 31
contents 190
property 780
goods 798
caribou 366
caricature
likeness 19
copy 21
exaggerate 549
misrepresent 555
ridicule 856
caricaturist 559, 844
caries 655
cariole 272
carious 653
cark 828
carking 828
- *care* 830
carle 876
carlock 352
carman 694
Carmelite 996
carminative 174, 662
carmine 434
carnage 361
carnal
intemperate 954
impure 961
irreligious 989
carnation 434
carnival 840
carnivorous 298
carol
music 415, 416
cheerful 836
rejoice 838
carom 276
caro sposo 897
carouse *feast* 298
festivity 840

defense 717
combatant 726
representative 759
championship 707
champlevé 847
chance
  absence of cause **156**
  absence of aim **621**
  as - would have it 152
  be one's - 151
  -s against one *danger* 665
  game of - 840
  great - 472
  small - 473
  stand a - *liable* 177
  possible 470
  take one's - 675
chancel 1000
chancellor
  president 745
  deputy 759
  judge 967
  - of the exchequer 801
chancery
  - suit *delay* 133
  court of - 966
chandelier 423
chandelle, le jeu ne vaut pas la -
  waste 638
  unimportant 643
  dear 814
chandler 797
change
  alteration **140**
  mart 799
  small coin 800
  - about 149
  - color 821
  - for 147
  - hands 783
  - of mind 607
  - of opinion 485
  - of place 264
  inter- 148
  radical - 146
  sudden - 146
changeableness
  mutable **149**
  irresolute 605
changeful
  fickle 607
changeling
  substitute 147
  fool 501
changer 797
channel
  furrow 259
  opening 260
  conduit 350
  way 627
chant *song* 415
  sing 416
  worship 990
chant du cygne 360
chanter 416
chanticleer 366
chantry 1000
chaomancy 511

chaos 59
chap *crack* 198
  jaw 231
  fellow 373
chaparajos 225
chaparral 367
chap book 593
chapeau 225
chapel 1000
chaperon 664
  guard 459
chapfallen 837, 878
chaplain 995, 996
chaplet *circle* 247
  trophy 733
  ornament 847
chapman 797
chapter *part* 51
  topic 454
  book 593
  council 696
  church 995
  - and verse
  evidence 467
  exact 494
  - of accidents 156, 621
chapter house 1000
chaque pays a sa guise 852
chaque saint sa chandelle 924
chaqueta 225
char 384
char-à-bancs 272
character
  nature 5
  state 7
  class 75
  oddity 83
  letter 561
  drama 599
  disposition 820
  - is higher than intellect 5
characteristic
  intrinsic 5
  special 79
  mark 550
characterize
  name 564
  describe 594
characterized 820
charade
  riddle 533
  drama 599
charcoal *fuel* 384, 388
  black 431
  drawing 556
charge *fill* 52
  contents 190
  business 625
  mandate 630
  direction 693
  advice 695
  precept 697
  attack 716
  order 741
  custody 751
  commission 755
  bargain for 794

  price 812
  accusation 938
  -d with
  possessed of 777
  - on *attribute* 155
  in - *prisoner* 754
  justifiable- 937
  take - of
  safe 664
  take in - 751
chargeable *debt* 806
  - on *duty* 926
chargé d'affaires 758
charger
  carrier 271
  fighter 726
chargeship 625
Charing Cross, proclaim at - 531
chariot 272
  drag at one's - wheels 749
charioteer
  driver 268
  pilot 694
charity *give* 784
  liberal 816
  beneficent 906
  pity 914
  - that begins at home 943
  Christian - 906
  cold as -
  insensible 823
charivari *loud* 404
  clatter 407
charlatan
  ignoramus 493
  impostor 548
  mountebank 844
  boaster 884
charlatanism
  ignorance 491
  falsehood 544
  affectation 855
Charles's wain 318
Charley 753
charm *motive* 615
  please 829
  beauty 845
  love 897
  conjure 992
  spell 993
  bear a -d life
  safe 664
  prosperous 734
charmer
  sorcerer 994
  not listen to voice of - 604
  voice of the -
  flattery 933
charnel house 363
chart *inform* 527
  represent 554
charter
  commission 755
  permit 760
  compact 769
  security 771
  privilege 924

chartered
  legal 963
  - accountant 811
  - libertine 962
charwoman
  worker 690
  servant 746
chary
  economical 817
  stingy 819
  cautious 864
Charybdis
  whirlpool 312
  danger 665
chase *emboss* 250
  drive away 289
  killing 361
  forest 367
  pursue 622
  ornament 847
  wild goose - 645
chaser 559
chasm *interval* 198
  opening 260
  (*discontinuity* 70)
chassemarée 273
chassepot 727
chasser 297
  - balancer 605
chasseur 726
chaste
  shapely 242
  language 576, 578
  simple 849
  good taste 850
  pure 960
  - as unsunn'd snow 960
chasten
  moderate 174
  punish 972
chastened
  subdued spirit 826
chastise
  censure 932
  punish 972
  - with scorpions 739
chastity
  - my brother chastity 960
chasuble 999
chat 588
château 189
  - en Espagne 858
châtelaine 847
chatoyant 440
chat qui dort 667, 668
chattels
  furniture 633
  property 780
chatter 584
chatterbox 584
chattering of teeth
  cold 383
chatti 191
chatty
  talkative 584
  sociable 892
chauffeur 268
chauki 752

chaunt
song 415
sing 416
worship 990
chaussé 225
Chautauqua 537
Chauvinism 884
chawbacon 876
cheap
worthless 643
low price 815
hold - 930
cheapen *haggle* 794
begrudge 819
cheapness 815
cheat *deceive* 545
deceiver 548
check
numerical 85
moderate 174
counteract 179
slacken 275
plaid 440
experiment 463
measure 466
evidence 468
ticket 550
dissuade 616
hinder 706
misfortune 735
restrain 751
money order 800
- oneself 826
- the growth 201
checkered
changeable 149
checkers 440
game 840
checkmate 731, 732
checkroll 86
checkstring
pull the - 142
cheek *side* 236
- by jowl *with* 88
near 197
cheeks *dual* 89
cheep 412
cheer *repast* 298
cry 411
aid 707
pleasure 827
relief 834
mirth 836
rejoicing 838
amusement 840
courage 861
sociality 892
welcome 894
applaud 931
(*please* 829)
good - *hope* 858
high living 957
cheerfulness 836
cheering 602
cheerless
unpleasing 830
dejected 837
cheeseparings
remains 40
dirt 653
economy 817

cheetah 440
chef de cuisine
proficient 700
servant 746
chef-d'œuvre
masterpiece 648
master stroke 698
chela 541
chemin faisant 270
chemise 225
chemistry 144
organic - 357
cheque 800
chequer 440
- roll 86
chercher une ai-
guille 471
chère amie 962
cherish *aid* 707
love 897
endearment 902
- a belief 484
- an idea &c. 451
- feelings &c. 821
cherry
two bites of a -
overrate 482
roundabout 629
clumsy 699
cherry-cheeked 845
cherry-colored 434
chersonese 342
cherub 977
Cheshire cat 838
chess 840
chessboard 440
chest *box* 191
money coffer 802
chestnut *stale* 532
chestnut-color 433
cheval-de-bataille
plea 617
plan 626
vanity 880
cheval glass 445
chevalier 875
-d'industrie 792
chevaux de frise
spikes 253
defense 717
chevron 550
chevronné 754
chew 298
tobacco 392
- the cud 451
chiaroscuro
light 420
gray 432
painting 556
chic
show 882
chicane
sophistry 477
deceit 545
cunning 702
chi-chi 563
chick 424
chickaree 274
chicken
young 129
fowl 366

reckon -s before
hatched
hope 858
rash 863
tender as a - *soft* 324
sensitive 822
compassionate 914
chicken-hearted 862
chicote 975
chide 932
chief *principal* 642
master 745
- part 31
evidence in - 467
chiefdom 737
Chief Justice 967
chieftain 745
chiffonnier 876
chiffonnière 191
chignon 225
child
infant 129
offspring 167
fool 501
- is father of the man
167
- of God 987
-'s play *trifling* 643
easy 705
childbirth 161
childhood 127
childish
credulous 486
foolish 499
feeble 575
- treble 581
chiliad 98
chill *cold* 383
render cold 385
indispose 616
Chiltern Hundreds
757
chime
repetition 104
roll 407
resonance 408
melody 413
- in with *agree* 23
conform 82
assent 488
concord 714
chimera
monster 83
imaginary 515
(*error* 495)
chimney
opening 260
airpipe 351
(*egress* 295)
- corner 189
china *ceramic* 384
art 557
- wedding 883
China to Peru 180
chinch 653
chine 235
chink *gap* 198
sound 408
money 800
-s that time has made
128

chinking 635
Chinook 349, 563
chip *small* 32
detach 44
bit 51
reduce 195
counter 550
- in 709
- of the old block
similar 17
copy 21
offspring 167
chipmunk 274
chipper 836
chippy 962
chirography 590
chirology 550
chiromancy 511
chirp
bird-note 412
sing 416
cheerful 836
rejoice 838
chirrup [see chirp]
chirurgery 662
chisel
fabricate 161
form 240
tool 262
sculpture 557
chiseling 558
chit *infant* 129
small 193
letter 592
chi tace accousente
488, 762
chit-chat 588
chitterlings 221
chivalry *war* 722
tenure 777
courage 861
philanthropy 910
honor 939
generosity 942
chivarras 225
chlamys 225
chloral 376
chloride
- of lime 652
- of sodium 336
chloroform
physical numbness
376
mental insensibility
823
chlorosis 655
chlorotic 655
chock full 52
chocolate
food 298
color 433
choice
election 609
excellent 648
absence of - **609a**
by - 600
- of words 569
- spirits 873
choir *sing* 416
church music 996
church 1000

392

choke *close* 261
  stifle 361
  redundant 641
  hinder 706
  -full *complete* 52
  replete 639
  - off 706
choke damp 663
chokidar 753
chokra 746
choky 752
choler 900
cholera 655
choleric 901
choose 609
  do what one -s 748
chop *disjoin* 44
  change 140
  indication 550
  - logic 476
  - up 201
chopfallen 837
chophouse 189
chopping
  large 192
  - sea 348
chops *mouth* 66
  jaws 231
  food 298
chop-suey 298
chor 792
choral 415
chord 413
chore 625, 746
  - boy 534
chorea 315, 655
choregus 694
chorister
  singer 416
  church singer 996
chorography 183
chorus
  shout 411
  song 415
  singers 416
  unanimity 488
  opera 599
  concord 714
chose
  - in action 780
  - in possession 777
chose qui plaît 796
chota hazri 298
chouse 545
choux gras, faire ses
  - 377
chowchow 41
chowder 298
  - head 501
chrestomathy 560
chrism 998
Christ 976
  Church of - 983a
  receive - 987
Christcross-row 561
christen
  name 564
  rite 998
Christendom 983a.
  995
Christian 983a, 987

- charity 906
- Science 984
Christmas
  period 138
  Church festival 998
Christmas box 784
chromatic
  color 428
  - scale *music* 413
chromatogenous 428
chromatography 428
chromatology 428
chromato pseudo-
  blepsis 443
chromatrope 445
chrome 436
chromolitho g r a p h
  558
chromosome 357
chromosphere 318
chronic 110
chronicle
  measure time 114
  annals 551
chronicler 553
chronogram 114
chronography
  measure time 114
  description 594
chronology 114
chronometry 114
chrononhotontho-
  logos 887
chrysalis 129
chrysolite
  perfection 650
  jewel 847
chrysology 800
chubby 192
chuck *throw* 284
  animal cry 412
  - under chin 902
chucker-out 297
chuck farthing 621
chuckle
  animal cry 412
  laugh 838
  exult 884
chucklehead 501
chudder 225
chuff 876
chum 890
chunk 51
chunky 201
chup! 403, 585
chupatty 298
Church
  infallible 474
  orthodox 983a
  Christendom 995
  temple 1000
  - of Christ 983a
  dignitaries of - 996
  go to - 990
  High -, Low -, &c.
  984
churchdom 995
churchman 996
churchwarden 996
churchyard
  burial 363

church 1000
- cough 655
churl *boor* 876
churlish
  niggard 819
  rude 895
  sulky 901a
  malevolent 907
churn
  agitate 315
  butter 352
chut! *silent* 403
  taciturn 585
chute 348
chutney 393
chyle 333
cibarious 298
cicatrix 551
  manet - 919
cicatrize 660
Cicero 587
cicerone 524, 527
Ciceronian 578, 582
cicisbeo 897
cicuration 370
cider 298
  all talk and no - 584
ci-devant 122
cienaga 345
cigar 392
ci-gît 363
cilia *hairs* 205
  rough 256
cimeter 727
Cimmerian 421
cinch 45, 705
cinchona 662
cincture 247
cinder
  combustion 384
  dirt 653
  (remains 40)
Cinderella
  servant 746
  commonalty 876
cinematograph 448
cinerary 363
cineration 384
cinereous 432
cineri gloria sera est
  873
cingle 230
cinnabar 434
cinnamon 433
cinque 98
cinquecento 114, 554
cipher
  unsubstantial 4
  number 84
  compute 85
  zero 101
  mark 550
  letter 561
  unimportant 643
  writing in - 590
Circe *seductor* 615
  sorcerer 994
Circean 992
  - cup *pleasure* 377
  intemperance 954
circination 312

circle *region* 181
  form 247
  party 712
  (*assemblage* 72)
  - of acquaintance 892
  - of the sciences 490
  describe a - 311
  great - sailing 628
circling
  convolution 248
circuit *region* 181
  outline 230
  winding 248
  tour 266
  indirect path 311
  indirect course 629
circuition 311
circuitous
  devious 279
  indirect 311
  - method 629
circular
  round 247
  publication 531
  letter 592
  pamphlet 593
  - note 805
  - saw 44
circularity 247
circulate
  circuit 311
  rotate 312
  publish 531
circulating medium
  800
circulation
  [see circulate]
  - of money 809
  in - *news* 532
circumambient 227
circumambulate
  travel 266
  go round 311
circumbendibus
  winding 248
  indirect method 629
  (*circuition* 311)
circumcision 44, 998
circumduction 552
circumference 230
circumferential 227
circumfluent
  lie round 227
  move round 311
circumforaneous
  traveling 266
  circuition 311
circumfuse 73
circumgyration 312
circumjacence 227
circumlocution
  periphrase 573
  (*phrase* 566)
circumnavigate
  navigation 267
  - *circuition* 311
circumrotation 312
circumscribe
  surround 229
  limit 761
circumscription 229

circumspection
  attention 457
  care 459
  caution 459
circumstance
  phase 8
  event 151
  blows of - 151
  - of glorious war 722
  my sins not those of -
    8
circumstances
  property 780
  bad - 804
  depend on - 475
  good - 803
  under the - 8
circumstantial 8
  - account 594
  - evidence 467
  probability 472
circumvallation
  inclosure 229, 232
  defense 717
  line of - 233
circumvent
  environ 227
  move round 311
  cheat 545
  cunning 702
  hinder 706
  checkmate 731
circumvest 225
circumvolution
  winding 248
  rotation 312
circus
  buildings 189
  drama 599
  arena 728
cirrocumulus 353
cirrostratus 353
cirrus 353
Cistercian 996
cistern
  receptacle 191
  store 636
cit 188
citadel
  defense 717
  (refuge 666)
cite
  quote as example 82
  as evidence 467
  summon 741
  accuse 938
  arraign 969
cithern 417
citizen
  inhabitant 188
  (man 373)
  - of the world 910
citrine 436
city 189
  in the - 794
civet 400
civic 372
  - crown 733
civil courteous 894
  laity 997
  - authorities 745
394

- crown 733
- law 963
- service list 86
- war 722
civilian lawyer 968
  layman 997
civilization
  improvement 658
  fashion 852
  courtesy 894
civilized life 852
civism 910
clack clatter 407
  animal cry 412
  talkative 584
clad 225
claim
  mandate 630
  demand 741
  property 780
  right 924
  lawsuit 969
  - the attention 457
claimant
  petitioner 767
  right 924
clair-obscur 420
clairvoyance 992
clairvoyant 994
clam 298
clamant 411
clambake 840
clamber 305
clammy 352
clamor cry 411
  wail 839
  - against 932
  - for 765
clamorous
  [see clamor]
  loud 404
  excitable 825
clamp fasten 43
  fastening 45
clan
  race 11
  class 75
  family 166
  party 712
clandestine 528
clangor 404
clank 410
clannishness 481
clanship 709
clap explosion 406
  applaud 931
  - on the back 931
  - on the shoulder 615
  - the hands rejoice
    838
  - together 43
  - up imprison 751
  thunder - prodigy 872
clapboard 223, 635
clapperclaw
  contention 720
  censure 932
claptrap
  pretense 546
  display 882
claquer 935

faire - son fouet 884
clarence 272
claret 298
  - color 434
clarify 652
clarinet 417
clarion music 417
  war 722
  pen became a - 590
clash disagree 24
  cross 179
  concussion 276
  sound 406
  oppose 708
  discord 713
  - of arms 720
clashing
  contrariety 14
  wrangle 24
clasp fasten 43
  fastening 45
  stick 46
  come close 197
  belt 230
  embrace 902
class arrange 60
  category 75
  learners 541
  school 542
  - fellow 890
classic old 124
  symmetry 242
classical
  elegant writing 578
  taste 850
  - education 537
classicism 578
classics 560
classify 60
classis 696
classman 873
  associate 890
clatter noise 404
  rattle 407
claudication
  slowness 275
  failure 732
clause part 51
  passage 593
  condition 770
clausis, januis - 528
claustral 1000
clavate 250
clavichord 417
clavier 417
claviform 250
clavis 522
claw hook 781
  grasp 789
  - back 935
clawhammer coat
  225
clay soft 324
  earth 342
  corpse 362
  material 635
clay-cold 383
claymore 727
clean
  entirely 52
  perfect 650

unstained 652
- bill of health 654
- breast
  disclose 529
- cut 494
- forgotten 506
- hand
  proficient 700
- out empty 297
- sweep
  revolution 146
  destruction 162
with - hands
  honesty 939
  innocence 946
cleanness 652
cleanse 652
clear simple 42
  sound 413
  light 420
  transparent 425
  visible 446
  certain 474
  intelligible 518
  manifest 525
  easy 705
  liberate 750
  profit 775
  vindicate 937
  innocent 946
  acquit 970
- articulation 580
- as day 474
- conscience 946
- cut 494
- for action
  prepare 673
- grit 604
- of distant 196
- off pay 807
- out empty 297
  clean 652
- sighted
  vision 441
  shrewd 498
- sky hope 858
- stage
  occasion 134
  easy 705
  right 922
- the course 302
- the ground
  facilitate 705
- the skirts of 937
- the throat 297
- up light 420
  intelligible 518
  interpret 522
coast - 664
get - off 671
keep - of 623
clearance 970
clear-headed 498
clearing 181
clear obscure 420
cleavage
  cutting 44
  structure 329
cleave sunder 44
  adhere 46
  bisect 91

COIN

in time 120
in place 199
in opinion 488
coiner *thief* 792
coistril 862
coition 43
cojuror 467
coke 388
colander 260
colature 652
cold *frigid* **383**
  color 429, 438
  style 575
  insensible 823
  indifferent 866
- comfort 832
- feet 862
- shoulder
  discourtesy 895
  contempt 930
- steel 727
- storage 387
- sweat *fear* 860
  dislike 867
- water cure 662
in - blood
  premeditated 611
  purposely 620
  unfeeling 823
  dispassionate 826
throw - water on
  dissuade 616
  hinder 706
  dull 843
cold-hearted
  unfeeling 823
  hostile 889
  malevolent 907
colic 378
Coliseum 728
collaborator 711
collapse
  prostration 158
  contract 195
  shortcoming 304
  deteriorate 659
  fatigue 688
  failure 732
collar *dress* 225
  circlet 247
  shackle 752
  seize 789
slip the - 750
collate 464
collateral
  relation 11
  lateral 236
- evidence 467
collation
  repast 298
  comparison 464
colleague
  accompany 88
  coöperation 709
  auxiliary 711
collect *assemble* 72
  opine 480
  understand 518
  acquire 775
  prayer 990
  (*take* 789)

COLO

- evidence 467
- knowledge 539
- one's thoughts 451
collectanea
  assemblage 72
  compendium 596
collected *calm* 826
collection
  assemblage 72
  (*store* 636)
collectively
  whole 50
  generality 78
  together 88
collectivism 737
collector
  director 694, 745
college 542
- education 537
go to - 539
collide 276
collie 366
collier 273
colligate 72
collimation 278
colliquation 335
collision *clash* 179
  percussion 276
  opposition 708
  encounter 720
collocate
  arrange 60
  assemble 72
  place 184
collocution 588
collogue
  wheedle 933
collop 51
colloquial
  figure of speech 521
  neology 563
  conversation 588
- meaning 516
colluctation 720
collusion
  deceit 545
  conspiring 709
collusive 544
colluvies 653
collyrium 662
colon 142
colonel 745
colonist 188
colonize 184
colonnade
  series 69
  houses 189
colony 184, 188
colophon 65
color *hue* **428**
  tone 431
  appearance 448
  probability 472
  disguise 544
  paint 556
  plea 617
  be angry 900
all -s 440
change -
  shame 879
- blindness 443

COMB

- printing 558
- sergeant 745
- too highly 549
- up *redden* 434
  blush 879
give a - to
  change 140
  qualify 469
  probable 472
  falsehood 544
lend a - to
  plea 617
  vindicate 937
man of - 431
show in true -s 543
colorable
  ostensible 472
  deceptive 545
Colorado beetle 913
coloration 428
coloring
  [*see* color]
  meaning 516
- matter 428
false - 523
colorless
  weak 160
  pale 429
  feeble 575
colors
  ensign 550
  decoration 877
false - 544, 545
flying -
  display 882
  celebration 883
lower one's - 735
nail one's - to the
  mast 604
show one's -
  manifest 525
  disclose 529
true to one's - 939
colossal 192
Colosseum 728
colossus *size* 192
  height 206
colporteur 797
colt *young* 129
  horse 271
  fool 501
colter 253
columbarium 189
columbine 599
columella 215
column *series* 69
  height 206
  support 215
  cylinder 249
  caravan 266
  monument 551
  printing 591
  troop 726
colures 318
coma *inactive* 683
  insensible 823
comb *teeth* 253
  clean 652
  punish 972
combat 720, 722
combat, hors de -

COME

  useless 645
  tired 688
combatant **726**
combe 252
combination **48**
  arithmetical 84
  party 712
- of fortuitous cir-
  cumstances 621
combine *unite* 48
  component 56
  partnership 712
  coöperate 709
combustible 388
combustion 384
come *happen* 151
  approach 286
  arrive 292
  cheer up! 836
  out upon! 932
- about 658
- across
  discover 480a
- after
  sequence 63
  posterior 117
- amiss
  disagreeable 24
  ill timed 135
- and go 314
- at one's call 743
- back 283
- before 116
- by **775**
- down with 807
- first *superior* 33
  precede 62
- forth
  egress 295
  appear 446
- forward 763
- from 154
- in *ingress* 294
  receipt 785
- in for
  property 778, 780
- into existence
  be 1
  begin 66
- into operation 170
- into the views of
  coöperate 709
- into the world 359
- into use 613
- into view 446
- near 286
- of 154
- of age 131
- off
  loose 44
  event 151
  loophole 617
  escape 671
- off well 731
- on *future* 121
  destiny 152
  I defy you 715
  attack 716
- out
  disclosure 529
  publication 531

on the stage 599
- *out of effect* 154
egress 295
- *out with*
disclose 529
speak 582
- *over*
influence 615
consent 762
- *round*
period 138
conversion 144
belief 484
assent 488
change of mind 607
influence 615
restoration 660
be pacified 723
consent 762
- *short of*
inferior 34
fall short 304
- *to equal* 27
whole 50
arithmetic 85
future 121
become 144
destiny 152
effect 154
inherit 777
money 800
price 812
- *to a determination* 604
- *to a head*
climax 33
complete 52
- *to a stand* 142
- *together*
assemble 72
converge 290
- *to hand* 785
- *to life* 359
- *to nothing*
unproductive 169
fail 732
- *to oneself* 660
- *to one's knowledge* 527
- *to one's senses* 502
- *to pass state* 7
event 151
- *to pieces* 44
- *to terms*
assent 488
contract 769
- *to the point*
speciality 79
attention 457
concise 572
- *to the front* 303
- *to the rescue* 672
- *to the same thing* 27
- *under* 76
- *upon*
unexpected 508
acquire 775
claim 924
- *what may* 474
cut and - *again* 639
it -s *to this*

398

concisely 572
comedown 735
comedy
drama 599
comic 853
comely 845
comestible 298
comet
wanderer 268
star 318
comfit 396
comfort
pleasure 377
delight 827
content 831
relief 834
a man of - 834
give - 906
comfortable
pleasing 829
Comforter 976
comfortless
painful 830
dejected 837
comic *wit* 842
ridiculous 853
coming [see come]
impending 152
- *events*
prediction 511
- *time* 121
comitia 696
comity 894
comma 142
command *high* 206
requirement 630
authority 737
order 741
possess 777
at one's -
obedient 743
- *a view of* 441
- *belief* 484
- *of language*
writing 574
speaking 582
- *of money* 803
- *one's passions* 944
- *one's temper* 826
- *respect* 928
commandant 745
commandeer 744,789
commanding
[see command]
important 642
comme deux gouttes
d'eau 17
comme il faut
taste 850
fashion 852
genteel 875
commemorate 883
commence 66
commencement de
la fin *end* 67
destruction 162
commend 931
- *the poisoned chalice* 544
commendable 944
commensurate

accordant 23
numeral 85
adequate 639
comment
reason 476
judgment 480
interpretation 522
commentary 595
commentator 524
commerce
conversation 588
barter 794
cards 840
commercial
- *arithmetic* 811
- *traveler* 758
commination 908, 909
commingle 41
comminute 330
commiserate 914
commissariat 637
commissary
consignee 758
commission
task 625
delegate **755**
- *of the peace* 965
commissioner 745, 758
commissionnaire
messenger 534
consignee 758
commissure 43
commis-voyageur 758
commit *do* 680
delegate 755
cards 840
arrest 969
- *an absurdity* 853
- *oneself*
clumsy 699
promise 768
- *oneself to a course* 609
- *to memory* 505
- *to prison* 751
- *to sin* 945
- *to the flames* 384
- *to writing* 551
committee
council 696
consignee 758
(director 694)
commix 41
commode 191
commodious 644
commodity 798
commodore 745
common
general 78
ordinary 82
plain 344
habitual 613
trifling 643
base 876
- *consent* 488
- *council* 966
- *course* 613
- *herd* 876

- *law old* 124
law 963
- *measure* 84
- *origin* 153
- *parlance* 576
- *place-book*
record 551
compendium 596
- *run* 78, 613
- *saying* 496
- *sense* 498
- *sewer* 653
- *stock* 778
- *weal*
mankind 372
good 618
utility 644
philanthropy 910
in - *related* 9
participate 778
make - *cause* 709
right of - 780
tenant in - 778
commonalty 876
commoner 876
commonplace
known 490
plain 576
habit 613
unimportant 643
dull 843
Common Pleas,
Court of - 966
commons 298
commonwealth 372, 644
commorant 188
commotion 315
commune
township 181
commune **pericu-**
lum concordiam
parit 714, 720
commune with 588
- *oneself* 451
communibus annis 29
communicant 990
communicate
join 43
tell 527
give 784
sacrament 998
communication
news 532
oral - 582, 588
communion
society 712
participation 778
sacrament 998
- *table* 1000
hold - *with* 888
communiqué 527
communist
rebel 742
participation 778
philanthropy 910
evil doer 913
community
party 712
- *at large* 372

concamerate 245
concatenation
  junction 43
  continuity 69
  - of circumstances
   621
concavity 252
conceal
  invisible 447
  hide 528
  cunning 702
concealment 528
concede
  assent 488
  admit 529
  permit 760
  consent 762
  give 784
conceit idea 453
  folly 499
  supposition 514
  imagination 515
  wit 842
  affectation 855
  vanity 880
conceited
  dogmatic 481
conceivable 470
conceive begin 66
  teem 168
  believe 484
  understand 490
  imagine 515
concent 413
concentrate
  assemble 72
  centrality 222
  converge 290
concentric 222
conception
  [see conceive]
  intellect 450
  idea 453
  guiding - 453
concern
  relation 9
  event 151
  business 625
  importance 642
  firm 797
  grief 828
  - oneself with 625
concerning
  relative to 9
  (topic 454)
concert
  agreement 23
  synchronous 120
  music 415
  act in - 709
  - measures 626
  in - musical 413
  concord 714
concertina 417
concerto 415
concert room 840
concession
  permission 760
  consent 762
  giving 784
  discount 813

concesso, ex -
  reasoning 476
  assent 488
concetto 842
conchoid 245
conchology 223
concierge 753
conciliate
  talk over 615
  pacify 723
  satisfy 831
  courtesy 894
  atonement 952
conciliatory [see con-
  ciliate]
  concord 714
  forgiving 918
conciliatrix 962
concinnity
  style 578
  beauty 845
conciseness 572
concision 201
conclave
  assembly 72
  council 696
  church 995
conclude
  end 67
  infer 480
  resolve 604
  complete 729
  compact 769
conclusion
  [see conclude]
  judgment 480
  foregone - 611
  hasty - 481
  try -s 476
conclusive
  [see conclude]
  answer 462
  certain 474
  proof 478
  - reasoning 476
concoct lie 544
  plan 626
  prepare 673
concomitant
  accompany 88
  same time 120
concord agree 23
  music 413
  assent 488
  harmony 714
  (amity 888)
  - born of contraries
   14
concordance
  dictionary 562
concordat 769
concordia discors
  disagree 24
  disorder 59
concours 720
concourse
  assemblage 72
  convergence 290
  - of atoms 621
concremation 384
concrete mass 46

density 321
  hardness 323
  materials 635
concubinage 961
concubine 926
concupiscence
  desire 865
  impurity 961
concur
  coexist 120
  causation 178
  converge 290
  assent 488
  concert 709
concurrence 178
  observance 772
concussion 276
condemnation
  censure 932
  conviction 971
condense
  compress 195
  dense 321
condensed 572
condescend 879
condign 924
condiment 393
condisciple 541
condition state 7
  modification 469
  supposition 514
  term 770
  repute 873
  rank 875
  in - plump 192
  in good - 648
  in perfect - 650
  on - 770
  physical - 316
conditional 8
conditions 770
condolence 914, 915
condone 918
condottiere
  traveler 268
  fighter 726
conduce
  contribute 153
  tend 176
  concur 178
  avail 644
conducive 631
conduct
  transfer 270
  procedure 692
  lead 693
  - an inquiry 461
  - to 278
  safe -
   passport 631
   safety 664
conductivity 157
conductor
  guard 268
  conveyer 271
  director 694
  lightning - 666
conduit 350
conduplicate 89
condyle 250
cone round 249

pointed 253
  - shaped 253
conestoga wagon 272
confabulation 588
confection 396
  confectionary 396
confederacy
  coöperation 709
  party 712
confederate 711
Confederates 712
confer advise 695
  give 784
  - benefit 648
  - power 157
  - privilege 760
  - right 924
  - with 588
conference [see con-
  fer]
  council 696
conferva 367
confess assent 488
  avow 529
  penitence 950
  - and avoid 937
confession [see con-
  fess]
  auricular - 998
  - of faith 983
confessional
  temple 1000
confessions
  biography 594
confessor 996
confidant 711
confidante
  servant 746
  friend 890
confidence
  trust 484
  expectation 507
  hope 858
  courage 861
  - trick 545
  in - 528
confident
  [see confidence]
  affirm 535
confiding 703
configuration 240
confine
  circumscribe 229
  border 231
  limit 233
  imprison 751
confined
  narrow judgment 481
  ill 655
confinement
  childbed 161
confines of
  on the - 197
confirm
  corroborate 467
  assent 488
  consent 762
  compact 769
  rite 998
confirmation 535
confirmed 150

- habit 613
confiscate *take* 789
  condemn 971
  penalty 974
confiture 396
conflagration 384
conflexure 245
conflict
  opposition 708
  discord 713
  contention 720
conflicting
  contrary 14
  counteracting 179
- evidence 468
confluence
  junction 43
  convergence 290
  river 348
conflux
  assemblage 72
  convergence 290
conform *assent* 488
conformable
  agreeing 23
conformation 240
conformity 82
- to rule 494
confound
  disorder 61
  destroy 162
  not discriminate
  465a
  perplex 475
  defeat 731
  astonish 870
  curse 908
confounded
  great 31
  bad 649
confraternity
  party 712
  friendship 888
confrère
  colleague 711
  friend 890
confrication 331
confront *face* 234
  compare 464
  oppose 708
  resist 719
- danger 861
- witnesses 467
Confucius 986
confuse *derange* 61
  perplex 458
  obscure 519
  not discriminate
  465a
  abash 879
confused *disorder* 59
  invisible 447
  uncertain 475
  style 571
  harmoniously - 81
confusion
  [see confuse]
- of tongues 560, 563
- of vision 443
- seize 908

- worse confounded 59
confutation 479
congé 756
- d'élire 995
congeal *dense* 321
  cold 385
congener
  similar 17
  included 76
congenial
  agreeing 23
  concord 714
  love 897
  (expedient 646)
congenital 5
  inborn 820
congeries 72
congestion 641
conglaciation 385
conglobation 72
conglomerate
  cohere 46
  assemblage 72
  dense 321
conglutinate 46
congratulate 896
- oneself 838
congratulation 896
congregation
  assemblage 72
  worshipers 990
  laity 997
Congregationalist 984
congress
  assembly 72
  convergence 290
  conference 588
  council 696
congressional 696
congressman 696
congreve *fuel* 388
- rocket 727
congruous
  agreeing 23
  (expedient 646)
conical *round* 249
  pointed 253
conjecture 514
conjoin 43
conjointly 37
conjugal 903
conjugate
  words 562
- in all its tenses &c. 104
conjugation
  junction 43
  pair 89
  phase 144
  grammar 567
conjunction 43
in - with 37
conjuncture
  contingency 8
  occasion 134
conjure *deceive* 545
  entreat 765
  sorcery 992
- up a vision 515

name to - with 873
conjuror
  deceiver 548
  sorcerer 994
connaître les dessous des cartes 490
connate *intrinsic* 5
  kindred 11
  cause 153
connatural
  uniform 16
  similar 17
connect *relate* 9
  link 43
connection 11, 46
connective 45
conned, well - 490
connexion
  [see connect]
- kin 11
in - with 9
connexions
  cards 840
connive
  overlook 460
  coöperate 709
  allow 760
connoisseur
  critic 480
  scholar 492
  taste 850
connotate 550
connote 550
connubial 903
conocidos muchos amigos pocos 890
conoscente 850
conquer 731
conquered
  (failure 732)
conquering hero comes 883
conqueror 731
conquest 749
consanguinity 11
conscia recti, mens -
  pride 878
  probity 939
  innocence 946
conscience
  knowledge 490
  moral sense 926
  awakened - 950
  clear - 946
in all - *great* 31
  affirmation 535
  qualms of - 603
  stricken - 950
  tender - 926
  honor 939
conscientious 926
  faithful 21
  scrupulous 939
  (veracious 543)
  (virtuous 944)
conscious
  intuitive 450
  knowledge 490
- of disgrace 874
- of glory 873

conscript 726
conscription 744
consecrate *use* 677
  dedicate 873
  sanctify 987
  holy orders 995
consecration
  rite 998
consectary 478
- reasoning 476
consecution 63
consecutive
  following 63
  continuous 69
consecutively
  slowly 275
consensus 488
consent *assent* 488
  compliance 762
with one - 178
consentaneous
  agreeing 23
  (expedient 646)
consequence
  event 151
  effect 154
  importance 642
in - 478
of no - 643
take the -s 154
consequent 63
consequential
  deducible 478
  arrogant 878
consequently
  reasoning 476
  effect 154
conservation
  permanence 141
  storage 636
  preservation 670
conservatism 141, 670
conservative 141
- policy 681
Conservatives 712
conservator of the peace 967
conservatory
  receptacle 191
  floriculture 371
  furnace 386
  store 636
conserve 396
consider *think* 451
  attend to 457
  examine 461
  adjudge 480
  believe 484
considerable
  in degree 31
  in size 192
  important 642
considerate
  careful 459
  judicious 498
consideration
  purchase money 147
  thought 451
  idea 453
  attention 457
  qualification 469

craichy 160
craig *height* 206
crake 884
cram *crowd* 72
  stuff 194
  choke 261
  teach 537
  learn 539
  gorge 957
  - down the throat
  induce belief 484
  compel 744
crambe repetita
  weariness 841
  satiety 869
crambo 597
crammed 52
  - to overflowing 641
crammer
  teacher 540
  lie 546
cramp
  fastening 45
  paralyze 158
  weaken 160
  little 193
  compress 195
  spasm 378
  hinder 706
cramped
  style 579
cramp iron 45
cran 191
cranch
  [see craunch]
crane *angle* 244
  elevate 307
  - neck 245
crane's-bill 845
craniology &c. 450
cranium 450
crank
  fanatic 504
  instrument 633
  wit 842
  treadmill 975
crankle *fold* 258
crankling
  rough 256
cranky *weak* 160
  ill health 655
cranny 198
crape
  crinkle 248
  mourning 839
craps 621
crapulence
  intemperance 954
  gluttony 957
  drunken 959
crash
  destruction 162
  collision 276
  sound 406
crasis *nature* 5
  coherence 48
  composition 54
crass 31
  - ignorance 491
crassamentum 321
crassitude

breadth 202
thickness 352
crate
  receptacle 191
  vehicle 272
crater *deep* 208
  hollow 252
craunch
  shatter 44
  chew 298
  pulverize 330
cravat 225
crave *ask* 765
  desire 865
craven *submit* 725
  cowardly 862
craw 191
crawfish
  recede 283
  apostatize 607
crawl *creep* 275
  withdraw 283
  apostatize 607
  servile 886
crayons 556
crazy *weak* 160
  mad 503
creak 410
cream
  emulsion 352
  oil 356
  important part 642
  best 648
  - color
  white 430
  yellow 436
  - of tartar 662
  - of the jest 842
creamy 352
crease 258
create *cause* 153
  produce 161
  imagine 515
created *being* 366
creation .
  [see create]
  effect 154
  world 318
creative 20
creativeness 18, 20
Creator 976
creature *thing* 3
  effect 154
  animal 271, 366
  man 372
  slave 746
  - comforts
  food 298
  pleasure 377
crèche 542
**credat Judæus
  Apella**
  unbelief 485
  absurdity 497
credence *belief* 484
  church 1000
credenda 484
credential 467
credible
  possible 470
  probable 472

belief 484
credit *belief* 484
  influence 737
  pecuniary **805**
  account 811
  repute 873
  approbation 931
  desert 944
  to one's -
  property 780
creditable *right* 924
credit mobilier 802
creditor 805
**credo quia impossi-
  bile** 486
credula res amor est
  897
credulity 486
  (*heterodoxy* 984)
credulous person
  dupe 547
creed *belief* 484
  theology 983
  Apostles' - 983a
  - bound 606
creek *interval* 198
  water 343
creel 191
creep *crawl* 275
  tingle 380
  (*inactivity* 683)
  - in 294
  - into a corner 893
  - into the good graces
    of 933
  - out 529
  - upon one 508
  - with
  multitude 102
  redundance 641
creeper 367
creeping
  sensation 380
  - thing 366
creese 727
cremation
  of corpses 363
  burning 384
crematorium 363
crême
  - de la crême 648
  - de menthe 435
Cremona 417
crenate 257
crenelle 257
crenulate 257
creole 57
crêpé 248
crepidam, ultra -
  471
crepitation 406
crepuscule
  dawn 125
  dusk 422
crescendo
  increase 35
  musical 415
crescent *street* 189
  curve 245
cresset *signal* 550
  (*luminary* 423)

crest *summit* 210
  pointed 253
  tuft 256
  sign 550
  armorial 877
  pride 878
crestate 253
crestfallen
  dejected 837
  humble 879
cretaceous 430
crevasse 198
crevice 198
crew *assemblage* 72
  inhabitants 188
  mariners 269
  party 712
crib *bed* 215
  translation 522
  steal 791
  parsimony 819
cribbage 840
**cribbed c o n f i n e d,
  cabined** - 751
cribble 260
cribriform 260
**Crichton, Admira-
  ble** -
  scholar 492
  perfect 650
  proficient 700
crick *pain* 378
cricket *game* 840
  - ground *level* 213
crier 534
  send round the - 531
crim. con. 961
crime *guilt* 947
criminal *vicious* 945
  culprit 949
  (- *conversation* 961)
  - law 963
criminality 947
criminate 938
criminologist 492
crimp *crinkle* 248
  notch 257
  brittle 328
  deceiver 548
  take 789
  steal 791
crimple 258
crimson 434
cringe *submit* 725
  servility 886
crinite 256
crinkle *angle* 244
  convolution 248
  fold 258
crinoline 225
cripple *disable* 158
  weaken 160
  injure 659
crippled
  disease 655
crisis
  conjuncture 8
  present time 118
  opportunity 134
  event 151
  strait 704

curriculum 537
curry *rub* 331
 condiment 393
 - favour with
 love 897
 flatter 933
curse *bane* 663
 adversity 735
 painful 830
 malediction 908
 (evil 619)
cursed *bad* 649
cursitor 968
cursory
 transient 111
 inattentive 458
 hasty 684
 take a - view of
 457
 neglect 460
curt *short* 201
 concise 572
 taciturn 585
curtæ nescio 832
curtail *retrench* 38
 shorten 201
 (decrease 36)
 (deprive 789)
 -ed of its fair propor-
 tions
 distorted 243
 ugly 846
curtain *shade* 424
 hide 528, 530
 theater 599
 fortification 717
 behind the -
 invisible 447
 inquiry 461
 knowledge 490
 close the - 528
 - lecture 932
 raise the - 529
 rising of the - 448
curtsy *stoop* 308, 314
 submit 725
 polite 894
curule 696
curvature 245
curvet *leap* 309
 turn 311
 oscillate 314
 agitate 315
curvilinear 245
 - motion 311
cushat 366
cushion *pillow* 215
 soft 324
 relief 834
cusp *angle* 244
 sharp 253
cuspidor 191
cussed 901*a*
cussedness 606
custodes? quis cus-
 todiet - 459
custodian 753
custody *safe* 664
 captive 751
 retention 781
 in - *prisoner* 754

accused 938
take into - 751
custom *old* 124
 habit 613
 barter 794
 sale 796
 tax 812
 fashion 852
 - honored in
 breach 614
customary
 [see custom]
 regular 80
customer 795
customhouse 799
 - officer 965
custos 753
 - rotulorum 553
cut *divide* 44
 bit 51
 discontinuity 70
 interval 198
 curtail 201
 layer 204
 form 240
 notch 257
 blow 276
 eject 297
 reap 371
 physical pain 378
 cold 385
 neglect 460
 carve 557
 engraving 558
 road 627
 attack 716
 affect 824
 mental pain 830
 ignore 893
 discourtesy 895
 tipsy 959
 - according to cloth
 economy 817
 caution 864
 - across 302
 - adrift 44
 - a figure
 appearance 448
 fashion 852
 repute 873
 display 882
 - along 274
 - and come again
 repeat 104
 enough 639
 - and dried
 arranged 60
 prepared 673
 - and run 623
 - and thrust 716
 - a poor figure 874
 - away 274
 - blocks with a razor
 sophistry 477
 waste 638
 misuse 679
 - both ways 468
 - capers 309
 - dead 893
 - direct 893
 - down *destroy* 162

shorten 201
fell 308
kill 361
 - in two 91
 - jokes 842
 - off *subduct* 38
 disjoin 44
 kill 361
 impede 706
 bereft 776
 secluded 893
 - off with a shilling
 789
 - of one's jib 448
 - one's own throat
 699
 - one's stick
 depart 293
 avoid 623
 - one's way through
 302
 - open 260
 - out *surpass* 33
 substitute 147
 plan 626
 - out for 698
 - out work
 prepare 673
 direct 693
 - short *stop* 142
 destroy 162
 shorten 201
 silence 581
 - the first turf 66
 - the ground from
 under one
 confute 479
 hinder 706
 - the knot 705
 - to pieces 162
 kill 361
 - to the heart 824, 308
 - to the quick 830
 - up root and branch
 162
 - up *divide* 44
 destroy 162
 pained 828
 give pain 830
 discontented 832
 dejected 837
 censure 932
 - up rough 900
 have a - at 716
 short - 628
 unkindest - of all
 pain 828
 malevolence 907
 what one will - up for
 78C
cutanéous 223
cutcherry 802, 965
cute 698, 850
cuteness 498
cuticle 223
cutlass 727
cutlery 253
cutpurse 792
cutter 273
 sleigh 272
cutthroat

killer 361
evil doer 913
-s with whisperings
 934
cutting *sharp* 253
 cold 383
 affecting 821
 painful 830
 reproachful 932
cuttings
 excerpta 596
 selections 609
cuttystool 950
cwt. *hundred* 98
 weight 319
cyanogen 438
cycle *period* 138
 circle 247
 vehicle 272
cyclist 268
cycloid 247
cyclone
 rotation 312
 wind 349
Cyclopean
 strong 159
 huge 31, 192
cyclopedia
 knowledge 490
 book 542, 593
Cyclops
 monster 83
 mighty 159
 huge 192
 dupe 547
cygne
 chant du - 360
 - noir 650
cygnet 366
cylindric 249
cymbal 417
cymbiform 245
cymophanous 440
cynanche 655
cynic
 misanthrope 911
 detractor 936
 ascetic 955
 closet -
 unsociable 893
cynical
 contemptuous 930
 censorious 932
 detracting 934
cynicism
 discourtesy 895
cynosure *sign* 550
 direction 693
 repute 873
Cynthia of the min-
 ute 149
cypher [see cipher]
cypress
 interment 363
 mourning 839
Cyprian 962
cyst 191
czar 745
Czarevna 745
Czarita 745
Czarowitz 745

D

dab
  paint 223
  morsel 32
  slap 276
  clever 700
dabble *water* 337
  dirty 653
  meddle 682
  fribble 683
dabbled *wet* 339
dabbler 493
dabster 700
da capo 104
dacker 605
dacoit 792
dactyl 597
dactyliomancy 511
dactylology 550
dactylonomy
  numeration 85
  symbol 550
dad 166
dado 211
dædal *various* 15
  variegated 440
dædalian
  convoluted 248
  artistic 698
dæva 980
daft 503
daffodil 845
dagger 727
  air drawn - 515
  at -s drawn
  opposed 708
  discord 713
  enmity 889
  hate 898
  - of the mind 860
  looks -s *anger* 900
  threat 909
  plant - in breast
  give pain 830
  speak -s 932
daggle *hang* 214
  dirty 653
Dago 57
dagobah 1000
Dagon 986
daguerreotype
  represent 554
  paint 556
dahabeah 273
daily
  frequent 136
  periodic 138
  newspaper 531
  - occurrence
  normal 82
  habitual 613
daimio 875
dainty *food* 298
  savoring 394
  pleasing 829

delicate 845
  tasty 850
  fastidious 868
dairy 191
dais *support* 215
  throne 747
daisy
  - pied 847
  fresh as a - 654
dak 534
  - bungalow 189
dalal 758
dale 252
  725, 745, 879
dally *delay* 133
  irresolute 605
  inactive 683
  amuse 640
  fondle 902
dalmatic 999
da locum melioribus
Daltonism 443
dam *parent* 166
  close 261
  pond 343
  obstruct 706
damage *evil* 619
  injure, spoil 659
  loss 776
  price 812
damages 974
damascene 440
damask 434
dame
  woman 374
  teacher 540
  lady 875
damn
  malediction 908
  condemn 971
  - with faint praise
  932, 934
damnable 649
damnatory
  disapprove 932
  condemn 971
damnify
  damage 649
  spoil 659
damnosa hereditas
  663
Damocles
  sword of - 667
Damon and Pythias
  890
damp
  moderate 174
  moist 339
  cold 385
  dissuade 616
  hinder 706
  depress 837
  dull 843
  - the sound 408a

damper 387
  cake 298
damsel
  youth 129
  female 374
damson 396
Danaë 803
Danaos, timeo -
  doubt 485
  caution 864
dance
  jump 309
  oscillate 314
  agitate 315
  rejoice 838
  sport 840
  - attendance
  waiting 133
  follow 281
  servant 746
  petition 765
  servility 886
  - the back step 283
  - the war dance 715
  - upon nothing 972
  lead one a -
  run away 623
  circuit 629
  difficult 704
  practical joke 929
  lead the - 175
dance music 415
dander 900
dandi 272
Dandie Dinmont 366
dandiprat 193
dandle 902
dandruff 653
dandy
  ship 273
  fop 854
dandyism 855
danger 665
  - past 664
  - signal 669
  in - *liable* 177
  source of - 667
dangerous
  [*see* danger]
  - classes 913
  - illness 655
  - person 667
dangle *hang* 214
  swing 314
  display 882
dangler 281
Daniel *sage* 500
  judge 967
  - come to judgment
  480
dank 339
danseuse 599
Dan to Beersheba
  complete 52

extent 180
dapper
  little 193
  elegant 845
dapple 433
dappled 440
Darby and Joan
  secluded 893
  married 903
dare *defy* 715
  face danger 861
  - not 860
  - say *probable* 472
  believe 484
  suppose 514
  I - do all 861
dare-devil
  rash 863
  bluster 887
dare pondus idonea
  fumo 32
daring 861
  - *imagination* 515
dark
  obscure 421
  dim 422
  black 431
  blind 442
  invisible 447
  unintelligible 519
  latent 526
  joyless 837
  insidious 940
  - ages 491
  - amid the blaze of
  noon 442
  - cloud 735
  - lantern 423
  - with excessive
  bright 420
  in the -
  ignorant 491
  keep - *hide* 528
  leap in the -
  experiment 463
  chance 621
  rash 863
  view with - eyes 932
darkie 431
darkly
  see through a glass -
  443
darkness [*see* dark]
  421
  children of - 988
  - of meaning 571
  no - but ignorance
  491
  powers of - 978
darling *beloved* 897
  favorite 599
darn 660
dart *swift* 274
  propel 284

411

Column 1 (DART)

missile 727
- to and fro 684
dartre 655
Darwinism 357
dash
　small quantity 32
　mix 41
　swift 276
　fling 284
　mark 550
　courage 861
　cut a - *repute* 873
　display 882
　- at *resolution* 604
　attack 716
　- cup from lips 761
　- down 308
　- hopes
　　disappoint 509
　　fail 732
　　dejected 837
　　despair 859
　- off *paint* 556
　　write 590
　　active 682
　　haste 684
　- of the pen 590
　- on 274
dashboard 666
dashed [see dash]
　humbled 879
dasher 666
dashing
　fashionable 852
　brave 861
　ostentatious 882
dastard 862
dasturi 973
data *evidence* 467
　reasoning 476
　supposition 514
date *time* 106
　chronology 114
　to this - 118
　up to - 123
daub *cover* 223
　bad painting 555
　dirt 653
daubing 635
daughter 167
daunt 860
dauntless 861
davenport 191
Davus sum non
　Œdipus
　unintelligent 499
　artless 703
　dull 843
dawdle *tardy* 133
　slow 275
　inactive 683
dawn
　precursor 64
　begin 66
　priority 116
　morning 125
　dim 422
　glimpse 490
dawplucker 936
day
　period 108

Column 2 (DE)

present time 118
light 420
all - 110
all in -'s work 625
clear as -
　certain 474
　intelligible 518
　manifest 525
close of - 126
- after day
　diuturnal 110
　frequent 136
- after the fair 135
- after to-morrow 121
- and night
　frequent 136
- before yesterday
　122
- blindness 443
- by day
　repeatedly 104
　time 106
　periodic 138
- for gods to stoop
　420
- of judgment 121
- of rest 686
- one's own 731
-s gone by 122
-s numbered
　transient 111
　death 360
-s of week 138
- star 423
decline of - 126
denizens of the - 366
happy as the - is long
　827, 836
have had its - 124
labor - and night 686
open as - 703
order of the - 613
red letter - 642
see the light of - 446
daybook *record* 551
　accounts 811
daybreak
　morning 125
　dim 422
daydream
　fancy 515
　hope 858
day-laborer 690
daylight 420
　see - *intelligible* 518
dayspring 125
daze 420, 870
　in a - 860
dazed 475
dazzle
　light 420
　blind 422, 443
　put out 458
　astonish 870
　awe 928
dazzling
　[see dazzle]
　beautiful 845
de: - die in diem
　time 106
　periodic 138

Column 3 (DEAD)

- facto 1
- fond en comble 52
- novo`104
- omnibus rebus 81
deacon 996
　juggle 545
　intone 990
deaconry 995
dead
　complete 52
　inert 172
　colorless 429
　lifeless 360
　insensible 376
- against
　contrary 14
　oppose 708
- asleep 683
- beat
　powerless 158
　sponger 886
- certainty 474
- color 556
- cut 893
- drunk 959
- failure 732
- flat 213
- heat 27
- languages 560
- letter
　impotent 158
　unmeaning 517
　useless 645
　laxity 738
　exempt 927
　illegal 964
- lift *exertion* 686
　difficulty 707
- lock *cease* 142
　stoppage 265
　difficulty 704
- march 363
- of night
　midnight 126
　dark 421
- reckoning
　numeration 85
　measurement 466
- secret 533
- set against 708
- set at
　attack 716
- shot 700
- silence 403
- sound 408a
- stop 142
- to 823
- wall
　hindrance 706
　defense 717
- water 343
- weight 706
more - than alive 688
deaden
　weaken 158
　moderate 174
　benumb 823
deadened 381
deadhead 815
deadhouse 363
deadlock 704

Column 4 (DEAT)

deadly *killing* 361
　pernicious 649
　unhealthy 657
- sin 947
- weapon 727
deads 645
deaf 419
　inattentive 458
- and dumb 581
- mute 581
- to *insensible* 823
- to advice 606
- to reason 901a
turn - ear to
　neglect 460
　unbelief 487
　refuse 764
deafen *loud* 404
deafness 419
deal *much* 31
　arrange 60
　compact 769
　allot 786
- a blow
　injure 659
　attack 716
　punish 972
- board 323
- in 794
- out *scatter* 73
　give 784
- with
　treat of 595
　handle 692
　barter 794
dealer 797
dealings *action* 680
　have - with
　trade 794
　friendly 888
dean 996
deanery *office* 995
　house 1000
dear
　high priced 814
　loved 897
　favorite 899
- at any price 646
- me *wonder* 870
O - ! *lament* 839
pay - for whistle
　647
dearborn 272
dearness 814
dearth 640
- of ideas 843
death 360
　be the - of one
- chair 975
　amuse 840
- in the pot
　unhealthy 657
　hidden danger 667
house of - 363
in at the -
　arrive 292
　kill 361
　persevere 604a
pale as -
　colorless 429
　fear 860

put to - 361
still as - 265
violent - 361
deathbed repent-
  ance 950
deathblow
  end 67
  killing 361
  failure 732
deathless
  perpetual 112
  fame 873
deathlike
  silent 403
  hideous 846
death-song 839
death-struggle 720
death-warrant 971
deathwatch 668
débâcle
  destruction 162
  violence 173
  downfall 306
  torrent 348
debar *hinder* 706
  restrain 751
  prohibit 761
debark 292
debase *depress* 308
  foul 653
  deteriorate 659
  degrade 874
debased
  lowered 207
  dishonored 940
debatable 475
debate *reason* 476
  talk 588
  hesitate 605
  dispute 720
debauch *spoil* 659
  intemperance 954
  impurity 961
debauchee 962
debenture
  security 771
  money 800
  credit 805
debility 160
debit *debt* 806
  accounts 811
debitor 806
débonnaire 836
debouch 293, 295
débris
  fragments 51
  crumbled 330
  useless 645
debt 806
  - of nature 360
  get out of - 807
  out of - 803
debtor 806
  - and creditor 811
début *beginning* 66
  essay 675
débutant
  learner 541
  drama 599
decade *ten* 98
  period 108

decadence 659
decagon 244
decalogue 926
decamp
  go away 293
  run away 623
decant 270
decanter 191
decapitate *kill* 361
  punish 972
decarbonized iron
  323
decay *decrease* 36
  shrivel 195
  unclean 653
  disease 655
  spoil 659
  adversity 735
  - of memory 506
  natural - 360
decayed
  [see decay]
  old 124
  rotten 160
decease 360
deceit 545
  falsehood 544
  deception 545
  cunning 702
deceived
  in error 495
  duped 547
deceiver 548
  gay - 962
decennium 108
decent
  mediocre 651
  pure 960
decentralize 49
deceptio visûs 443
deception 545
deceptive reasoning
  477
decession 293
dechristianize 989
decide
  turn the scale 153
  judge 480
  choose 609
decided *great* 31
  ended 67
  certain 474
  resolved 604
  take a - step 609
deciduous
  transitory 111
  falling 306
  spoiled 659
decies repetita place-
  bit 829
decimal
  numeration 84
  tenth 98, 99
decimate
  subtract 38
  tenth 99
  few 103
  weaken 160
  kill 361
  play havoc 659
  punish 972

decipimur specie
  recti 545
decipher 522
decision
  judgment 480
  resolution 604
  intention 620
  law case 969
decisive
  certain 474
  proof 478
  take a - step 609
deck *floor* 211
  cards 840
  beautify 847
deckle-edged 674
declaim 582
  - against 932
declamatory
  style 577
  speech 582
declaration
  affirmation 535
  law pleadings 969
  - of faith
  belief 484
  theology 983
  - of war 713
declaratory
  meaning 516
  inform 527
declension
  [see decline]
  grammar 567
  backsliding 988
declensions 5
declination
  [see decline]
  deviation 279
  measurement 466
  rejection 610
declinature 764
decline *decrease* 36
  old 124
  weaken 160
  be unwilling 603
  reject 610
  disease 655
  become worse 659
  adversity 735
  refuse 764
  - of day 126
  - of life 128
declivity *slope* 217
  descent 306
decoction 384
decollate 972
decoloration 429
decolorize 429
decomposition 49
decompound 49
deconsecrate 756
decoration
  insignia 747
  ornament 847
  title 877
Decoration Day 840
decorous
  [see decorum]
  proper 924
  respectful 928

decorticate 226
decorum
  fashion 852
  duty 926
  purity 960
décousu
  discontinuous 70
  failure 732
decoy *deceive* 545
  deceiver 548
  entice 615
decrassify 652, 658
decrease
  in degree 36
  in size 195
decree
  judgment 480
  order 741
  law 963, 969
decrement
  decrease 36
  thing deducted **40a**
  contraction 195
decrepit *old* 128
  weak 160
  disease 655
  decayed 659
decrepitate 406
decretal 741
decry *underrate* 483
  censure 932
  detract 934
decumbent 213
decuple 98
decursive 306
decurtation 201
decussation 219
dedecorous
  disreputable 874
  discourteous 895
dedicate *use* 677
  inscribe 873
deduce *deduct* 38
  infer 480
deducible
  evidence 467
  proof 478
deduct *retrench* 38
  deprive 789
deduction
  [see deduce]
  decrement 40a
  reasoning 476
deed *evidence* 467
  record 551
  act 680
  security 771
  -s of arms 720
  - without a name 947
  would the - were
  good 947
deem 484
deep *great* 31
  profound 208
  sea 341
  sonorous 404
  cunning 702
  - color 428
  - game 702
  - in debt 806
  - knowledge 490

delicto, in flagrante - 947
delictum 947
delight
　pleasure 827
　pleasing 829
　weighing - and dole 922
Delilah 962
delineate
　represent 554
　describe 594
delineavit 556
delinquency 947
delinquent 949
deliquation 335
deliquesce 335
deliquium
　paralysis 158
　fatigue 688
delirant reges plectuntur Achivi 739
delirium
　raving 503
　passion 825
　- *tremens* 959
delitescence
　invisible 447
　latency 526
　seclusion 893
deliver
　transfer 270
　utter 580, 582
　rescue 672
　liberate 750
　give 784
　relieve 834
　- *as one's act and deed* 467
　- *a speech* 582
　- *judgment* 480
deliverance 672
delivery
　[see deliver]
　bring forth 161
dell 252
Delphic oracle
　prophetic 513
　equivocal 520
　latent 526
delta 342
delude *error* 495
　deceive 545
deluge *crowd* 72
　water 337
　flood 348
　redundance 641
delusion
　[see delude]
　insane 503
　self - credulous 486
delve *dig* 252
　till 371
　- *into inquire* 461
demagogue
　director 694
　malcontent 710
　rebel 742
demagogy 737
demand

inquire 461
order 741
ask 765
price 812
claim 924
in - *require* 630
　desire 865
demarcation 233
demean oneself
　conduct 692
　humble 879
　dishonor 940
demeanor ·
　aid 448
　conduct 692
　fashion 852
démêlé 713
demency 503
démenti 536
dementia 503
demerit 945
demesne
　abode 189
　property 780
demi- 91
demigod *hero* 861
　angel 948
　- *Authority* 737
demigration 266
demijohn 191
demi-jour 422
demimonde
　plebeian 876
　licentious 962
demirep 962
demise *death* 360
　transfer 783
　lease 787
demisemiquaver 413
demission 756
demiurge *agent* 690
　deity 979
demivolt 309
democracy *rule* 737
　commonalty 876
Democrats 912
Democritus 838
demoiselle 129
demolish 479
demon *violent* 173
　bane 663
　devil 980
　- *in human shape* 913, 949
　- *worship* 991
demonetize 800
　wicked 945
demoniacal
　malevolent 907
　·*furious* 824
demonology
　demons 980
　sorcery 992
demonophobia 898
demonstration
　number 85
　proof 478
　manifest 525
　ostentation 882
　ocular - 441, 446
demonstrative

manifest 525
　indicative 550
　vehement 825
demonstrator 524
demoralize
　unnerve 158
　spoil 659
　vicious 945
de mortuis nil nisi bonum 360, 906
δῆμος 876
Demosthenes 582
demulcent
　mild 174
　soothing 662
demur
　disbelieve 485
　dissent 489
　unwilling 603
　hesitate 605
demure *grave* 826
　sad 837
　affected 855
　modest 881
demurrer 969
den *abode* 189
　study 191
　sty 653
　prison 752
　- *of thieves* 791
denary 98
denaturalize
　corrupt 659
denaturalized
　abnormal 83
dendriform 242
dendrology 369
dengue fever 655
denial
　negation 536
　refusal 764
　self - 953
denigrate 431
denization 748
denizen
　inhabitant 188
　freeman 748
　-s *of the air* 979
　-s *of the day* 366
Denmark, rotten in the state of - 526
denominate 566
denomination
　class 75
　name 564
　sect 712
　religious - 983
denominational
　dissent 489
　theological 983
　- *education* 537
denominator 84
denote 79, 550
dénouement
　end 67
　result 154
　disclosure 529
　completion 729
denounce
　curse 908
　disapprove 932

accuse 938
de novo 104
dense
　crowded 72
　close 321
density 321
dent
　hollow 252
　notch 257
dental 561
denticulated
　sharp 253
　notched 257
dentifrice 652
dentistry 662
denude 226
denuded *loss* 776
　- *of*
　insufficient 640
denunciation 909
　[see denounce]
deny *dissent* 489
　negative 536
　refuse 764
　- *oneself*
　avoid 623
　seclude 893
　temperate 953
　ascetic 990
deobstruct 705
deobstruent 652, 662
deodand 974
deodorant 399
deodorize 399
　clean 652
deontology 926
deoppilation 705
deorganization 61
deosculation 902
deos fortioribus adesse 33
Deo volente 470
deoxidization 140
depart 293
　- *from*
　deviate 279
　relinquish 624
　- *this life* 360
departed
　nonexistent 2
department
　class 75
　region 181
　business 625
　bureau 965
　- *store* 799
departmental 737
departure 293
　new - 66
　point of - 293
depend *hang* 214
　contingent 475
　- *on circumstances* 475
　- *upon*
　be the effect of 154
　evidence 467
　trust 484
depended on, to be -
　certain 474
　reliable 484

415

honorable 939
dependence 46
dependency
  relation 9
  property 777, 780
dependent
  effect 154
  liable 177
  hanging 214
  servant 746
  subject 749
deperdition 776
dephlegmation 340
depict 554, 556
  describe 594
depilation 226
depilatory 662
depletion 640
deplorable *bad* 649
  disastrous 735
  painful 830
deplore *regret* 833
  complain 839
  remorse 950
deploy 194
depone 535 .
deponent 467
depopulate
  eject 297
  desert 893
deportation
  removal 270
  emigration 297
deportment 692
depose
  evidence 467
  declare 535
  dethrone 738, 756
deposit *place* 184
  precipitate 321
  store 636
  security 771
  payment 809
depositary 801
deposition
  [*see* depose, deposit]
  record 551
depository 636
depot
  station 266
  store 636
  shop 799
deprave *spoil* 659
depraved *bad* 649
  vicious 945
deprecation 766
  pity 914
  disapprove 932
depreciation
  decrease 36
  underestimate 483
  discount 8.3
  cheap 815
  censure 932
  detraction 934
  accusation 938
depredation 791
depredator 792
deprehension 789
depressing
  painful 830

depression
  lowness 207
  depth 208
  concavity 252
  dent 257
  lowering 308
  dejection 837
  dullness 843
deprive *subduct* 38
  take 789
  - of life 361
  - of power 158
  - of property 789
  - of strength 160
deprived of 776
depth *physical* **208**
  mental 498
  - of misery 828
  - of thought 451
  - of winter 383
  out of one's - 304, 310
depurate *clean* 652
  improve 658
depuratory 662
deputation 755
depute 755
deputies, chamber
  of - 696
deputy 759
  - commissioner 745
dequantitate 36
derail 142
deranged 503
derangement 61
  mental - 503
Derby-day 720
derelict *land* 342
  relinquished 782
  outcast 893
dereliction
  relinquishment 624,
    782
  guilt 947
  - of duty **927**
deride
  ridicule 856
  disrespect 929
  contempt 930
derivation
  origin 153, 154, 155
  verbal 562
derive
  attribute 155
  deduce 480
  acquire 775
  income 810
dermal 223
dermatoid 223
dermatology 223
dernier ressort 601
dérobée, à la - 528
derogate
  underrate 483
  disparage 934
  dishonor 940
  - from 874
derogatory
  shame 874
  dishonor 940
derrick 307
derring-do 861

dervish 996
désagrément 830
descant *music* 415
  diffuseness 573
  loquacity 584
  dissert 595
descend *slope* 217
  go down 306
  - to particulars
    special 79
    describe 594
descendant 167
descensus Averni, fa-
  cilis - 665
descent 69
  lineage 166
  fall **306**
  inheritance 775
description
  kind 75
  name 564
  narration **594** ·
descry 441
desecrate
  misuse 679
  disrespect 929
  profane 988
desert
  unproductive 169
  empty 187
  plain 344
  run away 623
  relinquish 624
  merit 944
  waste sweetness on -
    air 638
deserted
  outcast 893
deserter 607
desertless 945
deserve
  be entitled to 924
  merit 944
  - belief 484
  - notice 642
désespoir, au -
  dejected 837
  hopeless 859
déshabille, en -
  not dressed 226
  unprepared 674
  homely 849
desiccate 340
desiderate
  need 630
  desire 865
desideratum
  inquiry 461
  requirement 630
  desire 865
design
  prototype 22
  delineation 554
  painting 556
  intention 620
  plan 626
designate
  specify 79
  call 564
  express 566
designation

  kind 75
designed
  aforethought 611
designer 559
designing
  cunning 702
designless 621
désillusionner 529
desinence *end* 67
  discontinuance 142
desipere in loco 840
desirable 646
desire 865
  will 600
  have no - for 866
desist
  discontinue 142
  relinquish 624
  inaction 681
desk *box* 191
  support 215
  school 542
  pulpit 1000
  the - 996
désobligeant
  carriage 272
désœuvre 683
desolate *alone* 87
  ravage 162
  afflicted 828
  dejected 837
  secluded 893
desolating
  painful 830
désolé 837
désorienté 475
despair *grief* 828
  hopeless 859
despatch *eject* 297
  kill 361
  news 532
  epistle 592
  expedition 682
  haste 684
  conduct 692
  complete 729
  command 741
  - food 298
  happy - 972
despect 930
desperado
  rash 863
  blusterer 887
  evil doer 913
desperate *great* **31**
  violent 173
  impossible 471
  resolved 604
  difficult 704
  excitable 825
  hopeless 859
  rash 863
  anger 900
despicable
  trifling 643
  shameful 874
  contemptible 930
despise 930
  - *danger* 861
despite 907
  in - 708

despoil *injure* 659
  take 789
  rob 791
despond
  dejected 837
  fear 860
despot 745
despotism
  authority 737
  severity 739
  arbitrary 964
despumate 652
desquamation 226
dess 204
dessert 298
dessous des cartes
  153
  cause 153
  latent 526
  secret 533
  connaître les - 490
dessus dessous, sens-
  (*disorder* 59)
  inverted 218
destination *end* 67
  arrival 292
  intention 620
destiny *chance* 152
  fate 601
  fight against - 606
destitute
  insufficient 640
  poor 804
  refuge for - 666
desto 415
destrier 726
destroy
  demolish 162
  injure 659
  - hopes 859
  - life 361
destroyed
  [*see destroy*]
  inexistent 2
  failure 732
destroyer 165
  naval 726
  evil doer 913
destructive
  bad 649
desuetude 614
  disuse 678
desultory
  disordered 59
  fitful 70
  multiform 81
  irregular in time 139
  changeable 149
  deviating 279
  agitated 315
desume 788
desunt inopiæ mul-
  ta 819
detach 44
detached
  irrelated 10
  loose 47
detachment
  part 51
  army 726
detail *item* 79

describe 594
  allot 786
  ornament 847
  attention to - 457,
  459
  in - 51
details
  minutiæ 32
  unimportant 643
detain 781
detect 480a
detective 527
detent 45
detention 781
  house of - 752
  in house of - 938
détenu 754
deter *dissuade* 616
  alarm 860
deterge *clean* 652
detergent
  remedy 662
deterioration 659
determinate
  special 79
  exact 474
  conclusive 480
  intended 620
determine *end* 67
  define 79
  cause 153
  direction 278
  satisfy 462
  make sure 474
  judge 480
  discover 480a
  resolve 604
determined
  resolute 604
deterration 529
detersion 652
detersive 662
detest *dislike* 867
  hate 898
detestable 649
dethronement
  anarchy 738
  abrogation 756
detonate
  explode 173
  sound 406
detortion *form* 243
  meaning 523
détour *curve* 245
  circuit 629
detract *subduct* 38
  underrate 483
  defame 934
  slander 938
detraction 934
detractor 936
detrain 292
detriment
  evil 619
  deterioration 659
detrimental 649
detrition 330
detritus
  fragments 51
  powder 330
detrude

  cast out 297
  cut down 308
detruncate 38
detrusive 308
deuce *two* 89
  devil 978
  - is in him 608
  play the - 825
deuced *great* 31
  painful 830
deus ex machinâ
  aid 707
  auxiliary 711
  deity 976
  sorcerer 994
deus nobis hæc otia
  fecit 265
Deus vult 600
deuterogamy 903
deva 979
Devanagari 590
devastate
  destroy 162
  havoc 659
develop
  increase 35
  produce 161
  expand 194
  evolve 313
development 154
devexity
  bending 217
  curvature 245
deviate *vary* 20a
  change 140
  turn 279
  diverge 291
  circuit 629
  - from rectitude 940
  - from virtue 945
deviation 279
device *motto* 550
  expedient 626
  artifice 702
devil
  seasoned food 392
  evil doer 913
  bad man 949
  Satan 978
  demon 980
  - in one
  headstrong 863
  temper 901
  - may care
  rash 863
  indifferent 866
  insolent 885
  -'s tattoo 407
  - take 908
  - take the hindmost
  run away 623
  haste 684
  cowardice 862
  - to pay
  disorder 59
  violence 173
  evil 619
  failure 732
  penalty 974
  fight like -s 722
  give the - his due

  right 922
  vindicate 937
  fair 939
  have a - 503
  machinations of the
  619
  play the - with
  injure 659
  malevolent 907
  printer's - 591
devilish *great* 31
  bad 649
  malevolent 907
  vicious 945
devious *curved* 245
  deviating 279
devise *imagine* 515
  plan 626
  bequeath 784
devised by the ene-
  my 546
devisee *possess* 779
  receive 785
devoid *absent* 187
  empty 640
  not having 777a
devoir *courtesy* 894
  respect 928
devolution 659, 783
devolve 783
  - on 926
devote *destine* 601
  employ 677
  consecrate 873
  - oneself to 604
  - the mind to 457
  - to destruction 908
devoted
  habit 613
  ill-fated 735
  obedient 743
  undone 828
  love 897
devotee
  zealot 682
  aspirant 865
  pious 987
  fanatic 988
devotion [*see devotee,*
  devoted]
  love 897
  piety 987
  worship 990
  self- 942
devour
  destroy 162
  eat 298
  gluttony 957
devoured by
  feeling 821
devouring element
  382
devout 987, 990
devoutless 989
devoutly 821
dew 339
  shake as -drops from
  lion's mane 483
Dewali 138
dewan 745
dewy eve 126

dissuade 616
dislike 867
disinclined 603
disinfect
  purify 652
  restore 660
disinfectant 662
disingenuous
  false 544
  dishonorable 940.
disinherit 783, 789
disintegrate
  separate 44
  pulverize 330
disintegration 49
disinter
  exhume 363
  discover 480a
disinterested 942
disjecta membra
  separate 44
  disorder 59
  dispersed 73
  - *poetæ* 597
disjoin 44
disjointed
  disorder 59
  powerless 158
disjunction 44
disjunctive 70
disk [*see* disc]
diskindness 907
dislike 867
  reluctance 603
  hate 898
dislimb 44
dislocate
  separate 44
  put out of joint
  · 61
dislocated
  disorder 59
dislodge
  displace 185
  eject 297
disloyal 940
dismal
  depressing 830
  dejected 837
  - *universal hiss* 930
dismantle
  destroy 162
  divest 226
  render useless 645
  injure 659
  disuse 678
dismask 529
dismast
  render useless 645
  injure 659
  disuse 678
dismay 860
dismember
  separate 44
  disperse 73
dismiss
  discard 678
  liberate 750
  abrogate 756
  relinquish 782
  punish 972

-- *from the mind* 452,
  458
dismount
  arrive 292
  descend 306
  render useless 645
disobedience 742
  nonobservance 773
disoblige 907
disomatous 90
disorder
  confusion **59**
  derange 61
  turbulent 173
  disease 655
  -ed *intellect* 503
disorderly
  unprincipled 945
disorganize
  derange 61
  destroy 162
  spoil 659
disorganized 59
disown 536
dispair 44
dispansion 194
disparage
  underrate 483
  disrespect 929
  dispraise 932
  detract 934
disparagement 908
disparity
  different 15
  dissimilar 18
  disagreeing 24
  unequal 28
  isolated 44
dispart 44
dispassionate 826
  - *opinion* 484
dispatch
  [*see* despatch]
dispel *scatter* 73
  destroy 162
  displace 185
  repel 289
dispensable
  useless 645
dispensary 662
dispensation
  [*see* dispense]
  command 741
  license 760
  relinquishment 782
  exemption 927a
  -s *of Providence* 976
dispense
  disperse 73
  give 784
  apportion 786
  retail 796
  cannot be -d *with*
    630
  - *with*
    disuse 678
    permit 760
    exempt 927a
dispeople
  eject 297
  expatriate. 893

dispermy 89
disperse
  separate 44
  scatter 73
  diverge 291
  waste 638
dispersion 73
  chromatic - 428
  - *of light* 420
dispirit
  discourage 616
  sadden 837
displacement
  derange 61
  remove **185**
  transfer 270
displacency
  dislike 867
  incivility 895
  disapprobation 932
displant 185
display *appear* 448
  show 525
  parade 882
displease 830
displeasure 828
  anger 900
displosion 173
displume 789
disport 840
disposal
  [*see* dispose]
  at one's - 777
dispose
  arrange 60
  tend 176
  induce 615
  -d *to doubt* 487
  - *of use* 677
  complete 729
  relinquish 782
  give 784
  sell 796
disposition
  temperament 5
  order 58
  arrangement 60
  inclination 602
  mind 820
dispossess
  transfer 783
  take away 789
  - *oneself of* 782
dispraise 932
dispread 73
disprize 483
disproof
  counter evidence 468
  confutation 479
disproportion
  irrelation 10
  disagreement 24
disprove 479
disputable
  uncertain 475
  doubt 485
disputant
  [*see* dispute]
  opponent 710
  combatant 726
disputare la verità fa

  errare, troppo ◄
  476
disputatious
  [*see* dispute]
  irritable 901
dispute
  discuss 476
  doubt 485
  deny 536
  discord 713
  in - 461
disqualification
  incapacitate 158
  useless 645
  unprepared 674
  unskillful 699
  disentitle 925
disquiet
  changeable 149
  agitation 315
  excitement 825
  uneasiness 828
  give pain 830
disquietude
  apprehension 860
disquiparant 10, 28
disquisition 595
disregard
  overlook 458
  neglect 460
  make light of 483
  insensible to 823,
  826
  disrespect **929**
  contempt 930
  - *of time* 115
disrelish
  dislike 867
  hate 889
disreputable 874
  vicious 945
disrepute 874
disrespect 929
  despise 930
disrobe 226
disruption
  disjunction 44
  destruction 162
  discord 713
dissatisfaction
  sorrow 828
  discontent 832
dissect
  anatomize 44, 49
  investigate 461
disseize 789
dissemblance 18
dissemble 544
dissembler 548
disseminate
  scatter 73
  pervade 186
  publish 531
  teach 537
dissension 713
  sow - 898
dissent
  disagree **489**
  refuse 764
  heterodoxy 984
dissepiment 228

dissertation 595
disservice
  disadvantage 619
  useless 645
disserviceable
  bad 649
dissever 44
  discontinue 70
dissidence
  disagreement 24
  dissent 489
  discord 713
  discontent 832
  heterodoxy 984
dissilience 173
dissimilarity 16a, **18**
dissimilitude 16a, 24
dissimulate 544
dissipate
  scatter 73
  destroy 162
  pleasure 377
  prodigality 818
  amusement 840
  intemperance 954
  dissolute 961
dissocial 893
dissociate 44
dissociation
  irrelation 10
  separation 44
dissogeny 161
dissolute
  profligate 945
  intemperate 954
  dissolute 961
dissolution
  [see dissolve]
  decomposition 49
  destruction 162
  death 360
dissolve *vanish* 2, 4
  liquefy 335
  disappear 449
  abrogate 756
dissolving views 448,
  449
dissonance
  disagreement 24
  unmusical 414
  discord 713
dissuasion 616
dissyllable 561
distain *dirty* 653
  ugly 846
distal 196
distance 196
  overtake 282
  go beyond 303
  defeat 731
  angular - 244
  - lends enchantment
    196
  - of time
  long time 110
  past 122
  keep at a -
  discourtesy 895
  keep one's -
  avoid 623
  modest 881

---

respect 928
teach one his - 879
distaste 867
distasteful 830
distemper
  color 428
  painting 556
  disease 655
distend 194
distended 192
distich 597
distichous 91
distil *come out* 295
  evaporate 336
  drop 348
distinct
  disjoined 44
  audible 402
  visible 446
  intelligible 518
  manifest 525
  express 535
  articulate 580
distinction
  difference 15
  discrimination 465
  fame 873
  rank 875
  - without a difference
    27
distinctive 15
  - feature 79
distingué
  fashion 852
  repute 873
distinguish
  perceive 441
  discriminate 465
  - by the name of 564
distinguishable 15
distinguished
  superior 33
  repute 873
distinguishing 15
distortion
  obliquity 217
  twist **243**
  of vision 443
  misinterpret 523
  falsehood 544
  misrepresent 555
  ugly 846
  (*misjudge* 481)
distract 458
distracted
  confused 475
  insane 503
  excited 824
distraction
  passion 825
  love to - 897
distrain *take* 789
  appraise 812
  attach 969
distrait 458
distraught 475
distress
  distraint 789
  poverty 804
  affliction 828
  cause pain 830

---

signal of - 669
distribute
  arrange 60
  disperse 73
  type 591
  allot 786
district 181
  - court 966
distrust
  disbelief 485
  fear 860
distrustful 487
disturb
  derange 61
  change 140
  agitate 315
  excite 824
  distress 828, 830
disturbance
  disorder 59
disunion
  separation 44
  disorder 59
  discord 713
disuse
  desuetude 614
  relinquish 624
  unemploy **678**
disvalue 932
ditch *inclosure* 232
  hollow 252
  trench 259
  water 343
  conduit 350
  defense 717
ditch water
  dirt 653
ditheism 984
dithyramb
  music 415
  poetry 597
dithyrambic
  wild 503
ditto 104
  say - to 488
ditty 415
  - bag 191
diurnal 138
diuturnity 110
divagate 279
divan *sofa* 215
  council 696
  throne 747
  tribunal 966
divaricate *differ* 15
  bifurcate 91
  diverge 291
divarication 16a
dive
  resort 189
  swim 267
  plunge 310
  - into *inquire* 461
divellicate 44
divergence
  nonuniformity 16a
  difference 15
  dissimilarity 18
  variation 20a
  disagreement 24
  deviation 279

---

separation **291**
divers *different* 15
  multiform 81
  many 102
  - colored 440
diverse 15
diversify
  [see diversity]
  vary 20a
  change 140
diversion
  change 140
  deviation 279
  amusement 840
diversity
  difference 15
  irregular 16a
  dissimilar 18
  multiform 81
  - of opinion 489
divert *turn* 279
  deceive 545
  amuse 840
  - the mind 452, **458**
divertissement
  drama 599
  amusement 840
Dives 803
divest *denude* 226
  take 789
  - oneself of
  abrogate 756
  relinquish 782
divestment 226
divide *separate* 44
  part 51
  arrange 60
  arithmetic 85
  bisect 91
  vote 609
  apportion 786
dividend *part* 51
  number 84
  portion 786
dividers 466
divina particula au-
  ræ 450
divination
  prediction 511
  sorcery 992
divine *predict* 511
  guess 514
  perfect 650
  of God 976, 983, 983a
  clergyman 996
  - right
  authority 737
  due 924
  - service 990
divining rod
  sign 550
  magic 993
Divinity *God* 976
  theology 983
divisible *number* 84
division
  [see divide]
  part 51
  class 75
  arithmetic 85
  discord 713

drabble 653
drachm 319
Draco *ruler* 694
  severe 739
draff 653
draft [*see also* draught]
  drawing 554, 556
  write 590
  abstract 596
  plan 626
  cheque 800, 805
  - off *displace* 185
  transfer 270
draft-horse 271
drag *carriage* 272
  crawl 275
  traction 285
  impediment 706
  - a chain
  tedious 110
  exertion 686
  subjection 749
  - into
  implicate 54
  compel 744
  - into open day 531
  - on *tedious* 110
  - slow length
  long 200
  weary 841
  - through mire
  disrepute 874
  disrespect 929
  - towards
  attract 288
  put on the - 275
draggle 653
drag-net
  all sorts 78
dragoman 524
dragon *monster* 83
  violent 173
  irascible 901
  -s of the night 684
dragonnade
  attack 716
  punish 972
dragoon *soldier* 726
  compel 744
  insolent 885
  worry 907
drain
  flow out 295
  empty 297
  dry 340
  conduit 350
  waste 638
  clean 652
  unclean 653
  exhaust 789
  dissipate 818
  - into 348
  - of resources 640
  - the cup
  drink 298
  drunken 959
  - the cup of misery 828
drake *male* 373
  fire - 423
dram *drink* 298
  pungent 392

stimulus 615
- drinking 959
drama 599
dramatic 599
  ostentation 882
- author 599
- poetry 597
dramatis personæ
  mankind 372
  play 599
  agents 690
  party 712
dramaturgy 599
drame comédie 599
drap d'or 847
draper 225
drapery 225
drastic 171
draught
  [*see also* draft]
  multitude 102
  depth 208
  traction 285
  drink 298
  stream of air 349
  delineation 554, 556
  plan 626
  physic 662
  troops 726
  - off 73
draughts
  game 840
draughtsman
  artist 559
draw *pull* 285
  delineate 554, 556
  money 800
- a bead on 716
- a curtain 424
- and quarter 972
- an inference 480
- a parallel 9
- a picture 594
- aside 279
- a straight furrow
  939
- back *regret* 283
  avoid 623
- breath
  refresh 689
  feeling 821
  relief 834
- down 153
- forth 677
- from 810
- in 195
- in one's horns
  tergiversation 607
  humility 879
- lots 621
- near *time* 121
  approach 286
- off *eject* 297
  hinder 706
  take 789
- off the attention 458
- on *time* 121
  event 151
  induce 615
- on futurity 132
- out

protract 110
late 133
prolong 200
extract 301
discover 480a
exhibit 525
diffuse style 573
- over *induce* 615
- poker 840
- profit 775
- the line 465
- the pen through 552
- the sword
  attack 716
  war 722
- the teeth of 158
- the veil 528
- together
  assemble 72
  coöperate 709
- towards 288
- up *order* 58
  stop 265
  write 590
- up a statement 594
- upon *money* 800
drawback *evil* 619
  imperfection 651
  hindrance 706
  discount 813
drawbridge
  way 627
  escape 671
drawcansir 887
drawee 800
drawer
  receptacle 191
  artist 559
- of water 690
drawers
  dress 225
drawing
  delineation 554, 556
drawing knife 253
drawing-room
  assembly 72
  room 191
  fashion 852
drawl *prolong* 200
  creep 275
  in speech 583
  sluggish 683
drawn *equated* 27
- battle
  pacification 723
  incomplete 730
dray 272
dray horse 271
drayman 268
dread 860
dreadful *great* 31
  bad 649
  dire 830
  depressing 837
  fearful 860
dreadless 861
dreadnought
  coat 225
  battleship 726
dream
  unsubstantial 4

error 495
fancy 515
sleep 683
- of *think* 451
  intend 620
- on other things 458
golden - 858
silently as a - 318
dreamer
  madman 504
  imaginative 515
dreamy
  unsubstantial 4
  inattentive 458
  sleepy 683
dreary
  solitary 87
  melancholy 830, 837
dredge *collect* 72
  extract 301
  raise 307
dredging machine
  307
dregs
  remainder 40
  refuse 645
  dirt 653
- of the people 876
- of vice 945
drench *drink* 298
  water 337
  redundance 641
- with physic 662
drenching rain 348
dress
  uniformity 16
  agree 23
  equalize 27
  clothes 225
  prepare 673
  ornament 847
  ostentation 882
- the ground 371
- to advantage 847
- up *falsehood* 544
  represent 554
- wounds 662
full - 852
dress coat 225
dresser
  sideboard 215
  surgeon 662
dressing
  reprimand 932
  punish 972
dressing gown 225
dressmaker 225
dribble
  flow out 295
  drop 348
driblet 32
drier 340
drift
  accumulate 72
  motion 264
  float 267
  transfer 270
  direction 278
  deviation 279
  approach 286
  wind 349

- time
  soon 132
- to
  cause and effect 154, 155
  give - weight 465
  give his - to
  right 922
  vindication 937
  fair 939
  in - course 109
  occasion 134
duel 720
duelist 726
duello 720
dueness 924
duenna
  teacher 540
  guardian 664
  keeper 753
dues 812
duet 415
due teste valgono 709
duffer
  bungler 701
  smuggler 792
du fort au faible 87, 159
dug 250
dugout
  dwelling 189
  boat 273
duke ruler 745
  noble 875
  -'s revenues on her back 878
dukedom
  volumes I prize above - 593
dulce
- domum 189
- est desipere 840
- et decorum 360, 926
dulcet sweet 396
  sound 405
  melodious 413
  agreeable 829
dulcify 174, 396
dulcimer 417
Dulcinea 897
dulcorate 396
dulia 990
dull weak 160
  unintelligent 32
  inert 172
  moderate 174
  blunt 254
  insensible 376
  sound 405
  dim 422
  colorless 429
  stolid 499
  style 575
  inactive 683
  unapt 699
  callous 823
  dejected 837
  weary 841
  prosing 843
  simple 849
  - of hearing 419

- sight 443
dullard 501
dullness 843
duly 924
dum
- loquimur 111
- Roma deliberat 162, 275
- vitant stulti 857
duma 696
dumb 581
- animal 366
- show 550
  strike -
  astonish 870
  humble 879
dumb-waiter 307
dumdum bullet 727
dumfounder
  disappoint 509
  silence 581
  astonish 870
  humble 879
dummodo sit dives 876
dummy
  substitute 147
  impotent 158
  speechless 581
  inactive 683
  cards 840
dump
  unload 297
  music 415
  lament 839
- cart 272
dumps
  discontent 832
  dejection 837
  sulk 901a
dumpy little 193
  short 201
  thick 202
dun dim 422
  colorless 429
  gray 432
  importune 765
  creditor 805
dunce
  ignoramus 493
  fool 501
dunderhead 501
dune 206
dung 653
dungeon 752
dunghill dirt 653
  cowardly 862
  baseborn 876
- cock 366
Dunker 984
duo 415
duodecimal 99
duodecimo
  little 193
  book 593
duodenary 98
duologue
  interlocution 588
  drama 599
dupe
  credulous 486

deceive 545
  deceived **547**
duplex 90
duplicate
  copy 21
  double 90
  tally 550
  record 551
  redundant 641
  pawn 805
duplication
  imitation 19
  doubling **90**
duplicature
  fold 258
duplicity
  duality 89
  falsehood 544
durability 141
durable
  long time 110
  stable 150
dura lex sed lex 926
durance 751
  in - 754
duration 106
  contingent - **108a**
durbar
  conference 588
  council 696
  tribunal 966
duress
  compulsion 744
  restraint 751
Durga 979
durham boat 273
during 106
- pleasure &c. 108a
durity 323
durwan 753
dusk
  evening 126
  half-light 422
dusky dark 421
  black 431
dust levity 320
  powder 330
  corpse 362
  trash 643
  dirt 653
  money 800
  come down with the - 807
  come to -
  die 360
- in the balance 643
- one's jacket 972
  humbled in the - 879
  kick up a - 885
  level with the - 162
  lick the -
  submit 725
  fail 732
  make to bite the - 731
  throw - in the eyes
  blind 442
  deceive 545
  plead 617
  turn to -
  deorganized 358
  die 360

duster 652
dust hole 519
  fit for the -
  useless 645
  dirty 653
  spoilt 659
dustman
  cleaner 652
dustoor 613
dustoori 973
dust storm 330
dusty
  powder 330
  dirt 653
Dutch
- auction 796
- courage 862
- oven 386
  high - 519
  it beats the - 508
Dutchman 57
  flying - 515
dutiable 812
dutiful 944
duty
  business 625
  work 686
  tax 812
  courtesy 894
  obligation **926**
  respect 928
  worship 990
  rite 998
  do one's -
  virtue 944
  on - 680, 682
duumvirate 737
Duval, Claude - 792
D. V. 470
dwarf lessen 36
  small 193
  elf 980
dwell
  reside 186
  abide 265
- upon
  descant 573
dweller 188
dwelling
  location 184
  abode 189
dwindle
  lessen 36
  shrink 195
dyadic 89
dye 428
  -d in the wool 709, 820
dying 360
dyke [see dike]
dynamic energy 157
dynamics 276
dynamitard 863
dynamite 727
dynamometer 466
dynasty 737
dysentery 299
dysmerogenesis 161
dysmeromorph 357
dyspepsia 655
dysphony 581
dyspnœa 688

E

spring **325**
elate *cheer* 836
  rejoice 838
  hope 858
  rain 880
  boast 884
elbow *angle* 244
  projection 250
  push 276
  at one's -
    near 197
    advice 695
  - one's way
    progress 282
    pursuit 622
    active 682
  out at -s
    undress 226
    poor 804
    disrepute 874
elbowchair 215
elbow grease 331
elbowroom
  space 180
  freedom 748
eld 122
elder *older* 124
  aged 128
  veteran 130
  clergy 996
El Dorado 803
elect *choose* 609
  good 648
  predestinate 976
  pious 987
election
  numerical 84
  necessity 601
electioneering 609
elective franchise 609
elector 745
electorate 737
electric *swift* 274
  sensation 821
  excitable 825
  - chair 975
  - light 423
electricity 157
electrify
  unexpected 508
  excite 824
  astonish 870
electro-biology 992
electrocution 972
electrocutioner 975
electrolier 423
electrolyze 49
electro-magnetism
  157
electrotype 591
electuary 662
eleemosynary 784
Elegance, Bank of -
  800
elegance
  in style 578
  beauty 845
  taste 850
elegy *interment* 363
  poetry 597
  lament 839

element
  substantiality 3
  component 56
  beginning 66
  cause 153
  matter 316
  devouring - 382
  in one's -
    facility 705
    content 831
  lowering - scowls 353
  out of its - 185
elementary
  simple 42
  - education 537
elements
  Eucharist 998
elench 477
elephant
  large 192
  carrier 271
  white - *bane* 663
elephantus non cap-
  it murem 643
eleutherian 748
elevated
  tipsy 959
elevation
  height 206
  vertical 212
  raising **307**
  plan 554
  angular - 244
  - of mind 942
  - of style 574
    improvement 658
    glory 873
elevator 307
élève 541
eleven 98
  representative 759
eleventh hour
  evening 126
  late 133
  opportune 134
elf *infant* 129
  little 193
  male 373
  imp 980
elicit *cause* 153
  draw out 301
  discover 480a
  manifest 525
eligible 646
eliminate
  subduct 38
  simplify 42
  exclude 55
  weed 103
  extract 301
elision
  separation 44
  shortening 201
élite *best* 648
  distinguished 873
  aristocratic 875
elixation 384
elixir 662
elk 366
ell 200
  take an -

take 789
  insolence 885
  wrong 923
  undue 925
  selfish 943
ellipse 247
ellipsis
  shorten 201
  style 572
ellipsoid 247, 249
elliptic 247
elocation
  displace 185
  transfer 270
elocution 582
éloge 931
elongation
  distance 196
  lengthening 200
elopement
  avoid 623
  escape 671
eloquence
  style 569
  speech 582
  action is - 582
  to try thy - 582
else 37
elsewhere 187
elucidate 82, 522
elude
  sophistry 477
  avoid 623
  escape 671
  succeed 731
  palter 773
elusive
  [see elude]
  deceptive 545
elusory
  untrue 546
elutriate 652
eluvium 349
elysian
  delightful 829
  heavenly 981
Elysium *bliss* 827
  paradise 981
elytron 223
Elzevir edition 193
emaciation
  shrinking 195
  thinness 203
emanate
  go out of 295
  excrete 299
  - from 544
emanation
  odor 398
emancipate
  deliver 672
  facilitate 705
  free 748, 750
emasculate
  impotent 158
  clean 652
  (*weaken* 160)
embalm
  interment 363
  perfume 400
  preserve 670

- in the memory
  505
embankment
  esplanade 189
  refuge 666
  fence 717
  (*inclosure* 232)
embargo
  stoppage 265
  prohibition 761
embark
  transfer 270
  depart 293
  - in *begin* 66
  engage in 676
embarquer sans bis-
  cuits, s'- 674
embarras de
  - choix 609
  - richesses
    redundance 641
    wealth 803
embarrass
  render difficult 704
  hinder 706
embarrassed
  poor 804
  in debt 806
embarrassing
  uncertain 475
embase 659
embassy
  errand 532
  commission 755
  consignee 758
embattled
  arranged 60
  leagued 712
  war array 722
embay 229
embed
  locate 184
  base 215
embellish 847
embers 384
embezzle 791
embitter
  deteriorate 659
  aggravate 835
  acerbate 900
emblazon
  color 428
  ornament 847
  display 882
emblem 550
  - of authority 747
embody *join* 43
  combine 48
  form a whole 50
  compose 54
  include 76
embogue 297
embolden
  hope 858
  encourage 861
embolism 228
embolus 261, 706
embonpoint 192
embosomed
  lodged 184
  interjacent 228

circumscribed 229
emboss *convex* 250
  ornament 847
embouchure 260
embowed 245
embowel 297
embrace
  compose 54
  include 76
  inclose 227
  choose 609
  take 789
  friendship 888
  sociality 892
  courtesy 894
  endearment 902
  - *an offer* 762
embrangle
  derange 61
embranglement
  discord 713
embrasure
  notch 257
  opening 260
embrocation 662
embroider
  variegate 440
  lie 544
  ornament 847
embroidery
  adjunct 39
  exaggeration 549
embroil *derange* 61
  discord 713
embroilment
  disorder 59
embrown 433
embryo
  beginning 66
  cause 153
  in - *destined* 152
  preparing 673
embryonic
  little 193
  immature 674
emendation 658
emerald *green* 435
  jewel 847
emerge 295
emergency
  circumstance 8
  event 151
  difficulty 704
emeritus *sage* 500
  respected 928
emersion 295
emery
  sharpener 253
  - *paper*
  smooth 255
emesis 297
emetic *remedy* 662
émeute 742
emication 420
emigrant
  stranger 57
  traveler 268
emigrate
  remove 266
  egress 295
eminence

height 206
  fame 873
  church dignitary 996
eminently 33
emir *master* 745
  noble 875
emissary
  messenger 534
  consignee 758
emission 297
emit *eject* 297
  publish 531
  - *vapor* 336
Emmanuel 976
emmeleia 413
emmet 193
emollient 662
emolument
  acquisition 775
  receipt 810
  remuneration 973
emotion 821
empale
  transfix 260
  execute 972
empanel 969
emperor 745
emphasis
  accent 580
emphatic
  positive assertion 535
  important 642
emphatically
  much 31
empierce
  perforate 260
  insert 300
empire
  dominion 737
  domain 780
empirema 476
empiric 548
empirical
  experiment 463
  essay 675
empiricism 463
emplastrum 662
employ
  business 625
  use 677
  servitude 749
  commission 755
  - *one's capital in* 794
  - *oneself* 680
  - *one's time in* 625
  in one's - 746
employé
  servant 746
  agent 758
employer 795
empoison 659
emporium 799
empower
  power 157
  commission 755
  permit 760
empress 745
empressement
  activity 682

emotion 821
  desire 865
emprise 676
empta dolore docet
  experientia 490
emption 795
emptor 795
  caveat - 769
empty *clear* 185
  vacant 187
  drain 297
  ignorant 491
  waste 638
  deficient 640
  useless 645
  beggarly account of - *boxes*
  poverty 804
  - *encomium* 894
  - *one's glass* 298
  - *purse* 804
  - *sound* 517
  - *stomach* 865
  - *title name* 564
  - *undue* 925
  - *words* 546
empty-handed 640
empty-headed 491
empurple 437
empyrean *sky* 318
  blissful 829
empyreuma 41
empyrosis 384
emulate *imitate* 19
  goodness 648
  rival 708
  compete 720
  glory 873
emulsion 352
emunctory 295, 350
en
  - *bloc* 50
  - *courroux* 593
  - *flûte* 210, 727
  - *foule* 102
  - *habiles gens* 159
  - *masse* 50
  - *passant parenthetical* 10
  transient 111
  àpropos 134
  - *rapport* 9
  - *règle order* 58
  conformity 82
  - *route*
  journey 266
  progress 282
  - *suivant la verité* 94
enable 157
enact *drama* 599
  action 680
  conduct 692
  complete 729
  order 741
  law 963
enallage
  metaphor 521
  (*substitute* 147)
enamel *coating* 223
  painting 556

porcelain 557
  ornament 847
enameler 559
enamor 897
enanthema 655
en avant 278
encage 751
encamp *locate* 184
  abode 189
encaustic painting 556
enceinte
  with child 161
  region 181
  inclosure 232
enchafe 830
enchain
  restrain 751
  (*join* 43)
enchant *please* 829
enchanted
  pleased 827
enchanting
  beautiful 845
  love 897
enchantment
  sorcery 992
enchase 43
enchymatous 194
enchyridion 593
encincture 229
encircle 227
  include 76
enclave *close* 181
  boundary 233
enclose [*see* inclose]
enclosure [*see* inclosure]
encomiast 935
encomium 931
encompass 227
  -ed *with difficulties* 704
encore *again* 104
  approbation 931
encounter
  undergo 151
  clash 276
  meet 292
  withstand 708
  contest 720
  - *danger* 665
  - *risk* 621
encourage
  animate 615
  aid 707
  comfort 834
  hope 858
  embolden 861
Encratism 953
Encratite 953
encroach
  transcursion 303
  do wrong 923
  infringe 925
  - *upon* 927
encuirassed 223
encumber
  difficulty 704
  hindrance 706
encyclical 531

encyclopedia
knowledge 490
book 542, 593
encyclopedical
general 78
- knowledge 490
encysted 229
end
termination **67**
effect 154
object 620
at an - 142
begin at the wrong - 699
come to its - 729
- in smoke 732
- of life 360
- of one's tether
sophistry 477
ignorant 491
insufficient 640
difficult 704
- one's days 360
-s of the earth 196
- to end *space* 180
touching 199
length 200
great - of life 680
on - 212
one's journey's - 292
put an - to
destroy 162
kill 361
endæmonism 910
endæmonist 910
endamage 649
endanger 665
endear 897
endearment 902
endeavor
pursue 622
attempt 675
- after 620
use one's best - 686
endemic
special 79
interior 221
disease 655
endenizen 184
endimanche
adorned 847
display 882
endless
multitudinous 102
infinite 105
perpetual 112
endlong 200
endogenous 567
endome 223
endophagy 945
endorse
[see indorse]
endorsement
[see indorsement]
endosmose 302
endow
confer power 157
endowed with
possessed of 777
endowment
intrinsic 5

power 157
talent 698
gift 784
endrogynous 83
endure 157
exist 1
time 106
last 110
continue 141
undergo 151
feel 821
submit to 826
- for ever 112
- pain 828
unable to - 867
yet I - 858
endwise 212
enema 300
enemy *time* 841
foe 891
- to society 891
the common - 978
thing devised by the - 546
put - in their mouths 959
energumen 504
energy *power* 157
strength 159
physical **171**
resolution 604
activity 682
passion 820
enervate
paralyze 158
weaken 160
enervated 575
enface 590
enfant
bon - 906
- gâté
prosperity 734
satiety 869
favorite 899
- perdu
hopeless 859
reckless 863
- terrible
artless 703
object of fear 860
enfeeble 160
enfeoffment 783
Enfield rifle 727
enfilade
lengthwise 200
pierce 260
pass through 302
enfold 229
enforce *urge* 615
advise 695
compel 744
require 924
enfranchise
free 748
liberate 750
permit 760
enfranchised
privileged 924
engage
bespeak 132
induce 615

undertake 676
do battle 722
commission 755
promise 768
compact 769
- the attention 457
- with 720
I'll -
affirmation 535
engaged
marriage 903
- in *attention* 457
engagement
business 625
battle 720
engaging
pleasing 829
amiable 897
engarrison 717
engender 161
engine 633
engine driver 268
engineer
engine driver 268
mechanician 690
military 726
engineering 633
engird 227
English
native 188
broken - 563
king's - 560
murder the king's - 568
plain -
intelligible 518
interpreted 522
style 576
engobe 223
engorge
swallow 296
gluttony 957
engorgement
too much 641
engrave
furrow 259
mark 550
- in the memory 505
engraver 559
engraving 558
engross *write* 590
possess 777
- the thoughts
thought 451
attention 457
engulf
destroy 162
plunge 310
swallow up 296
enhance
increase 35
improve 658
enharmonic 413
enigma
question 461
secret 533
enigmatic
uncertain 475
obscure 519
(*hidden* 528)
enigmatical 520

enigme, mot d'- 522
enjoin 600
advise 695
command 741
prescribe 926
enjoy
physically 377
possess 777
morally 827
- a state 7
- health 654
enkindle *heat* 384
excite 824
(*induce* 615)
enlarge
increase 35
swell 194
in writing 573
liberate 750
- the mind 537
enlarged views 498
enleague 712
enlighten
illumine 420
inform 527
teach 537
enlightened
knowledge 490
enlist *engage* 615
war 722
commission 755
- into the service 677
- under the banners of 707
enliven
delight 829
inspirit 834
cheer 836
amuse 840
enmesh 704
enmity 889
ennoble 873
ennui 841
enormity
crime 947
enormous *great* 31
bid 192
- number 102
enough *much* 31
no more! 142
sufficient 639
moderately 651
satiety 869
- and to spare 639
- in all conscience 641
- to drive one mad 830
know when one has had - 953
enrage
provoke 830
aggravate 835
incense 900
enragé 865
enrapture
excite 824
beatify 829
love 897
enraptured 827
enravish

EVER

- other 138
- whit 52
in - mouth
  assent 488
  news 532
  repute 873
in - quarter 180
in - respect 494
on - side 227
everybody 78
everyone 78
- his due 922
- in his turn 148
everywhere
  space 180
  presence 186
evict 297
evidence 467
  ocular - 446
évidence, en - 446
evident
  visible 446
  certain 474
  manifest 525
evil *harm* 619
  badness 649
  impious 988
- day
  adversity 735
- eye *vision* 441
  malevolence 907
  disapprobation 932
  demon 980
  spell 993
- favored 846
- fortune 735
- genius 980
- hour 135
- one 978
- plight 735
- star 649
prepare for - 673
through - report &c.
  604a
evil doer 913
evil doing 945
evil-minded
  malevolent 907
  vicious 945
evil speaking
  malediction 908
  censure 932
  detraction 934
evince *show* 467
  prove 478
eviscerate
  eject 297
  extract 301
eviscerated 4
evoke *cause* 153
  call upon 765
  excite 824
evolution
  numerical 85
  production 161
  motion 264
  extraction 301
  circuition 311
  turning out **313**
  training 673
  action 680

EXAL

  military -s 722
evolve
  discover 480a
evolved from 154
  [*and see* evolution]
evolvement 313
evulgate 531
evulsion 301
evviva! 931
ewe *sheep* 366
  female 374
ewer 191
ex
- animo 602
- dono 784
- facto jus oritur 494
- more 613
- nihilo nihil 161
- officio 494
- parte 467
- pede Herculem 82
- post facto 122, 133
- quovis ligno 134
- tempore
  instant 113
  occasion 134
- vi termini 159
- voto 768
exacerbate
  increase 35
  exasperate 173
  aggravate 835
exact *similar* 17
  true 494
  style 572
  require 741
  tax 812
  insolence 885
  claim 924, 926
- meaning 516
- memory 505
- observance 772
- truth 494
exacting
  severe 739
  discontented 832
  grasping 865
exaction
  [*see* exact]
  undue 925
exactly
  literally 19
  just so 488
exaggeration
  increase 35
  expand 194
  overestimate 482
  magnify **549**
  misrepresent 555
exalt
  increase 35
  elevate 307
  extol 931
  (*boast* 884)
- one's horn 873
exalté 504
  tête -e 503
exalted *high* 206
  repute 873
  noble 875
  magnanimous 942

EXCE

examination
  [*see* examine]
  evidence 467
  undergo - 461
examine
  attend to 457
  inquire 461
example
  pattern 22
  instance 82
  bad - 949
  good - 948
  make an - of 974
  set a good - 944
exanimate
  dead 360
  supine 683
exanthema 655
exarch 745
exasperate
  exacerbate 173
  aggravate 835
  enrage 900
excavate 252
excecation 442
exceed *surpass* 33
  remain 40
  transgress 303
  intemperance 954
exceedingly
  (*greatly* 31)
excel *surpass* 33
- in *skillful* 698
excellence
  goodness 648
  virtue 944
excellence, par - 642
excellency
  title 877
excelsior 305
excentric 220 [*and see*
  eccentric]
except *subduct* 38
  exclude 55
  reject 610
exception
  unconformity 83
  qualification 469
  exemption 777a
  disapproval 932
  take -
  qualify 469
  resent 900
exceptionable
  bad 649
  guilty 947
exceptional
  unimitated 20
  extraneous 57
  unconformable 83
  in an - degree 31
exceptions 901, 901a
exceptis excipiendis
  469
excern 297
excerpta *parts* 51
  compendium 596
  selections 609
excerption 609
excess
  remainder 40

EXCR

  redundance 641
  intemperance 954
excessive
  great 31
exchange
  reciprocity 12
  interchange 148
  saloon 189
  transfer 783
  barter 794
  mart 799
  bill of - 771
- blows &c.
  retaliation 718
  battle 720
Exchequer 802
  Baron of - 967
  Court of - 966
- bill 800
excise 812
exciseman 965
excision 38
**excitabat enim fluc-
  tus in simpulo**
  549
excitability
  excitement **825**
  irascibility 901
excitation 824
excite *energy* 171
  violence 173
- morally 824
- an impression 375
- attention 457
- desire 865
- hope 811
- love 897
excited fancy 515
excitement 824, 825
  anger 900
exclaim 411
- against 932
exclamation 580
exclude
  sift 42
  leave out 55
  reject 610
  prohibit 761
  banish 893
exclusion **55,** 57
exclusive
  simple 42
  omitting 55
  special 79
  irregular 83
  forbidding 761
- of 38
- possession 777
- thought 457
excogitate
  thought 451
  imagination 515
excommunicate
  banish 893
  curse 908
  rite 998
  (*exclude* 55)
excoriate 226
excrement
  excretion 299
  dirt 653

(*inform* 527)
(*teach* 537)
- away 523
- wrongly 523
explainer 524
expletive
diffuse 573
redundant 641
explication 522
explicit *clear* 518
potent 525
explicitness 570
explode *burst* 173
confute 479
failure 732
passion 825
exploded *past* 122
antiquated 124
error 495
blown upon 932
[*and see* explosion]
exploit
action 680
courage 861
exploitation 461
explore
investigate 461
experiment 463
explorer 268
explosion
[*see* explode]
revolution 146
violence 173
sound 406
anger 900
explosive 727
dangerous 665
exponent
numerical 84
interpreter 524
informant 527
index 550
export 295
expose
denude 226
confute 479
disclose 529
censure 932
- oneself
disreputable 874
- to danger 665
- to view
visible 446
manifest 525
exposé
disclosure 529
description 594
exposed to
liable 177
exposition
[*see* expose]
explanation 522
exhibition 882
expositor
interpreter 524
teacher 540
expository
explaining 522
informing 527
disserting 595
expostulate

438

dissuade 616
advise 695
deprecate 766
reprehend 932
exposure [*see* expose]
appearance 448
- to weather 338
expound
interpret 522
teach 537
expounder 524
express
carrier 271
rapid 274
squeeze out 301
mean 516
declare 525
inform 527
intentional 620
transit 627
haste 684
- by words 566
- car 272
- sympathy for 915
- train 272
expressed, well - 578
expression [*see* express]
musical - 416
aspect 448
nomenclature 564
phrase 566
mode of - 569
new fangled - 563
expressive
meaning 516
sensibility 822
expressman 271
exprobation
censure 932
accusation 938
expropriation 782
expugnable 665
expugnation
success 731
(*taking* 789)
expuition 297
expulsion
[*see* expel]
exclusion 55
expunge
destroy 162
efface 552
expurgate 652
expurgatorius, index
- 761
exquisite
savory 394
excellent 648
pleasurable 829
fop 854
exquisitely
very 31
exsiccate 340
exspuition 297
exsudation 299
exsufflation 993
exsuscitate
stimulate 824
(*move* 615)
extant 1

extasy [*see* ecstasy]
extemporaneous
[*see* extempore]
transient 111
extempore
instant 113
early 132
occasion 134
off-hand 612
unprepared 674
extend
expand 194
prolong 200
(*increase* 35)
- to 196
extended 202
spacious 180
extensibility 324
extensile 324
extension [*see* extend]
increase 35
space 180
- of time 110
extensive
great 31
wide 180
- knowledge 490
extenso, in -
whole 50
diffuse 573
extent
degree 26
space 180
extenuate
decrease 36
weaken 160
excuse 937
extenuated 203
**extenuating circum-
stances**
qualification 469
excuse 937
exteriority 220
exterminate 162
extermination 301
exterminator 165
external 220
- evidence 467
- senses 375
extinct
inexistent 2
past 122
destroyed 162
darkness 421
extincteur 385
extinction
obliteration 552
- of life 360
extinguish
destroy 162
blow out 385
darken 421
extinguisher 165
put an - upon
hinder 706
defeat 731
extinguishment 2
extirpate 2, 301
extispicious 511
extispicy 511
extol

over-estimate 482
praise 931
extort *extract* 301
compel 744
despoil 789
extorted
dissent 489
extortion
dearness 814
rapacity 819
extortionate
severe 739
grasping 865
extra
additional 37
supernumerary 641
ab - 220
extract .
take out 301
quotation 596
extraction 301
paternity 166
- of roots 85
extractor 301
extradition
deportation 270
expulsion 297
extrados 220
extrajudicial 964
extralimitary 220
extramundane 220,
317
extramural 220
extraneous
extrinsic 6
not related 10
foreign 57
extraneousness 57
extraordinary
great 31
exceptional 83
extraregarding 220
extravagant
inordinate 31
violent 173
absurd 497
foolish 499
fanciful 515
exaggerated 549
excessive 641
high-priced 814
prodigal 818
vulgar 851
ridiculous 853
extravaganza
fanciful 515
drama 599
extravagation 303
extravasate
egress 295
ejection 297
extreme
inordinate 31
end 67
- unction 998
extremis, in -
dying 360
difficulty 704
extremity *end* 67
adversity 735
tribulation 828

at the last - 665
  drive matters to an - 604
extricate
  take out 301
  deliver 672
  facilitate 705
  liberate 750
extrinsicality 6
extrinsic evidence 467
extrusion
  eject 297
  excrete 299
exuberant
  - *style* 573
  redundant 639
exudation
  egress 295
  excretion 299
exulcerate 659
exult *rejoice* 838
  boast 884
exultant
  hopeful 858
exulting
  cheerful 836
exunge 356
exuviæ *dirt* 653

(remains 40)
eye *circle* 247
  opening 260
  organ of sight 441
appear to one's - 446
before one's -s
  front 234
  visible 446
  manifest 525
cast the -s on
  see 441
cast the -s over
  attend to 457
catch the - 457
close the -s
  blind 442
  death 360
  sleep 683
dry -s 823
- askance 860
- glistening 824
- like Mars 441
- of a needle 260
- of the master 693
-s draw straws 683
-s in flood with laugh-
  ter 838
-s open

attention 457
care 459
intention 620
-s opened
  disclosure 529
-s out 442
fix the -s on 457
have an - to
  attention 457
  intention 620
  desire 865
have one's -s about
  one 459
her -s are homes of
  silent prayer 441
in one's -
  visible 446
  expectant 507
in the - of the law 963
in the -s of
  appearance 448
  belief 484
keep an - upon 459
look with one's own
  -s 459
mind's - 515
open the -s to 480a
set one's -s upon 865

shut one's -s to
  inattention 458
  permit 760
to the -s 448
under the -s of 186
up to one's -s 641
with moistened -s 839
with open -s 870
eyeglass 445
eyeless 442
eyelet 260
eye opener 508
eyesight 441
eyesore
  ugly 846
  blemish 848
eyeteeth
have cut one's -
  adolescence 131
  skill 698
  cunning 702
eyewater 662
eyewitness
  spectator 444
  evidence 467
eyot 346
eyre 966
eyry 189

heavy - 599
Father, God the - 976
fatherhood 166
fatherland 189
fatherless 158
fatherly 906
fathership 166
Fathers, the - 983
fathom
length 200
investigate 461
solve 462
measure 466
discover 480a
knowledge 490
fathomless 208
fatidical 511
fatigation 688
fatigue 688
(*weariness* 841)
fatihah 66
fatiloquent 511
fatling 298
fatras 643
fatten
expand 194
improve 658
prosperous 734
- on *parasite* 886
- upon
feed 298
fatuity 499
fat-witted 499
faubourg 227
fauces 231
faugh! 867
fault
break 70
error 495
imperfection 651
failure 732
vice 945
guilt 947
at -
uncertain 475
ignorant 491
unskillful 699
find - with 932
fault-finder 832
faultless
perfect 650
innocent 946
faulty
imperfect 651
faun 980
fauna 366
faut: comme il -
taste 850
fashion 852
il s'en - bien 489
tant s'en - 536
faute 732
- de mieux
substitution 147
necessity 601
fauteuil 215
fautor 890
faux pas
failure 732
misconduct 947

intrigue 961
favaginous 252
faveolate 252
favillous 432
favor
resemble 17
badge 550
letter 592
aid 707
indulgence 740
permit 760
gift 784
partiality 923
appearances in - of 472
- with 784
get into -
friendship 888
love 897
in - *repute* 873
approbation 931
in - of
approve 931
under - of 760
view with - 906
favorable
occasion 134
willing 602
good 648
aid 707
- *prospect* 472
- to 709
take a - turn
improve 658
prosperity 734
favorably
well 618
favorer 890
favorite
pleasing 829
beloved 897, **899**
favoritism
friendship 888
wrong 923
favose 252
fawn
cringe 886
flatter 933
fawn-colored 433
fax mentis incendium gloriæ 615
fay 979
faze
disconcert 706
bother 830
daunt 860
fealty
obedience 743
duty 926
respect 928
fear 860
- is the parent of cruelty 860
fearful
painful 830
timid 862
fearfully
much 31
wonderfully 870
fearless
hope 858

courage 861
feasible
possible 470
easy 705
feast *period* 138
repast 298
pleasure 377
revel 840
rite 998
- one's eyes 897
feast of reason
conversation 588
- and flow of soul
sociality 892
feat *action* 680
courage 861
- of arms 720
- of strength 159
feather *class* 75
tuft 256
light 320
trifle 643
ornament 847
decoration 877
- in one's cap
honor 873
- *decoration* 877
- in the scale 643
- one's nest
prepare 673
prosperity 734
wealth 803
economy 817
selfish 943
- the oar 698
hear a - drop 403
in full -
prepared 673
prosperous 734
rich 803
in high -
health 654
cheerful 884
pleased with a - 840
feather bed 324
feathered tribes 366
feathery 256
featly 682
feature
character 5
component 56
form 240
appearance 448
lineament 550
feaze 60 [see also faze]
febrifuge 662
febrile 825
fecal 653
fecit 556
fecula 653
feculence 653
fecund 168
fecundate 161
federal currency 800
federalists 712
federation 712
fee *possession* 777
property 780
pay 809
reward 973
feeble *weak* 160

illogical 477
(*scanty* 32)
feeble-minded
imbecile 499
irresolute 605
feebleness
style 575
feed *eat* 298
supply 637
- the flame 707
fee-faw-fum
bugbear 860
spell 993
feel *sense* 375
touch 379
emotion 821
- for *try* 463
benevolence 906
pity 914
- *grief* 915
- one's way
essay 675
caution 864
- the pulse 461
- the want of 865
feeler 379
inquiry 461
experiment 463
feeling 821
- of sense 916
feet *low* 207
walkers 266
at one's -
near 197
subjection 749
humility 879
fall at one's -
submit 725
fall on one's -
prosper 734
lick the - of
servile 886
light upon one's -
safe 664
spring to one's - 307
throw oneself at the -
of *entreat* 765
feign 544
feigned 545
feint 545
felicitas, curiosa - 698
felicitas multos habet amicos 734
felicitate 896
felicitous
agreeing 23
- *style* 23
skillful 698
successful 731
pleasant 829
felicity
happiness 827
feline *cat* 366
stealthy 528
cunning 702
felix
- qui potuit 153
- se nescit amari 734
fell *destroy* 162
mountain 206

hot 382
strong feeling 821
excitable 825
angry 900
irascible 901
- cross 550
- furnace 386
- imagination 515
- ordeal 828
fiesta 840
fife 417
fifer 416
fifth 98, 99
fifty 98
fig
  unimportance 643
- out 857
in the name of the
  prophet -s! 497
fight
  contention 720
  warfare 722
- against destiny 606
- it out 722
- one's battles again
  594
- one's way
- shy *avoid* 623
  coward 862
  pursue 622
  active 682
  exertion 686
- the good fight 944
show -
  defense 717
  courage 861
fighter 726
fighting cock
  combatant 726
  courage 861
fighting man 726
figment 515
figurante 599
figurate number 84
figuration 240
figurative
  metaphorical 521
  representing 554
- *style* 577
figure
  number 84
  form 240
  appearance 448
  metaphor 521
  indicate 550
  represent 554
  price 812
  ugly 846
cut a -
  repute 873
  display 882
- to oneself 515
- of speech 521
  exaggeration 549
poor - 874
figure flinger 994
figurehead
  sign 550
  representativn 554
figurine 554
figuriste 559

filaceous 205
filament 205
filamentiferous 205
filamentous 256
filch 791
filcher 762
file *subduct* 38
  arrange 60
  row 69
  assemblage 72
  list 86
  reduce 195
  smooth 255
  pulverize 330
  store 636
  soldiers 726
- a claim &c. 969
- leader 694
- off *march* 266
  diverge 291
file-fire 716
filgurate 420
filial 167
filiation
  consanguinity 11
  attribution 155
  posterity 167
filibeg 225
filibuster
  impede 706
  obstructionist 710
  plunder 791
  thief 792
filibustering 791
filiciform 242
filicoid 242
filiform 205
filigree 219
filings 330
filius nullius 925
filius terræ 876
fill *complete* 52
  occupy 186
  contents 190
  stuff 224
  provision 637
eat one's - 957
- an office
  business 625
  government 737
-ed to overflowing
  641
- one's pocket 803
- out
  expand 194
- the bill 729
- time 106
- up *compensate* 30
  compose 54
  close 261
  restore 660
- up the time
  inaction 681
have one's -
  enough 639
  satiety 869
fille
- de chambre 746
- de joie 962
filled
- to overflowing 641

fillet *band* 45
  filament 205
  circle 247
  ornament 847
filling
  stuffing 224
fillip
  impulse 276
  propulsion 284
  stimulus 615
  excite 824
filly 271
film *layer* 204
  opaque 426
  semitransparent 427
- over the eyes
  dim sight 443
  ignorant 491
filmy *texture* 329
filter *percolate* 295
  clean 652
filth 653
filtrate 652
fimbriæ 256
fimbriated 256
fimetarious 653
fimicolous 653
fin 267
- contre - 702
il faut considérer la -
  67
final *ending* 67
  completing 729
  court of - appeal 474
- cause 620
- stroke 729
- touch 729
finale *end* 67
  completion 729
finality 67, 729
finally
  for good 141
  on the whole 476
finance
  money 800
  account 811
minister of - 801
financier 801
finch 366
find
  eventuality 151
  adjudge 480
  discover 480a
  acquire 775
- a clue to 480a
- credence 484
- in *provide* 637
- it in one's heart 602
- means 632
- one's account in 644
- oneself *be* 1
  present 186
- one's way 731
- one's way into 294
- out 480a
- the cause of 522
- the key of 522
- the meaning 522
- to one's cost 509
- vent 671
finding

judgment 480
- store 799
fine
  small 32
  large 192
  thin 203
  rare 322
  not raining 340
  exact 494
  good 648
  beautiful 845
  adorned 847
  proud 878
  mulct 974
- air 656
- arts 554
- by degrees 30
- feather
  strong 159
  healthy 654
- feeling 850
- frenzy 515
- gentleman
  fop 854
  proud 878
- grain 329
- lady 854, 878
- powder 330
- talking
  overrate 482
  boast 884
- time of it 734
- voice 580
- writing 577
in - end 67
  after all 476
one - morning 106
some - morning 119
finedraw 660
fine-fingered 698
finem respice 67, 457
finem, respicere - 510
finery
  ornament 847
  vulgarity 851
fine-spoken
  courtesy 894
  flattery 933
finespun *thin* 203
  sophistry 477
finesse *tact* 698
  artifice 702
  taste 850
  (*deception* 545)
finestill 336
fine-toned 413
finger *touch* 379
  hold 781
at one's -s' end
  near 197
  know 490
  remember 505
- in the pie
  cause 153
  interfere 228
  act 680
  active 682
  coöperate 709
- on the lips
  aphony 581
  taciturnity 585

fola 258
flibbertigibbet 980
flicker
  changing 149
  waver 314
  flutter 315
  light 420
  dim 422
flickering
  irregular 139
flies *theater* 599
flight *flock* 102
  volitation 267
  swiftness 274
  departure 293
  avoidance 623
  escape 671
  - of fancy 515
  - of stairs
  ascent 305
  way 627
  - of time 109
  put to -
  propel 284
  repel 717
  vanquish 731
flighty *mad* 503
  fanciful 515
flimflam *lie* 544
  caprice 608
flimsy *weak* 160
  rarity 322
  soft 324
  sophistical 477
  trifling 643
flinch *swerve* 607
  avoid 623
  fear 860
  cowardice 862
fling *propel* 284
  jig 840
  jeer 929
  - aside 782
  - away *reject* 610
  waste 638
  relinquish 782
  - down 308
  - to the winds
  destroy 162
  not observe 773
  have a - at
  attack 716
  resent 900
  disrespect 929
  censure 932
  have one's -
  active 682
  laxity 738
  freedom 748
  amusement 840
flint *hard* 323
flint-hearted 907
flip *beverage* 298
flippant *fluent* 584
  pert 885
flipper *paddle* 267
flirt *propel* 284
  love 897
  endearment 902
  - a fan
  affectation 855

flit *elapse* 109
  changeable 149
  move 264
  travel 266
  swift 274
  depart 293
  run away 623
flitter
  small part 32
  changeable 149
  flutter 315
flitting
  evanescent 111
float
  establish 150
  navigate 267
  boat 273
  buoy up 305
  lightness 320
  before the -s
  on the stage 599
  - before the eyes 446
  - in the mind
  thought 451
  imagination 515
  - on the air 405
floater 702
floating
  [see float]
  rumored 532
  - battery 726
  - capital 805
  - debt 806
  - hotel 273
Flobert rifle 727
floccillation 315
flocculent
  woolly 256
  soft 324
  pulverulent 330
flock
  assemblage 72
  multitude 102
  laity 997
  -s and herds 366
  - together 72
floe *ice* 383
flog 972
flood *much* 31
  crowd 72
  river 348
  abundance 639
  redundance 641
  prosperity 734
  - of light 420
  - of tears 839
  stem the - 708
flood gate
  limit 233
  egress 295
  conduit 350
  open the -s
  eject 297
  permit 760
flood mark 466
flood tide
  increase 35
  complete 52
  height 206
  advance 282
  water 337

floor *level* 204
  base 211
  horizontal 213
  support 215
  overthrow 731
  ground - 191
flop 315
flora 369
floral 367
floret 367
floriculture 371
florid *color* 428
  red 434
  - style 577
  health 654
florist 371
flosculi sententia-
  rum 498
floss 256
flotilla *ships* 273
  navy 726
flotsam and jetsam
  73
flounce
  trimming 231
  jump 309
  agitation 315
  (*move quickly* 274)
flounder
  change 149
  toss 315
  uncertain 475
  bungle 699
  difficulty 704
  fail 732
  (*blunder* 495)
flour 330
flourish
  brandish 314, 315
  exaggerate 549
  language 577
  speech 582
  healthy 654
  prosperous 734
  ornament 847
  repute 873
  display 882
  boast 884
  (*succeed* 731)
  - in immortal youth
  112
  - of trumpets
  loud 404
  publish 531
  ostentation 882
  celebrate 883
  boast 884
flout
  disrespect 929
  contempt 930
  (*ridicule* 856)
flow *course* 109
  hang 214
  motion 264
  stream 348
  murmur 405
  abundance 639
  - from
  result 154
  - in 294
  - into *river* 348

- of ideas 451
- of soul
  conversation 588
  affections 820
  cheerful 836
  social 892
- of time 109
- of words 582, 584
- out 295
- over 641
- with the tide 705
flower *produce* 161
  vegetable 367
  prosper 734
  beauty 845
  ornament 847
  repute 873
- of age 131
- of flock 648
- of life 127
- painting 556, 559
  full many a - 447
flowering plant 367
flowers
  anthology 596
- of rhetoric 577
- preach if we will
  hear 845
flowing
  [see flow]
- periods 578
fluctuate
  change 149
  oscillate 314
  irresolute 605
flue *opening* 260
  air-pipe 351
  down 320
  dust 653
fluent
  differential 84
  fluid 333
  stream 348
- language 578
  speech 584
fluff 256
flugelman 694
fluid 333
- in motion 347
fluidity 333
fluke *hook* 244
  chance 621
flume 350
flummery
  unmeaning 517
  flattery 933
flump 406
flunk 732
flunker 732
flunkey
  servant 746
  servile 886
flunkeyism 933
fluorescence 425
flurry *hurry* 684
  agitation 821
  excitability 825
flush *flat* 251
  flood 348
  heat 382
  light 420

- one's good opinion 932
forfeiture
  disfranchisement 925
forfend
  hinder 706
  defend 717
forgather 72
forge produce 161
  furnace 368
  trump up 544
  workshop 691
  - ahead 282
  - fetters 751
forged
  false 546
forger
  maker 690
  thief 792
forgery
  deception 545
forget 506
  - benefits 917
  - injury 918
  - oneself 945
  hand - cunning 699
forgive 918
forgo [see forego]
forgotten
  past 122
  ingratitude 917
  - by the world 893
fork bifid 91
  pointed 244
  - lightning 423
  - out
  give 784
  pay 807
  expenditure 809
forking 291
forlorn
  dejected 837
  hopeless 859
  deserted 893
  - hope
  danger 665
  rashness 863
form state 7
  likeness 21
  make up 54
  order 58
  arrange 60
  convert 144
  produce 161
  bench 215
  shape **240**
  educate 537
  pupils 541
  manner 627
  beauty 845
  fashion 852
  etiquette 882
  law 963
  rite 998
  - a party 712
  - a resolution 604
  - part of 56
formal [see form]
  regular 82
  definitive 535
  - style 579

affected 855
  stately 882
  - speech 582
formalism 988
formality [see formal]
  ceremony 852
  affectation 855
  law 963
formation
  composition 54
  production 161
  shape 240
formative 240
  - notion 453
formed [see form]
  attempered 820
former
  in order 62
  prior in time 116
  past 122
formication 380
formidable
  difficult 704
  terrible 860
formless 241
formosa facies 234
formula rule 80
  arithmetic 84
  maxim 496
  precept 697
  law 963
formulary 998
formulate 590
fornication 961
fornicator 962
foro conscientiæ
  veracity 543
  duty 926
  probity 939
forsake 624
forsaken 898
forsooth 535
forswear lie 544
  tergiversation 607
  refuse 764
  transgress 927
  improbity 940
fort refuge 666
  defense 717
fort
  le droit du plus -
  compulsion 744
  illegality 964
  un peu - 641
fortalice 717
forte 698
fortelage 717
fortes fortuna adjuvat 861
forth 282
  come -
  egress 295
  visible 446
  go - depart 293
  the decree has gone - 741
forthcoming
  destiny 152
  preparing 673
forthwith 132
fortification

defense 717
fortify
  strengthen 159
fortiori, a -
  evidence 467
  reasoning 476
fortis cadere 157
fortiter in re 171
fortitude
  endurance 826
  courage 861
fortnightly 138
fortress
  defense 717
  prison 752
fortuitous
  adventitious 6
  chance 156
  undesigned 621
  - combination of circumstances 621
  - concourse of atoms 59
fortuna
  - favet fatuis 501
  - multis dat 641
fortunate
  opportune 134
  successful 731
  prosperous 734
Fortunatus's - cap
  wish 865
  spell 993
  - purse 803
fortune
  chance 156
  fate 601
  wealth 803
  be one's - 151
  chacun est l'artisan de sa - 731
  evil - 735
  -s narrative 594
  good -.734
  make one's -
  succeed 731
  wealth 803
  tempt -
  hazard 621
  essay 675
  trick of - 509
  try one's - 675
  wheel of - 601
fortune hunter
  servile 886
  selfish 943
fortuneless 804
fortune teller 513
fortune telling 51
forty 98
  - winks 683
forum
  school 542
  tribunal 966
forward early 132
  transmit 270
  advance 282
  interjection 286
  willing 602
  improve 658
  active 682

help 707
  vain 880
  insolent 885
  uncourteous 895
  bend - 234
  come -
  in sight 446
  offer 763
  display 882
  - in knowledge 490
  move - 282
  press - haste 684
  put - aid 707
  offer 763
  put oneself - 88
  set - 676
foss 348
fosse
  inclosure 232
  ditch 259
  defense 717
  (interval 198)
fossil
  ancient 124
  hard 323
  organic 357
  dry bones 362
  giant -s of my past 593
foster aid 707
  excite 824
  caress 902
  - a belief 484
fou 959
foul
  collide 276
  bad 649
  dirty 653
  ugly 846
  base 940
  vicious 945
  fall - of
  oppose 708
  quarrel 713
  attack 716
  fight 720
  censure 932
  - fiend 978
  - invective 908
  - language
  malediction 908
  - odor 401
  - play evil 619
  cunning 702
  wrong 923
  improbity 940
  - whisperings are abroad 584, 934
  run - of
  impede 706
foul-mouthed
  uncourteous 895
foul-spoken
  detraction 934
found cause 153
  support 215
foundation
  stability 150
  base 211
  support 215
  lay the -s 673

sandy - 667
shake to its -s 315
founded
  - on *base* 211
  evidence 467
  well - 472
founder
  originator 164
  sink 310
  fail 732
  religious -s 986
foundling
  vagrant 268
  trover 775
  derelict 782
  outcast 893
foundry 691
fount *type* 591
fountain
  source 153
  river 348
  store 636
  - head 210
four 95
  - in hand 272
  - score &c. 98
  - times 96
  from the - winds 278
  on all -s
    identity 13
    agreement 23
    horizontal 213
    easy 705
    prosperous 734
    humble 879
four-flush 545, 884
fourfold 96
Four Hundred 852, 875
Fourierism 910
fourmart 401
four-oar 273
four-poster 215
foursquare 244
fourth 96, 97
  musical 413
four-wheeler 272
fous: les - font les festins 501, 818
fowl 366
fowling piece 727
fox *animal* 366
  cunning 702
  - chase 622
foxhound 366
foxy *brown* 433
  red 434
fox terrier 366
fracas
  disorder 59
  noise 404
  discord 713
  contention 720
fraction *part* 51
  numerical 84
  less than one **100a**
Foxy Quiller 804
fractional 100a
  - currency 800
fractious 901
fracture

---

disjunction 44
discontinuity 70
  (*fissure* 198)
fragile *weak* 160
  brittle 328
fragment
  small 32
  part 51
  little 193
fragmentary 100a
fragrance 400
fragrant weed 392
frail *weak* 160
  brittle 328
  irresolute 605
  imperfect 651
  failing 945
  impure 961
  - sisterhood 962
frais, à grands - 814
frame
  condition 7
  make 161
  support 215
  border 231
  form 240
  substance 316
  structure 329
  contrive 626
  - of mind
    inclination 602
    disposition 820
  have -d and glazed 822
frame house 189
framework
  support 215
  structure 329
franchise
  freedom 748
  right 924
  exemption 927a
Franciscan 996
franc-tireur 726
frangas non flectes 604
frangible 328
frank *open* 525
  sincere 543
  artless 703
  honorable 939
  - as rain 703
frankalmoigne 748
Frankenstein
  evil doer 913
  demon 980
frankincense 400
frantic
  violent 173
  delirious 503
  excited 824
fraternal
  brother 11
  concord 714
  friendly 888
  (*benevolent* 906)
fraternity
  brothers 11
  party 712
  friends 888
fraternize

---

coöperate 709
agree 714
sympathize 888
associate 892
fratricide 361
Frau 374
fraud
  falsehood 544
  deception 545
  impostor 548
  dishonor 940
  pious - 988
fraught *full* 52
  pregnant 151
  possessing 777
  (*sufficient* 639)
  - with danger 665
fraus est celare fraudem 545
fray *rub* 331
  battle 720
  in the thick of the - 722
frayed
  worn 659
freak 608
  - of Nature 83
freckle 848
freckled 440
fredaine 840
free
  detached 44, 47
  unconditional 52
  unobstructed 705
  at liberty 748, 750
  gratis 815
  liberal 816
  insolent 885
  exempt 927a
  impure 961
  - and easy
    cheerful 836
    adventurous 863
    vain 880
    insolent 885
    friendly 888
    sociable 892
  - companion 726
  - fight 720
  - from
    simple 42
  - from imperfection 650
  - gift 784
  - lance 726, 748
  - land 748
  - liver 954a
  - living 954
  - love 897, 961
  - play 170, 748
  - quarters
    cheap 815
    hospitality 892
  - space 180
  - stage 748
  - trade
    commerce 794
  - translation 522
  - will 600
  make - of 748
  make - with

---

frank 703
  take 789
  sociable 892
  uncourteous 895
freebooter 792
freeborn 748
freedman 748
freedom 748
free-handed 816
freehold 780
freely
  willingly 602
freeman 748
freemasonry
  unintelligible 519
  secret 528
  sign 550
  coöperation 709
  party 712
free-spoken 703
freethinker 748, 989
free trader 748
freeze 385
  - the blood 830
freezing 383
  - mixture 387
freight *lade* 184
  cargo 190
  transfer 270
  - train 272
freightage 812
French
  - and English 840
  - horn 417
  - leave *avoid* 623
    freedom 748
  - polish 847
  peddler's - 563
frenetic 503
frenzy
  madness 503
  imagination 515
  excitement 825
frequency 136
frequent
  in number 104
  in time 136
  in space 186
  habitual 613
fresco *cold* 383
  painting 556
  al -
    out of doors 220
    in the air 338
fresh *new* 123
  flood 348
  cold 383
  color 428
  remembered 505
  novice 541
  good 648
  healthy 654
  pert 885
  tipsy 959
  - breeze 349
  - color 434
  - news 532
  - plucked from bowers 451
freshen up 689
freshet 348

- blown
  expanded 194
  glorious 873
- colored 428
- cry *aloud* 404
  bark 412
  pursuit 622
- dress
  dress 225
  ornament 847
  fashion 852
  show 882
- drive 274
- feather
  prepared 673
- force 159
- gallop 274
- heart 820
- house *cards* 840
- many 102
- measure 639
- of business 682
- of incident 151
- of meaning 516
- of people 186
- of point 842
- of sound and fury
  &c. *unmeaning* 517
- of whims 608
- play
  facility 705
  freedom 748
- scope 748
- score 415
- size 912
- speed 274
- stop
  cease 142
  rest 265
- swing
  strong 159
  active 682
  successful 731
  free 748
- tide 348
- tilt *active* 682
  haste 684
- view 446
  hands -
  active 682
  receipt in - 807
full-fed 954
full-flavored 392
full-grown
  adolescent 131
  large 192
  (*expanded* 194)
full-handed
  liberal 816
  prodigal 818
full-length 556
full-mouthed 412
fullness [*see* full]
  in the - of time 109
full-toned 413
fully 31
fulminate
  violent 173
  propel 284
  loud 404
  malediction 908

454

threat 909
- against
  accuse 932
fulsome
  nauseous 395
  fetid 401
  bad 649
  abhorrent 867
  adulatory 933
  impure 961
fulvid 436
fulvous 436
fumble
  derange 61
  handle 379
  grope 463
  awkward 699
fumbler 701
fume *violent* 173
  exhalation 334, 336
  heat 382
  odor 398
  excitement 824, 825
  anger 900
  -s of fancy 515
  in a -
  discontented 832
fumid 426
fumigate
  vaporize 336
  cleanse 652
fumo, dare pondus -
  481
fun
  amusement 840
  humor 842
  make - of 856
funambulist 700
function
  algebra 84
  office 170
  business 625
  utility 644
  pomp 882
  duty 926
  rite 998
functionary
  director 694
  consignee 758
functus officio 756
fund *store* 636
  (*abundance* 639)
  sinking - 802
fundamental
  intrinsic 5
  base 211
  support 215
  - bass 413
  - note 413
fundamentally
  very 31
funds 800
  in - 803
  public - 802
funebrial 363
funeral 363
  - pace 275
funereal
  interment 363
  dismal 837
fungiform 249

fungology 369
fungosity
  projection 250
fungus
  projection 250
  vegetable 367
  fetor 401
  bane 663
funicle 205
funk *fear* 860
  cowardice 862
funnel *opening* 260
  conduit 350
  air pipe 351
funnel-shaped 252
funny
  odd 83
  boat 273
  humorous 842
  comic 853
fur *covering* 223
  hair 256
  warm 384
  dirt 653
furacious 791
furbelow 231
furbish
  improve 658
  prepare 673
  adorn 847
furcated 244
furcula 993
furcular 91, 244
furfur 653
furfuraceous 330
Furies *anger* 900
  evil doers 913
furious *violent* 173
  haste 684
  passion 825
  anger 900
furiously *much* 31
furl 312
furlong 200
furlough 760
furnace 386
  workshop 691
  like a - *hot* 382
  sighing like -
  lament 839
  in love 902
furnish
  provide 637
  prepare 673
  give 784
- a handle 617
- aid 707
- its quota 784
furniture 633
  (*property* 780)
furor
  insanity 503
  passion 825
- arma ministrat 173,
  900
- loquendi 584
- poeticus 597
- scribendi 592, 594
furore
  emotion 820, 821
  passion 825

desire 865
furrow 259
Fürst 745
further
  added 37
  distant 196
  aid 707
  go - and fare worse
  worse 659
  bungle 699
  not let it go - 528
furthermore 37
furtive
  clandestine 528
  stealing 791
  (*false* 544)
furuncle 250
fury *violence* 173
  excitation 825
  anger 900
  demon 980
  filled with - 825
furze 367
fuscous 433
fuse *join* 43
  combine 48
  heat 384
  torch 388
  (*melt* 335)
fusel oil 356
fusiform
  angular 244
  pointed 253
fusil 727
fusileer 726
fusillade
  killing 361
  attack 716
fusion *union* 48
  heat 384
  coöperation 709
fuss *agitation* 315
  activity 682
  haste 684
  excitement 825
  ostentation 882
  make a - about
  importance 642
  lament 839
  disapprove 932
fussy *crochety* 481
  bustling 682
  excitable 825
fustee 41
fustian *absurd* 497
  unmeaning 517
  - style 577, 579
fustigate 972
fusty *fetid* 401
  dirty 653
futile 645
future 121
  eye to the - 510
  - possession 777
  - state
  destiny 152
  heaven 981
futurity 121
fuzzle 959
fuzzy 447
fylfot 993

G

tutelary - 711
genre
  painting 556
gent *vulgar* 851
  commonalty 876
genteel
  fashion 852
  rank 875
  (*polite* 894)
- comedy 599
gentile
  heterodox 984
  without religion 989
gentilhomme 939
gentility
  fashion 852
  rank 875
  politeness 894
gentium, jus - 963
gentle *moderate* 174
  slow 275
  faint sound 405
  lenient 740
  meek 826
  cool down 826
  courteous 894
- blood 875
- hint 527
- slope 217
gentlefolk 875
gentleman
  male 373
  squire 875
  man of honor 939
  the old - 978
  walking - 599
gentlemanly
  fashionable 852
Gentoo 984
gentry 875
  landed - 779
genuflexion
  bowing 308
  submission 725
  servility 886
  courtesy 894
  respect 928
  worship 990
genuine *true* 494
  good 648
genus 75
  - irritabile vatum 597
genus est mortis 945
geodesy &c. 466
geography 183
geology &c. 358
geomancer 513
geomancy 511
geometry 466
geophilous 342
geoponics 371
georama 448
Georgics 371
geotic 318
geranium 845
gerfalcon 913
germ 153
german 11
  - silver 430, 545
  - tinder 388
germane

---

relevant 23
(*related* 9)
germinal 153
- matter 357
germinate 194
- from 154
germination 161
gerontic 128
gerrymander 702
gest 680
geste 515
gestation
  propagation 161
  carriage 270
  maturation 673
gesticulate 550
gesture *hint* 527
  indication 550
get *become* 144
  beget 161
  acquire 775
- ahead 35
- ahead of 33
- along 282
- along with you
  ejection 297
  dismissal 756
- a sight of
  see 441
  comprehend 490
- at 480a
- away 287
- back
  retire 283
  regain 775
- better 658
- by heart 505
- down
  swallow 298
  descend 306
- for one's pains 973
- home 292
- in *collect* 72
  gather 775
- into harness 673
- into the way of 613
- into trouble 732
- loose 44
- near 286
- off *depart* 293
  escape 671
- on *advance* 282
  prosper 734
- out *eject* 297
  extract 301
  publish 531
- over
  recover from 660
  succeed 731
  be content 831
- over the ground 274
- ready 673
- rid of 42, 672
- the best of 731
- there 731
- the wrong pig by
  the tail 699, 732
- through
  end 67
  transact 692
  complete 729

---

expend 809
- to
  extend to 196
  arrive 292
- together 72
- up *ascend* 305
  raise 307
  learn 539
  fabricate 544
  prepare 673
  rise early 682
  foment 824
- you gone 297
gewgaw
  trifle 643
  ornament 847
  vulgar 851
geyser 384
gharry-wallah 268
ghastly
  pale 429
  hideous 846
  frightful 860
ghaut 203
ghazal 597
ghee 356
ghetto 189
ghost *shade* 362
  fallacy of vision 443
  soul 450
  writer 593
  apparition 980
- dance 992
- of a chance 473
give up the - 360
needs no - to tell us
  525
pale as a -
  colorless 429
  fear 860
Ghost, Holy - 976
ghostlike
  ugly 846
ghostly
  intellectual 450
  supernatural   976,
  980
ghoul
  evil doer 913
  demon 980
ghurry 108, 114
ghyll 348
giant
  large 192
  tall 206
- refreshed
  strong 159
  refreshed 689
-'s strides
  distance 196
  swift 274
giaour
  heterodox 984
  irreligion 989
gibber
  stammer 583
gibberish
  nonsense 517
  neology 563
gibbet
  stigmatize 932

---

execute 972
  gallows 975
gibble-gabble 584
gibbous
  globose 249
  convex 250
gib-cat *male* 373
gibe *disrespect* 929
  (*ridicule* 856)
gibier de potence 949
giddy
  inattentive 458
  vertiginous 503
  irresolute 605
  capricious 608
  bungling 699
giddy-head 501
giddy-paced 315
gift *power* 157
  talent 698
  given 784
- of the gab 582
look a - horse in   the
  mouth
  fastidious 868
  ungrateful 917
gifted 698
gig 273
gigantic
  strong 159
  large 192
  tall 206
giggle 838
Gilbertine 996
gild *coat* 223
  color 439
  ornament 847
-ed rooster 875
- refined gold 641
- the pill
  deceive 545
  tempt 615
  please 829
  flatter 933
gilding [see gild]
Gilead, balm in -
  relief 834
  hope 858
Giles's Greek, St. -
  563
gill 348
  -s *respiration* 349
gillie 746
gilt 847
- edged *excellent* 648
gimbals 312
gimcrack
  weak 160
  brittle 328
  trifling 643
  ornament 847
  ridiculous 853
  (*useless* 645)
gimlet 262
gimp *clean* 652
  pretty 845
gin *trap* 545
  instrument 633
  intoxicating 959
  demon 980
gingerbread

weak 160
vulgar 851
  (*ornament* 847)
gingerly
  moderately 174
  carefully 459
  (*slowly* 275)
gingle 408
gin palace 189
giovane santo dia-
  volo vecchio 988
gipsy
  wanderer 268
  cheat 548
  wag 844
  - *lingo* 563
giraffe 206
girandole 423
girasol 847
girasol look 441
gird *bind* 43
  strengthen 159
  surround 227
  jeer 929
  - up one's loins
  brace 159
  prepare 673
girder *bond* 45
  beam 215
girdle *bond* 45
  circumference 230
  circle 247
  put a - round about
    the earth 274, 311
girl *young* 129
  female 374
girl bachelor 904
girlhood 127
girth *bond* 45
  circumference 230
gisarme 727
gist *essence* 5
  meaning 516
  important 642
gît, ci - 363
gite 265
gittern 417
give
  yield 324
  melt 382
  bestow 784
  discount 813
  - a horse his head 748
  - and take
  compensation 30
  interchange 148
  retaliation 718
  compromise 774
  barter 794
  equity 922
  honor 939
  - a turn to 140
  - away 782, 784
  in marriage 903
  - back 790
  - birth to 161
  - chase 622
  - consent 762
  - ear 418
  - every man thine ear
    695
  - expression to 566

- forth 531
- in *submit* 725
- in charge
  restratn 751
- in custody 751
- into *consent* 762
- it one
  censure 932
  punish 972
- light 420
- notice
  inform 527
  warn 668
- one credit for 484
- one the slip 671
- one to understand
  527
- out *emit* 297
  publish 531
  bestow 784
- over *cease* 142
  relinquish 624
  lose hope 859
- place to
  substitute 147
  avoid 623
- play to the imagina-
  tion 515
- points to 27
- quarter 740
- rise to 153
- security 771
- the go by 623
- the lie 536
- the mind to 457
- tongue 531
- up
  not understand 519
  reject 610
  relinquish 624
  submit 725
  resign 757
  surrender 782
  restore 790
  hopeless 859
- up the ghost 360
- way *weak* 160
  brittle 328
  submit 725
  pine 828
  despond 837
  modest 881
given
  [*see* give]
  circumstances 8
  supposition 514
  received 785
- over *dying* 360
- time 143
- to 613
giving 784
gizzard 191
  stick in one's - 900
glabrous 255
glacial 383
glaciarum 840
glaciate 385
glacier 383
glacis 717
glad
  pleased 827

  pleasing 829
- tidings 532
  would be - of 865
gladden 834, 836
glade *hollow* 252
  opening 260
  shade 424
gladiate 253
gladiator 726
gladiatorial 713, 720
gladsome 827, 829
glair 352
glaive 727
glamor 992
glance *look* 441
  sign 550
- at
  take notice of 457
  allude to 527
  censure 932
- off *deviate* 279
  diverge 291
- coal 388
  see at a - 498
glanders 655
glare
  light 420
  stare 441
  imperfect vision 443
  visible 446
glaring
  [*see* glare]
  great 31
  color 428
  visible 446
  manifest 525
glass *vessel* 191
  smooth 255
  brittle 328
  transparent 425
  lens 445
- of fashion 852
- too much 959
  live in a - house
  brittle 328
  visible 446
  danger 665
  musical -es 47
  see through a - dark-
    ly 491
glass-coach 272
Glassite 984
glassy
  [*see* glass]
  shining 420
  colorless 429
glaucous 435
glave 727
glaver 933
glaze 255
  ice 383
gleam *small* 32
  light 420
glean *choose* 609
  acquire 775
glebe *land* 342
  ecclesiastical 995
  church 1000
glee *music* 415
  satisfaction 827
  merriment 836

gleek 929
glen 252
glib *voluble* 584
  facile 705
glide *lapse* 109
  move 264
  travel 266
  (*slow* 275)
- into
  conversion 144
glimmer
  light 420
  dim 422
  visible 446
  slight knowledge 490,
    491
glimpse
  sight 441
  knowledge 490
glint 420, 441
glisten 420
glitter
  shine 420
  illustrious 882
glittering
  ornament 847
  display 882
gloam 901a
gloaming 126
gloar *look* 441
  wonder 870
gloat - on
  look 441
- over
  pleasure 377
  delight 827
globated 249
globe
  sphere 249
  world 318
  on the face of the -
    318
globe-trotter 268
globule
  small 32
  spherule 249
glomeration 72
gloom
  darkness 421
  sadness 837
gloomy horizon 859
gloriation 884
glories
- of the possible 470
glorify
  honor 873
  approve 931
  worship 990
glorious
  illustrious 873
  tipsy 959
glory *light* 420
  honor 873
  heaven 981
- be to God 990
- dies not 873
- in 878
  King of - 976
gloss *smooth* 255
  sheen 420
  interpretation 522

Godspeed
farewell 293
hope 858
courtesy 894
benevolence 906
approbation 931
goer *horse* 271
goes [*see* go]
as one - 270
here - 676
Gog and Magog 192
goggle 441
- eyes 443
goggles 445
going [*see* go]
general 78
rumor 532
- on
incomplete 53, 730
current 151
transacting 625
- to happen 152
goiter 655
Golconda 803
gold *yellow* 436
orange 439
money 800
all is not - 486
worth its weight in -
648
write in letters of -
642
golden [*see* gold]
- age
prosperity 734
pleasure 827
- apple 615
- calf
wealth 803
idol 985
idolatry 991
- dream
imagination 515
hope 858
- mean
moderation 174
mid-course 628
- opinions 931
- opportunity 134
- rule
precept 697
- season of life 127
- wedding 883
music's - tongue 415
golf 840
Golgotha
burial 363
churchyard 1000
Goliath
strength 159
size 192
goloshes 225
gomashta 758
gondola 273
gondolier 269
gone [*see* go]
past 122
absent 187
dead 360
hopeless 859
- bad 653

460

- by
antiquated 124
- case 859
- coon 859
- out of one's recol-
lection 506
- where the woodbine
twineth 771
goneness 688
goner 859
gonfalon 550
gong 417
goniometer
angle 244
measure 466
gonorrhea 655
good
complete 52
palatable 394
assent 488
benefit **618**
beneficial 648
right 922
virtuous 944
pious 987
as - as 197
be - enough 765
be so - as 765
dc - 906
for -
diuturnal 110
permanent 141
- actions 944
- as one's word
veracity 543
observance 772
probity 939
- at 698
- at the price 815
- auspices 858
- behavior
contingent 108a
duty 926
virtue 944
- bye 293
- chance 472
- cheer *food* 298
cheerful 826
- circumstances 803
- condition 192
- day
arrival 292
departure 293
courtesy 894
- effect
goodness 648
beauty 845
- enough
not perfect 651
- fellow 892
- fight *war* 722
virtue 944
- for
useful 644
salubrious 656
- for nothing
impotence 158
useless 645
- fortune 734
- Friday 998
- genius

friend 890
benefactor 912
god 979
- hand 700
- humor
concord 714
cheerfulness 836
amuse 840
courtesy 894
kindly 906
- intention 906
- judgment 498
- lack! 870
- living
food 298
gluttony 957
- look out 459
- looks 845
- luck 734
- man *man* 373
husband 903
worthy **948**
- manners 894
- morrow 292
- name 873
- nature 906
- offices
mediation 724
kind 906
- old time 122
- omen 858
- opinion 931
- pennyworth 815
- repute 873
- sense 498
- society 852
- taste 850
- temper 894
- thing 648
- time *early* 132
opportune 134
prosperous 734
- turn
kindness 906
- understanding 714
- wife
woman 374
spouse 903
- will
willingness 602
benevolence 906
- word
approval 931
vindication 927
- works 906
in - case 192
in - odor
repute 873
approbation 931
in one's - books 888
in one's - graces 888
make -
evidence 467
provide 637
restore 660
complete 729
substantiate 924
vindicate 937
atone for 952
much - may it do 906
put a - face upon

cheerful 836
proud 878
so far so - 931
take in - part
pleased 827
courteous 894
kind 906
think - 931
to - purpose 731
to the - 780
turn to - account 731
what's the - 645
goodly
great 31
large 192
handsome 845
what a - outside false-
hood hath 544
goodness
[*see* good] **648**
virtue 944
- gracious! 870
- of heart 906
have the -
request 765
long may such - live
648
goods *effects* 780
merchandise 798
Goodwin sands 667
goody 374
goose *hiss* 409
game of - 840
giddy as a - 458
- grass 253
kill the - with golden
eggs
bungler 699
prodigal 818
gooseberry:
yarn 549
- eyes 441, 443
old - 978
goosecap 501
goosequill 590
goose-skin 383
Gordian knot
tangled 59
difficulty 704
(*problem* 461)
gore
gusset 43
stab 260
blood 361
gorge *ravine* 198
fill 641
satiety 869
gluttony 957
(*eat* 298)
- the hook 602
raise one's - 900
gorge de pigeon 440
gorgeous
color 428
beauty 845
ornament 847
Gorgon 860
-s and hydras 860
gorilla 913
gormandize
eat 298

active 682
grasshopper 309
grate *rub* 330
  physical pain 378
  stove 386
- on the ear
  harsh sound 410
- on the feelings 830
grated
  barred 219
grateful
  physically pleasant 377
  agreeable 829
  thankful 916
grater 330
gratification
  animal - 377
  moral - 827
gratify *permit* 760
  please 829
grating [see grate]
  lattice 219
gratior ac pulchro 845
gratis 815
gratitude 916
gratuitous
  inconsequent 477
  supposititious 514
  voluntary 602
  payless 815
  - *service* 602
gratuity
  gift 784
  gratis 815
gratulate 896
gravamen 642
- of a charge 938
grave *great* 31
  tomb 363
  engrave 558
  important 642
  composed 826
  distressing 830
  sad 837
  heinous 945
  cities have their -s 189
- in the memory 505
- note 408
  look -
  disapprove 932
  on this side of the - 359
  rise from the - 660
  silent as the - 403
  sink into the - 360
  without a - 363
gravel
  earth 342
  puzzle 704
graven image 991
graveolent 398
graver 558
gravis ira regum est semper 972
gravitate
  descend 306
  weigh 319
  - towards 176

gravity *force* 157
  weight **319**
  vigor 574
  importance 642
  sedateness 826
  seriousness 827
  center of - 222
  specific -
  weight 319
  density 321
gravy 333
gray 432 [*and see* grey]
graze *touch* 199
  browze 298
  rub 331
grazier 370
gré, savoir - 916
grease
  lubricate 332
  oil 356
  graft 784
- the palm
  tempt 615
  give 784
  pay 807
greasy 355
great *much* 31
  big 192
  glorious 873
  magnanimous 942
  (*important* 642)
- bear 318
- circle sailing 628
- coat 225
- doings
  importance 642
  bustle 682
- folks 875
- gun 626, 875
- hearted 942
- is the glory 873
- Mogul 745
- number 102
- quantity 31
- Spirit 979
  some are born - 31
greater 33
- number 102
- part 31
  nearly all 50
greatest 33
- good 618
greatness 31
- knows itself 31
greave 225
greed
  desire 865
  gluttony 957
greedy
  avaricious 819
Greek
  unintelligible 519
  sharper 792
- Church 984
- Kalends 107
  St. Giles's - 563
green *new* 123
  young 127
  lawn 344
  color 435
  credulous 486

novice 491
  unused 614
  healthy 654
  immature 674
  unskilled 699
  board of - cloth 966
- goods 545
- memory 505
- old age 128
- sickness 655
greenback 800
green-eyed monster 920
greenhorn
  novice 493
  dupe 547
  bungler 701
greenhouse
  receptacle 191
  horticulture 371
greenness 435
greenroom 599
greensward 344
greenwood 367
greet *weep* 839
  hail 894
greeting
  sociality 892
gregarious 892
grenade 727
grenadier
  tall 206
  soldier 726
grey 432
  bring - hairs to the grave
  adversity 735
  harass 830
- beard 130
- friar 996
- hairs 128
- mare
  ruler 737
  master 745
  wife 903
greyhound
  swift 274
  animal 366
griddlecake 298
gridelin 437
gridiron
  crossing 219
  stove 386
grief 828
  come to - 735
grievance *evil* 619
  painful 830
  wrong 923
grieve *mourn* 828
  pain 830
  dejected 837
  complain 839
grievous *bad* 649
  painful 830
grievously
  very 31
griffe 41
griffin 83
griffo 41
griffonage 590
grig *merry* 836

grill 384
grille 219
grill room 189
grim
  painful 830
  doleful 837
  ugly 846
  discourteous 895
  sullen 901a
- faced 914a
- visaged war 722
grimace
  distortion 243
  affectation 855
grimac-er, -ier
  actor 599
  humorist 844
  affected 855
grimalkin 366
grimy 652
grin *laugh* 838
  ridicule 856
- a ghastly smile
  dejected 837
  ugly 846
- and abide 725
grind
  reduce 195
  sharpen 253
  pulverize 330
  learn 539
  oppress 907
- one's teeth 900
- the organ 416
grinder
  teacher 330
grindery warehouse 799
grinding
  severe 739
  distressing 830
grindstone
  sharpener 253
  pulverizer 330
grip
  bag 191
  power 737
  retention 781
  clutch 789
- of the hand 894
gripe [see grip]
  pain 378
  parsimony 819
grippe 655
gripsack 191
grisaille
  grey 432
  painting 556
grisette
  woman 374
  commonalty 876
  libertine 962
grisly 846
grist
  materials 635
  provision 637
- to the mill
  useful 644
  acquire 775
gristle
  dense 321

H

habeas corpus 963
haberdasher 225
habergeon 717
habiliment 225
habilitation 698
habilité
  une grande - 698
habit *essence* 5
  coat 225
  custom **613**
  - of mind 820
  -s of business 682
  want of - 614
habitant 188, 371
habitat 189
habitation 189
habit maker 225
habitual
  ordinary 82
  customary 613
habituate
  train 537
  accustom 613
habituation 82
habitude
  state 7
  habit 613
habitué 613
hachure 550
hacienda
  abode 189
  property 780
hack *cut* 44
  shorten 201
  horse 271
  vehicle 272
  worker 690
  literary - 593
hackamore 752
hackbut 727
hackee 274
hackery 272
hackle 44
  comb 253
hackman 268
hackney coach 272
hackneyed
  known 490
  trite 496
  habitual 613
  experienced 698
Hades 982
Hadji *traveler* 268
  priest 996
hæmatobious 5, 161
h æ m o r r h a g e [see
  hemorrhage]
hæret lateri lethalis
  arundo
  displeasure 828
  anger 900
hæ tibi erunt artes
  627
haft 633
hag *ugly* 846

wretch 913
witch 994
haggard
  insane 503
  tired 688
  wild 824
  ugly 846
haggle *cut* 44
  chaffer 794
hagiographa 985
hagiology 983, 985
hagioscope 260
haguebut 727
ha-ha *ditch* 198
  defense 717
haik 225
hail *welcome* 292
  ice 383
  call 586
  rejoicing 838
  honor to 873
  celebration 883
  courtesy 894
  salute 928
  approve 931
  - fellow well met
  friendship 888
  sociality 892
  - from 293
hailstone 383
hair *small* 32
  filament 205
  roughness 256
  - breadth escape
  danger 665
  escape 671
  -'s breadth
  near 197
  narrow 203
  -s on the head
  multitude 102
  make one's - stand
  on end
  distressing 830
  fear 860
  wonder 870
  to a - 494
hairif 253
hairless 226
hairy *rough* 256
hajj 266
halberd 727
halberdier 726
halcyon *calm* 174
  peace 721
  prosperous 734
  joyful 827, 829
hale 654
half 91
  - a dozen *six* 98
  several 102
  - a gale 349
  - a hundred 98
  - and half
  equal 27

mixed 41
incomplete 53
- distance 68
- light 422
- measures
  incomplete 53
  vacillating 605
  mid-course 628
- moon 245
- price 815
- rations 640
- scholar 493
- seas over 959
- sight 443
- speed
  moderate 174
  slow 275
- the battle
  important 642
  success 731
- truth 546
see with - an eye
  intelligent 498
  intelligible 518
  manifest 525
half-baked 499
half-blind 443
half blood
  mixture 41
  unconformity 83
  imperfect 651
half-frozen 352
half-hearted
  irresolute 605
  insensible 823
  indifferent 866
half-learned 491
half-melted 352
halfpenny
  trifle 643
half-starved
  insufficient 640
  fasting 956
half-tone 558
half-way
  small 32
  middle 68
  between 228
  go - *irresolute* 605
  mid-course 628
  meet -
  willing 602
  compromise 774
half-witted 499, 501
hall *chamber* 189
  receptacle 191
  mart 799
  - mark 550
  - of audience 588
  music - 599
hallelujah 990
halloo *cry* 411
  look here! 457
  call 586
  wonder 870

hallow
  celebrate 883
  respect 928
hallowed 976
Halloween 138
Hallowmas 138
hallucination
  error 495
  insanity 503
halo *light* 420
  glory 873
  - hovering round de-
  cay 36
halomancy 511
halser 45
halt *cease* 142
  weak 160
  rest 265
  go slowly 275
  lame 655
  fail 732
  at the - 265
halter *rope* 45
  restraint 752
  punishment 975
  wear a - 874
  with a - round one's
  neck 665
halting
  style 579
  - place 292
halve [see half]
halves
  do by -
  neglect 460
  not complete 730
  go - 778
  not do by - 729
ham *house* 189
hamadryad 979
hamal 746
hamfatter 599
hamiform 245
hamlet 189
hammer
  repeat 104
  knock 276
  stammer 583
  between the - and the
  anvil 665
  - at *think* 451
  work 686
  - out *form* 240
  prepare 673
  complete 729
  under the -
  auction 796
hammock 215
hamous 245
hamper
  basket 191
  obstruct 706
hamstring
  incapacitate 158
  injure 659

465

happen 151
- as it may
  chance 621
- what may
  certain 474
  reckless 863
happiness
  [see happy]
- our being's end 827
  the greatest - of the
  greatest number
  910
happy *fit* 23
  opportune 134
  style 578
  glad 827
  cheerful 836
- as a clam 827
- dispatch 972
- go lucky 674
- he with such a
  mother 166
- hunting grounds
  981
- returns of the day
  896
- thought 842
- valley
  imagination 515
  delight 827
harakiri 972
harangue 582
harass
  fatigue 688
  vex 830
  worry 907
harbinger
  precursor 64
  omen 512
harbor
  abode 189
  haven 292
  refuge 666
  cherish 821
- a design 620
- an idea 451
- revenge 919
  natural - 343
harborless 665
hard
  strong 159
  dense 323
  physically insensible
  376
  sour 397
  difficult 704
  severe 739
  morally insensible
  823
  grievous 830
  impenitent 951
  blow - 349
  go -
  difficult 704
  failure 732
  adversity 735
  pain 828
- a-lee 273
- and fast rule 80
- a-port 273
- at it 682

- at work 682
- bargain 819
- by 197
- case 735
- cash 800
- earned 704
- fought 704
- frost 383
- heart
  malevolent 907
  vicious 945
  impenitent 951
- hit 732
- knocks 720
- life 735
- lines
  adversity 735
  severity 739
- liver 954a
- lot 735
- master 739
- measure 739
- names 932
- necessity 601
- nut to crack 704
- of belief 487
- of hearing 419
- pressed
  haste 684
  difficulty 704
  hindrance 706
- put to it 704
- set 704
- tack 298
- task 703
- time 704
- to believe 485
- to please 868
- up
  difficulty 704
  poor 804
- upon
  nearness 197
  attack 715
  severe 739
  censure 932
- winter 383
- words
  obscure 571
  rude 895
  censure 932
- work 686
  hit - 276
  look - at 441
  not be too - upon 918
  strike -
  energy 171
  impulse 276
  try - 675
  work - 686
harden [see hard]
  strengthen 159
  accustom 613
- the heart
  insensible 823
  enmity 889
  impenitence 951
hardened
  impious 988
- front
  insolent 885

hardening
  habit 613
hard-favored 846
hard-featured 846
hard-fisted 819
hard-handed 739
hard-headed 498
hardihood
  courage 861
  insolence 885
hardly
  scarcely 32
  deal - with 739
- any *few* 103
- anything
  small 32
  unimportant 643
- ever 137
hard-mouthed 606
hardness 323
hardpan 211
hard-shell 739
hardship 735
hard-visaged 846
hardware 323
hardy
  strong 159
  healthy 654
  brave 861
hare 274
  hold with the - and
  run with the
  hounds
  fickle 607
  servile 886
harebrained
  giddy 458
  rash 863
  (*foolish* 499)
  (*mad* 503)
harelip 243
harem
  household 189
  impurity 961
hariff 253
hariolation 511
hark
  hear 418
  attention 457
- back 283
harlequin
  changeable 149
  nimble 274
  motley 440
  pantomimic 599
  humorist 844
harlequinade 599
harlot 962
harlotry 961
harm
  evil 619
  badness 649
  malevolence 907
harmattan 349
harmless
  impotent 158
  good 648
  perfect 650
  salubrious 656
  safe 664
  innocent 946

  bear - 717
harmonica 417
harmonics 413
harmoniphone 417
harmonist 413
harmonium 417
harmony
  agreement 23
  music 413
  color 428
  concord 714
  peace 721
  friendship 888
  want of - 414
harness
  fasten 43
  fastening 45
  accouterment 225
  instrument 633
  restraint 752
  in -
  prepared 673
  in action 680
  active 682
  subjection 749
harp
  repeat 104
  musical instrument
  417
  weary 841
Harpagon 819
harper 416
harpoon 727
harpsichord 417
harpy
  relentless 739
  thief 792
  miser 819
  evil doer 913
  demon 980
harquebuss 727
harridan
  hag 846
  trollop 962
harrier 366
harrow
  agriculture 371
- up the soul 860
harrowing 830
harry *pain* 830
  attack 716
  persecute 907
Harry, old - 978
harsh
  acrid 171
  sound 410
  style 579
  severe 739
  disagreeable 830
  morose 895
  malevolent 907
- voice 581
hart *deer* 366
  male 373
hartshorn 392
harum-scarum
  disorder 59
  inattentive 458
haruspice 513
haruspicy 511
harvest

take into one's -
 thought 451
 caprice 608
 intention 620
trouble one's - about 457
turn the - 824
with - erect 878
headache 378
head center 694
headdress 225
header 310
headforemost
 violent 173
 rash 863
headgear 225
heading *prefix* 64
 beginning 66
 indication 550
 title 564
headland
 height 206
 projection 250
 (*land* 342)
headlight 550
headline 590
headlong
 hurry 684
 rush 863
rush -
 violence 173
headman 694
headmost
 front 234
 precession 280
headpiece
 intellect 450
 helmet 717
 ornament 847
headquarters
 focus 74
 abode 189
 authority 737
headrace 350
heads
 compendium 596
 - I win tails you lose
  unfair 940
 - or tails 156, 621
 lay - together
  advice 695
  coöperate 709
headship 737
headsman 975
headstall 752
headstone 215, 363
headstrong
 violent 173
 obstinate 606
 rash 863
headway
 navigation 267
 progression 282
head wind 708
headwork 451
heady 606
heal *restore* 660
 - the breach
  pacify 723
 let the wound -
  forgive 918

heald 633
healing art 662
health 654
healthiness 655
healthy 656
heap *quantity* 31
 collection 72
 store 636
 too many 641
 rubbish - 645
hear
 audition 418
 be informed 527
 - a cause
  adjudge 480
  lawsuit 969
 - and obey 743
 - hear! 931
 - out 457
 not - of
  refuse 764
hearer 418
hearing 418
 [*see* hear]
 gain a - 175
 give a - 418
 hard of - 419
 out of - 196
 within - 197
hearken 457
hearsay 532
 - *evidence* 467
hearse 363
heart
 intrinsicality 5
 interior 221
 center 222
 mind 450
 willingness 602
 essential 642
 affections 820
 courage 861
 love 897
 a - *untainted* 939
 at - 820, 821
 beating - 821, 824
 break the - 830
 by -
  memory 505
 do one's - good 829
 from bottom of - 543
 go to one's - 824
 have a place in the - 897
 - and soul
  completely 52
  willing 602
  resolute 604
  exertion 686
  feeling 821
 - bleeding for 914
 - expanding 821
 - failing one
  dejection 837
  fear 860
 - far from fraud 939
 - in hand 602
 - in right place 906
 - leaping into one's mouth 824
 - leaping with joy

 pleasure 827
 rejoicing 838
 - of grace 858
 - of oak
  strong 159
  hard 323
 - of stone
  insensible 823
  malevolent 907
 -'s core
  mind 450
  affections 820
 - sinking *fear* 860
 - to conceive 698
 - with room for joy 831
 in good - 858
 know by - 490
 lay to - 837
 learn by - 539
 lift up the - 990
 lose - 837
 lose one's - 897
 man after one's own - 899
 nearest to one's - 897
 not find it in one's - 603
 put one's - into 604
 set one's - upon 604
 take -
  content 831
  hope 858
  courage 861
 take to -
  sensibility 822
  discontent 832
  dejection 837
  anger 900
 to one's -'s content
  willing 602
  enough 639
  success 731
  content 831
 warm - 822
 wind round the - 897
 with a heavy - 603
 with all one's - 602
heartache 828
heartbreaking
 affecting 821
 painful 830
heartbroken 828
heartburn 655
heartburning
 discontent 832
 regret 833
 enmity 889
 anger 900
heart-corroding 830
heartfelt
 emotion 821
 pleasure 829
hearth *home* 189
 fireplace 386
heartless
 insensible 823
 vicious 945
heartquake 860
heartrending 830
heart-robbing 829

heart's-ease 831
heartshaped 245
heartsick
 dejection 837
 dislike 867
 satiety 869
heart-sickening 830
heart-sinking 860
heartsome 858
heart-stirring 824
heartstricken 828
heartstrings, tear the - 830
heartswelling
 excitation 824
 resentment 900
hearty
 willing 602
 healthy 654
 feeling 821
 cheerful 836
 friendly 888
 social 892
 - laugh 838
 - meal 298
 - reception 892
heat *warmth* 382
 make hot 384
 contest 720
 excitement 824, 825
 dead - 27
 - of passion 900
heat engine 633
heated imagination 515
heater 386
heath *moor* 344
 plant 367
heathen
 pagan 984
 irreligious 989
 - *mythology* 979
heathenish
 vulgar 851
heather *moor* 344
 plant 367
heaume 717
heautontimoreumenos
 croaker 837
 ascetic 955
heave *raise* 307
 emotion 821
 - a sigh 839
 - in sight 446
 - the lead
  depth 208
  measure 466
 - to 265
heaven
 bliss 827
 paradise 981
 call - to witness 535
 for -'s sake 765
 - be praised
  rejoicing 838
  gratitude 916
 - forfend! 766
 - knows
  uncertain 475
  ignorant 491

in the face of - 525
light of - 420
marriages made in -
  903
move - and earth 686
will of - 601
heaven-born
  wise 498
  repute 873
  virtue 944
heaven-directed 498
heaven-kissing 206
heavenly
  celestial 318
  rapturous 829
  divine 976
  of heaven 981
  - bodies 318
  - host 977
  - kingdom 981
heavenly-minded
  987
heavens 318
  - and earth! 870
heave offering 990
heaves 655
heavy *great* 31
  inert 172
  weighty 319
  stupid 499
  sleepy 683
  dull 843
  brutish 851
  - affliction 828
  - cost 814
  - dragoon 726
  - father 599
  - gun 727
  - hand
  clumsy 699
  severe 739
  - heart *loth* 603
  pain 828
  dejection 837
  - hours 841
  - news 830
  - on hand 641
  - on the mind 837
  - sea
  agitation 315
  waves 348
  - sleep 683
  - wet 298
heavy-laden
  hindrance 706
  trouble 828
hebdomadal 138
Hebe 845
hebetate 823, 826
hebetic 127
hebetude
  imbecile 499
  insensible 823
  inexcitable 826
hebetudinous 499
Hebraist 492
Hebrew
  unintelligible 519
  Jew 984
hecatomb
  number 98

470

sacrifice 991
heckle *comb* 253
  harry 830
hectic *hot* 382
  flush 821
Hector *brave* 861
  rash 863
  bully 885, 887
heddle 633
hedge
  compensate 30
  inclosure 232
  - in
  circumscribe 229
  hinder 706
  conditions 770
hedgehog 253
hedgerow 232
hedonic 827, 836
hedonism 377, 827
hedonist 954*a*
heed *attend* 457
  care 459
  beware 668
  caution 864
heedfulness 457
heedless
  inattentive 458
  neglectful 460
  forgetful 506
  rash 863
heel *support* 215
  lean 217
  deviate 279
  go round 311
  - of Achilles 665
  iron - 975
  turn on one's -
  go back 283
  go round 311
  avoid 623
heeler 886
heelpiece *sequel* 65
  back 235
  repair 660
heeltap
  remainder 40
  dress 653
heels *lowness* 207
  at the - of
  near 197
  behind 235
  cool one's - 681
  follow on the - of 281
  - over head
  inverted 218
  hasty 684
  rash 863
  laid by the - 751
  lay by the - 789
  show a light pair of -
  623
  take to one's - 623
  tread on the - of
  near 197
  follow 281
  approach 286
heft *handle* 633
  exertion 686
hegemony
  influence 175

direction 693
authority 737
heifer 366
heigho! 839
height *degree* 26
  altitude 206
  summit 210
  at its-
  great 31
  supreme 33
  draw oneself up to his
  full - 307
heighten
  increase 35
  elevate 307
  exaggerate 549
  aggravate 835
heinous 945
heir *futurity* 121
  posterity 167
  inheritor 779
heirloom 780
heirship 777
Hejira 293
heliacal 318
helical 248
Helicon 597
Heliogabalus 954*a*
heliograph
  signal 550
  picture 556
heliography
  light 420
  painting 556
heliolatry 991
heliometer 466
heliophagous 420
helioscope 445
heliotrope 847
heliotype 437, 558
helix 248
hell *abyss* 208
  gaming house 621
  gehenna **982**
  - broke loose 59
  - paved with good
  resolutions 620
  - upon earth
  misfortune 735
  pain 828
  - within 926
hellborn
  vicious 945
  satanic 978
hellebore 663
hell-cat 949
hellhag 913
hellhound
  evil-doer 913
  bad man 949
hellish
  malevolent 907
  vicious 945
  hell 982
  (bad 649)
helluo librorum 492
helm *handle* 633
  scepter 747
  (authority 737)
  answer the - 743
  at the - 693

obey the - 705
take the - 693
helmet *hat* 225
  armor 717
helminth 663
helminthagogue 662
helminthology 368
helmsman 694
helot 746
help *utility* 644
  remedy 662
  aid 707
  servant 746
  give 784
  - oneself to 789
  it can't be -ed
  submission 725
  never mind 823
  content 831
  God - you 914
  so - me God 535
helper 711
helpless
  incapable 158
  exposed 665
helpmate
  auxiliary 711
  wife 903
helter-skelter
  disorder 59
  haste 684
**helve after the
  hatchet, throw
  the** - 818
hem *edge* 231
  fold 258
  indeed! 870
  - in *inclose* 229
  restrain 751
  kiss the - of one's garment 886
hematite 847
hemeralopia 443
hemi- 91
hemiplegia 376
hemisphere 181
hemispheric 250
hemlock 663
hemorrhage 299
hemorrhoids 655
hemp 205
hen *bird* 366
  female 374
  - with one chicken
  busy 682
henbane 663
hence
  arising from 155
  departure 293
  deduction 476
  - loathed melancholy
  836
henceforth 121
henchman 746
hencoop 370
hen-hearted 862
henhussy 374, 501
hen party 892
henpecked
  obedient 743
  subject 749

in - feather
strong 159
health 654
cheerful 836
boasting 884
in - quarters 875
in - spirits 836
on - 206
on one's - ropes
excitation 824
pride 878
anger 900
on the - road to
way 627
hope 858
ride the - horse 878
think -ly of 931
highball 959
highbinder 361
highborn 875
higher 33
highest 210
- heaven 981
highfaluting 884
high-fed 954
high-flavored 392
highflier
madman 504
proud 878
high-flown
imaginative 515
style 577
proud 878
vain 880
insolent 885
highflying
inattentive 458
exaggerated 549
ostentatious 822
highlands 206
high-low 225
high-mettled
excitable 825
brave 861
high-minded
honorable 939
magnanimous 942
highness title 877
high-pitched 410
high-plumed 878
high-reaching 206,
865
high-roller 818
high-seasoned 392
high-souled 878
high-sounding
loud 404
words 577
display 882
high-spirited
brave 861
honorable 939
high-strung 825
hight 564
high-toned 410, 878
highwater
completeness 52
height 206
crater 337
- mark
measure 466

highway 627
-s and byways 627
highwayman 792
high-wrought
good 648
prepared 673
excited 824
hilarity 836
hill height 206
convexity 250
ascent 305
descent 306
hillock 206
hilt 633
hinc illæ lachrymæ
155
hind back 235
clown 876
on one's - legs
elevation 307
anger 900
hinder impede 706
(counteract 179)
(prohibit 761)
hindermost end 67
back 235
hind quarters 235
Hinduism 984
Hindustani 563
hindrance 706
hinge fasten 43
fastening 45
cause 153
depend upon 154
rotate 312
hinny 271
hint reminder 505
suppose 514
inform 527
- a fault &c. 932
take a - 498
hinterland 235
hip 236
have on the -
confute 479
success 731
authority 737
subjection 749
hippocentaur 80
Hippocrates 662
hippocratic 360
hippodrome
drama 599
arena 728
hippogriff 83
Hippolytus 960
hippophagy 298
hippopotamus 192
hip rafter 215
hirdy-girdy 218
hire
commission 755
borrowing 788
price 812
reward 973
(purchase 795)
on - 763
hireling 746
hirsute 256
hispid 256
hiss sound 409

animal cry 412
disrespect 929
contempt 930
disapprobation 932
hist
hush! 585, 586
histology 329
historian 553
historic 594
historical
- painter 559
- painting 556
historiette 594
historiographer 553
historiography 594
history
record 551
narrative 594
read their - in a na-
tion's eyes 551
history, natural - 357
histrionic 599
hit chance 156
strike 276
reach 292
succeed 731
- censure 932
(punish 972)
good - 626
- off 554
- one's fancy 829
- on the raw 900
- the mark 731
- upon
discover 480a
plan 626
make a - 731
palpable - 276
hitch
fasten 43
hang 214
jerk 315
difficulty 704
hindrance 706
hither
direction 278
arrival 292
come - 286
hitherto 122
hive
multitude 102
location 184
abode 189
apiary 370
workshop 691
H. M. S. 726
hoar aged 128
white 430
- frost 383
hoard 636
-s after -s 819
hoarse husky 405
harsh 410
voiceless 581
talk oneself - 584
hoary [see hoar]
- head is a crown of
glory 128
hoax 545
hob support 215
stove 386

- and nob
celebration 883
courtesy 894
hobble
limp 275
awkward 699
difficulty 704
fail 732
shackle 751
hobbledehoy 129
hobby
crotchet 481
pursuit 622
desire 865
hobbyhorse 272
hobgoblin
fearful 860
demon 980
hobnail 876
hobo 268
hoboism 266
Hobson's choice
necessity 601
no choice 609a
compulsion 744
**hoc erat in more ma-
jorum** 122, 613
hoc genus omne 876
hockey 840
hocus 545
hocus-pocus
interchange 148
unmeaning 517
cheat 545
conjuration 992
hod
receptacle 191
vehicle 272
hoddy-doddy 501
hodgepodge 59
hoe vehicle 272
agriculture 371
hoecake 298
hog animal 366
sensualist 954a
glutton 957
go the whole - 604
greedy as a - 865
hog's back 206
hog wallow 343
hog wash 653
hoist 307
- a flag 550
- on one's own petard
retaliation 718
failure 732
- the black flag 722
hoity-toity
defiance 715
wonder 870
hold cohere 46
contain 54
remain 141
cease 142
go on 143
happen 151
receptacle 191
cellar 207
base 211
support 215
halt 265

homunculus 193
hone 253
honest
 veracious 543
 honorable 939
 pure 960
 - *meaning* 516
 - *truth* 494
 turn an - penny 775
honesta mors turpi
 360
honey
 sweet 396
 favorite 899
 milk and - 734
honeybee 366
honeycomb
 concave 252
 opening 260
 deterioration 659
honeyed
 - *phrases* 894
 - *words*
  allurement 615
  flattery 933
honeymoon
 pleasure 827
 endearment 902
 marriage 903
honey-mouthed
 courteous 894
 flatter 933
honeysuckle 396
honneur: tout est
 perdu hors l'-
 732
honorarium
 gift 784
 reward 973
honorary 815
honor
 demesne 780
 glory 873
 title 877
 respect 928
 approbation 931
 probity 939
 affair of - 720
 do - to 883
 do the -s
  sociality 892
  courtesy 894
  respect 928
 his - *judge* 967
 - a bill 807
 - be to 873
 - bright
  veracity 543
  probity 939
 - in the breach 923
 - pricks me on 928
 in - of 883
 man of - 939
 upon my - 535
 word of - 768
honores mutant mo-
 res 149, 882
honor virtutis præ-
 mium 873, 973
honos habet onus
 926

honte, mauvaise -
 881
hood *cap* 225
 cowl 999
hooded 223
hoodlum 887, 913
hoodoo
 bane 649
 sorcery 992
 wizard 994
hoodooed 735
hoodwink
 ignore 491
 blind 442
 hide 528
 deceive 545
hoof 211
hook *fasten* 43
 fastening 45
 hang 214
 curve 245
 deceive 545
 retain 781
 take 789
 by - or by crook 631
hooked 244, 245
hooker *ship* 273
hookey, blind - 840
hooks, go off the -
 360
hooligan 887, 913
hoop *circle* 247
 cry 411
Hoosier 565
hoot *cry* 411
 deride 929
 contempt 930
 censure 932
hop *leap* 309
 dance 840
 - skip and jump
  leap 309
  agitation 315
  haste 684
  game 840
 - the twig 360
hope 858
 band of - 958
 beyond all - 734
 dash one's -s 837
 excite - 511
 foster - 858
 - against hope 859
 - deferred
  dejection 837
  lamentation 859
 - for *expect* 507
  desire 865
 - for the best 858
 - thou nurse of desire
  858
 well grounded - 472
hopeful *infant* 129
 probable 472
 hope 858
hopelessness 471, 859
hop garden 371
Hop-o'-my-thumb
 193
hopper 191
hopple 751

hopples 752
hopscotch 840
horary 108
horde
 assemblage 72
 party 712
 commonalty 876
horehound 400
horizon
 distance 196
 view 441
 expectation 507
 (*future* 121)
 gloomy - 859
horizontality 213
horn
 receptacle 191
 pommel 215, 249
 sharp 253
 music 417
 draw in one's -s
  recant 607
  submit 725
  humility 879
 exalt one's - 873
 - mad 920
 - of plenty 639
 -s of a dilemma
  reasoning 476
  difficulty 704
 wear the -s 905
hornbook 542
hornet
 evil doer 913
 -'s nest
  pitfall 667
  difficulty 704
  adversity 735
  painful 830
  resentment 900
  censure 932
hornpipe 840
hornwork 717
horny 323
Horny, old - 978
horology 114
horoscope 511
horresco referens
 860
horrible *great* 31
 noxious 649
 dire 830
 ugly 846
 fearful 860
horrid [see horrible]
 vulgar 851
horrida bella 722
horrific [see horrible]
horrified
 pain 828
 fear 860
horrify
 pain 830
 terrify 860
horripilation 383
horrisonous 410
horror
 fear 860
 dislike 867
 view with - 898
horrors

 dejection 837
 cup full of - 828
horror-stricken 828
hors de combat
 impotent 158
 useless 645
 tired out 688
 put - 731
hors d'œuvre 298
horse
 hang on 214
 stand 215
 carrier 271
 animal 366
 male 373
 cavalry 726
 - and foot 726
 - artillery 726
 - coper 548
 - doctor 370
 - guards 726
 - laugh 838
 - leech 370
 - marine 701
 - racing
  pastime 840
  contention 720
 - sense 498
 - soldier 726
 - track 627
 like a - in a mill 613
 put the -s to 673
 put up one's -s at 184
 put up one's -s to-
  gether
  concord 714
  friendship 888
 ride the high - 885
 take - 266
 war - 726
 work like a - 686
horseback 266
horse car 272
horse cloth 225
horseman 268
horsemanship
 riding 266
 skill 698
horseplay 856
horse power 466
horseshoe 245
horsewhip 972
hortation
 persuasion 615
 advice 695
horticulture 371
hortus siccus 369
hosanna
 praise 931
 worship 990
hose *stockings* 225
 pipe 350
hosier 225
hospice *house* 189
 hospital 662
hospitable
 liberal 816
 social 892
hospital 662
 in - 655
hospitality

HOSP

[see hospitable]
Hospitaller 996
hospodar 745
host collection 72
  multitude 102
  army 726
  friend 890
  rite 998
- in himself 175
- of heaven 977
reckon without one's -
  error 495
  unskillful 699
  rash 863
hostage 771
hostel 189
hostelry 189
hostile disagreeing 24
  opposed 708
  enmity 889
- meeting 720
in - array 708
hostilities 722
hostility 889
hostler 746
hot violent 173
  warm 382
  pungent 392
  red 434
  orange 439
  excited 824
  irascible 901
blow - and cold
  inconsistent 477
  falsehood 544
  tergiversation 607
  caprice 608
- air bombast 884
- blood rash 863
  angry 900
  irascible 901
- water
  difficulty 704
  quarrel 713
  painful 830
in - haste 684
in - pursuit 622
make - 384
hotbed cause 153
  center 222
  workshop 691
hot-brained 863
hotchpot
  mixture 41
  confusion 59
  participation 778
hotel 189
- keeper 188
- runner 767
Hôtel des Invalides
  662
hot-headed
  hasty 684
  excitable 825
hothouse
  conservatory 371
  furnace 386
  workshop 691
hotpress 255
Hotspur 863
Hottentot 876

HOUS

hough 659
hound animal 366
  hunt 622
  persecute 907
  wretch 949
hold with the hare but
  run with the -s 607
- on 615
houppelande 225
hour period 108
  point of time 113
  present time 118
blessed - of our din-
  ners 299
- after hour 110
improve the shining -
  682
one's - is come
  occasion 134
  death 360
the long -s 106
hourglass
  chronometer 114
  contraction 195
  narrow 203
Houri 845
hourly time 106
  frequent 136
  periodical 138
house lineage 69
  family 166
  locate 184
  abode 189
  theater 599
  make safe 664
  council 696
  firm 712
bring the - about one's
  ears 699
eat out of - and home
  prodigal 818
  gluttony 957
- divided against it-
  self 713
- of cards 160
- of Commons 966
- of correction
  prison 752
  punishment 975
- of death 363
- of detention 752
- of God 1000
- of Lords 875, 966
- of peers 875
- of prayer 1000
- of Representatives
  696
keep - 184
set one's - in order
  952
turn - out of window
  713
turn out of - and home
  297
housebreaker 792
housebreaking 791
house dog 366
household
  inhabitants 188
  abode 189
- gods 189

HUDD

- stuff 635
- troops 726
- words
  known 490
  language 560
  plain 576, 849
householder 188
housekeeper 694
housekeeping 692
houseless 185
housemaid 746
house raising 892
houseroom 180
house top
  summit 210
proclaim from - 531
housewarming 892
housewife 682
  bag 191
housewifery
  conduct 692
  economy 817
housing
  lodging 189
  covering 223
  horse-cloth 225
hovel 189
hover high 206
  rove 266
  soar 267
  ascend 305
  irresolute 605
- about
  move 264
- over
  near 197
how way 627
  means 632
- comes it?
  attribution 155
  inquiry 461
- now 870
howbeit 30
however
  degree 26
  notwithstanding 30
  except 83
howitzer 727
howker 273
howl human cry 411
  animal cry 412
  lamentation 839
howling wilderness
  unproductive 169
  secluded 893
hoy 273
hoyden girl 129
  rude 851
hub 247, 250
hubbub stir 315
  noise 404
  outcry 411
  discord 713
hubby 250
huckster
  barter 794
  merchant 797
huddle
  disorder 59
  derange 61
  collect 72

HUMA

hug 197
- on 225
Hudibrastic 856
- verse 597
hue 428
- and cry cry 411
  proclaim 531
  pursuit 622
  alarm 669
- of dungeons 982
raise a - and cry 932
hueless 429
huff insolence 885
  anger 900
huffy 901
hug cohere 46
  border on 197
  retain 781
  courtesy 894
  love 897
  endearment 902
- a belief 606
- a sin 945
- oneself
  pleasure 827
  content 831
  rejoicing 838
  pride 878
- the shore
  navigation 267
  approach 286
huge in degree 31
  in size 192
hugger-mugger 528
Huguenot 984
huis clos, à - 528
huissier 965
huke 225
hukm 741, 760
hulk body 50
  ship 273
hulks 752
hulky big 192
  unwieldy 647
  ugly 846
hull 50
hullabaloo
  noise 404
  shout 411
hum faint sound 405
  continued sound 407
  animal sound 412
  sing 416
  deceive 545, 546
busy - of men 682
- and haw
  stammer 583
  irresolute 605
human 372
- face divine 234
- race 372
- sacrifices 991
- system 364
humane
  benevolent 906
  philanthropic 910
  merciful 914
humanitarian
  mankind 372
  philanthropic 910
humanities

letters 560
humanize 894
**humano capiti cer-
vicem j u n g e r e
equinam** 24
humation 363
humble *meek* 879
  modest 881
  pious 987
  eat - pie 725
  - oneself
  meek 879
  penitent 950
  worship 990
  -r classes 876
  your - servant
  dissent 489
  refusal 764
humble-minded 879
humbug
  falsehood 544
  deception 545
  deceiver 548
  trifle 643
humdrum
  weary 841
  dull 843
  (*prose* 598)
humectate
  water 337
  moisture 339
humid 339
humiliation
  disrepute 874
  sense of shame 879
  worship 990
  self - 950
humility
  meekness **879**
  piety 987
hummer 682
humming top 417
hummock *hill* 206
  hump 250
humor *essence* 5
  tendency 176
  liquid 333
  disposition 602
  caprice 608
  aid 707
  indulge 760
  affections 820
  please 829
  wit 842
  flatter 933
  (*fun* 840)
  in the - 602
  out of - 901a
  peccant -
  unclean 653
  disease 655
humorist 844
humorous 842
humorsome
  capricious 608
  sulky 901a
hump 250
humpbacked 243
Humph! 870
**Humphrey, dine
with Duke** - 956

hunch 250
hunchbacked 243
hundi 800
hundred *number* 98
  many 102
  region 181
hundredth 99
hundredweight 319
hunger 865
hunks 819
hunt *inquiry* 461
  pursuit 622
  - after 622
  - down 907
  - in couples 709
  - out *inquiry* 461
  discover 480a
  - the slipper 840
hunter *horse* 271
  killer 361
  pursuer 622
  place &c. - 767
hunting
  killing 361
  sporting 622
hunting ground 840
huntsman 361
hurdle 272
hurdy-gurdy 417
hurl 284
  - against 716
  - defiance 715
hurler avec les loups
  conformity 82
  concord 714
Hurlothrumbo 860
hurly-burly 315
hurrah 836, 838
hurricane
  tempest 349
  (*violence* 173)
  - deck 210
hurry *haste* 684
  excite 825
  - forward 684
  - off with 789
  - of spirits 821
  - on 615
  - skurry 825
hurst 367
hurt
  physical pain 378
  evil 619
  maltreat 649
  injure 659
  - the feelings
  pain 830
  anger 900
  more frightened than
  - 860
hurtful 649
hurtle 276
hurtless 648
husband *store* 636
  director 694
  spouse 903
husbandman 371
husbandry
  agriculture 371
  conduct 692
  economy 817

hush *moderate* 174
  stop 265
  silence 403
  taciturn 585
  - up
  conceal 528
  pacify 723
hush money
  compensation 30
  reward 973
husk 223
husking bee 892
husky *dry* 340
  faint sound 405
  hoarse 581
hussar 726
hussif 191
hussy 962
hustings
  school 542
  arena 728
  tribunal 966
hustle *perturb* 61
  push 276
  agitate 315
  hinder 706
hustler 682
hut 189
hutch 189
huzza 838
hyacinth
  jewel 847
hyaline 425
hyaloid 425
hybernation 683
hybrid
  mixture 41
  exception 83
hydra
  monster 83
  productive 168
hydrant 348
hydrargyrum 274
hydrate of amyl 356
hydraulics 348
hydrocephalus 194
hydrocyanic acid 663
hydrocyanide 663
hydrodynamics
  fluid 333
  stream 348
hydrography 341
hydrology 333
hydromancy 511
hydromel 396
hydrometer 321
hydropathy
  remedy 662
hydrophobia 867
hydrophthalmus 194
hydroplane 273
hydropot 953, 958
hydrostatics 333
hydrous 337
hyemal 383
hyena 913
hyetology 348
hygeian 656
hygiantics 670
hygiene 656
hygienic

  healthy 656
  preservative 670
hygre 348
hygrometry 339
hyle 316
hylotheism
  heterodoxy 984
  irreligion 989
Hymen 903
hymeneal 903
hymn *song* 415
  worship 990
hymn book 998
hypallage 218
hyperbaton 218
hyperbola 245
hyperbole 549
hyperborean
  far 196
  cold 383
hypercriticism
  misjudgment 481
  discontent 832
  fastidiousness 868
  censure 932
hyperdulia 990
Hyperion 845
  - to a satyr 14
hyperorthodoxy 984
hyperphysical 450
  976
hypertrophy 194
hyphen 45
hypnology 683
hypnotic
  remedy 662
  sleep 683
hypocaust 386
hypochondriac
  madman 504
  low spirits 837
hypochondriasis 837
hypocrisy
  falsehood 544
  religious - 988
hypocrite 548
  play the - 544
hypostasis 3
hypostatic union 976
hypothecate 771
hypothenuse 217
hypothesis 514
hypothetical
  uncertain 475
  supposed 514
hypped *insane* 503
  dejected 837
hypsometry 466
Hyrcynian wood 533
hysteria *insanity* 503
hysteric
  violent 173
hysterical
  spasmodic 608
  emotional 821
  excitable 825
hysterics
  in - *excited* 824
  frightened 860
hysteron proteron
  218

- for
  undertake 676
  promise 768
-s and outs 182
in: - *articulo* 111
- *extenso whole* 50
  diffuse 573
- *limine* 66
- *loco* 23
- *medias res* 68
- *propriâ personâ* 79
- *re* 9
- *statu pupillari* 127
- *statu quo* 141
- *statu quo ante bel-*
  lum 140
- *toto* 52
- *transitu*
  transient 111
  transfer 270
inability
  want of power 158
  want of skill 699
inabstinent 954
inaccessible
  distant 196
  impossible 471
inaccurate *error* 495
· *solecism* 568
inaction
  inertness 172
  not doing **681**
inactivity 683
  inertness 172
inadequate
  powerless 158
  insufficient 640
  useless 645
  imperfect 651
  (*weak* 160)
inadmissible
  incongruous 24
  excluded 55
  extraneous 57
  inexpedient 647
inadvertence 458
inadvisable 647
inaffable 895
inalienable
  retention 781
  right 924
inamorata 897
inane *void* 4
  unmeaning 517
  insufficient 640
  trivial 643
  useless 645
inanimate 360
- *matter* 358
inanition 158
inanity [see *inane*]
inappetency
  insensibility 823
  indifference 866
inapplicable
  irrelation 10
  disagreement 24
inapposite
  irrelation 10
  disagreement 24
inappreciable

in degree 32
in size 193
  unimportant 643
inapprehensible
  stolid 499
  unintelligible 519
inappropriate
  unconsonant 24
  inexpedient 647
inapt
  incongruous 24
  impotent 158
  useless 645
  inexpedient 647
  unskillful 699
inarticulate 581, 583
inartificial 703
inartistic 846
inasmuch *whereas* 9
  however, 26
  because 476
inattention 458
inaudible
  silence 403
  faint sound 405
  deaf 419
  voiceless 581
inaugural
  precursor 64
inaugurate
  begin 66
  install 755
  celebrate 883
inauspicious
  untimely 135
  untoward 649
  hopeless 859
inbeing 5
inborn, inbred
  intrinsic 5
  affections 820
  (*habit* 613)
- *proclivity* 601
inca 745
incage 751
incalculable
  much 31
  infinite 105
incalescence 382
incandescence 382
incantation
  invocation 765
  spell 993
incantatory 992
incapable
  impotent 158
  (*weak* 160)
incapacious 203
incapacitate 158
incapacity
  impotence 158
  ignorance 491
  stupidity 499
  (*weakness* 160)
incarcerate
  imprison 751
  (*surround* 229)
incarnadine 434
incarnate
  intrinsic 5
  vicious 945

devil -
  bad man 949
  Satan 978
incarnation 976
incase *cover* 223
  surround 229
incautious *rash* 863
  (*neglect* 460)
incendiary
  destroy 162
  burn 384
  influence 615
  malevolent 907
  evil doer 913
  bad man 949
incense *fuel* 388
  fragrant 400
  hate 898
  anger 900
  flatter 933
  worship 990
  rite 998
- *breathing morn* 125
incension
  burning 384
incentive 615
incept 66, 537
inception 66
inceptor 541
incertitude 475
incessant
  repeated 104
  ceaseless 112
  frequent 136
incest 961
inch *small* 32
  length 200
by -es 275
give an - and take an
  ell 789
- by inch
  by degrees 26
  in parts 51
  slowly 275
not see an - beyond
  one's nose 699
not yield an - 606
to an - 494
inchoation
  beginning 66
  preparation 673
incide 44
incidence 278
incident 151
  full of - 151
incidental
  extrinsic 6
  circumstance 8
  irrelative 10
  occurring 151
  casual 156
  liable 177
  chance 621
incinerate 384
incipience 66
incircumspect 460
incision *cut* 44
  furrow 259
incisive *energy* 171
  vigor 574
  feeling 821

incite
  exasperate 173
  urge 615
incivility 895
incivism 911
inclasp 229
inclement
  violent 173
  cold 383
  severe 739
  pitiless 914a
inclination
  [see *incline*]
  affection 820
  desire 865
  love 897
incline *tendency* 176
  slope 217
  direction 278
  willing 602
  induce 615
- an ear to 457
inclined
- *plane* 633
inclose
  place within 221
  surround 227
  hem in 229
inclosure
  region 181
  envelope **232**
  fence 752
include
  composition 54
- *in a class* 76
inclusion 76
inclusive
  additive 37
  component 56
  class 76
incogitancy 452
incognita, terra
  491
incognito 528
incognizable 519
incoherence
  physical 47
  mental 503
incombustible 385
income *profit* 775
  property 780
  wealth 803
  receipt 810
incoming
  ingress 294
  receipt 810
incommensurable
  irrelation 10
  (*disagreeing* 24)
- *quantity* 84, 85
incommode
  hinder 706
  (*trouble* 830)
  (*incommodious* 647)
incommunicable
  unmeaning 517
  unintelligible 519
  retention 781
incommutable 150
incomparable
  superior 33

(*good* 648)
incompassionate
  914a
incompatible 24
incompetence
  inability 158
  incapacity 499
  unskillful 699
incompleteness 53
  noncompletion 730
incomplex 42
incompliance 764
incomprehensible
  infinite 105
  unintelligible 519
incomprehension
  491
incompressible 321
inconcealable 525
inconceivable
  impossible 471
  improbable 473
  incredible 485
  unintelligible 519
  wonder 870
inconceptible 519
inconcinnity
  disagreement 24
  ugliness 846
inconclusive 477
inconcoction 674
incondite 851
incongruous 24, 568
inconnection
  irrelation 10
  disjunction 44
inconsequence
  irrelation 10
inconsequential
  illogical 477
inconsiderable
  small 32
  fractional 100a
  unimportant 643
inconsiderate
  thoughtless 452
  inattentive 458
  neglectful 460
  foolish 699
inconsistent
  contrary 14
  disagreeing 24
  illogical 477
  absurd 497
  foolish 499
  capricious 608
inconsolable 837
inconsonant
  disagreeing 24
  fitful 149
inconspicuous 447
inconstant 149
incontestable
  strong 159
  certain 474
incontiguous 196
incontinent 961
incontinently 132
incontrollable 173
incontrovertible
  stable 15G

---

  certain 474
inconvenience 647
  put to - 706
inconversable
  taciturn 585
  unsociable 893
inconvertible
  continuing 143
  (*stable* 150)
inconvincible 487
incorporate 48, 317
incorporeal 317
  - *hereditaments* 780
incorrect
  illogical 477
  erroneous 495
  solecism 568
  vicious 945
incorrigible
  obstinate 606
  hopeless 859
  vicious 945
  impenitent 951
incorruptible
  honorable 939
incorruption
  probity 939
  innocence 946
  (*health* 654)
incrassate
  increase 194
  density 321
  - *fluids* 352
  (*thick* 202)
increase
  - *in degree* 35
  - *in number* 102
  - *in size* 194
incredible
  great 31
  impossible 471
  improbable 473
  doubtful 485
  wonderful 870
incredulity
  unbelief **487**
  religious - 989
increment
  increase 35
  addition 37
  adjunct 39
  expansion 194
increpation 932
incriminate 938
incrust *coat* 223
  line 224
incubation 673
incubus
  hindrance 706
  pain 828
  demon 980
inculcate 537
inculcated 6
inculpable 946
inculpate 938
inculture 674
incumbency
  business 625
  churchdom 995
incumbent
  inhabitant 188

---

  high 206
  weight 319
  duty 926
  clergyman 996
incumber 706
incumbered 806
incunabula 127
incur 177
  - *a debt* 806
  - *a loss* 776
  - *blame* 932
  - *danger* 665
  - *disgrace* 874
  - *the risk* 621
incurable
  ingrained 5
  disease 655
  hopeless 859
incuriam, per - 458,
  460
incuriosity 456
incursion
  ingress 294
  attack 716
incurvation 245
indagation 461
indebted
  owing 806
  gratitude 916
  duty 926
indecent 961
indeciduous 150
indecipherable 519
indecision 605
indecisive 475
indeclinable 150
indecorous
  vulgar 851
  vicious 945
  impure 961
indeed *existing* 1
  very 31
  assent 488
  truly 494
  assertion 535
  wonder 870
indefatigable
  persevering 604a
  active 682
indefeasible
  stable 150
  due 924
indefectible 650
indefensible
  powerless 158
  submission 725
  accusable 938
  wrong 945
indeficient 650
indefinite
  great 31
  infinite 105
  aoristic 119
  misty 447
  uncertain 475
  inexact 495
  vague 519
indeliberate 612
indelible *stable* 150
  memory 505
  mark 550

---

  feeling 821
indelicate 961
indemnification 790,
  952
indemnity
  compensation **30**
  forgiveness 918
  reward 973
  deed of - 771
indent *scollop* 248
indentation 252, 257
indenture
  compact 769
  security 771
  (*evidence* 467)
  (*record* 551)
independence
  irrelation 10
  freedom 748
  wealth 803
Independence Day
  840
Independent 984
indescribable
  great 31
  wonderful 870
indesinent 112
indestructible 150
indeterminate
  chance 156
  uncertain 475
  equivocal 520
  irresolute 605
indevotion 989
index
  arrangement 60
  exponent 84
  list 86
  sign 550
  words 562
index expurgatoriu
  761
indexterity 699
Indian:
  - *file* 69
  - *gift* 794
  - *giver* 702
  - *rubber* 325
  - *sage* 662
  - *summer* 126
  - *weed* 392
indicate
  specify 79
  direct attention t
  457
  mean 516
  mark 550
indication 75, **550**
indicative
  evidence 467
indicolite 438
indict *accuse* 938
  arraign 969
indiction 531
indifference
  incuriosity 456
  unwillingness 603
  no choice 609a
  insensibility 823
  unconcern **866**
  matter of - 643

inferential
demonstrative 478
latent 526
inferiority
in degree **34**
in size 195
imperfection 651
personal - 34
infernal *bad* 649
malevolent 907
wicked 945
satanic 978
- *machine* 727
- *regions* 982
infertility 169
infest 830
infestivity *sad* 837
dull 843
infibulation 43
infidel 989
- I have thee on the hip 919
infidelity
dishonor 940
irreligion 989
infiltrate *mix* 41
intervene 228
interpenetrate 294
moisten 337, 339
teach 537
infiltration
passage 302
infinite 105
- *goodness* 976
Infinite, the - 976
infinitely *great* 31
infinitesimal
small 32
little 193
- *calculus* 85
infinity 105
infirm *weak* 160
disease 655
vicious 945
- *of purpose* 605
infirmary 662
infirmity
[see *infirm*]
infix 537
inflame
render violent 173
burn 384
excite 824
anger 900
(*incite* 615)
inflammable
burn 384
fuel 388
inflammation
heating 384
disease 655
inflate *expand* 194
blow 349
inflated
style 573, 577
ridiculous 853
vain 880
inflation
[see *inflate*]
rarefaction 322
inflect 245

inflection
change 140
curvature 245
grammar 567
inflexible *hard* 323
resolved 604
obstinate 606
stern 739
a well - 906
- *in faith* 159
inflexion [see inflection]
inflict *act upon* 680
severity 739
- *evil* 649
- *pain*
bodily pain 378
mental pain 830
- *punishment* 972
infliction
adversity 735
mental pain 828, 830
punishment 972
inflorescence 161
influence
cause 153
change 140
physical - **175**
inducement 615
authority 737
(*importance* 642)
absence of - **175a**
sphere of - 780
influx 294
infold 232
inform 527
- *against*
accuse 938
go to law 969
informal
irregular 83
lawless 964
informality
nonobservance 773
informant 527
information
knowledge 490
communication **527**
lawsuit 969
pick up - 539
wide - 539
informity 241
infra dignitatem
inglorious 874
dishonorable 940
infraction
disobedience 742
nonobservance 773
exemption 927
- *of usage &c.*
unconformity 83
desuetude 614
infrangible
combined 46
dense 321
infrequency **137**
infrigidation 385
infringe
transgress 303
disobey 742
not observe 773

undueness 925
dereliction 927
- *a law &c.* 83
infumate 673
infundibular
concave 252
hole 260
infuriate
violent 173
excite 824
anger 900
infuscate 431
infuse *mix* 41
insert 300
teach 537
- *courage* 861
- *life into* 824
- *new blood* 658
infused 6
infusible 321
infusion
[see *infuse*]
liquefaction 335
infusoria 193
ingannation 545
ingate 350
ingathering 72
ingemination 90
ingenerate 5
ingenious 698
ingenite 5
ingenium, perfervidum - 682
ingentes stupent curæ 735
ingénu *artless* 703
ingénue *actress* 599
ingenuity 698
ingenuous
artless 703
(*sincere* 543)
(*honorable* 939)
ingesta 298
ingestion 296
ingle 388
ingle side 189
inglorious
disreputable 874
dishonorable 940
ingot 800
ingraft *add* 37
join 43
insert 300
teach 537
ingrafted
extrinsic 6
habit 613
ingrain
insinuate 228
color 428
ingrained
intrinsic 5
combined 48
habit 613
character 820
ingrate 917
ingratiate 897
ingratiating 894
ingratitude 917
- *thou marble-hearted fiend* 917

ingredient 56
ingress 294
forcible - 300
ingurgitate 296
ingustible 391
inhabile 699
inhabit 186
inhabitant **188**
inhale *receive* 296
smell 398
inharmonious:
- *color* 428
- *sound* 414
inhere in 56
inherence 5
inherent 820
inherit *acquire* 775
possess 777
inheritance
property 780
- *of the saints* 981
inherited
intrinsic 5
inheritor 779
inhesion 5
inhibit *hinder* 706
restrain 751
prohibit 761
(*restrain* 615)
inhospitable 893
inhuman 907
inhumanum verbum est ultio 919
inhume 363
inimaginable
impossible 471
improbable 473
wonderful 870
inimical
opposition 708
enmity 889
inimitable
nonimitation 20
supreme 33
very good 648
perfect 650
iniquity *wrong* 923
vice 945
worker of - 949
inirritability 826
initial 66
- *letter* 558
initiate *begin* 66
teach 537
initiated *skillful* 698
inject 300
fluid 337
injudicial 964
injudicious 499
injunction
command 630
advice 695
command 741
prohibition 761
injure *damage* 659
spite 907
injuria formæ, spretæ -
ugly 846
contempt 930
injurious 923

instinctive
  inborn 5
institute cause 153
  produce 161
  academy 542
  society 712
  - an inquiry 461
institution
  academy 542
  society 712
  political - 963
  church 995
institutor 540
instruct teach 537
  advise 695
  precept 697
  order 741
instructed 490
instructor 540
instrument
  implement 633
  security 771
  mighty - of little men 590
  musical - 417
  optical - 445
instrumental 631
  - music 415
instrumentalist 416
instrumentality 631
insuavity 895
insubordinate 742
insubstantial 2, 3, 4
  - pageant 882
insufferable
  painful 830
  dislike 867
insufficiency 640
insufflation 349
insular unrelated 10
  detached 44
  single 87
  island 346
insulate 44
insulse stupid 499
  dull 843
insult rudeness 895
  offense 900
  disrespect 929
insulting 898
insuperable 471
  - obstacle 706
insupportable 830
insuppressible 173
insurance 768
insure
  make sure 474
  obtain security 771
insurgent 742
insurmountable 471
insurrection
  resistance 719
  disobedience 742
insusceptible 823
  - of change 150
intact
  permanent 141
  perfect 650
  preserved 670
intaglio mold 22
  concave 252

sculpture 557
intangible little 193
  numb 381
integer whole 50
  number 84
integer vitæ sceleris-
  que purus 939
integral 50
  - calculus 85
  - part 56
integrate
  consolidate 50
  (complete 52)
integrity whole 50
  probity 939
  virtue 944
integument 223
intellect 450
  absence of - 450a
  exercise of the - 451
intellection 450, 451
intellectual 450
  - force 574
  - powers 450
intelligence
  mind 450
  capacity 498
  news 532
intelligencer 527
intelligibility 518
  (perspicuity 570)
intemperance 954
  drunkenness 959
intempestivity 135
intend 620
intendant 694
intended will 600
  predetermined 611
intense great 31
  energetic 171
  - color 428
  - thought 457
intensify
  increase 35
  stimulate 171
intensity degree 26
  greatness 31
  energy 171
intent attention 457
  design 620
  active 682
  - upon desire 865
  resolved 604
intention 620
  bad - 607
  good - 906
intently, look - 441
intents and pur-
  poses, to all - 27, 52
inter 363
inter: - alia 82
  - nos 528
interaction
  working 170
  (intermedium 228)
intercalate 228
intercede
  mediate 724
  deprecate 766
intercept

hinder 706
  take 789
intercession
  [see intercede]
  worship 990
Intercessor 976
intercessor 714
interchange 148
  barter 794
  - visits &c. 892
interchangeable 12
intercipient 706
interclude 706
intercommunica-
  tion 527
intercommunity 892
intercourse
  friendship 888
  sociality 892
  verbal - 582, 588
intercurrence
  interchange 148
  interjacence 228
  passage 302
interdependence 12
interdict 761
interdigitate
  intersect 219
  intervene 228
interdum lacrymæ
  839
interest concern 9
  influence 175
  curiosity 455
  advantage 618
  importance 642
  property 780
  debt 806
  excite 824
  please 829
  amuse 840
  devoid of - 841
  feel an - in 906
  make - for 707
  not know one's own - 699
  place out at -
  lend 787
  economy 817
  take an - in
  curiosity 455
  love 897
  take no - in
  insensibility 823
  indifference 866
  want of - 866
interested
  selfish 943
interesting
  lovable 897
interfere disagree 24
  counteract 179
  intervene 228
  activity 682
  thwart 706
  mediate 724
interferometer 466
interim time 106
  same time 120
interiority 221
interjacence

middle 68
  coming between 228
interject
  interpose 228
  insert 300
interlace join 43
  twine 219
interlard mix 41
  interpolate 228
interleave 228
interline
  interpolate 288
  write 590
interlink join 43
  twine 219
interlocation 228
interlocution 588
interlocutor 582
interloper
  extraneous 57
  intervene 228
  obstruct 706
interlude time 106
  dramatic 599
intermarriage 903
intermeddle
  interfere 682
  hinder 706
intermeddling 724
intermediate
  mean 29
  middle 68
  intervening 228
  ministerial 631
  - time 106
intermedium
  mean 29
  link 45
  intervention 228
  instrument 631
  (means 632)
interment 363
  insertion 300
intermigration 266
interminable
  infinite 105
  eternal 112
  long 200
intermingle 41
intermission
  time 106
  discontinuance 142
intermit
  interrupt 70
  recur 138
  discontinue 142
intermittence
  time 106
intermix 41
intermutation 148
intern 221
internal intrinsic 5
  interior 221
  - evidence 467
international
  reciprocal 12
  sociality 892
  - law 963
internecine 361
  - war 722
internuncio

hatred 898
spite 907
envy 921
invigorate
  strengthen 159
  inspirit 834
invigorating
  healthy 656
invincible 159
inviolable
  secret 528
  right 924
  honor 939
inviolate
  permanent 141
  secret 528
  honorable 939
invious *closed* 261
  pathless 704
invisibility 447
invisible *small* 193
  not to be seen 447
  concealed 526
  - helpers 977
invitâ Minervâ
  unwilling 603
  difficult 704
invite *induce* 615
  offer 763
  ask 765
  - the attention 457
inviting
  [*see* invite]
  pleasing 829
invoice 86
invoke *address* 586
  implore 765
  pray 990
  - curses 908
  - saints 998
involucrum 223
involuntary
  necessary 601
  unwilling 603
  - servitude 749
involution [*see* in-
  volve]
  algebra 85
involve *include* 54
  derange 61
  wrap 225
  evince 467
  mean 516
  latency 526
involved
  disorder 59
  convoluted 248
  secret 533
  obscure style 571
  in debt 806
involvement 61, 704
invulnerable 664
inward *intrinsic* 5
  inside 221
  - monitor 926
inweave 219
inwrap 225
inwrought 5
Ionic 597
iota *small* 32
  (*minute* 193)

io triumphe!
  rejoicing 838
  celebration 883
I. O. U. *security* 771
  money 800
ipecacuanha 662
ipse dixit
  certainty 474
  affirmation 535
ipsissima verba 494
ipso facto 1
iræ
  amantium - 918
  tantæne animis cœ-
  lestibus - 900
ira furor brevis est
  503, 900
irascibility 901
irate 900
ire 900
iridescent 440
Iris *traveler* 268
  messenger 534
iris *rainbow* 440
  eye 441
irisated 440
Irish 188
Irishism 497
irk 688, 830
irksome
  tiresome 688
  difficult 704
  painful 830
  weary 841
iron *strength* 159
  smooth 255
  hard 323
  resolution 604
  - age *adversity* 735
  pain 828
  - cross 733
  - entering into the
   soul 828, 830
  - gray 432
  - grip 159
  - gripe 781
  - heel 739
  - necessity 601
  - rule 739
  - sway 739
  - will 604
  rule with a rod of-
   739
iron-bound coast
  land 342
  danger 667
ironclad
  covering 223
  defense 717
  man of war. 726
iron-handed 739
iron-hearted 861
iron mold 434
irons 752
  fire - 386
  - in the fire
   business 625
   redundance 641
   active 682
   unskillful 699
  put in - 751

irony
  figure of speech 521
  untruth 546
  ridicule 856
irradiate 420
irrational
  number 84
  illogical 477
  silly 499
irreclaimable
  hopeless 859
  vicious 945
  impenitent 951
irreconcilable
  unrelated 10
  discordant 24
  enmity 889
irrecoverable
  past 122
  hopeless 859
  (*lost* 776)
irredeemable
  hopeless 859
  (*lost* 776)
irreducible
  discordant 24
  out of order 59
  unchangeable 150
irrefragable 478
irrefutable
  certain 474
  proved 478
irregular
  diverse 16a
  out of order 59
  multiform 81
  against rule 83
  - in recurrence 139
  distorted 243
  combatant 726
irregularity 139
irrelation 10
irrelevant
  unrelated 10
  unaccordant 24
  sophistical 477
irreligion 989
irremediable
  bad 649
  hopeless 859
  (*spoiled* 659)
  (*lost* 776)
irremissible 945
irremovable 150
irreparable
  hopeless 859
  (*bad* 649)
  (*spoiled* 659)
  (*lost* 776)
irrepentance 951
irreprehensible 946
irrepressible
  violent 173
  free 748
  excitable 825
irreproachable 946
irreprovable 946
irresilient 326
irresistible
  strong 159
  demonstration 478

necessary 601
irresoluble 150
irresolution 605
irresolvable 87
irresolvedly 605
irrespective 10
irresponsible
  exempt 927a
  arbitrary 964
irretrievable
  stable 150
  lost 776
  hopeless 859
irrevealable 528
irreverence
  disrespect 929
  impiety 988
irreversible
  stable 150
  hopeless 859
  (*past* 122)
irrevocable
  stable 150
  necessary 601
  hopeless 859
irrigate 337
irriguous 339
irrision *ridicule* 856
  disrespect 929
irritabile, genus-
  901
irritable
  excitable 825
  irascible 901
irritate *violent* 173
  excite 824
  pain 830
  provoke 898
  incense 900
irritating
  [*see* irritate]
  stringent 171
irritation
  [*see* irritate]
  pain 828
  source of - 830
irruption
  ingress 294
  invasion 716
Irvingite 984
is: - to be 152
  that - 118
ischiagra 378
isinglass 352
Isis 979
Islamism 984
island 44, **346**
islander 188
isle 346
isobar 338
isobath 27
ischeimal 383
isochronal 27
isochronous 120
isogamy 17, 357
isolate *detach* 44
  seclude 893
isolated
  unrelated 10
  single 87
isomorphism 240

J

jab 276
jabber
  unmeaning 517
  stammer 583
  chatter 584
jacal 189
jacent 213
jacet, hic - 363
jacinth 847
jack *rotation* 312
  ensign 550
  cards 840
Jack
  before one can say
   '- Robinson' 132
  - at a pinch 711
  - Cade 742
  - in office
   director 694
   bully 887
  - Ketch 975
  - of all trades 700
  - o' lantern 423
  - Pudding
   actor 599
   humorist 844
   boaster 884
  - tar 269
jack-a-dandy
  buffoon 844
  fop 854
jackal *provision* 637
  auxiliary 711
jackanapes *fop* 854
  blusterer 887
jackass 271
jack boot 225
**jackdaw in pea-
  cock's feathers**
  701
jacket 225
  cork - 666
jackleg 792
jackpot 840
jackstones 840
Jacobin 710
Jacquerie
  attack 716
  tumult 719
jacta est alea 601
jactitation
  tossing 315
  boasting 884
jaculation 284
jade *horse* 271
  worn-out 659
  fatigue 688
  low woman 876
  scamp 949
  drab 962
jag 257
  burden 190
  dent 257
jäger 726
jagged 244

jaguar 913
jahannan 982
Jahre lehren 490
jail 752
  - bird
   prisoner 754
   bad man 949
jailer *keeper* 753
  punisher 975
jakes 653
jaldi 682
jalousie de métier
  921
jam *squeeze* 43
  pulp 354
  sweet 396
  - in *interpose* 228
Jamaica pepper 393
jamb 215
jamboree 840
jammed in
  restraint 751
jangle
  harsh sound 410
  quarrel 713
janissary 726
janitor 263
Jansenist 984
janty
  [see jaunty]
January 138
januis clausis 528
Janus *deceiver* 607
  tergiversation 607
  close the temple of -
   723
Janus-faced 544
jao 297
japan *coat* 223
  resin 356a
  ornament 847
jaquima 752
jar *clash* 24
  vessel 191
  agitation 315
  stridor 410
  discord 713
  - upon the feelings
   830
jardinière 191
jargon
  absurdity 497
  no meaning 517
  unintelligible 519
  neology 563
jarring 414
jasper 847
jaundiced
  yellow 436
  prejudiced 481
  dejected 837
  jealous 920
  view with - eyes
   disapprove 932
jaunt 266

jaunting car 272
jaunty
  gay 836
  pretty 845
  stylish 852
  rash 863
  showy 882
  insolent 885
javelin 727
jaw *chatter* 584
  scold 932
jaw-fallen 837
jaws *mouth* 231
  eating 298
  - of death 360
jay 584
  dupe 547
jealous of honor 939
jealousy 920
  suspicion 485
jecur, difficili bile -
  900
jeer *flout* 929
  (*joke* 842)
  (*banter* 856)
Jehovah 976
Jehu *traveler* 268
  director 694
jejune *style* 575
  scanty 640
**jejunus raro stom-
  achus** 957
jelly 352
  beat to a - 972
jemidar 745
jemmy *lever* 633
  dandy 854
je ne sais quoi
  exceptional 83
  what d'ye call 'em
   563
  beauty 845
jennet 271
jenny 633
jeopardy 665
jerboa 309
jereed 727
jeremiad
  lament 839
  invective 932
  (*accusation* 938)
Jericho, send to -
  297
jerk *start* 146
  throw 284
  pull 285
  agitate 315
jerkin 225
jerks, by - 70
  the - 315
jerry building 545
Jerry Sneak
  coward 862
  knave 941
jersey 225

Jessamy, Jemmy -
  854
jest *trifle* 643
  wit 842
jest book 842
jester 844
jesting stock 857
Jesuit *deceiver* 548
  priest 996
jesuitical
  sophistical 477
  deceitful 544
Jesus 976
jet *stream* 348
  - black 431
jetsam 782
jettison 782
jetty
  projection 250
  harbor 666
jeu
  - de mots 842
  - d'esprit 842
  - de théâtre 599
  le - ne vaut pas la
   chandelle
   waste 638
   unimportant 643
   dear 814
jeune
  - premier 599
  - veuve 599
Jew *cunning* 702
  rich 803
  extortioner 819
  heretic 984
  -'s harp 417
  worth a -'s eye
   good 648
   costly 814
jewel *gem* 648
  ornament 847
  favorite 899
  -s five words long 648
jewelry, false - 545
Jezebel *wicked* 913
  wretch 949
  courtesan 962
jhil 345
jhilmil 351
jhuth 546
jib
  front 234
  regression 283
  cut of one's -
   form 240
   appearance 448
jiffy 113
jig *dance* 840
  (*music* 415)
jigger 215, 272
jilt *disappoint* 509
  deceive 545
  deceiver 548
  dishonor 940

489

jilted 898
jimp 845
jingal 727
jingle 408
jingo 887
jinks, high - 840
jinn 980
jinrikisha 272
jiujitsu 720
jiva 157
job *business* 625
 action 680
 unfair 940
 tough - 704
Job
 -'s comforter
 dejection 837
 hopeless 859
 patience of - 826
 poor as - 804
jobation 932
jobber *deceiver* 548
 tactician 700
 merchant 797
 trickster 943
jobbernowl 501
jobbery
 cunning 702
 improbity 940
jobbing *barter* 794
jockey *rider* 268
 deceive 545
 deceiver 548
 servant 746
jocose *gay* 836
 witty 842
jocoseness *fun* 840
jocular *gay* 836
 droll 842
jocund *gay* 836
 sportive 840
Joe Miller *wit* 842
 humorist 844
jog *push* 276
 shake 315
 - on *continue* 143
 trudge 266
 slow 275
 advance 282
 mediocrity 736
 - the memory 505
joggle 315
jog trot *trudge* 266
 slow 275
 habit 613
John Doe and Rich-
 ard Roe 4
Johnsonian 577
joie, feu de - 883
join *connect* 43
 assemble 72
 contiguous 199
 arrive 272
 party 712
 sociality 892
 marry 903
 - battle 722
 - forces 708
 - hands 708
 - in 778
 - in the chorus 488
490

- issue *discuss* 476
 deny 536
 quarrel 713
 contend 720
 lawsuit 969
 - the majority 360
 - with 709
joint *junction* 43
 part 51
 accompanying 88
 meat 298
 low resort 621, 945
 - concern 712
joint stock
 coöperation 709
 participation 778
joint tenancy 778
jointure 780
joist 215
joke *trifle* 643
 wit 842
 ridicule 856
 in - 842
 mere - 643
 no - *existing* 1
 important 642
 practical -
 deception 545
 ridicule 856
 disrespect 929
 take a - 498
joker 844
 cards 840
joking apart
 affirmation 535
 resolution 604
jole 236
jollification
 amusement 840
 intemperance 954
jollity
 amusement 840
 sociality 892
jolly *plump* 192
 marine 269
 gay 836
 flattery 933
 - boat 273
 - fellow 892
jolt *impulse* 276
 agitation 315
jolthead 501
Jonah 649
Jones
 Davy -'s locker 360
 Paul - 792
jonquil 662
jornada 200
jorum 191
Joseph 960
 -'s coat 440
joss, - house 1000
jostle *rush* 276
 jog 315
 clash 713
 (*disagree* 24)
jot *small* 32
 unimportant 643
jotting
 indication 550
 record 551

jounce 315
jour de ma vie 827
journal *annals* 114
 newspaper 531
 record 551
 magazine 593
 narrative 594
 accounts 811
journalism 551
journalist
 recorder 553
 author 593
journey 266
 -'s end 292
journeyman
 artisan 690
 servant 746
joust 720
Jove 979
 sub -
 out of doors 220
 air 338
jovial *gay* 836
 amusement 840
 social 892
Jovinianist 984
jowl 236
joy 827
 give one - 896
 I wish you all the -
  827
 - ambition finds 865
joyful 836
joyless *painful* 830
 sad 837
J. P. 967
Juan, Don - 962
jubbah 225
jube 1000
jubeo, sic volo sic -
  741
jubilant *gay* 836
 rejoicing 838
 boastful 884
jubilee
 anniversary 138
 celebration 883
jucundity 829
Judæus Apella, cre-
 dat -
 disbelief 485
 absurdity 497
Judaism 984
Judas *deceiver* 548
 knave 941
 - kiss
 hypocrisy 544
 base 940
judge *decide* 480
 master 745
 taste 850
 magistrate **967**
Judge *deity* 976
Judgment
 Day of - 67
judgment
 intellect 450
 discrimination 465
 decision 480
 wisdom 498
 condemnation 971

 sentence 972
judgment seat 966
judicata, res-
 certain 474
 judgment 480
judication 480
judicatory 965, 966
judicature 965
Judicature, High
 Court of - 966
judice: coram -
 jurisdiction 965
 lawsuit 969
 me - 481
 sub - *inquiry* 461
 lawsuit 969
judicial 965
 - astrology 511
 - murder 361
 - separation 905
judicious 498
jug 191
juggernath
 kill 361
 god 979
 idolatry 991
juggle *deceive* 545
 cunning 702
juggler 548
jugulate 361
juice 333
juiceless 340
juicy 339
jujube 396
julep 396
jumble *mixture* 41
 confusion 59
 derange 61
jument 271
jump
 sudden change 146
 leap 309
 neglect 460
 at one - 113
 - about 315
 - at *willing* 602
 pursue 622
 hasten 684
 consent 762
 seize 789
 desire 865
 - over 460
 - to a conclusion
 misjudge 481
 credulous 486
 - up 307, 309
jumper 272
junction 43
juncture
 circumstance 8
 junction 43
 period 134
jungle *disorder* 59
 vegetation 367
junior 127
junk 273
 lumber 645
junket *dish* 298
 merrymaking 840
Juno 920
junta 696

K

L

laager 717
labarum 550
labefy 659
label 550
labent 306
labial *lip* 231
 letter 561
labitur et labetur
 perpetuity 112
 continuance 143
labor
 parturition 161
 work 680
 exertion 686
 hard -
 punishment 972
 - Day 840
 - for 620
 - has summit in
  Heaven 686
 - in one's vocation
  625
 - in vain
  fall short 304
  useless 645
 - of love
  willing 602
  amusement 840
  disinterested 942
 - under *state* 7
  disease 655
  difficulty 704
  feeling 821
  affliction 828
 mountain in - 638
laboratory 691
labored
 style 579
 prepared 673
 - study 457
laborer 690
labor hoc opus, hic -
 704
laboring
 - man 690
 - oar 686
laborious
 active 682
 exertion 686
 difficult 704
labor omnia vincit
 686
labyrinth
 disorder 59
 convolution 248
 secret 533
 (*difficulty* 704)
lac *number* 98
 resin 356a
 - of rupees 800
lace *stitch* 43
 netting 219
 ornament 847
 - one's jacket 972
lacerable 328

lacerate 44, 378
 - the heart 830
laches *neglect* 460
 nonobservance 773
lachrymæ, hinc illæ
 - 830
lachrymation 839
lachrymis, quis tem-
 peret a - 914
lachrymose 837
laciniate 256
lack *require* 630
 insufficient 640
 destitute 804
 - faith 989
 - of contrition 951
 - preparation 674
 - wit 501
lackadaisical
 inactive 683
 melancholy 837
 indifferent 866
lackadaisy!
 lament 839
 wonder 870
lackaday 839
lackbrain 499, 501
lacker [*see* lacquer]
lackey 746
lackluster 422, 429
laconic 572
lacquer
 covering 223
 resin 356a
 adorn 847
lacrosse 840
lacteal 352
lactescence 430
lacuna *gap* 198
 pit 252
lacustrine 343
 - *dwelling* 189
lad 129
ladder *ascent* 305
 way 627
 kick down the - 604
lade *load* 184
 transfer 185
 contents 190
 - out 297
laden 52
 heavy - 828
 - with 777
lading *contents* 190
 property 780
 bill of - *list* 86
ladino 41, 271
ladle
 receptacle 191
 transfer 270
 vehicle 272
lady *woman* 374
 rank 875
 wife 903
 - help 746

 -'s maid 746
 lovely - gar m e n t ed
  374
Lady day 138
ladylike
 womanly 374
 fashionable 852
 (*courteous* 894)
ladylove 897
lætificant 829
lag *linger* 275
 follow 281
 dawdle 683
lager-beer 298
laggard
 unwilling 603
 inactive 683
lagoon 343
lagniappe 784
laical 997
laid: - by the heels 751
 - low 160
 - on one's back 158
 - up 655
lair *den* 189
 sty 653
laird *master* 745
 proprietor 779
 nobility 875
Lais 962
laisse manger, cela
 se - 394
laisser: - aller, - faire
 neglect 460
 inaction 681
 laxity 738
 freedom 748
 inexcitable 826
laity 997
lake *water* 343
 pink 434
 - *dwelling* 189
 - of fire and brim-
  stone 982
Lama *ruler* 745
 prince 996
Lamarckism 357
lamb *infant* 129
 animal 366
 gentle 826
 innocent 946
 go out like a - 174
 lion lies down with -
  721
lamba-chauki 215
lambaste 972
lambent
 touching 379
 - flame *heat* 382
 light 420
Lambeth 1000
Lamb of God 976
lame *incomplete* 53
 impotent 158
 weak 160

 imperfect 651
 disease 655
 injury 659
 failing 732
 (*bad* 649)
 (*lax* 738)
 help a - dog over a
  stile *aid* 707
 vindicate 937
 - conclusion
  illogical 477
  failure 732
 - duck 808
 - excuse 617
 O most - conclusion
  480
lamellar 204
lamentable *bad* 649
 painful 830
 sad 837
lamentably *very* 31
lamentation 839
 (*regret* 833)
lamia *demon* 980
 sorcerer 994
lamina *part* 51
 layer 204
Lammas 998
lamp 423
 rub the - 992
 safety - 666
 smell of the -
  style 577
  prepared 673
lamplighter
 quick 682
lampoon
 censure 932
 detraction 934
lampooner 936
lanâ caprinâ, de -
 643
lanate 255, 256
lance *pierce* 260
 throw 284
 spear 727
 break a - with
  attack 716
  warfare 722
 couch one's - 720
 - corporal 745
lanceolate 253
lancer 726
lancet *sharp* 253
 piercer 262
lanciform 253
lancinate
 bodily pain 378
 mental pain 830
land
 arrive 292
 ground 342
 estate 780
 how the - lies
  circumstance 8

experiment 463
foresight 510
hug the - 286
in the - of the living
  359
- covered with water
  343
- flowing with milk
  and honey 168
make the - 286
on - 342
see - 858
landamman 745
landau 272
landed
  property 780
  - gentry 779
  - estate 780
landgrave 745
landholder 779
landingplace
  stage 215
  arrive 292
landlady 779
landlocked 229
landloper 268
landlord 779
landlubber 701
landmark
  limit 233
  indication 550
landreeve 694
landscape
  prospect 448
  - gardening
  agriculture 371
  beauty 845
  - painter 559
  - painting 556
landshark 792
landslip 306
landsman 342
Landsturm 726
landsurveying 466
Landwehr 726
lane *street* 189
  way 627
langrage shot 727
langrel 727
langsyne 122
language 560
  command of - 582
  strong -
   vigor 574
   malediction 908
languid *weak* 160
  inert 172
  slow 275
  - *style* 575
  inactive 683
  torpid 823
languish
  decrease 36
  ill 655'
  inactive 683
  repine 828
  - for 865
languishing 160
languishment
  lament 839
languor

[*see* languid]
laniate 162 •
lanky *thin* 203
  tall 206
lantern
  window 260
  lamp 423
  - jaws 203
  - of Diogenes 461
  magic - 448
lanterne, à la - 972
lanuginous 256
Laocoön 557
lap *abode* 189
  support 215
  interior 221
  wrap 225
  encompass 227, 229
  drink 298
  - of luxury
  pleasure 377
  inactivity 683
  voluptuousness 954
lapdog *animal* 366
  servile 886
lapel 258
lapidate *kill* 361
  attack 716
  punish 972
lapidescence 323
lapis lazuli
  blue 438
  jewel 847
lappet 39
lapse *course* 109
  past 122
  conversion 144
  fall 306
  degeneracy 659
  relapse 661
  loss 776
  vice 945
  guilt 947
  - of memory 506
  - of time 109
lapsus linguæ
  mistake 495
  solecism 568
  stammering 583
Laputa, college of -
  538
larboard 239
larceny 791
lard 356
lardaceous 355
larder 636
  contents of the - 298
lares et penates
  - *home* 189
  idols 991
large *quantity* 31
  size 192
  at - *diffuse* 573
  free 748
  become - 194
  - number 102
  - type 642
large-hearted
  liberal 816
  benevolent 906
  disinterested 942

larger 194
largess 785
largest 784
largest portion 192
larghetto
  slow 275
  music 415
largiloquent
  verbose 573
  loquacious 584
largo *slow* 275
  music 415
lariat 45
larigo 45
lark *ascent* 305
  spree 840
  with the -
  morning 125
larmes
  fondre en - 839
  - aux yeux 839
larmoyante, comé-
  die - 599
larrigan 225
larrikin 887, 913
larrup 972
larum *loud* 404
  alarm 669
larva 129
larynx 351
lasciate ogni spe-
  ranza 859
lascivious 961
lash *tie together* 43
  violence 173
  incite 615
  censure 932
  punish 972
  scourge 975
  - into fury 900
  - the waves 645
  under the - *compelled*
  744
  subject 749
lass *girl* 129
  (*woman* 374)
lassitude
  fatigue 688
  weariness 841
lasso *tie* 45
  loop 247
last
  abide 1
  model 22
  - *in order* 67
  endure 106
  durable 110
  - *in time* 122
  continue 141
  at - 133
  at the - *extremity* 665
  breathe one's - 360
  die in the - ditch 604a
  game to the - 604a
  go to one's - home 360
  - but one &c. 67
  - finish 729
  - for ever 112
  - gasp 360
  - resort 666
  - shift 601

  - sleep 360
  - stage 67
  - straw 153
  - stroke 729
  - touch 729
  - word
   affirmation 535
   obstinacy 606
  - year &c. 122
  never hear the - of
  104
  on - legs *weak* 160
   dying 360
   spoiled 659
   adversity 735
latch *fasten* 43
  fastening 45
latchet 45
latchkey 631
latchstring
  find the - out 892
  have the - out 888
late *past* 122
  new 123
  tardy 133
  dead 360
  too - 135
lately *formerly* 122
  recently 123
latency 526
lateness 133
latent *inert* 172
  concealed 526
later 117
laterality 236
lateritious 434
latet anguis in herbâ
  667
lateward 132
lath 205
  thin as a - 203
lathe *region* 181
  machine 633
lather
  lubrication 332
  bubble 353
lathi 215
latifoliate 202
Latin
  au bout de son - 704
  lash'd into - 539
  perdre son - 704
  small - and less Greek
  491
  thieves' - 563
latitancy 528
latitat 969
latitude *extent* 180
  region 181
  breadth 202
  measurement 466
  freedom 748
  - and longitude
  situation 183
latitudinarian
  heterodox 984
  irreligious 989
latration 412
latria 990
latrines 653
latrocinium 791

latrociny 791
latter *sequent* 63
  past 122
Latter-day Saint 984
latterly 123
lattice *crossing* 219
  opening 260
laud *praise* 931
  worship 990
laudable 944
laudanum 174
laudari à laudato
  viro 931
laudator 935
 - *temporis acti*
  past 122
  habit 613
  discontent 832
  detractor 936
laudatory 931
laugh 838
 - *at ridicule* 856
  sneer 929
  (*undervalue* 483)
 - in one's sleeve
  latent 526
  ridicule 856
  disrespect 929
  contempt 930
 - on the wrong side of
  one's mouth
  disappointed 509
  dejected 837
  in disrepute 874
 - to scorn *defy* 715
  despise 930
make one - 853
raise a - 840
laughable 853
laughing
 - gas 376
no - matter 642
laughingstock 857
laughter [*see* laugh]
 - holding both his
  sides 838
laughter-loving 836
launch *begin* 66
 boat 273
 propel 284
 - forth 676
 - into 676
 - into eternity 360,
  361
 - out 573
 - out against 716
laundress
 washerwoman 652
 servant 746
laundry *room* 191
 heat 386
 clean 652
laundryman 652
laureate 875
 poet - 597
laurel-*trophy* 733
 glory 873
 decoration 877
 (*reward* 973)
repose on one's -s 265
lava *excretion* 299

semiliquid 352
lavage 300
lavatory 652
lave *water* 337
 clean 652
lavement 300
lavender
 color 437
laver la tête 932
lavish *profuse* 641
 give 784
 squander 818
 - of praise 931
law *regularity* 80
 statute 697
 permission 760
 legality 963
 court of - 966
 give the - 737
 go to - 969
 Jewish - 985
 - of the Medes and
  Persians 80
 lay down the -
  certainty 474
  affirm 535
  command 741
 learned in the - 968
 set the - at defiance
  964
 so many -s 947
 take the - into one's
  own hands
  war 722
  disobedience 742
 take the - of 969
lawful
 permitted 760
 due 924
 legal 963
lawgiver
 director 694
 (*master* 745)
lawless
 irregular 83
 mutinous 742
 nonobservant 773
 vicious 945
 arbitrary 964
lawn *plain* 344
 agriculture 371
 - sleeves 999
 - tennis 840
lawsuit 969
lawyer 968
lax *incoherent* 47
 soft 324
 error 495
 - *style* 575
 remiss 738
 nonobservance 773
 dishonorable 940
 licentious 945
 irreligious 989
laxative 652
 remedial 662
laxity 738
lay *moderate* 174
 place 184
 ley 344
 music 415

poetry 597
bet 621
secular 997
- about one
active 682
exertion 686
attack 716
contend 720
punish 972
- apart
exclude 55
relinquish 782
- aside
neglect 460
reject 610
disuse 678
give up 782
- at one's feet 763
- at the door of
  155
- bare 529
- before 527
- brother 996
- by *store* 636
sickness 655
disuse 678
- claim to 924
- down [*see* below]
- eggs 161
- figure *model* 22
representation 554
- hands on
use 677
take 789
rite 998
- heads together
advise 695
coöperate 709
- in *eat* 298
store 636
provide 637
- in ruins 162
- in the dust 162
- it on thick
cover 223
too much 641
flatter 933
- on 972
- one's account for
  484
- oneself open to 177
- oneself out for 673
- one's finger upon
  480a
- one's head on the
  block 942
- open *divest* 226
opening 260
show 525
disclose 529
- out
horizontal 213
- *corpse* 363
plan 626
expend 809
- over 133
- siege to 716
- stress on 642
- the axe at the root
  of tree 162
- the first stone 66

- the flattering unc-
  tion to one's soul
content 831
relief 834
- the foundations
originate 153
prepare 673
- to *attribute* 155
rest 265
- together 43
- to one's charge 938
- train 626
- under hatches 751
- under restraint 751
- up *store* 636
sickness 655
disuse 678
- waste 162
lay down *locate* 184
 horizontal 213
 assert 535
 renounce 757
 relinquish 782
 pay 807
 - a plan 626
 - one's arms
  pacification 723
  submission 725
 - one's life 360
 - the law
  certain 474
  assert 535
  command 741
  insolence 885
layer 204
layette 225
layman 997
laystall 653
lazar house 662
lazy
 inactive 683
 (slow 275)
lazzarone 683
lb 319
lea *land* 342
 plain 344
lead
 supremacy 33
 in order 62
 tend 176
 soundings 208
 - in motion 280
 heavy 319
 induce 615
 direct 693
 authority 737
heave the - 466
- a dance
run away 623
circuit 629
difficulty 704
disrespect 929
- a life 692
- astray 495
- by the nose 737
- captive
subject 749
restraint 751
- on 693
- one to expect 511
- the choir 990

- the dance 280
-- the way
  precedence 62
  begin 66
  precession 280
  importance 642
  direction 693
  repute 873
- to no end 645
- to the altar 903
red - 434
take the -
  influence 175
  importance 642
  authority 737
leaden *dim* 422
  colorless 429
  gray 432
  inactive 683
leader
  precursor 64
  dissertation 595
  director 694
  counsel 968
leading
  beginning 66
  important 642
- article 595
- note *music* 413
- part 175
- question 461
- strings
  childhood **127**
  child 129
  pupil 541
  subject 749
  restraint 751, **752**
leads 223
leaf *part* 51
  layer 204
  plant 367
- *of a book* 593
turn over a new - 658
leafless 226
leafy 256
league *length* 200
  coöperation 709
  party 712
leak *crack* 198
  dribble 295
  waste 638
- out
  disclosure 529
spring a -
  injury 659
leaky
  imperfect 651
lean *thin* 203
  oblique 217
- on 215
- to *shed* 191
  willing 602
- towards
  favor 923
- upon *belief* **484**
  subjection 749
  hope 858
leaning
  tendency 176
  willingness 602
  desire 865

friendship 888
favoritism 923
lean-witted 499
leap
  sudden change 146
  ascent 305
  jump **309**
- in the dark
  experiment 463
  uncertain 475
  chance 621
  rash 863
- with joy 838
make a - at 622
leapfrog 840
**leaps and bounds,
  by -** 274
leap year 138
learn 539
- by experience 950
- by heart 505
learned 490
- man 492
learner 541
learning
  knowledge 490
  acquisition of - **539**
lease *property* 780
  lending 787
  grant a - 771
- and release 783
take a new - of life
  654
leash *tie* 43
  three 92
hold in - 751
leasehold 780
least
- *in quantity* 34
- *in size* 193
at the - 32
leather *skin* 223
  tough 327
  beat 972
- or prunello 643
nothing like - 481
leave *remainder* 40
  part company 44
  relinquish 624
  permission 760
  bequeathe 784
French - 623
give me - to say 535
- ad referendum 605
- alone
  inaction 681
  freedom 748
  permit 760
- a loophole 705
- an inference 526
- a place 293
- in the lurch
  pass 303
  decisive 545
- it to one 760
- no trace
  disappear 449
  obliterate 552
- off *cease* 142
  desuetude 614
  relinquish 624

disuse 678
- out 55
- out of one's calcula-
  tion 460
- the beaten track 83
- to chance 621
- to oneself 748
- undecided 609a
- undone 730
- void *regret* 833
- word 527
live in hearts we -
  behind 505
take - *depart* 293
  freedom 748
leaven
  component 56
  cause 153
  lighten 320
  qualify 469
  unclean 653
  deterioration 659
  bane 663
leavings
  remainder 40
  useless 645
lecher 962
lechery 961
lectern 1000
lection *special* 79
  interpretation 522
lectionary 998
lecture *teach* 537
  speak 582
  dissertation 595
  censure 932
  sermon 998
- room 542
lecturer
  teacher 540
  preacher 996
lectureship 542
led - captain
  follower 746
  servile 886
  favorite 899
- by the nose 749
ledge *height* 206
  horizontal 213
  shelf 215
  projection 250
ledger *list* 86
  record 551
  accounts 811
lee *front* 234
  side 236
leech *remedy* 662
  physician 695
Lee Enfield rifle 727
leef 829
leek
  eat the - *recant* 607
  submit 725
Lee-Metford rifle 727
leer *stare* 441
  dumb show 550
leery 702
lees 653
lee shore
  danger 665, 667
leet, court - 966

lee wall 666
leeward 236
leeway *tardy* 133
  navigation 267
  progression 282
  shortcoming 304
left *residuary* 40
  sinistral 239
- alone 748
- bower 840
- in the lurch 732
- to shift for oneself
  893
over the - 545
pay over the - shoul-
  der 808
left-handed
  clumsy 699
- compliment 932
- marriage 903
leg *support* 215
  walker 266
  thief 792
best - foremost 686
fast as -s will carry
  274
keep on one's -s 654
last -s *spoiled* 659
  fatigue 688
- bail 623
light on one's -s 734
make a - 894
not a - to stand on
  illogical 477
  confuted 479
  failure 732
off one's -s
  propulsion 284
on one's -s
  upright 212
  elevation 307
  speaking 582
  in health 654
  active 682
  free 748
set on one's -s 660
legacy *property* 780
  gift 784
legadero 45
legal *permitted* 760
  legitimate 924
  relating to law **963**
- adviser 968
- estate 780
- pledge 535
legality 963
legate 534
legatee
  possessor 779
  receiver 785
legation 755
legato 415
legend *record* 551
  description 594
legendary
  imaginary 515
legerdemain
  change 146
  trick 545
  (*cunning* 702)
légèreté 605

liar 548
libadist 984
libation
  potation 298
  drunkenness 959
  worship 990
libel *detraction* 934
  accusation 938
libeler 936
liberal *ample* 639
  generous 816
  disinterested 942
  - education
  knowledge 490
  teaching 537
  over - 818
liberalism
  freedom 748
liberality
  giving 784
  generosity **816**
Liberals 712
liberation 750
  (*disjunction* 44)
liberavi animam
  meam 703
libertinage 961
libertine 962
libertinism 961
liberty *freedom* 748
  permission 760
  right 924
  exemption 927a
  gain one's - 750
  set at - *free* 750
  exempt 927a
  take a -
  arrogate 739
  make free 748
  insolence 885
  discourtesy 895
liberum arbitrium
  600
libidinous 961
libitum, ad -
  at will 600
  enough 639
  freely 748
librarian 593
library *room* 191
  books 593
librate 314
libretto *book* 593
  opera 599
license *laxity* 738
  permission 760
  right 924
  exemption 927a
  - to plunder 791
licentiate 492
licentia vatum 597
licentious *lax* 738
  dissolute 954
  debauched 961
lichen 367
lich gate 363
licit *permitted* 760
  due 924
lick *lap* 298
  conquer 731
  punish 972

500

- into shape 240
- the dust 933
lickerish
  savory 394
  desirous 865
  fastidious 868
  licentious 961
lickpenny 819
lick-spittle
  servile 886
  (*flatterer* 935)
licorice 396
lictor 965
lid 223
lie *situation* 183
  presence 186
  recline 213
  falsehood 544
  untruth 546
  awkward at a - 544
  give the - to 536
  - at one's door 926
  - at the root of 153
  - by 681
  - down *flat* 213
  rest 687
  - fallow 674
  - hid 528
  - in *be* 1
  give birth 161
  - in ambush 528
  - in a nutshell 32
  - in one's power 157
  - in wait for
  expect 507
  inaction 681
  - on 215
  - over *defer* 133
  destiny 152
  - still 265
  - to
  quiescence 265
  inaction 681
  - under 177
  - under a necessity
  601
  white - 617
liedertafel 416
lief *pleasant* 829
  as - *willing* 602
  choice 609
liege 745
liegeman 746
lien *security* 771
  credit 805
lienteria 653
lieu 182
  in - of 147
lieutenant
  officer 745
  deputy 759
  lord - 965
life *events* 151
  vitality **359**
  biography 594
  activity 682
  conduct 692
  cheerful 836
  animal - 364
  battle of - 682
  come to - 660

infuse - into
  excite 824
learnt - from the
  poets 597
- and spirit 682
- beyond the grave
  152
- or death
  need 630
  important 642
  contention 720
- to come 152
put - into 359
recall to - 660
see - 840
support - 359
take away - 361
tenant for - 779
Life, the 976
lifeblood
  intrinsic 5
  vital 359
lifeboat *boat* 273
  safety 666
life-giving 168
life guards 726
lifeless *inert* 172
  dead 360
lifelike 17
lifelong 110
life-preserver 727
life-size 192
lifetime 108
life-weary 841
lift *raise* 307
  aid 707
- a finger 680
- cattle 791
- hand against 716
- one's head 734
- the mask 529
- the voice
  shout 411
  speak 582
- up the eyes 441
- up the heart 990
lift smoke 840
ligament 45
ligation 43
ligature 45
light
  state 7
  small 32
  window 260
  velocity 274
  arrive 292
  descend 306
  levity 320
  kindle 384
  match 388
  luminosity **420**
  luminary 423
  - *in color* 429
  white 430
  aspect 448
  knowledge 490
  interpretation 522
  unimportant 643
  easy 705
  gay 836
  loose 961

a - breaks in upon
  one 529
blue - *signal* 550
bring to -
  discover 480a
  manifest 525
  disclose 529
children of - 987
come to - 529
false -s 443
foot -s 599
half - 422
in one's own - 699
- and shade 420
- comedy 599
- fantastic toe 309
- heart 836
- horse 726
- infantry 726
- mingled with the
  gloom 30
- of heel 274
- of truth 543
- purse 804
- under a bushel
  hide 528
  not hide 878
  modesty 881
- up *illumine* 420
  excite 824
  cheer 836
- upon one's feet 664
- upon *chance* 156
  arrive at 292
  discover 480a
  acquire 775
make - of
  underrate 483
  easy 705
  inexcitable 826
  despise 930
obstruct the - 426
see the - *life* 359
  publication 531
throw - upon 522
transmit - 425
lighten
  make light 320
  illume 420
  facilitate 705
lighter *boat* 273
lighterman 269
light-fingered 791,
  792
light-footed
  fleet 274
  active 682
light-headed 503
lighthouse 550
lightless 421
light-minded 605
lightning
  velocity 274
  flash 420
  spark 423
brief as the - 421
- express 272
Light of the World
  976
lightsome
  luminous 420

letter 561
word 562
- meaning 516
- translation 522
literarum
  homo multarum - 492
  homo trium - 792
literary 560
- hack 593
- man 492
- power 569
literati 492
literatim [see literal]
literature
  learning 490
  language 560
lithagogue 662
lithe 324
lithic 323
lithograph 558
lithoidal 358
lithology 358
lithomancy 511
lithotint 558
litigant
  litigious 713
  combatant 726
  accusation 938
litigation
  quarrel 713
  contention 730
  lawsuit 969
litigious 713
litter *disorder* 59
  derange 61
  multitude 102
  brood 167
  support 215
  vehicle 272
  useless 645
littéraire, la morgue
  - 569
littera scripta manet
  150
littérateur
  scholar 492
  author 593
little
  - *in degree* 32
  - *in size* 193
  darling 897
  mean 940
  cost - 815
  do - 683
  - by little
    degree 26
    slowly 275
  - did one think 508
  - one 129
  make - of 483
  signify - 643
  think - of 458
  to - purpose
    useless 645
    failure 732
littleness 193
littoral 342
liturgy 998
live *exist* 1
  continue 141
  dwell 186

life 359
  glowing 382
  activity 682
  repute 873
- and let live
  inaction 681
  freedom 748
  inexcitability 826
- by one's wits 545
- circuit 157
- from hand to mouth
  674
- hard 954
- in hope 858
- in the memory 505
- man 682
- matter 591
- on 298
- rail 157
- to explain 485
- to fight again 110
- upon nothing 819
we - in deeds 680
livelihood 803
livelong 110
lively *keen* 375
- *style* 574
  active 682
  acute 821
  sensitive 822
  sprightly 836
- *imagination* 515
- *pace* 274
liver
  hard - 954*a*
  white - 862
liver-colored 433
livery *suit* 225
  color 428
  badge 550
  decoration 877
- *servant* 746
liveryman 748
livid *dark* 431
  gray 432
  purple 437
living *life* 359
  business 625
  benefice 995
  good - 957
- *beings* 357
- *soul* 372
- *thing* 366
livraison 593
livret 593
lixiviate 652
lixivium 335
llama 271
llano 344
Lloyd's register 86
lo! *attention* 457
  wonder 870
load *quantity* 31
  fill 52
  lade 184
  cargo 190
  weight 319
  store 636
  redundance 641
  hindrance 706
  adversity 735

anxiety 828
  oppress 830
- the memory 505
- with 607
- with reproaches 932
prime and - 673
take off a - of care 834
loadstar
  attraction 288
  indication 550
  direction 693
loadstone
  attraction 288
  motive 615
loaf *mass* 192
  dawdle 683
loafer *stroller* 268
  inactive 683
  bad man 949
loam 342
loan 787
loath 603
loathe *dislike* 867
  hate 898
loathing
  [see loathe]
  weariness 841
loathsome
  unsavory 395
  painful 830
  dislike 867
loaves and fishes
  prosperity 734
  acquisition 775
  wealth 803
lobby *chamber* 191
  way 627
lobbyism 615
lobe 51
lobiform 245
Lob's pound, in - 751
local 183
- board 696
- habitation
  location 184
  abode 189
locale 183
locality 182, 183
localize 184
location 184
loch 343
Lochaber axe 727
loci, genius - 664
lock *fasten* 43
  fastening 45
  tuft 256
  canal 350
  hindrance 706
  prison 752
dead - 265
in the - up 938
- hospital 662
- out 719
- stock and barrel 50
- the stable door
  too late 135
  useless 645
  unskillful 699
- up *hide* 528
  imprison 751
- weir 350

under - and key
  safe 664
  restraint 751
  prisoner 754
locker 191
locket 847
lockjaw 655
locksmith 690
lockup *prison* 752
loco, in -
  agreeing 23
  situation 183
  expedience 646
locofoco 388
locomotion 264
- by air 267
- by land 266
- by water 267
locomotive
  travel 266
  carriage 271
locos y ninos 450
locular 191
locum tenens
  substitute 147
  inhabitant 188
  deputy 759
locus
- *pœnitentiæ* 937
- *standi*
  support 215
  plea 617
  social rank 873
locust *prodigal* 818
  evil doer 913
  swarm like -s 102
locution 582
lode 636
lodestar, &c.
  [see loadstar &c.]
lodge *place* 184
  presence 186
  dwelling 189
- a complaint 938
lodgement 184
lodger
  inhabitant 188
  possessor 779
lodging 189
loft *garret* 191
  top 210
lofty *high* 206
- *style* 574
  proud 878
  insolent 885
  magnanimous 942
log *velocity* 274
  fuel 388
  record 551
- canoe 273
- house 189
heave the - 466
sleep like a - 683
logan 314
logarithm 84
loggerhead 501
at -s *discord* 713
  contention 720
  hate 898
logic 476
- of facts 467

logician 476
logography 590
logogriph 533
logomachy
 discussion 476
 words 588
 dispute 720
logometer 85
logometric 84
Logos 976
logotype 591
logrolling 709
logy 843
loin *back* 235
 side 236
 gird up one's -s
 strong 159
 prepare 673
loisir, impromptu
 fait à - 673
loiter *tardy* 133
 slow 275
 inactive 683
 (*temporize* 110)
Loki 980
loll *sprawl* 213
 recline 215
 inactive 683
lollipop 396
lollop 683
lolly 383
loma 206
Lombard Street to a
 China orange 472
lone 87
lonesome 893
long
 - *in time* 110
 - *in space* 200
 diffuse 573
 draw the - *bow* 549
 go to one's - account
  360
 - ago 122
 - and the short
 whole 50
 concise 572
 - bit 800
 - boat 273
 - clothes 129
 - drawn out 573
 - duration 110
 - expected 507
 - face
 discontent 832
 dejection 837
 - for 865
 - headed *wise* 498
 - life to *glory* 873
 approval 931
 - lived 110
 - odds *chance* 156
 improbability 473
 difficulty 704
 - pending 110
 - pull and strong pull
  285
 - range 196
 - robe 968
 - run *average* 29
 whole 50

destiny 152
- sea 348
- sighted
 dim-sighted 443
 wise 498
 foresight 518
- since 122
- spun 573
- standing
 diuturnal 110
 old 124
- suffering
 lenity 740
 inexcitable 826
 pity 914
 - time 110
- winded 573
make a - arm
 exertion 686
 seize 789
take a - breath
 refreshment 689
 relief 834
longanimity
 inexcitable 826
 forgiving 918
long chair 215
longevity
 diuturnal 110
 age 128
long head
 wise man 500
longing 865
- lingering look be-
 hind 833
nor cast one - look
 behind 831
longinquity 196
longitude
 situation 183
 length 200
 measurement 466
longitudinal 200
longo intervallo
 discontinuity 70
 diuturnity 110
 distance 196
 interval 198
longshoreman
 waterman 269
 plebeian 876
longways 217
loo 840
looby *fool* 501
 bungler 701
 clown 876
look
 small degree 32
 see 441
 appearance 448
 attend to 457
 - about
 take care 459
 seek 461
 - after *care* 459
 direction 693
 - ahead 510
 - another way 442
 - back 122
 - before one leaps 864
 - beyond 510

- black *or* blue
 feeling 821
 discontent 832
 dejection 837
- down upon 930
- foolish 874
- for *seek* 461
 expect 507
- forwards
 future 121
 foresight 510
- here 457
- in the face
 sincerity 703
 courage 861
 pride 878
- in thy heart and
 write 593
- into
 attend to 457
 inquire 461
- like
 similarity 17
 appearance 448
 - on 186
- out *view* 448
 care 459
 seek 461
 expect 507
 intention 620
 business 625
- over *examine* 461
- round *seek* 461
- sharp 682
- through
 seek 461
- to *care* 459
 duty 926
- up *prosper* 734
 high price 814
 hope 858
 visit 892
- upon as
 adjudge 480
 believe 484
- up to *repute* 873
 respect 928
 approbation 931
looker-on 444
looking
- before and after 441,
 673
- forward to 507
looking-glass 445
lookout 668
loom *destiny* 152
 dim 422
 dim sight 443
 come in sight 446
 weave 691
- of the land 342
loon *fool* 501
 clown 876
 rascal 949
loop *curve* 245
 circle 247
 circuit 629
loophole
 opening 260
 vista 441
 plea 617

device 626
 escape 671
 fortification 717
loose
 detach 44
 incoherent 47
 pendent 214
 desultory 279
 illogical 477
 vague 519
 - *style* 575
 lax 738
 free 748
 liberate 750
 debauched 961
 at a - end 685
 give a - to
 - *imagination* 515
 laxity 738
 permit 760
 indulgence 954
 let - 750
 - character 961
 - fish *bad man* 949
 libertine 962
 - morals 945
 - rein 738
 - suggestion 514
 - thread 495
 leave a - 460
 take up a - 664
 on the - 961
 screw - 713
loosen
 make loose 47
 let loose 750
looseness 573
loot *steal* 791
 booty 793
lop 201
 - and top 371
lopped
 incomplete 53
lopper 321
lop-sided 28
loquacity 584
loquendi
 cacoëthes - 584
 jus et norma - 567
 usus - 582
lorcha 273
Lord, lord
 ruler 745
 nobleman 875
 God 976
 - Chancellor 967
 - it over
 authority 737
 insolence 885
 - Justices 966, 967
 - lieutenant 965
 - of Lords 976
 - of the creation 372
 - of the manor 779
 - of thy presence 745
 -'s day 687
 -'s prayer 990
 -'s supper 998
 -'s table 1000
 O - *worship* 990
 the - knows 491

lordling 875
lordly *repute* 873
   pride 878
Lord Mayor 745
  -'s show 883
lordship
  authority 737
  property 780
  title 877
  judge 967
lore 490, 539
lorette 962
Lorettine 996
lorgnette 445
loricated
  clothed 223
lorication
  armor 717
lorn 893
lorry 272
lose
  forget 506
  unintelligible 519
  fail 732
  loss 776
  - an opportunity 135
  - breath 688
  - caste
  disrepute 874
  dishonor 940
  - color 429
  - flesh 195
  - ground
  slow 275
  regression 283
  shortcoming 304
  - heart 837
  - hope 859
  - labor 732
  - no time
  active 682
  haste 684
  - one's balance 732
  - one's cunning 699
  - one's head
  bewildered 475
  - one's heart 897
  - one's life 360
  - oneself
  uncertain 475
  - one's reason 503
  - one's temper 900
  - one's way
  - sight of
  blind 442
  disappear 449
  neglect 460
  oblivion 506
  not complete 730
  - the clew
  uncertain 475
  unintelligible 519
  - the day 732
  - time 683
  wander 279
  unskillful 699
  difficulty 704
  no time to - 684
losel 818
losing game
  failure 732

misfortune 735
loss
  decrement 40a
  death 360
  evil 619
  deterioration 659
  privation **776**
  at a -
  uncertain 475
  at a - for
  desiring 865
  - of fortune 804
  -of health 655
  - of life 360
  - of right 925
  - of strength 160
lost
  nonexisting 2
  absent 187
  invisible 449
  abstracted 458
  uncertain 475
  failure 732
  loss 776
  over-excited 824
  pain 828
  dejection 837
  impenitent 951
  - in admiration 931
  - in astonishment 870
  - in iniquity 945
  - in thought 458
  - labor 645
  - to shame
  insolent 885
  improbity 940
  bad man 949
  - to sight 449
  - to view 449
  - to virtue 945
lot
  state 7
  quantity 25
  group 72
  multitude 102
  necessity 601
  chance 621
  sufficient 639
  allotment 786
  be one's - 151
  cast in one's - with
  choose 609
  coöperate 709
  cast -s 621
  fall to one's - 156
  in -s 51
  where one's - is cast
   189
lota 191
loth *unwilling* 603
  dislike 867
Lothario *lover* 897
  libertine 962
lotion *liquid* 337
  clean 652
  remedy 662
loto 840
lotto 840
lottery *chance* 156
  cards 840
  put into a - 621

lotus-eater 683
loudness 404
lough 343
lounge
  chamber 191
  inactive 683
  (*quiet* 275)
loup
  hurler avec les -s 714
  - garou 980
louse 653
lout *fool* 501
  clown 876
louvre 351
lovable 897
love
  desire 865
  courtesy 894
  affection **897**
  favorite 899
  abode of - 897
  God's - 906
  labor of -
  willing 602
  inexpensive 815
  amusement 840
  disinterested 942
  - affair 897
  - all trust a few 864
  - of country 910
  make - 902
  no - lost 713
  not for - or money
  scarce 640
  dear 814
love knot *token* 550
lovelock 256
lovelorn 898
lovely
  beautiful 845
  lovable 897
love making 902
love pot 959
lover [*see love*]
love-sick 897, 902
love story 897, 902
love token 897, 902
loving cup
  social 892
  courteous 894
loving-kindness 906
low
  small 32
  not high 207
  - sound 405
  moo 412
  vulgar 851
  disreputable 874
  common 876
  at a - ebb
  small 32
  inferior 34
  depressed 308
  waste 638
  deteriorated 659
  bring - 308
  - comedy 599
  - condition 876
  - fellow 876
  - life 851
  - note 408

- origin 876
- price 815
- spirits 837
- tide 207
- tone *black* 431
  mutter 581
- water *low* 207
  dry 340
  insufficient 640
  poor 804
lowborn 876
lower
  inferior 34
  decrease 36
  depress 308
  dark 421
  dim 422
  predict 511
  sad 837
  irate 900
  sulky 901a
  - case 591
  - one's flag 725
  - one's note 879
  - orders 876
  - quality 34
lowlands 207
lowly 879
low-minded
  vulgar 876
  base 940
lown *fool* 501
  knave 949
lowness [*see low*] 207
  humility 879
loy 272
loyal *obedient* 743
  observant 772
  honorable 939
loyauté
  - m'oblige 926
  - n'a honte 939
lozenge 244
L. s. d. 800
lubbard [*see lubber*]
lubber *slow* 683
  bungler 701
lubberly *huge* 192
  awkward 699
lubrication
  smooth 255
  oil **332**
lubricity
  slippery 255
  unctuous 355
  impure 961
lubricous 332
lucent 420
lucid
  luminous 420
  transparent 425
  intelligible 518
  rational 502
  - style 570
- interval 502
lucidus ordo 58
lucifer 388
Lucifer 423, 978
lucimeter 445
luck *chance* 156, 621
  prosperity 734

M

main part 31, 50
mainpernor 771
mainspring
  cause 153
  instrument 633
  (*motive* 615)
mainstay
  support 215
  refuge 666
  hope 858
maintain
  permanence 141
  continue 143
  sustain 170
  support 215
  assert 535
  preserve 670
  - one's course
  persevere 604a
  - one's ground 717
  - the even tenor of
    one's way 623
maintenance
  [*see* maintain]
  wealth 803
maintien 692
maison de santé 662
maître: coup de -
  goodness 648
  skill 698
  l'œil de - 459
majesté, lèse - 742
majestic
  grand 31
  glorious 873
  stately 882
majesty *king* 745
  rank 873
  deity 976
major *greater* 33
  officer 745
  - domo
  director 694
  retainer 746
  - general 745
  - key 413
  - part *great* 31
  all 50
majority
  superiority 33
  plurality 100
  multitude 102
  age 131
  join the - 360
majusculæ 561
make
  constitute 54, 56
  render 144
  produce 161
  form 240
  arrive at 292
  complete 729
  compel 744
  - acquainted with
  inform 527
  learn 539
  - after 622
  - a fuss
  importance 642
  activity 682
  - a go of it 731

- a piece of work 832
- a present 784
- a push 682
- a requisition
  demand 741
  ask for 765
- a speech 582
- a splurge 882
- away with
  destroy 162
  kill 361
- a wry face 867
- believe 544, 545, 546
- choice of 609
- fast 43
- for 278
- fun of *wit* 842
  ridicule 856
- good
  compensation 30
  complete 52, 729
  establish 150
  evidence 467
  demonstrate 478
  provide 637
  restore 660
- haste 684
- hay while the sun
    shines 134
- interest 765
- its appearance 446
- known 527
- light of
  underestimate 483
  easy 705
- money 775
- much of
  exaggerate 549
  importance 642
- no doubt 484
- no secret of 525
- no sign
  latent 526
  hidden 528
- nothing of
  unintelligible 519
  not wonder 871
- of 902
- off
  run away 623
  escape 671
- off with 791
- oneself master of
    539
- one's escape 671
- one's fortune 734
- one's way
  go on 302
  prosper 734
- one's word 772
- out *see* 441
  evidence 467
  demonstrate 478
  discover 480a
  know 490
  intelligible 518
  interpret 522
  due 924
- over
  transfer 783
  give 784

- peace 723, 724
- public 531
- ready 673
- sure *stable* 150
  prepare 673
- terms 769
- the best of 725
- the land 292
- things pleasant 702
- time 110
- towards 278
- up [*see below*]
- use of 677, 788
- way
  progress 282
  (*improve* 658)
- way for
  substitution 147
  avoid 623
maker *artificer* 690
  (*producer* 164)
Maker, the - 976
makeshift
  substitute 147
  excuse 617
make up
  complete 52
  compose 54
  printing 591
- accounts 811
- a quarrel 723
- a sum 809
- for 30
- matters 952
- one's mind
  judgment 480
  belief 484
  resolve 604
- to *approach* 286
  address 586
makeweight
  inequality 28
  compensation 30
  completeness 52
making of, be the -
  utility 644
  goodness 648
  aid 707
malachite 435
malacology 368
malade imaginaire
    837
maladie
  la - sans maladie 837
  - du pays 833
maladministration
    699
maladroit 699
malady 655
mala fides 940
malaise
  bodily pain 378
  mental pain 828
mala mens malus
    animus 907, 945
malapert 885, 887
Malaprop, Mrs. - 565
mal à propos
  discordant 24
  inopportune 135
malaria

  unhealthy 657
  poison 663
malarial fever 655
malconformation
    243
malcontent
  opposition 710
  discontent 832
mal du pays 833
male *strong* 159
  man 373
  - animal 373
malediction 908
malefaction 947
malefactor 949
malefic 649
maleficent 907
  - being 913
mal entendu 499
male vincetis sed
    vincite 861
malevolence 907
malevolus animus
    919
malfeasance 647
malformation
  distortion 243
  (*ugliness* 846)
malgré soi 603
malice *hate* 898
  spite 907
  bear - *revenge* 919
  - prepense 907
malign *bad* 649
  malevolent 907
  detract 934
malignant 649, 907
malignity
  violence 173
malinger 544
malison 908
malkin
  mop 652
  slattern 653
mall *walk* 189
  club 276
malleable *soft* 324
  (*facile* 705)
mallet 276
malodor 401
malpractice 947
malt liquor 298
maltreat
  injure 649
  aggrieve 830
  molest 907
malum
  - in se 923
  - prohibitum 925
malversation
  prodigal 818
  guilt 947
mamelon 250
Mameluke 726
mamma 166
mammal 366
mammalogy 368
mammet 554
mammiform 250
mammilla 250
Mammon 803

mammoth 192
man *adult* 131
  mankind 372
  male **373**
  prepare 673
  workman 690
  servant 746
  courage 861
  husband 903
  make a - of
    good 648
    brave 861
  - among men 948
  - and a brother 372
  - and wife 903
  - at-arms 726
  - in office 745
  - in the street 876
  - of straw 548
  -of-war *ship* 273
    combatant 726
  -of-war's man 269
  - 's estate 131
  one's - of business
    758
  Son of - 976
  to a - 488
manacle
  restraint 751
  fetter 752
manage 693
  - to *succeed* 731
manageable
  easy 705
management
  conduct 692
  skill 698
manager
  stage - 599
  director 694
managery 693
man bird 269
manche après la
  cognée, jeter le -
  859
mancipation 751
manciple 637
mandamus 741
mandarin 745
mandate
  requirement 630
  command 741
mandible 298
mandola 417
mandolin 417
mandragora 174
mandrel 312
manduction 298
mane 256
man-eater 361
manège *riding* 266
  equestration 370
manes 362
manet: - altâ mente
  repostum
  memory 505
  - cicatrix
  revenge 919
maneuver
  operation 680
  stratagem 702

  (*scheme* 626)
manful *strong* 159
  resolute 604
  brave 861
mange 655
manger 191
manger
  cela se laisse - 394
  - son blé en herbe 818
mangle
  separate 44
  smooth 255
  injure 659
mango 298
mangosteen 298
mangy 655
man hater 911
manhood 131, 861
mania *insanity* 503
  desire 865
  - a potu 959
maniac 504
manibus   pedibus-
  que 686
manicheism 978
manichord 417
manicure 662
manie 865
maniéré 855
manifest
  visible 446
  obvious 525
  (*appear* 448)
  (*intelligible* 518)
manifestation 525
manifesto 531
manifold
  multiform 81
  multitude 102
  writing 590
  - *linguist* 492
manikin *dwarf* 193
  image 554
maniple 103
manipulate
  handle 379
  use 677
  conduct 692
manito 980
mankind **372**
manly
  adolescent 131
  strong 159
  male 373
  brave 861
manna *food* 396
  - in the wilderness
  aid 707
  pleasing 829
manner *kind* 75
  style 569
  way 627
  conduct 692
  by all - of means 536
  by no - of means 602
  in a - 32
  to the - born 5
mannered 579
mannerism
  special 79
  unconformity 83

  affectation 855
  vanity 880
mannerly 894
manners
  breeding 852
  politeness 894
manor 780
  lord of the - 779
  - house 189
manorial 780
mansard roof 244
manse 1000
mansion 189
manslaughter 361
mansuetude 894
mantelpiece 215
mantilla 225
mantle *spread* 194
  dress 225
  foam 353
  shade 424
  redden 434
  robes 747
  flush 821, 824
  anger 900
mantlet *cloak* 225
  defense 717
mantology 511
manual *guide* 527
  schoolbook 542
  book 593
  advice 695
  - labor 686
manubial 793
manufactory 691
manufacture 161,680
manufacturer 690
manu forti 604, 686,
  739
manumission 750
manumotor 272
manure
  agriculture 371
  dirt 653
  aid 707
manuscript 590
many 102
  for - a day 110
  - irons in the fire 682
  - men many minds
    489
  - times
    repeated 104
    frequent 136
  the - 876
many-colored 440
many-sided
  multiform 81
  sides 236
many-tongued 532
map
  information 527
  representation 554
  - of days outworn 236
  - out 626
maple
  - sugar 396
  - syrup 396
mar
  deface 241
  spoil 659

  obstruct 706
marabou 41
marabout 1000
marah 395
maranatha 908
marasmus
  shrinking 195
  atrophy 655
  deterioration 659
maraud 791
marauder 792
marble *ball* 249
  hard 323
  sculpture 557
  tablet 590
  insensible 823
marble-constant 939
marbled 440
marble-hearted 907
march
  region 181
  journey 266
  progression 282
  music 415
  dead - 363
  forced - 684
  - against 716
  - of events 151
  - off 293
  - of intellect
    knowledge 490
    improvement 658
  - of time 109
  - on a point 278
  - past 882
  - with 199
  on the - 264
  steal a -
    advance 280
    go beyond 303
    deceive 545
    active 682
    cunning 702
March, Ides of - 601
marches 233
marchioness 875
marcid 203
marconigram 532
marcor 203
Mardi gras 840
mare *horse* 271
  female 374
  -'s nest 497, 546
  -'s tail *wind* 349
    cloud 353
marechal 745
marescent 659
margin *space* 180
  edge 231
  redundance 641
  latitude 748
margrave
  master 745
  nobility 875
mariage de con-
  venance 903
marigraph 466
marine *fleet* 273
  sailor 269
  oceanic 341
  soldier 726

Column 1 (MARI)

- painter 559
- painting 556
tell it to the -s 497
mariner 269
marinism 579
Mariolatry 991
marionette
  representation 554
  drama 599
marish 345
marital 903
maritime
  navigation 267
  oceanic 341
mark
  degree 26
  term 71
  take cognizance 450
  attend to 457
  indication 550
  record 551
  object 620
  importance 642
  repute 873
beyond the - 303
leave one's - 873
.man of -
  repute 873
  rank 875
- off 551
- of recognition 894
- out *choose* 609
  plan 626
  command 741
- time
  chronometry 114
  halt 265
- with a red letter 883
- with a white stone 931
near the - 197
overshoot the - 699
put a - upon 457
save the - 870
up to the -
  enough 639
  good 648
  skill 698
  due 924
wide of the -
  distant 196
  error 495
within the - 304
marked [*see* mark]
  great 31
  affirmed 535
in a - degree 31
well - 446
market *buy* 795
  mart 799
bring to - 796
buy in the cheapest &c. - 794
in the -
  offered 763
  barter 794
  sale 796
- garden 371
- overt
  manifest 525

Column 2 (MART)

mart 799
- place *street* 189
mart 799
- price 812
rig the - 794
marketable 794, 796
marksman 700
marksmanship 698
marl 342
marmalade 396
marmot 683
maroon
  brown 433
  red 434
  fugitive 623
  abandon 782
  outlaw 893
marplot
  bungler 701
  obstacle 706
  malicious 913
marque, letters of - 791
marquee 223
marquetry
  variegated 440
marquis 875
marriage 903
ill-assorted - 904
- bell 836
- broken 903
marriageable
  adolescent 131
  nubile 903
marrow *essence* 5
  interior 221
  central 222
  (*meaning* 516)
  (*importance* 642)
chill to the - 385
marrowbones, on one's -
  submit 725
  beg 765
  humble 879
  servile 886
  atonement 952
marrowless 158
marrubium 400
marry *combine* 48
  assertion 535
  wed 903
- come up
  defiance 715
  anger 900
  censure 932
Mars 722
- *gravior sub pace latet* 713
- orange 439
marsh 345
- gas 663
marshal
  arrange 60
  messenger 534
  auxiliary 711
  officer 745
Marshalsea 752
marsupial 191
mart 799
Marte, suo -

Column 3 (MASS)

exertion 686
skill 698
martello tower 717
martial 722
  court - 966
- law *severe* 739
  compulsory 744
  illegal 964
- music 415
martinet 739
martingale 752
Martinmas 998
martyr
  bodily pain 378
  mental pain 828
  ascetic 955
- to disease 655
martyrdom
  killing 361
  agony 378, 828
  unselfish 942
  punishment 972
marvel *wonder* 870
  prodigy 872
- whether 514
marvelous
  great 31
  wonderful 870
deal in the - 549
Masaniello 742
mascot 621, 993
masculine
  strong 159
  male 373
mash *mix* 41
  disorder 59
  soft 324
  semiliquid 352
masher 854
masjid 1000
mask *dress* 225
  shade 424
  concealment 528
  ambush 530
  deceit 545
  shield 717
put on the - 544
masker 599
masochism 659
mason 690
Masorah 985
masque 599
masqué, bal - 840
masquerade
  dress 225
  concealment 528
  deception 545
  frolic 840
- dress 530
mass *quantity* 25
  much 31
  whole 50
  heap 72
  size 192
  gravity 319
  density 321
  worship 990
  rite 998
  attend - 990
in the - 50
- book 998

Column 4 (MATA)

- of society 876
massacre 361
massage 331, 379
masse, en - 712
masses, the - 876
massive *huge* 192
  heavy 319
  dense 321
mastaba 363
master, Master
  boy 129
  man 373
  know 490
  understand 518
  learn 539
  teacher 540
  director 694
  proficient 698, 700
  succeed, conquer 731
  ruler **745**
  possession 777
  possessor 779
  title 877
eye of the - 693
hard - 739
- hand 700
- key *open* 260
  instrument 631
- mind *sage* 500
  proficient 700
- of Arts 492
- of one's time 685
- of self 604
- of the position 731
- of the revels 840
- of the Rolls
  recorder 553
  judge 967
- of the situation
  success 731
  authority 737
- one's feelings 826
- one's passions 944
- passion 820
- spirit of the age
  sage 500
  repute 873
past - 700
masterdom 737
masterpiece
  good 648
  perfect 650
  skill 698
master stroke
  plan 626
  success 731
mastery
  success 731
  authority 737
masthead
  punish 972
mastic *viscid* 352
  resin 356a
masticate 298
mastiff 366
mastology 368
más vale saber que haber 498
mat *support* 215
  woven 219
matador 361

509

menticulture 490, 658
mention 527
  above -ed 104
  not worth - ing 643
mentira: la - tiene las piernas cortas 544
mentis gratissimus error 481, 495
mentor *teacher* 540
  adviser 695
menu *list* 86
  food 298
Mephistopheles 980
Mephistophelian 945
mephitic *fetid* 401
  deleterious 657
mephitis 663
mer
  il a le - à boire, 471
meracious 392
mercantile 794
mercatoria, lex - 963
mercature 794
mercenary
  soldier 726
  servant 746
  price 812
  parsimonious 819
  selfish 943
mercer 225
merchandise 798
merchant 797
merchantman 273
merciful 914
merciless 914*a*
mercurial
  mobile 264
  quick 274
  excitable 825
mercurous chloride 662
Mercury
  traveler 268
  quick 274
  messenger 534
  -'s rod 747
mercy *lenity* 740
  pity 914
  at the - of
  liable 177
  subject 749
  cry you - 766
  for -'s sake 765
  have no - 914*a*
  - on us! 870
  - seat 966
mere *simple* 32
  lake 343
  trifling 643
  buy for a - nothing 815
  > nothing
  small 32
  trifle 643
  - pretext 617
  - words 477
  - wreck 659
merelles 840
merestead 780

meretricious
  false 495
  vulgar 851
  licentious 961
merfolk 980
merge *combine* 48
  include 76
  insert 300
  plunge 337
  - in 56
  - into *become* 144
merged 228
meridian
  region 181
  room 125
  summit 210
  light 420
  - of life 131
merit
  goodness 648
  due 924
  virtue 944
  make a - of 884
  - notice 642
merito, e - 944
meritorious
  praiseworthy 931
mermaid
  monster 83
  mythology 979, 980
merogenesis 161
mero motu, ex - 600
merriment
  cheerful 836
  amusement 840
merry *cheerful* 836
  drunk 959
  make - *sport* 840
  make - with
  wit 842
  ridicule 856
  - and wise 842
  - as the day is long 836
  - heart 836
  wish a - Christmas &c. 896
merry-andrew 844
merry-go-round 840
merrymaking
  revel 840
  sociality 892
merrythought 842, 993
mersion 337
meruit ferat, pal- mam qui - 873
merveille, à - 731
mesa 344
mésalliance
  ill-assorted 24
  marriage 903
meseems 484
mesh
  interstices 198
  crossing 219
meshes *trap* 545
  difficulty 704
  - or sophistry 477
mesial *middle* 68
  (*central* 222)

mesilla 344
mesmerism 992
mesmerist 994
mesne lord 779
mess *mixture* 41
  disorder 59
  meal 298
  difficulty 704
  portion 786
  make a -
  unskillful 699
  fail 732
message
  intelligence 532
  command 741
Messalina 962
messenger
  cloud 353
  envoy **534**
  servant 746
  - balloon 463
Messiah 976
messmate 890
messuage 189, 780
mestee 41
mestizo 41
metabolism 357
metacenter 222
metachronism 115
metage 466
metagenesis 140
metagrammatism 561
metal 635
  Britannia - 545
metalepsis 521
metallurgy 358
metamorphosis 140
metaphor
  comparison 464
  figure **521**
  (*analogy* 17)
metaphrase 522
metaphrast 524
metaphysics 450
metaplasm 357
metastasis
  change 140
  inversion 218
  displacement 270
metathesis
  inversion 218
  displacement 270
mete *measure* 466
  distribute 786
  - out *give* 784
metempirical 519
metempsychosis 140
meteor
  heavenly body 318
  luminary 423
meteoric
  violent 173
  light 420
meteorite 318
meteorology 338
meteoromancy 466
meter 466, 597
metheglin 396
methinks 484
method *order* 58

  way **627**
  want of - 59
methodical 60, 80
methodist *formalist* 988
Methodist 984
methodize 58, 60
Methuselah 130
  old as - 128
  since the days of - 124
métis 83
metogenesis 161
metonymy 521
metoposcopy
  appearance 44
  front 234
  interpret 522
metrical
  measured 466
  verse 597
metrology 466
μέτρον, ἄριστον
  moderation 174
  mid-course 628
metropolis 189
metropolitan
  archbishop 996
mettle *spirit* 820
  courage 861
  man of - 861
  on one's -
  resolved 604
  put on one's -
  excite 824
  encourage 861
mettlesome
  sensitive 822
  excitable 825
  brave 861
mettre de l'eau dans son vin 160
meum et tuum 777, 780
  disregard distinction between - 791
mew *molt* 226
  cry 412
  - up 751
mewed up 229
mewl 412
mews 189
mezzanine floor
  house 191
  theater 599
Mezzofanti 492
mezzo rilievo
  convex 250
  sculpture 557
mezzo termine
  middle 68
  mid-course 628
  compromise 774
mezzotint 558
miasm 663
mica 427
micaceous 204
mi-carême 840
Micawber 460
Michaelmas 998
Micomicon 51z

microbe 193
microcosm 193
microgamete 357
micrography 193
micrometer 193
microphone 418
microscope
little 193
optics 445
microscopic 32, 193
microzoa 193
mid 68
Midas 803
mid-course 29, **628**
midday 125
midden 653
middle
- *in degree* 29
- *in order* **68**
- *in space* 222
- classes 736
- constriction 203
- course 628
- man *director* 694
agent 758
- state 29
- term 68
compromise 774
middle-aged 131
middlemost 222
middling *small* 32
imperfect 651
middy 269
Midgard 318
midge 193
midland 342
midnight *night* 126
dark 421
- oil 539
mid progress 282
midriff *middle* 68
interjacence 228
midshipman 269
midships 68
midst
- *in order* 68
central 222
interjacent 228
in the - of
mixed with 41
doing 680
midsummer 125
- day 138
midway 68
midwife
instrument 631
remedy 662
auxiliary 711
midwifery
production 161
surgery 662
mien 448
miff 900
might *power* 157
violence 173
energy 686
mighty *much* 31
strong 159
large 192
haughty 878
migrate 266

mihi cura futuri 510
mikado 745
milch cow
productive 168
animal 366
store 636
mild *moderate* 174
warm 382
insipid 391
lenient 740
calm 826
courteous 894
mildew *dirt* 653
bane 663
mildewed
spoiled 659
mile 200
mileage 200, 973
- ticket 550
milestone 550
whistle jigs to a - 645
milieu, juste -
moderation 174
mid-course 628
militant 722
military
warfare 722
soldiers 726
- authorities 745
- education 537
- power 737
- school 542
- time 132
- train 726
militate against 708
militat omnis ama-
sius 897
militia 726
milk *moderate* 174
semiliquid 352
white 430
mild 740
flow with - and honey
plenty 639
prosperity 734
pleasant 829
- a he-goat into a
sieve 471
- and water
weak 160
insipid 391
unimportant 643
imperfect 651
- of human kindness
906
- sickness 655
- the ram 645
milk-livered 862
milksop *fool* 501
coward 862
milky [*see* milk]
semitransparent 427
- way 318
mill 330
machine 633
unimportance 643
workshop 691
fight 720
like a horse in a - 312
millennium
period 108

futurity 121
utopia 515
hope 858
millesimal 99
millet seed 193
milliard 98
milliary 550
milliner 225
man - 854
millinery *dress* 225
ornament 847
display 882
man - 855
million 98
multitude 102
people 372
populace 876
for the -
intelligible 518
easy 705
millionaire 803
mill pond *level* 213
pond 343
store 636
mime *player* 599
buffoon 844
mimeography 19
mimic 19
mimmation 560
minacity 909
minaret 206
minauderie 855
mince *cut up* 44
slow 275
food 298
stammer 583
affected 855
extenuate 937
- the matter 868
- the truth 544
not - the matter
affirm 525
artless 703
mince-meat
make - of 162
mince pie 298
mincing 855
- steps 275
mind
intellect 450
attend to 457
take care 459
believe 484
remember 505
will 600
willing 602
purpose 620
warning 668
desire 865
dislike 867
bear in -
thought 451
attention 457
bit of one's - 527
food for the - 454
give the - to 457
have a - to
willing 602
desire 865
in the -
thought 451

topic 454
willing 602
make one's - easy 826
make up one's -
opinion 484
resolve 604
- at ease 827
- one's book 539
- one's business
incurious 456
attentive 457
-'s eye 515
- what one is about 864
my - is my kingdom
450
never - *neglect* 460
unimportant 643
not - 866
out of - 506
set one's - upon 604
speak one's -
say 582
blunt 703
to one's - *taste* 850
love 897
the music - breathing
- 450
the poet's - 597
the public - 488
willing - 602
minded *willing* 602
intending 620
mindful
attentive 457
memory 505
mindless
inattentive 458
imbecile 499
forgetful 506
insensible 823
mine *sap* 162
hollow 252
open 260
snare 545
store 636
abundance 639
damage 659
attack 716
dig a - *plan* 626
prepare 673
- of wealth 803
spring a -
unexpected 508
attack 716
miner 252
sapper and - 726
mineral 358
- oil 356
mineralogy 358
Minervâ, invitâ
unwilling 603
difficult 704
Minerva press
fustian 577
fiction 594
mingle 41
miniature *small* 193
portrait 556
- painter 559
Minié rifle 727
minikin 193

minim *small* 32
  music 413
minimize 483
minimum *small* 32
  inferior 34
  - decet libere cui mul-
    tum licet 31
minion 899
minister
  instrumentality 631
  remedy 662
  director 694
  aid 707
  deputy 759
  give 784
  clergy 996
  rites 998
ministerial
  clerical 995
ministering spirit
  977
ministration
  direction 693
  aid 707
  rite 998
ministry
  direction 693
  aid 707
  church 995
  clergy 996
minium 434
minnesinger 597
minnow 193
minor *inferior* 34
  infant 129
  - key 413
Minorites 996
minority *few* 103
  youth 127
Minos 694
minotaur 83
minster 1000
minstrel
  musician 416
  poet 597
minstrelsy 415
mint *mold* 22
  fragrance 400
  workshop 691
  wealth 803
  - julep 298
minuend 38
minuet *music* 415
  dance 840
minus *less* 84
  subtracted 38
  absent 187
  deficient 304
  loss 776
  in debt 806
  nonpayment 808
minusculæ 561
minute
  - *in degree* 32
  - *of time* 108
  instant 113
  - *in size* 193
  record 551
  compendium 596
  (*unimportant* 643)
  - account 594

- attention 457
to the - 132
minutemen 726
minuteness
  care 459
minutiæ *small* 32
  details 79
  unimportant 643
minx *malapert* 887
  wanton 962
mir 188
mirabile
  - dictu &c. 870
mirabilis, annus -
  872
miracle
  exceptional 83
  prodigy 872
  - play 599
miraculous
  wonderful 870
mirage 443
mire 653
mirror *imitate* 19
  reflector 445
  perfection 650
  glory 873
  hold the - up to na-
    ture 554
  hold up the - 525
  magic - 443
mirth 836
misacceptation 523
misadventure
  adversity 735
  (*evil* 619)
  (*failure* 732)
misadvised 699
misanthropy 911
misapply
  misinterpret 523
  misuse 679
  mismanage 699
misapprehend
  mistake 495
  misinterpret 523
misappropriate 679
misarrange 61
misbecome 925
misbegotten
  crooked 243
  vicious 945
misbehave
  vulgar 851
  vice 945
misbehavior
  discourtesy 895
  guilt 947
misbelief 485
misbeliever 487
miscalculate
  misjudge 481
  err 495
  disappoint 509
miscall 565
miscarry 732
miscegenation 41,
  903
miscellany
  mixture 41
  collection 72

  generality 78
misce stultitiam
  consiliis brevem
  840
mischance *evil* 619
  misfortune 735
  (*failure* 732)
mischief 619
  do - 649
  make - 649
mischief-maker
  evil doer 913
  knave 941
miscible 41
miscite 544
miscompute
  misjudge 481
  mistake 495
misconceive
  mistake 495
  misinterpret 523
misconduct
  bungling 699
  guilt 947
  - oneself 945
misconjecture 481
misconstrue 523
miscorrect 538
miscount 495
miscreance 485
miscreant 949
miscreated 945
misdate 115
misdeed 947
misdemean 945
misdemeanant 949
misdemeanor 947
misdescribe 538
misdevotion 988
misdirect
  misteach 538
  unskillful 699
misdo 945
misdoing 947
misdoubt 485
mise en scéne
  appearance 448
  drama 599
  display 882
misemploy 679
miser 819
miserabile dictu 839
miserable *small* 32
  contemptible 943
  unhappy 828
miserably *very* 31
misère 840
miserere, sing - 950
misericordia Domini
  470
misericordiam, ar-
  gumentum ad
  - 914
miseries of human
  life 828
miseris succurrere
  disco 914
miserly 819
misery 828
  put out of one's - 914
misestimate

  misjudge 481
  (*mistake* 495)
misfeasance
  bungling 699
  guilt 947
misfortune
  adversity 735
  unhappiness 830
  (*evil* 619)
  (*failure* 732)
misgiving
  doubt 485
  fear 860
misgovern 699
misguide *error* 495
  misteaching 538
misguided 699
mishap *evil* 619
  failure 732
  misfortune 735
  painful 830
mishmash 59
Mishna 985
misinform 538
misinformed 491
misinstruct 538
misintelligence 538
misinterpretation
  523
misjoined 24
misjudgment
  sophistry 477
  misjudge 481
  (*error* 495)
mislay *derange* 61
  lose 776
mislead *error* 495
  misteach 538
  deceive 545
mislike 867
mismanage 699
mismatch
  difference 15
  disagreement 24
misname 565
misnomer 565
misogamist
  celibacy 904
  misanthropy 911
misogyny 904
mispersuasion 538
misplace
  derange 61
misplaced
  intrusive 24
  unconformable 83
  displaced 185
  (*disorder* 59)
misprint 495
misprison
  concealment 528
  guilt 947
  - of treason 742
misprize
  underrate 483
  disrespect 929
mispronounce 582
misproportioned
  distortion 243
  ugly 846
misquote 544

moldy 653, 659
  (fetid 401)
mole *wound* 206
  prominence 250
  refuge 666
  defense 717
  spot 848
molecular 32
molecule 193
mole-eyed 443
molehill *little* 193
  low 207
  trifling 643
molest *trouble* 830
molestation
  damage 649
  malevolence 907
mollah *judge* 967
mollia tempora 134
  - fandi 588
mollify *allay* 174
  soften 324
  (mental calm 826)
mollusk 366
mollycoddle 158, 372
Moloch
  slaughter 361
  demon 980
  heathen deity 986
molt 226
molten
  liquefied 384
  (heated 335)
moment
  - of *time* 113
  importance 642
  for the - 111
  lose not a - 684
  not have a - 682
  on the spur of the -
    612
momentous 151
momentum 276
Momus 838
monachism 995
monad 193
monarch 745
monarchy 737
monastery 1000
monastic 995
monde 852
monetary 800
  - arithmetic 811
monetize 800
money 800
  wealth 803
  bad - 800
  command of - 803
  for one's - 609
  made of - 803
  make - 775
  - burning one's pock-
    et 818
  - coming in 810
  - down 807
  - going out 809
  - market 800
  - matters 811
  - paid 809
  -'s worth
    useful 644

price 812
  cheap 815
  raise - 788
  save - 817
  throw away one's - 818
money bag 802
money broker 797
money changer
  merchant 797
  treasurer 801
moneyed 803
moneyer 797
money-grubbing 775
moneyless 804
monger 797
mongrel
  mixture 41
  anomalous 83
  dog 366
  base 949
moniliform 249
monition
  information 527
  warning 668
  (advice 695)
monitor *oracle* 513
  pupil teacher 540
  director 694
  adviser 695
  war ship 726
  inward - 926
monitory
  prediction 511
  dissuasion 616
  warning 668
monk 904, 996
monkery 984
monkey
  imitative 19
  support 215
  catapult 276
  ridiculous 857
  - trick
  absurdity 497
  sport 840
  - up 900
  play the - 499
monkhood 995
monkish Latin 553
monochord 417
monochrome
  no color 429
  painting 556
monoclinous 83
monocracy 737
monoculous 443
monodrame 599
monody *poem* 597
  lament 839
monogamist 904
monogamy 903
monogram
  cipher 533
  diagram 554
  letter 561
monograph
  writing 590
  description 594
monolith 551
monolithic 983a
monologue

soliloquy 589
  drama 599
monomachy 720
monomania
  insanity 503
  obstinacy 606
monomaniac 504
monoplane 273
monopolist 943
monopoly
  restraint 751
  possession 777
monospermous 87
monostich 572
monosyllable 561
monotheism 983
monotonous
  uniform 16
  equal 27
  repetition 104
  permanent 141
  - *style* 575
  weary 841
  dull 843
monotype 591
Monroe Doctrine 748
monsoon 349
monster
  exception 83
  large 192
  ugly 846
  prodigy 872
  evil doer 913
  ruffian 949
monstrosity
  [see monster]
  distortion 243
monstrous
  excessive 31
  exceptional 83
  huge 192
  ugly 846
  vulgar 851
  ridiculous 853
  wonderful 870
montagne Russe
  slope 217
  sport 840
mont de piété 787
monte 840
Montgolfier 273
month 108
monthly 138
  - *nurse* 662
monticle 206
monument *tall* 206
  tomb 363
  record 551
monumentum ære
  perennius 733
moo 412
mood *nature* 5
  state 7
  change 140
  tendency 176
  willingness 602
  temper 820
moodish
  rude 895
  irascible 901
moods and tenses

difference 15
  variation 20a
moody *furious* 825
  sad 837
  sullen 901a
moon
  period 108
  changes 149
  world 318
  bay the - 645
  jump over the - 309
  man in the - 515
  - glade 422
  - of green cheese
  credulity 486
  - shaped 245
moonbeam
  light 420
  dim 422
mooncalf 501
moon-eyed 443
moonshine
  unsubstantial 4
  dim 422
  absurdity 497
  unmeaning 517
  untrue 546
  excuse 617
  - *revelers* 979
moonstone 847
moonstruck
  insane 503
  wonder 870
moor *fasten* 43
  open space 180
  locate 184
  highland 206
  plain 344
Moore, Old - 513
moored *firm* 150
moorings
  connection 45
  location 184
moorish
  marshy 345
moorland 180, 206
moose 366
moot *inquire* 461
  argue 476
  - point *topic* 454
  question 461
mooted
  supposed 514
mop 652
mopboard 211
mope 837
mope-eyed 443
moppet 899
mopsy 962
mopus *dreamer* 515
  drone 683
  money 800
  sad 837
mora nec requies,
  nec - 682
moral *judgment* 480
  maxim 496
  right 922
  duty 926
  virtuous 944
  - *certainty* 474

- courage 604
- education 537
- obligation 926
- support 707
- tuition 537
- turpitude 940
point a - 537
moralize 476
moral philosophy
  mind 450
  duty 926
morals *duty* 926
  virtue 944
morass 345
morbid 655
morbific 657
morceau 32, 415
mordacity 907
mordant *keen* 171
  pungent 392
  color 428
more *superior* 33
  added 37
- last words 65
- or less
  quantity 25
  small 32
  inexact 495
- than a match for
  superior 33
  strong 159
- than enough 641
- than flesh and blood
  can bear 830
- than meets the eye
  526
- than one 100
more:
- *majorum* 82
- *solito*
  conformable 82
  habitual 613
- *suo* 613
morem fecerat usus
  613
moreover 37
mores, O - 932
Moresque 847
Morgana, Fata - 423
morganatic mar-
  riage 903
morgue 363
- *littéraire* 569
mori, memento -
  363
moribund
  dying 360
  sick 655
morient 360
morion 717
morisco 840
mormo 860
Mormon 984
Mormonism
  polygamy 903
  heterodoxy 984
morning 125
- dress 225
- noon and night
  diuturnal 110
  frequent 136

- star 423, 977
morose *rude* 895
  sulky 901a
morphea 653
Morpheus 683
morphology 357
  form 240
  zoölogy 368
morra 840
morris,
  nine men's - 840
morris-chair 215
morris dance 840
morrow 121
mors aux dents,
  prendre le - 719
morsel *small* 32
  portion 51
  food 298
mors ultima linea
  rerum est 360
mort, guerre à - 722
mortal
  transient 111
  fatal 361
  man 372
  wearisome 841
- antipathy 867
- blow 619
- coil 362
- funk 860
- remains 362
- sin 947
mortality
  evanescence 111
  death 360
  mankind 372
  bills of - 360
mortar *cement* 45
  pulverizer 330
  cannon 727
mortem, post - 360,
  363
mortgage
  security 771
  lend 787
  sale 796
  credit 805
mortgagee
  possessor 779
  creditor 805
mortgagor
  possessor 779
  debtor 806
mortiferous
  fatal 361
  (*unhealthy* 657)
mortification
  disease 655
  pain 828
  vexation 830
  discontent 832
  humiliation 879
  asceticism 955
mortise *unite* 43
  intersect 219
  interjacence 228
  printing 591
mortmain 748
  in - 781
| **mortuary**

death 360
  interment 363
mosaic *mixture* 41
  multiform 81
  variegation 440
  painting 556
Moslem 984
mosque 1000
mosquito 913
moss *tuft* 256
  marsh 345
  vegetation 367
  money 800
moss-grown 659
mosstrooper
  fighter 726
  thief 792
most 31
  at - 32
  for the - part
  generally 78
  habit 613
  make the - of
  overestimate 482
  exaggerate 549
  improve 658
  use 677
  skill 698
  make the - of one's
  time 682
- often 136
  the - 33
mot 496
- à mot 19
- d'énigme 522
- de passe 550
- d'ordre 741
- du guet 550
- pour rire 842
Motazilite 984
mote *small* 32
  light 320
- in the eye
  dim-sighted 443
  misjudging 481
motet 990
moth *bane* 663
moth-eaten
  unclean 653
  deteriorated 659
mother *parent* 166
  mold 653
  -of-pearl 427, 440
- tongue 560
- wit 498
motherly *love* 897
  kind 906
motion
  change of place 264
  topic 454
  plan 626
  proposal 763
  request 765
  make a - 763
- downwards 306
- from
  recession 287
  repulsion 289
- into *ingress* 294
  reception 296
- out of 295

- through 302
- towards
  approach 286
  attraction 288
- upwards 305
put in - 284
put oneself in - 680
set in - 677
motionless 265
motive 615
  absence of - **615a**
- power 264
motley
  multiform 81
  variegated 440
  wearer of the - 844
motor 271
- paralysis 376
motor car 272
motocycle 272
motory 264
motte 367
mottled 440
motto *maxim* 496
  device 550
  phrase 566
motu: ex mero - 737
  suo - 600
mouchard 527
mould [*see* mold]
moulin
- à paroles 584
  se battre contre des
  -s 645
mound *large* 192
  hill 206
  defense 717
mount
  greatness 31
  hill 206
  ascend 305
  raise 307
  display 882
- guard *care* 459
  safety 664
- up to *money* 800
  price 812
mountain *large* 192
  hill 206
  weight 319
  make -s of molehills
  482
- brought forth mouse
  disappoint 509
- flax 385
- in labor
  waste 638
mountaineer 268
mountainous 206
mountebank
  quack 548
  drama 599
  buffoon 844
mounted rifles 726
mourn *grieve* 828
  lament 839
mourners' bench
  1000
mournful
  afflicting 830
  sad 837

munch 298
Munchausen 549
munchil 272
mundane
  world 318
  selfish 943
  irreligious 989
mundation 652
mundivagant 266
munerary 973
munerate 973
municipal 965
munificent 816
muniment
  record 551
  defense 717
  security 771
munition
  materials 635
  defense 717
munshi
  learned man 493
  teacher 540
mural 717
murder 361
  - the King's English
  solecism 568
  stammering 583
  the - is out 529
murderer 361
muricated 253
murky *dark* 421
  opaque 426
  black 431
  gloomy 837
murmur *purl* 348
  sound 405
  complain 839
murmurer 832
murrain 655
Murray *travel* 266
  Lindley - 542
murrey 434
murrion 717
murus æneus con-
  scientia sana 946
mus, nascitur ridi-
  culus -
  disappoint 509
  unimportant 643
musæo contingens
  c u n c t a lepore
  515
muscadine 400
muscle 159
muscular 159
muse 451
  [*and see* musing]
Muse *poetry* 597
  historic - 594

- of fire 597
unlettered - 579
museology 72
Muses, the - 416
musette 417
museum
  collection 72
  store 636
mushroom *new* 123
  fungus 367
  upstart 734
  lowborn 876
  spring up like -s 163
music 415
  - arose 415
  - of a dream 415
  - of the spheres
  order 58
  universe 318
  set to - 416
musical 413, 415, 416
  - ear
  musician 416
  hearing 418
  - instruments 417
  - note 413
  - voice 580
music hall
  playhouse 599
  amusement 840
musician 416
musing
  thought 451
  - on other things 458
  thick-eyed - 837
musk 400
  - ox 366
musket 727
  shoulder a - 722
musketeer 726
musketry 727
muskrat 400
muslin
  semitransparent 427
musnud
  support 215
  council 696
  scepter 747
muss 59, 61
mussuk 191, 348
Mussulman 984
mussy 61, 653
must *necessity* 601
  mucor 653
  compulsion 744
  I - say 535
  it - follow 478
mustache 256
mustang 271
mustard

pungent 392
  condiment 393
  after meat - 135
mustard seed 193
muster *collect* 72
  numeration 85
  - courage 861
  not pass - 651
  pass - 639
muster roll *list* 86
  (*record* 551)
musty 961
  smelling 401
  foul 653
mutable
  changeable 149
  (*irresolute* 605)
mutation 140
mutatis mutandis
  correlation 12
  change 140
  interchange 148
mutato nomine de
  te &c.
  parable 521
  retaliation 718
mute *funeral* 363
  silent 403
  sordine 417
  letter 561
  speechless 581
  taciturn 585
  d r a m a t i s persona
  599
  deaf - 419
  render - 581
mutilate
  retrench 38
  deform 241
  injure 659
mutilated
  incomplete 53
mutilation
  evil 619
mutineer 742
mutiny
  disobedience 742
  (*resistance* 719)
mutter
  faint sound 405
  imperfect speech 583
  grumble 839
  threaten 909
mutton 298
  - head 501
  - headed 499
mutual
  correlative 12
  interchange 148
  - concession 774

- understanding 23
mutum est pictura
  poema 556, 597
muzzle
  powerless 158
  edge 231
  opening 260
  silence 403
  render speechless 581
  restrain 751
  gag 752
muzzle-loader 727
muzzy
  confused 458
  in liquor 959
my: all - eye 546
  - stars! 870
myatism 560
mycology 369
mynheer 877
myology 329
myomancy 511
myopia 443
myriad
  ten thousand 98
  multitude 102
myrmidon 726
myrrh 400
myrtle 897
myself *I* 79
  immateriality 317
mysterious
  invisible 447
  obscure 519
  concealed 528
mystery
  [*see* mysterious]
  latency 526
  secret 533
  play 599
  craft 625
  into the supreme - 528
  - of folded sleep 683
mystic
  uncertain 475
  obscure 519
  concealed 528
  sorcery 992
  - bond of brotherhood
  888
mystify *falsify* 477
  hide 528
  misteach 538
  deceive 545
myth *fancy* 515
  untruth 546
mythogenesis 515
mythology
  gods 979
  heathen 984

soon 132
impending 152
approach 286
stingy 819
bring - 17
come - 286
draw - 197
- at hand 132
- one's end 360
- run 32
- side 239
- sight 443
- the mark 32
- the truth 480a
- upon 32
sail - the wind
skillful 698
rash 863
nearly 32
- all 50
nearness 197
neat simple 42
order 58
in writing 572, 576, 578
clean 652
spruce 845
-'s foot oil 356
neat-handed 698
neatherd 370
neb 250
nebula stars 318
mist 353
nebular dim 422
nebulous misty 353
obscure 519
necessarian 601
necessaries 630
necessarily
cause and effect 154
necessitas non habet legem 630
necessitate 630
necessity fate 601
predetermination 611
requirement 630
compulsion 744
indigence 804
make a virtue of - 698
neck
contraction 195
narrow 203
break one's - 360
- and crop
completely 52
turn out - 297
-- and neck 27
- of land 342
- or nothing
resolute 604
rash 863
neckcloth 225
necklace
circle 247
ornament 847
necrology
obituary 360
biography 594
necromancer 994
necromancy 992

necropolis 363
necropsy 363
necroscopic 363
necrosis 655
nec scire fas est omnia 490
nectar
savory 394
sweet 396
need necessity 601
requirement 630
insufficiency 640
indigence 804
desire 865
friend in - 711
in one's utmost - 735
needful
necessary 601
requisite 630
money 800
do the - pay 807
needle sharp 253
perforator 262
compass 693
as the - to the pole
veracity 543
observance 772
honor 939
- in a bottle of hay 475
touch'd - trembles 375
needle gun 727
needle-shaped 253
needless 641
needle-witted 498
needlewoman 690
ne e quovis legno 82
ne'er-do-well 949
nefarious 945
negation 536
negative
inexisting 2
contrary 14
prototype 22
quantity 84
confute 479
deny 536
photograph 558
refuse 764
prove a - 468
neglect 460
disuse 678
leave undone 730
omit 773
evade 927
disrespect 929
- of time 115
négligé 225
negligence 460
negotiate
mediate 724
bargain 769
transfer 783
traffic 794
negotiator
go-between 724
agent 758
negro black 431
slave 746
negro head 392

negrophobia 898
negus 298
neif 781
neigh cry 412
boast 884
neighbor
near 197
friend 890
neighborhood 197, 227
neighborly
aid 707
friendly 888
social 892
courteous 894
neither 610
- here nor there
irrelevant 10
absent 187
- more nor less
equal 27
true 494
- one thing nor another 83
ne Jupiter quidem 832
nem. con. 488
Nemesis
vengeance 919
justice 922
punishment 972
nemine contradicente 488
nemo bis punitur 970
nemo me impune lacessit 715
nemo repente fuit turpissimus 945
nemo solus sapit 498
nenia 839
neogamist 903
neo-Lamarckism 357
neology 563, 989
neophyte 541
Neoplatonism 984
neoteric 123
Nepenthe
remedy 662
cheer 836
nephalism 955
nephelognosy 353
nephew 11
nephograph 353
nephology 353
nepotism
nephew 11
wrong 923
dishonest 940
selfish 943
Neptune 341
Nereid ocean 341
mythology 979
nerve
strength 159
courage 861
nerveless 158
nervos belli pecuniam infinitam 727, 800

nervous weak 160
style 574
timid 860
modest 881
nescience 491
nescit vox missa reverti 864
ness 250
nessun maggior dolere 828
multitude 102
nest
cradle 153
lodging 189
- of boxes 204
nest egg 636
nestle lodge 186
safety 664
endearment 902
nestling 129
Nestor veteran 130
sage 500
advice 695
net remainder 40
receptacle 191
intersection 219
inclosure 232
snare 545
difficulty 704
gain 775
- profit gain 775
receipt 810
nether 207
nethermost 211
netting 219
nettle bane 663
sting 830
incense 900
network
disorder 59
crossing 219
neuralgia 378
neurology 329
neurotic 662
neuter matter 316
no choice 609a
remain -
irresolute 605
stand -
indifferent 866
neutral mean 29
no choice 609a
avoidance 623
pacific 721
- tint
colorless 429
gray 432
neutrality
mid-course 628
peace 721
insensibility 823
indifference 866
neutralize
compensate 30
counteract 179
nevée 383
never 107
it will - do
inexpedient 647
prohibit 761
discontent 832

and - mistake 474
at - great distance 197
at - hand 32
at - time 107
give - quarter 361
have - business there
  83
have - end
  perpetual 112
have - notion of 489
in - degree 32
make - scruple of 602
- chicken
  aged 128
  grown up 131
- choice
  necessary 601
  neutral 609a
-conjuror
  fool 501
  bungler 701
- consequence 643
- doubt
  certain 474
  assent 488
- end of *great* 31
  multitude 102
  length 200
- go
  shortcoming 304
  failure 732
- great shakes
  small 32
  trifling 643
  imperfect 651
- less 639
- longer 122
- love lost between
  them 898
- matter
  neglect 460
  unimportant 643
- more
  inexistent 2
  past 122
  dead 360
- more than 32
- object 643
- one 4
- one knows who 876
- other *same* 13
  one 87
- scholar 493
- sooner said than
  done
  instantaneous 113
  early 132
- stranger to 490.
- such thing
  nonexistent 2
  unsubstantial 4
  contrary 14
  dissimilar 18
- surrender
  obstinate 606
  defense 717
- thank you 764
- wonder 871
on - account 761
to - purpose
  shortcoming 304

useless 645
failure 732
unable to say - 605
with - interval 199
Noah's ark
  mixture 41
  assemblage 72
nob 210
nobilitate 873
nobility 875
noble *great* 31
  important 642
  rank 873
  peer 875
  disinterested 942
  virtuous 944
  - liver 948
  - scorn 919
noblesse 875
noblesse oblige 875
nobody
  unsubstantial 4
  zero 101
  absence 187
  lowborn 876
  - knows
  ignorance 491
  - knows where
  distance 196
  - present 187
  - would think 508
noctambulation 266
noctambulist 268
noctivagant
  travel 266
  dark 421
noctograph 442
nocturnal
  night 126
  dark 421
  black 431
nocuous 649
nod *wag* 314
  assent 488
  signal 550
  sleep 683
  command 741
  bow 894
  (*hint* 527)
  - of approbation 931
  - of assent 488
nodding to its fall
  destruction 162
  descent 306
noddle *summit* 210
  head 450
noddy 501
node 250
nodosity
  convex 250
  rough 256
nods and becks and
  wreathed smiles
  894
nodule 250
nodus, dignus vin-
  dice - 704
νοήματα 454
no es oro todo 486
noggin 191
noise *sound* 402

loud 404
make a - in the world
  873
- abroad 531
noiseless 403
noisome
  fetid 401
  bad 649
  unhealthy 657
nolens volens 601
noli irritare leones
  864
noli me tangere
  defiance 715
  excitable 825
  fastidious 868
nolition 603
nolleity 603
nolle prosequi 624
nolumus leges An-
  gliæ mutari
  permanence 141
  continuance 143
  preservation 670
nomad 268
nomadic 266
Nomancy 511
nom de: - guerre 565
  - plume 565
nomenclature 564
nominal
  unsubstantial 4
  word 562
  name 564
  - price 815
nomina stultorum
  501, 531
nomination
  naming 564
  appointment 755
nominee 758
nominis umbra 4
nomology 963
non
  lex - scripta 963
  - compos mentis 503
  - constat 477
  - deficit alter 100
  - ens 2
  - est inventus 187
  - est vivere 359, 654
  - hæc in fœdera
  deny 536
  reject 610
  - libet 867
  - nobis Domine 990
  - nostrum tantas
  componere lites
  impossible 471
  discord 713
  - numero hæc judi-
  cantur 5
  - obstante 707
  - omnia possumus
  omnes 699
  - possimus
  impossible 471
  obstinate 606
  refusal 764
  - semper erit ætas 111
  - sequitur 477

- sum qualis eram
  change 140
  weak 160
- vobis solum 942
nonaddition 38
nonadmission 55
nonage 127
nonagenarian 130
nonappearance 447
nonassemblage 73
nonattendance 187
nonbeing 2
non-Biblical
  - prophets 986
nonce 118
  for the -
  present 118
  occasion 134
nonchalance
  neglect 460
  insensibility 823
  indifference 866
noncohesive 47
noncoincidence 14
noncommissioned
  officer 745
noncompletion 730
noncompliance
  disobedience 742
  refusal 764
nonconformity
  exception 83
  dissent 489
  sectarianism 984
noncontent 489
nondescript 83
none 101
  - else 87
  - in the world 4
  - such
  superior 33
  exceptional 83
  very good 648
  - the worse 660
  - to spare 640
nonendurance 825
nonentity
  inexistence 2
  unsubstantial 4
  unimportant 643
nonessential
  extrinsic 6
  unimportant 643
nonexistence 2
nonexpectance 508
nonextension 180a
nonfulfillment 730,
  732
  - of one's hopes 509
nonillion 102
nonimitation 20
noninclusion 55
noninterference
  inaction 681
  freedom 748
nonius 466
nonjuror
  dissent 489
  heterodox 984
nonnaturals 657
nonny 501

non objective 317
non observance
  inattention 458
  desuetude 614
  infraction **773**
  dereliction 927
nonpareil 648
nonpayment 808
nonperformance
  noncompletion 730
  dereliction 927
nonpertinence 10
nonplus
  uncertain 475
  difficulty 704
  conquer 731
nonpreparation **674**
nonprevalence 614
nonresidence 187
nonresistance
  submission 725
  obedience 743
nonresonance **408a**
nonsense
  absurdity 497
  unmeaning 517
  trash 643
  talk - *folly* 499
  to varnish - 499
nonsubjective 316
nonsubsistence 2
nonsuccess 732
nonsuch [*see* none]
nonsuit
  defeat 731
  fail 732
  condemn 971
nonum prematur in
  annum 133
nonuniformity 16a
noodle 501
nook *place* 182
  receptacle 191
  corner 244
noon *midday* 125
noonday *light* 420
  clear as -
  intelligible 518
  manifest 525
  - quiet holds the hill
  265
nooning 125
noontide 420
nooscopic 450
noose *ligature* 45
  loop 247
  snare 545
  gallows 975
N or M 78
norm 697
normal
  intrinsic 5
  regular 82
  perpendicular 212
  - condition
  rule 80
norma loquendi 567
Normand, répondre
  en - 544
North 278
  - and South **237**

norther 349
Northern 237
  - lights 423
  - star
  constant 939
Northwest passage
  311
nosce te 498
nosce tempus 134
noscitur a sociis 82,
  88
nose *prominence* 250
  curiosity 455, 461
  smell 398
  lead by the -
  induce 615
  govern 737
  led by the - 749
  not see beyond one's -
  misjudge 481
  folly 499
  unskillful 699
  put one's - out of
  joint *defeat* 731
  disrepute 874
  (*supplant* 147)
  speak through the -
  583
  thrust one's - in
  interjacence 228
  busy 682
  under one's -
  present 186
  near 197
  manifest 525
  defy 715
nosegay
  fragrance 400
  ornament 847
nosology 655
nostalgia 833
nostology 128
nostril 351
  breath of one's -s 359
  stink in the -s 401
nostrum
  contrivance 626
  remedy 662
not *negation* 536
  (*dissent* 489)
  it will - do 923
  - a bit 536
  - a few 102
  - a leg to stand on 158
  - a little 31
  - allowed 964
  - amiss *good* 618
  médiocre 651
  pretty 845
  - any 101
  - a particle 4
  - a pin to choose 27
  - a soul 101
  - at all 32
  - bad 651
  - bargain for 508
  - come up to 34
  - expect 508
  - fail 939
  - far from 197
  - fit to be seen 846

- following 477
- for the world
  unwilling 603
  refusal 764
- grant 764
- guilty 946
- hardened 950
- having
  absent 187
  exempt 777a
- hear of 764
- included 55
- know what to make
  of 519
- matter
  unimportant 643
- mind
  insensible 823
  contempt 930
- often 137
- of the earth 987
- one 101
- on speaking terms
  889
- on your life 764
- particular 831
- pay 808
- quite 32
- reach 304
- right 503
- sorry 827
- the thing 925
- to be borne 830
- to be despised 642
- to be had
  impossible 471
  insufficient 640
- to mention
  together with 37
- to be put down 604
- to be thought of
  incogitancy 452
  impossible 471
  refusal 764
  hopeless 859
  undue 925
  disapprobation 932
- trouble oneself
  about 460
- understand 519
- vote 609a
- within previous ex-
  perience 137
- wonder 871
- worth
  trifling 643
  useless 645
  what is - 546
  what ought - 923
nota bene 457
notabilia 642
notabilities 875
notable
  manifest 525
  important 642
  active 682
  distinguished 873
notables 875
notably 31
notary *recorder* 553
  lawyer 968

notation 85
notch
  gully 198
  nick **257**
  mark 550
note *music* 413
  take cognizance 450
  remark 457
  explanation 522
  sign 550
  record 551
  printing 591
  epistle 592
  minute 596
  money 800
  fame 873
  change one's - 607
  make a - of 551
  - of admiration 870
  - of alarm 669
  - of preparation 673
  -s by distance 415
  of - 873
  take - of 457
notebook
  record 551
  compendium 569
noted *known* 490
  famous 873
noteworthy
  great 31
  exceptional 83
  important 642
nothing *nihility* 4
  zero 101
  trifle 643
  come to -
  fall short 304
  fail 732
  do - 681
  for - 815
  go for - 643
  good for - 646
  make - of
  underestimate 483
nothingness 2
  fail 732
  - comes amiss 831
  - in it 4
  - loth 602
  - more to be said 478
  - of the kind
  unlike 18
  negation 536
  - on 226
  - to do 681
  - to do with 764
  - to go upon 471
  - to signify 643
  take - by 732
  think of - 930
  worse than - 808
notice *intellect* 450
  observe 457
  review 480
  information 527
  warning 668
  bring into - 525
  deserve - 642
  give -
  manifest 525

inform 527
indicate 550
- is hereby given
  publication 531
- to quit 782
short - 111
take - of 450
this is to give - 457
worthy of - 642
notification
  information 527
  (*publication* 531)
notion *idea* 453
  (*belief* 484)
  (*knowledge* 490)
notional
  fanciful 515
notoriety
  publication 531
  fame 873
notorious
  known 490
  public 531
  famous 873
  infamous 874
Notre Dame 987
notturno 415
notwithstanding 30
nought
  [*see* naught]
noun 564
nourish 707
nourishment
  food 298
nous 498
nous avons changé
  tout cela 140
nousle 545
nous verrons 870
novaculite 253
novation 609
Nova Zembla 383
novel
  dissimilar 18
  new 123
  unknown 491
  tale 594
  (*romance* 515)
  (*fiction* 546)
novelist 594
novello: di - tutto par
  bello 123
novice
  ignoramus 493
  learner 541
  bungler 701
  religious 996
novitiate
  learning 539
  training 673
novus homo
  stranger 57
  upstart 87¢
now 118
- and then 136

- or never 134
noways 32
nowhere 187
nowise *small* 32
  negation 536
noxious *bad* 649
  unhealthy 657
noyade *kill* 361
  punish 972
noyerait dans une
  goutte d'eau, il
  se - 699
nozzle
  projection 250
  opening 260
  air pipe 351
nuance
  difference 15
  discrimination
  465
nubibus, in -
  inexistent 2
  imaginary 515
nubiferous 426
nubile
  adolescent 131
  marriage 903
nucleus *middle* 68
  cause 153
  center 222
  kernel 642
nuda veritas 494
nude 226
nudge 550
nudity 226
nugacity
  absurdity 497
  folly 499
  inutility 645
nugæ canoræ
  unmeaning 517
  wit 842
nugas, magno co-
  natu magnas -
  643
nugatory
  powerless 158
  (*useless* 645)
nuggah 273
nugget *mass* 192
  money 800
nuisance *evil* 619
  annoyance 830
null 4
  declare - and void
  abrogation 756
  nonobservance 773
- and void
  powerless 158
  unproductive 169
  illegal 964
  (*inexistence* 2)
nulla dies sine lineâ
  682
nullâ pallescere cul-

pâ, nil conscire
  sibi - 946
nullibiety 187
nulli est homini per-
  petuum bonum
  734
nullify *inexistence* 2
  compensate 30
  destroy 162
  abrogate 756
  not observe 773
  not pay 808
nulli secundus 33
nullity
  inexistence 2
  unsubstantiality 4
nullius jurare in
  verba magistri
  487
nullum est jam dic-
  tum 104, 123
nullum magnum in-
  genium 498
numb
  physically insensible
  376, 381
  morally insensible
  823
number
  abstract - **84**
  count 85
  plural 100
  - *of a magazine* &c.
  593
- among 76
- of times 104
take care of - one
  943
numbered: days -
  kill 361
  necessity 601
  hopeless 859
. - with the dead 360
numberless 105
numbers *many* 102
  verse 597
numbness **381**
numdah 223
numerable 85
numeral 84, 85
numeration 85
numerator 84
numerical 85
numerose
  many 102
  elegant writing
  578
numerous 102
- *as glittering gems*
  102
numismatics 800
nummary 800
numps 501
numskull 493, 501
nun 904, 996

nunc aut nunquam
  134
nunc dimittis 990
nuncio
  messenger 534
  diplomatist 758
nuncupation
  naming 564
nuncupative 527, 582
nuncupatory
  informing 527
nundination 794
nunnation 560
nunnery 1000
nuptials 903
nurse *remedy* 662
  preserve 670
  help 707
  servant 746
  custodian 753
  put to - 537
nursling 129
nursery *infancy* 127
  nest 153
  room 191
  garden 371
  school 542
  workshop 691
- rhymes 597
- tale *fiction* 546
  narrative 594
nurture *feed* 298
  educate 537
  prepare 673
  aid 707
- a belief 484
- an idea 451
nusquam est qui
  ubique est 186
nut: - to crack
  riddle 533
  difficulty 704
- oil 365
nutation 314
nut-brown 433
nutmeg grater 330
nuts *good* 618
  pleasing 829
nutshell *small* 32
  lie in a -
  little 193
  compendium 596
nutriment 298
nutrition 707
nutritious *food* 298
  healthy 656
  remedy 662
nux vomica 663
nuzzle 902
nyctalopia 443
nymph *woman* 374
  mythology. 979
  sea - 341
nympha 129
nystagmus 443

O

O! *wonder* 870
  discontent 932
  - for *desire* 865
oaf *fool* 501
oak *strong* 159
  heart of -
    hard 323
    brave 861
oakum 205
oar *paddle* 267
  oarsman 269
  instrument 633
  laboring - 686
  lie upon one's -s 681
  ply the -
    navigate 267
    exert 686
  pull an - 680
  put in an -
    interpose 228
    busy 682
  rest on one's -
    cease 142
    quiescence 265
    repose 687
  spread the thin - 267
  stroke - 693
oar-shaped 245
oarsman 269
oasis *separate* 44
  exceptional 83
  land 342
oath *assertion* 535
  bad language 908
  rap out -s 885
  upon - 768
oatmeal 298
obbligato
  accompaniment 88
  music 415
obduction 223
obdurate
  obstinate 606
  severe 739
  malevolent 907
  graceless 945
  impenitent 951
obedience 743
obeisance *bow* 308
  submission 725
  courtesy 894
  reverence 928
obelisk *tall* 206
  monument 551
Oberon 979
obese 194
obesity 192
obey 743
  be subject to 749
  - a call 615
  - rules 82
  - the helm 705
obfuscate *dark* 421
  opaque 426
obfuscated

  drunk 959
obi 992
obiism 992
obit *death* 360
  interment 363
  post - 360, 363
obiter dictum
  irrelevant 10
  occasion 134
  interjacent 228
obituary *death* 360
  biography 594
object *thing* 3
  matter 316
  intention 620
  ugly 846
  disapprove 932
  be an -
    important 642
  - lesson 82
  - to *dislike* 867
objection
  hindrance 706
  disapproval 932
  no - 762
objectionable
  inexpedient 647
  wrong 923
objective
  extrinsic 6
  material 316
objurgate 932
oblate 201
  - spheroid 249
oblation *gift* 784
  religious - 990
  (*offer* 763)
oblectation 827
obligation
  necessity 601
  promise 768
  conditions 770
  debt 806
  confer an -
    good 648
  feeling of - 916
  under an -
    gratitude 916
    duty 926
oblige *benefit* 707
  compel 744
  duty 926
obligé, bien -
  refusal 764
obliged
  grateful 916
  duty 926
obligee 800
obliging
  helping 707
  courteous 894
  kind 906
obliquation 279
obliquity
  slope 217

  vice 945
  - of judgment 481
  - of vision 443
obliterate 2
obliteration 552
  - of the past 506
oblivion 506
  inexistence 2
  forgiveness 918
  - of benefits 917
  - of time 115
  redeem from - 505
oblivious 506
oblong 200
  - spheroid 249
obloquy
  disrepute 874
  disapprobation 932
  detraction 934
obmutescence
  voiceless 581
  taciturn 585
obnoxious
  pernicious 649
  unpleasing 830
  hateful 898
  - to *liable* 177
obnubilated 422
oboe 417
obreption 528, 775
obscene
  dirty 653
  indecent 961
obscure *dark* 421
  dim 422
  unseen 447
  unintelligible 519
  eclipse 874
  ignoble 876
obscurity
  style 571
obscurum per ob-
  scurius 519
obsecration 765
obsecratory 765
obsequies 363
obsequious
  servile 886
  courteous 894
  respectful 928
obsequiousness 933
observance *rule* 82
  attention 457
  habit 613
  practice 692
  fulfillment **772**
  duty 926
  rite 998
Observant
  friar 996
observation
  intellect 450
  idea 453
  attention 457
  assertion 535

observatory 318
observe [*see* observ-
  ance, observation]
  - a duty 926
  - rules 82
observer 444
obsession 716
obsidional 716
obsolescence 614
obsolete *old* 124
  words 563
  effete 645
obstacle
  moral - 706
  (*physical* - 179)
obstant, Fata - 601
obstetrician 631
obstetrics
  production 161
  surgery 662
obstinacy 606
  prejudice 481
obstipation 261
obstreperous
  violent 173
  loud 404
obstruct *close* 261
  hinder 706
  - the passage of light
    426
obstructionist 710
obstructive
  opponent 710
obstruent 706
obstupefaction 823
obstupui steterunt-
  que comæ 860
obtain *exist* 1
  get 775
  - under false pretense
    791
obtainable 470
obtenebration 421
obtestation
  injunction 695
  entreaty 765
obtrectation 934
obtrude
  interfere 228
  insert 300
  meddle 682
  (*obstruct* 706)
obtruncate 201
obtrusion
  interference 228
  obstruction 706
obtrusive
  interfering 228
  vulgar 851
  rude 895
obtund *mitigate* 174
  blunt 254
  deaden 376
  paralyze 823
obtuse *blunt* 253

526

insensible 376
imbecile 499
dull 823
- angle 244
obumbrate 421
obverse 234
obviate 706
obvious *visible* 446
  clear 518
  manifest 525
ocarina 417
occasion *juncture* 8
  opportunity **134**
  cause 153
  befit the - 646
  have - for 630
  on the present - 118
  on the spur of - 612
occasional 475
occasionally 136
occidental 236
occiput 235
occision 361
occlusion 261
occult
  unintelligible 519
  latent 526
  hidden 528
  - art 992
occultation
  disappearance 449
  concealment 528
occupancy
  presence 186
  possession 777
  (*property* 780)
  - in common 778
occupant
  inhabitant 188
  proprietor 779
occupation
  business 625
  in the - of 188
  - road 627
occupied 682
  - by 188
  - with
    attention 457
    business 625
occupier
  dweller 188
  possessor 779
occupy
  presence 186
  possess 777
  - a post 737
  - oneself with
    attend 457
    business 625
  - the chair 693
  - the mind
    thought 451
    attention 457
  - time 106
occur *exist* 1
  follow 117
  happen 151
  - in a place 186
  - to the mind 451
occurrence 151
  circumstance 8

of daily - 613
occurrent nubes 706
occursion 276
ocean 341
  - greyhound 273
  - of dreams 4
  plough the - 267
ocelot 440
ocher *brown* 433
  orange 439
  yellow - 436
ochlocracy 737
o'clock 114
  know what's - 698
octagon 244
octahedron 244
Octateuch 985
octave *music* 413
octavo 593
octifid 99
octodecimo 593
octogenarian 130
octopus 846, 913
octoroon 41
octroi 812
octuple 98
ocular 441
  - demonstration
    see 441
    visible 446
  - inspection 441
oculi pictura tenen-
  tur 850
oculis subjecta fidel-
  ibus 446
oculist 662
odalisque 746
odd *remaining* 40
  exception 83
  single 87
  insane 503
  vulgar 851
  ridiculous 853
  - fish 857
oddity
  laughingstock 857
oddments 51
odds *inequality* 28
  chance 156
  discord 713
  at -
    disagreement 24
    discord 713
  long - 704
  - against one 665
  - and ends
    remainder 40
    mixture 41
    part 51
    useless 645
  the - are 472
  what's the - 643
ode 597
od force 992
Odin 979
odious
  disagreeable 830
  ugly 846
  hateful 898
  comparisons   are -
    464

odi profanum vul-
  gus 878
odium *disgrace* 874
  hatred 898
  blame 932
odium theologicum
  pedantry 481
  pietism 988
  church 995
odometer 466
odontalgia 378
odontoid
  prominent 250
  sharp 253
odor 398
  in bad - 932
  - of sanctity 987
odylic force 992
odzookens 870
œcology 357
œcumenical 78
œdematous
  swollen 194
  soft 324
Œdipus
  answer 462
  expounder 524
  Davus sum non - 703
œil de maître 459
œnomancy 511
o'er [*see* over]
œuvre 161
of: - all things 33
  - a piece
    uniform 16
    similar 17
    agreeing 23
  - course
    conformity 82
    effect 154
  - late 123
  - no effect 169
  - old 122
  - one mind 23
off 196
  be - 623
  keep - 623
  make - with 791
  move - 287
  - and on
    periodical 138
    changeable 149
    irresolute 605
  - one's balance 605
  - one's guard
    neglect 260
    inexpectant 508
  - one's hands 776
  - one's head 503
  - one's legs
    carry one - 284
    dance one - 309
  - one's mind 452
  - side 238
  - the track 475
  - with you 297
  sheer - 287
  stand - 287
  start - 293
  take - one's hands
    785

  throw - one's center
    874
  throw - the scent
    uncertain 475
    avoid 623
offal 653
offend *pain* 830
  vice 945
  - against the law 964
offender
  - never pardons 918
offense *attack* 716
  anger 900
  guilt 947
offensive
  unsavory 395
  fetid 401
  foul 653
  aggressive 716
  displeasing 830
  distasteful 867
  obnoxious 898
  - and defensive alli-
    ance 712
  - to ears polite 579
offer *proposal* **763**
  - a choice 609
  - for sale 796
  - of marriage 902
  - oneself 763
  - sacrifice 990
  - the alternative 609
  - up prayers 990
offering *gift* 784
  burnt - 990
  sin - 952
offertory *gift* 784
  worship 990
  rite 998
offhand *soon* 132
  inattentive 458
  careless 460
  spontaneous 612
  (*unprepared* 674)
office *doing* 170
  room 191
  business 625
  mart 799
  worship 990
  a dog's obeyed in -
    737
  do an ill - 907
  do one's - 772
  good -s
    mediate 724
    kind 906
  hold - 693
  kind -s 906
  man in - 694
officer *director* 694
  commander 745
  constable 965
offices
  kitchen &c. 191
official
  certain 474
  true 494
  business 625
  man in office 694
  authoritative 737
  master 745

servant 746
fficialism 739
fficiate
  business 625
  instrumentality 631
  act 680
  conduct 692
  religious 998
officio, ex –
  officer 694
  authority 737
  duly 924
officious 682
offing *distance* 196
  ocean 341
offscourings
  useless 645
  dirt 653
offset
  compensation 30
  offspring 167
  printing 591
offshoot
  adjunct 39
  part 51
  effect 154
  offspring 167
offspring
  posterity 167
offuscate *dark* 421
  opaque 426
often
  repeated 104
  frequent 136
  most – 613
Ogham 590
ogle *look* 441
  desire 865
  rude 895
  endearment 902
ogre *bugbear* 860
  evil doer 913
  demon 980
**ohne Hast aber ohne
  Rast** 112, 684
oil *lubricate* 332
  grease 355, **356**
  – on the troubled wa-
    ters 174
  pour – on
  relieve 834
oil painting 556
oilskins 225
oily *smooth* 255
  greasy 355
  servile 886
  courteous 894
  flattery 933
oinomania 959
ointment
  grease 356
  remedy 662
old 124
  die of – *age* 729
  of – 122
  – age 128
  – bachelor 904
  – clothes 225
  – fogy *fool* 501
  laughingstock 857
  – glory 550

528

– joke 842
– maid *cards* 840
  spinster 904
– man *veteran* 130
  husband 903
– man of the sea 706
– Nick 978
– school
  antiquated 124
  obstinate 606
  habit 613
– soldier 392
– song
  repetition 104
  trifle 643
  cheap 815
– stager
  veteran 130
  proficient 700
– story
  repetition 104
  stale news 532
  love 897
– times 122
– woman *fool* 501
  effeminacy 374
  wife 903
– womanish 499
one's – *way* 613
pay off – *scores* 718
Oldbuck 122
older 128
oldest inhabitant
  not in memory of –
    137
old-fashioned 124
oldness 124
old world 124
oleagine 356
oleaginous 355
**oleum addere cam-
  ino**
  increase 35
  violent 173
olfactory 398
olibanum 400
olid 401
oligarch 745
oligarchy 737
olio 41
olive branch
  infant 129
  offspring 167
  pacification 723
olive green 435
olla podrida 41
Olympus 981
Om 993
omber 840
ombres chinoises 448
ombrometer 466
omega *end* 67
omelet 298
omen 512
ominate 511
ominous
  predicting 511
  danger 665
omission
  incomplete 53
  exclusion 55

neglect 460
failure 732
nonobservance 773
guilt 947
omitted
  inexistent 2
  absent 187
**omne ignotum pro
  magnifico** 486
**omnem movere la-
  pidem** 52
**omne solum forti
  patria** 861, 910
**omnes stultos in-
  sanire** 503
omne tulit punctum
  731
omnia
– *mors æquat* 360
– *tuta timens* 860
– *vincit amor* 731, 897
omnibus 272
omnifarious 81
omnific 168
omniform 81
omnigenous 81
omnipotence
  power 157 .
  God 976
omnipresence
  presence 186
  God 976
omniscience
  knowledge 490
  God 976
omnium gatherum
  mixture 41
  confusion 59
  assemblage 72
**omnium rerum
  principia parva
  sunt** 66
omnivorous
  eating 298
  desire 865
  gluttony 957
omophagic 298
omphalos 68
on *forwards* 282
– account of 155
– a large scale 31
– all accounts 52
– all fours
  identity 13
  agreement 23
– an average 29
– a par 27
– foot *duration* 106
  event 151
  doing 170
– no account 32
– no occasion 107
– one's head 218
– one's travels 57
– that account 155
– the brink of 32
– the cards 152
– the increase 35
– the moment 113
– the move 264
– the nail 118

– the other hand 30
– the part of 9
– the point of 111
– the present occa-
  sion 118
– the whole 50
once *past* 122
  seldom 137
at –
  instantaneously 113
  soon 132
– for all *final* 67
  infrequency 137
  tell one – 527
  determine – 604
  choose 609
– in a blue moon 137
– in a way 137
– more *twice* 90
  again 104
– upon a time
  time 106
  different time 119
  formerly 122
Ondine 979
on dit *news* 532
  talk 588
one *identical* 13
  whole 50
  unity 87
  somebody 372
  married 903
all – to 823
as – man
  unanimous 488
  coöperation 709
at – with *agree* 23
  concur 178
  concord 714
both the – and the
  other 80
from – to another
  transfer 783
make – of 186
neither – nor the other
  610
of – *accord* 488
on – side
  oblique 217
  lateral 236
– and a half 87
– and all
  whole 50
  general 78
  unanimous 488
– and the same 13
– at a time 87
– bone and one flesh
  903
– by one
  separately 44
  respectively 79
  unity 87
– consent
  concur 178
  assent 488
– fell swoop
  instantaneous 113
  violent 173
– fine morning 106
– idea

optime! 931
optimism
  overestimation 482
  hopeful 858
optimist
  flatterer 935
option 609
optional 600
opulence 803
**opum furiata cupi-
  do** 803
opuscule 593
or *yellow* 436
  orange 439
  alternative 609
oracle *sage* 500
  prophet 513
Oracle, Sir -
  positive 474
  vanity 880
  blusterer 887
oracular
  ambiguous 475
  wise 498
  prediction 511
ora e sempre 112
ora et labora 686, 990
oral *voice* 580
  speech 582
  - communication 588
  - evidence 467
orange *round* 249
  color **439**
orangery 371
oration 582
  funeral - 363
orator 582
oratorio 415
oratory
  speaking 582
  place of prayer 1000
orb *region* 181
  circle 247
  luminary 423
  eye 441
  sphere of action 625
  - of day *sun* 318
  luminary 423
  - of night 318
orbicular 247
orbit *circle* 247
  heavens 318
  path 627
orchard 371
orchestra
  music 415
  musicians 416
  instruments 417
  theater 599
orchotomy 158
ordain
  command **741**
  commission 755
  due 924
  legal 963
  God 976
  church 99**5**
ordained *due* 924
  clergy 996
ordeal
  experiment 463

trouble 828
sorcery 992
- of battle 722
order
  regularity **58**
  class 75
  requirement 630
  direct 693
  command 741
  money 800
  rank 873
  quality 875
  decoration 877
  law 963
  at one's - 743
  call to - 932
  in - 620
  in working - 673
  keep in - 693
  money - 800
  - from disorder sprung
    58
  - is heaven's first law
    58
  - of the day
    conformity 82
    events 151
    habit 613
    plan 636
    command 741
  - of your going 684
  out of - 651
  pass to the - of the
    day 624
  put in - 60
  recur in regular - 138
  set in - 60
  set one's house in -
    673
  standing - 613
orderless 59
orderly
  regular 58, 80
  arrange 60
  conformable 82
  servant 746
  - of succession 63
  - of things 80
orders, holy - 995
  in - 996
ordinal 998
ordinance
  command 741
  law 963
  rite 998
ordinary *usual* 82
  meal 298
  habitual 613
  imperfect 651
  ugly 846
  simple 849
  in - *store* 636
  lay up in - 678
  lie in - 681
  - condition
    rule 80
  - course of things 613
ordinate 466
ordination
  measurement 466
  command 741

commission **755**
church 995
rite 998
ordnance 727
**ordo est parium dis-
  pariumque** &c. 58
ordonnance 963
ordure 653
ore 635
oread 979
ore rotundo 577
organ *music* 417
  voice 580
  instrument 633
  - of the soul 580
organic *state* 7
  structural 329
  protoplastic 357
  - change 146
  - chemistry 357
  - remains 357
  dead 362
organism 329
organist 416
organization
  arrangement 60
  production 161
  structure 329
  animated nature **357**
organize
  arrange 60
  produce 161
  plan 626
  (*prepare* 673)
organized hypocrisy
  544
organology 329
orgasm 173
orgies 954
oriel *recess* 191
  corner 244
  window 260
  chapel 1000
Orient *East* 236
  sunrise 420
orientate 236
orifice
  beginning 66
  opening 260
oriflamme 550
Origenism 984
origin
  beginning 66
  cause 153
  derive its - 154
original
  dissimilar 18
  not imitated 20
  model 22
  individual 79
  exceptional 83
  cause 153
  invented 515
  laughingstock 857
  return to - *state* 660
originality
  will 600
  want of - 843
originate *begin* 66
  cause 153
  invent 515

  - in 154
originator 164
Orion's belt 318
orismology
  word 562
  name 564
orison *request* 765
  worship 990
ormolu
  sham 545
  ornament 847
Ormuzd 979
ornament
  in writing **577**
  adornment **847**
  glory 873
  excess of - 851
ornamental art 847
  painting 556
ornate
  - *writing* 577
  ornamental 847
**ornavit, nihil tetigit
  quod non -** 850
orniscopy 511
ornithology 368
ornithomancy 511
orotund 577
orphan 129
Orpheus 416
orpiment 436
orrery 318
orthodox
  conformable 82
  - *religion* 983a
  - dissenter 984
orthodoxy 983a
orthoepy 580
orthogonal 212
orthography 561
orthology 494
orthometry
  measurement 466
  prosody 597
orthopædy 662
orthopraxy 662
orts *remnants* 40
  useless 645
  (*trifles* 643)
oryctology
  minerals 358
  organic remains 368
O Salutaris 990
oscillation
  change 149
  motion **314**
  center of - 222
oscitancy
  opening 260
  sleepy 683
osculation
  contact 199
  endearment 902
Osiris 979
Osmanli 984
Ossa on Pelion
  heap 72
  weight 319
osseous 323
ossify 323
ossuary 363

put - sight
  invisible 447
  neglect 460
  conceal 528
turn - doors 297
outogeny 357
outpost *distant* 196
  circumjacent 227
  front 234
  - of advancing day
    126
outpouring
  egress 295
  information 527
  abundance 639
output *egress* 295
  produce 775
outrage
  violence 173
  evil 619
  badness 649
  injury to 659
  resentment 900
  malevolence 907
  disrespect 929
  guilt 947
outrageous
  excessive 31
  violent 173
  scandalous 874
outrance: à -
  great 31
  complete 52
  violent 173
  guerre - 722
outrank 33
outré
  exceptional 83
  exaggerate 549
  ridiculous 853
outreach 545
outreckon 482
outre mer 196
outride 303
outrider 64
outrigger
  support 215
  boat 273
outright 52
outrival
  superior 33
  surpass 303
  fame 873
outrun 303
  - the constable
  debt 806
  prodigal 818
outscourings 653
outset
  beginning 66
  departure 293
outshine *glory* 873
  eclipse 874
outside
  exterior 220
  appearance 448
  clean the - of the
    platter
  ostentation 882
  mere - 544
  - car 272

outsider 57
outskirts
  distant 196
  environs 227
outspan 292
outspeak 582
outspoken *say* 582
  artless 703
  be - *censure* 932
outspread 202
outstanding
  remaining 40
  outside 220
  - accounts 811
  - debt 806
outstare 885
outstep 303
outstretched 202
  with - arms 894
outstrip 303
outtalk 584
outvie *contend* 720
  shine 873
outvote 731
outward 220
  - bound 293
outweigh
  exceed 33
  predominate 175
  (*unequal* 28)
outwit *deceive* 545
  defeat 731
outwork
  defense 717
oval 247
ovary 357
ovate 247
ovation
  triumph 883
  (*trophy* 733)
oven 386
  like an - *hot* 382
over *more* 33
  remainder 40
  end 67
  past 122
  high 206
  too much 641
  all - *completed* 729
  all - with
  destroyed 162
  dead 360
  failure 732
  adversity 735
  danger - 664
  fight one's battles
    again 594
  get - 660
  hand - 783
  make - 784
  - again
  repeatedly 104
  - against 237
  - and above
  superior 33
  added 37
  remainder 40
  redundance 641
  - head and ears
  complete 52
  height 206

  feeling 821
  - the border 196
  - the hills and far
    away 196
  - the mark 33
  - the way 237
  set - 755
  turn - 218
overabound 641
overact *bustle* 682
  affect 855
overall 225
overanxiety 865
overarch 223
overawe *sway* 737
  intimidate 860
  respect 928
overbalance
  unequal 28
  compensation 30
  superior 33
overbear
  influence 175
overbearing 885
overboard, throw -
  eject 297
  reject 610
  disuse 678
  abrogate 756
  relinquish 782
overborne
  failure 732
  subjection 749
overburden
  redundant 641
  bad 649
  fatigue 688
overcast *cloudy* 353
  dark 421
  dim 422
overcautious 864
overcharge
  exaggerate 549
  style 577
  redundance 641
  dearness 814
overcoat 225
overcolor 549
overcome
  induce 615
  conquer 731
  sad 837
  disgraced 874
  tipsy 959
  - an obstacle 731
overconfident
  credulous 486
  rash 863
overcredulous 486
overcurious 455
overdate 115
overdistention 194
overdo
  redundance 641
  bustle 682
  affectation 855
overdose 641
overdraw
  exaggerate 549
  misrepresent 555
  prodigal 818

overdrawn account
  808.
overdue 115
overeager 865
overeat oneself 957
overestimation 482
overfatigued 688
overfed 957
overfeed 641
overflow *stream* 348
  redundance 641
  - with gratitude 916
overgo 303
overgorged
  satiety 869
  gluttony 957
overgrown *much* 31
  large 192
  expanded 194
overhang *high* 206
overhanging
  destiny 152
  pendency 214
overhasty 901
overhaul *count* 85
  attend to 457
  inquire 461
  censure 932
overhead 206
overhear *hear* 418
  be informed 527
overjoyed 827
overjump 303
overlap
  inwrap 225
  go beyond 303
overlay *cover* 223
  exaggerate 549
  excess 641
  overdo 682
  hinder 706
  - with ornament
  writing 577
overleap 303
overliberal 818
overlie 223
overload
  redundance 641
  hinder 706
overlook *slight* 458
  neglect 460
  superintend 693
  forgive 918
  disparage 929
overlooked 642
  not to be - 642
overlooker 694
overlying 206
overmaster 731
overmatch
  unequal 28
  superior 33
  strength 159
  conquer 731
overmeasure 641
overmodest 881
overmuch 641
overnight 122
overofficious 682
overpaid 816
overpass

exceed 33
transgress 303
overpersuade 615
overplus
　remainder 40
　excess 641
overpoise 179
overpower
　subdue 731
　emotion 824
overpowering
　strong 159
overpraise
　overrate 482
　exaggerate 549
　flatter 933
overprize 482
overrate 482
overreach *pass* 303
　deceive 545
　baffle 545
overreckon 482
overrefinement 477
over-religious 955
override
　superior 33
　influence 175
　pass 303
　hinder 706
　defeat 731
　authority 737
　severity 739
　abrogate 756
overrighteous 988
overrule
　control 737
　cancel 756
overruling
　important 642
overrun
　presence 186
　spread 194
　printing 591
　redundance 641
　despoil 659
overscrupulous 939
oversea 57
overseer 694
oversensitive 822
overset *invert* 218
　level 308
　subvert 731
overshadow
　darken 421
　repute 873
　disrepute 874
overshoot the mark

go beyond 303
exaggerate 549
overdo 682
clumsy 699
oversight
　inattention 458
　error 495
　superintendence 693
　failure 732
overskip 303
oversleep 683
overspent 688
overspread
　disperse 73
　be present 186
　cover 233
overstate 549
overstep 303
overstock 641
overstrain
　extol 482
　fatigue 688
oversupply 641
overt 525
　- act 680
overtake 292
overtaken
　tipsy 959
overtask }
overtax }
　misuse 679
　fatigue 688
overthrow
　destroy 162
　level 308
　confute 479
　vanquish 751
overthrown
　vanquished 732
overthwart 708
overtired 688
overtop *surpass* 33
　height 206
　(perfection 650)
overtrustful 486
overture
　precursor 64
　music 415
　offer 763
　request 765
overturn
　destroy 162
　invert 218
　level 308
　confute 479
overvalue 482
overweening

excess 641
rash 863
pride 878
conceit 880
insolence 885
overweigh
　exceed 33
　influence 175
　overrate 482
overwhelm
　ruin 162
　redundant 641
　affect 824
overwhelmed
　defeated 732
　subjection 749
overwhelming
　strong 159
　wonderful 870
overwise 880
overwork
　misuse 679
　fatigue 688
overwrought
　exaggerated 549
　emotion 824
　affectation 855
overzealous 825
oviform 249
ovo, in - 153
ovoid 249
ovule 247
ovum 357
owe 806
　- it to oneself 926
owing *debt* 806
　attribution 155
owl *fool* 501
　-'s light 422
　-s to Athens 641
　screech - 412
own *assent* 488
　divulge 529
　possess 777
　property 780
　act on one's - respon-
　　sibility 738
　after one's - heart
　　897
　at one's - risk 926
　come by one's - 775
　condemned out of
　　one's - mouth 479
　consult one's - pleas-
　　ure 943
　have one's - way
　　will 600

easy 705
succeed 731
authority 737
freedom 748
hold one's - 737
know one's - mind
　604
look after one's - in-
　terest 943
look with one's - eyes
　459
not know one's - in-
　terest 699
not know one's -
　mind 605
of one's - accord
　will 600
　willing 602
out of one's - head
　600
- flesh and blood
　11
- oneself in the wrong
　950
pay in one's - coin
　718
stand in one's - light
　699
take the law into
　one's - hands
　war 722
　lawless 964
throw a stone in one's
　- garden
　clumsy 699
　retaliation 718
will of one's - 604
owner *possessor* 779
　without an - 777a
ownership
　property 780
ox *animal* 366
　male 373
　hot enough to roast
　　an - 382
Oxford school 984
oxgoad 727
oxidation 357, 659
oxreim 45
oxygen 359
oxygon 244
**oyer and terminer,
　court of** - 966
oyes 531
oyez! *hear* 418
　publication 531
oyster 298

P

P: - coat 225
  mind one's -'s and Q's
  care 459
  polite 894
  duty 926
pabulum
  food 298
  material 316
  mental - 454
  - *pictura pascit inani*
  452
pace *walk* 264
  journey 266
  measure 466
  keep - with
  concur 178
  velocity 274
  - up and down 266
  put through one's -s
  525
  show one's -s
  ostentation 882
pace *permission* 760
  - *tanti nominis* 928
pachydermatous
  physically - 376
  morally - 823
pacific 721
pacification 723
pacify *allay* 174
  (*compose* 823)
  (*forgive* 918)
pack *arrange* 60
  assemblage 72
  locate 184
  squeeze 195
  prepare 673
  burden 706
  - off *depart* 293
  eject 297
  - of nonsense 643
  - up 229
  send -ing 297
package
  assemblage 72
  location 184
packer 673
packet
  assemblage 72
  ship 273
pack horse 271
pack saddle 215
pack thread 205
pact 769
Pactolus 803
pad *thicken* 194
  line 224
  horse 271
padding
  lining 224
  stopper 263
  soft 324
paddle *walk* 266
  row 267
  oar 633

534

- one's own canoe
  conduct 692
  free 748
  - steamer 273
paddock 232
paddy 330
padishah 745
padlock
  fastening 45
  fetter 752
  put a - on one's lips
  585
padre 996
padrone 745
pæan
  rejoicing 838
  celebration 883
  gratitude 916
  approbation 931
  worship 990
paganism 984
page
  numeration 85
  printing 591
  book 593
  attendant 746
pageant
  spectacle 448
  show 882
pagination 85
pagoda 1000
pagri 225
pah 717
pail 191
paillard 962
paillasse 215
pain *physical* - **378**
  moral - **828**
  penalty 974
painfulness 830
painfully *very* 31
painless 827
pains 686
  get for one's - 973
  - and penalties 974
  take - 686
painstaking
  active 682
  laborious 686
paint *coat* 223
  color 428
  deceive 545
  delineate 556
  ornament 847
  - the lily 641
  - the town red 840
painter *rope* 45
  artist 559
painting 556
pair *similar* 17
  couple 89
  - off *average* 29
  marry 903
pair-oar 273
pairs *cards* 840

pajamas 225
paktong 545
pal *ally* 711
  chum 890
palace 89
  bishop's - 1000
Paladin
  defense 717
  combatant 726
palæocrystic 124
palæology [*see*
  paleology &c.]
palæstra
  school 542
  arena 728
  [*and see* palestric]
palais de vérité 703
palang 215
palanquin 272
palatable
  savory 394
  pleasant 829
palate 390
  tickle the - 394
palatial *palace* 189
  ostentatious 882
palatine 745
Palatine Court 966
palaver
  unmeaning 517
  speech 582
  loquacity 584
  colloquy 588
  council 696
pale *region* 181
  inclosure 232
  limit 233
  dim 422
  colorless 429
  frightened 860
  - its ineffectual fire
  dim 422
  out of repute 874
  - of the church 995
  turn -
  lose color 429
  emotion 821
  fear 860
pale-faced 429
paleoanthropic 124
paleography
  past 122
  Philology 560
paleology *past* 122
  language 160
paleontology 368
paleozoic 124
palestric
  exertion 686
  contention 720
paletot 225
palette 556
palfrey 271
palimpsest 147
palindrome

  inversion 218
  neology 563
paling *fence* 232
  prison 752
palingenesis 163, 660
palinody 607
palisade
  defense 717
  prison 752
palki 272
pall *mantle* 225
  funeral 363
  disgust 395
  insignia 747
  weary 841
  dislike 867
  satiety 869
  canonicals 999
palladium
  safety 664
  (*defense* 717)
pallet *support* 215
  painter's - 556
palliament 225
palliate
  moderate 174
  mind 658
  .*relieve* 834
  extenuate 937
palliative 174
  remedy 662
pallid 429
pallium 999
pall-mall 840
pallone 840
pallor 429
palm
  measure of length 200
  trophy 733
  steal 791
  laurel 877
  bear the - 873
  for authors nobler -s
  remain 593
  grease the -
  induce 615
  give 784
  itching - 865
  - off, - upon 545
  win the - 731
palmated 257
palmer
  traveler 268
  clergy 996
palmiped 219
palmistry 511
palmy
  prosperous 734
  pleasant 829
  joyous 836
  - days
  prosperity 734
  pleasure 827
palpable
  material 316

perfervidum inge-
  nium 682
perfidy 940
perflate 349
perforate 260
perforator 262
perforce
  necessity 601
  compulsion 744
perform
  produce 161
  do 170
  - *music* 416
  action 680
  achieve 729
  fulfill 772
  - a *circuit* 629
  - a *duty* 926
  - a *function* 644
  - a *funeral* 363
  - an *obligation* 772
  - a *part*
    drama 599
    action 680
  - a *service* 998
  - the *duties of* 625
performable 470
performance
  [see *perform*]
  effect 154
performer
  musician 416
  stageplayer 599
  agent 690
  affectation 855
perfume 400
perfunctory
  incomplete 53
  neglect 460
perhaps
  possibly 470
  supposition 514
  (*chance* 156)
peri
  beauty 845
  mythology 979
periapt 993
pericarp 191
pericranium 450
periculous 665
peridot 847
perihelion 197
peril 665
  at your - 909
  take heed at one's -
    668
perilepsis 476
perimeter 230
period *end* 67
  point 71
  - *of time* 106, **108**
  recurrence 138
  at fixed -s 138
  well rounded -s 577,
    578
periodical
  recurring 138
  book 593
periodicity 138
peripatetic
  journey 266

traveler 268
periphery 230
periphrase
  phrase 566
  diffuse 573
periplus 267
periscope 441
periscopic 446
  - *lens* 445
perish
  cease to exist 2
  be destroyed 162
  die 360
  decay 659
  - *with cold* 383
  - *with hunger* 956
perishable 111
perissology
  diffuseness 573
  (*loquacity* 584)
peristaltic 248
peristyle 189
periwig 225
perjured 940
perjurer 548
perjury 544
perk *dress* 225
  - *up elevate* 307
  revive 689
  cheer 836
perked up
  proud 878
perlustration 441
permanence
  durability 110
  unchanging **141**
  unchangeable 150
permanent
  habitual 613
permeable 260
permeate
  insinuate 228
  pervade 186
  pass through 302
permissible
  permitted 760
  (*lawful* 924)
permission 760
permissive 760
permit 760
permitting
  weather &c. - 469,
    470
permutation
  numerical - 84
  change 140
  interchange 148
pernicious 649
pernicity 274
perorate
  diffuse style 573
peroration
  sequel 65
  end 67
  speech 582
perpend *think* 451
perpendicular 212
perpension
  attention 457
perpetrate 680
  - a *pun* &c. 842

perpetrator 690
perpetua, esto -
  respect 928
  approbation 931
perpetual 112
  frequent 136
  - *curate* 996
perpetuate 112
  continue 143
  establish 150
perpetuity 112
perplex *derange* 61
  distract 458
  uncertainty 475
  bother 830
perplexed
  confused 59
  convoluted 248
perplexity
  disorder 59
  uncertainty 475
  unintelligibility 519
  difficulty 704
  (*ignorance* 491)
perquisite 973
perquisition 461
perron 627
perscrutation 461
persecute
  oppress 649
  annoy 830
  malevolence 907
perseverance
  continuance 143
  persistence **604a**
Persides 215
persiflage 856
persifleur 844
persist *duration* 106
  permanence 141
  continue 143
  persevere 604a
persistence
  diuturnity 110
person
  substantiality 3
  man 372
  without distinction of
    -s 922
personable 845
personæ, dramatis -
  drama 599
  doer 690
personage 372
persona grata
  friend 890
  favorite 899
personal
  [see *person*]
  special 79
  subjective 317
  - *narrative* 594
  - *properly* 780
  - *security* 771
personality
  [see *personal*]
  discourtesy 895
  disrespect 929
  censure 932
  detraction 934
personalty 780

personate
  imitate 19
  represent 554
personify
  allegory 521
  represent 554
personnel
  constituent 56
  doer 690
perspective
  view 448
  expectation 507
  painting 556
  aerial - 428
  in - 200
perspicacity
  sight 441
  intelligence 498
perspicuity
  intelligibility 518
  style **470**
perspiration
  exudation 295
  excretion 299
  in a - 382
perstringe 457
persuadable 602
persuade *belief* 484
  induce 615
  (*advise* 695)
persuasibility
  willingness 602
persuasion
  opinion 484
  teaching 537
  inducement 615
  religious - 983
persuasive r e a s o n-
  ing 476
pert *vain* 880
  insolent 885
  discourteous 895
pertain to
  relate to 9
  included under 76
  power 157
  belong 777
  property 780
  duty 926
perte de vue, à -
  distant 196
  invisible 447
pertinacity 604a
pertinent
  relative 9
  congruous 23
  (*applicable* 644)
pertingent 199
perturbation
  derange 61
  ferment 171
  agitation 315
  emotion 821
  excitation 824, 825
  fear 860
  O polished - 459
pertusion 260
pertussis 655
peruke 225
peruse 539
Peruvian bark 662

physiognomy
face 234
appearance 448
interpret 522
physiology
organization 357
life 359
vegetable - 369
physique
strength 159
animality 364
phytivorous 298
phytology 369
phytotomy 369
phytozoaria 193
pi 591
piacere, al - 600
piacular 952
pianino 417
pianissimo 415
pianist 416
piano *gentle* 174
slow 275
music 415
pianoforte 417
piazza 189, 191
pibroch *music* 415
war 722
pica 591
picacho 206
picaresco, gusto - 945
picaroon 792
picayune 643
piccolo 417
pick *axe* 253
eat 298
select 609
best 648
clean 652
gain 775
- a quarrel 713
- holes
censure 932, 934
- one's steps 459
- one's way 675
- out *extract* 301
select 609
- the brains of 461
- the lock 480a
- to pieces
separate 44
destroy 162
find fault 932
- up *learn* 539
get better 658
gain 775
pickaninny 129
pickaxe 253
picked 648
- men 700
pickeer 720
pickeerer 792
pickelhaube
armor 717
picket
join 43
locate 184
fence 229
guard 668
defense 717

soldiers 726
restrain 751
imprison 752
torture 972
pickings *gain* 775
booty 793
pickle *condition* 7
macerate 337
pungent 392
condiment 393
preserve 670
difficulty 704
have a rod in - 673
pickle-herring 844
pick-me-up 662
pickpocket 792
abuse like a - 932
pickthank
busy 682
servile 886
picnic *food* 298
participation 778
amusement 840
picquet 840
pictorial
painting 556
beauty 845
picture
appearance 448
representation 554
painting 556
description 594
- post card 592
- to oneself 515
picture gallery 556
picturesque
painting 556
beauty 845
piddle *dawdle* 683
piddling
trivial 642
pie *food* 298
sweet 396
printing 591
piebald 440
piece
adjunct 39
bit 51
painting 556
drama 599
cannon 727
coin 800
courtesan 962
fall to -s 162
give a - of advice 695
in -s 330
make a - of work
about 642
of a - 42
- of a good fortune 618
- of music 415
- of news 532
- of work
discord 713
- out 52
- together 43
pull to -s 162
piéce
- de résistance 298
- justificative 467

piecemeal 51
pied 440
pied de la lettre, au - 494
pie-poudre, court of - 966
pier 666
pierce
perforate 260
bodily pain 378
chill 385
hurt 649
wound 659
affect 824
mental pain 830
- the head 410
- the heart 830
piercer 262
piercing *cold* 383
loud 404
shrill 410
intelligent 498
feeling 821
- eye 441
- pain 378
pier glass 445
Pierian spring 597
Pierides 416
pierre fendre, à - 383
pietas 998
piété, mont de - 787
pietism 988
pietist 987, 988
pietra mossa 149
piety 987
pig *animal* 366
sensual 954a
- in a poke
uncertain 475
chance 621
rash 863
- together 72
pigeon *dupe* 547
steal 791
gorge de - 440
pigeon English 563
pigeon-hearted 862
pigeon hole
receptacle 191
hole 260
shelve 460
piggin 191
piggish 954
pig-headed
foolish 499
obstinate 606
pigment 428
pigmy 193
pignoration 771
pig-sticking 361
pigsty 653
pigtail 214
pigwidgeon
dwarf 193
imp 980
pike *hill* 206
sharp 253
weapon 727
pikeman 726
pikestaff *tall* 206
plain 525

pilaster
support 215
projection 250
ornament 847
pile *heap* 72
edifice 161
velvet 256
money 800
(*house* 189)
funeral - 363
- on the agony 860
- up
exaggeration 549
redundance 641
pile-driving engine 276
pile-dwelling 189
pileous 256
piles 655
pilfer *steal* 791
pilferer 792
pilgarlic
outcast 893
pilgrim
traveler 268
palmer 996
pilgrimage
journey 266
undertaking 676
pill *sphere* 249
medicine 662
bore 841
bitter - 735
pillage *injury* 659
theft 791
pillager 792
pillar *stable* 150
lofty 206
support 215
monument 551
tablet 590
from - to post
transfer 270
agitation 315
irresolute 505
circuit 629
- of the state &c. 873
-s of Hercules 550
pillarist 996
pillion 215
pillory 975
pillow
support 215
soft 324
consult one's -
temporize 133
reflect 451
pillowcase 223
pilon 784
pilose 256
pilot *mariner* 269
inform 527
guide 693
director 694
pilot balloon
experiment 463
pilot boat 273
pilot bread 298
pilot jacket 225
Pilsener beer 298
pimento 393

pimp 962
pimple *tumor* 250
  blemish 848
pin *fasten* 43
  fastening 45
  locate 184
  sharp 253
  axis 312
  trifle 643
  might hear a - drop 403
  not a - to choose
  equal 27
  no choice 609a
  - down
  compulsion 744
  restraint 751
  - oneself upon
  serve 746
  servile 886
  - one's faith upon 484
  point of a - 193
pinacotheca 556
pinafore 225
pince-nez 445
pincers 781
pinch *emergency* 8
  contract 195
  pain 378
  chill 385
  need 630
  difficulty 704
  grudge 819
  hurt morally 830
  (*insufficiency* 640)
  at a - 704
  jack at a - 711
  - of snuff 643
  where the shoe -s 830
pinchbeck *sham* 545
  jewelry 847
pinched [see pinch]
  poor 804
  - with hunger 865
pinchfist 819
pinching *cold* 383
  miserly 819
Pindaric 597
pine *disease* 655
  dejection 837
  suffer in mind 828
  - away 837
  - for 865
pineapple 298
pinery 371
pingpong 840
pin grass 367
pinguid 355
pin hole 260
pinion *fasten* 43
  wing 267
  instrument 633
  restrain 751
  fetter 752
pink *pierce* 260
  thrust 276
  color 434
  perfection 650
  glory 873
pink of *beauty* 845
  - courtesy 894

- fashion 852
- perfection 650
- politeness 894
pin money 800
pinnace 273
pinnacle 210
pins *legs* 266
- and needles
  bodily pain 378
  numb 381
  mental pain 828
Pinto, Fernam Mendez - 548
pioneer
  precursor 64
  leader 234
  teacher 540
  prepare 673
pious 987
- fraud
  untruth 546
  false piety 988
pipe *tube* 260
  conduit 350
  vent 351
  sound 410
  cry 411
  music 416, 417
  weep 839
  no - no dance 812
- of peace 721
- one's eye 839
pipe clay *habit* 613
  strictness 739
piped 260
pipelaying 626
piper 416
  pay the - *aid* 707
  payment 807
piping - hot 382
- time *peace* 721
  prosperity 734
pipkin 191
piquant
  pungent 392
- *style* 574
  impressive 821
piquante, sauce -
  condiment 393
  pleasing 829
pique *excite* 824
  pain 830
  hate 898
  anger 900
- oneself
  pride 878
piqueerer 792
piquet *defense* 717
  soldiers 726
piracy 773
pirate *steal* 791
  thief 792
pirogue 273
pirouette
  inversion 218
  evolution 312
  turn a - 607
Pisa, tower of - 217
pis-aller
  substitute 147
piscatorial 366

pisces natare docere
  misteaching 538
  redundance 641
pisciculture 370
piscina
  drain 350
  altar 1000
pish! *absurd* 497
  trifling 643
  excitable 825
  irascible 901
pistareen 643
piste 551
pistol 727
Pistol 887
pistol shot 197
piston 263
pit *deep* 208
  hole 252
  opening 260
  grave 363
  theater 599
  bottomless - 982
- against
  opposition 708
  discord 713
- against one another 464
- of Acheron 982
pitapat
  agitation 315
  rattle 407
  feeling 821
  excitation 824
pitch *degree* 26
  . *term* 71
  location 184
  height 206
  summit 210
  throw 284
  descent 306
  depression 308
  reel 314
  resin 356a
  musical - 413
  black 431
  - and toss 621
  - dark 421
  - into *attack* 716
  contend 720
  punish 972
  - of one's breath 411
  - one's tent 292
  - overboard 782
  - upon *reach* 292
  discover 480a
  choose 609
  get 775
  touch - 653
pitched battle 720
pitcher 191
pitchfork
  vehicle 273
  throw 284
  rain -s 348
pitch pipe 417
piteous
  painful 830
piteously *much* 31
pitfall *snare* 545
  danger 667

pith *gist* 5
  strength 159
  interior 221
  center 222
  meaning 516
  important part 642
pithless 158
pithy *meaning* 516
  concise 572
  vigorous 574
pitiable *bad* 649
  painful 830
  contemptible 930
pitied, to be - 828
pitiful
  unimportant 643
  bad 649
  disrepute 874
  pity 914
pitiless 914a
  revengeful 919
  (*malevolent* 907)
pittance *dole* 640
  allotment 786
  income 810
pitted 848
pituitous 352
pity 914
  express - 915
  for -'s sake 914
  what a -
  regret 833
  lament 839
pivot *junction* 43
  cause 153
  support 215
  axis 312
pix *box* 191
  assay 463
  rites 998
pixy 980
pizzicato 415
placable 918
placard 531
placate *pacify* 723
  forgive 918
place
  circumstances 8
  order 58
  arrange 60
  term 71
  situation 182, 183
  locate 184
  abode 189
  office 625
  rank 873
  give - to 623
  have - 1
  in - 183
  in - of 147
  make a - for 184
  out of - 185
  - in order 60
  - itself 58
  - to one's credit 805
  - upon record 551
  - under
  include 76
  take - 151
placebit, decies repetita - 829

placebo 933
place hunter 767
placeman 758
placenta 63
placid 826
placit 741
placket 260
plafond 223
plagiarism
  imitation 19
  borrowing 788
  theft 791
plagiarist 792
Plagiary, Sir Fretful
  - 901
plagihedral 217
plague *disease* 655
  pain 828
  worry 830
- of sighing and grief
  837
plague spot 657
plaguy
  difficult 704
  troublesome 830
plaid *shawl* 225
  variegation 440
plaidoyer 476
plain
  horizontal 213
  country 344
  obvious 446
  meaning 518
  manifest 525
  style 576
  artless 703
  ugly 846
  simple 849
- dealing 543
- English 576
- interpretation 522
- question 461
- sailing 705
- sense 498
- speaking
  manifest 525
  frank 703
- terms
  intelligible 518
  interpreted 522
  language 576
- truth 494
- words 703
lainly, tell one -
  527
plainness 576
plain song 990
plain-spoken
  manifest 525
  frank 703
plaint *cry* 411
  lament 839
plaintiff 938
plaintive 839
plaisance
  demesne 189
  pleasure ground 840
plaisanterie 842
plaister 223
plait *weave* 219
  fold 258

plan *itinerary* 266
  information 527
  representation 554
  scheme **626**
planchment 223
plane *horizontal* 213
  flat 251
  smooth 255
  soar 305
inclined - 633
planet *world* 318
  fate 601
-s in their station 423
planetarium 318
planet-struck
  adversity 735
  wonder 870
plank *board* 204
  platform 586, 626
  path 627
  safety 666
plant *place* 184
  insert 300
  vegetable 367
  agriculture 371
  trick 545
  tools 633
  property 780
- a battery 716
- a dagger in the
  breast 830
- a thorn in the side
  830
- oneself 184
plantation
  location 184
  agriculture 371
  estate 780
planter 188, 779
planter ses choux,
  aller - 893
plant louse 659
plash *lake* 343
  stream 348
  sound 408
plashy 345
plasm 22
plasma 847
plasmature 240
plasmic 240
plaster *cement* 45
  covering 223
  remedy 662
- up *repair* 660
plastic *alterable* 149
  form 240
  soft 324
  (*facile* 705)
plat *weave* 219
  ground 344
plate *dish* 191
  layer 204
  covering 223
  flat 251
  food 298
  engraving 558
- printing 558, 591
plateau *level* 213
  plain 344
plated 545
plate layer 690

platform
  horizontal 213
  support 215
  stage 542
  scheme 626
  arena 728
- orator 582
platitude
  unmeaning 517
  dull 843
  (*absurdity* 497)
Platonic
  contemplative 451
  inexcitable 826
  chaste 960
- bodies 244
Platonism 451
platoon *army* 726
  (*assemblage* 72)
- fire 716
platter
  receptacle 191
  layer 204
  flat 251
clean the outside of
  the - 544
plaudit 931
plausible
  probable 472
  sophistical 477
  false 544
  approbation 931
  flattery 933
  vindication 937
play *operation* 170
  influence 175
  scope 180
  oscillation 314
  music 416
  drama 599
  use 677
  action 680
  freedom 748
  amusement 840
at - 840
bring into - 677
full of - 836
full - 175
give - to the imagina-
  tion 515
in - 842
- a deep game 702
- a game
  pursue 622
  conduct 692
  pastime 840
- a part
  false 544
  drama 599
  action 680
- at cross purposes
  confusion 59
  misinterpret 523
- fast and loose
  falsehood 544
  irresolute 605
  tergiversation 607
  caprice 608
- first fiddle
  importance 642
  repute 873

- for *chance* 621
- gooseberry 459
- havoc 659
- hide and seek
  hide 528
  avoid 623
- into the hands of
  709
- of colors 440
- off 545
- of light 420
- one a trick
  disappoint 509
  deceive 545
- one false
  disappoint 509
  falsehood 544
  deception 545
- one's best card
  exertion 686
  skill 698
- one's part
  business 625
  conduct 692
- on the feelings 824
- possum 544
- second fiddle
  inferior 34
  subject 749
-'s the thing 599
- the deuce
  excitement 825
- the devil with
  malevolence 907
- the fool
  folly 499
  clumsy 699
  amusement 840
  ridiculous 853
  ridicule 856
- the monkey 499
- tricks with
  unskillful 699
  cunning 702
- truant 623
- upon
  deceive 545
  ridicule 856
- upon words
  misinterpret 523
  neology 563
  wit 842
- with 460
playa 342, 344
playday 840
played out
  end 67
  fatigue 688
  completion 729
  failure 732
player
  musician 416
  actor 599
playfellow 890
playful 836
- imagination 515
playground
  arena 728
  games 840
playhouse 599
playmate 890

record 551
fame 873
postern *portal* 66
  back 235
  opening 260
postexistence 152
posthaste
  swift 274
  haste 684
  rash 863
post-horse 271
posthumous
  subsequent 117
  late 133
- fame 873
postilion
  rider 268
  guide 694
postliminious
  subsequent 117
  late 133
postmeridian 126
post-mortem
  death 360
  interment 363
postnate 117
post-obit 360, 363
post office 534
- order 800
postpone 133
postprandial 117
postscript 65
postulant
  asking 765
  petitioner 767
  nun 996
postulate
  reasoning 476
  axiom 496
  supposition 514
postulation
  supposition 514
  request 765
posture
  circumstances 8
  situation 183
  form 240
posture master
  player 599
  buffoon 844
posy *motto* 550
  poem 597
  flowers 847
pot *much* 31
  mug 191
  heat 384
  saucepan 386
  preserve 670
  stakes 775
  death in the - 657
  go to -
    destruction 162
    failure 732
  keep the - boiling
    continue 143
    active 682
  le - au lait
    imagination 515
    hope 858
  make the - boil 775
potable 298

potage 298
potager 191
Potomac
  all quiet on - 721
potation
  beverage 298
  tippling 959
pot-bellied 194
pot companion 890
potency 157
potent 157, 159
potentate 745
potential
  inexistent 2
potentiality
  power 157
  possibility 470
pother *disorder* 59
  feeling 821
  excitement 825
  annoyance 830
pot herbs 393
pothooks 590
pothouse 189
pot hunter 767
potion
  beverage 298
  medicine 662
potluck
  eating 298
  chance 621
Potosi 803
potpourri
  mixture 41
  fragrance 400
  music 415
pottage 298
pottering
  busy 682
  faddling 683
potter's field 363
pottery *baked* 384
  art 557
pottle 191
potulent *drink* 298
  drunken 959
pot-valiant 959
pot-walloper 746, 876
pouch 191
poudre:
  jeter de la - aux yeux 442
  qui n'a pas inventé la -
    fool 501
    bungler 701
poultice *pulp* 354
  remedy 662
  relief 834
poultry 366
pounce upon
  unexpected 508
  attack 716
  seize 789
pound
  inclose 232
  weight 319
  bruise 330
  imprison 752
- together 41
poundage 813

pounds, shillings, and pence 800
pour *emerge* 295
  stream 348
  sufficient 639
  it never rains but it -s 641
- a broadside into 716
- forth *eject* 297
  speak 582
  loquacity 584
- forth like water 818
- in *converge* 290
  ingress 294
  sufficiency 639
- on *lavish* 784
- out 295, 297
- out blood like water 361
- water into a sieve
  waste 638
  prodigality 818
- with rain 348
pourboire 784
pourparler
  interlocution 588
  advice 695
  council 696
  ποῦ στῶ 215
pout *project* 250
  sad 837
  discourteous 895
  irate 900
  sulky 901a
poverty
  insufficiency 640
  unimportance 643
  indigence 804
- of blood 160
- of intellect 499
powder 330
  food for - 726
  gun - 727
  keep one's - dry 673
  not worth - 645
- and shot 727
  smell - 722
  waste - 638
powdered
  variegated 440
powdering
  ornament 847
power *much* 31
  numerical 84
  efficacy 157
  loud 404
- of style 574
  authority 737
  do all in one's - 686
  give - 760
  in the - of
    authority 737
    subjection 749
  knowledge is - 490
  literary - 569
- of attorney 755
- of money 800
-s by deepest calms are fed 31
powerful
  strong 159

- voice 580
powerless
  impotent 158
  weak 160
powerlessness 175a
powers that be 745
powwow 696
  palaver 588
pox 655
praam 273
practicable
  possible 470
  (easy 705)
practical
  acting 170
  executive 692
- joke
  deception 545
  ridicule 856
  disrespect 929
- knowledge 698
practically
  intrinsically 5
practice
  arithmetic 85
  training 537
  habit 613
  conduct 692
  in - prepared 673
  skilled 698
  out of - 699
  put in - use 677
    action 680
    conduct 692
    complete 729
practice *train* 537
  use 677
  act 680
- at the bar 968
- on one's credulity 545
- upon
  experiment 463
  deceive 545
practiced
  skilled 698
- eye 700
- hand 700
practitioner
  medical - 662
  doer 690
præcognita 467
prænomen 564
prætor 967
pragmatical
  pedantic 855
  vain 880
Pragmatic Sanction 769
prahu 273
prairie *plain* 344
  vegetation 367
- schooner 272
praise *thanks* 916
  commendation 931
  worship 990
praiseworthy
  commendable 931
  virtue 944
prame 273
prance *move* 266

appearance 448
prediction 511
manifestation 525
premunire
disobedience 742
penalty 974
prendre la balle au bond 134
prenotion
misjudgment 481
foresight 510
prensation 789
prentice 541
prenticeship 539
preoccupancy
possession 777
preoccupation
inattention 458
preoption 609
preordain 611
destiny 152
necessity 601
preparation 673
music 413
instruction 537
in course of –
plan 626
preparatory
preceding 62
prepared *ready* 698
prepare the way
facilitate 705
preparing
destined 152
prepense
spontaneous 600
predetermined 611
intended 620
malice – 907
prepollence 157
πρέπον, τὸ –
taste 850
propriety 926
preponderance
superiority 33
influence 175
dominance 737
(*importance* 642)
prepossessed
obstinate 606
prepossessing 829
prepossession
prejudice 481
possession 777
preposterous
great 31
absurd 497
exaggerated 549
ridiculous 853
undue 925
prepotency 157
Pre-Raphaelite 122, 124
prerequire 630
preresolve 611
prerogative
authority 737
right 924
presage
predict 511
omen 512

presbyopia 443
presbyter 996
Presbyterian 984
presbytery 995, 996, 1000
prescience 510
prescious 511
prescribe
direct 693
advice 695
order 741
entitle 924
enjoin 926
prescript
precept 697
decree 741
prescription
remedy 662
prescriptive
old 124
unchanged 141
habitual 613
due 924
presence
in space **186**
appearance 448
breeding 894
in the – of
near 197
– of God 981
– of mind
calm 826
cautious 864
real – 998
saving one's – 928
presence chamber 191
present
– *in time* 118
– *in space* 186
offer 763
give 784
church preferment 995
at – 118
– a bold front 861
– a front 719
– arms
courtesy 894
respect 928
– hour alone is man's 118
– in spirit 187
– itself *event* 151
visible 446
thought 451
– oneself
presence 186
offer 763
courtesy 894
– time **118**
instant 113
– to the mind
attention 457
memory 505
– to the view 448
these –s
writing 590
epistle 592
presentable 852
presentation

[*see* present]
celebration 883
courtesy 894
presentiment
instinct 477
prejudgment 481
foresight 510
presently 132
presentment
information 527
law proceeding 969
preservation
continuance 141
conservation **670**
Divine attributes 976
preserve *sweets* 396
– a middle course 628
preserver
safeguard 664
preshow 511
preside
– at the board
direction 693
– over
authority 737
presidency 737
president
director 694
master 745
–'s message 695
press *crowd* 72
closet 191
weight 319
public – 531
printing 591
book 593
move 615
compel 744
offer 763
solicit 765
go to – 591
– agent's yarn 546
– in 300
– into the service
use 677
aid 707
– of business 682
– on *course* 109
progression 282
haste 684
– one hard 716
– out 301
– proof 591
– to the bosom 902
under – of 744
writer for the – 593
pressed: hard – 704
– for time 684
pressgang 965
pressing *need* 630
urgent 642
press room 591
pressure
power 157
influence 175
weight 319
urgency 642
adversity 735
center of – 222
high – 824
presswork 591

Prester John 515
prestidigitation 545
prestidigitator 548
prestige *bias* 481
authority 737
fascination 865
fame 873
prestigiation 545
prestissimo 415
presto
instantly 113
music 415
prestriction 442
presumable 472
presume
misjudge 481
believe 484
suppose 514
hope 858
pride 878
presumption
[*see* presume]
probability 472
expectation 607
rashness 863
arrogance 885
unlawfulness 925
presumptive
probable 472
supposed 514
due 924
heir – 779
– evidence
evidence 467
probability 472
presumptuous 885
presuppose
misjudge 481
suppose 514
presurmise
foresee 510
suppose 514
pretend *assert* 535
simulate 544
pretended 545
pretender
deceiver 548
braggart 884
unentitled 925
pretending 544
pretense
falsehood 544
untruth 546
excuse 617
ostentation 882
boast 884
pretension
ornament 577
affectation 855
due 924
pretentious
affected 855
vain 880
ostentatious 882
boasting 884
undue 925
preterition 122
preterlapsed 122
pretermit 460
preternatural 83
preterperfect 122

pretext
  untruth 546
  plea 617
pretty *much* 31
  imperfectly 651
  beautiful 845
  - fellow 501
  - good 651
  - kettle of fish, pass, &c.
  disorder 59
  difficulty 704
  - quarrel 720
  - well *much* 31
  little 32
  trifling 643
preux chevalier 939
prevail *exist* 1
  superior 33
  general 78
  influence 175
  habit 613
  succeed 731
  - upon 615
prevailing 78
  - taste 852
prevalence
  [*see* prevail]
prevaricate
  falsehood 544
  (*equivocate* 520)
prévenance 894
prevenient
  precedent 62
  early 132
prevention
  prejudice 481
  hindrance 706
  - of waste 817
previous
  - *in time* 116
  (- *in order* 62)
  move the - question 624
  not within - experience 137
prevision 510
prewarn 668
prey *food* 298
  quarry 620
  booty 793
  victim 828
  fall a - to
  be defeated 732
  subjection 749
  - on the mind
  excite 824
  regret 833
  fear 860
  - on the spirits 837
  - to grief 828
  - to melancholy 837
price
  consideration 147
  value 648
  money 812
  at any - 604*a*
  beyond - 814
  cheap at the - 815
  have one's - 812
  of great -

  good 648
  dear 814
  reward 973
price current 812
priceless
  valueless 645
  valuable 648
  dear 814
prick *sharp* 253
  hole 260
  sting 378
  sensation of touch 380
  incite 615
  mental suffering 830
  kick against the -s
  useless 645
  resistance 719
  - up one's ears
  hear 418
  curiosity 455
  attention 457
  expect 507
prickle *sharp* 253
  sensation of touch 380
prickly 253
pride
  ornament 847
  loftiness 878
  take a - in 878
priest 996
priestcraft 995
priesthood 995, 996
priest-ridden
  false piety 988
  churchdom 995
prig *steal* 791
  puppy 854
  affected 855
  blusterer 887
priggish
  affected 855
  vain 880
prim *affected* 855
  proud 878
prima: - donna
  actress 599
  important 642
  proficient 700
  - facie *sight* 441
  appearance 448
  probable 472
  - *meaning* 516
  manifest 525
primacy
  celebrity 873
  church 995
primary
  cause 153
  important 642
  assembly 696
  - color 428
  - education 537
primate 996
primates 875
prime
  primeval 124
  early 132
  teach 537
  important 642

  excellent 648
  prepare 673
  in one's - 131
  - and load 673
  - cost *price* 812
  cheap 815
  - minister 694
  - mover 153, 164
  - number 84
  - of life *youth* 127
  adolescence 131
  - of the morning 125
primed
  skilled 698
  tipsy 959
primer 542
primeval 124
primices 154
primigenous 124
priming 556
primitive *old* 124
  cause 153
  - color 428
primo avulso non deficit alter 30
primogenial
  beginning 66
primogeniture
  old 124
  age 128
  posterity 167
  heritage 777
primordial *old* 124
  cause 153
primordinate 124
primrose-colored 436
primum mobile
  cause 153
  motive 615
primus inter pares 33
prince
  perfection 650
  master 745
  nobility 875
  - of darkness 978
Prince Albert coat 225
princely
  authoritative 737
  liberal 816
  famous 873
  noble 875
  generous 942
princess 745, 875
principal
  important 642
  director 694
  - part *great* 31
  whole 50
principality
  region 181
  property 780
principally 33
principia 496
principiis obstare 673
principle
  intrinsic 5
  rule 80

  cause 153
  element 316
  reasoning 476
  tenet 484
  maxim 496
  motive 615
  probity 939
  on - 615
  want of - 945
principled, high - 939
prink *adorn* 847
  show off 882
print *mark* 550
  engraving 558
  letterpress 591
  out of - 552
printer 591
printing 591
prior
  - *in order* 62
  - *in time* 116
  clergy 996
priori reasoning, a - 476
priority 116
prior tempore prior jure 62, 116
priory 1000
Priscian's head, break - 568
prism
  angularity 244
  optical instrument 445
  see through a - 443
prismatic
  color 428
  variegated 440
prison 752
  cast into - 751
  in - 754
prisoner
  captive 754
  accused 938
  take -
  restrain 751
  seize 789
prison house
  secrets of the -
  reveal 529
  secret 533
pristine 122
prithee 765
prittle-prattle 588
privacy
  conceal 528
  seclude 893
private *special* 79
  hidden 528
  secluded 893
  in - 528
  keep - 881
  - road 627
  - soldier 726
  talk to in - 586, 588
  to gain some - ends 943
privateer
  combatant 726

robber 792
privateering 791
privately 881
privation *loss* 776
  poverty 804
privative 789
privilege
  permission 760
  exemption 777a
  due 924
privity 490
privy *hidden* 528
  latrines 653
  - to 490
Privy Council
  tribunal 966
prize *good* 618
  palm 733
  gain 775
  booty 793
  love 897
  approve 931
  - open 173
  win the - 731
prizer 767
prize fighter 726
prize fighting 720
prizeman 700
pro: - and con
  reasoning 476
  motive 615
  - formâ 82
  - hâc vice
  special 79
  present time 118
  occasion 134
  seldom 137
  - re natâ
  circumstances 8
  relation 9
  special 79
  occasion 134
  conditions 770
  - tanto *degree* 26
  small 32
  - tempore 111
proa 273
probability
  chance 156
  likelihood **472**
probable
  hopeful 858
probate
  security 771
  (*evidence* 467)
Probate, Court of -
  966
probation
  trial 463
  demonstration 478
probationary 463
  essay 675
probationer 541
probative 478
probatum est
  proof 478
  approval 931
probe *depth* 208
  perforator 262
  investigate 461
  measure 466

probitas laudatur et
  alget 939
probity 939
problem *topic* 454
  question 461
  enigma 533
problematical
  uncertain 475
  (*hidden* 528)
proboscis 250
procacity
  insolence 885
  rudeness 895
  irascibility 901
procedure
  method 627
  action 680
  conduct 692
proceed *time* 109
  advance 282
  - from 154
  - with 692
proceeding
  incomplete 53
  event 151
  action 680
  not finished 730
  course of - 692
Proceedings of -
  551
proceeds *gain* 775
  money 800
  receipts 810
procerity 206
process
  projection 250
  conduct 692
  (*action* 680)
  in - of time
  posterior 117
  legal - 963
  - of time
  course 109
procession
  continuity 69
  march 266
  ceremony 882
processional
  rite 998
procès verbal
  record 551
  law proceeding 969
prochronism 115
proclaim 531
proclivity
  tendency 176
  proneness 820
  (*disposition* 602)
proconsul 759
proconsulship 737
procrastination
  delay 133
  inactivity 683
procreant 168
procreate
  produce 161
  productive 168
procreator 166
procrustean 82
  - law 80
Procrustes:

stretch on the bed of -
  27
proctor *officer* 694
  consignee 758
  lawyer 968
proctorship 693
procumbent 213
procuration 755
procurator 694
procure *cause* 153
  induce 615
  get 775
  buy 795
procurement 170
procuress 962
prod 276
prodigal *lavish* 641
  extravagant 818
prodigality 818
prodigious
  much 31
  wonderful 870
prodigy
  exception 83
  élite 648
  wonderful **872**
  - of learning 700
prodition 940
prodrome 64
produce
  increase 35
  cause 153
  effect 154
  create 161
  prolong 200
  show 525
  fruit 775
  merchandise 798
  - itself 446
producer 164
product
  multiple 84
  effect 154
  gain 775
production 161
  [*and see* produce]
productive
  power 157
productiveness 168
proem 64
proemial
  preceding in order 62
  beginning 66
profane
  desecrate 679
  impious 988
  laical 997
  - swearing 908
profanum vulgus 876
profession
  assertion 535
  pretense 546
  business 625
  promise 768
  enter a - 625
  - of faith
  belief 484
  theology 983
professor
  learned man 492
  teacher 540

professorship 542
proffer 763
proficient
  knowledge 490
  skill 698
  adept **700**
proficuous 644
profile
  outline 230
  side 236
  appearance 448
  portraiture 556
profit
  increase 35
  advantage 618
  utility 644
  acquisition 775
  - and loss account 811
  - by *use* 677
profitable
  useful 644
  good 648
  gainful 775
  (*receipts* 810)
profitless 646
profligacy 945
profluent
  progressive 282
  stream 348
profound
  great 31
  deep 208
  learned 490
  wise 498
  sagacious 702
  feeling 821
  - attention 457
  - knowledge 490
  - secret 533
profundis, de -
  lamentation 839
  penitence 950
profundity
  [*see* profound]
profuse
  diffuse style 573
  redundant 641
  prodigal 818
profusion
  multitude 102
  plenty 639
prog 298
progenerate 161
progenitor 166
progeny 167
prognosis 510, 511
prognostic 512
prognosticate 511
programme
  catalogue 86
  plan 626
progress
  growth 144
  motion 264
  advance 282
  (*improvement* 658)
  in - *incomplete* 53, 730
  in mid - 270
  make - 282
  - of science 490
  - of time 109

progression
gradation 58
series 69
numerical - 84
motion **282**

progressive
continuous 69
course 109
advancing 282
improving 658

prohibition 761
exclusion 55
temperance 953

prohibitionist 958

project *bulge* 250
impel 284
intend 620
plan 626

projectile 727

projecting 214

projection *map* 554

projector 626

prolation
voice 580
speech 582

prole, sine - 169

prolegomena 64

prolepsis
precursor 64
anachronism 115

proletarian 876

prolific 168

prolix 573

prolocutor
interpreter 524
teacher 540
speaker 582

prologue
precursor 64
drama 599
what's past is - 122

prolong
protract 110
late 133
lengthen 200

prolongation 143

prolusion 64

promenade
walk 266
display 882

Promethean 359

prominent
convex 250
manifest 525
important 642
eminent 873

prominently
much 31
more 33

promiscuous
mixed 41
irregular 59
indiscriminate 465a
casual 621

promise
predict 511
engage **768**
hope 858
keep one's - 939
keep - to ear and
break to hope 545

- of celestial worth 511
- oneself
expect 507
hope 858

promissory 768
- note
security 771
money 800

promontory
height 206
projection 250
land 342

promote
improve 658
aid 707

promoter
planner 626

promotion 658

prompt *early* 132
remind 505
tell 527
induce 615
active 682
advise 695
(*quick* 274)
- book 505
- memory 505

prompter
drama 599
motive 615
adviser 695

promptuary 636

promulgate 531
- a decree 741

pronation and supination 218

prone
horizontal 213

proneness
tendency 176
disposition 820

prôner
ostentation 882
praise 931

prôneur 935

prong 91

pronounce
judge 480
assert 535
voice 580
speak 582

pronounced 525

pronouncement 535

pronunciation 580

pronunciative 535

pronunziamento 531

proof *hard* 323
insensible 376
test 463
demonstration 478
printing 591
draft 626
ocular - 446
- against
strong 159
resolute 604
safe 664
defense 717
esistance 719
nsensible 823

prop *support* 215
help 707

propædeutic 537

propædeutics 537

propagable 168

propaganda
teaching 537
school 542

propagandism 537

propagandist
teacher 540
priest 996

propagate
produce 161
be productive 168
publish 531

propel 284

propeller 284

propend 602

propendency
predetermination 611
inclination 820

propense 602

propension 820

propensity
tendency 176
inclination 820

proper *special* 79
expedient 646
handsome 845
due 924
(*right* 922)
in its - place 58
- name 564
- time 134
show a - spirit 939
the - thing
duty 926

properties, theatrical -
costume 225
drama 599

property *power* 157
possessions **780**
wealth 803

property-man 599

prophasis 510

prophecy 511

prophet *seer* 513
priest 996
in the name of the -
figs! 497
non-Biblical -s 986

prophetic
predict 511
revelation 985

Prophets, the - 985

prophylactic
healthful 656
remedy 662
preservative 670
hindrance 706

prophylaxis 670

propinquity 197

propitiate
pacify 723
calm 826
content 831
love 897
pity 914

forgive 918
atone 952
worship 990

propitiator 724

propitious
timely 134
beneficial 648
helping 707
prosperous 734
auspicious 858

proplasm 22

proportion
relation 9
mathematical 84
symmetry 242
allotment 786

proportionate
agreeing 23

proportions
space 180
size 192

proposal 765
plan 626

propose
suggest 514
broach 535
intend 620
offer 763
offer marriage 902
- a question 461

proposition
supposition 454
reasoning 476
project 626
suggestion 514
offer 763
request 765

propound
suggest 514
broach 535
- a question 461

propriâ personâ
in - *speciality* 79
presence 186

proprietary 779

proprietor 779

proprietorship 780

propriety
agreement 23
expedience 646
fashion 852
right 922
duty 926

proprio motu 600

propter hoc 155

propugn
resist 717
vindicate 937

propulsion 284

propylon 66

prore 234

prorogue 133

proruption 295

prosaic - *style* 575
dry 576
dull 843

prosaism *prose* 598

prosal 598

proscenium
front 234
theater 599

proscribe
　interdict 761
　banish 893
　curse 908
　condemn 971
　(*exclude* 77)
prose
　diffuse style 573
　prate 584
　not verse **598**
　- *run mad*
　ornate 577
　poetical 597
　- *writer* 598
prosecute
　pursue 622
　act 680
　accuse 938
　arraign 969
　- *an inquiry* 461
prosecutor 938
proselyte
　learner 541
　convert 607
proselytism 537
proser 841
prosody 597
prosopopœia 521
prospect
　futurity 121
　view 448
　probability 472
　expectation 507
　landscape painting
　　556
　good - 858
　in - *intended* 620
prospectively 121
prospectus *list* 86
　foresight 510
　compendium 596
　scheme 626
prosperity 734
prospicience 510
prosternation
　dejection 837
　servility 886
prostitute
　corrupt 659
　misuse 679
　impure 961
　courtesan 962
prostrate
　powerless 158
　destroyed 162
　low 207
　horizontal 213
　depress 308
　laid up 655
　exhausted 688
　dejected 837
　servile 886
　fall - 306
　- *oneself*
　servile 886
　obeisance 928
　worship 990
prostration
　[*see* prostrate]
　submission 725
　pain 828

prosy *weary* 841
　dull 843
prosyllogism 476
protagonist
　actor 599
　proficient 700
protasis
　precursor 64
　maxim 496
protean 149
protect *safe* 664
protected cruiser 726
protection
　influence 175
　defense 717
　restrain 751
protector 664, 717
　master 745
　keeper 753
protectorate 737
　realm 780
protégé *servant* 746
　friend 890
proteiform 149
protein
　semiliquid 352
　organic 357
protervity 901
protest *dissent* 489
　assert 535
　deny 536
　refuse 764
　deprecate 766
　not observe 773
　not pay 808
　counter - 468
　enter a - 766
　- *against*
　oppose 708
　disapprove 932
　under -
　unwilling 603
　compulsion 744
protestant
　dissenting 489
Protestant 984
protested bills 808
Proteus 149
prothesis 1000
prothonotary 553
protocol *scheme* 626
　compact 769
　(*record* 551)
　(*warrant* 771)
protogenal 153
protohistoric 124
protoplasm
　prototype 22
　productive 168
　organization 357
protoplast 22
prototype 22
　prediction 511
protoxide of nitro-
　gen 376
protozoa 357
protract *time* 110
　late 133
　lengthen 200
　diffuse style 573
protreptical 615

protrude 250
protuberance 250
protypify 511
proud
　dignified 873
　lofty 878
　- *flesh* 250
prove
　arithmetic 85
　turn out 151
　try 463
　demonstrate 478
　affect 821
　- *one's case*
　vindication 937
　- *true* 494
provender *food* 298
　provision 637
proverb *maxim* 496
　(*phrase* 566)
proverbe *acting* 599
proverbial 490
provide
　furnish 637
　- *against*
　prepare 673
　- *against a rainy day*
　　817
provided
　conditionally 8
　qualification 469
　supposition 514
　(*conditions* 770)
　- *for* 803
　well - 639
providence
　foresight 510
　preparation 673
　divine government
　　976
Providence 976
　waiter on -
　idle 683
　contented 831
provident
　careful 459
　wise 498
　prepared 673
providential
　opportune 134
　fortunate 734
province
　department 75
　region 181
　abode 189
　office 625
　(*duty* 926)
provincial
　[*see* province]
　vulgar 851
provincialism
　neology 563
provision *food* 298
　supply **637**
　preparation 673
　wealth 803
　(*materials* 635)
provisional 475
　circumstances 8
　temporary 111
　uncertain 475

　preparing 673
provisions
　conditions 770
proviso
　qualification 469
　condition 770
provisory 111
provocateur, agent
　- 615
provoke *cause* 153
　incite 615
　excite 824
　vex 830
　aggravate 835
　anger 900
　- *desire* 865
　- *hatred* 898
provoquant 824
provost *master* 745
　deputy 759
prow 234
prowess 861
prowl *walk* 266
　lurk 528
　- *after* 622
proximate
　next 63
　near 197
　- *cause* 153
proximity *near* 197
　adjacent 199
proximo 121
proximus ardet
　danger 665, 667
　proxy 759
prude *affected* 855
　chaste 960
prudent
　careful 459
　wise 498
　cautious 864
　(*skillful* 698)
prudery
　affectation 855
　fastidiousness 868
pruina 383
prune
　take away 38
　lop 201
　repair 658
prunello, leather or
　- 643
prurience
　desire 865
　lust 961
Prussian blue 438
Prussic acid 663
pry *look* 441
　curiosity 455
　inquire 461
　- *into the future* 510
Prytaneum 931
psalm *music* 415
　worship 990
psalm book 998
psalmody 415
psalter 998
psaltery 417
psammous 330
psephomancy 511
pseudo

- the proof 463
- the question 830
- the rack 830
- the sword 361
- the vote 609
- use 677
putty 45
put up *assemble* 72
   locate 184
   store 636
- a petition ⎱
- a prayer ⎰
   request 765
   worship 990
- a shutter 424

- for 865
- for sale 796
- the sword 723
- to 615
- to auction 796
- with
   substitute 147
   bear 826
puzzle *uncertain* 475
   conceal 528
   enigma 533
puzzled 475, 533
   (*ignorant* 491)
puzzle-headed 499
puzzling

   unintelligible 519
pyæmia 655
Pylades and Orestes
   890
pyramid *heap* 72
   point 253
pyramids
   billiards 840
pyre 363
pyriform 249
pyrology 282
pyromancy 511
pyromaniac 913
pyrometer 389
pyrosis 655

pyrotechnics 423
pyrotechnic sponge
   388
pyrotechny 382
pyrotic 830
pyroxyline 727
pyrrhonism
   incredulity 487
   irreligion 989
Pythagorean 953
Pythia *oracle* 513
Python, -ess 513
pyx *vessel* 191
   rites 998
   temple 1000

Q

R

R's, three - 537
rabat 225
rabbet 43
Rabbi 996
Rabbist 984
rabbit
  productive 168
rabble *assemblage* 72
  mob 876
rabid *insane* 502
  emotion 821
  eager 865
  angry 900
rabies 503
raccroc 156
race *relation* 11
  sequence 69
  kind 75
  lineage 166
  run 274
  stream 348
  conduit 350
  pungency 392
  course 622
  business 625
  culture 658
  carree 692
  opposition 708
  contention 720
  one's - is run 360
  - by vigor won 171,
    731
  run a - 720
  run in a - 680
  run one's - 729
race course 728
race horse
  horse 271
  swift 274
rachidian 222
rachitis 655
raciness 574
rack *receptacle* 191
  frame 215
  cloud 353
  physical pain 378
  purify 652
  moral pain 828
  torture 830
  punish 972
  instrument of torture
    975
  go to - and ruin 735
  - one's brains
    thought 451
    imagination 515
  - rent 810
rackabones 659
racket
  agitation 315
  loud 404
  roll 407
  discord 713
racket court 840
racketing

  active 682
  amusements 840
rackets 840
rackety *loud* 404
raconteur 594
racy *strong* 171
  pungent 392
  - *style* 574
  feeling 821
raddle *weave* 219
raddled *tipsy* 959
radiance *light* 420
  beauty 845
radiant
  diverging 291
  glorious 873
radiate 291
radical
  essential 5
  complete 52
  algebraic root 84
  cause 153
  important 642
  reformer 658
  - *change* 146
  - *cure* 662
  - *reform* 658
radically
  greatly 31
radication 613
radicle 153
radio-active 171, 384
radiograph 554
radiometer
  light 420
  optical instrument
    445
  measurement 466
radium 384
radius *length* 200
  width 202
radix 153
radoter 499
radoteur 501
raff *refuse* 653
  rabble 876
  (*miscreant* 949)
raffle 621
raft 273
rafter 215
rag *small* 32
  (*part* 51)
ragamuffin 876
rage *violence* 173
  influence 175
  excitement 824, 825
  fashion 852
  desire 865
  wrath 900
  the battle -s 722
ragged 226
ragoût 298
rags *clothes* 225
  useless 645
  do to - 384

  tear to - 162
  worn to - 659
rag tag
  - and bobtail 876
raid *attack* 716
  theft 791
rail *inclosure* 232
  prison 752
  - at 932
  - in
    circumscribe 229
    restrain 751
railing 232
**raillerie, ne pas en-
  tendre** - 900
raillery 856
rail-riding 972
railroad 627
  expedite 684
railway 627
  - *speed* 274
  - *station* 266
raiment 225
rain *stream* 348
  sufficient 639
  - or shine
    certain 474
    at all hazards 604
rainbow 440
rain gauge 466
rainless 340
**rains but it pours,
  never** - 641
rainy day 735
  provide against a -
    prepare 673
    economy 817
raise *increase* 35
  produce 161
  elevate 307
  excite 824
  - a cry 531
  - a dust 682
  - a hue and cry against
    932
  - alarm 860
  - a laugh 840
  - anger 900
  - a question
    inquire 461
    doubt 485
  - a report 531
  - a siege 723
  - a storm 173
  - Cain 900
  - expectations 858
  - funds 775
  - hope 511
  - money 788
  - one's banner 722
  - one's head
    improve 658
    refresh 689
    prosperity 734
    repute 873

  - one's voice
    affirm 535
  - one's voice against
    932
  - spirits from the dead
    992
  - the finger 550
  - the mask 529
  - the spirits 836
  - the voice
    shout 441
  - the wind
    gain 775
    borrow 788
  - troops 722
  - up *vertical* 212
    excite 824
raised *convex* 250
raison
  - d'être 620
  - de plus 467
rajah 745, 875
rajput 726
rake *drag* 285
  gardening 371
  clean 652
  profligate 949
  intemperance 954
  libertine 962
  - out 301
  - up *collect* 72
    extract 301
    recall 505
    excite 824
  - up evidence 467
rakehell 949, 962
raking fire 716
rakish
  intemperate 954
  licentious 961
rallentando 415
rally *arrange* 60
  improve 658
  restore 660
  ridicule 856
  encourage 861
  - round *order* 58
    coöperate 709
rallying: - cry
  indication 550
  encouragement 861
  - point 74
ram *impulse* 276
  sheep 366
  male 373
  man-of-war 726
  milk the - 645
  - down *close* 261
    dense 321
  - in 300
Ramadan
  fasting 956
  rite 998
ramage 367
Ramazan

560

[see Rámadan]
amble *stroll* 266
  wander 279
  folly 499
  delirium 503
  digress 573
rambler 269
rambling
  irregularity 139
ramification *part* 51
  bisection 91
  posterity 167
  filament 205
  symmetry 242
  divergence 291
rammer *plug* 263
  impeller 276
ramose 242
  (*rough* 256)
ramp *climb* 305
  leap 309
rampage 173
rampant
  violent 173
  prevalent 175
  vertical 212
  raised 307
  free 748
  vehement 825
  licentious 961
rampart 717
ramrod 263
ramshackle 665
ranch 780
rancid *fetid* 401
  unclean 653
rancour
  enmity 889
  malevolence 907
  rerenge 919
randan 273
random *casual* 156
  carriage 272
  uncertain 475
  aimless 621
  talk at -
    sophistry 477
    exaggerate 549
    loquacity 584
  - *experiment* 463
  chance 621
randy 840
range *extent* 26
  collocate 60
  series 69
  term 71
  class 75
  space 180
  distance 196
  roam 266
  direction 278
  stove 386
  freedom 748
  long - 196
  - itself 58
  - under, - with **76**
  within - 177
ranger
  director 694
  keeper 753
  thief 792

rani 374, 745, 875
rank *degree* 26
  thorough 31
  collocate 60
  row 69
  term 71
  vegetation 365
  fetid 401
  estimate 480
  bad 649
  soldiers 726
  glory 873
  nobility 875
  man of - 875
  - and file
    continuity 69
    soldiers 726
    commonalty 876
rankle *unclean* 653
  corrupt 659
  painful 830
  animosity 900
  malevolence 907
  revenge 919
ranks
  fill up the - 660
  risen from the - 876
ransack *seek* 461
  deliver 672
  plunder 791
  price 812
  atonement 952
  - one's brains
    thought 451
    imagination 515
ransom 952
rant
  unmeaning 517
  exaggeration 549
  diffuse style 573
  turgescence 577
  speech 582
  acting 599
  excitement 825
ranter *talker* 584
  false piety 988
rantipole 458
ranunculus 845
rap *blow* 276
  sound 406
  trifle 643
  money 800
  not worth a - 804
  - on the knuckles
    angry 900
    censure 932
    punish 972
  - out *affirm* 535
    voice 580
    speak 582
  - out oaths
    insolence 885
    malediction 908
rapacity
  taking 789
  stealing 791
  avarice 819
  greed 865
rape *seizure* 791
  violation 961
rape oil 356

rapid 274
  - slope 217
  - strides
    progress 282
    velocity 274
  - *succession* 136
rapids 348
rapier 727
rapine 791
rapparee 792
rappee 392
rappel 722
rapping, spirit - 992
rapport, en - 9
rapports, sous tous
  les - 494
rapprochement
  concord 714
  friendship 888
rapscallion 949
rapt *attention* 457
  inattention 458
  emotion 821
raptorial
  taking 789
  stealing 791
raptors 739
rapture *bliss* 827
  love 897
rapturous 221, 827
rara avis
  exceptional 83
  good 648
  famous 873
rare
  unexampled 20
  exceptional 83
  few 103
  infrequent 137
  light 322
  excellent 648
raree show
  appearance 448
  amusement 840
rarefaction
  expand 194
  render light 322
rari nantes 103
rarity 322
rasa, tabula - 552
rascal *knave* 941
  bad man 949
rascality 940
rase *obliterate* 552
rash
  skin disease 655
  reckless 863
  (*careless* 460)
rasher 204
rashness 863
rasorial 366
rasp *powder* 330
  rub 331
rasper *difficult* 704
rasure 552
rat *recant* 607
  smell a -
    discover 480a
    doubt 485
rataplan 407
ratatat 407

ratchet 253
rate *degree* 26
  motion 264
  measure 466
  estimation 480
  price, tax 812
  abuse 932
  at a great - 274
rath *early* 132
  fort 717
rather
  a little 32
  trifling 643
  have - 609
  have - not 867
  - good 651
ratification
  confirm 467
  affirm 488
  consent 762
  compact 769
ratio *relation* 9
  degree 26
  proportion 84
  apportionment 786
ratiocination 476
ration *food* 298
  allotment 786
rational
  - *quantity* 84
  intellectual 450
  judicious 498
  sane 502
rationale *cause* 153
  attribution 155
  answer 462
  interpretation 522
rationalism
  reasoning 476
  irreligion 989
ratlings 215
ratsbane 663
rats in the upper
  story 503
rattan 975
ratten 158
rattle *noise* 407
  music 417
  prattle 584
  death - 360
  - on 584
rattle-brained 499
rattle-headed 499
rattlesnake 913
rattletraps 780
rattling 836
  - pace 274
raucity
  faintness 405
raucous *hoarse* 581
ravage *destroy* 162
  despoil 659
ravages of time 659
rave *madness* 503
  excitement 824, 825
  - against 932
ravel *untwist* 60
  derange 61
  entangle 219
  difficulty 704
raveled 59

ravelin 717
raven *black* 431
  hoarse 581
  gorge 957
  - for 865
ravening
  violent 173
  desire 865
ravenous
  grasping 789
  desirous 865
raver 504
ravine *interval* 198
  narrow 203
  dike 259
raving *mad* 503
  feeling 821
  excitement 824, 825
ravish *seize* 789
  please 829
ravished
  pleased 827
ravishment 824
raw *immature* 123
  sensitive 378
  cold 383
  color 428
  unprepared 674
  unskilled 699
  - head and bloody
   bones 860
  - levies 726
  - material 635
rawboned 203
rawhide 975
ray 420
  - of comfort 831
  thou living - 450
rayah 745
rayless 421
raze *destroy* 162
  - to the ground
  lower 308
razor 253
  cut blocks with a -
  waste 638
  misuse 679
  unskillful 699
  keen as a - 821
razzia
  destruction 162
  attack 716
  plunder 791
re, in - 9
reabsorb 296
reach *degree* 26
  equal 27
  distance 196
  fetch 270
  arrive at 292
  river 348
  deceive 545
  grasp 737
  take 789
  - of thought 498
  - the ear
  hearing 418
  information 527
  - to *distance* 196
  length 200
  within - *near* 197

possible 470
reaction
  compensation 30
  counteraction 179
  recoil 277
  restoration 660
reactionary
  reversion 145
  tergiversation 607
reactionist
  opponent 710
read *interpret* 522
  learn 539
  - a lecture 537
  well - 490
readable 578
reader *teacher* 540
  printer 591
  clergyman 996
readership 542
readily 705
reading
  speciality 79
  knowledge 490
  interpretation 522
  learning 539
  - in 995
reading desk 1000
readjust *agree* 23
  equalize 27
readmit 296
ready
  expecting 507
  willing 602
  useful 644
  prepare 673
  active 682
  skillful 698
  cash 800
  get - 673
  make - 673
  - made 673
  - memory 505
  - money 800
  - pen 569
  - to burst forth 825
  - to sink 824
  - wit 842
reaffirm 535
reagent 463
real *existing* 1
  - *number* 84
  true 494
  - estate 780
  - property 780
  - security 771
realgar 434
realism 494
realize
  speciality 79
  intellect 450
  think 451
  discover 480a
  believe 484
  conceive 490
  imagine 515
  accomplish 729
  acquire 775
  sell 796
really *wonder* 870
  (*very* 31)

realm *region* 181
  people 372
  government 737
  property 780
reality 780
ream 593
reanimate
  reproduce 163
  life 359
  resuscitate 660
reap *shorten* 201
  agriculture 371
  take 789
  - and carry 775
  - the benefit of
  be better for 658
  - the fruits
  succeed 731
  acquire 775
  reward 973
  - the whirlwind
  product 154
  failure 732
  - where one has not
   sown 923
reappear
  repetition 104
  reproduce 163
  visible 446
  restore 660
  (*frequent* 136)
rear *sequel* 65
  end 67
  bring up 161
  erect 212
  back **235**
  elevate 307
  teach 537
  in the - 281
  - its head
  manifest 525
  - one's head
  pride 878
rear admiral 745
reason *cause* 153
  intellect 450
  argue 476
  wisdom 498
  motive 615
  by - of 615
  feast of - 588
  in - *moderate* 174
  right 922
  listen to - 498
  - in a circle 477
  - why *cause* 153
  motive 615
  stand to -
  certain 474
  proof 478
  manifest 525
  what's the - ? 461
  without rhyme or -
   615a
reasonable
  moderate 174
  probable 472
  judicious 498
  sane 502
  cheap 815
  right 922

- prospect 472
reasoner 476
reasoning 476
  - faculties 450
reasonless 499
reasons 476
reassemble 72
reassert 535
reassure *hope* 858
  courage 861
reasty *fetid* 401
  unclean 653
reave 789
rebate
  moderate 174
  discount 813
rebeck 417
rebel
  disobedience 742
  (*resistance* 719)
rebellow 412
reboation 412
rebound *recoil* 277
  regression 283
  (*counteraction* 179)
rebours, à -
  reversion 145
  regression 283
  difficult 704
rebuff *recoil* 277
  resist 719
  repulse 732
  refuse 764
  discourtesy 895
  censure 932
rebuild 660
rebuke 932
rebus 533
rebut *answer* 462
  counter evidence 468
  confute 479
  deny 536
rebutter
  answer 462
  law pleadings 969
recalcitrant 742
recalcitrate
  recoil 277
  resist 719
recalesce 382
recall
  recollect 505
  recant 607
  cancel 756
  - to life 660
recant *deny* 536
  retract 607
  resign 756
recapitulate
  enumerate 85
  repeat 104
  describe 594
  summarize 596
recapper 633
recast
  revolution 146
  scheme 626
recede
  move back 283
  move from 287
  - into the shade 874

563

not consent 764
- assent 489
- to associate with 893
- to believe 487
- to hear 460
refute 479
refuted 495
regain 775
- breath 689
regal 737
regale *feast* 298
  physical pleasure 377
  refresh 689
  pleasing 829
  amusement 840
regalia 747
regality 737
regard
  relation 9
  view 441
  attention 457
  judge 480
  credit 873
  love 897
  respect 928
  approbation 931
  have - to 457
  merit - 642
  pay - to
    believe 484
    honor 873
  - as 484
regardful
  attentive 457
  careful 459
regardless
  inattentive 458
  insensible 823
regards
  courtesy 894
  respect 928
regatta
  contention 720
  amusement 840
regelate 385
regency 755
regenerate
  reproduce 163
  restore 660
  piety 987
regeneration
  divine function 976
  baptismal - 998
regent
  governor 745
  deputy 759
regibus esse manus 737
regicide 361
régime
  circumstances 8
  conduct 692
  authority 737
  ancien - 875
regimen *diet* 298
  remedy 662
regiment
  assemblage 72
  army 726

regimentals 225
region 181
regional 181
register
  arrange 60
  list 86
  chronicle 114
  record 551
  recorder 553
registrar 553
registration 551
registry 114
  record 551
règle: en - 924
reglet 591
regnant
  influence 175
  authority 737
regnant populi 737
regni, anno - 106
regorge 790
regrade 283
regrate 777
regrater 797
regression 283
regret *sorrow* **833**
  penitence 950
regretted, to be - 833
regrowth 163
reguerdon 973
regular
  uniform 16
  complete 52
  order 58
  arrangement 60
  rule 80
  conformity 82
  periodic 138
  symmetric 242
  habitual 613
  by - intervals 58
  - return 138
regulars 726
regulate
  adjust 23
  order 58
  arrange 60
  direct 693
regulated by
  conformity 82
regulation
  precept 697
  law 963
  (*command* 741)
regulative principle 453
regurgitate
  return 283
  flow 348
  restore 790
rehabilitate
  reconstruct 660
  restore 790
rehearse
  repeat 104
  try 463
  describe 594
  drama 599
  prepare 673
Reichsrath 696
reign *influence* 175

government 737
- of terror
  severity 739
  fear 860
- of violence 738
reimburse
  restore 790
  pay 807
rein
  means of restraint 752
  (*moderate* 174)
  (*counteract* 179)
  - in *retard* 275
  restrain 751
reindeer 271
re infectâ
  shortening 304
  inaction 681
reinforce [*see* reên-force]
reinforcement [*see* reênforcement]
reinless 738
reins [*see* rein]
  direction 693
  give - to the imagination 515
  give the - to
    facilitate 705
    lax 738
    permit 760
  hold the - 693
  take the -
    authority 737
reinstall 660
reinstate 660
reinvest 790
reinvigorate 689
Reis Effendi 694
reiterate 104
reject
  exclude 55
  eject 297
  refuse 764
rejected
  hateful 898
rejection 610
rejoice *exult* 838
  amuse 840
  - in 827
  - in the name of 564
  - the heart
    gratify 829
    cheer 836
rejoicing 838
rejoin *assemble* 72
  arrive 292
rejoinder
  answer 462
  law pleadings 969
rejuvenescence 660
rekindle
  ignite 384
  excite 824
  (*incite* 615)
relapse
  turn back 145
  fall back **661**
relate *narrate* 594
- to *refer* 9

related *kin* 11
relation 9
  kin 11
  narrative 594
relationship 9
relative position 9
relator
  accuser 938
relax *loose* 47
  weaken 160
  moderate 174
  slacken speed 275
  soften 324
  inactive 683
  repose 687
  misrule 738
  liberate 750
  relent 914
- one's efforts 681
- the mind 452
relaxation
  [*see* relax]
  amusement 840
  dereliction 927
relaxed *weak* 160
relay *materials* 635
  provision 637
release *death* 360
  liberate 750
  exempt 760
  from engagement **768a**
  security 771
  exemption 777a
  restore 790
  repay 807
  forgive 918
  exempt 927a
  discharge 970
  deed of - 723
relegate *banish* 55
  transfer 270
  remove **297**
relent *moderate* 174
  soften 324
  pity 914
relentless
  resolute 604
  severe 739
  wrathful 900
  malevolent 907
  revenge 919
  impenitent 951
relessee
  possessor 779
  receiver 785
relevancy
  pertinence 9
  congruity 23
relevé 298
reliable
  certain 474
reliance
  confidence 484
  expectation 507
  hope 858
relic *remainder* 40
  reminiscence 505
  token 551
relics *corpse* 362
  sacred 998

convolution 248
reticule 191
retiform 219
retina 441
retinue *followers* 65
  series 69
  servants 746
retire *move back* 283
  recede 287
  resign 757
  modest 881
  seclusion 893
  - from sight
  disappear 449
  hide 528
  - into the shade
  inferior 34
  decrease 36
retiring
  concave 252
  - *color* 438
  - *disposition* 881
retold 104
retort
  crucible 144
  receptacle 191
  vaporizer 336
  boiler 386
  answer 462
  confutation 479
  retaliation 718
  wit 842
  - *courteous* 718
retouch *restore* 660
  (*improve* 658)
retrace 505
  - one's steps 607
retract
  recant 607
  annul 756
  abjure 757
  violate 773
  (*deny* 536)
retreat
  resort 74
  abode 189
  regression 283
  recede 287
  ambush 530
  refuge 666
  escape 671
  give way 725
  beat a - 623
retreating
  concave 252
retrench *subduct* 38
  shorten 201
  lose 789
  economize 817
retribution
  retaliation 718
  payment 807
  punishment 972
  reward 973
retrieve *restore* 660
  acquire 775
retriever *dog* 366
retroaction
  counteraction 179
  recoil 277
  regression 283

retroactive
  past 122
retrocession
  regression 283
  recession 287
retrograde
  moving back 283
  deteriorated 659
  relapsing 661
retrogression
  regression 283
  deterioration 659
  relapse 661
retrorse 145
retrospection
  past 122
  thought 451
  memory 505
retroussé 201
retroversion 218
retrude 289
return *list* 86
  repeat 104
  periodic 138
  reverse 145
  recoil 277
  regression 283
  arrival 292
  answer 462
  report 551
  relapse 661
  appoint 755
  profit 775
  restore 790
  proceeds 810
  reward 973
  in -
  compensation 30
  - thanks
  gratitude 916
  worship 990
  - the compliment
  interchange 148
  retaliate 718
  - to the original state
  660
reunion *junction* 43
réunion
  assemblage 72
  concord 714
  point de - 74
  social - 892
revanche, en - 718
reveal 529
  - itself 446
reveille 550
reveiller le chat qui
  dort, ne pas -
  warning 668
  caution 864
revel *amuse* 840
  dissipation 954
  - in *enjoy* 377
revelation
  discovery 480a
  disclosure 529
  theological 985
Revelations 985
reveler 840
  drunkard 959
reveling

disorder 59
rejoicing 838
revenant 980
revendicate
  claim 741
  acquisition 775
  due 924
revenge 919
  breathe -
  anger 900
revenons à nos mou-
  tons
  regression 283
  restoration 660
revenue 810
  means 632
reverberate
  recoil 277
  sound 408
reverberatory 386
revere *love* 897
  respect 928
  piety 987
reverence *title* 877
  respect 928
  piety 987
  clergy 996
reverenced 500
reverend *title* 877
  clergy 996
reverent *pious* 987
  worship 990
reverential
  respectful 928
reverie
  train of thought 451
  inattention 458
  imagination 515
reversal
  inversion 218
  revolution 607
reversible
  irresolute 605
reverse *contrary* 14
  inversion 218
  - *of a medal* 235
  anteposition 237
  adversity 735
  abrogate 756
  cards 840
  - of the shield 468
reverseless 150
reversion
  [*see reverse*]
  posteriority 117
  return 145
  possession 777
  property 780
  succession 783
  remitter 790
reversioner 779
reversis 840
revert *repeat* 104
  return 145
  turn back 283
  revest 790
  - to 457
revest 790
reviction 660
review *consider* 457
  inquiry 461

judge 480
recall 505
dissertation 595
compendium 596
revise 658
parade 882
reviewer 480
revile *abuse* 932
  blaspheme 988
reviler 936
revise *copy* 21
  consider 457
  printing 591
  plan 626
  improve 658
revising barrister 967
revision, under - 673
revisit 186
revival
  reproduction 163
  restoration 660
  worship 990
revivalist 996
revive
  reproduce 163
  resuscitate 660
  excite 824
revivify
  reproduce 163
  life 359
  resuscitate 660
revocable 605
revoir, au - 293
revoke *recant* 607
  cancel 756
  (*deny* 536)
  (*refuse* 764)
revolt *resist* 719
  disobey 742
  shock 830
  disapproval 932
  - against *hate* 898
  - at the idea
  dissent 489
revolting
  painful 830
revolution
  periodicity 138
  change **146**
  rotation 312
revolutionary 146
revolutionize 146
revolve
  [*see revolution*]
  - in the mind 451
revolver
  weapon 727
revulsion
  reversion 145
  revolution 146
  inversion 218
  recoil 277
reward 973
reword 104
Reynard
  animal 366
  cunning 702
rez de chaussée
  room 191
  low 207
rhabdology 85

rhabdomancy 511
rhadamanthus
  judge 967
  hell 982
rhamphoid 245
rhapsodical
  irregular 139
rhapsodist
  fanatic 504
rhapsody
  discontinuity 70
  nonsense 497
  fancy 515
rheometer 466
rhetoric *speech* 582
  flowers of - 577
rheum
  excretion 299
  fluidity 333
  water 337
rheumatism 378
rhino 800
rhinoceros hide
  physically insensible 376
  morally insensible 823
rhipidate 194
rhododendron 845
rhomb 244
rhumb 278
rhyme
  similarity 17
  verse 597
  without - or reason
  absurd 497
  caprice 608
  motiveless 615a
rhymeless
  prose 598
rhymester 597
rhythm
  periodicity 138
  melody 413
  verse 597
rhythmical
  - *style* 578
riant 836
rib *support* 215
  ridge 250
  wife 903
ribald *vulgar* 851
  disreputable 874
  impure 961
ribaldry 908
riband
  [see ribbon]
ribbed
  furrowed 259
ribbon *tie* 45
  filament 205
  decoration 877
ribbons *reins* 752
ribroast 972
rice 330
rich *savory* 394
  color 428
  language 577
  abundant 639
  wealthy 803
  beautiful 845

  ornament 847
  - gifts wax poor 907
  - man 803
riches 803
richesses, embarras de -
  redundance 641
  wealth 803
richly *much* 31
  - deserve 924
rick
  accumulation 72
  store 636
rickety *weak* 160
  ugly 846
  imperfect 651
ricksha 272
ricochet 277
ricordo, non mi - 506
rid *deliver* 672
  get - of *eject* 297
  liberation 750
  loose 776
  relinquish 782
riddance 672, 776, 782
riddle *arrange* 60
  sieve 260
  secret 533
  clean 652
  (*question* 461)
ride *get above* 206
  move 266
  - and tie
  periodicity 138
  journey 266
  - at anchor 265
  - full tilt at
  pursue 622
  attack 716
  - hard 274
  - in the whirlwind
  will 604
  rule 737
  - one's hobby 622
  - out the storm 664
  - rough shod
  violence 173
  severity 739
  insolence 885
  illegality 964
rideau, lever de - 599
ridentem dicere verum
  cheerful 836
  wit 842
rider *appendix* 39
  equestrian 268
rideret Heraclitus 853
ride si sapis 377
ridge *narrow* 203
  height 206
  prominence 250
ridicule 856
  disrespect 929
ridiculous
  absurd 497
  foolish 499
  trifling 643
  grotesque 853
ridiculousness 853

riding *district* 181
  journey 266
ridotto *gala* 840
  rout 892
rifacimento
  repetition 104
  resuscitation 660
rife *general* 78
  influence 175
riffle 348
riffraff *dirt* 653
  commonalty 876
  bad folk 949
rifle *musket* 727
  plunder 791
rifled cannon 727
rifleman 726
rifler 792
rifles 726
rifle shooting 840
rift *separation* 44
  fissure 198
rig *dress* 225
  vehicle 272
  prepare 673
  frolic 840
  strumpet 962
  - the market 794
  run the - upon 929
rigadoon 840
rigging *ropes* 45
  gear 225
  instrument 633
riggish 961
right *dextral* 238
  straight 246
  true 494
  property 780
  just **922**
  privilege 924
  duty 926
  honor 939
  virtuous 944
  bill of - 969
  by - 924
  have a - to 924
  hit the - nail on the head
    discover 480a
    skill 698
  in one's - mind
    wise 498
    sane 502
  in the - place 646
  keep the - path 944
  - about
    [see below]
  - ahead 234
  - and left
    space 180
    circumjacence 227
    lateral 236
  - angle 212
  - as a trevet 650
  - ascension 466
  - away 113, 143
  - bower 840
  - divine of kings 737
  - establishment 478
  - hand [see below]
  - itself 660

  - line 246
  - man in the right place 23
  - owner 779
  - thing to do 926
  - word in the right place 578
  set - *inform* 527
    disclose 529
  step in the - direction 644
  that's - 931
right about
  go to the -
    circuit 311
    tergiversation 607
  send to the -
    eject 297
    reject 610
    refuse 764
  to the - 283
  turn to the -
    inversion 218
    deviation 279
righteous
  virtuous 944
  - overmuch 988
  the - 987
Righteousness:
  Lord our - 976
  Sun of - 976
rightful 922
  - owner 779
right hand
  power 157
  dextrality 238
  help 711
  not let the - know what the left is doing 528
  - of friendship 888
rightly served, be - 972
right-minded
  probity 939
  virtue 944
rights: put to -
  restore 660
  set to -
  arrange 60
  stand on one's - 748
rigid *regular* 82
  hard 328
  exact 494
  severe 739
  (*stubborn* 606)
rigmarole
  unmeaning 517
  (*absurd* 497)
rigor 383, 494, 739
  (*compulsion* 744)
  - mortis 360
rigorous *exact* 494
  severe 739
  revengeful 919
  - establishment 478
Rigsdag 696
rigueur, de 744
riksdag 696
rile *annoy* 830
  hate 898

anger 900
rilievo *convex* 250
　sculpture 557
rill 348
rim 231
rime *chink* 198
　frost 283
rimer 262
rimiform 259
rimose 198
rimple 258
rimulose 198
rind 223
rinderpest 655
ring *pendency* 214
　circle 247
　loud 404
　resonance 408
　test 463
　clique 712
　arena 728
　have the true - 494
　in a - fence
　　circumscription 229
　　inclosure 232
　- dove 366
　- in the ear 408
　- the changes
　　repeat 104
　　change 140
　　changeable 149
　- the tocsin 669
　- with the praises of
　　931
　rub the - 902
ringer *impostor* 548
ringleader
　director 694
　mutineer 742
ringlet *circling* 247
　hair 256
ringworm 655
rink 840
rinse 652
rinsings 653
riot *confusion* 59
　derangement 61
　violence 173
　discord 713
　resist 719
　mutiny 742
　- *in pleasure* 742
　run - *activity* 682
　　excitement 825
　　intemperance 954
rioter 742
riotous 173
rip *bad man* 949
　libertine 962
　- open 260
　- up *tear* 44
　　recall the past 505
　　excite 824
riparian 342
ripe 673
　- age *old* 128
　　grown up 131
ripen *perfect* 650
　improve 658
　prepare 673
　complete 729

- into 144
ripicolous 342
riposte 462
ripple *ruffle* 256
　shake 315
　water 348
　murmur 405
riprap 215
rire, pour - 853
rise *grow* 35
　begin 66
　slope 217
　progress 282
　ascend 305
　stir 682
　revolt 742
　- again 660
　- from 154
　- in arms 722
　- in price 814
　- in the world 734
　- up *elevation* 307
risible
　laughable 838
　ridiculous 853
　(*wit* 842)
rising [see rise]
　- generation
　　youth 127
　　posterity 167
　- ground
　　height 206
　　slope 217
　- of the curtain
　　beginning 66
　　appearance 448
　worship the - sun 886
risk *chance* 621
　danger 665
　at any - 604
risqué 961
**risum teneatis ami-
　ci?** 853
rit: il - bien 864
rite *law* 963
　religious **998**
　funeral - 363
ritornello 104
ritual
　ostentation 882
　rite 998
ritualism
　religious sect 984
rival *emulate* 648
　oppose 708
　opponent 710
　compete 720
　combatant 726
　outshine 873
rivalry *envy* 921
rive 44
rivel 258
river 348
rivet *fasten* 43
　fastening 45
　- in the memory 505
　- the attention
　　attend 457
　　excite 824
　- the eyes upon 441
　- the yoke 739

riveted *firm* 150
rivulation 219, 248
rivulet 348
rivulose 248
rixation 713
rixiform 249
road *street* 189
　direction 278
　way 627
　on the -
　　transference 270
　　progression 282
　　approach 286
　on the high - to 278
　- to ruin
　　destruction 162
　　danger 665
　　adversity 735
road book 266
roads *lake* 343
roadstead
　abode 189
　refuge 666
roadster 271
roadway 627
roam 266
roan *horse* 271
　color 432
roanoke 800
roar *violence* 173
　sound 404
　bellow 411, 412
　laugh 838
　weep 839
roarer 887
roaring *great* 31
　- trade 731, 734
roast *heat* 384
　ridicule 856
　rib - 972
　- and boiled 298
　- an ox 883
　rule the - 737
rob *pulp* 354
　plunder 791
　- Peter to pay Paul
　　30
robber 792
robbery 791
robe
　covering 223
　dress 225
　canonicals 999
robes - of state 747
R o b i n Goodfellow
　980
Robinson, say Jack
　- 132
roborant 662
robust *strong* 159
　healthy 654
roc 83
Rocinante 271
rock *firm* 150
　oscillate 314
　hard 323
　land 342
　danger 667
　attack 716
　money 800
　build on a - 150

- ahead 665
- oil 356
split upon a - 732
rockaway 272
rocket *rapid* 274
　rise 305
　light 423
　signal 550
　arms 727
　go up like a - and
　　come down like
　　the stick 732
rocking-chair 215
rocking-stone 314
rococo 124
rod *support* 215
　measure 466
　scourge 975
　divining 993
　kiss the - 725
　- in pickle
　　prepared 673
　　accusation 938
　　punishment 972
　　scourge 975
　- of empire 747
　sounding - 208
rodomontade
　unmeaning 517
　boast 884
　(*absurdity* 497)
roe *deer* 366
　female 374
rogation
　request 765
　worship 990
rogue *cheat* 548
　knave 941
　scamp 949
　-'s march 297
roguery 940
roguish
　playful 840
roi
　le - est mort, vive le
　　roi 838
　le - le veut 737
Roi le veut, le - 741
roister 885
roisterer 887
Roland for an Oliver
　retaliation 718
　barter 794
rôle *drama* 599
　business 625
　plan 626
　conduct 692
roll *list* 86
　fillet 205
　convolution 248
　rotundity 249
　make smooth 255
　move 264
　rotate 312
　rock 314
　flow 348
　sound **407**
　record 551
　- along 312
　- in *plenty* 639

- a corner 311
- and round
  periodic 138
  rotation 312
- assertion 535
- game 840
- like a horse in a mill 613
- number
  number 84
  multitude 102
- of life 151
- of pleasures
  pleasure 377
  amusement 840
- of the ladder 71
- of visits 892
- pace 274
- robin
  information 527
  petition 765
  censure 932
- sum 800
- terms 566
- trot 274
run the - of
  active 682
turn - invert 218
  retreat 283
  revolve 311
round about
  circumjacent 227
  deviation 279
  circuit 311
  amusement 840
- phrases 573
- way 629
rounded periods 577, 578
roundelay 597
rounder 949
rounders 840
roundhouse 752
roundlet 247
round-shouldered 243
round-up 72
roup 796
rouse
  stimulate 615
  excite 824
- oneself 682
rouser 83
rousing 171
roustabout 690
rout agitation 315
  printing 591
  overcome 731
  discomfit 732
  rabble 876
  assembly 892
  put to the - 731
- out 652
route 627
  en - 270
  en - for 282
routine
  uniform 16
  order 58
  rule 80
  periodic 138

custom 613
business 625
rove travel 266
  deviate 279
rover traveler 268
  pirate 792
roving commission 475
row disorder 59
  series 69
  violence 173
  street 189
  navigate 267
  discord 713
- in the same boat 88
rowdy vulgar 851
  blusterer 887
  bad man 949
rowel sharp 253
  stimulus 615
rowen 168
rower 269
rowlock 215
royal 737
- road way 627
  easy 705
Royal Academician 559
royalist 737
royaliste que le roi, plus - 33
royalty 737
royne 298
ruade impulse 276
  attack 716
ruat cœlum 908
rub friction 331
  difficulty 704
  adversity 735
  painful 830
- down lessen 195
  powder 330
- down with an oaken towel 972
- off 552
- off corners 82
- on slow 275
  progress 282
  inexcitable 826
- one's eyes 870
- one's hands 838
- on the raw 900
- out 552
- up 658
- up the memory 505
rubadub 407
rubber whist 840
rubberneck 444, 455
rubbers 225
rubbish
  unmeaning 517
  trifling 643
  useless 645
rubble 645
rube 501, 876
rubeola 655
rubescence 434
Rubicon limit 233
  pass the -
  begin 66
  cross 303

choose 609
rubicose 434
rubicund 434
rubiform 434
rubify 434
rubigo 653
rubric precept 697
  liturgy 998
rubricate
  redden 434
ruby red 434
  gem 648
  ornament 847
ruck 258
ructation 297
rudder 693
rudderless 158
ruddle 434
ruddy red 434
  beautiful 845
rude violent 173
  shapeless 241
  ignorant 491
  inelegant 579
  ugly 846
  vulgar 851
  uncivilized 876
  uncivil 895
  disrespect 929
- health 654
- reproach 908
rudera 645
rudiment
  beginning 66
  cause 153
rudimental
  small 193
  immature 674
rudiments
  knowledge 490
  school 542
rudis indigestaque moles disorder 59
  amorphous 241
rue bitter 395
  regret 833
  repent 950
rueful painful 830
  sad 837
ruff 225
ruffian
  maleficent 913
  scoundrel 949
ruffianism 907
ruffle disorder 59
  derange 61
  roughen 256
  fold 258
  feeling 821
  excite 824, 825
  pain 830
  anger 900
rufous 434
rufulous 434
rug support 215
  covering 223
rugged
  shapeless 241
  rough 256
  difficult 704
  ugly 846

churlish 895
rugose 256
ruin destruction 162
  evil 619
  failure 732
  adversity 735
  poverty 804
  (decay 659)
ruined hopeless 859
ruinous
  painful 830
ruins remains 40
rule regularity 80
  length 200
  measure 466
  decide 480
  custom 613
  precept 697
  government 737
  law 963
  absence of - 699
  as a - 613
  by - 82
  golden - 697
  obey -s 82
- of three 85
- of thumb
  experiment 463
  unreasoning 477
  essay 675
  unskilled 699
ruler 745
ruling passion
  obstinacy 606
  character 820
rum queer 853
  drink 959
rumal 225
rumble 407
ruminate chew 298
  think 451
rummage 461
rummer 191
rumor
  publicity 531
  report 532
rump 235
rumple
  disorder 59
  derange 61
  roughen 256
  fold 258
rumpus
  confusion 59
  violence 173
  discord 713
  (contention 720)
run generality 78
  repetition 104
  course 109
  continuance 143
  eventuality 151
  motion 264
  speed 274
  liquefy 335
  flow 348
  habit 613
  smuggle 791
  contraband 964
  have a -
  fashion 852

repute 873
have - of 748
he that -s may read 525
near - 197
race is - 729
- abreast 27
- a chance
  probable 472
  chance 621
- after pursue 622
  in repute 873
- against
  impact 276
  oppose 708
  attack 716
- amuck
  violent 173
  kill 361
  attack 716
- a race speed 274
  conduct 692
  contend 720
- a rig 840
- a risk 665
- at 716
- a tilt at
  attack 716
  contend 720
- away avoid 623
  (escape 671)
- away with
  take 789
  steal 791
- away with a notion
  misjudge 481
  credulous 486
- back 283
- counter to 708
- down
  pursue 622
  bad 649
  attack 716
  depreciate 932
  detract 934
- dry waste 638
  insufficient 640
- foul of 276
- hard danger 665
  difficult 704
  success 731
- high great 31
  violent 173
- in introduce 228
- in a race
  act 680
- in the head
  think 451
  remember 505
- into
  conversion 144
  insert 300
- into danger 665

- into debt 806
- its course
  course 109
  complete 729
  past 122
- like mad 274
- low 36
- mad insane 503
  passion 825
- mad after 865
- of luck
  fortune 156
  prosperity 734
- of one's teeth 815
- of things 151
- on 143
- on in a groove 613
- out end 67
  course 109
  past 122
  antiquated 124
  egress 295
  prodigal 818
- out on 573
- over count 85
  - in the mind 451
  examine 457
  describe 594
  synopsis 596
  overflow 641
- parallel 178
- riot violent 173
  exaggerate 549
  redundance 641
  active 682
  disobey 742
  intemperance 954
- rusty 603
- smooth
  easy 705
  prosperous 734
- the eye over
  see 441
  learn 539
- the fingers over 379
- the gauntlet 861
- the rig upon 929
- through
  uniform 16
  influence 175
  be present 186
  kill 361
  expend 809
  prodigal 818
- to seed age 128
  deterioration 659
- to waste 638
- up increase 25
  build 161
- up an account
  credit 805
  debt 806

  charge 812
- up bills
  not pay 808
- upon
  require 630
- upon a bank
  bankrupt 808
  expenditure 809
- wild 173
time -s 106
runabout 268
  vehicle 272
runagate
  fugitive 623
  disobey 742
  bad man 949
runaway 623
rundle circle 247
  convolution 248
  rotundity 249
rundlet 191
runer 597
Runes writing 590
  poetry 597
  spell 993
rung 215
runnel 348
runner
  branch 51
  courier 268
  conduit 350
  messenger 534
  petitioner 767
running
  continuous 69
- account 811
- commentary 595
- fight 720
- hand 590
- over 641
- water 348
the mind - upon 451
the mind - upon other things 458
runnion 949
runt 193
rupture
  disjunction 44
  disease 655
  quarrel 713
rural village 189
  agricultural 371
- dean 893
ruralist 893
ruse cunning 702
  (deception 545)
rush crowd 72
  vigor 171
  violence 173
  velocity 274
  water 348
  plant 367
  trifle 643

  haste 684
make a - at 716
- in medias res 604
- into print 591
- on destruction 863
- to a conclusion
  misjudge 481
  credulous 486
- upon 622
Rush, Friar - 980
rus in urbe
  abode 189
  secluded 893
rushlight dim 422
  candle 423
rusk 298
Russe, montagne 840
russet gray 432
  brown 433
  red 434
Russian bath 386
rust red 434
  decay 659
  canker 663
  inaction 683
moth and - 659
- of antiquity 122
rustic
  village 189
  agricultural 371
  vulgar 851
  clown 876
rusticate
  punish 972
  seclude 893
rusticity
  impolite 895
rusticus expectat dum defluat amnis 858
rustle 409
rusty dirty 653
  decayed 659
  sluggish 683
  unskillful 699
  sulky 901a
  (old 128)
  (unserviceable 645)
run - averse 603
rut furrow 259
  habit 613
ruth 914
ruthless
  savage 907
  pitiless 914a
  revengeful 919
rutilant 420
ruttish 961
rye 959
ryot servant 746
  possessor 779
  commonalty 876

worth one's - 644
saltation 309
saltatory 315
saltimbanco 548
saltpeter
  pungent 392
  gunpowder 727
saltum, per - 315
saluiority 656
salutary
  healthful 656
  (*remedial* 662)
salutatory 582
salute
  allocution 586
  celebration 883
  courtesy 894
  kiss 902
  respect 928
salutiferous
  [see *salutary*]
salva:
  - res est 664
  - sit reverentia 928
salvable 946
salvage
  acquisition 775
  tax 812
  discount 813
  reward 973
salvation
  preservation 670
  deliverance 672
  religious 976
  piety 987
  work out one's - 990
salve *remedy* 662
  relieve 834
salver 191
salvo *exception* 83
  explosion 406
  qualification 469
  plea 617
  excuse 937
  (*condition* 770)
  - of artillery
  celebration 883
sal-volatile 392
Samael 978
Samaritan, good -
  benevolent 906
  benefactor 912
sambar 366
sambo 431
same 13
  all the - to 823
  at the - time
  compensatory 30
  synchronous 120
  go over the - ground
    104
  in the - boat 709
  in the - breath
  instantaneous 113
  synchronous 120
  of the - mind 488
  on the - tack 709
samiel 349
samo 720
sampan 273
sample 82

Samson 159
samurai 875
sana, mens - 502
  - in corpore sano 827
sanation
  restoration 660
sanative
  remedial 662
sanatorium 662
sanctification
  divine attribute 976
sanctify
  authorize 926
  piety 987
sanctimony 988
sanction
  permission 760
  dueness 924
  approbation 931
  to - vice 945
sanctitude 987
sanctity 987
sanctuary
  refuge 666
  altar 1000
sanctum
  chamber 191
  - sanctorum
  abode 189
  privacy 893
  temple 1000
sanctus 900
  - bell 550
sand *powder* 330
  resolution 604
  built upon - 665
  sow the - 645
sandal 225
sandbag 727, 972
sandbagger 792
sand-blind 442
Sandemanian 984
sandpaper 255
sands *danger* 667
  - on the seashore
  multitude 102
sand storm 330
sandwich-wise 228
sandy *yellow* 436
sane 502
sangar 717
sang froid
  insensibility 823
  inexcitability 826
  presence of mind 864
sangraal 998
sanguinary 361
sanguine *red* 434
  hopeful 858
  - expectation
  expect 507
  hope 858
  - imagination 515
sanguisage 662
sanhedrim
  council 696
  churchdom 995
sanies 333
sanitaire, cordon -
  670
sanitarian 656

sanitarium 656
sanitary 656
sanity *mental* 502
  bodily - 654
sans 187
  - cérémonie
  friendly 888
  social 892
  - façon
  simple 849
  modest 881
  social 892
  - pareil 33
  - peur et sans re-
    proche
  perfect 650
  heroic 873
  honorable 939
  - souci
  insensible 823
  pleasure 827
  content 831
sans-culotte
  rebel 742
  commonalty 876
sans Dieu rien 976
Sanskrit 124
Sanskritist 492
santé, maison de -
  662
santon hermit 893
  priest 996
sanyasi 955, 996
sap *essence* 5
  destroy 162
  excavate 252
  juice 333
  damage 659
  attack 716
  - the foundations 162,
    659
sapere aude 498
sapid 390
sapient 498
sapless *weak* 160
  dry 340
sapling 129
saponaceous 355
saporific 390
sapper
  excavator 252
  soldier 726
sappers and miners
  preparerers 673
  preparers 673
Sapphic 597
sapphire *blue* 438
  gem 847
sapphism 961
sapphist 962
sappy *young* 127
  juicy 333
  foolish 499
saprogenie 653
sapromyiophyllous
  362
saraband 840
sarà sarà, che - 601
sarcasm
  disrespect 929
  censure 932

  detraction 934
sarcastic
  ridicule 856
  discourteous 895
sarcology 662
sarcoma 250
sarcophagus 363
sarculation 103
sard 847
Sardanapalus 954a
sardonic
  censure 932
  detraction 934
  - grin
  laughter 838
  ridicule 856
  discontent 932
sardonyx 847
sark 225
sarmentum 51
sartorial 225
Sarum, Old - 893
sash 247
sassafras 662
Sastra 986
Satan 978
satanic
  malevolent 907
  vicious 945
  diabolic 978
satchel 191
sate 869
satellite
  companion 88
  follower 281
  heavenly body 318
  auxiliary 711
  servant 746
satiety
  sufficient 639
  pleasant 829
  cloy 869
  (*redundance* 641)
satin 255
satire *ridicule* 856
  censure 932
satirical 932
  detraction 934
satirist
  detractor 936
satis: jam - 869
  - superque 641
satisfaction
  [see *satisfy*]
  duel 720
  pleasure 827
  atonement 952
  hail with - 931
satisfactorily 618
satisfactory
  [see *satisfy*]
  good 648
satisfy *answer* 462
  convince 484
  sufficient 639
  consent 762
  observance 772
  pay 807
  gratify 829
  content 831
  satiate 869

come to the -
contention 720
courage 861
mere - 209
old - 978
- out 552
- the head 461
up to the - 861
scrawl 590
scrawny 203
screak 411
scream *cry* 411
wail 839
screaming 853
screech 411, 412
screech owl 412
screen *sift* 60
sieve 260
shade 424
hide 528
hider 530
side scene 599
clean 652
safety 664
shelter 666
defense 717
- from sight 442
screw *fasten* 43
fastening 45
oar 267
propeller 284
rotation 312
instrument 633
miser 819
put on the -
severity 739
compel 744
- loose *insane* 503
imperfect 651
unskillful 699
hindrance 706
attack 713
- one's courage to the
sticking place 861
- shaped 248
- up *fasten* 43
strengthen 159
prepare 673
- up the eyes 443
screw-driver 633
screwed
drunk 959
screw steamer 273
scribble 590
scribbler 593
scribe *recorder* 553
writer 590
priest 996
scribendi, cacoëthes
- 590
scribendi recte sa-
pere 590
scrimmage
discord 713
contention 720
scrimp *short* 201
insufficient 640
stingy 819
scrip 191
script 590
scripta, lex - 963

scriptæ, literæ - 590
scriptural
orthodox 983a
Scripture
certain 474
revelation 895
-s of the skies 423
scrivener *writer* 590
lawyer 968
scrofula 655
scroll 551
scrub *rub* 331
bush 367
clean 652
dirty person 653
commonalty 876
scrubby *small* 193
trifling 643
stingy 819
disreputable 874
vulgar 876
shabby 940
scruple
small quantity 32
weight 319
doubt 485
reluctance 603
probity 939
scrupulous
careful 459
incredulous 487
exact 494
reluctant 603
fastidious 868
punctilious 939
scrutator 461
scrutinizer 461
scrutiny
attention 457
inquiry 461
scrutoire 191
scud *sail* 267
speed 274
shower 348
cloud 353
- under bare poles
704
scuffle 720
scull *row* 267
brain 450
scullery 191
scullion 746
sculpsit 558
sculptor 559
sculpture *form* 240
carving 557
scum *dirt* 653
- of the earth 949
- of society 876
scupper 350
scurf 653
scurrility 908
scurrilous
ridicule 856
disrespect 929
detraction 934
scurvy
insufficient 640
unimportant 643
base 940
wicked 945

scut 235
scutate 245
scutcheon
standard 550
honor 877
scutiform 251
scuttle *destroy* 162
receptacle 191
speed 274
- along *haste* 684
scutum 717
Scylla and Charyb-
dis, between -
danger 665
difficulty 704
Scyllam, incidit in -
699
scyphiform 252
scytho *pointed* 244
sharp 253
sdeath! *wonder* 870
anger 900
disapprobation 932
sea *multitude* 102
ocean 341
at - 341
uncertain 475
go to - 293
heavy - 315
- hath bounds 865
- of doubt 475
- of troubles
difficulty 704
adversity 735
- of upturned faces
234
seaboard 342
seafarer 269
seafaring 267
sea fight 720
seagirt 346
seagoing 267, 341
sea green 435
sea king 791
seal *matrix* 22
close 261
evidence 467
mark 550
resolve 604
complete 729
compact 769
security 771
marriage 903
break the - 529
- of secrecy 528
- one's infamy 940
- the doom of 162
- the lips 585
- up *restrain* 751
under - 769
sealed:
hermetically - 261
one's fate is - 601
- book
ignorance 491
unintelligible 519
secret 533
sealing 903
sealing wax 747
seals
insignia 747

seam 43
sea-maid 979
seaman 269
seamanship
conduct 692
skill 698
seamark 550
seamless 50
seamstress 690
seamy side 651
séance 696
seapiece 556
seaport 666
sear *dry* 340
burn 384
deaden 823
- and yellow leaf
age 128
wither 659
search *inquire* 461
searching
severe 739
painful 830
searchless 519
seared conscience
951
sea serpent 83
seasickness 655
seaside 342
sea slug 298
season *mix* 41
time 106
pungent 392
accustom 613
preserve 670
prepare 673
seasonable *fit* 23
early 132
opportune 134
sea song 597
seasoning
condiment 393
seat *place* 183
locate 184
abode 189
support 215
judgment - 966
- of government 737
- of war 728
seated, firmly - 150
seawant 800
seaworthy 664
sebacious 355
secant 44, 219
secede *dissent* 489
relinquish 624
disobey 742
seceder
heterodox 984
secern 297
seclusion 893
second
duplication 90
- *of time* 108
instant 113
- in music 413, 415
abet 707
one's - self 17
play or sing a - 416
play - fiddle
obey 743

subject 749
disrepute 874
- best
imperfect 651
failure 732
- childhood
age 128
imbecility 499
- crop
fertile 168
profit 775
- edition 104
- nature 613
- sight
foresight 510
sorcery 992
- thoughts
sequel 65
thought 451
improvement 658
- to none 33
- youth 660
secondary
inferior 34
following 63
imperfect 651
deputy 759
- education 537
- evidence 467
seconder 711
secondhand
imitation 19
old 124
deteriorated 659
received 785
secondly 90
second-rate 651
secret key 522
latent 526
hidden 528
riddle **533**
in the - 490
keep a -
silent 585
- motive 615
- passage 627
- place 530
- writing 590
secrétaire 191
secretariat 965
secretary
recorder 553
writer 590
director 694
auxiliary 711
servant 746
consignee 758
secrete excrete 297
conceal 528
secretion 299
secretive 528
sect 75
religious - 983, 984
sectarian
dissent 489
ally 711
heterodox 984
section division 44
part 51
class 75
chapter 593

troops 726
sector part 51
circle 247
secular
centenary 98
periodic 138
laity 997
- education 537
secularism 984
secula seculorum, in
- 112
secundines 63 -
secundum artem
conformable 82
skillful 698
secure fasten 43
bespeak 132
belief 484
safe 664
restrain 751
engage 768
gain 775
confident 858
- an object
success 731
securities 805
security safety 664
pledge **771**
hope 858
lend on - 787
sedan chair 272
sedate
thoughtful 451
calm 826
grave 837
sedative
calming 174
remedy 662
sedentary 265
sedge 367
sedile 1000
sediment dregs 653
sedimentary
remainder 40
sedition 742
seditiosissimus quis-
que ignavus 742
seduce entice 615
love 897
debauch 961
seducer 962
seduction
pleasing 829
desire 865
sedulous
active 682
desirous 865
see view 441
look 457
believe 484
know 490
bishopric 995
- after 459
- at a glance 498
- daylight 480a
- double 959
- fit 600, 602
- justice done 922
- life
amusement 840
- one's way

foresight 510
intelligible 518
skill 698
easy 705
- service 722
- sights 455
- the light
born 359
published 531
- through
discover 480a
intelligence 498
- to attention 457
care 459
direction 693
we shall - 507
seed small 32
cause 153
posterity 167
grain 330
run to - age 128
lose health 659
sow the - 673
seedling 129
seed plot
productive 168
agriculture 371
seedtime of life 127
seedy weak 160
disease 655
deteriorated 659
exhausted 688
needy 804
seeing that
circumstance 8
reasoning 476 -
seek inquire 461
pursue 622
offer 763
request 765
- safety 664
seek-sorrow 837
seel 217
seem 448
as it -s good to 600
seeming 488
seemingly 472
seemless
ugly 846
undue 925
seemliness
duty 926
seemly
expedient 646
handsome 845
due 924
seer veteran 130
madman 504
oracle 513
sorcerer 994
seesaw 314
seethe hot 382
make hot 384
excitement 824
seething caldron 386
segar 392
segment 51
segnitude 683
s'égosiller 411
segregate
not related 10

separate 44
exclude 55
segregated
incoherent 47
seigneur, grand -
pride 878
insolence 885
seignior
master 745
nobility 875
seigniority
authority 737
possession 777
property 780
seigniory 737
seine net 232
seisin
possession 777
estate 780
seismometer 276
seize take 789
rob 791
- an opportunity 134
- the present hour 134
seized with
disease 655
feeling 821
seizure 925
se judice nemo 947
sejunction 44
seldom 137
select
specify 79
choose 609
good 648
selection 75
selectman 965
self identity 13
speciality 79
- abasement 879
- accusing 950
- admiration 880
- annulling 497
- applause 880
- called 565
- command
resolution 604
caution 864
(temperance 953)
- communing 451
- complacency
cheerful 836
vanity 880
- confidence 880
- conquest
resolution 604
(temperance 953)
- conscious 855
- consultation 451
- contradictory 471,
497
- control 604
- conviction
belief 484
penitent 950
condemned 971
- council 451
- deceit error 495
- deception
credulity 486
- defense 717

- delusion 486, 347
- denial
  disinterested 942
  temperance 953
  penance 990
- discipline 990
- esteem 880
- evident
  certain 474
  manifest 525
- examination 990
- existing 1
- government
  freedom 748
  (*virtue* 944)
- help 698
- immolation 991
- indulgence
  selfishness 943
  intemperance 954
- instruction 539
- interest 943
- knowledge 881
- love 943
- luminous 423
- opinioned
  narrow-minded 481
  (*foolish* 499)
  (*obstinate* 606)
- possession
  sanity 502
  resolution 604
  inexcitability 826
  caution 864
- praise 880
- preservation 717
- reliance
  resolution 604
  hope 858
  courage 861
- reproach 950
- respect
  pride 878
- restraint 953
- sacrifice 942
- satisfied 880
- seeking 943
- styled 565
- sufficient 880
- taught 490
- tormentor 837
- will 606
selfishness 943
selfsame 13
self-trust
- essence of heroism
  861
sell *absurdity* 497
  deception 545
  untruth 546
  sale 796
- for 812
- off 796
- oneself 940
- one's life dearly
  resist 719
  fight 722
- out 796
seller 796
selliform 250
selon les règles 82

selvedge 231
semaphore 550
sematic 668
semblance
  similarity 17
  imitation 19
  copy 21
  probability 472
  wear the - of
  appearance 448
semeiology
  interpretation 522
semeiotics
  signs 550
semel emissum volat irrevocabile verbum 531
semen 153
semi - 91
semibarbarian 913
semibreve 413
semicircle 247
semicircular 245
semicolon 142
semidiaphanous 427
semifluid 352
semiliquidity 352
semilunar 245
seminal
  causing 153
seminar 542
seminary 542
semination
  preparation 673
semiopaque 427
semipellucid 427
semiquaver 413
semitone 413
semitransparency 427
semper avarus eget 640
sempervirid 110, 123
sempiternal 112
sempstress
  dressmaker 225
  workwoman 690
senary 98
senate 696
senate house 966
senator
  counsel 695
  councillor 696
  green-robed -s of
  mighty woods 367
senatorship 693
senatus consultum 741
send *transfer* 270
  propel 284
- adrift 597
- a letter to 592
- away
  repel 289
  eject 297
  refuse 764
- for 741
- forth
  propel 284
  publish 531

- off 284
- out *eject* 297
  commission 755
- word 527
seneca-oil 356
senescence 128
seneschal
  director 694
  master 745
  servant 746
seneschalship 737
senile 128
senior *age* 128
  master 745
seniores priores
  precedence 62
  precession 380
seniority
  oldness 124
  age 128
se non e vero e ben trovato 546
señor 877
sensation
  physical sensibility 375
  emotion 821
  wonder 870
sensational
  language 574
  exciting 824
sensation drama 599
sensations of touch 380
sense *wisdom* 498
  meaning 516
  accept in a particular - 522
  deep - 821
  in no - 565
- of duty 926
senseless
  insensible 376
  absurd 497
  foolish 499
  unmeaning 517
senses
  external - 375
  intellect 450
  sanity 502
sensibility
  physical - **375**
  moral **822**
sensible
  material 316
  wise 498
sensitive 375, 822
sensorial 821
sensorium 450
sensual
  pleasure 377
  intemperate 954
sensualist 954a
sensuous
  sensibility 375
  pleasure 377
  feeling 821
sentence
  decision 480
  maxim 496
  affirmation 535

  phrase 566
  condemnation 971
  my - is for war 722
sententious
  concise 572
- language 574, 577
sentient
- *physically* 375
- *morally* 821
sentiment *idea* 453
  (*opinion* 484)
  (*maxim* 496)
sentimental
  sensitive 822
  affected 855
sentinel }
sentry }
  guardian 664
  watch 668
  keeper 753
separable 44
separate
  disjoin 44
  exclude 55
  bisect 91
  diverge 291
  divorce 905
- into elements 49
- maintenance 905
- the chaff from the wheat
  discriminate 465
  select 609
separatist 489, 984
  disjunction 44
separative 49
sepia 433
seposition
  disjunction 44
  exclusion 55
sepoy 726
seppuku 972
sept *kin* 11
  class 75
  clan 166
Septentrional 237
septett 415
septic 657
septicity 655
Septuagint 985
septum 228
septuple 98
sepulcher 363
  whited - 545
sepulchral
  interment 363
  resonance 408
  stridor 410
  hoarse 581
sepulture 363
sequacious
  following 63
sequacity *soft* 324
  tenacity 327
sequel
  following **65**
- in time 117
  (*addition* 39)
sequela 65
sequence
- in order **63**

shaggy 256
shagreen 223
shah 745
shaitan 980
shake *totter* 149
  weak 160
  vibrate 314
  agitation 315
  shiver 383
  trill 407
  music 416
  dissuade 616
  shingle 635
  injure 659
  impress 821
  excited 824
  fear 860
 - hands
  pacification 723
  friendship 888
  courtesy 894
  forgive 918
 - off 297
 - off the yoke 750
 - one's faith 485
 - one's sides 838
 - the head
  dissent 489
  deny 536
  refuse 764
  disapprove 932
 - to pieces 162
 - up 315
shakedown *bed* 215
shaker 984
shakes, no great -
  trifling 643
  imperfect 651
shaking prairie 344
shako *hat* 225
  helmet 717
shaky *weak* 160
  in danger 665
  fearful 860
shallop 273
shallow
  unintelligent 32
  not deep 209
  ignorant 491
  ignoramus 493
  foolish 499
  trifling 643
 - pretext 617
 - profundity 855
shallow-brain
  fool 501
shallowness 209
shallow-pated 499
shallows
  danger 667
sham *falsehood* 544
  deception 545
 - fight 720
shaman 994
shamanism 992
shamble
  dawdle 275
  stagger 315
shambles 361
shame
  disrepute 874

584

  wrong 923
  censure 932
  chastity 960
 cry - upon 932
 false - 855
 for - 874
 sense of - 879
 - the devil 939
 to one's - be it spoken
  874
shamefaced 881
shameful
  disgraceful 874
  profligate 945
shameless
  impudent 885
  profligate 945
  indecent 961
shamrock 92
shandredhan 272
shanghai 545
shank *support* 215
  printing 591
  instrument 633
shanks's mare 266
shanty 189
shape *form* 240
  aspect 448
  (*state* 7)
  (*convert* 144)
 - one's course
  direction 278
  pursuit 622
  conduct 692
 - out a course
  plan 626
shapeless
  amorphous 241
  ugly 846
shapely
  symmetrical 242
  comely 845
share *part* 51
  participate 778
  allotted portion 786
 - and share alike 778
 - one's sorrow 915
shareholder 778
shark *thief* 792
  (*cheat* 548)
sharp *energetic* 171
  violent 173
  acute 253
  sensible 375
  pungent 392
 - sound 410
  musical tone 413
  intelligent 498
  active 682
  clever 698
  cunning 702
  feeling 821
  painful 830
  rude 895
  censorious 932
 look -
  take care 459
  be active 682
 - appetite 865
 - contest 720
 - ear 418

 - eye 441
 - fellow
  active 682
  proficient 700
 - frost 383
 - lookout
  vigilance 459
  expectation 507
 - pain 378
 - practice
  cunning 702
  severity 739
  improbity 940
 - set 865
 - toothed *unkindness*
  907
sharpen
  [*see* sharp]
  excite 824
 - one's tools 673
 - one's wits 537
sharpener 253
sharper *thief* 792
  (*cheat* 548)
sharpness 253
sharpshooter 726
sharpshooting 716
Shastra 986
shatter *disjoin* 44
  render powerless 158
  destroy 162
shatter-brained 503
shattered *weak* 160
  fatigued 688
shave *reduce* 195
  shorten 201
  layer 204
  smooth 255
  grate 330
  lie 546
shaving *small* 32
  layer 204
  filament 205
  (*part* 51)
shawl 225
shay 272
she 374
sheaf 72
shear *reduce* 195
  shorten 201
  take 789
shears 253
sheath
  receptacle 191
  envelope 223
sheathe
  moderate 174
  clothe 225
 - the sword 723
sheathing 223
shebeen 189
shed *scatter* 73
  building 189
  emit 297
  give 784
 - a luster on 873
 - blood 361
 - light upon 420
 - tears 839
Shedim 980
sheen 420

sheep 366
sheep dog 366
sheepfold 232
sheepish 881
sheep's eye, cast a
  desire 865
  modest 881
  endearment 902
sheer
  mere 32
  simple 42
  complete 52
 - off *avoid* 623
  (*depart* 293)
sheet *layer* 204
  covering 223
  paper 593
 - of fire 382
 - of water 343
 white -
  penance 952
 winding - 363
sheet anchor
  safety 666
  hope 858
sheet lightning 423
sheet work 591
sheik *ruler* 745
  priest 996
shelf
  support 215
  rock 667
 on the -
  powerless 158
  disused 678
  inaction 681
shell *cover* 223
  coffin 363
  bombard 716
  bomb 727
 - game 545
 - out 807, 809
shellfish 366
shelter *safety* 664
  refuge 666
 - oneself under plea
  of 617
sheltie 271
shelve *locate* 184
  slope 217
  neglect 460
  disuse 678
shelving beach 217
shenanigan 842
shend 659
sheol 982
shepherd
  tender of sheep 370
  director 694
  pastor 996
Shepherd, the Good
  - 976
shepherd's dog 366
Sheppard, Jack - 792
sheriff 965
sherry 959
Shiah 984
shibboleth 550
shield
  heraldry 550
  safety 664

siccity 340
sick *ill* 655
　make one -
　　painful 830
　　aversion 867
　-- at heart 837
　- of *weary* 841
　　dislike 867
　　satiated 869
　visitation of the - 998
sick chamber 655
sicken *nauseate* 395
　disease 655
　pain 830
　weary 841
　disgust 867
sickener
　too much 641
sickle *pointed* 244
　sharp 253
　- shaped 245
sickly *weak* 160
sick room 655
side
　consanguinity 11
　edge 231
　laterality 236
　party 712
　at one's - 197
　from - to side 314
　look only at one - of
　　the shield 481
　on every - 227
　on one - 243
　on one's - 714
　pass from one - to
　　another 607
　- by side
　　accompaniment 88
　　near 197
　　laterality 236
　　party 712
　- issue 39
　- with *aid* 707
　　coöperate 709
　　concord 714
　take up a - 476
　wrong - up 218
side arms 727
side blow 702
sideboard 191
side drum 417
sideling 279
sidelong 236
sideration 318
sidereal 318
siderite 288
sideromancy 511
sidesaddle 215
side scene 599
sidesman 996
sidetrack 279
sidewalk 627
sideways
　oblique 217
　lateral 236
side wind
　oblique 217
　circuit 629
　cunning 702
sidewinder 276

sidewipe 276
sidle *oblique* 217
　lateral 236
　deviate 279
siege 716
　lay - to 716
　state of - 722
siege cap 717
siege train 727
siesta 683
sieve *sort* 60
　perforate 260
　clean 652
　pour water into a -
　　waste 638
　lavish 818
　stop one hole in a -
　　819
sift *simplify* 42
　sort 60
　inquire 461
　discriminate 465
　clean 652
　- the chaff from the
　　wheat 609
sigh 839
　and -ed again 833
　- for 865
sighing like furnace
　902
sight *much* 31
　multitude 102
　vision 441
　appearance 448
　ugly 846
　prodigy 872
　at - *soon* 132
　seeing 441
　charms strike the -
　　829
　dim - 443
　in - 446
　in - of *near* 197
　seen 441
　keep in - 457
　within - of shore 858
sightless
　blind 442
　invisible 447
　ugly 846
sightly 845
sights, see - 455
sight-seeing 441
sight-seer
　spectator 444
　curiosity 455
sigil *seal* 550
　evidence 769
sigmoidal 248
sign *attest* 467
　omen 512
　indication 550
　record 551
　write 590
　compact 769
　prodigy 872
　give - of 525
　make no - 585
　-s of the times
　　omen 512
　warning 668

-s of the zodiac 318
signal *great* 31
　eventful 151
　sign 550
　important 642
　give the - 741
　- of distress 669
signalize
　indicate 550
　glory 873
　celebrate 883
signally 31
signal post 668
signature
　mark, identification
　　550
　writing 590
　printing 591
　compact 769
　security 771
signboard 550
signet
　mark, identification
　　550
　sign of authority 747
　compact 769
　(evidence 467)
　writer to the - 968
significant
　[see *signify*]
　important 642
　(clear 518)
signifies, what - 643
signify
　forebode 511
　mean 516
　inform 527
signior 875
sign manual 550, 590
signo
　in hoc - spes mea 858
　in hoc - vinces 858
signor 877
sign painter 559
sign painting 555
signpost 550
signum, ecce - 550
sike 348
Sikes, Bill - 792
silence *disable* 158
　no sound **403**
　confute 479
　latency 526
　concealment 528
　aphony 581
　taciturn 585
　check 731
　le - du peuple 668
　- more musical than
　　song 403
silencer 408a
silentio, sub -
　silent 403
　inattention 458
　latent 526
**silent leges inter
　arma** 722
silhouette
　outline 230
　portrait 556
siliquose 192

silk *smooth* 255
　soft 324
　make a - purse out of
　　a sow's ear 471
　rustling in unpaid-for
　　- 880
　- gown
　　barrister 968
silken repose 687
silkiness
　voluptuousness 954
sill 215
silly
　credulous 486
　imbecile 499
　insane 503
silt *dirt* 653
　(remainder 40)
silvan 367
silver *bright* 420
　white 430
　gray 432
　money 800
　bait with a - hook 615
　German - 545
　- footed queen 318
　- lining of the cloud
　　858
　- livery of advised
　　age 128
　- wedding 883
silver-toned 413
simagrée 855
similarity 17
　- of form 240
simile
　similarity 17
　comparison 464
　metaphor 521
similitude
　likeness 17
　copy 21
simious 499
simmer
　agitation 315
　boil 382, 384
　excitement 824
simmering 825
Simon, Simple - 547
Simon Pure
　the real - 494
Simon Stylites 893
simony 964
simoon 349, 382
simous 243
simper *smile* 838
　affectation 855
simple *mere* 32
　unmixed 42
　credulous 486
　silly 499
　- *language* 576
　herb 662
　artless 703
　unadorned 849
　- *duty* 926
　- *meaning* 516
simple-hearted
　true 543
simpleness 42
Simple Simon 547

simpleton 501
simplex munditiis 849
simplicity
  [see simple] **849**
  ignorance 491
simplify
  [see simple]
  elucidate 518
simply *little* 32
  singly 87
  more -
   interpreted 522
simulate
  resemble 17
  imitate 19
  cheat 544
simultaneous 120
sin *vice* 945
  guilt 947
sinapism 662
since *under the circum-*
  stances 8
  after 117
  cause 155
  reason 476
sincere
  veracious 543
  ingenuous 703
  feeling 821
sine 217
sine: - curâ 831
  - die *never* 107
  defer 133
  - ictu 158
  - quâ non
   required 630
   important 642
   condition 770
sinecure 681
  no - 682
sinew 159
sinewless 158
sinews of war
  money 800
sinful 945
sing *music* 416
  poetry 597
  rejoice 838
  - because I must 597
  - Io triumphe 884
  - out 411
  - praises
   approve 931
   worship 990
  - small 879
  - the savageness 415
singe 384
singer 416
single *unmixed* 42
  unit 87
  secluded 893
  unmarried 904
  ride at - anchor 863
  - combat 720
  - file 69
  - out 609
single-handed
  one 87
  easy 705
  unassisted 706

single-minded 703
singleness
  [see single]
  - of heart
   artless 703
   probity 939
  - of purpose
   perseverance 604a
   artless 703
singlestick 720
singsong 414
singular
  special 79
  exceptional 83
  one 87
singularly *very* 31
sinister *left* 239
  bad 649
  vicious 945
  bar -
   imperfect 651
   disrepute 874
sinistrality 239
sinistrorsal 239
sinistrous
  sullen 901a
sink *destroy* 162
  descend 306
  lower 308
  submerge 310
  neglect 460
  conceal 528
  cloaca 653
  fatigue 688
  vanquish 731
  fail 732
  adversity 735
  pain 828
  depressed 837
  (decay 659)
  - back 661
  - in the mind
   thought 451
   memory 505
   excite 824
  - into oblivion 506
  - into the grave 360
  - money 809
  - of corruption 653
  - of iniquity 945
  - or swim
   certainty 474
   perseverance 604a
sinking
  heart - 837
  - fund 802
sinless 946
sinned against than
  sinning, more -
  946
sinner 949
sin offering 952
sinologist 492
sinuous 248
sinus 252
sip *small* 32
  drink 298
siphon 350
sippet 298
si qua voles apte 905
sir *man* 373

  title 877
  - Oracle 887
sircar 745
sirdar 745
sire 166
siren
  sea nymph 341
  musician 416
  seducing 615
  warning 668
  evil doer 913
  demon 980
  sorcerer 994
  - strains 415
  song of the -s 615
sirene *musical instru-*
  ment 417
siriasis 503
sirius 423
sirkar 745
sirocco *wind* 349
  heat 382
sirrah! 949
siskin 366
sister *kin* 11
  likeness 17
  nurse 662
sisterhood
  party 712
  frail - 962
sisterly 906
sisters:
  - three 601
  weird - 994
Sisyphus, task of -
  useless 645
  difficult 704
  (not complete 730)
sit 308
  - down *settle* 184
  lie 213
  stoop 308
  - in judgment
   adjudge 480
   jurisdiction 965
   lawsuit 969
  - on 215
  - on thorns
   annoyance 828
   fear 860
site 183
sith
  circumstance 8
  reason 476
sitting *[see sit]*
  incubation 673
  convocation 696
  - up *late* 133
  work 686
sitting room 191
situ, in -
  situation 183
  quiescence 265
situation
  circumstances 8
  place **183**
  location 184
  business 625
  out of a - 185
Siva 979
si vis amari ama 897

si vis pacem para
  bellum 673, 722
six 98
  - of one and half a
   dozen of the other
   27
sixes and sevens, at
  - *disorder* 59
  discord 713
six-shooter 727
sixty 98
sizar 746
size *magnitude* 31
  glue 45
  arrange 60
  dimensions **192**
  viscid 352
  - up 480
sizzle 409
sjambok 975
skald 597
skate
  locomotion 266
  vehicle 272
  deterioration 659
skating 840
skating rink 840
skean 727
skean dhu 727
skedaddle 623
skeel 191
skeezix 949
skein 219
  tangled - 59
skeleton
  remains 40
  essential part 50
  thin 203
  support 215
  corpse 362
  plan 626
  reduced to a - 659
  - in the closet
   bad 649
   painful 830
skepticism
  doubt 485
  incredulity 487
  irreligion 989
sketch *form* 240
  represent 554
  paint 556
  describe 594
  plan 626
sketcher 559
sketchy
  incomplete 53
  feeble 575
  unfinished 730
skew 217
skewer 45
ski 272
skiagraphy 554, 556
skid *support* 215
  hindrance 706
skies:
  exalt to the - 873
  praise to the - 933
skiff 273
skill 698
  acquisition of - 539

game of - 840
skillet 191
skim *move* 266
  navigate 267
  rapid 274
  neglect 460
  summarize 596
skin *outside* 220
  tegument 223
  peel 226
  thief 792
  mere - and bone 203
  - a flint
  impossible 471
  parsimony 819
  - game 545
  - over 660
  wet to the - 339
  with a whole - 670
  without - 822
skin-deep
  shallow 209
  external 220
skinned: thick - 376
  thin - 375
skinny *thin* 203
  all skin 223
skip *jump* 309
  neglect 460
  rejoice 838
  (*amusement* 840)
skipjack
  prosperous 734
  lowborn 876
skipper
  sea captain 269
  captain 745
skippet 191
skippingly 70
skips, by - 70
skirmish 720
skirmisher 726
skirt *appendix* 39
  pendent 214
  dress 225
  surrounding 227
  edge 231
  side 236
skirt-dance 840
skirting 231
skirts of
  hang upon the -
  sequence 281
  on the - of
  near 197
  - happy chance 156
skit *ridicule* 856
  detraction 934
  prostitute 962
skittish
  capricious 608
  excitable 825
  timid 862
  bashful 881
skittles 840
skittle sharper 792
skulk *hide* 528
  cowardly 862
skull 450
skullcap 225
skunk 401

skurry 684
sky *summit* 210
  world 318
  air 338
  necessity 601
sky-aspiring 865
sky-blue 438
skylark 305
skylarking 840
skylight 260
skyrocket 305
sky scraper 210
slab *layer* 204
  support 215
  flat 251
  puddle 343
  viscous 352
  record 551
slabber *slaver* 297
  unclean 653
slack *loose* 47
  weak 160
  inert 172
  slow 275
  cool 385
  coal 388
  unwilling 603
  insufficient 640
  inactive 683
  lax 738
slacken
  loosen 47
  moderate 174
  repose 687
  hinder 706
  one's pace 275
slade 252
slag *embers* 384
  dirt 653
  (*remains* 40)
slake *quench* 174
  gratify 829
  satiate 869
  (*content* 831)
  - one's appetite
  intemperance 954
slam *slap* 276
  snap 406
  - the door in one's
  face *oppose* 708
  refuse 764
slammerkin 653
slammock 653
slander 934
slanderer 936
slang 563
slang-whanger 887
slant 217
slap *instantly* 113
  strike 276
  censure 932
  punish 972
  - in the face
  opposition 708
  attack 716
  anger 900
  disrespect 929
  disapprobation 932
  - the forehead 461
slap-dash 684
slash 44

slashing
  style 574
slate
  writing tablet 590
  plan 626
  - loose *mad* 503
slate-colored 432
slates *roof* 223
slattern
  disorder 59
  dirty 653
  bungler 701
  vulgar 851
  (*negligent* 460)
slatternly
  unskillful 699
slaughter 361
slaughterhouse 361
slave *toil* 686
  servant 746
  a - to 749
  - to no sect 984
  - trade 795
slaver *ship* 273
  slobber 297
  dirt 653
  flatter 933
slavery *toil* 686
  subjection 749
slavish 886
slay 361
sleave 59
sled 272
sledge 272
sledge hammer 276
  with a -
  destroy 162
  exertion 686
sleek *smooth* 255
  pretty 845
sleep
  inactivity 683
  balmy - 683
  last - 360
  not have a wink of -
  825
  rock to -
  smoothe 174
  send to - 841
  - at one's post 683
  - upon *defer* 133
  consider 451
  - with one eye open
  459
  the tides of - 683
sleeper
  support 215
  wake the seven -s404
sleeping car 272
sleeping partner 683
sleepless
  active 682
sleepwalker 268
sleepy 683
sleet 383
sleeve *skein* 219
  dress 225
  hang on the - of 746
  in one's -
  hidden 528
  laugh in one's -

  rejoice 838
  hope 856
  wear one's heart upon
  his -
  manifest 525
  artless 703
sleeveless
  foolish 499
  unreasonable 608
  - errand
  useless 645
  unskillful 699
sleigh 272
sleight *skill* 698
  - of hand
  deception 545
  (*interchange* 146)
slender *small* 32
  thin 203
  trifling 643
  - means 804
sleuth 527
  - hound 913
slice *cut* 44
  piece 51
  layer 204
slick *smooth* 255
  smart 698
slide *elapse* 109
  smooth 255
  pass 264
  locomotion 266
  descend 306
  - back 661
  - in 228
  - into 144
slide valve 263
sliding
  amusement 840
sliding panel 545
sliding rule 85
slight *small* 32
  shallow 209
  rare 322
  neglect 460
  disparage 483
  feeble 575
  trifle 643
  dereliction 927
  disrespect 929
  contempt 930
slight-made 203
slily
  surreptitiously 544
  craftily 702
slim 203
  cunning 702
slime *viscous* 352
  dirt 653
sling *hang* 214
  project 284
  weapon 727
  drink 959
slink *hide* 528
  cowardice 862
  - away *avoid* 623
  disrepute 874
  (*escape* 671)
slinky 203
slip *small* 32
  elapse 109

strip 205
descend 306
error 495
workshop 691
fail 732
false coin 800
vice 945
guilt 947
give one the - 671
let - *liberate* 750
lose 776
relinquish 782
let - the dogs of war 722
- away 623
- cable 623
- in (*or* - into) 294
- of the pen 568
- of the tongue
solecism 568
stammering 583
- on 225
- over *neglect* 460
- the collar
escape 671
free oneself 750
- the memory 506
- through the fingers
miss an opportunity 135
escape 671
fail 732
- 'twixt cup and lip 509
slipper 225
hunt the - 840
slippery
transient 111
smooth 255
greasy 355
uncertain 475
vacillating 607
dangerous 665
facile 705
faithless 940
- ground 667
slipshod 575
slipslop
absurdity 497
solecism 568
weak language 575
slit *divide* 44
chink 198
furrow 259
sliver 51
slobber *drivel* 297
slop 337
dirt 653
sloe *black* 431
slogan 722
sloop 273
--of-war 726
slop *spill* 297
water 337
dirt 653
slope *oblique* 217
run away 623
sloppy *moist* 339
marsh 345
slops *clothes* 225
slosh 653

590

slot 260
sloth 683
slouch *low* 207
oblique 217
move slowly 275
inactive 683
slouching *ugly* 846
slough
quagmire 345
dirt 653
difficulty 704
adversity 735
(*remains* 40)
- of Despond 859
sloven *bungler* 701
vehicle 272
slovenly *untidy* 59
careless 460
style 575
dirty 653
awkward 699
vulgar 851
slow *tardy* 133
inert 172
moderate 174
motion 275
inactive 683
wearisome 841
dull 843
be - to
unwilling 603
not finish 730
refuse 764
by - degrees 26
march in - time 275
- movement
music 415
slow coach 701
slowness 275
sloyd 537
slubber
unclean 653
(*inactive* 683)
slubberdegullion 876
sludge 653
slug *slow* 275
printing 591
inaction 681
inactivity 683
bullet 727
money 800
sluggard 275, 683
sluggish *inert* 172
callous 823
sluice *limit* 233
egress 295
river 348
conduit 350
open the -s 297
slum 653
slumber 683
slummock 653
slump 306
slung shot 727
slur *stigma* 874
gloss over 937
reproach 938
- over *neglect* 460
slight 483
(*exclude* 55)
(*inattention* 458)

(*conceal* 528)
slush *marsh* 345
semiliquid 352
dirt 653
slut *untidy* 59
dirty 653
unchaste 962
(*neglect* 460)
sly *stealthy* 528
cunning 702
(*false* 544)
slyboots 702
smack
small quantity 32
mixture 41
boat 273
impulse 276
taste 390
kiss 902
strike 972
- of *resemble* 17
- the lips
pleasure 277
taste 390
savory 394
rejoice 838
small
- in degree 32
- in size 193
become - 195
esteem of - account 930
feel - 879
not think - beer of oneself 880
of - account 643
on a - scale 32, 193
- arms 727
- beer 643
- chance 473
- coin 800
- fry
littleness 193
unimportant 643
commonalty 876
- hours 125
- matter 643
- number 103
- part 51
- sands the mountain 32
- talk 588
think no - beer of oneself 878
think - beer of 930
small bore 727
smallclothes 225
smaller
in degree 34
in size 195
smallness 32
smalls 225
smalt 438
smart *pain* 378
active 682
clever 698
feel 821
grief 828
witty 842
pretty 845
ornamental 847

- pace 274
- saying 842
- set 852
- under 821
smarten 847
smart money 973
smash
destruction 162
failure 732
smasher 792
smatch 390
smatterer 493
smattering 491
smear *cover* 223
soil 653
smell 398
bad - 401
- a rat 485
- of the lamp
ornate style 577
prepared 673
- powder 722
smell-feast 886
smelling bottle 400
smelt *heat* 384
prepare 673
smicker 838
smile *cheerful* 836
rejoice 838
raise a - 840
- at 856
- of contempt 930
- of fortune 734
- upon *aid* 707
courtesy 894
endearment 902
smirch
blacken 431
dirty 653
smirk 838
smite *maltreat* 649
excite 824
afflict 830
punish 972
(*strike* 276)
smith 690
smitten *love* 897
- with *moved* 615
smock 225
smock-faced 862
smock frock 225
smoke *dust* 330
vapor 336
heat 382
tobacco 392
discover 480a
suspect 485
unimportant 643
dirt 653
disrespect 929
end in -
shortcoming 304
failure 732
- the calumet of peace 723
smoker *concert* 892
smokestack 260, 351
smoking hot 382
smoking room 191
smoky *opaque* 426
dirty 653

SQUA

pay 807
account 811
put a - thing into a
  round hole 699
- inches 180
- the circle 471
- up 556
- with 23
- yards 180
square-toes 857
squash *destroy* 162
  blow 276
  soft 324
  marsh 345
  semiliquid 352
  hiss 409
squashy 345, 352
squat
  locate oneself 184
  little 193
  short 201
  thick 202
  low 207
  sit 308
  (*ugly* 846)
squatter 188
squaw *woman* **374**
  wife 903
squeak }
squeal }
  human cry 411
  animal cry 412
  disclosure 529
  (*weep* 839)
squealer 941
squeamish
  unwilling 603
  sick 655
  fastidious 868
  (*censorious* 932)
squeasy 868
squeezable 762
squeeze
  contract 195
  condense 321
  embrace 894
  (*narrow* 203)
squeeze out
  extract 301
  give 784
squeezers 840
squelch 162
squib *sound* 406
  lampoon 856
squiffy 959
squint *look* 441
  defective sight 443
squirarchy 875
squire *aid* 707
  attendant 746
  gentry 875
squireen 875
squirm 315
squirrel *swift* 274
  nimble 682
squirt *eject* 297
  sport 348
S. S. C. 968
stab *pierce* 260
  kill 361
  pain 649

STAG

injure 659
stability 150
  (*quiescence* 265)
  (*perseverance* 604a)
stable *firm* 150
  house 189
  lock the - door when
  the steed is stolen
  too late 135
  useless 645
  bungling 699
- companion 890
- equilibrium 150
staccato 415
stack *assemblage* 72
  store 636
staddle 215
  infant 129
stadtholder 745
staff *support* 215
  music 413
  signal 550
  council 696
  party 712
  weapon 727
  chief 745
  retinue 746
  (*directors* 694)
  (*hope* 858)
  pastoral - 999
- officer 745
- of honor 128
- of life 298
- of office 747
stag *deer* 366
  male 373
  defaulter 808
  sociality 892
- the market 794
stag dance 840
stage *degree* 26
  term 71
  time 106
  position 183
  layer 204
  platform 215
  forum 542
  drama 599
  arena 728
  come upon the - 446
  go off the -
  depart 293
  on the -
  manifest 525
  theatrical 599
- business 599
- coach 272
- direction 697
- effect
  display 882
- manager 599
- play 599
- player 599
- whisper 580
stager *player* 599
  doer 690
  old - 130
stagger *slow* 275
  totter 314
  agitate 315
  unexpected 508

STAM

dissuade 616
affect 824
astonish 870
- belief *doubt* 485
- like a drunken man
  irresolute 605
staggers 315
stagirite 850
stagnant
  quiescent 265
stagnate 265
  (*persist* 141)
stagy *drama* 599
  affected 855
staid *wise* 498
  calm 826
  grave 837
stain *color* 428
  dirt 653
  spoil 659
  blemish 848
  disgrace 874
  (*deface* 846)
  (*dishonor* 940)
- paper *writing* 590
stained, travel - 266
stainless *clean* 652
  honorable 939
  innocent 946
stair 627
stake *fastening* 45
  wager 621
  danger 665
  security 771
  property 780
  lay down 807
  execution 975
at - *intended* 620
  in danger 665
stalactite 224
stalagmite 224
stale *old* 124
  insipid 391
  deteriorated 659
  (*undesired* 866)
- flat and unprofit-
  able 645
- news 532
stalemate 731, 732
stalk *walk* 266
- abroad
  generality 78
  proud 878
stalking-horse
  ambush 530
  plea 617
stall *abode* 189
  receptacle 191
  support 215
  play-house 599
  mart 799
  churchdom 995
  cathedral 1000
finger - 223
stallion *horse* 271
  male 373
stalwart *strong* 159
  large 192
  (*tall* 206)
stamina
  strength 159

STAN

perseverance 604a
stammel 434
stammering **583**
stamp
  character 7
  prototype 22
  kind 75
  form 240
  mark 550
  engraving 558
  complete 729
  security 771
  (*record* 551)
- in the memory 505
- out *destroy* 162
  extinguish 385
- the foot
  anger 900
stampede 860
stanch - *a flow* 348
  persevering 604a
  health 654
  reinstate 660
  honest 939
- belief 484
stanchion 215
stanchless 825
stand *exist* 1
  rank 71
  long time 110
  permanent 141
  support 215
  quiescence 265
  difficulty 704
  resistance 719
  brook 821
  patience 826
  brave 861
at a - 681
come to a - 704
make a -
  oppose 708
  resist 719
- a chance
  possible 470
  probable 472
- aghast 870
- aloof
  avoidance 623
  inaction 681
- at attention 507
- at ease 458
- by *near* 197
  aid 707
  defend 717
- committed 754
- fair for 472
- fire 861
- firm
  stability 150
  resist 719
- first 66
- for *indicate* 550
  deputy 759
  candidate 763
- forth
  visible 446
- in need of 630
- in one's own light
  699
- in the shoes of 147

throw a - in one's own
  garden 699
throw -s at
  malevolent 907
tomb- 363
stone-blind 442
stone-colored 432
stone-deaf 419
stone's throw 197
stoneware 384
stony 323
stony-hearted
  malevolent 907
  revengeful 919
stook 72
stool 215
  between two -s 704
  - of repentance 950
stool pigeon 548
stoop
  receptacle 191
  slope 217
  lower 308
  humble 879
  servile 886
  dishonorable 940
  - to conquer
  cunning 702
stop *end* 67
  cease 142
  close 261
  rest 265
  silent 403
  inaction 681
  hinder 706
  prohibit 761
  put a - to 142
  - a flow 348
  - a gap
  repair 660
  - payment 808
  - short
  discontinue 142
  cease to move 265
  - short of 304
  - the breath 361
  - the ears 419
  - the mouth
  confute 479
  gag 581
  - the sound 408*a*
  - the way 706
  - to consider 485
  - up 261
stopcock 263
stop-gap
  substitute 147
  stopper 263
stoppage
  cessation 142
  hindrance 706
stopper 263
store *stock* 636
  shop 799
  (*collection* 72)
  (*abundance* 639)
  in - *destiny* 152
  preparing 673
  lay in a - 637
  set no - 483
  set - by

important 642
commend 931
  - in the memory 505
  - of knowledge 490
storehouse 636
storeship *ship* 273
  ship of war 726
στοργή 897
storied
  descriptive 594
storm *crowd* 72
  convulsion 146
  violence 173
  agitation 315
  wind 349
  attack 716
  passion 825
  anger 900
  He mounts the - 976
  ride the - 267
  - brewing 665
  - in a teacup
  overrate 482
  exaggerate 549
  - is up 349
  take by -
  conquer 731
  seize 789
storthing 696
story *rooms* 191
  layer 204
  lie 546
  history 594
  as the - goes 532
  the old - 897
story-teller 548
stot 366
stound 870
stoup *cup* 191
  altar 1000
stour 59
  large 192
stout *strong* 159
stout-hearted 861
stove *fireplace* 386
  - in 252
stow *locate* 184
  pack close 195
  store 636
stowage *space* 180
  location 184
stowaway 528
strabism 443
straddle 266
  tergiversation 607
straggle *stroll* 266
  deviate 279
straggler 268
straggling
  disjunction 44
  disorder 59
straight
  vertical 212
  rectilinear 246
  direction 278
  cards 840
  all - *rich* 803
  solvent 807
  - course 628
  - descent 167
  - poker 840

  - sailing 705
  - shoot 278
  - ticket 609
straighten 246
  - out 774
straightforward 278
  truthful 543
  artless 703
  honorable 939
straightness 246
straightway 132
strain
  race 11
  continuity 69
  weaken 160
  operation 170
  violence 173
  percolate 295
  transgress 303
  sound 402
  melody 415
  overrate 482
  exaggerate 549
  style 569
  voice 580
  poetry 597
  clean 652
  effort 686
  fatigue 688
  - a point
  go beyond 303
  exaggerate 549
  not observe 773
  undue 925
  - at a gnat and swal-
  low a camel 608
  - every nerve 686
  - in the arms 902
  - one's eyes 441
  - one's invention 515
  - the meaning 523
  - the throat 411
strait
  interval 198
  water 343
  difficulty 704
straitened
  poor 804
strait-handed 819
strait-laced
  severe 739
  restraint 751
  fastidious 868
  haughty 878
strait-waistcoat
  restrain 751
  means of restraint
  752
stramash 720
strand 342
  thread 205
stranded
  stuck fast 150
  in difficulty 704
  failure 732
  pain 828
strange
  unrelated 10
  exceptional 83
  ridiculous 853
  wonderful 870

  - bedfellows 713
  - to say 870
strangely *much* 31
stranger
  extraneous 57
  a - to
  ignorant 491
strangle
  render powerless 158
  contract 195
  kill 361
strap *fasten* 43
  fastening 45
  punish 972
  instrument of pun-
  ishment 975
strappado 972
strapping
  strong 159
  big 192
  - *pace* 274
strapwork 847
stratagem
  deception 545
  plan 626
  artifice 702
strategic *plan* 626
  artifice 702
strategist
  planner 626
  director 694
  proficient 700
strategy
  conduct 692
  warfare 722
  (*skill* 698)
strath 252
strathspey 840
stratification
  layers 204
  structure 329
stratocracy 737
stratum 204
stratus 353
straw *scatter* 73
  light 320
  unimportant 643
  catch at -s
  overrate 482
  credulous 486
  - *misuse* 679
  unskillful 699
  hope 858
  rash 863
  care not a -
  indifference 866
  despise 930
  in the - 161
  man of -
  unsubstantial 4
  cheat 548
  insolent 808
  low person 876
  not worth a -
  trifling 643
  useless 645
  - bail 545
  - bid 545
  - bidder 548
  - to show the wind
  463

- accent 580
- and great, a hero 861
- argument 476
- arm man 792
- box 802
- language 574
- point 476
- pull 686
with a - hand
  resolution 604
  exertion 686
  severity 739
strong-headed 498
stronghold
  defense 717
  prison 752
strong-minded
  wisdom 498
  courage 861
strong-room 802
strong-scented 398
strong-willed 604
strop 253
strophe 597
strow 73
struck [see stricken, strike]
awe - 860
- all of a heap
  emotion 821
  wonder 870
- down
  defeated 732
- with love 897
structural state 7
structure
  production 161
  form 240
  texture 329
  organization 357
  (house 189)
struggle
  essay 675
  exert 686
  difficulty 704
  contend 720
strum 416
struma 655
strumpet 962
strut walk 266
  pride 878
  parade 882
  boast 884
- and fret one's hour upon a stage life 359
  drama 599
strychnine 663
stubbed 201
stubble remains 40
  useless 645
stubborn
  strong 159
  hard 323
  obstinate 606
  resistance 719
stubby 201
stucco cement 45
  covering 223
stuck [see stick]

= fast firm 150
  difficulty 704
stuck-up 878
stud hanging peg 214
  knob 250
  horses 271
- poker 840
studded many 102
  spiked 253
  variegated 440
student 541
studied
  predetermined 611
  (willful 600)
studio room 191
  painting 556
  workshop 691
studious
  thoughtful 451
  docile 539
  intending 620
study copy 21
  room 191
  thought 451
  attention 457
  research 461
  learning 539
  painting 556
  intention 620
stuff substance 3
  contents 190
  expand 194
  line 224
  matter 316
  texture 329
  absurdity 497
  unmeaning 517
  deceive 545
  material 635
  trifle 643
  overeat 957
- and nonsense
  unsubstantial 4
  unmeaning 517
- in 300
- the memory with 505
- up close 261
  hoax 545
such - as dreams are made of 515
stuffing contents 190
  lining 224
  stopper 263
stuffy dense 321
  sultry 382
stultified
  failure 732
stultify oneself 699
stultiloquy 497
stultorum plena sunt omnia 501
stumble fall 306
  flounder 315
  error 495
  unskillful 699
  failure 732
- on chance 556
  discover 480a
stumbling-block
  difficulty 704

  hindrance 706
stump
  remainder 40
  trunk 51
  walk 266
  drawing 556
  speak 582
stir your -s
  active 682
- along slow 275
worn to the - 659
stump orator 582
stumpy short 201
stun physically insensible 376
  loud 404
  deafen 419
  unexpected 508
  morally insensible 823
  affect 824
  astonish 870
Stundist 984
stung [see sting]
- to the quick 824
stunt shorten 201
stunted small 193
  contracted 195
stupa 363
stupe 834
stupefaction 826
stupefy
- physically 376
- morally 823
  astonish 870
stupendous
  great 31
  large 192
  wonderful 870
stupid
  misjudging 481
  credulous 486
  unintelligent 499
  tiresome 841
  dull 843
stupor
  insensibility 823
  wonder 870
stupration 961
sturdy strong 159
  persevering 604a
- beggar
  beggar 767
  thief 792
sturgeon 298
stutter 583
sty house 189
  dirt 653
Stygian dark 421
  diabolic 945
  infernal 982
cross the - ferry
  die 360
- shore
  death 360
style state 7
  time 114
  painting 556
  graver 558
  name 564
  phrase 566

  diction 569
  writing 590
  beauty 845
  fashion 852
le - est l'homme 79, 569, 590
- the dress of thought 569
stylet awl 262
  dagger 727
stylite 996
Stylites, Simon - 893
styptic 397
Styx 982
suanpan 85
suant 705
suasible 602
suasion 615
suave mari magno 664
suaviter in modo
  calm 826
  courteous 894
suavity 894
sub 34
subacid 397
subaction 330
subahdar 745
subalpine 206
subaltern
  inferior 34
  soldier 726
  officer 745
  servant 746
  plebeian 876
subaqueous 208
subarborescent 242
subastral 318
subaudition 527
subclavate 250
subcommittee 696
subconscious 450
subcontrary 237
subcutaneous 221
subdean 996
subdichotomy 91
subdititious 147
subdivide 44
subdivision
  part 51
  military 726
subdolous 702
subdominant 413
subdual 731
subduction
  subtraction **38**
  (taking 789)
subdue calm **174**
  succeed 731
subdued
  morally 826
subeditor 593
suberose 320
subitaneous 113
subito 113
subjacent 207
subject liable 177
  topic 454
  meaning 516
  servant 746
  enthrall 749

- of dispute 713
- to *examination* 461
- of *inquiry* 461
- of *thought* 454
- to *qualification* 469
uncertain 475
subjection 749
subjective
intrinsic 5
immaterial 317
intellectual 450
subjoin 37
subjugate
conquer 731
subject 749
subjugation
defeat 732
moral impression 824
subjunctive 37
Sublapsarian 984
sublation 38
sublevation 307
sublieutenant 745
sublimate
elevate 307
lighten 320
vaporize 336
sublime
greatness 31
high 206
language 574
beauty 845
glory 873
magnanimous 942
du - au ridicule 853
from the - to the ridiculous 853
Sublime Porte 745
sublimi feriam sidera vertice 620
subliminal 450
- consciousness 450
sublineation 550
sublunary 318
submarine 208
boat 726
submediant 413
submerge
destroy 162
immerse 300
plunge 310
steep 337
submersion
depth 208
subministration 707
submission 725
obedience 743
with - 928
submissive
tractable 705
enduring 826
humble 879
(penitent 950)
submit
propound 514
- to *arbitration* 774
submonish 695
submultiple 84
subordinate
inferior 34

unimportant 643
subject 749
subordination
order 58
(*obedience* 743)
suborn *induce* 615
purchase 795
(*bribe* 784)
subpanation 998
subpœna
command 741
lawsuit 969
subreption
falsehood 544
acquisition 775
subscribe
assent 488
aid 707
agree to 769
give 784
subscription
gift 784
subsequent
- *in order* 63
- *in time* 117
- time 121
subserviency
servility 886
subservient
instrumental 631
aid 707
subside *decrease* 36
sink 306
subsidiary *aid* 707
servant 746
(*tending* 176)
subsidy *gift* 784
pay 809
subsist *exist* 1
continue 141
live 359
subsistence
food 298
subsoil
interior 221
earth 342
sub spe rati 475
substance *thing* 3
quantity 25
inside 221
matter 316
texture 329
important part 642
wealth 803
in - 596
man of - 803
substantial
existing 1
hypostatic 3
material 316
dense 321
true 494
- meaning 516
substantiality 3
substantially
intrinsically 5
- true 494
substantiate
evidence 467
make good 924
substantive

existing 1
substantial 3
substitute
change 147
means **634**
deputy 759
substitution 147
substratum
substance 3
layer 204
base 211
support 215
interior 221
materiality 316
substructure 211
subsultory 315
subsultus 315
subtend 237
subterfuge
sophistry 477
lie 546
cunning 702
subterranean 208
subtile *light* 320
rare 322
- *texture* 329
subtilize *rarefy* 322
sophistry 477
subtilty 322
subtle *slight* 32
cunning 702
- point 704
- reasoning 476
subtlety
sophistry 477
wisdom 498
subtraction
subduction 38
arithmetic 85
taking 789
subtrahend
subtract 38
number 84
subulate 253
suburb *town* 189
near 197
environs 227
subvention
support 215
aid 707
gift 784
subversion
revolution 146
subvert *destroy* 162
invert 218
depress 308
succedaneum 147
succeed *follow* 63
posterior 117
success 731
transfer 783
- to *acquire* 775
succès d'estime 873
success 731
succession
sequence 63
continuity 69
repetition 104
posteriority 117
transfer 783
in quick - 136

in regular - 138
- of ideas 451
- of time 109
successless 732
successor *sequel* 65
posterior 117
succinct 572
succor 707
succotash 298
succubus 980
succulent
nutritive 298
juicy 333
semiliquid 352
succumb *fatigue* 688
yield 725
fail 732
(*obey* 743)
succussion 315
such: - a one 372
- as 17
- being the case 8
- like 17
suchwise 8
suck *draw off* 297
drink 298
take 789
- in 296
- the blood of 789
sucker 260
dupe 547
servility 886
suckle 707
suckling
infant 129
suction *force* 157
reception 296
sudarium 993
sudary 652
sudation 299
sudatory 386
sudden
transient 111
instantaneous 113
soon 132
unexpected 508
- and quick in quarrel 901
- burst 508
- death 360
- thought 612
sudorific 382
suds *froth* 353
in the -
difficulty 704
dejected 837
sue *demand* 765
go to law 969
suerte 786
suet 356
suffer physical pain 378
disease 655
allow 760
feel 821
endure 826
moral pain 828
- for 972
- punishment 972
sufferance, tenant on - 779

superlatively good
648
supernal
summit 210
heavenly 981
supernatant
high 206
ascent 305
supernatural
deity 976
demon 980
- aid 707
supernumerary
adjunct 39
theatrical 599
reserve 636
redundant 641
(remainder 40)
superphysical 450
superplus 40
superpose add 37
cover 223
supersaturate 641
superscription
mark 550
writing 590
(evidence 467)
supersede
substitute 147
disuse 678
relinquish 782
supersensible
into the realms - 528
- regions 317, 318
superstition
(credulity 486)
religious - 984
superstitione tollen-
dâ 984
superstratum 220
superstructure 729
supertonic 413
supervacaneous
redundant 641
(useless 645)
supervene
be added 37
succeed 117
happen 151
supervise 693
supervisor 694
supination 213
supine
horizontal 213
inverted 218
sluggish 683
mentally torpid 823
suppeditate 637
supper 298
full of - 954a
supplant 147
supple soft 324
servile 886
supplement
addition 37
adjunct 39
completion 52
suppletory 37
suppliant
begging 765
beggar 767

supplicate beg 765
pity 914
worship 990
supplies
materials 635
aid 707
money 800
supply store 636
provide 637
give 784
- aid 707
- deficiencies 52
- the place of 147
support perform 170
sustain 215
evidence 467
preserve 670
aid 707
feel 821
endure 826
vindicate 937
- life 359
supporters
heraldic 550
suppose 514
supposing
provided 469
supposition 514
supposititious
unattested 468
untrue 546
suppress
destroy 162
conceal 528
silent 581
restrain 751
suppression of truth
544
suppuration 653
suppute 85
supralapsarian 984
supramundane 939
supremacy
superior 33
authority 737
supreme 33
summit 210
authority 737
in a - degree 31
- good 618
- principle 450
Supreme Being 976
surbate 659
surbated 688
surcease 142
surcharge
redundance 641
(dear 814)
- and falsify 811
surcingle 45
surcoat 225
surd number 84
deaf 419
sure certain 474
belief 484
safe 664
make - against 673
make - of
inquire 461
take 789
on - ground 664

security 771
to be - assent 488
you may be -
affirmation 535
sure-footed
careful 459
skillful 698
cautious 864
surely 870
surety
certainty 474
safety 664
surf tide 348
foam 353
surface outside 220
texture 329
lie on the -
intelligible 518
manifest 525
skim the -
slur over 460
- car 272
Surface, Joseph - 548
surfeit
redundance 641
satiety 869
surge swarm 72
swell 305
rotation 312
wave 348
surgeon 662
surgery 662
surgit amari aliquid
651
surly gruff 895
sullen 901a
unkind 907
surmise 514
surmount tower 206
transcursion 303
ascent 305
- a difficulty
overcome 731
surmountable 470
surname 564
surpass
be superior 33
grow 194
go beyond 303
outshine 873
surplice 999
surplus
remainder 40
redundance 641
surplusage 641
surprise
nonexpectation 508
wonder 870
- party 892
surprisingly 31
surrebutter &c
answer 462
pleadings 969
surrejoinder 462
surrender
submit 725
relinquish 782
(obey 743)
- one's life 360
surreptitious
furtive 528

deceptive 545
untrue 546
surrogate 759
surround
circumjacent 227
circumscribe 229
surroundings
amidst such and such
- 183
sursum corda 990
surtout coat 225
surveillance
care 459
direction 693
under - 938
survene 151
survey view 441
measure 466
surveyor
director 694
survive remain 40
long time 110
permanent 141
susceptibility
power 157
tendency 176
liability 177
motive 615
impressibility 822
irascibility 901
suscipient 785
suscitate cause 153
produce 161
stir up 173
excite 824
suspect doubt 485
suppose 514
suspected
accused 938
suspectless 484
suspend defer 133
discontinue 142
hang 214
suspended anima-
tion 823
suspenders 45
suspense
cessation 142
uncertainty 475
expectation 507
irresolution 605
in - inert 172
suspension
cessation 142
hanging 214
music 413
- of arms 723
suspicion doubt 485
incredulity 487
knowledge 490
supposition 514
fear 860
jealousy 920
under - 938
suspiration 839
sustain
continue 143
strength 159
perform 170
support 215
preserve 670

put to the - 361
- of Damocles 667
- in hand
  prepare 673
  war 722
turn -s into plow-
  shares 723
sword-shaped 253
swordsman 726
Sybarite 954a
sybaritism 954
syce 268
sycophancy
  flattery 933
sycophant
  servile 886
  flatterer 935
syenite
  blue 438
syllabicate 567
syllable 561
  breathe not a -
  528
  -s govern the world
  560
syllabus *list* 86
  compendium 596
syllogism 476
sylph 979
sylvan 367
symbol

mathematical - 84
  sign 550
symbolize 550
  represent 554
symmetry
  equality 27
  order 58
  conformity 82
  centrality 222
  regular form **242**
  beauty 845
want of - 846
sympathetic
  [see sympahy]
- *tear* 906
sympathizer
  partisan 890
sympathy
  concord 714
  friendship 888
  love 897
  kindness 906
  pity 914
  condolence 915
symphonious 413
symphony
  overture 64
  music 415
  concord 714
symphysis 43
symposium

festival 840
  (*meal* 298)
  (*drunken* 959)
symptom 550
symptomatology
  522
synagogue 1000
synchronism 120
synchysis 218
syncope
  impotence 158
  musical 413
  rhetoric 572
  fatigue 688
syncretic
  derangement 61
syncretism
  disagreement 24
  heterodoxy 984
syndic *ruler* 745
  judge 967
syndicate 696
  league 712
synecdoche 521
synergy 709
syngenic 5
synod *council* 696
  church 995
  (*assemblage* 72)
synonym
  meaning 516

interpretation 522
  (*nomenclature* 564)
synopsis
  arrangement 60
  list 86
  compendium 596
synovia
  lubrication 332
  oil 356
syntagma 60
syntax 567
syntectic 655
syntexis 655
synthesis
  combination 48
  reasoning 476
syringe *water* 337
  stream 348
syrt 667
syrup 396
system *order* 58
  rule 80
  plan 626
- of knowledge 490
- of opinions 484
systematize
  order 58
  arrange 60
  plan 626
systole 195
syzygy 199

T

bad man 949
tickle *touch* 380
  please 829
  amuse 840
  (*physical pleasure* 377)
  - the fancy 829, 840
  - the palate 394
  - the palm
  give 784
  pay 807
ticklish
  uncertain 475
  dangerous 665
  difficult 704
tidbit *good* 648
  pleasing 829
tide *ocean* 341
  wave 348
  abundance 639
  prosperity 734
  against the - 708
  drift with the -
  facile 705
  go with the -
  conformity 82
  high &c. - 348
  stem the - 708
  swim with the -
  prosperity 734
  - of eloquence 582
  - of events 151
  - of time 109
  - over *time* 106
  defer 133
  safe 664
  inaction 681
  succeed 731
  turn of the - 210
tidings 532
tidy *orderly* 58
  covering 223
  good 648
  clean 652
  pretty 845
tie *relation* 9
  equality 27
  fasten 43
  fastening 45
  neckcloth 225
  security 771
  obligation 926
  nuptial - 903
  ride and - 266
  - down
  hinder 706
  compel 744
  restrain 751
  - oneself
  promise 768
  - the hands
  render powerless 158
  restrain 751
  -s of blood 11
  - up *restrain* 751
  condition 770
  entail 771
tiebeam 45
tied up
  in debt 806
tienoscope 445

tier *continuity* 69
  layer 204
tierce
  triality 92
  worship 990
  carte and - 716
tiff *quarrel* 713
  anger 900
tiffin 298
tigella 367
tiger *violent* 173
  servant 746
  cheer 838
  courage 861
  savage 907
  evil doer 913
  bad man 949
tight *fast* 43
  closed 261
  smart 845
  drunk 959
  keep a - hand on 751
  on one's - ropes 878
  - grasp 739
  - hand 739
tighten 43
  contract 195
tight-fisted 819
tights 225
tigress 374
tike 876
tilbury 272
tilde 550
tile *roof* 223
  hat 225
  - loose *insane* 503
till *up to the time* 106
  coffer 191
  cultivate 371
  treasury 802
  - doomsday 112
  - now 122
  - the soil
  prepare 673
tiller
  instrument 633
  money-box 802
  - of the soil
  agriculture 371
  clown 876
tilmus 315
tilpah 223
tilt *slope* 217
  cover 223
  propel 284
  fall 306
  contention 720
  full - *direct* 278
  active 682
  haste 684
  ride full - at
  pursue 622
  attack 716
  run a - at 716
  - over 218
  - up 307
  - with 720
tilting at the ring 840
tilt-yard 728
timber *trees* 367

materials 635
timbre 413
timbrel 417
timbrology 550
time 106
  instant 113
  leisure 685
  against -
  haste 684
  at -s 136
  course of - 109
  employ one's - in 625
  glass of - 106
  in - *course* 109
  early 132
  destiny 152
  measure - 114
  no - *instantly* 113
  soon 132
  no - to lose
  need 630
  haste 684
  no - to spare 684
  ravages of - 659
  slow - 275
  take - *slow* 275
  inaction 681
  inactive 683
  there being -s when 136
  - after time 104
  - and again 104
  - being 118
  - drawing on 121
  - enough 132
  - gone by 135
  - hanging on one's hands
  inaction 681
  leisure 685
  weariness 841
  - has been 122
  - immemorial 122
  - is out of joint 106
  - of day 113
  - of life
  duration 106
  now 118
  age 128
  - out of mind 122
  - rolls his ceaseless course 106
  - the foe of man's dominion 106
  - to come 121
  - to spare 685
  - up *transient* 111
  occasion 134
  - was 122
  - wasted 106
  true - 113
  waste - 683
timeful 134
time-honored
  old 124
  repute 873
  respected 928
timekeeper 114
timeless 135
timely *early* 132
  opportune 134

- dew of sleep 683
timeo Danaos
  disbelief 485
  caution 864
timepiece 114
timepleaser 607, 943
times *present* 118
  events 151
  hard - 735
  many - 136
timeserving
  tergiversation 607
  cunning 702
  servility 886
  improbity 940
  selfishness 943
time-worn *old* 124
  age 128
  deteriorated 659
timid *fearful* 860
  cowardly 862
  humble 881
timist 607
Timocracy 803
Timon of Athens
  wealth 803
  seclusion 893
  misanthrope 911
timorous
  [see timid]
timothy 367
tin *preserve* 670
  money 800
  - wedding 883
tinct 428
tinctorial 428
tincture
  small quantity 32
  mixture 41
  color 428
tinctured
  disposition 820
tinder *fuel* 388
  irascible 901
tine 253
tinge
  small quantity 32
  mix 41
  color 428
tingent 428
tingible 428
tingle *pain* 378
  touch 380
  emotion 821
  make the ears - 900
tink 408
tinker
  restore to health 654
  repair 660
  (*improve* 658)
tinkle
  faint sound 405
  resonance 408
tinkling cymbal 517
tinned goods 670
tinnient 408
tinsel *glitter* 420
  sham 545
  ornament 847
  frippery 851
tint 428

tintamarre 404
tintinnabulary 408
tiny 193
tip *end* 67
 summit 210
 cover 223
 give 784
 (*pay* 807)
 on -toe *high* 206
  expect 507
 - the wink 550
tipcat 840
tippet 225
tipple *drink* 298
 tope 959
tippler 959
tippybob 803
tipstaff 965
tipsy 959
tiptop *summit* 210
 good 648
tirade *speech* 582
 censure 932
tirailleur 726
tire *fatigue* 688
 worry 830
 weary 841
tiré à quatre épin-
 gles 850
tirer d'affaire 672
 se - 731
Tiresias 513
tiresome [*see* tire]
Tisiphone 173
tissue *whole* 50
 assemblage 72
 matted 219
 texture 329
tit *small* 193
 pony 271
Titan 980
titbit *savory* 394
 pleasing 829
tit for tat 718
tithe *tenth* 99
 tax 812
tithing 181
tithingman 965
titillate *amuse* 840
 provoke desire 865
titillation
 pleasure 377
 touch 380
titivate 847
title *indication* 550
 name 564
 right to property 780
 distinction **877**
 right 924
titled 875
title-deed 771
title-page 66
titter 838
tittle
 small quantity 32
 to a - 494
tittle-tattle
 news 532
 small talk 588
titubancy 583
titubate *fall* 306

fail 732
titular *word* 562
 nomenclature 564
tivoli 840
tmesis 218
to *direction* 278
 lie - 681
 - a certain degree 32
 - a great extent 31
 - all intents and pur-
  poses
  equally 27
  whole 52
 - a man 78
 - and fro 314
 - a small extent 32
 - be sure 488
 - come *future* 121
  destiny 152
 - crown all 33, 642
 - do 59
 - some extent 26
 - the credit of 805
 - the end of the chap-
  ter 52
 - the end of time 112
 - the full 52
 - the letter 19
 - the point 23
 - the purpose 23
 - this day 118
 - wit 79
toad *hateful* 649
 ugly 846
 - under a harrow 378
toadeater
 servile 886
 sycophant 935
toadeating
 flattery 933
toadstool 367
toast *roast* 384
 celebrate 883
tobacco 392
toboggan 272
tobogganing 840
toby 191
toccata 415
tocogony 161
tocology 662
tocsin 669
tod 319
to-day 118
toddle *walk* 266
 limp 275
toddy 298
toe 211
 on the light fantastic -
  jump 309
  dance 840
toes turn up the -
 die 360
toft 189, 780
toga *coat* 225
 robes 747
 assume the - virilis
  131
together
 accompanying 88
 same time 120
 come - 290

get - 72
hang - 709
lay heads - 695
- with
 added to 37
 accompanied by 88
toggery 225
toil *activity* 682
 exertion 686
 - of a pleasure 682
 -s *trap* 545
  (*danger* 667)
  (*wile* 702)
toilet 225
toilette 225
 en grande - 847
toilsome 686
 difficult 704
toilworn 688
token 550
 give -
  manifest 525
 - of remembrance 505
told, do what one is
 - 743
tolderolloll 838
Toledo 727
tolerable
 a little 32
 trifling 643
 pretty good 648
 not perfect 651
 satisfactory 831
tolerably, get on -
 736
toleration
 laxity 738
 lenity 740
 permission 760
 feeling 821
 calmness 826
 benevolence 906
toll *sound* 407
 tax 812
 - the knell 363
tollbooth
 prison 752
 market 799
tomahawk 727
tomb 363
 lay in the - 363
 - of the Capulets 506
tombé des nues
 exception 83
 wonder 870
tombola 156
tomboy 851
tombstone 363
tomcat 373
tome 593
tomentose 256
tomfool 501
tomfoolery
 absurdity 497
 amusement 840
 wit 842
 ostentation 882
Tommy Atkins 726
Tom Noddy 501
Tom o' Bedlam 504
to-morrow 121

- and to-morrow
 repetition 104
 course of time 109
tompion 263
tomtit 193
Tom Thumb 193
tom-tom *music* 417
 military 722
ton *weight* 319
 fashion 852
tonality
 music 413
 light and shade 420
tone *state* 7
 strength 159
 tendency 176
 sound 402
 music 413
 color 428
 blackness 431
 method 627
 disposition 820
 give a - to 852
 - down
  moderate 174
  darken 421
  discolor 429
 - of voice 580
tong 712
tonga 272
tongs
 fire irons 386
 retention 781
tongue
 projection 250
 taste 390
 language 560
 bite the - 392
 bridle one's - 585
 give - 580
 have a - in one's head
  582
 hold one's - 403
 keep one's - between
  one's teeth 585
 on the tip of one's -
  near 197
  forget 506
  latent 526
  speech 582
 slip of the -
  error 495
  solecism 568
 - *stammering* 583
 - cleave to the roof of
  one's mouth 870
 - of land 342
 - running loose 584
 wag the - 582
tongueless 581
tongue-shaped 245
tongue-tied 581
tonic
 musical note 413
 healthy 656
 medicine 662
tonicity
 strength 159
tonjon 272
tonnage 192
tonsilitis 655

tonsils 351
tonsure 999
tontine 810
tony 501
Tony Lumpkin 876
too *also* 37
  excess 641
  in a - great degree 31
  - bad
  disreputable 874
  wrong 923
  censure 932
  - clever by half 702
  - far 641
  - hot to hold one 830
  - late 133
  - late for 135
  - little 640
  - many 641
  - much [*see below*]
  - soon 132
  - soon for 135
  - true *regret* 833
  lamentation 839
too much
  redundance 641
  intemperance 954
  have - of 869
  make - of 482
  - for 471
  - of a good thing 869
tool *instrument* 633
  steer 693
  catspaw 711
  servile 886
  edge - 253
  mere - 690
tooling 847
tooth *fastening* 45
  projection 250
  sharp 253
  roughness 256
  notch 257
  texture 329
  taste 390
  sweet -
  desire 865
  fastidious 868
  - and nail
  violence 173
  exertion 686
  attack 716
  - of time 106, 551
toothache 378
toothed 253
toothless 254
toothsome 394
top *supreme* 33
  summit 210
  .*roof* 223
  spin 312
  at the - of one's speed
  274
  at the - of one's voice
  loud 404
  shout 411
  at the - of the tree
  873
  fool to the - of one's
  bent 545
  from - to toe 200

sleep like a - 683
- of the ladder 873
- to bottom
  completely 52
topaz *yellow* 436
  jewel 847
top-boot 225
tope *tomb* 363
  trees 367
  drink 959
  temple 1000
topek 189
toper 959
topfull 52
top-gallant mast
  height 206
  summit 210
top-heavy
  unbalanced 28
  inverted 218
  dangerous 665
  tipsy 959
Tophet 982
topiary 847
topic 454
  - of the day 532
topical 183
topmast 206
topmost 210
topography 183
topple
  unbalanced 28
  perish 162
  decay 659
  - down *fall* 306
  - over 28, 306
topsail schooner 273
top sawyer
  important 642
  proficient 700
topsy-turvy 218
tor 206
torch *fuel* 388
  luminary 423
  apply the - 824
  light the - of war 722
  - of Hymen 903
Tories 712
torment
  physical 378
  moral 828, 830
  place of - 982
Tormes, Lazarillo de
  - 941
tormina 378
torminous 378
torn [*see* tear]
  discord 713
tornado
  whirl 312
  wind 349
  (*violence* 173)
torose 250
torpedinous 823
torpedo *bane* 663
  sluggish 683
  weapon 727
  evil doer 913
torpedo boat 726
torpid, torpor
  inert 172

inactive 683
insensible 823
torpids 720
torporific 823
torque 847
torrefy 384
torrent
  violence 173
  rapid 274
  flow 348
  rain in -s 348
torrid 382
torsion 248
torso 50
tort 925
tort et à travers, à
  - *disagreement* 24
  .*absurdity* 497
  resolution 604
torticollis 378
tortile 248
tortious 925
tortive 248
tortoise 275
tortoise shell 440
tortuous
  twisted 248
  concealed 528
  dishonorable 940
torture
  physical 378
  moral 828, 830
  cruelty 907
  punishment 972
  - a question 476
torvity 901a
toss *derange* 61
  throw 284
  oscillate 314
  agitate 315
  - in a blanket 929
  - off *drink* 298
  - on one's pillow 825
  - overboard 610
  - the head
  pride 878
  insolence 885
  contempt 930
  - up 156, 621
tosspot 959
total 50
  - abstinence
  temperate 953
  ascetic 955
  - eclipse 421
  sum - 800
totalizator 621
totally 52
tote 270
totem 550
totidem verbis
  imitation 19
  exactness 494
totient 84
toties quoties 136
totis viribus 686
totitive 84
toto: in - 52
  - cœlo 52
totter
  changeable 149

weak 160
limp 275
oscillate 314
agitate 315
decay 659
danger 665
- to its fall 162
touch *relate to* 9
  small quantity 32
  mixture 41
  contact 199
  sensation **379, 380**
  music 416
  test 463
  indication 550
  act 680
  receive 785
  excite 824
  pity 914
  in - with 9
  some - of n a t u r e's
  glow 318
  - and go
  instant 113
  soon 132
  changeable 149
  easy 705
  - on 516
  - on the raw 822
  - the guitar 416
  - the hat 894
  - the heart 824
  - to the quick 822
  - up 658
  - upon
  treat on 595
touched
  crazy 503
  tainted 653
  compassion 914
  - in the wind 655
  - with *feeling* 821
touching 830
touchstone 463
touchwood
  fuel 388
  irascible 901
touchy 901
tough *coherent* 46
  tenacious 327
  difficult 704
  larrikin 887
  bully 913
toujours perdrix
  repetition 104
  weary 841
  satiety 869
toupee 256
tour 266
tour de force
  skill 698
  stratagem 702
  display 882
tourist 268
tournament 720
tourner casaque 608
tourniquet 263
tournure
  outline 230
  appearance 448
  belle - 845

transfer 270
- the sense of 522

transgress
go beyond 303
infringe 773
violate 927
sin 945

transgression
guilt 947

transi de froid 383

transient 111
changeable 149

transientness 111

transilience
revolution 146
transcursion 303

transit
conversion 144
motion 264
transference 270

transit gloria mundi, sic -
adversity 735
disrepute 874

transition 144, 270

transitional
change 140

transitory 111

transitu, in -
transient 111
journey 266
transference 270

translate
interpret 522
promote 995

translation
transference 270
resurrection 981

translocation 270

translucence 425

translumination 425

transmarine 196

transmigration
change 140
conversion 144

transmission
moving 270
passage 302
- *of property* 783

transmit light 425

transmogrify 140

transmutation
change 140
conversion 144

transom 215

transparency 425

transparent
transmitting light 425
obvious 518

transpicuous
transmitting light 425
obvious 518

transpierce 260

transpire
evaporate 336
appear 525
be disclosed 529

transplace 270

transplant 270

620

transplendent 420

transpontine 196

transport
transfer 270
ship 273
war vessel 726
excitement 825
delight 827
please 829
punish 972
(emotion 821, 824)
- *of love* 897

transportation 144

transposal 218

transpose
exchange 148
displace 185
invert 218
transfer 270
- *music* 413

transubstantiation
change 140
sacrament 998

transude
ooze 295
pass 302
(stream 348)

transume
change 140

transumption
transfer 270

transverse
oblique 217
crossing 219

tranter 271

trap *closure* 261
gig 272
snare 545
stage - 599
pitfall 667
fall into a -
dupe 547
clumsy 699
lay a - for 545

trapan 545

trap bat and ball 840

trapdoor
opening 260
snare 545
pitfall 667

trapes 701

trappings
adjunct 39
clothes 225
equipment 633
ornament 847

Trappist 996

traps *clothes* 225
baggage 780

trash
unmeaning 517
trifling 643
useless 645
riffraff 876

trashy - *style* 575

traulism 583

traumatic 662

travail
childbirth 161
labor 686
le - du corps 686

trave 215

travel 215
- *out of the record* 10, 477

traveler 268
bagman 758
tricks upon -s
deception 545
cunning 702
-'s tale
untruth 546
exaggeration 549

traverse
contravene 179
move 266
pass 302
negative 536
obstruct 706

travestie *copy* 21
ridicule 856

travesty
imitate 19
misinterpret 523
misrepresentation 555
ridicule 856

travis 215

trawl 463

trawler 273

tray 191

treacherous 940
- *memory* 506

treachery
deception 545
dishonesty 940

treacle
thick 352
sweet 396

tread *motion* 264
walk 266
- a path
journey 266
pursuit 622
- *down harsh* 739
humble 879
- in the steps of 19
- on the heels of 281
- the beaten track
conformity 82
habit 613
- the boards 599
- the stage 599
- under foot
destroy 162
subjection 749
disrepute 874
insolence 885
contempt 930
- upon
persecute 649

treadle 633

treadmill 975

treason *revolt* 742
treachery 940

treasure *store* 636
goodness 648
money 800
- trove 618
- up in the memory 505

treasurer 801

treasury 802
- of everlasting joy 981

treat *physical pleasure* 377
manage 692
bargain 769
delight 827, 829
amusement 840
- of 595
- oneself to 827
- well 906

treatise 595

treatment
painting 556
conduct 692
ill - 649
medical - 662

treaty 769

treble *three* 93
shrill 410
(music 413)
childish - 581

trebucket 727, 975

trecento 114, 554

trecker 268

tree *pedigree* 166
plant 367
gallows 975
as the - falls 151
top of the - 210
- of knowledge 493
up a - 704

treenail 45

trefoil 92

trek 266

trekker 268

trellis 219

tremble
fluctuate 149
weakness 160
shake 315
cold 383
emotion 821
fear 860
make one - 860

trembling:
- in the balance
uncertain 475
danger 665
- prairie 344
- to its fall
destruction 160

tremblingly alive 822

tremellose 352

tremendous
painful 830
fearful 860

tremendously 31

tremor
agitation 315
emotion 821
fearful 860

tremulous
agitated 315
- *voice* 583
irresolute 605
fear 860

trench *furrow* 259
- on *near* 197

trespass 303
  moral trespass 925
- upon 927
trenchant
  energetic 171
  assertive 535
  concise style 572
  vigorous language 574
  important 642
  emotion 821
  discourteous 895
  censure 932
trencher plate 191
  layer 204
trenches, open the - 716
trend tendency 176
  bend 278
  deviate 279
trennel 45
trepan borer 262
  snare 545
trepang 298
trepidation
  agitation 315
  emotion 821
  excitement 825
  fear 860
trespass
  go beyond 303
  vice 945
  guilt 947
tress 256
trestle 215
trevet 215
  [and see trivet]
trey 92
triad 92
triadelphous 94
triagonal 244
tria juncta in uno 43, 92
trial inquiry 461
  experiment 463
  essay 675
  difficulty 704
  adversity 735
  suffering 828, 830
  lawsuit 969
  punishment 972
- of temper 824
triality 92
trialogue 588
triangle
  triality 92, 244
  music 417
  punishment 975
triangular 94
- duel 720
triarch 92
triarchy 737
tribe
  race 11
  assemblage 72
  class 75
  clan 166
tribulation 828
tribunal 966
tribune
  rostrum 542

judge 967
tributary river 348
  giving 784
tribute
  donation 784
  money paid 809
  reward 973
pay - to
  respect 928
  approbation 931
tricapsular 94
trice 113
- up 43
trichogenous 256
trichoid 256
trichosis 226
trichotomy 94
trichroism 440
trick deception 545
  habit 613
  contrivance 626
  skill 698
  artifice 702
- at cards 775
play -s
  bungle 699
  cunning 702
  amusement 840
  ridicule 856
- of fortune 509
- out adorn 847
  vulgar 851
-s of the trade 702
trickery
  deceit 545
  finery 851
trickle ooze 295
  stream 348
trickster
  deceiver 548
  rogue 792
tricksy cheery 836
  pretty 845
  ornamented 847
tricolor
  variegated 440
  flag 550
tricuspid 94
tricycle 272
trident 92, 341
tridental 94
triennial
  periodical 138
  plant 367
triennium 92
trifid 94
trifle small 32
  neglect 460
  folly 499
  unimportant 643
not stick at -s 604
not to be -d with 744
- time away 683
- with neglect 460
  deceive 545
  disrespect 929
trifler 460
  fool 501
trifling 499, 643
  wit 842
trifoliate 94

triform 92
trifurcate 94
trig 652, 845
trigamy 903
trigger 633
  draw the - 722
Trigger, Sir Lucius O' - 887
trigon 92, 244
trigonal 94
trigonometry 244
trigrammatic 94
trigraph 561
τρικυμία 33
trilateral sides 236
  angles 244
trilogistic
  triple 93
trilogy drama 599
trill stream 348
  sound 407
  music 416
thousand -s 402
trillion 98
trim state 7
  adjust 27
  dress 225
  form 240
  lie 544
  waver 605
  change sides 607
  clean 652
  beautify 845
  adorn 847
  scold 932
  flog 972
  (prepare 673)
in - order 58
trimmer fickle 607
  apostate 941
  timeserver 943
trimming
  border 231
  ornament 847
  dishonesty 940
trinal 92
trine 93
trinity 92
Trinity, Holy - 976
trinket trifle 643
  ornament 847
trinkgeld 784
trinomial 92
trio three 92
  music 415
trionym 92
trip jaunt 266
  run 274
  fall 306
  leap 309
  mistake 495
  bungle 699
  fail 732
  vice 945
  guilt 947
- up deceive 545
  overthrow 731
tripartition 94
tripetalous 94
triphthong 561
triplane 273

triple 93
- crown 999
triplet three 92
  verse 597
triplication 93
triplopia 92
tripod 92, 215
tripodal 94
tripotage 588
tripping [see trip]
  style 578
  nimble 682
  caught - 491
trippingly on the tongue 584
tripsis 330
Triptolemus 371
triquetral 94
trireme 92, 273
Trisagion 900
triseme 92
trisection 94
triskelion 92, 993
trismus 655
triste 837
tristful 837
trisula 92
trisulcate
  trisected 94
  furrow 259
trite known 490
  conventional 613
- saying 496
tritheism 984
Triton sea 341
- among the minnows
  superior 33
  huge 192
  important 642
trituration 330
trium literarum, homo - 792
triumph
  success 731
  trophy 733
  exult 838
  celebrate 883
  boast 884
triumvirate 737
triune 93
Triune God 976
triunity 92
trivet support 215
  stove 386
right as a -
  perfect 650
  due 924
trivial
  unmeaning 517
  trifling 643
  useless 645
  (small 32)
troat 412
trocar 262
trocha 706
trochaic 597
trochee 597
trochilic 312
trodden: down- 749
well -
  habitual 613

used 677
croglodyte 893
troll *move fast* 274
  roll 312
  fairy 980
trolley 266
  - *car* 272
trollop 962
trombone 417
troop
  assemblage 72
  soldiers 726
  raise -s 722
trooper 726
  lie like a - 544
  swear like a - 908
troopship 726
trop, de - 641
trope 521
Trophonius, cave of
  - 837
trophoplasm 357
trophy *record* 551
  palm **733**
tropical 382
  metaphorical 521
trot *run* 266
  velocity 274
  - *out manifest* 525
  display 882
troth *belief* 484
  veracity 543
  promise 768
  by my - 535
  plight one's - 902
trothless *false* 544
  dishonorable 940
trotters 266
trottoir 627
troubadour 597
trouble *disorder* 59
  derange 61
  exertion 686
  difficulty 704
  adversity 735
  pain 828
  painful 830
  bring into - 649
  get into - 732
  in - *evil* 619
  adversity 735
  take - 686
  - *one for* 765
  - *oneself* 686
  - *one's head about*
  682
troubled waters, fish
  in - 704
troublesome 686, 704,
  830
troublous 59
  violent 173
  - *times* 713
trough *hollow* 252
  trench 259
  conduit 350
trounce *censure* 932
  punish 972
troupe 72
trousers 225
trousseau 225

trout 366
trouvaille 775
trouvère 597
trover
  acquisition 775
  unlawful 964
trow *think* 451
  believe 484
  know 490
trowel 191
trowsers 225
troy weight 319
truant *absent* 187
  runaway 623
  idle 682
  apostate 941
truce *cessation* 142
  peace 721
  pacification 723
  flag of - 724
trucidation 361
truck *summit* 210
  vehicle 272
  barter 794
truckle-bed 215
truckler 886
truckle to
  submit 725
  servile 886
  flatter 933
truckman 268
truculent 907
trudge *walk* 266
  move slowly 275
truditur dies die 106,
  109
true *real* 1
  straight 246
  assent 488
  accurate 494
  veracious 543
  faithful 772
  honorable 939
  orthodox 983a
  see in its - *colors* 480a
  - *bill*
  vindicate 937
  accuse 938
  lawsuit 969
  - *faith* 983a
  - *meaning* 516
  - *to nature* 17
  - *to oneself* 604a
  - *saying* 496
true-hearted 543, 939
truelove 897
truelover's knot
  love 897
  endearment 902
true-penny 939
truism *axiom* 496
  unmeaning 517
trull 962
truly *very* 31
  assent 488
  really 494
  indeed 535
trump *perfect* 650
  cards 840
  honorable 939
  good man 948

- *card device* 626
  success 731
- *up falsehood* 544
  accuse 938
  turn up -s 731
trumped up 545, 546
trumpery
  unmeaning 517
  trifling 643
trumpet *music* 417
  war cry 722
  boast 884
  ear- 418
  flourish of -s
    ostentation 882
    celebration 883
    boasting 884
  penny -
    skill 410
  sound of -
    alarm 669
  speaking - 418
  - *blast* 404
  - *call signal* 550
    command 741
  - *forth* 531
trumpeter
  musician 416
  messenger 534
  boaster 884
trumpet-toned
  shrill 410
trumpet-tongued
  loud 404
  public 531
truncate
  shorten 201
  formless 241
truncated
  incomplete 53
truncheon
  weapon 727
  staff of office 747
  instrument of pun-
    ishment 975
trundle *propel* 284
  roll 312
trunk *whole* 50
  origin 153
  paternity 166
  box 191
trunk hose 225
trunnion
  support 215
  projection 250
truss *tie* 43
  pack, packet 72
  support 215
trust *belief* 484
  property 780
  credit 805
  hope 858
  - *to a broken reed* 699
  - *to the chapter of*
    accidents 621
trustee
  consignee 758
  possessor 779
  treasurer 801
trustless 940
trustworthy

certain 474
  belief 484
  - *memory* 505
  veracious 543
  honorable 939
truth *exactness* **494**
  veracity 543
  probity 939
  arrive at the - 480a
  in - *certainly* 474
  love of - 543
  of a -
    affirmation 535
    veraciously 543
  prove the - *of* 937
  religious - 983a
  speak the -
    disclose 529
    veracity 543
Truth, Spirit of - 976
truthless 544
truth-loving 543
trutination 319
try *experiment* 463
  adjudge 480
  endeavor 675
  use 677
  lawsuit 969
  - *a case* 967
  - *a cause* 480
  - *a prisoner* 967
  - *conclusions*
    discuss 476
    quarrel 713
    contend 720
  - *one*
    difficulty 704
  - *one's hand* 675
  - *one's luck* 621
  - *one's temper* 824
  - *one's utmost* 686
  - *the patience* 830
trying *fatigue* 688
  difficulty 704
tryst 892
trysting place 74
tsar 745
Tsung-li Yamen 759
tub 191
  - *to a whale*
    deception 545
    excuse 617
tuba 417
tubam trepidat,
  ante - *fear* 860
  cowardice 862
tubate 260
tube 260
tubercle 250
tuberosity 250
tubman 968
tubular 260
tubulated 260
tubule 260
tuck *fold* 258
  dagger 727
  - *in locate* 184
  eat 298
  insert 300
tucker 225
tuft *collection* 72

unimpeached 931, 946
unimpelled (616)
unimportance 643
unimpressed 838
unimpressible 823
unimproved 659
unincited (616)
unincreased 36
unincumbered
  easy 705
  exempt 927a
uninduced 616
uninfected 652
uninfectious 656
uninflammable 385
uninfluenced
  obstinate 606
  unactuated 616
uninfluential
  inert 172
  no influence 175a
uninformed 491
uningenuous 544
uninhabit -able, -ed
  absence 187
  secluded 893
uninitiated
  ignorant 491
  unskillful 699
uninjured
  perfect 650
  healthy 654
  preserved 670
uninjurious 656
uninquisitive 456
uninspired
  unexcited 823
  (unactuated 616)
uninstructed 491
unintellectual
  incogitant 452
  imbecile 499
unintelligent 32, 499
unintelligibility 519
unintelligible 519
  - style 571
render - 538
unintentional
  necessary 601
  undesigned 621
uninterested
  incurious 456
  weary 841
  dull 843
unintermitting
  unbroken 69
  durable 110
  continuing 143
  persevering 604a
uninterrupted
  continuous 69
  perpetual 112
  unremitting 893
- existence 112
unintroduced 893
uninured
  unaccustomed 614
  (unprepared 674)
uninvented 526
uninvestigated 491

uninvited 893
uninviting 830
union
  agreement 23
  junction 43
  combination 48
  concurrence 178
  party 712
  concord 714
  marriage 903
dark - of insensate
  dust 363
union jack 550
union pipes 417
unique
  dissimilar 18
  original 20
  exceptional 83
  alone 87
unirritating 174
unison
  agreement 23
  melody 413
  concord 714
  (uniform 16)
unisulcate 259
unit 87
Unitarian 984
unite join 43
  combine 48
  component 56
  assemble 72
  concur 178
  converge 290
  party 712
  (agree 23)
- in pairs 89
- one's efforts 709
- with
  coöperate 709
united coherent 46
  concord 714
unity whole 50
  complete 52
  single 87
  concord 714
- of time 120
Unity, Trinity in - 976
universal 78
music the - language 415
- Church 983a
- concept 450
- favorite 899
- ly present 186
- predicament 25
universe 318
university 542
go to the - 539
- education 537
unjust wrong 923
  impious 988
unjustifiable
  wrong 923
  inexcusable 938
  wicked 945
unjustified 923
  undue 925
unkempt
  unclean 653

  vulgar 851
unkennel eject 297
  disclose 529
unkind 907
-est cut of all 828
unkindness
  hard - 907
unknightly 940
unknit (44)
unknowable 519
unknowing 491
unknown
  ignorant 491
  latent 526
- quantities 491
- to fame
  inglorious 874
  lowborn 876
unlabored
  - style 578
  unprepared 674
unlace (44)
unlade 297
unladylike
  vulgar 851
  rude 895
unlamented
  hated 898
  disapproved 932
unlatch 44
unlawful
  undue 925
  illegal 964
unlearn 506
unlearned 491
unleavened 674
unless
  circumstances 8
  except 83
  qualification 469
  (condition 770)
unlettered 491
- Muse 579
- small knowing soul 491
unlicensed 761
unlicked
  unprepared 674
  vulgar 851
  clownish 876
- cub
  shapeless 241
  unmannerly 895
unlike 18
unlikely 471, 473
unlimber 323
unlimited great 31
  infinite 105
  free 748
- space 180
unlink (44)
unliquefied 321
unlively
  grave 837
  dull 843
unload
  displace 185
  eject 297
  disencumber 705
unlock unfasten 44
  discover 480a

  (explain 462)
unlooked for 508
unloose
  unfasten 44
  liberate 750
unloved 898
unlovely 846
unlucky
  inopportune 135
  bad 649
  ·unfortunate 735
  in·pain 830
unmade 2
unmaimed 654
unmake 145
unman
  render powerless 158
  madden 837
  frighten 860
unmanageable
  unwieldy 647
  perverse 704
unmanly
  effeminate 374
  dishonorable 940
unmanned
  dejected 837
  cowardly 862
unmannered 895
unmannerly 895
unmarked 460
unmarred
  sound 654
  preserved 670
unmarried 904
unmask
  disclose 529
  (show 525)
unmatched
  different 15
  dissimilar 18
  unparalleled 20
unmeaningness 517
unmeant 517
unmeasured
  infinite 105
  undistinguished 465a
  abundant 639
unmeditated
  impulsive 612
  (undesigned 621)
unmeet 925
unmellowed 674
unmelodious 414
unmelted 321
unmentionable 874
unmentioned (526)
unmerciful
  pitiless 914a
  (malevolent 907)
unmerited 925
unmethodical 59
unmindful
  inattentive 458
  neglectful 460
  ungrateful 917
unmingled 42
unmissed 460
unmistakable
  certain 474
  intelligible 518

Column 1 (UNMI)

manifest 525
(*visible* 446)
unmitigable 173
unmitigated
  great 31
  complete 52
  violent 173
unmixed 42
unmodified (141)
unmolested *safe* 664
  content 831
unmoneyed 804
unmoral 823
unmourned 898
unmoved
  quiescent 265
  obstinate 606
  insensible 823
  (*resolute* 604)
  (*uninduced* 616)
unmusical 414
  - *voice* 581
unmuzzled 748
unnamed 565
unnatural
  exceptional 83
  affected 855
  spiteful 907
unnecessary
  redundant 641
  useless 645
  inexpedient 647
unneeded 645
unneighborly 895
unnerved
  powerless 158
  weak 160
  dejected 837
unnoted }
unnoticed }
  neglected 460
  ignoble 874
unnumbered 105
unnurtured 674
unobeyed 742
unobjectionable
  good 648
  pretty good 651
  innocent 946
unobnoxious 648
unobscured 420
unobservant 458
unobserved 460
unobstructed
  clear 705
  free 749
  (*unopposed* 709)
unobtainable 471
unobtained 777a
unobtrusive 881
unoccupied
  vacant 187
  unthinking 452
  doing nothing 681
  inactive 683
unoffended
  enduring 826
  humble 879
unofficial 964
unoften 137
unopened 261

Column 2 (UNPI)

unopposed 709
unorganized
  unprepared 674
  - *matter* 358
unornamental 846
unornamented
  - *style* 576
  simple 849
unorthodox 984
uno saltu 113
unostentatious 881
unowed 807
unowned 782
unpacific
  discordant 713
  warfare 722
unpacified 713
unpack
  unfasten 44
  take out 297
unpaid *debt* 806
  honorary 815
unpalatable
  unsavory 395
  disagreeable 830
  (*dislike* 867)
unparagoned
  supreme 33
  best 648
  perfect 650
unparalleled
  unimitated 20
  supreme 33
  exceptional 83
unpardonable
  inexcusable 938
  wicked 945
unparliamentary
  language
  discourteous 895
  cursing 908
unpassable 261
unpassionate 826
unpatriotic 911
unpeaceful
  contention 720
  war 722
unpeople
  emigration 297
  banishment 893
  (*displace* 185)
unperceived
  neglected 460
  unknown 491
  (*latent* 526)
unperformed 730
unperjured
  truthful 543
  honorable 939
unperplexed 498
unpersuadable
  obstinate 606
unpersuaded 616
unperturbed 826
unphilosophical 499
unpierced 261
unpin (44)
unpitied 932
unpitying
  pitiless 914a
  (*angry* 900)

Column 3 (UNPR)

  (*malevolent* 907)
unplaced 185
unplagued 831
unpleasant 830
unpleasing 830
unpoetical
  prose 598
  matter of fact 703
unpolished
  rough 256
  inelegant 579
  unprepared 674
  vulgar 851
  rude 895
unpolite 895
unpolluted
  good 648
  perfect 650
unpopular
  disagreeable 830
  dislike 867
unpopularity
  hatred 898
unportioned 804
unpossessed 777a
unpracticed (699)
unprecedented
  exceptional 83
  rare 137
unprejudiced 498
unpremeditated
  impulsive 612
  undesigned 621
  unprepared 674
unprepared 674
unprepossessed 498
unprepossessing 846
unpresentable 851
unpretending 881
unprevented 748
unprincipled 945
unprivileged 925
unprized 483
unproclaimed 526
unproduced
  inexistent 2
unproductive
  useless 645
unproductiveness
  169
unproficiency 699
unprofitable
  unproductive 169
  useless 645
  inexpedient 647
  bad 649
unprolific 169
unpromising 859
unprompted 612
unpronounced
  (*latent* 526)
unpropitious
  ill-timed 135
  opposed 708
  hopeless 859
unproportioned
  (*disagreeing* 24)
unprosperous 735
unprotected 665
unproved 477
unprovided

Column 4 (UNRE)

scanty 640
unprepared 674
unprovoked (616)
unpublished 526
unpunctual
  tardy 133
  untimely 135
  irregular 139
unpunished 970
unpurchased 796
unpurified 653
unpurposed 621
unpursued 624
unqualified
  incomplete 52
  impotent 158
  certain 474
  unprepared 674
  inexpert 699
  unentitled 925
  - *truth* 494
unquelled 173
unquenchable
  strong 159
  desire 865
unquenched
  violence 173
  heat 382
unquestionable
  certain 474
unquestionably
  assent 488
unquestioned 474
  agreed upon 488
unquiet
  motion 264
  agitation 315
  excitable 825
unravel *untie* 44
  arrange 60
  straighten 246
  evolve 313
  discover 480a
  interpret 522
  disembarrass 705
  (*solve* 462)
unreached 304
unread
  ignorant 491
unready 674
unreal
  not existing 2
  unsubstantial 4
  erroneous 495
  imaginary 515
unreasonable
  impossible 471
  illogical 477
  misjudging 481
  foolish 499
  exorbitant 814
  unjust 923
unreclaimed 951
unrecognizable 146
unreconciled 713
unrecorded 552
unrecounted 55
unrecovered (659)
unreduced 31
unrefined 851
unreflecting 458

unreformed 951
unrefreshed 688
- **unrefuted**
  proved 478
  true 494
unregarded
  neglected 460
  unrespected 929
unregenerate 988
unregistered 552
unreined 748
unrelated 10
unrelenting
  pitiless 914a
  revengeful 919
  (malevolent 907)
unreliable 475
unrelieved 835
unremarked 460
unremembered 506
unremitting
  continuous 69
  continuing 110
  persevering 604a
  (industrious 682)
unremoved 184
unremunerated 808
unrenewed 141
unrepaid (806)
unrepealed 141
unrepeated *single* 87
  few 103
unrepentant 951
unrepining 831
unreplenished 640
unreported (526)
unrepressed 173
unreproached 946
unreproved 946
unrequited
  owing 806
  ingratitude 917
unresented
  forgiven 918
unresenting
  enduring 826
unreserved
  manifest 525
  veracious 543
  artless 703
unresisted 743
unresisting 725
unresolved 605
unrespected 929
unrespited 971
unrest
  changeable 149
  moving 264
unrestored
  fatigue 688
unrestrained
  unencumbered 705
  free 748
unrestricted
  undiminished 31
  free 748
unretracted 535
unrevealed (528)
unrevenged 918
unreversed 143
unrevoked 143

unrewarded
  unpaid 806
  ingratitude 917
unrhymed 598
unriddle
  find out 480a
  disclose 529
  (interpret 522)
unrig 645
unrighteous 945
unrip 260
unripe 674
unrivaled,
  supreme 33
  (good 648)
unrivet (44)
unrobe (226)
unroll *evolve* 313
  display 525
  (unravel 47)
  (straighten 246)
unromantic 494
unroof (226)
unroot
  extract 301
  (destroy 162)
unruffled *calm* 174
  quiet 265
  unaffected 823
  placid 826
  (in order 58)
unruly *violent* 173
  obstinate 606
  disobedient 742
unsaddle 756
unsafe 665
unsaid 526
unsaleable
  useless 645
  selling 796
  cheap 815
unsaluted 929
unsanctified
  impiety 988
  irreligion 989
unsanctioned 925
unsated 865
unsatisfactory
  inexpedient 647
  bad 649
  displeasing 830
  discontent 832
unsatisfied
  discontented 832
  desirous 865
unsavoriness 395
unsay *recant* 607
  (negation 536)
unscanned 460
unscathed 654
unscattered (72)
unschooled
  ignorant 491
  (unskillful 699)
unscientific
  illogical 477
  (erroneous 495)
unscoured 653
unscreened (665)
unscrew (44)
unscriptural 984

unscrupulous 940
unseal 529
unsearched 460
unseasonable
  inappropriate 24
  ill-timed 135
  (inexpedient 647)
unseasoned
  unaccustomed 614
  unprepared 674
unseat 756
unseconded
  (unassisted 706)
unseemly
  inexpedient 647
  ugly 846
  vulgar 851
  undue 925
  vicious 945
unseen
  invisible 447
  neglected 460
  latent 526
unsegmentic 357
unseldom 136
unselfish 816, 942
unseparated 46
unserviceable 645
unservient 645
unsettle *derange* 61
unsettled
  mutable 149
  displaced 185
  uncertain 475
  - *in one's mind* 503
unsevered 50
unsex 146
unshackle (*untie* 44)
  (liberate 750)
unshackled
  (free 748)
unshaded
  manifest 525
unshaken
  strong 159
  (resolute 604)
  - *belief* 484
unshapely 846
unshapen
  amorphous 241
  (ugly 846)
unshared 777
unsheathe
  (uncover 266)
  - *the sword*
  war 722
unsheltered (655)
unshielded 665
unshifting 143
unship 297
unshocked 823
unshorn 50
unshortened 200
unshrinking
  determined 604
  courageous 861
unsifted 460
unsightly 846
unsinged 670
unskillfulness 699
unslaked 865

unsleeping
  persevering 604a
  active 682
unsmooth 256
unsociable 893
unsocial 893
unsoiled 652
unsold 777
unsolder
  (disjoin 44)
  (incoherence 47)
unsoldierlike 862
unsolicitous 866
unsolved 526
unsophisticated
  simple 42
  genuine 494
  artless 703
  (good 648)
unsorted 59
unsought
  avoided 623
  unrequested 766
unsound
  illogical 477
  erroneous 495
  deceptive 545
  imperfect 651
  (unhealthy 655)
  - *heaps of miser's treasures* 819
  - *mind* 503
unsown 674
unsparing
  abundant 639
  severe 739
  liberal 816
  with an - hand 818
unspeakable
  great 31
  wonderful 870
unspecified 78
unspent 678
unspied 526
unspiritual 316
unspoiled
  (good 648)
unspoken (581)
unspotted
  clean 652
  beautiful 845
  innocent 946
unstable
  changeable 149
  precarious 665
  - *equilibrium* 149
unstaid 149
unstained
  clean 652
  honorable 939
unstatesmanlike 699
unsteadfast 605
unsteady
  mutable 149
  irresolute 605
  in danger 665
  (fickle 607)
unstinted 639
unstirred 823, 826
unstopped
  continuing 143

open 260
unstored 640
unstrained
  turbid 653
  relaxed 687
  - meaning 516
unstrengthened 160
unstruck 823
unstrung 160
unstudied 460
unsubject 748
unsubmissive 742
unsubservient
  useless 645
  inexpedient 647
unsubstantial 4
  weak 160
  rare 322
  erroneous 495
  imaginary 515
unsubstantiality 4
unsuccessful 732
unsuccessive 70
unsuitable
  incongruous 24
  (inexpedient 647)
  - time 135
unsullied *clean* 652
  honorable 939
  (guiltless 946)
unsung 526
unsupplied 640
unsupported
  weak 160
  (unassisted 706)
  - by evidence 468
unsuppressed 141
unsurmountable
  471
unsurpassed 33
unsusceptible 823
unsuspected
  belief 484
  latent 526
unsuspecting
  hopeful 858
unsuspicious
  belief 484
  artless 703
  hope 858
unsustainable
  erroneous 495
unsustained
  (weak 160)
  (unassisted 706)
unswayed (616)
unsweet 395
unswept 653
unswerving
  straight 246
  direct 278
  persevering 604a
unsymmetric
  unconformable 83
unsymmetrical
  irregular 59
  distorted 243
unsympathetic 24
unsystematic 59
untack (44)
untainted *pure* 652

healthy 654
  honorable 939
untalked of 526
untamed *rude* 851
  ferocious 907
untangled (58)
untarnished
  honorable 939
  (innocent 946)
untasted 391
untaught
  ignorant 491
  untrained 674
untaxed 815
unteach 538
unteachable
  foolish 499
  unskillful 699
untempted (616)
untenable
  powerless 158
  illogical 477
  undefended 725
untenanted 187
unthanked 917
unthankful 917
unthankfulness 915
unthawed
  solid 321
  cold 383
unthinkable 471
unthinking
  unconsidered 452
  involuntary 601
unthought of
  unconsidered 452
  neglected 460
unthread: - rude eye
  of rebellion 742
unthreatened 664
unthrifty
  unprepared 674
  prodigal 818
unthrone 756
untidy
  in disorder 59
  slovenly 653
untie *liberate* 750
  (loose 44)
  - the knot 705
until 106, (108)
  - now 118
untilled 674
untimely 135
  - end 360
untinged *simple* 42
  (uncolored 429)
untired 689
untiring 604a
untitled 876
untold
  countless 105
  uncertain 475
  latent 526
  secret 528
untouched
  disused 678
  insensible 823
untoward
  ill-timed 135
  bad 649

unprosperous 735
  unpleasant 830
untraced 526
untracked 526
untractable
  obstinate 606
  unskillful 699
untrained
  unaccustomed 614
  unprepared 674
  unskilled 699
untrammeled
  easy 705
  free 748
untranslatable 523
untranslated 20, 523
untraveled 265
untreasured 640
untried *new* 123
  not decided 461
untrimmed
  unprepared 674
  simple 849
untrodden *new* 123
  impervious 261
  not used 678
untroubled
  calm 174
  peaceful 721
untrue
  erroneous 495
  unveracious 546
untrustworthy
  uncertain 475
  erroneous 495
  danger 665
  dishonorable 940
untruth 546
untunable 414
unturned 246
untutored
  ignorant 491
  unprepared 674
  artless 703
untwine 313
untwist
  evolve 313
  (separate 44, 47)
  (straighten 246)
unused
  unaccustomed 614
  unskillful 699
unusual 83
unusually *very* 31
unutterable
  great 31
  wonderful 870
unvalued
  underrated 483
  undesired 866
  disliked 898
unvanquished 748
unvaried
  uniform 16
  monotonous 104
  continuing 143
  - style 575, 576
unvarnished
  true 494
  - style 576
  simple 849

- tale *true* 494
  veracious 543
unvarying 143
unveil *disclose* 529
  (manifest 525)
unventilated 261
unveracious 544
unversed
  ignorant 491
  (unskilled 699)
unvexed 831
unviolated 939
unvisited 893
unvitiated (648)
unwakened 683
unwarlike 862
unwarmed 383
unwarned
  unexpected 508
  danger 665
unwarped judgment
  498
unwarrantable
  wrong 923
unwarranted 923
  illogical 477
  undue 925
  illegal 964
unwary
  neglectful 460
  (rash 863)
unwashed 653
  great - 876
unwaste (639)
unwatchful 460
unwavering 604a
unweakened 159
unwearied
  persevering 604a
  indefatigable 682
  refreshed 689
unwedded 904
unweeded   garden
  674
unweeting 491
unweighed 460
unwelcome
  disagreeable 830
  unsocial 893
unwell 655
unwept 831
unwholesome 657
unwieldy *large* 192
  heavy 319
  cumbersome 647
  difficult 704
  ugly 846
unwilling
  dissent 489
unwillingness 603
unwind *evolve* 313
  (straighten 246)
unwiped 653
unwise 499
unwished 866
unwithered 159
unwitnessed (526)
unwitting
  ignorant 491
  involuntary 601
unwittingly

V

vacant *void* 4
  absent 187
  thoughtless 452
  unmeaning 517
  scanty 640
  - hour 685
  - mind *folly* 499
vacate *displace* 185
  absent 187
  depart 293
  resign 757
vacation
  repose 687
  (*leisure* 685)
vacatur 756
vaccine 366
vache 191
vacillate
  changeable 149
  undulate 314
  waver 605
vacuity 187, 452
vacuolar 357
vacuolization 161
vacuometer 466
vacuous
  unsubstantial 4
  absent 187
  (*inexistent* 2)
vacuum
  absence 187
vade mecum
  information 527
  schoolbook 542
vadium 771
væ victis! *war* 722
  adversity 735
  threat 909
vagabond
  wanderer 268
  low person 876
  rogue 949
vagabondage 266
vagary
  absurdity 497
  imagination 515
  whim 608
  antic 840
vagas 999
vaginate 223
vagitus 129
vagrant
  changeable 149
  roving 266
  traveler 268
  deviating 279
vague
  uncertain 475
  unreasoning 477
  obscure 519
  - *language* 571
  - *suggestion* 514
vail
  donation 784
  reward 973

(*expenditure* 809)
vain *unreal* 2
  unprofitable 645
  unvalued 866
  conceited 880
  in - *failure* 732
  labor in -
   come short 304
   useless 645
   fail 732
  take a name in - 895
  use - efforts 645
  - attempt 732
  - expectation 509
vainglorious
  haughty 878
  vain 880
  boasting 884
vakas 999
vakil 968
valance 231
vale 252
  - of years 128
valeat quantum 467
valeat quantum va-
  lere protest 465a
valediction
  adieu 293
  courtesy 894
valedictorian 293
valedictory 582
valentine 902
valet 746
  - de chambre 746
  - de place
   interpreter 524
   guide 527
valet anchora virtus
  666
valetudinarian
  invalid 655
  salubrity 656
Valhalla 981
valiant 861
valid *confirmed* 150
  powerful 157
  strong 159
  true 494
  sufficient 639
  (*influential* 179)
  - reasoning 476
valise 191
vallation 717
valley 252
  - of the shadow of
   death 360
vallum 717
valoir, se faire - 884
valor 861
  for - 733
valorem, ad - 812
valorization 480
valuable
  useful 644
  good 648

value
  color 428
  measure 466
  estimate 480
  importance 642
  utility 644 ·
  goodness 648
  price 812
  approbation 931
  of priceless - 814
  set a - upon 482
  - received 810
valueless 646
valve *stop* 263
  conduit 350
  safety - *safety* 664
  refuge 666
  escape 671
vambrace 717
vamose 293
vamp *change* 140
  - up *improve* 658
  restore 660
  prepare 673
vampire
  evil doer 913
  demon 980
vampirism
  extortion 789
  sorcery 992
van *beginning* 66
  front 234
  wagon 272
  in the - 234
  precession 280
van-courier 64
Vandal *vulgar* 851
  commonalty 876
  evil doer 913
vandalism 851
vandyke 257
vandyke brown 433
vane *wind* 349
  indication 550
vanfos 717
vanguard 234
vanilla 298
vanish
  unsubstantial 4
  transient 111
  disappear 449
  (*cease to exist* 2)
vanishing *small* 32
  little 193
vanity *useless* 645
  conceit 880
Vanity Fair 852
vanquish 731
vantage ground
  superiority 33
  power 157
  influence 175
  height 206
vapid *insipid* 391
  - *style* 575

(*unattractive* 866)
vaporarium 386
vaporization 336
vapor *gas* 334
  bubbles 353
  fancy 515
  boast 884
  insolence 885
  - bath 386
vaporer 887
vaporous
  (*opaque* 426)
vapors
  dejection 837
vaquero 370
vargueno 191
variable
  irregular 139
  changeable 149
  irresolute 605
variance
  difference 15
  disagreement 24
  discord 713
  at - *enmity* 889
  at - with 489
variation
  difference 15
  dissimilarity 18
  diverseness **20a**
  number 84
  chance 140
  music 415
varicella 655
varicose 655
varied 15
  - *assortment* 81
variegation 440
variety
  difference 15
  class 75
  multiformity 81
  exception 83
  - the spice of life 81
variform 81
variola 655
variometer 466
variorum 596
various
  different 15
  many 102
  - places 182
  - times 119
varium et mutabile
  149, 374
varlet 949
varnish
  overlay 223
  resin 356a
  sophistry 477
  falsehood 544
  painting 556
  decorate 847
  excuse 937
Varuna 318, 979

victoria
  carriage 272
Victoria Cross 733
victory 731
victrix fortunæ sa-
  pientia 498
victual *provide* 637
victuals 298
vide et crede 484
videlicet
  specification 79
  namely 522
  (*example* 82)
vide ut supra 550
viduity 905
vie *good* 648
  - with
  contend 720
  (*oppose* 708)
vielle 417
vi et armis
  violence 173
  exertion 686
  compulsion 744
vieux: - comptes 901
  peu de gens savent
  être - 128
view *sight* 441
  appearance 448
  attend to 457
  opinion 484
  landscape painting
  556
  intention 620
  bring into - 525
  come into - 446
  commanding - 441
  in - *visible* 446
  intended 420
  expected 507
  keep in - 457
  on - 448
  present to the - 448
  - as 484
  - in a new light 658
  with a - to 620
viewless 447
vigesimal 98
vigeur de dessus 981
vigil *care* 459
vigilance *care* 459
  wisdom 498
  activity 682
vigilant 864
vigils *worship* 990
vigneron 371
vignette
  engraving 558
  embellishment 847
vigor *strength* 159
  energy 171
  style **574**
  resolution 604
  health 654
  activity 682
viking 792
vile *valueless* 643
  bad 649
  painful 830
  disgraceful 874
  plebeian 876

dishonorable 940
vicious 945
vilification 908
vilify *shame* 874
  censure 932
  detract 934
  (*disrespect* 929)
  (*contempt* 930)
vilipend
  disrespect 929
  censure 932
  detract 934
vilipendency 930
villa 189
village 189
  - talk 588
villager 188
villain *servant* 746
  serf 876
  rascal 949
villanous *bad* 648
  wicked 945
  - saltpeter 727
villany 940
villein [*see* villain]
villenage
  subjection 749
  tenure 777
villi 256
villous 256
vim 682
vin: - d'honneur
  arrival 292
  courtesy 894
  not think - ordinaire
  of oneself 880
vina 417
vinaigrette 400
vincible
  impotent 158
  (*weak* 160)
vincit
  - qui patitur 731
  - qui se vincit 731
vincture 43
vinculo matrimonii,
  separatio a - 905
vinculum 45
  - matrimonii 903
vindicate
  avenge 919
  justify 937
  - a right 924
vindication 937
vindicator
  revenge 919
vindictive
  irascible 901
  revengeful 919
vinegar 397
  - aspect 846
vinegrub 659
vineyard
  tillage 371
  workshop 691
vingt-un 840
vino tortus et irâ 901
vintage
  agriculture 371
  store 636
vintner 797

viol 417
violate
  disobey 742
  nonobservance 773
  undue 925
  dereliction 927
  ravish 961
  - a law 83
  - a usage 614
  - the law 964
violence 173
  arbitrary 964
  do - to *bad* 649
  nonobservance 773
  undue 925
violent 173
  excitable 825
  in a - degree 31
  lay - hands on 789
  - death *death* 360
  kill 361
violet 437
violin 417
violinist 416
violoncello 417
violone 417
viper
  snake 366
  bane 663
  evil doer 913
  bad man 949
virago 901
virent 435
vires acquirit eundo
  increase 35
  energy 171
  velocity 274
virescence 435
virgate 246
Virgilianæ, sortes -
  621
virgin *new* 123
  girl 129
  spinster 904
  pure 960
  - soil
  ignorance 491
  untilled 674
virginal 900
virginals 417
Virginia
  crooked as - fence
  243
  - reel 840
virginibus puerisque
  960
viribus, totis - 686
viridity 435
virile
  adolescent 131
  strong 159
  manly 373
virtù 850
virtual
  inexistent 2
  unsubstantial 5
  - image 443
virtually
  (*truly* 494)
virtue *power* 157
  courage 861

goodness **944**
  purity 960
by - of *power* 157
  instrumentality 631
in - of
  authority 737
make a - of necessity
  no choice 609a
  skill 698
  submit 725
  compromise 774
  bear 826
  - greatest of all mon
  archies 944
virtueless 945
virtuoso 850
virtuous *virtue* 944
  purity 960
virtus
  - ariete fortior 861
  - laudatur et alget
  944
  - vincit invidiam 944
virtutis fortuna co-
  mes 88
virulence
  energy 171
  noxiousness 649
  insalubrity 657
  discourtesy 895
  anger 900
  malevolence 907
virum volitare per
  ora 531
virus *disease* 655
  poison 663
vis: - a tergo 284
  - comica 842
  - conservatrix 670
  - inertiæ
  power 157
  inertness 172
  insensibility 823
  - medicatrix
  restoration 660
  remedy 662
  - mortua 157
  - viva 157
visa 488
visage *front* 234
  appearance 148
vis-à-vis *front* 234
  opposite 237
  carriage 272
viscera 221
viscid 352
viscidity 327
viscount 875
viscous 352
viscum 45
vise 752
Vishnu 979
visibility 446
visible 446
  (*intelligible* 518)
  become - 448
  be - 448
  darkness - 421
vision *sight* 441
  phantasm 443
  dream 515

W

weigh *influence* **175**
　lift 307
　heavy 319
　ponder 451
under -
　[see way]
　- anchor 293
　- carefully
　　discriminate 465
　- down
　　aggrieve 649
　　subjection 749
　- on the heart 830
　- heavy on 649
　- on the mind
　　regret 833
　　dejection 837
　　fear 860
　　- with 615
weighbridge 319
weighed and found
　wanting
　inferior 34
　disapproved 932
weight 535
　influence 175
　gravity 319
　importance 642
attach - to 484
carry - 175
drag - 706
have -
　evidence 467
throw one's - into the
　scale 175
weightless 320
weights and meas-
　ures 466
weir *conduit* 350
　hindrance 706
weird *demon* 980
　mystic 992
　spell 993
　- sisters 994
Weismannism 357
weiss: was ich nicht -
　490
welcome
　arrival 292
　grateful 829
　friendly 888
　sociality 892
　reception 894
weld *join* 43
　cohere 46
welfare 734
welkin *worlds* **318**
　air 338
well *much* **31**
　origin 153
　deep 208
　exude 295
　pool 343
　flow 348
　assent 488
　good 618
　store 636
　healthy 654
　spa 662
act - 944
all's - 664

644

drop a bucket into an
　empty - 645
get - 660
go on - 734
let - alone
　quiescence 265
　inaction 681
think - of 931
treat - 906
turn out - 731
- and good
　assent 488
　consent 762
　content 831
- done! 931
- enough
　not much 32
　imperfect 651
- out 295
- over 641
- up in 698
- with 888
work - 731
welladay
　lament 839
　wonder 870
well-advised 498
well-affected 888
well-behaved
　genteel 852
　courteous 894
well-being
　prosperous 734
　happy 827
well-beloved 897
well-born 875
well-bred
　genteel 852
　(*courteous* 894)
well-composed 845
well-defined
　visible 446
　exact 494
　predetermined 611
　(*plan* 626)
well-devised 611
well-disposed 707
welldoing 944
well-favored 845
well-formed 845
well-fed 192
well-founded
　existent 1
　probable 472
　certain 474
　- belief 484
　true 494
well-grounded
　existent 1
　informed 490
　- hope 858
well-grouped 845
well-informed 490
Wellington boots
　225
well-intentioned
　benevolent 906
　virtuous 944
well-knit
　strong 159
well-known

knowledge 490
　habitual 613
well-laid 611
well-made
　beauty 845
well-mannered 894
well-marked 446
well-meaning 906
well-meant 906
well-met 894
well-natured 906
well-nigh
　almost 32
　near 197
well-off
　prosperous 734
　rich 803
well-proportioned
　845
well-provided 639
well-regulated
　order 58
　conformity 82
　circumspect 864
well-set 242
well-spent
　successful 731
　virtuous 944
wellspring 636
well-tasted 394
well-timed 134
well to do
　prosperous 734
　rich 803
well-turned periods
　578
well-weighed 611
wellwisher 890, 914
Welsh 188
welsher
　swindler 792
　nonpayment 808
welt 321
welter
　plunge 310
　roll 312
　- in one's blood 361
Weltgeschichte 966
　- ist das Weltgesicht
　318
wem 848
wen 250
wench *girl* 129
　woman 374
　impure 962
wenching 961
wend 266
were, as you - 660
wergild 974
werowance 745
Wesleyan 984
west *lateral* 236
　direction 278
Westminster
　superior courts of -
　966
westward
　- the course of empire
　282
wet *water* 337
　moist 339

just enough to - **one's**
　feet 209
- blanket
　dissuade 616
　hindrance 706
　sadden 837
　weary 841
　dull 843
- one's whistle
　drink 298
　tipple 959
whack 276
whacking
　large 192
whale *large* **192**
sprat to catch a - 699
tub to a -
　deception 545
　excuse 617
whalebone 325
whaler 273
whap 276
wharf *houses* **189**
　workshop 691
　mart 799
wharfage 812
wharf boat 273
what *inquiry* **461**
　wonder 870
and - not 81
know -'s what
　discriminate 465
　intelligent 498
　skill 698
- d'ye call 'em 563
- in the world
　singular 83
　wonderful 870
- is the reason? 461
- next 455
- on earth
　singular 83
-'s his name 563
- signifies 643
whatever 78
- may happen 474
wheal 250
wheat
winnow the chaff from
　the - 609
wheedle *coax* **615**
　endearment 902
　flatter 933
wheel *circle* **247**
　bicycle 272
　deviate 279
　turn back 283
　circuition 311
　rotation 312
　rack 975
break on the -
　pain 378
　punish 972
get the - out of the rut
　rut 672
scotch the - 706
- about 279
- and axle 633
- of Fortune
　changeable 149
　chance 156

X

Y

Z